U.S. FOREIGN RELATIONS LAW

CASES, MATERIALS, AND PRACTICE EXERCISES

Fifth Edition

■ ■ ■

Sean D. Murphy
Manatt/Ahn Professor of International Law
George Washington University Law School
Member, U.N. International Law Commission

Edward T. Swaine
Professor of Law
George Washington University Law School

Ingrid Wuerth
Helen Strong Curry Professor of International Law
Vanderbilt Law School

AMERICAN CASEBOOK SERIES®

444 Cedar Street, Suite 700
St. Paul, MN 55101
1-877-888-1330

Printed in the United States of America

ISBN: 978-1-68328-426-0

This edition is dedicated to

Michael J. Glennon

Scholar, colleague, mentor, and friend

PREFACE

Every decade seems to present a cataclysm in the field of U.S. foreign relations, whether it be the dramatic withdrawal of U.S. forces from Vietnam, the collapse of communism in the Soviet Union and Eastern Europe, the horrific terrorist attacks of September 11, the ensuing U.S. interventions in Afghanistan and Iraq, or the revolutionary wave of uprisings in the Arab world since 2011, triggering in part military intervention in Libya and waves of refugees from Syria.

Between those cataclysms, less dramatic transnational events also occur that can deeply affect the U.S. polity, such as adherence to or withdrawal from trade agreements that both help and hurt U.S. industry; pursuit of litigation in U.S. courts that seeks to promote respect for human rights abroad; enactment of state-level sanctions directed at foreign governments, which might also impede federal policy; or invocation of immunities by States or State officials to preclude the jurisdiction of U.S. courts for allegedly wrongful acts.

This course book introduces law students, and upper-level undergraduate students, to the constitutional rules, principal statutes, and landmark judicial decisions applicable to such cataclysms and events in the field of U.S. "foreign relations law." The seven Chapters cover the core areas of substantive law and procedure, addressing the manner in which international law (the law of nations and treaties) becomes a part of U.S. law, and the manner in which power is allocated within the federal government and between the federal government and the several states. Each Chapter is further sub-divided into topics appropriate for coverage during one or two classes. The cases and materials are designed to inform the reader and to provoke discussion about *de lege lata* (the law as it is) and *de lege ferenda* (the law as it should be). Detailed notes guide the reader through the major thematic elements, pose questions for further analysis, and provide suggestions for additional reading. An appendix sets forth various practice exercises related to the readings that may be used to enhance the classroom experience, by having students play particular roles for addressing fictitious (but realistic) problems.

Why use this particular course book? Course books in constitutional, criminal, and international law touch upon various aspects of the field of U.S. foreign relations law, but largely in a hit-or-miss fashion. Course books on particular subjects of transnational affairs, such as on trade law, terrorism, or human rights, provide a detailed look at a slice of the field, but at the expense of the broader range of substance and structure. By contrast, this course book provides a comprehensive overview of the field of U.S. foreign relations law, thereby laying the groundwork for more detailed study. The issues addressed in this course book are of enormous importance—perhaps the most monumental that any lawyer ever confronts. In times of national emergency, such as a large-scale terrorist attack, how should one think about the relative allocation of the powers of Congress and the president? What are the effects on U.S. law and policy when the United States adheres to a treaty that, for example, prohibits torture? Should rules developed through the practice of nations worldwide be used as a part of internal U.S. law, including for interpretation of the U.S. Constitution? When can the president introduce U.S. armed forces into hostilities without congressional authorization? What role can the courts play in adjudicating such disputes?

Such questions have been hotly debated, of course, since the earliest days of the Republic, and many contemporary arguments are but replays of previous disputes. Consequently materials once written on parchment retain an enduring relevance. Yet, as the nation moves forward in this twenty-first century, old controversies do take on new forms. Unprecedented threats are posed not only to the nation, but also to the values at the heart of our legal structure. These cases and materials provide students an opportunity to confront these difficult choices of law, policy, and social values in both an historical and contemporary context.

Please note that cases have been edited to omit most citations and footnotes. For materials relating to this casebook, visit our website at: http://www.foreignrelationslaw.com. We welcome the comments of instructors and students who use this book. Subsequent editions will benefit greatly from your advice and counsel.

SEAN D. MURPHY
EDWARD T. SWAINE
INGRID WUERTH

September 2017

ACKNOWLEDGMENTS

The authors wish to acknowledge the invaluable help of the following research assistants: Marta Bylica, Jeremiah Cioffi, Alden DiIanni-Morton, Clayton Mark, and Elle Ross. The authors' students at George Washington University and Vanderbilt University made helpful comments on ways of improving the prior editions, as did instructors at other colleges and universities who taught from those editions. Finally, the authors acknowledge, with appreciation, the permission granted to reprint copyrighted material contained herein.

ACKNOWLEDGMENTS

[illegible]

SUMMARY OF CONTENTS

TABLE OF CONTENTS

TABLE OF CASES

The principal cases are in bold type.

U.S. FOREIGN RELATIONS LAW

CASES, MATERIALS, AND PRACTICE EXERCISES

Fifth Edition

CHAPTER 1

FOREIGN RELATIONS LAW: NATURE AND CONSTITUTIONAL STRUCTURE

■ ■ ■

1. ORIGINS AND NATURE OF U.S. FOREIGN RELATIONS LAW

Constitutional history plays an important role in modern U.S. foreign relations law for several reasons. The Constitution's text relating to foreign relations uses some language drawn from 18th Century international law and practice; the study of historical sources thus helps us understand the meaning of those terms at the time the Constitution was enacted. Second, to understand the types of powers accorded to the federal government under the U.S. Constitution, it is useful to know what governmental powers existed under the Articles of Confederation and why those powers were regarded as deficient. After all, the U.S. Constitution was written against the backdrop of the Articles of Confederation. The framers were trying to fix certain problems of the previous government. By understanding these problems, we can better understand what the framers were trying to accomplish—and what they were trying to avoid—in creating certain federal foreign affairs powers.

Related to the foregoing is a third reason that constitutional history plays an especially prominent role in foreign relations law: the text of the Constitution—famed for its brevity—includes an impressive (if sometimes baffling) list of foreign relations-related powers. Constitutional text and the historical meaning of that text is thus potentially more important to modern foreign relations law than it is to some other areas of constitutional interpretation. Fourth, although constitutional theorists employ different interpretive approaches to the Constitution, all accept that constitutional text and its meaning when the Constitution was adopted is at least relevant to contemporary constitutional interpretation, even if not dispositive. Finally, the Supreme Court has relied on constitutional history in many of its important foreign relations cases, including *Curtiss-Wright* and *Zivotofsky*.

As you read the materials below, consider the following. The ability to represent the American colonies in matters of foreign relations resided with the British government up until 1776. Where did that foreign relations power reside after the U.S. Declaration of Independence? Where did it reside after the formation of the new government under the U.S. Constitution in 1789? To the extent that concern about foreign affairs powers was one impetus to shift from the Articles of Confederation to the U.S. Constitution, what exactly were the problems under the Articles of Confederation? Was it a concern with the division of powers within the central government or the division of powers between the central government and the states?

ANDREW C. MCLAUGHLIN, A CONSTITUTIONAL HISTORY OF THE UNITED STATES

125–146 (1935).

. . . The powers granted to Congress [under the Articles of Confederation, which were ratified in 1781,] bear a general resemblance to those exercised by the Crown and Parliament in the old colonial system in which the colonies had grown to maturity; and if one compares the Articles with the Constitution adopted at Philadelphia in 1787, he will find a considerable similarity in the scheme of distribution. Time was to show the defects of the system; but the actual merits of the system agreed upon are noteworthy. No power to lay taxes was bestowed on Congress, and no power to regulate commerce, the two things about which there had been so much dispute in the preceding decade. These omissions were largely instrumental in bringing into existence the Constitutional Convention of 1787.

Without the consent of Congress, the states were expressly forbidden to send an embassy to a foreign state, receive an embassy, enter into any agreement with a foreign power, form any treaty of combination among themselves, maintain ships of war or troops in time of peace—though a militia must be provided and sufficiently armed—, or engage in war unless actually invaded or in immediate danger of Indian attack. All charges of war and other expenses incurred for the common defense and general welfare were to be defrayed out of a common treasury supplied by the several states. To Congress was given, among other powers, the general powers of determining on war and peace, carrying on foreign affairs, though with some restrictions, regulating the alloy and value of coin, fixing the standard of weights and measures, regulating the trade and managing all the affairs with the Indians "not members of any of the States", establishing and regulating post offices from one state to another, appointing important army officers and all naval officers, borrowing money, building and equipping a navy, and making requisitions upon the states for troops. . . .

While the Articles granted to Congress considerable authority, its powers were qualified, in some respects carefully, for the protection of the states' rights. Although Congress was given power to enter into treaties, the states were not totally forbidden to lay imposts, but they were forbidden to levy such duties as might interfere with "stipulations in treaties entered into by the United States . . . in pursuance of any treaties already proposed by Congress to the courts of France and Spain." Congress could make no treaty of commerce whereby the states should be restrained from imposing such imposts on foreigners as their own people were subjected to; and apparently the states could freely prohibit the exportation or importation of any kind of goods. The failure to grant Congress complete power to regulate commerce rendered it difficult or impossible to make a commercial treaty with a foreign nation and to have assurance that the states would comply with its provisions. The years that followed disclosed the fact that the want of authority to make treaties which would bind the states was one of the cardinal defects of the system. . . .

The industrial and commercial conditions after the [revolutionary] war were in considerable confusion. Readjustments were necessary, especially for the resuscitation of the New England shipping industry. Some improvement came fairly quickly, and there is evidence that by 1786 the clouds of depression were beginning to lift. But it was hard to make much headway, especially as Britain was not ready to treat her former colonies as if they deserved particular favors or consideration; they had made their own beds, now let them lie there—a condition of retirement not suited to the restless spirit of the New England skippers whose ships were soon plowing the seas, even on to the Orient as well as to the ports of continental Europe. Commercial treaties were desirable, and some steps were taken in that direction; but it was hard to do anything effectively as long as the individual states could not be relied on to fulfill their obligations. Foreign nations naturally queried whether America was one or many, or, perhaps, one to-day and thirteen to-morrow.

The [1783 U.S.-Great Britain] treaty of peace was not carried out. Britain still held the western posts from Lake Champlain to Mackinaw and thus retained control of the northern fur trade and influence over the Indians. Spain holding the mouth of the Mississippi was unwilling to allow free navigation through her territory. Trouble was brewing because of American treatment of loyalists and because the stipulation in the treaty, that there should be no unlawful impediment to the collection of debts due British creditors, received no particular attention. John Jay declared in 1786 that the treaty had been constantly violated by one state or another from the time of its signing and ratification. The Barbary powers, eager to take advantage of a helpless country, to seize American seamen, and to hold them for ransom, entered upon the game with lusty vigor. A nation which was not yet a nation in terms of law and political authority could do nothing to resist scorn and humiliation. . . .

But what was the very center of the difficulty? What was the chief problem of the time? The trouble and confusion were manifestly caused by the failure of the states to abide by their obligations. The problem was to find a method, if union was to subsist at all, for overcoming the difficulty, to find therefore some arrangement, some scheme or plan of organization wherein there would be reasonable assurance that the states would fulfill their obligations and play their part under established articles of union and not make mockery of union by willful disregard or negligent delay. That was the *chief problem* of the day. . . .

THE FEDERALIST PAPERS NO. 41 (MADISON)

255–59 (Clinton Rossiter ed., 1961).

The Constitution proposed by the convention may be considered under two general points of view. The first relates to the sum or quantity of power which it vests in the government, including the restraints imposed on the States. The second, to the particular structure of the government and the distribution of this power among its several branches.

Under the first view of the subject, two important questions arise: 1. Whether any part of the powers transferred to the general government be unnecessary or improper? 2. Whether the entire mass of them be dangerous to the portion of jurisdiction left in the several States? . . .

It cannot have escaped those who have attended with candor to the arguments employed against the extensive powers of the government that the authors of them have very little considered how far these powers were necessary means of attaining a necessary end. They have chosen rather to dwell on the inconveniences which must be unavoidably blended with all political advantages; and on the possible abuses which must be incident to every power or trust of which a beneficial use can be made. . . .

That we may form a correct judgment on this subject, it will be proper to review the several powers conferred on the government of the Union; and that this may be the more conveniently done they may be reduced into different classes as they relate to the following different objects: 1. Security against foreign danger; 2. Regulation of the intercourse with foreign nations; 3. Maintenance of harmony and proper intercourse among the States; 4. Certain miscellaneous objects of general utility; 5. Restraint of the States from certain injurious acts; 6. Provisions for giving due efficacy to all these powers. . . .

Security against foreign danger is one of the primitive objects of civil society. It is an avowed and essential object of the American Union. The powers requisite for attaining it must be effectually confided to the federal councils. . . .

The Union itself, which it cements and secures, destroys every pretext for a military establishment which could be dangerous. America united, with a handful of troops, or without a single soldier, exhibits a more forbidding posture to foreign ambition than America disunited, with a hundred thousand veterans ready for combat. . . . Instead of deriving from our situation the precious advantage which Great Britain has derived from hers, the face of America [in the absence of union] will be but a copy of that of the continent of Europe. It will present liberty everywhere crushed between standing armies and perpetual taxes. The fortunes of disunited America will be even more disastrous than those of Europe. The sources of evil in the latter are confined to her own limits. No superior powers of another quarter of the globe intrigue among her rival nations, inflame their mutual animosities, and render them the instruments of foreign ambition, jealousy, and revenge. In America the miseries springing from her internal jealousies, contentions, and wars would form a part only of her lot. A plentiful addition of evils would have their source in that relation in which Europe stands to this quarter of the earth, and which no other quarter of the earth bears to Europe.

THE FEDERALIST PAPERS NO. 42 (MADISON)

264–65 (Clinton Rossiter ed., 1961).

The *second* class of powers lodged in the general government consist of those which regulate the intercourse with foreign nations, to wit: to make treaties; to send and receive ambassadors, other public ministers, and consuls;[1] to define and punish piracies and felonies committed on the high seas, and offenses against the law of nations; to regulate foreign commerce. . . .[2]

This class of powers forms an obvious and essential branch of federal administration. If we are to be one nation in any respect, it clearly ought to be in respect to other nations.

The powers to make treaties and to send and receive ambassadors speak their own propriety. Both of them are comprised in the Articles of Confederation, with this difference only, that the former is disembarrassed by the plan of the convention, of an exception under which treaties might be substantially frustrated by regulations of the States; and that a power of appointing and receiving "other public ministers and consuls" is expressly and very properly added to the former provision concerning ambassadors. . . .

The power to define and punish piracies and felonies committed on the high seas and offenses against the law of nations belongs with equal propriety to the general government, and is a still greater improvement on the Articles of Confederation. These articles contain no provision for the case of offenses against the law of nations; and consequently leave it in the

1 [Authors' Note: *See* U.S. CONST. art. II, § 2, cl. 2.]

2 [Authors' Note: *See* U.S. CONST. art. I, § 8.]

power of any indiscreet member to embroil the Confederacy with foreign nations. . . .

THE FEDERALIST PAPERS NO. 44 (MADISON)

280–86 (Clinton Rossiter ed., 1961).

A *fifth* class of provisions in favor of the federal authority consists of the following restrictions on the authority of the several States.

1. "No State shall enter into any treaty, alliance, or confederation; [or] grant letters of marque and reprisal. . . ."[1]

The prohibition against treaties, alliances, and confederations makes a part of the existing [Articles of Confederation]; and for reasons which need no explanation, is copied into the new Constitution. The prohibition of letters of marque is another part of the old system, but is somewhat extended in the new. According to the former, letters of marque could be granted by the States after a declaration of war; according to the latter, these licenses must be obtained, as well during war as previous to its declaration, from the government of the United States. This alteration is fully justified by the advantage of uniformity in all points which relate to foreign powers; and of immediate responsibility to the nation in all those for whose conduct the nation itself is to be responsible. . . .

2. "No state shall, without the consent of Congress, lay any imposts or duties on imports or exports, except what may be absolutely necessary for executing its inspection laws, and the net produce of all duties and imposts laid by any State on imports or exports shall be for the use of the treasury of the United States; and all such laws shall be subject to the revision and control of the Congress. No State shall, without the consent of Congress, lay any duty on tonnage, keep troops or ships of war in time of peace, enter into any agreement or compact with another State, or with a foreign power, or engage in war unless actually invaded, or in such imminent danger as will not admit of delay."[2]

The restraint on the power of the States over imports and exports is enforced by all the arguments which prove the necessity of submitting the regulation of trade to the federal councils. It is needless, therefore, to remark further on this head, than that the manner in which the restraint is qualified seems well calculated at once to secure to the States a reasonable discretion in providing for the conveniency of their imports and exports, and to the United States a reasonable check against the abuse of this discretion. The remaining particulars of this clause fall within reasonings which are either so obvious, or have been so fully developed, that they may be passed over without remark.

---

1 [Authors' Note: U.S. CONST. art. I, § 10, cl. 1.]

2 [Authors' Note: U.S. CONST. art. I, § 10, cl. 2 & 3.]

The *sixth* and last class consists of the several powers and provisions by which efficacy is given to all the rest.

1. Of these the first is the "power to make all laws which shall be necessary and proper for carrying into execution the foregoing powers, and all other powers vested by this Constitution in the government of the United States, or in any department or officer thereof."[3]

Few parts of the Constitution have been assailed with more intemperance than this; yet on a fair investigation of it, as has been elsewhere shown, no part can appear more completely invulnerable. Without the *substance* of this power, the whole Constitution would be a dead letter. . . .

2. "This Constitution and the laws of the United States which shall be made in pursuance thereof, and all treaties made, or which shall be made, under the authority of the United States, shall be the supreme law of the land, and the judges in every State shall be bound thereby, anything in the constitution or laws of any State to the contrary notwithstanding."[4]

The indiscreet zeal of the adversaries to the Constitution has betrayed them into an attack on this part of it also, without which it would have been evidently and radically defective. To be fully sensible of this, we need only to suppose for a moment that the supremacy of the State constitutions had been left complete by a saving clause in their favor.

CHAE CHAN PING V. UNITED STATES [THE CHINESE EXCLUSION CASE]

130 U.S. 581 (1889).

[Following the anti-Chinese riots of 1885–86 in San Francisco, the United States and China took measures to limit emigration from China to America. Under the Bayard-Zhang Treaty (1888), China agreed to suspend immigration for twenty years. In return, the American government pledged to protect Chinese assets in the United States. Massive protests erupted in China following the signing of the Bayard-Zhang Treaty, and the agreement was never formally ratified by the Chinese government. Congress proceeded legislatively, enacting the Scott Act in 1888, which permanently banned the immigration or return of Chinese to the United States. In 1889, the Supreme Court considered the legality of the Scott Act.]

MR. JUSTICE FIELD delivered the opinion of the Court. . . .

There being nothing in the treaties between China and the United States to impair the validity of the act of Congress of October 1, 1888, was it on any other ground beyond the competency of Congress to pass it? If so,

---

[3] [Authors' Note: U.S. CONST. art. I, § 8, cl. 18.]

[4] [Authors' Note: *See* U.S. CONST. art. VI, cl. 2.]

it must be because it was not within the power of Congress to prohibit Chinese laborers who had at the time departed from the United States, or should subsequently depart, from returning to the United States. Those laborers are not citizens of the United States; they are aliens. That the government of the United States, through the action of the legislative department, can exclude aliens from its territory is a proposition which we do not think open to controversy. Jurisdiction over its own territory to that extent is an incident of every independent nation. It is a part of its independence. If it could not exclude aliens it would be to that extent subject to the control of another power. . . .

While under our Constitution and form of government the great mass of local matters is controlled by local authorities, the United States, in their relation to foreign countries and their subjects or citizens are one nation, invested with powers which belong to independent nations, the exercise of which can be invoked for the maintenance of its absolute independence and security throughout its entire territory. The powers to declare war, make treaties, suppress insurrection, repel invasion, regulate foreign commerce, secure republican governments to the States, and admit subjects of other nations to citizenship, are all sovereign powers, restricted in their exercise only by the Constitution itself and considerations of public policy and justice which control, more or less, the conduct of all civilized nations. . . .

To preserve its independence, and give security against foreign aggression and encroachment, is the highest duty of every nation, and to attain these ends nearly all other considerations are to be subordinated. It matters not in what form such aggression and encroachment come, whether from the foreign nation acting in its national character, or from vast hordes of its people crowding in upon us. The government, possessing the powers which are to be exercised for protection and security, is clothed with authority to determine the occasion on which the powers shall be called forth; and its determinations, so far as the subjects affected are concerned, are necessarily conclusive upon all its departments and officers. If, therefore, the government of the United States, through its legislative department, considers the presence of foreigners of a different race in this country, who will not assimilate with us, to be dangerous to its peace and security, their exclusion is not to be stayed because at the time there are no actual hostilities with the nation of which the foreigners are subjects. The existence of war would render the necessity of the proceeding only more obvious and pressing. The same necessity, in a less pressing degree, may arise when war does not exist, and the same authority which adjudges the necessity in one case must also determine it in the other. In both cases its determination is conclusive upon the judiciary. If the government of the country of which the foreigners excluded are subjects is dissatisfied with this action, it can make complaint to the executive head of our government, or resort to any other measure which, in its judgment, its interests or dignity may demand; and there lies its only remedy.

UNITED STATES V. CURTISS-WRIGHT EXPORT CORP.

299 U.S. 304 (1936).

[From 1932 to 1935, Bolivia and Paraguay fought a war for control of a large part of the Chaco region of South America, which was thought to contain vast oil resources. In 1934, Congress enacted and the president signed into law a joint resolution providing that, if the president made certain findings and issued a proclamation to the effect that a ban on arms sales to Bolivia and Paraguay would serve the cause of regional peace, then such arms sales would be illegal. Thereafter, the president made the findings and issued the proclamation. Upon being charged in 1936 with violating the law by selling arms to Bolivia, defendant Curtiss-Wright Corporation challenged the law's constitutionality inter alia on a theory that it invalidly delegated legislative power to the executive.]

MR. JUSTICE SUTHERLAND delivered the opinion of the Court. . . .

Whether, if the Joint Resolution had related solely to internal affairs it would be open to the challenge that it constituted an unlawful delegation of legislative power to the Executive, we find it unnecessary to determine. The whole aim of the resolution is to affect a situation entirely external to the United States, and falling within the category of foreign affairs. The determination which we are called to make, therefore, is whether the Joint Resolution, as applied to that situation, is vulnerable to attack under the rule that forbids a delegation of the law-making power. In other words, assuming (but not deciding) that the challenged delegation, if it were confined to internal affairs, would be invalid, may it nevertheless be sustained on the ground that its exclusive aim is to afford a remedy for a hurtful condition within foreign territory?

It will contribute to the elucidation of the question if we first consider the differences between the powers of the federal government in respect of foreign or external affairs and those in respect of domestic or internal affairs. That there are differences between them, and that these differences are fundamental, may not be doubted.

The two classes of powers are different, both in respect of their origin and their nature. The broad statement that the federal government can exercise no powers except those specifically enumerated in the Constitution, and such implied powers as are necessary and proper to carry into effect the enumerated powers, is categorically true only in respect of our internal affairs. In that field, the primary purpose of the Constitution was to carve from the general mass of legislative powers *then possessed by the states* such portions as it was thought desirable to vest in the federal government, leaving those not included in the enumeration still in the states. *Carter v. Carter Coal Co.*, 298 U.S. 238, 294. That this doctrine applies only to powers which the states had, is self evident. And since the states severally never possessed international powers, such powers could not have been carved from the mass of state powers but obviously were transmitted to the United States from some other source. During the colonial period, those powers were possessed exclusively by and were entirely under the control of the Crown. By the Declaration of Independence, "the Representatives of the United States of America" declared the United [not the several] Colonies to be free and independent states, and as such to have "full Power to levy War, conclude Peace, contract Alliances, establish Commerce and to do all other Acts and Things which Independent States may of right do."

As a result of the separation from Great Britain by the colonies acting as a unit, the powers of external sovereignty passed from the Crown not to the colonies severally, but to the colonies in their collective and corporate capacity as the United States of America. Even before the Declaration, the colonies were a unit in foreign affairs, acting through a common agency—namely, the Continental Congress, composed of delegates from the thirteen colonies. That agency exercised the powers of war and peace, raised an army, created a navy, and finally adopted the Declaration of Independence. Rulers come and go; governments end and forms of government change; but sovereignty survives. A political society cannot endure without a supreme will somewhere. Sovereignty is never held in suspense. When, therefore, the external sovereignty of Great Britain in respect of the colonies ceased, it immediately passed to the Union. *See Penhallow v. Doane*, 3 Dall. 54, 80–81. That fact was given practical application almost at once. The treaty of peace, made on September 23, 1783, was concluded between his Brittanic Majesty and the "United States of America."

The Union existed before the Constitution, which was ordained and established among other things to form "a more perfect Union." Prior to that event, it is clear that the Union, declared by the Articles of Confederation to be "perpetual," was the sole possessor of external sovereignty and in the Union it remained without change save in so far as the Constitution in express terms qualified its exercise. The Framers' Convention was called and exerted its powers upon the irrefutable postulate that though the states were several their people in respect of foreign affairs were one. Compare *The Chinese Exclusion Case*, 130 U.S. 581, 604, 606. In that convention, the entire absence of state power to deal with those affairs was thus forcefully stated by Rufus King:

> "The states were not 'sovereigns' in the sense contended for by some. They did not possess the peculiar features of sovereignty,—they could not make war, nor peace, nor alliances, nor treaties. Considering them as political beings, they were dumb, for they could not speak to any foreign sovereign whatever.

They were deaf, for they could not hear any propositions from such sovereign. They had not even the organs or faculties of defence or offence, for they could not of themselves raise troops, or equip vessels, for war." 5 Elliot's Debates 212.

It results that the investment of the federal government with the powers of external sovereignty did not depend upon the affirmative grants of the Constitution. The powers to declare and wage war, to conclude peace, to make treaties, to maintain diplomatic relations with other sovereignties, if they had never been mentioned in the Constitution, would have vested in the federal government as necessary concomitants of nationality. Neither the Constitution nor the laws passed in pursuance of it have any force in foreign territory unless in respect of our own citizens; and operations of the nation in such territory must be governed by treaties, international understandings and compacts, and the principles of international law. As a member of the family of nations, the right and power of the United States in that field are equal to the right and power of the other members of the international family. Otherwise, the United States is not completely sovereign. The power to acquire territory by discovery and occupation, the power to expel undesirable aliens, the power to make such international agreements as do not constitute treaties in the constitutional sense, none of which is expressly affirmed by the Constitution, nevertheless exist as inherently inseparable from the conception of nationality. This the court recognized, and in each of the cases cited found the warrant for its conclusions not in the provisions of the Constitution, but in the law of nations. . . .

Not only, as we have shown, is the federal power over external affairs in origin and essential character different from that over internal affairs, but participation in the exercise of the power is significantly limited. In this vast external realm, with its important, complicated, delicate and manifold problems, the President alone has the power to speak or listen as a representative of the nation. He *makes* treaties with the advice and consent of the Senate; but he alone negotiates. Into the field of negotiation the Senate cannot intrude; and Congress itself is powerless to invade it. As Marshall said in his great argument of March 7, 1800, in the House of Representatives, "The President is the sole organ of the nation in its external relations, and its sole representative with foreign nations." Annals, 6th Cong., col. 613. The Senate Committee on Foreign Relations at a very early day in our history (February 15, 1816), reported to the Senate, among other things, as follows:

"The President is the constitutional representative of the United States with regard to foreign nations. He manages our concerns with foreign nations and must necessarily be most competent to determine when, how, and upon what subjects negotiation may be urged with the greatest prospect of success.

> For his conduct he is responsible to the Constitution. The committee considers this responsibility the surest pledge for the faithful discharge of his duty. They think the interference of the Senate in the direction of foreign negotiations calculated to diminish that responsibility and thereby to impair the best security for the national safety. The nature of transactions with foreign nations, moreover, requires caution and unity of design, and their success frequently depends on secrecy and dispatch." U.S. Senate, Reports, Committee on Foreign Relations, vol. 8, p. 24.

It is important to bear in mind that we are here dealing not alone with an authority vested in the President by an exertion of legislative power, but with such an authority plus the very delicate, plenary and exclusive power of the President as the sole organ of the federal government in the field of international relations—a power which does not require as a basis for its exercise an act of Congress, but which, of course, like every other governmental power, must be exercised in subordination to the applicable provisions of the Constitution. It is quite apparent that if, in the maintenance of our international relations, embarrassment—perhaps serious embarrassment—is to be avoided and success for our aims achieved, congressional legislation which is to be made effective through negotiation and inquiry within the international field must often accord to the President a degree of discretion and freedom from statutory restriction which would not be admissible were domestic affairs alone involved. Moreover, he, not Congress, has the better opportunity of knowing the conditions which prevail in foreign countries, and especially is this true in time of war. He has his confidential sources of information. He has his agents in the form of diplomatic, consular and other officials. Secrecy in respect of information gathered by them may be highly necessary, and the premature disclosure of it productive of harmful results. Indeed, so clearly is this true that the first President refused to accede to a request to lay before the House of Representatives the instructions, correspondence and documents relating to the negotiation of the Jay Treaty—a refusal the wisdom of which was recognized by the House itself and has never since been doubted. In his reply to the request, President Washington said:

> "The nature of foreign negotiations requires caution, and their success must often depend on secrecy; and even when brought to a conclusion a full disclosure of all the measures, demands, or eventual concessions which may have been proposed or contemplated would be extremely impolitic; for this might have a pernicious influence on future negotiations, or produce immediate inconveniences, perhaps danger and mischief, in relation to other powers. The necessity of such caution and secrecy was one cogent reason for vesting the power of making treaties in

the President, with the advice and consent of the Senate, the principle on which that body was formed confining it to a small number of members. To admit, then, a right in the House of Representatives to demand and to have as a matter of course all the papers respecting a negotiation with a foreign power would be to establish a dangerous precedent." 1 Messages and Papers of the Presidents, p. 144.

The marked difference between foreign affairs and domestic affairs in this respect is recognized by both houses of Congress in the very form of their requisitions for information from the executive departments. In the case of every department except the Department of State, the resolution *directs* the official to furnish the information. In the case of the State Department, dealing with foreign affairs, the President is *requested* to furnish the information "if not incompatible with the public interest." A statement that to furnish the information is not compatible with the public interest rarely, if ever, is questioned.

When the President is to be authorized by legislation to act in respect of a matter intended to affect a situation in foreign territory, the legislator properly bears in mind the important consideration that the form of the President's action—or, indeed, whether he shall act at all—may well depend, among other things, upon the nature of the confidential information which he has or may thereafter receive, or upon the effect which his action may have upon our foreign relations. This consideration, in connection with what we have already said on the subject, discloses the unwisdom of requiring Congress in this field of governmental power to lay down narrowly definite standards by which the President is to be governed. As this court said in *Mackenzie v. Hare*, 239 U.S. 299, 311, "As a government, the United States is invested with all the attributes of sovereignty. As it has the character of nationality it has the powers of nationality, especially those which concern its relations and intercourse with other countries. *We should hesitate long before limiting or embarrassing such powers*." (Italics supplied.)

In the light of the foregoing observations, it is evident that this court should not be in haste to apply a general rule which will have the effect of condemning legislation like that under review as constituting an unlawful delegation of legislative power. The principles which justify such legislation find overwhelming support in the unbroken legislative practice which has prevailed almost from the inception of the national government to the present day. . . .

The uniform, long-continued and undisputed legislative practice just disclosed rests upon an admissible view of the Constitution which, even if the practice found far less support in principle than we think it does, we should not feel at liberty at this late day to disturb.

We deem it unnecessary to consider, *seriatim*, the several clauses which are said to evidence the unconstitutionality of the Joint Resolution as involving an unlawful delegation of legislative power. It is enough to summarize by saying that, both upon principle and in accordance with precedent, we conclude there is sufficient warrant for the broad discretion vested in the President to determine whether the enforcement of the statute will have a beneficial effect upon the reestablishment of peace in the affected countries; whether he shall make proclamation to bring the resolution into operation; whether and when the resolution shall cease to operate and to make proclamation accordingly; and to prescribe limitations and exceptions to which the enforcement of the resolution shall be subject. . . .

Reversed.

MR. JUSTICE MCREYNOLDS does not agree. He is of opinion that the court below reached the right conclusion and its judgment ought to be affirmed.

MR. JUSTICE STONE took no part in the consideration or decision of this case.

NOTES

1. *Content of U.S. Foreign Relations Powers.* At the end of this casebook, the U.S. Constitution is appended. (*See* Appendix 1). Look through the Constitution and identify what powers relating to foreign affairs have been expressly allocated to the federal government. In doing so, you may wish to divide them up based on whether they were allocated to the legislative, executive, or judicial branches. To which branch are the most powers accorded? To which the least? Note that in some instances specific foreign affairs powers (such as the power to make treaties) were expressly denied to the several states. Are any significant foreign affairs powers left unaddressed? Do any appear to have been allocated to the several states? What arguments were made in the Federalist Papers in favor of the centralization of foreign affairs powers in the federal government? The division of power between the federal government and the states in the area of foreign affairs remains an important issue today. For cases and commentary, see Chapter 6.

2. *Nature of U.S. Foreign Relations Powers.* Do you think the foreign relations powers of the United States emanate solely from the U.S. Constitution or are they also drawn from other sources? Do you see in the *Chinese Exclusion Case* a reliance upon sovereignty as a source of extra-constitutional congressional authority? Or is sovereignty a source of authority that comes from the Constitution, albeit one that is not specified in the text? Does the sovereignty-based reasoning in *Curtiss-Wright* and the *Chinese Exclusion Case* mean that the powers of the federal government change based on developments in international or comparative law?

In *Curtiss-Wright*, the Court explicitly reasoned that the federal government's power over foreign affairs has an extra-constitutional source. Does either the *Chinese Exclusion Case* or *Curtiss-Wright* suggest that the foreign relations power trumps protections that might otherwise exist for individuals, or must the foreign relations power be read consonant with individual rights and liberties, as they existed at the founding and as they have evolved over time? *See* Louis Henkin, *Essays Commemorating the One Hundredth Anniversary of the Harvard Law Review: The Constitution and United States Sovereignty: A Century of* Chinese Exclusion *and Its Progeny*, 100 HARV. L. REV. 853, 862–63 (1987); David A. Martin, *Why Immigration's Plenary Power Doctrine Endures*, 68 OK. L. REV. 29 (2015).

3. *Methodology*. How important is constitutional history to contemporary constitutional interpretation? One family of theories called originalism (or, more broadly, formalism), posits that the original meaning of the Constitution's text is controlling unless that meaning is ambiguous or otherwise does not provide a clear answer. Another family of theories, functionalism, generally holds that the contemporary practice of the political branches should be relevant to constitutional interpretation in separation of powers cases and that constitutional policy or goals are relevant to interpretation generally. Professor Harlan Cohen, quoting from William Eskridge, has described the distinction in this way:

> . . . [T]he tension between these two visions, one formalist and the other functionalist, can take a number of forms in judicial opinions. One manifestation is the choice between rules and standards. 'Formalism might be associated with bright-line rules that seek to place determinate, readily enforceable limits on public actors. Functionalism, at least as an antipode, might be associated with standards or balancing tests that seek to provide public actors with greater flexibility.' A different manifestation is in the forms of reasoning we might use to answer hard questions. 'Formalism might be understood as deduction from authoritative constitutional text, structure, original intent, or all three working together. Functionalism might be understood as induction from constitutional policy and practice, with practice typically being examined over time.' Finally, a third manifestation might be with regard to goals. 'Formalism might be understood as giving priority to rule of law values such as transparency, predictability, and continuity in law. Functionalism, in turn, might be understood as emphasizing pragmatic values like adaptability, efficacy, and justice in law.' Formalism is essentially backward-looking, tethering interpretations to existing doctrines, prior precedents, and original text. Functionalism looks to the present and future, asking what rule will lead to the best results (understood, of course, within the general constitutional design).

Harlan Grant Cohen, *Formalism and Distrust: Foreign Affairs Law in the Roberts Court*, 83 GEO. WASH. L. REV. 380, 392 (2015). Over the past century, the Supreme Court's reasoning in separation of powers and foreign relations cases has oscillated between various kinds of formalism and functionalism. The Court has generally failed to "articulate a consistent theoretical framework for determining the significance" of various interpretative tools such as constitutional text, structure, original intent or meaning, subsequent practice, and other potential sources of constitutional meaning. *See Michael J. Glennon, Constitutional Diplomacy* 35–36 (1990).

4. *Foreign Affairs Exceptionalism.* Are foreign affairs issues and cases "exceptional," meaning that they involve different tools of constitutional interpretation, different constraints on judicial decision-making, or especially compelling arguments in favor of federal and presidential power? The *Curtiss-Wright* opinion reasons that foreign affairs are exceptional for both historical and functional reasons. Since the *Curtiss-Wright* decision, the Court has sometimes suggested that foreign relations cases are exceptional and at other times has reasoned that they should be treated like other cases. *See* Ganesh Sitaraman & Ingrid Wuerth, *The Normalization of Foreign Relations Law*, 128 HARV. L. REV. 1897 (2015). How compelling are Justice Southerland's functional reasons in favor of foreign relations exceptionalism?

5. *Hindsight.* Is Justice Sutherland's view of history correct? For the view that sovereignty resided in the states for at least some period of time between 1776 and 1789, see Akhil Reed Amar, *America's Constitution: A Biography* (2005) (arguing, based in part on comparisons to Dutch and Swiss confederacies from the eighteenth century, that the each state was sovereign notwithstanding their agreement to "what the Articles [of Confederation] called a 'perpetual' 'union' "); Merrill Jensen, *The Articles of Confederation* 176 (1970) ("according to the constitution which united the thirteen states from 1781 to 1789, the several states were *de facto* and *de jure* sovereign"); Claude H. Van Tyne, *Sovereignty in the American Revolution: An Historical Study*, 12 AM. HIST. REV. 529 (1907) (arguing that both psychologically and legally the states were regarded as sovereign throughout the period).

6. *International Law.* What role should international law play in interpreting the Constitution's allocation of foreign affairs authority? In analyzing *Curtiss-Wright*, Professor Sarah Cleveland notes, "the Court has also relied on inherent sovereign powers derived from international law to establish national quasi-constitutional or extra-constitutional authority in a variety of areas, including immigration and the governance of Native American tribes and territorial inhabitants, as well as the power of eminent domain. . . . In each of these contexts, the Court has looked to international law, not to inform constitutional text, but to supplant it." Sarah H. Cleveland, *Our International Constitution*, 31 YALE J. INT'L L. 1, 39 (2006).

7. *Sole Organ.* Does the president "alone ha[ve] the power to speak or listen as a representative of the nation," as *Curtiss-Wright* reasons? What does the opinion cite in support of this claim? The phrase is attributed to John Marshall's speech in 1800 before the House of Representatives. But at issue there was only President Adams' authority to turn over to Britain an individual

charged with murder. Marshall took to the floor of the House to argue against efforts to impeach Adams. Louis Fisher, *Congressional Abdication on War and Spending* 31 (2000). Does the "sole organ" argument mean that the president has exclusive control over the conduct of diplomacy? The Office of Legal Counsel (OLC) has reasoned that an appropriations bill that purported to prohibit funds from being used to pay the expenses of U.S. delegations to certain international meetings was unconstitutional. *See* Constitutionality of Section 7054 of the Fiscal Year 2009 Foreign Appropriations Act (June 1, 2009), available at https://www.justice.gov/sites/default/files/olc/opinions/2009/06/31/section7054.pdf, [http://perma.cc/RD6W-6277]. The OLC's Memorandum discusses many statutes in which Congress has attempted to control the conduct of diplomacy. Does this practice suggest that the issue is unsettled? (*See generally* Chapter 5).

8. *Delegation Theory.* In *Curtiss-Wright,* Congress and the president were marching in lockstep. Does the case present a significant constitutional issue? Is it surprising that the Supreme Court should take the case? Part of the explanation lies in cases decided during the year before *Curtiss-Wright* was handed down. In these cases, the Supreme Court struck down key pieces of New Deal legislation on the theory that the statutes unconstitutionally delegated legislative power to the Executive. *See Panama Refining Co. v. Ryan*, 293 U.S. 388, 421 (1935); *A.L.A. Schechter Poultry Corp. v. United States*, 295 U.S. 495 (1935). Arguably, some clarification was required concerning the extent to which the "non-delegation doctrine" applied in the realm of foreign affairs.

9. *An Executive Stalwart.* The *Curtiss-Wright* case is often cited by the executive branch to support wide-ranging presidential powers in the field of foreign affairs, even though in that case Congress fully supported the executive action. Was it necessary for the Court to discuss the scope of the president's "inherent" powers? Is the discussion of sovereignty and its effect on executive power holding or dictum? The case gives important functional reasons in favor of executive power in foreign relations cases. Are they convincing? Does the answer change depending upon the military and economic strength of the nation?

2. SEPARATION OF POWERS

The Constitution's division of foreign relations powers between the president and Congress has framed the conduct of U.S. foreign policy since the late eighteenth century. From the 1790s through today, Congress has enacted legislation related to many foreign policy issues including the capture of enemy vessels, trade and commerce, the assets and immunity of foreign nations, sanctions, international human rights, the treatment of prisoners, foreign aid, and other topics. Many of these statutes delegate power to the president. Most of them rarely give rise to litigation. In practice, many foreign relations powers are shared or concurrent. Studying court cases that address the separation of powers between the president and Congress accordingly presents a somewhat distorted view of that relationship which can often function without difficulty. Nevertheless, there are seminal separation of powers cases that have set limits on presidential and congressional action. This Section addresses four especially significant ones. As you read them, keep in mind that they also raise, whether implicitly or explicitly, the question of how and under what circumstances courts should demarcate the boundaries between executive and legislative power.

LITTLE V. BARREME

6 U.S. (2 Cranch) 170 (1804).

[Relations between the United States and France, two allies during the American Revolutionary War, deteriorated rapidly following ratification of the Jay Treaty between America and Britain in 1795. Within just a few years, French privateers were raiding U.S. vessels, including in the Chesapeake Bay. Consequently, during 1798–1800, the United States fought an undeclared naval war with France.

Little v. Barreme was one of three Supreme Court cases to address this so-called "quasi-war" with France. In this case, U.S. frigates in 1799 captured a Danish vessel (the *Flying Fish*) near the island of Hispaniola (a large island that is now home to the countries of Haiti and the Dominican Republic). The *Flying Fish* was en route from Jeremie (a port on the French-controlled part of Hispaniola, now in Haiti) to the island of St. Thomas (part of the Virgin Islands then under Danish control). The U.S. captain (Little) brought the vessel to Boston, thinking that he was acting in accordance with a 1799 statute entitled "an act further to suspend the commercial intercourse between the United States and France, and the dependencies thereof." That statute suspended all U.S. seaborne trade with France (section 1) and allowed for seizure on the high seas of U.S. vessels bound for France if thought to be carrying cargo for France (section 5).]

February 27. MARSHALL, CHIEF JUSTICE, now delivered the opinion of the Court.

The *Flying-Fish*, a Danish vessel, having on board Danish and neutral property, was captured on the 2d of December 1799, on a voyage from Jeremie to St. Thomas's, by the United States frigate *Boston*, commanded by Captain Little, and brought into the port of Boston, where she was libelled as an American vessel that had violated the non-intercourse law.

The judge before whom the cause was tried, directed a restoration of the vessel and cargo as neutral property, but refused to award damages for the capture and detention, because in his opinion, there was probable cause to suspect the vessel to be American.

On an appeal to the circuit court this sentence was reversed, because the *Flying-Fish* was on a voyage *from*, not *to*, a French port, and was therefore, had she even been an American vessel, not liable to capture on the high seas.

During the hostilities between the United States and France, an act for the suspension of all intercourse between the two nations was annually passed. That under which the *Flying-Fish* was condemned, declared every vessel, owned, hired or employed wholly or in part by an American, which should be employed in any traffic or commerce with or for any person resident within the jurisdiction or under the authority of the French republic, to be forfeited together with her cargo; the one half to accrue to the United States, and the other to any person or persons, citizens of the United States, who will inform and prosecute for the same.

The 5th section of this act authorizes the president of the United States, to instruct the commanders of armed vessels, "to stop and examine any ship or vessel of the United States on the high seas, which there may be reason to suspect to be engaged in any traffic or commerce contrary to the true tenor of the act, and if upon examination it should appear that such ship or vessel is bound, or sailing *to* any port or place within the territory of the French republic or her dependencies, it is rendered lawful to seize such vessel, and send her into the United States for adjudication."

It is by no means clear that the president of the United States whose high duty it is to "take care that the laws be faithfully executed," and who is commander in chief of the armies and navies of the United States, might not, without any special authority for that purpose, in the then existing state of things, have empowered the officers commanding the armed vessels of the United States, to seize and send into port for adjudication, American vessels which were forfeited by being engaged in this illicit commerce. But when it is observed that the general clause of the first section of the "act, which declares that such vessels may be seized, and may be prosecuted in any district or circuit court, which shall be holden within or for the district where the seizure shall be made," obviously contemplates a seizure within the United States; and that the 5th section gives a special authority to seize on the high seas, and limits that authority to the seizure of vessels bound or sailing *to* a French port, the legislature seems to have prescribed that the manner in which this law shall be carried into execution, was to exclude a seizure of any vessel not bound *to* a French port. Of consequence, however strong the circumstances might be, which induced Captain Little to suspect the *Flying-Fish* to be an American vessel, they could not excuse the detention of her, since he would not have been authorised to detain her had she been really American.

It was so obvious, that if only vessels sailing to a French port could be seized on the high seas, that the law would be very often evaded, that this act of congress appears to have received a different construction from the executive of the United States; a construction much better calculated to give it effect.

A copy of this act was transmitted by the secretary of the navy, to the captains of the armed vessels, who were ordered to consider the 5th section as a part of their instructions. The same letter contained the following clause. "A proper discharge of the important duties enjoined on you, arising out of this act, will require the exercise of a sound and an impartial judgment. You are not only to do all that in you lies, to prevent all intercourse, whether direct or circuitous, between the ports of the United States and those of France or her dependencies, where the vessels *are apparently as well as really* American, and protected by American papers only, but you are to be vigilant that vessels or cargoes really American, but covered by Danish or other foreign papers, and bound *to* or *from* French ports, do not escape you."

These orders given by the executive under the construction of the act of congress made by the department to which its execution was assigned, enjoin the seizure of American vessels sailing from a French port. Is the officer who obeys them liable for damages sustained by this misconstruction of the act, or will his orders excuse him? If his instructions afford him no protection, then the law must take its course, and he must pay such damages as are legally awarded against him; if they excuse an act not otherwise excusable, it would then be necessary to inquire whether this is a case in which the probable cause which existed to induce a suspicion that the vessel was American, would excuse the captor from damages when the vessel appeared in fact to be neutral.

I confess the first bias of my mind was very strong in favor of the opinion that though the instructions of the executive could not give a right, they might yet excuse from damages. I was much inclined to think that a distinction ought to be taken between acts of civil and those of military officers; and between proceedings within the body of the country and those on the high seas. That implicit obedience which military men usually pay to the orders of their superiors, which indeed is indispensably necessary to every military system, appeared to me strongly to imply the principle that those orders, if not to perform a prohibited act, ought to justify the person whose general duty it is to obey them, and who is placed by the laws of his country in a situation which in general requires that he should obey them. I was strongly inclined to think that where, in consequence of orders from the legitimate authority, a vessel is seized with pure intention, the claim of the injured party for damages would be against that government from which the orders proceeded, and would be a proper subject for negotiation. But I have been convinced that I was mistaken, and I have receded from this first opinion. I acquiesce in that of my brethren, which is, that the instructions cannot change the nature of the transaction, or legalize an act which without those instructions would have been a plain trespass.

It becomes therefore unnecessary to inquire whether the probable cause afforded by the conduct of the *Flying-Fish* to suspect her of being an American, would excuse Captain Little from damages for having seized and sent her into port, since had she actually been an American, the seizure would have been unlawful.

Captain Little then must be answerable in damages to the owner of this neutral vessel, and as the account taken by order of the circuit court is not objectionable on its face, and has not been excepted to by council before the proper tribunal, this court can receive no objection to it.

There appears then to be no error in the judgment of the circuit court, and it must be affirmed with costs.

NOTES

1. *Congressional Power.* What constitutional power of Congress was at play in *Little v. Barreme*? The power to declare war? To make rules concerning captures on water? To make rules for the governing and regulation of naval forces? To regulate foreign commerce?

2. *Presidential Power.* Is there any constitutional power of the president that should have been relevant in *Little v. Barreme*? Of what significance is it that the Court does not discuss whether the president has "inherent" or "independent" power to conduct U.S. foreign policy, especially in the context of an informal war? Why does the Court not discuss the constitutionality of the statute in question, *i.e.*, the ability of Congress to inhibit the president's conduct in waging an informal war?

3. *Relating Congressional Power to Executive Power.* What specific act of the executive was challenged in *Little v. Barreme*? With respect to that challenged act, what was the posture of Congress? Did Congress approve of the act? Oppose it? Neither? Does the constitutionality of the president's act turn on how you answer that question? Would the president's act have been constitutional if Congress had been silent?

4. *Implying Congressional Approval.* Assuming that the non-intercourse statute is the relevant source of law, might the Secretary of the Navy have *implied* a broader congressional restriction on trade with France from the statute? Is Justice Marshall's interpretation the only viable one? What if Congress had appropriated funding for naval patrols off the coast of Port-au-Prince? The question of implied congressional authorization is one that has arisen repeatedly and will be revisited in the materials to come.

5. *Precedential Value. Little v. Barreme* is frequently cited as a case dealing with the distribution of war powers between Congress and the president, one that helps define the scope of presidential power in the face of congressional disapproval. How significant is it that the congressional statute

at issue authorized the seizure of American vessels engaged in *commerce* with France, given Congress's express constitutional power to regulate foreign commerce? Further, should the case be read narrowly as concerning merely the liability of a military official for damages during a period of hostilities? One scholar has suggested that "the Court instead viewed the provisions of the act as primarily pertaining to Congress's power to regulate commerce with other nations," Gregory J. Sidak, *The Quasi-War Cases*, 28 HARV. J.L. & PUB. POL'Y 465, 493 (2005), while another has argued that *Barreme* does not reach the issue of presidential war powers because the Court was asked only to consider Captain Little's liability. *See* John C. Yoo, *The Continuation of Politics by Other Means: The Original Understanding of War Powers*, 84 CAL. L. REV. 167, 294–95 n.584 (1996). Do you agree?

YOUNGSTOWN SHEET & TUBE CO. V. SAWYER

343 U.S. 579 (1952).

MR. JUSTICE BLACK delivered the opinion of the Court.

We are asked to decide whether the President was acting within his constitutional power when he issued an order directing the Secretary of Commerce to take possession of and operate most of the Nation's steel mills. The mill owners argue that the President's order amounts to lawmaking, a legislative function which the Constitution has expressly confided to the Congress and not to the President. The Government's position is that the order was made on findings of the President that his action was necessary to avert a national catastrophe which would inevitably result from a stoppage of steel production, and that in meeting this grave emergency the President was acting within the aggregate of his constitutional powers as the Nation's Chief Executive and the Commander in Chief of the Armed Forces of the United States. The issue emerges here from the following series of events:

In the latter part of 1951, a dispute arose between the steel companies and their employees over terms and conditions that should be included in new collective bargaining agreements. Long-continued conferences failed to resolve the dispute. On April 4, 1952, the Union gave notice of a nation-wide strike called to begin at 12:01 a.m. April 9. The indispensability of steel as a component of substantially all weapons and other war materials led the President to believe that the proposed work stoppage would immediately jeopardize our national defense and that governmental seizure of the steel mills was necessary in order to assure the continued availability of steel Reciting these considerations for his action, the President, a few hours before the strike was to begin, issued Executive Order 10340. The order directed the Secretary of Commerce to take possession of most of the steel mills and keep them running. The Secretary immediately issued his own possessory orders, calling upon the presidents of the various seized companies to serve as operating managers for the

United States. They were directed to carry on their activities in accordance with regulations and directions of the Secretary. The next morning the President sent a message to Congress reporting his action. Twelve days later he sent a second message. Congress has taken no action.

Obeying the Secretary's orders under protest, the companies brought proceedings against him in the District Court. Their complaints charged that the seizure was not authorized by an act of Congress or by any constitutional provisions. The District Court was asked to declare the orders of the President and the Secretary invalid and to issue preliminary and permanent injunctions restraining their enforcement. Opposing the motion for preliminary injunction, the United States asserted that a strike disrupting steel production for even a brief period would so endanger the well-being and safety of the Nation that the President had "inherent power" to do what he had done—power "supported by the Constitution, by historical precedent, and by court decisions." . . .

The President's power, if any, to issue the order must stem either from an act of Congress or from the Constitution itself. There is no statute that expressly authorizes the President to take possession of property as he did here. Nor is there any act of Congress to which our attention has been directed from which such a power can fairly be implied. Indeed, we do not understand the Government to rely on statutory authorization for this seizure. There are two statutes which do authorize the President to take both personal and real property under certain conditions. However, the Government admits that these conditions were not met and that the President's order was not rooted in either of the statutes. The Government refers to the seizure provisions of one of these statutes as "much too cumbersome, involved, and time-consuming for the crisis which was at hand."

Moreover, the use of the seizure technique to solve labor disputes in order to prevent work stoppages was not only unauthorized by any congressional enactment; prior to this controversy, Congress had refused to adopt that method of settling labor disputes. When the Taft-Hartley Act was under consideration in 1947, Congress rejected an amendment which would have authorized such governmental seizures in cases of emergency. Apparently it was thought that the technique of seizure, like that of compulsory arbitration, would interfere with the process of collective bargaining. Consequently, the plan Congress adopted in that Act did not provide for seizure under any circumstances. Instead, the plan sought to bring about settlements by use of the customary devices of mediation, conciliation, investigation by boards of inquiry, and public reports.

It is clear that if the President had authority to issue the order he did, it must be found in some provisions of the Constitution. And it is not claimed that express constitutional language grants this power to the

President. The contention is that presidential power should be implied from the aggregate of his powers under the Constitution. Particular reliance is placed on provisions in Article II which say that "The executive Power shall be vested in a President . . ."; that "he shall take Care that the Laws be faithfully executed"; and that he "shall be Commander in Chief of the Army and Navy of the United States."

The order cannot properly be sustained as an exercise of the President's military power as Commander in Chief of the Armed Forces. The Government attempts to do so by citing a number of cases upholding broad powers in military commanders engaged in day-to-day fighting in a theater of war. Such cases need not concern us here. Even though "theater of war" be an expanding concept, we cannot with faithfulness to our constitutional system hold that the Commander in Chief of the Armed Forces has the ultimate power as such to take possession of private property in order to keep labor disputes from stopping production. This is a job for the Nation's lawmakers, not for its military authorities.

Nor can the seizure order be sustained because of the several constitutional provisions that grant executive power to the President. In the framework of our Constitution, the President's power to see that the laws are faithfully executed refutes the idea that he is to be a lawmaker. The Constitution limits his functions in the lawmaking process to the recommending of laws he thinks wise and the vetoing of laws he thinks bad. And the Constitution is neither silent nor equivocal about who shall make laws which the President is to execute. The first section of the first article says that "All legislative Powers herein granted shall be vested in a Congress of the United States. . . ." After granting many powers to the Congress, Article I goes on to provide that Congress may "make all Laws which shall be necessary and proper for carrying into Execution the foregoing Powers, and all other Powers vested by this Constitution in the Government of the United States, or in any Department or Officer thereof."

The President's order does not direct that a congressional policy be executed in a manner prescribed by Congress—it directs that a presidential policy be executed in a manner prescribed by the President. The preamble of the order itself, like that of many statutes, sets out reasons why the President believes certain policies should be adopted, proclaims these policies as rules of conduct to be followed, and again, like a statute, authorizes a government official to promulgate additional rules and regulations consistent with the policy proclaimed and needed to carry that policy into execution. The power of Congress to adopt such public policies as those proclaimed by the order is beyond question. It can authorize the taking of private property for public use. It can make laws regulating the relationships between employers and employees, prescribing rules designed to settle labor disputes, and fixing wages and working conditions in certain fields of our economy. The Constitution does not subject this lawmaking power of Congress to presidential or military supervision or control.

It is said that other Presidents without congressional authority have taken possession of private business enterprises in order to settle labor disputes. But even if this be true, Congress has not thereby lost its exclusive constitutional authority to make laws necessary and proper to carry out the powers vested by the Constitution "in the Government of the United States, or in any Department or Officer thereof."

The Founders of this Nation entrusted the lawmaking power to the Congress alone in both good and bad times. It would do no good to recall the historical events, the fears of power and the hopes for freedom that lay behind their choice. Such a review would but confirm our holding that this seizure order cannot stand.

The judgment of the District Court is

Affirmed. . . .

MR. JUSTICE JACKSON, concurring in the judgment and opinion of the Court.

That comprehensive and undefined presidential powers hold both practical advantages and grave dangers for the country will impress anyone who has served as legal adviser to a President in time of transition and public anxiety. While an interval of detached reflection may temper teachings of that experience, they probably are a more realistic influence on my views than the conventional materials of judicial decision which seem unduly to accentuate doctrine and legal fiction. But as we approach the question of presidential power, we half overcome mental hazards by recognizing them. The opinions of judges, no less than executives and publicists, often suffer the infirmity of confusing the issue of a power's validity with the cause it is invoked to promote, of confounding the permanent executive office with its temporary occupant. The tendency is strong to emphasize transient results upon policies—such as wages or stabilization—and lose sight of enduring consequences upon the balanced power structure of our Republic.

A judge, like an executive adviser, may be surprised at the poverty of really useful and unambiguous authority applicable to concrete problems of executive power as they actually present themselves. Just what our forefathers did envision, or would have envisioned had they foreseen modern conditions, must be divined from materials almost as enigmatic as the dreams Joseph was called upon to interpret for Pharaoh. A century and a half of partisan debate and scholarly speculation yields no net result but only supplies more or less apt quotations from respected sources on each side of any question. They largely cancel each other.[1] And court decisions are indecisive because of the judicial practice of dealing with the largest questions in the most narrow way.

The actual art of governing under our Constitution does not and cannot conform to judicial definitions of the power of any of its branches based on isolated clauses or even single Articles torn from context. While the Constitution diffuses power the better to secure liberty, it also contemplates that practice will integrate the dispersed powers into a workable government. It enjoins upon its branches separateness but interdependence, autonomy but reciprocity. Presidential powers are not fixed but fluctuate, depending upon their disjunction or conjunction with those of Congress. We may well begin by a somewhat over-simplified grouping of practical situations in which a President may doubt, or others may challenge, his powers, and by distinguishing roughly the legal consequences of this factor of relativity.

1. When the President acts pursuant to an express or implied authorization of Congress, his authority is at its maximum, for it includes all that he possesses in his own right plus all that Congress can delegate.[2] In these circumstances, and in these only, may he be said (for what it may be worth), to personify the federal sovereignty. If his act is held unconstitutional under these circumstances, it usually means that the Federal Government as an undivided whole lacks power. A seizure executed by the President pursuant to an Act of Congress would be supported by the strongest of presumptions and the widest latitude of judicial interpretation, and the burden of persuasion would rest heavily upon any who might attack it.

2. When the President acts in absence of either a congressional grant or denial of authority, he can only rely upon his own independent powers, but there is a zone of twilight in which he and Congress may have concurrent authority, or in which its distribution is uncertain. Therefore, congressional inertia, indifference or quiescence may sometimes, at least

[1] A Hamilton may be matched against a Madison. 7 The Works of Alexander Hamilton, 76–117; 1 Madison, Letters and Other Writings, 611–654. Professor Taft is counterbalanced by Theodore Roosevelt. Taft, Our Chief Magistrate and His Powers, 139–140; Theodore Roosevelt, Autobiography, 388–389. It even seems that President Taft cancels out Professor Taft. Compare his "Temporary Petroleum Withdrawal No. 5" of September 27, 1909, *United States v. Midwest Oil Co.*, 236 U.S. 459, 467, 468, with his appraisal of executive power in "Our Chief Magistrate and His Powers" 139–140.

[2] It is in this class of cases that we find the broadest recent statements of presidential power, including those relied on here. *United States v. Curtiss-Wright Export Corp.*, 299 U.S. 304, involved, not the question of the President's power to act without congressional authority, but the question of his right to act under and in accord with an Act of Congress. . . .

That case does not solve the present controversy. It recognized internal and external affairs as being in separate categories, and held that the strict limitation upon congressional delegations of power to the President over internal affairs does not apply with respect to delegations of power in external affairs. It was intimated that the President might act in external affairs without congressional authority, but not that he might act contrary to an Act of Congress.

as a practical matter, enable, if not invite, measures on independent presidential responsibility. In this area, any actual test of power is likely to depend on the imperatives of events and contemporary imponderables rather than on abstract theories of law.

3. When the President takes measures incompatible with the expressed or implied will of Congress, his power is at its lowest ebb, for then he can rely only upon his own constitutional powers minus any constitutional powers of Congress over the matter. Courts can sustain exclusive presidential control in such a case only by disabling the Congress from acting upon the subject. Presidential claim to a power at once so conclusive and preclusive must be scrutinized with caution, for what is at stake is the equilibrium established by our constitutional system.

Into which of these classifications does this executive seizure of the steel industry fit? It is eliminated from the first by admission, for it is conceded that no congressional authorization exists for this seizure. That takes away also the support of the many precedents and declarations which were made in relation, and must be confined, to this category.[5]

Can it then be defended under flexible tests available to the second category? It seems clearly eliminated from that class because Congress has not left seizure of private property an open field. . . .

This leaves the current seizure to be justified only by the severe tests under the third grouping, where it can be supported only by any remainder of executive power after subtraction of such powers as Congress may have over the subject. In short, we can sustain the President only by holding that seizure of such strike-bound industries is within his domain and beyond control by Congress. Thus, this Court's first review of such seizures occurs under circumstances which leave presidential power most vulnerable to attack and in the least favorable of possible constitutional postures.

I did not suppose, and I am not persuaded, that history leaves it open to question, at least in the courts, that the executive branch, like the Federal Government as a whole, possesses only delegated powers. The purpose of the Constitution was not only to grant power, but to keep it from getting out of hand. However, because the President does not enjoy unmentioned powers does not mean that the mentioned ones should be narrowed by a niggardly construction. Some clauses could be made almost unworkable, as well as immutable, by refusal to indulge some latitude of interpretation for changing times. I have heretofore, and do now, give to

5 The oft-cited Louisiana Purchase had nothing to do with the separation of powers as between the President and Congress, but only with state and federal power. The Louisiana Purchase was subject to rather academic criticism, not upon the ground that Mr. Jefferson acted without authority from Congress, but that neither had express authority to expand the boundaries of the United States by purchase or annexation. Mr. Jefferson himself had strongly opposed the doctrine that the State's delegation of powers to the Federal Government could be enlarged by resort to implied powers.

the enumerated powers the scope and elasticity afforded by what seem to be reasonable practical implications instead of the rigidity dictated by a doctrinaire textualism.

The Solicitor General seeks the power of seizure in three clauses of the Executive Article, the first reading, "The executive Power shall be vested in a President of the United States of America." Lest I be thought to exaggerate, I quote the interpretation which his brief puts upon it: "In our view, this clause constitutes a grant of all the executive powers of which the Government is capable." If that be true, it is difficult to see why the forefathers bothered to add several specific items, including some trifling ones.[9]

The example of such unlimited executive power that must have most impressed the forefathers was the prerogative exercised by George III, and the description of its evils in the Declaration of Independence leads me to doubt that they were creating their new Executive in his image. Continental European examples were no more appealing. And if we seek instruction from our own times, we can match it only from the executive powers in those governments we disparagingly describe as totalitarian. I cannot accept the view that this clause is a grant in bulk of all conceivable executive power but regard it as an allocation to the presidential office of the generic powers thereafter stated.

The clause on which the Government next relies is that "The President shall be Commander in Chief of the Army and Navy of the United States. . . ." These cryptic words have given rise to some of the most persistent controversies in our constitutional history. Of course, they imply something more than an empty title. But just what authority goes with the name has plagued presidential advisers who would not waive or narrow it by nonassertion yet cannot say where it begins or ends. It undoubtedly puts the Nation's armed forces under presidential command. Hence, this loose appellation is sometimes advanced as support for any presidential action, internal or external, involving use of force, the idea being that it vests power to do anything, anywhere, that can be done with an army or navy.

That seems to be the logic of an argument tendered at our bar—that the President having, on his own responsibility, sent American troops abroad derives from that act "affirmative power" to seize the means of producing a supply of steel for them. To quote, "Perhaps the most forceful illustrations of the scope of Presidential power in this connection is the fact that American troops in Korea, whose safety and effectiveness are so directly involved here, were sent to the field by an exercise of the

9 ". . . he may require the Opinion, in writing, of the principal Officer in each of the executive Departments, upon any Subject relating to the Duties of their respective Offices. . . ." U.S. Const., Art. II, § 2. He ". . . shall Commission all the Officers of the United States." U.S. Const., Art. II, § 3. Matters such as those would seem to be inherent in the Executive if anything is.

President's constitutional powers." Thus, it is said, he has invested himself with "war powers."

I cannot foresee all that it might entail if the Court should indorse this argument. Nothing in our Constitution is plainer than that declaration of a war is entrusted only to Congress. Of course, a state of war may in fact exist without a formal declaration. But no doctrine that the Court could promulgate would seem to me more sinister and alarming than that a President whose conduct of foreign affairs is so largely uncontrolled, and often even is unknown, can vastly enlarge his mastery over the internal affairs of the country by his own commitment of the Nation's armed forces to some foreign venture.[10] I do not, however, find it necessary or appropriate to consider the legal status of the Korean enterprise to discountenance argument based on it.

Assuming that we are in a war *de facto,* whether it is or is not a war *de jure,* does that empower the Commander in Chief to seize industries he thinks necessary to supply our army? The Constitution expressly places in Congress power "to raise and *support* Armies" and "to *provide* and *maintain* a Navy." (Emphasis supplied.) This certainly lays upon Congress primary responsibility for supplying the armed forces. Congress alone controls the raising of revenues and their appropriation and may determine in what manner and by what means they shall be spent for military and naval procurement. I suppose no one would doubt that Congress can take over war supply as a Government enterprise. On the other hand, if Congress sees fit to rely on free private enterprise collectively bargaining with free labor for support and maintenance of our armed forces, can the Executive, because of lawful disagreements incidental to that process, seize the facility for operation upon Government-imposed terms?

---

[10] How widely this doctrine espoused by the President's counsel departs from the early view of presidential power is shown by a comparison. President Jefferson, without authority from Congress, sent the American fleet into the Mediterranean, where it engaged in a naval battle with the Tripolitan fleet. He sent a message to Congress on December 8, 1801, in which he said:

> "Tripoli, the least considerable of the Barbary States, had come forward with demands unfounded either in right or in compact, and had permitted itself to denounce war on our failure to comply before a given day. The style of the demand admitted but one answer. I sent a small squadron of frigates into the Mediterranean . . . with orders to protect our commerce against the threatened attack. . . . Our commerce in the Mediterranean was blockaded and that of the Atlantic in peril. . . . One of the Tripolitan cruisers having fallen in with and engaged the small schooner *Enterprise,* . . . was captured, after a heavy slaughter of her men. . . . Unauthorized by the Constitution, without the sanction of Congress, to go beyond the line of defense, the vessel being disabled from committing further hostilities, was liberated with its crew. The Legislature will doubtless consider whether, by authorizing measures of offense also, they will place our force on an equal footing with that of its adversaries. I communicate all material information on this subject, that in the exercise of the important function confided by the Constitution to the Legislature exclusively their judgment may form itself on a knowledge and consideration of every circumstance of weight." I Richardson, Messages and Papers of the Presidents, 314.

There are indications that the Constitution did not contemplate that the title Commander in Chief *of the Army and Navy* will constitute him also Commander in Chief of the country, its industries and its inhabitants. He has no monopoly of "war powers," whatever they are. While Congress cannot deprive the President of the command of the army and navy, only Congress can provide him an army or navy to command. It is also empowered to make rules for the "Government and Regulation of land and naval Forces," by which it may to some unknown extent impinge upon even command functions.

That military powers of the Commander in Chief were not to supersede representative government of internal affairs seems obvious from the Constitution and from elementary American history. Time out of mind, and even now in many parts of the world, a military commander can seize private housing to shelter his troops. Not so, however, in the United States, for the Third Amendment says, "No Soldier shall, in time of peace be quartered in any house, without the consent of the Owner, nor in time of war, but in a manner to be prescribed by law." Thus, even in war time, his seizure of needed military housing must be authorized by Congress. It also was expressly left to Congress to "provide for calling forth the Militia to execute the Laws of the Union, suppress Insurrections and repel Invasions. . . ." Such a limitation on the command power, written at a time when the militia rather than a standing army was contemplated as the military weapon of the Republic, underscores the Constitution's policy that Congress, not the Executive, should control utilization of the war power as an instrument of domestic policy.

We should not use this occasion to circumscribe, much less to contract, the lawful role of the President as Commander in Chief. I should indulge the widest latitude of interpretation to sustain his exclusive function to command the instruments of national force, at least when turned against the outside world for the security of our society. But, when it is turned inward, not because of rebellion but because of a lawful economic struggle between industry and labor, it should have no such indulgence. His command power is not such an absolute as might be implied from that office in a militaristic system but is subject to limitations consistent with a constitutional Republic whose law and policy-making branch is a representative Congress. The purpose of lodging dual titles in one man was to insure that the civilian would control the military, not to enable the military to subordinate the presidential office. No penance would ever expiate the sin against free government of holding that a President can escape control of executive powers by law through assuming his military role. What the power of command may include I do not try to envision, but I think it is not a military prerogative, without support of law, to seize persons or property because they are important or even essential for the military and naval establishment.

The third clause in which the Solicitor General finds seizure powers is that "he shall take Care that the Laws be faithfully executed. . . ." That authority must be matched against words of the Fifth Amendment that "No person shall be . . . deprived of life, liberty or property, without due process of law. . . ." One gives a governmental authority that reaches so far as there is law, the other gives a private right that authority shall go no farther. These signify about all there is of the principle that ours is a government of laws, not of men, and that we submit ourselves to rulers only if under rules.

The Solicitor General lastly grounds support of the seizure upon nebulous, inherent powers never expressly granted but said to have accrued to the office from the customs and claims of preceding administrations. The plea is for a resulting power to deal with a crisis or an emergency according to the necessities of the case, the unarticulated assumption being that necessity knows no law.

Loose and irresponsible use of adjectives colors all non-legal and much legal discussion of presidential powers. "Inherent" powers, "implied" powers, "incidental" powers, "plenary" powers, "war" powers and "emergency" powers are used, often interchangeably and without fixed or ascertainable meanings.

The vagueness and generality of the clauses that set forth presidential powers afford a plausible basis for pressures within and without an administration for presidential action beyond that supported by those whose responsibility it is to defend his actions in court. The claim of inherent and unrestricted presidential powers has long been a persuasive dialectical weapon in political controversy. While it is not surprising that counsel should grasp support from such unadjudicated claims of power, a judge cannot accept self-serving press statements of the attorney for one of the interested parties as authority in answering a constitutional question, even if the advocate was himself. But prudence has counseled that actual reliance on such nebulous claims stop short of provoking a judicial test. . . .

Germany, after the First World War, framed the Weimar Constitution, designed to secure her liberties in the Western tradition. However, the President of the Republic, without concurrence of the Reichstag, was empowered temporarily to suspend any or all individual rights if public safety and order were seriously disturbed or endangered. This proved a temptation to every government, whatever its shade of opinion, and in 13 years suspension of rights was invoked on more than 250 occasions. Finally, Hitler persuaded President Von Hindenberg to suspend all such rights, and they were never restored.

The French Republic provided for a very different kind of emergency government known as the "state of siege." It differed from the German emergency dictatorship, particularly in that emergency powers could not be assumed at will by the Executive but could only be granted as a parliamentary measure. And it did not, as in Germany, result in a suspension or abrogation of law but was a legal institution governed by special legal rules and terminable by parliamentary authority.

Great Britain also has fought both World Wars under a sort of temporary dictatorship created by legislation.[22] As Parliament is not bound by written constitutional limitations, it established a crisis government simply by delegation to its Ministers of a larger measure than usual of its own unlimited power, which is exercised under its supervision by Ministers whom it may dismiss.

This contemporary foreign experience may be inconclusive as to the wisdom of lodging emergency powers somewhere in a modern government. But it suggests that emergency powers are consistent with free government only when their control is lodged elsewhere than in the Executive who exercises them. That is the safeguard that would be nullified by our adoption of the "inherent powers" formula. Nothing in my experience convinces me that such risks are warranted by any real necessity, although such powers would, of course, be an executive convenience.

In the practical working of our Government we already have evolved a technique within the framework of the Constitution by which normal executive powers may be considerably expanded to meet an emergency. Congress may and has granted extraordinary authorities which lie dormant in normal times but may be called into play by the Executive in war or upon proclamation of a national emergency. In 1939, upon congressional request, the Attorney General listed ninety-nine such separate statutory grants by Congress of emergency or wartime executive powers. They were invoked from time to time as need appeared. Under this procedure we retain Government by law—special, temporary law, perhaps, but law nonetheless. The public may know the extent and limitations of the powers that can be asserted, and persons affected may be informed from the statute of their rights and duties.

In view of the ease, expedition and safety with which Congress can grant and has granted large emergency powers, certainly ample to embrace this crisis, I am quite unimpressed with the argument that we should affirm possession of them without statute. Such power either has no beginning or it has no end. If it exists, it need submit to no legal restraint. I am not alarmed that it would plunge us straightway into dictatorship, but it is at least a step in that wrong direction. . . .

The essence of our free Government is "leave to live by no man's leave, underneath the law"—to be governed by those impersonal forces which we call law. Our Government is fashioned to fulfill this concept so far as

[22] Defense of the Realm Act, 1914, 4 & 5, Geo. V. c. 29, as amended, c. 63; Emergency Powers (Defence) Act, 1939, 2 & 3 Geo. VI, c. 62; Rossiter, Constitutional Dictatorship, 135–184.

humanly possible. The Executive, except for recommendation and veto, has no legislative power. The executive action we have here originates in the individual will of the President and represents an exercise of authority without law. . . . With all its defects, delays and inconveniences, men have discovered no technique for long preserving free government except that the Executive be under the law, and that the law be made by parliamentary deliberations.

Such institutions may be destined to pass away. But it is the duty of the Court to be last, not first, to give them up.

NOTES

1. *The Majority's Reasoning on Presidential Power.* Justice Black wrote for the Court that the president had engaged in a lawmaking function, one that the Constitution assigns to Congress. What standard does Justice Black apply to distinguish a "legislative act" from an "executive act"? What guidance is provided by the Constitution? Is the distinction useful? Do you think that the result would have been different if substantial United States casualties in Korea had been directly traceable to the strike against the steel companies? Should it? *See* Harry S. Truman, II *Memoirs* 465–71 (1955). Viewed in this light, should the president's conduct have been seen as an exercise of executive power to address a growing national security crisis?

2. *Wither Curtiss-Wright?* Justice Black makes no reference to *Curtiss-Wright*—even though it had been decided only sixteen years earlier. Could not the president's seizure of the steel mills have been justified under the *Curtiss-Wright* wide-ranging "sovereignty" theory? Does Justice Black mean to repudiate the theory when he writes, that "[t]he President's power, if any, . . . must stem either from an act of Congress or from the Constitution itself"? What does Justice Jackson say about *Curtiss-Wright*?

3. *Justice Jackson's Approach.* Although set forth in a concurring opinion, Justice Jackson's tripartite framework has proven very influential. Many of the separation of powers cases in this book apply that framework. Is Justice Jackson correct in placing the executive act in *Youngstown* in category three? Why should it not be placed in the "zone of twilight"? As Justice Rehnquist (a former clerk of Justice Jackson) wrote in *Dames & Moore*, "Justice Jackson himself recognized that his three categories represented 'a somewhat oversimplified grouping,' and it is doubtless the case that executive action in any particular instance falls, not neatly in one of three pigeonholes, but rather at some point along a spectrum running from explicit congressional authorization to explicit congressional prohibition." 453 U.S. 654, 669 (1981). What do you think Justice Rehnquist means?

Note that if Congress prohibits an action taken by the president, Jackson reasons that the president's power is "at its lowest ebb," not that the president is then without any power to act. Under these circumstances, a second inquiry is necessary: whether the act in question falls within the exclusive powers of the president—whether, in Justice Jackson's calculus, the "constitutional powers of Congress over the matter" amount to zero? If this second level of inquiry is necessary, Justice Jackson leaves open which method of constitutional interpretation should be applied to determine the existence of an exclusive presidential power.

4. *Political Question Doctrine*. Why didn't *Youngstown* present a non-justiciable "political question"? If Congress had been silent, would such a question have presented itself? What is the relationship between the "zone of twilight" and the political question doctrine? (*See* Chapter 7).

5. *Playing with Jackson's Categories*. Into which of Justice Jackson's three categories does the particular executive act in *Little v. Barreme* fall? The executive act in *Curtiss-Wright*? Note the parallel between Justice Jackson's third category and the reasoning of Chief Justice Marshall in *Little v. Barreme*. Does Chief Justice Marshall also suggest that the president's powers fluctuate as a function of action taken by Congress? Yet, conceptually, how can a statute alter the scope of a constitutional power? Do these opinions discuss constitutional power or statutory power—or some amalgam of the two? In cases applying Justice Jackson' framework, often the most important issue is determining into which category the president's action falls. As you read *Dames & Moore v. Regan* in Chapter 3, Sec. 7 and *Hamdi v. Rumsfeld* in Chapter 4, Sec., 7, consider how the Court addresses this issue. In *Medellín v. Texas*, the Supreme Court was asked to enforce a memorandum by President George W. Bush ordering Texas state courts to implement a decision of the International Court of Justice. The president argued that the memorandum was authorized by two treaties which made the ICJ judgment binding on the United States. The treaties were not, however, self-executing and could not be directly enforced in U.S. Courts. The Supreme Court reasoned that

> The responsibility for transforming an international obligation arising from a non-self-executing treaty into domestic law falls to Congress, not the Executive. *Foster,* 2 Pet., at 315. It is a fundamental constitutional principle that " '[t]he power to make the necessary laws is in Congress; the power to execute in the President.' " *Hamdan v. Rumsfeld*, 548 U.S. 557, 591. A non-self-executing treaty, by definition, is one that was ratified with the understanding that it is not to have domestic effect of its own force. That understanding precludes the assertion that Congress has implicitly authorized the President—acting on his own—to achieve precisely the same result. Accordingly, the President's Memorandum does not fall within the first category of the *Youngstown* framework. Indeed, because the non-self-executing character of the relevant treaties not only refutes the notion that the ratifying parties vested the President with the authority to unilaterally make treaty obligations binding on domestic courts, but also implicitly prohibits him from doing so, the President's assertion of authority is within *Youngstown*'s third category, not the first or even the second.

Is this reasoning convincing? Is it relevant to note that treaty self-execution was an unclear area of law when the treaties were ratified? (*See* Chapter 3, Sec. 4).

6. *The Commander-in-Chief Clause*. Why wasn't the seizure of the steel mills a lawful exercise of the president's power as Commander in Chief? How is Justice Jackson's reasoning about the Commander-in-Chief Clause different from Justice Black's reasoning in the majority opinion? Justice Jackson notes that the Clause "undoubtably puts the Nation's armed forces under presidential command." In other words, a statute purporting to put the military under the command of someone other than the president would be unconstitutional. What other powers are exclusive to the president under the Commander-in-Chief Clause? Do they depend upon designations such as "theater of war" or "internal" and "external"? What does *Little v. Barreme* suggest? These questions are revisited in Chapter 4.

7. *The Executive Vesting Clause*. How is the Executive Vesting Clause in Article II of the Constitution different than the Legislative Vesting Clause of Article I? What did the government argue about the Executive Vesting Clause in the *Youngstown* case? Why do the majority and Justice Jackson reject this argument? The Executive Vesting Clause thesis was advanced by Alexander Hamilton in defense of President Washington's Neutrality Proclamation in 1793. *See William R. Casto, Foreign Relations and the U.S. Constitution in the Age of Fighting Sail* (2006). For a modern defense of the theory, see Saikrishna B. Prakash & Michael D. Ramsey, *The Executive Power over Foreign Affairs*, 111 YALE L.J. 231, 312–13 (2001). Justice Jackson's opinion in *Youngstown* lays out the most important objections to the theory.

8. *The Distinction Between Domestic and Foreign*. The *Youngstown* opinions reason that separation of powers questions can be resolved in part by distinguishing between domestic and foreign conduct. The *Curtiss-Wright* case drew a similar distinction. The application of the Constitution and of various federal statutes to external or foreign events has generated a number of important and closely-divided Supreme Court cases including *Boumediene v. Bush*, 553 U.S. 723 (2008) (application of the privilege of *habeas corpus* to Guantánamo detainees) (*see* Chapter 4, Sec. 7); *Kiobel v. Royal Dutch Petroleum*, 133 S.Ct. 1659 (2013) (extraterritorial application of the Alien Tort Statute) (*see* Chapter 2, Sec. 6); *RJR Nabisco, Inc. v. European Community*, 136 S.Ct. 2090 (2016) (extraterritorial application of the Racketeer Influenced and Corrupt Organizations Act) (*see* Chapter 2, Sec. 5). Should the Constitution and federal statutes be interpreted to apply differently (or not at all) to extraterritorial events? How clear is the distinction between domestic and foreign? Are globalization, digitalization, and new forms of armed conflict making boundaries less relevant and conduct more difficult to characterize?

9. *The Non-Delegation Doctrine*. As discussed in the notes following the *Curtiss-Wright* case, the non-delegation doctrine in U.S. constitutional law is the principle that the Congress, being vested with "all legislative powers" by Article I, Section 1 of the Constitution, cannot delegate that power to anyone

else. Yet when one looks at the foreign affairs powers accorded to the Congress under the Constitution and the foreign affairs powers exercised by the president in practice, it seems that there is a considerable amount of delegation to the president. What is the current viability of this doctrine and to what extent does it apply to foreign affairs legislation? If a significant amount of delegation to the president is permissible for reasons of convenience and efficiency, are there ways for Congress to "claw back" some of its authority when it disagrees with the president's action?"

INS v. CHADHA

462 U.S. 919 (1983).

CHIEF JUSTICE BURGER delivered the opinion of the Court. . . .

I

Chadha is an East Indian who was born in Kenya and holds a British passport. He was lawfully admitted to the United States in 1966 on a nonimmigrant student visa. His visa expired on June 30, 1972. On October 11, 1973, the District Director of the Immigration and Naturalization Service ordered Chadha to show cause why he should not be deported for having "remained in the United States for a longer time than permitted." . . . [A] deportation hearing was held before an Immigration Judge on January 11, 1974. Chadha conceded that he was deportable for overstaying his visa and the hearing was adjourned to enable him to file an application for suspension of deportation. . . .

Pursuant to § 244(c)(1) of the Act, the Immigration Judge suspended Chadha's deportation and a report of the suspension was transmitted to Congress. . . .

Once the Attorney General's recommendation for suspension of Chadha's deportation was conveyed to Congress, Congress had the power under [the Act] to veto the Attorney General's determination that Chadha should not be deported. . . .

On December 12, 1975, Representative Eilberg, Chairman of the Judiciary Subcommittee on Immigration, Citizenship, and International Law, introduced a resolution opposing "the granting of permanent residence in the United States to [six] aliens," including Chadha. . . . The resolution was passed without debate or recorded vote. Since the House action was pursuant to § 244(c)(2), the resolution was not treated as an Art. I legislative act; it was not submitted to the Senate or presented to the President for his action.

. . . We begin, of course, with the presumption that the challenged statute is valid. Its wisdom is not the concern of the courts; if a challenged action does not violate the Constitution, it must be sustained. . . .

By the same token, the fact that a given law or procedure is efficient, convenient, and useful in facilitating functions of government, standing alone, will not save it if it is contrary to the Constitution. Convenience and efficiency are not the primary objectives—or the hallmarks—of democratic government and our inquiry is sharpened rather than blunted by the fact that congressional veto provisions are appearing with increasing frequency in statutes which delegate authority to executive and independent agencies:

> "Since 1932, when the first veto provision was enacted into law, 295 congressional veto-type procedures have been inserted in 196 different statutes as follows: from 1932 to 1939, five statutes were affected; from 1940–49, nineteen statutes; between 1950–59, thirty-four statutes; and from 1960–69, forty-nine. From the year 1970 through 1975, at least one hundred sixty-three such provisions were included in eighty-nine laws." Abourezk, The Congressional Veto: A Contemporary Response to Executive Encroachment on Legislative Prerogatives, 52 Ind. L. Rev. 323, 324 (1977). . . .

JUSTICE WHITE undertakes to make a case for the proposition that the one-House veto is a useful "political invention," and we need not challenge that assertion. We can even concede this utilitarian argument although the long-range political wisdom of this "invention" is arguable. It has been vigorously debated, and it is instructive to compare the views of the protagonists. But policy arguments supporting even useful "political inventions" are subject to the demands of the Constitution which defines powers and, with respect to this subject, sets out just how those powers are to be exercised.

Explicit and unambiguous provisions of the Constitution prescribe and define the respective functions of the Congress and of the Executive in the legislative process. Since the precise terms of those familiar provisions are critical to the resolution of these cases, we set them out verbatim. Article I provides:

> "All legislative Powers herein granted shall be vested in a Congress of the United States, which shall consist of a Senate *and* House of Representatives." Art. I, § 1. (Emphasis added.)
>
> "Every Bill which shall have passed the House of Representatives *and* the Senate, *shall,* before it becomes a law, be presented to the President of the United States. . . ." Art. I, § 7, cl. 2. (Emphasis added.)
>
> "*Every* Order, Resolution, or Vote to which the Concurrence of the Senate and House of Representatives may be necessary (except on a question of Adjournment) *shall be* presented to the President of the United States; and before the Same shall take

Effect, *shall be* approved by him, or being disapproved by him, *shall be* repassed by two thirds of the Senate and House of Representatives, according to the Rules and Limitations prescribed in the Case of a Bill." Art. I, § 7, cl. 3. (Emphasis added.)

These provisions of Art. I are integral parts of the constitutional design for the separation of powers. . . .

We see therefore that the Framers were acutely conscious that the bicameral requirement and the Presentment Clauses would serve essential constitutional functions. The President's participation in the legislative process was to protect the Executive Branch from Congress and to protect the whole people from improvident laws. The division of the Congress into two distinctive bodies assures that the legislative power would be exercised only after opportunity for full study and debate in separate settings. The President's unilateral veto power, in turn, was limited by the power of two-thirds of both Houses of Congress to overrule a veto thereby precluding final arbitrary action of one person. . . . It emerges clearly that the prescription for legislative action in Art. I, §§ 1, 7, represents the Framers' decision that the legislative power of the Federal Government be exercised in accord with a single, finely wrought and exhaustively considered, procedure. . . .

Not every action taken by either House is subject to the bicameralism and presentment requirements of Art. I. See *infra* . . . nn. 20, 21. Whether actions taken by either House are, in law and fact, an exercise of legislative power depends not on their form but upon "whether they contain matter which is properly to be regarded as legislative in its character and effect." S. Rep. No. 1335, 54th Cong., 2d Sess., 8 (1897).

Examination of the action taken here by one House pursuant to § 244(c)(2) reveals that it was essentially legislative in purpose and effect. In purporting to exercise power defined in Art. I, § 8, cl. 4, to "establish an uniform Rule of Naturalization," the House took action that had the purpose and effect of altering the legal rights, duties, and relations of persons, including the Attorney General, Executive Branch officials and Chadha, all outside the Legislative Branch. Section 244(c)(2) purports to authorize one House of Congress to require the Attorney General to deport an individual alien whose deportation otherwise would be canceled under § 244. The one-House veto operated in these cases to overrule the Attorney General and mandate Chadha's deportation; absent the House action, Chadha would remain in the United States. Congress has *acted* and its action has altered Chadha's status.

The legislative character of the one-House veto in these cases is confirmed by the character of the congressional action it supplants. Neither the House of Representatives nor the Senate contends that, absent the veto provision in § 244(c)(2), either of them, or both of them acting together, could effectively require the Attorney General to deport an alien once the Attorney General, in the exercise of legislatively delegated authority, had determined the alien should remain in the United States. Without the challenged provision in § 244(c)(2), this could have been achieved, if at all, only by legislation requiring deportation. Similarly, a veto by one House of Congress under § 244(c)(2) cannot be justified as an attempt at amending the standards set out in § 244(a)(1), or as a repeal of § 244 as applied to Chadha. Amendment and repeal of statutes, no less than enactment, must conform with Art. I.

The nature of the decision implemented by the one-House veto in these cases further manifests its legislative character. After long experience with the clumsy, time-consuming private bill procedure, Congress made a deliberate choice to delegate to the Executive Branch, and specifically to the Attorney General, the authority to allow deportable aliens to remain in this country in certain specified circumstances. It is not disputed that this choice to delegate authority is precisely the kind of decision that can be implemented only in accordance with the procedures set out in Art. I. Disagreement with the Attorney General's decision on Chadha's deportation—that is, Congress' decision to deport Chadha—no less than Congress' original choice to delegate to the Attorney General the authority to make that decision, involves determinations of policy that Congress can implement in only one way; bicameral passage followed by presentment to the President. Congress must abide by its delegation of authority until that delegation is legislatively altered or revoked.

Finally, we see that when the Framers intended to authorize either House of Congress to act alone and outside of its prescribed bicameral legislative role, they narrowly and precisely defined the procedure for such action. [The Court then discusses four constitutional provisions by which one House may act alone, such as according to the House of Representatives the sole power to initiate impeachments. *See* U.S. CONST. Art. I, § 2, cl. 5.] . . .

Since it is clear that the action by the House under § 244(c)(2) was not within any of the express constitutional exceptions authorizing one House to act alone, and equally clear that it was an exercise of legislative power, that action was subject to the standards prescribed in Art. I. The bicameral requirement, the Presentment Clauses, the President's veto, and Congress' power to override a veto were intended to erect enduring checks on each Branch and to protect the people from the improvident exercise of power by mandating certain prescribed steps. To preserve those checks, and maintain the separation of powers, the carefully defined limits on the power of each Branch must not be eroded. To accomplish what has been attempted by one House of Congress in this case requires action in conformity with the express procedures of the Constitution's prescription for legislative action: passage by a majority of both Houses and presentment to the President. . . .

The choices we discern as having been made in the Constitutional Convention impose burdens on governmental processes that often seem clumsy, inefficient, even unworkable, but those hard choices were consciously made by men who had lived under a form of government that permitted arbitrary governmental acts to go unchecked. There is no support in the Constitution or decisions of this Court for the proposition that the cumbersomeness and delays often encountered in complying with explicit constitutional standards may be avoided, either by the Congress or by the President. *See Youngstown Sheet & Tube Co. v. Sawyer,* 343 U.S. 579 (1952). With all the obvious flaws of delay, untidiness, and potential for abuse, we have not yet found a better way to preserve freedom than by making the exercise of power subject to the carefully crafted restraints spelled out in the Constitution.

Affirmed. . . .

JUSTICE WHITE, dissenting.

Today the Court not only invalidates § 244(c)(2) of the Immigration and Nationality Act, but also sounds the death knell for nearly 200 other statutory provisions in which Congress has reserved a "legislative veto." For this reason, the Court's decision is of surpassing importance. And it is for this reason that the Court would have been well advised to decide the cases, if possible, on the narrower grounds of separation of powers, leaving for full consideration the constitutionality of other congressional review statutes operating on such varied matters as war powers and agency rulemaking, some of which concern the independent regulatory agencies.

The prominence of the legislative veto mechanism in our contemporary political system and its importance to Congress can hardly be overstated. It has become a central means by which Congress secures the accountability of executive and independent agencies. Without the legislative veto, Congress is faced with a Hobson's choice: either to refrain from delegating the necessary authority, leaving itself with a hopeless task of writing laws with the requisite specificity to cover endless special circumstances across the entire policy landscape, or in the alternative, to abdicate its law-making function to the Executive Branch and independent agencies. To choose the former leaves major national problems unresolved; to opt for the latter risks unaccountable policymaking by those not elected to fill that role. Accordingly, over the past five decades, the legislative veto has been placed in nearly 200 statutes.[2] The device is known in every field of governmental concern: reorganization, budgets, foreign affairs, war

[2] A selected list and brief description of these provisions is appended to this opinion.

powers, and regulation of trade, safety, energy, the environment, and the economy. . . .

During the 1970's the legislative veto was important in resolving a series of major constitutional disputes between the President and Congress over claims of the President to broad impoundment, war, and national emergency powers. The key provision of the War Powers Resolution authorizes the termination by concurrent resolution of the use of armed forces in hostilities. . . .

Even this brief review suffices to demonstrate that the legislative veto is more than "efficient, convenient, and useful." It is an important if not indispensable political invention that allows the President and Congress to resolve major constitutional and policy differences, assures the accountability of independent regulatory agencies, and preserves Congress' control over lawmaking. Perhaps there are other means of accommodation and accountability, but the increasing reliance of Congress upon the legislative veto suggests that the alternatives to which Congress must now turn are not entirely satisfactory. . . .

APPENDIX TO OPINION OF WHITE, J., DISSENTING, STATUTES WITH PROVISIONS AUTHORIZING CONGRESSIONAL REVIEW

This compilation, reprinted from the Brief for the United States Senate, identifies and describes briefly current statutory provisions for a legislative veto by one or both Houses of Congress. . . .

A.

FOREIGN AFFAIRS AND NATIONAL SECURITY

1. Act for International Development of 1961 (Funds made available for foreign assistance under the Act may be terminated by concurrent resolution).

2. War Powers Resolution (Absent declaration of war, President may be directed by concurrent resolution to remove United States armed forces engaged in foreign hostilities.)

[the remaining statutes on Justice White's list are omitted]

NOTES

1. *Thwarting a Congressional Claw-Back.* As indicated in *Chadha*, the increased effort to use legislative vetoes was probably the result of an increased delegation of power from Congress to the president over the past 70 years. As a matter of constitutional theory, why is the Court willing to tolerate extensive delegation of power to the president that is legislative in nature, but is unwilling to allow Congress to try to maintain some kind of check on that power through a legislative veto? Do you think *Chadha* is constitutionally sound or does it rely upon an overly rigid conception of separation of powers?

2. *Types of Congressional Measures*. Four kinds of measures are used by Congress: bills, joint resolutions, concurrent resolutions, and simple resolutions. A *bill* is passed by both houses and presented to the president for his signature or veto. If enacted, it has the force of law. A *joint resolution* is different in name only: it too is passed by both houses and presented to the president for his signature or veto. The two can be used interchangeably, although proposals to amend the Constitution typically are set forth in joint resolutions. A *concurrent resolution* is passed by both houses, but not sent to the president. Consequently, it does not have the force and effect of law. Concurrent resolutions often are used for "sense-of-the-Congress" statements. A *simple resolution* is passed by only one house and thus also lacks the force of law. It is used to amend the standing rules of that house and for "sense-of-the-House" or "sense-of-the-Senate" declarations. *Chadha* involved use of a simple resolution. Does the reasoning of the Court apply equally to a legislative veto consisting of a concurrent resolution? Should it matter that the one-House veto in *Chadha* was not enacted as a "bolt out of the blue" but was incorporated in an otherwise valid statute?

3. *Convenience and Efficiency*. Is the Court correct in assuming that congressional use of the legislative veto is motivated by concerns of "convenience and efficiency"? Could not the alternative—a statute spelling out specific limits on executive discretion—actually be more convenient and efficient, inasmuch as it would involve no subsequent congressional approval or disapproval procedure? Is not the real reason for the legislative veto, or at least some legislative vetoes, a belief that certain executive activities require regulation but cannot be regulated with specific, *prospective* statutory limitation?

4. *Post-Enactment Contingencies*. There are numerous statutes that delegate authority to an executive official so long as certain statutorily-specified contingencies occur after enactment. That contingency is often a finding by the president that a certain event has (or has not) occurred. The contingency need not turn solely on an executive branch determination, however. For example, in January 2004 Congress passed and President George W. Bush signed into law the Millennium Challenge Act of 2003 (MCA). *See* 22 U.S.C. § § 7701–18 (2006). Under the statute, a developing country may qualify for foreign aid if it demonstrates commitment to three broad criteria: good governance; health and education for its people; and sound economic policies. A "Millennium Challenge Corporation" (MCC) was established as a government corporation to administer the MCA. The MCC uses sixteen "indicators" drawn from reputable sources (*e.g.*, Freedom House, the World Bank Institute, the Heritage Foundation) to measure developing country performance on the three criteria. Based on these indicators, the MCC selects those countries eligible for MCA assistance. If the MCC decides that the criteria have not been met for a country seeking aid, then that country cannot receive aid under the MCA.

The Supreme Court has previously upheld the constitutionality of statutes which condition the authority granted therein upon the occurrence or nonoccurrence of a specified contingent event. *See, e.g., J. W. Hampton & Co. v. United States*, 276 U.S. 394 (1927) (statute authorizing the president to raise tariff rates if he determines it necessary to equalize foreign and domestic production costs); *Hirabayashi v. United States*, 320 U.S. 81 (1943) (statute authorizing a military commander to determine that danger existed warranting imposition of a curfew).

Why is it that the effectiveness of action legislative in character may be conditioned upon decisions by organizations such as Freedom House or the Heritage Foundation, but under *Chadha,* may not be conditioned on the vote of the two legislative bodies of the Congress? Is it sufficient to say that the effect accorded to Freedom House or the Heritage Foundation is not governed by the Presentment Clause?

5. *Functional Effects of* Chadha. In considering this issue it may be useful to examine the functional effect of the *Chadha* decision. A good vehicle for illustrating that effect is the Arms Export Control Act, Pub. L. No. 94–329, 90 Stat. 729 (1976), as amended. In 1976, following concerns about arms sales abuses, the Senate Foreign Relations Committee proposed sweeping revisions of the Foreign Military Sales Act, including renaming it the "Arms Export Control Act." President Ford vetoed the original version of the Act, objecting, *inter alia,* to various legislative veto provisions. *See* President's Message to the Senate Returning S. 2662 Without His Approval, 12 WEEKLY COMP. PRES. DOC. 828 (May 7, 1976). A new version was considered and several of the legislative vetoes were dropped, but the Act continued to provide, in section 36(b), that Congress could disapprove certain presidentially-proposed arms sales in excess of $25 million in value through the use of a concurrent resolution. After *Chadha,* such use of the concurrent resolution is no longer permissible, and the Act was amended to preclude such sales when prohibited by joint resolution. *See* 22 U.S.C. § 2753 (2006).

Clearly, however, the Act could have been re-written to permit presidential arms sales in excess of $25 million only if approved by a bill or joint resolution. Under such circumstances, to make the proposed sale, the president would have to persuade a majority in each house of Congress to vote for the proposed sale. In other words, where before it took *two* houses of Congress to block presidential action, after *Chadha* a majority of only *one* house might be required to do so. It thus seems doubtful that the decision in all circumstances benefits the president. Moreover, could it not be argued that, viewed functionally, certain pre-*Chadha* procedures better served principles of bicameralism than those now required by the Court?

6. *Interpretive Theory.* Why should the Court's inquiry be "sharpened rather than blunted by the fact that Congressional veto provisions are appearing with greater frequency . . ."? Does not practice provide a "gloss" on the constitutional text? The original version of the Arms Export Control Act (discussed in the prior note) included seven legislative veto provisions. *See* S. 2662, 94th Cong., 1st Sess. (1975). In justifying those provisions constitutionally, the Senate Foreign Relations Committee said that, "[i]f

custom has tended to validate otherwise questionable practices engaged in by the executive branch, custom would seem just as surely to have validated the congressional practice embodied in the legislative veto." S. Rep. No. 94–605, 94th Cong., 2d Sess., at 15 (1976).

7. *Relation to War Powers Resolution*. Should it matter whether the presidential act subject to the veto is authorized by the Constitution rather than by a statute? See the materials concerning the legislative veto in section 5(c) of the War Powers Resolution set forth in Chapter 4, Sec. 4.

ZIVOTOFSKY EX REL. ZIVOTOFSKY V. KERRY

135 S.Ct. 2076 (2015).

JUSTICE KENNEDY delivered the opinion of the Court.

A delicate subject lies in the background of this case. That subject is Jerusalem. Questions touching upon the history of the ancient city and its present legal and international status are among the most difficult and complex in international affairs. In our constitutional system these matters are committed to the Legislature and the Executive, not the Judiciary. As a result, in this opinion the Court does no more, and must do no more, than note the existence of international debate and tensions respecting Jerusalem. Those matters are for Congress and the President to discuss and consider as they seek to shape the Nation's foreign policies.

The Court addresses two questions to resolve the inter-branch dispute now before it. First, it must determine whether the President has the exclusive power to grant formal recognition to a foreign sovereign. Second, if he has that power, the Court must determine whether Congress can command the President and his Secretary of State to issue a formal statement that contradicts the earlier recognition. The statement in question here is a congressional mandate that allows a United States citizen born in Jerusalem to direct the President and Secretary of State, when issuing his passport, to state that his place of birth is "Israel."

I

A

Jerusalem's political standing has long been, and remains, one of the most sensitive issues in American foreign policy, and indeed it is one of the most delicate issues in current international affairs. In 1948, President Truman formally recognized Israel in a signed statement of "recognition." That statement did not recognize Israeli sovereignty over Jerusalem. Over the last 60 years, various actors have sought to assert full or partial sovereignty over the city, including Israel, Jordan, and the Palestinians. Yet, in contrast to a consistent policy of formal recognition of Israel, neither President Truman nor any later United States President has issued an official statement or declaration acknowledging any country's sovereignty over Jerusalem. Instead, the Executive Branch has maintained that " 'the status of Jerusalem ... should be decided not unilaterally but in consultation with all concerned.' " ... The President's position on Jerusalem is reflected in State Department policy regarding passports and consular reports of birth abroad. Understanding that passports will be construed as reflections of American policy, the State Department's Foreign Affairs Manual instructs its employees, in general, to record the place of birth on a passport as the "country [having] present sovereignty over the actual area of birth." Dept. of State, 7 Foreign Affairs Manual (FAM) § 1383.4 (1987). If a citizen objects to the country listed as sovereign by the State Department, he or she may list the city or town of birth rather than the country. See id., § 1383.6. The FAM, however, does not allow citizens to list a sovereign that conflicts with Executive Branch policy. See generally id., § 1383. Because the United States does not recognize any country as having sovereignty over Jerusalem, the FAM instructs employees to record the place of birth for citizens born there as "Jerusalem."

In 2002, Congress passed the Act at issue here, the Foreign Relations Authorization Act, Fiscal Year 2003, 116 Stat. 1350. Section 214 of the Act is titled "United States Policy with Respect to Jerusalem as the Capital of Israel." Id., at 1365. The subsection that lies at the heart of this case, § 214(d), addresses passports. That subsection seeks to override the FAM by allowing citizens born in Jerusalem to list their place of birth as "Israel." Titled "Record of Place of Birth as Israel for Passport Purposes," § 214(d) states "[f]or purposes of the registration of birth, certification of nationality, or issuance of a passport of a United States citizen born in the city of Jerusalem, the Secretary shall, upon the request of the citizen or the citizen's legal guardian, record the place of birth as Israel." Id., at 1366.

When he signed the Act into law, President George W. Bush issued a statement declaring his position that § 214 would, "if construed as mandatory rather than advisory, impermissibly interfere with the President's constitutional authority to formulate the position of the United States, speak for the Nation in international affairs, and determine the terms on which recognition is given to foreign states." Statement on Signing the Foreign Relations Authorization Act, Fiscal Year 2003, Public Papers of the Presidents, George W. Bush, Vol. 2, Sept. 30, 2002, p. 1698 (2005). The President concluded, "U. S. policy regarding Jerusalem has not changed." Ibid.

Some parties were not reassured by the President's statement. A cable from the United States Consulate in Jerusalem noted that the Palestine Liberation Organization Executive Committee, Fatah Central Committee, and the Palestinian Authority Cabinet had all issued statements claiming that the Act " 'undermines the role of the U. S. as a sponsor of the peace process.' " In the Gaza Strip and elsewhere residents marched in protest.

In response the Secretary of State advised diplomats to express their understanding of "Jerusalem's importance to both sides and to many others around the world." He noted his belief that America's "policy towards Jerusalem" had not changed.

B

In 2002, petitioner Menachem Binyamin Zivotofsky was born to United States citizens living in Jerusalem. In December 2002, Zivotofsky's mother visited the American Embassy in Tel Aviv to request both a passport and a consular report of birth abroad for her son. She asked that his place of birth be listed as " 'Jerusalem, Israel.' " The Embassy clerks explained that, pursuant to State Department policy, the passport would list only "Jerusalem." Zivotofsky's parents objected and, as his guardians, brought suit on his behalf in the United States District Court for the District of Columbia, seeking to enforce § 214(d).

Pursuant to § 214(d), Zivotofsky claims the right to have "Israel" recorded as his place of birth in his passport. . . .

II

In considering claims of Presidential power this Court refers to Justice Jackson's familiar tripartite framework from *Youngstown Sheet & Tube Co. v. Sawyer,* 343 U. S. 579, 635–638 (1952) (concurring opinion). . . .

In this case the Secretary contends that § 214(d) infringes on the President's exclusive recognition power by "requiring the President to contradict his recognition position regarding Jerusalem in official communications with foreign sovereigns." In so doing the Secretary acknowledges the President's power is "at its lowest ebb." *Youngstown*, 343 U. S., at 637. Because the President's refusal to implement § 214(d) falls into Justice Jackson's third category, his claim must be "scrutinized with caution," and he may rely solely on powers the Constitution grants to him alone.

To determine whether the President possesses the exclusive power of recognition the Court examines the Constitution's text and structure, as well as precedent and history bearing on the question.

A

Recognition is a "formal acknowledgement" that a particular "entity possesses the qualifications for statehood" or "that a particular regime is the effective government of a state." Restatement (Third) of Foreign Relations Law of the United States § 203, Comment a, p. 84 (1986). It may also involve the determination of a state's territorial bounds. See 2 M. Whiteman, Digest of International Law § 1, p. 1 (1963) (Whiteman) ("[S]tates may recognize or decline to recognize territory as belonging to, or under the sovereignty of, or having been acquired or lost by, other states").

Recognition is often effected by an express "written or oral declaration." 1 J. Moore, Digest of International Law § 27, p. 73 (1906) (Moore). It may also be implied—for example, by concluding a bilateral treaty or by sending or receiving diplomatic agents. Ibid.; I. Brownlie, Principles of Public International Law 93 (7th ed. 2008) (Brownlie).

Legal consequences follow formal recognition. Recognized sovereigns may sue in United States courts, *see Guaranty Trust Co. v. United States*, 304 U. S. 126, 137 (1938), and may benefit from sovereign immunity when they are sued, *see National City Bank of N. Y. v. Republic of China*, 348 U. S. 356, 358–359 (1955). The actions of a recognized sovereign committed within its own territory also receive deference in domestic courts under the act of state doctrine. *See Oetjen v. Central Leather Co.*, 246 U. S. 297, 302–303 (1918). Recognition at international law, furthermore, is a precondition of regular diplomatic relations. Recognition is thus "useful, even necessary," to the existence of a state. Ibid.

Despite the importance of the recognition power in foreign relations, the Constitution does not use the term "recognition," either in Article II or elsewhere. The Secretary asserts that the President exercises the recognition power based on the Reception Clause, which directs that the President "shall receive Ambassadors and other public Ministers." Art. II, § 3. As Zivotofsky notes, the Reception Clause received little attention at the Constitutional Convention. In fact, during the ratification debates, Alexander Hamilton claimed that the power to receive ambassadors was "more a matter of dignity than of authority," a ministerial duty largely "without consequence." The Federalist No. 69, p. 420 (C. Rossiter ed. 1961).

At the time of the founding, however, prominent international scholars suggested that receiving an ambassador was tantamount to recognizing the sovereignty of the sending state. See E. de Vattel, The Law of Nations § 78, p. 461 (1758) (J. Chitty ed. 1853) ("[E]very state, truly possessed of sovereignty, has a right to send ambassadors" and "to contest their right in this instance" is equivalent to "contesting their sovereign dignity"). . . . It is a logical and proper inference, then, that a Clause directing the President alone to receive ambassadors would be understood to acknowledge his power to recognize other nations.

This in fact occurred early in the Nation's history when President Washington recognized the French Revolutionary Government by receiving its ambassador. After this incident the import of the Reception Clause became clear—causing Hamilton to change his earlier view. He wrote that the Reception Clause "includes th[e power] of judging, in the case of a revolution of government in a foreign country, whether the new rulers are competent organs of the national will, and ought to be recognised, or not." As a result, the Reception Clause provides support, although not the sole authority, for the President's power to recognize other nations. The inference that the President exercises the recognition power is further supported by his additional Article II powers. It is for the President, "by and with the Advice and Consent of the Senate," to "make Treaties, provided two thirds of the Senators present concur." Art. II, § 2, cl. 2. In addition, "he shall nominate, and by and with the Advice and Consent of the Senate, shall appoint Ambassadors" as well as "other public Ministers and Consuls."

As a matter of constitutional structure, these additional powers give the President control over recognition decisions. At international law, recognition may be effected by different means, but each means is dependent upon Presidential power. In addition to receiving an ambassador, recognition may occur on "the conclusion of a bilateral treaty," or the "formal initiation of diplomatic relations," including the dispatch of an ambassador. The President has the sole power to negotiate treaties, see *United States* v. *Curtiss-Wright Export Corp.*, 299 U. S. 304, 319 (1936), and the Senate may not conclude or ratify a treaty without Presidential action. The President, too, nominates the Nation's ambassadors and dispatches other diplomatic agents. Congress may not send an ambassador without his involvement. Beyond that, the President himself has the power to open diplomatic channels simply by engaging in direct diplomacy with foreign heads of state and their ministers. The Constitution thus assigns the President means to effect recognition on his own initiative. Congress, by contrast, has no constitutional power that would enable it to initiate diplomatic relations with a foreign nation. Because these specific Clauses confer the recognition power on the President, the Court need not consider whether or to what extent the Vesting Clause, which provides that the "executive Power" shall be vested in the President, provides further support for the President's action here. Art. II, § 1, cl. 1.

The text and structure of the Constitution grant the President the power to recognize foreign nations and governments. The question then becomes whether that power is exclusive. The various ways in which the President may unilaterally effect recognition—and the lack of any similar power vested in Congress—suggest that it is. So, too, do functional considerations. Put simply, the Nation must have a single policy regarding which governments are legitimate in the eyes of the United States and which are not. Foreign countries need to know, before entering into diplomatic relations or commerce with the United States, whether their ambassadors will be received; whether their officials will be immune from suit in federal court; and whether they may initiate lawsuits here to vindicate their rights. These assurances cannot be equivocal.

Recognition is a topic on which the Nation must " 'speak . . . with one voice.' " *American Ins. Assn.* v. *Garamendi*, 539 U. S. 396, 424 (2003) (quoting *Crosby* v. *National Foreign Trade Council*, 530 U. S. 363, 381 (2000)). That voice must be the President's. Between the two political branches, only the Executive has the characteristic of unity at all times. And with unity comes the ability to exercise, to a greater degree, "[d]ecision, activity, secrecy, and dispatch." The Federalist No. 70, p. 424 (A. Hamilton). The President is capable, in ways Congress is not, of engaging in the delicate and often secret diplomatic contacts that may lead to a decision on recognition. He is also better positioned to take the decisive, unequivocal action necessary to recognize other states at international law. 1 Oppenheim's International Law § 50, p. 169 (R. Jennings & A. Watts eds., 9th ed. 1992) (act of recognition must "leave no doubt as to the intention to grant it"). These qualities explain why the Framers listed the traditional avenues of recognition—receiving ambassadors, making treaties, and sending ambassadors—as among the President's Article II powers. . . .

It remains true, of course, that many decisions affecting foreign relations—including decisions that may determine the course of our relations with recognized countries—require congressional action. . . .

In foreign affairs, as in the domestic realm, the Constitution "enjoins upon its branches separateness but interdependence, autonomy but reciprocity." *Youngstown*, 343 U. S., at 635 (Jackson, J., concurring). Although the President alone effects the formal act of recognition, Congress' powers, and its central role in making laws, give it substantial authority regarding many of the policy determinations that precede and follow the act of recognition itself. If Congress disagrees with the President's recognition policy, there may be consequences. Formal recognition may seem a hollow act if it is not accompanied by the dispatch of an ambassador, the easing of trade restrictions, and the conclusion of treaties. And those decisions require action by the Senate or the whole Congress.

In practice, then, the President's recognition determination is just one part of a political process that may require Congress to make laws. The President's exclusive recognition power encompasses the authority to acknowledge, in a formal sense, the legitimacy of other states and governments, including their territorial bounds. Albeit limited, the exclusive recognition power is essential to the conduct of Presidential duties. The formal act of recognition is an executive power that Congress may not qualify. If the President is to be effective in negotiations over a formal recognition determination, it must be evident to his counterparts abroad that he speaks for the Nation on that precise question.

A clear rule that the formal power to recognize a foreign government subsists in the President therefore serves a necessary purpose in diplomatic relations. All this, of course, underscores that Congress has an important role in other aspects of foreign policy, and the President may be bound by any number of laws Congress enacts. In this way ambition counters ambition, ensuring that the democratic will of the people is observed and respected in foreign affairs as in the domestic realm. See The Federalist No. 51, p. 322 (J. Madison).

B

No single precedent resolves the question whether the President has exclusive recognition authority and, if so, how far that power extends. In part that is because, until today, the political branches have resolved their disputes over questions of recognition. The relevant cases, though providing important instruction, address the division of recognition power between the Federal Government and the States, see, *e.g., Pink*, 315 U. S. 203, or between the courts and the political branches, see, *e.g., Banco Nacional de Cuba*, 376 U. S., at 410—not between the President and Congress. As the parties acknowledge, some isolated statements in those cases lend support to the position that Congress has a role in the recognition process. In the end, however, a fair reading of the cases shows that the President's role in the recognition process is both central and exclusive.

. . . [D]uring the 1930's and 1940's, the Court addressed issues surrounding President Roosevelt's decision to recognize the Soviet Government of Russia. In *United States* v. *Belmont,* 301 U. S. 324 (1937), and *Pink*, 315 U. S. 203, New York state courts declined to give full effect to the terms of executive agreements the President had concluded in negotiations over recognition of the Soviet regime. In particular the state courts, based on New York public policy, did not treat assets that had been seized by the Soviet Government as property of Russia and declined to turn those assets over to the United States. The Court stated that it "may not be doubted" that "recognition, establishment of diplomatic relations, . . . and agreements with respect thereto" are "within the competence of the President." In these matters, "the Executive ha[s] authority to speak as the sole organ of th[e] government." The Court added that the President's authority "is not limited to a determination of the government to be recognized. It includes the power to determine the policy which is to govern the question of recognition." Thus, New York state courts were required to respect the executive agreements.

It is true, of course, that *Belmont* and *Pink* are not direct holdings that the recognition power is exclusive. Those cases considered the validity of executive agreements, not the initial act of recognition. The President's determination in those cases did not contradict an Act of Congress. And the primary issue was whether the executive agreements could supersede state law. Still, the language in *Pink* and *Belmont*, which confirms the President's competence to determine questions of recognition, is strong support for the conclusion that it is for the President alone to determine which foreign governments are legitimate.

Banco Nacional de Cuba contains even stronger statements regarding the President's authority over recognition. There, the status of Cuba's Government and its acts as a sovereign were at issue. As the Court explained, "Political recognition is exclusively a function of the Executive." 376 U. S., at 410. Because the Executive had recognized the Cuban Government, the Court held that it should be treated as sovereign and could benefit from the "act of state" doctrine. . . As these cases illustrate, the Court has long considered recognition to be the exclusive prerogative of the Executive.

The Secretary now urges the Court to define the executive power over foreign relations in even broader terms. He contends that under the Court's precedent the President has "exclusive authority to conduct diplomatic relations," along with "the bulk of foreign-affairs powers." In support of his submission that the President has broad, undefined powers over foreign affairs, the Secretary quotes *United States* v. *Curtiss-Wright Export Corp.*, which described the President as "the sole organ of the federal government in the field of international relations." 299 U. S., at 320. This Court declines to acknowledge that unbounded power. A formulation broader than the rule that the President alone determines what nations to formally recognize as legitimate—and that he consequently controls his statements on matters of recognition—presents different issues and is unnecessary to the resolution of this case. . . .

Th[e] description of the President's exclusive power was not necessary to the holding of *Curtiss-Wright*—which, after all, dealt with congressionally authorized action, not a unilateral Presidential determination. Indeed, *Curtiss-Wright* did not hold that the President is free from Congress' lawmaking power in the field of international relations. . . . [W]hether the realm is foreign or domestic, it is still the Legislative Branch, not the Executive Branch, that makes the law.

In a world that is ever more compressed and interdependent, it is essential the congressional role in foreign affairs be understood and respected. For it is Congress that makes laws, and in countless ways its laws will and should shape the Nation's course. The Executive is not free from the ordinary controls and checks of Congress merely because foreign affairs are at issue. . . .

That said, judicial precedent and historical practice teach that it is for the President alone to make the specific decision of what foreign power he will recognize as legitimate, both for the Nation as a whole and for the purpose of making his own position clear within the context of recognition in discussions and negotiations with foreign nations. Recognition is an act with immediate and powerful significance for international relations, so the President's position must be clear. Congress cannot require him to contradict his own statement regarding a determination of formal recognition. . . .

C

Having examined the Constitution's text and this Court's precedent, it is appropriate to turn to accepted understandings and practice. In separation-of-powers cases this Court has often "put significant weight upon historical practice." *NLRB* v. *Noel Canning*, 573 U. S. ___, ___, 134 S.Ct. 2550, 2559 (2014) (emphasis deleted). Here, history is not all on one side, but on balance it provides strong support for the conclusion that the recognition power is the President's alone. As Zivotofsky argues, certain historical incidents can be interpreted to support the position that recognition is a shared power. But the weight of historical evidence supports the opposite view, which is that the formal determination of recognition is a power to be exercised only by the President. . . .

[E]ven a brief survey of the major historical examples, with an emphasis on those said to favor Zivotofsky, establishes no more than that some Presidents have chosen to cooperate with Congress, not that Congress itself has exercised the recognition power.

The first debate over the recognition power arose in 1793, after France had been torn by revolution. . . . [T]he new French Government proposed to send an ambassador, Citizen Genet, to the United States. . . . Members of the President's Cabinet agreed that receiving Genet would be a binding and public act of recognition. . . . They decided, however, both that Genet should be received and that consultation with Congress was not necessary. . . . Congress expressed no disagreement with this position, and Genet's reception marked the Nation's first act of recognition—one made by the President alone. . . . For the most part, Congress has respected the Executive's policies and positions as to formal recognition. At times, Congress itself has defended the President's constitutional prerogative. Over the last 100 years, there has been scarcely any debate over the President's power to recognize foreign states. In this respect the Legislature, in the narrow context of recognition, on balance has acknowledged the importance of speaking "with one voice." The weight of historical evidence indicates Congress has accepted that the power to recognize foreign states and governments and their territorial bounds is exclusive to the Presidency.

III

As the power to recognize foreign states resides in the President alone, the question becomes whether § 214(d) infringes on the Executive's consistent decision to withhold recognition with respect to Jerusalem. . . .

Section 214(d) requires that, in a passport or consular report of birth abroad, "the Secretary shall, upon the request of the citizen or the citizen's legal guardian, record the place of birth as Israel" for a "United States citizen born in the city of Jerusalem." 116 Stat. 1366. That is, § 214(d) requires the President, through the Secretary, to identify citizens born in Jerusalem who so request as being born in Israel. But according to the President, those citizens were not born in Israel. As a matter of United States policy, neither Israel nor any other country is acknowledged as having sovereignty over Jerusalem. In this way, § 214(d) "directly contradicts" the "carefully calibrated and longstanding Executive branch policy of neutrality toward Jerusalem."

If the power over recognition is to mean anything, it must mean that the President not only makes the initial, formal recognition determination but also that he may maintain that determination in his and his agent's statements. This conclusion is a matter of both common sense and necessity. If Congress could command the President to state a recognition position inconsistent with his own, Congress could override the President's recognition determination. Under international law, recognition may be effected by "written or oral declaration of the recognizing state." 1 Moore § 27, at 73. In addition an act of recognition must "leave no doubt as to the intention to grant it." 1 Oppenheim's International Law § 50, at 169. Thus, if Congress could alter the President's statements on matters of recognition or force him to contradict them, Congress in effect would exercise the recognition power. . . .

If Congress may not pass a law, speaking in its own voice, that effects formal recognition, then it follows that it may not force the President himself to contradict his earlier statement. That congressional command would not only prevent the Nation from speaking with one voice but also prevent the Executive itself from doing so in conducting foreign relations.

Although the statement required by § 214(d) would not itself constitute a formal act of recognition, it is a mandate that the Executive contradict his prior recognition determination in an official document issued by the Secretary of State. See *Urtetiqui* v. *D'Arcy*, 9 Pet. 692, 699 (1835) (a passport "from its nature and object, is addressed to foreign powers" and "is to be considered . . . in the character of a political document"). As a result, it is unconstitutional. This is all the more clear in light of the longstanding treatment of a passport's place-of-birth section as an official executive statement implicating recognition. The Secretary's position on this point has been consistent: He will not place information in the place-of-birth section of a passport that contradicts the President's recognition policy. See 7 FAM § 1383. If a citizen objects to the country listed as sovereign over his place of birth, then the Secretary will accommodate him by listing the city or town of birth rather than the country. See *id.*, § 1383.6. But the Secretary will not list a sovereign that contradicts the President's recognition policy in a passport. Thus, the

Secretary will not list "Israel" in a passport as the country containing Jerusalem.

The flaw in § 214(d) is further underscored by the undoubted fact that that the purpose of the statute was to infringe on the recognition power—a power the Court now holds is the sole prerogative of the President. The statute is titled "United States Policy with Respect to Jerusalem as the Capital of Israel." § 214, 116 Stat. 1365. The House Conference Report proclaimed that § 214 "contains four provisions related to the recognition of Jerusalem as Israel's capital." H. R. Conf. Rep. No. 107–671, p. 123 (2002). And, indeed, observers interpreted § 214 as altering United States policy regarding Jerusalem—which led to protests across the region. . .

It is true, as Zivotofsky notes, that Congress has substantial authority over passports. . . . In *Kent* v. *Dulles*, for example, the Court held that if a person's " 'liberty' " to travel "is to be regulated" through a passport, "it must be pursuant to the law-making functions of the Congress." Later cases, such as *Zemel* v. *Rusk* and *Haig* v. *Agee*, also proceeded on the assumption that Congress must authorize the grounds on which passports may be approved or denied. See *Zemel*, at 7–13; *Haig*, *supra*, at 289–306. This is consistent with the extensive lawmaking power the Constitution vests in Congress over the Nation's foreign affairs.

The problem with § 214(d), however, lies in how Congress exercised its authority over passports. It was an improper act for Congress to "aggrandiz[e] its power at the expense of another branch" by requiring the President to contradict an earlier recognition determination in an official document issued by the Executive Branch. *Freytag* v. *Commissioner*, 501 U.S. 868, 878 (1991). To allow Congress to control the President's communication in the context of a formal recognition determination is to allow Congress to exercise that exclusive power itself. As a result, the statute is unconstitutional. . . .

In holding § 214(d) invalid the Court does not question the substantial powers of Congress over foreign affairs in general or passports in particular. This case is confined solely to the exclusive power of the President to control recognition determinations, including formal statements by the Executive Branch acknowledging the legitimacy of a state or government and its territorial bounds. Congress cannot command the President to contradict an earlier recognition determination in the issuance of passports. . . .

CHIEF JUSTICE ROBERTS, with whom JUSTICE ALITO joins, dissenting.

Today's decision is a first: Never before has this Court accepted a President's direct defiance of an Act of Congress in the field of foreign affairs. We have instead stressed that the President's power reaches "its lowest ebb" when he contravenes the express will of Congress, "for what is at stake is the equilibrium established by our constitutional system." *Youngstown Sheet & Tube Co.* v. *Sawyer*, 343 U.S. 579, 637–638 (1952) (Jackson, J., concurring). . . .

In this case, the President claims the exclusive and preclusive power to recognize foreign sovereigns. The Court devotes much of its analysis to accepting the Executive's contention. I have serious doubts about that position. The majority places great weight on the Reception Clause, which directs that the Executive "shall receive Ambassadors and other public Ministers." Art. II, § 3. But that provision, framed as an obligation rather than an authorization, appears alongside the *duties* imposed on the President by Article II, Section 3, not the *powers* granted to him by Article II, Section 2. Indeed, the People ratified the Constitution with Alexander Hamilton's assurance that executive reception of ambassadors "is more a matter of dignity than of authority" and "will be without consequence in the administration of the government." The Federalist No. 69, p. 420 (C. Rossiter ed. 1961). In short, at the time of the founding, "there was no reason to view the reception clause as a source of discretionary authority for the president." Adler, The President's Recognition Power: Ministerial or Discretionary? 25 Presidential Studies Q. 267, 269 (1995). . . .

Precedent and history lend no more weight to the Court's position. The majority cites dicta suggesting an exclusive executive recognition power, but acknowledges contrary dicta suggesting that the power is shared. . . . When the best you can muster is conflicting dicta, precedent can hardly be said to support your side.

As for history, the majority admits that it too points in both directions. Some Presidents have claimed an exclusive recognition power, but others have expressed uncertainty about whether such preclusive authority exists. . . .

In sum, although the President has authority over recognition, I am not convinced that the Constitution provides the "conclusive and preclusive" power required to justify defiance of an express legislative mandate. *Youngstown*, 343 U. S., at 638 (Jackson, J., concurring). As the leading scholar on this issue has concluded, the "text, original understanding, post-ratification history, and structure of the Constitution do not support the . . . expansive claim that this executive power is plenary." Reinstein, Is the President's Recognition Power Exclusive? 86 Temp. L. Rev. 1, 60 (2013).

But even if the President does have exclusive recognition power, he still cannot prevail in this case, because the statute at issue *does not implicate recognition*. The relevant provision, § 214(d), simply gives an American citizen born in Jerusalem the option to designate his place of birth as Israel "[f]or purposes of" passports and other documents. Foreign Relations Authorization Act, Fiscal Year 2003, 116 Stat. 1366. The State

Department itself has explained that "identification"—not recognition—"is the principal reason that U. S. passports require 'place of birth.' " Congress has not disputed the Executive's assurances that § 214(d) does not alter the longstanding United States position on Jerusalem. And the annals of diplomatic history record no examples of official recognition accomplished via optional passport designation.

The majority acknowledges both that the "Executive's exclusive power extends no further than his formal recognition determination" and that § 214(d) does "not itself constitute a formal act of recognition." Taken together, these statements come close to a confession of error. The majority attempts to reconcile its position by reconceiving § 214(d) as a "mandate that the Executive contradict his prior recognition determination in an official document issued by the Secretary of State." But as just noted, neither Congress nor the Executive Branch regards § 214(d) as a recognition determination, so it is hard to see how the statute could contradict any such determination.

At most, the majority worries that there may be a *perceived* contradiction based on a *mistaken* understanding of the effect of § 214(d), insisting that some "observers interpreted § 214 as altering United States policy regarding Jerusalem." To afford controlling weight to such impressions, however, is essentially to subject a duly enacted statute to an international heckler's veto.

Moreover, expanding the President's purportedly exclusive recognition power to include authority to avoid potential misunderstandings of legislative enactments proves far too much. Congress could validly exercise its enumerated powers in countless ways that would create more severe perceived contradictions with Presidential recognition decisions than does § 214(d). If, for example, the President recognized a particular country in opposition to Congress's wishes, Congress could declare war or impose a trade embargo on that country. A neutral observer might well conclude that these legislative actions had, to put it mildly, created a perceived contradiction with the President's recognition decision. And yet each of them would undoubtedly be constitutional. So too would statements by nonlegislative actors that might be seen to contradict the President's recognition positions, such as the declaration in a political party platform that "Jerusalem is and will remain the capital of Israel."

Ultimately, the only power that could support the President's position is the one the majority purports to reject: the "exclusive authority to conduct diplomatic relations." The Government offers a single citation for this allegedly exclusive power: *United States* v. *Curtiss-Wright Export Corp.*, 299 U.S. 304, 319–320 (1936). But as the majority rightly acknowledges, *Curtiss-Wright* did not involve a claim that the Executive could contravene a statute; it held only that he could act pursuant to a legislative delegation. . . .

JUSTICE SCALIA, with whom THE CHIEF JUSTICE and JUSTICE ALITO join, dissenting.

Before this country declared independence, the law of England entrusted the King with the exclusive care of his kingdom's foreign affairs. The royal prerogative included the "sole power of sending ambassadors to foreign states, and receiving them at home," the sole authority to "make treaties, leagues, and alliances with foreign states and princes," "the sole prerogative of making war and peace," and the "sole power of raising and regulating fleets and armies." 1 W. Blackstone, Commentaries *253, *257, *262. The People of the United States had other ideas when they organized our Government. They considered a sound structure of balanced powers essential to the preservation of just government, and international relations formed no exception to that principle.

The People therefore adopted a Constitution that divides responsibility for the Nation's foreign concerns between the legislative and executive departments. The Constitution gave the President the "executive Power," authority to send and responsibility to receive ambassadors, power to make treaties, and command of the Army and Navy—though they qualified some of these powers by requiring consent of the Senate. Art. II, §§ 1–3. At the same time, they gave Congress powers over war, foreign commerce, naturalization, and more. Art. I, § 8. "Fully eleven of the powers that Article I, § 8 grants Congress deal in some way with foreign affairs." L. Tribe, American Constitutional Law, § 5–18, p. 965.

This case arises out of a dispute between the Executive and Legislative Branches about whether the United States should treat Jerusalem as a part of Israel. The Constitution contemplates that the political branches will make policy about the territorial claims of foreign nations the same way they make policy about other international matters: The President will exercise his powers on the basis of his views, Congress its powers on the basis of its views. That is just what has happened here.

Before turning to Presidential power under Article II, I think it well to establish the statute's basis in congressional power under Article I. Congress's power to "establish an uniform Rule of Naturalization," Art. I, § 8, cl. 4, enables it to grant American citizenship to someone born abroad. The naturalization power also enables Congress to furnish the people it makes citizens with papers verifying their citizenship—say a consular report of birth abroad (which certifies citizenship of an American born outside the United States) or a passport (which certifies citizenship for purposes of international travel). . . .

One would think that if Congress may grant Zivotofsky a passport and a birth report, it may also require these papers to record his birthplace as

"Israel." The birthplace specification promotes the document's citizenship-authenticating function by identifying the bearer, distinguishing people with similar names but different birthplaces from each other, helping authorities uncover identity fraud, and facilitating retrieval of the Government's citizenship records. To be sure, recording Zivotovsky's birthplace as "Jerusalem" rather than "Israel" would fulfill these objectives, but when faced with alternative ways to carry its powers into execution, Congress has the "discretion" to choose the one it deems "most beneficial to the people." *McCulloch v. Maryland*, 4 Wheat. 316, 421 (1819). It thus has the right to decide that recording birthplaces as "Israel" makes for better foreign policy. Or that regardless of international politics, a passport or birth report should respect its bearer's conscientious belief that Jerusalem belongs to Israel.

No doubt congressional discretion in executing legislative powers has its limits; Congress's chosen approach must be not only "necessary" to carrying its powers into execution, but also "proper." Congress thus may not transcend boundaries upon legislative authority stated or implied elsewhere in the Constitution. But as we shall see, § 214(d) does not transgress any such restriction.

The Court frames this case as a debate about recognition. . . . The Court holds that the Constitution makes the President alone responsible for recognition and that § 214(d) invades this exclusive power. I agree that the Constitution *empowers* the President to extend recognition on behalf of the United States, but I find it a much harder question whether it makes that power exclusive. The Court tells us that "the weight of historical evidence" supports exclusive executive authority over "the formal determination of recognition." But even with its attention confined to formal recognition, the Court is forced to admit that "history is not all on one side." To take a stark example, Congress legislated in 1934 to grant independence to the Philippines, which were then an American colony. In the course of doing so, Congress directed the President to "recognize the independence of the Philippine Islands as a separate and self-governing nation" and to "acknowledge the authority and control over the same of the government instituted by the people thereof." Constitutional? And if Congress may control recognition when exercising its power "to dispose of . . . the Territory or other Property belonging to the United States," Art. IV, § 3, cl. 2, why not when exercising other enumerated powers? Neither text nor history nor precedent yields a clear answer to these questions. Fortunately, I have no need to confront these matters today—nor does the Court—because § 214(d) plainly does not concern recognition.

Recognition is more than an announcement of a policy. Like the ratification of an international agreement or the termination of a treaty, it is a formal legal act with effects under international law. It signifies acceptance of an international status, and it makes a commitment to continued acceptance of that status and respect for any attendant rights. See, e.g., Convention on the Rights and Duties of States, Art. 6, Dec. 26, 1933, 49 Stat. 3100, T. S. No. 881. "Its legal effect is to create an estoppel. By granting recognition, [states] debar themselves from challenging in future whatever they have previously acknowledged." 1 G. Schwarzenberger, International Law 127 (3d ed. 1957). In order to extend recognition, a state must perform an act that unequivocally manifests that intention. Whiteman § 3. That act can consist of an express conferral of recognition, or one of a handful of acts that by international custom imply recognition—chiefly, entering into a bilateral treaty, and sending or receiving an ambassador.

To know all this is to realize at once that § 214(d) has nothing to do with recognition. Section 214(d) does not require the Secretary to make a formal declaration about Israel's sovereignty over Jerusalem. And nobody suggests that international custom infers acceptance of sovereignty from the birthplace designation on a passport or birth report, as it does from bilateral treaties or exchanges of ambassadors. Recognition would preclude the United States (as a matter of international law) from later contesting Israeli sovereignty over Jerusalem. But making a notation in a passport or birth report does not encumber the Republic with any international obligations. It leaves the Nation free (so far as international law is concerned) to change its mind in the future. That would be true even if the statute required all passports to list "Israel." But in fact it requires only those passports to list "Israel" for which the citizen (or his guardian) requests "Israel"; all the rest, under the Secretary's policy, list "Jerusalem." It is utterly impossible for this deference to private requests to constitute an act that unequivocally manifests an intention to grant recognition. . . .

The best indication that § 214(d) does not concern recognition comes from the State Department's policies concerning Taiwan. According to the Solicitor General, the United States "acknowledges the Chinese position" that Taiwan is a part of China, but "does not take a position" of its own on that issue. Even so, the State Department has for a long time recorded the birthplace of a citizen born in Taiwan as "China." It indeed insisted on doing so until Congress passed a law (on which § 214(d) was modeled) giving citizens the option to have their birthplaces recorded as "Taiwan." The Solicitor General explains that the designation "China" "involves a geographic description, not an assertion that Taiwan is . . . part of sovereign China." Quite so. Section 214(d) likewise calls for nothing beyond a "geographic description"; it does not require the Executive even to assert, never mind formally recognize, that Jerusalem is a part of sovereign Israel. Since birthplace specifications in citizenship documents are matters within Congress's control, Congress may treat Jerusalem as a part of Israel when regulating the recording of birthplaces, even if the President does not do so when extending recognition. Section 214(d), by the way, expressly directs the Secretary to "record the place of birth as Israel" "[f]*or purposes of* the registration of birth, certification of nationality, or issuance of a passport." (Emphasis added.) And the law bears the caption, "Record of Place of Birth as Israel *for Passport Purposes*." (Emphasis added.) Finding recognition in this provision is rather like finding admission to the Union in a provision that treats American Samoa as a State for purposes of a federal highway safety program, 23 U. S. C. § 401.

The Court complains that § 214(d) requires the Secretary of State to issue official documents implying that Jerusalem is a part of Israel; that it appears in a section of the statute bearing the title "United States Policy with Respect to Jerusalem as the Capital of Israel"; and that foreign "observers interpreted [it] as altering United States policy regarding Jerusalem." But these features do not show that § 214(d) recognizes Israel's sovereignty over Jerusalem. They show only that the law displays symbolic support for Israel's territorial claim. That symbolism may have tremendous significance as a matter of international diplomacy, but it makes no difference as a matter of constitutional law.

Even if the Constitution gives the President sole power to extend recognition, it does not give him sole power to make all decisions relating to foreign disputes over sovereignty. To the contrary, a fair reading of Article I allows Congress to decide for itself how its laws should handle these controversies. Read naturally, power to "regulate Commerce with foreign Nations," § 8, cl. 3, includes power to regulate imports from Gibraltar as British goods or as Spanish goods. Read naturally, power to "regulate the Value . . . of foreign Coin," § 8, cl. 5, includes power to honor (or not) currency issued by Taiwan. And so on for the other enumerated powers. These are not airy hypotheticals. A trade statute from 1800, for example, provided that "the whole of the island of Hispaniola"—whose status was then in controversy—"shall for purposes of [the] act be considered as a dependency of the French Republic." In 1938, Congress allowed admission of the Vatican City's public records in federal courts, decades before the United States extended formal recognition. The Taiwan Relations Act of 1979 grants Taiwan capacity to sue and be sued, even though the United States does not recognize it as a state. 22 U. S. C. § 3303(b)(7). Section 214(d) continues in the same tradition. . . .

The Court [ ]announces a rule that is blatantly gerrymandered to the facts of this case. It concludes that, in addition to the exclusive power to make the "formal recognition determination," the President holds an ancillary exclusive power "to control . . . formal statements by the Executive Branch acknowledging the legitimacy of a state or government and its territorial bounds." It follows, the Court explains, that Congress may not "requir[e] the President to contradict an earlier recognition determination in an official document issued by the Executive Branch." So requiring imports from Jerusalem to be taxed like goods from Israel is fine, but requiring Customs to issue an official invoice to that effect is not? Nonsense. . . .

To the extent doubts linger about whether the United States recognizes Israel's sovereignty over Jerusalem, § 214(d) leaves the President free to dispel them by issuing a disclaimer of intent to recognize. A disclaimer always suffices to prevent an act from effecting recognition. Restatement (Second) of Foreign Relations Law of the United States § 104(1) (1962). Recall that an earlier law grants citizens born in Taiwan the right to have their birthplaces recorded as "Taiwan." The State Department has complied with the law, but states in its Foreign Affairs Manual: "The United States does not officially recognize Taiwan as a 'state' or 'country,' although passport issuing officers may enter 'Taiwan' as a place of birth." 7 FAM § 1300, App. D, § 1340(d)(6). Nothing stops a similar disclaimer here.

At other times, the Court seems concerned with Congress's failure to give effect to a recognition decision that the President has already made. The Court protests, for instance, that § 214(d) "directly contradicts" the President's refusal to recognize Israel's sovereignty over Jerusalem. But even if the Constitution empowers the President alone to extend recognition, it nowhere obliges Congress to align its laws with the President's recognition decisions. Because the President and Congress are "perfectly coordinate by the terms of their common commission," The Federalist No. 49, p. 314 (C. Rossiter ed. 1961) (Madison), the President's use of the recognition power does not constrain Congress's use of its legislative powers.

Congress has legislated without regard to recognition for a long time and in a range of settings. For example, responding in 1817 and 1818 to revolutions in Latin America, Congress amended federal neutrality laws—which originally prohibited private military action for or against recognized states—to prohibit private hostilities against unrecognized states too. *See The Three Friends*, 166 U. S. 1, 52–59 (1897). . . . Federal law today prohibits murdering a foreign government's officials, 18 U. S. C. § 1116, counterfeiting a foreign government's bonds, § 478, and using American vessels to smuggle goods in violation of a foreign government's laws, § 546—all "irrespective of recognition by the United States," §§ 11, 1116. Just as Congress may legislate independently of recognition in all of those areas, so too may it legislate independently of recognition when regulating the recording of birthplaces.

The Court elsewhere objects that § 214(d) interferes with the autonomy and unity of the Executive Branch, setting the branch against itself. The Court suggests, for instance, that the law prevents the President from maintaining his neutrality about Jerusalem in "his and his agent's statements." That is of no constitutional significance. As just shown,

Congress has power to legislate without regard to recognition, and where Congress has the power to legislate, the President has a duty to "take Care" that its legislation "be faithfully executed," Art. II, § 3. It is likewise "the duty of the secretary of state to conform to the law"; where Congress imposes a responsibility on him, "he is so far the officer of the law; is amenable to the laws for his conduct; and cannot at his discretion sport away the vested rights of others." *Marbury v. Madison*, 1 Cranch 137, 158, 166 (1803). The Executive's involvement in carrying out this law does not affect its constitutionality; the Executive carries out every law.

In the end, the Court's decision does not rest on text or history or precedent. It instead comes down to "functional considerations"—principally the Court's perception that the Nation "must speak with one voice" about the status of Jerusalem. The vices of this mode of analysis go beyond mere lack of footing in the Constitution. Functionalism of the sort the Court practices today will systematically favor the unitary President over the plural Congress in disputes involving foreign affairs. It is possible that this approach will make for more effective foreign policy, perhaps as effective as that of a monarchy. It is certain that, in the long run, it will erode the structure of separated powers that the People established for the protection of their liberty.

NOTES

1. Youngstown *Category III. Zivotofsky II* was an unusual and important case because it addressed a conflict between the political branches over an issue of foreign relations law. Such conflicts are unusual in part because Congress has delegated significant power over foreign relations to the president, and in part because the Court has sometimes inferred congressional authorization or relied upon congressional acquiescence to uphold actions by the president. The political question doctrine and standing have also limited the justiciability of potential conflicts between the political branches. In *Zivotofsky II*, however, the conflict was unavoidable and the Court reached the merits. Justice Breyer argued in *Zivotofsky I* that the case should be dismissed as presenting a political question. Was he correct? (*See* Chapter 7, Sec. 1). *Zivotofsky II* is also an important case because the Court held for the executive branch. Was Chief Justice Roberts right to urge greater caution in doing so? How important is the reasoning and holding of *Zivotofsky II*? *See* Jack L. Goldsmith, Zivotofsky II *as Precedent in the Executive Branch,* 129 HARV. L. REV. 112 (2015) and Ingrid Wuerth, Zivotofsky v. Kerry: *A Foreign Relations Law Bonanza*, 109 AM. J. INT'L L. 636 (2015).

2. *International Law.* For what purposes do the majority and the dissenting opinions cite to international law? Is modern international law relevant to the interpretation of the Constitution? Why or why not? Does your answer vary depending upon the constitutional issue with which courts are confronted? These questions arise throughout the course and are specifically addressed in Chapter 2, Sec. 4.

3. *A Loss for the "Sole Organ" Doctrine*? Is the majority's analysis of the relationship between section 214(d) and the recognition power convincing? What do the dissenting opinions argue on this point? Note that the majority could have reached the same result without addressing the relationship between section 214(d) and recognition if it had held that the president has the exclusive power to conduct diplomacy. As the majority opinion notes, *United States* v. *Curtiss-Wright Export Corp.* describes the president as "the sole organ of the federal government in the field of international relations." Why did the Court reject this argument?

4. *Methodology*. To what extent do the dissenting and majority opinions disagree about the proper method of constitutional interpretation? What roles do constitutional text, constitutional history, post-constitutional practice of Congress and the executive branch, prior cases, and functional reasoning play in each opinion? How important is each? Are functional concerns central to the majority opinion?

3. INDIVIDUAL LIBERTY AND FOREIGN RELATIONS

JOHN LOCKE, SECOND TREATISE OF GOVERNMENT

84 (C.B. Macpherson ed., 1980).

. . . This power to act according to discretion, for the public good, without the prescription of the law, and sometimes even against it, *is* that which is called *prerogative*: for since in some governments the lawmaking power is not always in being, and is usually too numerous, and so too slow, for the dispatch requisite to execution; and because also it is impossible to foresee, and so by laws to provide for, all accidents and necessities that may concern the public, or make such laws as will do no harm, if they are executed with an inflexible rigour, on all occasions, and upon all persons that may come in their way; therefore there is a latitude left to the executive power, to do many things of choice which the laws do not prescribe.

EX PARTE MERRYMAN

17 F. Cas. 144 (C.C.D. Md. 1861).

[After the 1861 bombardment of Fort Sumter by Confederate troops, President Lincoln called for reinforcements to defend Washington, D.C. Riots erupted as Union soldiers from Massachusetts traveled through Maryland, a slave state. President Lincoln ordered his officers to suspend the writ of *habeas corpus* along the "military line" between Philadelphia and Washington. John Merryman, an officer of the Maryland cavalry, was imprisoned on suspicion of sabotage. Merryman petitioned for a writ of *habeas corpus*.]

TANEY, CIRCUIT JUSTICE. . . .

As the case comes before me, therefore, I understand that the president not only claims the right to suspend the writ of habeas corpus himself, at his discretion, but to delegate that discretionary power to a military officer, and to leave it to him to determine whether he will or will not obey judicial process that may be served upon him. No official notice has been given to the courts of justice, or to the public, by proclamation or otherwise, that the president claimed this power, and had exercised it in the manner stated in the return. And I certainly listened to it with some surprise, for I had supposed it to be one of those points of constitutional law upon which there was no difference of opinion, and that it was admitted on all hands, that the privilege of the writ could not be suspended, except by act of congress. . . .

The clause of the constitution, which authorizes the suspension of the privilege of the writ of habeas corpus, is in the 9th section of the first article. This article is devoted to the legislative department of the United States, and has not the slightest reference to the executive department. . . .

It is the second article of the constitution that provides for the organization of the executive department, enumerates the powers conferred on it, and prescribes its duties. And if the high power over the liberty of the citizen now claimed, was intended to be conferred on the president, it would undoubtedly be found in plain words in this article; but there is not a word in it that can furnish the slightest ground to justify the exercise of the power. . . .

With such provisions in the constitution, expressed in language too clear to be misunderstood by any one, I can see no ground whatever for supposing that the president, in any emergency, or in any state of things, can authorize the suspension of the privileges of the writ of habeas corpus, or the arrest of a citizen, except in aid of the judicial power. He certainly does not faithfully execute the laws, if he takes upon himself legislative power, by suspending the writ of habeas corpus, and the judicial power also, by arresting and imprisoning a person without due process of law. . . .

[Following the circuit court's decision, Merryman was released on bail. He was never tried.]

NOTES

1. *Locke and Load.* Do you think John Locke is correct that there are times when governmental authorities must be allowed to act "without the prescription of the law, and sometimes even against it," when society is severely threatened? Is the field of foreign relations and national security law one where this is most likely to happen? What are the dangers of allowing such action? Of prohibiting it?

2. *State of Emergency and the U.S. Constitution*. The U.S. Constitution, unlike the constitutions of some other countries, does not contain a "state of emergency" provision. Nor is there any notion of "derogable" rights in United States constitutional jurisprudence. The only provision of the Constitution that expressly provides for its own suspension is the *Habeas Corpus* Clause, article I, section 9, clause 2, which provides that the writ "shall not be suspended, unless when in cases of rebellion or invasion the public safety may require it." Does this mean that the scope of the president's constitutional power is constant, or does it expand during a national emergency? If the latter, does this mean that the power of the president and Congress, acting together, also expands so that what would otherwise be unconstitutional (even though within Justice Jackson's first category) is rendered permissible?

3. *Judicial Complicity*. Is the "bending" process greater if the courts consider and legitimate what would otherwise be a transgression? In *The Imperial Presidency*, Arthur Schlesinger writes that, while the Founding Fathers did not rule out the possibility that "crisis might require the executive to act outside the Constitution," neither did they intend to confer constitutional legitimacy on such acts, believing that the "legal order would be better preserved if departures from it were frankly identified as such than if they were anointed with a factitious legality and thereby enabled to serve as constitutional precedents for future action." Arthur Schlesinger, Jr., *The Imperial Presidency* 8 (1973). In this connection, consider in particular the dissent of Justice Jackson in the following case.

KOREMATSU V. UNITED STATES

323 U.S. 214 (1944).

MR. JUSTICE BLACK delivered the opinion of the Court.

The petitioner, an American citizen of Japanese descent, was convicted in a federal district court for remaining in San Leandro, California, a "Military Area", contrary to Civilian Exclusion Order No. 34 of the Commanding General of the Western Command, U.S. Army, which directed that after May 9, 1942, all persons of Japanese ancestry should be excluded from that area. No question was raised as to petitioner's loyalty to the United States. The Circuit Court of Appeals affirmed, and the importance of the constitutional question involved caused us to grant certiorari. . . .

It should be noted, to begin with, that all legal restrictions which curtail the civil rights of a single racial group are immediately suspect. That is not to say that all such restrictions are unconstitutional. It is to say that courts must subject them to the most rigid scrutiny. Pressing public necessity may sometimes justify the existence of such restrictions; racial antagonism never can.

In the instant case prosecution of the petitioner was begun by information charging violation of an Act of Congress, of March 21, 1942, 56 Stat. 173, which provides that

". . . whoever shall enter, remain in, leave, or commit any act in any military area or military zone prescribed, under the authority of an Executive order of the President, by the Secretary of War, or by any military commander designated by the Secretary of War, contrary to the restrictions applicable to any such area or zone or contrary to the order of the Secretary of War or any such military commander, shall, if it appears that he knew or should have known of the existence and extent of the restrictions or order and that his act was in violation thereof, be guilty of a misdemeanor and upon conviction shall be liable to a fine of not to exceed $5,000 or to imprisonment for not more than one year, or both, for each offense."

Exclusion Order No. 34, which the petitioner knowingly and admittedly violated, was one of a number of military orders and proclamations, all of which were substantially based upon Executive Order No. 9066, 7 Fed. Reg. 1407. That order, issued after we were at war with Japan, declared that "the successful prosecution of the war requires every possible protection against espionage and against sabotage to national-defense material, national-defense premises, and national-defense utilities. . . ."

One of the series of orders and proclamations, a curfew order, which like the exclusion order here was promulgated pursuant to Executive Order 9066, subjected all persons of Japanese ancestry in prescribed West Coast military areas to remain in their residences from 8 p.m. to 6 a.m. As is the case with the exclusion order here, that prior curfew order was designed as a "protection against espionage and against sabotage." In *Hirabayashi v. United States*, 320 U.S. 81, we sustained a conviction obtained for violation of the curfew order. The *Hirabayashi* conviction and this one thus rest on the same 1942 Congressional Act and the same basic executive and military orders, all of which orders were aimed at the twin dangers of espionage and sabotage.

The 1942 Act was attacked in the *Hirabayashi* case as an unconstitutional delegation of power; it was contended that the curfew order and other orders on which it rested were beyond the war powers of the Congress, the military authorities and of the President, as Commander in Chief of the Army; and finally that to apply the curfew order against none but citizens of Japanese ancestry amounted to a constitutionally prohibited discrimination solely on account of race. To these questions, we gave the serious consideration which their importance justified. We upheld the curfew order as an exercise of the power of the government to take steps necessary to prevent espionage and sabotage in an area threatened by Japanese attack.

In the light of the principles we announced in the *Hirabayashi* case, we are unable to conclude that it was beyond the war power of Congress and the Executive to exclude those of Japanese ancestry from the West Coast war area at the time they did. True, exclusion from the area in which one's home is located is a far greater deprivation than constant confinement to the home from 8 p.m. to 6 a.m. Nothing short of apprehension by the proper military authorities of the gravest imminent danger to the public safety can constitutionally justify either. But exclusion from a threatened area, no less than curfew, has a definite and close relationship to the prevention of espionage and sabotage. The military authorities, charged with the primary responsibility of defending our shores, concluded that curfew provided inadequate protection and ordered exclusion. They did so, as pointed out in our *Hirabayashi* opinion, in accordance with Congressional authority to the military to say who should, and who should not, remain in the threatened areas.

In this case the petitioner challenges the assumptions upon which we rested our conclusions in the *Hirabayashi* case. He also urges that by May 1942, when Order No. 34 was promulgated, all danger of Japanese invasion of the West Coast had disappeared. After careful consideration of these contentions we are compelled to reject them.

Here, as in the *Hirabayashi* case, *supra*, at p. 99, ". . . we cannot reject as unfounded the judgment of the military authorities and of Congress that there were disloyal members of that population, whose number and strength could not be precisely and quickly ascertained. We cannot say that the war-making branches of the Government did not have ground for believing that in a critical hour such persons could not readily be isolated and separately dealt with, and constituted a menace to the national defense and safety, which demanded that prompt and adequate measures be taken to guard against it."

Like curfew, exclusion of those of Japanese origin was deemed necessary because of the presence of an unascertained number of disloyal members of the group, most of whom we have no doubt were loyal to this country. It was because we could not reject the finding of the military authorities that it was impossible to bring about an immediate segregation of the disloyal from the loyal that we sustained the validity of the curfew order as applying to the whole group. In the instant case, temporary exclusion of the entire group was rested by the military on the same ground. The judgment that exclusion of the whole group was for the same reason a military imperative answers the contention that the exclusion was in the nature of group punishment based on antagonism to those of Japanese origin. That there were members of the group who retained loyalties to Japan has been confirmed by investigations made subsequent to the exclusion. Approximately five thousand American citizens of Japanese ancestry refused to swear unqualified allegiance to the United States and to renounce allegiance to the Japanese Emperor, and several thousand evacuees requested repatriation to Japan.[2]

We uphold the exclusion order as of the time it was made and when the petitioner violated it. . . . In doing so, we are not unmindful of the hardships imposed by it upon a large group of American citizens. . . . But hardships are part of war, and war is an aggregation of hardships. All citizens alike, both in and out of uniform, feel the impact of war in greater or lesser measure. Citizenship has its responsibilities as well as its privileges, and in time of war the burden is always heavier. Compulsory exclusion of large groups of citizens from their homes, except under circumstances of direst emergency and peril, is inconsistent with our basic governmental institutions. But when under conditions of modern warfare our shores are threatened by hostile forces, the power to protect must be commensurate with the threatened danger. . . .

It is said that we are dealing here with the case of imprisonment of a citizen in a concentration camp solely because of his ancestry, without evidence or inquiry concerning his loyalty and good disposition towards the United States. Our task would be simple, our duty clear, were this a case involving the imprisonment of a loyal citizen in a concentration camp because of racial prejudice. Regardless of the true nature of the assembly and relocation centers—and we deem it unjustifiable to call them concentration camps with all the ugly connotations that term implies—we are dealing specifically with nothing but an exclusion order. To cast this case into outlines of racial prejudice, without reference to the real military dangers which were presented, merely confuses the issue. Korematsu was not excluded from the Military Area because of hostility to him or his race. He *was* excluded because we are at war with the Japanese Empire, because the properly constituted military authorities feared an invasion of our West Coast and felt constrained to take proper security measures, because they decided that the military urgency of the situation demanded that all citizens of Japanese ancestry be segregated from the West Coast temporarily, and finally, because Congress, reposing its confidence in this time of war in our military leaders—as inevitably it must—determined that they should have the power to do just this. There was evidence of disloyalty on the part of some, the military authorities considered that the need for action was great, and time was short. We cannot—by availing

[2] Hearings before the Subcommittee on the National War Agencies Appropriation Bill for 1945, Part II, 608–726; Final Report, Japanese Evacuation from the West Coast, 1942, 309–327; Hearings before the Committee on Immigration and Naturalization, House of Representatives, 78th Cong., 2d Sess., on H.R. 2701 and other bills to expatriate certain nationals of the United States, pp. 37–42, 49–58.

ourselves of the calm perspective of hindsight—now say that at that time these actions were unjustified.

Affirmed.

MR. JUSTICE FRANKFURTER, concurring. . . .

The provisions of the Constitution which confer on the Congress and the President powers to enable this country to wage war are as much part of the Constitution as provisions looking to a nation at peace. And we have had recent occasion to quote approvingly the statement of former Chief Justice Hughes that the war power of the Government is "the power to wage war successfully." *Hirabayashi v. United States, supra* at 93. Therefore, the validity of action under the war power must be judged wholly in the context of war. That action is not to be stigmatized as lawless because like action in times of peace would be lawless. To talk about a military order that expresses an allowable judgment of war needs by those entrusted with the duty of conducting war as "an unconstitutional order" is to suffuse a part of the Constitution with an atmosphere of unconstitutionality. The respective spheres of action of military authorities and of judges are of course very different. But within their sphere, military authorities are no more outside the bounds of obedience to the Constitution than are judges within theirs. "The war power of the United States, like its other powers . . . is subject to applicable constitutional limitations". *Hamilton v. Kentucky Distilleries Co.*, 251 U.S. 146, 156. To recognize that military orders are "reasonably expedient military precautions" in time of war and yet to deny them constitutional legitimacy makes of the Constitution an instrument for dialectic subtleties not reasonably to be attributed to the hard-headed Framers, of whom a majority had had actual participation in war. If a military order such as that under review does not transcend the means appropriate for conducting war, such action by the military is as constitutional as would be any authorized action by the Interstate Commerce Commission within the limits of the constitutional power to regulate commerce. And being an exercise of the war power explicitly granted by the Constitution for safeguarding the national life by prosecuting war effectively, I find nothing in the Constitution which denies to Congress the power to enforce such a valid military order by making its violation an offense triable in the civil courts. Compare *Interstate Commerce Commission v. Brimson,* 154 U.S. 447; 155 U.S. 3, and *Monongahela Bridge Co. v. United States,* 216 U.S. 177. To find that the Constitution does not forbid the military measures now complained of does not carry with it approval of that which Congress and the Executive did. That is their business, not ours.

MR. JUSTICE ROBERTS.

I dissent, because I think the indisputable facts exhibit a clear violation of Constitutional rights.

This is not a case of keeping people off the streets at night as was *Hirabayashi v. United States*, 320 U.S. 81, nor a case of temporary exclusion of a citizen from an area for his own safety or that of the community, nor a case of offering him an opportunity to go temporarily out of an area where his presence might cause danger to himself or to his fellows. On the contrary, it is the case of convicting a citizen as a punishment for not submitting to imprisonment in a concentration camp, based on his ancestry, and solely because of his ancestry, without evidence or inquiry concerning his loyalty and good disposition towards the United States. If this be a correct statement of the facts disclosed by this record, and facts of which we take judicial notice, I need hardly labor the conclusion that Constitutional rights have been violated. . . .

I would reverse the judgment of conviction.

MR. JUSTICE MURPHY, dissenting.

This exclusion of "all persons of Japanese ancestry, both alien and non-alien," from the Pacific Coast area on a plea of military necessity in the absence of martial law ought not to be approved. Such exclusion goes over "the very brink of constitutional power" and falls into the ugly abyss of racism.

In dealing with matters relating to the prosecution and progress of a war, we must accord great respect and consideration to the judgments of the military authorities who are on the scene and who have full knowledge of the military facts. The scope of their discretion must, as a matter of necessity and common sense, be wide. And their judgments ought not to be overruled lightly by those whose training and duties ill-equip them to deal intelligently with matters so vital to the physical security of the nation.

At the same time, however, it is essential that there be definite limits to military discretion, especially where martial law has not been declared. Individuals must not be left impoverished of their constitutional rights on a plea of military necessity that has neither substance nor support. Thus, like other claims conflicting with the asserted constitutional rights of the individual, the military claim must subject itself to the judicial process of having its reasonableness determined and its conflicts with other interests reconciled. "What are the allowable limits of military discretion, and whether or not they have been overstepped in a particular case, are judicial questions." *Sterling v. Constantin*, 287 U.S. 378, 401.

The judicial test of whether the Government, on a plea of military necessity, can validly deprive an individual of any of his constitutional rights is whether the deprivation is reasonably related to a public danger that is so "immediate, imminent, and impending" as not to admit of delay and not to permit the intervention of ordinary constitutional processes to alleviate the danger. *United States v. Russell*, 13 Wall. 623, 627, 628; *Mitchell v. Harmony*, 13 How. 115, 134, 135; *Raymond v. Thomas*, 91 U.S.

712, 716. Civilian Exclusion Order No. 34, banishing from a prescribed area of the Pacific Coast "all persons of Japanese ancestry, both alien and non-alien," clearly does not meet that test. Being an obvious racial discrimination, the order deprives all those within its scope of the equal protection of the laws as guaranteed by the Fifth Amendment. It further deprives these individuals of their constitutional rights to live and work where they will, to establish a home where they choose and to move about freely. In excommunicating them without benefit of hearings, this order also deprives them of all their constitutional rights to procedural due process. Yet no reasonable relation to an "immediate, imminent, and impending" public danger is evident to support this racial restriction which is one of the most sweeping and complete deprivations of constitutional rights in the history of this nation in the absence of martial law.

It must be conceded that the military and naval situation in the spring of 1942 was such as to generate a very real fear of invasion of the Pacific Coast, accompanied by fears of sabotage and espionage in that area. The military command was therefore justified in adopting all reasonable means necessary to combat these dangers. In adjudging the military action taken in light of the then apparent dangers, we must not erect too high or too meticulous standards; it is necessary only that the action have some reasonable relation to the removal of the dangers of invasion, sabotage and espionage. But the exclusion, either temporarily or permanently, of all persons with Japanese blood in their veins has no such reasonable relation. And that relation is lacking because the exclusion order necessarily must rely for its reasonableness upon the assumption that *all* persons of Japanese ancestry may have a dangerous tendency to commit sabotage and espionage and to aid our Japanese enemy in other ways. It is difficult to believe that reason, logic or experience could be marshalled in support of such an assumption.

That this forced exclusion was the result in good measure of this erroneous assumption of racial guilt rather than bona fide military necessity is evidenced by the Commanding General's Final Report on the evacuation from the Pacific Coast area. In it he refers to all individuals of Japanese descent as "subversive," as belonging to "an enemy race" whose "racial strains are undiluted," and as constituting "over 112,000 potential enemies . . . at large today" along the Pacific Coast. In support of this blanket condemnation of all persons of Japanese descent, however, no reliable evidence is cited to show that such individuals were generally disloyal, or had generally so conducted themselves in this area as to constitute a special menace to defense installations or war industries, or had otherwise by their behavior furnished reasonable ground for their exclusion as a group.

Justification for the exclusion is sought, instead, mainly upon questionable racial and sociological grounds not ordinarily within the realm of expert military judgment, supplemented by certain semi-military conclusions drawn from an unwarranted use of circumstantial evidence. Individuals of Japanese ancestry are condemned because they are said to be "a large, unassimilated, tightly knit racial group, bound to an enemy nation by strong ties of race, culture, custom and religion." They are claimed to be given to "emperor worshipping ceremonies" and to "dual citizenship." Japanese language schools and allegedly pro-Japanese organizations are cited as evidence of possible group disloyalty, together with facts as to certain persons being educated and residing at length in Japan. It is intimated that many of these individuals deliberately resided "adjacent to strategic points," thus enabling them "to carry into execution a tremendous program of sabotage on a mass scale should any considerable number of them have been inclined to do so." The need for protective custody is also asserted. The report refers without identity to "numerous incidents of violence" as well as to other admittedly unverified or cumulative incidents. . . .

The main reasons relied upon by those responsible for the forced evacuation, therefore, do not prove a reasonable relation between the group characteristics of Japanese Americans and the dangers of invasion, sabotage and espionage. The reasons appear, instead, to be largely an accumulation of much of the misinformation, half-truths and insinuations that for years have been directed against Japanese Americans by people with racial and economic prejudices—the same people who have been among the foremost advocates of the evacuation. A military judgment based upon such racial and sociological considerations is not entitled to the great weight ordinarily given the judgments based upon strictly military considerations. Especially is this so when every charge relative to race, religion, culture, geographical location, and legal and economic status has been substantially discredited by independent studies made by experts in these matters. . . .

MR. JUSTICE JACKSON, dissenting.

Korematsu was born on our soil, of parents born in Japan. The Constitution makes him a citizen of the United States by nativity and a citizen of California by residence. No claim is made that he is not loyal to this country. There is no suggestion that apart from the matter involved here he is not law-abiding and well disposed. Korematsu, however, has been convicted of an act not commonly a crime. It consists merely of being present in the state whereof he is a citizen, near the place where he was born, and where all his life he has lived.

Even more unusual is the series of military orders which made this conduct a crime. They forbid such a one to remain, and they also forbid him to leave. They were so drawn that the only way Korematsu could avoid violation was to give himself up to the military authority. This meant submission to custody, examination, and transportation out of the territory, to be followed by indeterminate confinement in detention camps. . . .

Neither the Act of Congress nor the Executive Order of the President, nor both together, would afford a basis for this conviction. It rests on the orders of General DeWitt. And it is said that if the military commander had reasonable military grounds for promulgating the orders, they are constitutional and become law, and the Court is required to enforce them. There are several reasons why I cannot subscribe to this doctrine.

It would be impracticable and dangerous idealism to expect or insist that each specific military command in an area of probable operations will conform to conventional tests of constitutionality. . . . But a commander in temporarily focusing the life of a community on defense is carrying out a military program; he is not making law in the sense the courts know the term. He issues orders, and they may have a certain authority as military commands, although they may be very bad as constitutional law.

But if we cannot confine military expedients by the Constitution, neither would I distort the Constitution to approve all that the military may deem expedient. That is what the Court appears to be doing, whether consciously or not. I cannot say, from any evidence before me, that the orders of General DeWitt were not reasonably expedient military precautions, nor could I say that they were. But even if they were permissible military procedures, I deny that it follows that they are constitutional. If, as the Court holds, it does follow, then we may as well say that any military order will be constitutional and have done with it.

The limitation under which courts always will labor in examining the necessity for a military order are illustrated by this case. How does the Court know that these orders have a reasonable basis in necessity? No evidence whatever on that subject has been taken by this or any other court. There is sharp controversy as to the credibility of the DeWitt report. So the Court, having no real evidence before it, has no choice but to accept General DeWitt's own unsworn, self-serving statement, untested by any cross-examination, that what he did was reasonable. And thus it will always be when courts try to look into the reasonableness of a military order.

In the very nature of things, military decisions are not susceptible of intelligent judicial appraisal. They do not pretend to rest on evidence, but are made on information that often would not be admissible and on assumptions that could not be proved. Information in support of an order could not be disclosed to courts without danger that it would reach the enemy. Neither can courts act on communications made in confidence. Hence courts can never have any real alternative to accepting the mere declaration of the authority that issued the order that it was reasonably necessary from a military viewpoint.

Much is said of the danger to liberty from the Army program for deporting and detaining these citizens of Japanese extraction. But a judicial construction of the due process clause that will sustain this order is a far more subtle blow to liberty than the promulgation of the order itself. A military order, however unconstitutional, is not apt to last longer than the military emergency. Even during that period a succeeding commander may revoke it all. But once a judicial opinion rationalizes such an order to show that it conforms to the Constitution, or rather rationalizes the Constitution to show that the Constitution sanctions such an order, the Court for all time has validated the principle of racial discrimination in criminal procedure and of transplanting American citizens. The principle then lies about like a loaded weapon ready for the hand of any authority that can bring forward a plausible claim of an urgent need. Every repetition imbeds that principle more deeply in our law and thinking and expands it to new purposes. All who observe the work of courts are familiar with what Judge Cardozo described as "the tendency of a principle to expand itself to the limit of its logic."[1] A military commander may overstep the bounds of constitutionality, and it is an incident. But if we review and approve, that passing incident becomes the doctrine of the Constitution. There it has a generative power of its own, and all that it creates will be in its own image. Nothing better illustrates this danger than does the Court's opinion in this case. . . .

I should hold that a civil court cannot be made to enforce an order which violates constitutional limitations even if it is a reasonable exercise of military authority. The courts can exercise only the judicial power, can apply only law, and must abide by the Constitution, or they cease to be civil courts and become instruments of military policy.

Of course the existence of a military power resting on force, so vagrant, so centralized, so necessarily heedless of the individual, is an inherent threat to liberty. But I would not lead people to rely on this Court for a review that seems to me wholly delusive. The military reasonableness of these orders can only be determined by military superiors. If the people ever let command of the war power fall into irresponsible and unscrupulous hands, the courts wield no power equal to its restraint. The chief restraint upon those who command the physical forces of the country, in the future as in the past, must be their responsibility to the political judgments of their contemporaries and to the moral judgments of history.

My duties as a justice as I see them do not require me to make a military judgment as to whether General DeWitt's evacuation and detention program was a reasonable military necessity. I do not suggest

[1] Nature of the Judicial Process, p. 51.

that the courts should have attempted to interfere with the Army in carrying out its task. But I do not think they may be asked to execute a military expedient that has no place in law under the Constitution. I would reverse the judgment and discharge the prisoner.

NOTES

1. *Detaining Americans as Threats to National Security*. To what extent might *Korematsu* serve as precedent for the detention without trial of other civilians thought to pose a threat to national security? How might such a group constitutionally be identified? If race can serve as the basis for detention, can expressive activity? Could the government properly take into account, for example, a person's contributions to certain charitable organizations in the Middle East? Could it consider one's membership in a religious congregation deemed to be "radical"?

2. *Applying Justice Jackson's Categories*. Would the challenged executive order have been constitutional if Congress had been silent? If Congress had opposed?

3. *Post-Script*. In 1980, a special commission appointed by President Jimmy Carter determined that the internment of Japanese-Americans during World War II occurred because of race prejudice, war hysteria, and a failure of political leadership. In 1984, Fred Korematsu petitioned the government for a writ of *coram nobis* to vacate his 1944 conviction on the grounds of governmental misconduct. A district court judge for the Northern District of California granted the writ, holding that "the government knowingly withheld information from the courts when they were considering the critical question of military necessity [as to the detention of Japanese-Americans]." 584 F.Supp. 1406 (N.D. Cal. 1984). In particular, the court cited the "erroneous" sabotage statistics included in the *Final Report of General DeWitt* (1943). In 1988, Congress apologized for the detentions and granted personal compensation of $20,000 to each surviving prisoner or their spouse/parent. *See* Civil Liberties Act of 1988, 50 U.S.C. § 1989b (2006). In 1998, President Clinton awarded Korematsu the Presidential Medal of Freedom, seven years before his death in 2005. Despite these measures, the Supreme Court's decision in *Korematsu v. United States* has never been overruled and remains valid law.

4. *Individual Liberties and the Armed Conflict with Al Qaeda*. After the terrorist attack of September 11, 2001, Congress enacted an Authorization for the Use of Military Force (AUMF or 2001 AUMF) which provides that:

> the President is authorized to use all necessary and appropriate force against those nations, organizations, or persons he determines planned, authorized, committed, or aided the terrorist attacks that occurred on September 11, 2001, or harbored such organizations or persons, in order to prevent any future acts of international terrorism against the United States by such nations, organizations or persons.

Pub. L. No. 107–40, § 2(a), 115 Stat. 224 (2001). The executive branch then embarked on an aggressive campaign against the terrorist organization al Qaeda by invading its stronghold in Afghanistan, toppling its allied Afghan government (the Taliban), and disrupting its activities in other countries, including Pakistan, the Philippines, and Yemen. (*See* Chapter 4, Sec. 5 (B)).

HAMDI V. RUMSFELD

542 U.S. 507 (2004).

JUSTICE O'CONNOR announced the judgment of the Court and delivered an opinion, in which THE CHIEF JUSTICE, JUSTICE KENNEDY, and JUSTICE BREYER join. . . .

This case arises out of the detention of a man whom the Government alleges took up arms with the Taliban during this conflict. His name is Yaser Esam Hamdi. Born in Louisiana in 1980, Hamdi moved with his family to Saudi Arabia as a child. By 2001, the parties agree, he resided in Afghanistan. At some point that year, he was seized by members of the Northern Alliance, a coalition of military groups opposed to the Taliban government, and eventually was turned over to the United States military. The Government asserts that it initially detained and interrogated Hamdi in Afghanistan before transferring him to the United States Naval Base in Guantanamo Bay in January 2002. In April 2002, upon learning that Hamdi is an American citizen, authorities transferred him to a naval brig in Norfolk, Virginia, where he remained until a recent transfer to a brig in Charleston, South Carolina. The Government contends that Hamdi is an "enemy combatant," and that this status justifies holding him in the United States indefinitely—without formal charges or proceedings—unless and until it makes the determination that access to counsel or further process is warranted. . . .

[The district court] ordered the Government to turn over numerous materials for *in camera* review, including copies of all of Hamdi's statements and the notes taken from interviews with him that related to his reasons for going to Afghanistan and his activities therein; a list of all interrogators who had questioned Hamdi and their names and addresses; statements by members of the Northern Alliance regarding Hamdi's surrender and capture; a list of the dates and locations of his capture and subsequent detentions; and the names and titles of the United States Government officials who made the determinations that Hamdi was an enemy combatant and that he should be moved to a naval brig. The court indicated that all of these materials were necessary for "meaningful judicial review" of whether Hamdi's detention was legally authorized and whether Hamdi had received sufficient process to satisfy the Due Process Clause of the Constitution and relevant treaties or military regulations. . . .

It is beyond question that substantial interests lie on both sides of the scale in this case. Hamdi's "private interest . . . affected by the official action" is the most elemental of liberty interests—the interest in being free from physical detention by one's own government. *Foucha v. Louisiana*, 504 U.S. 71, 80 (1992) ("Freedom from bodily restraint has always been at the core of the liberty protected by the Due Process Clause from arbitrary governmental action"); *see also Parham v. J. R.*, 442 U.S. 584, 600 (1979) (noting the "substantial liberty interest in not being confined unnecessarily"). . . .

On the other side of the scale are the weighty and sensitive governmental interests in ensuring that those who have in fact fought with the enemy during a war do not return to battle against the United States. As discussed above, the law of war and the realities of combat may render such detentions both necessary and appropriate, and our due process analysis need not blink at those realities. Without doubt, our Constitution recognizes that core strategic matters of warmaking belong in the hands of those who are best positioned and most politically accountable for making them. *Department of Navy v. Egan*, 484 U.S. 518, 530 (1988) (noting the reluctance of the courts "to intrude upon the authority of the Executive in military and national security affairs"); *Youngstown Sheet & Tube Co. v. Sawyer*, 343 U.S. 579, 587 (1952) (acknowledging "broad powers in military commanders engaged in day-to-day fighting in a theater of war"). . . .

With due recognition of these competing concerns, we believe that neither the process proposed by the Government nor the process apparently envisioned by the District Court below strikes the proper constitutional balance when a United States citizen is detained in the United States as an enemy combatant. That is, "the risk of erroneous deprivation" of a detainee's liberty interest is unacceptably high under the Government's proposed rule, while some of the "additional or substitute procedural safeguards" suggested by the District Court are unwarranted in light of their limited "probable value" and the burdens they may impose on the military in such cases. *Mathews*, 424 U.S., at 335.

We therefore hold that a citizen-detainee seeking to challenge his classification as an enemy combatant must receive notice of the factual basis for his classification, and a fair opportunity to rebut the Government's factual assertions before a neutral decisionmaker. . . . "For more than a century the central meaning of procedural due process has been clear: 'Parties whose rights are to be affected are entitled to be heard; and in order that they may enjoy that right they must first be notified.' It is equally fundamental that the right to notice and an opportunity to be heard 'must be granted at a meaningful time and in a meaningful manner.'" *Fuentes v. Shevin*, 407 U.S. 67, 80 (1972) (quoting *Baldwin v. Hale*, 1 Wall. 223, 233 (1864)). . . . These essential constitutional promises may not be eroded.

At the same time, the exigencies of the circumstances may demand that, aside from these core elements, enemy-combatant proceedings may be tailored to alleviate their uncommon potential to burden the Executive at a time of ongoing military conflict. Hearsay, for example, may need to be accepted as the most reliable available evidence from the Government in such a proceeding. Likewise, the Constitution would not be offended by a presumption in favor of the Government's evidence, so long as that presumption remained a rebuttable one and fair opportunity for rebuttal were provided. Thus, once the Government puts forth credible evidence that the habeas petitioner meets the enemy-combatant criteria, the onus could shift to the petitioner to rebut that evidence with more persuasive evidence that he falls outside the criteria. A burden-shifting scheme of this sort would meet the goal of ensuring that the errant tourist, embedded journalist, or local aid worker has a chance to prove military error while giving due regard to the Executive once it has put forth meaningful support for its conclusion that the detainee is in fact an enemy combatant. In the words of *Mathews*, process of this sort would sufficiently address the "risk of erroneous deprivation" of a detainee's liberty interest while eliminating certain procedures that have questionable additional value in light of the burden on the Government. 424 U.S., at 335.

We think it unlikely that this basic process will have the dire impact on the central functions of warmaking that the Government forecasts. The parties agree that initial captures on the battlefield need not receive the process we have discussed here; that process is due only when the determination is made to *continue* to hold those who have been seized. The Government has made clear in its briefing that documentation regarding battlefield detainees already is kept in the ordinary course of military affairs. Any factfinding imposition created by requiring a knowledgeable affiant to summarize these records to an independent tribunal is a minimal one. Likewise, arguments that military officers ought not have to wage war under the threat of litigation lose much of their steam when factual disputes at enemy-combatant hearings are limited to the alleged combatant's acts. This focus meddles little, if at all, in the strategy or conduct of war, inquiring only into the appropriateness of continuing to detain an individual claimed to have taken up arms against the United States. While we accord the greatest respect and consideration to the judgments of military authorities in matters relating to the actual prosecution of a war, and recognize that the scope of that discretion necessarily is wide, it does not infringe on the core role of the military for the courts to exercise their own time-honored and constitutionally mandated roles of reviewing and resolving claims like those presented here. Cf. *Korematsu v. United States*, 323 U.S. 214, 233–234 (1944) (Murphy, J., dissenting) ("[L]ike other claims conflicting with the asserted constitutional rights of the individual, the military claim must subject itself to the judicial process of having its reasonableness determined and its conflicts with other interests reconciled"). . . .

In sum, while the full protections that accompany challenges to detentions in other settings may prove unworkable and inappropriate in the enemy-combatant setting, the threats to military operations posed by a basic system of independent review are not so weighty as to trump a citizen's core rights to challenge meaningfully the Government's case and to be heard by an impartial adjudicator. . . .

In so holding, we necessarily reject the Government's assertion that separation of powers principles mandate a heavily circumscribed role for the courts in such circumstances. Indeed, the position that the courts must forgo any examination of the individual case and focus exclusively on the legality of the broader detention scheme cannot be mandated by any reasonable view of separation of powers, as this approach serves only to *condense* power into a single branch of government. We have long since made clear that a state of war is not a blank check for the President when it comes to the rights of the Nation's citizens. *Youngstown Sheet & Tube*, 343 U.S., at 587. Whatever power the United States Constitution envisions for the Executive in its exchanges with other nations or with enemy organizations in times of conflict, it most assuredly envisions a role for all three branches when individual liberties are at stake. *Mistretta v. United States*, 488 U.S. 361, 380 (1989) (it was "the central judgment of the Framers of the Constitution that, within our political scheme, the separation of governmental powers into three coordinate Branches is essential to the preservation of liberty"); *Home Building & Loan Assn. v. Blaisdell*, 290 U.S. 398, 426 (1934) (The war power "is a power to wage war successfully, and thus it permits the harnessing of the entire energies of the people in a supreme cooperative effort to preserve the nation. But even the war power does not remove constitutional limitations safeguarding essential liberties"). Likewise, we have made clear that, unless Congress acts to suspend it, the Great Writ of habeas corpus allows the Judicial Branch to play a necessary role in maintaining this delicate balance of governance, serving as an important judicial check on the Executive's discretion in the realm of detentions. . . .

The judgment of the United States Court of Appeals for the Fourth Circuit is vacated, and the case is remanded for further proceedings.

It is so ordered.

JUSTICE THOMAS, dissenting.

The Executive Branch, acting pursuant to the powers vested in the President by the Constitution and with explicit congressional approval, has determined that Yaser Hamdi is an enemy combatant and should be detained. This detention falls squarely within the Federal Government's war powers, and we lack the expertise and capacity to second-guess that decision. As such, petitioners' habeas challenge should fail, and there is no reason to remand the case. The plurality reaches a contrary conclusion by failing adequately to consider basic principles of the constitutional structure as it relates to national security and foreign affairs and by using the balancing scheme of *Mathews v. Eldridge*, 424 U.S. 319 (1976). I do not think that the Federal Government's war powers can be balanced away by this Court. Arguably, Congress could provide for additional procedural protections, but until it does, we have no right to insist upon them. But even if I were to agree with the general approach the plurality takes, I could not accept the particulars. The plurality utterly fails to account for the Government's compelling interests and for our own institutional inability to weigh competing concerns correctly. I respectfully dissent. . . .

"It is 'obvious and unarguable' that no governmental interest is more compelling than the security of the Nation." *Haig v. Agee*, 453 U.S. 280, 307 (1981) (quoting *Aptheker v. Secretary of State*, 378 U.S. 500, 509 (1964)). The national security, after all, is the primary responsibility and purpose of the Federal Government. . . . But because the Founders understood that they could not foresee the myriad potential threats to national security that might later arise, they chose to create a Federal Government that necessarily possesses sufficient power to handle any threat to the security of the Nation. The power to protect the Nation

> "ought to exist without limitation . . . *[b]ecause it is impossible to foresee or define the extent and variety of national exigencies, or the correspondent extent & variety of the means which may be necessary to satisfy them.* The circumstances that endanger the safety of nations are infinite; and for this reason no constitutional shackles can wisely be imposed on the power to which the care of it is committed." [The Federalist No. 23, p. 147 (J. Cooke ed. 1961) (A. Hamilton)]. . . .

The Founders intended that the President have primary responsibility—along with the necessary power—to protect the national security and to conduct the Nation's foreign relations. They did so principally because the structural advantages of a unitary Executive are essential in these domains. "Energy in the executive is a leading character in the definition of good government. It is essential to the protection of the community against foreign attacks." *Id.,* No. 70, at 471 (A. Hamilton). The principle "ingredient[t]" for "energy in the executive" is "unity." *Id.,* at 472. This is because "[d]ecision, activity, secrecy, and dispatch will generally characterise the proceedings of one man, in a much more eminent degree, than the proceedings of any greater number." *Ibid.*

These structural advantages are most important in the national-security and foreign-affairs contexts. "Of all the cares or concerns of government, the direction of war most peculiarly demands those qualities which distinguish the exercise of power by a single hand." *Id.*, No. 74, at 500 (A. Hamilton). Also for these reasons, John Marshall explained that "[t]he President is the sole organ of the nation in its external relations, and its sole representative with foreign nations." 10 Annals of Cong. 613 (1800); see *id.,* at 613–614. To this end, the Constitution vests in the President "[t]he executive Power," Art. II, § 1, provides that he "shall be Commander in Chief of the" Armed Forces, § 2, and places in him the power to recognize foreign governments, § 3.

This Court has long recognized these features and has accordingly held that the President has *constitutional* authority to protect the national security and that this authority carries with it broad discretion.

> "If a war be made by invasion of a foreign nation, the President is not only authorized but bound to resist force by force. He does not initiate the war, but is bound to accept the challenge without waiting for any special legislative authority. . . . Whether the President in fulfilling his duties, as Commander in-chief, in suppressing an insurrection, has met with such armed hostile resistance . . . is a question to be decided *by him*." *Prize Cases*, 2 Black 635, 668, 670 (1863).

The Court has acknowledged that the President has the authority to "employ [the Nation's Armed Forces] in the manner he may deem most effectual to harass and conquer and subdue the enemy." *Fleming v. Page*, 9 How. 603, 615 (1850). With respect to foreign affairs as well, the Court has recognized the President's independent authority and need to be free from interference. See, *e.g., United States v. Curtiss-Wright Export Corp.*, 299 U.S. 304, 320 (1936) (explaining that the President "has his confidential sources of information. He has his agents in the form of diplomatic, consular and other officials. Secrecy in respect of information gathered by them may be highly necessary, and the premature disclosure of it productive of harmful results"); *Chicago & Southern Air Lines, Inc. v. Waterman S. S. Corp.,* 333 U.S. 103, 111 (1948). . . .

[W]here "the President acts pursuant to an express or implied authorization from Congress, he exercises not only his powers but also those delegated by Congress[, and i]n such a case the executive action 'would be supported by the strongest of presumptions and the widest latitude of judicial interpretation, and the burden of persuasion would rest heavily upon any who might attack it.' " *Dames & Moore,* 453 U.S. 654, 668 (1981) (quoting *Youngstown, supra,* at 637 (Jackson, J., concurring)). That is why the Court has explained, in a case analogous to this one, that "the detention[,] ordered by the President in the declared exercise of his powers as Commander in Chief of the Army in time of war and of grave public danger[, is] not to be set aside by the courts without the clear conviction that [it is] in conflict with the Constitution or laws of Congress constitutionally enacted." *Ex parte Quirin*, 317 U.S. 1, 25 (1942). See also *Ex parte Milligan,* 4 Wall. 2, 133 (1866) (Chase, C. J., concurring in judgment) (stating that a sentence imposed by a military commission "must not be set aside except upon the clearest conviction that it cannot be reconciled with the Constitution and the constitutional legislation of Congress"). This deference extends to the President's determination of all the factual predicates necessary to conclude that a given action is appropriate. . . .

Although the President very well may have inherent authority to detain those arrayed against our troops, I agree with the plurality that we need not decide that question because Congress has authorized the President to do so. The Authorization for Use of Military Force (AUMF), 115 Stat. 224, authorizes the President to "use all necessary and appropriate force against those nations, organizations, or persons he determines planned, authorized, committed, or aided the terrorist attacks" of September 11, 2001. . . .

NOTES

1. *War Powers and Individual Liberties. Hamdi v. Rumsfeld*, 542 U.S. 507 (2004) is a significant case for the study of both war powers and individual liberties. As discussed in Chapter 4 on war powers, the Court considered in *Hamdi* how to interpret the AUMF, including its relationship to international law. Writing for the plurality, Justice O'Connor determined that "Congress has in fact authorized Hamdi's detention" through the AUMF. 542 U.S. at 517. (*See* Chapter 4, Sec.7). In the excerpt above, the Court considered whether Congress and the president, even when working together in the field of foreign relations, are limited by due process concerns. The plurality held that due process required that Hamdi be given the opportunity to contest the factual basis for his detention. Do you agree with the plurality's analysis or do you find Justice Thomas's dissent compelling?

2. *The Least Dangerous Branch*. The *Hamdi* case reminds us that while foreign affairs powers are largely exercised concurrently by the two political branches, the judicial branch can play a pivotal role as well, even when the two political branches are acting in apparent harmony. In times of extremis, should courts be more deferential to the political branches, or is that the situation where judicial oversight is most needed?

3. *Deferring to the President*. How much deference should a court give to the executive branch's determination that Yaser Hamdi is an enemy combatant? By what standards would a court determine that the executive branch is mistaken? Are courts equipped to make such judgments? Recall the Court's treatment of the *Final Report of General DeWitt* (1943) in *Korematsu;* would that deference be more appropriate? Or are you troubled by what happened in the *Korematsu* case? Given that the executive branch makes such

determinations based in part on highly classified information, how could that information be properly shared with the court and with the alleged terrorist?

4. *Interpreting Congressional Action.* Does the existence of a statute authorizing the use of force by the executive mean that courts should be more deferential to executive detention of U.S. citizens without charge? Note that Justice Thomas places the president's authority to detain U.S. citizens as enemy combatants in Justice Jackson's first category where "the President acts pursuant to an express or implied authorization of Congress" and "his authority is at its maximum." Do you agree with the plurality, and with Justice Thomas, that Congress authorized the detention of U.S. citizens when it enacted the AUMF?

5. *Never Mind.* The Supreme Court's decision in *Hamdi* remanded the case for further proceedings on the issue of what procedures would be implemented in order to ensure Yaser Hamdi's due process rights. However, this issue was never resolved. Rather than granting Hamdi a hearing, in the fall of 2004 the U.S. government brokered a deal in which Hamdi—a U.S. citizen raised in Saudi Arabia—was freed from detention in exchange for agreeing to return to Saudi Arabia, renouncing his American citizenship, and adhering to prescribed travel restrictions. *See* Eric Lichtblau, *U.S., Bowing to Court Ruling, Will Free "Enemy Combatant,"* N.Y. TIMES, Sept. 23, 2004.

6. *Preventive Detentions.* Separate from the detention of certain U.S. citizens, in the aftermath of the September 11 attacks the executive branch embarked on an aggressive domestic law enforcement campaign that involved the detention of thousands of aliens in the United States as a preventive strategy against future terrorist activity. Consider the following description:

> Such arrests—which were on a scale not seen in the United States since the Second World War—were conducted under great secrecy. Gag orders and other rules (including rules relating to the grand jury and to the detainees' privacy) prevented officials from discussing the detainees, and defense lawyers were sometimes allowed to see documents only at the courthouse. A *Washington Post* analysis of 235 detainees revealed that the largest groups came from Egypt, Pakistan, and Saudi Arabia; virtually all were men in their twenties and thirties; and the greatest concentration were in U.S. states with large Islamic populations that included what law enforcement officials identified as Al Qaeda sympathizers: California, Florida, Michigan, New Jersey, New York, and Texas. Many were arrested because they were in the same places or engaged in the same kinds of activities as the hijackers (for example, taking flying lessons); many others apparently were detained because they came from certain countries or had violated U.S. immigration law. Further, the Justice Department announced a new policy that it would monitor communications between lawyers and persons being held on suspicion of being terrorists.

Sean D. Murphy, *United States Practice in International Law, Vol. 1: 1999–2001* 437 (2002) (footnotes omitted). When combined with the detention of some U.S. citizens as "enemy combatants," does this development suggest that a new approach should be considered for handling foreign relations law in times of crisis? By trying to adhere to the normal rules, do we risk watering down those rules by trying to make them fit extreme circumstances? By shifting to another model, do we risk jettisoning core values just when they are needed most?

7. *Extra-Legal Measures and Emergencies.* Should executive branch officials ever respond to emergency situations by defying legal restraints on their authority? If a court believes the executive branch might ignore its ruling, how, if at all, should that possibility factor into the court's decision-making? Oren Gross has written that "The dilemma confronting a constitutional democracy having to respond to emergencies has been famously captured by Abraham Lincoln's rhetorical question: '[A]re all the laws *but* one to go unexecuted, and the Government itself go to pieces, lest that one be violated?' " Gross goes on to argue that "there may be circumstances where the appropriate method of tackling grave dangers and threats entails going outside the constitutional order, at times even violating otherwise accepted constitutional principles, rules, and norms. Such a response, if pursued in appropriate circumstances and properly applied, may strengthen rather than weaken, and result in more rather than less, long-term constitutional fidelity and commitment to the rule of law." How might "going outside the legal order" promote "ethical concepts of political and popular responsibility, political morality, and candor"? *See* Oren Gross, *Chaos and Rules: Should Responses to Violent Crises Always Be Constitutional*? 112 YALE L.J. 1011, 1014–15, 1023–24 (2003).

CHAPTER 2

CUSTOMARY INTERNATIONAL LAW

■ ■ ■

1. INTRODUCTION TO CUSTOMARY INTERNATIONAL LAW

This book is not a treatise on international law, a discipline that has produced a vast literature in its own right. Mastering some basic concepts in international law, however, is key for any student of U.S. foreign relations law. This Section will introduce several of those concepts, including that of customary international law, the subject of this Chapter as a whole.

"International law," as the name suggests, is traditionally described as rules that govern relations between States—though that term, and its perceived limitations, have not always been with us. William Blackstone's influential *Commentaries on the Laws of England* described a "law of nations" that concerned not just the rights and obligations of States to one another, but also the law governing intercourse between individuals of different States.[1] In 1789, Jeremy Bentham invented the term "international law" to describe the rights and obligations of States to one another, but apparently not to address transnational relations of individuals.[2] Today, the term "international law" is broadly used to address various types of international rules that govern States, international organizations, and individuals; its main subject, though, remains the state.

Modern international law is generally understood to derive from two main sources: treaties and customary international law.[3] While treaties have proliferated in recent years and now constitute the dominant form of international lawmaking, customary international law predominated for many centuries and today retains an important role in the international system, including as a "gap-filler" in areas where a recognizable custom

---

[1] William Blackstone, *Commentaries on the Laws of England* [1765–1769] (1979 ed., University of Chicago Press, 4 vols.).

[2] *See* Mark Janis, *The American Tradition of International Law: Great Expectations, 1789–1914*, at 11–15 (2004).

[3] A third source of international law is "general principles of law." *See* Statute of the International Court of Justice, art. 38(1), June 26, 1945, 59 Stat. 1055. While these play a role in the jurisprudence of international tribunals, they have had little relevance to the foreign relations law of the United States. In addition, judicial decisions and the teachings of highly qualified publicists may be invoked, on a subsidiary basis, as a means of understanding these three basic sources. *Id.*

has evolved but has not yet been codified by treaty. The role of treaties in U.S. foreign relations law will be examined in Chapter 3; this Chapter is concerned with customary international law.

In discussing customary international law, this Chapter will consider numerous questions hearkening back to the "law of nations," a term that retains considerable significance. As suggested, Blackstone used that term broadly to encompass all of what is now known as international law, including (among other things) what we now call treaties and customary international law. The same usage was adopted by others: hence, in cases such as *Ware v. Hylton* (*infra*, this Chapter, Sec. 2), reference is made broadly to the "law of nations," even though what is actually at issue is the interpretation of a treaty (in that case, the 1783 Treaty of Paris ending the U.S. Revolutionary War). More often the term "law of nations" was used to refer to international law *other than treaties*. Thus, in the First Judiciary Act of 1789, Congress adopted a statute that refers to violations of "the law of nations *or* a treaty of the United States."[4] In this sense, the term "law of nations" is a synonym for customary international law, rather than international law generally. As the *Restatement (Third)* puts it: "The term 'law of nations' was used to describe the customary rules and obligations that regulated conduct between states and certain aspects of state conduct towards individuals." *See Restatement of the Law (Third), The Foreign Relations Law of the United States* § 111, introductory note (1987).

While treaties, as explored in Chapter 3, are ordinarily expressed as formally-adopted, written documents—with relatively clear principles, themselves set out in a treaty—customary international law is more elusive. How does one determine when it exists, and what it is? The *Restatement (Third)* summarizes the typical criteria: "Customary international law results from a general and consistent practice of states followed by them from a sense of legal obligation." *Id.* § 102(2). As that quote suggests, there are two components to customary international law: (1) a general and consistent practice of States and (2) some sense of legal obligation to engage in that practice, otherwise known as *opinio juris*. A State that does not agree with an emergent trend in customary international law may register its dissent and thereby gain the status of "persistent objector," in which case that State is not bound by the particular rule.

A key threshold question for U.S. foreign relations law is how international law becomes part of the U.S. legal system. Two types of approaches may be contrasted. *Monism* contends that all law is part of the same system and constitutes a spectrum wherein domestic law is hierarchically inferior to and governed by international law. *Dualism*, on the other hand, rejects this ordering and views both systems as entirely

[4] Alien Tort Statute, 28 U.S.C. § 1350 (2012) (emphasis added), discussed in Sec. 6 of this Chapter.

separate; it allows, however, that a domestic legal system can adopt rules (such as in a constitution) that incorporate any aspects of international law to which the domestic system wishes to adhere. Most countries in the world today, the United States included, fall somewhere along the spectrum between these extremes, but they tend more toward dualism. *See, e.g.*, *Restatement (Third)*, Part I, Chapter 2, introductory note ("International law and the law of the United States are two different and discrete bodies of law, but often they impinge on the same conduct, relations, and interests.").

The next Section addresses U.S. incorporation of international law into the domestic U.S. legal system. While the Chapter as a whole focuses on customary international law, you will note that much of the material—primarily, but not solely, older case law—addresses international law and related concepts more generally. As you review the material, try to assess the strengths and weaknesses of that approach.

2. INCORPORATION OF INTERNATIONAL CUSTOM INTO U.S. LAW

RESTATEMENT OF THE LAW (THIRD), THE FOREIGN RELATIONS LAW OF THE UNITED STATES §§ 111, 114*

(1987).

§ 111. *International Law and Agreements as Law of the United States*

(1) International law and international agreements of the United States are law of the United States and supreme over the law of the several States.

(2) Cases arising under international law or international agreements of the United States are within the Judicial Power of the United States and, subject to Constitutional and statutory limitations and requirements of justiciability, are within the jurisdiction of the federal courts. . . .

Comment to § 111:

d. *International law and agreements as supreme federal law.* Treaties made under the authority of the United States, like the Constitution itself and the laws of the United States, are expressly declared to be "supreme Law of the Land" by Article VI of the Constitution. International agreements of the United States other than treaties . . . , and customary international law, while not mentioned explicitly in the Supremacy Clause, are also federal law and as such are supreme over State law. Interpretations of international agreements by the United

States Supreme Court are binding on the States. Customary international law is considered to be like common law in the United States, but it is federal law. A determination of international law by the Supreme Court is binding on the States and on State courts. . . .

§ 114. *Interpretation of Federal Statute in Light of International Law or Agreement*

Where fairly possible, a United States statute is to be construed so as not to conflict with international law or with an international agreement of the United States.

NOTE: STATUS OF CUSTOMARY INTERNATIONAL LAW IN U.S. LAW

Section 111 of the *Restatement (Third)* sets out a common view of customary international law's place within the domestic hierarchy of U.S. law, though in recent years this ordering has become subject to some dispute. The debate is due in part to the relative silence of the Constitution itself and its disparate treatment of international law's two main sources, treaties and custom. As Section 111 indicates, the Supremacy Clause explicitly addresses treaties, but neither the Supremacy Clause or any other constitutional provision addresses "customary international law." This is unsurprising, given that this precise term had not yet been coined when the framers met in Philadelphia in 1787; more revealingly, the Constitution only once refers to the "law of nations"— potentially encompassing treaties as well as custom—in Article 1, § 8, clause 10 of the Constitution, which authorizes Congress to "define and punish . . . Offenses against the Law of Nations."

Nonetheless, it is possible to see traces of customary international law in U.S. law. You have probably learned in previous courses some relevant forms of federal law and their hierarchy: the Constitution is the highest form of law in the United States, and precludes application of any other laws inconsistent with it; federal statutes and treaties come next; federal common law, a body of law greatly circumscribed since the decision of the Supreme Court in *Erie R. Co. v. Tompkins*, 304 U.S. 64 (1938), is inferior in status to other forms of federal law, but still superior to state law, including but not limited to state common law.

How does customary international law fit into this scheme? As just noted, the Constitution does not directly and automatically confer any particular status on customary international law. (Sec. 4 of this Chapter addresses, however, the possibility that custom may inform the interpretation of constitutional provisions.) The Constitution does suggest in the Offenses Clause that Congress may incorporate customary international law, and this Section considers the possibility of statutory incorporation more generally. Finally, as this Section also explores, U.S. courts have long expressed the view that the common law incorporates customary international law. This tendency can be traced back to pre-revolutionary English and American cases.[5] It was this history that the *Paquete Habana* case, excerpted below, recalled when pronouncing that "international law is part of our law."[6] And, notwithstanding the Erie-led revolution in federal common law, the Court's more recent decision in *Sosa v. Alvarez-Machain* (addressed further *infra*, this Chapter, Sec. 6) observed that "[f]or two centuries we have affirmed that the domestic law of the United States recognizes the law of nations," and identified such law as one of the "limited enclaves in which federal courts may derive some substantive law in a common law way."[7]

This Section examines how customary international law has been understood to become part of our law, beginning with selected excerpts from the early case law. In the first excerpt, Chief Justice John Jay—performing a role unknown to today's Supreme Court, but not uncommon at the time—delivered a much-quoted charge to the grand jury empanelled in Richmond, Virginia, in connection with an alleged illegal enlisting of Gideon Henfield for service with a French privateer.

TRIAL OF GIDEON HENFIELD

U.S. Circuit Court for the Pennsylvania District, 1793.
Reprinted in Wharton, State Trials 49, 52–53 (1849).

CHIEF JUSTICE JAY:

That you may perceive more clearly the extent and objects of your inquiries, it may be proper to observe, that the laws of the United States admit of being classed under three heads of descriptions.

1st. All treaties made under the authority of the United States.

2d. The laws of nations.

3dly. The constitution, and statutes of the United States.

Treaties between independent nations, are contracts or bargains which derive all their force and obligation from mutual consent and agreement; and consequently, when once fairly made and properly concluded, cannot be altered or annulled by one of the parties, without the consent and concurrence of the other. Wide is the difference between treaties and statutes—we may negotiate and make contracts with other nations, but we can neither legislate for them, nor they for us; we may repeal or alter our statutes, but no nation can have authority to vacate or modify treaties at discretion. Treaties, therefore, necessarily become the

---

[5] *See, e.g.*, *Triquet v. Bath*, 3 Burr. 1478 (K.B. 1764) (upholding diplomatic immunity because the law of nations was a part of the law of England); *Republica v. De Longchamps*, Court of Oyer and Terminer (Pa.), 11 (1784) (holding that the case "must be determined on the principles of the law of nations, which form a part of the municipal law of Pennsylvania.").

[6] 175 U.S. 677, 700 (1900).

[7] 542 U.S. 692, 729 (2004).

supreme law of the land, and so they are very properly declared to be by the sixth article of the constitution.

Whenever doubts and questions arise relative to the validity, operation or construction of treaties, or of any articles in them, those doubts and questions must be settled according to the maxims and principles of the laws of nations applicable to the case.

The peace, prosperity, and reputation of the United States, will always greatly depend on their fidelity to their engagements; and every virtuous citizen (for every citizen is a party to them) will concur in observing and executing them with honour and good faith; and that, whether they be made with nations respectable and important, or with nations weak and inconsiderable, our obligation to keep our faith results from our having pledged it, and not from the character or description of the state or people, to whom, neither impunity nor the right of retaliation can sanctify perfidy; for although perfidy may deserve chastisement, yet it can never merit imitation.

As to the laws of nations—they are those laws by which nations are bound to regulate their conduct towards each other, both in peace and war. Providence has been pleased to place the United States among the nations of the earth, and therefore, all those duties, as well as rights, which spring from the relation of nation to nation, have devolved upon us. We are with other nations, tenants in common of the sea—it is a highway for all, and all are bound to exercise that common right, and use that common highway in the manner which the laws of nations and treaties require.

On this occasion, it is proper to observe to you, gentlemen, that various circumstances and considerations now unite in urging the people of the United States to be particularly exact and circumspect in observing the obligation of treaties, and the laws of nations, which, as has been already remarked, form a very important part of the laws of our nation. I allude to the facts and injunctions specified in the President's late proclamation; it is in these words:

> "Whereas, it appears that a state of war exists between Austria, Prussia, Sardinia, Great Britain, and the United Netherlands of the one part, and France of the other, and the duty and interest of the United States, require that they should with sincerity and good faith, adopt and pursue a conduct friendly and impartial towards the belligerent powers:
>
> "I have, therefore, thought fit by these presents, to declare the disposition of the United States to observe the conduct aforesaid towards these powers respectively, and to exhort and warn the citizens of the United States, carefully to avoid all acts and proceedings whatsoever, which may in any manner tend to contravene such disposition.

"And I do hereby also make known, that whosoever of the citizens of the United States, shall render himself liable to punishment or forfeiture, under the law of nations, by committing, aiding, or abetting hostilities against any of the said powers, or by carrying to them those articles which are deemed contraband, by the modern usage of nations, will not receive the protection of the United States against such punishment or forfeiture: and further, that I have given instructions to those officers to whom it belongs, to cause prosecutions to be instituted against all persons who shall within the cognizance of the Courts of the United States, violate the law of nations, with respect to the powers at war, or any of them."

WARE V. HYLTON

3 U.S. (3 Dall.) 199 (1796).

[The 1783 Treaty of Paris, which ended the U.S. Revolutionary War, provided that British creditors would meet with no impediment to the recovery of their debts. After the U.S. Constitution took effect, a case arose concerning the refusal of a Virginian to pay a debt owed to a British subject. While the case is important on the issue of whether, under the new Constitution, the Treaty of Paris could override an otherwise valid state law (*see* Chapter 6, Sec. 3), Justice Wilson in his separate opinion spoke broadly to the role of the law of nations in U.S. law.]

JUSTICE WILSON:

. . . When the United States declared their independence, they were bound to receive the law of nations, in its modern state of purity and refinement. By every nation, whatever is its form of government, the confiscation of debts has long been considered disreputable: and, we know, that not a single confiscation of that kind stained the code of any of the European powers, who were engaged in the war, which our revolution produced. Nor did any authority for the confiscation of debts proceed from Congress (that body, which clearly possessed the right of confiscation, as an incident of the powers of war and peace) and, therefore, in no instance can the act of confiscation be considered as an act of the nation.

MURRAY V. THE SCHOONER CHARMING BETSY

6 U.S. (2 Cranch) 64 (1804).

[During 1798–1800, the United States and France faced off in an undeclared war (or "quasi-war") involving attacks and seizures of each other's vessels on the high seas. By statute enacted in February 1800, Congress prohibited all commercial intercourse by U.S. nationals with France. In this case, that prohibition was interpreted by the Supreme

Court in light of the rule under the law of nations obliging belligerents not to seize the persons and property of neutral countries.]

MR. CHIEF JUSTICE MARSHALL delivered the opinion of the court:

The *Charming Betsy* was an American built vessel, belonging to citizens of the United States, and sailed from Baltimore, under the name of the *Jane*, on the 10th of April, 1800, with a cargo of flour for St. Bartholomew's; she was sent out for the purpose of being sold. The cargo was disposed of at St. Bartholomew's; but finding it impossible to sell the vessel at that place, the captain proceeded with her to the island of St. Thomas, where she was disposed of to Jared Shattuck, who changed her name to that of the *Charming Betsy*, and having put on board her a cargo consisting of American produce, cleared her out, as a Danish vessel, for the island of Guadaloupe.

On her voyage, she was captured by a French privateer, and eight hands were put on board her for the purpose of taking her into Guadaloupe as a prize. She was afterwards re-captured by Captain Murray, commander of the *Constellation* frigate, and carried into Martinique. It appears, that the captain of the *Charming Betsy* was not willing to be taken into that island; but when there, he claimed to have his vessel and cargo restored, as being the property of Jared Shattuck, a Danish burgher.

Jared Shattuck was born in the United States, but had removed to the island of St. Thomas while an infant, and was proved to have resided there ever since the year 1789 or 1790. He had been accustomed to carry on trade as a Danish subject; had married a wife and acquired real property in the island, and also taken the oath of allegiance to the crown of Denmark in 1797.

Considering him as an American citizen, who was violating the law prohibiting all intercourse between the United States and France or its dependencies, or the sale of the vessel as a mere cover to evade that law, Captain Murray sold the cargo of the *Charming Betsy*, which consisted of American produce, in Martinique, and brought the vessel into the port of Philadelphia, where she was libelled under what is termed the non-intercourse law. The vessel and cargo were claimed by the consul of Denmark as being the *bonâ fide* property of a Danish subject. . . .

. . . Is the *Charming Betsy* subject to seizure and condemnation for having violated a law of the United States?

The libel claims this forfeiture under the act passed in February, 1800, further to suspend the commercial intercourse between the United States and France and the dependencies thereof.

That act declares "that all commercial intercourse," & c. It has been very properly observed, in argument, that the building of vessels in the United States for sale to neutrals, in the islands, is, during war, a profitable business, which Congress cannot be intended to have prohibited, unless that intent be manifested by express words or a very plain and necessary implication.

It has also been observed that an act of Congress ought never to be construed to violate the law of nations if any other possible construction remains, and consequently can never be construed to violate neutral rights, or to affect neutral commerce, further than is warranted by the law of nations as understood in this country.

These principles are believed to be correct, and they ought to be kept in view, in construing the act now under consideration.

The first sentence of the act which describes the persons whose commercial intercourse with France or her dependencies is to be prohibited, names any person or persons, resident within the United States or under their protection. Commerce carried on by persons within this description is declared to be illicit.

From persons the act proceeds to things, and declares explicitly the cases in which the vessels employed in this illicit commerce shall be forfeited. Any vessel owned, hired or employed wholly or in part by any person residing within the United States, or by any citizen thereof residing elsewhere, which shall perform certain acts recited in the law, becomes liable to forfeiture. It seems to the court to be a correct construction of these words to say, that the vessel must be of this description, not at the time of the passage of the law, but at the time when the act of forfeiture shall be committed. . . .

The *Jane* having been completely transferred in the island of St. Thomas, by a *bonâ fide* sale to Jared Shattuck, and the forfeiture alleged to have accrued on a fact subsequent to that transfer, the liability of the vessel to forfeiture must depend on the inquiry whether the purchaser was within the description of the act.

Jared Shattuck having been born within the United States, and not being proved to have expatriated himself according to any form prescribed by law, is said to remain a citizen, entitled to the benefit and subject to the disabilities imposed upon American citizens; and, therefore, to come expressly within the description of the act which comprehends American citizens residing elsewhere.

Whether a person born within the United States, or becoming a citizen according to the established laws of the country, can divest himself absolutely of that character otherwise than in such manner as may be prescribed by law, is a question which it is not necessary at present to decide. The cases cited at bar and the arguments drawn from the general conduct of the United States on this interesting subject, seem completely to establish the principle that an American citizen may acquire in a foreign country, the commercial privileges attached to his domicil, and be exempted from the operation of an act expressed in such general terms as that now under consideration. Indeed the very expressions of the act would seem to exclude a person under the circumstances of Jared Shattuck. He is not a person under the protection of the United States. The American citizen who goes into a foreign country, although he owes local and temporary allegiance to that country, is yet, if he performs no other act changing his condition, entitled to the protection of our government; and if, without the violation of any municipal law, he should be oppressed unjustly, he would have a right to claim that protection, and the interposition of the American government in his favor, would be considered as a justifiable interposition. But his situation is completely changed, where by his own act he has made himself the subject of a foreign power. Although this act may not be sufficient to rescue him from punishment for any crime committed against the United States, a point not intended to be decided, yet it certainly places him out of the protection of the United States while within the territory of the sovereign to whom he has sworn allegiance, and consequently takes him out of the description of the act.

It is therefore the opinion of the court, that the *Charming Betsy*, with her cargo, being at the time of her re-capture the *bonâ fide* property of a Danish burgher, is not forfeitable, in consequence of her being employed in carrying on trade and commerce with a French island.

THE NEREIDE

13 U.S. (9 Cranch) 388 (1815).

[In 1813, during the War of 1812, a Spanish subject named Pinto contracted to have goods transported on a British vessel, *The Nereide*, from London to Buenos Aires. On the voyage, *The Nereide* was separated from her convoy, captured by an American privateer, and brought into the port of New York, where the vessel and cargo were libeled and condemned as a prize of war, including the cargo owned by Pinto and other Spanish subjects. The captors argued that neutral property forfeits that character when put on board an enemy's armed ship. The Spaniards argued that the property of a neutral country and its nationals (in this case, Spain) was not liable to condemnation under the law of nations.]

MARSHALL, CH. J. after stating the facts of the case, delivered the opinion of the court as follows:

. . . The rule that the goods of an enemy found in the vessel of a friend are prize of war, and that the goods of a friend found in the vessel of an enemy are to be restored, is believed to be a part of the original law of nations, as generally, perhaps universally, acknowledged. Certainly it has been fully and unequivocally recognized by the United States. This rule is founded on the simple and intelligible principle that war gives a full right to capture the goods of an enemy, but gives no right to capture the goods of a friend. In the practical application of this principle, so as to form the rule, the propositions that the neutral flag constitutes no protection to enemy property, and that the belligerent flag communicates no hostile character to neutral property, are necessarily admitted. The character of the property, taken distinctly and separately from all other considerations, depends in no degree upon the character of the vehicle in which it is found. . . .

The . . . captors [argue that] the ordinances of [the Spanish] government would subject American property, under similar circumstances, to confiscation, and therefore the property, claimed by Spanish subjects in this case, ought to be condemned as prize of war.

The ordinances themselves have not been produced, nor has the Court received such information respecting them as would enable it to decide certainly either on their permanent existence, or on their application to the United States. But be this as it may, the Court is decidedly of opinion that reciprocating to the subjects of a nation, or retaliating on them, its unjust proceedings towards our citizens, is a political not a legal measure. It is for the consideration of the government not of its Courts. The degree and the kind of retaliation depend entirely on considerations foreign to this tribunal. It may be the policy of the nation to avenge its wrongs in a manner having no affinity to the injury sustained, or it may be its policy to recede from its full rights and not to avenge them at all. It is not for its Courts to interfere with the proceedings of the nation and to thwart its views. It is not for us to depart from the beaten track prescribed for us, and to tread the devious and intricate path of politics. Even in the case of salvage, a case peculiarly within the discretion of Courts, because no fixed rule is prescribed by the law of nations, congress has not left it to this department to say whether the rule of foreign nations shall be applied to them, but has by law applied that rule. If it be the will of the government to apply to Spain any rule respecting captures which Spain is supposed to apply to us, the government will manifest that will by passing an act for the purpose. Till such an act be passed, the Court is bound by the law of nations which is a part of the law of the land.

THE LOTTAWANNA

88 U.S. (21 Wall.) 558 (1874).

[In an 1819 case called *The General Smith*, the Supreme Court decided that when repairs or other services are furnished to a ship in the port of a state to which she belongs, no lien is implied unless it is recognized by the local law of the state; by contrast, when such services are furnished to a foreign vessel, maritime and admiralty law recognizes a lien for the party providing the service on the vessel so as to secure payment for the services provided. In this case, a Louisiana vessel called the *Lottawanna* was provided repairs in the port of New Orleans and then became the subject of a lien, even though Louisiana law did not provide for such a lien. Despite the Supreme Court's earlier finding in *The General Smith*, the lower court upheld the lien.]

JUSTICE BRADLEY:

. . . The ground on which we are asked to overrule the judgment in the case of *The General Smith* is, that by the general maritime law, those who furnish necessary materials, repairs, and supplies to a vessel, upon her credit, have a lien on such a vessel therefor, as well when furnished in her home port as when furnished in a foreign port, and that the courts of admiralty are bound to give effect to that lien.

The proposition assumes that the general maritime law governs this case, and is binding on the courts of the United States.

But it is hardly necessary to argue that the maritime law is only so far operative as law in any country as it is adopted by the laws and usages of that country. In this respect it is like international law or the laws of war, which have the effect of law in no country any further than they are accepted and received as such; or, like the case of the civil law, which forms the basis of most European laws, but which has the force of law in each state only so far as it is adopted therein, and with such modifications as are deemed expedient. The adoption of the common law by the several States of this Union also presents an analogous case. It is the basis of all the State laws; but is modified as each sees fit. Perhaps the maritime law is more uniformly followed by commercial nations than the civil and common laws are by those who use them. But, like those laws, however fixed, definite, and beneficial the theoretical code of maritime law may be, it can have only so far the effect of law in any country as it is permitted to have. But the actual maritime law can hardly be said to have a fixed and definite form as to all the subjects which may be embraced within its scope. Whilst it is true that the great mass of maritime law is the same in all commercial countries, yet, in each country, peculiarities exist either as to some of the rules, or in the mode of enforcing them. Especially is this the case on the outside boundaries of the law, where it comes in contact with, or shades off into the local or municipal law of the particular country and affects only its own merchants or people in their relations to each other. Whereas, in matters affecting the stranger or foreigner, the commonly received law of the whole commercial world is more assiduously observed—as, in justice, it should be. No one doubts that every nation may adopt its own maritime code. France may adopt one; England another; the United States a third; still, the convenience of the commercial world, bound together, as it is, by mutual relations of trade and intercourse, demands that, in all essential things wherein those relations bring them in contact, there should be a uniform law founded on natural reason and justice. Hence the adoption by all commercial nations (our own included) of the general maritime law as the basis and groundwork of all their maritime regulations. But no nation regards itself as precluded from making occasional modifications suited to its locality and the genius of its own people and institutions, especially in matters that are of merely local and municipal consequence and do not affect other nations. . . . Thus adopted and thus qualified in each case, it becomes the maritime law of the particular nation that adopts it. And without such voluntary adoption it would not be law. And thus it happens, that, from the general practice of commercial nations in making the same general law the basis and groundwork of their respective maritime systems, the great mass of maritime law which is thus received by these nations in common, comes to be the common maritime law of the world.

. . . The government of one country may be willing to give to its citizens, who supply a ship with provisions at her home port where the owner himself resides, a lien on the ship; whilst that of another country may take a contrary view as to the expediency of such a rule. The difference between them in a matter that concerns only their own citizens, in each case, cannot seriously affect the harmony and consistency of the common maritime law which each adopts and observes. . . .

. . . [A]ccording to the maritime law as accepted and received in this country, we feel bound to declare that no such lien exists as is claimed by the appellees in this case. . . .

UNITED STATES V. ARJONA

120 U.S. 479 (1887).

[In this case, the Supreme Court considered the constitutionality of a law by which Congress had declared it a punishable offense to counterfeit notes of a foreign bank or corporation. Although the law did not state that this was "an offense against the Law of Nations" the Supreme Court nevertheless found it to be so.]

CHIEF JUSTICE WAITE

. . . The law of nations requires every national government to use "due diligence" to prevent a wrong being done within its own dominion to another nation with which it is at peace, or to the people thereof; and because of this the obligation of one nation to punish those who within its own jurisdiction counterfeit the money of another nation has long been recognized. Vattel, in his Law of Nations, which was first printed at Neuchâtel in 1758, and was translated into English and published in England in 1760, uses this language: "From the principles thus laid down, it is easy to conclude, that if one nation counterfeits the money of another, or if she allows and protects false coiners who presume to do it, she does that nation an injury." . . .

This rule was established for the protection of nations in their intercourse with each other. If there were no such intercourse, it would be a matter of no special moment to one nation that its money was counterfeited in another. Its own people could not be defrauded if the false coin did not come among them, and its own sovereignty would not be violated if the counterfeit could not under any circumstances be made to take the place of the true money. But national intercourse includes commercial intercourse between the people of different nations. It is as much the duty of a nation to protect such an intercourse as it is any other, and that is what Vattel meant when he said: "For the same reason that sovereigns are obliged to protect commerce, they are obliged to support this custom;" "namely, *exchange,* or the traffic of bankers, by means of which a merchant remits immense sums from one end of the world to the other," "by good laws, in which every merchant, whether citizen or foreigner, may find security." . . .

No nation can be more interested in this question than the United States. Their money is practically composed of treasury notes or certificates issued by themselves, or of bank bills issued by banks created under their authority and subject to their control. Their own securities, and those of the states, the cities, and the public corporations, whose interests abroad they alone have the power to guard against foreign national neglect, are found on sale in the principal money markets of Europe. If these securities, whether national, municipal, or corporate, are forged and counterfeited with impunity at the places where they are sold, it is easy to see that a great wrong will be done to the United States and their people. Any uncertainty about the genuineness of the security necessarily depreciates its value as a merchantable commodity, and against this international comity requires that national protection shall, as far as possible, be afforded. If there is neglect in that, the United States may, with propriety, call on the proper government to provide for the punishment of such an offence, and thus secure the restraining influences of a fear of the consequences of wrong doing. A refusal may not, perhaps, furnish sufficient cause for war, but it would certainly give just ground of complaint, and thus disturb that harmony between the governments which each is bound to cultivate and promote.

But if the United States can require this of another, that other may require it of them, because international obligations are of necessity reciprocal in their nature. The right, if it exists at all, is given by the law of nations, and what is law for one is, under the same circumstances, law for the other. A right secured by the law of nations to a nation, or its people, is one the United States as the representatives of this nation are bound to protect. Consequently, a law which is necessary and proper to afford this protection is one that Congress may enact, because it is one that is needed to carry into execution a power conferred by the Constitution on the Government of the United States exclusively. There is no authority in the United States to require the passage and enforcement of such a law by the states. Therefore the United States must have the power to pass it and enforce it themselves, or be unable to perform a duty which they may owe to another nation, and which the law of nations has imposed on them as part of their international obligations. . . .

It remains only to consider those questions which present the point whether, in enacting a statute to define and punish an offence against the law of nations, it is necessary, in order "to define" the offence, that it be declared in the statute itself to be "an offence against the law of nations." This statute defines the offence, and if the thing made punishable is one which the United States are required by their international obligations to use due diligence to prevent, it is an offence against the law of nations. Such being the case, there is no more need of declaring in the statute that it is such an offence than there would be in any other criminal statute to declare that it was enacted to carry into execution any other particular power vested by the Constitution in the Government of the United States. Whether the offence as defined is an offence against the law of nations depends on the thing done, not on any declaration to that effect by Congress. As has already been seen, it was incumbent on the United States as a nation to use due diligence to prevent any injury to another nation or its people by counterfeiting its money, or its public or *quasi* public securities. This statute was enacted as a means to that end, that is to say, as a means of performing a duty which had been cast on the United States by the law of nations, and it was clearly appropriate legislation for that purpose. Upon its face, therefore, it defines an offence against the law of nations as clearly as if Congress had in express terms so declared. Criminal statutes passed for enforcing and preserving the neutral relations of the United States with other nations were passed by Congress at a very early date; June 5, 1794, c. 50, 1 Stat. 381; June 14, 1797, c. 1, 1 Stat. 520; March 3, 1817, c. 58, 3 Stat. 370; April 20, 1818, c. 88, 3 Stat. 447: and those now in force are found in Title LXVII of the Revised Statutes. These all rest on the same power of Congress that is here invoked, and it has never been supposed they were invalid because they did not expressly declare that the offences there defined were offences against the law of nations.

THE PAQUETE HABANA

175 U.S. 677 (1900).

MR. JUSTICE GRAY delivered the opinion of the court.

These are two appeals from decrees of the District Court of the United States for the Southern District of Florida, condemning two fishing vessels and their cargoes as prize of war.

Each vessel [*Paquete Habana* and the *Lola*] was a fishing smack, running in and out of Havana, and regularly engaged in fishing on the coast of Cuba; sailed under the Spanish flag; was owned by a Spanish subject of Cuban birth, living in the city of Havana; was commanded by a subject of Spain, also residing in Havana; and her master and crew had no interest in the vessel, but were entitled to shares, amounting in all to two thirds, of her catch, the other third belonging to her owner. Her cargo consisted of fresh fish, caught by her crew from the sea, put on board as they were caught, and kept and sold alive. Until stopped by the blockading squadron, she had no knowledge of the existence of the war, or of any blockade. She had no arms or ammunition on board, and made no attempt to run the blockade after she knew of its existence, nor any resistance at the time of the capture. . . .

Both the fishing vessels were brought by their captors into Key West. A libel for the condemnation of each vessel and her cargo as prize of war was there filed . . . [O]n May 30, 1898, a final decree of condemnation and sale was entered, "the court not being satisfied that as a matter of law, without any ordinance, treaty or proclamation, fishing vessels of this class are exempt from seizure." . . .

We are then brought to the consideration of the question whether, upon the facts appearing in these records, the fishing smacks were subject to capture by the armed vessels of the United States during the recent war with Spain.

By an ancient usage among civilized nations, beginning centuries ago, and gradually ripening into a rule of international law, coast fishing vessels, pursuing their vocation of catching and bringing in fresh fish, have been recognized as exempt, with their cargoes and crews, from capture as prize of war.

This doctrine, however, has been earnestly contested at the bar; and no complete collection of the instances illustrating it is to be found, so far as we are aware, in a single published work although many are referred to and discussed by the writers on international law . . . It is therefore worth the while to trace the history of the rule, from the earliest accessible sources, through the increasing recognition of it, with occasional setbacks, to what we may now justly consider as its final establishment in our own country and generally throughout the civilized world. . . .

Since the English orders in council of 1806 and 1810, before quoted, in favor of fishing vessels employed in catching and bringing to market fresh fish, no instance has been found in which the exemption from capture of private coast fishing vessels, honestly pursuing their peaceful industry, has been denied by England, or by any other nation. And the Empire of Japan, (the last state admitted into the rank of civilized nations,) by an ordinance promulgated at the beginning of its war with China in August, 1894, established prize courts, and ordained that "the following enemy's vessels are exempt from detention"—including in the exemption "boats engaged in coast fisheries," as well as "ships engaged exclusively on a voyage of scientific discovery, philanthropy or religious mission." Takahashi, International Law, 11, 178.

International law is part of our law, and must be ascertained and administered by the courts of justice of appropriate jurisdiction, as often as questions of right depending upon it are duly presented for their determination. For this purpose, where there is no treaty, and no controlling executive or legislative act or judicial decision, resort must be had to the customs and usages of civilized nations; and, as evidence of these, to the works of jurists and commentators, who by years of labor, research and experience, have made themselves peculiarly well acquainted with the subjects of which they treat. Such works are resorted to by judicial tribunals, not for the speculations of their authors concerning what the law ought to be, but for trustworthy evidence of what the law really is. *Hilton v. Guyot,* 159 U.S. 113, 163, 164, 214, 215. . . .

This review of the precedents and authorities on the subject appears to us abundantly to demonstrate that at the present day, by the general consent of the civilized nations of the world, and independently of any express treaty or other public act, it is an established rule of international law, founded on considerations of humanity to a poor and industrious order of men, and of the mutual convenience of belligerent States, that coast fishing vessels, with their implements and supplies, cargoes and crews, unarmed, and honestly pursuing their peaceful calling of catching and bringing in fresh fish, are exempt from capture as prize of war.

The exemption, of course, does not apply to coast fishermen or their vessels if employed for a warlike purpose, or in such a way as to give aid or information to the enemy; nor when military or naval operations create a necessity to which all private interests must give way.

Nor has the exemption been extended to ships or vessels employed on the high sea in taking whales or seals, or cod or other fish which are not brought fresh to market, but are salted or otherwise cured and made a regular article of commerce.

This rule of international law is one which prize courts, administering the law of nations, are bound to take judicial notice of, and to give effect to, in the absence of any treaty or other public act of their own government in relation to the matter. . . .

By the practice of all civilized nations, vessels employed only for the purposes of discovery or science are considered as exempt from the contingencies of war, and therefore not subject to capture. It has been usual for the government sending out such an expedition to give notice to other powers; but it is not essential. 1 Kent Com. 91, note; Halleck, c. 20, § 22; Calvo, § 2376; Hall, § 138. . . .

To this subject, in more than one aspect, are singularly applicable the words uttered by Mr. Justice Strong, speaking for this court: "Undoubtedly, no single nation can change the law of the sea. The law is of universal obligation, and no statute of one or two nations can create obligations for the world. Like all the laws of nations, it rests upon the common consent of civilized communities. It is of force, not because it was prescribed by any superior power, but because it has been generally accepted as a rule of conduct. Whatever may have been its origin, whether in the usages of navigation, or in the ordinances of maritime States, or in both, it has become the law of the sea only by the concurrent sanction of those nations who may be said to constitute the commercial world. Many of the usages which prevail, and which have the force of law, doubtless originated in the positive prescriptions of some single State, which were at first of limited effect, but which, when generally accepted, became of universal obligation." "This is not giving to the statutes of any nation extraterritorial effect. It is not treating them as general maritime laws; but it is recognition of the historical fact that by common consent of mankind these rules have been acquiesced in as of general obligation. Of that fact, we think, we may take judicial notice. Foreign municipal laws must indeed be proved as facts, but it is not so with the law of nations." *The Scotia*, 14 Wall. 170, 187, 188.

The position taken by the United States during the recent war with Spain was quite in accord with the rule of international law, now generally recognized by civilized nations, in regard to coast fishing vessels.

On April 21, 1898, the Secretary of the Navy gave instructions to Admiral Sampson, commanding the North Atlantic Squadron, to "immediately institute a blockade of the north coast of Cuba, extending from Cardenas on the east to Bahia Honda on the west." Bureau of Navigation Report of 1898, appx. 175. The blockade was immediately instituted accordingly. On April 22, the President issued a proclamation, declaring that the United States had instituted and would maintain that blockade, "in pursuance of the laws of the United States, and the law of nations applicable to such cases." 30 Stat. 1769. And by the act of Congress of April 25, 1898, c. 189, it was declared that the war between the United States and Spain existed on that day, and had existed since and including April 21. 30 Stat. 364.

On April 26, 1898, the President issued another proclamation, which, after reciting the existence of the war, as declared by Congress, contained this further recital: "It being desirable that such war should be conducted upon principles in harmony with the present views of nations and sanctioned by their recent practice." This recital was followed by specific declarations of certain rules for the conduct of the war by sea, making no mention of fishing vessels. 30 Stat. 1770. But the proclamation clearly manifests the general policy of the Government to conduct the war in accordance with the principles of international law sanctioned by the recent practice of nations.

On April 28, 1898, (after the capture of the two fishing vessels now in question,) Admiral Sampson telegraphed to the Secretary of the Navy as follows: "I find that a large number of fishing schooners are attempting to get into Havana from their fishing grounds near the Florida reefs and coasts. They are generally manned by excellent seamen, belonging to the maritime inscription of Spain, who have already served in the Spanish navy, and who are liable to further service. As these trained men are naval reserves, have a semi-military character, and would be most valuable to the Spaniards as artillerymen, either afloat or ashore, I recommend that they should be detained prisoners of war, and that I should be authorized to deliver them to the commanding officer of the army at Key West." To that communication the Secretary of the Navy, on April 30, 1898, guardedly answered: "Spanish fishing vessels attempting to violate blockade are subject, with crew, to capture, and any such vessel or crew considered likely to aid enemy may be detained." Bureau of Navigation Report of 1898, appx. 178. The Admiral's despatch assumed that he was not authorized, without express order, to arrest coast fishermen peaceably pursuing their calling; and the necessary implication and evident intent of the response of the Navy Department were that Spanish coast fishing vessels and their crews should not be interfered with, so long as they neither attempted to violate the blockade, nor were considered likely to aid the enemy. . . .

Upon the facts proved in either case, it is the duty of this court, sitting as the highest prize court of the United States, and administering the law of nations, to declare and adjudge that the capture was unlawful, and without probable cause; and it is therefore, in each case, *Ordered, that the decree of the District Court be reversed*, and the proceeds of the sale of the vessel, together with the proceeds of any sale of her cargo, be restored to the claimant, with damages and costs.

NOTES

1. *The Obligations of International Law*. Early cases addressing the incorporation of customary international law into U.S. law—such as Chief Justice Jay's charge to the jury in the *Trial of Gideon Henfield* or Justice

Wilson's language in *Ware v. Hylton*—emphasize the indispensability of accepting international law as a component of national sovereignty. At the same time, Jay's jury charge noted incorporation by the Constitution and the president, and Wilson noted the lack of any derogation by Congress. What do these pronouncements suggest to you about the commitment of the United States to customary international law?

2. *Three Faces of Customary International Law in U.S. Law*. The cases above suggest three important ways that customary international law can affect U.S. law. First, as demonstrated in cases such as *The Nereide* and *The Paquete Habana*, norms contained in customary international law can directly serve as a part of the law of the United States. Thus, even without enactment of a statute, customary international law can be the basis for a governing rule in a particular case. Second, as demonstrated in the *Arjona* case, Congress may adopt a statute that explicitly or implicitly seeks to implement a norm of customary international law. Third, as demonstrated in *The Schooner Charming Betsy*, customary international law may give rise to an interpretive presumption, which U.S. courts will apply when construing U.S. statutory or executive exercises of authority.

3. *Direct Incorporation of Customary International Law*. Cases like *The Paquete Habana* are sometimes read to suggest a seamless transition from the international plane to the domestic plane, such that neither incorporation nor translation of customary international law is required. Do the excerpted cases genuinely support this? For one thing, international law may permit, or U.S. law may require, adaptation to domestic circumstances. Does *The Lottawanna* help explain when such variation is permissible? Does *The Nereide* express a view as to whether reciprocity is essential?

A second potential qualification is that "direct" incorporation appears in fact to require assistance from courts, and as previously noted, their role has changed over time. For 150 years, U.S. courts applied the law of nations as a matter of general common law. Students of U.S. civil procedure will recall that during the period marked by *Swift v. Tyson*, 41 U.S. (16 Pet.) 1 (1842), federal judges in diversity cases were free to develop a body of common law distinct from and unbound by the common law of the states in which they sat. Judges by and large believed that legal principles could be discerned and applied even absent explicit legislation. Thus, during this time, customary international law was applied as common law by both federal and state courts independently of one another.

Then, in *Erie R. Co. v. Tompkins*, the Supreme Court declared that thenceforth, "[e]xcept in matters governed by the Federal Constitution or by acts of Congress"—basically, in diversity cases—"the law to be applied in any case is the law of the state." 304 U.S. 64, 78 (1938). That decision left open the question of how the law of nations should be properly applied. Would the law of nations now be treated as state law or its equivalent? Would it be applied only in limited circumstances where a constitutional or statutory grant of authority was conferred? Or did questions on the law of nations "arise under" the Constitution, as per Article III, such that they were appropriately decided by the federal courts?

In the immediate aftermath of *Erie*, Professor Philip Jessup, later judge of the International Court of Justice, urged that *Erie* not be read as granting states the exclusive power to apply the law of nations. Professor Jessup argued that the United States—and not the fifty states—was the relevant entity under international law, and that therefore federal law was inherently a better repository for law of nations. He wrote:

> [A]ny attempt to extend the doctrine of [*Erie*] to international law should be repudiated by the Supreme Court. . . . Any question of applying international law in our courts involves the foreign relations of the United States and can thus be brought within a federal power. . . . The several states of the Union are entities unknown to international law. It would be as unsound as it would be unwise to make our state courts our ultimate authority for pronouncing the rules of international law.

Philip C. Jessup, *The Doctrine of Erie Railroad v. Tompkins Applied to International Law*, 33 AM. J. INT'L L 740, 743 (1939). Professor Jessup's view proved influential in subsequent jurisprudence. In *Banco Nacional de Cuba v. Sabbatino*, 376 U.S. 398 (1964) (excerpted Chapter 7, Sec. 8), Justice Harlan, writing for the Court and citing Professor Jessup, upheld the proposition that international law was rightly within the province of federal law.

Nonetheless, the academic debate rekindled in the 1990s, establishing a "revisionist" position—opposed to what it described as the "modern position" that had been favored by Jessup, the *Restatement (Third)*, and others. *See, e.g.*, Louis Henkin, *International Law as Law in the United States*, 82 MICH. L. REV. 1555 (1984). Revisionists argued that customary international law should not provide a federal rule of decision unless incorporated into U.S. law by the political branches. *See* Curtis A. Bradley and & Jack L. Goldsmith, *Customary International Law as Federal Common Law: A Critique of the Modern Position*, 110 HARV. L. REV. 815 (1997); Curtis A. Bradley, Jack L. Goldsmith & David H. Moore, Sosa*, Customary International Law, and the Continuing Relevance of Erie,* 120 HARV. L. REV. 869 (2007). Those associated with the "modern position" responded, see, e.g., Gerald L. Neuman, *Sense and Nonsense About Customary International Law: A Response to Professors Bradley and Goldsmith*, 66 FORDHAM L. REV. 371 (1997); Harold Hongju Koh, *Is International Law Really State Law?*, 111 HARV. L. REV. 1824 (1998); and yet other variants were advanced. *See, e.g.*, Julian Ku & John Yoo, *Beyond Formalism in Foreign Affairs: A Functional Approach to the Alien Tort Statute*, 2004 SUP. CT. REV. 153 (advocating a "state-led" system of customary international law development, subject to federal preemption by the executive). *See generally* Anthony J. Bellia, Jr. & Bradford R. Clark, *The Law of Nations and the United States Constitution* (2017).

Much of this debate was abstract, with the notable exception of its application in human rights litigation concerning the Alien Tort Statute—in which the Supreme Court affirmed, in 2004, that federal courts retain jurisdiction for certain claims under the law of nations and can decide such cases as an element of federal common law. *Sosa v. Alvarez-Machain*, 542 U.S. 692 (2004). This decision, and critical reactions to it, are discussed further in Sec. 6 below. Several other opinions have ventured views on the broader question. *See, e.g.*, *Al-Bihani v. Obama*, 619 F.3d 1, 16–19 (D.C. Cir. 2010) (Kavanaugh, J., concurring in the denial of rehearing en banc) (siding with objections to the "modern position"). *But cf. Al-Bihani*, 619 F.3d at 53–56 (statement of Williams, J., respecting the denial of rehearing en banc) (distinguishing use of customary international law as a tool for statutory construction); *Al-Bihani,* 619 F.3d at 1 (Sentelle, C.J., and Ginsburg, Henderson, Rogers, Tatel, Garland, and Griffith, JJ., concurring in the denial of rehearing en banc) (indicating that discussions of international law principles in the panel opinion by Judge Kavanaugh and others were dicta).

4. *Statutory Incorporation of Customary International Law.* A customary international law norm may also be incorporated into U.S. law by means of a statute, as opposed to simply being recognized by judges as a part of U.S. law. Critics of direct incorporation frequently distinguish circumstances in which there is political branch authorization for incorporating customary international law, and statutory incorporation is the clearest (and most clearly legitimate) means of providing such authorization. Yet statutory incorporation is not invariably clear. Congress may allude to customary international law without providing clear guidance as to the metes and bounds of that inquiry; as considered in the remainder of this Chapter, this has bedeviled domestic application of the international law of war, piracy, and human rights (perhaps particularly in relation to the Alien Tort Statute). In other instances, U.S. statutes may depend on terms or concepts that have resonance in international law, at least arguably inviting courts to rely on those terms or concepts in applying the statutes. *See, e.g.*, *Republic of Argentina v. Weltover, Inc.*, 504 U.S. 607, 612 (1992) (reckoning that the term "commercial" in the Foreign Sovereign Immunities Act should be construed in light of Congress's incorporation of the theory of restrictive immunity as it then prevailed). Does it suffice when, as in the *Arjona* case, Congress is only implicitly adverting to the status of a wrong under international law? Do you think that the act of forgery in *Arjona* would have been treated as illegal under federal common law (thereby permitting seizure of the forgers' plates by treasury officials, for example) in the *absence* of a law by Congress specifically making such forgery illegal?

The *Arjona* case is in some respects at the extreme, insofar as the Supreme Court indicated that the law of nations (not directly invoked by Congress) might provide the constitutional basis for federal authority. (The Court also cited the Foreign Commerce Clause, U.S. Const. art. I, § 8, cl. 3, as part of the panoply of international authorities vested in the federal government. *See* 120 U.S. at 483. Today, that authority—which, while it has not been carefully detailed, is likely broader than its domestic Commerce Clause authority—would likely suffice. *See, e.g.*, *United States v. Baston*, 818 F.3d 651, 667–68

(11th Cir. 2016).) The Offenses Clause, and customary international law, were more directly employed as the potential basis for establishing military commissions. *See Hamdan v. Rumsfeld*, 548 U.S. 557, 592 & n.22 (2006) (identifying "substantially identical" successor provision to former Article 15 of the Articles of War, held in *Ex parte Quirin*, 317 U.S. 1, 28, 30 (1942), to be based in the define-and-punish authority); *id.* at 601–02 (plurality op.) (relating to alleged war crime of conspiracy); *id.* at 631–35 (plurality op.) (applying, as customary international law, Article 75 of Protocol I to the 1949 Geneva Conventions). How far does the Offenses Clause go? It appears to permit Congress to criminally and civilly regulate individuals for violations of the law of nations, and it has been argued that it extends a regulatory authority over foreign and domestic states as well. J. Andrew Kent, *Congress' Under-Appreciated Power to Define and Punish Offenses Against the Law of Nations*, 85 TEX. L. REV. 843 (2007). Others argue that it extends to treaty violations; note how this relates to the broader original understanding of the "law of nations" discussed at the beginning of this Chapter. Sarah H. Cleveland & William S. Dodge, *Defining and Punishing Offenses Under Treaties*, 124 YALE L.J. 2202 (2014–2015).

5. *Interpretive Presumption Based on Customary International Law.* The idea "that an act of congress ought never to be construed to violate the law of nations, if any other possible construction remains," as enunciated by Chief Justice Marshall in *Charming Betsy*, has remained a guiding principle in U.S jurisprudence. *See, e.g., F. Hoffman-La Roche Ltd. v. Empagran*, 542 U.S. 155, 164–65 (2004). Indeed, you will encounter aspects of this principle in this Chapter's Sec. 3 (concerning limits on incorporation) and Sec. 5 (concerning jurisdiction), as well as in relation to treaties (Chapter 3, Sec. 4). It may be helpful to contemplate its rationale from the outset: If a law can be interpreted either in congruity, or in conflict, with international law, why precisely should courts strive for congruity? Perhaps Congress, as a predictive matter, is unlikely to have intended to conflict with international law; perhaps, regardless of congressional intent, courts are well advised to avoid unnecessary conflicts with other nations as a matter of comity; or perhaps courts should avoid creating unnecessary conflicts between Congress and the president, since it is the latter's responsibility to direct U.S. foreign relations and to respond to claims that the United States has violated customary international law. *See* Curtis A. Bradley, *The* Charming Betsy *Canon and Separation of Powers: Rethinking the Interpretive Role of International Law*, 86 GEO. L.J. 479 (1998). When Congress itself expresses the interpretive presumption, of course, the line between statutory incorporation and the *Charming Betsy* canon is blurred. *See, e.g.*, 33 U.S.C. § 1902(i) (2012) (describing ships subject to preventive measures, subject to savings clause providing that "[n]othing in this section shall be construed to restrict in a manner inconsistent with international law navigational rights and freedoms as defined by United States law, treaty, convention, or customary international law").

6. *Evidence of Customary International Law (and Presidential Incorporation).* Customary international law is widely considered to be more

difficult to ascertain than some of other forms of law, and the more controversial the means for establishing that law, the more questions may be raised about its status in U.S. law. Naturally, questions of method are considered more extensively and authoritatively on the international plane. *See, e.g.*, Int'l Law Ass'n, Comm. on the Formation of Customary (Gen.) Int'l Law, Statement of Principles Applicable to the Formation of General Customary International Law 27 (2000); Draft Conclusions on the Identification of Customary International Law, with Commentary, Report of the International Law Commission on the Work of Its Sixty-Eighth Session, UN GAOR, 71st Sess., Supp. No. 10, at 80-117, UN Doc. A/71/10 (Sept. 19, 2016). Reviewing the above U.S. cases (particularly the excerpts from *The Paquete Habana*, which describe at least part of the Court's reasoning), what evidence seemed to you most probative? Note, and evaluate, references in the cases to U.S. positions concerning the establishment and meaning of international law, even though—as a matter of international law—State consent is not a precondition for customary international law obligations. Does this raise concerns? Does it matter whether the position is established primarily by the executive branch?

Speaking of State consent and the political branches, note that a longstanding issue in international law is the degree to which multilateral treaties count as evidence of customary international, something which is most likely to be germane when a State is not itself a party to the treaty in question. Is this also problematic as a matter of U.S. foreign relations law? Suppose the Senate has not provided its advice and consent to a widely ratified treaty, and the president declares that a portion of the treaty reflects customary international law binding upon the United States. Would the president's action subvert the constitutional process for ratification of treaty obligations, and should that bear on the weight given to that law in U.S. courts? As discussed in Chapter 3, Sec. 8, the United States has not ratified the U.N. Convention on the Law of the Sea, Dec. 10, 1982, 1833 U.N.T.S. 3, due to its concerns about particular provisions. Nonetheless, the executive branch has asserted that other provisions restate or clarify customary law and provide a basis for U.S. law, even where inconsistent with prior treaty obligations. Is that problematic?

7. *Relevance for Inter-State Conflicts*. Customary international law that regulates *inter-country* matters may be invoked when considering *inter-state* matters in the United States. For example, the customary international law concerning *thalwegs* has been invoked to resolve river boundaries between U.S. states. *See, e.g., Louisiana v. Mississippi*, 466 U.S. 96, 101 (1984); *New Jersey v. Delaware,* 291 U.S. 361, 379 (1934); *Iowa v. Illinois,* 147 U.S. 1, 7–11 (1893). Is a different approach appropriate?

3. LIMITATIONS ON INCORPORATION

As Sec. 2 indicated, customary international law is often addressed as having an obligatory character not only internationally, but also domestically: *Ware v. Hylton* said that the United States, like other nations, was "bound to receive the law of nations," and over a century later *The Paquete Habana* famously declared that "international law is part of our law." How does it relate, though, to other parts of U.S. law? As previously discussed, the primacy of the U.S. Constitution does not seem open to question, though the relationship between customary international law and the Constitution is explored further in Sec. 4. What of other forms of law, and legal actors?

The Paquete Habana tendered a possible answer. In another oft-quoted passage, Justice Gray suggested that a "controlling executive or legislative act or judicial decision" might override the "customs and usages of civilized nations." Technically that was merely dictum, as no party in the case at bar claimed that such a controlling act existed. Yet the concept of some "controlling" authority in U.S. law defeating the application of customary international law has persisted, and it has given rise to sharp debates as to whether, and when, U.S. actors may disobey customary international law.

With regard to Congress, the notion of statutory incorporation implies, at a minimum, that Congress might sometimes choose *not* to incorporate customary international law. Cases like *The Nereide* and *The Lottawanna* also hinted at the role the legislature might have in refining and adapting customary international law to the needs of the United States. Finally, the interpretive principle of *The Charming Betsy* suggested that where an act of Congress *cannot* be construed so as to avoid violating international law, something would have to give. Should Congress be able to adopt a statute that places the United States in violation of customary international law?

What about the president? Should he or she be able to issue an executive order or decision, or adopt a policy, that places the United States in violation of customary international law? Bear in mind not only that "international law is a part of our law," but also that the president is charged under Article 2, § 3 of the U.S. Constitution with taking care that the laws be "faithfully executed."

What about the courts? Can U.S. courts choose to apply or not to apply customary international law as they wish? Justice Blackmun's remarks, excerpted below, suggest that the Supreme Court at least exercises considerable discretion (not always in the manner he would have preferred). If customary international law is like federal common law, then should federal courts be allowed to construe it in whatever manner they see appropriate? Or is customary international law different because it is not formed by U.S. federal courts, but rather through the practice of countries worldwide, such that federal courts do not have the same discretion as they do for "normal" federal common law? Regardless of whether federal courts have discretion, are state courts absolutely bound to apply customary international law when it arises in cases before them, just as they would any federal common law?

The excerpts below from the *Restatement (Third)*, which continues to be the most authoritative statement on the place of customary international law in U.S. law, set out some of the basics. Excerpts from the Eleventh Circuit's decision in *Garcia-Mir v. Meese* then give an example of congressional, executive, and judicial limits on incorporation, though (as the accompanying commentary suggest) its positions were controversial. Finally, Justice Blackmun reflects further on the role of the judiciary.

RESTATEMENT OF THE LAW (THIRD), THE FOREIGN RELATIONS LAW OF THE UNITED STATES §§ 111, 115*

(1987).

§ 111. *International Law and Agreements as Law of the United States*

Comment c. International law and agreements as law of the United States. The proposition that international law and agreements are law in the United States is addressed largely to the courts. In appropriate cases they apply international law or agreements without the need of enactment by Congress or proclamation by the President. . . . Much customary law and many international agreements, however, do not have the quality of law for the courts in that they do not regulate activities, relations, or interests in the United States. . . .

That international law and agreements of the United States are law of the United States means also that the President has the obligation and the necessary authority to take care that they be faithfully executed. United States Constitution, Article II, Section 2. But under the President's constitutional authority, as "sole organ of the nation in its external relations" or as Commander in Chief . . . , the President has the power to take various measures including some that might constitute violations of international law by the United States. . . .

§ 115. *Inconsistency Between International Law or Agreement and Domestic Law: Law of the United States*

(1)(a) An act of Congress supersedes an earlier rule of international law or a provision of an international agreement as law of the United States if the purpose of the act to supersede the earlier rule or provision is clear or if the act and the earlier rule or provision cannot be fairly reconciled.

(b) That a rule of international law or a provision of an international agreement is superseded as domestic law does not relieve the United States of its international obligation or of the consequences of a violation of that obligation.

(2) A provision of a treaty of the United States that becomes effective as law of the United States supersedes as domestic law any inconsistent preexisting provision of a law or treaty of the United States.

(3) A rule of international law or a provision of an international agreement of the United States will not be given effect as law in the United States if it is inconsistent with the United States Constitution.

GARCIA-MIR V. MEESE

788 F.2d 1446 (11th Cir. 1986).

JOHNSON, CIRCUIT JUDGE:

These cases pose the question whether unadmitted aliens properly may claim the protection of the Due Process Clause of the United States Constitution to secure parole revocation hearings. We earlier determined that, for unadmitted aliens, the right to such hearings is not resident in the core values of the Due Process Clause *per se*. . . . It is our opinion that, assuming that undocumented aliens may have actionable nonconstitutionally-based liberty interests, these particular aliens have not stated a viable claim for relief under the Due Process Clause. We also determine that customary international law [prohibiting prolonged arbitrary detention] does not afford these aliens a remedy in American courts.

I.

. . . The appellees-cross appellants ["appellees" or "aliens" or "Mariels"] are a certified class of Mariel Cuban refugees who were accorded a special immigration parole status by the Refugee Education Assistance Act of 1980, Pub.L. No. 96–422, § 501(e), 94 Stat. 1799 (1980), *reprinted at* 8 U.S.C.A. § 1522 note (1985).[2] The district court has broken the class into

---

[2] The Act defines a "Cuban and Haitian entrant" as:

(1) any individual granted parole status as a Cuban/Haitian Entrant (Status Pending) or granted any other special status subsequently established under the immigration laws for nationals of Cuba or Haiti, regardless of the status of the individual at the time assistance or services are provided; and

(2) any other national of Cuba or Haiti

(A) who

(i) was paroled into the United States and has not acquired any other status under the Immigration and Nationality Act;

(ii) is the subject of exclusion or deportation proceedings under the Immigration and Nationality Act; or

(iii) has an application pending with the Immigration and Naturalization Service; and

(B) with respect to whom a final, nonappealable, and legally enforceable order of deportation or exclusion has not been entered.

two sub-classes. The "First Group" includes those who are guilty of crimes committed in Cuba before the boat lift or who are mentally incompetent. They have never been paroled into this country. The "Second Group" consists of all other Mariels—those who, because there was no evidence of criminal or mental defect, were paroled under the provisions of the general alien parole statute, 8 U.S.C.A. § 1182(d)(5) (1985), but whose parole was subsequently revoked. All are currently detained in the Atlanta Penitentiary. . . .

II.

. . . The public law of nations was long ago incorporated into the common law of the United States. . . . To the extent possible, courts must construe American law so as to avoid violating principles of public international law. . . . But public international law is controlling only "where there is no treaty and no controlling executive or legislative act or judicial decision. . . ." [*The Paquete Habana*, 175 U.S. 677, 700 (1900)]. Appellees argue that, because general principles of international law forbid prolonged arbitrary detention, we should hold that their current detention is unlawful.

We have previously determined that the general deportation statute, 8 U.S.C.A. § 1227(a) (1985), does not *restrict* the power of the Attorney General to detain aliens indefinitely. *Fernandez-Roque II*, 734 F.2d at 580 n. 6. But this does not resolve the question whether there has been an *affirmative legislative grant* of authority to detain. As to the First Group there is sufficiently express evidence of congressional intent as to interdict the application of international law: Pub. L. No. 96–533, Title VII, § 716, 94 Stat. 3162 (1980), *reprinted at* 8 U.S.C.A. § 1522 note.[9]

The trial court found, correctly, that there has been no affirmative legislative grant to the Justice Department to detain the Second Group without hearings because 8 U.S.C.A. § 1227(c) does not expressly authorize indefinite detention. Thus we must look for a controlling executive act. The trial court found that there was such a controlling act in the Attorney General's termination of the status review plan and in his decision to

---

[9] That enactment provides:

> The Congress finds that the United States Government has already incarcerated recently arrived Cubans who are admitted criminals, are security threats, or have incited civil disturbances in Federal processing facilities. The Congress urges the Executive branch, consistent with United States law, to seek the deportation of such individuals.

Admittedly, the legislation encourages the Executive Branch to act in accordance with United States law. That would implicitly incorporate international law prohibiting detention without a hearing, assuming for argument's sake that the international norm appellees invoke actually applies to circumstances of this sort. But the language suggests that Congress clearly anticipated that the First Group was being and would continue to be held until they could be deported. Congress made no attempt to undo what the Justice Department has already done. In fact they encouraged it to deport these persons. We hold that the First Group is subject to a controlling legislative enactment and hence unprotected by international law.

incarcerate indefinitely pending efforts to deport. The appellees and the *amicus* challenge this by arguing that a controlling executive act can only come from an act by or expressly sanctioned by the President himself, not one of his subordinates. They rely for that proposition upon *The Paquete Habana* and upon the *Restatement of the Law of Foreign Relations Law of the United States (Revised)* § 131 comment c (Tent. Draft No. 1, 1980) [hereinafter cited as "*Restatement 1*"].

As to *The Paquete Habana*. . . . The Court held that the ships were seized in violation of international law because they were used solely for fishing. It was the *admiral* who acted in excess of the clearly delimited authority granted by the Secretary, who instructed him to act only consistent with international law. Thus *The Paquete Habana* does not support the proposition that the acts of cabinet officers cannot constitute controlling executive acts. At best it suggests that lower level officials cannot by their acts render international law inapplicable. That is not an issue in this case, where the challenge is to the acts of the Attorney General.

[The *Restatement 1*] notes that the President, "acting within his constitutional authority, may have the power under the Constitution to act in ways that constitute violations of international law by the United States." The Constitution provides for the creation of executive departments, *U.S. Const.* art. 2, § 2, and the power of the President to delegate his authority to those departments to act on his behalf is unquestioned. Likewise, in [Restatement of the Law of Foreign Relations Law of the United States (Revised) (Tent. Draft No. 6, 1985)], § 135 Reporter's Note 3, the power of the President to disregard international law in service of domestic needs is reaffirmed. Thus we hold that the executive acts here evident constitute a sufficient basis for affirming the trial court's finding that international law does not control.

Even if we were to accept, *arguendo*, the appellees' interpretation of "controlling executive act," *The Paquete Habana* also provides that the reach of international law will be interdicted by a controlling judicial decision. In *Jean v. Nelson*, we interpreted the Supreme Court's decision in *Mezei* to hold that even an indefinitely incarcerated alien "could not challenge his continued detention without a hearing." 727 F.2d at 974–75. This reflects the obligation of the courts to avoid any ruling that would "inhibit the flexibility of the political branches of government to respond to changing world conditions. . . ." *Mathews v. Diaz*, 426 U.S. 67, 81 (1976). We find this decision sufficient to meet the test of *The Paquete Habana*. . . .

AGORA: MAY THE PRESIDENT VIOLATE CUSTOMARY INTERNATIONAL LAW?*

80 AM. J. INT'L L. 913 (1986).

[Following *Garcia-Mir v. Meese*, the *American Journal of International Law* published a symposium on the relationship between customary international law and presidential authority. Excerpts follow.]

- Jonathan I. Charney, *The Power of the Executive Branch of the United States Government to Violate Customary International Law*

. . . The Supreme Court may now face the difficult question of determining the meaning of "controlling executive . . . act" as used in *The Paquete Habana*. The answer to that question will determine the extent to which the United States is bound under domestic law to abide by rules of customary international law. . . .

. . . In the international system, the United States must have the power to engage in the lawmaking process. This participation may involve actions that put the United States in violation of existing customary international law. If the executive branch is restrained by the rule that customary international law is domestic law of the United States and that it may not be violated, U.S. participation in the international system will be handicapped. The alternative solution that the executive branch has no domestic legal obligation to conform to customary international law is equally unpalatable and is contrary to the holding in *The Paquete Habana*.

Some writers maintain that the Executive is obligated under domestic law to conform to customary law, but may be exempted by statute only. Thus, a proposed violation would require the approval of Congress. In the *Garcia-Mir* case, the Eleventh Circuit found such combined action of Congress and the Executive sufficient to establish a controlling action that was determinative for some, but not all, of the issues before it.

. . . But in the present system, required congressional approval would place unacceptable obstacles in the way of U.S. participation in the international legal system. The evolution of the community law system would not be amenable to case-by-case authorization by Congress. Just as the international system requires that the President be able to enter into executive agreements and, apparently, to terminate treaties unilaterally, so must the President have the unilateral power to enter into the international lawmaking process. The Supreme Court appeared to have assumed that this power resides in the President when, in *The Paquete Habana,* it spoke of a "controlling executive or legislative act." Compared to making and terminating international agreements, this process is more subtle. Thus, it requires greater executive flexibility.

The plaintiffs and amicus in the *Garcia-Mir* case have argued that the Executive is bound under domestic law by customary international law unless the President officially declares that the United States no longer will be bound by it. This approach would permit the Executive to interact in the international system, but at a price. The President must squarely address the legal obligations of the United States and declare that they will be abrogated. Such direct abrogation would be extremely difficult. In fact, it would never be done. . . .

[T]here are several considerations that ought to be taken into account in a search for the appropriate solution to this debate over the power to take a "controlling . . . act." First, customary international law is law of the United States and is binding as such on all, including members of the executive branch. Second, the United States must have the power to engage effectively in the customary lawmaking process; this process requires that, from time to time, the United States break that law. Third, restrictions on those branches of the Government charged with conducting U.S. foreign relations that inhibit this function are not tolerable; members of the executive branch cannot be subject to enforcement as violators of domestic law if they are participating in the legitimate process of developing customary international law. Fourth, the authority of the executive branch to participate in legitimate customary lawmaking activities should not be so broad that, in fact, it is not bound by customary law in the domestic legal system.

Certainly, if congressional approval were given by statute for an action, that approval would eliminate any domestic law questions so long as there was no violation of the U.S. Constitution. Furthermore, violations of customary law by the President, in the face of a contrary statute, would be unacceptable. Even though an official declaration by the President might be appropriate, more flexibility in the Executive is necessary. That flexibility, however, should not extend either to all members of the executive branch or to all actions by high officials. . . .

The President's special role in the United States Government, including the conduct of the nation's foreign relations, suggests that the President, acting alone, may have the authority under domestic law to place the United States in violation of customary international law. The President sits at the intersection of the domestic and international responsibilities of the United States. Other officers, such as the Attorney General, the Secretary of State and the Secretary of the Navy, do not have the same combination of domestic and international responsibilities that would permit them to authorize U.S. violations of international and domestic law in the circumstances under consideration here. . . .

- Michael J. Glennon, *Can the President Do No Wrong?*

. . . Suppose, for example, that under the facts of *The Paquete Habana,* the President had ordered the seizure of coastal fishing vessels, and suppose that that act lay within his plenary power as commander-in-chief; would his act not be legal?

. . . As the question is posed, it answers itself: the exercise of a plenary power *by definition* is not susceptible of abridgment. . . .

We know, however, from the constitutional text that the President has no plenary power to act in violation of international law. Article I, section 8, clause 10 explicitly confers upon Congress the power to define and punish offenses against the law of nations. Congress in clear terms is directly empowered to prohibit violations of international law. It simply cannot be, therefore, that the Constitution gives the President plenary power to carry out an act that violates international law. An act of Congress that prohibits him from doing so will prevail. . . .

Recognition that no plenary power inheres in the Executive to breach customary international law also removes any rationale for giving subordinates immunity. . . . [T]he Chief Executive cannot give what he does not have: *no one* in the executive branch has the authority to breach customary international law in the absence of congressional authorization. . . .

. . . Changes in customary international law ordinarily involve many acts by many states, carried out over an extended period of time. The result may be a gradual alteration of existing norms, or it may be a series of acts that fall short of a new custom (or lack *opinio juris*) and thus represent violations. But the point is that the process normally is gradual. Participation in that process thus admits of little need for sole executive action. . . .

. . . If it is imperative that the United States violate customary international law, then the President should have no difficulty in persuading Congress that it is in our national interest to authorize that violation. If he cannot persuade Congress, then the United States should continue to honor international law. . . .

This does not mean that the President can *never* act alone. The Executive, for example, may indicate its dissent while a customary rule is being developed. That nascent rule, should it develop into a customary norm, would then have no application to acts of the United States, either internationally or domestically. This measure of discretion is permitted because, at the time the Executive objects, the rule is not yet part of customary international law, and a fortiori not yet part of federal common law, thus lacking wide acceptance and perhaps even clear definition. . . .

- Louis Henkin, *The President and International Law*

. . . The President's duty to take care that the laws be faithfully executed includes not only statutes of Congress and judge-made law, but also treaties and principles of customary law. As with any other law, however, the President need not take care that international law be faithfully executed if (1) it has ceased to be law, or (2) it is superseded by some other law and it is his duty to execute the superseding law.

1. . . . When a treaty or a principle of law terminates as a result of circumstances, or of an action by another state, it ceases to be an international obligation for the United States, and ceases to be law in the United States. . . .

In either case, I stress, the constitutional question is not whether the President has authority to violate international law; the question is whether he has constitutional authority to do the act that terminated the treaty or superseded the customary principle. . . .

2. The President need not, may not, execute a principle of international law or a provision in a treaty if it is superseded in United States law by another law that has higher or equal status. Thus, the President will not execute a treaty or customary principle that conflicts with the Constitution. The President will not execute a principle of international law if it is superseded by an intervening treaty provision or a new principle of international law. Under established doctrine, he may not execute a treaty provision if it is superseded by an intervening act of Congress and, as indicated, the same principle would probably apply to require the President to give effect to an act of Congress that is inconsistent with a preexisting principle of customary law.

A case can be made also that, in some cases, the President can supersede a principle of international law or a treaty by law made under his own authority, in those special circumstances when the President has constitutional authority to make law in the United States. For example, the courts have found that he has such "legislative authority" to determine sovereign immunity. . . .

. . . It is argued that, in his conduct of the foreign relations of the United States, the President may decide that it is in the interest of the United States to take some action without regard to international law, e.g., to overfly foreign territory without the state's consent, bring down a foreign airplane, violate a diplomat's immunity. Such acts, contrary to international law, do not ordinarily impinge on international law incorporated as domestic law in the United States. . . .

A presidential act that terminates the obligation of the United States and therefore its place in the law of the United States, or a presidential act that makes law in the United States and supersedes a principle of customary law as United States law, is a "controlling executive act" within the meaning of *The Paquete Habana.* Perhaps, an act within the President's constitutional authority as sole organ or as commander-in-chief is controlling and will not be enjoined even if it violates a treaty or principle of law. I know of no other kind of acts that would relieve the Executive of the duty to take care that international law be faithfully executed. . . .

Joseph Modeste Sweeney commented on the above *Agora* as follows:

[T]here are many scholars willing to write at length about *The Paquete Habana,* but few disposed to read the case from beginning to end. . . . [This] helps to perpetuate a totally unfounded, yet slavishly honored misinterpretation of the short, but notorious clause "*where there is no treaty, and no controlling executive or legislative act or judicial decision.*"

. . . [L]ook at the second paragraph of the dissenting opinion by Chief Justice Fuller, in which two of his brethren concurred. It is a succinct, and what we may reasonably presume to be an accurate, summary of the position of the majority. He wrote: "This court holds . . . [fishing vessels exempt from seizure] not because such exemption is to be found in *any treaty, legislation, proclamation or instruction, granting it*, but on the ground that the vessels were exempt by reason of an established rule of international law applicable to them. . . ."

The Chief Justice disagreed with the majority because he was unwilling to hold fishing vessels exempt from capture *unless the exemption could be found in some treaty, legislation, proclamation or instruction.* Justice Gray, writing for the majority, obviously could have held the vessels exempt from capture had an exemption been provided by a treaty or other public act. But there was no such treaty or other public act and it is to this fact that the notorious clause refers, albeit by implication rather than expressly. Properly understood, it means: where there is no treaty, and no executive or legislative act or judicial opinion, *exempting fishing vessels from capture. . . .*

It is the difference between the two views of international law that explains the meaning of the clause, and its presence in the sentence where it appears. As far as Chief Justice Fuller was concerned, fishing vessels were not exempted from capture by customary international law. Hence, such vessels were subject to capture unless there was a treaty, or controlling executive or legislative act or judicial precedent, exempting them. As far as Justice Gray was concerned, it was just the reverse. Where there was no such treaty, or controlling executive or legislative act or judicial decision, they were exempted from capture nevertheless, by a rule of customary international law. . . .

Letter to the Editor, 81 AM. J. INT'L L. 637 (1987) (reprinted with permission of the American Society of International Law; permission conveyed through Copyright Clearance Center, Inc.).

HARRY A. BLACKMUN, THE SUPREME COURT AND THE LAW OF NATIONS*

104 Yale L.J. 39 (1994).

I. FIRST PRINCIPLES

The Declaration of Independence opens with the following memorable passage:

> When in the Course of human Events, it becomes necessary for one People to dissolve the Political Bands which have connected them with another, and to assume among the Powers of the Earth, the separate and equal Station to which the Laws of Nature and of Nature's God entitle them, *a decent Respect to the Opinions of Mankind* requires that they should declare the causes which impel them to the Separation.

As Professor Louis Henkin has noted, the early architects of our Nation understood that the customs of nations—the global opinions of mankind—would be binding upon the newly forged union. John Jay, the first Chief Justice of the United States, observed in *Chisolm v. Georgia* that the United States "had, by taking a place among the nations of the earth, become amenable to the laws of nations." Although the Constitution gives Congress the power to "define and punish . . . Offenses against the Law of Nations" and identifies treaties as part of "the supreme Law of the Land," the task of further defining the role of international law in the nation's legal fabric has fallen to the federal courts. . . .

The Paquete Habana left many questions unanswered, and courts since have backed away from some of that decision's more sweeping promises. . . .

II. CONSTRUING INTERNATIONAL INSTRUMENTS

A. *United States v. Alvarez-Machain*

[I]n the case of *United States v. Alvarez-Machain* [504 U.S. 655 (1992)], the Supreme Court was asked to consider whether the forced abduction of a Mexican national by United States agents violated a U.S.-Mexico extradition treaty. Over the vehement protest of the Mexican government, Dr. Humberto Alvarez-Machain was kidnaped in Mexico and brought to the United States to stand charges for the kidnaping, torture, and murder of a U.S. Drug Enforcement Administration agent. The district court

* Reprinted with permission of the Yale Law Journal; permission conveyed through Copyright Clearance Center, Inc.

dismissed the charges, concluding that the abduction violated the U.S.-Mexico extradition treaty.

The Supreme Court disagreed, holding, by a 6–3 vote, that the abduction had not violated the extradition treaty. . . . In the absence of an express prohibition, the majority reasoned, the kidnaping must be allowed. Ignoring the hornbook principle that a treaty shall be interpreted according to its ordinary meaning and in light of its object and purpose, the majority rejected the contention that its interpretation would eviscerate the treaty's purpose, even while acknowledging that the abduction "may be in violation of general international law principles." . . . .

In so doing, the Supreme Court also ignored customary international law. . . . [T]he dissenting opinion observed that with or without an extradition treaty, abducting a person from a foreign country without the foreign government's consent " 'is a gross violation of international law and gross disrespect for a norm high in the opinion of mankind. It is a blatant violation of the territorial integrity of another state; [and] it eviscerates the [global] extradition system.' " Even *with* the consent of the foreign sovereign, kidnaping a foreign national flagrantly violates peremptory human rights norms. . . .

We perhaps can take some comfort in the fact that although the Supreme Court is the highest court in the land, its rulings are not necessarily the final word on questions of international law. The *Alvarez-Machain* decision provoked domestic and international outcry and was deemed by the Inter-American Juridical Committee to be "contrary to the rules of international law." And the decision and its aftermath inspired a searching reexamination, in both Congress and the Justice Department, of the Government's kidnapping policy. In June 1993, the United States and Mexico formally agreed to negotiate a ban on the practice of transborder kidnapping. Thus, as is often the case, it appears to have taken a troublesome Supreme Court decision to launch the process of bringing domestic law in line with international practice.

B. *Sale v. Haitian Centers Council, Inc.*

. . . *Sale v. Haitian Centers Council, Inc.* [509 U.S. 155 (1993)] concerned a challenge by Haitian refugees to the U.S. policy of interdicting all Haitians who fled Haiti on the high seas and summarily returning them to Haiti, without any inquiry into their asylum claims or even their intended destination. Central to the Haitian plaintiffs' challenge was Article 33.1 of the United Nations Convention Relating to the Status of Refugees. That Article provides: "No Contracting State shall expel or return *('refouler')* a refugee in any manner whatsoever to the frontiers of territories where his life or freedom would be threatened." The principle of *nonrefoulement* expressed in Article 33.1—that no refugee may be returned to a country where he will suffer persecution—guarantees one of the most fundamental international rights of refugees. More than 120 nations, including the United States, have acceded to the binding obligations of Article 33.1. In 1980, Congress adopted § 243(h) of the Immigration and Nationality Act, which mirrors the language of Article 33.1, in order to bring U.S. law expressly into compliance with the Refugee Convention.

In construing § 243(h) and Article 33.1 in *Haitian Centers Council,* the Court once again failed to respect its first principles of international law. Turning first to the statute, the Court remarkably applied a presumption against extraterritoriality to § 243(h) without considering the fact that the statute was enacted pursuant to a multilateral treaty, and without acknowledging the primacy of the principle of *nonrefoulement* in customary international law. The Court thus ignored a maxim recognized since *Schooner Charming Betsy:* An Act of Congress—and particularly a statute enacted pursuant to a treaty—ought never to be construed to violate a coextensive treaty or otherwise to contradict customary international law. . . .

Do not the decisions in the *Alvarez-Machain* and *Haitian Centers Council* cases reflect a disturbing disregard on the part of the Supreme Court of its obligations when construing international law? Treaties are contracts among nations and thus must be interpreted with sensitivity toward the customs of the world community. In each of these cases, however, the Court ignored its first principles and construed the challenged treaty in a manner directly contrary to the opinions of mankind. . . .

IV. CONCLUSION

Professor Henkin poignantly has observed that "almost all nations observe almost all principles of international law and almost all of their obligations almost all of the time." Unfortunately, as the cases I have discussed illustrate, the Supreme Court's own recent record in the area is somewhat more qualified. At best, I would say that the present Supreme Court enforces *some* principles of international law and *some* of its obligations *some* of the time. . . .

NOTES

1. *Statutes and Customary International Law.* As noted in Sec. 2 of this Chapter, the Constitution's Supremacy Clause does not address the status of customary international law in the U.S. legal system, let alone in relation to the forms of law it does address. You will learn in Chapter 3, Sec. 6, that for treaties (a class of them, at least), the relationship with statutes is governed by the later-in-time doctrine. Does that same principle apply to the relationship between customary international law and statutes? Section 115 of the *Restatement (Third)* suggested as much, insofar as it said that "[a]n act of Congress supersedes an *earlier* rule of international law" (emphasis added), but that is probably a byproduct of the fact that the rule purports to speak to

international law generically. Whatever the original meaning of *The Paquete Habana*, case law seems to accept the superiority of constitutionally-enacted statutes irrespective of the enactment's timing relative to the (often uncertain) time at which a customary international law rule came to bind the United States. This is especially evident in cases dealing with jurisdictional issues, as explored in Sec. 5 of this Chapter. *See, e.g.*, *TMR Energy Ltd. v. State Prop. Fund of Ukr.*, 411 F.3d 296, 302 (D.C. Cir. 2005) ("Never does customary international law prevail over a contrary federal statute.").

2. *The President and Customary International Law*. The president may be confronted with a norm of customary international law in many different areas; later, for example, we will explore constraints imposed by human rights law and the laws of war. In some instances, customary international law is just part of the overall context. For example, customary international law may appear to temper the exercise of presidential authority under a statute. On other occasions, customary international law is entangled with treaty-related obligations. (For the United States, this confusion is probably inevitable. The rule of *pacta sunt servanda* (agreements must be kept) is part of the Vienna Convention on the Law of Treaties, May 23, 1969, 1155 U.N.T.S. 331; while the United States has not yet joined that convention, it does regard *pacta sunt servanda* as a rule of customary international law, and it is indeed one of the most fundamental. This means that U.S. obligations to perform treaty obligations likely arise under both treaty law and customary international law.)

To the extent an obligation arises only under customary international law, is the president authorized, or even required, to see that these obligations are given effect? Does this entail the capacity to ask state and local governments, and their courts, to comply? If she or he wishes not to comply with such obligations, must the United States first take the position that its international obligation has ceased? Assuming that hurdle is crossed, must the decision be one taken by the president, or may it be taken by a lower-ranked official acting with her or his delegated authority?

3. *The Courts and Customary International Law*. As the above excerpt from Justice Blackmun suggests, U.S. courts have a somewhat inconsistent track record when it comes to embracing customary international law. The materials in Sec. 2 highlighted pronouncements that international law, including customary international law, is a part of U.S. law. Sometimes, though, these pronouncements are not necessary to the decision at hand—even the landmark decision in *The Paquete Habana* might have been decided on the basis of the applicable presidential proclamation, without direct recourse to the law of nations—which both illustrates the enthusiasm of the judicial pronouncements and their uncertain value as precedent. On other occasions, courts have avoided pronouncing on customary international law, or even gone out of their way to express skepticism about it. Why do you think customary international law is such a vexed subject for U.S. judges? Should it be a last resort, as is suggested (on one reading) by *The Paquete Habana*? What do you make of the suggestion in *Garcia-Mir*, at least, that customary international

law may be ignored if there is contrary judicial precedent, even if it is lower-court precedent that has limited binding effect in the U.S. legal system, and none whatsoever in international terms?

4. USE OF INTERNATIONAL CUSTOM FOR CONSTITUTIONAL INTERPRETATION

As we have just examined, U.S. courts will (at least sometimes) turn to customary international law in interpreting statutes. To what extent should Congress, the president, or U.S. courts use customary international law when interpreting the U.S. Constitution? If there is an open-textured term in the Constitution, one that appears to invite reasoning based on broad notions of justice, equity, or humanity, is it appropriate to look to the norms that regulate relations among countries? Or is it wholly inappropriate to use the views of other countries to inform our understanding of an instrument drafted by Americans to govern Americans—given that the Constitution is not only hierarchically superior to customary international law, but also to decisions by the political branches that U.S. courts have held may themselves trump international law?

HARRY A. BLACKMUN, THE SUPREME COURT AND THE LAW OF NATIONS*

104 Yale L.J. 39 (1994).

III. RESPECT FOR THE LAW OF NATIONS IN CONSTITUTIONAL LAW

Although questions of international law typically arise before the Court in cases involving the construction of international conventions, the law of nations is implicated in Supreme Court jurisprudence in other situations as well. International law can and should inform the interpretation of various clauses of the Constitution, notably the Due Process Clause and the Eighth Amendment prohibition against cruel and unusual punishments. I thus turn to a second area where the Court has failed to inform its decisions with a "decent respect to the opinions of mankind": the execution of juvenile offenders.

For nearly half a century, the Supreme Court has acknowledged that the Eighth Amendment's Cruel and Unusual Punishments Clause "must draw its meaning from evolving standards of decency that mark the progress of a maturing society."[43] The drafters of the Amendment were concerned, at root, with "the dignity of man,"[44] and understood that "evolving standards of decency" should be measured, in part, against

43 *Trop v. Dulles*, 356 U.S. 86, 101 (1958) (plurality opinion).

44 *Id.* at 100.

international norms. Thus, in cases striking down the death penalty as a punishment for rape[45] or for unintentional killings,[46] the Court has looked to both domestic custom and the "climate of international opinion" to determine what punishments are cruel and unusual.[47]

Taking international law seriously where the death penalty is concerned, of course, draws into question the United States' entire capital punishment enterprise. According to Amnesty International, more than fifty countries (including almost all of Western Europe) have abolished the death penalty entirely, and thirty-seven others either have ceased imposing it or have limited its imposition to extraordinary crimes.[48] Even those countries that continue to impose the death penalty almost universally condemn the execution of juvenile offenders.[49] They do so in recognition of the fact that juveniles are too young, and too capable of growth and development, to act with the culpability necessary to justify society's ultimate punishment. The United States, however, persistently has defended its "right" to sentence juvenile offenders to death. . . .

Refusing to consider international practice in construing the Eighth Amendment is convenient for a Court that wishes to avoid conflict between the death penalty and the Constitution. But it is not consistent with this Court's established construction of the Eighth Amendment. If the substance of the Eighth Amendment is to turn on the "evolving standards of decency" of the civilized world, there can be no justification for limiting judicial inquiry to the opinions of the United States. Under the principles set forth in *The Paquete Habana,* interpretation of the Eighth Amendment, no less than interpretations of treaties and statutes, should be informed by a decent respect for the global opinions of mankind.

I am confident, however, that at some point the courts and the country will come to appreciate that the execution of juvenile offenders—and the imposition of the death penalty generally—is no more tolerable than other violations of international law.

ROPER V. SIMMONS

543 U.S. 551 (2005).

JUSTICE KENNEDY delivered the opinion of the Court.

This case requires us to address, for the second time in a decade and a half, whether it is permissible under the Eighth and Fourteenth

---

45 *Coker v. Georgia*, 433 U.S. 584 (1977).

46 *Enmund v. Florida*, 458 U.S. 782 (1982).

47 *Coker*, 433 U.S. at 596 n.10.

48 *See* INTERNATIONAL SECRETARIAT, AMNESTY INT'L, THE DEATH PENALTY: LIST OF ABOLITIONIST AND RETENTIONIST COUNTRIES 1 (1994).

49 *See* INTERNATIONAL SECRETARIAT, AMNESTY, INT'L, OPEN LETTER TO THE PRESIDENT ON THE DEATH PENALTY 8 (1994) [hereinafter OPEN LETTER].

Amendments to the Constitution of the United States to execute a juvenile offender who was older than 15 but younger than 18 when he committed a capital crime. In *Stanford v. Kentucky*, 492 U.S. 361 (1989), a divided Court rejected the proposition that the Constitution bars capital punishment for juvenile offenders in this age group. We reconsider the question. . . .

II

. . . The prohibition against "cruel and unusual punishments," like other expansive language in the Constitution, must be interpreted according to its text, by considering history, tradition, and precedent, and with due regard for its purpose and function in the constitutional design. To implement this framework we have established the propriety and affirmed the necessity of referring to "the evolving standards of decency that mark the progress of a maturing society" to determine which punishments are so disproportionate as to be cruel and unusual. *Trop v. Dulles*, 356 U.S. 86, 100–101 (1958) (plurality opinion).

In *Thompson v. Oklahoma*, 487 U.S. 815 (1988), a plurality of the Court determined that our standards of decency do not permit the execution of any offender under the age of 16 at the time of the crime. *Id.*, at 818–838 (opinion of STEVENS, J., joined by Brennan, Marshall, and Blackmun, JJ.). The plurality opinion explained that no death penalty State that had given express consideration to a minimum age for the death penalty had set the age lower than 16. *Id.*, at 826–829. The plurality also observed that "[t]he conclusion that it would offend civilized standards of decency to execute a person who was less than 16 years old at the time of his or her offense is consistent with the views that have been expressed by respected professional organizations, by other nations that share our Anglo-American heritage, and by the leading members of the Western European community." *Id.*, at 830. The opinion further noted that juries imposed the death penalty on offenders under 16 with exceeding rarity; the last execution of an offender for a crime committed under the age of 16 had been carried out in 1948, 40 years prior. *Id.*, at 832–833.

Bringing its independent judgment to bear on the permissibility of the death penalty for a 15-year-old offender, the *Thompson* plurality stressed that "[t]he reasons why juveniles are not trusted with the privileges and responsibilities of an adult also explain why their irresponsible conduct is not as morally reprehensible as that of an adult." *Id.*, at 835. . . .

The next year, in *Stanford v. Kentucky*, 492 U.S. 361 (1989), the Court, over a dissenting opinion joined by four Justices, referred to contemporary standards of decency in this country and concluded the Eighth and Fourteenth Amendments did not proscribe the execution of juvenile offenders over 15 but under 18. The Court noted that 22 of the 37 death penalty States permitted the death penalty for 16-year-old offenders, and, among these 37 States, 25 permitted it for 17-year-old offenders. These numbers, in the Court's view, indicated there was no national consensus "sufficient to label a particular punishment cruel and unusual." *Id.*, at 370–371. . . .

III

A

The evidence of national consensus against the death penalty for juveniles is similar, and in some respects parallel, to the evidence *Atkins* [*v. Virginia*, 536 U.S. 304 (2002)] held sufficient to demonstrate a national consensus against the death penalty for the mentally retarded. . . . 30 States prohibit the juvenile death penalty, comprising 12 that have rejected the death penalty altogether and 18 that maintain it but, by express provision or judicial interpretation, exclude juveniles from its reach. . . . In the present case, too, even in the 20 States without a formal prohibition on executing juveniles, the practice is infrequent. Since *Stanford*, six States have executed prisoners for crimes committed as juveniles. In the past 10 years, only three have done so: Oklahoma, Texas, and Virginia. . . .

Petitioner cannot show national consensus in favor of capital punishment for juveniles but still resists the conclusion that any consensus exists against it. Petitioner supports this position with, in particular, the observation that when the Senate ratified the International Covenant on Civil and Political Rights (ICCPR), Dec. 19, 1966, 999 U.N.T.S. 171 (entered into force Mar. 23, 1976), it did so subject to the President's proposed reservation regarding Article 6(5) of that treaty, which prohibits capital punishment for juveniles. Brief for Petitioner 27. This reservation at best provides only faint support for petitioner's argument. First, the reservation was passed in 1992; since then, five States have abandoned capital punishment for juveniles. Second, Congress considered the issue when enacting the Federal Death Penalty Act in 1994, and determined that the death penalty should not extend to juveniles. See 18 U.S.C. § 3591. The reservation to Article 6(5) of the ICCPR provides minimal evidence that there is not now a national consensus against juvenile executions.

As in *Atkins*, the objective indicia of consensus in this case—the rejection of the juvenile death penalty in the majority of States; the infrequency of its use even where it remains on the books; and the consistency in the trend toward abolition of the practice—provide sufficient evidence that today our society views juveniles, in the words *Atkins* used respecting the mentally retarded, as "categorically less culpable than the average criminal." 536 U.S., at 316.

B

[The Court separately reviewed social science literature suggesting differences in terms of criminal responsibility between juveniles and adults, in that youth are more inclined to "impetuous and ill-considered actions and decisions," that they "are more vulnerable or susceptible to negative influences and outside pressures, including peer pressure," and that "personality traits of juveniles are more transitory, less fixed."]

IV

Our determination that the death penalty is disproportionate punishment for offenders under 18 finds confirmation in the stark reality that the United States is the only country in the world that continues to give official sanction to the juvenile death penalty. This reality does not become controlling, for the task of interpreting the Eighth Amendment remains our responsibility. Yet at least from the time of the Court's decision in *Trop*, the Court has referred to the laws of other countries and to international authorities as instructive for its interpretation of the Eighth Amendment's prohibition of "cruel and unusual punishments." . . .

As respondent and a number of *amici* emphasize, Article 37 of the United Nations Convention on the Rights of the Child, which every country in the world has ratified save for the United States and Somalia, contains an express prohibition on capital punishment for crimes committed by juveniles under 18. . . . No ratifying country has entered a reservation to the provision prohibiting the execution of juvenile offenders. Parallel prohibitions are contained in other significant international covenants. See ICCPR, Art. 6(5), 999 U.N.T.S., at 175 (prohibiting capital punishment for anyone under 18 at the time of offense) (signed and ratified by the United States subject to a reservation regarding Article 6(5), as noted, *supra*); American Convention on Human Rights: Pact of San Jose, Costa Rica, Art. 4(5), Nov. 22, 1969, 1144 U.N.T.S. 146 (entered into force July 19, 1978) (same); African Charter on the Rights and Welfare of the Child, Art. 5(3), OAU Doc. CAB/LEG/ 24.9/49 (1990) (entered into force Nov. 29, 1999) (same).

Respondent and his *amici* have submitted, and petitioner does not contest, that only seven countries other than the United States have executed juvenile offenders since 1990: Iran, Pakistan, Saudi Arabia, Yemen, Nigeria, the Democratic Republic of Congo, and China. Since then each of these countries has either abolished capital punishment for juveniles or made public disavowal of the practice. Brief for Respondent 49–50. In sum, it is fair to say that the United States now stands alone in a world that has turned its face against the juvenile death penalty.

Though the international covenants prohibiting the juvenile death penalty are of more recent date, it is instructive to note that the United Kingdom abolished the juvenile death penalty before these covenants came into being. The United Kingdom's experience bears particular relevance here in light of the historic ties between our countries and in light of the Eighth Amendment's own origins. The Amendment was modeled on a parallel provision in the English Declaration of Rights of 1689, which provided: "[E]xcessive Bail ought not to be required nor excessive Fines imposed; nor cruel and unusual Punishments inflicted." 1 W. & M., ch. 2, § 10, in 3 Eng. Stat. at Large 441 (1770); see also *Trop, supra*, at 100 (plurality opinion). As of now, the United Kingdom has abolished the death penalty in its entirety; but, decades before it took this step, it recognized the disproportionate nature of the juvenile death penalty; and it abolished that penalty as a separate matter. . . .

It is proper that we acknowledge the overwhelming weight of international opinion against the juvenile death penalty, resting in large part on the understanding that the instability and emotional imbalance of young people may often be a factor in the crime. See Brief for Human Rights Committee of the Bar of England and Wales et al. as *Amici Curiae* 10–11. The opinion of the world community, while not controlling our outcome, does provide respected and significant confirmation for our own conclusions.

. . . It does not lessen our fidelity to the Constitution or our pride in its origins to acknowledge that the express affirmation of certain fundamental rights by other nations and peoples simply underscores the centrality of those same rights within our own heritage of freedom.

* * *

The Eighth and Fourteenth Amendments forbid imposition of the death penalty on offenders who were under the age of 18 when their crimes were committed. The judgment of the Missouri Supreme Court setting aside the sentence of death imposed upon Christopher Simmons is affirmed.

It is so ordered. . . .

JUSTICE SCALIA, with whom THE CHIEF JUSTICE and JUSTICE THOMAS join, dissenting. . . .

Though the views of our own citizens are essentially irrelevant to the Court's decision today, the views of other countries and the so-called international community take center stage.

The Court begins by noting that "Article 37 of the United Nations Convention on the Rights of the Child, [1577 U.N.T.S. 3, 28 I.L.M. 1448, 1468–1470, entered into force Sept. 2, 1990,] which every country in the world has ratified *save for the United States* and Somalia, contains an express prohibition on capital punishment for crimes committed by juveniles under 18." *Ante* (emphasis added). The Court also discusses the International Covenant on Civil and Political Rights (ICCPR), December 19, 1966, 999 U.N.T.S. 175, *ante*, which the Senate ratified only subject to a reservation that reads:

> "The United States reserves the right, subject to its Constitutional constraints, to impose capital punishment on any person (other than a pregnant woman) duly convicted under existing or future laws permitting the imposition of capital punishment, including such punishment for crimes committed by persons below eighteen years of age." Senate Committee on Foreign Relations, International Covenant on Civil and Political Rights, S. Exec. Rep. No. 102–23, 11 (1992).

Unless the Court has added to its arsenal the power to join and ratify treaties on behalf of the United States, I cannot see how this evidence favors, rather than refutes, its position. That the Senate and the President—those actors our Constitution empowers to enter into treaties, see Art. II, § 2—have declined to join and ratify treaties prohibiting execution of under-18 offenders can only suggest that *our country* has either not reached a national consensus on the question, or has reached a consensus contrary to what the Court announces. That the reservation to the ICCPR was made in 1992 does not suggest otherwise, since the reservation still remains in place today. It is also worth noting that, in addition to barring the execution of under-18 offenders, the United Nations Convention on the Rights of the Child prohibits punishing them with life in prison without the possibility of release. If we are truly going to get in line with the international community, then the Court's reassurance that the death penalty is really not needed, since "the punishment of life imprisonment without the possibility of parole is itself a severe sanction," *ante*, gives little comfort.

It is interesting that whereas the Court is not content to accept what the States of our Federal Union *say*, but insists on inquiring into what they *do* (specifically, whether they in fact *apply* the juvenile death penalty that their laws allow), the Court is quite willing to believe that every foreign nation—of whatever tyrannical political makeup and with however subservient or incompetent a court system—in fact *adheres* to a rule of no death penalty for offenders under 18. Nor does the Court inquire into how many of the countries that have the death penalty, but have forsworn (on paper at least) imposing that penalty on offenders under 18, have what no State of this country can constitutionally have: a *mandatory* death penalty for certain crimes, with no possibility of mitigation by the sentencing authority, for youth or any other reason. I suspect it is most of them. See, *e.g.,* R. Simon & D. Blaskovich, A Comparative Analysis of Capital Punishment: Statutes, Policies, Frequencies, and Public Attitudes the World Over 25, 26, 29 (2002). . . . The foreign authorities, in other words, do not even speak to the issue before us here.

More fundamentally, however, the basic premise of the Court's argument—that American law should conform to the laws of the rest of the world—ought to be rejected out of hand. In fact the Court itself does not believe it. In many significant respects the laws of most other countries differ from our law—including not only such explicit provisions of our Constitution as the right to jury trial and grand jury indictment, but even many interpretations of the Constitution prescribed by this Court itself. The Court-pronounced exclusionary rule, for example, is distinctively American. . . .

The Court has been oblivious to the views of other countries when deciding how to interpret our Constitution's requirement that "Congress shall make no law respecting an establishment of religion. . . ." Amdt. 1. Most other countries—including those committed to religious neutrality—do not insist on the degree of separation between church and state that this Court requires. . . .

And let us not forget the Court's abortion jurisprudence, which makes us one of only six countries that allow abortion on demand until the point of viability. . . .

The Court's special reliance on the laws of the United Kingdom is perhaps the most indefensible part of its opinion. . . . As we explained in *Harmelin v. Michigan*, 501 U.S. 957, 973–974 (1991), the "Cruell and Unusuall Punishments" provision of the English Declaration of Rights was originally meant to describe those punishments " 'out of [the Judges'] Power' "—that is, those punishments that were not authorized by common law or statute, but that were nonetheless administered by the Crown or the Crown's judges. Under that reasoning, the death penalty for under-18 offenders would easily survive this challenge. The Court has, however—I think wrongly—long rejected a purely originalist approach to our Eighth Amendment, and that is certainly not the approach the Court takes today. Instead, the Court undertakes the majestic task of determining (and thereby prescribing) *our* Nation's *current* standards of decency. It is beyond comprehension why we should look, for that purpose, to a country that has developed, in the centuries since the Revolutionary War—and with increasing speed since the United Kingdom's recent submission to the jurisprudence of European courts dominated by continental jurists—a legal, political, and social culture quite different from our own. . . .

The Court should either profess its willingness to reconsider all these matters in light of the views of foreigners, or else it should cease putting forth foreigners' views as part of the *reasoned basis* of its decisions. To invoke alien law when it agrees with one's own thinking, and ignore it otherwise, is not reasoned decisionmaking, but sophistry.

The Court responds that "[i]t does not lessen our fidelity to the Constitution or our pride in its origins to acknowledge that the express affirmation of certain fundamental rights by other nations and peoples simply underscores the centrality of those same rights within our own heritage of freedom." *Ante*. To begin with, I do not believe that approval by "other nations and peoples" should buttress our commitment to American principles any more than (what should logically follow) disapproval by "other nations and peoples" should weaken that commitment. More importantly, however, the Court's statement flatly misdescribes what is going on here. Foreign sources are cited today, *not* to underscore our "fidelity" to the Constitution, our "pride in its origins," and "our own [American] heritage." To the contrary, they are cited to *set aside* the centuries-old American practice—a practice still engaged in by a large majority of the relevant States—of letting a jury of 12 citizens decide whether, in the particular case, youth should be the basis for withholding the death penalty. What these foreign sources "affirm," rather than repudiate, is the Justices' own notion of how the world ought to be, and their diktat that it shall be so henceforth in America. The Court's parting attempt to downplay the significance of its extensive discussion of foreign law is unconvincing. "Acknowledgment" of foreign approval has no place in the legal opinion of this Court *unless it is part of the basis for the Court's judgment*—which is surely what it parades as today.

HAROLD HONGJU KOH, INTERNATIONAL LAW AS PART OF OUR LAW*

98 Am. J. Int'l L. 43 (2004).

. . . When is it appropriate for the Supreme Court to construe our Constitution in light of foreign and international law? History suggests that over the years, the Court has regularly looked to foreign and international precedents as an aid to constitutional interpretation in at least three situations, which for simplicity's sake I will call "parallel rules," "empirical light," and "community standard." First, the Court has noted when American legal rules seem to parallel those of other nations, particularly those with similar legal and social traditions.[13] As the Court has repeatedly recognized, the concept of "ordered liberty" is not uniquely American but, rather, is "enshrined" in the legal history of "English-speaking peoples," as well as other legal systems.[14]

Second, as Justice Stephen Breyer recently noted, the "Court has long considered as relevant and informative the way in which foreign courts have applied standards roughly comparable to our own constitutional standards in roughly comparable circumstances."[15] In *Printz v. United States*, he elaborated . . . "[T]he experience [of nations with differing

* Reprinted with permission of the American Society of International Law; permission conveyed through Copyright Clearance Center, Inc.

13 *See, e.g., Reynolds v. United States*, 98 U.S. 145, 164 (1878) (pointing out that "[p]olygamy has always been odious among the northern and western nations of Europe").

14 *See, e.g., Ingraham v. Wright*, 430 U.S. 651, 673 n.42 (1977). . . .

15 *Knight v. Florida*, 528 U.S. 990, 997 (1999) (Breyer, J., dissenting from denial of certiorari).

constitutions] may nonetheless cast an empirical light on the consequences of different solutions to a common legal problem . . ."

Third, in addition to situations involving parallel rules and empirical lessons, the Court has looked outside the United States when a U.S. constitutional concept, by its own terms, implicitly refers to a *community standard*—e.g., "cruel and *unusual*," "*due* process of law," "*unreasonable* searches and seizures." In such cases, the Court has long since recognized that the relevant communities to be consulted include those outside our shores. . . .

[T]he last Supreme Court Term confirms that two distinct approaches now uncomfortably coexist within our own Supreme Court's global jurisprudence. The first is a "nationalist jurisprudence," exemplified by the opinions of Justices Scalia and Clarence Thomas. That jurisprudence is characterized by commitments to territoriality, extreme deference to national executive power and political institutions, and resistance to comity or international law as meaningful constraints on national prerogatives. . . . When advised of foreign legal precedents, these decisions have treated them as irrelevant, or worse yet, an impermissible imposition on the exercise of American sovereignty.

A second, more venerable strand of "transnationalist jurisprudence," [is] now being carried forward by Justices Breyer and Ginsburg. . . .

Unlike nationalist jurisprudence, which rejects foreign and international precedents and looks for guidance primarily to national territory, political institutions, and executive power, the transnationalist jurisprudence assumes America's political and economic interdependence with other nations operating within the international legal system. Nor, significantly, do these Justices distinguish sharply between the relevance of foreign and international law, recognizing that one prominent feature of a globalizing world is the emergence of a transnational law, particularly in the area of human rights, that merges the national and the international. Addressing the American Society of International Law, Justice O'Connor noted that, increasingly, foreign and international law issues are coming before U.S. courts "because international law is no longer confined in relevance to a few treaties and business agreements. Rather, it has taken on the character of transnational law—what Philip Jessup has defined as law that regulates actions or events that transcend national frontiers." Similarly, Justice Breyer has noted, time has blurred

> the differences between what my law professors used to call comparative law and public international law. . . . Formally speaking, state law is state law, but practically speaking, much of that law is national, if not international, in scope. Analogous developments internationally, including the emergence of regional or specialized international legal bodies, tend similarly

to produce *cross-country results that resemble each other more and more, exhibiting common, if not universal, principles in a variety of legal areas.*

In such a transnationalist system, as Justice Breyer has noted, understanding and making reference to foreign constitutional precedents aids U.S. constitutional interpretation, "simply because of the enormous value in any discipline of trying to learn from the similar experience of others." Under this view, domestic courts must play a key role in coordinating U.S. domestic constitutional rules with rules of foreign and international law, not simply to promote American aims, but to advance the broader development of a well-functioning international judicial system. In Justice Blackmun's words, U.S. courts must look beyond narrow U.S. interests to the "mutual interests of all nations in a smoothly functioning international legal regime" and, whenever possible, should "consider if there is a course that furthers, rather than impedes, the development of an ordered international system."

The nationalist justices reject the transnationalist views on the ground that comparative and international analysis is appropriate only to legislative and constitutional *drafting*, not to the task of judicial constitutional *interpretation*. Yet on reflection, this distinction makes no sense. . . . Construing U.S. constitutional law by referring to other nations' constitutional drafters, but not their constitutional interpreters, would be akin to operating a building by examining the blueprints of others on which it was modeled, while ignoring all subsequent progress reports on how well those other buildings actually functioned over time. . . .

Nationalist academics add a second objection, which one dubs the "international countermajoritarian difficulty": the claim that U.S. constitutional protections that are responsive to "national consensus giving expression to the sovereign will of the American people" cannot "be interpreted to give expression to the international majoritarian impulse to protect the individual from democratic governance." Yet this argument assumes that the job of judges construing the Constitution is to give expression to majoritarian impulses, when their long-settled role (which, of course, gives rise to the *domestic* countermajoritarian difficulty) has been to apply enduring principles of law to evolving circumstance without regard to the will of shifting democratic majorities. . . .

Nor is there anything necessarily antidemocratic about construing U.S. constitutional law in light of transnational law. As Justice Breyer recently noted:

> [T]he transnational law that is being created is not simply a product of treaty-writers, legislatures, or courts. We in America know full well that in a democracy, law, perhaps most law, is not decreed from on high but bubbles up from the interested publics,

> affected groups, specialists, legislatures, and others, all interacting through meetings, journal articles, the popular press, legislative hearings, and in many other ways. *That is the democratic process in action*. Legislation typically comes long after this process has been underway. Judicial decisions, particularly from our Court, work best when they come last, after experience has made the consequences of legislation apparent.

What Justice Breyer describes is what I have elsewhere called "transnational legal process," the process whereby domestic systems incorporate international rules into domestic law through a three-part process of interaction, interpretation, and norm internalization. . . .

In this transnational legal process, the several states, foreign governments, and international bodies do not represent competing sovereigns, all vying for the right to control America's judicial destiny. Rather, a transnationalist jurisprudence suggests, the United States expresses its national sovereignty not by blocking out all foreign influence but by vigorous "participation in the various regimes that regulate and order the international system." The nationalists' suggestion that U.S. courts should disregard the rest of the civilized world by ignoring parallel foreign precedents only invites charges of parochialism, and undermines U.S. influence over the global development of human rights.

Nationalist academics charge that American human rights advocates have used international and foreign legal materials selectively; in one commentator's words, refusing to "take the bitter with the sweet," or in another's view, proposing "international sources . . . for comparison only if they are viewed as rights enhancing." Bizarrely, these scholars assume that United States judges should construe a national bill of rights that the framers thought was the model for the world in light of the world's worst practices. What this claim misunderstands is that those who advocate the use of international and foreign sources in U.S. constitutional interpretation are not urging U.S. courts to defer automatically to some kind of global "nose count." Instead, they are suggesting that the practices of other mature democracies—not those that lag behind developmentally—constitute the most relevant evidence of what Eighth Amendment jurisprudence calls the "evolving standards of decency that mark the progress of a maturing society."

. . . When phrases like "due process of law," "equal protection," and "cruel and unusual punishments" are illuminated by parallel rules, empirical evidence, or community standards found in other mature legal systems, that evidence should not simply be ignored. Wise American judges did not do so at the beginning of the Republic, and there is no warrant for them to start now.

CONFIRMATION HEARING ON THE NOMINATION OF HON. SONIA SOTOMAYOR, TO BE AN ASSOCIATE JUSTICE OF THE SUPREME COURT OF THE UNITED STATES

Hearing Before the S. Comm. on the Judiciary, 111th Cong. 349 (2009).

SENATOR COBURN. So you stand by it. There is no authority for a Supreme Court Justice to utilize foreign law in terms of making decisions based on the Constitution or statutes?

JUDGE SOTOMAYOR. Unless the statute requires you or directs you to look at foreign law, and some do by the way, the answer is no. Foreign law cannot be used as a holding or a precedent or to bind or to influence the outcome of a legal decision interpreting the Constitution or American law that doesn't direct you to that law.

CONFIRMATION HEARING ON THE NOMINATION OF ELENA KAGAN TO BE AN ASSOCIATE JUSTICE OF THE SUPREME COURT OF THE UNITED STATES

Hearing Before the S. Comm. on the Judiciary, 111th Cong. 259 (2010).

MS. KAGAN. Well, Senator Grassley, I guess I'm in favor of good ideas coming from wherever you can get them, so in that sense I think for a judge to read a law review article or to read a book about legal issues or to read the decision of a State court, even though there's no binding effect of that State court, or to read the decision of a foreign court, to the extent that you learn about how different people might approach and have thought about approaching legal issues. But I don't think that foreign law should have independent precedential effect in any but a very, very, narrow set of circumstances. . . . Fundamentally, we have an American Constitution. Our Constitution is our own.

CONFIRMATION HEARING ON THE NOMINATION OF HON. NEIL GORSUCH, TO BE AN ASSOCIATE JUSTICE OF THE SUPREME COURT OF THE UNITED STATES

Hearing Before the S. Comm. on the Judiciary (March 22, 2017), available at http://www.wsj.com/livecoverage/supreme-court-nominee-neil-gorsuch-hearing-senate-judiciary-committee, [https://perma.cc/T6DX-57UW].

JUDGE GORSUCH. [A]s a general matter, [S]enator [Sasse], I would say it[']s improper to look abroad when interpreting the Constitution—as a general matter. . . We're talking about interpreting the Constitution of the United States. We have our own tradition and our own history. I don't know why we would look to the experience other countries rather than our own when everybody else looks to us.

NOTES

1. *International Law Versus Foreign Law.* In reading these excerpts, note the often indiscriminate references to "international law," "foreign law," and decisions by international (or foreign) courts and tribunals. Put most simply, international law covers matters such as treaties and international custom, whereas foreign law has to do with the domestic laws of foreign countries, including their constitutions, statutes, and case law; a decision by an international or foreign court or tribunal may have either kind of law as its legal basis, and may or may not bind the United States in the case at hand. Should these be treated distinctly for purposes of interpreting U.S. law? Are you persuaded by Justice Breyer's view, excerpted in the article by Professor Koh, that such distinctions are overblown?

2. *Supreme Court Practice.* As reflected in the *Roper v. Simmons* and other death penalty opinions, there has been a heated debate in recent years about the appropriate role for international and foreign jurisprudence in the opinions of U.S. judges. In some of the Supreme Court's most controversial cases, its members have referred to one or the other as lending support to their conclusions. These include not only other sentencing cases, see *Graham v. Florida*, 560 U.S. 48, 80–82 (2010) (noting that only the United States authorized life without parole for juvenile non-homicide offenders, and that U.S. practice would violate the United Nations Convention on the Rights of the Child), but also the right to engage in intimate sexual conduct, see *Lawrence v. Texas*, 539 U.S. 558, 577–78 (2003) (noting that "[t]he right the petitioners seek in this case has been accepted as an integral part of human freedom in many other countries"); affirmative action, see *Grutter v. Bollinger*, 539 U.S. 306, 344 (2003) (Ginsburg, J., concurring) (explaining that the Court's view that "race-conscious programs 'must have a logical end point' accords with the international understanding of the office of affirmative action"); and assisted suicide, see *Washington v. Glucksberg*, 521 U.S. 702, 785 (1997) (Souter, J., concurring) (reporting that "Respondents' proposals . . . sound much like the guidelines now in place in the Netherlands"). However, in many of the same subject areas, the Supreme Court has refrained from citing, let alone relying on, foreign and international authorities, despite being invited to do so by parties or amici. *See, e.g.*, *Miller v. Alabama*, 567 U.S. 460 (2012) (holding unconstitutional mandatory life imprisonment without parole for those under the age of 18 at the time of their crimes, but ignoring international practices cited by amici); *Fisher v. University of Texas at Austin*, 133 S. Ct. 2411 (2013) (refraining, in affirmative action case, from citing treaties and international practices invoked by amici); *Hollingsworth v. Perry*, 133 S. Ct. 2652 (2013) (refraining, in same-sex marriage case, from relying on foreign practices and international norms invoked by amici); *see also Glossip v. Gross*, 135 S. Ct. 2726, 2775–76 (2015) (Breyer, J., dissenting) (citing international practices, ignored by other opinions, in lethal injection case).

What role does this track record suggest? Do you think foreign and international law play a constructive role in U.S. constitutional adjudication? What variables affect your analysis? Does the nature of the foreign or international source matter? Are your concerns, if any, mollified when it is cited in an opinion other than the majority opinion, or when it is cited with a caveat to the effect that it is "by no means dispositive"? *Atkins v. Virginia*, 536 U.S. 304, 316 n.21 (2002). Reviewing the testimony of the last three nominees for the Supreme Court (as of mid-2017), what do you foresee as the likely practice in the future?

For other reflections on this topic, see Stephen Breyer, *The Court and the World: American Law and the New Global Realities* 244–45 (2015); the discussion between Justice Stephen Breyer and Justice Antonin Scalia, "The Constitutional Relevance of Foreign Court Decisions," American University, January 13, 2005, available at http://www.c-span.org/video/?185122-1/constitutional-relevance-foreign-court-decisions, [http://perma.cc/7EQR-F2WU]; and Hon. Patricia M. Wald, *The Use of International Law in the American Adjudicative Process,* 27 HARV. J.L. & PUB. POL'Y 431 (2004). For a guide to prior judicial approaches, see Sarah H. Cleveland, *Our International Constitution*, 31 YALE J. INT'L 1 (2006). And for a small slice of a huge secondary literature, see Symposium, *The Debate Over Foreign Law in* Roper v. Simmons, 119 HARV. L. REV. 103 (2005); Symposium, *The United States Constitution and International Law*, 98 AM. J. INT'L L. 42 (2004).

3. *Prohibiting the Use of International/Foreign Law by U.S. Courts.* Would you support adoption of a statute that limits the use by U.S. courts of international or foreign law? The Military Commissions Act of 2006, discussed in Chapter 4, Sec. 7, provided:

> No foreign or international source of law shall supply a basis for a rule of decision in the courts of the United States in interpreting the prohibitions enumerated in subsection (d) of such section 2441.

Pub. L. No. 109–366, § 6(a)(2), 120 Stat. 2600 (2006). The purpose of that provision (and of § 6 in general) appears to be to preclude U.S. courts from interpreting the meaning of "grave breaches" of the 1949 Geneva Conventions by reference to any foreign or international source of law. Presumably this category includes foreign and international courts' decisions as to the meaning of the Conventions, as well as the Conventions themselves and their negotiating history, and by reference to foreign and state practice. The constitutionality of this provision remains as yet untested.

Similar efforts have been made within Congress that disapprove of the use of international and foreign law to interpret the U.S. Constitution. These range from resolutions that would discourage such reliance, see, e.g., H.R. Res. 473, 111th Cong. (2009), to repeated suggestions that the Constitution be amended to prevent reliance on international law, international agreements, or religious laws. *See, e.g.*, H.R.J. Res. 54, 113th Cong. (2013). A notable example is the failed "Constitution Restoration Act," introduced on several occasions in reaction to cases like *Roper v. Simmons* and *Lawrence v. Texas*. The bill would have precluded U.S. courts, when engaged in constitutional interpretation, from relying on any legal materials—including constitutions, laws, and judicial decisions—of any foreign State or international organization or agency; further, it would have deemed judicial engagement in such activities an impeachable offense. *See, e.g.*, S. 520, 109th Cong. §§ 201, 302 (2005).

Do these attempts to regulate the judicial process raise issues that are different from the underlying judicial practices? Does legislation of this kind improperly intrude upon the judicial function of U.S. courts? What do you make, in that regard, of now-routine attempts to extract from Supreme Court nominees commitments that they will generally refrain from using foreign and international law?

Occasionally similar efforts have been attempted in state legislatures. In 2010, an Oklahoma referendum approved the "Save Our State Amendment," which provided in relevant part that "[t]he courts shall not look to the legal precepts of other nations or cultures"—"[s]pecifically, the courts shall not consider international law or Sharia law." Certification of the referendum was enjoined, preliminarily and later permanently, on the ground that it violated the Establishment Clause of the U.S. Constitution. *See Awad v. Ziriax*, 670 F.3d 1111 (10th Cir. 2010); *Awad v. Ziriax*, 966 F.Supp.2d 1198 (W.D. Okla. 2013). Does the regulation (by state voters) of state courts pose a different question than the regulation of federal courts by Congress, or self-regulation of federal courts? As you reflect later on the preemption issues posed in Chapter 6, consider whether—putting aside any Establishment Clause issues—the Save Our State Amendment also violates, or vindicates, principles of constitutional federalism.

4. *Next Steps*. The remaining Sections of this Chapter explore the areas where the law of nations has been most frequently applied (or not applied) by U.S. courts. In some, Congress has defined specific offenses against the law of nations. In others, it has passed laws that simply incorporated "offenses against the law of nations," leaving it to the courts to define them. In still other instances, the courts have acted in the absence of statutory incorporation to bring international customary law into U.S. law. In addition to general maritime and admiralty matters (several of which are noted in Sec. 2 above), U.S. courts have focused on customary international law in areas like jurisdiction (Sec. 5), human rights (Sec. 6), and piracy and terrorism (Sec. 7 and Sec. 8); other important areas include war-related crimes (Chapter 4, Sec. 7) and immunities for States, diplomats, and their property (Chapter 7, Sec. 7).

5. SCOPE OF U.S. EXTRATERRITORIAL JURISDICTION

As evident from maritime and admiralty cases like *The Schooner Charming Betsy* and *The Paquete Habana*, courts have often confronted the question whether the exercise of U.S. authority is consistent with customary international law. At a more general level, similar problems are presented as problems of "prescriptive jurisdiction"—which the American Law Institute's *Restatement (Fourth)* defines as "the authority of a state to make laws applicable to persons, property, or conduct." *See Restatement of the Law (Fourth), The Foreign Relations Law of the United States: Jurisdiction*, Part II, introductory note at 29 (Tentative Draft No. 2, 2016); *id.* (distinguishing "jurisdiction to adjudicate," concerning a State's authority to "subject particular persons or things to its judicial process," and "jurisdiction to enforce," which concerns its authority to "compel compliance with law").

United States foreign relations law mediates between customary international law and prescriptive jurisdiction in at least two ways. First, courts may scrutinize whether Congress, when legislating, has purposefully heeded or exceeded the established bases for prescriptive jurisdiction recognized under international law—or, at least, has intended to regulate matters beyond U.S. territory. The former inquiry will be familiar from *The Schooner Charming Betsy*. The latter, known as the presumption against extraterritoriality, may produce different results, and is explored at greater length below.

The second issue, broadly familiar from Sec. 3 of this Chapter, concerns the result if a congressional statute conflicts with customary international law norms of prescriptive jurisdiction. Should Congress be able to adopt a statute that places the United States in violation of customary international law? Should courts be concerned with whether this might have the effect of licensing other States to extend their laws beyond their borders, and to Americans?

The excerpts below, beginning with the Second Circuit's decision in *United States v. Yousef*, address these issues. For purposes of understanding these materials, it is useful to understand the basic principles that States have developed through their practice (and in some instances, through treaties) as to acceptable exercises of prescriptive jurisdiction. Generally, these rules view the permissible scope of a State's jurisdiction over persons or conduct as a function of the State's linkages with those persons or conduct. *Yousef* itself summarized the available justifications as follows:

> (1) the "objective territorial principle," which provides for jurisdiction over conduct committed outside a State's borders that has, or is intended to have, a substantial effect within its territory;
>
> (2) the "nationality principle," which provides for jurisdiction over extraterritorial acts committed by a State's own citizen;
>
> (3) the "protective principle," which provides for jurisdiction over acts committed outside the State that harm the State's interests;

(4) the "passive personality principle," which provides for jurisdiction over acts that harm a State's citizens abroad; and

(5) the "universality principle," which provides for jurisdiction over extraterritorial acts by a citizen or non-citizen that are so heinous as to be universally condemned by all civilized nations.

327 F.3d 56, 91 n.24 (2d Cir. 2003); *see Restatement of the Law (Fourth), The Foreign Relations Law of the United States: Jurisdiction* §§ 212–7 (Tentative Draft No. 2, 2016) (dividing principles into "territory," "effects" (within territory), "active personality" (nationality), "passive personality," the "protective principle," and "universal jurisdiction"). Where the link between the State and the person or conduct is weak or unreasonable, U.S. courts are more likely—based on customary international law, comity, or some other basis—to preclude or interpret narrowly the exercise of the jurisdiction. *Id.* at § 204.

UNITED STATES V. YOUSEF

327 F.3d 56 (2d Cir. 2003).

INTRODUCTION

. . . In the first trial, Yousef, Murad, and Wali Khan Amin Shah were tried on charges relating to a conspiracy to bomb United States commercial airliners in Southeast Asia. In the second trial, Yousef and Ismoil were tried for their involvement in the February 1993 bombing of the World Trade Center in New York City. . . . [The following excerpts relate solely to their convictions on Counts Twelve through Nineteen, which charged Yousef, Murad, and Shah with various crimes relating to their conspiracy to bomb United States airliners in Southeast Asia in 1994 and 1995.]

GENERAL BACKGROUND

. . . A year and a half after the World Trade Center bombing, Yousef entered Manila, the capital of the Philippines, under an assumed name. By September 1994, Yousef had devised a plan to attack United States airliners. According to the plan, five individuals would place bombs aboard twelve United States-flag aircraft that served routes in Southeast Asia. The conspirators would board an airliner in Southeast Asia, assemble a bomb on the plane, and then exit the plane during its first layover. As the planes continued on toward their next destinations, the time-bombs would detonate. Eleven of the twelve flights targeted were ultimately destined for cities in the United States.

Yousef and his co-conspirators performed several tests in preparation for the airline bombings. In December 1994, Yousef and Wali Khan Amin Shah placed one of the bombs they had constructed in a Manila movie theater. The bomb exploded, injuring several patrons of the theater. Ten days later, Yousef planted another test bomb under a passenger's seat during the first leg of a Philippine Airlines flight from Manila to Japan. Yousef disembarked from the plane during the stopover and then made his way back to Manila. During the second leg of the flight, the bomb exploded, killing one passenger, a Japanese national, and injuring others.

The plot to bomb the United States-flag airliners was uncovered in January 1995, only two weeks before the conspirators intended to carry it out. . . . Philippine authorities arrested Murad and Shah, though Shah escaped and was not recaptured until nearly a year later. Yousef fled the country, but was captured in Pakistan the next month.

* * *

DISCUSSION

. . . Yousef contends that the Government exceeded its authority by trying him in the United States for his conduct in the aircraft bombing case. In particular, he asserts that the charges alleged in Counts Twelve, Thirteen, Fourteen and Nineteen should be dismissed because 18 U.S.C. § 32 cannot be applied to conduct outside the United States.[1] He further claims that he cannot be convicted of the charge set forth in Count Nineteen because he was not "found" within the United States as required by 18 U.S.C. § 32(b).[2] Yousef also contends that his prosecution violates customary international law limiting a nation's jurisdiction to proscribe conduct outside its borders. . . .

---

1 [Authors' Note: 18 U.S.C. § 32(a)(2006) provided that whoever willfully

> (1) sets fire to, damages, destroys, disables, or wrecks any aircraft in the special aircraft jurisdiction of the United States or any civil aircraft used, operated, or employed in interstate, overseas, or foreign air commerce; [or]
>
> (2) places or causes to be placed a destructive device or substance in, upon, or in proximity to, or otherwise makes or causes to be made unworkable or unusable or hazardous to work or use, any such aircraft, or any part or other materials used or intended to be used in connection with the operation of such aircraft, if such placing or causing to be placed or such making or causing to be made is likely to endanger the safety of any such aircraft . . .

shall be fined under this title or imprisoned not more than twenty years or both.]

2 [Authors' Note: 18 U.S.C. § 32(b)(3) (2006) provided that whoever willfully

> places or causes to be placed on a civil aircraft registered in a country other than the United States while such aircraft is in service, a device or substance which is likely to destroy that aircraft, or to cause damage to that aircraft which renders that aircraft incapable of flight or which is likely to endanger that aircraft's safety in flight . . . shall be fined under this title or imprisoned not more than twenty years, or both. There is jurisdiction over an offense under this subsection if a national of the United States was on board, or would have been on board, the aircraft; an offender is a national of the United States; or an offender is afterwards found in the United States.]

A. Jurisdiction to Prosecute Defendants' Extraterritorial Conduct Under Federal Law

1. Applicable Law

It is beyond doubt that, as a general proposition, Congress has the authority to "enforce its laws beyond the territorial boundaries of the United States." *EEOC v. Arabian Am. Oil Co.*, 499 U.S. 244, 248 (1991). Although there is a presumption that Congress does not intend a statute to apply to conduct outside the territorial jurisdiction of the United States, *see Foley Bros. v. Filardo,* 336 U.S. 281, 285 (1949), that presumption can be overcome when Congress clearly expresses its intent to do so . . . As long as Congress has indicated its intent to reach such conduct, a United States court is "bound to follow the Congressional direction unless this would violate the due process clause of the Fifth Amendment." *United States v. Pinto-Mejia*, 720 F.2d 248, 259 (2d Cir. 1983) (internal quotation marks omitted). Moreover, the presumption against extraterritorial application does not apply to those "criminal statutes which are, as a class, not logically dependent on their locality for the Government's jurisdiction." *United States v. Bowman*, 260 U.S. 94, 98 (1922).

In determining whether Congress intended a federal statute to apply to overseas conduct, "an act of Congress ought never to be construed to violate the law of nations if any other possible construction remains." *McCulloch v. Sociedad Nacional de Marineros de Honduras*, 372 U.S. 10, 21 (1963) (internal quotation marks omitted). Nonetheless, in fashioning the reach of our criminal law, "Congress is not bound by international law." *Pinto-Mejia*, 720 F.2d at 259. "If it chooses to do so, it may legislate with respect to conduct outside the United States, in excess of the limits posed by international law." *Id.* . . .

2. Counts Thirteen and Fourteen

Counts Thirteen and Fourteen charged Yousef, Murad and Shah with violating 18 U.S.C. § 32(a). . . .

Section 32(a)(1) prohibits damaging "any aircraft in the special aircraft jurisdiction of the United States" or "any civil aircraft used, operated, or employed in interstate, overseas, or foreign air commerce." Section 32(a)(2) makes it a crime to place a destructive device on board any such aircraft if it would be likely to endanger the aircraft's safety. Section 32(a)(7) prohibits an attempt or conspiracy to do anything forbidden under § 32(a).

The text of the applicable federal statutes makes it clear that Congress intended § 32(a) to apply extraterritorially. Under 49 U.S.C. § 46501(2)(A) the "special aircraft jurisdiction of the United States" is defined to include any "civil aircraft of the United States" while that aircraft is in flight. "Civil aircraft of the United States," in turn, is defined in 49 U.S.C. § 40102(a)(17) as "an aircraft registered under Chapter 441" of Title 49, which requires registration of any United States-flag aircraft. See 49 U.S.C. §§ 44101–44103. Accordingly, § 32(a) covers any United States-flag aircraft while in flight, wherever in the world it may be. In addition, Congress defined "foreign air commerce" to cover "the transportation of passengers or property by aircraft . . . between a place in the United States and a place outside the United States." 49 U.S.C. § 40102(a)(22).

The District Court was correct to hold that the twelve aircraft targeted in the instant case fell within one or another category of craft protected by United States law. . . . Accordingly, it was proper for the District Court to exercise jurisdiction over the extraterritorial crimes charged in Counts Thirteen and Fourteen.

3. Count Twelve

In Count Twelve, the defendants were charged with violating 18 U.S.C. § 371 by conspiring to place bombs on board aircraft and destroy aircraft, in violation of 18 U.S.C. § 32(a)(1) and (2). The District Court concluded that, because it had jurisdiction over the substantive crimes charged—including attempted destruction of aircraft in the special aircraft jurisdiction of the United States—it also had derivative jurisdiction over the conspiracy charges. . . .

We agree. Indeed, this conclusion is a simple application of the rule enunciated by the Supreme Court as long ago as 1922 in *Bowman*, that Congress is presumed to intend extraterritorial application of criminal statutes where the nature of the crime does not depend on the locality of the defendants' acts and where restricting the statute to United States territory would severely diminish the statute's effectiveness. . . . In the instant case, if Congress intended United States courts to have jurisdiction over the substantive crime of placing bombs on board the aircraft at issue, it is reasonable to conclude that Congress also intended to vest in United States courts the requisite jurisdiction over an extraterritorial conspiracy to commit that crime. . . .

4. Count Nineteen

In Count Nineteen, Yousef alone was charged with violating 18 U.S.C. § 32(b)(3) for placing a bomb on a civil aircraft registered in another country. Specifically, Yousef was charged with planting a bomb on board a Philippine Airlines flight traveling from the Philippines to Japan on December 11, 1994. The aircraft was a civil aircraft registered in the Philippines.

There is no dispute that Congress intended § 32(b) to apply to attacks on non-United States-flag aircraft. The statute applies expressly to placing a bomb on aircraft registered in other countries while in flight, no matter where the attack is committed, and provides for jurisdiction over such extraterritorial crimes whenever, inter alia, "an offender is afterwards found in the United States." 18 U.S.C. § 32(b). . . .

B. Exercise of United States Extraterritorial Jurisdiction and Customary International Law

On appeal, Yousef challenges the District Court's jurisdiction over Counts Twelve through Nineteen of the indictment by arguing that customary international law does not provide a basis for jurisdiction over these counts and that United States law is subordinate to customary international law and therefore cannot provide a basis for jurisdiction. . . . He particularly contests the District Court's conclusion that customary international law permits the United States to prosecute him under the so-called universality principle for the bombing of Philippine Airline Flight 434 charged in Count Nineteen. Yousef claims that, absent a universally agreed-upon definition of "terrorism" and an international consensus that terrorism is a subject matter over which universal jurisdiction may be exercised, the United States cannot rest jurisdiction over him for this "terrorist" act *either* on the universality principle or on any United States positive law, which, he claims, necessarily is subordinate to customary international law.

Yousef's arguments fail. First, irrespective of whether customary international law provides a basis for jurisdiction over Yousef for Counts Twelve through Nineteen, United States law provides a separate and complete basis for jurisdiction over each of these counts and, contrary to Yousef's assertions, United States law is not subordinate to customary international law or necessarily subordinate to treaty-based international law and, in fact, may conflict with both. Further contrary to Yousef's claims, customary international law *does* provide a substantial basis for jurisdiction by the United States over each of these counts, although not (as the District Court held) under the universality principle. . . .

1. Bases of Jurisdiction over the Counts Charged

a. Relationship between Domestic and International Law in Yousef's Prosecution

Jurisdiction over Yousef on Counts Twelve through Nineteen was based on 18 U.S.C. § 32. Yousef argues that this statute cannot give rise to jurisdiction because his prosecution thereunder conflicts with established principles of customary international law. Yousef's argument fails because, while customary international law may inform the judgment of our courts in an appropriate case, it cannot alter or constrain the making of law by the political branches of the government as ordained by the Constitution.

Principles of customary international law reflect the practices and customs of States in the international arena that are applied in a consistent fashion and that are generally recognized by what used to be called "civilized states." That is, principles of customary international law consist of the "*settled* rule[s] of international law" as recognized through "the general assent of civilized nations."[25] *The Paquete Habana,* 175 U.S. 677, 694 (1900) (emphasis added); *id.* at 686 . . .

It has long been established that customary international law is part of the law of the United States to the limited extent that "where there is *no treaty,* and *no controlling executive or legislative act or judicial decision,* resort must be had to the customs and usages of civilized nations." *The Paquete Habana,* 175 U.S. at 700 (emphasis added); *see also Garcia-Mir v. Meese,* 788 F.2d 1446, 1453 (11th Cir. 1986) (noting that "public international law is controlling only" in the absence of controlling positive law or judicial precedent).

While it is permissible for United States law to conflict with customary international law, where legislation is susceptible to multiple interpretations, the interpretation that does not conflict with "the law of nations" is preferred. . . .

If a statute makes plain Congress's intent (instead of employing ambiguous or "general" words), then Article III courts, which can overrule Congressional enactments only when such enactments conflict with the Constitution, *see, e.g., Sinclair Refining Co. v. Atkinson,* 370 U.S. 195, 215 (1962) (stating that, "[i]n dealing with problems of interpretation and application of federal statutes, we have no power to change deliberate choices of legislative policy that Congress has made within its constitutional powers"), must enforce the intent of Congress irrespective of whether the statute conforms to customary international law. Thus the Supreme Court stated in *The Nereide,* 13 U.S. (9 Cranch) 388 (1815) (Marshall, C.J.), that while courts are "bound by the law of nations which is a part of the law of the land," Congress may "manifest [its] will" to apply a different rule "by passing an act for the purpose." *Id.* at 423. . . . It also is established that Congress "may legislate with respect to conduct outside the United States, in excess of the limits posed by international law." *United States v. Pinto-Mejia,* 720 F.2d 248, 259 (2d Cir. 1983).

In the event that there is no "controlling executive or legislative act or judicial decision" that the court must apply, *The Paquete Habana,* 175 U.S. at 700, a court should identify the norms of customary international law by looking to "the general usage and practice of nations[,] or by [looking to] judicial decisions recognizing and enforcing that law . . . [, or by] consulting the works of jurists writing professedly on public law," *United States v.*

[25] While it is not possible to claim that the practice or policies of any one country, including the United States, has such authority that the contours of customary international law may be determined by reference only to that country, it is highly unlikely that a purported principle of customary international law in direct conflict with the recognized practices and customs of the United States and/or other prominent players in the community of States could be deemed to qualify as a *bona fide* customary international law principle.

Smith, 18 U.S. (5 Wheat.) 153 (1820) (Story, J.). However, materials beyond the laws and practices of States, such as the writings of jurists, may serve only as "evidence" of these principles of customary international law, to which courts may look "not for the speculations of their authors concerning what the law *ought to be,* but for trustworthy evidence of *what the law really is.*" *The Paquete Habana,* 175 U.S. at 700 (emphasis added); *see also Tel-Oren v. Libyan Arab Republic,* 726 F.2d 774, 789 (D.C. Cir. 1984) (Edwards, J., concurring) (relying on *The Paquete Habana* for the proposition that courts should identify the "law of nations" primarily from the official acts and practices of States and, secondarily, as "evidence" of existing state practices, from the writings of scholars). . . .

b. Treaty-Based Jurisdiction: The Hague and Montreal Conventions

Treaty law also may provide a basis for a State's action independent of the principles of customary international law. A treaty creates obligations in States parties to it that may differ from those of customary international law, and it generally is immaterial whether customary international law points in the same or in a different direction than the treaty obligation. . . .

The express purpose of the [Montreal] Convention is to ensure that terrorists who commit crimes on or against aircraft cannot take refuge in countries whose courts otherwise might have lacked jurisdiction over an offense against a foreign-flag aircraft that transpired either in another State or in international airspace. See Montreal Conv., art. 5, 24 U.S.T. at 565.

The Montreal Convention, unlike the customary international law principles of criminal jurisdiction (including universal jurisdiction), creates a basis for the assertion of jurisdiction that is moored in a process of formal lawmaking and that is binding only on the States that accede to it. The jurisdiction thus created is not a species of universal jurisdiction, but a jurisdictional agreement among contracting States to extradite or prosecute offenders who commit the acts proscribed by the treaty—that is, the agreements between contracting States create *aut dedere aut punire* ("extradite or prosecute") jurisdiction. . . .

2. Jurisdiction over Counts Twelve through Eighteen

Jurisdiction over Counts Twelve through Eighteen is straight-forward, and we affirm both the District Court's finding of jurisdiction and its reasoning. . . .

First, jurisdiction over Counts Twelve through Eighteen is consistent with the "passive personality principle" of customary international jurisdiction because each of these counts involved a plot to bomb United States-flag aircraft that would have been carrying United States citizens and crews and that were destined for cities in the United States. Moreover, assertion of jurisdiction is appropriate under the "objective territorial principle" because the purpose of the attack was to influence United States foreign policy and the defendants intended their actions to have an effect—in this case, a devastating effect—on and within the United States. Finally, there is no doubt that jurisdiction is proper under the "protective principle" because the planned attacks were intended to affect the United States and to alter its foreign policy.

3. Jurisdiction over Count Nineteen

. . . .

a. The District Court's Holding and Yousef's Challenges on Appeal

Count Nineteen, the bombing of Philippine Airlines Flight 434, appears to present a less straight-forward jurisdictional issue because the airplane that was bombed was not a United States-flag aircraft, it was flying between two destinations outside of the United States, and there is no evidence that any United States citizens were aboard the flight or were targets of the bombing. The District Court nevertheless concluded that jurisdiction over Yousef for the offenses charged in Count Nineteen was proper, inter alia, under the principle of "universal jurisdiction." *Yousef*, 927 F. Supp. at 681–82.

Yousef makes a two-part argument on appeal challenging the District Court's holding with respect to the Court's jurisdiction over Count Nineteen. First, he claims that the District Court erred in holding that the universality principle provides jurisdiction over Count Nineteen. He bases this claim on the argument that, if his placing the bomb on the Philippine Airlines plane constituted terrorism, then jurisdiction under the universality principle is improper because terrorism is not universally condemned by the community of States and, therefore, is not subject to universal jurisdiction under customary international law. Second, he argues that because customary international law does not provide for the punishment of terrorist acts under the universality principle, such failure precludes or invalidates United States laws that provide for the prosecution of such acts that occur extraterritorially.

. . . We hold that the District Court erred as a matter of law in relying upon the universality principle as a basis for jurisdiction over the acts charged in Count Nineteen and further hold that customary international law currently does not provide for the prosecution of "terrorist" acts under the universality principle, in part due to the failure of States to achieve anything like consensus on the definition of terrorism. However, . . . we hold that Yousef's conduct charged in Count Nineteen—regardless of whether it is termed "terrorist"—constitutes the core conduct proscribed by the Montreal Convention and its implementing legislation. Accordingly, Yousef's prosecution and conviction on this Count is both consistent with and required by the United States' treaty obligations and domestic laws.

We therefore reject Yousef's claim that jurisdiction over Count Nineteen was lacking and affirm the substance of the District Court's ruling. . . .

To summarize our conclusions, with respect to the airline bombing trial we hold: . . . The District Court had jurisdiction over the defendants' extraterritorial conduct pursuant to federal law.

MORRISON V. NATIONAL AUSTRALIA BANK LTD.

561 U.S. 247 (2010).

[National Australia Bank (National), a foreign company the shares of which were not traded on any U.S. exchange, purchased HomeSide Lending, a Florida mortgage service company. National's share price later fell after it wrote down HomeSide's assets. Australian shareholders of National sued National and others for violating the Securities and Exchange Act of 1934 and SEC Rule 10b–5, claiming that HomeSide had inflated its value and that National and its chief executive officer were aware of it. The defendants moved to dismiss for lack of subject-matter jurisdiction under Federal Rule of Civil Procedure 12(b)(1) and for failure to state a claim under Rule 12(b)(6). The district court granted the Rule 12(b)(1) motion on the ground that the securities fraud was concluded abroad. The Second Circuit affirmed.]

JUSTICE SCALIA delivered the opinion of the Court.

We decide whether § 10(b) of the Securities Exchange Act of 1934 provides a cause of action to foreign plaintiffs suing foreign and American defendants for misconduct in connection with securities traded on foreign exchanges. . . .

II

Before addressing the question presented, we must correct a threshold error in the Second Circuit's analysis. It considered the extraterritorial reach of § 10(b) to raise a question of subject-matter jurisdiction. . . .

But to ask what conduct § 10(b) reaches is to ask what conduct § 10(b) prohibits, which is a merits question. Subject-matter jurisdiction, by contrast, "refers to a tribunal's ' "power to hear a case." ' " . . . [N]othing in the analysis of the courts below turned on the mistake. . . .

III

A

It is a "longstanding principle of American law 'that legislation of Congress, unless a contrary intent appears, is meant to apply only within the territorial jurisdiction of the United States.' " *EEOC v. Arabian American Oil Co.*, 499 U.S. 244, 248 (1991) (*Aramco*) (quoting *Foley Bros., Inc. v. Filardo*, 336 U.S. 281, 285 (1949)). This principle represents a canon of construction, or a presumption about a statute's meaning, rather than a limit upon Congress's power to legislate, see *Blackmer v. United States*, 284 U.S. 421, 437 (1932). It rests on the perception that Congress ordinarily legislates with respect to domestic, not foreign matters. *Smith v. United States*, 507 U.S. 197, 204, n. 5 (1993). Thus, "unless there is the affirmative intention of the Congress clearly expressed" to give a statute extraterritorial effect, "we must presume it is primarily concerned with domestic conditions." Aramco, supra, at 248 (internal quotation marks omitted). The canon or presumption applies regardless of whether there is a risk of conflict between the American statute and a foreign law, see *Sale v. Haitian Centers Council, Inc.*, 509 U.S. 155, 173–174 (1993). When a statute gives no clear indication of an extraterritorial application, it has none. . . .

The Second Circuit . . . formalized . . . (1) an "effects test," "whether the wrongful conduct had a substantial effect in the United States or upon United States citizens," and (2) a "conduct test," "whether the wrongful conduct occurred in the United States." . . .

As they developed, these tests were not easy to administer. The conduct test was held to apply differently depending on whether the harmed investors were Americans or foreigners: When the alleged damages consisted of losses to American investors abroad, it was enough that acts "of material importance" performed in the United States "significantly contributed" to that result; whereas those acts must have "directly caused" the result when losses to foreigners abroad were at issue. See *Bersch*, 519 F.2d, at 993. And "merely preparatory activities in the United States" did not suffice "to trigger application of the securities laws for injury to foreigners located abroad." *Id.*, at 992. This required the court to distinguish between mere preparation and using the United States as a "base" for fraudulent activities in other countries. *Vencap, supra*, at 1017–1018. But merely satisfying the conduct test was sometimes insufficient without " 'some additional factor tipping the scales' " in favor of the application of American law. . . . There is no more damning indictment of the "conduct" and "effects" tests than the Second Circuit's own declaration that "the presence or absence of any single factor which was considered significant in other cases . . . is not necessarily dispositive in future cases." *IIT v. Cornfeld*, 619 F.2d 909, 918 (1980). . . .

The criticisms seem to us justified. The results of judicial-speculation-made-law—divining what Congress would have wanted if it had thought of the situation before the court—demonstrate the wisdom of the presumption against extraterritoriality. Rather than guess anew in each case, we apply the presumption in all cases, preserving a stable background against which Congress can legislate with predictable effects.

B

Rule 10b–5, the regulation under which petitioners have brought suit, was promulgated under § 10(b), and "does not extend beyond conduct encompassed by § 10(b)'s prohibition." *United States v. O'Hagan*, 521 U.S. 642, 651 (1997). Therefore, if § 10(b) is not extraterritorial, neither is Rule 10b–5.

On its face, § 10(b) contains nothing to suggest it applies abroad:

> "It shall be unlawful for any person, directly or indirectly, by the use of any means or instrumentality of interstate commerce or of the mails, or of any facility of any national securities exchange . . . [t]o use or employ, in connection with the purchase or sale of any security registered on a national securities exchange or any security not so registered, . . . any manipulative or deceptive device or contrivance in contravention of such rules and regulations as the [Securities and Exchange] Commission may prescribe . . . ." 15 U.S.C. 78j(b).

. . . [T]here is § 30(b) of the Exchange Act, 15 U.S.C. § 78dd(b), which does mention the Act's extraterritorial application: "The provisions of [the Exchange Act] or of any rule or regulation thereunder shall not apply to any person insofar as he transacts a business in securities without the jurisdiction of the United States," unless he does so in violation of regulations promulgated by the Securities and Exchange Commission "to prevent . . . evasion of [the Act]." (The parties have pointed us to no regulation promulgated pursuant to § 30(b).) The Solicitor General argues that "[this] exemption would have no function if the Act did not apply in the first instance to securities transactions that occur abroad." Brief for United States as Amicus Curiae 14.

We are not convinced. . . . The provision seems to us directed at actions abroad that might conceal a domestic violation, or might cause what would otherwise be a domestic violation to escape on a technicality. At most, the Solicitor General's proposed inference is possible; but possible interpretations of statutory language do not override the presumption against extraterritoriality. See *Aramco*, *supra*, at 253.

The Solicitor General also fails to account for § 30(a), which reads in relevant part as follows:

> "It shall be unlawful for any broker or dealer . . . to make use of the mails or of any means or instrumentality of interstate commerce for the purpose of effecting on an exchange not within or subject to the jurisdiction of the United States, any transaction in any security the issuer of which is a resident of, or is organized under the laws of, or has its principal place of business in, a place within or subject to the jurisdiction of the United States, in

contravention of such rules and regulations as the Commission may prescribe. . . ." 15 U.S.C. § 78dd(a).

Subsection 30(a) contains what § 10(b) lacks: a clear statement of extraterritorial effect. Its explicit provision for a specific extraterritorial application would be quite superfluous if the rest of the Exchange Act already applied to transactions on foreign exchanges—and its limitation of that application to securities of domestic issuers would be inoperative. Even if that were not true, when a statute provides for some extraterritorial application, the presumption against extraterritoriality operates to limit that provision to its terms. *See Microsoft Corp. v. AT&T Corp.*, 550 U.S. 437, 455–456 (2007). No one claims that § 30(a) applies here.

The concurrence claims we have impermissibly narrowed the inquiry in evaluating whether a statute applies abroad, citing for that point the dissent in Aramco, see post, at 2891. But we do not say, as the concurrence seems to think, that the presumption against extraterritoriality is a "clear statement rule," ibid., if by that is meant a requirement that a statute say "this law applies abroad." Assuredly context can be consulted as well. But whatever sources of statutory meaning one consults to give "the most faithful reading" of the text, post, at 2892, there is no clear indication of extraterritoriality here. The concurrence does not even try to refute that conclusion, but merely puts forward the same (at best) uncertain indications relied upon by petitioners and the Solicitor General. As the opinion for the Court in Aramco (which we prefer to the dissent) shows, those uncertain indications do not suffice.[8]

In short, there is no affirmative indication in the Exchange Act that § 10(b) applies extraterritorially, and we therefore conclude that it does not.

IV

A

Petitioners argue that the conclusion that § 10(b) does not apply extraterritorially does not resolve this case. They contend that they seek no more than domestic application anyway, since Florida is where HomeSide and its senior executives engaged in the deceptive conduct of manipulating HomeSide's financial models; their complaint also alleged that Race and Hughes made misleading public statements there. This is less an answer to the presumption against extraterritorial application than it is an assertion—a quite valid assertion—that that presumption here (as

[8] The concurrence notes that, post-*Aramco*, Congress provided explicitly for extraterritorial application of Title VII, the statute at issue in *Aramco*. Post, at 2891, n. 6. All this shows is that Congress knows how to give a statute explicit extraterritorial effect—and how to limit that effect to particular applications, which is what the cited amendment did. See Civil Rights Act of 1991, § 109, 105 Stat. 1077.

often) is not self-evidently dispositive, but its application requires further analysis. For it is a rare case of prohibited extraterritorial application that lacks all contact with the territory of the United States. But the presumption against extraterritorial application would be a craven watchdog indeed if it retreated to its kennel whenever some domestic activity is involved in the case. . . .

Applying the same mode of analysis here, we think that the focus of the Exchange Act is not upon the place where the deception originated, but upon purchases and sales of securities in the United States. . . .

The primacy of the domestic exchange is suggested by the very prologue of the Exchange Act, which sets forth as its object "[t]o provide for the regulation of securities exchanges . . . operating in interstate and foreign commerce and through the mails, to prevent inequitable and unfair practices on such exchanges. . ." 48 Stat. 881. We know of no one who thought that the Act was intended to "regulat[e]" foreign securities exchanges—or indeed who even believed that under established principles of international law Congress had the power to do so. The Act's registration requirements apply only to securities listed on national securities exchanges. 15 U.S.C. § 78l (a).

With regard to securities not registered on domestic exchanges, the exclusive focus on domestic purchases and sales is strongly confirmed by § 30(a) and (b), discussed earlier. . . . Under both provisions it is the foreign location of the transaction that establishes (or reflects the presumption of) the Act's inapplicability, absent regulations by the Commission. . . .

Finally, we reject the notion that the Exchange Act reaches conduct in this country affecting exchanges or transactions abroad for the same reason that *Aramco* rejected overseas application of Title VII to all domestically concluded employment contracts or all employment contracts with American employers: The probability of incompatibility with the applicable laws of other countries is so obvious that if Congress intended such foreign application "it would have addressed the subject of conflicts with foreign laws and procedures." 499 U.S., at 256. [The Court noted that the Commonwealth of Australia, the United Kingdom of Great Britain and Northern Ireland, and the Republic of France, and a number of international and foreign organizations had filed amicus briefs opposing extraterritorial application.]

B

The Solicitor General suggests a different test, which petitioners also endorse: "[A] transnational securities fraud violates [§]10(b) when the fraud involves significant conduct in the United States that is material to the fraud's success." Brief for United States as Amicus Curiae 16; see Brief for Petitioners 26. Neither the Solicitor General nor petitioners provide any textual support for this test. . . . It is our function to give the statute the effect its language suggests, however modest that may be; not to extend it to admirable purposes it might be used to achieve. . . .

The Solicitor General points out that the "significant and material conduct" test is in accord with prevailing notions of international comity. If so, that proves that if the United States asserted prescriptive jurisdiction pursuant to the "significant and material conduct" test it would not violate customary international law; but it in no way tends to prove that that is what Congress has done.

Finally, the Solicitor General argues that the Commission has adopted an interpretation similar to the "significant and material conduct" test, and that we should defer to that. . . . Since the Commission's interpretations relied on cases we disapprove, which ignored or discarded the presumption against extraterritoriality, we owe them no deference.

* * *

Section 10(b) reaches the use of a manipulative or deceptive device or contrivance only in connection with the purchase or sale of a security listed on an American stock exchange, and the purchase or sale of any other security in the United States. This case involves no securities listed on a domestic exchange, and all aspects of the purchases complained of by those petitioners who still have live claims occurred outside the United States. Petitioners have therefore failed to state a claim on which relief can be granted. We affirm the dismissal of petitioners' complaint on this ground.

It is so ordered.

[JUSTICE SOTOMAYOR took no part in the consideration or decision of the case. JUSTICE BREYER concurred in part and concurred in the judgment. JUSTICE STEVENS, joined by JUSTICE GINSBURG, concurred in the judgment.]

NOTES

1. *Roots of the Presumption Against Extraterritoriality.* The introduction to this Section distinguished between the *Charming Betsy* principle and the presumption against extraterritoriality. That distinction was not always apparent, and it appears as though what is now recognized as the presumption against extraterritoriality was once more a presumption against "extrajurisdictionality"—rooted in a desire to conform U.S. law to international law restrictions on jurisdiction. John H. Knox, *A Presumption Against Extrajurisdictionality*, 104 AM. J. INT'L L. 351, 362–64 (2010); *see also Hartford Fire Ins. Co. v. California*, 509 U.S. 764, 815 (1993) (Scalia, J., dissenting) ("Though it clearly has constitutional authority to do so, Congress is generally presumed not to have exceeded those customary international-law limits on jurisdiction to prescribe.").

In *Morrison*, while the Supreme Court was willing to note the lack of evident authority under international law as an additional reason to doubt that Congress intended to regulate foreign securities exchanges, it clearly distinguished between what "Congress has done" and what Congress could do "that would not violate customary international law." What, then, is the purpose or purposes of the presumption against extraterritoriality, and does it make a difference? Does that rationale, or rationales, make sense, and promote an appropriate relationship between the United States and international law?

2. *Further Developments in the Presumption—Judicial and Legislative.* Although *Morrison* was decided fairly recently, understanding of the Supreme Court's approach to extraterritoriality was further advanced in *Kiobel v. Royal Dutch Petroleum Co.*, 133 S. Ct. 1659 (2013)—discussed *infra*, this Chapter, Sec. 6—and then in *RJR Nabisco v. European Community*, 136 S. Ct. 2090 (2016). *RJR Nabisco* was distinctive largely in holding that the private right of action under the Racketeer Influenced and Corrupt Organizations Act (RICO) must itself overcome the presumption, even if it sought to vindicate substantive provisions that were extraterritorial in nature. *Id.* at 2105–11. But it also clarified the Court's two-step approach to extraterritoriality. At the first step, courts are to ask—with regard to all manners of statute—whether the presumption has been rebutted by some clear, affirmative indication that it is to apply extraterritoriality. If not, then at the second step, courts are to decide whether the case entails (merely) a domestic application of the statute, in the sense that the relevant conduct occurred in the United States. *Id.* at 2099–2101.

Morrison defended the presumption it described against any inference that might be drawn from the congressional override of its holding in *Aramco* that Title VII lacked extraterritorial effect, suggesting that merely showed that Congress knew how to indicate extraterritorial application. On at least one reading, the holding in *Morrison* was also revisited by Congress. *See SEC v. Traffic Monsoon, LLC*, 245 F.Supp.3d 1275, 1288–94 (D. Utah 2017) (indicating that Congress provided for extraterritorial application of sections of the Securities Exchange Act and Rule 10b–5 immediately in the aftermath of *Morrison*). If Congress frequently provides such indications after a contrary judicial interpretation, does that vindicate or undermine the Court's approach?

3. *Capacity to Override Customary International Law (Redux).* Congress's capacity to override customary international law, introduced *supra*, this Chapter, Sec. 3, is frequently exhibited in the jurisdictional context because the United States has, historically, taken a relatively aggressive view of its jurisdiction. *See L. Littlejohn & Co. v. United States*, 270 U.S. 215, 226–27 (1926) (affirming the power of Congress to make laws permitting the seizure of enemy ships even in contravention of recognized international law); *United States v. Ballestas*, 795 F.3d 138 (D.C. Cir. 2015) (applying the Maritime Drug Law Enforcement Act extraterritorially); *United States v. Ali*, 718 F.3d 929 (D.C. Cir. 2013) (applying Hostage Taking Act extraterritorially). In these and other cases, courts have expressed unwillingness to apply the *Charming Betsy* canon to provisions that were clearly extraterritorial, and paid (probably for

similar reasons) little or no attention to the presumption against extraterritoriality. Suppose you represented the United States, a frequent participant in such cases, and had flexibility to argue that a U.S. court should resolve a defense based on (a) the language of the statute, regardless of customary international law; (b) a modest reading of customary international law's constraints; or (c) an obligation under international law to extend U.S. jurisdiction; or (d) some or all of these. Which would you prefer? If these arguments were presented to you as a judge, which would be most appealing as a basis for decision?

6. HUMAN RIGHTS

International law regarding human rights has become sufficiently complex and diverse—consisting not only of traditionally-derived forms of customary international law, but also multiple widely-ratified, multilateral treaties that influence custom and establish independent treaty-based systems—that it is often the subject of separate law school courses.

The *Restatement (Third)*, excerpted below, provides an influential—but non-exhaustive, and now dated—list of human rights norms established by customary international law, while noting the importance of relating such wrongdoing to State policies or practices. The material that follows then provides a leading example—again, entirely non-exhaustive—of how U.S. statutory and case law incorporates those norms as part of domestic law.

RESTATEMENT OF THE LAW (THIRD), THE FOREIGN RELATIONS LAW OF THE UNITED STATES § 702*

(1987).

§ 702. *Customary International Law of Human Rights*

A state violates international law if, as a matter of state policy, it practices, encourages, or condones

(a) genocide,

(b) slavery or slave trade,

(c) the murder or causing the disappearance of individuals,

(d) torture or other cruel, inhuman, or degrading treatment or punishment,

(e) prolonged arbitrary detention,

(f) systematic racial discrimination, or

(g) a consistent pattern of gross violations of internationally recognized human rights.

Comment:

a. *Scope of customary law of human rights*. This section includes as customary law only those human rights whose status as customary law is generally accepted (as of 1987) and whose scope and content are generally agreed. . . . The list is not necessarily complete, and is not closed: human rights not listed in this section may have achieved the status of customary law, and some rights might achieve that status in the future. . . .

b. *State policy as violation of customary law*. In general, a state is responsible for acts of officials or official bodies, national or local, even if the acts were not authorized by or known to the responsible national authorities, indeed even if expressly forbidden by law, decree or instruction. . . . The violations of human rights cited in this section, however, are violations of customary international law only if practiced, encouraged, or condoned by the government of a state as official policy. . . .

A government may be presumed to have encouraged or condoned acts prohibited by this section if such acts, especially by its officials, have been repeated or notorious and no steps have been taken to prevent them or to punish the perpetrators. That state law prohibits the violation and provides generally effective remedies is strong evidence that the violation is not state policy. A state is not ordinarily responsible under this section for violations of human rights by individuals, such as individual acts of torture or of racial discrimination. A state would be responsible if, as a matter of state policy, it required, encouraged, or condoned such private violations, but mere failure to enact laws prohibiting private violations of human rights would not ordinarily constitute encouragement or condonation. International law requires a state to outlaw genocide, slavery, and the slave trade, and the state would be responsible under this section if it failed to prohibit them or to enforce the prohibition.

Even when a state is not responsible under this section because a violation is not state policy, the state may be responsible under some international agreement that requires the state to prevent the violation. For example, under the Covenant on Civil and Political Rights, a state party is guilty of a violation if any of the acts listed in this section is perpetrated by officials, persons acting under color of law, or other persons for whose acts the state is responsible . . . , even when their acts are contrary to state law or policy.

ALIEN TORT STATUTE

28 U.S.C. § 1350 (2012).

The district courts shall have original jurisdiction of any civil action by an alien for a tort only, committed in violation of the law of nations or a treaty of the United States.

FILARTIGA V. PENA-IRALA

630 F.2d 876 (2d Cir. 1980).

IRVING R. KAUFMAN, CIRCUIT JUDGE:

Upon ratification of the Constitution, the thirteen former colonies were fused into a single nation, one which, in its relations with foreign states, is bound both to observe and construe the accepted norms of international law, formerly known as the law of nations. Under the Articles of Confederation, the several states had interpreted and applied this body of doctrine as a part of their common law, but with the founding of the "more perfect Union" of 1789, the law of nations became preeminently a federal concern.

Implementing the constitutional mandate for national control over foreign relations, the First Congress established original district court jurisdiction over "all causes where an alien sues for a tort only [committed] in violation of the law of nations." Judiciary Act of 1789, ch. 20, § 9(b), 1 Stat. 73, 77 (1789), *codified at* 28 U.S.C. § 1350. Construing this rarely-invoked provision, we hold that deliberate torture perpetrated under color of official authority violates universally accepted norms of the international law of human rights, regardless of the nationality of the parties. Thus, whenever an alleged torturer is found and served with process by an alien within our borders, § 1350 provides federal jurisdiction. Accordingly, we reverse the judgment of the district court dismissing the complaint for want of federal jurisdiction.

I

The appellants, plaintiffs below, are citizens of the Republic of Paraguay. Dr. Joel Filartiga, a physician, describes himself as a longstanding opponent of the government of President Alfredo Stroessner, which has held power in Paraguay since 1954. His daughter, Dolly Filartiga, arrived in the United States in 1978 under a visitor's visa, and has since applied for permanent political asylum. The Filartigas brought this action in the Eastern District of New York against Americo Norberto Pena-Irala (Pena), also a citizen of Paraguay, for wrongfully causing the death of Dr. Filartiga's seventeen-year old son, Joelito. Because the district court dismissed the action for want of subject matter jurisdiction, we must accept as true the allegations contained in the Filartigas' complaint and affidavits for purposes of this appeal.

The appellants contend that on March 29, 1976, Joelito Filartiga was kidnapped and tortured to death by Pena, who was then Inspector General of Police in Asuncion, Paraguay. Later that day, the police brought Dolly Filartiga to Pena's home where she was confronted with the body of her brother, which evidenced marks of severe torture. As she fled, horrified, from the house, Pena followed after her shouting, "Here you have what you have been looking for for so long and what you deserve. Now shut up." The Filartigas claim that Joelito was tortured and killed in retaliation for his father's political activities and beliefs.

Shortly thereafter, Dr. Filartiga commenced a criminal action in the Paraguayan courts against Pena and the police for the murder of his son. As a result, Dr. Filartiga's attorney was arrested and brought to police headquarters where, shackled to a wall, Pena threatened him with death. This attorney, it is alleged, has since been disbarred without just cause.

During the course of the Paraguayan criminal proceeding, which is apparently still pending after four years, another man, Hugo Duarte, confessed to the murder. Duarte, who was a member of the Pena household, claimed that he had discovered his wife and Joelito *in flagrante delicto,* and that the crime was one of passion. The Filartigas have submitted a photograph of Joelito's corpse showing injuries they believe refute this claim. Dolly Filartiga, moreover, has stated that she will offer evidence of three independent autopsies demonstrating that her brother's death "was the result of professional methods of torture." Despite his confession, Duarte, we are told, has never been convicted or sentenced in connection with the crime.

In July of 1978, Pena sold his house in Paraguay and entered the United States under a visitor's visa. He was accompanied by Juana Bautista Fernandez Villalba, who had lived with him in Paraguay. The couple remained in the United States beyond the term of their visas, and were living in Brooklyn, New York, when Dolly Filartiga, who was then living in Washington, D.C., learned of their presence. Acting on information provided by Dolly, the Immigration and Naturalization Service arrested Pena and his companion, both of whom were subsequently ordered deported on April 5, 1979 following a hearing. They had then resided in the United States for more than nine months.

Almost immediately, Dolly caused Pena to be served with a summons and civil complaint at the Brooklyn Navy Yard, where he was being held pending deportation. The complaint alleged that Pena had wrongfully caused Joelito's death by torture and sought compensatory and punitive damages of $10,000,000. The Filartigas also sought to enjoin Pena's deportation to ensure his availability for testimony at trial. The cause of action is stated as arising under "wrongful death statutes; the U.N. Charter; the Universal Declaration on Human Rights; the U.N.

Declaration Against Torture; the American Declaration of the Rights and Duties of Man; and other pertinent declarations, documents and practices constituting the customary international law of human rights and the law of nations," as well as 28 U.S.C. § 1350, Article II, sec. 2 and the Supremacy Clause of the U.S. Constitution. Jurisdiction is claimed under the general federal question provision, 28 U.S.C. § 1331 and, principally on this appeal, under the Alien Tort Statute, 28 U.S.C. § 1350.

Judge Nickerson stayed the order of deportation, and Pena immediately moved to dismiss the complaint on the grounds that subject matter jurisdiction was absent and for *forum non conveniens.* On the jurisdictional issue, there has been no suggestion that Pena claims diplomatic immunity from suit. The Filartigas submitted the affidavits of a number of distinguished international legal scholars, who stated unanimously that the law of nations prohibits absolutely the use of torture as alleged in the complaint. Pena, in support of his motion to dismiss on the ground of *forum non conveniens,* submitted the affidavit of his Paraguayan counsel, Jose Emilio Gorostiaga, who averred that Paraguayan law provides a full and adequate civil remedy for the wrong alleged. Dr. Filartiga has not commenced such an action, however, believing that further resort to the courts of his own country would be futile.

Judge Nickerson heard argument on the motion to dismiss on May 14, 1979, and on May 15 dismissed the complaint on jurisdictional grounds. The district judge recognized the strength of appellants' argument that official torture violates an emerging norm of customary international law. Nonetheless, he felt constrained by dicta contained in two recent opinions of this Court, *Dreyfus v. von Finck,* 534 F.2d 24 (2d Cir.), *cert. denied,* 429 U.S. 835 (1976); *IIT v. Vencap, Ltd.,* 519 F.2d 1001 (2d Cir.1975), to construe narrowly "the law of nations," as employed in § 1350, as excluding that law which governs a state's treatment of its own citizens.

The district court continued the stay of deportation for forty-eight hours while appellants applied for further stays. These applications were denied by a panel of this Court on May 22, 1979, and by the Supreme Court two days later. Shortly thereafter, Pena and his companion returned to Paraguay.

II

Appellants rest their principal argument in support of federal jurisdiction upon the Alien Tort Statute, 28 U.S.C. § 1350, which provides: "The district courts shall have original jurisdiction of any civil action by an alien for a tort only, committed in violation of the law of nations or a treaty of the United States." Since appellants do not contend that their action arises directly under a treaty of the United States,[7] a threshold question on the jurisdictional issue is whether the conduct alleged violates the law of nations. In light of the universal condemnation of torture in numerous international agreements, and the renunciation of torture as an instrument of official policy by virtually all of the nations of the world (in principle if not in practice), we find that an act of torture committed by a state official against one held in detention violates established norms of the international law of human rights, and hence the law of nations.

The Supreme Court has enumerated the appropriate sources of international law. The law of nations "may be ascertained by consulting the works of jurists, writing professedly on public law; or by the general usage and practice of nations; or by judicial decisions recognizing and enforcing that law." *United States v. Smith,* 18 U.S. (5 Wheat.) 153, 160–61 (1820). . . .

The requirement [indicated in *The Paquete Habana,* 175 U.S. 677, 694 (1900)] that a rule command the "general assent of civilized nations" to become binding upon them all is a stringent one. Were this not so, the courts of one nation might feel free to impose idiosyncratic legal rules upon others, in the name of applying international law. Thus, in *Banco Nacional de Cuba v. Sabbatino,* 376 U.S. 398 (1964), the Court declined to pass on the validity of the Cuban government's expropriation of a foreign-owned corporation's assets, noting the sharply conflicting views on the issue propounded by the capital-exporting, capital-importing, socialist and capitalist nations. *Id.* at 428–30.

The case at bar presents us with a situation diametrically opposed to the conflicted state of law that confronted the *Sabbatino* Court. Indeed, to paraphrase that Court's statement, *id.* at 428, there are few, if any, issues in international law today on which opinion seems to be so united as the limitations on a state's power to torture persons held in its custody.

The United Nations Charter (a treaty of the United States, *see* 59 Stat. 1033 (1945)) makes it clear that in this modern age a state's treatment of its own citizens is a matter of international concern. It provides:

> With a view to the creation of conditions of stability and well-being which are necessary for peaceful and friendly relations among nations . . . the United Nations shall promote . . . universal respect for, and observance of, human rights and fundamental freedoms for all without distinctions as to race, sex, language or religion.

---

[7] Appellants "associate themselves with" the argument of some of the *amici curiae* that their claim arises directly under a treaty of the United States, Brief for Appellants at 23 n.*, but nonetheless primarily rely upon treaties and other international instruments as evidence of an emerging norm of customary international law, rather then independent sources of law.

Id. Art. 55. And further:

> All members pledge themselves to take joint and separate action in cooperation with the Organization for the achievement of the purposes set forth in Article 55.

Id. Art. 56.

While this broad mandate has been held not to be wholly self-executing, *Hitai v. Immigration and Naturalization Service,* 343 F.2d 466, 468 (2d Cir. 1965), this observation alone does not end our inquiry. For although there is no universal agreement as to the precise extent of the "human rights and fundamental freedoms" guaranteed to all by the Charter, there is at present no dissent from the view that the guaranties include, at a bare minimum, the right to be free from torture. This prohibition has become part of customary international law, as evidenced and defined by the Universal Declaration of Human Rights, General Assembly Resolution 217 (III)(A) (Dec. 10, 1948) which states, in the plainest of terms, "no one shall be subjected to torture."[10] The General Assembly has declared that the Charter precepts embodied in this Universal Declaration "constitute basic principles of international law." G.A. Res. 2625 (XXV) (Oct. 24, 1970).

Particularly relevant is the Declaration on the Protection of All Persons from Being Subjected to Torture, General Assembly Resolution 3452, 30 U.N. GAOR Supp. (No. 34) 91, U.N.Doc. A/1034 (1975). . . . The Declaration expressly prohibits any state from permitting the dastardly and totally inhuman act of torture. . . .

These U.N. declarations are significant because they specify with great precision the obligations of member nations under the Charter. Since their adoption, "[m]embers can no longer contend that they do not know what human rights they promised in the Charter to promote." Sohn, "A Short History of United Nations Documents on Human Rights," in *The United Nations and Human Rights, 18th Report of the Commission* (Commission to Study the Organization of Peace ed. 1968). Moreover, a U.N. Declaration is, according to one authoritative definition, "a formal and solemn instrument, suitable for rare occasions when principles of great and lasting importance are being enunciated." 34 U.N. ESCOR, Supp. (No. 8) 15, U.N. Doc. E/cn.4/1/610 (1962) (memorandum of Office of Legal Affairs, U.N. Secretariat). Accordingly, it has been observed that the Universal Declaration of Human Rights "no longer fits into the dichotomy of 'binding treaty' against 'non-binding pronouncement,' but is rather an authoritative statement of the international community." E. Schwelb, *Human Rights and the International Community* 70 (1964). Thus, a Declaration creates an expectation of adherence, and "insofar as the expectation is gradually

---

[10] Eighteen nations have incorporated the Universal Declaration into their own constitutions. 48 *Revue Internationale de Droit Penal* Nos. 3 & 4, at 211 (1977).

justified by State practice, a declaration may by custom become recognized as laying down rules binding upon the States." 34 U.N. ESCOR, *supra.* Indeed, several commentators have concluded that the Universal Declaration has become, *in toto,* a part of binding, customary international law. Nayar, *supra,* at 816–17; Waldock, "Human Rights in Contemporary International Law and the Significance of the European Convention," *Int'l & Comp. L.Q.,* Supp. Publ. No. 11 at 15 (1965).

Turning to the act of torture, we have little difficulty discerning its universal renunciation in the modern usage and practice of nations. *Smith, supra,* 18 U.S. (5 Wheat.) at 160–61. The international consensus surrounding torture has found expression in numerous international treaties and accords. *E.g., American Convention on Human Rights,* Art. 5, OAS Treaty Series No. 36 at 1, OAS Off. Rec. OEA/Ser 4 v/II 23, doc. 21, rev. 2 (English ed., 1975) ("No one shall be subjected to torture or to cruel, inhuman or degrading punishment or treatment"); International Covenant on Civil and Political Rights, U.N. General Assembly Res. 2200 (XXI)A, U.N. Doc. A/6316 (Dec. 16, 1966) (identical language); European Convention for the Protection of Human Rights and Fundamental Freedoms, Art. 3, Council of Europe, European Treaty Series No. 5 (1968), 213 U.N.T.S. 211 (*semble*). The substance of these international agreements is reflected in modern municipal i.e. national law as well. Although torture was once a routine concomitant of criminal interrogations in many nations, during the modern and hopefully more enlightened era it has been universally renounced. . . . "There is no doubt that these rights are often violated; but virtually all governments acknowledge their validity." Department of State, Country Reports on Human Rights for 1979, published as Joint Comm. Print, House Comm. on Foreign Affairs, and Senate Comm. on Foreign Relations, 96th Cong. 2d Sess. (Feb. 4, 1980), Introduction at 1. We have been directed to no assertion by any contemporary state of a right to torture its own or another nation's citizens. Indeed, United States diplomatic contacts confirm the universal abhorrence with which torture is viewed:

> In exchanges between United States embassies and all foreign states with which the United States maintains relations, it has been the Department of State's general experience that no government has asserted a right to torture its own nationals. Where reports of torture elicit some credence, a state usually responds by denial or, less frequently, by asserting that the conduct was unauthorized or constituted rough treatment short of torture.[15]

[15] The fact that the prohibition of torture is often honored in the breach does not diminish its binding effect as a norm of international law. As one commentator has put it, "The best evidence for the existence of international law is that every actual State recognizes that it does exist and that it is itself under an obligation to observe it. States often violate international law, just as individuals often violate municipal law; but no more than individuals do States defend their

Memorandum of the United States as Amicus Curiae at 16 n.34.

Having examined the sources from which customary international law is derived—the usage of nations, judicial opinions and the works of jurists—we conclude that official torture is now prohibited by the law of nations. The prohibition is clear and unambiguous, and admits of no distinction between treatment of aliens and citizens. Accordingly, we must conclude that the dictum in *Dreyfus v. von Finck, supra,* 534 F.2d at 31, to the effect that "violations of international law do not occur when the aggrieved parties are nationals of the acting state," is clearly out of tune with the current usage and practice of international law. The treaties and accords cited above, as well as the express foreign policy of our own government, all make it clear that international law confers fundamental rights upon all people vis-a-vis their own governments. While the ultimate scope of those rights will be a subject for continuing refinement and elaboration, we hold that the right to be free from torture is now among them. We therefore turn to the question whether the other requirements for jurisdiction are met.

III

Appellee submits that even if the tort alleged is a violation of modern international law, federal jurisdiction may not be exercised consistent with the dictates of Article III of the Constitution. The claim is without merit. Common law courts of general jurisdiction regularly adjudicate transitory tort claims between individuals over whom they exercise personal jurisdiction, wherever the tort occurred. Moreover, as part of an articulated scheme of federal control over external affairs, Congress provided, in the first Judiciary Act, § 9(b), 1 Stat. 73, 77 (1789), for federal jurisdiction over suits by aliens where principles of international law are in issue. The constitutional basis for the Alien Tort Statute is the law of nations, which has always been part of the federal common law. . . .

. . . A case properly "aris(es) under the . . . laws of the United States" for Article III purposes if grounded upon statutes enacted by Congress or upon the common law of the United States. . . . The law of nations forms an integral part of the common law, and a review of the history surrounding the adoption of the Constitution demonstrates that it became a part of the common law *of the United States* upon the adoption of the Constitution. Therefore, the enactment of the Alien Tort Statute was authorized by Article III. . . .

As ratified, the judiciary article contained no express reference to cases arising under the law of nations. Indeed, the only express reference to that body of law is contained in Article I, sec. 8, cl. 10, which grants to the Congress the power to "define and punish . . . offenses against the law of

violations by claiming that they are above the law." J. Brierly, The Outlook for International Law 4–5 (Oxford 1944).

nations." Appellees seize upon this circumstance and advance the proposition that the law of nations forms a part of the laws of the United States only to the extent that Congress has acted to define it. This extravagant claim is amply refuted by the numerous decisions applying rules of international law uncodified in any act of Congress. *E. g., Ware v. Hylton*, 3 U.S. (3 Dall.) 199 (1796); *The Paquete Habana, supra*, 175 U.S. 677; *Sabbatino, supra*, 376 U.S. 398 (1964). A similar argument was offered to and rejected by the Supreme Court in *United States v. Smith, supra,* 18 U.S. (5 Wheat.) 153, 158–60, and we reject it today. As John Jay wrote in *The Federalist* No. 3, at 22 (1 Bourne ed. 1901), "Under the national government, treaties and articles of treaties, as well as the laws of nations, will always be expounded in one sense and executed in the same manner, whereas adjudications on the same points and questions in the thirteen states will not always accord or be consistent." Federal jurisdiction over cases involving international law is clear.

Thus, it was hardly a radical initiative for Chief Justice Marshall to state in *The Nereide*, 13 U.S. (9 Cranch) 388, 422 (1815), that in the absence of a congressional enactment, United States courts are "bound by the law of nations, which is a part of the law of the land." These words were echoed in *The Paquete Habana, supra*, 175 U.S. at 700: "(i)nternational law is part of our law, and must be ascertained and administered by the courts of justice of appropriate jurisdiction, as often as questions of right depending upon it are duly presented for their determination."

The Filartigas urge that 28 U.S.C. § 1350 be treated as an exercise of Congress's power to define offenses against the law of nations. While such a reading is possible, *see Lincoln Mills v. Textile Workers*, 353 U.S. 448 (1957) (jurisdictional statute authorizes judicial explication of federal common law), we believe it is sufficient here to construe the Alien Tort Statute, not as granting new rights to aliens, but simply as opening the federal courts for adjudication of the rights already recognized by international law. The statute nonetheless does inform our analysis of Article III, for we recognize that questions of jurisdiction "must be considered part of an organic growth—part of an evolutionary process," and that the history of the judiciary article gives meaning to its pithy phrases. *Romero v. International Terminal Operating Co.*, 358 U.S. 354, 360 (1959). The Framers' overarching concern that control over international affairs be vested in the new national government to safeguard the standing of the United States among the nations of the world therefore reinforces the result we reach today.

Although the Alien Tort Statute has rarely been the basis for jurisdiction during its long history, in light of the foregoing discussion, there can be little doubt that this action is properly brought in federal court.[22] This is undeniably an action by an alien, for a tort only, committed in violation of the law of nations. The paucity of suits successfully maintained under the section is readily attributable to the statute's requirement of alleging a "*violation* of the law of nations" (emphasis supplied) at the jurisdictional threshold. Courts have, accordingly, engaged in a more searching preliminary review of the merits than is required, for example, under the more flexible "arising under" formulation. . . . Thus, the narrowing construction that the Alien Tort Statute has previously received reflects the fact that earlier cases did not involve such well-established, universally recognized norms of international law that are here at issue. . . .

Since federal jurisdiction may properly be exercised over the Filartigas' claim, the action must be remanded for further proceedings.

NOTES

1. *Rediscovery of the Alien Tort Statute.* The Alien Tort Statute, or ATS (also known as the Alien Tort Claims Act or ATCA), was a provision of the First Judiciary Act of 1789, ch. 20, § 9, 1 Stat. 73, 77 (1789). Today it is codified at 28 U.S.C. § 1350 (2012). Prior to the *Filartiga* case, the ATS had almost never been invoked. Judge Friendly famously referred to the ATS as "a kind of legal Lohengrin," *IIT v. Vencap, Ltd.*, 519 F.2d 1001 (2d Cir. 1975), meaning that, although it has been with us since the founding of the republic, no one seems to know from whence it came. For efforts to explain its origins, see Anne-Marie Burley, *The Alien Tort Statute and the Judiciary Act of 1789: A Badge of Honor*, 83 AM. J. INT'L L. 461 (1989); William R. Casto, *The Federal Courts' Protective Jurisdiction Over Torts Committed in Violation of the Law of Nations*, 18 CONN. L. REV. 467 (1986). What explanation does *Filartiga* provide for the statute's long neglect? Do you find that explanation persuasive?

The *Filartiga* case infused the ATS with renewed importance, signaling a watershed moment for the human rights movement by raising the possibility of using U.S. courts to bring individuals to account for egregious human rights crimes committed anywhere in the world. In *Filartiga*, the plaintiffs were aliens, the defendant was an alien, and the conduct at issue occurred abroad; the only direct connection to the United States was that, at the time the case was filed, both the plaintiffs and the defendant were present in the United States. This signaled both the potential of the ATS and its potential vulnerability.

2. *Treaties, Custom, and Post-*Filartiga *Cases.* The ATS refers to violations of either treaties of the United States or the "law of nations." While *Filartiga* noted (in its footnote 10) the possibility of basing a claim on a treaty, the action was filed before the United States ratified the Convention Against

[22] We recognize that our reasoning might also sustain jurisdiction under the general federal question provision, 28 U.S.C. § 1331. We prefer, however, to rest our decision upon the Alien Tort Statute, in light of that provision's close coincidence with the jurisdictional facts presented in this case. *See Romero v. International Terminal Operating Co.,* 358 U.S. 354 (1959).

Torture and Other Cruel, Inhuman, or Degrading Treatment or Punishment, Dec. 10, 1984, S. Treaty Doc. No. 100–20 (1988), 1465 U.N.T.S. 85. Following Chapter 3, try to reflect on the relative strengths and weaknesses of relying on treaties rather than customary international law.

As to customary international law, do you think the Second Circuit engaged in a careful analysis of whether customary international law prohibited State-sponsored torture, or do you see flaws in the approach? Note the different sources relied upon by the court. Does this provide a template for how U.S. courts can engage in an analysis of customary human rights law? Does it seem similar to the Supreme Court's approach in *The Paquete Habana*?

Following *Filartiga*, numerous ATS cases were filed, some resulting in the award of civil damages. The courts generally required that the international norms alleged to have been violated be specific, universal, and mandatory; some invoked the *Restatement (Third)* § 702, excerpted above, in evaluating whether a human rights norm was firmly embedded in customary international law, a starting point not available at the time of the *Filartiga* decision. For each of the human rights listed in § 702, it was possible to find a U.S. court case construing that right under the ATS, including genocide, see, e.g., *Kadic v. Karadzic*, 70 F.3d 232 (2d Cir. 1995); slavery or forced labor, see, e.g., *Doe I v. Unocal Corp.*, 395 F.3d 932 (9th Cir. 2002), *vacated by consent of parties*, 403 F.3d 708 (9th Cir. 2005) (Mem); disappearance of persons, see, e.g., *Forti v. Suarez-Mason*, 694 F. Supp. 707 (N.D. Cal. 1988); cruel, degrading, or inhuman treatment, see, e.g., *Abebe-Jira v. Negewo*, 72 F.3d 844 (11th Cir. 1996); and arbitrary detention, see, e.g., *Paul v. Avril*, 901 F. Supp. 330 (S.D. Fla. 1994). Consistent with § 702, the comments to which indicated that the "list is not necessarily complete, and is not closed," U.S. courts also considered ATS actions for violations of other widely recognized human rights, such as war crimes, see, e.g., *Mehinovic v. Vuckovic*, 198 F. Supp. 2d 1322 (N.D. Ga. 2002), and crimes against humanity, see, e.g., *Estate of Cabello v. Fernandez-Larios*, 157 F. Supp. 2d 1345 (S.D. Fla. 2001).

3. *Human Rights Violations by Private Actors*. As § 702 of the *Restatement (Third)* cautioned, some human rights norms may only be invoked directly against government actors; *Filartiga* itself involved the conduct of a government official. Nonetheless, U.S. courts have held that ATS claims may sometimes be brought against private actors. For example, in *Kadic v. Karadzic*, 70 F.3d 232 (2d Cir. 1995), the Second Circuit found certain heinous acts to be of such "universal concern" that they constitute violations of customary international law not only when they are committed by State actors, but also when they are committed by private individuals. *Id.* at 239–40. In particular, the Second Circuit determined that acts of piracy, slave trading, war crimes, and genocide violate customary international law regardless of whether they are undertaken by State or private actors, whereas acts of torture and "summary execution" constitute violations of customary international law only when committed by State officials or under color of law. *Id.* at 239–43. As noted below, the liability of private actors is also affected by lingering questions concerning corporate and secondary liability, as well as extraterritoriality.

4. *Resistance to ATS Claims.* In the wake of *Filartiga,* some courts and scholars balked at what they viewed as an objectionable breadth to the resurrected statute. *See, e.g., Tel-Oren v. Libyan Arab Republic,* 726 F.2d 774 (D.C. Cir. 1984) (per curiam); Curtis Bradley, *The Costs of International Human Rights Litigation,* 2 CHI. J. INT'L L. 457 (2001).

To some extent, concerns were addressed through the use of conventional defenses employed in foreign-relations and other litigation. For example, some claims were dismissed as time-barred, see, e.g., *Iwanowa v. Ford Motor Co.*, 67 F.Supp.2d 424 (D.N.J. 1999); on grounds of forum non conveniens, see, e.g., *Flores v. Southern Peru Copper Corp.*, 253 F.Supp.2d 510 (S.D.N.Y. 2002); based on the political question doctrine, see, e.g., *United States v. Noriega,* 746 F.Supp. 1506 (S.D. Fla. 1990); the Act of State doctrine, see, e.g., *Sarei v. Rio Tinto PLC,* 221 F.Supp.2d 1116 (C.D.Cal. 2002), *vacated for further consideration,* 487 F.3d 1193 (9th Cir. 2007); diplomatic immunity, see, e.g., *Ahmed v. Hoque,* 2002 WL 1964806 (S.D.N.Y. Aug. 23, 2002); or sovereign immunity. *See, e.g., Argentine Republic v. Amerada Hess Shipping Corp.*, 488 U.S. 428 (1989); *Hwang Geum Joo v. Japan,* 332 F.3d 679 (D.C. Cir. 2003). Chapter 7 addresses some of these issues in greater depth. On the merits, courts proved willing to challenge whether an alleged norm of customary international law genuinely existed. *See, e.g., Hamid v. Price Waterhouse,* 51 F.3d 1411, 1418 (9th Cir. 1995) (determining that "garden variety" fraud was not a violation of the law of nations); *Flores v. Southern Peru Copper Corp.*, 343 F.3d 140, 172 (2d Cir. 2003) (determining that environmental torts are not a violation of customary international law).

Within this case law lurked fundamental, unresolved questions regarding the scope of the ATS. One issue concerned whether the ATS was solely a jurisdictional statute or whether it also created a private cause of action. For some taking the jurisdictional view, this entailed a further requirement that Congress needed to have adopted additional legislation implementing the relevant human rights norm. *See Tel-Oren v. Libya,* 726 F.2d 774, 798–99 (D.C. Cir. 1984) (Bork, J., concurring); *Al Odah v. United States,* 321 F.3d 1134, 1145–47 (D.C. Cir. 2003) (Randolph, J., concurring) (suggesting that implying a cause of action "would be to grant aliens greater rights in the nation's courts than American citizens enjoy"), *rev'd on other grounds, Rasul v. Bush,* 542 U.S. 466 (2004). *But see, e.g., In re Estate of Ferdinand Marcos, Human Rights Litig.*, 25 F.3d 1467, 1475 (9th Cir. 1994) ("We thus join the Second Circuit in concluding that the [ATCA] creates a cause of action for violations of specific, universal and obligatory international human rights standards[.]").

A related question—particularly relevant if the ATS was deemed to be jurisdictional only—was whether the "law of nations" was a part of U.S. law that could provide such a cause of action. Here a key issue was the effect of the Supreme Court's decision in *Erie R. Co. v. Tompkins,* 304 U.S. 64 (1938), on the "law of nations" in U.S. law. As noted *supra,* this Chapter Sec. 2, some commentators observed that in *Erie* the Court denied the existence of any "general" federal common law, leading them to the view that federal courts could apply the law of nations only when properly authorized, such as in the context of federal maritime jurisdiction. Others saw customary international law as firmly grounded in U.S. law and as one of the areas of federal common law that survived *Erie*.

These issues were addressed by the Supreme Court in 2004 and then, much more indirectly, in 2013.

SOSA V. ALVAREZ-MACHAIN

542 U.S. 692 (2004).

[Humberto Alvarez-Machain (Alvarez) was indicted by a federal grand jury for the torture and murder in Mexico of a U.S. Drug Enforcement Administration (DEA) agent. After attempts by the U.S. government to secure the assistance of the Mexican government failed, the DEA arranged for Mexican nationals, including defendant Jose Francisco Sosa, to kidnap and deliver Alvarez to the United States to stand trial. Alvarez was brought to Texas and turned over to DEA agents. In 1992, the Supreme Court rejected Alvarez's argument that the kidnapping violated an extradition treaty between the United States and Mexico, and remanded the case for trial. *United States v. Alvarez-Machain*, 504 U.S. 655 (1992).

Alvarez was acquitted in the ensuing criminal trial. He subsequently brought suit against the United States under the Federal Tort Claims Act, or FTCA. (This was dismissed by the district court, which dismissal was then reversed by the court of appeals, but the Supreme Court ultimately determined the clam should be dismissed.) He also sued Sosa for violating the law of nations under the ATS. The district court found for Alvarez on the ATS claim. A three-judge panel affirmed, 266 F.3d 1045 (9th Cir. 2001), and the court sitting *en banc* agreed, 331 F.3d 604 (9th Cir. 2003).]

JUSTICE SOUTER delivered the opinion of the Court.

The two issues are whether respondent Alvarez-Machain's allegation that the Drug Enforcement Administration instigated his abduction from Mexico for criminal trial in the United States supports a claim against the Government under the Federal Tort Claims Act (FTCA or Act), 28 U.S.C. §§ 1346(b)(1), 2671–2680, and whether he may recover under the Alien Tort Statute (ATS), 28 U.S.C. § 1350. We hold that he is not entitled to a remedy under either statute. . . .

III

Alvarez . . . brought an action under the ATS against petitioner, Sosa, who argues (as does the United States supporting him) that there is no relief under the ATS because the statute does no more than vest federal courts with jurisdiction, neither creating nor authorizing the courts to recognize any particular right of action without further congressional action. Although we agree the statute is in terms only jurisdictional, we think that at the time of enactment the jurisdiction enabled federal courts to hear claims in a very limited category defined by the law of nations and recognized at common law. We do not believe, however, that the limited, implicit sanction to entertain the handful of international law *cum* common law claims understood in 1789 should be taken as authority to recognize the right of action asserted by Alvarez here.

A

. . . The first Congress passed [the ATS] as part of the Judiciary Act of 1789, in providing that the new federal district courts "shall also have cognizance, concurrent with the courts of the several States, or the circuit courts, as the case may be, of all causes where an alien sues for a tort only in violation of the law of nations or a treaty of the United States." Act of Sept. 24, 1789, ch. 20, § 9, 1 Stat. 79.[10]

The parties and *amici* here advance radically different historical interpretations of this terse provision. Alvarez says that the ATS was creation of a new cause of action for torts in violation of international law. We think that reading is implausible. As enacted in 1789, the ATS gave the district courts "cognizance" of certain causes of action, and the term bespoke a grant of jurisdiction, not power to mold substantive law. *See, e.g.,* The Federalist No. 81, pp. 447, 451 (J. Cooke ed. 1961) (A. Hamilton) (using "jurisdiction" interchangeably with "cognizance"). The fact that the ATS was placed in § 9 of the Judiciary Act, a statute otherwise exclusively concerned with federal-court jurisdiction, is itself support for its strictly jurisdictional nature. Nor would the distinction between jurisdiction and cause of action have been elided by the drafters of the Act or those who voted on it. . . . In sum, we think the statute was intended as jurisdictional in the sense of addressing the power of the courts to entertain cases concerned with a certain subject.

But holding the ATS jurisdictional raises a new question, this one about the interaction between the ATS at the time of its enactment and the ambient law of the era. Sosa would have it that the ATS was stillborn because there could be no claim for relief without a further statute expressly authorizing adoption of causes of action. *Amici* professors of federal jurisdiction and legal history take a different tack, that federal courts could entertain claims once the jurisdictional grant was on the books, because torts in violation of the law of nations would have been recognized within the common law of the time. . . . We think history and practice give the edge to this latter position.

---

[10] The statute has been slightly modified on a number of occasions since its original enactment. It now reads in its entirety: "The district courts shall have original jurisdiction of any civil action by an alien for a tort only, committed in violation of the law of nations or a treaty of the United States." 28 U.S.C. § 1350.

1

"When the *United States* declared their independence, they were bound to receive the law of nations, in its modern state of purity and refinement." *Ware v. Hylton,* 3 U.S. (3 Dall.) 199, 281 . . . (1796) (Wilson, J.). In the years of the early Republic, this law of nations comprised two principal elements, the first covering the general norms governing the behavior of national states with each other: *"the science which teaches the rights subsisting between nations or states, and the obligations correspondent to those rights,"* E. de Vattel, The Law of Nations, Preliminaries § 3 (J. Chitty et al. transl. and ed. 1883) (hereinafter Vattel) (footnote omitted), or "that code of public instruction which defines the rights and prescribes the duties of nations, in their intercourse with each other," 1 Kent Commentaries on American Law *1. This aspect of the law of nations thus occupied the executive and legislative domains, not the judicial. *See* 4 W. Blackstone, Commentaries on the Laws of England 68 (1769) (hereinafter Commentaries) ("[O]ffenses against" the law of nations are "principally incident to whole states or nations").

The law of nations included a second, more pedestrian element, however, that did fall within the judicial sphere, as a body of judge-made law regulating the conduct of individuals situated outside domestic boundaries and consequently carrying an international savor. To Blackstone, the law of nations in this sense was implicated "in mercantile questions, such as bills of exchange and the like; in all marine causes, relating to freight, average, demurrage, insurances, bottomry . . .; [and] in all disputes relating to prizes, to shipwrecks, to hostages, and ransom bills." *Id.,* at 67. The law merchant emerged from the customary practices of international traders and admiralty required its own transnational regulation. And it was the law of nations in this sense that our precursors spoke about when the Court explained the status of coast fishing vessels in wartime grew from "ancient usage among civilized nations, beginning centuries ago, and gradually ripening into a rule of international law. . . ." *The Paquete Habana,* 175 U.S. 677, 686 . . . (1900).

There was, finally, a sphere in which these rules binding individuals for the benefit of other individuals overlapped with the norms of state relationships. Blackstone referred to it when he mentioned three specific offenses against the law of nations addressed by the criminal law of England: violation of safe conducts, infringement of the rights of ambassadors, and piracy. 4 Commentaries 68. An assault against an ambassador, for example, impinged upon the sovereignty of the foreign nation and if not adequately redressed could rise to an issue of war. *See* Vattel 463–464. It was this narrow set of violations of the law of nations, admitting of a judicial remedy and at the same time threatening serious consequences in international affairs, that was probably on [the] minds of the men who drafted the ATS with its reference to tort. . . .

3

Although Congress modified the draft of what became the Judiciary Act, *see generally* Warren, New Light on the History of the Federal Judiciary Act of 1789, 37 Harv. L. Rev. 49 (1923), it made hardly any changes to the provisions on aliens, including what became the ATS, *see* Casto, Law of Nations 498. There is no record of congressional discussion about private actions that might be subject to the jurisdictional provision, or about any need for further legislation to create private remedies; there is no record even of debate on the section. Given the poverty of drafting history, modern commentators have necessarily concentrated on the text, remarking on the innovative use of the word "tort," *see, e.g.,* Sweeney, A Tort only in Violation of the Law of Nations, 18 Hastings Int'l & Comp. L. Rev. 445 (1995) (arguing that "tort" refers to the law of prize), and the statute's mixture of terms expansive ("all suits"), *see, e.g.,* Casto, Law of Nations 500, and restrictive ("for a tort only"), *see, e.g.,* Randall, at 28–31 (limiting suits to torts, as opposed to commercial actions, especially by British plaintiffs).[12] The historical scholarship has also placed the ATS within the competition between federalist and antifederalist forces over the national role in foreign relations. *Id.,* at 22–23 (nonexclusiveness of federal jurisdiction under the ATS may reflect compromise). But despite considerable scholarly attention, it is fair to say that a consensus understanding of what Congress intended has proven elusive.

Still, the history does tend to support two propositions. First, there is every reason to suppose that the First Congress did not pass the ATS as a jurisdictional convenience to be placed on the shelf for use by a future Congress or state legislature that might, someday, authorize the creation of causes of action or itself decide to make some element of the law of nations actionable for the benefit of foreigners. The anxieties of the preconstitutional period cannot be ignored easily enough to think that the statute was not meant to have a practical effect. Consider that the principal draftsman of the ATS was apparently Oliver Ellsworth,[13] previously a member of the Continental Congress that had passed the 1781 resolution [calling on the States to enact laws punishing "infractions of the immunities of ambassadors and other public ministers, authorised and received as such by the United States in Congress assembled," targeting in particular "violence offered to their persons, houses, carriages and property," 21 Journal of the Continental Cong. 1136–37 (1784) (G. Hunt ed. 1912),] and a member of the Connecticut Legislature that made good on

[12] The restriction may have served the different purpose of putting foreigners on notice that they would no longer be able to prosecute their own criminal cases in federal court. *Compare, e.g.,* 3 Commentaries 160 (victims could start prosecutions) with the Judiciary Act § 35. (creating the office of the district attorney). *Cf.* 1 Op. Atty. Gen. 41, 42 (1794) (British consul could not himself initiate criminal prosecution, but could provide evidence to the grand jury.)

[13] The ATS appears in Ellsworth's handwriting in the original version of the bill in the National Archives. Casto, Law of Nations 498, n. 169.

that congressional request. *See generally* W. Brown, The Life of Oliver Ellsworth (1905). Consider, too, that the First Congress was attentive enough to the law of nations to recognize certain offenses expressly as criminal, including the three mentioned by Blackstone. *See* An Act for the Punishment of Certain Crimes Against the United States, § 8, 1 Stat. 113–114 (murder or robbery, or other capital crimes, punishable as piracy if committed on the high seas), and § 28, *id.,* at 118 (violation of safe conducts and assaults against ambassadors punished by imprisonment and fines described as "infract[ions of] the law of nations"). It would have been passing strange for Ellsworth and this very Congress to vest federal courts expressly with jurisdiction to entertain civil causes brought by aliens alleging violations of the law of nations, but to no effect whatever until the Congress should take further action. There is too much in the historical record to believe that Congress would have enacted the ATS only to leave it lying fallow indefinitely.

The second inference to be drawn from the history is that Congress intended the ATS to furnish jurisdiction for a relatively modest set of actions alleging violations of the law of nations. Uppermost in the legislative mind appears to have been offenses against ambassadors, *see id.,* at 118; violations of safe conduct were probably understood to be actionable, *ibid.,* and individual actions arising out of prize captures and piracy may well have also been contemplated, *id.,* at 113–114. But the common law appears to have understood only those three of the hybrid variety as definite and actionable, or at any rate, to have assumed only a very limited set of claims. As Blackstone had put it, "offences against this law [of nations] are principally incident to whole states or nations," and not individuals seeking relief in court. 4 Commentaries 68. . . .

In sum, although the ATS is a jurisdictional statute creating no new causes of action, the reasonable inference from the historical materials is that the statute was intended to have practical effect the moment it became law. The jurisdictional grant is best read as having been enacted on the understanding that the common law would provide a cause of action for the modest number of international law violations with a potential for personal liability at the time.

IV

We think it is correct, then, to assume that the First Congress understood that the district courts would recognize private causes of action for certain torts in violation of the law of nations, though we have found no basis to suspect Congress had any examples in mind beyond those torts corresponding to Blackstone's three primary offenses: violation of safe conducts, infringement of the rights of ambassadors, and piracy. We assume, too, that no development in the two centuries from the enactment of § 1350 to the birth of the modern line of cases beginning with *Filartiga v. Pena-Irala,* 630 F.2d 876 (2d Cir. 1980), has categorically precluded federal courts from recognizing a claim under the law of nations as an element of common law; Congress has not in any relevant way amended § 1350 or limited civil common law power by another statute. Still, there are good reasons for a restrained conception of the discretion a federal court should exercise in considering a new cause of action of this kind. Accordingly, we think courts should require any claim based on the present-day law of nations to rest on a norm of international character accepted by the civilized world and defined with a specificity comparable to the features of the 18th-century paradigms we have recognized. This requirement is fatal to Alvarez's claim.

A

A series of reasons argue for judicial caution when considering the kinds of individual claims that might implement the jurisdiction conferred by the early statute. First, the prevailing conception of the common law has changed since 1789 in a way that counsels restraint in judicially applying internationally generated norms. When § 1350 was enacted, the accepted conception was of the common law as "a transcendental body of law outside of any particular State but obligatory within it unless and until changed by statute." *Black and White Taxicab & Transfer Co. v. Brown and Yellow Taxicab & Transfer Co.,* 276 U.S. 518, 533 (1928) (Holmes, J., dissenting). Now, however, in most cases where a court is asked to state or formulate a common law principle in a new context, there is a general understanding that the law is not so much found or discovered as it is either made or created. . . .

Second, along with, and in part driven by, that conceptual development in understanding common law has come an equally significant rethinking of the role of the federal courts in making it. *Erie R. Co. v. Tompkins,* 304 U.S. 64 . . . (1938), was the watershed in which we denied the existence of any federal "general" common law, *id.,* at 78, which largely withdrew to havens of specialty, some of them defined by express congressional authorization to devise a body of law directly, *e.g., Textile Workers v. Lincoln Mills of Ala.,* 353 U.S. 448 . . . (1957) (interpretation of collective-bargaining agreements); Fed. Rule Evid. 501 (evidentiary privileges in federal-question cases). Elsewhere, this Court has thought it was in order to create federal common law rules in interstitial areas of particular federal interest. . . . And although we have even assumed competence to make judicial rules of decision of particular importance to foreign relations, such as the act of state doctrine, *see Banco Nacional de Cuba v. Sabbatino,* 376 U.S. 398, 427 . . . (1964), the general practice has been to look for legislative guidance before exercising innovative authority over substantive law. It would be remarkable to take a more aggressive role in exercising a jurisdiction that remained largely in shadow for much of the prior two centuries.

Third, this Court has recently and repeatedly said that a decision to create a private right of action is one better left to legislative judgment in the great majority of cases. . . . The creation of a private right of action raises issues beyond the mere consideration whether underlying primary conduct should be allowed or not, entailing, for example, a decision to permit enforcement without the check imposed by prosecutorial discretion. Accordingly, even when Congress has made it clear by statute that a rule applies to purely domestic conduct, we are reluctant to infer intent to provide a private cause of action where the statute does not supply one expressly. While the absence of congressional action addressing private rights of action under an international norm is more equivocal than its failure to provide such a right when it creates a statute, the possible collateral consequences of making international rules privately actionable argue for judicial caution.

Fourth, the subject of those collateral consequences is itself a reason for a high bar to new private causes of action for violating international law, for the potential implications for the foreign relations of the United States of recognizing such causes should make courts particularly wary of impinging on the discretion of the Legislative and Executive Branches in managing foreign affairs. It is one thing for American courts to enforce constitutional limits on our own State and Federal Governments' power, but quite another to consider suits under rules that would go so far as to claim a limit on the power of foreign governments over their own citizens, and to hold that a foreign government or its agent has transgressed those limits. *Cf. Sabbatino, supra,* at 431–432. Yet modern international law is very much concerned with just such questions, and apt to stimulate calls for vindicating private interests in § 1350 cases. Since many attempts by federal courts to craft remedies for the violation of new norms of international law would raise risks of adverse foreign policy consequences, they should be undertaken, if at all, with great caution. *Cf. Tel-Oren v. Libyan Arab Republic,* 726 F.2d 774, 813 (D.C. Cir. 1984) (Bork, J., concurring) (expressing doubt that § 1350 should be read to require "our courts [to] sit in judgment of the conduct of foreign officials in their own countries with respect to their own citizens").

The fifth reason is particularly important in light of the first four. We have no congressional mandate to seek out and define new and debatable violations of the law of nations, and modern indications of congressional understanding of the judicial role in the field have not affirmatively encouraged greater judicial creativity. It is true that a clear mandate appears in the Torture Victim Protection Act of 1991, 106 Stat. 73, providing authority that "establish[es] an unambiguous and modern basis for" federal claims of torture and extrajudicial killing, H.R.Rep. No. 102–367, pt. 1, p. 3 (1991). But that affirmative authority is confined to specific subject matter, and although the legislative history includes the remark that § 1350 should "remain intact to permit suits based on other norms that already exist or may ripen in the future into rules of customary international law," *id.,* at 4, Congress as a body has done nothing to promote such suits. Several times, indeed, the Senate has expressly declined to give the federal courts the task of interpreting and applying international human rights law, as when its ratification of the International Covenant on Civil and Political Rights declared that the substantive provisions of the document were not self-executing. 138 Cong. Rec. 8071 (1992).

B

These reasons argue for great caution in adapting the law of nations to private rights. Justice SCALIA, *post,* (opinion concurring in part and concurring in judgment) concludes that caution is too hospitable, and a word is in order to summarize where we have come so far and to focus our difference with him on whether some norms of today's law of nations may ever be recognized legitimately by federal courts in the absence of congressional action beyond § 1350. All Members of the Court agree that § 1350 is only jurisdictional. We also agree, or at least Justice SCALIA does not dispute, *post,* that the jurisdiction was originally understood to be available to enforce a small number of international norms that a federal court could properly recognize as within the common law enforceable without further statutory authority. Justice Scalia concludes, however, that two subsequent developments should be understood to preclude federal courts from recognizing any further international norms as judicially enforceable today, absent further congressional action. As described before, we now tend to understand common law not as a discoverable reflection of universal reason but, in a positivistic way, as a product of human choice. And we now adhere to a conception of limited judicial power first expressed in reorienting federal diversity jurisdiction, *see Erie R. Co. v. Tompkins,* 304 U.S. 64 . . . (1938), that federal courts have no authority to derive "general" common law.

Whereas JUSTICE SCALIA sees these developments as sufficient to close the door to further independent judicial recognition of actionable international norms, other considerations persuade us that the judicial power should be exercised on the understanding that the door is still ajar subject to vigilant doorkeeping, and thus open to a narrow class of international norms today. *Erie* did not in terms bar any judicial recognition of new substantive rules, no matter what the circumstances, and post-*Erie* understanding has identified limited enclaves in which federal courts may derive some substantive law in a common law way. For two centuries we have affirmed that the domestic law of the United States recognizes the law of nations. *See, e.g., Sabbatino,* 376 U.S., at 423 ("[I]t is, of course, true that United States courts apply international law as a part of our own in appropriate circumstances");[18] . . . It would take some explaining to say now that federal courts must avert their gaze entirely from any international norm intended to protect individuals.

We think an attempt to justify such a position would be particularly unconvincing in light of what we know about congressional understanding bearing on this issue lying at the intersection of the judicial and legislative powers. The First Congress, which reflected the understanding of the framing generation and included some of the Framers, assumed that federal courts could properly identify some international norms as enforceable in the exercise of § 1350 jurisdiction. We think it would be unreasonable to assume that the First Congress would have expected federal courts to lose all capacity to recognize enforceable international norms simply because the common law might lose some metaphysical cachet on the road to modern realism. Later Congresses seem to have shared our view. The position we take today has been assumed by some federal courts for 24 years, ever since the Second Circuit decided *Filartiga v. Pena-Irala,* 630 F.2d 876 (2d Cir. 1980), and for practical purposes the point of today's disagreement has been focused since the exchange between Judge Edwards and Judge Bork in *Tel-Oren v. Libyan Arab Republic,* 726 F.2d 774 (D.C. Cir. 1984), Congress, however, has not only expressed no disagreement with our view of the proper exercise of the judicial power, but has responded to its most notable instance by enacting legislation supplementing the judicial determination in some detail. *See supra* (discussing the Torture Victim Protection Act).

While we agree with Justice SCALIA to the point that we would welcome any congressional guidance in exercising jurisdiction with such obvious potential to affect foreign relations, nothing Congress has done is a reason for us to shut the door to the law of nations entirely. It is enough to say that Congress may do that at any time (explicitly, or implicitly by treaties or statutes that occupy the field), just as it may modify or cancel any judicial decision so far as it rests on recognizing an international norm as such.[19]

---

[18] *Sabbatino* itself did not directly apply international law, *see* 376 U.S., at 421–423, but neither did it question the application of that law in appropriate cases, and it further endorsed the reasoning of a noted commentator who had argued that *Erie* should not preclude the continued application of international law in federal courts. 376 U.S., at 425 (citing Jessup, The Doctrine of Erie Railroad v. Tompkins Applied to International Law, 33 Am. J. Int'l L. 740 (1939)).

[19] Our position does not, as Justice SCALIA suggests, imply that every grant of jurisdiction to a federal court carries with it an opportunity to develop common law (so that the grant of federal-question jurisdiction would be equally as good for our purposes as § 1350), *see post,* n. 1. Section 1350 was enacted on the congressional understanding that courts would exercise jurisdiction by entertaining some common law claims derived from the law of nations; and we know of no reason to think that federal-question jurisdiction was extended subject to any comparable congressional assumption. Further, our holding today is consistent with the division of responsibilities between federal and state courts after *Erie, see supra,* as a more expansive common law power related to 28 U.S.C. § 1331 might not be.

C

We must still, however, derive a standard or set of standards for assessing the particular claim Alvarez raises, and for this action it suffices to look to the historical antecedents. Whatever the ultimate criteria for accepting a cause of action subject to jurisdiction under § 1350, we are persuaded that federal courts should not recognize private claims under federal common law for violations of any international law norm with less definite content and acceptance among civilized nations than the historical paradigms familiar when § 1350 was enacted. *See, e.g., United States v. Smith,* 5 Wheat. 153, 163–180, n. a (1820) (illustrating the specificity with which the law of nations defined piracy). This limit upon judicial recognition is generally consistent with the reasoning of many of the courts and judges who faced the issue before it reached this Court. See *Filartiga, supra,* at 890 ("[F]or purposes of civil liability, the torturer has become—like the pirate and slave trader before him—hostis humani generis, an enemy of all mankind"); *Tel-Oren, supra,* at 781 (Edwards, J., concurring) (suggesting that the "limits of section 1350's reach" be defined by "a handful of heinous actions—each of which violates definable, universal and obligatory norms"); *see also In re Estate of Marcos, Human Rights Litigation,* 25 F.3d 1467, 1475 (9th Cir. 1994) ("Actionable violations of international law must be of a norm that is specific, universal, and obligatory"). And the determination whether a norm is sufficiently definite to support a cause of action[20] should (and, indeed, inevitably must) involve an element of judgment about the practical consequences of making that cause available to litigants in the federal courts.[21]

---

20 A related consideration is whether international law extends the scope of liability for a violation of a given norm to the perpetrator being sued, if the defendant is a private actor such as a corporation or individual. *Compare Tel-Oren v. Libyan Arab Republic,* 726 F.2d 774, 791–795 (D.C. Cir.1984) (Edwards, J., concurring) (insufficient consensus in 1984 that torture by private actors violates international law), with *Kadic v. Karadzic,* 70 F.3d 232, 239–241 (2d Cir. 1995) (sufficient consensus in 1995 that genocide by private actors violates international law).

21 This requirement of clear definition is not meant to be the only principle limiting the availability of relief in the federal courts for violations of customary international law, though it disposes of this case. For example, the European Commission argues as *amicus curiae* that basic principles of international law require that before asserting a claim in a foreign forum, the claimant must have exhausted any remedies available in the domestic legal system, and perhaps in other fora such as international claims tribunals. *See* Brief for European Commission as *Amicus Curiae* 24, n. 54 (citing I. Brownlie, Principles of Public International Law 472–481 (6th ed.2003)); cf. Torture Victim Protection Act of 1991, § 2(b), 106 Stat. 73 (exhaustion requirement). We would certainly consider this requirement in an appropriate case. Another possible limitation that we need not apply here is a policy of case-specific deference to the political branches. For example, there are now pending in federal district court several class actions seeking damages from various corporations alleged to have participated in, or abetted, the regime of apartheid that formerly controlled South Africa. *See In re South African Apartheid Litigation,* 238 F. Supp. 2d 1379 (J.P.M.L. 2002) (granting a motion to transfer the cases to the Southern District of New York). The Government of South Africa has said that these cases interfere with the policy embodied by its Truth and Reconciliation Commission, which "deliberately avoided a 'victors' justice' approach to the crimes of apartheid and chose instead one based on confession and absolution, informed by the principles of reconciliation, reconstruction, reparation and goodwill." Declaration of Penuell Mpapa Maduna, Minister of Justice and Constitutional Development, Republic of South Africa, reprinted in App. to Brief for Government of Commonwealth of Australia et al. as Amici Curiae

Thus, Alvarez's detention claim must be gauged against the current state of international law, looking to those sources we have long, albeit cautiously, recognized. . . .

To begin with, Alvarez cites two well-known international agreements that, despite their moral authority, have little utility under the standard set out in this opinion. He says that his abduction by Sosa was an "arbitrary arrest" within the meaning of the Universal Declaration of Human Rights (Declaration), G.A. Res. 217A (III), U.N. Doc. A/810 (1948). And he traces the rule against arbitrary arrest not only to the Declaration, but also to article nine of the International Covenant on Civil and Political Rights (Covenant), Dec. 16, 1966, 999 U.N.T.S. 171,[22] to which the United States is a party, and to various other conventions to which it is not. But the Declaration does not of its own force impose obligations as a matter of international law. *See* Humphrey, The UN Charter and the Universal Declaration of Human Rights, in The International Protection of Human Rights 39, 50 (E. Luard ed. 1967) (quoting Eleanor Roosevelt calling the Declaration " 'a statement of principles . . . setting up a common standard of achievement for all peoples and all nations' " and " 'not a treaty or international agreement . . . impos[ing] legal obligations' ").[23] And, although the Covenant does bind the United States as a matter of international law, the United States ratified the Covenant on the express understanding that it was not self-executing and so did not itself create obligations enforceable in the federal courts. *See supra*. Accordingly, Alvarez cannot say that the Declaration and Covenant themselves establish the relevant and applicable rule of international law. He instead attempts to show that prohibition of arbitrary arrest has attained the status of binding customary international law.

Here, it is useful to examine Alvarez's complaint in greater detail. As he presently argues it, the claim does not rest on the cross-border feature of his abduction. Although the District Court granted relief in part on finding a violation of international law in taking Alvarez across the border from Mexico to the United States, the Court of Appeals rejected that ground of liability for failure to identify a norm of requisite force prohibiting a forcible abduction across a border. Instead, it relied on the conclusion that the law of the United States did not authorize Alvarez's arrest, because the

---

7a, ¶ 3.2.1 (emphasis deleted). The United States has agreed. *See* Letter of William H. Taft IV, Legal Adviser, U.S. Dept. of State, to Shannen W. Coffin, Deputy Asst. Atty. Gen., Oct. 27, 2003, *reprinted in id.*, at 2a. In such cases, there is a strong argument that federal courts should give serious weight to the Executive Branch's view of the case's impact on foreign policy. . . .

[22] Article nine provides that "[n]o one shall be subjected to arbitrary arrest or detention," that "[n]o one shall be deprived of his liberty except on such grounds and in accordance with such procedure as are established by law," and that "[a]nyone who has been the victim of unlawful arrest or detention shall have an enforceable right to compensation." 999 U.N.T. S., at 175–176.

[23] It has nevertheless had substantial indirect effect on international law. *See* Brownlie, *supra*, at 535 (calling the Declaration a "good example of an informal prescription given legal significance by the actions of authoritative decision-makers").

DEA lacked extraterritorial authority under 21 U.S.C. § 878, and because Federal Rule of Criminal Procedure 4(d)(2) limited the warrant for Alvarez's arrest to "the jurisdiction of the United States." It is this position that Alvarez takes now: that his arrest was arbitrary and as such forbidden by international law not because it infringed the prerogatives of Mexico, but because no applicable law authorized it.

Alvarez thus invokes a general prohibition of "arbitrary" detention defined as officially sanctioned action exceeding positive authorization to detain under the domestic law of some government, regardless of the circumstances. Whether or not this is an accurate reading of the Covenant, Alvarez cites little authority that a rule so broad has the status of a binding customary norm today.[27] He certainly cites nothing to justify the federal courts in taking his broad rule as the predicate for a federal lawsuit, for its implications would be breathtaking. His rule would support a cause of action in federal court for any arrest, anywhere in the world, unauthorized by the law of the jurisdiction in which it took place, and would create a cause of action for any seizure of an alien in violation of the Fourth Amendment, supplanting the actions under Rev. Stat. § 1979, 42 U.S.C. § 1983, and *Bivens v. Six Unknown Fed. Narcotics Agents*, 403 U.S. 388 . . . (1971), that now provide damages remedies for such violations. It would create an action in federal court for arrests by state officers who simply exceed their authority; and for the violation of any limit that the law of any country might place on the authority of its own officers to arrest. And all of this assumes that Alvarez could establish that Sosa was acting on behalf of a government when he made the arrest, for otherwise he would need a rule broader still.

Alvarez's failure to marshal support for his proposed rule is underscored by the Restatement (Third) of Foreign Relations Law of the United States (1986), which says in its discussion of customary international human rights law that a "state violates international law if, as a matter of state policy, it practices, encourages, or condones . . . prolonged arbitrary detention." 2 *Id.*, § 702. Although the Restatement does not explain its requirements of a "state policy" and of "prolonged" detention, the implication is clear. Any credible invocation of a principle

---

27 Specifically, he relies on a survey of national constitutions, Bassiouni, Human Rights in the Context of Criminal Justice: Identifying International Procedural Protections and Equivalent Protections in National Constitutions, 3 Duke J. Comp. & Int'l L. 235, 260–261 (1993); a case from the International Court of Justice, *United States v. Iran*, 1980 I.C.J. 3, 42; and some authority drawn from the federal courts. None of these suffice. The Bassiouni survey does show that many nations recognize a norm against arbitrary detention, but that consensus is at a high level of generality. The *Iran* case, in which the United States sought relief for the taking of its diplomatic and consular staff as hostages, involved a different set of international norms and mentioned the problem of arbitrary detention only in passing; the detention in that case was, moreover, far longer and harsher than Alvarez's. *See* 1980 I.C. J., at 42, ¶ 91 ("detention of [United States] staff by a group of armed militants" lasted "many months"). And the authority from the federal courts, to the extent it supports Alvarez's position, reflects a more assertive view of federal judicial discretion over claims based on customary international law than the position we take today.

against arbitrary detention that the civilized world accepts as binding customary international law requires a factual basis beyond relatively brief detention in excess of positive authority. Even the Restatement's limits are only the beginning of the enquiry, because although it is easy to say that some policies of prolonged arbitrary detentions are so bad that those who enforce them become enemies of the human race, it may be harder to say which policies cross that line with the certainty afforded by Blackstone's three common law offenses. In any event, the label would never fit the reckless policeman who botches his warrant, even though that same officer might pay damages under municipal law. *E.g.*, *Groh v. Ramirez*, 540 U.S. 551 . . . (2004).[28]

Whatever may be said for the broad principle Alvarez advances, in the present, imperfect world, it expresses an aspiration that exceeds any binding customary rule having the specificity we require.[29] Creating a private cause of action to further that aspiration would go beyond any residual common law discretion we think it appropriate to exercise.[30] It is enough to hold that a single illegal detention of less than a day, followed by the transfer of custody to lawful authorities and a prompt arraignment, violates no norm of customary international law so well defined as to support the creation of a federal remedy.

The judgment of the Court of Appeals is

Reversed.

JUSTICE SCALIA, with whom the CHIEF JUSTICE and JUSTICE THOMAS join, concurring in part and concurring in the judgment. . . .

III.

The analysis in the Court's opinion departs from my own in this respect: After concluding in Part III that "the ATS is a jurisdictional statute

---

[28] In this action, Sosa might well have been liable under Mexican law. Alvarez asserted such a claim, but the District Court concluded that the applicable law was the law of California, and that under California law Sosa had been privileged to make a citizen's arrest in Mexico. Whether this was correct is not now before us, though we discern tension between the court's simultaneous conclusions that the detention so lacked any legal basis as to violate international law, yet was privileged by state law against ordinary tort recovery.

[29] It is not that violations of a rule logically foreclose the existence of that rule as international law. *Cf. Filartiga v. Pena-Irala,* 630 F.2d 876, 884, n. 15 (2d Cir. 1980) ("The fact that the prohibition of torture is often honored in the breach does not diminish its binding effect as a norm of international law"). Nevertheless, that a rule as stated is as far from full realization as the one Alvarez urges is evidence against its status as binding law; and an even clearer point against the creation by judges of a private cause of action to enforce the aspiration behind the rule claimed.

[30] Alvarez also cites Brief for Respondent Alvarez-Machain 49–50, a finding by a United Nations working group that his detention was arbitrary under the Declaration, the Covenant, and customary international law. *See* Report of the United Nations Working Group on Arbitrary Detention, U.N. Doc. E/CN.4/1994/27, pp. 139–140 (Dec. 17, 1993). That finding is not addressed, however, to our demanding standard of definition, which must be met to raise even the possibility of a private cause of action. If Alvarez wishes to seek compensation on the basis of the working group's finding, he must address his request to Congress.

creating no new causes of action," *ante,* the Court addresses at length in Part IV the "good reasons for a restrained conception of the *discretion* a federal court should exercise in considering a new cause of action" under the ATS. *Ibid.* (emphasis added). By framing the issue as one of "discretion," the Court skips over the antecedent question of authority. This neglects the "lesson of *Erie*," that "grants of jurisdiction alone" (which the Court has acknowledged the ATS to be) "are not themselves grants of lawmaking authority." *Meltzer, supra.* On this point, the Court observes only that no development between the enactment of the ATS (in 1789) and the birth of modern international human rights litigation under that statute (in 1980) "has categorically *precluded* federal courts from recognizing a claim under the law of nations as an element of common law." *Ante* (emphasis added). This turns our jurisprudence regarding federal common law on its head. The question is not what case or congressional action *prevents* federal courts from applying the law of nations as part of the general common law; it is what *authorizes* that peculiar exception from *Erie*'s fundamental holding that a general common law *does not exist*. . . .

Because today's federal common law is not our Framers' general common law, the question presented by the suggestion of discretionary authority to enforce the law of nations is not whether to extend old-school general-common-law adjudication. Rather, it is whether to create new federal common law. The Court masks the novelty of its approach when it suggests that the difference between us is that I would "close the door to further independent judicial recognition of actionable international norms," whereas the Court would permit the exercise of judicial power "on the understanding that the door is still ajar subject to vigilant doorkeeping." *Ante.* The general common law was the old door. We do not close that door today, for the deed was done in *Erie*. Federal common law is a *new* door. The question is not whether that door will be left ajar, but whether this Court will open it. . . .

To be sure, today's opinion does not itself precipitate a direct confrontation with Congress by creating a cause of action that Congress has not. But it invites precisely that action by the lower courts, even while recognizing (1) that Congress understood the difference between granting jurisdiction and creating a federal cause of action in 1789, (2) that Congress understands that difference today, and (3) that the ATS itself supplies only jurisdiction. *Ante.* In holding open the possibility that judges may create rights where Congress has not authorized them to do so, the Court countenances judicial occupation of a domain that belongs to the people's representatives. One does not need a crystal ball to predict that this occupation will not be long in coming, since the Court endorses the reasoning of "many of the courts and judges who faced the issue before it reached this Court," including the Second and Ninth Circuits. *Ante.*

The Ninth Circuit brought us the judgment that the Court reverses today. Perhaps its decision in this particular case, like the decisions of other lower federal courts that receive passing attention in the Court's opinion, "reflects a more assertive view of federal judicial discretion over claims based on customary international law than the position we take today." *Ante.* But the verbal formula it applied is the same verbal formula that the Court explicitly endorses. . . . Endorsing the very formula that led the Ninth Circuit to its result in this action hardly seems to be a recipe for restraint in the future.

The Second Circuit, which started the Judiciary down the path the Court today tries to hedge in, is a good indicator of where that path leads us: directly into confrontation with the political branches. *Kadic v. Karadzíc*, 70 F.3d 232 (2d Cir. 1995), provides a case in point. One of the norms at issue in that case was a norm against genocide set forth in the Convention on the Prevention and Punishment of the Crime of Genocide, Dec. 9, 1948, 78 U.N.T.S. 278. The Second Circuit held that the norm was actionable under the ATS after applying Circuit case law that the Court today endorses. 70 F.3d, at 238–239, 241–242. The Court of Appeals then did something that is perfectly logical and yet truly remarkable: It dismissed the determination by Congress and the Executive that this norm should *not* give rise to a private cause of action. We *know* that Congress and the Executive made this determination, because Congress inscribed it into the Genocide Convention Implementation Act of 1987, 18 U.S.C. § 1091 *et seq.*, a law signed by the President attaching criminal penalties to the norm against genocide. The Act, Congress said, shall not "be construed as creating any substantive or procedural right enforceable by law by any party in any proceeding." § 1092. Undeterred, the Second Circuit reasoned that this "decision not to create a *new* private remedy" could hardly be construed as *repealing* by implication the cause of action supplied by the ATS. 70 F.3d, at 242 (emphasis added). Does this Court truly wish to encourage the use of a jurisdiction-granting statute with respect to which there is "no record of congressional discussion about private actions that might be subject to the jurisdictional provision, or about any need for further legislation to create private remedies; [and] no record even of debate on the section," *ante,* to override a clear indication from the political branches that a "specific, universal, and obligatory" norm against genocide is *not* to be enforced through a private damages action? Today's opinion leads the lower courts right down that perilous path. . . .

We Americans have a method for making the laws that are over us. We elect representatives to two Houses of Congress, each of which must enact the new law and present it for the approval of a President, whom we also elect. For over two decades now, unelected federal judges have been usurping this lawmaking power by converting what they regard as norms of international law into American law. Today's opinion approves that process in principle, though urging the lower courts to be more restrained.

. . . In today's latest victory for its Never Say Never Jurisprudence, the Court ignores its own conclusion that the ATS provides only jurisdiction, wags a finger at the lower courts for going too far, and then—repeating the same formula the ambitious lower courts *themselves* have used—invites them to try again.

JUSTICE BREYER, concurring in part and concurring in the judgment.

. . . I would add one further consideration. Since enforcement of an international norm by one nation's courts implies that other nations' courts may do the same, I would ask whether the exercise of jurisdiction under the ATS is consistent with those notions of comity that lead each nation to respect the sovereign rights of other nations by limiting the reach of its laws and their enforcement. In applying those principles, courts help ensure that "the potentially conflicting laws of different nations" will "work together in harmony," a matter of increasing importance in an ever more interdependent world. *F. Hoffmann-La Roche Ltd. v. Empagran S. A.*, ante, 542 U.S., at 164; *cf.* Murray v. Schooner Charming Betsy, 2 Cranch 64 (1804). Such consideration is necessary to ensure that ATS litigation does not undermine the very harmony that it was intended to promote. . . .

These comity concerns normally do not arise (or at least are mitigated) if the conduct in question takes place in the country that provides the cause of action or if that conduct involves that country's own national—where, say, an American assaults a foreign diplomat and the diplomat brings suit in an American court. . . . They do arise, however, when foreign persons injured abroad bring suit in the United States under the ATS, asking the courts to recognize a claim that a certain kind of foreign conduct violates an international norm. . . .

. . . [R]ecognition of universal jurisdiction in respect to a limited set of norms [such as torture, genocide, crimes against humanity, and war crimes] is consistent with principles of international comity. That is, allowing every nation's courts to adjudicate foreign conduct involving foreign parties in such cases will not significantly threaten the practical harmony that comity principles seek to protect. That consensus concerns criminal jurisdiction, but consensus as to universal criminal jurisdiction itself suggests that universal tort jurisdiction would be no more threatening. . . .

Taking these matters into account, as I believe courts should, I can find no similar procedural consensus supporting the exercise of jurisdiction in these cases. That lack of consensus provides additional support for the Court's conclusion that the ATS does not recognize the claim at issue here—where the underlying substantive claim concerns arbitrary arrest, outside the United States, of a citizen of one foreign country by another.

KIOBEL V. ROYAL DUTCH PETROLEUM CO.

569 U.S. 108 (2013).

CHIEF JUSTICE ROBERTS delivered the opinion of the Court.

Petitioners, a group of Nigerian nationals residing in the United States, filed suit in federal court against certain Dutch, British, and Nigerian corporations. Petitioners sued under the Alien Tort Statute, 28 U.S.C. § 1350, alleging that the corporations aided and abetted the Nigerian Government in committing violations of the law of nations in Nigeria. The question presented is whether and under what circumstances courts may recognize a cause of action under the Alien Tort Statute, for violations of the law of nations occurring within the territory of a sovereign other than the United States.

I

Petitioners were residents of Ogoniland, an area of 250 square miles located in the Niger delta area of Nigeria and populated by roughly half a million people. . . . [R]espondents Royal Dutch Petroleum Company and Shell Transport and Trading Company, p.l.c., were holding companies incorporated in the Netherlands and England, respectively. Their joint subsidiary, respondent Shell Petroleum Development Company of Nigeria, Ltd. (SPDC), was incorporated in Nigeria, and engaged in oil exploration and production in Ogoniland. According to the complaint, after concerned residents of Ogoniland began protesting the environmental effects of SPDC's practices, respondents enlisted the Nigerian Government to violently suppress the burgeoning demonstrations. Throughout the early 1990's, the complaint alleges, Nigerian military and police forces attacked Ogoni villages, beating, raping, killing, and arresting residents and destroying or looting property. Petitioners further allege that respondents aided and abetted these atrocities by, among other things, providing the Nigerian forces with food, transportation, and compensation, as well as by allowing the Nigerian military to use respondents' property as a staging ground for attacks.

Following the alleged atrocities, petitioners moved to the United States where they have been granted political asylum and now reside as legal residents. . . . They filed suit in the United States District Court for the Southern District of New York, alleging jurisdiction under the Alien Tort Statute and requesting relief under customary international law. . . . According to petitioners, respondents violated the law of nations by aiding and abetting the Nigerian Government in committing (1) extrajudicial killings; (2) crimes against humanity; (3) torture and cruel treatment; (4) arbitrary arrest and detention; (5) violations of the rights to life, liberty, security, and association; (6) forced exile; and (7) property destruction. The District Court dismissed the first, fifth, sixth, and seventh claims, reasoning that the facts alleged to support those claims did not give rise to a violation of the law of nations. . . .

The Second Circuit dismissed the entire complaint, reasoning that the law of nations does not recognize corporate liability. . . . We granted certiorari to consider that question. . . . After oral argument, we directed the parties to file supplemental briefs addressing an additional question: "Whether and under what circumstances the [ATS] allows courts to recognize a cause of action for violations of the law of nations occurring within the territory of a sovereign other than the United States." . . . .

II

. . . The question here is not whether petitioners have stated a proper claim under the ATS, but whether a claim may reach conduct occurring in the territory of a foreign sovereign. Respondents contend that claims under the ATS do not, relying primarily on a canon of statutory interpretation known as the presumption against extraterritorial application. That canon provides that "[w]hen a statute gives no clear indication of an extraterritorial application, it has none," *Morrison v. National Australia Bank Ltd.*, 130 S. Ct. 2869, 2878 (2010), and reflects the "presumption that United States law governs domestically but does not rule the world," *Microsoft Corp. v. AT&T Corp.*, 550 U.S. 437, 454 (2007).

This presumption "serves to protect against unintended clashes between our laws and those of other nations which could result in international discord." *EEOC v. Arabian American Oil Co.*, 499 U.S. 244, 248 (1991) (*Aramco*). . . .

We typically apply the presumption to discern whether an Act of Congress regulating conduct applies abroad. . . . The ATS, on the other hand, is "strictly jurisdictional." *Sosa*, 542 U.S., at 713. It does not directly regulate conduct or afford relief. It instead allows federal courts to recognize certain causes of action based on sufficiently definite norms of international law. But we think the principles underlying the canon of interpretation similarly constrain courts considering causes of action that may be brought under the ATS.

Indeed, the danger of unwarranted judicial interference in the conduct of foreign policy is magnified in the context of the ATS, because the question is not what Congress has done but instead what courts may do. This Court in *Sosa* repeatedly stressed the need for judicial caution in considering which claims could be brought under the ATS, in light of foreign policy concerns. As the Court explained, "the potential [foreign policy] implications . . . of recognizing. . . . causes [under the ATS] should make courts particularly wary of impinging on the discretion of the Legislative and Executive Branches in managing foreign affairs." . . . These concerns, which are implicated in any case arising under the ATS, are all the more pressing when the question is whether a cause of action under the ATS reaches conduct within the territory of another sovereign.

These concerns are not diminished by the fact that *Sosa* limited federal courts to recognizing causes of action only for alleged violations of international law norms that are " 'specific, universal, and obligatory.' " . . . As demonstrated by Congress's enactment of the Torture Victim Protection Act of 1991 . . . identifying such a norm is only the beginning of defining a cause of action. See id., § 3 (providing detailed definitions for extrajudicial killing and torture); id., § 2 (specifying who may be liable, creating a rule of exhaustion, and establishing a statute of limitations). Each of these decisions carries with it significant foreign policy implications.

The principles underlying the presumption against extraterritoriality thus constrain courts exercising their power under the ATS.

III

Petitioners contend that even if the presumption applies, the text, history, and purposes of the ATS rebut it for causes of action brought under that statute. It is true that Congress, even in a jurisdictional provision, can indicate that it intends federal law to apply to conduct occurring abroad. See, e.g., 18 U.S.C. § 1091(e) (2006 ed., Supp. V) (providing jurisdiction over the offense of genocide "regardless of where the offense is committed" if the alleged offender is, among other things, "present in the United States"). But to rebut the presumption, the ATS would need to evince a "clear indication of extraterritoriality." *Morrison*, 130 S. Ct. at 2883. It does not.

To begin, nothing in the text of the statute suggests that Congress intended causes of action recognized under it to have extraterritorial reach. The ATS covers actions by aliens for violations of the law of nations, but that does not imply extraterritorial reach—such violations affecting aliens can occur either within or outside the United States. Nor does the fact that the text reaches "any civil action" suggest application to torts committed abroad; it is well established that generic terms like "any" or "every" do not rebut the presumption against extraterritoriality. . . .

Petitioners make much of the fact that the ATS provides jurisdiction over civil actions for "torts" in violation of the law of nations. They claim that in using that word, the First Congress "necessarily meant to provide for jurisdiction over extraterritorial transitory torts that could arise on foreign soil." Supp. Brief for Petitioners 18. For support, they cite the common-law doctrine that allowed courts to assume jurisdiction over such "transitory torts," including actions for personal injury, arising abroad. . . .

Under the transitory torts doctrine . . . "the only justification for allowing a party to recover when the cause of action arose in another civilized jurisdiction is a well founded belief that it was a cause of action in that place." . . . . The question under *Sosa* is not whether a federal court has jurisdiction to entertain a cause of action provided by foreign or even international law. The question is instead whether the court has authority to recognize a cause of action under U.S. law to enforce a norm of international law. The reference to "tort" does not demonstrate that the First Congress "necessarily meant" for those causes of action to reach conduct in the territory of a foreign sovereign. In the end, nothing in the text of the ATS evinces the requisite clear indication of extraterritoriality.

Nor does the historical background against which the ATS was enacted overcome the presumption against application to conduct in the territory of another sovereign. . . . We explained in *Sosa* that when Congress passed the ATS, "three principal offenses against the law of nations" had been identified by Blackstone: violation of safe conducts, infringement of the rights of ambassadors, and piracy. . . . The first two offenses have no necessary extraterritorial application. Indeed, Blackstone—in describing them—did so in terms of conduct occurring within the forum nation. . . .

Two notorious episodes involving violations of the law of nations occurred in the United States shortly before passage of the ATS. Each concerned the rights of ambassadors, and each involved conduct within the Union. In 1784, a French adventurer verbally and physically assaulted Francis Barbe Marbois—the Secretary of the French Legion—in Philadelphia. The assault led the French Minister Plenipotentiary to lodge a formal protest with the Continental Congress and threaten to leave the country unless an adequate remedy were provided. . . . And in 1787, a New York constable entered the Dutch Ambassador's house and arrested one of his domestic servants. . . . At the request of Secretary of Foreign Affairs John Jay, the Mayor of New York City arrested the constable in turn, but cautioned that because " 'neither Congress nor our [State] Legislature have yet passed any act respecting a breach of the privileges of Ambassadors,' " the extent of any available relief would depend on the common law. . . . The two cases in which the ATS was invoked shortly after its passage also concerned conduct within the territory of the United States. See *Bolchos*, 3 F. Cas. 810 (wrongful seizure of slaves from a vessel while in port in the United States); *Moxon*, 17 F. Cas. 942 (wrongful seizure in United States territorial waters). . . .

The third example of a violation of the law of nations familiar to the Congress that enacted the ATS was piracy. Piracy typically occurs on the high seas, beyond the territorial jurisdiction of the United States or any other country. See 4 Blackstone, supra, at 72 ("The offence of piracy, by common law, consists of committing those acts of robbery and depredation upon the high seas, which, if committed upon land, would have amounted to felony there"). This Court has generally treated the high seas the same as foreign soil for purposes of the presumption against extraterritorial application. . . . Petitioners contend that because Congress surely intended the ATS to provide jurisdiction for actions against pirates, it necessarily anticipated the statute would apply to conduct occurring abroad.

Applying U.S. law to pirates, however, does not typically impose the sovereign will of the United States onto conduct occurring within the territorial jurisdiction of another sovereign, and therefore carries less direct foreign policy consequences. Pirates were fair game wherever found, by any nation, because they generally did not operate within any jurisdiction. See 4 Blackstone, supra, at 71. We do not think that the existence of a cause of action against them is a sufficient basis for concluding that other causes of action under the ATS reach conduct that does occur within the territory of another sovereign; pirates may well be a category unto themselves. . . .

Petitioners also point to a 1795 opinion authored by Attorney General William Bradford. See Breach of Neutrality, 1 Op. Atty. Gen. 57. In 1794, in the midst of war between France and Great Britain, and notwithstanding the American official policy of neutrality, several U.S. citizens joined a French privateer fleet and attacked and plundered the British colony of Sierra Leone. In response to a protest from the British Ambassador, Attorney General Bradford responded as follows:

> So far . . . as the transactions complained of originated or took place in a foreign country, they are not within the cognizance of our courts; nor can the actors be legally prosecuted or punished for them by the United States. But crimes committed on the high seas are within the jurisdiction of the . . . courts of the United States; and, so far as the offence was committed thereon, I am inclined to think that it may be legally prosecuted in . . . those courts. . . . But some doubt rests on this point, in consequence of the terms in which the [applicable criminal law] is expressed. But there can be no doubt that the company or individuals who have been injured by these acts of hostility have a remedy by a civil suit in the courts of the United States; jurisdiction being expressly given to these courts in all cases where an alien sues for a tort only, in violation of the laws of nations, or a treaty of the United States. . . ." Id., at 58–59.

Petitioners read the last sentence as confirming that "the Founding generation understood the ATS to apply to law of nations violations committed on the territory of a foreign sovereign." . . . Respondents counter that when Attorney General Bradford referred to "these acts of hostility," he meant the acts only insofar as they took place on the high seas, and even if his conclusion were broader, it was only because the applicable treaty had extraterritorial reach. . . . The Solicitor General, having once read the opinion to stand for the proposition that an "ATS suit could be brought against American citizens for breaching neutrality with Britain only if acts did not take place in a foreign country," . . . now suggests the opinion "could have been meant to encompass . . . conduct [occurring within the foreign territory]," . . .

Attorney General Bradford's opinion defies a definitive reading and we need not adopt one here. Whatever its precise meaning, it deals with U.S. citizens who, by participating in an attack taking place both on the high seas and on a foreign shore, violated a treaty between the United States and Great Britain. The opinion hardly suffices to counter the weighty concerns underlying the presumption against extraterritoriality.

Finally, there is no indication that the ATS was passed to make the United States a uniquely hospitable forum for the enforcement of international norms. As Justice Story put it, "No nation has ever yet pretended to be the custos morum of the whole world. . . ." *United States v. The La Jeune Eugenie*, 26 F. Cas. 832, 847 (No. 15,551) (C.C. Mass. 1822). It is implausible to suppose that the First Congress wanted their fledgling Republic—struggling to receive international recognition—to be the first. Indeed, the parties offer no evidence that any nation, meek or mighty, presumed to do such a thing.

The United States was, however, embarrassed by its potential inability to provide judicial relief to foreign officials injured in the United States. . . . Such offenses against ambassadors violated the law of nations, "and if not adequately redressed could rise to an issue of war." . . . The ATS ensured that the United States could provide a forum for adjudicating such incidents. . . . Nothing about this historical context suggests that Congress also intended federal common law under the ATS to provide a cause of action for conduct occurring in the territory of another sovereign.

Indeed, far from avoiding diplomatic strife, providing such a cause of action could have generated it. Recent experience bears this out. See *Doe v. Exxon Mobil Corp.*, 654 F.3d 11, 77–78 (C.A.D.C.2011) (Kavanaugh, J., dissenting in part) (listing recent objections to extraterritorial applications of the ATS by Canada, Germany, Indonesia, Papua New Guinea, South Africa, Switzerland, and the United Kingdom). Moreover, accepting petitioners' view would imply that other nations, also applying the law of nations, could hale our citizens into their courts for alleged violations of the law of nations occurring in the United States, or anywhere else in the world. The presumption against extraterritoriality guards against our courts triggering such serious foreign policy consequences, and instead defers such decisions, quite appropriately, to the political branches.

We therefore conclude that the presumption against extraterritoriality applies to claims under the ATS, and that nothing in the statute rebuts that presumption. . . . [P]etitioners' case seeking relief for violations of the law of nations occurring outside the United States is barred.

IV

On these facts, all the relevant conduct took place outside the United States. And even where the claims touch and concern the territory of the United States, they must do so with sufficient force to displace the presumption against extraterritorial application. See *Morrison*, 561 U.S. 247, 130 S. Ct., at 2883–2888. Corporations are often present in many countries, and it would reach too far to say that mere corporate presence suffices. If Congress were to determine otherwise, a statute more specific than the ATS would be required.

The judgment of the Court of Appeals is affirmed.

JUSTICE KENNEDY, concurring.

The opinion for the Court is careful to leave open a number of significant questions regarding the reach and interpretation of the Alien Tort Statute. In my view that is a proper disposition. Many serious concerns with respect to human rights abuses committed abroad have been addressed by Congress in statutes such as the Torture Victim Protection Act of 1991 (TVPA) . . . and that class of cases will be determined in the future according to the detailed statutory scheme Congress has enacted. Other cases may arise with allegations of serious violations of international law principles protecting persons, cases covered neither by the TVPA nor by the reasoning and holding of today's case; and in those disputes the proper implementation of the presumption against extraterritorial application may require some further elaboration and explanation.

JUSTICE ALITO, with whom JUSTICE THOMAS joins, concurring.

I concur in the judgment and join the opinion of the Court as far as it goes. Specifically, I agree that when Alien Tort Statute (ATS) "claims touch and concern the territory of the United States, they must do so with sufficient force to displace the presumption against extraterritorial application." . . . [O]nly conduct that satisfies *Sosa*'s requirements of definiteness and acceptance among civilized nations can be said to have been "the 'focus' of congressional concern," . . . when Congress enacted the ATS. As a result, a putative ATS cause of action will fall within the scope of the presumption against extraterritoriality—and will therefore be barred—unless the domestic conduct is sufficient to violate an international law norm that satisfies *Sosa*'s requirements of definiteness and acceptance among civilized nations.

JUSTICE BREYER, with whom JUSTICE GINSBURG, JUSTICE SOTOMAYOR and JUSTICE KAGAN join, concurring in the judgment.

I agree with the Court's conclusion but not with its reasoning. . . .

Unlike the Court, I would not invoke the presumption against extraterritoriality. . . . In this case, however, the parties and relevant conduct lack sufficient ties to the United States for the ATS to provide jurisdiction.

I

A

. . . Recognizing that Congress enacted the ATS to permit recovery of damages from pirates and others who violated basic international law norms as understood in 1789, *Sosa* essentially leads today's judges to ask: Who are today's pirates? . . .

In this case we must decide the extent to which this jurisdictional statute opens a federal court's doors to those harmed by activities belonging to the limited class that *Sosa* set forth when those activities take place abroad. . . .

B

In my view the majority's effort to answer the question by referring to the "presumption against extraterritoriality" does not work well. That presumption "rests on the perception that Congress ordinarily legislates with respect to domestic, not foreign matters." *Morrison v. National Australia Bank Ltd.* . . . The ATS, however, was enacted with "foreign matters" in mind. The statute's text refers explicitly to "alien[s]," "treat[ies]," and "the law of nations." 28 U.S.C. § 1350. The statute's purpose was to address "violations of the law of nations, admitting of a judicial remedy and at the same time threatening serious consequences in international affairs." . . . . And at least one of the three kinds of activities that we found to fall within the statute's scope, namely piracy, ibid., normally takes place abroad. See 4 W. Blackstone, Commentaries on the Law of England 72 (1769).

The majority cannot wish this piracy example away by emphasizing that piracy takes place on the high seas. . . . That is because the robbery and murder that make up piracy do not normally take place in the water; they take place on a ship. And a ship is like land, in that it falls within the jurisdiction of the nation whose flag it flies. . . . Indeed, in the early 19th century Chief Justice Marshall described piracy as an "offenc[e] against the nation under whose flag the vessel sails, and within whose particular jurisdiction all on board the vessel are." . . .

The majority also writes, "Pirates were fair game wherever found, by any nation, because they generally did not operate within any jurisdiction." Ibid. I very much agree that pirates were fair game "wherever found." Indeed, that is the point. That is why we asked, in *Sosa*, who are today's pirates? Certainly today's pirates include torturers and perpetrators of genocide. And today, like the pirates of old, they are "fair game" where they are found. Like those pirates, they are "common enemies of all mankind and all nations have an equal interest in their apprehension and punishment." . . . And just as a nation that harbored pirates provoked the concern of other nations in past centuries . . . so harboring "common enemies of all mankind" provokes similar concerns today. . . .

II

In applying the ATS to acts "occurring within the territory of a[nother] sovereign," I would assume that Congress intended the statute's jurisdictional reach to match the statute's underlying substantive grasp. That grasp, defined by the statute's purposes set forth in *Sosa*, includes compensation for those injured by piracy and its modern-day equivalents, at least where allowing such compensation avoids "serious" negative international "consequences" for the United States. . . . And just as we have looked to established international substantive norms to help determine the statute's substantive reach . . . so we should look to international jurisdictional norms to help determine the statute's jurisdictional scope.

The Restatement (Third) of Foreign Relations Law is helpful. Section 402 recognizes that, subject to § 403's "reasonableness" requirement, a nation may apply its law (for example, federal common law . . .) not only (1) to "conduct" that "takes place [or to persons or things] within its territory" but also (2) to the "activities, interests, status, or relations of its nationals outside as well as within its territory," (3) to "conduct outside its territory that has or is intended to have substantial effect within its territory," and (4) to certain foreign "conduct outside its territory . . . that is directed against the security of the state or against a limited class of other state interests." In addition, § 404 of the Restatement explains that a "state has jurisdiction to define and prescribe punishment for certain offenses recognized by the community of nations as of universal concern, such as piracy, slave trade," and analogous behavior.

Considering these jurisdictional norms in light of both the ATS's basic purpose (to provide compensation for those injured by today's pirates) and *Sosa*'s basic caution (to avoid international friction), I believe that the statute provides jurisdiction where (1) the alleged tort occurs on American soil, (2) the defendant is an American national, or (3) the defendant's conduct substantially and adversely affects an important American national interest, and that includes a distinct interest in preventing the United States from becoming a safe harbor (free of civil as well as criminal liability) for a torturer or other common enemy of mankind. . . .

III

Applying these jurisdictional principles to this case, however, I agree with the Court that jurisdiction does not lie. The defendants are two foreign corporations. Their shares, like those of many foreign corporations, are traded on the New York Stock Exchange. Their only presence in the United States consists of an office in New York City (actually owned by a separate but affiliated company) that helps to explain their business to potential investors. . . . The plaintiffs are not United States nationals but nationals of other nations. The conduct at issue took place abroad. And the plaintiffs allege, not that the defendants directly engaged in acts of torture, genocide, or the equivalent, but that they helped others (who are not American nationals) to do so.

Under these circumstances . . . it would be farfetched to believe, based solely upon the defendants' minimal and indirect American presence, that this legal action helps to vindicate a distinct American interest, such as in not providing a safe harbor for an "enemy of all mankind." Thus I agree with the Court that here it would "reach too far to say" that such "mere corporate presence suffices." . . .

I consequently join the Court's judgment but not its opinion.

NOTES

1. Sosa *and the Nature of the ATS.* One key issue that *Sosa* decided was that the ATS is solely a jurisdictional statute; it does not itself provide a cause of action. Nonetheless, the Court concluded that a cause of action could be found in either treaties or customary international law, notwithstanding *Erie.* Although the Court rejected the plaintiff's claim that he had been subjected to a violation of the law of nations, the Court accepted that the ATS encompassed torts existing under contemporary international law, and cited *Filartiga* favorably in the course of its decision. What standards did the Court set for the type of international norm that must be established by a plaintiff, and how (if at all) did it differ from the approach in *Filartiga*?

Following *Sosa*—and prior to *Kiobel*—the ATS remained the subject of considerable dispute. Was the Supreme Court right to reject the idea that further congressional action was necessary to create causes of action under the ATS? Was it reasonable, and internally consistent, to accept actionable torts under the law of nations other than Blackstone's three specific offenses? Do you agree with Justice Scalia that little guidance was provided, or share concerns that its holding reflected a realistic assessment of modern international law and the discretionary power of federal judges?

As you may recall, the law of nations is just one of two potential bases for an ATS claim. After U.S. ratification of the Convention Against Torture (CAT) in 1994, it was even clearer than in *Filartiga* that a treaty-based norm prohibiting State-sponsored torture bound the United States under international law. Yet when ratifying the CAT, the United States filed a declaration asserting that the operative provisions of the convention were not "self-executing" in the United States. The meaning of this doctrine, and that declaration, is addressed more completely in Chapter 3, Sec. 4. At first blush, though, do you think that U.S. ratification, with that declaration, enhances or detracts from an ATS claim relating to the prohibition on State-sponsored torture contained in the CAT? Is that consistent with the *Sosa* majority's treatment of the ICCPR, and Justice Scalia's critique of the Second Circuit's decision in *Kadic v. Karadzic?*

2. *Corporate Complicity and the ATS.* Courts and commentators observed that ATS defendants shifted over time. *Filartiga* and *Sosa* considered ATS claims against individuals, neither of whom was serving at the time in an official capacity. Claims concerning the acts of governments and their officials frequently provoke immunities-based defenses, considered in greater depth in Chapter 7, Sec. 7. Unsurprisingly, plaintiffs increasingly sought to sue corporate actors for complicity in human rights abuses—in the typical case, when a corporation engaged in a joint venture with a foreign government, which itself committed human rights violations in furtherance of the venture. Such claims might bypass immunity-related defenses and, not incidentally, more easily surmount potential obstacles in terms of service, personal jurisdiction, and amenability to money damages.

For example, in 1996 villagers from Myanmar (Burma) filed a class action lawsuit in U.S. federal court against, *inter alia*, a U.S. corporation (Unocal), alleging that Unocal was responsible under the ATS for international human rights violations, including forced labor perpetrated by the Burmese military in furtherance of the pipeline portion of a natural gas joint venture with the Myanmar government. A Ninth Circuit Court of Appeals panel held that the district court erred in requiring that the plaintiffs must show that Unocal controlled the Burmese military's actions in order to establish Unocal's liability; rather, it was only necessary to show that Unocal "knowingly assisted" the military in perpetrating the abuses, and they had produced sufficient evidence under this standard for the case to proceed to trial on the forced labor claim (but not for claims of torture). *See Doe I v. Unocal Corp.*, 395 F.3d 932 (9th Cir. 2002). That decision was vacated preliminary to en banc rehearing, see *Doe I v. Unocal Corp.*, 395 F.3d 978 (9th Cir. 2003). Before the Ninth Circuit could issue a final decision, however, the parties settled. Although the terms of the settlement were not released publicly, Unocal stated that it would pay the plaintiffs an unspecified amount of money and fund programs to improve the living conditions of people who lived in the region surrounding the pipeline and who may have suffered hardships.

The Second Circuit, home of *Filartiga*, has been especially active in wrestling with the issues posed by corporate liability under the ATS, sometimes in conflict with other courts. On one of the issues in the Unocal litigation, aiding and abetting liability, the Second Circuit held that actionable conduct must be done with the intention of violating the law of nations. *Presbyterian Church of Sudan v. Talisman Energy*, 582 F.3d 244 (2d Cir. 2009). *Compare Aziz v. Alcolac, Inc.*, 658 F.3d 388, 401 (4th Cir. 2011) (requiring "substantial assistance with the purpose of facilitating the alleged violation"), *with Doe v. Exxon Mobil Corp.*, 654 F.3d 11 (D.C. Cir. 2011) (adopting less demanding "knowledge" standard, based on customary international law, but suggesting that "[f]or all practical purposes" the federal common law standard was identical and could be applied), *vacated on other grounds*, 527 Fed.Appx. 7 (Mem) (D.C. Cir. 2013); *cf. Doe I v. Nestle, USA*, 766 F.3d 1013, 1024 (9th

Circ. 2104) (reviewing precedent, but declining to decide between purpose or knowledge standards).

Later, another Second Circuit panel held *sua sponte* that the ATS does not confer jurisdiction over claims against corporations at all; because corporations were not subject to liability under customary international law, they were not liable under the ATS. *Kiobel v. Royal Dutch Petroleum*, 621 F.3d 111 (2d Cir. 2010). *But see id.* at 149, 174–76 (Leval, J., concurring in the judgment) (accepting that international law may in theory resolve whether corporations should be held liable for violations of customary international law, but in fact leaves the question to domestic law). This question was left unresolved by the Supreme Court, which instead resolved that case on grounds of extraterritoriality, as excerpted above. Subsequent to the Supreme Court's decision in *Kiobel*, the Second Circuit held that the non-liability of corporations under the ATS was dictated by circuit precedent, acknowledging a split with other courts. *See In re Arab Bank, PLC Alien Tort Statute Litigation*, 808 F.3d 144, 156 (2d Cir. 2015) (citing, *inter alia*, *Doe I v. Nestle USA, Inc.*, 766 F.3d 1013, 1022 (9th Cir. 2014); *Doe VIII v. Exxon Mobil Corp.*, 654 F.3d 11, 57 (D.C. Cir. 2011), *vacated on other grounds*, 527 Fed. Appx. 7 (D.C. Cir. 2013); *Flomo v. Firestone Nat. Rubber Co.*, 643 F.3d 1013, 1021 (7th Cir. 2011); *Romero v. Drummond Co.*, 552 F.3d 1303, 1315 (11th Cir. 2008)).

In 2017, the Supreme Court granted certiorari on the issue of corporate liability, with briefing and argument early in October Term 2018. *Jesner v. Arab Bank, PLC*, 137 S. Ct. 1432 (2017). One issue the Court appears to confront is whether courts should look for resolution of questions like corporate liability in international law (and what to conclude, for example, from the fact that customary international law rarely addresses the liability of corporations, and what weight to give to their treatment in the statutes of international criminal tribunals) or instead to domestic law principles (as for the imposition of civil liability by the ATS in the first place). Under *Sosa*, which approach is correct? Would you apply international law to some questions, but not others? If domestic law governs, should it be the law of the forum State (the United States), or the law of the State where the underlying events occurred? *See Wiwa v. Royal Dutch Petroleum Co.*, 226 F.3d 88, 105 n.12 (2d Cir. 2000) (noting ATS cases applying international law, forum State law, and foreign law to address comparable questions); Chimène I. Keitner, *Conceptualizing Complicity in Alien Tort Cases*, 60 HASTINGS L.J. 61 (2008) (distinguishing between conduct-regulating rules, like accomplice liability, that are defined by international law, as opposed to ancillary questions governed by domestic law).

3. *Extraterritoriality and the Future of the ATS.* The continuing proceedings in *Jesner* suggest that issues like corporate liability under the ATS remain pertinent, but their significance was changed dramatically following *Kiobel v. Royal Dutch Petroleum Co.* How dramatically, of course, depends on how that decision is read. The *Kiobel* majority suggested in closing that future ATS claims may "touch and concern the territory of the United States . . . with sufficient force to displace the presumption against extraterritorial application" (133 S. Ct. 1659, 1669 (2013)), but what exactly does that mean?

Justice Kennedy's concurrence provides little guidance, see *id.* at 1669 (Kennedy, J., concurring), and Justice Alito would bar an ATS claim "unless the domestic conduct is sufficient to violate an international law norm that satisfies *Sosa*'s requirements of definiteness and acceptance among civilized nations." *Id.* at 1669–70 (Alito, J., concurring). Do you understand these to be different standards? To what extent might the factors indicated by Justice Breyer indicate whether a claim was sufficiently domestic? Analysis may be affected by the subsequent decision in *RJR Nabisco, Inc. v. European Community*, 136 S. Ct. 2090 (2016) (noted *supra*, this Chapter, Sec. 3). *See* Edward T. Swaine, Kiobel *and Extraterritoriality: Here, (Not) There, (Not Even) Everywhere*, 69 OKLA. L. REV. 23 (2016).

4. *Congress and ATS Reform*. There have been periodic calls for a new statute to replace the ATS, see, e.g., Ralph G. Steinhardt, *Laying One Bankrupt Critique to Rest:* Sosa v. Alvarez-Machain *and the Future of International Human Rights Litigation*, 57 VAND. L. REV. 2241, 2294 (2004), but little by way of legislative initiatives—save for more technical amendments (see footnote 10 in *Sosa*) and a short-lived alternative that articulated a limited number of actionable torts, largely so as to increase certainty for U.S.-based multinational corporations. Alien Tort Statute Reform Act, S. 1874, 109th Cong. (1st Sess. 2005); 151 CONG. REC. 22,858 (2005).

5. *Torture Victim Protection Act (TVPA).* Although it has resisted revisiting the ATS, Congress has pursued more targeted problems. For example, as noted in *Sosa*, Congress in 1992 adopted the Torture Victim Protection Act, 28 U.S.C. § 1350 note (2012). The TVPA imposes civil liability on any "individual who, under actual or apparent authority, or color of law, of any foreign nation . . . subjects an individual to torture . . . or . . . to extrajudicial killing." TVPA § 2(a). Rather than making a direct cross-reference to the "law of nations," the statute defines torture using language virtually identical to that found in the CAT. The TVPA differs from the ATS insofar as the claim must concern action under the authority of a foreign government, the claimant need not be an alien, and that, in order to bring a claim under the statute, a claimant must have "exhausted [any] adequate and available remedies in the place in which the conduct giving rise to the claim occurred." *Id.* § 2(b). The Supreme Court has also held that it only supports liability of natural persons, not organizations, resolving an issue temporarily sidestepped in *Kiobel. See Mohamad v. Palestinian Authority*, 566 U.S. 449 (2012). For further text of the statute, see Chapter 3, Sec. 3.

The Senate report on the TVPA states that the statute was intended to "establish an unambiguous basis for a cause of action that has been successfully maintained under [the ATS,] . . . which permits Federal district courts to hear claims by aliens for torts committed 'in violation of the law of nations.' " S. REP. NO. 102–249, at 4 (1991). The report specifically noted that "[t]he *Filartiga* case has met with general approval." Recognizing that "[a]t least one Federal judge . . . has questioned whether [the ATS] can be used by victims of torture committed in foreign nations absent an explicit grant of a cause of action by Congress," *id.* (citing *Tel-Oren*, 726 F.2d at 774 (Bork, J., concurring)), the Senate report concluded that "[t]he TVPA would provide such a grant," *id.* at 5.

Does the TVPA provide a superior template for the incorporation of human rights norms, or is it categorically different in its objectives and methods? For another leading example of congressional action in human rights—also known, confusingly, as the TVPA—consider the Trafficking Victims Protection Act. When passed initially, the Act defined (without reference to any international law) the offense of trafficking and established that as a criminal offense; later, during reauthorization, Congress added a civil action for damages. Pub.L. 108–193, 117 Stat. 2878 (2003), codified at 18 U.S.C. § 1595(a) (2012).

7. PIRACY

UNITED STATES V. SMITH

18 U.S. (5 Wheat.) 153 (1820).

[A jury found that, in March 1819, the defendant Thomas Smith and others were part of the crew of a private armed vessel called the *Creollo*. The *Creollo* had been commissioned by the government of Buenos Ayres (a Spanish colony then at war with Spain). While the vessel was lying in the port of Margaritta, the defendant and other crew members mutinied, confined their officer, left the vessel, and seized by violence another private-armed vessel called the *Irresistible*. The mutineers then took the *Irresistible* to sea, where they engaged in the plunder and robbery of a Spanish vessel. The jury determined that such conduct violated a U.S. criminal statute on piracy that was enacted on March 3, 1819 and that referenced the "law of nations."]

MR. JUSTICE STORY delivered the opinion of the court.

The act of Congress upon which this indictment is founded provides, "that if any person or persons whatsoever, shall, upon the high seas, commit the crime of piracy, as defined by the law of nations, and such offender or offenders shall be brought into, or found in the United States, every such offender or offenders shall, upon conviction thereof, & c. be punished with death." . . . .

It is . . . to be considered, whether the crime of piracy is defined by the law of nations with reasonable certainty. What the law of nations on this subject is, may be ascertained by consulting the works of jurists, writing professedly on public law; or by the general usage and practice of nations; or by judicial decisions recognising and enforcing that law. There is scarcely a writer on the law of nations, who does not allude to piracy as a crime of a settled and determinate nature; and whatever may be the diversity of definitions, in other respects, all writers concur, in holding, that robbery, or forcible depredations upon the sea, *animo furandi,* is

piracy. The same doctrine is held by all the great writers on maritime law, in terms that admit of no reasonable doubt. The common law, too, recognises and punishes piracy as an offence, not against its own municipal code, but as an offence against the law of nations, (which is part of the common law,), as an offence against the universal law of society, a pirate being deemed an enemy of the human race. . . . Sir Charles Hedges, in his charge at the Admiralty sessions, in the case of *Rex v. Dawson*, (5 *State Trials,*) declared in emphatic terms, that "piracy is only a sea term for robbery, piracy being a robbery committed within the jurisdiction of the admiralty." Sir Leoline Jenkins, too, on a like occasion, declared that "a robbery, when committed upon the sea, is what we call piracy;" and he cited the civil law writers, in proof. And it is manifest from the language of Sir William Blackstone, in his comments on piracy, that he considered the common law definition as distinguishable in no essential respect from that of the law of nations. So that, whether we advert to writers on the common law, or the maritime law, or the law of nations, we shall find that they universally treat of piracy as an offence against the law of nations, and that its true definition by that law is robbery upon the sea. And the general practice of all nations in punishing all persons, whether natives or foreigners, who have committed this offence against any person whatsoever, with whom they are in amity, is a conclusive proof that the offence is supposed to depend, not upon the particular provisions of any municipal code, but upon the law of nations, both for its definition and punishment. We have, therefore, no hesitation in declaring, that piracy, by the law of nations, is robbery upon the sea, and that it is sufficiently and constitutionally defined by the fifth section of the act of 1819. . . .

It is to be certified to the Circuit Court, that upon the facts stated, the case is piracy, as defined by the law of nations, so as to be punishable under the act of Congress of the 3d of March, 1819.

MR. JUSTICE LIVINGSTON dissented.

In a case affecting life, no apology can be necessary for expressing my dissent from the opinion which has just been delivered.

The only question of any importance in this case is, whether the act of the 3d of March, 1819, be a constitutional exercise of the power delegated to Congress of "defining and punishing piracies?" The act declares, that any person who shall commit on the high seas the crime of piracy as *defined by the law of nations,* shall be punished with death. The special power here given to define piracy, can be attributed to no other cause, than to the uncertainty which it was known existed on this subject in the law of nations, and which it must have been the intention of the framers of the constitution to remove, by conferring on the national legislature the power which has been mentioned. It was well known to the members of the Federal Convention, that in treatises on the law of nations, or in some of them at least, definitions of piracy might be found; but it must have been as well known to them that there was not such a coincidence on this subject, as to render a reference to that code a desirable or safe mode of proceeding in a criminal, and especially in a capital case. If it had been intended to adopt the definition or definitions of this crime, so far as they were to be collected from the different commentators on this code, with all the uncertainty and difficulty attending a research for that purpose, it might as well at once have been adopted as a standard by the constitution itself. The object, therefore, of referring its definition to Congress was, and could have been no other than, to enable that body, to select from sources it might think proper, and then to declare, and with reasonable precision to define, what act or acts should constitute this crime; and having done so, to annex to it such punishment as might be thought proper. Such a mode of proceeding would be consonant with the universal practice in this country, and with those feelings of humanity which are ever opposed to the putting in jeopardy the life of a fellow-being, unless for the contravention of a rule which has been previously prescribed, and in language so plain and explicit as not to be misunderstood by any one. . . . [I]t is the duty of Congress to incorporate into their own statutes a definition in *terms,* and not to refer the citizens of the United States for rules of conduct to the statutes or laws of any foreign country, with which it is not to be presumed that they are acquainted. Nor does it make any difference in this case, that the law of nations forms part of the law of every civilized country. This may be the case to a certain extent; but as to criminal cases, and as to the offence of piracy in particular, the law of nations could not be supposed of itself to form a rule of action; and, therefore, a reference to it in this instance, must be regarded in the same light, as a reference to any other foreign code. . . . Congress have power to punish offences against the law of nations, and yet it would hardly be deemed a fair and legitimate execution of this authority, to declare, that all offences against the law of nations, without defining any one of them, should be punished with death. Such mode of legislation is but badly calculated to furnish that precise and accurate information in criminal cases, which it is the duty, and ought to be the object, of every legislature to impart.

Upon the whole, my opinion is, that there is not to be found in the act that definition of piracy which the constitution requires, and that, therefore, judgment on the special verdict ought to be rendered for the prisoner.

CONTEMPORARY PIRACY AND PRIVATEERING STATUTES

18 U.S.C. Ch. 81, §§ 1651–1654 (2012).

§ 1651. Piracy under law of nations

Whoever, on the high seas, commits the crime of piracy as defined by the law of nations, and is afterwards brought into or found in the United States, shall be imprisoned for life.

§ 1652. Citizens as pirates

Whoever, being a citizen of the United States, commits any murder or robbery, or any act of hostility against the United States, or against any citizen thereof, on the high seas, under color of any commission from any foreign prince, or state, or on pretense of authority from any person, is a pirate, and shall be imprisoned for life.

§ 1653. Aliens as pirates

Whoever, being a citizen or subject of any foreign state, is found and taken on the sea making war upon the United States, or cruising against the vessels and property thereof, or of the citizens of the same, contrary to the provisions of any treaty existing between the United States and the state of which the offender is a citizen or subject, when by such treaty such acts are declared to be piracy, is a pirate, and shall be imprisoned for life.

§ 1654. Arming or serving on privateers

Whoever, being a citizen of the United States, without the limits thereof, fits out and arms, or attempts to fit out and arm or is concerned in furnishing, fitting out, or arming any private vessel of war or privateer, with intent that such vessel shall be employed to cruise or commit hostilities upon the citizens of the United States or their property; or

Whoever takes the command of or enters on board of any such vessel with such intent; or

Whoever purchases any interest in any such vessel with a view to share in the profits thereof—

Shall be fined under this title or imprisoned not more than ten years, or both.

SAMUEL PYEATT MENEFEE, "YO HEAVE HO!": UPDATING AMERICA'S PIRACY LAWS*

21 Cal. W. Int'l L.J. 151 (1990).

I. GENERAL BACKGROUND

. . . While subsequent years have seen revisions in the *arrangement* of these statutes, their general *content* has remained largely unchanged for over a century and a half! At the same time, this period, particularly the half-century since the Second World War, has seen important changes in occurrences of violence at sea. The 1856 Declaration of Paris, for example, virtually put an end to privateering. While the United States did not accede to this document, it has generally followed its provisions, and the overall disappearance of privateering from international law itself points up the obsolescent nature of much of Chapter 81. As some scholars have pointed out, an *emerging* problem has been the takeover of vessels by passengers for political purposes. The problem of localized piracy, seemingly confined to the Aegean, the South China Sea, and Malay Archipelago after the Caribbean "campaign" of the 1820s and 1930s, has broken out anew in the post-War years. Clusters of piratical activity are found in West Africa, the Malaccan Straits area, the Philippines, and the Caribbean, not to mention in ports such as Santos, Brazil. Often, the objects of the assaults are United States vessels, cargos, or nationals. At the very least, these activities should call for a *review* of Chapter 81, as the issue is not a *theoretical* one, but a contemporary problem affecting American lives and property.

Finally, there are developments undreamed of by the drafters of the Code's piracy statutes. Submarines, offshore platforms, pipelines and cables have widened the sphere of potential maritime operations. Bombs allow for "remote-controlled mayhem," while telephones have opened the floodgates to *threatened* actions. The rise of environmental issues (and, unfortunately, of environmental extremists) have provided new incentives for maritime violence. In the last fifteen years, for example, six whaling vessels have been attacked (and five sunk) in protests against depletion of cetaceans. Sealing, fishing, ocean dumping, and nuclear energy provide lightning-rods for similar potential outbursts. The international law of piracy has been at least *partially* codified in the 1958 Geneva Convention on the High Seas and in its successor, the 1982 Convention on the Law of the Sea.[50] But, during this century and a half of change and development, the United States Code provisions on piracy have remained frozen.

---

* Reprinted with permission of the California Western International Law Journal.

[50] *See* Convention on the High Seas, Apr. 29, 1958, 13 U.S.T. 2312, T.I.A.S. No. 5200; 450 U.N.T.S. 82 (arts. 14–22) [hereinafter Convention on the High Seas]; United Nations Convention on the Law of Sea, Dec. 10, 1982, U.N. Doc. A/CONF.62/122, *reprinted in* UNITED NATIONS CONVENTION ON THE LAW OF THE SEA 1982: A COMMENTARY 206, 248–49 (M. Nordquist ed. 1985) (arts. 100–107) [hereinafter Convention on the Law of the Sea]. . . .

II. CHAPTER 81 AND ITS PROBLEMS

In examining Chapter 81 and its problems, it seems most useful to proceed with a section-by-section review of the law as it now stands. The criticisms and comments offered herein do not pretend to be complete, but should indicate some problems with the Code provisions as they exist, and will, hopefully, provide a basis for future discussion.

A. Section 1651: Piracy Under Law of Nations

This section is obviously derived from section 5 of the Act of March 3, 1819. The only major difference is that life imprisonment has been substituted for the death penalty. The provision raises two questions. First, if the 1958 Convention on the High Seas and its successor, the 1982 Convention, are judged to be the *complete and exclusive* codification of the intended crime of piracy, section 1651 would *not* cover all cases of piracy "against a ship, aircraft, persons or property in a place outside the jurisdiction of any State."[53] Similarly, the specified high seas nexus might well *omit* some acts "of voluntary participation in the operation of a ship or of an aircraft with knowledge of facts making it a pirate ship or aircraft"[54] or acts "of inciting or of intentionally facilitating" piratical acts.[55]

If the two Conventions are *not* considered to be a definitive codification of the international law of piracy, the question arises as to what constitutes piracy "as defined by the law of nations." . . .

The worst problem with this section appears to be the use of the term "high seas." As used in section 1651, this does not appear to have the jurisdictional meaning which it has acquired in international law, but rather to attach to *any* waters beyond the low water mark.[58] It would therefore seem appropriate for the term to be used in its correct treaty sense or, alternately, to be dropped in any revision of section 1651.

B. Section 1652: Citizens as Pirates

This section derives from section 9 of the Act of April 30, 1790. Its purpose was to cover acts of privateering by American citizens, but it has been wrenched out of context and this, plus a number of changes in circumstance, has resulted in several problems. The most obvious is the demise of privateering; people simply do not cruise on the seas "under color of any commission" to commit hostile acts against the United States or its citizens, to murder, or to rob. . . . At the same time, bearing in mind the

---

[53] . . . The quotation comes from Article 101 of the 1982 Convention. . . .

[54] *See* Convention on the Law of the Sea, *supra* note 50, art. 101(b); Convention on the High Seas, *supra* note 50, art. 15(2). . . .

[55] *See* Convention on the Law of the Sea, art. 101(c), *supra* note 50; Convention on the High Seas, art. 15(3), *supra* note 50. . . .

[58] *See United States v. Pirates*, 18 U.S. (5 Wheat.) 184 (1820); *United States v. Wilson*, 28 Fed. Cas. no. 16,731 (S.D.N.Y. 1856); *United States v. Gourlay*, 25 Fed. Cas. no. 15,241 (S.D.N.Y. 1823); *United States v. Ross*, Fed. Cas. no. 16,196 (C.C.R.I. 1813). . . .

possibility of ideological crimes which are *non-political* in nature, thought should be given to a more expansive description of the criminal mind-set involved.

Another tangle arises from the reference to "any murder or robbery, or any act of hostility against the United States, or against any citizen thereof." As currently phrased, *all murders or robberies* by U.S. citizens falling under the terms of the statute would be included, but *only those other acts of hostility directed against the United States or its citizens* are covered by this section. The murder or robbery of a British passenger by an American for political purposes would thus appear to be covered by this section of the Code, but *not* his kidnap or torture. A decision should be made as to whether only political crimes by Americans against the United States or fellow citizens should be covered, or whether it is desirable that maritime political crimes against *any* nation or national by an American should fall within the Code's ambit.

There are again questions of jurisdiction. In addition to the problems of terminology, the extension of territorial waters and Exclusive Economic Zones means that fewer crimes will be committed *outside* national jurisdiction. It must therefore be decided whether cases occurring *within* national jurisdiction should be left to the jurisdiction of the coastal state, or whether the United States should preserve at least the *option* of exerting its own jurisdiction. Finally, one must consider whether only citizens should be covered by this section, or whether others, such as resident aliens, should be included as well.

C. *Section 1653: Aliens as Pirates*

Section 1653 is a direct descendent of the Act of March 3, 1847. While its title and positioning suggest that it is intended as a counter-point to section 1652, several differences prevent the two statutes from serving as mirror images. First, the provision that the individual must be "a citizen or subject of [a] foreign state" could allow a *stateless* alien to escape punishment. Next, the requirement that the individual be "found and taken on the sea" disallows any possibility of later capture on land, regardless of whether the national's country assents to extradition, the individual is apprehended in a third county, or capture occurs within the territorial (dry land) confines of the United States itself! Finally, there may (or may not) be a difference between the term "high seas" and "sea."[72]

Again returning to changed concepts, "making war upon the United States, or cruising against the vessels and property thereof, or of the citizens of the same," has a nineteenth-century flavor which has not "kept" well. It would be far more to the point to speak of ideologically or politically motivated actions. Similarly, the *absence* of a bilateral (or multilateral)

[72] . . . There appears to be no case law discussing this issue, but it is at least arguable that "sea" could refer to *all* waters subject to tidal ebb and flow. . . .

treaty declaring certain acts to be piracy should not permit the citizens of any particular state to "cruise" with impunity. Following such logic, the term "Barbary pirates" would be an oxymoron! As in prior sections, the *extent* of jurisdiction is also open to question. Should the current "high seas" jurisdiction (assuming that is what is meant by "sea") be retained, or should a different scope of potential jurisdiction be contemplated?

D. Section 1654: Arming or Serving as Privateers

This section is based on section 4 of the Act of 1818. Like section 1652, it deals with the problem of privateering by U.S. nationals under color of a commission, and suffers from similar defects. In addition to problems with "privateering" itself, and the limitation of the section to "citizen[s] of the United States," section 1654, unlike section 1652, does *not* apply within U.S. territorial waters. Thus, some privateering activities by American citizens in American waters would be covered by the Code while *others* would not. . . .

CONCLUSION

A general review of the background to 18 U.S.C. Chapter 81 has shown that the laws on piracy do *not* reflect recent developments in maritime law. Additionally, reactions to *prior* developments have resulted in a composite chapter of laws which, as the reviser noted, cry out for "a fundamental reconsideration and complete restatement," including "drastic changes by way of modification and expansion." . . .

UNITED STATES V. DIRE

680 F.3d 446 (4th Cir. 2012).

KING, CIRCUIT JUDGE:

In the early morning hours of April 1, 2010, on the high seas between Somalia and the Seychelles (in the Indian Ocean off the east coast of Africa), the defendants . . . imprudently launched an attack on the USS Nicholas, having confused that mighty Navy frigate for a vulnerable merchant ship. The defendants, all Somalis, were swiftly apprehended and then transported to the Eastern District of Virginia, where they were convicted of the crime of piracy, as proscribed by 18 U.S.C. § 1651 . . . In this appeal, the defendants challenge their convictions and life-plus-eighty-year sentences on several grounds, including that their fleeting and fruitless strike on the Nicholas did not, as a matter of law, amount to a § 1651 piracy offense. As explained below, we reject their contentions and affirm. . . .

II.

In these consolidated appeals, the defendants . . . contend that their ill-fated attack on the USS Nicholas did not constitute piracy under 18 U.S.C. § 1651, which provides in full:

Whoever, on the high seas, commits the crime of piracy as defined by the law of nations, and is afterwards brought into or found in the United States, shall be imprisoned for life.

According to the defendants, the crime of piracy has been narrowly defined for purposes of § 1651 as robbery at sea, i.e., seizing or otherwise robbing a vessel. Because they boarded the Nicholas only as captives and indisputably took no property, the defendants contest their convictions on Count One, as well as the affixed life sentences.

A.

. . . [T]he [district] court concluded—contrary to the defendants' posited robbery requirement—that piracy as defined by § 1651's incorporated law of nations encompasses, inter alia, acts of violence committed on the high seas for private ends. See [*United States v. Hasan*, 747 F.Supp.2d 599, 640–42 (E.D. Va. 2010)]. . . .

Th[at] . . . opinion was issued on the heels of the August 17, 2010 published opinion in *United States v. Said*, 757 F.Supp.2d 554 (E.D.Va.2010) (Jackson, J.), wherein a different judge of the Eastern District of Virginia essentially took these defendants' view of the piracy offense by recognizing a robbery element. Like these defendants, the *Said* defendants have been charged with piracy under 18 U.S.C. § 1651 for attacking—but not seizing or otherwise robbing—a United States Navy ship. . . .

Invoking the principle that a court "must interpret a statute by its ordinary meaning at the time of its enactment," the *Said* court deemed [United States v.] Smith to be the definitive authority on the meaning of piracy under 18 U.S.C. § 1651. . . . Looking to courts that have addressed the piracy statute post-Smith in other contexts, the *Said* court concluded that "the discernible definition of piracy as 'robbery or forcible depredations committed on the high seas' under § 1651 has remained consistent and has reached a level of concrete consensus in United S[t]ates law." Id. at 560. . . .

The crux of the defendants' position is now, as it was in the district court, that the definition of general piracy was fixed in the early Nineteenth Century, when Congress passed the Act of 1819 first authorizing the exercise of universal jurisdiction by United States courts to adjudicate charges of "piracy as defined by the law of nations." Most notably, the defendants assert that the "law of nations," as understood in 1819, is not conterminous with the "customary international law" of today. The defendants rely on Chief Justice Marshall's observation that "[t]he law of nations is a law founded on the great and immutable principles of equity and natural justice," *The Venus*, 12 U.S. (8 Cranch) 253, 297 (1814) (Marshall, C.J., dissenting), to support their theory that "[t]he Congress that enacted the [Act of 1819] did not view the universal law of nations as an evolving body of law." . . .

The defendants' view is thoroughly refuted, however, by a bevy of precedent, including the Supreme Court's 2004 decision in *Sosa v. Alvarez-Machain*. . . . [T]he Sosa Court did not regard the [Alien Tort Statute] as incorporating some stagnant notion of the law of nations. Rather, the Court concluded that, while the first Congress probably understood the ATS to confer jurisdiction over only the three paradigmatic law-of-nations torts of the time—including piracy—the door was open to ATS jurisdiction over additional "claim[s] based on the present-day law of nations," albeit in narrow circumstances. See id. at 724–25. Those circumstances were lacking in the case of Alvarez, whose ATS claim could not withstand being "gauged against the current state of international law." See id. at 733.

Although, as the defendants point out, the ATS involves civil claims and the general piracy statute entails criminal prosecutions, there is no reason to believe that the "law of nations" evolves in the civil context but stands immobile in the criminal context. Moreover, if the Congress of 1819 had believed either the law of nations generally or its piracy definition specifically to be inflexible, the Act of 1819 could easily have been drafted to specify that piracy consisted of "piracy as defined on March 3, 1819 [the date of enactment], by the law of nations," or solely of, as the defendants would have it, "robbery upon the sea." . . .

Additional theories posited by the defendants of a static piracy definition are no more persuasive. For example, the defendants contend that giving "piracy" an evolving definition would violate the principle that there are no federal common law crimes. See Br. of Appellants 32 (citing *United States v. Hudson*, 11 U.S. (7 Cranch) 32, 34 (1812), for the proposition "that federal courts have no power to exercise 'criminal jurisdiction in common-law cases' "). The 18 U.S.C. § 1651 piracy offense cannot be considered a common law crime, however, because Congress properly "ma[de] an act a crime, affix[ed] a punishment to it, and declare[d] the court that shall have jurisdiction of the offence." *See Hudson*, 11 U.S. (7 Cranch) at 34. Moreover, in its 1820 *Smith* decision, the Supreme Court unhesitatingly approved of the piracy statute's incorporation of the law of nations, looking to various sources to ascertain how piracy was defined under the law of nations. *See Smith*, 18 U.S. (5 Wheat.) at 159–61.

The defendants would have us believe that, since the *Smith* era, the United States' proscription of general piracy has been limited to "robbery upon the sea." But that interpretation of our law would render it incongruous with the modern law of nations and prevent us from exercising universal jurisdiction in piracy cases. . . . At bottom, then, the defendants' position is irreconcilable with the noncontroversial notion that Congress intended in § 1651 to define piracy as a universal jurisdiction crime. In these circumstances, we are constrained to agree with the district court that § 1651 incorporates a definition of piracy that changes with advancements in the law of nations.

We also agree with the district court that the definition of piracy under the law of nations, at the time of the defendants' attack on the USS Nicholas and continuing today, had for decades encompassed their violent conduct. That definition, spelled out in the UNCLOS, as well as the High Seas Convention before it, has only been reaffirmed in recent years as nations around the world have banded together to combat the escalating scourge of piracy. For example, in November 2011, the United Nations Security Council adopted Resolution 2020, recalling a series of prior resolutions approved between 2008 and 2011 "concerning the situation in Somalia"; expressing "grave[ ] concern[ ] [about] the ongoing threat that piracy and armed robbery at sea against vessels pose"; and emphasizing "the need for a comprehensive response by the international community to repress piracy and armed robbery at sea and tackle its underlying causes." Of the utmost significance, Resolution 2020 reaffirmed "that international law, as reflected in the [UNCLOS], sets out the legal framework applicable to combating piracy and armed robbery at sea."[15] Because the district court correctly applied the UNCLOS definition of piracy as customary international law, we reject the defendants' challenge to their Count One piracy convictions, as well as their mandatory life sentences. . . .

Pursuant to the foregoing, we affirm the convictions and sentences of each of the defendants.

INSTITUTE OF CETACEAN RESEARCH V. SEA SHEPHERD CONSERVATION SOCIETY

725 F.3d 940 (9th Cir. 2013).

KOZINSKI, CHIEF JUDGE:

You don't need a peg leg or an eye patch. When you ram ships; hurl glass containers of acid; drag metal-reinforced ropes in the water to damage propellers and rudders; launch smoke bombs and flares with hooks; and point high-powered lasers at other ships, you are, without a doubt, a pirate, no matter how high-minded you believe your purpose to be.

Plaintiffs-Appellants (collectively, "Cetacean") are Japanese researchers who hunt whales in the Southern Ocean. The United States, Japan and many other nations are signatories to the International

[15] Notably, as one of the permanent members of the Security Council, the United States supported the adoption of Resolution 2020, which was approved by a unanimous Security Council.

Convention for the Regulation of Whaling art. VIII, Dec. 2, 1946, 62 Stat. 1716, 161 U.N.T.S. 74, which authorizes whale hunting when conducted in compliance with a research permit issued by a signatory. Cetacean has such a permit from Japan. Nonetheless, it has been hounded on the high seas for years by a group calling itself Sea Shepherd Conservation Society and its eccentric founder, Paul Watson (collectively "Sea Shepherd"). Sea Shepherd's tactics include all of those listed in the previous paragraph.

Cetacean sued under the Alien Tort Statute, 28 U.S.C. § 1350, for injunctive and declaratory relief. The statute provides a cause of action for "a tort . . . committed in violation of the law of nations or a treaty of the United States." 28 U.S.C. § 1350. Cetacean argues that Sea Shepherd's acts amount to piracy and violate international agreements regulating conduct on the high seas. . . .

. . . "[T]he definition of piracy under the law of nations . . . [is] spelled out in the UNCLOS, as well as the High Seas Convention," which provide almost identical definitions. *United States v. Dire,* 680 F.3d 446, 469 (4th Cir. 2012); *see* United Nations Convention on the Law of the Sea ("UNCLOS"), art. 101, Dec. 10, 1982, 1833 U.N.T.S. 397; Convention on the High Seas, art. 15, Apr. 29, 1958, 13 U.S.T. 2312, 450 U.N.T.S. 82. The UNCLOS defines "piracy" as "illegal acts of *violence* or detention, or any act of depredation, committed for *private ends* by the crew or the passengers of a private ship . . . and directed . . . on the high seas, against another ship . . . or against persons or property on board such ship." UNCLOS art. 101 (emphasis added); *see also* Convention on the High Seas art. 15.

The district court's analysis turns on an erroneous interpretation of "private ends" and "violence." The district court construed "private ends" as limited to those pursued for "financial enrichment." But the common understanding of "private" is far broader. The term is normally used as an antonym to "public" (e.g., private attorney general) and often refers to matters of a personal nature that are not necessarily connected to finance (e.g., private property, private entrance, private understanding and invasion of privacy). *See Webster's New Int'l Dictionary* 1969 (2d. ed.1939) (defining "private" to mean "[b]elonging to, or concerning, an individual person, company, or interest").

We give words their ordinary meaning unless the context requires otherwise. . . . The context here is provided by the rich history of piracy law, which defines acts taken for private ends as those not taken on behalf of a state. . . . Belgian courts, perhaps the only ones to have previously considered the issue, have held that environmental activism qualifies as a private end. *See* Cour de Cassation [Cass.] [Court of Cassation] *Castle John v. NV Mabeco,* Dec. 19, 1986, 77 I.L.R. 537 (Belg.). This interpretation is "entitled to considerable weight." *Abbott v. Abbott,* 560 U.S. 1, 130 S. Ct.

1983, 1993 (2010) (internal quotation marks omitted). We conclude that "private ends" include those pursued on personal, moral or philosophical grounds, such as Sea Shepherd's professed environmental goals. That the perpetrators believe themselves to be serving the public good does not render their ends public.

The district court's interpretation of "violence" was equally off-base. Citing no precedent, it held that Sea Shepherd's conduct is not violent because it targets ships and equipment rather than people. This runs afoul of the UNCLOS itself, which prohibits "violence . . . against another ship" and "violence . . . against persons or property." UNCLOS art. 101. Reading "violence" as extending to malicious acts against inanimate objects also comports with the commonsense understanding of the term, *see Webster's New Int'l Dictionary* 2846, as when a man violently pounds a table with his fist. Ramming ships, fouling propellers and hurling fiery and acid-filled projectiles easily qualify as violent activities, even if they could somehow be directed only at inanimate objects.

Regardless, Sea Shepherd's acts fit even the district court's constricted definition. The projectiles directly endanger Cetacean's crew, as the district court itself recognized. And damaging Cetacean's ships could cause them to sink or become stranded in glacier-filled, Antarctic waters, jeopardizing the safety of the crew.

The activities that Cetacean alleges Sea Shepherd has engaged in are clear instances of violent acts for private ends, the very embodiment of piracy. The district court erred in dismissing Cetacean's piracy claims. . . .

UNITED STATES V. SUERTE

291 F.3d 366 (5th Cir. 2002).

RHESA HAWKINS BARKSDALE, CIRCUIT JUDGE:

At issue is whether, for extraterritorial application of the Maritime Drug Law Enforcement Act, 46 U.S.C.App. § 1901 *et seq.*, the Fifth Amendment's Due Process Clause requires a nexus between a foreign citizen and the United States, where the flag nation for his vessel "has consented or waived objection to the enforcement of United States law by the United States". *Id.* § 1903(c)(1)(C). Requiring such a nexus, the district court dismissed the indictment for lack of jurisdiction. *Vacated* and *remanded.*

I.

Defendant Nestor Suerte, a Philippine national and resident of Colombia, has apparently never entered the United States. The Government alleges the following.

Suerte was captain of a freighter registered in Malta and owned by a member of a Colombian/Venezuelan drug trafficking organization (DTO); he met in Venezuela with DTO members in July and August 2000 to coordinate loading the freighter, off the northern coast of Venezuela, with 4900 kilograms of cocaine for transport to, and distribution in, Europe; the freighter apparently departed Venezuela on 11 August; the next day, an attempt was made, using speed boats, to transport the cocaine to it; after Venezuelan law enforcement detected the boats, they took evasive action. . . .

The DTO telexed Suerte plans for the second attempt, . . . however, Venezuelan authorities arrested some of the DTO members, thwarting the second attempt; but, nevertheless, on 17 August, the freighter was at the vicinity of the designated rendezvous point, in international waters.

The United States requested, and received, permission from Malta (the flag nation) to board and search the freighter. . . . A search by the Coast Guard did not find cocaine.

Approximately a week later, Malta waived objection to the enforcement of United States laws over the freighter and its crew. The Government towed the vessel to the Port of Houston, Texas; on 2 September, it was searched by United States Customs Special Agents; found in Suerte's cabin was a torn copy of the above-referenced telex giving the date, time, and coordinates for the second attempt to load cocaine; and also found was an attache case containing $3500 in $100 bills.

Suerte was arrested and indicted for *conspiracy* . . . to possess, with intent to distribute, more than five kilograms of cocaine on board a vessel subject to United States jurisdiction, in violation of the Maritime Drug Law Enforcement Act (MDLEA), 46 U.S.C.App. § 1903. The Act provides, in pertinent part:

> (a) It is unlawful for any person . . . *on board a vessel subject to the jurisdiction of the United States* . . . to knowingly or intentionally . . . possess with intent to . . . distribute[ ] a controlled substance. . . .
>
> (c)(1) For purposes of this section, a "vessel subject to the jurisdiction of the United States" includes—. . . .
>
> > (C) a vessel registered in a foreign nation where the *flag nation has consented or waived objection* to the enforcement of United States law by the United States; . . . .
>
> (j) Any person who attempts or *conspires* to commit any offense defined in this chapter shall be subject to the same penalties as those prescribed for the offense, the commission of which was the object of the attempt or conspiracy.

Id. (emphasis added). . . .

II.

B.

. . . [S]everal sources of law . . . provide us great assurance that, "where the flag nation has consented or waived objection to the enforcement of United States law by the United States", § 1903(c)(1)(C), due process does not require a nexus for the MDLEA's extraterritorial application. Those sources include: the Constitutional Convention debate surrounding the Piracies and Felonies Clause ("The Congress shall have Power . . . [t]o define and punish Piracies and Felonies committed on the high Seas, and Offenses against the Law of Nations"); the earliest exercise of Congressional power under the clause; and Supreme Court opinions reviewing that exercise.

1.

Concerning the Piracies and Felonies Clause, the Committee of Detail's draft Constitution, submitted to the Convention on 6 August 1787, would have empowered Congress "[t]o *declare* the law and punishment of piracies and felonies committed on the high seas, and the punishment of counterfeiting the coin of the United States, and of offences against the law of nations". 2 RECORDS OF THE FEDERAL CONVENTION OF 1787 182 (Max Farrand ed., 1999) (emphasis added). Subsequent debate over the clause primarily concerned the propriety of granting the power to both punish *and* declare and whether the latter power should read "declare", "designate", or "define". *See id.* at 315–16.

There was apparently no debate regarding constraints *vel non* on the clause's extraterritorial reach. It would seem that, had they been of concern, the matter would have been discussed, especially because the clause contains "the only specific grant of power to be found in the Constitution for the punishment of offenses outside the territorial limits of the United States". CONGRESSIONAL RESEARCH SERVICE, LIBRARY OF CONGRESS, THE CONSTITUTION OF THE UNITED STATES, ANALYSIS AND INTERPRETATION, S. Doc. No. 103–6, at 304 (Johnny H. Killian & George A. Costello eds., 1992) (S. Doc. No. 103–6).

The First Congress promptly enacted far-reaching legislation under the Piracies and Felonies power. In April 1790, approximately seven months *after* proposing the Bill of Rights to the States (25 September 1789), Congress approved An Act for the Punishment of Certain Crimes Against the United States (1790 Act). It provides, in part: in § 8, "[t]hat if *any person or persons* shall commit upon the high seas . . . murder or robbery, . . . every such offender shall be . . . adjudged . . . a pirate and felon, and being thereof convicted, shall suffer death"; and, in § 12, "[t]hat if *any* . . . *person* shall commit manslaughter upon the high seas, . . . such person . . .

so offending, and being thereof convicted, shall be imprisoned not exceeding three years, and fined not exceeding one thousand dollars". Act of 30 Apr. 1790, ch. 9, 1 Stat. 112, 113–15 (emphasis added).

For purposes of this appeal, perhaps the most striking aspect of the 1790 Act is that many of its provisions regarding crimes on the high seas apply to "*any* person". (Emphasis added.) It is important to note, especially in a case in which at issue is the constitutionality of another exercise of the Piracies and Felonies power, that, at the time it passed the 1790 Act, the First Congress had already drafted the Fifth Amendment and proposed it to the States.

While that Amendment was not ratified until 15 December 1791, during "[t]he debates [in August 1789 for] what became the Fifth Amendment . . . there was no hint . . . of any intention, by the adoption of that amendment, to deprive Congress of this [Piracies and Felonies] power expressly and uncontroversially granted to it by the Convention". A. Mark Weisburd, *Due Process Limits on Federal Extraterritorial Legislation?,* 35 COLUM. J. TRANSNAT'L L. 379, 421 (1997) (citing 1 ANNALS OF CONG. 753 (Joseph Gales ed., 1789)). In this regard, the First Congress, which drafted the 1790 Act and the Amendment, "included 20 Members who had been delegates to the [Constitutional] Convention". *Bowsher v. Synar*, 478 U.S. 714, 724 n. 3 (1986).

2.

Early Supreme Court opinions addressing extraterritorial applications of the 1790 Act intimate that the Fifth Amendment imposes no nexus requirement on the reach of statutes criminalizing felonious conduct by foreign citizens on the high seas. In *United States v. Palmer*, 16 U.S. (3 Wheat.) 610 (1818), the Court considered, *inter alia,* whether the United States had jurisdiction, pursuant to § 8 of the 1790 Act, to try, and punish, foreign citizens who had, on the high seas, boarded and robbed a foreign-owned vessel manned by a Spanish crew.

In answering "whether th[e] act extends farther than to American citizens, or to persons on board American vessels, or to offences committed against citizens of the United States", *id.* at 630, Chief Justice Marshall stated for the Court:

> *The constitution having conferred on congress the power of defining and punishing piracy,* there can be no doubt of the right of the legislature to enact laws punishing pirates, *although they may be foreigners, and may have committed no particular offence against the United States. The only question is, has the legislature enacted such a law?* Do the words of the act authorize the courts of the Union to inflict its penalties on persons who are not citizens of the United States, nor sailing under their flag, nor offending particularly against them?

Id. at 630–31 (emphasis added).

The Court answered in the negative. After emphasizing the generality of the language employed by the 1790 Act in setting its reach (*e.g.,* "any captain, or mariner of any ship or vessel"; "any seaman"; "any person or persons"), the Court stated: "Every nation provides for such offense[s] the punishment its own policy may dictate, and *no general words of a statute ought to be construed* to embrace them when committed by foreigners against a foreign government". *Id.* at 632–33 (emphasis added). Therefore, the Court concluded that, as a *statutory* matter, "the crime of robbery, committed by a person on the high seas, on board of any ship or vessel belonging exclusively to subjects of a foreign state, on persons within a vessel belonging exclusively to subjects of a foreign state, *is not a piracy within the true intent and meaning of the act*". *Id.* at 633–34 (emphasis added).

Palmer is an illustration of the well-established canon of construction espoused by Chief Justice Marshall in *Murray v. The Schooner Charming Betsy,* 6 U.S. (2 Cranch) 64 (1804): "[A]n act of Congress ought never to be construed to violate the law of nations if any other possible construction remains. . . ." *Id.* at 118. Later, the Court emphasized in *Lauritzen v. Larsen*, 345 U.S. 571 (1953), however, that this canon "is not, as sometimes is implied, any impairment of our own sovereignty, or limitation of the power of Congress". *Id.* at 578.

While the constraints *vel non* imposed by the Fifth Amendment on extraterritorial application of laws enacted pursuant to the Piracies and Felonies Clause may not have been directly at issue in *Palmer*, Chief Justice Marshall's assessment of the relevant inquiry regarding extraterritorial applications—"The constitution having conferred on congress the power of defining and punishing piracy, . . . [t]he only question is, has the legislature enacted such a law?"—arguably removes any doubt that such enactments comport with the Fifth Amendment. And while at issue was Congress' power to define and punish *piracies,* Chief Justice Marshall's assessment should apply with equal weight to *felonies* such as at issue here, a parallel provision within the same constitutional clause.

Other case law interpreting the 1790 Act suggests international law principles are in some way inherent in the Piracies and Felonies Clause. In *United States v. Furlong,* 18 U.S. (5 Wheat.) 184 (1820), the Court considered, in *dictum,* whether Congress could punish a murder, committed upon the high seas, by one foreign crew member against another aboard a foreign vessel. *Id.* at 193–98. Justice Johnson opined for the Court: "I am led to the conclusion, that [§ 8 of the 1790 Act] does not extend the punishment for murder to the case of that offence committed by a foreigner upon a foreigner in a foreign ship. But otherwise as to piracy, *for that is a crime within the acknowledged reach of the punishing power of Congress*". *Id.* at 197 (emphasis added).

Addressing the fact that, in § 8 of the 1790 Act, Congress had declared murder committed upon the high seas to be piracy, Justice Johnson further concluded: "[Murder and piracy] are things so essentially different in their nature, that not even the omnipotence of legislative power can confound or identify them". *Id.* at 198. He continued:

> If, by calling murder *piracy,* it might assert a jurisdiction over that offence committed by a foreigner in a foreign vessel, what offence might not be brought within their power by the same device? *The most offensive interference with the governments of other nations might be defended on the precedent.* Upon the whole, I am satisfied that Congress [did not] intend [ ] to punish murder *in cases with which they had no right to interfere. . . .*

Id. at 198 (first emphasis in original).

In short, it appears Justice Johnson thought Congress' Piracies and Felonies power extends *only so far* as permitted by international law. That position may be at loggerheads, however, with more recent pronouncements by the Court. . . .

The opinions addressing the reach of the 1790 Act are of significance to our consideration of the MDLEA's reach. Those opinions concern an exercise of power, pursuant to the Piracies and Felonies Clause, by a Congress which, as noted, had some members who had drafted that clause, the 1790 Act, *and* the Fifth Amendment. While none of these cases addresses whether the Fifth Amendment has any applicability to exercises of power under the Piracies and Felonies Clause, neither the Fifth Amendment generally, nor its Due Process Clause specifically, was flagged as an issue in any of them. In fact, in addressing an 1819 law providing for the punishment of piracy on the high seas, the Court noted that, "notwithstanding a series of contested adjudications on [§ 8 of the 1790 Act], *no doubt has hitherto been breathed of its conformity to the constitution*". *United States v. Smith*, 18 U.S. (5 Wheat.) 153, 158 (1820) (emphasis added).

3.

In the light of this rich history, and for the issue at hand, it is not necessary to decide whether the Due Process Clause imposes *no* constraints on the extraterritorial application of the MDLEA. . . .

Accordingly, we hold that, for the MDLEA issue at hand, and to the extent the Due Process Clause may constrain the MDLEA's extraterritorial reach, that clause does not impose a nexus requirement, in that Congress has acted pursuant to the Piracies and Felonies Clause. Again, that clause is "the only specific grant of power to be found in the Constitution for the punishment of offenses outside the territorial limits of the United States". S. DOC. NO. 103–6, at 304.

C.

Assuming, *arguendo,* that resolution of this issue does require consulting international law, the MDLEA's application to Suerte still passes constitutional muster because, on these facts, international law does not require a nexus.

1.

Malta, under whose flag Suerte's vessel was registered, consented to the boarding and search of his vessel, as well as to the application of United States law. A flag nation's consent to a seizure on the high seas constitutes a waiver of that nation's rights under international law. . . .

Along this line, and as noted, the MDLEA provides: "[A] 'vessel subject to the jurisdiction of the United States' includes . . . a vessel registered in a foreign nation where the flag nation has consented or waived objection to the enforcement of United States law by the United States". 46 U.S.C.App. § 1903(c)(1)(C). This codifies the above-described generally accepted principle of international law: a flag nation may consent to another's jurisdiction. . . . Such an agreement between the United States and a flag nation to apply United States law on a flag-nation vessel may be made informally. . . .

2.

. . . In this light, application of the MDLEA to Suerte is permissible; a nexus between his conduct and the United States is not required. Rejecting a nexus requirement will not result in the unrestrained, global law enforcement by the United States decried by Suerte.

Again, the power "to define and punish Piracies and Felonies committed on the high seas, and Offenses against the Law of Nations" is "the *only* specific grant of power to be found in the Constitution for the punishment of offenses outside the territorial limits of the United States". S. DOC. NO. 103–6, at 304 (emphasis added). The MDLEA represents an extremely limited exercise of that power. For certain persons not aboard United States vessels or in United States customs waters, it proscribes drug trafficking only aboard a stateless vessel or, as in the case at hand, a vessel whose flag nation consents to enforcement of United States law.

Enforcement of the MDLEA in these circumstances is neither arbitrary nor fundamentally unfair (the due process standard agreed upon by Suerte and the Government). Those subject to its reach are on notice. In addition to finding "that trafficking in controlled substances aboard vessels . . . presents a specific threat to the security and societal well-being of the United States", Congress has also found that such activity "is a serious *international* problem and is *universally* condemned". 46 U.S.C.App. § 1902 (emphasis added). Along this line, the United Nations Convention Against Illicit Traffic in Narcotic Drugs and Psychotropic Substances, *opened for signature* 20 Dec. 1988, 28 I.L.M. 493, to which Malta and the United States are signatories, provides as its purpose: "to promote cooperation among the Parties so that they may address more effectively the various aspects of illicit traffic in narcotic drugs and psychotropic substances having an international dimension". *Id.* art. 2.

III.

For the foregoing reasons, we *vacate* the dismissal of the indictment in this case and *remand* for further proceedings.

NOTES

1. *Contemporary Piracy.* Although piracy is associated with days of yore (as Samuel Menefee and Judge Kozinski suggest), it persists as a concern on today's oceans. The rate of piracy in traditionally vulnerable areas, like in Southeast Asia and around the Horn of Africa, depends as much on onshore political capacity and economic conditions as it does on preventive measures on the waters. The objective of today's pirates is often kidnapping and ransom, which can yield millions per ship. *See* Congressional Research Service, *Piracy Off the Horn of Africa*, CRS Rep. R40528 (Apr. 27, 2011). "Live" reports of piracy incidents are maintained by the International Chamber of Commerce (available at https://www.icc-ccs.org/piracy-reporting-centre/live-piracy-report, [https://perma.cc/F4A9-UW22]) and the International Maritime Organization (available at http://www.imo.org/en/OurWork/Security/PiracyArmedRobbery/Reports/Pages/Default.aspx, [https://perma.cc/89NJ-Z7QE]).

2. *Evolving Piracy and Evolving International Law.* The opinions in *United States v. Dire* and *Sea Shepherd* provide interesting and controversial glimpses into the evolution capacity of piracy law. The former, addressing whether pirates seized before they succeed in obtaining property or ransom have actually committed "piracy," resolved a contemporary divergence of views by district courts; the full opinion provides a more extensive response to *United States v. Said*, 757 F.Supp. 2d 554 (E.D. Va. 2010), which had concluded that section 1651's reference to "the crime of piracy as defined by the law of nations" excluded mere armed attacks and would, if resolved differently, violate constitutional due process. *Sea Shepherd*, concerning the meaning of "private ends" and "violence," prompted a vigorous debate concerning the inclusion of politically-motivated acts of violence on the high seas. *See* Kevin Jon Heller, *Why Political Ends Are Public Ends, Not Private Ends*, Opinio Juris, March 1, 2013 (available at http://opiniojuris.org/2013/03/01/a-final-word-about-politically-motivated-piracy/, [https://perma.cc/DE22-Z8YN]) (criticizing *Sea Shepherd*, and linking to prior exchanges). How do their inquiries resemble one another, and how do they differ? In each case, consider the context in which the court examines the customary international law of piracy, and contemplate the degree to which it constitutes congressional incorporation.

3. *Jurisdiction over Piracy-Like Offenses and the Constitution.* In *United States v. Suerte*, the court of appeals addresses a constitutional challenge that bears on the entire congressional power to "define and punish Piracies and Felonies committed on the high Seas." U.S. Const. art. I, § 8, cl. 10. Dismissing the challenge, the court nearly takes the view that—where Congress has exercised power pursuant to that clause—the Due Process Clause requires no nexus between a foreign citizen and the United States. To what extent does the court's analysis rely upon, or reject, the relevance of international law? Does its analysis provide an example of using international law to interpret the Constitution, or is something different at work?

4. *Further Reading.* For analysis of contemporary legal issues relating to piracy, see *Prosecuting Maritime Piracy: Domestic Solutions to International Crimes* (Michael P. Scharf, Michael A. Newton & Milena Sterio eds., 2015); Alfred P. Rubin, *The Law of Piracy* (2d ed.1998); Agora: *Piracy Prosecutions*, 104 AM. J. INT'L L. 397 (2010). For a perspective on the relationship of piracy to other contemporary legal controversies, including the ATS, see Eugene Kontorovich, *The "Define and Punish" Clause and the Limits of Universal Jurisdiction*, 103 NW. U. L. REV. 149 (2009); Eugene Kontorovich, *The Piracy Analogy: Modern Universal Jurisdiction's Hollow Foundation*, 45 HARV. INT'L L.J. 183 (2004); for a comparison to terrorism, the focus of the next Section, see Eugene Kontorovich, *"A Guantánamo on the Sea": The Difficulty of Prosecuting Pirates and Terrorists*, 98 CAL. L. REV. 243 (2010).

8. TERRORISM

Various U.S. statutes—of relatively recent vintage, compared to piracy—can be employed to address the threat of terrorism. There are general federal criminal law statutes that can be of relevance, such as those relating to murder, unlawful use of explosive materials, and even civil rights. There are also more specific statutes. The Hostage Taking Act and Aircraft Piracy Act (excerpted below) were enacted to implement treaty obligations entered into by the United States in the 1970s. The Omnibus Diplomatic Security and Antiterrorism Act of 1986 created the terrorist homicide statute (18 U.S.C. § 2332 below) and further legislation in the early 1990s established the terrorist definitions (18 U.S.C. § 2331 below). Other statutes (not reproduced below) are also important. In 1994, Congress criminalized the provision of material support to terrorists (18 U.S.C. § 2339A). The Antiterrorism and Effective Death Penalty Act of 1996 prohibited acts of terrorism "transcending national boundaries" (18 U.S.C. § 2332b) and further prohibited material support to groups designated as terrorist organizations (18 U.S.C. § 2339B).

These statutes are something of a patchwork, and their interaction with customary international law has been a feature of important U.S. prosecutions. As you read them, and the *Yunis* case that follows, consider how these statutes relate to contemporary customary international law on the extraterritorial application of national jurisdiction. When is it acceptable for the United States to regulate conduct abroad that it regards as terrorist in nature? When does such regulation run afoul of customary international law?

HOSTAGE TAKING ACT

18 U.S.C. § 1203 (2012).

(a) [W]hoever, whether inside or outside the United States, seizes or detains and threatens to kill, to injure, or to continue to detain another person in order to compel a third person or a governmental organization to do or to abstain from doing any act . . . shall be punished by imprisonment by any term of years or for life. . . .

(b)(1) It is not an offense under this section if the conduct required for the offense occurred outside the United States unless—

(A) the offender or the person seized or detained is a national of the United States;

(B) the offender is found in the United States; or

(C) the governmental organization sought to be compelled is the Government of the United States.

AIRCRAFT PIRACY ACT

49 U.S.C. § 46502(b) (2012).

Outside Special Aircraft Jurisdiction.—

(1) An individual committing or conspiring to commit an offense (as defined in the Convention for the Suppression of Unlawful Seizure of Aircraft) on an aircraft in flight outside the special aircraft jurisdiction of the United States—

(A) shall be imprisoned for at least 20 years; or

(B) notwithstanding section 3559(b) of title 18, if the death of another individual results from the commission or attempt, shall be put to death or imprisoned for life.

(2) There is jurisdiction over the offense in paragraph (1) if—

(A) a national of the United States was aboard the aircraft;

(B) an offender is a national of the United States; or

(C) an offender is afterwards found in the United States. . . .

TERRORISM DEFINITIONS AND CRIMINAL PENALTIES

18 U.S.C. §§ 2331–32 (2012).

§ 2331. Definitions

As used in this chapter—

(1) the term "international terrorism" means activities that—

(A) involve violent acts or acts dangerous to human life that are a violation of the criminal laws of the United States or of any State, or that would be a criminal violation if committed within the jurisdiction of the United States or of any State;

(B) appear to be intended—

(i) to intimidate or coerce a civilian population;

(ii) to influence the policy of a government by intimidation or coercion; or

(iii) to affect the conduct of a government by mass destruction, assassination, or kidnapping; and

(C) occur primarily outside the territorial jurisdiction of the United States, or transcend national boundaries in terms of the means by which they are accomplished, the persons they appear intended to intimidate or coerce, or the locale in which their perpetrators operate or seek asylum; . . .

(5) the term "domestic terrorism" means activities that—

(A) involve acts dangerous to human life that are a violation of the criminal laws of the United States or of any State;

(B) appear to be intended—

(i) to intimidate or coerce a civilian population;

(ii) to influence the policy of a government by intimidation or coercion; or

(iii) to affect the conduct of a government by mass destruction, assassination, or kidnapping; and

(C) occur primarily within the territorial jurisdiction of the United States.

§ 2332. Criminal penalties

(a) Homicide.—Whoever kills a national of the United States, while such national is outside the United States, shall—

(1) if the killing is murder (as defined in section 1111(a)), be fined under this title, punished by death or imprisonment for any term of years or for life, or both;

(2) if the killing is a voluntary manslaughter . . . , be fined under this title or imprisoned not more than ten years, or both; and

(3) if the killing is an involuntary manslaughter . . . , be fined under this title or imprisoned not more than three years, or both.

(b) Attempt or conspiracy with respect to homicide.—Whoever outside the United States attempts to kill, or engages in a conspiracy to kill, a national of the United States shall—

(1) in the case of an attempt to commit a killing that is a murder as defined in this chapter, be fined under this title or imprisoned not more than 20 years, or both; and

(2) in the case of a conspiracy by two or more persons to commit a killing that is a murder as defined in section 1111(a) of this title, if one or more of such persons do any overt act to effect the object of the conspiracy, be fined under this title or imprisoned for any term of years or for life, or both so fined and so imprisoned.

(c) Other conduct.—Whoever outside the United States engages in physical violence—

(1) with intent to cause serious bodily injury to a national of the United States; or

(2) with the result that serious bodily injury is caused to a national of the United States;

shall be fined under this title or imprisoned not more than ten years, or both.

(d) Limitation on prosecution.—No prosecution for any offense described in this section shall be undertaken by the United States except on written certification of the Attorney General or the highest ranking subordinate of the Attorney General with responsibility for criminal prosecutions that, in the judgment of the certifying official, such offense was intended to coerce, intimidate, or retaliate against a government or a civilian population.

UNITED STATES V. YUNIS

681 F.Supp. 896 (D.D.C. 1988).

BARRINGTON D. PARKER, DISTRICT JUDGE.

Defendant's motion to dismiss, presenting interesting and novel legal issues, challenges the authority for and the limits to which the United States government may extend its prosecutorial arm over certain crimes allegedly committed by a nonresident alien on foreign soil. . . .

I.

BACKGROUND

This criminal proceeding and indictment arise from the hijacking of a Jordanian civil aircraft, Royal Jordanian Airlines ("ALIA") Flight 402, on June 11, and 12, 1985. There is no dispute that the only nexus to the United States was the presence of several American nationals on board the flight. The airplane was registered in Jordan, flew the Jordanian flag and never landed on American soil or flew over American airspace.

On the morning of June 11, the aircraft was positioned at the Beirut International Airport, Beirut, Lebanon, for a scheduled departure to Amman, Jordan. As the 50–60 passengers boarded, several Arab men, one allegedly the defendant, stormed the plane and ordered the pilot to fly to Tunis, Tunisia where a meeting of the Arab League Conference was underway. The airplane departed from Beirut with all passengers, including the Americans, held hostage. The plane made a short landing in Larnaco, Cyprus where additional fuel was obtained. It then proceeded to Tunis where landing privileges were denied. The airplane flew to Palermo, Sicily, where it was allowed to replenish its fuel and food supply. Thereafter, it lifted off, destined once more for Tunis. Again, entry was denied and the pilot returned to Beirut. On the morning of June 12th, it took off for Damascus, Syria. However, the Syrian authorities also denied landing privileges. Thus after crisscrossing the Mediterranean Sea area for more than 30 hours, the hijackers were forced to return to Beirut, their point of initial departure.

After landing, the hostages were directed to exit the aircraft. The hijackers then called an impromptu press conference and the defendant Yunis allegedly read a speech, which he originally intended to give to the delegates of the Arab League Conference then meeting in Tunis. Following the speech, the hijackers blew up the Jordanian aircraft, quickly left the scene and vanished into the Beirut landscape.

Between June 11 and 12, 1985, ALIA flight 402 never landed on or flew over American space. Its flight path was limited to an area within and around the Mediterranean Sea. Based on the absence of any nexus to United States territory, Yunis has moved to dismiss the entire indictment, arguing that no United States federal court has jurisdiction to prosecute a foreign national for crimes committed in foreign airspace and on foreign soil. He further claims that the presence of the American nationals on board the aircraft is an insufficient basis for exercising jurisdiction under principles of international law.

Defendant's motion raises several threshold inquiries: whether or not there is a basis for jurisdiction under international law, and if so, whether Congress intended to and had authority to extend jurisdiction of our federal courts over criminal offenses and events which were committed and occurred overseas and out of the territorial jurisdiction of such courts.

II.

ANALYSIS

A. *Jurisdiction Under International Law*

The parties agree that there are five traditional bases of jurisdiction over extraterritorial crimes under international law:

> *Territorial,* wherein jurisdiction is based on the place where the offense is committed;
>
> *National,* wherein jurisdiction is based on the nationality of the offender;
>
> *Protective,* wherein jurisdiction is based on whether the national interest is injured;
>
> *Universal,* wherein jurisdiction is conferred in any forum that obtains physical custody of the perpetuator [sic] of certain offenses considered particularly heinous and harmful to humanity;
>
> *Passive personal,* wherein jurisdiction is based on the nationality of the victim.

These general principles were developed in 1935 by a Harvard Research Project in an effort to codify principles of jurisdiction under international law. . . .

The Universal and the Passive Personal principle appear to offer potential bases for asserting jurisdiction over the hostage-taking and aircraft piracy charges against Yunis. However, his counsel argues that the Universal principle is not applicable because neither hostage-taking nor aircraft piracy are heinous crimes encompassed by the doctrine. He urges further, that the United States does not recognize the Passive Personal as a legitimate source of jurisdiction. The government flatly disagrees and maintains that jurisdiction is appropriate under both.

1. *Universal Principle*

The Universal principle recognizes that certain offenses are so heinous and so widely condemned that "any state if it captures the offender may prosecute and punish that person on behalf of the world community regardless of the nationality of the offender or victim or where the crime was committed." M. Bassiouini, II *International Criminal Law*, Ch. 6 at 298 (ed. 1986). The crucial question for purposes of the defendant's motion is how crimes are classified as "heinous" and whether aircraft piracy and hostage taking fit into this category.

Those crimes that are condemned by the world community and subject to prosecution under the Universal principle are often a matter of international conventions or treaties. *See Demjanjuk v. Petrovsky,* 776 F.2d 571, 582 (6th Cir. 1985) (Treaty against genocide signed by a significant number of states made that crime heinous; therefore, Israel had proper jurisdiction over [N]azi war criminal under the Universal principle).

Both offenses are the subject of international agreements. A majority of states in the world community, including Lebanon, have signed three treaties condemning aircraft piracy: The Tokyo Convention,[2] The Hague Convention,[3] and The Montreal Convention.[4] The Hague and Montreal Conventions explicitly rely on the principle of Universal jurisdiction in mandating that all states "take such measures as may be necessary to establish its jurisdiction over the offences where the alleged offender is present in its territory." Hague Convention Art. 4 § 2; Montreal Convention Art. 5 § 2. Further, those treaties direct that all "contracting states . . . of which the alleged offender is found, . . . shall, be obliged, *without exception whatsoever and whether or not the offense was committed in its territory,* to submit the case to its competent authorities for the purpose of prosecution." Hague Convention Art. 7; Montreal Convention Art. 7. (emphasis added). These two provisions together demonstrate the international community's strong commitment to punish aircraft hijackers irrespective of where the hijacking occurred.

The global community has also joined together and adopted the International Convention for the Taking of Hostages,[5] an agreement which condemns and criminalizes the offense of hostage taking. Like the conventions denouncing aircraft piracy, this treaty requires signatory states to prosecute any alleged offenders "present in its territory."[6]

In light of the global efforts to punish aircraft piracy and hostage taking, international legal scholars unanimously agree that these crimes fit within the category of heinous crimes for purposes of asserting universal jurisdiction. . . . In The Restatement (Revised) of Foreign Relations Law of the United States, a source heavily relied upon by the defendant, aircraft hijacking is specifically identified as a universal crime over which all states should exercise jurisdiction.

---

[2] Convention on Offenses and Certain Other Acts Committed on Board Aircraft, Sept. 14, 1963, T.I.A.S. No. 159.

[3] Convention for the Suppression of Unlawful Seizure of Aircraft, Dec. 16, 1970, T.I.A.S. No. 7192.

[4] Convention for the Suppression of Unlawful Acts against the Safety of Civil Aviation, Sept. 23, 1971. T.I.A.S. No. 7570.

[5] 34 U.N. GAOR Supp. (No. 39) at 23, U.N. Doc. A/34/39 (1979), reprinted in 18 I.L.M. 1456 (1979) [hereinafter Hostage Taking Convention].

[6] Art. V. § 2 states "each state *shall* establish jurisdiction in cases where the alleged offender is present in its territory."

Our Circuit has cited the Restatement with approval and determined that the Universal principle, standing alone, provides sufficient basis for asserting jurisdiction over an alleged offender. *See Tel-Oren v. Libyan Arab Republic,* 726 F.2d at 781, n. 7, ("The premise of universal jurisdiction is that a state 'may exercise jurisdiction to define and punish certain offenses recognized by the community of nations as of universal concern,' . . . even where no other recognized basis of jurisdiction is present.") Therefore, under recognized principles of international law, and the law of this Circuit, there is clear authority to assert jurisdiction over Yunis for the offenses of aircraft piracy and hostage taking.

2. Passive Personal Principle

This principle authorizes states to assert jurisdiction over offenses committed against their citizens abroad. It recognizes that each state has a legitimate interest in protecting the safety of its citizens when they journey outside national boundaries. Because American nationals were on board the Jordanian aircraft, the government contends that the Court may exercise jurisdiction over Yunis under this principle. Defendant argues that this theory of jurisdiction is neither recognized by the international community nor the United States and is an insufficient basis for sustaining jurisdiction over Yunis.

Although many international legal scholars agree that the principle is the most controversial of the five sources of jurisdiction, they also agree that the international community recognizes its legitimacy. . . . More importantly, the international community explicitly approved of the principle as a basis for asserting jurisdiction over hostage takers. As noted above, the Hostage Taking Convention set forth certain mandatory sources of jurisdiction. But it also gave each signatory country discretion to exercise extraterritorial jurisdiction when the offense was committed "with respect to a hostage who is a national of that state if that state considers it appropriate." Art. 5(a)(d). Therefore, even if there are doubts regarding the international community's acceptance, there can be no doubt concerning the application of this principle to the offense of hostage taking, an offense for which Yunis is charged. *See* M. Bassiouini, II *International Criminal Law*, Ch. 4 at 120.

Defendant's counsel correctly notes that the Passive Personal principle traditionally has been an anathema to United States lawmakers. . . . In the past, the United States has protested any assertion of such jurisdiction for fear that it could lead to indefinite criminal liability for its own citizens. This objection was based on the belief that foreigners visiting the United States should comply with our laws and should not be permitted to carry their laws with them. Otherwise Americans would face criminal prosecutions for actions unknown to them as illegal. However, in the most recent draft of the Restatement, the authors noted that the theory "has been increasingly accepted when applied to terrorist and other organized attacks on a state's nationals by reason of their nationality, or to assassinations of a state's ambassadors, or government officials." Restatement (Revised) § 402, comment g (Tent. Draft No. 6). . . . The authors retreated from their wholesale rejection of the principle, recognizing that perpetrators of crimes unanimously condemned by members of the international community, should be aware of the illegality of their actions.[11] Therefore, qualified application of the doctrine to serious and universally condemned crimes will not raise the specter of unlimited and unexpected criminal liability.

Finally, this case does not present the first time that the United States has invoked the principle to assert jurisdiction over a hijacker who seized an American hostage on foreign soil. The government relied on this very principle when it sought extradition of Muhammed Abbas Zaiden, the leader of the terrorists who hijacked the *Achillo Lauro* vessel in Egyptian waters and subsequently killed Leon Klinghoffer, an American citizen. As here, the only connection to the United States was Klinghoffer's American citizenship. Based on that link, an arrest warrant was issued charging Abbas with hostage taking, conspiracy and piracy. *Id.* at 719; *See also* N.Y. TIMES, Oct. 16, 1985 § 1 at 1, col. 6.[13]

Thus the Universal and Passive Personality principles, together, provide ample grounds for this Court to assert jurisdiction over Yunis. In fact, reliance on both strengthens the basis for asserting jurisdiction. Not only is the United States acting on behalf of the world community to punish alleged offenders of crimes that threaten the very foundations of world order, but the United States has its own interest in protecting its nationals.[14]

---

[11] While it might be too much to expect the average citizen to be familiar with all of the criminal laws of every country, it is not unrealistic to assume that he would realize that committing a terrorist act might subject him to foreign prosecution. See Note, Bringing the Terrorist to Justice, 11 Cornell Int'l L.J. 71 (1978).

[13] Only recently, the Justice Department announced it had withdrawn the arrest warrant issued against Abbas after reviewing the outstanding indictment and weighing the fact that the defendant had been convicted and sentenced in absentia in an Italian Court. *See* Wash. Post, Jan. 17, 1988.

[14] The government also argues that a third doctrine, the Protective principle, offers grounds for asserting jurisdiction over Yunis. Because this principle gives states wide latitude in defining the parameters of their jurisdiction, the international community has strictly construed the reach of this doctrine to those offenses posing a direct, specific threat to national security. *See* Blakesley, United States Jurisdiction Over Extraterritorial Crime, 73 J.Crim.L & Criminology at 1136; Bassiouini, II International Criminal Law ch. 2 at 21. Recently, some academicians have urged a more liberal interpretation of the protective principle when applied to terroristic activities. Given "the increase in the number of terroristic threats against United States nationals abroad, there can be no doubt that the United States has significant security and protective interests at stake." Paust, Federal Jurisdiction Over Extraterritorial Acts of Terrorism, 23 Va. J. Int'l Law 191, 210 (1983). . . .

UNITED STATES V. YUNIS

924 F.2d 1086 (D.C. Cir. 1991).

[Once the motion to dismiss for lack of jurisdiction was denied by the district court (*United States v. Yunis*, 681 F.Supp. 896 (D.D.C. 1988), *supra* this Section),the jury convicted Yunis of conspiracy, hostage taking, and air piracy, but they acquitted him of violence against people on board an aircraft, aircraft damage, and placing a destructive device on board an aircraft. He received concurrent sentences of five years for conspiracy, thirty years for hostage taking, and twenty years for air piracy. The Court of Appeals for the D.C. Circuit affirmed both the district court's jurisdiction and the conviction. It had the following to say about jurisdiction under customary international law:]

Nor is jurisdiction precluded by norms of customary international law. The district court concluded that two jurisdictional theories of international law, the "universal principle" and the "passive personal principle," supported assertion of U.S. jurisdiction to prosecute Yunis on hijacking and hostage-taking charges. *See Yunis,* 681 F.Supp. at 899–903. . . .

Relying primarily on the RESTATEMENT, Yunis argues that hostage taking has not been recognized as a universal crime and that the passive personal principle authorizes assertion of jurisdiction over alleged hostage takers only where the victims were seized because they were nationals of the prosecuting state. Whatever merit appellant's claims may have as a matter of international law, they cannot prevail before this court. Yunis seeks to portray international law as a self-executing code that trumps domestic law whenever the two conflict. That effort misconceives the role of judges as appliers of international law and as participants in the federal system. Our duty is to enforce the Constitution, laws, and treaties of the United States, not to conform the law of the land to norms of customary international law. *See* U.S. CONST. art. VI. As we said in *Committee of U.S. Citizens Living in Nicaragua v. Reagan,* 859 F.2d 929 (D.C. Cir. 1988): "Statutes inconsistent with principles of customary international law may well lead to international law violations. But within the domestic legal realm, that inconsistent statute simply modifies or supersedes customary international law to the extent of the inconsistency." *Id.* at 938. . . .

To be sure, courts should hesitate to give penal statutes extraterritorial effect absent a clear congressional directive. . . . Similarly, courts will not blind themselves to potential violations of international law where legislative intent is ambiguous. . . . But the statute in question reflects an unmistakable congressional intent, consistent with treaty obligations of the United States, to authorize prosecution of those who take Americans hostage abroad no matter where the offense occurs or where the offender is found. Our inquiry can go no further.

UNITED STATES V. BIN LADEN

92 F.Supp.2d 189 (S.D.N.Y. 2000).

[In this case, fifteen defendants were charged with various counts related to the 1998 U.S. embassy bombings in Kenya and Tanzania as well as subsequent obstructions of the investigation; among the charges were 223 counts of murder.]

Odeh argues that the Counts based on 18 U.S.C. §§ 2332 . . . and 2332a . . . must be dismissed because these statutes are unconstitutional in that they exceed Congress's authority to legislate under the Constitution. . . . Subsection 2332(b) provides in relevant part that "[w]hoever outside the United States . . . engages in a conspiracy to kill[ ] a national of the United States shall [be punished as further provided]," 18 U.S.C. § 2332(b); and Section 2332a(a) provides in relevant part that, "[a] person who . . . uses, threatens, or attempts or conspires to use, a weapon of mass destruction . . . (1) against a national of the United States while such national is outside of the United States; . . . or (3) against any property that is owned, leased or used by the United States . . . , whether the property is within or outside of the United States, shall [be punished as further provided]." 18 U.S.C. § 2332a(a).

Odeh suggests that there is but one constitutional grant of authority to legislate that could support these two statutory provisions: Article I, Section 8, Clause 10. . . . Clause 10 grants Congress the authority "[t]o define and punish Piracies and Felonies committed on the high Seas, and Offenses against the Law of Nations." U.S. Const. art. I, § 8, cl. 10. Odeh argues that, as "[t]he acts described in these two statutes . . . are not widely regarded as offenses 'against the law of nations,' " these statutes exceed Congress's authority under Clause 10.

There are two problems with this argument. First, even assuming that the acts described in Section 2332 and 2332a are not *widely* regarded as violations of international law, it does not necessarily follow that these provisions exceed Congress's authority under Clause 10. Clause 10 does not merely give Congress the authority to punish offenses against the law of nations; it also gives Congress the power to "define" such offenses. Hence, provided that the acts in question are recognized by at least some members of the international community as being offenses against the law of nations,[56] Congress arguably has the power to criminalize these acts pursuant to its power *to define* offenses against the law of nations. *See United States v. Smith,* 18 U.S. (5 Wheat.) 153, 159 . . . (1820) (Story, J.) ("Offenses . . . against the law of nations, cannot, with any accuracy, be said to be completely ascertained and defined in any public code recognized by

---

56 And this would appear to be the case. . . .

the common consent of nations. . . . [T]herefore . . . , there is a peculiar fitness in giving the power to define as well as to punish.") . . .

Second, and more important, it is not the case that Clause 10 provides the only basis for Sections 2332 and 2332a. The Supreme Court has recognized that, with regard to foreign affairs legislation, "investment of the federal Government with the powers of external sovereignty did not depend upon the affirmative grants of the Constitution." *United States v. Curtiss-Wright Export Corp.,* 299 U.S. 304 . . . (1936). Rather, Congress's authority to regulate foreign affairs "exist[s] as inherently inseparable from the conception of nationality." *Id.* (citations omitted). More specifically, this "concept of essential sovereignty of a free nation clearly requires the existence and recognition of an inherent power in the state to protect itself from destruction." *United States v. Rodriguez,* 182 F.Supp. 479, 491 (S.D. Cal. 1960), *aff'd in part, rev'd in part sub nom. Rocha v. United States,* 288 F.2d 545 (9th Cir.), *cert. denied,* 366 U.S. 948 (1961).

In penalizing extraterritorial conspiracies to kill nationals of the United States, Section 2332(b) is clearly designed to protect a vital United States interest. And, indeed, Congress expressly identified this protective function as the chief purpose of Section 2332. *See* 132 Cong. Rec. S1382–88, § 2331 (1986) (finding that "it is an accepted principle of international law that a country may prosecute crimes committed outside its boundaries that are directed against its own security or the operation of its government functions . . . [and] terrorist attacks on Americans abroad threaten a fundamental function of our Government: that of protecting its citizens"); *see also* 132 Cong. Rec. S1057 (1986) (statement of Sen. Specter) (stating that Section 2332 is justified by the protective principle). Similarly, in penalizing attacks on United States property, Section 2332a(a)(3) is clearly designed to protect a vital United States interest. See H.R. Conf. Rep. No. 102–405, at 6 (1991) ("The Congress finds that the use and threatened use of weapons of mass destruction . . . gravely harm the national security and foreign relations interests of the United States. . . ."). Therefore, we conclude, under *Curtiss-Wright,* that Congress acted within its authority in enacting these provisions.

In view of the foregoing, we deny Odeh's motion to dismiss the counts based on Sections 2332 and 2332a (viz., Counts 1, 4, 9, and 10) insofar as this motion depends on his "lack of constitutional authority" argument.

NOTES

1. *International Law Jurisdictional Principles and Terrorism*. Section 5 began by introducing the theories of prescriptive jurisdiction on which the *Yunis* and *Bin Laden* cases relied. You may also recall that in *United States v. Yousef*, 327 F.3d 56 (2d Cir. 2003), the defendants claimed that the United States lacked jurisdiction over charges of conspiracy to bomb commercial airliners in Southeast Asia and the World Trade Center in 1993. The court

upheld jurisdiction under the protective principle (on the basis that the planned attacks were intended to affect the United States and alter its foreign policy); the passive personality principle (on the basis that the plot, if executed, would have bombed U.S. aircrafts carrying U.S. nationals); and the objective territorial principle/effects doctrine (on the basis that the plot was intended to have an impact in the United States). Count 19, however, involved a "test run" bombing of a non-U.S. aircraft, carrying no U.S. citizens, whose flight path was entirely within Southeast Asia. While the district court had upheld jurisdiction over this count under the universality principle, the Second Circuit rejected its reasoning, finding:

> The universality principle permits jurisdiction over only a limited set of crimes that cannot be expanded judicially. . . . We emphasize that the indefinite category of " 'terrorism' " is not subject to universal jurisdiction. . . . Unlike those offenses supporting universal jurisdiction under customary international law—that is, piracy, war crimes, and crimes against humanity—that now have fairly precise definitions and that have achieved universal condemnation, "terrorism" is a term as loosely deployed as it is powerfully charged.

327 F.3d at 103–06. The court nonetheless upheld jurisdiction over count 19 under both a treaty, the Montreal Convention, as well as the protective principle of customary international law.

Does the potential (and actual) overlap among these theories suggest a principle of judicial economy? If so, is there a particular theory that should be read more narrowly than others? *Yousef*, as just noted, might point toward universal jurisdiction; the district court in *Yunis*, on the other hand, showed (in its note 14) reluctance to embrace the protective principle. Was their reasoning similar? Should the passive personality theory (to which some commentators have been less receptive, as the *Yunis* district court also noted) be read narrowly so as to apply only when there is specific intent to harm a U.S. national, rather than any time there is an effect on U.S. nationals? Do these alternative theories erode the focus on territoriality, on which cases like *Morrison* and *Kiobel* (*excerpted supra*, this Chapter, Sec. 5 and Sec. 6, respectively) dwell? *See, e.g.*, Abraham Abramovsky, *Extraterritorial Jurisdiction: The United States' Unwarranted Attempt to Alter International Law in* United States v. Yunis, 125 YALE J. INT'L L. 121 (1990); Andreas F. Lowenfeld, *U.S. Law Abroad: The Constitution and International Law,* 83 AM. J. INT'L L. 880 (1989); Andreas F. Lowenfeld, *U.S. Law Enforcement Abroad: The Constitution and International Law, Continued,* 84 AM. J. INT'L L. 444 (1990).

2. *International Law Jurisdictional Principles and U.S. Law.* Section 7 explored the relationship between the modern law of piracy and the scope of congressional power under one of its Article I powers. What kind of relationship does *Bin Laden* propose between terrorism and congressional authority?

While the above excerpt focuses on the constitutional question, *Bin Laden* also opined at length about a number of jurisdiction-related issues. Another somewhat controversial aspect of the district court opinion was its narrow approach to the presumption against extraterritoriality. The Second Circuit specifically disagreed, for example, with the district court's assertion that the presumption was designed to apply to substantive statutory provisions, not jurisdictional statutes. *United States v. Gatlin*, 216 F.3d 207, 212 n.6 (2d Cir. 2000) (noting disagreement with *United States v. Bin Laden*, 92 F.Supp.2d 189, 206 n. 32 (S.D.N.Y. 2000); *see also Bin Laden*, 92 F. Supp. 2d at 193–97 (describing approach to extraterritoriality). The later decision in *Kiobel*, though relating to the ATS, seemed to confirm the Second Circuit's approach in this regard.

3. *Civil Remedies*. In his separate concurrence in *Tel-Oren v. Libyan Arab Republic*, Judge Edwards, while broadly endorsing the approach taken in *Filartiga*, concluded that there was an insufficient consensus on terrorism to support liability under the Alien Tort Statute. 726 F.2d 774, 795–96 (D.C. Cir. 1984) (Edwards, J., concurring). This remains the general view, following *Sosa*, even putting extraterritoriality aside. *See, e.g., In re Chiquita Brands Intern., Inc. Alien Tort Statute and Shareholder Derivative Litigation*, 792 F.Supp.2d 1301, 1304–22 (S.D. Fla. 2011).

The ATS is not, however, the only basis for civil liability. Title 18, section 2333(a), adopted as part of the Anti-Terrorism Act, establishes jurisdiction in federal district court and a treble damages remedy for "[a]ny national of the United States injured in his or her person, property, or business by reason of an act of international terrorism, or his or her estate, survivors, or heirs" to sue for treble damages, attorneys' fees, and costs. 18 U.S.C. § 2333(a) (2016). Civil suits brought by victims of terrorism soon proliferated against a variety of actors. *See, e.g., Ungar v. Palestine Liberation Organization*, 402 F.3d 274 (1st Cir. 2005) (estate and survivors of American citizen killed in a terrorist attack in Israel granted damages under 18 U.S.C. § 2333); *Smith v. Islamic Emirate of Afghanistan*, 262 F.Supp.2d 217 (S.D.N.Y. 2003) (attacks of September 11, 2001 constitute "international terrorism" under § 2333 and can be the basis of suit for damages by victim's family under § 2333); *Boim v. Quranic Literacy Institute & Holy Land Foundation for Relief & Development*, 291 F.3d 1000 (7th Cir. 2002) (suit for civil damages brought by parents of 17-year-old boy killed in terrorist attack on bus stop in Israel).

Surveying these and other actions, which by now are quite numerous, it is immediately apparent that most claims are not against sovereign States—undoubtedly reflecting the fact that the Foreign Sovereign Immunities Act generally precludes civil suits against sovereign States for acts of international terrorism. However, an exception codified by the 1996 Antiterrorism and Effective Death Penalty Act denies such immunity to States that have been designated by the United States as sponsors of terrorism. *See* 28 U.S.C. § 1605A (2006); *see also* Chapter 7, Sec. 7. In 2016, Congress amended section 2333 to provide for liability "as to any person who . . . conspires with the person who committed [ ]an act of international terrorism." 18 U.S.C. § 2333(d); *see*

Justice Against Sponsors of Terrorism Act ("JASTA"), Pub. L. 114–222, 130 Stat. 852 (2016). Do civil remedies such as these create greater or lesser challenges to international principles of jurisdiction?

4. *Commentary.* For an overview of the issue of extraterritorial jurisdiction, see Anthony J. Colangelo, *Constitutional Limits on Extraterritorial Jurisdiction: Terrorism and the Intersection of National and International Law*, 48 HARV. INT'L L.J. 1216 (2007). For an appraisal of the fluid area of civil remedies for acts of terrorism, see Harold Hongju Koh, *Civil Remedies for Uncivil Wrongs: Combatting Terrorism Through Transnational Public Law Litigation*, 50 TEX. INT'L L.J. 661 (2016).

CHAPTER 3

TREATIES AND OTHER INTERNATIONAL AGREEMENTS

■ ■ ■

1. HISTORICAL CONTEXT OF THE TREATY POWER

Article II, Section 2, of the Constitution states that the president "shall have power, by and with the advice and consent of the Senate, to make treaties, provided two-thirds of the senators present concur. . . ." The origins of this clause shed some light on its contemporary meaning.

British Treaty-Making Power

In founding the American Republic, the framers both reacted against and drew inspiration from their former colonizers, who boasted the most successful constitutional system of the time. Alexander Hamilton remarked at the Constitutional Convention in Philadelphia "that the British government was the best in the world," and expressed the hope that other Americans would come to share his regard for it.[1]

A key feature of the British system—one first exercised on behalf of the colonies, and later in tandem with them—was its approach to treaties. William Blackstone, an authority well known to the framers and to subsequent generations, famously wrote that "[i]t is . . . the king's prerogative to make treaties, leagues, and alliances with foreign states and princes. . . . Whatever contracts therefore he engages in, no other power in the kingdom can legally delay, resist, or annul."[2] It was the crown's prerogative, in other words, to conduct foreign affairs and to make international agreements that bound the nation. Blackstone did not explicitly address the distinct question of the effect treaties had on British domestic law, but that prerogative was one generally belonging to

---

1 *Debates on the Adoption of the Federal Constitution in the Convention Held at Philadelphia, reprinted in* 5 *The Debates in the Several State Conventions, on the Adoption of the Federal Constitution, as Recommended by the General Convention at Philadelphia, in 1787*, at 202 (Jonathan Elliot ed., 2d ed. 1996) (1891) [hereinafter "5 *Elliot's Debates*"].

2 William Blackstone, 1 Commentaries *257; *see also* Alpheus Todd, 1 *Parliamentary Government in England: Its Origins, Development, and Practical Operation* 132 (1892); William R. Anson, *The Law and Custom of the Constitution* pt. 2, at 279 (Richard H. Leach ed., 1970) (1892).

Parliament—which under the British constitution remained responsible for exercising legislative power.[3]

While Hamilton, among others, may have been enamored of the Crown's role in making treaties,[4] those responsible for developing the U.S. Constitution had to develop a mechanism for implementing them as well.

Treaty-Making in the U.S. Colonies

Though prior to U.S. independence the treaty-making power resided with Britain, many of the colonies, so distant from London, conducted their own foreign relations—including at times written agreements, usually with Indian tribes. Colonial action reflected not only interests divergent from those of Britain, but also among the colonies themselves, given substantial differences among them in commercial interests, trade, and proximity to foreign partners.[5]

Colonial foreign relations concerned the British—who found, for example, that they made it difficult to coordinate an approach to the Iroquois, thereby benefiting French interests in North America. This led the London Board of Trade to propose in 1753 that a meeting of representatives of the colonies be held in New York to develop a single treaty, to be made in the name of the Crown, to settle affairs with the Iroquois. The resulting "Albany Congress" of 1754 resulted in a treaty with the tribes represented (though it failed prevent the outbreak of the French and Indian War in 1756). In addition, though, the gathering instructed several colonial delegations to investigate a union of the colonies to better coordinate their external relations. Benjamin Franklin (representing Pennsylvania) compiled ideas for a union into a single document, which was then referred to the colonial governments and to the Crown. This Albany Plan was rejected by Britain and by the assemblies in several of the colonies, but it presaged the later movement toward independence.[6]

Treaty-Making Under the Articles of Confederation

The Articles of Confederation, adopted by the Continental Congress in 1777 and ratified by the states in 1781, governed treaty-making by the United States before the Constitution took effect in 1789. Article IX of the Articles of Confederation conferred upon Congress "the sole and exclusive right and power" of "sending and receiving ambassadors" and "entering

---

[3] *See* Vasan Kesavan, *The Three Tiers of Federal Law*, 100 NW. U. L. REV. 1479, 1515–29 (2006) (relating British practice to contemporary understanding among the framers); *e.g.*, W.S. Holdsworth, *The Treaty-Making Power of the Crown*, 58 L. Q. REV. 175 (1942) (depicting parliamentary limitations on the crown prerogative).

[4] 5 *Elliot's Debates*, *supra* note 1, at 203 (expressing Hamilton's general belief that "[A]s to the executive . . . [t]he English model was the only good one. . . .").

[5] John Ferling, *A Leap in the Dark: The Struggle to Create the American Republic* 15–16 (2003).

[6] *See* Timothy J. Shannon, *Indians and Colonists at the Crossroads of Empire: The Albany Congress of 1754* (2002).

into treaties and alliances"; Article VI reinforced this by denying to the states any power, without the consent of Congress, to "send any embassy to, or receive any embassy from, or enter into any conference, agreement, alliance or treaty with any King, Prince or State." At the same time, the states sought to retain the commercial freedom and political control they had gained as a result of the 1776 revolution. Article 2 thus stipulated that "each State retains its sovereignty, freedom, and independence, and every power, jurisdiction, and right, which is not by this Confederation expressly delegated to the United States in Congress assembled." More explicitly, Article IX prohibited certain commercial treaties that would limit state authority.

Whatever the formal authority enjoyed by the central government, that authority was exercised by the Confederation Congress—through which the states continued to pursue distinct objectives. The lack of an executive came to be perceived as a serious structural deficiency. Hamilton, assessing the nation's ills in 1780, famously observed:

> Another defect in our system, is want of method and energy in the administration. This has partly resulted from the other defect [the weakness of Congress]; but in a great degree from prejudice, and the want of a proper executive. Congress have kept the power too much in their own hands, and have meddled too much with details of every sort. Congress is, properly, a deliberative corps; and it forgets itself when it attempts to play the executive. It is impossible such a body, numerous as it is, constantly fluctuating, can ever act with sufficient decision, or with system. . . .[7]

Jefferson, writing later that decade, added that "[n]othing is so embarrassing nor so mischievous" as distracting Congress with the task of execution, explaining that "I have ever viewed the executive details as the greatest cause of evil to us, because they in fact place us as if we had no federal head, by diverting the attention of that head from great to small subjects; and should this division of power not be recommended by the convention, it is my opinion Congress should make it itself, by establishing an executive committee.[8]

The creation and strengthening—during John Jay's tenure—of the position of Secretary of Foreign Affairs, the precursor to the Secretary of State, was a partial but incomplete improvement. That post, filled by a member of Congress, also remained subject to congressional oversight. While this created a potential for micro-management, some contemporary

[7] Letter from Alexander Hamilton to James Duane (Sept. 3, 1780), in 1 *The Works of Alexander Hamilton* 150, 154 (John C. Hamilton ed., 1850).

[8] Letter from Thomas Jefferson to Edward Carrington (Aug. 4, 1787), in *The Best Letters of Thomas Jefferson* 30, 31 (J. G. de Roulhac Hamilton ed., 1926).

observers (like the French, in internal correspondence) perceived that it actually created a power vacuum that left Jay with free rein:

> The little stability of congress, my lord, insensibly gives to the ministers of the different departments a power incompatible with the spirit of liberty and of jealousy which prevails in this country.... Mr. Jay especially has acquired a peculiar ascendancy over the members of congress. All important business passes through his hands. He makes his report on it, and congress seldom has an opinion different from his. Instead of appointing committees, they will insensibly become accustomed to seeing only through the eyes of Mr. Jay....[9]

Perhaps the clearest diplomatic challenge for the young United States and its Articles lay in resolving the terms of independence. As the war drew to a close, the United States confronted the awesome task of negotiating a multilateral peace settlement. Congress corresponded with its plenipotentiaries at Paris but, while conducting its deliberations, found it difficult to keep information classified—at one point allowing the accidental disclosure and publication of the preliminary articles of the draft agreement, causing the French to distrust the motives of their recent allies.[10] Congress also delayed in setting its terms and faced defiance by the commissioners it was instructing. Despite this, and despite additional delay in approving the final pact, the treaty was ultimately concluded in September 1783. *See* Definitive Treaty of Peace, Sept. 3, 1783, U.S.-Gr. Brit., *reprinted in* 2 *Treaties and Other International Agreements of the United States of America* 151 (Hunter Miller ed., 1931).

Congress then faced a new challenge: the failure of some states to comply with the Treaty of Peace, particularly article IV's stipulation that neither country would enact laws that would prevent the collection of debts. In his October 1783 report to Congress, Secretary Jay included a letter from the British Secretary of State for Foreign Affairs, Lord Carmarthen, complaining of U.S. violations:

> The little attention paid to the fulfilling [of] this engagement on the part of the subjects of the United States in general, and the direct breach of it in many particular instances, have already reduced many of the king's subjects to the utmost degree of difficulty and distress....
>
> The engagements entered into by treaty ought to be mutual and equally binding on the respective contracting parties. It would therefore be the height of folly as well as injustice, to suppose one party alone obliged to a strict observance of the publick faith,

---

9 Letter from Otto to Vergennes (Dec. 25, 1785), in George Bancroft, 1 *History of the Formation of the Constitution of the United States of America* 473, 474 (1882).

10 5 *Elliot's Debates*, *supra* note 1, at 66.

> while the other might remain free to deviate from its own engagements, as often as convenience might render such deviation necessary, though at the expense of its own national credit and importance.[11]

Advised by Jay of the need to restore U.S. credibility, Congress passed a resolution on March 21, 1787 addressing state compliance with treaties. That resolution pushed the central government's authority about as far as the Articles of Confederation would bear. Congress resolved:

> That the legislatures of the several States cannot of right pass any act or acts for interpreting, explaining, or construing a national treaty or any part or clause of it; nor for restraining, limiting or in any manner impeding, retarding or counteracting the operation and execution of the same for that on being constitutionally made ratified and published, they become in virtue of the confederation part of the law of the land and are not only independent of the will and power of such legislatures but also binding and obligatory upon them.[12]

At the same time, the resolution appeared to recognize that state cooperation was essential, requesting that state acts "repugnant to the treaty of peace ought to be forthwith repealed, as well to prevent their continuing to be regarded as violations of that treaty as to avoid the disagreeable necessity there might otherwise be of raising and discussing questions touching their validity and obligation," and suggesting that states provide for judicial resolution of treaty-based claims despite any conflicting state laws—acknowledging, indirectly, that national treaties required state cooperation in order to be implemented.[13]

With all of these problems in mind, the delegates went on to the Convention at Philadelphia anxious to revise the *status quo*.

Debates at the Federal Convention of 1787 and Thereafter

The Treaty Clause. The Virginia Resolutions presented by Edmund Randolph were the first proposals made to the Convention. They did not constitute a comprehensive plan and did not specifically mention treaty-making. They did, however, resolve "that a national executive be instituted . . . and that, besides a general authority to execute the national laws, it ought to enjoy the executive rights vested in Congress by the Confederation."[14] This provision was designed, *inter alia*, to remedy the problems created by Congress's management of foreign affairs. Charles Pickney next laid before the Convention a different proposal that

11 4 *Secret Journals of the Acts and Proceedings of Congress* 188 (1821).

12 32 *Journals of the Continental Congress* 124–25 (1787).

13 *Id.*

14 5 *Elliot's Debates*, *supra* note 1, at 128.

stipulated that the "Senate shall have the sole and exclusive power to declare war, and to make treaties. . . ."[15]

The Convention began to consider more radical remedies in a speech made by Alexander Hamilton on June 18. At the conclusion of his remarks, he submitted some "amendments which he should probably propose to the plan of Mr. Randolph. . . ."[16] In regard to treaty-making, he suggested that the "supreme executive authority of the United States to be vested in a governor . . . have, with the advice and approbation of the senate, the power of making all treaties. . . ."[17]

Despite this, until late in the Convention, there was little inclination to alter legislative preeminence in treaty-making. Some preferred to strengthen, rather than undermine, it. For example, Mr. Wilson of Pennsylvania stressed that the Senate ought "to be made respectable in the eyes of foreign nations"[18] and urged that this be accomplished through longer senatorial terms of office.[19]

On August 6, however, John Mercer renewed earlier challenges, arguing "that the Senate ought not to have the power of treaties. This power belonged to the executive department. . . ."[20] On August 23, the floor was opened for discussion of the proposed clause: "The Senate . . . shall have power to make treaties. . . ."[21] James Madison, stressing the propensity of Senators (who were to be appointed by the state legislatures) to favor local interests, stated "that for this, as well as other obvious reasons, it was proper that the President should be an agent in treaties."[22] Governeur Morris of Pennsylvania "did not know that he should agree to refer the making of treaties to the Senate at all but for the present would move to add, as an amendment . . .: 'But no treaty shall be binding on the United States which is not ratified by law.' "[23] At the end of the day Madison, in connection with legislative assent, "hinted, for consideration, whether a distinction might not be made between different sorts of treaties. . . ."[24]

The business of deciding upon this issue was referred to a committee of eleven who reported on September 4 that "The President, by and with the advice and consent of the Senate, shall have power to make treaties. . . . But no treaty shall be made without the consent of two-thirds of the

15 *Id.* at 131.

16 *Id.* at 205.

17 *Id.*

18 *Id.* at 245.

19 *See id.*

20 *Id.* at 428.

21 *Id.* at 469.

22 *Id.*

23 *Id.*

24 *Id.* at 470.

members present."[25] This wording remained practically unaltered in the final draft.

The nature of the treaty power remained open to dispute during ratification. John Jay, in *The Federalist Papers* No. 64, pointed from experience to defects in treaty negotiation as primary reasons for vesting the treaty-making power with the president and Senate, stating that "So often and so essentially have we heretofore suffered from the want of secrecy and dispatch that the Constitution would have been inexcusably defective if no attention had been paid to those objects."[26] On the other hand, a dissenting minority of the Pennsylvania's ratifying convention warned of "uncorseted corruption" as a result of blurring the delineation between the branches of government in the process of treaty-making and expressed concern that it would "destroy all independency and purity in the executive department,"[27] while Elbridge Gerry of Massachusetts thought the treaty power would give the Executive "undue influence over the legislature."[28] Cato suspected that a division of powers would destroy accountability, explaining that: "If treaties are erroneously or wickedly made who is there to punish—the executive can always cover himself with the plea, that he was advised by the senate; and the senate being a collective body are not easily made accountable for mal-administration."[29]

Responding to some of these concerns in *The Federalist Papers* No. 75, Hamilton defended collaboration between the executive and the Senate as an appropriate response to the special nature of treaties, since it was not strictly legislative or executive in character:

> The essence of the legislative authority is to enact laws, or, in other words, to prescribe rules for the regulation of the society; while the execution of the laws and the employment of the common strength . . . seem to comprise all the functions of the executive magistrate. The power of making treaties is, plainly, neither the one nor the other. It relates neither to the execution of the subsisting laws nor to the enaction of new ones; and still less to an exertion of the common strength. Its objects are CONTRACTS with foreign nations which have the force of law, but derive it from the obligations of good faith. They are not rules prescribed by the sovereign to the subject, but agreements between sovereign and sovereign. The power in question seems therefore to form a

---

25 *Id.* at 507.

26 *The Federalist Papers* No. 64, at 392–93 (Jay) (Clinton Rossiter ed., 1961).

27 *The Address and Reasons of Dissent of the Minority of the Convention of Pennsylvania to Their Constituents* (PENN. PACKET and DAILY ADVERTISER, Dec. 18, 1787), *reprinted in* 3 *The Complete Anti-federalist* 145, 161–62 (Herbert J. Storing ed., 1981) [hereinafter cited as "Storing"].

28 *Hon. Mr. Gerry's objections to signing the National Constitution* (MASS. CENTINEL, Nov. 3, 1787), *reprinted in* 2 Storing, *supra* note 34, at 6–7.

29 Letters of Cato (NEW YORK JOURNAL, Sept. 1787–Jan. 1788), *reprinted in* 2 Storing, *supra* note 27, at 123.

distinct department, and to belong, properly, neither to the legislative nor to the executive. The qualities elsewhere detailed as indispensable in the management of foreign negotiations point out the executive as the most fit agent in those transactions; while the vast importance of the trust and the operation of treaties as laws plead strongly for the participation of the whole or a portion of the legislative body in the office of making them.[30]

The Supremacy Clause. As Hamilton's description suggested, the Convention also had to address the force of treaties as law. On July 17, Luther Martin of Maryland proposed: "That the legislative acts of the United States, made by virtue and in pursuance of the Articles of Union, and all treaties made and ratified under the authority of the United States, shall be the supreme law of the respective states. . . ."[31] In the prevailing spirit of nationalism, which induced the transfer of power from state to federal government, Mr. Martin's motion passed. This shift in the distribution of legislative authority was facilitated by Madison's insistence that the states, otherwise, would "pass laws which will accomplish their injurious objects before they can be repealed by the general [federal] legislature,"[32] and that "confidence cannot be put in the state tribunals as guardians of the national authority and interests."[33] He urged that federal preeminence in the conduct of foreign relations was essential "to the efficacy and security of the general government."[34]

Martin's resolution remained substantially unaltered in the Convention's final draft. Yet the resulting Supremacy Clause, including as it applied to treaties, was not without controversy. George Mason, who attended the federal Convention as a deputy from Virginia, detailed his objections to this and other provisions during Convention's final days. Unmoved by the lessons others purported to derive from treaty-making during the confederate period, Mason thought treaty supremacy was afforded too broadly, and that requiring the assent of the House would be appropriate for such a legislative power.[35]

In the months following the Convention, critics focused both on the centralizing effect of treaty supremacy in relation to state power and on the legal validity and effect of instruments not adopted through legislative means. John Jay, in *The Federalist Papers* No. 64, noted that other binding sovereign acts, like the judgments of courts, were not by virtue of that fact

---

30 *The Federalist Papers* No. 75, *supra* note 26, at 450–51 (Hamilton).

31 5 *Elliot's Debates*, *supra* note 1, at 322.

32 *Id.* at 321.

33 *Id.*

34 *Id.*

35 George Mason, *Objections to the Constitution of Government formed by the Convention* (1787), *reprinted in* 2 Storing, *supra* note 27, at 11, 12.

alone thought appropriate to the legislature.[36] But others continued to argue that, if treaties were to be "law of the land," they should be enacted more in accordance with the legislative provisions of the Constitution. The lack of limitations on the content of international agreements provoked another controversy, emanating from suspicion that this power would eventually be abused. The *Federal Farmer* regarded the provision as a loophole for creating unjust laws because (unlike the statutes also addressed by the Supremacy Clause) "[i]t is not said that these treaties shall be made in pursuance of the Constitution—nor are there any constitutional bounds set to those who shall make them. . . ."[37] An antifederalist using the pseudonym Brutus complained: "I do not find any limitation, or restriction, to the exercise of this power."[38]

Attempts are often made to explain why the framers insisted on a two-thirds majority in the Senate to approve a treaty. Historians like Samuel Bemis sometimes attribute this requirement to dissatisfaction with John Jay's recently-evidenced willingness to abandon navigation privileges on the Mississippi River that had been held for thirty years in negotiations with Spain concerning Florida. Bemis says:

> A few months later when the delegates to the Philadelphia Convention of 1787 were drawing up the new Constitution the men from the southern states remembered the dangers, so recently presented to them, of any constitution which would allow a bare majority to ratify a treaty, either with a foreign nation or with Indian tribes. The Jay-Gardoqui negotiations are responsible for that clause in the Constitution of 1787 which requires a two-thirds majority of senators present for the ratification of any treaty.[39]

This undoubtedly played a role. But another substantial factor giving rise to the two-thirds provision, certainly, was the founding fathers' wish to avoid unnecessary, dangerous alliances. Washington, in his Farewell Address, gave voice to these concerns when he asked: "Why, by interweaving our own destiny with that of any part of Europe, entangle our peace and prosperity in the toils of European ambition, rivalship, interest, humor, or caprice?"[40]

---

36 *The Federalist Papers* No. 64, *supra* note 26, at 393–94.

37 *Letters from The Federal Farmer* (No. IV: Oct. 12, 1787), *reprinted in* 2 Storing, *supra* note 27, at 245, 246–47.

38 *Essays of Brutus* (No. II: Nov. 1, 1787), *reprinted in* 2 Storing, *supra* note 27, at 372, 377.

39 Samuel F. Bemis, *A Diplomatic History of the United States* 79–80 (1938).

40 Washington's Farewell Address (Sept. 17, 1796), *reprinted in Documents of American History* 169, 174 (Henry Steele Commager ed., 1968).

Treaty-Making Under the Constitution

Since 1789, the United States has concluded thousands of treaties at the bilateral, regional, and global level. Important early treaties ended wars (such as the 1814 Treaty of Ghent, ending the War of 1812) and established U.S. boundaries, such as the 1817 Rush-Bagot Treaty (demilitarizing the Great Lakes), the 1819 Adams-Onís Treaty (purchasing Florida from Spain), the 1842 Webster-Ashburton Treaty (settling the boundary with Canada), and the 1867 treaty purchasing Alaska from Russia. Other treaties focused on core interests of the United States in areas of trade and immigration, such as the 1855 U.S.-Canadian Reciprocity Treaty on trade and tariffs, the 1858 U.S.-Japan Treaty of Amity and Commerce, and the 1868 Burlingame Treaty establishing relations with China. By the latter part of the nineteenth century, multilateral treaties became increasingly important, such as the 1883 Paris Convention for the Protection of Industrial Property and the 1899 Hague Conventions on the laws of war.

Although the role of treaties changed during the twentieth century, as we will see, the United States nonetheless concluded major multilateral and bilateral treaties covering a wide array of subjects (including dispute settlement, arms control, terrorism, human rights, oceans, environment, criminal law, family law, and immunities) and establishing major international organizations (such as the United Nations, the Organization of American States, the World Bank, the International Monetary Fund, and the World Trade Organization). While treaty basics have remained much the same, the process for making treaties, and the key legal issues they present, have continued to evolve.

2. SENATORIAL ADVICE AND CONSENT FUNCTION

Article II, Section 2 of the U.S. Constitution provides that the president "shall have Power, by and with the Advice and Consent of the Senate, to make Treaties, provided two thirds of the Senators present concur. . . ." This language, and its presence in Article II, makes clear that it is the president, not the Senate, who "makes" treaties, typically by depositing an instrument of ratification.

At the same time, Section 2 says that before the president "makes" a treaty, the Senate must give its "advice" and "consent," thus suggesting that the Senate is expected to provide counsel to the president in addition to a final stamp of approval.[41] Nonetheless, executive branch practice is generally to keep the Senate out of the process until final consent is needed, unless its involvement at an earlier stage is necessary to secure political

[41] *See* Arthur Bestor, *"Advice" From the Very Beginning, "Consent" When the End Is Achieved*, 83 AM. J. INT'L. L. 718 (1989).

support for the treaty. The following excerpt sets forth the basic treaty-making process.

TREATIES AND OTHER INTERNATIONAL AGREEMENTS: THE ROLE OF THE UNITED STATES SENATE

S. Prt. 106–71, at 6–12 (2001).

NEGOTIATION AND CONCLUSION

The first phase of treatymaking, negotiation and conclusion, is widely considered an exclusive prerogative of the President. . . . The President chooses and instructs the negotiators and decides whether to sign an agreement after its terms have been negotiated. Nevertheless, the Senate or Congress sometimes proposes negotiations and influences them through advice and consultation. In addition, the executive branch is supposed to advise appropriate congressional leaders and committees of the intention to negotiate significant new agreements and consult them as to the form of the agreement.

Steps in the negotiating phase follow.

(1) *Initiation.*—The executive branch formally initiates the negotiations. The original concept or proposal for a treaty on a particular subject, however, may come from Congress.

(2) *Appointment of negotiators.*—The President selects the negotiators of international agreements, but appointments may be subject to the advice and consent of the Senate. Negotiations are often conducted by ambassadors or foreign service officers in a relevant post who have already been confirmed by the Senate.

(3) *Issuance of full powers and instructions.*—The President issues full power documents to the negotiators, authorizing them officially to represent the United States. Similarly, he issues instructions as to the objectives to be sought and positions to be taken. On occasion the Senate participates in setting the objectives during the confirmation process, or Congress contributes to defining the objectives through hearings or resolutions.

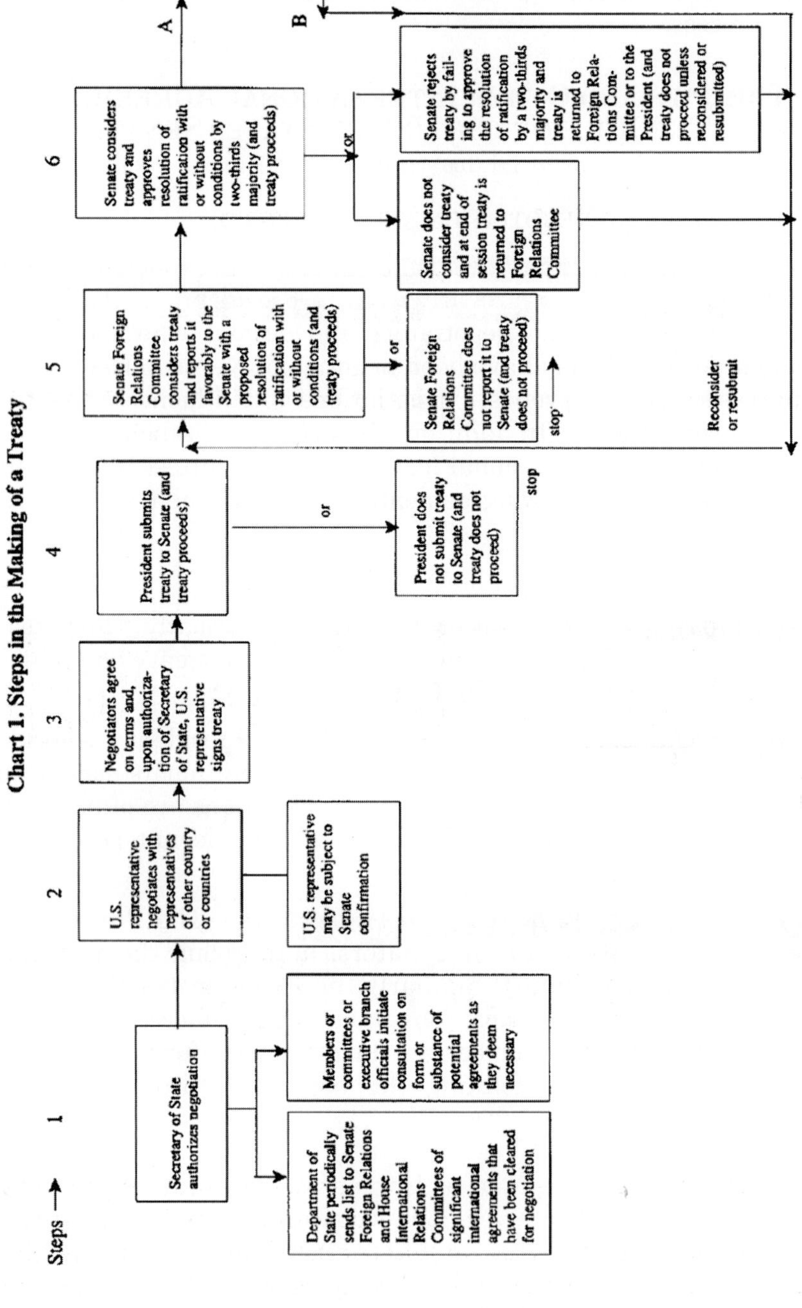

Chart 1. Steps in the Making of a Treaty

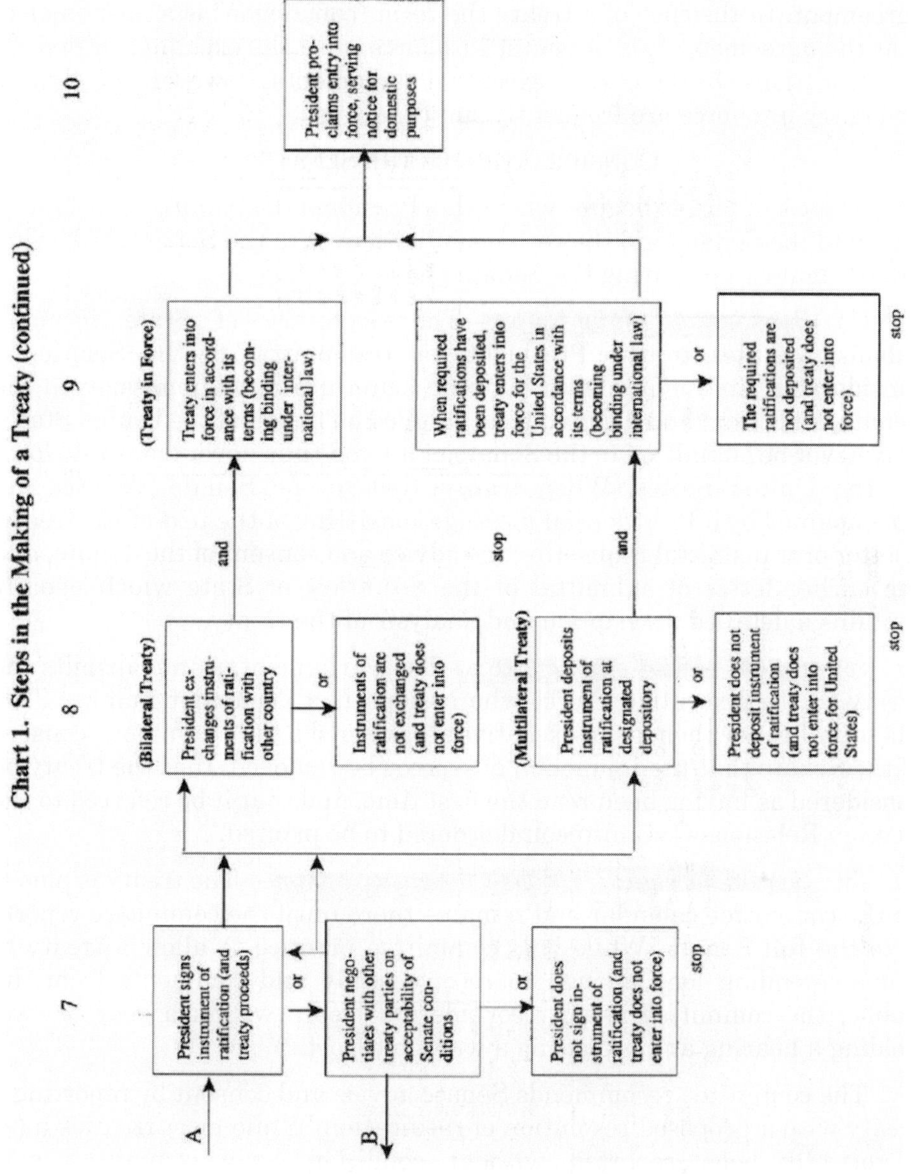

Chart 1. Steps in the Making of a Treaty (continued)

(4) *Negotiation*.—Negotiation is the process by which representatives of the President and other governments concerned agree on the substance, terms, wording, and form of an international agreement. Members of Congress sometimes provide advice through consultations arranged either by Congress or the executive branch, and through their statements and writings. Members of Congress or their staff have served as members or advisers of delegations and as observers at international negotiations.

(5) *Conclusion*.—The conclusion or signing marks the end of the negotiating process and indicates that the negotiators have reached

agreement. In the case of a treaty the term "conclusion" is a misnomer in that the agreement does not enter into force until the exchange or deposit of ratifications. In the case of executive agreements, however, the signing and entry into force are frequently simultaneous.

CONSIDERATION BY THE SENATE

A second phase begins when the President transmits a concluded treaty to the Senate and the responsibility moves to the Senate. Following are the main steps during the Senate phase.

(1) *Presidential submission.*—The Secretary of State formally submits treaties to the President for transmittal to the Senate. A considerable time may elapse between signature and submission to the Senate, and on rare occasions a treaty signed on behalf of the United States may never be submitted to the Senate at all and thus never enter into force for the United States. When transmitted to the Senate, treaties are accompanied by a Presidential message consisting of the text of the treaty, a letter of transmittal requesting the advice and consent of the Senate, and the earlier letter of submittal of the Secretary of State which usually contains a detailed description and analysis of the treaty.

(2) *Senate receipt and referral.*—The Parliamentarian transmits the treaty to the Executive Clerk, who assigns it a document number. The Majority Leader then, as in executive session, asks the unanimous consent of the Senate that the injunction of secrecy be removed, that the treaty be considered as having been read the first time, and that it be referred to the Foreign Relations Committee and ordered to be printed. . . .

(3) *Senate Foreign Relations Committee action.*—The treaty is placed on the committee calendar and remains there until the committee reports it to the full Senate. While it is committee practice to allow a treaty to remain pending long enough to receive study and comments from the public, the committee usually considers a treaty within a year or two, holding a hearing and preparing a written report.

The committee recommends Senate advice and consent by reporting a treaty with a proposed resolution of ratification. While most treaties have historically been reported without conditions, the committee may recommend that the Senate approve a treaty subject to conditions incorporated in the resolution of ratification.

(4) *Conditional approval.*—The conditions traditionally have been grouped into categories described in the following way.

— Amendments to a treaty change the text of the treaty and require the consent of the other party or parties. (Note that in Senate debate the term may refer to an amendment of the resolution of ratification, not the treaty itself, and therefore be comprised of some other type of condition.)

— Reservations change U.S. obligations without necessarily changing the text, and they require the acceptance of the other party.

— Understandings are interpretive statements that clarify or elaborate provisions but do not alter them.

— Declarations are statements expressing the Senate's position or opinion on matters relating to issues raised by the treaty rather than to specific provisions.

— Provisos relate to issues of U.S. law or procedure and are not intended to be included in the instruments of ratification to be deposited or exchanged with other countries.

Whatever name a condition is given by the Senate, if a condition alters an international obligation under the treaty, the President is expected to transmit it to the other party. In recent years, the Senate on occasion has explicitly designated that some conditions were to be transmitted to the other party or parties and, in some cases, formally agreed to by them. It has also designated that some conditions need not be formally communicated to the other party, that some conditions were binding on the President, and that some conditions expressed the intent of the Senate.

(5) *Action by the full Senate.*—After a treaty is reported by the Foreign Relations Committee, it is placed on the Senate's Executive Calendar and the Majority Leader arranges for the Senate to consider it. . . .

The Senate then considers amendments to the resolution of ratification, which would incorporate any amendments to the treaty itself that the Senate had agreed to in the first stage, as well as conditions recommended by the Foreign Relations Committee. Senators may then offer reservations, understandings, and other conditions to be placed in the resolution of ratification. Votes on these conditions, as well as other motions, are determined by a simple majority. Finally, the Senate votes on the resolution of ratification, as it has been amended. The final vote on the resolution of ratification requires, for approval, a two-thirds majority of the Senators present. Although the number of Senators who must be present is not specified, the Senate's practice with respect to major treaties is to conduct the final treaty vote at a time when most Senators are available. After approval of a controversial treaty, a Senator may offer a motion to reconsider which is usually laid on the table (defeated). In the case of a treaty that has failed to receive a two-thirds majority, if the motion to reconsider is not taken up, the treaty is returned to the Foreign Relations Committee. . . .

(6) *Return to committee.*—Treaties reported by the committee but neither approved nor formally returned to the President by the Senate are

automatically returned to the committee calendar at the end of a Congress; the committee must report them out again in order for the Senate to consider them.

(7) *Return to President or withdrawal*.—The President may request the return of a treaty, or the Foreign Relations Committee may report and the Senate adopt a simple resolution directing the Secretary of the Senate to return a treaty to the President. Otherwise, treaties that do not receive the advice and consent of the Senate remain pending on the committee calendar indefinitely.

Presidential Action After Senate Action

After the Senate gives its advice and consent to a treaty, the Senate sends it to the President. He resumes control and decides whether to take further action to complete the treaty.

(1) *Ratification*.—The President ratifies a treaty by signing an instrument of ratification, thus declaring the consent of the United States to be bound. If the Senate has consented with reservations or conditions that the President deems unacceptable, he may at a later date resubmit the original treaty to the Senate for further consideration, or he may renegotiate it with the other parties prior to resubmission. Or the President may decide not to ratify the treaty because of the conditions or for any other reason.

(2) *Exchange or deposit of instruments of ratification and entry into force*.—If he ratifies the treaty, the President then directs the Secretary of State to take any action necessary for the treaty to enter into force. A bilateral treaty usually enters into force when the parties exchange instruments of ratification. A multilateral treaty enters into force when the number of parties specified in the treaty deposit the instruments of ratification at a specified location. Once a treaty enters into force, it is binding in international law on the parties who have ratified it. . . .

NOTE ON THE FAILURE OF THE SENATE TO GIVE CONSENT

As indicated above, treaties that do not receive advice and consent do not—unlike proposed legislation—necessarily expire; a deferred or defeated treaty may remain with the Senate, enabling future consideration. *See Unperfected Treaties of the United States of America, 1776–1976* (Christian L. Wiktor ed., 1976).

Regardless of whether a failed treaty remains with the Senate, it may have continuing consequences under the international law of treaties and, consequently, foreign relations law. Such a treaty cannot (and will not) be ratified by the president, and absent such ratification does not bind the United States as such. However, if the United States has already *signed* the treaty—which may occur well prior to ratification or even Senate submission—that creates an obligation on it not to "defeat" the treaty's "object and purpose . . .

until it shall have made its intention clear not to become a party to the treaty." Vienna Convention on the Law of Treaties art. 18, May 23, 1969, 1155 U.N.T.S. 331, 336. The scope of this interim obligation is not wholly clear, but it at least requires avoiding acts that would make the agreement impossible to perform.

As Article 18 suggests, international law also permits a signing State to notify the depositary that it has no further intention of seeking ratification (sometimes referred to by non-lawyers as "unsigning" a treaty). For example, just prior to entry into force of the Rome Statute of the International Criminal Court, July 17, 1998, 2187 U.N.T.S. 3, the United States decided that it had no intention of pursuing ratification, and so notified the Secretary-General. *See* U.S. Department of State Press Release on International Criminal Court: Letter to UN Secretary-General Kofi Annan (May 6, 2002). If the Senate withholds consent to a treaty (or, in a more extreme case, votes against a resolution of advice and consent), should the president inform the depositary that the United States does not intend to become a party? Otherwise, has not the president bound the Senate to aspects of the treaty without the Senate's consent? For discussion, see Curtis A. Bradley, *Unratified Treaties, Domestic Politics, and the U.S. Constitution*, 48 HARV. INT'L L. J. 307 (2007); David H. Moore, *The President's Unconstitutional Treatymaking*, 59 U.C.L.A. L. REV. 598 (2012).

NOTE: CASE STUDY ON SENATORIAL ADVICE AND CONSENT TO THE CONVENTION AGAINST TORTURE

To demonstrate the Senate's advice and consent role, the materials below depict the United States' process for considering the Convention Against Torture and Other Cruel, Inhuman or Degrading Treatment or Punishment, Dec. 10, 1984, S. TREATY DOC. NO. 100–20 (1988), 1465 U.N.T.S. 85 (Convention Against Torture, or CAT). The Convention was adopted by unanimous agreement of the United Nations General Assembly (including by the United States) on December 10, 1984; the Convention entered into force on June 26, 1987, after having received the requisite number of approvals by States Parties; the United States signed it on April 18, 1988; and it entered into force for the United States on November 20, 1994, following its deposit of an instrument of ratification in October 21. *See* 18 U.N.T.S. 320.

International law specifies, in principle, the significance of each of these steps, but U.S. foreign relations law supplies important nuances—including the terms on which the United States would join the Convention. The executive branch played the main role in the negotiating process, which largely took place in Geneva at the U.N. Commission on Human Rights, and signed the Convention on behalf of the United States. Even so, the United States still had to decide whether to ratify and thereby assume the Convention as an international treaty obligation for the United States. When considering that question, some contended that aspects of the treaty conflicted with U.S. legal and policy preferences, including traditional divisions of responsibility between the federal government and the states.

What might be done? The United States could swallow hard and change its preferences, including federal and state law, but potential treaty supporters may not wish to do so. (And changing the Constitution would require a cumbersome amendment process that has never been undertaken to accommodate a treaty.) In such circumstances, the United States often considers, during the advice and consent process, adopting reservations, understandings, or declarations ("RUDs") to accompany U.S. ratification and align U.S. obligations with U.S. policy preferences and national legal requirements. RUDs can be proposed to the Senate by the president or may be demanded by the Senate as a condition for its consent. *See Haver v. Yaker*, 76 U.S. (9 Wall.) 32, 35 (1869) (acknowledging the Senate's broad power to demand changes between signing and ratification).

As you read these particular materials, imagine that you are the Attorney General, the Secretary of State, or a senator who must decide whether the United States should join the already-negotiated Convention and on what terms. You might well have concerns about the following issues:

- The United States follows a federal system, in which state and local units have important responsibilities for enforcement of criminal law. How should this be taken into account in adhering to a treaty that calls for the United States to punish certain behavior?
- The treaty calls for punishing persons who commit torture, but what is "torture"? What acts must be criminalized? U.S. law enforcement officers, judges, and others will want to know.
- What should be done if the treaty uses one standard, such as whether "there are substantial grounds for believing" something, but U.S. law historically has used a different standard, such as "it is more likely than not" that something will happen? Or the treaty uses a broad standard, such as "cruel, inhuman, or degrading treatment," which may or may not be consistent with analogous standards in U.S. law?
- Should the principal provisions of the treaty have direct effect as a part of U.S. law (because they are "self-executing"), or should the United States clarify by some means that they only have force of law when implemented by statute or other means (because they are "non-self-executing")? (These confusing terms will be explored in Sec. 4 of this Chapter, but for the time being, consider that the Senate can play a critical role in determining whether a treaty's provisions are self-executing.)

As the following materials indicate, the answers to these questions were not controlled by the executive branch, and the Senate was far from a "rubber stamp" on the president's preferred approach. The initial RUDs proposed by the president were revised following criticisms from various interest groups, including human rights organizations. Some changes were attributable to the change in presidential administration (from that of President Ronald Reagan to that of President George H.W. Bush), illustrating political dynamics that can arise over the course of the advice and consent process. Further changes were made on the floor of the Senate to accommodate the views of a senator. Note, finally, how at each stage of the process, important statements were made by the executive branch or Senate that can assist in understanding the meaning of a treaty or of the RUDs.

CONVENTION AGAINST TORTURE AND OTHER CRUEL, INHUMAN OR DEGRADING TREATMENT OR PUNISHMENT

Dec. 10, 1984, S. Treaty Doc. No. 100–20 (1988), 1465 U.N.T.S. 85.

The States Parties to this Convention . . . .

Having regard also to the Declaration . . . adopted by the General Assembly on 9 December 1975,

Desiring to make more effective the struggle against torture and other cruel, inhuman or degrading treatment or punishment throughout the world,

Have agreed as follows: . . . .

Article 1. 1. For the purposes of this Convention, the term "torture" means any act by which severe pain or suffering, whether physical or mental, is intentionally inflicted on a person for such purposes as obtaining from him or a third person information or a confession, punishing him for an act he or a third person has committed or is suspected of having committed, or intimidating or coercing him or a third person, or for any reason based on discrimination of any kind, when such pain or suffering is inflicted by or at the instigation of or with the consent or acquiescence of a public official or other person acting in an official capacity. It does not include pain or suffering arising only from, inherent in or incidental to lawful sanctions.

2. This article is without prejudice to any international instrument or national legislation which does or may contain provisions of wider application.

Article 2. 1. Each State Party shall take effective legislative, administrative, judicial or other measures to prevent acts of torture in any territory under its jurisdiction.

2. No exceptional circumstances whatsoever, whether a state of war or a threat of war, internal political instability or any other public emergency, may be invoked as a justification of torture. . . .

Article 3. 1. No State Party shall expel, return (*refouler*) or extradite a person to another State where there are substantial grounds for believing that he would be in danger of being subjected to torture.

2. For the purpose of determining whether there are such grounds, the competent authorities shall take into account all relevant considerations including, where applicable, the existence in the State concerned of a consistent pattern of gross, flagrant or mass violations of human rights.

Article 4. 1. Each State Party shall ensure that all acts of torture are offences under its criminal law. The same shall apply to an attempt to commit torture and to an act by any person which constitutes complicity or participation in torture.

2. Each State Party shall make these offences punishable by appropriate penalties which take into account their grave nature.

Article 5. 1. Each State Party shall take such measures as may be necessary to establish its jurisdiction over the offences referred to in article 4 in the following cases:

(a) When the offences are committed in any territory under its jurisdiction or on board a ship or aircraft registered in that State;

(b) When the alleged offender is a national of that State;

(c) When the victim is a national of that State if that State considers it appropriate.

2. Each State Party shall likewise take such measures as may be necessary to establish its jurisdiction over such offences in cases where the alleged offender is present in any territory under its jurisdiction and it does not extradite him. . . .

Article 7. 1. The State Party in the territory under whose jurisdiction a person alleged to have committed any offence referred to in article 4 is found shall in the cases contemplated in article 5, if it does not extradite him, submit the case to its competent authorities for the purpose of prosecution. . . .

Article 14. 1. Each State Party shall ensure in its legal system that the victim of an act of torture obtains redress and has an enforceable right to fair and adequate compensation, including the means for as full rehabilitation as possible. . . .

Article 16. 1. Each State Party shall undertake to prevent in any territory under its jurisdiction other acts of cruel, inhuman or degrading treatment or punishment which do not amount to torture as defined in article 1, when such acts are committed by or at the instigation of or with the consent or acquiescence of a public official or other person acting in an official capacity. . . .

U.S. DEPARTMENT OF STATE SUMMARY AND ANALYSIS OF THE CONVENTION AGAINST TORTURE

S. Treaty Doc. No. 100–20, at 2–18 (1988).

Although the terms of the Convention, with the suggested reservations and understandings, are consonant with U.S. law, it is nevertheless preferable to leave any further implementation that may be desired to the domestic legislature and judicial process. The following declaration is therefore recommended, to clarify that the provisions of the Convention would not of themselves become effective as domestic law:

> "The United States declares that the provisions of Articles 1 through 16 are not self-executing." . . . .

Given the decentralized distribution of police and other governmental authority at federal, state and local levels, it is desirable to make [t]he following federal-state reservation:

> "The United States shall implement the Convention to the extent that the Federal Government exercises legislative and judicial jurisdiction over the matters covered therein; to the extent that constituent units exercise jurisdiction over such matters, the Federal Government shall take appropriate measures to the end that the competent authorities of the constituent units of the United States of America may take appropriate measures for the fulfillment of the Convention." . . . .

The requirement that torture be an extreme form of cruel and inhuman treatment is expressed in Article 16, which refers to "other acts of cruel, inhuman or degrading treatment or punishment *which do not amount to torture. . . .*" The negotiating history indicates that the underlined portion of this description was adopted in order to emphasize that torture is at the extreme end of cruel, inhuman and degrading treatment or punishment and that Article 1 should be construed with this in mind. . . .

The following understandings are recommended to reflect the United States understanding of Article 1 as explained above. These understandings are intended to guard against the improper application of the Convention to legitimate law enforcement actions and thereby would protect U.S. law enforcement interests.

> "The United States understands that, in order to constitute torture, an act must be a deliberate and calculated act of an extremely cruel and inhuman nature, specifically intended to

inflict excruciating and agonizing physical or mental pain or suffering."

> "The United States understands that the definition of torture in Article 1 is intended to apply only to acts directed against persons in the offender's custody or physical control.". . . .

Although no circumstances justify torture, legitimate acts of self-defense or defense of others do not constitute torture as defined by Article 1, since they are not performed with the specific intent to cause excruciating and agonizing pain or suffering. To clarify that Article 2 does not affect the availability of these common-law defenses, the following understanding is recommended:

> "The United States understands that paragraph 2 of Article 2 does not preclude the availability of relevant common law defenses, including but not limited to self-defense and defense of others." . . . .

Under current U.S. law, an individual may not normally be expelled or returned where his "life or freedom would be threatened . . . on account of race, religion, nationality, membership in a particular social group, or political opinion." 8 U.S.C. § 1253(h)(1). The U.S. Supreme Court has interpreted this provision to mean that a person entitled to its protections may not be deported to a country where it is more likely than not that he would be persecuted. *INS v. Stevic*, 467 U.S. 407 (1984). To clarify that Article 3 is not intended to alter this standard of proof, the following understanding is recommended:

> "The United States understands the phrase, 'where there are substantial grounds for believing that he would be in danger of being subjected to torture,' as used in Article 3 of the Convention, to mean 'if it is more likely than not that he would be tortured.' "

. . . Article 16 is arguably broader than existing U.S. law. The phrase "cruel, inhuman or degrading treatment or punishment" is a standard formula in international instruments and is found in the Universal Declaration of Human Rights, the International Covenant on Civil and Political Rights, and the European Convention on Human Rights. To the extent the phrase has been interpreted in the context of those agreements, "cruel" and "inhuman" treatment or punishment appears to be roughly equivalent to the treatment or punishment barred in the United States by the Fifth, Eighth and Fourteenth Amendments. "Degrading" treatment or punishment, however, has been interpreted as potentially including treatment that would probably not be prohibited by the U.S. Constitution. *See, e.g.,* European Commission of Human Rights, *Dec. on Adm.,* Dec. 15, 1977, *Case of X v. Federal Republic of Germany* (No. 6694/74), 11 Dec. & Rep. 16 (refusal of authorities to give formal recognition to an individual's change of sex might constitute "degrading" treatment). To make clear that the United States construes the phrase to be coextensive with its constitutional guarantees against cruel, unusual, and inhumane treatment, the following understanding is recommended:

> "The United States understands the term 'cruel, inhuman or degrading treatment or punishment,' as used in Article 16 of the Convention, to mean cruel, unusual, and inhumane treatment or punishment prohibited by the Fifth, Eighth and/or Fourteenth Amendments to the Constitution of the United States."

LETTER OF TRANSMITTAL TO THE SENATE FROM PRESIDENT RONALD REAGAN (MAY 20, 1988)

S. Treaty Doc. No. 100–20, at iii–iv (1988).

THE WHITE HOUSE, *May 20, 1988.*

To the Senate of the United States:

With a view to receiving the advice and consent of the Senate to ratification, subject to certain reservations, understandings, and declarations, I transmit herewith the Convention against Torture. . . . I also transmit, for the information of the Senate, the report of the Department of State on the Convention. . . .

In view of the large number of States concerned, it was not possible to negotiate a treaty that was acceptable to the United States in all respects. Accordingly, certain reservations, understandings, and declarations have been drafted, which are discussed in the report of the Department of State. With the inclusion of these reservations, understandings, and declarations, I believe there are no constitutional or other legal obstacles to United States ratification. The recommended legislation necessary to implement the Convention will be submitted to the Congress separately. . . .

By giving its advice and consent to ratification of this Convention, the Senate of the United States will demonstrate unequivocally our desire to bring an end to the abhorrent practice of torture.

RONALD REAGAN.

LETTER FROM JANET G. MULLINS, ASSISTANT SECRETARY, LEGISLATIVE AFFAIRS, DEPARTMENT OF STATE, TO SENATOR PELL

S. Exec. Rep. No. 101–30, at 35–36 (1990).

U.S. DEPARTMENT OF STATE
WASHINGTON, DC.,
December 10, 1989.

HON. CLAIBORNE PELL
Chairman, Committee on Foreign Relations
U.S. Senate, Washington, D.C.

DEAR MR. CHAIRMAN:

. . . In your letter to the Secretary of State dated July 24, 1989, you expressed concern that the administration's proposed package [of reservations, understandings, and declarations] faced substantial opposition from human rights groups and other interested parties. . . .

. . . Reflecting our consultations with various interested groups in the private sector, the [enclosed revised] package now contains a revised understanding to the definition of torture, which would not raise the high threshold of pain already required under international law, clarifies the definition of mental pain and suffering, and maintains our position that specific intent is required for torture. The revised package also eliminates the understanding relating to "common law" defenses, makes it clear that the United States does not regard authorized sanctions that unquestionably violate international law as "lawful sanctions" exempt from the prohibition on torture. . . .

JANET G. MULLINS
ASSISTANT SECRETARY, LEGISLATIVE AFFAIRS

CONVENTION AGAINST TORTURE: HEARING ON S. TREATY DOC. 100–20 BEFORE THE SENATE FOREIGN RELATIONS COMMITTEE

101st Cong. 9–18 (Jan. 30, 1990).

PREPARED STATEMENT OF ABRAHAM D. SOFAER, LEGAL ADVISER, U.S. STATE DEPARTMENT

. . . [An] important revision we propose concerns the definition of "torture" under Article I. The original package proposed an understanding to the effect that, in order to constitute "torture," an act must be a deliberate and calculated act of an extremely cruel and inhuman nature, specifically intended to inflict excruciating and agonizing physical or mental pain or suffering. This proposal was criticized by some as possibly setting a higher, more difficult evidentiary standard than the Convention required. Substantial concern was expressed that the effect of this understanding might be to undercut the central feature of the Convention, at least as codified in U.S. law, and to encourage other States also to adopt higher domestic standards, thereby limiting the effectiveness of the Convention.

Although no higher standard was intended, we recognized the concern raised by this criticism. At the same time, our colleagues at the Justice Department felt that, since the definition of "torture" will constitute the basis for a criminal punishment under U.S. law, some clarification of the Convention's definition was constitutionally required.

Accordingly, and on the basis of extensive discussions with concerned representatives in the human rights community, we prepared a codified proposal which does not raise the high threshold of pain already required under international law, but clarifies the definition of mental pain and suffering, and maintains the position that specific intent is required for torture. . . .

Mr. Chairman, I want to emphasize my firm and considered opinion that the death penalty does not violate international law, nor does international law require abolition of the death penalty. . . .

Moreover, international law could not develop a prohibition against capital punishment applicable to the United States, as long as the United States continues to impose the death penalty and to object to development of such a norm.

Nonetheless, some concerns have been expressed that the United States should take no risks in this regard. To allay these concerns, the administration has decided to propose an additional understanding, addressed explicitly to the death penalty issue. Since the death penalty is clearly not a violation of international law, this in no way derogates from the Convention. . . .

The Convention deals primarily with "torture." In Article 16, however, the Parties also undertake to prohibit lesser forms of ill-treatment under the rubric of "cruel, inhuman or degrading treatment or punishment." The revised package retains a statement to the effect that the United States considers itself bound, under Article 16, to prevent "cruel, inhuman or degrading treatment or punishment" not amounting to torture only insofar as those words mean the cruel and unusual punishment prohibited by the Fifth, Eighth and/or Fourteenth Amendments to the Constitution. In fact, the revised package upgrades this point to a reservation from the status of an understanding.

The reason for this reservation is straightforward. The formulation used by Article 16 is ambiguous, particularly its reference to "degrading treatment." Of course, our own 8th Amendment to the Constitution protects against cruel and unusual punishment. Our courts have interpreted this prohibition to protect against a broad range of practices that involve the unnecessary and wanton infliction of pain. . . .

. . . [I]t is prudent that the U.S. specify that, because the Constitution of the United States directly addresses this area of the law, and because of the ambiguity of the phrase "degrading," we would limit our obligations under this Convention to the proscriptions already covered in our Constitution.

PREPARED STATEMENT OF MARK RICHARD,
DEPUTY ASSISTANT ATTORNEY GENERAL,
CRIMINAL DIVISION, DEPARTMENT OF JUSTICE

At the outset, I note with some pride that torture, as understood by most persons, committed by public officials does not often occur within this country and when, if it does, the Department of Justice is committed to seeing that appropriate prosecutions are instituted. . . .

Having said such, one might wonder why we found it necessary to propose a number of reservations, understandings, or declarations in regard to a well intended convention against torture. The basic problem with the Torture Convention—one which permeates all our concerns—is its imprecise definition of torture, especially as that term is applied to actions which result solely in mental anguish. This definitional vagueness makes it very doubtful that the United States can, consistent with Constitutional due process constraints, fulfill its obligation under the Convention to adequately engraft the definition of torture into the domestic criminal law of the United States. Further, unless this definitional problem is addressed, the Torture Convention we fear will have the effect of fostering unwarranted litigation in numerous areas of law enforcement.

The potentially adverse impact of the definitional imprecision of the term torture is compounded when considered in the context of the international jurisdiction created by the Convention. The Convention places U.S. law enforcement officials, when traveling overseas, at risk of arrest and prosecution in foreign jurisdictions, or even extradition to a third country, for purported violations committed within the United States. . . .

As applied to physical torture, there appears to be some degree of consensus that the concept involves conduct the mere mention of which sends chills down one's spine: the needle under the fingernail, the application of electrical shock to the genital area, the piercing of eyeballs, etc. Techniques which inflict such excruciating and agonizing physical pain are recognized as the essence of torture. Hence, the Convention chose the [word] "severe" to indicate the high level of the pain required to support a finding of torture. Moreover, to constitute torture the action must be done in a deliberate and calculated manner, or, to put it in customary United

States legal terminology, it must be done with specific intent to inflict such a high level of pain. Therefore, insofar as physical pain is concerned, the boundaries of torture as defined by the Convention appear to have satisfactory clarity.

It is, however, in regard to the area of mental pain that the definition poses the greatest problem. Mental pain is by its nature subjective. Action that causes one person severe mental suffering may seem inconsequential to another person. Moreover, mental suffering is often transitory, causing no lasting harm. . . .

In an effort to overcome [the] unacceptable element of vagueness in Article 1 of the Convention, we have proposed an understanding which defines severe mental pain constituting torture with sufficient specificity to protect innocent persons and meet Constitutional due process requirements. In formulating this understanding, we have drawn on international case law and treaties as well as on international law scholars. Our proposed understanding encompasses conduct calculated to generate severe and prolonged mental suffering of the type which can properly be viewed as rising to the level of torture. As such, it properly condemns as torture intentional acts such as those designed to damage and destroy the human personality. In contrast, it does not encompass the normal legal compulsions which are properly a part of the criminal justice system interrogation, incarceration, prosecution, compelled testimony against a friend, etc.—notwithstanding the fact that they may have the incidental effect of producing a mental strain.

COMMENTS OF THE SENATE COMMITTEE ON FOREIGN RELATIONS

S. Exec. Rep. No. 101–30, at 3–4 (1990).

The committee regards the Convention Against Torture as a major step forward in the international community's efforts to eliminate torture and other cruel, inhuman or degrading treatment or punishment. The Convention codifies international law as it has evolved, particularly in the 1970's, on the subject of torture and takes a comprehensive approach to the problem of combating torture. The strength of the Convention lies in the obligation of States Parties to make torture a crime and to prosecute or extradite alleged torturers found in their territory.

Ratification of the Convention Against Torture will demonstrate clearly and unequivocally U.S. opposition to torture and U.S. determination to take steps to eradicate it. Ratification is a natural follow-on to the active role that the United States played in the negotiating process for the Convention and is consistent with longstanding U.S. efforts to promote and protect basic human rights and fundamental freedoms throughout the world. As a party to the Convention, the United States will be in a stronger position to prosecute alleged torturers and to bring to task those countries in the international arena that continue to engage in this heinous and inhumane practice. . . .

SENATE FLOOR DEBATE ON CONVENTION AGAINST TORTURE

136 Cong. Rec. 36193–99 (1990).

Mr. PELL. Mr. President, this convention is the product of some 7 years of intense negotiation in which the United States played an active role. The convention was unanimously adopted by the U.N. General Assembly on December 10, 1984. . . . It has now been ratified by or acceded to by 51 States and signed by 21 others.

The Convention . . . represents a major step forward in the international community's campaign to combat torture because it makes torture a criminally punishable offense and obligates each State party to prosecute alleged torturers or extradite them for prosecution elsewhere. . . .

The Foreign Relations Committee held a hearing on the treaty on January 30 of this year. On July 19, the committee voted 10 to 0 to report favorably the convention with a resolution of ratification containing the reservations, understandings and declarations proposed by the Bush administration.

In categorizing the treaties pending before the Senate, the administration listed the Convention Against Torture as one for which there is an urgent need for Senate action. At the appropriate time, I will be offering four amendments en bloc on behalf of myself and Senator HELMS. The first three amendments would make changes in the language of the resolution of ratification dealing with the issue of Federal-State relations as it impacts on our obligations under the treaty and the lawful sanctions issue in article 1. These have been worked out with the administration and the administration supports their adoption. The fourth amendment would add a new proviso to the resolution of ratification regarding deposition of the instrument of ratification by the President. This proviso will not be included in the instrument. The administration accepts this amendment. The administration strongly supports ratification of the convention with its proposed conditions, as modified by the committee amendments. . . .

THE PRESIDING OFFICER. The question is on agreeing to the amendments, en bloc.

Those in favor of the amendments will rise and stand until counted. (After a pause.) Those opposed will rise and stand until counted.

The amendments . . . were agreed to. . . .

THE PRESIDING OFFICER. A division is requested. Senators in favor of the resolution of ratification will rise and stand until counted. (After a pause.) Those opposed will rise and stand until counted.

On a division, two-thirds of the Senators present and voting have voted in the affirmative, the resolution of ratification is agreed to.

The resolution of ratification, as agreed to, is as follows:

Resolved (two-thirds of the Senators present concurring therein), That the Senate advise and consent to the ratification of the Convention Against Torture . . . : *Provided,* That:

I. The Senate's advice and consent is subject to the following reservations:

(1) That the United States considers itself bound by the obligation under Article 16 to prevent "cruel, inhuman or degrading treatment or punishment," only insofar as the term "cruel, inhuman or degrading treatment or punishment" means the cruel, unusual and inhumane treatment or punishment prohibited by the Fifth, Eighth, and/or Fourteenth Amendments to the Constitution of the United States.

(2) That pursuant to Article 30(2) the United States declares that it does not consider itself bound by Article 30(1) [providing for the referral to the International Court of Justice of disputes between States Parties concerning interpretation or application of the Convention], but reserves the right specifically to agree to follow this or any other procedure for arbitration in a particular case.

II. The Senate's advice and consent is subject to the following understandings, which shall apply to the obligations of the United States under this Convention:

(1) (a) That with reference to Article 1, the United States understands that, in order to constitute torture, an act must be specifically intended to inflict severe physical or mental pain or suffering and that mental pain or suffering refers to prolonged mental harm caused by or resulting from: (1) the intentional infliction or threatened infliction of severe physical pain or suffering; (2) the administration or application, or threatened administration or application, of mind altering substances or other procedures calculated to disrupt profoundly the senses or the personality; (3) the threat of imminent death; or (4) the threat that another person will imminently be subjected to death, severe physical pain or suffering, or the administration or application of mind altering substances or other procedures calculated to disrupt profoundly the senses or personality.

(b) That the United States understands that the definition of torture in Article 1 is intended to apply only to acts directed against persons in the offender's custody or physical control. . . .

(2) That the United States understands the phrase, "where there are substantial grounds for believing that he would be in danger of being subjected to torture," as used in Article 3 of the Convention, to mean "if it is more likely than not that he would be tortured."

(3) That it is the understanding of the United States that Article 14 requires a State Party to provide a private right of action for damages only for acts of torture committed in territory under the jurisdiction of that State Party.

(4) That the United States understands that international law does not prohibit the death penalty, and does not consider this Convention to restrict or prohibit the United States from applying the death penalty consistent with the Fifth, Eighth and/or Fourteenth Amendments to the Constitution of the United States, including any constitutional period of confinement prior to the imposition of the death penalty.

(5) That the United States understands that this Convention shall be implemented by the United States Government to the extent that it exercises legislative and judicial jurisdiction over the matters covered by the Convention and otherwise by the state and local governments. Accordingly, in implementing Articles 10–14 and 16, the United States Government shall take measures appropriate to the Federal system to the end that the competent authorities of the constituent units of the United States of America may take appropriate measures for the fulfillment of the Convention.

III. The Senate's advice and consent is subject to the following declarations:

(1) That the United States declares that the provisions of Articles 1 through 16 of the Convention are not self-executing. . . .

IV. The Senate's advice and consent is subject to the following proviso, which shall not be included in the instrument of ratification to be deposited by the President:

> The President of the United States shall not deposit the instrument of ratification until such time as he has notified all present and prospective ratifying parties to this Convention that nothing in this Convention requires or authorizes legislation, or other action, by the United States of America prohibited by the Constitution of the United States as interpreted by the United States.

NOTES

1. *RUDs*. Why do you think the various U.S. conditions were classified as "reservations," "understandings," "declarations," or "provisos"? (You may wish to review the description of these categories.) What was the significance

of upgrading one of the conditions from "understanding" to "reservation"? Why include an understanding on a punishment (the death penalty) that the U.S. government regarded as outside the scope of the prohibitions in the Convention? Regarding the concerns by Deputy Assistant Attorney General Richard about the potential prosecution of U.S. officials abroad, is filing a U.S. reservation regarding the meaning of "torture" likely to have any impact?

The precise effect of RUDs upon U.S. domestic law has been disputed in bilateral contexts, where tacit acceptance by the other party (absent an agreed amendment) is required. Former executive branch officials John Bolton and John Yoo asserted that any reservations and understandings included in the Senate's resolution approving the New START treaty would not be legally binding, invoking a comment by Eugene Rostow (a former Undersecretary of State, speaking in relation to a strategic arms agreement with the Soviet Union) that "a reservation has the same legal effect as a letter from my mother." *See* John R. Bolton & John Yoo, *Why Rush to Cut Nukes?*, N.Y. TIMES, Nov. 9, 2010, at A35. Former legal counsel to the Senate Foreign Relations Committee Michael Glennon responded:

> When the Senate approves a treaty, it can condition its consent (by reservation, understanding or whatever—the label doesn't matter) either by requiring the president to get the other party to agree to a change in the treaty's text, or simply by including its condition in the resolution of ratification.
>
> After the Senate acts, the president decides whether to bring the treaty into force. If he wishes to do so, he is constitutionally required to respect the Senate's conditions, regardless of which method the Senate has used. Each is equally binding in international law as well as law of the land, and each has been used on numerous occasions for over 200 years without raising any legal concern.

Michael Glennon, *What the New Arms Treaty Would Do*, N.Y. TIMES, Nov. 16, 2010, at A32. Which view seems sounder, and why?

RUDs are much more common in multilateral treaties, and there (at least), it is accepted that if the president ratifies a treaty after obtaining the Senate's advice and consent, this accepts any (valid) conditions attached by the Senate. *See Restatement of the Law (Fourth), The Foreign Relations Law of the United States: Treaties* § 105 (Tentative Draft No. 2, 2017). United States courts have also given effect to such conditions, including in relation to the Torture Convention. *See, e.g.*, *Oxygene v. Lynch*, 831 F.3d 541, 546 (4th Cir. 2016) (understanding relating to specific intent); *Auguste v. Ridge*, 395 F.3d 123, 131, 149 (3d Cir. 2005) (understandings relating to specific intent and substantial grounds for believing risk of torture).

2. *RUDs by Other States*. Other countries have also filed RUDs to the Convention against Torture (for a complete listing, including reactions by other states, see https://treaties.un.org/pages/ViewDetails.aspx?src=TREATY&mtd

sg_no=IV-9&chapter=4&clang=_en). Do the following alter your view of U.S. RUDs?

- "The Government of the Republic of Botswana considers itself bound by Article 1 of the Convention to the extent that 'torture' means the torture and inhuman or degrading punishment or other treatment prohibited by Section 7 of the Constitution of the Republic of Botswana."
- "Ecuador declares that, in accordance with the provisions of article 42 of its Political Constitution, it will not permit extradition of its nationals."
- Germany: Article 3 "prohibits the transfer of a person directly to a State where this person is exposed to a concrete danger of being subjected to torture. In the opinion of the Federal Republic of Germany, article 3 as well as the other provisions of the Convention exclusively establish State obligations that are met by the Federal Republic of Germany in conformity with the provisions of its domestic law which is in accordance with the Convention."
- "The Government of New Zealand reserves the right to award compensation to torture victims referred to in article 14 of the Convention Against Torture only at the discretion of the Attorney-General of New Zealand."

3. *Reaction to U.S. RUDs.* Other countries are also entitled to object to the United States' RUDs and, if they do, to indicate whether (1) the treaty does not enter into force as between the two states; or (2) the treaty does enter into force, in which case the provision to which the reservation relates do not apply between the states to the extent of the reservation. Consider the following objections filed in response to U.S. RUDs:

> *Objection by Finland.* A reservation which consists of a general reference to national law without specifying its contents does not clearly define to the other Parties of the Convention the extent to which the reserving State commits itself to the Convention and therefore may cast doubts about the commitment of the reserving State to fulfil its obligations under the Convention. Such a reservation is also, in the view of the Government of Finland, subject to the general principle to treaty interpretation according to which a party may not invoke the provisions of its internal law as justification for failure to perform a treaty.
>
> The Government of Finland therefore objects to the reservation made by the United States to article 16 of the Convention. . . .
>
> *Objection by the Netherlands.* The Government of the Netherlands considers the reservation made by the United States of America regarding the article 16 of [the Convention] to be incompatible with the object and purpose of the Convention, to which

> the obligation laid down in article 16 is essential. . . . This objection shall not preclude the entry into force of the Convention between the Kingdom of the Netherlands and the United States of America.
>
> The Government of the Kingdom of the Netherlands considers the following understandings to have no impact on the obligations of the United States of America under the Convention:
>
> II.1 (a) This understanding appears to restrict the scope of the definition of torture under article 1 of the Convention. . . .
>
> The Government of the Kingdom of the Netherlands reserves its position with regard to the understandings II. 1b . . . and 2 as the contents thereof are insufficiently clear.

Sometimes states react to objections by withdrawing in whole or in part their RUDs—as Pakistan and Qatar did when states objected to reservations that (among other things) limited their Torture Convention obligations when incompatible with, respectively, Sharia laws or Islamic law. Under what circumstances should the executive branch do likewise? What roles should the president and the Senate play in reacting to other states' RUDs?

4. *Incorporation of Senate Conditions*. If a condition approved by the Senate seeks to modify the legal effect of a treaty, the president must (if electing to proceed with the treaty afterward) include that condition in the instrument of ratification or accession or otherwise manifest the condition to other states parties. *Restatement of the Law (Fourth), The Foreign Relations Law of the United States: Treaties* § 105 (Tentative Draft No. 2, 2017). On one occasion, because the State Department believed a Senate-adopted declaration—commenting on the state of democracy in Spain—might endanger Spanish ratification, it attached the declaration to the instrument of ratification solely by means of an annex (where it was ignored). *See* U.S. Department of State, *Digest of United States Practice in International Law 1976*, at 216 (E. McDowell ed., 1977). Two years later, when considering the Panama Canal Treaties, the Senate recalled the incident and required that its conditions be included within the instrument of ratification. *See* S. EXEC. REP. NO. 95–12, at 10–11 (1978). As you will have seen, the president and the Senate agreed regarding the presentation of Torture Convention RUDs.

5. *Invalidity of Senate Condition Under U.S. Law*. If the Senate imposes a reservation that is essentially unrelated to the bilateral concerns addressed by a treaty, does the reservation become "supreme law of the land," or is it invalid? If invalid, what is the effect on U.S. ratification?

The issue was most fully explored in relation to the Treaty on Uses of Waters of Niagara River, Can.-U.S., 1 U.S.T. 694. The Senate conditioned its consent on the right to provide by subsequent law for development of the U.S. share of the Niagara River waters. S. EXEC. REP. No. 81–11, at 7 (1950). When the New York Power Authority applied for a license to utilize the Niagara River waters, the Federal Power Commission rejected the application, stating that it had to give effect to the Senate's reservation, and that Congress had not adopted the described legislation. The New York Power Authority then sued, claiming that the reservation was invalid. A divided D.C. Circuit Court of Appeals agreed, finding that the reservation, to which the Canadian government had formally agreed, was a mere "expression of domestic policy." *Power Auth. v. Federal Power Comm'n*, 247 F.2d 538 (D.C. Cir. 1957).

> The purported reservation to the 1950 treaty makes no change in the relationship between the United States and Canada under the treaty and has nothing at all to do with the rights or obligations of either party. To the extent here relevant, the treaty was wholly executed on its effective date. Each party became entitled to divert its half of the agreed quantum of water. Neither party had any interest in how the share of the other would be exploited, nor any obligation to the other as to how it would exploit its own share.

Id. at 541–42. The Supreme Court, however, vacated the D.C. Circuit's decision as moot after Congress adopted legislation. Am. Public Power Ass'n v. Power Auth., 355 U.S. 64 (1957). Contemporaries disputed the D.C. Circuit's premises, see Louis Henkin, *The Treaty Makers and the Law Makers: The Niagara Reservation*, 56 COLUM. L. REV. 1151 (1956), and the distinction between domestic and non-domestic conditions has not been pursued—for example, in relation to declarations that provisions of a treaty are non-self-executing, and thus lack immediate effect as domestic law. *See Iguarta v. United States*, 626 F.3d 592, 624–28 (1st Cir. 2010) (Torruella, J., concurring in part and dissenting in part) (disagreeing with majority concerning the significance of such a declaration, and citing D.C. Circuit opinion in *Power Authority*). Instead, it has been suggested that Senate conditions must at least relate to the treaty in question and conform with the Constitution. *See Restatement of the Law (Fourth), The Foreign Relations Law of the United States: Treaties* § 105 (Tentative Draft No. 2, 2017). Do those limitations make sense, and seem administrable? How would they apply to the Torture Convention?

If a RUD is invalid, the question arises whether the treaty is still in force for the United States. In other words, is the reservation severable from the instrument of ratification even though the Senate's consent was predicated on the reservation? The dissenting judge in the *Power Authority* decision notes that "[i]f it is beyond the power of the Senate, then not just the reservation falls, but the entire treaty. How can it be otherwise when the Senate has made it abundantly clear that without the reservation it would not have consented to the treaty?" 247 F.2d at 546 (Bastian, J., dissenting). Is that persuasive?

6. *Treaty Prohibitions of Reservations*. In addition to the general prohibition on reservations that defeat a treaty's object and purpose, some treaties limit or prohibit reservations outright, such as the U.N. Convention on the Law of the Sea art. 309, Dec. 10, 1982, 1833 U.N.T.S. 3, and the Rome Statute for the International Criminal Court art. 120, July 17, 1998, 2187 U.N.T.S. 3. This presents the Senate with a "take it or leave it" situation: it can either consent to or reject the treaty, but it cannot seek to modify U.S.

obligations thereunder. Since this deprives the Senate of an important opportunity to participate in treaty-making, the Senate Foreign Relations Committee has periodically expressed its view that no-reservation clauses are inconsistent with the Senate's "constitutional prerogatives." *See, e.g.*, U.S. Department of State, 1 *Digest of United States Practice in International Law, 1991–1999*, at 732 (2005).

7. *Consequences of an Invalid Reservation Under International Law.* Suppose an international court or some other authoritative body determines that the United States, in ratifying a treaty, included a reservation that is invalid (because it was prohibited, or defeats the object and purpose of the treaty). Is the implication (or actual consequence) that the United States is not a party to the treaty—or that it is a party to the treaty, but without the benefit of the reservation? Does it matter whether the treaty is one with broader significance, such as protecting human rights? Does it matter whether the United States indicated expressly or implicitly, when joining the treaty, what consequences would flow from an invalid reservation?

In 1994, the U.N. Human Rights Committee issued Comment No. 24 which stated, among other things, that a reserving State would remain a party to the International Covenant on Civil and Political Rights without the benefit of its invalid reservation. *See* Human Rights Committee, General Comment No. 24, Issues Relating to Reservations Made Upon Ratification or Accession to the Covenant or the Optional Protocols Thereto, or in Relation to Declarations under Article 41 of the Covenant, 52d Sess., U.N. Doc. CCPR/C/21/Rev.1/Add.6 (Apr. 10, 1994), *reprinted in* 34 I.L.M. 839 (1994). The United States reacted by asserting that the Human Rights Committee was not empowered to speak authoritatively on this issue and that, in any event, was wrong as to the consequences of an invalid reservation. *See* Observations by the United States of America on General Comment No. 24, U.N. Doc. A/50/40, annex VI, at 131–59 (1995). (For other appraisals, see Ryan Goodman, *Human Rights Treaties, Invalid Reservations, and State Consent*, 96 AM. J. INT'L L. 531 (2002); Roberto Baratta, *Should Invalid Reservations to Human Rights Treaties Be Disregarded?,* 11 EUR. J. INT'L L. 413 (2000); Curtis A. Bradley & Jack L. Goldsmith, *Treaties, Human Rights, and Conditional Consent*, 149 U. PA. L. REV. 399 (2000); Catherine Redgwell, *Reservations to Treaties and Human Rights Committee General Comment No. 24*, 46 INT'L & COMP. L.Q. 390 (1997).) The International Law Commission's Guide to Practice has since advised that the effect of an impermissible reservation depends on whether the reserving State intends to be bound by the treaty without the benefit of the reservation or whether it considers that it is not bound by the treaty; it is presumed to be bound unless is expresses a contrary intent, but it may manifest that intent at any time. Report of the Int'l Law Comm'n to the General Assembly, § 4.5.3, U.N. GAOR Supp. No. 10, 63rd Sess., U.N. Doc. A/66/10/Add.1 (2011), *reprinted in* [2011] 2 Y.B. INT'L L. COMM'N 2.

3. NATIONAL IMPLEMENTATION OF TREATIES BY STATUTES/REGULATIONS

When a country ratifies or accedes to a treaty, it may find that the obligations undertaken require no further implementation under national law. Thus, a treaty obliging a country to make periodic reports to an international organization probably can be fulfilled by the country's government without any further enactment under national law.

Many treaties, however, require states parties to conform their national legal systems, such as when criminalizing or regulating the conduct of persons. When a treaty requires such measures, a country may determine that its existing national law is sufficient to ensure compliance, in which case no further steps are needed. If existing national law is insufficient, there are then two possibilities. First, the country might enact new laws or regulations that allow for compliance with the treaty. Second, the country might regard the new treaty itself as having the force of law within its national legal system (*i.e.*, regard the treaty as "self-executing").

This Section considers the first possibility, while Sec. 4 considers the second. The following materials illustrate how the United States implemented the Convention Against Torture through existing U.S. laws, new statutes and regulations, interpretations and reinterpretations of the executive branch, interpretations by U.S. courts, and, in one instance, a legislative fix to an executive branch interpretation. Materials dated after September 2001 should be considered in the context of the United States' detention and interrogation of suspected terrorists, and the tension between the requirements of the Convention and the desire for obtaining information on terrorist networks. As you review these materials, you may wish to revisit some of the materials excerpted in Sec. 2 relating to the Convention's ratification process.

U.S. DEPARTMENT OF STATE SUMMARY AND ANALYSIS OF THE CONVENTION AGAINST TORTURE (MAY 10, 1988)

S. Treaty Doc. No. 100–20, at 8–10 (1988).

Acts of torture committed in the United States, . . . as well as acts in the United States constituting an attempt or conspiracy to torture, would appear to violate criminal statutes under existing state or federal law. When such acts are subject to state jurisdiction, the offense would presumably be a common crime such as assault or murder. In particular cases, the nature of the activity or persons involved could give rise to a federal offense as well, such as interstate kidnapping or hostage-taking. *See, e.g.*, 18 U.S.C. § 112, § 114, § 115, § 878, § 1201 and § 1203.

Where the acts are subject to federal jurisdiction, similar common crimes are defined under federal criminal law, for example, assault, maiming, murder, manslaughter, attempt to commit murder or manslaughter, and rape. 18 U.S.C. § 113, § 114, § 1111, § 1112, § 1113, and § 2031. Conspiracy to commit the above crimes and being an accessory after the fact are also offenses. 18 U.S.C. § 3, § 371 and § 1117. Moreover, where acts are committed within the special maritime and territorial jurisdiction located within a state, federal law incorporates criminal offenses as defined by state law. 18 U.S.C. § 13. . . .

In general, protection against torture is afforded by the Eighth, Fifth and Fourteenth Amendments to the U.S. Constitution. The Eighth Amendment prohibition of cruel and unusual punishment is, of the three, the most limited in scope, as this amendment has consistently been interpreted as protecting only "those convicted of crimes." *Ingraham v. Wright*, 430 U.S. 651, 664 (1977). The Eighth Amendment does, however, afford protection against torture and ill-treatment of persons in prison and similar situations of criminal punishment.

In other situations, the Fifth and Fourteenth Amendments provide protection against torture. Such protection is afforded most generally by substantive due process protection of the right to personal security. . . . The prohibition against self-incrimination also provides more specific protection against torture being used to coerce a confession. . . .

. . . [E]xisting federal and state law appears sufficient to establish jurisdiction when the offense has allegedly been committed in any territory under U.S. jurisdiction or on board a ship or aircraft registered in the United States. *See* 18 U.S.C. § 7; 49 U.S.C. App. §§ 1301(38), 1472. Implementing legislation is therefore needed only to establish Article 5(1)(b) jurisdiction over offenses committed by U.S. nationals outside the United States, and to establish Article 5(2) jurisdiction over foreign offenders committing torture abroad who are later found in territory under U.S. jurisdiction. Recommended legislation will be transmitted to Congress by the Department of Justice. . . .

STATUTE CRIMINALIZING TORTURE OUTSIDE THE UNITED STATES

18 U.S.C. §§ 2340, 2340A, & 2340B (2012).

§ 2340. Definitions

As used in this chapter—

(1) "torture" means an act committed by a person acting under the color of law specifically intended to inflict severe physical or mental pain or suffering (other than pain or suffering incidental to lawful sanctions) upon another person within his custody or physical control;

(2) "severe mental pain or suffering" means the prolonged mental harm caused by or resulting from—

(A) the intentional infliction or threatened infliction of severe physical pain or suffering;

(B) the administration or application, or threatened administration or application, of mind-altering substances or other procedures calculated to disrupt profoundly the senses or the personality;

(C) the threat of imminent death; or

(D) the threat that another person will imminently be subjected to death, severe physical pain or suffering, or the administration or application of mind-altering substances or other procedures calculated to disrupt profoundly the senses or personality; and

(3) "United States" means the several States of the United States, the District of Columbia, and the commonwealths, territories, and possessions of the United States.[1]

§ 2340A. Torture

(a) OFFENSE.—Whoever outside the United States commits or attempts to commit torture shall be fined under this title or imprisoned not more than 20 years, or both, and if death results to any person from conduct prohibited by this subsection, shall be punished by death or imprisoned for any term of years or for life.

(b) JURISDICTION.—There is jurisdiction over the activity prohibited in subsection (a) if—

(1) the alleged offender is a national of the United States; or

(2) the alleged offender is present in the United States, irrespective of the nationality of the victim or alleged offender.

(c) CONSPIRACY.—A person who conspires to commit an offense under this section shall be subject to the same penalties (other than the penalty of death) as the penalties prescribed for the offense, the commission of which was the object of the conspiracy.[2]

§ 2340B. Exclusive remedies

Nothing in this chapter shall be construed as precluding the application of State or local laws on the same subject, nor shall anything in

---

[1] [Authors' Note: Originally, this definition embraced all areas within the U.S. "special maritime and territorial jurisdiction," which includes military bases and buildings abroad. As such, the original statute did not cover torture committed at those facilities since they were not "outside the United States." The definition was changed to the provision shown above by Pub. L. No. 108–375, § 1089, 118 Stat. 1811, 2067 (2004), such that those facilities are now covered by this statute.]

[2] [Authors' Note: Subsection (c) was added by the USA Patriot Act, Pub. L. No. 107–56, § 811(g) (2001).]

this chapter be construed as creating any substantive or procedural right enforceable by law by any party in any civil proceeding.

TORTURE VICTIM PROTECTION ACT

28 U.S.C. § 1350 note (2012).

[When ratifying the Convention Against Torture, the United States filed an understanding that Article 14 did not require the United States to create a private right of action in U.S. courts for torture occurring outside the United States. Nevertheless, in 1991, Congress enacted the Torture Victim Protection Act (TVPA), which provides for a right of action, with "torture" defined in a manner similar to that in Article 1 of the Convention.]

Section 1. Short Title

This Act may be cited as the "Torture Victim Protection Act of 1991".

Section 2. Establishment of Civil Action

(a) LIABILITY.—An individual who, under actual or apparent authority, or color of law, of any foreign nation—

(1) subjects an individual to torture shall, in a civil action, be liable for damages to that individual; or

(2) subjects an individual to extrajudicial killing shall, in a civil action, be liable for damages to the individual's legal representative, or to any person who may be a claimant in an action for wrongful death.

(b) EXHAUSTION OF REMEDIES.—A court shall decline to hear a claim under this section if the claimant has not exhausted adequate and available remedies in the place in which the conduct giving rise to the claim occurred.

(c) STATUTE OF LIMITATIONS.—No action shall be maintained under this section unless it is commenced within 10 years after the cause of action arose.

Section 3. Definitions

(a) EXTRAJUDICIAL KILLING.—For the purposes of this Act, the term "extrajudicial killing" means a deliberated killing not authorized by a previous judgment pronounced by a regularly constituted court affording all the judicial guarantees which are recognized as indispensable by civilized peoples. Such term, however, does not include any such killing that, under international law, is lawfully carried out under the authority of a foreign nation.

(b) TORTURE.—For the purposes of this Act—

(1) the term "torture" means any act, directed against an individual in the offender's custody or physical control, by which severe pain or suffering (other than pain or suffering arising only from or inherent in, or incidental to, lawful sanctions), whether physical or mental, is intentionally inflicted on that individual for such purposes as obtaining from that individual or a third person information or a confession, punishing that individual for an act that individual or a third person has committed or is suspected of having committed, intimidating or coercing that individual or a third person, or for any reason based on discrimination of any kind; and

(2) mental pain or suffering refers to prolonged mental harm caused by or resulting from—

(A) the intentional infliction or threatened infliction of severe physical pain or suffering;

(B) the administration or application, or threatened administration or application, of mind altering substances or other procedures calculated to disrupt profoundly the senses or the personality;

(C) the threat of imminent death; or

(D) the threat that another individual will imminently be subjected to death, severe physical pain or suffering, or the administration or application of mind altering substances or other procedures calculated to disrupt profoundly the senses or personality.

NOTE ON INTERROGATION OF GUANTÁNAMO DETAINEES

In late 2001 to 2002, hundreds of suspected Al Qaeda and Taliban operatives were captured by the United States in Afghanistan and elsewhere, and transported to the U.S. Naval Base at Guantánamo in Cuba. The Bush Administration engaged in "enhanced" interrogation techniques in an effort to uncover information about Al Qaeda and its plans for terrorist attacks. Military and intelligence interrogators wished to know what kinds of techniques, if any, were criminalized by the statute (then, 18 U.S.C. §§ 2340–2340A (2000)). Consequently, advice was sought from the Office of Legal Counsel (OLC) of the U.S. Department of Justice. An initial memorandum was issued by OLC in August 2002 advancing a permissive interpretation, which was then walked back in December 2004 and January 2009. Separately, questions were also raised as to whether such techniques ran afoul of the U.S. obligation under Article 16 of the Convention Against Torture to prevent "in any territory under its jurisdiction" conduct not constituting torture, but that is still cruel, inhuman or degrading treatment. If you had been asked to "draw the line" for a U.S. interrogator as to what acts were impermissible torture or inhuman treatment, and what acts were not, what advice would you have given?

DEPARTMENT OF JUSTICE, OFFICE OF LEGAL COUNSEL, MEMORANDUM FOR COUNSEL TO THE PRESIDENT

available at http://www.justice.gov/olc/docs/memo-gonzales-aug2002.pdf, [https://perma.cc/NJ4D-TB5D].

August 1, 2002

Memorandum for Alberto R. Gonzales
Counsel to the President

Re: Standards of Conduct for Interrogation Under 18 U.S.C. §§ 2340–2340A

You have asked for our Office's views regarding the standards of conduct under the Convention Against Torture . . . as implemented by Sections 2340–2340A of title 18 of the United States Code. As we understand it, this question has arisen in the context of the conduct of interrogations outside of the United States. . . .

Each component of the definition [of torture in Section 2340] emphasizes that torture is not the mere infliction of pain or suffering on another, but is instead a step well removed. The victim must experience intense pain or suffering of the kind that is equivalent to the pain that would be associated with serious physical injury so severe that death, organ failure, or permanent damage resulting in a loss of significant body function will likely result. If that pain or suffering is psychological, that suffering must result from one of the acts set forth in the statute. In addition, these acts must cause long-term mental harm. . . . In short, reading the definition of torture as a whole, it is plain that the term encompasses only extreme acts. . . .

Even if an interrogation method arguably were to violate Section 2340A, the statute would be unconstitutional if it impermissibly encroached on the President's constitutional power to conduct a military campaign. As Commander-in-Chief, the President has the constitutional authority to order interrogations of enemy combatants to gain intelligence information concerning the military plans of the enemy. The demands of the Commander-in-Chief power are especially pronounced in the middle of a war in which the nation has already suffered a direct attack. In such a case, the information gained from interrogations may prevent future attacks by foreign enemies. Any effort to apply Section 2340A in a manner that interferes with the President's direction of such core war matters as the detention and interrogation of enemy combatants thus would be unconstitutional. . . .

JAY S. BYBEE
Assistant Attorney General

DEPARTMENT OF JUSTICE, OFFICE OF LEGAL COUNSEL, MEMORANDUM OPINION FOR THE ATTORNEY GENERAL

Definition of Torture Under 18 U.S.C. §§ 2340–2340A, 2004 WL 3554701
available at https://www.justice.gov/file/18791/download,
[https://perma.cc/48QK-Z9BT].

December 30, 2004

Memorandum for James B. Comey
Deputy Attorney General

Re: Legal Standards Applicable Under 18 U.S.C. §§ 2340–2340A

Torture is abhorrent both to American law and values and to international norms. This universal repudiation of torture is reflected in our criminal law, for example, 18 U.S.C. §§ 2340–2340A; international agreements, exemplified by the United Nations Convention Against Torture (the "CAT"); customary international law; centuries of Anglo-American law; and the longstanding policy of the United States, repeatedly and recently reaffirmed by the President.

This Office interpreted the federal criminal prohibition against torture—codified at 18 U.S.C. §§ 2340–2340A—in *Standards of Conduct for Interrogation under 18 U.S.C. §§ 2340–2340A* (Aug. 1, 2002) ("August 2002 Memorandum"). The August 2002 Memorandum also addressed a number of issues beyond interpretation of those statutory provisions. . . .

Questions have since been raised, both by this Office and by others, about the appropriateness and relevance of the non-statutory discussion in the August 2002 Memorandum, and also about various aspects of the statutory analysis, in particular the statement that "severe" pain under the statute was limited to pain "equivalent in intensity to the pain accompanying serious physical injury, such as organ failure, impairment of bodily function, or even death." . . . We decided to withdraw the August 2002 Memorandum, a decision you announced in June 2004. . . .

This memorandum supersedes the August 2002 Memorandum in its entirety. . . .

Although Congress defined "torture" under sections 2340–2340A to require conduct specifically intended to cause "severe" pain or suffering, we do not believe Congress intended to reach only conduct involving "excruciating and agonizing" pain or suffering. Although there is some support for this formulation in the ratification history of the CAT, a proposed express understanding to that effect was "criticized for setting too high a threshold of pain," S. Exec. Rep. No. 101–30 at 9, and was not adopted. We are not aware of any evidence suggesting that the standard was raised in the statute and we do not believe that it was.

Drawing distinctions among gradations of pain (for example, severe, mild, moderate, substantial, extreme, intense, excruciating, or agonizing) is obviously not an easy task, especially given the lack of any precise, objective scientific criteria for measuring pain. We are, however, aided in this task by judicial interpretations of the Torture Victims Protection Act ("TVPA"), 28 U.S.C. § 1350 note (2000). The TVPA, also enacted to implement the CAT, provides a civil remedy to victims of torture. The TVPA defines "torture" to include:

> any act, directed against an individual in the offender's custody or physical control, by which *severe pain or suffering . . . whether physical or mental*, is intentionally inflicted. . . .

. . . The emphasized language is similar to section 2340's "severe physical or mental pain or suffering." As the Court of Appeals for the District of Columbia Circuit has explained:

> The severity requirement is crucial to ensuring that the conduct proscribed by the [CAT] and the TVPA is sufficiently extreme and outrageous to warrant the universal condemnation that the term "torture" both connotes and invokes. The drafters of the [CAT], as well as the Reagan Administration that signed it, the Bush Administration that submitted it to Congress, and the Senate that ultimately ratified it, therefore all sought to ensure that "only acts of a certain gravity shall be considered to constitute torture."
>
> The critical issue is the degree of pain and suffering that the alleged torturer intended to, and actually did, inflict upon the victim. The more intense, lasting, or heinous the agony, the more likely it is to be torture.

Price v. Socialist People's Libyan Arab Jamahiriya, 294 F.3d 82, 92–93 (D.C. Cir. 2002) (citations omitted). That court concluded that a complaint that alleged beatings at the hands of police but that did not provide details concerning "the severity of plaintiffs' alleged beatings, including their frequency, duration, the parts of the body at which they were aimed, and the weapons used to carry them out," did not suffice "to ensure that [it] satisf[ied] the TVPA's rigorous definition of torture." *Id.* at 93.

In *Simpson v. Socialist People's Libyan Arab Jamahiriya*, 326 F.3d 230 (D.C. Cir. 2003), the D.C. Circuit again considered the types of acts that constitute torture under the TVPA definition. The plaintiff alleged, among other things, that Libyan authorities had held her incommunicado and threatened to kill her if she tried to leave. *See id.* at 232, 234. The court acknowledged that "these alleged acts certainly reflect a bent toward cruelty on the part of their perpetrators," but, reversing the district court, went on to hold that "they are not in themselves so unusually cruel or sufficiently extreme and outrageous as to constitute torture within the meaning of the [TVPA]." *Id.* at 234. Cases in which courts have found torture suggest the nature of the extreme conduct that falls within the statutory definition. *See, e.g., Hilao v. Estate of Marcos*, 103 F.3d 789, 790–91, 795 (9th Cir. 1996) (concluding that a course of conduct that included, among other things, severe beatings of plaintiff, repeated threats of death and electric shock, sleep deprivation, extended shackling to a cot (at times with a towel over his nose and mouth and water poured down his nostrils), seven months of confinement in a "suffocatingly hot" and cramped cell, and eight years of solitary or near-solitary confinement, constituted torture); *Mehinovic v. Vuckovic*, 198 F.Supp.2d 1332–40, 1345–46 (N.D.Ga.2002) (concluding that a course of conduct that included, among other things, severe beatings to the genitals, head, and other parts of the body with metal pipes, brass knuckles, batons, a baseball bat, and various other items; removal of teeth with pliers; kicking in the face and ribs; breaking of bones and ribs and dislocation of fingers; cutting a figure into the victim's forehead; hanging the victim and beating him; extreme limitations of food and water; and subjection to games of "Russian roulette," constituted torture); *Daliberti v. Republic of Iraq*, 146 F. Supp. 2d 19, 22–23 (D.D.C. 2001) (entering default judgment against Iraq where plaintiffs alleged, among other things, threats of "physical torture, such as cutting off . . . fingers, pulling out . . . fingernails," and electric shocks to the testicles); *Cicippio v. Islamic Republic of Iran*, 18 F. Supp. 2d 62, 64–66 (D.D.C. 1998) (concluding that a course of conduct that included frequent beatings, pistol whipping, threats of imminent death, electric shocks, and attempts to force confessions by playing Russian roulette and pulling the trigger at each denial, constituted torture). . . .

DANIEL LEVIN
Acting Assistant Attorney General

DEPARTMENT OF JUSTICE, OFFICE OF LEGAL COUNSEL, INTERNAL MEMORANDUM

2009 WL 1267352, available at
https://www.justice.gov/sites/default/files/opa/legacy/2009/03/09/memostatusolcopinions01152009.pdf, [https://perma.cc/VS5U-8C5V].

January 15, 2009

Memorandum for the Files

Re: Status of Certain OLC Opinions Issued in the Aftermath of the Terrorist Attacks of September 11, 2001

It is well established that the President has broad authority as Commander in Chief to take military actions in defense of the country. . . .

At the same time, Article I, Section 8 of the Constitution also grants significant war powers to Congress. We recognize that a law that is constitutional in general may still raise serious constitutional issues if applied in particular circumstances to frustrate the President's ability to fulfill his essential responsibilities under Article II. Nevertheless, the sweeping assertions in the [August 1, 2002, as well as other] opinions . . . that the President's Commander in Chief authority categorically precludes Congress from enacting any legislation concerning the detention, interrogation, prosecution, and transfer of enemy combatants are not sustainable.

Congress's power to "define and punish . . . Offences against the Law of Nations," U.S. Const., art. I, § 8, cl. 10, provides a basis for Congress to establish the federal crime of torture, in accordance with U.S. treaty obligations under the Convention Against Torture, and the War Crimes Act offenses, in accordance, for example, with the "grave breach" provisions of the Geneva Conventions. This grant of authority also provides a basis for Congress to establish a statutory framework, such as that set forth in the Military Commissions Act of 2006 ("MCA"), for trying and punishing unlawful enemy combatants for violations of the law of war and other hostile acts in support of terrorism. . . .

We have advised the Attorney General, the Counsel to the President, the Legal Adviser to the National Security Council, the Principal Deputy General Counsel of the Department of Defense, and appropriate offices within the Department of Justice of these conclusions.

STEVEN G. BRADBURY
Principal Deputy Assistant Attorney General

RESPONSE OF ALBERTO R. GONZALES, U.S. ATTORNEY GENERAL-DESIGNATE, TO A WRITTEN QUESTION OF SENATOR RICHARD J. DURBIN ON THE GEOGRAPHICAL LIMITATION OF TORTURE CONVENTION ARTICLE 16

(January 2005).

[B]ecause of the Senate's reservation to Article 16 of the Convention Against Torture and the jurisdictional and other limitations of Article 16 and of the Fifth, Eighth and Fourteenth Amendments, which have been held not to apply to aliens overseas who are not being punished within the meaning of the Eighth Amendment, Article 16 has a limited reach. However, we also want to be in compliance with the relevant substantive constitutional standard incorporated into Article 16 by virtue of the Senate's reservation, even where it may not be legally required. I have been advised that approved interrogation techniques were analyzed under that standard and satisfied it.

LETTER FROM ABRAHAM D. SOFAER, FORMER STATE DEPARTMENT LEGAL ADVISER, TO SENATOR PATRICK J. LEAHY

(January 21, 2005).

Dear Senator Leahy:

. . . I do not hesitate to say that I disagree with the merits and wisdom of the conclusion reached by the Department of Justice and cited in the response of Judge Gonzales concerning the geographical reach of Article 16 of the Convention Against Torture. . . . Article 16 on its face limits the obligation of the United States to undertake to prevent cruel, inhuman, or degrading acts not amounting to torture to "territory under its jurisdiction." Within such territory, the US is obliged to undertake to prevent such "other" acts, even if they do not amount to torture.

. . . [T]he Senate agreed to ratify the Torture Convention at the urging of the Reagan and Bush Administrations, and one of its reservations was that in applying Article 16 the US government would not be obliged to undertake to enforce its provisions, anywhere, in a manner inconsistent with the US interpretation of its almost identically worded Eighth Amendment prohibiting cruel and unusual punishment. As I testified at the time, in writing and orally, the purpose of this reservation was to prevent any tribunal or state from claiming that the US would have to follow a different and broader meaning of the language of Article 16 than the meaning of those same words in the Eighth Amendment. The words of the reservation support this understanding, in that they relate to the meaning of the terms involved, not their geographic application. . . . The Department of Justice at the time characterized this reservation as "modest," and explained its purpose as being to use established meanings under the Eighth Amendment instead of the Treaty's vague terms that had not yet evolved under international law. No evidence of which I am aware indicates that the reservation was intended to enable the US to refuse to enforce Article 16 in any territory "under its jurisdiction."

. . . On the basis of my understanding of the purposes of the Convention, and of the purpose of the reservation related to Article 16 and the Eighth Amendment, I disagree with the Department's view and would urge the Attorney General Designate to accept a different view. . . .

Sincerely,

ABE SOFAER

DETAINEE TREATMENT ACT OF 2005

42 U.S.C. 2000dd note (2012).

PROHIBITION ON CRUEL, INHUMAN, OR DEGRADING TREATMENT OR PUNISHMENT OF PERSONS UNDER CUSTODY OR CONTROL OF THE UNITED STATES GOVERNMENT.

(a) IN GENERAL.—No individual in the custody or under the physical control of the United States Government, regardless of nationality or physical location, shall be subject to cruel, inhuman, or degrading treatment or punishment.

(b) CONSTRUCTION.—Nothing in this section shall be construed to impose any geographical limitation on the applicability of the prohibition against cruel, inhuman, or degrading treatment or punishment under this section.

(c) LIMITATION ON SUPERSEDURE.—The provisions of this section shall not be superseded, except by a provision of law enacted after December 30, 2005, which specifically repeals, modifies, or supersedes the provisions of this section.

(d) CRUEL, INHUMAN, OR DEGRADING TREATMENT OR PUNISHMENT DEFINED.—In this section, the term "cruel, inhuman, or degrading treatment or punishment" means the cruel, unusual, and inhumane treatment or punishment prohibited by the Fifth, Eighth, and Fourteenth Amendments to the Constitution of the United States, as defined in the United States Reservations, Declarations and Understandings to the United Nations Convention Against Torture. . . .

NOTE ON DEPORTATION OF ALIENS

Article 3 of the Convention Against Torture requires the United States not to "expel, return (*refouler*) or extradite a person to another State where there are substantial grounds for believing that he would be in danger of being subjected to torture." Recall that in the course of ratifying the Convention, the

United States issued an "understanding" regarding the meaning of the phrase "substantial grounds for believing." To implement its obligation, Congress adopted a statute, the Foreign Affairs Reform and Restructuring (FARR) Act, 8 U.S.C. § 1231 note (2012), which addressed both the issue of deportation of aliens and extradition of persons. With respect to deportation of aliens, the FARR Act required the executive branch to adopt implementing regulations, which appear below. In what way do the regulations incorporate the Convention into U.S. law? In what way do they alter the Convention obligation based on the RUDs asserted by the United States? In what way do they help clarify the obligation, providing more detailed guidance to executive and judicial branch officials?

U.S. IMMIGRATION AND NATURALIZATION SERVICE (INS) 1999 REGULATIONS IMPLEMENTING THE FARR ACT

8 C.F.R. §§ 208.16(c) & 208.18 (2016).

§ 208.16 Withholding of removal under section 241(b)(3)(B) of the Act and withholding of removal under the Convention Against Torture

(c) *Eligibility for withholding of removal under the Convention Against Torture.* (1) For purposes of regulations under Title II of the [Immigration and Naturalization] Act, "Convention Against Torture" shall refer to the United Nations Convention Against Torture . . . , subject to any reservations, understandings, declarations, and provisos contained in the United States Senate resolution of ratification of the Convention, as implemented by section 2242 of the Foreign Affairs Reform and Restructuring Act of 1998 (Pub. L. 105–277, 112 Stat. 2681, 2681–821). The definition of torture contained in § 208.18(a) of this part shall govern all decisions made under regulations under Title II of the Act about the applicability of Article 3 of the Convention Against Torture.

(2) The burden of proof is on the applicant for withholding of removal under this paragraph to establish that it is more likely than not that he or she would be tortured if removed to the proposed country of removal. The testimony of the applicant, if credible, may be sufficient to sustain the burden of proof without corroboration.

(3) In assessing whether it is more likely than not that an applicant would be tortured in the proposed country of removal, all evidence relevant to the possibility of future torture shall be considered, including, but not limited to:

(i) Evidence of past torture inflicted upon the applicant;

(ii) Evidence that the applicant could relocate to a part of the country of removal where he or she is not likely to be tortured;

(iii) Evidence of gross, flagrant or mass violations of human rights within the country of removal, where applicable; and

(iv) Other relevant information regarding conditions in the country of removal.

(4) In considering an application for withholding of removal under the Convention Against Torture, the immigration judge shall first determine whether the alien is more likely than not to be tortured in the country of removal. If the immigration judge determines that the alien is more likely than not to be tortured in the country of removal, the alien is entitled to protection under the Convention Against Torture. Protection under the Convention Against Torture will be granted either in the form of withholding of removal or in the form of deferral of removal. An alien entitled to such protection shall be granted withholding of removal unless the alien is subject to mandatory denial of withholding of removal. . . .[1]

§ 208.18 Implementation of the Convention Against Torture

(a) *Definitions*. The definitions in this subsection incorporate the definition of torture contained in Article 1 of the Convention Against Torture, subject to the reservations, understandings, declarations, and provisos contained in the United States Senate resolution of ratification of the Convention.

(1) Torture is defined as any act by which severe pain or suffering, whether physical or mental, is intentionally inflicted on a person for such purposes as obtaining from him or her or a third person information or a confession, punishing him or her for an act he or she or a third person has committed or is suspected of having committed, or intimidating or coercing him or her or a third person, or for any reason based on discrimination of any kind, when such pain or suffering is inflicted by or at the instigation of or with the consent or acquiescence of a public official or other person acting in an official capacity.

(2) Torture is an extreme form of cruel and inhuman treatment and does not include lesser forms of cruel, inhuman or degrading treatment or punishment that do not amount to torture.

(3) Torture does not include pain or suffering arising only from, inherent in or incidental to lawful sanctions. Lawful sanctions include judicially imposed sanctions and other enforcement actions authorized

---

[1] [Authors' Note: If the alien's removal is deferred, various outcomes are possible. The alien may remain in detention in the United States for periods prescribed by regulation (8 C.F.R. §§ 208.17(c), 241.13–14), or he may be removed to a different country where he will not be tortured (8 C.F.R. §§ 208.17(a), (b)(2)). In addition, the alien may request that the deferral be terminated, or an immigration judge may determine that the alien would no longer likely be tortured if removed, in which case the removal could go forward (8 C.F.R. § 208.17(d)–(e)).]

by law, including the death penalty, but do not include sanctions that defeat the object and purpose of the Convention Against Torture to prohibit torture.

(4) In order to constitute torture, mental pain or suffering must be prolonged mental harm caused by or resulting from:

(i) The intentional infliction or threatened infliction of severe physical pain or suffering;

(ii) The administration or application, or threatened administration or application, of mind altering substances or other procedures calculated to disrupt profoundly the senses or the personality;

(iii) The threat of imminent death; or

(iv) The threat that another person will imminently be subjected to death, severe physical pain or suffering, or the administration or application of mind altering substances or other procedures calculated to disrupt profoundly the sense or personality.

(5) In order to constitute torture, an act must be specifically intended to inflict severe physical or mental pain or suffering. An act that results in unanticipated or unintended severity of pain and suffering is not torture.

(6) In order to constitute torture an act must be directed against a person in the offender's custody or physical control.

(7) Acquiescence of a public official requires that the public official, prior to the activity constituting torture, have awareness of such activity and thereafter breach his or her legal responsibility to intervene to prevent such activity.

(8) Noncompliance with applicable legal procedural standards does not *per se* constitute torture. . . .

(c) *Diplomatic assurances against torture obtained by the Secretary of State.*

(1) The Secretary of State may forward to the Attorney General assurances that the Secretary has obtained from the government of a specific country that an alien would not be tortured there if the alien were removed to that country.

(2) If the Secretary of State forwards assurances described in paragraph (c)(1) of this section to the Attorney General for consideration by the Attorney General or her delegates under this paragraph, the Attorney General shall determine, in consultation with the Secretary of State, whether the assurances are sufficiently reliable

to allow the alien's removal to that country consistent with Article 3 of the Convention Against Torture. . . .

(3) Once assurances are provided under paragraph (c)(2) of this section, the alien's claim for protection under the Convention Against Torture shall not be considered further by an immigration judge, the Board of Immigration Appeals, or an asylum officer.

AL-SAHER V. INS

268 F.3d 1143, 1144–48 (9th Cir. 2001).

HUG, CIRCUIT JUDGE:

Mudher Jassim Mohamed Al-Saher, a native and citizen of Iraq, petitions for review of the Board of Immigration Appeals' ("BIA")[1] dismissal of his appeal from the Immigration Judge's ("IJ") denial of his application for asylum and withholding of removal and for protection under the Convention against Torture. . . .

Al-Saher arrived at Los Angeles International Airport seeking admission to the United States as a non-immigrant visitor. He presented no valid entry document and the INS issued a Notice to Appear (NTA) charging him with removability as an immigrant not in possession of a valid travel or entry document.

At his hearing he presented the following testimony. He was in the Iraqi military from 1984 until 1992 and thereafter until he left Iraq he was a civilian government worker assigned to work with the military. When he initially applied for military service in 1984 he claimed to be a Sunni Muslim from Baghdad even though he was a Shiite Muslim from Al-Bashra. He stated he misrepresented his religion and place of birth because there was discrimination against Shiite Muslims. In 1997, the truth was revealed when his father completed a census form stating that his family was Shiite.

Al-Saher was arrested in 1997 for misrepresenting his religion and place of birth. He was detained, interrogated and beaten for one month. He described the type of beatings he received stating that two people came in, blindfolded him, tied his hands behind his back, ["]and the only thing I felt was getting beaten up. They just kept beating me. . . . It kept on this way somewhere between 10 days to 2 weeks.["]

He explained that at that time his father was trying to get in contact with high authority so that he would not be beaten up. He stated that he stayed two weeks after the first period of beatings. During that time every three or four days an officer would come in at night and beat him up until

[1] [Authors' Note: The BIA, part of the U.S. Department of Justice, is the highest administrative body for interpreting and applying U.S. immigration law.]

his father paid a half million dinar to someone in the office of Saddam Hussein. As he left they told him that he was to tell no one about his experience, stating "if we ever heard anything that you have talked, you're going to come back and do the same thing again. Same room will be reserved for you." When asked at the hearing what he was being beaten with he stated it was with their hands and feet and a thick electrical cable.

He went back to work on his job and in December he was instructed to take a number of men to construct a fence that was to be built in a sensitive location, somewhere near the president. When he asked exactly where the fence was to be built, he was arrested. He stated that this time the beating was more severe and "had lots of monstrosities in it." He was again blindfolded with his hands tied behind him and beaten like before. This time they burned him with cigarettes. His parents got a hold of a friend who got him out after 8 to 10 days.

In April 1998 he was arrested again after he was heard talking with friends about how the elite Iraqi eat well while the poor go hungry. He and his friends were detained for 5 or 6 days until they escaped. He stated he found out it was not going to be the last time because anyone who has been accused and suspected twice that's going to be it for him—"it's impossible to let him go." . . .

The BIA addressed Al-Saher's torture claim and concluded that the arrests did not amount to torture as defined in the regulations. Accepting Al-Saher's testimony as true, we must disagree. Al-Saher testified that he was subjected to sustained beatings for a month on the first arrest. On the second arrest he suffered severe beatings and was burned with cigarettes over an 8 to 10 day period. These are not practices "inherent in or incidental to lawful sanction." These actions were specifically intended by officials to inflict severe physical pain on Al-Saher.

The Country Reports on Human Rights and Practices for 1997 for Iraq tell of the torture routinely administered to those detained or imprisoned. . .

The BIA must take this into consideration when assessing whether an applicant qualifies under the Convention. . . . Al-Saher was informed that if he told anyone about the beatings he would be arrested again and suffer the same consequences.

When officials detained Al-Saher for the third time based on an imputed political opinion, Al-Saher managed to escape from custody and avoid the possibility of further severe beatings and physical abuse. He then fled the country. If forced to return to Iraq, it is likely that Al-Saher would be tortured again. The Iraqi officials would correctly assume he has told of the beatings in making his claims in this proceeding. Based on these facts, we find that Al-Saher is entitled to withholding of removal under the

Convention Against Torture. We grant Al-Saher's petition for review and remand to the BIA for entry of an order granting withholding of removal.

Petition for review GRANTED and case REMANDED.

OPENING STATEMENT BY MARY E. MCLEOD, ACTING LEGAL ADVISER, U.S. DEPARTMENT OF STATE, BEFORE THE COMMITTEE AGAINST TORTURE

(November 12–13, 2014—Geneva)
available at https://geneva.usmission.gov/2014/11/12/acting-legal-adviser-mcleod-u-s-affirms-torture-is-prohibited-at-all-times-in-all-places/, [https://perma.cc/FY2B-4LGC].

Distinguished Chair, Members of the Committee, on behalf of the United States, it is my honor and privilege to address the Committee Against Torture and to present the Third Periodic Report of the United States . . .

. . . [I]n the wake of the 9/11 attacks, we regrettably did not always live up to our own values, including those reflected in the Convention. As President Obama has acknowledged, we crossed the line and we take responsibility for that.

The United States has taken important steps to ensure adherence to its legal obligations. We have engaged in ongoing efforts to determine why lapses occurred, and we have taken concrete measures to prevent them from happening again. . . . For example, immediately upon taking office in 2009, President Obama issued Executive Order 13491 on ensuring lawful interrogations. This Executive Order was clear: consistent with the Convention Against Torture and Common Article 3 of the 1949 Geneva Conventions, as well as U.S. law, any individual detained in armed conflict by the United States or within a facility owned, operated, or controlled by the United States, in all circumstances, must be treated humanely and must not be tortured or subjected to cruel, inhuman, or degrading treatment or punishment. The Executive Order directed all U.S. officials to rely only on the U.S. Army Field Manual in conducting interrogations in armed conflict. And it revoked all previous executive directives that were inconsistent with the Order including legal opinions regarding the definition of torture. Executive Order 13491 also created a Special Task Force on Interrogations and Transfer Policies Issues, which helped strengthen U.S. policies so that individuals transferred to other countries would not be subjected to torture.

. . . We have made public a number of investigations of the treatment of detainees in the post 9/11 time-period. We are expecting the public release of the Findings and Conclusions of a detailed congressional investigation into the former detention and interrogation program that was put in place in the immediate aftermath of 9/11. President Obama has made clear that this document should be released, with appropriate redactions to protect national security.

... [T]he United States has carefully reviewed the extent to which certain obligations under the Convention apply beyond the sovereign territory of the United States and is prepared to clarify its views on these issues for the Committee today.

In brief, we understand that where the text of the Convention provides that obligations apply to a State Party in "any territory under its jurisdiction," such obligations, including the obligations in Articles 2 and 16 to prevent torture and cruel, inhuman or degrading treatment or punishment, extend to certain areas beyond the sovereign territory of the State Party, and more specifically to "all places that the State Party controls as a governmental authority." We have determined that the United States currently exercises such control at the U.S. Naval Station at Guantanamo Bay, Cuba, and with respect to U.S. registered ships and aircraft. . . .

There should be no doubt, the United States affirms that torture and cruel, inhuman, and degrading treatment and punishment are prohibited at all times in all places, and we remain resolute in our adherence to these prohibitions. . . .

NOTES

1. *Fidelity of Implementing Statutes.* As indicated in the above materials, there already existed in the United States various constitutional and statutory provisions at the federal and state level allowing the United States to implement most of its obligations under the Convention Against Torture. The United States also adopted additional provisions to implement its obligations, including 18 U.S.C. § 2340A (2012), which allows prosecution of anyone involved in torture who is present in the United States, regardless of nationality or location of the crime. In its first prosecution under that provision, the United States alleged that the son of former Liberian president Charles Taylor used a hot iron, scalding water, and an electrical device to shock and burn one of his father's political opponents in Liberia; after his father's fall from power, the son had attempted to enter the United States using a false passport. Taylor was convicted and sentenced to 97 years in prison. On appeal, Taylor argued (among other things) that the statute was an invalid exercise of congressional power because the statute's definition of torture was broader than that of the Convention. The court of appeals, however, found that "slight variances between a treaty and its congressional implementing legislation do not make the enactment unconstitutional; identicality is not required." *United States v. Belfast*, 611 F.3d 783, 806 (11th Cir. 2010); *see* William J. Aceves, *United States v. George Tenet: A Federal Indictment for Torture*, 48 N.Y.U. J. INT'L L. & POL. 1, 34 (2015).

2. *Fidelity of Governmental Interpretation and Application.* The memoranda by the Justice Department's Office of Legal Counsel sought to determine the meaning of "severe pain or suffering, whether physical or mental," through an interpretation of the Convention's ratification history, U.S. implementing legislation, and case law. The 2002 Memorandum, issued shortly after the September 11, 2001, terrorist attacks, takes a very limited view as to what constitutes "torture," while the 2004 Memorandum takes a broader view. Is it predictable—or, rather, surprising—that this broader, more prohibitory view would be adopted following revelations of abuses by U.S. personnel?

A 2004 investigation by the U.S. Central Command into abuses at Abu Ghraib (the largest U.S. detention facility in Iraq) concluded, based in part on detailed witness statements and graphic photographs, that in late 2003 "numerous incidents of sadistic, blatant, and wanton criminal abuses were inflicted on several detainees. This systemic and illegal abuse of detainees was intentionally perpetrated by several members of the military police guard force." *Article 15–6 Investigation of the 800th Military Police Brigade* pt. 1 (*Findings and Recommendations*), ¶ 5, at 16; *see generally The Torture Papers: The Road to Abu Ghraib* (Karen J. Greenberg & Joshua T. Dratel eds., 2005). Thereafter, the U.S. Army charged multiple U.S. military personnel with the abuse of prisoners at Abu Ghraib; this eventually resulted in some being subject to courts-martial, sentenced to military prison, and dishonorably discharged from service.

Reports also emerged regarding harsh treatment of persons detained by the U.S. government at Guantánamo Bay Naval Base in Cuba. For example, a Saudi national, Mohammed al-Qahtani, was reportedly treated by U.S. interrogators in late 2001/early 2002 as follows:

> Qahtani had been subjected to a hundred and sixty days of isolation in a pen perpetually flooded with artificial light. He was interrogated on forty-eight of fifty-four days for eighteen to twenty hours at a stretch. He had been stripped naked; straddled by taunting female guards, in an exercise called "invasion of space by a female"; forced to wear women's underwear on his head, and to put on a bra; threatened by dogs; placed on a leash; and told that his mother was a whore. By December, Qahtani had been subjected to a phony kidnapping, deprived of heat, given large quantities of intravenous liquids without access to a toilet, and deprived of sleep for three days. . . . Qahtani's heart rate had dropped so precipitately, to thirty-five beats a minute, that he required cardiac monitoring. . . .
>
> [By January 2002], Qahtani had been stripped and shaved and told to bark like a dog. He'd been forced to listen to pop music at ear-splitting volume, deprived of sleep, and kept in a painfully cold room. Between confessing to and then recanting various terrorist plots, he had begged to be allowed to commit suicide.

Jane Mayer, *The Memo*, THE NEW YORKER, Feb. 27, 2006, at 32, 34, 37; *see also* Jane Mayer, *The Black Sites*, THE NEW YORKER, Aug. 8, 2007, at 46 (recounting tactics used on Khalid Sheik Mohammad, the alleged mastermind of the September 11 terrorist attacks).

Were such interrogation tactics "torture" within the meaning of the Convention Against Torture and its U.S. implementation? Within the meaning of one or both Justice Department memoranda? The subject continued to be evaluated by the U.S. government. In 2012, the bipartisan United States Senate Select Committee on Intelligence (SSCI) approved a report on the Central Intelligence Agency (CIA)'s Detention and Interrogation Program in its relation to detainees between 2001 and 2006. The executive summary and key findings have been released, along with associated materials (available at https://www.intelligence.senate.gov/press/committee-releases-study-cias-detention-and-interrogation-program, [https://perma.cc/JV3Y-T33H]), but the vast majority of the report remains classified as of this writing. Among the key findings were that the CIA's enhanced interrogation techniques were ineffective and resulted in "brutal" interrogations and harsh conditions of confinement, and that the CIA had misled others within the government and impeded oversight. Individual members of the Select Committee provided supportive and minority views.

Abu Ghraib and Guantánamo allegations were acknowledged in the next periodic report of the United States to the Committee Against Torture, a group of experts established under Article 17 of the Convention; the United States also reported the change in OLC views and reaffirmed the U.S. prohibition and the president's commitment to investigating allegations and prosecuting violations. Second Periodic Report of the United States of America to the Committee Against Torture (May 6, 2005), available at https://www.state.gov/documents/organization/62175.pdf, [https://perma.cc/W5PP-6F9D]. Later developments were noted in 2014 in the opening remarks by Acting Legal Adviser Mary E. McLeod before the Committee, excerpted above, and the other proceedings associated with the United States' submission of its (combined) third through fifth periodic reports. What role do you think these reports and proceedings play in articulating and refining U.S. positions concerning its Convention obligations?

3. *Implementation by Other States*. The 2004 Memorandum drew upon the standards used by U.S. courts to address torture claims arising from the conduct of foreign governments toward U.S. nationals. More generally, should the United States approach be shaped by how other States parties implement the Convention, or how the United States would like them to implement it, including (but not solely) when the well-being of U.S. nationals is at stake? One source of information on other States' efforts are their periodic reports to the Committee Against Torture; these reports typically describe their relevant legislation and case law. Implementation by other States may also be evaluated via Article 22 of the Convention, according to which some States (but not the United States) have permitted the Committee to hear complaints brought against them by individuals. Examining foreign laws would reveal, for

example, that to implement the Convention, the United Kingdom adopted the Criminal Justice Act, 1988, c. 33, §§ 134–38 (Eng.); among other things (and as relevant to the following note), the statute criminalizes torture wherever in the world it may be committed.

4. *Extraterritorial Application of the Convention*. As with some other human rights treaties, the United States has raised questions whether the Convention imposes obligations upon the U.S. government with respect to actions taken outside U.S. territory. Article 2 imposes on a State party the obligation to prevent torture "in any territory under its jurisdiction." Does this mean that U.S. authorities are not restricted by the CAT when engaging in interrogations abroad? Article 3 imposes the obligation not to "expel, return or extradite" a person to another State where he might be tortured, but does not expressly state whether this only covers expulsion, return, or extradition from U.S. territory. In *Sale v. Haitian Centers Council, Inc.*, 509 U.S. 155, 187–88 (1993), the Supreme Court held that a comparable *non-refoulement* requirement in Article 33 of the Refugee Convention, July 28, 1951, 189 U.N.T.S. 150, did not apply to the interdiction and return of Haitians apprehended on the high seas prior to their arrival in the United States. Does *Sale* suggest that CAT Article 3 does not apply to actions taken outside U.S. territory?

The materials excerpted above considered the similar question whether, in accepting Article 16 of the Convention Against Torture, the United States undertook a legal obligation to refrain from cruel and inhuman treatment outside U.S. territory. According to then Attorney General-Designate Alberto Gonzales, the U.S. understanding filed with respect to that Article limited its scope to conduct within the United States. Former U.S. State Department Legal Adviser Abraham Sofaer, who had testified during the advice-and-consent process, disagreed with that interpretation. To resolve the matter, Senator John McCain, a Vietnam veteran who was tortured as a prisoner of war, spearheaded the adoption of a statutory amendment. Later still, Acting Legal Adviser Mary E. McLeod explained the revised U.S. position to the Committee Against Torture. Reviewing these materials, which strikes you as having a better legal foundation? Which is the most authoritative?

Adoption of the Detainee Treatment Act (sometimes referred to as the McCain Amendment) also provoked a broader interpretive question. President George W. Bush, who had resisted passage of the amendment but faced a veto-proof majority in both Houses of Congress, issued the following statement while signing it into law:

> The executive branch shall construe Title X in Division A of the Act, relating to detainees, in a manner consistent with the constitutional authority of the President to supervise the unitary executive branch and as Commander in Chief and consistent with the constitutional limitations on the judicial power, which will assist in achieving the shared objective of the Congress and the President, evidenced in Title X, of protecting the American people from further terrorist attacks.

Statement on Signing the Department of Defense, Emergency Supplemental Appropriations to Address Hurricanes in the Gulf of Mexico, and Pandemic Influenza Act, 2006, 41 WEEKLY COMP. PRES. DOC. 1918–19 (Dec. 30, 2005). What do you think this statement means? Does it have any legal significance?

5. *Deportation of Aliens.* The materials above, including *Al-Saher v. INS*, provide a sense of how the Convention Against Torture has been implemented with respect to the deportation (or "removal") of aliens. Article 3 of the Convention has had the most significant day-to-day impact upon U.S. law enforcement activity, though most claims seeking withholding or deferral of an alien's removal based on a risk of torture are unsuccessful. Congressional Research Service, The U.N. Convention Against Torture: Overview of U.S. Implementation Policy Concerning the Removal of Aliens, CRS Doc. RL32276, at 7 (Jan. 21, 2009). According to the most recent report, immigration courts adjudicated 37,060 torture-related applications during Fiscal Year (FY) 2016, and of those, immigration judges granted 621, the majority of which were withholdings. U.S. Department of Justice, Executive Office of Immigration Review, FY 2016 Statistics Yearbook, at M1 (March 2017), available at https://www.justice.gov/eoir/page/file/fysb16/download, [https://perma.cc/S8DW-UUWG].

Note that if the Secretary of State obtains diplomatic assurances that an alien will not be tortured and forwards the assurances to the Attorney General, then the alien may be removed without further administrative or judicial review. The Committee Against Torture has voiced its concern about the reliability and transparency of such assurances, see U.N. Comm. Against Torture, 36th Sess., Conclusions and Recommendations of the Committee Against Torture, May 1–19, 2006, ¶ 21, U.N. Doc. CAT/C/USA/CO/2 (May 18, 2006), and the jurisprudence of some other States Parties and that of the European Court of Human Rights permits judicial review of such assurances for violation of human rights obligations. *See, e.g., Othman (Abu Qatada) v. United Kingdom*, 2012-I Eur. Ct. H.R. 159 (holding that, under the particular circumstances, formal assurances by Jordan to the United Kingdom were sufficient to provide adequate protection against torture, despite past practices, but that deportation was nonetheless unlawful because of the risk that evidence obtained by torture might be used).

6. *Extradition of Persons.* Article 3 of the Convention Against Torture also imposes an obligation not to extradite persons to a country where they may be tortured. Here, too, the basic U.S. extradition statute, 18 U.S.C. §§ 3184–86 (2012) has been augmented with regulations implementing the Convention's obligation. *See* 22 C.F.R. §§ 95.2–.4 (2016). However, the "rule of non-inquiry" in extradition law—by which U.S. courts refrain from examining the penal systems of the foreign country and instead defer to the Secretary of State's determination of whether the extradited person will likely be mistreated by the foreign country—typically bars review. *But see Trinidad y Garcia v. Thomas*, 683 F.3d 952, 956–57 (9th Cir. 2012) (per curiam) (requiring that Secretary of State provide formal declaration demonstrating necessary findings concerning non-likelihood of torture, while noting that deference to

any such declaration was required). *Cf. Munaf v. Geren*, 553 U.S. 674, 702–03 (2008) (holding that in *habeas* proceedings not presenting FARR Act claims, the decision to surrender a detainee held by U.S. forces in Iraq to the Government of Iraq for criminal prosecution, including determination by the Secretary of State that the detainee was not likely to be tortured, should not be second-guessed by the judiciary).

7. *Extraordinary Rendition*. One U.S. response to the September 2001 terrorist attacks has been the practice of "extraordinary rendition," whereby persons suspected of having information about terrorist activities are handed over by the United States to foreign governments for interrogation. Such practices may implicate the Convention Against Torture. For example, in January 2004, a Canadian national, Maher Arar, sued various U.S. government officials, alleging that they had detained him in 2002 while he was transiting through JFK Airport in New York for a flight to Canada. The defendants then allegedly sent Arar to Syria for interrogation, because he was suspected of being involved with terrorists; there, the Syrian government subjected him to physical and mental torture, causing him to confess to acts (such as training with terrorists) that he did not do, which information was then provided to U.S. authorities. According to Arar, since Syria could not genuinely link him to terrorist activity, he was eventually allowed to return to Canada. Thereafter, Arar filed a *Bivens* action against U.S. government officials, claiming both a violation of the TVPA and a denial of his constitutional right to substantive due process under the Fifth Amendment of the Constitution. Though it noted the confirmation of Arar's factual assertions by a commission established by the Canadian government, as well as that government's apology (and millions of dollars in compensation) for having provided exaggerated and false information to the United States identifying Arar as a terrorist, the Second Circuit affirmed the dismissal of Arar's complaint, stating that if a civil remedy in damages is to be created for extraordinary rendition, it must be expressly done by Congress. *See Arar v. Ashcroft*, 585 F.3d 559 (2d Cir. 2009).

4. NATIONAL IMPLEMENTATION BY SELF-EXECUTION

FOSTER & ELAM V. NEILSON

27 U.S. (2 Pet.) 253, 299–317 (1829).

MR. CHIEF JUSTICE MARSHALL delivered the opinion of the Court.

This suit was brought by the plaintiffs in error in the court of the United States, for the eastern district of Louisiana, to recover a tract of land lying in that district, about thirty miles east of the Mississippi, and in the possession of the defendant. The plaintiffs claimed under a grant for 40,000 arpents[1] of land, made by the Spanish governor, on the 2d of

[1] [Authors' Note: An arpent is a pre-metric French unit, about 0.85 English acres.]

January 1804, to Jayme Joydra, and ratified by the king of Spain on the 29th of May 1804. The petition and order of survey are dated in September 1803, and the return of the survey itself was made on the 27th of October in the same year. The defendant excepted to the petition of the plaintiffs, alleging that it does not show a title on which they can recover; that the territory, within which the land claimed is situated, had been ceded, before the grant, to France, and by France to the United States; and that the grant is void, being made by persons who had no authority to make it. The court sustained the exception, and dismissed the petition. The cause is brought before this Court by a writ of error.

The case presents this very intricate, and at one time very interesting question: To whom did the country between the Iberville and the Perdido rightfully belong, when the title now asserted by the plaintiffs was acquired?

[The Court accepted the argument of the United States "that by the Treaty of St Ildefonso, made on the 1st of October in the year 1800, Spain ceded the disputed territory as part of Louisiana to France; and that France, by the treaty of Paris, signed on the 30th of April 1803, and ratified on the 21st of October in the same year, ceded it to the United States."].

If the rights of the parties are in any degree changed, that change must be produced by the subsequent arrangements made between the two governments.

A "treaty of amity, settlement, and limits, between the United States of America and the king of Spain," was signed at Washington on the 22d day of February 1819. By the 2d article, "his catholic majesty cedes to the United States in full property and sovereignty, all the territories which belong to him, situated to the eastward of the Mississippi, known by the name of East and West Florida."

The 8th article stipulates, that "all the grants of land made before the 24th of January 1818 by his catholic majesty, or by his lawful authorities, in the said territories ceded by his majesty to the United States, shall be ratified and confirmed to the persons in possession of the lands, to the same extent that the same grants would be valid if the territories had remained under the dominion of his catholic majesty." . . . .

[W]e think the sound construction of the eighth article will not enable this Court to apply its provisions to the present case. The words of the article are, that "all the grants of land made before the 24th of January 1818, by his catholic majesty, & c. shall be ratified and confirmed to the persons in possession of the lands, to the same extent that the same grants would be valid if the territories had remained under the dominion of his catholic majesty." Do these words act directly on the grants, so as to give validity to those not otherwise valid; or do they pledge the faith of the United States to pass acts which shall ratify and confirm them?

A treaty is in its nature a contract between two nations, not a legislative act. It does not generally effect, of itself, the object to be accomplished, especially so far as its operation is infra-territorial; but is carried into execution by the sovereign power of the respective parties to the instrument.

In the United States a different principle is established. Our constitution declares a treaty to be the law of the land. It is, consequently, to be regarded in courts of justice as equivalent to an act of the legislature, whenever it operates of itself without the aid of any legislative provision. But when the terms of the stipulation import a contract, when either of the parties engages to perform a particular act, the treaty addresses itself to the political, not the judicial department; and the legislature must execute the contract before it can become a rule for the Court.

The article under consideration does not declare that all the grants made by his catholic majesty before the 24th of January 1818, shall be valid to the same extent as if the ceded territories had remained under his dominion. It does not say that those grants are hereby confirmed. Had such been its language, it would have acted directly on the subject, and would have repealed those acts of congress which were repugnant to it; but its language is that those grants shall be ratified and confirmed to the persons in possession, & c. By whom shall they be ratified and confirmed? This seems to be the language of contract; and if it is, the ratification and confirmation which are promised must be the act of the legislature. Until such act shall be passed, the Court is not at liberty to disregard the existing laws on the subject. Congress appears to have understood this article as it is understood by the Court. Boards of commissioners have been appointed for East and West Florida, to receive claims for lands; and on their reports titles to lands not exceeding _______ acres have been confirmed, and to a very large amount. . . .

The act of 1804, erecting Louisiana into two territories, . . . annuls all grants for lands in the ceded territories, the title whereof was at the date of the treaty of St Ildefonso in the crown of Spain. The grant in controversy is not brought within any of the exceptions from the enacting clause.

The legislature has passed many subsequent acts previous to the treaty of 1819, the object of which was to adjust the titles to lands in the country acquired by the treaty of 1803.

They cautiously confirm to residents all incomplete titles to lands, for which a warrant or order of survey had been obtained previous to the 1st of October 1800. . . .

Congress has reserved to itself the supervision of the titles reported by its commissioners, and has confirmed those which the commissioners have approved, but has passed no law, withdrawing grants generally for lands west of the Perdido from the operation of the . . . act of 1804. . . .

We are of opinion then, that the court committed no error in dismissing the petition of the plaintiff, and that the judgment ought to be affirmed with costs.

HEAD MONEY CASES (EDYE & ANOTHER V. ROBERTSON)

112 U.S. 580, 586–99 (1884).

MR. JUSTICE MILLER delivered the opinion of the court. . . .

The suit is brought to recover from Robertson the sum of money received by him, as collector of the port of New York, from plaintiffs, on account of their landing in that port passengers from foreign ports, not citizens of the United States, at the rate of fifty cents for each of such passengers, under the act of Congress of August 3, 1882, entitled "An Act to regulate immigration." . . .

An[ ] objection to the validity of this act of Congress, is that it violates provisions contained in numerous treaties of our government with friendly nations. And several of the articles of these treaties are annexed to the careful brief of counsel. We are not satisfied that this act of Congress violates any of these treaties, on any just construction of them. Though laws similar to this have long been enforced by the State of New York in the great metropolis of foreign trade, where four-fifths of these passengers have been landed, no complaint has been made by any foreign nation to ours, of the violation of treaty obligations by the enforcement of those laws. . . .

A treaty is primarily a compact between independent nations. It depends for the enforcement of its provisions on the interest and the honor of the governments which are parties to it. If these fail, its infraction becomes the subject of international negotiations and reclamations, so far as the injured party chooses to seek redress which may in the end, be enforced by actual war. It is obvious that with all this the judicial courts have nothing to do and can give no redress. But a treaty may also contain provisions which confer certain rights upon the citizens or subjects of one of the nations residing in the territorial limits of the other, which partake of the nature of municipal law, and which are capable of enforcement as between private parties in the courts of the country. An illustration of this character is found in treaties, which regulate the mutual rights of citizens and subjects of the contracting nations in regard to rights of property by descent or inheritance, when the individuals concerned are aliens. The Constitution of the United States places such provisions as these in the same category as other laws of Congress by its declaration that "this Constitution and the laws made in pursuance thereof, and all treaties made or which shall be made under authority of the United States, shall be the supreme law of the land." A treaty, then, is a law of the land as an act of Congress is, whenever its provisions prescribe a rule by which the rights of the private citizen or subject may be determined. And when such rights are of a nature to be enforced in a court of justice, that court resorts to the treaty for a rule of decision for the case before it as it would to a statute.

[The Court proceeded to determine that the provisions of the treaty had been superseded by a later-in-time statute. (*See infra,* this Chapter, Sec. 6)].

ASAKURA V. CITY OF SEATTLE

265 U.S. 332, 339–44 (1924).

MR. JUSTICE BUTLER delivered the opinion of the Court.

Plaintiff in error is a subject of the Emperor of Japan, and, since 1904, has resided in Seattle, Washington. Since July, 1915, he has been engaged in business there as a pawnbroker. The city passed an ordinance, which took effect July 2, 1921, regulating the business of pawnbroker and repealing former ordinances on the same subject. It makes it unlawful for any person to engage in the business unless he shall have a license, and the ordinance provides "that no such license shall be granted unless the applicant be a citizen of the United States." Violations of the ordinance are punishable by fine or imprisonment or both. Plaintiff in error . . . attacked the ordinance on the ground that it violates the treaty between the United States and the Empire of Japan, proclaimed April 5, 1911, 37 Stat. 1504; violates the constitution of the State of Washington, and also the due process and equal protection clauses of the Fourteenth Amendment of the Constitution of the United States. . . . On appeal, the Supreme Court of the State held the ordinance valid and reversed the decree. . . .

Does the ordinance violate the treaty? Plaintiff in error invokes and relies upon the following provisions: "The citizens or subjects of each of the High Contracting Parties shall have liberty to enter, travel and reside in the territories of the other to carry on trade, wholesale and retail, to own or lease and occupy houses, manufactories, warehouses and shops, to employ agents of their choice, to lease land for residential and commercial purposes, and generally to do anything incident to or necessary for trade upon the same terms as native citizens or subjects, submitting themselves to the laws and regulations there established. . . . The citizens or subjects of each . . . shall receive, in the territories of the other, the most constant protection and security for their persons and property. . . ."

A treaty made under the authority of the United States "shall be the supreme law of the land; and the judges in every State shall be bound thereby, any thing in the Constitution or laws of any State to the contrary notwithstanding." Constitution, Art. VI, § 2.

The treaty-making power of the United States is not limited by any express provision of the Constitution, and, though it does not extend "so far as to authorize what the Constitution forbids," it does extend to all proper subjects of negotiation between our government and other nations. *De Geofroy v. Riggs*, 133 U.S. 258, 266, 267; *In re Ross*, 140 U.S. 453, 463; *Missouri v. Holland*, 252 U.S. 416. The treaty was made to strengthen friendly relations between the two nations. As to the things covered by it, the provision quoted establishes the rule of equality between Japanese subjects while in this country and native citizens. Treaties for the protection of citizens of one country residing in the territory of another are numerous, and make for good understanding between nations. The treaty is binding within the State of Washington. *Baldwin v. Franks*, 120 U.S. 678, 682–683. The rule of equality established by it cannot be rendered nugatory in any part of the United States by municipal ordinances or state laws. It stands on the same footing of supremacy as do the provisions of the Constitution and laws of the United States. It operates of itself without the aid of any legislation, state or national; and it will be applied and given authoritative effect by the courts. . . .

The purpose of the ordinance complained of is to regulate, not to prohibit, the business of pawnbroker. But it makes it impossible for aliens to carry on the business. It need not be considered whether the State, if it sees fit, may forbid and destroy the business generally. Such a law would apply equally to aliens and citizens, and no question of conflict with the treaty would arise. The grievance here alleged is that plaintiff in error, in violation of the treaty, is denied equal opportunity. . . .

Decree reversed.

MEDELLÍN V. TEXAS

552 U.S. 491 (2008).

CHIEF JUSTICE ROBERTS delivered the opinion of the Court.

The International Court of Justice (ICJ), located in the Hague, is a tribunal established pursuant to the United Nations Charter to adjudicate disputes between member states. In the *Case Concerning Avena and Other Mexican Nationals* (Mex. v. U.S.), 2004 I.C.J. 12 (Judgment of Mar. 31) (*Avena*), that tribunal considered a claim brought by Mexico against the United States. The ICJ held that, based on violations of the Vienna Convention [on Consular Relations], 51 named Mexican nationals were entitled to review and reconsideration of their state-court convictions and sentences in the United States. This was so regardless of any forfeiture of the right to raise Vienna Convention claims because of a failure to comply with generally applicable state rules governing challenges to criminal convictions.

In *Sanchez-Llamas v. Oregon*, 548 U.S. 331 (2006)—issued after *Avena* but involving individuals who were not named in the *Avena* judgment—we held that, contrary to the ICJ's determination, the Vienna Convention did not preclude the application of state default rules. . . .

Petitioner José Ernesto Medellín, who had been convicted and sentenced in Texas state court for murder, is one of the 51 Mexican nationals named in the *Avena* decision. Relying on the ICJ's decision . . . , Medellín filed an application for a writ of *habeas corpus* in state court. The Texas Court of Criminal Appeals dismissed Medellín's application as an abuse of the writ under state law, given Medellín's failure to raise his Vienna Convention claim in a timely manner under state law. We granted certiorari to decide[:] . . . is the ICJ's judgment in *Avena* directly enforceable as domestic law in a state court in the United States? . . .

I

A

In 1969, the United States, upon the advice and consent of the Senate, ratified the Vienna Convention on Consular Relations (Vienna Convention or Convention), Apr. 24, 1963, and the Optional Protocol Concerning the Compulsory Settlement of Disputes to the Vienna Convention (Optional Protocol or Protocol), Apr. 24, 1963. . . . Article 36 of the Convention . . . provides that if a person detained by a foreign country "so requests, the competent authorities of the receiving State shall, without delay, inform the consular post of the sending State" of such detention, and "inform the [detainee] of his righ[t]" to request assistance from the consul of his own state. Art. 36(1)(b).

The Optional Protocol provides a venue for the resolution of disputes arising out of the interpretation or application of the Vienna Convention. Under the Protocol, such disputes "shall lie within the compulsory jurisdiction of the International Court of Justice" and "may accordingly be brought before the [ICJ] . . . by any party to the dispute being a Party to the present Protocol."

The ICJ . . . was established in 1945 pursuant to the United Nations Charter. The ICJ Statute—annexed to the U.N. Charter—provides the organizational framework and governing procedures for cases brought before the ICJ. Statute of the International Court of Justice (ICJ Statute).

Under Article 94(1) of the U.N. Charter, "[e]ach Member of the United Nations undertakes to comply with the decision of the [ICJ] in any case to which it is a party." The ICJ's jurisdiction in any particular case, however, is dependent upon the consent of the parties. . . . By ratifying the Optional Protocol to the Vienna Convention, the United States consented to the specific jurisdiction of the ICJ with respect to claims arising out of the Vienna Convention. On March 7, 2005, subsequent to the ICJ's judgment in *Avena*, the United States gave notice of withdrawal from the Optional Protocol to the Vienna Convention.

B

[Medellín and fellow gang members raped and murdered two teenage girls. A few days later, Medellín was arrested and, after receiving Miranda warnings, signed a written waiver and gave a detailed written confession—but "[l]ocal law enforcement officers did not, however, inform Medellín of his Vienna Convention right to notify the Mexican consulate of his detention.]

Medellín first raised his Vienna Convention claim in his first application for state post-conviction relief. The state trial court held that the claim was procedurally defaulted because Medellín had failed to raise it at trial or on direct review. The trial court also rejected the Vienna Convention claim on the merits, finding that Medellín had "fail[ed] to show that any non-notification of the Mexican authorities impacted on the validity of his conviction or punishment.". . .

Medellín then filed a *habeas* petition in Federal District Court. The District Court denied relief, holding that Medellín's Vienna Convention claim was procedurally defaulted and that Medellín had failed to show prejudice arising from the Vienna Convention violation.

While Medellín's application for a certificate of appealability was pending in the Fifth Circuit, the ICJ issued its decision in *Avena*. . . .

The Fifth Circuit denied a certificate of appealability. *Medellín v. Dretke*, 371 F. 3d 270, 281 (2004). The court concluded that the Vienna Convention did not confer individually enforceable rights. The court further ruled that it was in any event bound by this Court's decision in *Breard v. Greene*, 523 U.S. 371, 375 (1998) (per curiam), which held that Vienna Convention claims are subject to procedural default rules, rather than by the ICJ's contrary decision in *Avena*. . . .

II

. . . No one disputes that the *Avena* decision—a decision that flows from the treaties through which the United States submitted to ICJ jurisdiction with respect to Vienna Convention disputes—constitutes an international law obligation on the part of the United States. But not all international law obligations automatically constitute binding federal law enforceable in United States courts. The question we confront here is whether the *Avena* judgment has automatic domestic legal effect such that the judgment of its own force applies in state and federal courts.

This Court has long recognized the distinction between treaties that automatically have effect as domestic law, and those that—while they constitute international law commitments—do not by themselves function as binding federal law. . . .

Medellín and his *amici* nonetheless contend that the Optional Protocol, United Nations Charter, and ICJ Statute supply the "relevant obligation" to give the *Avena* judgment binding effect in the domestic courts of the United States. Because none of these treaty sources creates binding federal law in the absence of implementing legislation, and because it is uncontested that no such legislation exists, we conclude that the *Avena* judgment is not automatically binding domestic law.

A

. . . As a signatory to the Optional Protocol, the United States agreed to submit disputes arising out of the Vienna Convention to the ICJ. . . .

The most natural reading of the Optional Protocol is as a bare grant of jurisdiction. . . . The Protocol says nothing about the effect of an ICJ decision and does not itself commit signatories to comply with an ICJ judgment. The Protocol is similarly silent as to any enforcement mechanism.

The obligation on the part of signatory nations to comply with ICJ judgments derives not from the Optional Protocol, but rather from Article 94 of the United Nations Charter—the provision that specifically addresses the effect of ICJ decisions. Article 94(1) provides that "[e]ach Member of the United Nations undertakes to comply with the decision of the [ICJ] in any case to which it is a party." The Executive Branch contends that the phrase "undertakes to comply" is not "an acknowledgment that an ICJ decision will have immediate legal effect in the courts of U.N. members," but rather "a commitment on the part of U.N. Members to take future action through their political branches to comply with an ICJ decision."

We agree with this construction of Article 94. The Article is not a directive to domestic courts. It does not provide that the United States "shall" or "must" comply with an ICJ decision, nor indicate that the Senate that ratified the U.N. Charter intended to vest ICJ decisions with immediate legal effect in domestic courts. Instead, "[t]he words of Article 94 . . . call upon governments to take certain action." *Committee of United States Citizens Living in Nicaragua v. Reagan*, 859 F. 2d 929, 938 (CADC 1988). . . . *See also Foster*. In other words, the U.N. Charter reads like "a compact between independent nations" that "depends for the enforcement of its provisions on the interest and the honor of the governments which are parties to it." *Head Money Cases*, 112 U.S., at 598.[5]

The remainder of Article 94 confirms that the U.N. Charter does not contemplate the automatic enforceability of ICJ decisions in domestic courts. Article 94(2)—the enforcement provision—provides the sole remedy for noncompliance: referral to the United Nations Security Council by an aggrieved state. . . .

This was the understanding of the Executive Branch when the President agreed to the U.N. Charter.... *See, e.g.*, The Charter of the United Nations for the Maintenance of International Peace and Security: Hearings before the Senate Committee on Foreign Relations, 79th Cong., 1st Sess., 124–125 (1945) ("[I]f a state fails to perform its obligations under a judgment of the [ICJ], the other party may have recourse to the Security Council"); *id.*, at 286 (statement of Leo Paslovsky, Special Assistant to the Secretary of State for International Organizations and Security Affairs) ("[W]hen the Court has rendered a judgment and one of the parties refuses to accept it, then the dispute becomes political rather than legal. It is as a political dispute that the matter is referred to the Security Council")....

If ICJ judgments were instead regarded as automatically enforceable domestic law, they would be immediately and directly binding on state and federal courts pursuant to the Supremacy Clause. Mexico or the ICJ would have no need to proceed to the Security Council to enforce the judgment in this case. Noncompliance with an ICJ judgment through exercise of the Security Council veto—always regarded as an option by the Executive and ratifying Senate during and after consideration of the U.N. Charter, Optional Protocol, and ICJ Statute—would no longer be a viable alternative. There would be nothing to veto. In light of the U.N. Charter's remedial scheme, there is no reason to believe that the President and Senate signed up for such a result.

In sum, Medellín's view that ICJ decisions are automatically enforceable as domestic law is fatally undermined by the enforcement structure established by Article 94....

The ICJ Statute, incorporated into the U.N. Charter, provides further evidence that the ICJ's judgment in *Avena* does not automatically constitute federal law judicially enforceable in United States courts. To begin with, the ICJ's "principal purpose" is said to be to "arbitrate particular disputes between national governments." *Sanchez-Llamas, supra*, at 355 (citing 59 Stat. 1055). Accordingly, the ICJ can hear disputes only between nations, not individuals. Art. 34(1), 59 Stat. 1059 ("Only states [i.e., countries] may be parties in cases before the [ICJ]"). More important, Article 59 of the statute provides that "[t]he decision of the [ICJ] has no binding force except between the parties and in respect of that particular case." *Id.*, at 1062 (emphasis added). The dissent does not explain how Medellín, an individual, can be a party to the ICJ proceeding....

It is, moreover, well settled that the United States' interpretation of a treaty "is entitled to great weight." *Sumitomo Shoji America, Inc. v. Avagliano*, 457 U.S. 176, 184–185 (1982). The Executive Branch has unfailingly adhered to its view that the relevant treaties do not create domestically enforceable federal law.

The pertinent international agreements, therefore, do not provide for implementation of ICJ judgments through direct enforcement in domestic courts, and "where a treaty does not provide a particular remedy, either expressly or implicitly, it is not for the federal courts to impose one on the States through lawmaking of their own." *Sanchez-Llamas*, 548 U.S., at 347.

B

The dissent faults our analysis because it "looks for the wrong thing (explicit textual expression about self-execution) using the wrong standard (clarity) in the wrong place (the treaty language)." Given our obligation to interpret treaty provisions to determine whether they are self-executing, we have to confess that we do think it rather important to look to the treaty language to see what it has to say about the issue. That is after all what the Senate looks to in deciding whether to approve the treaty.

The interpretive approach employed by the Court today—resorting to the text—is hardly novel. . . .

As against this time-honored textual approach, the dissent proposes a multifactor, judgment-by-judgment analysis that would "jettiso[n] relative predictability for the open-ended rough-and-tumble of factors." *Jerome B. Grubart, Inc. v. Great Lakes Dredge & Dock Co.*, 513 U.S. 527, 547 (1995). The dissent's novel approach to deciding which (or, more accurately, when) treaties give rise to directly enforceable federal law is arrestingly indeterminate. . . .

The dissent's approach risks the United States' involvement in international agreements. It is hard to believe that the United States would enter into treaties that are sometimes enforceable and sometimes not. Such a treaty would be the equivalent of writing a blank check to the judiciary. Senators could never be quite sure what the treaties on which they were voting meant. Only a judge could say for sure and only at some future date. This uncertainty could hobble the United States' efforts to negotiate and sign international agreements. . . .

C

Our conclusion that *Avena* does not by itself constitute binding federal law is confirmed by the "postratification understanding" of signatory nations. There are currently 47 nations that are parties to the Optional Protocol and 171 nations that are parties to the Vienna Convention. Yet neither Medellín nor his *amici* have identified a single nation that treats ICJ judgments as binding in domestic courts. . . .

Our conclusion is further supported by general principles of interpretation. To begin with, . . . "'absent a clear and express statement to the contrary, the procedural rules of the forum State govern the implementation of the treaty in that State.'" 548 U.S., at 351. Given that ICJ judgments may interfere with state procedural rules, one would expect the ratifying parties to the relevant treaties to have clearly stated their intent to give those judgments domestic effect, if they had so intended. Here there is no statement in the Optional Protocol, the U.N. Charter, or the ICJ Statute that supports the notion that ICJ judgments displace state procedural rules.

Moreover, the consequences of Medellín's argument give pause. An ICJ judgment, the argument goes, is not only binding domestic law but is also unassailable. As a result, neither Texas nor this Court may look behind a judgment and quarrel with its reasoning or result. . . . And there is nothing to prevent the ICJ from ordering state courts to annul criminal convictions and sentences, for any reason deemed sufficient by the ICJ. Indeed, that is precisely the relief Mexico requested. . . .

D

Our holding does not call into question the ordinary enforcement of foreign judgments or international arbitral agreements. . . . The point is that the particular treaty obligations on which Medellín relies do not of their own force create domestic law.

. . . Again, under our established precedent, some treaties are self-executing and some are not, depending on the treaty. . . .

. . . Congress is up to the task of implementing non-self-executing treaties, even those involving complex commercial disputes. The judgments of a number of international tribunals enjoy a different status because of implementing legislation enacted by Congress. *See, e.g.*, 22 U.S.C. § 1650a(a) ("An award of an arbitral tribunal rendered pursuant to chapter IV of the [Convention on the Settlement of Investment Disputes] shall create a right arising under a treaty of the United States. The pecuniary obligations imposed by such an award shall be enforced and shall be given the same full faith and credit as if the award were a final judgment of a court of general jurisdiction of one of the several States"); 9 U.S.C. §§ 201–208 ("The [U.N.] Convention on the Recognition and Enforcement of Foreign Arbitral Awards of June 10, 1958, shall be enforced in United States courts in accordance with this chapter," § 201). Such language demonstrates that Congress knows how to accord domestic effect to international obligations when it desires such a result. . . .

JUSTICE BREYER, with whom JUSTICE SOUTER and JUSTICE GINSBURG join, dissenting.

. . . The majority places too much weight upon treaty language that says little about the matter. The words "undertak[e] to comply," for example, do not tell us whether an ICJ judgment rendered pursuant to the parties' consent to compulsory ICJ jurisdiction does, or does not, automatically become part of our domestic law. To answer that question we must look instead to our own domestic law, in particular, to the many treaty-related cases interpreting the Supremacy Clause. Those cases, including some written by Justices well aware of the Founders' original intent, lead to the conclusion that the ICJ judgment before us is enforceable as a matter of domestic law without further legislation. . . .

The case law provides no simple magic answer to the question whether a particular treaty provision is self-executing. But the case law does make clear that, insofar as today's majority looks for language about "self-execution" in the treaty itself and insofar as it erects "clear statement" presumptions designed to help find an answer, it is misguided.

The many treaty provisions that this Court has found self-executing contain no textual language on the point. Few, if any, of these provisions are clear. Those that displace state law in respect to such quintessential state matters as, say, property, inheritance, or debt repayment, lack the "clea[r] state[ment]" that the Court today apparently requires. . . . These many Supreme Court cases finding treaty provisions to be self-executing cannot be reconciled with the majority's demand for textual clarity.

Indeed, the majority does not point to a single ratified United States treaty that contains the kind of "clea[r]" or "plai[n]" textual indication for which the majority searches. . . . Rather, it is because the issue whether further legislative action is required before a treaty provision takes domestic effect in a signatory nation is often a matter of how that Nation's domestic law regards the provision's legal status. And that domestic status-determining law differs markedly from one nation to another. *See generally* Hollis, Comparative Approach to Treaty Law and Practice, in National Treaty Law and Practice 1, 9–50 (D. Hollis, M. Blakeslee, & L. Ederington eds. 2005) (hereinafter Hollis). . . .

The case law also suggests practical, context-specific criteria that this Court has previously used to help determine whether, for Supremacy Clause purposes, a treaty provision is self-executing. The provision's text matters very much. But that is not because it contains language that explicitly refers to self-execution. For reasons I have already explained, one should not expect that kind of textual statement. Drafting history is also relevant. But, again, that is not because it will explicitly address the relevant question. Instead text and history, along with subject matter and related characteristics will help our courts determine whether, as Chief Justice Marshall put it, the treaty provision "addresses itself to the political . . . department[s]" for further action or to "the judicial department" for direct enforcement. *Foster*, 2 Pet., at 314. . . .

In making this determination, this Court has found the provision's subject matter of particular importance. Does the treaty provision declare peace? Does it promise not to engage in hostilities? If so, it addresses itself to the political branches. Alternatively, does it concern the adjudication of traditional private legal rights such as rights to own property, to conduct a business, or to obtain civil tort recovery? If so, it may well address itself to the Judiciary. Enforcing such rights and setting their boundaries is the bread-and-butter work of the courts.

One might also ask whether the treaty provision confers specific, detailed individual legal rights. Does it set forth definite standards that judges can readily enforce? Other things being equal, where rights are specific and readily enforceable, the treaty provision more likely "addresses" the judiciary.

Alternatively, would direct enforcement require the courts to create a new cause of action? Would such enforcement engender constitutional controversy? Would it create constitutionally undesirable conflict with the other branches? In such circumstances, it is not likely that the provision contemplates direct judicial enforcement. . . .

Such questions, drawn from case law stretching back 200 years, do not create a simple test, let alone a magic formula. But they do help to constitute a practical, context-specific judicial approach, seeking to separate run-of-the-mill judicial matters from other matters. . . .

Applying the approach just described, I would find the relevant treaty provisions self-executing as applied to the ICJ judgment before us (giving that judgment domestic legal effect) for the following reasons, taken together.

First, the language of the relevant treaties strongly supports direct judicial enforceability, at least of judgments of the kind at issue here. The Optional Protocol bears the title "Compulsory Settlement of Disputes," thereby emphasizing the mandatory and binding nature of the procedures it sets forth. . . .

Moreover, in accepting Article 94(1) of the Charter, "[e]ach Member . . . undertakes to comply with the decision" of the ICJ "in any case to which it is a party." And the ICJ Statute (part of the U.N. Charter) makes clear that, a decision of the ICJ between parties that have consented to the ICJ's compulsory jurisdiction has "binding force . . . between the parties and in respect of that particular case." Enforcement of a court's judgment that has "binding force" involves quintessential judicial activity. . . .

The upshot is that treaty language says that an ICJ decision is legally binding, but it leaves the implementation of that binding legal obligation to the domestic law of each signatory nation. In this Nation, the Supremacy Clause, as long and consistently interpreted, indicates that ICJ decisions rendered pursuant to provisions for binding adjudication must be domestically legally binding and enforceable in domestic courts at least sometimes. And for purposes of this argument, that conclusion is all that I need. The remainder of the discussion will explain why, if ICJ judgments sometimes bind domestic courts, then they have that effect here.

Second, the Optional Protocol here applies to a dispute about the meaning of a Vienna Convention provision that is itself self-executing and judicially enforceable. The Convention provision is about an individual's "rights," namely, his right upon being arrested to be informed of his separate right to contact his nation's consul. *See* Art. 36(1)(b), 21 U.S.T., at 101. The provision language is precise. The dispute arises at the intersection of an individual right with ordinary rules of criminal procedure; it consequently concerns the kind of matter with which judges are familiar. The provisions contain judicially enforceable standards. See Art. 36(2), ibid. (providing for exercise of rights "in conformity with the laws and regulations" of the arresting nation provided that the "laws and regulations . . . enable full effect to be given to the purposes for which the rights accorded under this Article are intended"). And the judgment itself requires a further hearing of a sort that is typically judicial. . . .

Third, logic suggests that a treaty provision providing for "final" and "binding" judgments that "settl[e]" treaty-based disputes is self-executing insofar as the judgment in question concerns the meaning of an underlying treaty provision that is itself self-executing. . . .

Fourth, the majority's very different approach has seriously negative practical implications. The United States has entered into at least 70 treaties that contain provisions for ICJ dispute settlement similar to the Protocol before us. . . . If the Optional Protocol here, taken together with the U.N. Charter and its annexed ICJ Statute, is insufficient to warrant enforcement of the ICJ judgment before us, it is difficult to see how one could reach a different conclusion in any of these other instances. And the consequence is to undermine longstanding efforts in those treaties to create an effective international system for interpreting and applying many, often commercial, self-executing treaty provisions. . . .

Nor can the majority look to congressional legislation for a quick fix. Congress is unlikely to authorize automatic judicial enforceability of all ICJ judgments, for that could include some politically sensitive judgments and others better suited for enforcement by other branches. . . .

Fifth, other factors, related to the particular judgment here at issue, make that judgment well suited to direct judicial enforcement. The specific issue before the ICJ concerned " 'review and reconsideration' " of the "possible prejudice" caused in each of the 51 affected cases by an arresting State's failure to provide the defendant with rights guaranteed by the Vienna Convention. . . . Judicial standards are readily available for working in this technical area. Legislative standards are not readily available. . . .

Sixth, to find the United States' treaty obligations self-executing as applied to the ICJ judgment (and consequently to find that judgment enforceable) does not threaten constitutional conflict with other branches;

it does not require us to engage in nonjudicial activity; and it does not require us to create a new cause of action. The only question before us concerns the application of the ICJ judgment as binding law applicable to the parties in a particular criminal proceeding that Texas law creates independently of the treaty. . . .

Seventh, neither the President nor Congress has expressed concern about direct judicial enforcement of the ICJ decision. . . .

For these seven reasons, I would find that the United States' treaty obligation to comply with the ICJ judgment in *Avena* is enforceable in court in this case without further congressional action beyond Senate ratification of the relevant treaties. The majority reaches a different conclusion because it looks for the wrong thing (explicit textual expression about self-execution) using the wrong standard (clarity) in the wrong place (the treaty language). Hunting for what the text cannot contain, it takes a wrong turn. It threatens to deprive individuals, including businesses, property owners, testamentary beneficiaries, consular officials, and others, of the workable dispute resolution procedures that many treaties, including commercially oriented treaties, provide. In a world where commerce, trade, and travel have become ever more international, that is a step in the wrong direction. . . .

For the reasons set forth, I respectfully dissent.

SENATE FOREIGN RELATIONS COMMITTEE REPORT ON EXTRADITION TREATIES WITH THE EUROPEAN UNION

S. Exec. Rep. No. 110–12, at 9–10 (2008).

[In recommending advice and consent to 49 extradition and mutual legal assistance treaties with the EU and its member states, the Senate Foreign Relations Committee stated as follows.]

In every resolution of advice and consent, the committee has included a proposed declaration that states that each treaty is self-executing. This declaration is consistent with statements made in the Letters of Submittal from the Secretary of State to the President on each of these instruments and with the historical practice of the committee in approving extradition treaties. Such a statement . . . has not generally been included in Resolutions of advice and consent. The committee, however, proposes making such a declaration in the Resolution of advice and consent in light of the recent Supreme Court decision, *Medellín v. Texas*, 128 S.Ct. 1346 (2008), which has highlighted the utility of a clear statement . . .

The committee believes it is of great importance that the United States complies with the treaty obligations it undertakes. In accordance with the Constitution, all treaties—whether self-executing or not—are the supreme law of the land, and the President shall take care that they be faithfully executed. In general, the committee does not recommend that the Senate give advice and consent to treaties unless it is satisfied that the United States will be able to implement them, either through implementing legislation, the exercise of relevant constitutional authorities, or through the direct application of the treaty itself in U.S. law. While situations may arise that were not contemplated when the treaty was concluded and ratified that raise questions about the authority of the United States to comply, the committee expects that such cases will be rare. Accordingly, in the committee's view, a strong presumption should exist against the conclusion in any particular case that the United States lacks the necessary authority in U.S. law to implement obligations it has assumed under treaties that have received the advice and consent of the Senate.

NOTES

1. *Self-Execution and Constitutional Text.* From the text of the U.S. Constitution, one might have the impression that treaties have the same effect under U.S. law as do statutes—a view suggested in *Asakura.* The Supremacy Clause (Article VI, Clause 2) states that "all Treaties made, or which shall be made, under Authority of the United States, shall"—like "the Laws of the United States which shall be made in Pursuance [of the Constitution]"—"be the supreme Law of the Land." This suggests that "all" Article II treaties duly approved by the Senate and ratified by the president (and which, on the international plane, have come into force and remain in force for the United States) have the same effect as domestic lawmaking pursuant to Article I.

Is that how the framers understood the Constitution? Professor Michael Ramsey writes:

> Both opponents and defenders of the Constitution plainly understood that Article VI's designation of the Constitution and statutes as "supreme Law of the Land" made them judicially enforceable. Further, in general both sides saw Article VI as giving the same effect to treaties, and this became a central point of contention. Former Convention delegate George Mason wrote, "By declaring all Treaties supreme Laws of the land, the Executive & Senate have, in many Cases, an exclusive power of legislation." Antifederalist pamphleteers complained that the "president and two thirds of the Senate have power to make laws in the form of treaties, independent of the legislature itself," and that "there is one of the most important duties [that] may be managed in the senate and executive alone, and to have all the force of the law paramount without the aid or interference of the house of representatives; that is the power of making treaties." The main Federalist response was not to dispute the premise, but to argue that the supermajority rule in the Senate provided sufficient protection.

Michael D. Ramsey, *Toward a Rule of Law in Foreign Affairs*, 106 COLUM. L. REV. 1450, 1470 (2006) (reprinted with permission of the Columbia Law Review; permission conveyed through Copyright Clearance Center, Inc.).

2. *The Doctrine of "Non-Self-Executing" Treaties*. Notwithstanding the Supremacy Clause, the Supreme Court has maintained—since *Foster v. Neilson*—that some treaty provisions do *not* automatically become the equivalent of statutory law, at least in the sense of being automatically enforceable in court. *Foster* allowed that the Supremacy Clause created for the United States the "different principle" that a treaty "is . . . to be regarded as in courts of justice as equivalent to an act of the legislature," but added that this was so "whenever [the treaty] operates of itself without the aid of any legislative provision"; otherwise, a treaty might instead "import a contract" that was to be executed by the legislature before judicial application. *Foster v. Neilson*, 27 U.S. (2 Pet.) 253, 314 (1829). The *Head Money Cases* also suggested that "[a] treaty . . . is a law of the land as an act of Congress is, whenever its provisions prescribe a rule by which the rights of the private citizen or subject may be determined." 112 U.S. 580, 598–99 (1884).

Relatively few Supreme Court cases have invoked the doctrine, leaving its compatibility with the Supremacy Clause, and its other contours, unclear. Some cases, like *Asakura*, relied expressly on the supremacy of treaty obligations over state law. In many other areas regulated by treaty—including recovery of monetary debts by aliens; alien land, property, and inheritance rights; rights of aliens to travel, engage in commerce, pursue a trade, and have access to the courts; property claims from territorial acquisition; extradition treaties and criminal jurisdiction; alcohol control conventions; civil air-carrier liability; trademark rights; and international civil discovery rules—the Court assumed treaties had domestic legal effect consistent with supremacy. *See Restatement of the Law (Fourth), The Foreign Relations Law of the United States: Treaties* § 110 reporters' note 1 (Tentative Draft No. 2, 2017); *see also Medellín v. Texas*, 552 U.S. 491, 568–69 (2008) (Breyer, J., dissenting) (appendix).

Medellín reached a different result, but without clarifying the underlying principles. The majority's language sometimes suggested that a non-self-executing treaty provision was simply not enforceable as such in court, and at other times that it was not domestic law at all, until Congress had taken steps to implement it. *See, e.g.*, 552 U.S. at 504, 510, 519, 523. Which position is more consistent with the Supremacy Clause? Does the distinction make a difference? Consider, for example, whether it is relevant to the question of the president's power to implement the treaty provisions at issue in *Medellín*, a subject addressed in Chapter 1.

The circumstances in which *Medellín* applies, unsurprisingly, are controverted. A joint task force of the ABA Section of International Law and the American Society of International Law suggested that the *Medellín* case may:

- Only affect the domestic enforceability of International Court of Justice decisions (a narrow interpretation);
- Only affect treaty provisions that contemplate future action by states parties and are not specifically addressed to the judiciary (an intermediate interpretation); or
- Affect all treaties not affirmatively providing for judicial enforceability that might otherwise have been treated as self-executing (a broad interpretation)

See ABA Section of International Law/American Society of International Law Joint Task Force on Treaties in U.S. Law, *Report* (Mar. 16, 2009). Which interpretation do you think is correct?

For further consideration of *Medellín* and its impact on non-self-execution doctrine, see (among many possibilities) Carlos Vázquez, *Treaties as the Law of the Land: The Supremacy Clause and the Judicial Enforcement of Treaties*, 122 HARV. L. REV. 599 (2008); David H. Moore, *Law (Makers) of the Land: The Doctrine of Treaty Non-Self-Execution*, 122 HARV. L. REV. FORUM 32 (2009); David L. Sloss, *The Death of Treaty Supremacy: An Invisible Constitutional Change* (2016). For an earlier, highly influential discussion, see Carlos Manuel Vázquez, *The Four Doctrines of Self-Executing Treaties*, 89 AM. J. INT'L L. 695 (1995).

3. *Factors in Finding a Treaty Self-Executing*. How does a court determine whether a treaty provision is self-executing? Is there a presumption one way or the other?

Initially, the Supreme Court focused on the treaty text. In *Foster*, for example, Chief Justice Marshall focused on "the terms of the stipulation," which might engage "either the parties . . . to perform a particular act." *Foster v. Neilson*, 27 U.S. (2 Pet.) 253, 314 (1829). As if to emphasize the potential difficulty of that inquiry, however, just four years later the Court concluded that the 1819 treaty with Spain *was* self-executing, since the Spanish version of the treaty should have been translated to read that land grants "shall remain ratified" rather than "shall be ratified." *United States v. Percheman*, 32 U.S. (7 Pet.) 51 (1833).) In *Medellín*, the Court relied on various evidence of the treaty's meaning: not only language in Article 94(1) of the U.N. Charter ("undertakes to comply"), but also the international enforcement structure, the negotiating and drafting history and the subsequent practice of other states. How persuasive do you find this, given that, as Justice Breyer wrote in his *Medellín* dissent, any treaty will have to accommodate the very different means by which states parties implement treaties? It is for this reason, among others, some have suggested that *Medellín* effectively created a presumption against self-execution. *See, e.g.*, *ESAB Group, Inc. v. Zurich Ins. PLC*, 685 F.3d 376, 387 (4th Cir. 2012). Or should the Supremacy Clause create the opposite presumption?

Increasingly, U.S. courts have focused on evidence concerning how the political branches understand a treaty obligation, including (as in *Medellín*) statements made by the executive branch during the advice and consent process and afterward. *See also Cheung v. United States*, 213 F.3d 82, 95 (2d Cir. 2000) (holding agreement between the United States and Hong Kong to be self-executing based partly on statements made by the executive branch, when transmitting the agreement to Senate, to the effect that "this Agreement will not require implementing legislation"). As noted below, the most conclusive evidence is a declaration attached to the Senate resolution of advice and consent indicating whether a treaty, or its particular provision, is self-executing.

In addition to international or domestic evidence regarding whether a treaty or its provisions were intended to operate of themselves, courts sometimes distinguish between treaty provisions that are hortatory or indeterminate, which may be difficult for courts to apply as such, and treaties expressing clear and detailed obligations—such as the treaty in *Asakura* (which simply called for application to Japanese aliens of standards applied to Americans). Less commonly, courts have treated as non-self-executing, and requiring statutory implementation, treaty provisions that require authority that the Constitution assigns exclusively to the House of Representatives or to Congress as a whole, such that approval by the Senate (and president) alone does not suffice. The clearest example is probably Congress's power to appropriate money (*see* U.S. Const., art. I, § 9, cl. 7), but it has also frequently been suggested that implementing legislation is required for treaty provisions obligating criminal prosecutions.

4. *Declarations of Non-Self-Execution (and Self-Execution).* Use by the United States of declaration of non-self-executinon became common with its ratification of multilateral human rights treaties—including, as we have seen, with the Convention Against Torture. *See also* U.S. reservations, declarations, and understandings, International Covenant on Civil and Political Rights, 138 CONG. REC. S4781–01 (daily ed. April 2, 1992). Courts have treated such declarations as highly influential or even conclusive. *See, e.g.*, *Renkel v. United States*, 456 F.3d 640, 644 (6th Cir. 2006) (Torture Convention declaration); *cf. Sosa v. Alvarez-Machain*, 542 U.S. 692, 728 (2004) (noting, in dicta, that the Senate had declined, through its non-self-execution declaration, to "give the federal courts the task of interpreting and applying international human rights law" under the International Covenant on Civil and Political Rights). Following *Medellín*, the Senate became increasingly interested in attaching declarations of self-execution instead, as seen in connection with the European Union extradition treaties; these have not yet been the subject of extensive litigation, though it can be expected that courts would defer to them.

Declarations of either form speak directly to the self-execution issue, and may clarify what would otherwise be difficult or ambiguous cases. What if they suggest an answer contrary to that indicated by the treaty itself? For example, is it constitutional for U.S. treaty-makers to consent to ratification of a treaty that is nominally part of the "supreme law of the land," but at the same time decide that the treaty is not self-executing? For a favorable appraisal, see

Curtis A. Bradley & Jack L. Goldsmith, *Treaties, Human Rights, and Conditional Consent*, 149 U. PA. L. REV. 399 (2000).

5. *Private Rights of Action.* If a treaty provision is self-executing, for what purposes may it be invoked? A number of lower-court decisions, and some legislative discussions, have addressed as non-self-executing a treaty provision that they consider unavailable to a litigant, but this may conflate issues. Treaties, like statutes, may have full effect as U.S. law without necessarily creating a private right of action. For example, a defendant in a criminal or civil matter might invoke a treaty as a basis for an immunity defense. *See, e.g., Brzak v. United Nations*, 597 F.3d 107 (2d Cir. 2010) (finding the U.N. Convention on Privileges and Immunities to be self-executing). Self-execution may then be a necessary, but not sufficient, condition to establishing a basis for suit or for the recovery of a particular remedy, such as damages.

In a footnote, the *Medellín* decision distinguished between self-execution and whether a treaty provision also creates private rights or remedies. *Medellín v. Texas*, 552 U.S. 491, 506 n.3 (2008). In the same passage, the Court stated that "the background presumption is that '[i]nternational agreements, even those directly benefiting private persons, generally do not create private rights or provide for a private cause of action in domestic courts.' " *Id.* (quoting 2 *Restatement of the Law (Third), The Foreign Relations Law of the United States* § 907, comment a (1987)). As the Court observed, a number of lower court decisions have applied such a presumption. *See, e.g., McKesson v. Islamic Republic of Iran*, 539 F.3d 485, 488–489 (D.C. Cir. 2008). In support of that position, it is common to invoke the Supreme Court's language in the *Head Money Cases* to the effect that "[a] treaty is primarily a compact between independent nations," and that "[i]t depends for the enforcement of its provisions on the interest and the honor of the governments which are parties to it." 112 U.S. 580, 598 (1884).

Is that a fair construction of *Head Money Cases*? Does *Medellín* convert a factual observation in the *Restatement (Third)*—that treaties do not often create private rights or causes of action—into a legal presumption, at least in describing the approach of lower courts? *Cf. Restatement of the Law (Fourth), The Foreign Relations Law of the United States: Treaties* § 111 reporters' note 1 (Tentative Draft No. 2, 2017). If there is a presumption against private rights (and further damages remedies, as are usually at issue in these cases), courts applying the presumption will yield given "express language to the contrary" (*Medellín*, 552 U.S. at 506 n.3). Is that likely, given that treaties often leaves to each State procedural and remedial matters? In support of the opposite presumption, consider the following view: although under traditional international law individuals do not have rights under treaties (rather, states do), did not the framers of the Constitution declare treaties to be part of the supreme law of the land precisely to make treaties enforceable by individuals in U.S. courts? *See* Carlos Manuel Vázquez, *Treaty-Based Rights and Remedies of Individuals*, 92 COLUM. L. REV. 1082 (1992).

When implementing treaties and other international agreements, Congress may of course provide its own instruction concerning private enforcement, and it may be broader than simply denying causes of action. Thus, when adhering to the Uruguay Round Agreements of the World Trade Organization (WTO), Congress enacted a statute stating:

> No person other than the United States—
>
> (A) shall have any cause of action or defense under any of the Uruguay Round Agreements or by virtue of congressional approval of such an agreement, or
>
> (B) may challenge . . . any action or inaction by any department, agency, or any other instrumentality of the United States, any State, or any political subdivision of a State on the ground that such action or inaction is inconsistent with any such agreement.

19 U.S.C. § 3512(c)(1) (2012). Such a provision does not, however, preclude reliance on the implementing statute, as opposed to the agreement. *See Canadian Lumber Free Trade Alliance v. United States*, 517 F.3d 1319, 1339–42 (Fed. Cir. 2008) (statute did not bar action brought by Canadian businesses challenging implementation of Continued Dumping and Subsidy Offset Act (CDSOA) based on alleged violation of Administrative Procedure Act and North American Free Trade Agreement Implementation Act (NIA)).

6. *Enforcing Non-Self-Executing Treaties.* If a treaty or one of its provisions is non-self-executing—and, as a result, cannot serve as a basis for a private right of action or as a defense in a judicial matter—does it have any significance as domestic law? As discussed in Chapter 1, Sec. 2, *Medellín* held that the president lacked authority to "unilaterally create federal law" by giving effect to the ICJ's decision, in large part because of its application of the *Youngstown* framework. *Medellín*, 552 U.S. at 523 n.13. The Court did not resolve, however, whether the ICJ decision (or another obligation imposed by a non-self-executing treaty provision) bound the president or the executive branch and required compliance short of overriding state law. Might the answer depend on the reason why a treaty provision is non-self-executing?

Non-self-execution has a more definite effect, seemingly, on the use of a treaty provision in courts of law. Even in that context, however, litigants may remain able to invoke the *Charming Betsy* principle (*see* Chapter 2, Sec. 2), which calls for construing U.S. statutes where possible to avoid treaty violations. *See, e.g., Ma v. Ashcroft*, 257 F.3d 1095, 1114 (9th Cir. 2001) (applying the canon to avoid a violation of the International Covenant on Civil and Political Rights, notwithstanding non-self-execution declaration); *Restatement of the Law (Fourth), The Foreign Relations Law of the United States: Treaties* § 109 comment b & reporters' note 1 (Tentative Draft No. 1, 2016) (suggesting that the canon applied by virtue of the international legal consequences of treaty obligations rather than their domestic legal effect). Does this significantly diminish the significance of non-self-execution?

7. *Practice in Other Countries*. In most common-law countries, treaty-making is the province of the executive. Nevertheless, Parliament typically remains the ultimate authority for creating national law, and thus often must adopt implementing legislation if the treaty requires domestic legal effect—even if such legislation simply mirrors the treaty text. *See* Joanna Harrington, *Scrutiny and Approval: The Role for Westminster-Style Parliaments in Treaty-Making*, 55 I.C.L.Q. 121 (2006) (reviewing the practice of Australia, Canada, South Africa, and the United Kingdom). Even so, a study of the law of treaties in nineteen countries worldwide (common law, civil law, and other systems) reveals that many allow for some type of direct effect in national law, suggesting that the United States may not be as distinctive as the Supremacy Clause, at least, may have suggested. It estimated that "[n]early two-thirds of the states surveyed considered treaties to operate directly as domestic law under certain circumstances"; this includes states (including Mexico and Switzerland) in which any constitutionally-authorized and internationally binding treaty automatically has domestic legal effect, and others (like Egypt, the Netherlands, France, Japan, and Chile) in which satisfying some separate domestic procedure (such as publication or a presidential decree) is a prerequisite. *See* Duncan B. Hollis, *A Comparative Approach to Treaty Law and Practice,* in *National Treaty Law and Practice* 1, 41–44 (Duncan B. Hollis, Merritt R. Blakeslee, & L. Benjamin Ederington eds., 2005).

5. DYNAMIC TREATY REGIMES

Most treaties create "static" obligations that stay essentially unchanged throughout the life of the treaty. Yet treaties can change also over time. The most subtle way that treaties change is through their interpretation—a process considered *infra*, this Chapter, Sec. 9, which also discusses more disruptive possibilities for "reinterpretation" by domestic actors. Treaties may also be amended, which requires that the parties agree on a change and then submit that change to the ratification process in the same way that they did the original treaty (including, in the United States at least, any preliminary domestic approval process).

Certain treaties are crafted so that they can change in an even more dynamic way. While more significant changes usually require amendments, a treaty may provide that certain changes can occur simply by agreement of the representatives of the parties. Such changes might occur at a regular meeting of the parties (or MOP) or conference of the parties (or COP), or through an affirmative vote of a particular organ of an international organization. These decisions often require consensus, but sometimes permit approval by a supermajority or even a simple majority; states that are in the minority might also be given a chance to opt out of the change, though a treaty need not provide that option. Multilateral environmental treaties, in particular, often feature a diverse set of means for adapting treaty obligations. *See* Robin R. Churchill & Geir Ulfstein, *Autonomous Institutional Arrangements in Multilateral Environmental*

Agreements: A Little Noticed Phenomenon in International Law 94 AM. J. INT'L L. 623 (2000); Annecoos Wiersema, *The New International Law-Makers? Conferences of the Parties to Multilateral Environmental Agreements*, 31 MICH. J. INT'L L. 231 (2009).

These "dynamic" treaty regimes raise interesting and important questions for U.S. foreign relations law. On the one hand, if the Senate (and president) have consented to a treaty regime that provides for dynamic changes, then U.S. constitutional requirements have at least nominally been satisfied. On the other hand, if they accord to a MOP, COP, or other international process the power to change legal obligations under a treaty, are they abdicating their constitutional role of "making" treaty obligations for the United States? To the extent that such treaty changes have direct effect under U.S. law (since treaties are part of the "supreme law of the land"), are the U.S. political branches of government unconstitutionally delegating power to other political bodies? If the treaty effectively allocates a veto to U.S. representatives, is any problem resolved, or does it remain a potentially unconstitutional loss of legislative authority?

Bear in mind that the whole point of dynamic treaty regimes is to permit more rapid adjustment to new technical developments than would be feasible through the formal amendment process. Making such changes binding avoids turning the treaty into a constellation of political commitments, promoting compliance. If one State (*e.g.*, the United States) fails to abide by its commitments or declares those commitments to be political in nature, other States may react in kind.

For example, consider the Montreal Protocol on Substances that Deplete the Ozone Layer, Sept. 16, 1987, S. TREATY DOC. 100–10 (1987), 1522 U.N.T.S. 3, *reprinted in* 26 I.L.M. 1550 (1987). States that joined the treaty have agreed to the progressive reduction by specified dates of certain types of ozone-depleting chemicals listing in the annexes to the Protocol. There are different ways that the Protocol may be changed.

- *Amendments.* For a new chemical to be listed in an annex, the Protocol requires that the parties *amend* the treaty through normal ratification processes. If a State does not ratify the amendment, the State incurs no obligation with respect to that chemical. For example, an amendment adopted by the COP in 1992 (as part of the "Copenhagen Amendment") added methyl bromide, a widely-used agricultural fumigant, as a covered chemical. The parties to the Protocol then underwent their normal ratification procedures. By 2006 about 175 States had ratified this change; as of 2017, all 197 States that had joined the Montreal Protocol had also adopted the Copenhagen Amendment.

- *Adjustments.* Once a chemical is added to the treaty, the target date for reducing or eliminating the chemical can be changed by an *adjustment*. An adjustment does not require normal ratification, but it does require at least a two-thirds vote of the MOP (preferably consensus), including support by states representing at least half of global consumption of the chemical in question. For example, while the Copenhagen Amendment initially provided only that states not exceed their 1991 levels of consumption and production of methyl bromide, a subsequent MOP (called the "London Adjustment") decided to *adjust* the obligation to require a complete phase-out of the chemical beginning in January 2005, with some latitude for developing countries.
- *Decisions.* An adjustment may contemplate a further decision by the MOP that would allow a state temporarily to avoid its obligations under the adjustment. For example, the London Adjustment provided that, despite the complete phase-out, the MOP could decide to permit production or consumption levels necessary to satisfy "critical uses." The MOP later issued a decision (called "Decision IX/6") setting general guidelines for when a methyl bromide "critical-use exemption" would be permitted and then issued a decision (called "Decision EX.I/3") granting the United States an exemption from the phase-out for certain amounts and uses of methyl bromide.

Since not all of these changes require consent by the U.S. Senate, do they create binding treaty obligations upon the United States? Do they have the effect of binding law within the United States?

NATURAL RESOURCES DEFENSE COUNCIL V. ENVIRONMENTAL PROTECTION AGENCY

464 F.3d 1, 1, 2–11 (D.C. Cir. 2006).

RANDOLPH, CIRCUIT JUDGE.

The United States and other countries entered into the Montreal Protocol on Substances that Deplete the Ozone Layer, Sept. 16, 1987, S. TREATY DOC. NO. 100–10, 1522 U.N.T.S. 29 ("Montreal Protocol"), a treaty in which the signatory nations agreed to reduce the use of certain substances, including methyl bromide, that degrade the stratospheric ozone layer. The Environmental Protection Agency issued a rule implementing "critical use" exemptions from the treaty's general ban on production and consumption of methyl bromide. Protection of Stratospheric Ozone: Process for Exempting Critical Uses From the Phaseout of Methyl

Bromide, 69 Fed. Reg. 76,982 (Dec. 23, 2004) (*codified at* 40 C.F.R. pt. 82) ("Final Rule"). . . .

Amidst growing international concern about ozone depletion, the United States and twenty-four other nations entered into the Montreal Protocol. The Protocol requires signatory nations—which now number 189—to reduce and eliminate their production and use of ozone-depleting chemicals in accordance with agreed-upon timetables. Montreal Protocol arts. 2–2I. The Senate ratified the treaty in 1988, and Congress incorporated its terms into domestic law through the Clean Air Act Amendments of 1990, Pub.L. No. 101–549, tit. VI, 104 Stat. 2399, 2648. Since then, the United States has reduced its use of methyl bromide to less than 39% of its 1991 baseline.

In 1997, the Parties "adjusted" the Protocol to require developed-country Parties to cease "production" and "consumption" of methyl bromide by 2005. *See* Montreal Protocol art. 2H(5). In response, Congress amended the Clean Air Act to require EPA to "promulgate rules for reductions in, and terminate the production, importation, and consumption of, methyl bromide under a schedule that is in accordance with, but not more stringent than, the phaseout schedule of the Montreal Protocol Treaty as in effect on October 21, 1998." 42 U.S.C. § 7671c(h). . . .

In light of methyl bromide's wide use and the lack of comparable substitute pesticides, *see* Final Rule, 69 Fed.Reg. at 76,985, the Protocol allows exemptions from the general ban "to the extent that the Parties decide to permit the level of production or consumption that is necessary to satisfy uses agreed by them to be critical uses." Montreal Protocol art. 2H(5); *see also* 42 U.S.C. § 7671c(d)(6) ("To the extent consistent with the Montreal Protocol, the [EPA] Administrator ... may exempt the production, importation, and consumption of methyl bromide for critical uses."). The Parties to the Protocol meet annually to "decide to permit the level of production or consumption that is necessary to satisfy uses agreed by them to be critical uses." Montreal Protocol art. 2H(5). At one of these meetings the Parties set general guidelines for implementing the critical-use exemptions ["Decision IX/6"], and at another the Parties approved exemptions for 2005. The United States formally began the process of establishing its 2005 critical-use exemptions in May 2002, when EPA published a notice in the *Federal Register* seeking applications for 2005 and 2006 critical uses of methyl bromide and the amounts of new production and consumption needed to satisfy those uses. *See* Protection of Stratospheric Ozone: Process for Exempting Critical Uses From the Phaseout of Methyl Bromide, 67 Fed.Reg. 31,798 (May 10, 2002). EPA teams composed of biologists and economists reviewed each application and decided which to include in the aggregate U.S. nomination to the Parties. The final U.S. nomination, submitted to the Montreal Protocol's administrative body (the "Ozone Secretariat") in February 2003, requested a total exemption of about ten-thousand metric tons of methyl bromide for sixteen different uses.

The process then moved to the international stage. Two working groups operating under the auspices of the Ozone Secretariat—the "Methyl Bromide Technical Options Committee" and the "Technology and Economic Assessment Panel"—evaluated each country's nomination and made a recommendation to the Parties at their November 2003 meeting. At that meeting, the Parties deadlocked over the proposed critical-use exemptions and called an "extraordinary meeting" to make the final decisions. . . .

The Parties reached agreement at their First Extraordinary Meeting in March 2004. They granted the United States critical uses in sixteen categories, amounting to 8,942 metric tons of methyl bromide. To satisfy these critical uses, the Parties authorized 7,659 metric tons of new production and consumption, with the remainder (1,283 metric tons) to be made up from existing stocks of methyl bromide ["Decision Ex.I/3"]. Decision Ex.I/3 noted that "each Party which has an agreed critical use should ensure that the criteria in paragraph 1 of decision IX/6 are applied when . . . authorizing the use of methyl bromide and that such procedures take into account available stocks." *Id.* ¶ 5.

With Decision Ex.I/3 in hand, EPA proposed rules to implement the critical-use exemption. *See* Protection of Stratospheric Ozone: Process for Exempting Critical Uses From the Phaseout of Methyl Bromide, 69 Fed.Reg. 52,366 (Aug. 25, 2004). Many parties, including NRDC, submitted comments. The Final Rule, issued in December 2004, authorized new production and consumption up to the limit established in Decision Ex.I/3. Final Rule, 69 Fed.Reg. at 76,990 tbl.1. It also authorized the use of stocks as permitted by the decision, *id.* at 76,986, 76,991 tbl.2, and permitted noncritical users to draw upon existing stocks, *id.* at 76,988. . . .

. . . Paragraph 1 of Decision IX/6 directs the Parties to authorize new production and consumption of methyl bromide only if it "is not available in sufficient quantity and quality from existing stocks," Decision IX/6 ¶ 1(b)(ii), and only after "[a]ll technically and economically feasible steps have been taken to minimize the critical use," *id.* ¶ 1(b)(I).

NRDC believes EPA's rule departs from these post-treaty agreements in three respects. First, the rule authorizes 7,659 metric tons of new production and consumption—the maximum agreed upon in Decision Ex.I/3—without offsetting this amount by existing stocks.[1] *See* Final Rule, 69 Fed.Reg. at 76,989. EPA declined to disclose the size of the total nationwide methyl bromide stockpile, *see id.* at 76,990—an action NRDC claims is itself a violation of the Clean Air Act, 42 U.S.C. § 7607(d)(4)(B)(i). Still, the record suggests that the stockpile is at least as large as the United

[1] [Authors' Note: In other words, the NRDC believed that EPA was required to first take account of existing methyl bromide stocks before authorizing any further production.]

States' total critical-use allocation for 2005. Second, EPA's rule allows noncritical users to draw down existing stocks. *See* Final Rule, 69 Fed.Reg. at 76,987–88. NRDC claims that the "decisions" implicitly reserve the stocks for critical users only. Third, EPA approved 8,942 metric tons of critical uses—again the maximum agreed upon in Decision Ex.I/3—without considering anew whether this was the minimum amount feasible. *Id.* at 76,989. EPA counters that it adhered to the agreed-upon critical-use and new production and consumption levels, and that the remainder of the decisions are "hortatory." *Id.* at 76,987.

NRDC fashions the entirety of its argument around the proposition that the "decisions" under the Protocol are "law." This premise is flawed. The "decisions" of the Parties—post-ratification side agreements reached by consensus among 189 nations—are not "law" within the meaning of the Clean Air Act and are not enforceable in federal court.

The Clean Air Act authorizes EPA to "exempt the production, importation, and consumption of methyl bromide for critical uses" only "[t]o the extent consistent with the Montreal Protocol." 42 U.S.C. § 7671c(d)(6); *see also id.* § 7671m(b). The Protocol bans the production or consumption of methyl bromide after December 31, 2004, except "to the extent that the Parties decide to permit the level of production or consumption that is necessary to satisfy uses agreed by them to be critical uses." Montreal Protocol art. 2H(5). NRDC argues that because the Clean Air Act requires EPA to abide by the Protocol, and because the Protocol authorizes future agreements concerning the scope of the critical-use exemption, those future agreements must "define the scope of EPA's Clean Air Act authority." . . .

NRDC's interpretation raises significant constitutional problems. If the "decisions" are "law"—enforceable in federal court like statutes or legislative rules—then Congress either has delegated lawmaking authority to an international body or authorized amendments to a treaty without presidential signature or Senate ratification, in violation of Article II of the Constitution. The Supreme Court has not determined whether decisions of an international body created by treaty are judicially enforceable. But there is a close analogy in this court. The United States is a party to a treaty establishing the International Court of Justice (ICJ). In *Committee of United States Citizens Living in Nicaragua v. Reagan*, 859 F.2d 929 (D.C.Cir.1988), we held that rulings of the ICJ do not provide "substantive legal standards for reviewing agency actions," *id.* at 942, because the rulings, though authorized by the ratified treaty, were not themselves self-executing treaties. *Id.* at 937–38; *see, e.g.*, *Medellín v. Dretke*, 544 U.S. 660, 682–84. . . . (2005) (O'Connor, J., dissenting).

Although *Committee of United States Citizens* is highly suggestive of the outcome in this case, several features of the Montreal Protocol "decisions" may distinguish them from ICJ "adjudications." For one thing,

Congress implemented the Montreal Protocol with a direction to EPA to abide by its terms. *See* 42 U.S.C. §§ 7671c(d)(6), 7671m(b). For another, Montreal Protocol "decisions" are not adjudications between parties; instead, they purport to set rules for implementing ongoing treaty commitments.

The legal status of "decisions" of this sort appears to be a question of first impression. There is significant debate over the constitutionality of assigning lawmaking functions to international bodies. *See, e.g.*, Julian G. Ku, *The Delegation of Federal Power to International Organizations: New Problems with Old Solutions*, 85 MINN. L. REV. 71 (2000); Edward T. Swaine, *The Constitutionality of International Delegations*, 104 COLUM. L. REV. 1492 (2004). A holding that the Parties' post-ratification side agreements were "law" would raise serious constitutional questions in light of the nondelegation doctrine, numerous constitutional procedural requirements for making law, and the separation of powers.

We need not confront the "serious likelihood that the statute will be held unconstitutional." *Almendarez-Torres v. United States*, 523 U.S. 224, 238 (1998) . . . It is far more plausible to interpret the Clean Air Act and Montreal Protocol as creating an ongoing international political commitment rather than a delegation of lawmaking authority to annual meetings of the Parties. . .

Nowhere does the Protocol suggest that the Parties' post-ratification consensus agreements about how to implement the critical-use exemption are binding in domestic courts. The only pertinent language in Article 2H(5) states that the Parties will "decide to permit" production and consumption necessary to satisfy those uses that they "agree[ ]" to be critical uses. The Protocol is silent on any specific conditions accompanying the critical-use exemption. Post-ratification agreements setting these conditions are not the Protocol.

To illustrate, suppose the president signed and the Senate ratified a treaty with Germany and France to conserve fossil fuel. How this is to be accomplished the treaty does not specify. In a later meeting of representatives of the signatory countries at the United Nations, a consensus is reached to lower the speed limits on all major highways of the signatory nations to a maximum of 45 miles per hour. No one would say that United States law has thus been made.

EPA characterizes the decisions as "subsequent consensus agreements of the Parties that address the interpretation and application of the critical use provision. . . ." Final Rule, 69 Fed.Reg. at 76,985. This may be so. Like any interpretive tool, however, the "decisions" are useful only to the extent they shed light on ambiguous terms in the Protocol. But the details of the critical-use exemption are not ambiguous. They are nonexistent. The "decisions" do not interpret treaty language. They fill in treaty gaps.

CAA

Article 2H(5) thus constitutes an "agreement to agree." The parties agree in the Protocol to reach an agreement concerning the types of uses for which new production and consumption will be permitted, and the amounts that will be permitted. "Agreements to agree" are usually not enforceable in contract. . . . *Foster v. Neilson*, 27 U.S. (2 Pet.) 253, 314 (1829) ("A treaty is in its nature a contract between . . . nations."). And the fruits of those agreements are enforceable only to the extent that they themselves are contracts. There is no doubt that the "decisions" are not treaties.

Leg. Intent

The Parties' post-ratification actions suggest their common understanding that the decisions are international political commitments rather than judicially enforceable domestic law . . . The Parties met to decide the 2006 critical-use exemptions well after EPA's rule went into effect. . . . Yet they did not invoke the Protocol's internal noncompliance procedure against the United States, *see* Montreal Protocol art. 8, nor did they admonish the United States to change its interpretation of the previous decisions. This course of dealing suggests that the Parties intended the side agreements to be enforceable as a political matter at the negotiating table.

Our holding in this case in no way diminishes the power of the Executive to enter into international agreements that constrain its own behavior within the confines of statutory and treaty law. The Executive has the power to implement ongoing collective endeavors with other countries. *See* Louis Henkin, *Foreign Affairs and the Constitution* 219–20 (2d ed.1996). Without congressional action, however, side agreements reached after a treaty has been ratified are not the law of the land; they are enforceable not through the federal courts, but through international negotiations. . . .

. . . Because the post-ratification agreements of the parties are not "law," EPA's rule—even if inconsistent with those agreements—is not in violation of any domestic law within the meaning of the Clean Air Act, 42 U.S.C. § 7607(d)(9)(A), the petition for review is denied.

NOTES

1. *Scope of the Court's Decision.* The D.C. Circuit addressed whether "decisions" by the MOP about how to implement the critical-use exemption are binding under U.S. law; it did not have before it the broader issue of the status of all post-ratification changes, such as MOP "adjustments." Indeed, the U.S. government took the position before the court that the Clean Air Act *did* accord legal effect under U.S. law to MOP "adjustments," but not to MOP "decisions." But doesn't the reasoning of the court suggest that *no* post-ratification change by the MOP, whether in the form of an "adjustment" or in the form of a "decision" for an exemption from an adjustment, can have the effect of law in the United States and be enforceable in U.S. courts?

2. *MOP Decisions as Political Commitments*. The D.C. Circuit took the position that the Clean Air Act and the Montreal Protocol simply created "an ongoing international political commitment rather than a delegation of lawmaking authority to annual meetings of the Parties." Further, the court characterizes the adjustments as "side agreements" and the adjustment process as an "agreement to agree." Is that right? The Montreal Protocol provides in Article 2(9)(d) that adjustment "decisions . . . shall be binding on all Parties" and "[u]nless otherwise provided in the decisions, they shall enter into force on the expiry of six months from the date of the circulation and communication by the Depositary." As such, it would appear that the Senate consented to a treaty that included a process for creating binding obligations on the United States. Since treaties are part of the supreme law of the land and the president is constitutionally obligated to faithfully execute the law, why should MOP decisions be viewed as creating mere political commitments? *See* Andrew D. Finkelman, Note, *The Post-Ratification Consensus Agreements of the Parties to the Montreal Protocol: Law or Politics? An Analysis of* Natural Resources Defense Council v. EPA, 93 IOWA L. REV. 665 (2008). What similarities or differences do you perceive in the court's hypothetical treaty among France, Germany, and the United States on highway speed limits?

3. *MOP Decisions as a Delegation of Power*. Assuming that the MOP adjustments do create binding obligations for the United States, does U.S. ratification of the Montreal Protocol constitute an unconstitutional delegation of power? The non-delegation doctrine arises from the "vesting clauses" of the U.S. Constitution, by which the legislative, executive, and judicial powers are vested respectively in the three branches. *See* U.S. CONST. art. I, § 1, art. II, § 1, & art. III, § 1. The doctrine states that these grants of power may not be reallocated, since doing so would interfere with constitutional checks and balances, but that the branches can "coordinate" their conduct where there is an "intelligible principle" for doing so. Since the 1930's, however, U.S. courts have largely avoided second-guessing congressional delegations of policymaking authority to the executive. *See EPA v. American Trucking Ass'n*, 531 U.S. 457, 473–75 (2001).

Should the doctrine have greater or (even) lesser vitality when it comes to delegations to a MOP, COP, or international organization? Are areas that turn on international decision-making best regarded as unconstitutional delegations—including, for example, a treaty that requires updating to reflect changes in endangered species? *See* 16 U.S.C. § 1538(c)(1) (2012) (criminalizing within U.S. jurisdiction trading any of the species protected under the Convention on the International Trade in Endangered Species (CITES), Mar. 3, 1973, 27 U.S.T. 1087, 993 U.N.T.S. 243, where those species are listed and de-listed based on decisions of the biennial meetings of the CITES parties). Or are these entities best regarded as engaged in international lawmaking of a kind that could not be performed by the United States alone, and therefore doing something not vested in the U.S. government?

For commentary, see John O. McGinnis, Medellín *and the Future of International Delegation*, 118 YALE L.J. 1712 (2009); Andrew T. Guzman &

Jennifer Landsidle, *The Myth of International Delegation*, 96 CAL. L. REV. 1693 (2008); Curtis A. Bradley & Judith G. Kelley, *The Concept of International Delegation*, 71 LAW & CONTEMP. PROBS. 1 (2008); Laurence R. Helfer, *Nonconsensual International Lawmaking*, 2008 U. ILL. L. REV. 71; Kristina Daugirdas, *International Delegations and Administrative Law*, 66 MD. L. REV. 707 (2007).

4. *MOP Decisions as Non-Self-Executing.* Rather than viewing such regimes as unconstitutional "delegations" of U.S. power and impermissible treaties, is it better to treat them as non-self-executing (*see supra*, this Chapter, Sec. 4)? That would require implementing legislation before any change could have effect in U.S. law. In the case of adjustment for the phase-out of methyl bromide, the D.C. Circuit correctly noted that Congress blessed the methyl bromide adjustment process by amending the Clean Air Act to require the EPA to "promulgate rules for reductions in, and terminate the production, importation, and consumption of, methyl bromide under a schedule that is in accordance with, but not more stringent than, the phaseout schedule of the Montreal Protocol Treaty as in effect on October 21, 1998," 42 U.S.C. § 7671c(h) (2012). What exactly is gained by having Congress authorize the EPA to follow decisions of the MOP—beyond the Senate's original consent to a treaty that contemplated decision-making by the MOP?

5. *Other Dynamic Decision-Making by International Organizations.* As previously noted, the dynamism required by environmental organizations has been particularly thorny—but, due to legal and political objections, U.S. ratification of many such treaties has been blocked. John H. Knox, *The United States, Environmental Agreements, and the Political Question Doctrine*, 40 N.C.J. INT'L L. & COM. REG. 933, 944–51 (2015). Other international organizations, however, make decisions that have effects within U.S. law. For example, in ratifying the 1944 Chicago Convention, the United States joined an International Civil Aviation Organization (ICAO) charged with creating rules for the safety of civil aviation worldwide. In addition to the rules contained in the Chicago Convention itself, ICAO's principal executive organ (the ICAO Council) adopts further rules (called "annexes" to the Chicago Convention) that bind ICAO's membership. Thus, Article 12 of the Chicago Convention requires that states adopt measures to ensure that aircraft of their nationality flying over the high seas conform with ICAO regulations on the "rules of the air." The United States implements this obligation by stating in the relevant FAA regulations that "[e]ach person operating a civil aircraft of U.S. registry outside of the United States shall . . . [w]hen over the high seas, comply with annex 2 (Rules of the Air) to the Convention on International Civil Aviation. . . ." 14 C.F.R. § 91.703(a) (2016); *see also id.* § 91.703(b) (incorporating Annex 2 and making "a part hereof"). Does this deference to the decision-making of the ICAO Council constitute an unconstitutional delegation of power?

6. *International Tribunal Decisions.* The D.C. Circuit referred to the situation where the United States ratifies a treaty that establishes an international court, and says that decisions by international courts cannot

have binding effect within U.S. law. Yet while some international tribunal decisions have not been enforced, there are situations where such decisions are regarded as creating binding obligations cognizable under U.S. law.

For example, the United States is a party to the Convention on the Settlement of Investment Disputes between States and Nationals of Other States, Mar. 18, 1965, 17 U.S.T. 1270, 575 U.N.T.S. 159 (ICSID Convention). The ICSID Convention allows for the rendering of arbitral awards by panels of arbitrators and provides, in Article 54(1), that each "Contracting State shall recognize an award rendered pursuant to this Convention as binding and enforce the pecuniary obligations imposed by that award within its territories as if it were a final judgment of a court in that State." Similarly, the Convention on the Recognition and Enforcement of Foreign Arbitral Awards (New York Convention), June 10, 1958, 21 U.S.T. 2517, 330 U.N.T.S. 38, obligates the United States (and some 134 other countries) to enforce a private contract to submit a dispute to arbitration. It further obligates the enforcement of foreign arbitral awards once rendered. (As indicated in *Medellín v. Texas*, 552 U.S. 491 (2008), U.S. implementing legislation instructs U.S. courts to heed those judgments. (*See supra*, this Chapter, Sec. 4.) The U.N. Convention on the Law of the Sea, which the United States has not yet ratified, states that "decisions of the [Seabed Disputes] Chamber shall be enforceable in the territories of the States Parties in the same manner as judgments or orders of the highest court of the State Party in whose territory the enforcement is sought." U.N. Convention on the Law of the Sea annex VI, art. 39, Dec. 10, 1982, 1833 U.N.T.S. 397, 570. Do you perceive any difference?

As discussed *infra*, this Chapter, Sec. 6, in the context of the North American Free Trade Agreement (NAFTA), Dec. 8, 1992, 32 I.L.M. 296, the United States has even accepted that an international dispute panel can—with final and legally binding effect, subject only to limited exceptions—overturn U.S. administrative decisions concerning antidumping or countervailing duties. To the extent that the United States joins such conventions, and enacts implementing legislation, are these unconstitutional delegations of power? Or is an inexorable process of "globalization" placing the United States in a position where such "delegation" must occur if the United States is to coordinate decision-making with other states in an effective manner?

7. *Further Reading. See Delegating State Powers: The Effect of Treaty Regimes on Democracy and Sovereignty* (Thomas M. Franck ed., 2000); Julian G. Ku, *The Delegation of Federal Power to International Organizations: New Problems with Old Solutions*, 85 MINN. L. REV. 71 (2000); Curtis A. Bradley, *International Delegations, the Structural Constitution, and Non-Self-Execution*, 55 STAN. L. REV. 1557 (2003); David Golove, *The New Confederalism: Treaty Delegations of Legislative, Executive, and Judicial Authority*, 55 STAN. L. REV. 1697 (2003); Ernest A. Young, *The Trouble with Global Constitutionalism*, 38 TEX. INT'L L.J. 527 (2003); Edward T. Swaine, *The Constitutionality of International Delegations*, 104 COLUM. L. REV. 1492 (2004); Oona A. Hathaway, *International Delegation and State Sovereignty*, 71 L. & CONTEMP. PROB. 115 (2008).

6. SCOPE AND HIERARCHICAL STATUS OF TREATIES IN U.S. LAW

Are there any substantive limits on the treaty power? We might distinguish between possible limits on the scope of the treaty power and limits on the hierarchical status of treaties. The first concerns whether a valid treaty can be concluded on any topic the president and Senate desire—or whether, for example, treaties must relate to matters in some sense "external" to the United States (as opposed to more internal matters, like the treatment of U.S. nationals in the United States by federal and state governments). The second possible limit, not always easily distinguished, assumes an otherwise valid treaty, but focuses on constraints imposed by other forms of domestic law; whether and to what extent treaties are constrained by the U.S. Constitution, including if they appear to give power to the Congress or the president that would otherwise be lacking, as well as the relationship between treaties and statutes that may conflict. This Section will consider both possibilities, starting with scope issues.

Ratification Debates. Concern about the scope of the treaty power dates back to the founding. John Jay argued in *The Federalist Papers* No. 64 that concerns about a broad scope of the treaty power should be allayed because of the political process that requires approval of a treaty: given the equal representation of states in the Senate, and developing sentiment that "the good of the whole can only be promoted by advancing the good of each of the parts,"

> "It will not be in the power of the President and the Senate to make any treaties by which they and their families and estates will not be equally bound and affected with the rest of the community; and, having no private interests distinct from that of the nation, they will be under no temptations to neglect the latter."[42]

Such assurances, however, did not satisfy opponents. In Virginia's ratifying convention, opponents expressed concern that the treaty power would be used by the federal government to affect important rights, such as by ceding territory west of the Mississippi to a foreign power or granting aliens a right (denied to them by Virginia common law) to own real property. Patrick Henry and George Mason led the opposition. Henry's intervention is recorded as follows:

> Mr. HENRY begged gentlemen to consider the condition this country would be in if two thirds of a quorum should be empowered to make a treaty: they might relinquish and alienate territorial rights, and our most valuable commercial advantages.

[42] *The Federalist Papers* No. 64, at 395 (Jay) (Clinton Rossiter ed., 1961).

> In short, if any thing should be left us, it would be because the President and senators were pleased to admit it. The power of making treaties, by this Constitution, ill-guarded as it is, extended farther than it did in any country in the world.... Treaties rest, says [Madison], on the laws and usages of nations. To say [under the proposed Constitution] that they are municipal is, to me, a doctrine totally novel. To make them paramount to the Constitution and laws of the states, is unprecedented.[43]

George Mason also opposed ratification, stating that if any such power existed, there should be certain subject-matter limitations placed upon it:

> Will any gentleman say that they may not make a treaty [under the proposed Constitution], whereby the subjects of France, England, and other powers, may buy what lands they please in this country? This would violate those principles which we have received from the mother country. The indiscriminate admission of all foreigners to the first rights of citizenship, without any permanent security for their attachment to the country, is repugnant to every principle of prudence and good policy. The President and Senate can make any treaty whatsoever. We wish not to refuse, but to guard, this power, as it is done in England. The empire there cannot be dismembered without the consent of the national Parliament. We wish an express and explicit declaration, in [the proposed Constitution], that the power which can make other treaties cannot, without the consent of the national Parliament—the national legislature—dismember the empire.... No treaty to dismember the empire ought to be made without the consent of three fourths of the legislature in all its branches. Nor ought such a treaty be made but in case of the most urgent and unavoidable necessity.[44]

Virginia Governor Edmund Randolph and James Madison responded in support of ratification. Randolph asserted:

> Mr. Chairman, I conceive that neither the life nor property of any citizen, nor the particular right of any state, can be affected by a treaty....
>
> The honorable gentleman says that, if you place treaties on the same footing here as they are in England, he will consent to the power, because the king is restrained in making treaties. Will not the President and Senate be restrained? Being creatures of that Constitution, can they destroy it? Can any particular body,

[43] *The Debates in the Several State Conventions, on the Adoption of the Federal Constitution, As Recommended by the General Convention at Philadelphia, in 1787,* at 500 (Jonathan Elliot ed., 2d ed. 1996) (1891) [hereinafter "3 *Elliot's Debates*"]

[44] *Id.* at 509.

> instituted for a particular purpose, destroy the existence of the society for whose benefit it is created?[45]

Meanwhile, Madison maintained:

> Does it follow, because this [treaty] power is given to Congress, that it is absolute and unlimited? I do not conceive that power is given to the President and Senate to dismember the empire, or to alienate any great, essential right. I do not think the whole legislative authority have this power. The exercise of the power must be consistent with the object of the delegation.
>
> . . . The object of treaties is the regulation of intercourse with foreign nations, and is external. I do not think it possible to enumerate all the cases in which such external regulations would be necessary. Would it be right to define all the cases in which Congress could exercise this authority? The definition might, and probably would, be defective. They might be restrained, by such a definition, from exercising the authority where it would be essential to the interest and safety of the community. It is most safe, therefore, to leave it to be exercised as contingencies may arise.[46]

Do the concerns voiced by Henry and Mason, which were not heeded, suggest that the treaty power as adopted has no subject-matter limits? In assuring their opponents that their fears were unfounded, do Randolph and Madison's comments establish that there are limits to the treaty power?

The Jay Treaty. The scope of the treaty power remained an issue of contention for the early American Republic. In 1794, John Jay negotiated with Great Britain a treaty for settling several outstanding disputes and regularizing commerce. Article IX of the Jay Treaty provided:

> that British Subjects who now hold Lands in the Territories of the United States . . . shall continue to hold them according to the nature and Tenure of their respective Estates and Titles therein, and may grant Sell or Devise the same to whom they please, in like manner as if they were Natives. . . .[47]

This provision conflicted with the common law of most of the states, which denied the right of aliens to own real property. The Jay Treaty thus sparked an extensive controversy between the emerging Federalist and Democratic-Republican parties, which in part concerned the scope of the treaty power.

---

45 *Id.* at 504.

46 *Id.* at 514–15.

47 The Jay Treaty, U.S.-Gr. Brit., art. IX, Nov. 19, 1794, *reprinted in* 2 *Treaties and Other International Acts of the United States of America* 245, 253–54 (Hunter Miller ed., 1931).

Robert Livingston wrote a series of essays (under the pseudonym Cato) arguing that treaties could not address subjects that Article I of the Constitution had assigned to Congress, unless the House of Representatives approved. Nor could treaties interfere in subjects *not* assigned to Congress, since those subjects were left to the states, unless the states agreed otherwise. Therefore, since Congress had not been accorded any power to regulate alien ownership of real property in the several states, that power was left to the states, which had not consented to it being addressed by treaty.[48]

The response of Federalists to such claims is best seen in a series of essays crafted by Alexander Hamilton in 1795–96 called *The Defence.* Hamilton asserted:

> It was impossible for words more comprehensive to be used than those which grant the power to make treaties. They are such as would naturally be employed to confer a *plenipotentiary* authority. A power "to make Treaties," granted in these indefinite terms, extends to all kinds of treaties and with all the latitude which such a power under any form of Government can possess. . . . With regard to the objects of the Treaty, there being no specification, there is of course a *charte blanche*. The general proposition must therefore be that whatever is a proper subject of compact between Nation & Nation may be embraced by a Treaty. . . .[49]

For Hamilton, the breadth of the Supremacy Clause was meant to ensure that the federal government did not have to rely on the states to pursue and secure compliance with U.S. treaty obligations.

Hamilton's position prevailed. After receiving the consent of the Senate, President Washington ratified the Jay Treaty, and even the House of Representatives voted to support it. Thereafter, a case came before the Supreme Court addressing the effect of the treaty on states' rights. In *Fairfax Devisee v. Hunter's Lessee*, the Supreme Court (per Justice Story) upheld application of the Jay Treaty notwithstanding Virginia state law, finding that Article IX, "being the supreme law of the land, confirmed the title to [a British subject, Denny Martin Fairfax], his heirs and assigns, and protected him from any forfeiture by reason of alienage."[50]

Jefferson's Manual. Nevertheless, states-rights advocates continued to lament the scope of the treaty power. After his Democratic-Republicans

---

48 *See* Robert Livingston, CATO No. XVI, *reprinted in* 3 *American Remembrancer* 63 (Mathew Carey ed., 1795).

49 Alexander Hamilton, *The Defence* No. XXXVI (Jan. 2, 1796), *reprinted in* 20 *The Papers of Alexander Hamilton* 3, 6 (Harold C. Syrett ed., 1974).

50 11 U.S. (7 Cranch) 603 (1812). Interestingly, one of the lawyers involved in this protracted litigation in support of Fairfax's title was none other than John Marshall, who became Chief Justice by the time of *Fairfax Devisee* and therefore did not sit in the case.

experienced considerable losses in the election of 1796 to the Federalists, Thomas Jefferson—serving as Vice President and presiding officer in the Senate—wrote a *Manual of Parliamentary Practice*. Published just prior to his ascent to the presidency in 1801, the *Manual* states in part:

> By the Constitution of the United States, this department of legislation [*i.e.*, treaty-making] is confined to two branches only of the ordinary Legislature—the President originating, and the Senate having a negative. To what subject this power extends, has not been defined in detail by the Constitution; nor are we entirely agreed among ourselves. 1. It is admitted that it must concern the foreign nation, party to the contract, or it would be a mere nullity, *res inter alias acta*. 2. By the general power to make treaties, the Constitution must have intended to comprehend only those objects which are usually regulated by treaty, and cannot be otherwise regulated. 3. It must have meant to except out of these the rights reserved to the States; for surely the President and Senate cannot do by treaty what the whole government is interdicted from doing in any way. 4. And also to except those subjects of legislation in which it gave a participation to the House of Representatives. This last exception is denied by some, on the ground that it would leave very little matter for the treaty power to work on. The less the better, say others.[51]

Does Jefferson's *Manual* evoke the same arguments as that of the earlier Cato? As Jefferson anticipates, if treaties may not address subjects within the scope of Congress's power or outside the scope of the federal government as a whole, then what is left of the treaty power?

After becoming president, Jefferson's views were put the test, when his administration used the Louisiana Purchase to acquire vast new territory and to incorporate its inhabitants into the United States, despite misgivings as to whether the treaty power permitted the U.S. government to accomplish a task not enumerated in Article I.[52]

---

[51] Thomas Jefferson, *A Manual of Parliamentary Practice* § 52 (1801), *reprinted in* 2 *The Writings of Thomas Jefferson* 335, 442 (Albert Ellery Bergh ed., 1904).

[52] Jefferson wrote to Secretary of State James Madison: "I infer that the less we say about constitutional difficulties respecting Louisiana the better, and that what is necessary for surmounting them must be done sub silentio." IV Dumas Malone, *Jefferson and His Time [Jefferson the President: First Term, 1801–1805]*, at 316 (1970); *see also* Robert Knowles, *The Balance of Forces and the Empire of Liberty: States' Rights and the Louisiana Purchase*, 88 IOWA L. REV. 343 (2003). The Supreme Court later expressed the view that territory could indeed be acquired by treaty (or by conquest). *American Ins. Co. v. Canter*, 26 U.S. (1 Pet.) 511, 542 (1828).

SANTOVINCENZO V. EGAN

284 U.S. 30 (1931).

[An 1878 U.S.-Italy consular convention provided that when an Italian national died intestate in the United States, the proceeds would be paid to the Italian Consul for distribution in accordance with Italian law (and vice versa for U.S. nationals in Italy). By contrast, New York law provided that the proceeds would escheat to the state. Upon the death intestate of an Italian national, the Italy's Consul General in New York sought the proceeds, but New York's Attorney General contested the claim. The U.S. Supreme Court found for the Consul General. In doing so, the Court discussed the scope of the treaty power.]

There can be no question as to the power of the Government of the United States to make the Treaty. . . . The treaty-making power is broad enough to cover all subjects that properly pertain to our foreign relations, and agreement with respect to the rights and privileges of citizens of the United States in foreign countries, and of the nationals of such countries within the United States, and the disposition of the property of aliens dying within the territory of the respective parties, is within the scope of the power, and any conflicting law of the State must yield. . . .

NOTES: ARE THERE LIMITS TO THE SCOPE OF THE TREATY POWER?

1. *The Persistent Question of Scope Limitations.* Founding era questions regarding the scope of the treaty power had not receded by the time of *Santovincenzo v. Egan*, nor have they since. One kind of limit, sometimes described as a "subject-matter" limit on treaties, relates to the international subject of a treaty. For example, Charles Evan Hughes, at the time a judge on the Permanent Court of International Justice, suggested that treaties must relate to matters of "international concern." Charles Evan Hughes, *Remarks on the Limitation of the Treaty-Making Power of the United States in Matters Coming Within the Jurisdiction of the States* (Apr. 26, 1929), 23 AM. SOC'Y INT'L L. PROC. 194, 194 (1929)). The Supreme Court has also suggested, in dicta, that treaties are limited to "all subjects that properly pertain to our foreign relations" (per *Santovincenzo*), those "properly the subject of negotiation with a foreign country" (*Geofroy v. Riggs*, 133 U.S. 258, 267 (1890)), or "all those objects which in the intercourse of nations had usually been regarded as the proper subjects of negotiation and treaty" (*Holden v. Joy*, 84 U.S. (17 Wall.) 211, 243 (1872)). Are these inquiries the same?

A second, related limit, urged by a number of commentators, suggests that a pretextual agreement, such as a "mock-marriage" designed to enhance the national government's domestic authority, would not fall within the treaty power. Louis Henkin, *Foreign Affairs and the United States Constitution* 185 (2d ed. 1996). The third proposed limit revolves around Article I, and suggests that the treaty power is limited to matters that could be subject to congressional legislation—respecting, accordingly, powers reserved to the states.

These limits appear to present nearly perennial questions. At the dawn of the twentieth century, for example, scholars disagreed vigorously concerning limits on the scope of the treaty power. *See, e.g.*, Edward S. Corwin, *National Supremacy: Treaty Power vs. State Power* (1913); Chandler P. Anderson, *The Extent and Limitations of the Treaty-Making Power Under the Constitution*, 1 AM. J. INT'L L. 636 (1907); William E. Mikell, *The Extent of the Treaty-Making Power of the President and Senate of the United States* (pts. 1 & 2), 57 U. PA. L. REV. 435, 528 (1909). The American Law Institute's Restatements have wavered as to whether there was an "international concern" limit. *Compare Restatement of the Law (Second), The Foreign Relations Law of the United States* § 117 (1965) (suggesting "international concern" limitation); 1 *Restatement of the Law (Third), The Foreign Relations Law of the United States* § 302 comment c (1987) (rejecting limitation); *Restatement of the Law (Fourth), The Foreign Relations Law of the United States: Treaties* § 112 reporters' notes 4, 8 (Tentative Draft No. 2, 2017) (declining to take position on existence of subject-matter limitations, giving lack of authority for a definitive position). And the possibility of Article I limits was recently revived. *See* Curtis A. Bradley, *The Treaty Power and American Federalism*, 97 MICH. L. REV. 390 (1998); Curtis Bradley, *The Treaty Power and American Federalism, Part II*, 99 MICH. L. REV. 98 (2000); David M. Golove, *Treaty-Making and the Nation: The Historical Foundations of the Nationalist Conception of the Treaty Power*, 98 MICH. L. REV. 1075, 1276 (2000). For a survey and discussion, see, e.g., Oona A. Hathaway *et al.*, *The Treaty Power: Its History, Scope, and Limits*, 98 CORNELL L. REV. 239, 279–304 (2013).

2. *U.S. Treaty Practice.* In *Santovincenzo*, a New York inheritance statute fell in the face of a consular treaty. Modern bilateral and multilateral treaties frequently address subjects that had once been the preserve of state regulation, sometimes in conjunction with federal implementing legislation. Consider the following:

- Numerous treaties grant foreign nationals the right to practice certain professions or provide certain services in the United States (and grant U.S. nationals reciprocal rights abroad), even though the professions or services are otherwise regulated by the several states. *See, e.g.*, Treaty of Friendship, Commerce and Consular Rights, U.S.-Hond., art. I, Dec. 7, 1927, T.S. No. 764, 87 L.N.T.S. 421; Treaty of Friendship, Commerce and Navigation, U.S.-Italy, art. I, Feb. 2, 1948, T.I.A.S. No. 1965, 79 U.N.T.S. 171; North American Free Trade Agreement, U.S.-Can.-Mex., chs. 12 (cross-border trade in services) & 14 (financial services), Dec. 17, 1992, 32 I.L.M. 289 & 605 (1993).

- Various treaties accord privileges and immunities to foreign nationals, such as exemption from state criminal prosecution or state taxes. *See, e.g.*, Treaty of Friendship, Commerce and

Consular Rights, U.S.-Austria, art. XV, June 19, 1928, T.S. No. 838, 118 L.N.T.S. 241; Vienna Convention on Diplomatic Relations, Apr. 18, 1961, 23 U.S.T. 3227, 500 U.N.T.S. 95.

- Several treaties regulate areas of "private international law," which deals with both private business and family-relations matters. For example, the Convention on the Recognition and Enforcement of Foreign Arbitral Awards, done at New York June 10, 1958, 21 U.S.T. 2517, 330 U.N.T.S. 38, obligates U.S. courts (with limited exceptions) to enforce certain contracts that provide for the submission of disputes to arbitration and enforcement of the arbitral award once rendered, regardless of conflicting state laws.
- Various treaties require the enactment of U.S. criminal statutes on issues such as narcotics, terrorism, or organized crime, which in turn preempt state law. *See, e.g.*, United Nations Convention Against the Illicit Traffic in Narcotic Drugs and Psychotropic Substances, Dec. 20, 1988, S. TREATY DOC. NO. 101–4 (1989), 1582 U.N.T.S. 95.

Are there ways the political branches might craft U.S. treaty obligations to avoid intruding upon core state functions? Consider the following reservation by the United States upon ratifying the U.N. Convention Against Transnational Organized Crime, United Nations Convention against Transnational Organized Crime (TOC Convention), Nov. 15, 2000, S. TREATY DOC. NO. 108–16 (2003):

> The United States of America reserves the right to assume obligations under the Convention in a manner consistent with its fundamental principles of federalism . . . Federal criminal law does not apply in the rare case where such criminal conduct does not so involve interstate or foreign commerce, or another federal interest. There are a small number of conceivable situations involving such rare offenses of a purely local character where U.S. federal and state criminal law may not be entirely adequate to satisfy an obligation under the Convention. The United States of America therefore reserves to the obligations set forth in the Convention to the extent they address conduct which would fall within this narrow category of highly localized activity . . .

available at https://treaties.un.org/pages/ViewDetails.aspx?src=TREATY&mtdsg_no=XVIII-12&chapter=18&clang=_en, [https://perma.cc/TPW7-DRJX]. Is this the way to embrace treaties while being sensitive to issues of federalism?

3. *Judicial Solutions*. While the Supreme Court has sometimes suggested standards for limiting the scope of the treaty power, they have never been used to limit it, even in cases posing federalism challenges. In *Missouri v. Holland*, excerpted later in this Section, the Court concluded with little

difficulty that the treaty in question was valid, as did the Court in *Bond v. United States*, also considered below. Justice Thomas's concurring opinion in *Bond*, joined in relevant part by Justices Scalia and Alito, discussed the question in detail. There, he distinguished between using treaties to "arrange intercourse with other nations," on the one hand, and those "regulat[ing] purely domestic affairs," on the other—arguing that dispensing with subject-matter limits, so as to permit addressing "matters without any nexus to foreign relations," would "destroy the basic constitutional distinction between domestic and foreign powers" and thus give the federal government a virtual "police power" over every aspect of life. 134 S. Ct. 2077, 2103 (2014) (Thomas, J., concurring in the judgment) (internal citations and quotations omitted).

Justice Thomas addressed the issue even though, as he acknowledged, the parties had not addressed issues of treaty scope or validity, and even though he appeared to agree that the treaty in question (the Chemical Weapons Convention) would not run afoul of his standard—given the possibility that a more appropriate case would come before the Court. *Id.* at 2103, 2110. He closed by suggesting that "[g]iven the increasing frequency with which treaties have begun to test the limits of the Treaty Power . . . that chance will come soon enough." *Id.* at 2111. Do you agree with that prediction?

NOTE ON THE HIERARCHICAL STATUS OF TREATIES IN U.S. LAW

Potential limits on the substantive scope of treaties are a threshold issue but not, as we have seen, easily applied. Two separate issues may be distinguished. The first concerns how to reconcile self-executing treaties with other U.S. law. (As noted *supra*, this Chapter, Sec. 4, perceived constitutional limitations may also influence the judgment as to whether a treaty provision is self-executing in the first place.) A second question arises when treaties are *not* self-executing: how does entering into a valid treaty affect the scope of domestic authority to implement it?

As you read the following materials, consider the following possibilities:

- Treaties are of an equivalent legal status to the U.S. Constitution. The Supremacy Clause in Article VI says that three things are "the supreme law of the Land": (1) the Constitution; (2) laws "made in Pursuance" of the Constitution; and (3) treaties made "under the Authority of the United States." This means that while laws enacted by Congress must conform to the Constitution, treaties need not, so long as they are made in accordance with Article II or otherwise properly authorized.

- Treaties are equivalent in legal status to a federal statute. A treaty that is inconsistent with the Constitution is invalid as a matter of U.S. law. A constitutionally valid treaty can repeal a pre-existing conflicting statute, and will always supersede conflicting federal common law or state law.

- Treaties are inferior to the Constitution and to federal statutes, since the latter—by involving both houses of Congress—are a more democratic form of legislation. Thus, a treaty does not repeal a conflicting pre-existing statute, even if it superior to inconsistent federal common law or state law.
- Treaties, even if non-self-executing, provide a basis for the exercise of federal legislative authority under the Necessary and Proper Clause. Treaty implementation is not, accordingly, limited by the need to identify another basis for federal authority, such as would be required in a purely domestic context.
- Treaties, when non-self-executing, cannot be understood to expand congressional authority, since that would in effect augment Article I, misconstrue the Necessary and Proper Clause, and violate the Tenth Amendment.

Which of these possibilities, if any, seem plausible to you?

MISSOURI V. HOLLAND

252 U.S. 416, 430–35 (1920).

MR. JUSTICE HOLMES delivered the opinion of the Court.

This is a bill in equity brought by the State of Missouri to prevent a game warden of the United States from attempting to enforce the Migratory Bird Treaty Act of July 3, 1918, c. 128, 40 Stat. 755, and the regulations made by the Secretary of Agriculture in pursuance of the same. The ground of the bill is that the statute is an unconstitutional interference with the rights reserved to the States by the Tenth Amendment, and that the acts of the defendant done and threatened under that authority invade the sovereign right of the State and contravene its will manifested in statutes. The State also alleges a pecuniary interest, as owner of the wild birds within its borders and otherwise. . . . A motion to dismiss was sustained by the District Court on the ground that the Act of Congress is constitutional. . . . The State appeals.

On December 8, 1916, a treaty between the United States and Great Britain was proclaimed by the President. It recited that many species of birds in their annual migrations traversed many parts of the United States and of Canada, that they were of great value as a source of food and in destroying insects injurious to vegetation, but were in danger of extermination through lack of adequate protection. It therefore provided for specified close[d] seasons and protection in other forms, and agreed that the two powers would take or propose to their law-making bodies the necessary measures for carrying the treaty out. 39 Stat. 1702. The above mentioned act of July 3, 1918, . . . [gave] effect to the convention, prohibited the killing, capturing or selling any of the migratory birds included in the terms of the treaty except as permitted by regulations compatible with those terms, to be made by the Secretary of Agriculture. Regulations were proclaimed on July 31, and October 25, 1918. 40 Stat. 1812, 1863. It is unnecessary to go into any details, because, as we have said, the question raised is the general one whether the treaty and statute are void as an interference with the rights reserved to the States.

To answer this question it is not enough to refer to the Tenth Amendment, reserving the powers not delegated to the United States, because by Article II, § 2, the power to make treaties is delegated expressly [to the federal government], and by Article VI treaties made under the authority of the United States, along with the Constitution and laws of the United States made in pursuance thereof, are declared the supreme law of the land. If the treaty is valid there can be no dispute about the validity of the statute under Article I, § 8, as a necessary and proper means to execute the powers of the Government. The language of the Constitution as to the supremacy of treaties being general, the question before us is narrowed to an inquiry into the ground upon which the present supposed exception is placed.

It is said that a treaty cannot be valid if it infringes the Constitution, that there are limits, therefore, to the treaty-making power, and that one such limit is that what an act of Congress could not do unaided, in derogation of the powers reserved to the States, a treaty cannot do. An earlier [1913] act of Congress that attempted by itself and not in pursuance of a treaty to regulate the killing of migratory birds within the States had been held bad in the District Court. *United States v. Shauver*, 214 Fed. Rep. 154. *United States v. McCullagh*, 221 Fed. Rep. 288. Those decisions were supported by arguments that migratory birds were owned by the States in their sovereign capacity for the benefit of their people, and that under cases like *Geer v. Connecticut*, 161 U.S. 519, this control was one that Congress had no power to displace. The same argument is supposed to apply now with equal force.

Whether the two cases cited were decided rightly or not they cannot be accepted as a test of the treaty power. Acts of Congress are the supreme law of the land only when made in pursuance of the Constitution, while treaties are declared to be so when made under the authority of the United States. It is open to question whether the authority of the United States means more than the formal acts prescribed to make the convention. We do not mean to imply that there are no qualifications to the treaty-making power; but they must be ascertained in a different way. It is obvious that there may be matters of the sharpest exigency for the national well being that an act of Congress could not deal with but that a treaty followed by such an act could, and it is not lightly to be assumed that, in matters requiring national action, "a power which must belong to and somewhere reside in every civilized government" is not to be found. *Andrews v.*

Andrews, 188 U.S. 14, 33. What was said in that case with regard to the powers of the States applies with equal force to the powers of the nation in cases where the States individually are incompetent to act. We are not yet discussing the particular case before us but only are considering the validity of the test proposed. With regard to that we may add that when we are dealing with words that also are a constituent act, like the Constitution of the United States, we must realize that they have called into life a being the development of which could not have been foreseen completely by the most gifted of its begetters. It was enough for them to realize or to hope that they had created an organism; it has taken a century and has cost their successors much sweat and blood to prove that they created a nation. The case before us must be considered in the light of our whole experience and not merely in that of what was said a hundred years ago. The treaty in question does not contravene any prohibitory words to be found in the Constitution. The only question is whether it is forbidden by some invisible radiation from the general terms of the Tenth Amendment. We must consider what this country has become in deciding what that Amendment has reserved.

The State as we have intimated founds its claim of exclusive authority upon an assertion of title to migratory birds, an assertion that is embodied in statute. No doubt it is true that as between a State and its inhabitants the State may regulate the killing and sale of such birds, but it does not follow that its authority is exclusive of paramount powers. To put the claim of the State upon title is to lean upon a slender reed. Wild birds are not in the possession of anyone; and possession is the beginning of ownership. The whole foundation of the State's rights is the presence within their jurisdiction of birds that yesterday had not arrived, tomorrow may be in another State and in a week a thousand miles away. If we are to be accurate we cannot put the case of the State upon higher ground than that the treaty deals with creatures that for the moment are within the state borders, that it must be carried out by officers of the United States within the same territory, and that but for the treaty the State would be free to regulate this subject itself.

As most of the laws of the United States are carried out within the States and as many of them deal with matters which in the silence of such laws the State might regulate, such general grounds are not enough to support Missouri's claim. Valid treaties of course "are as binding within the territorial limits of the States as they are elsewhere throughout the dominion of the United States." *Baldwin v. Franks*, 120 U.S. 678, 683. No doubt the great body of private relations usually fall within the control of the State, but a treaty may override its power. We do not have to invoke the later developments of constitutional law for this proposition; it was recognized as early as *Hopkirk v. Bell*, 3 Cranch, 454, with regard to statutes of limitation, and even earlier, as to confiscation, in *Ware v.*

Hylton, 3 Dall. 199. It was assumed by Chief Justice Marshall with regard to the escheat of land to the State in *Chirac v. Chirac*, 2 Wheat. 259, 275; *Hauenstein v. Lynham*, 100 U.S. 483; *De Geofroy v. Riggs*, 133 U.S. 258; *Blythe v. Hinckley*, 180 U.S. 333, 340. So as to a limited jurisdiction of foreign consuls within a State. *Wildenhus' Case*, 120 U.S. 1. *See Ross v. McIntyre*, 140 U.S. 453. Further illustration seems unnecessary, and it only remains to consider the application of established rules to the present case.

Here a national interest of very nearly the first magnitude is involved. It can be protected only by national action in concert with that of another power. The subject-matter is only transitorily within the State and has no permanent habitat therein. But for the treaty and the statute there soon might be no birds for any powers to deal with. We see nothing in the Constitution that compels the Government to sit by while a food supply is cut off and the protectors of our forests and our crops are destroyed. It is not sufficient to rely upon the States. The reliance is vain, and were it otherwise, the question is whether the United States is forbidden to act. We are of opinion that the treaty and statute must be upheld. . . .

Decree affirmed.

REID V. COVERT

354 U.S. 1, 3–19 (1957).

[Two spouses of U.S. soldiers, one in the United Kingdom (Clarice Covert) and one in Japan (Dorothy Smith), murdered their husbands. The United States was accorded jurisdiction over the spouses pursuant to bilateral agreements: Executive Agreement, U.S.-U.K., July 27, 1942, 57 Stat. 1193; Administrative Agreement, U.S.-Japan, Feb. 28, 1952, T.I.A.S. 2492, 3 U.S.T. 3341. Although the spouses were not members of the U.S. armed services, they were tried and convicted by court martial under the Uniform Code of Military Justice (UCMJ), which, among other things, did not provide for an indictment by a grand jury or a trial by jury. The spouses challenged the convictions as violating their rights under Article III, Section 2 and the Fifth and Sixth Amendments of the U.S. Constitution.]

MR. JUSTICE BLACK announced the judgment of the Court and delivered an opinion, in which THE CHIEF JUSTICE, MR. JUSTICE DOUGLAS, and MR. JUSTICE BRENNAN join.

These cases raise basic constitutional issues of the utmost concern. They call into question the role of the military under our system of government. They involve the power of Congress to expose civilians to trial by military tribunals, under military regulations and procedures, for offenses against the United States thereby depriving them of trial in civilian courts, under civilian laws and procedures and with all the safeguards of the Bill of Rights. . . .

At the beginning we reject the idea that when the United States acts against citizens abroad it can do so free of the Bill of Rights. The United States is entirely a creature of the Constitution. Its power and authority have no other source. It can only act in accordance with all the limitations imposed by the Constitution. When the Government reaches out to punish a citizen who is abroad, the shield which the Bill of Rights and other parts of the Constitution provide to protect his life and liberty should not be stripped away just because he happens to be in another land. . . .

At the time of Mrs. Covert's alleged offense, an executive agreement was in effect between the United States and Great Britain which permitted United States' military courts to exercise exclusive jurisdiction over offenses committed in Great Britain by American servicemen or their dependents. For its part, the United States agreed that these military courts would be willing and able to try and to punish all offenses against the laws of Great Britain by such persons. In all material respects, the same situation existed in Japan when Mrs. Smith killed her husband. Even though a court-martial does not give an accused trial by jury and other Bill of Rights protections, the Government contends that Art. 2 (11) of the UCMJ, insofar as it provides for the military trial of dependents accompanying the armed forces in Great Britain and Japan, can be sustained as legislation which is necessary and proper to carry out the United States' obligations under the international agreements made with those countries. The obvious and decisive answer to this, of course, is that no agreement with a foreign nation can confer power on the Congress, or on any other branch of Government, which is free from the restraints of the Constitution.

Article VI, the Supremacy Clause of the Constitution, declares:

> "This Constitution, and the Laws of the United States which shall be made in Pursuance thereof; and all Treaties made, or which shall be made, under the Authority of the United States, shall be the supreme Law of the Land; . . ."

There is nothing in this language which intimates that treaties and laws enacted pursuant to them do not have to comply with the provisions of the Constitution. Nor is there anything in the debates which accompanied the drafting and ratification of the Constitution which even suggests such a result. These debates as well as the history that surrounds the adoption of the treaty provision in Article VI make it clear that the reason treaties were not limited to those made in "pursuance" of the Constitution was so that agreements made by the United States under the Articles of Confederation, including the important peace treaties which concluded the Revolutionary War, would remain in effect. It would be manifestly contrary to the objectives of those who created the Constitution, as well as those who were responsible for the Bill of Rights—let alone alien to our entire constitutional history and tradition—to construe Article VI as permitting the United States to exercise power under an international agreement without observing constitutional prohibitions. In effect, such construction would permit amendment of that document in a manner not sanctioned by Article V. The prohibitions of the Constitution were designed to apply to all branches of the National Government and they cannot be nullified by the Executive or by the Executive and the Senate combined. . . .

There is nothing in *Missouri v. Holland*, 252 U.S. 416, which is contrary to the position taken here. There the Court carefully noted that the treaty involved was not inconsistent with any specific provision of the Constitution. The Court was concerned with the Tenth Amendment which reserves to the States or the people all power not delegated to the National Government. To the extent that the United States can validly make treaties, the people and the States have delegated their power to the National Government and the Tenth Amendment is no barrier.

In summary, we conclude that the Constitution in its entirety applied to the trials of Mrs. Smith and Mrs. Covert. . . . [The plurality decision further found that the Necessary and Proper Clause of Article 1, Section 8, could not be stretched to validate military jurisdiction over a person not a member of the class described in Clause 14, *i.e.*, "land and naval Forces."]

BOND V. UNITED STATES

134 S.Ct. 2077 (2014).

CHIEF JUSTICE ROBERTS delivered the opinion of the Court. . . .

I

A

In 1997, the President of the United States, upon the advice and consent of the Senate, ratified the Convention on the Prohibition of the Development, Production, Stockpiling, and Use of Chemical Weapons and on Their Destruction, S. Treaty Doc. No. 103–21, 1974 U.N.T.S. 317. . . .

Although the Convention is a binding international agreement, it is "not self-executing." W. Krutzsch & R. Trapp, A Commentary on the Chemical Weapons Convention 109 (1994). . . . It instead provides that "[e]ach State Party shall, in accordance with its constitutional processes, adopt the necessary measures to implement its obligations under this Convention." Art. VII(1), 1974 U.N.T.S. 331. "In particular," each State Party shall "[p]rohibit natural and legal persons anywhere . . . under its jurisdiction . . . from undertaking any activity prohibited to a State Party under this Convention, including enacting penal legislation with respect to such activity." Art. VII(1)(a), *id.*, at 331–332.

Congress gave the Convention domestic effect in 1998 when it passed the Chemical Weapons Convention Implementation Act. See 112 Stat. 2681–856. The Act closely tracks the text of the treaty: It forbids any person knowingly "to develop, produce, otherwise acquire, transfer directly or indirectly, receive, stockpile, retain, own, possess, or use, or threaten to use, any chemical weapon." 18 U.S.C. § 229(a)(1). It defines "chemical weapon" in relevant part as "[a] toxic chemical and its precursors, except where intended for a purpose not prohibited under this chapter as long as the type and quantity is consistent with such a purpose." § 229F(1)(A). "Toxic chemical," in turn, is defined in general as "any chemical which through its chemical action on life processes can cause death, temporary incapacitation or permanent harm to humans or animals. The term includes all such chemicals, regardless of their origin or of their method of production, and regardless of whether they are produced in facilities, in munitions or elsewhere." § 229F(8)(A). Finally, "purposes not prohibited by this chapter" is defined as "[a]ny peaceful purpose related to an industrial, agricultural, research, medical, or pharmaceutical activity or other activity," and other specific purposes. § 229F(7). A person who violates section 229 may be subject to severe punishment: imprisonment "for any term of years," or if a victim's death results, the death penalty or imprisonment "for life." § 229A(a).

B

Petitioner Carol Anne Bond is a microbiologist from Lansdale, Pennsylvania. In 2006, Bond's closest friend, Myrlinda Haynes, announced that she was pregnant. When Bond discovered that her husband was the child's father, she sought revenge against Haynes. Bond stole a quantity of 10-chloro-10H-phenoxarsine (an arsenic-based compound) from her employer, a chemical manufacturer. She also ordered a vial of potassium dichromate (a chemical commonly used in printing photographs or cleaning laboratory equipment) on Amazon.com. Both chemicals are toxic to humans and, in high enough doses, potentially lethal. It is undisputed, however, that Bond did not intend to kill Haynes. She instead hoped that Haynes would touch the chemicals and develop an uncomfortable rash.

Between November 2006 and June 2007, Bond went to Haynes's home on at least 24 occasions and spread the chemicals on her car door, mailbox, and door knob. These attempted assaults were almost entirely unsuccessful. . . . Haynes repeatedly called the local police to report the suspicious substances, but they took no action. When Haynes found powder on her mailbox, she called the police again, who told her to call the post office. Haynes did so, and postal inspectors placed surveillance cameras around her home. The cameras caught Bond opening Haynes's mailbox, stealing an envelope, and stuffing potassium dichromate inside the muffler of Haynes's car.

Federal prosecutors naturally charged Bond with two counts of mail theft, in violation of 18 U.S.C. § 1708. More surprising, they also charged her with two counts of possessing and using a chemical weapon, in violation of section 229(a). . . . The District Court sentenced Bond to six years in federal prison plus five years of supervised release, and ordered her to pay a $2,000 fine and $9,902.79 in restitution. . . .

II

. . . The Federal Government . . . "can exercise only the powers granted to it," McCulloch v. Maryland, 17 U.S. (4 Wheat.) 316, 405 (1819), including the power to make "all Laws which shall be necessary and proper for carrying into Execution" the enumerated powers, U.S. Const., Art. I, § 8, cl. 18. For nearly two centuries it has been "clear" that, lacking a police power, "Congress cannot punish felonies generally." Cohens v. Virginia, 19 U.S. 264 (6 Wheat.) 428 (1821). A criminal act committed wholly within a State "cannot be made an offence against the United States, unless it have some relation to the execution of a power of Congress, or to some matter within the jurisdiction of the United States." United States v. Fox, 95 U.S. 670, 672 (1878).

The Government frequently defends federal criminal legislation on the ground that the legislation is authorized pursuant to Congress's power to regulate interstate commerce. In this case, however, the Court of Appeals held that the Government had explicitly disavowed that argument before the District Court. As a result, in this Court the parties have devoted significant effort to arguing whether section 229, as applied to Bond's offense, is a necessary and proper means of executing the National Government's power to make treaties. Bond argues that the lower court's reading of *Missouri* v. *Holland* would remove all limits on federal authority, so long as the Federal Government ratifies a treaty first. She insists that to effectively afford the Government a police power whenever it implements a treaty would be contrary to the Framers' careful decision to divide power between the States and the National Government as a means of preserving liberty. To the extent that *Holland* authorizes such usurpation of traditional state authority, Bond says, it must be either limited or overruled.

The Government replies that this Court has never held that a statute implementing a valid treaty exceeds Congress's enumerated powers. To do so here, the Government says, would contravene another deliberate choice of the Framers: to avoid placing subject matter limitations on the National Government's power to make treaties. And it might also undermine confidence in the United States as an international treaty partner.

Notwithstanding this debate, it is "a well-established principle governing the prudent exercise of this Court's jurisdiction that normally the Court will not decide a constitutional question if there is some other ground upon which to dispose of the case." . . . Bond argues that section 229 does not cover her conduct. So we consider that argument first.

III

Section 229 exists to implement the Convention . . . [T]he Convention's drafters intended for it to be a comprehensive ban on chemical weapons. But even with its broadly worded definitions, we have doubts that a treaty about *chemical weapons* has anything to do with Bond's conduct. The Convention, a product of years of worldwide study, analysis, and multinational negotiation, arose in response to war crimes and acts of terrorism. There is no reason to think the sovereign nations that ratified the Convention were interested in anything like Bond's common law assault.

Even if the treaty does reach that far, nothing prevents Congress from implementing the Convention in the same manner it legislates with respect to innumerable other matters—observing the Constitution's division of responsibility between sovereigns and leaving the prosecution of purely local crimes to the States. The Convention, after all, is agnostic between enforcement at the state versus federal level: It provides that "[e]ach State Party shall, *in accordance with its constitutional processes*, adopt the necessary measures to implement its obligations under this Convention." Art. VII(1) (emphasis added) . . .

Fortunately, we have no need to interpret the scope of the Convention in this case. Bond was prosecuted under section 229, and the statute—unlike the Convention—must be read consistent with principles of federalism inherent in our constitutional structure.

A

In the Government's view, the conclusion that Bond "knowingly" "use[d]" a "chemical weapon" in violation of section 229(a) is simple: The chemicals that Bond placed on Haynes's home and car are "toxic chemical[s]" as defined by the statute, and Bond's attempt to assault Haynes was not a "peaceful purpose." The problem with this interpretation is that it would "dramatically intrude[ ] upon traditional state criminal jurisdiction," and we avoid reading statutes to have such reach in the absence of a clear indication that they do. United States v. Bass, 404 U.S. 336, 350 (1971). . . .

[Our] precedents make clear that it is appropriate to refer to basic principles of federalism embodied in the Constitution to resolve ambiguity in a federal statute. In this case, the ambiguity derives from the improbably broad reach of the key statutory definition given the term—"chemical weapon"—being defined; the deeply serious consequences of adopting such a boundless reading; and the lack of any apparent need to do so in light of the context from which the statute arose—a treaty about chemical warfare and terrorism. We conclude that, in this curious case, we can insist on a clear indication that Congress meant to reach purely local crimes, before interpreting the statute's expansive language in a way that intrudes on the police power of the States. . . .

B

. . . [A] fair reading of section 229 suggests that it does not have as expansive a scope as might at first appear. To begin, as a matter of natural meaning, an educated user of English would not describe Bond's crime as involving a "chemical weapon." Saying that a person "used a chemical weapon" conveys a very different idea than saying the person "used a chemical in a way that caused some harm." The natural meaning of "chemical weapon" takes account of both the particular chemicals that the defendant used and the circumstances in which she used them.

When used in the manner here, the chemicals in this case are not of the sort that an ordinary person would associate with instruments of chemical warfare. . . .

The Government would have us brush aside the ordinary meaning and adopt a reading of section 229 that would sweep in everything from the detergent under the kitchen sink to the stain remover in the laundry room. . . . Any parent would be guilty of a serious federal offense—possession of a chemical weapon—when, exasperated by the children's repeated failure to clean the goldfish tank, he considers poisoning the fish with a few drops of vinegar. We are reluctant to ignore the ordinary meaning of "chemical weapon" when doing so would transform a statute passed to implement the international Convention on Chemical Weapons into one that also makes it a federal offense to poison goldfish. . . .

This case is unusual, and our analysis is appropriately limited. Our disagreement with our colleagues reduces to whether section 229 is "utterly clear." . . . We think it is not. . . .

JUSTICE SCALIA, with whom JUSTICE THOMAS joins, and with whom JUSTICE ALITO joins as to Part I, concurring in the judgment. . . .

I. The Statutory Question

. . . Applying th[e] [Act's] provisions to this case is hardly complicated. Bond possessed and used "chemical[s] which through [their] chemical action on life processes can cause death, temporary incapacitation or permanent harm." Thus, she possessed "toxic chemicals." And, because they were not possessed or used only for a "purpose not prohibited," they were "chemical weapons." Ergo, Bond violated the Act. End of statutory analysis, I would have thought. . . .

I suspect the Act will not survive today's gruesome surgery. A criminal statute must clearly define the conduct it proscribes. If it does not " 'give a person of ordinary intelligence fair notice' " of its scope, United States v. Batchelder, 442 U.S. 114, 123 (1979), it denies due process. . . .

II. The Constitutional Question

Since the Act is clear, the *real* question this case presents is whether the Act is constitutional as applied to petitioner. An unreasoned and citation-less sentence from our opinion in Missouri v. Holland, 252 U.S. 416 (1920), purported to furnish the answer: "If the treaty is valid"—and no one argues that the Convention is not—"there can be no dispute about the validity of the statute under Article I, § 8, as a necessary and proper means to execute the powers of the Government." *Id.* at 432. Petitioner and her *amici* press us to consider whether there is anything to this *ipse dixit.* The Constitution's text and structure show that there is not.

A. Text

Under Article I, § 8, cl. 18, Congress has the power "[t]o make all Laws which shall be necessary and proper for carrying into Execution the foregoing Powers and all other Powers vested by this Constitution in the Government of the United States, or in any Department or Officer thereof." One such "other Powe[r]" appears in Article II, § 2, cl. 2: "[The President] shall have Power, by and with the Advice and Consent of the Senate, to make Treaties, provided two thirds of the Senators present concur." Read together, the two Clauses empower Congress to pass laws "necessary and proper for carrying into Execution . . . [the] Power . . . to make Treaties."

It is obvious what the Clauses, read together, do not say. They do not authorize Congress to enact laws for carrying into execution "Treaties," even treaties that do not execute themselves, such as the Chemical Weapons Convention. Surely it makes sense, the Government contends, that Congress would have the power to carry out the obligations to which the President and the Senate have committed the Nation. The power to "carry into Execution" the "Power . . . to make Treaties," it insists, has to mean the power to execute the treaties themselves.

That argument, which makes no pretense of resting on text, unsurprisingly misconstrues it. Start with the phrase "to make Treaties." . . . Upon the President's agreement and the Senate's ratification, a treaty—no matter what kind—has been made and is not susceptible of any more making.

How might Congress have helped "carr[y]" the power to make the treaty—here, the Chemical Weapons Convention—"into Execution"? In any number of ways. It could have appropriated money for hiring treaty negotiators, empowered the Department of State to appoint those negotiators, formed a commission to study the benefits and risks of entering into the agreement, or paid for a bevy of spies to monitor the treaty-related deliberations of other potential signatories. . . .

But a power to help the President make treaties is not a power to implement treaties already made. See generally Nicholas Quinn Rosenkranz, Executing the Treaty Power, 118 Harv. L. Rev. 1867 (2005). Once a treaty has been made, Congress's power to do what is "necessary and proper" to assist the making of treaties drops out of the picture. To legislate compliance with the United States' treaty obligations, Congress must rely upon its independent (though quite robust) Article I, § 8, powers.

B. Structure

. . . Though *Holland*'s change to the Constitution's text appears minor (the power to carry into execution the *power to make treaties* becomes the power to carry into execution *treaties*), the change to its structure is seismic.

To see why vast expansion of congressional power is not just a remote possibility, consider two features of the modern practice of treaty making. . . . [B]eginning in the last half of the last century, many treaties were "detailed multilateral instruments negotiated and drafted at international conferences," *ibid.*, and they sought to regulate states' treatment of their own citizens, or even "the activities of individuals and private entities," Abram Chayes & Antonia Chandler Chayes, The New Sovereignty: Compliance with International Regulatory Agreements 14 (1995). "[O]ften vague and open-ended," such treaties "touch on almost every aspect of domestic civil, political, and cultural life." Curtis A. Bradley & Jack L. Goldsmith, *Treaties, Human Rights, and Conditional Consent*, 149 U. Pa. L. Rev. 399, 400 (2000).

Consider also that, at least according to some scholars, the Treaty Clause comes with no implied subject-matter limitations. On this view, "[t]he Tenth Amendment . . . does not limit the power to make treaties or other agreements," Restatement (Third) of Foreign Relations Law of the United States § 302, Comment *d*, p. 154 (1986), and the treaty power can be used to regulate matters of strictly domestic concern.

If that is true, then the possibilities of what the Federal Government may accomplish, with the right treaty in hand, are endless and hardly farfetched. It could begin, as some scholars have suggested, with abrogation of this Court's constitutional rulings. For example, the holding that a statute prohibiting the carrying of firearms near schools went beyond Congress's enumerated powers, *United States v. Lopez*, 514 U.S. 549, 551 (1995), could be reversed by negotiating a treaty with Latvia providing that neither sovereign would permit the carrying of guns near schools. . . .

The Government raises a functionalist objection: If the Constitution does not limit a *self-executing treaty* to the subject matter delineated in Article I, § 8, then it makes no sense to impose that limitation upon a statute implementing a *non-self-executing treaty*. The premise of the objection (that the power to make self-executing treaties is limitless) is, to say the least, arguable. But even if it is correct, refusing to extend that proposition to non-self-executing treaties makes a great deal of sense. Suppose, for example, that the self-aggrandizing Federal Government wishes to take over the law of intestacy. If the President and the Senate find in some foreign state a ready accomplice, they have two options. First, they can enter into a treaty with "stipulations" specific enough that they "require no legislation to make them operative," *Whitney v. Robertson*, 124 U.S. 190, 194 (1888), which would mean in this example something like a comprehensive probate code. But for that to succeed, the President and a supermajority of the Senate would need to reach agreement on all the details—which, when once embodied in the treaty, could not be altered or superseded by ordinary legislation. The second option—far the better one—is for Congress to gain lasting and flexible control over the law of intestacy by means of a non-self-executing treaty. "[Implementing] legislation is as much subject to modification and repeal by Congress as legislation upon any other subject." *Ibid.* And to make such a treaty, the President and Senate would need to agree only that they desire power over the law of intestacy. . . .

We have here a supposedly "narrow" opinion which, in order to be "narrow," sets forth interpretive principles never before imagined that will bedevil our jurisprudence (and proliferate litigation) for years to come. . . .

NOTES

1. *The Bricker Amendment.* In the early 1950s, a conservative Ohio Republican, Senator John W. Bricker, sponsored an amendment to the Constitution designed to counter *Missouri v. Holland* and prevent what he and others perceived as dangers posed by multilateral treaties. Various version of the amendment were considered, but among the various proposals were commitments that (1) treaties conflicting with the Constitution would lack force or effect; (2) treaties could become effective as U.S. law only through legislation which would be valid in the absence of treaty; and (3) all executive and other agreements with foreign powers or international organizations would be subject to the same limitations as treaties and subject as well to congressional control. *See* S. Rep. No. 412, at 1 (1953) (version adopted by Judiciary Committee); *see also* S.J. Res. 1, 83d Cong. (1953) (revised proposal from Sen. Bricker); S.J. Res. 43, 83d Cong. (1953) (proposal by Sen. Watkins). Among the concerns were a loss of individual rights, states' rights, world government and the loss of U.S. sovereignty, and communist influence—and domestic issues relating to these themes, like the possible collision between

states' rights and support for civil rights derived from the U.N. Charter and future human rights treaties. *See* Natalie Hevener Kaufman, *Human Rights Treaties and the Senate* 106 (1990); Duane Tananbaum, *The Bricker Amendment Controversy: A Test of Eisenhower's Political Leadership* (1988); for focus on the civil rights issue, in particular, see Carol Anderson, *Eyes off the Prize: The United Nations and the African American Struggle for Human Rights*, 1944–1955 (2003).

The final version submitted for a floor vote in February 1954 read:

> Section 1. A provision of a treaty or other international agreement which conflicts with this Constitution shall not be of any force or effect.
>
> Section 2. An international agreement other than a treaty shall become effective as internal law in the United States only by an act of the Congress.

See 100 CONG. REC. 853, 2358 (1954). It was defeated in a tally of 60 to 31 in favor, which fell one vote short of the two-thirds requirement for Senate passage of a proposed amendment. *Id.* at 2374–75. Afterwards, the effort flagged, especially in the wake of the Supreme Court's finding in *Reid v. Covert* that a treaty may not operate in a manner inconsistent with the U.S. Constitution. Even so, the Bricker Amendment illustrates potentially influential misgivings about the treaty power, and has since been invoked to criticize, for example, the use of RUDs in U.S. ratifications of human rights treaties. *See* Louis Henkin, *U.S. Ratification of Human Rights Conventions: The Ghost of Senator Bricker*, 89 AM. J. INT'L L. 341 (1995).

2. *The Principle of* Reid v. Covert. One of the Bricker Amendment's principles—that international agreements must be consistent with the U.S. Constitution—was confirmed in *Reid v. Covert.* To be sure, it was announced as a plurality decision, with only four justices joined in its legal reasoning. However, neither the concurring opinions nor the dissent suggested a different understanding of the relationship between agreements and the Constitution. Rather, they focused on whether and when it would be permissible for civilian dependents of members of the armed forces to be tried overseas by court martial based on Congress's power under Article I, Section 8, Clause 14, to "make Rules for the Government and Regulation of the land and naval Forces."

Technically, too, the international agreements at issue in *Reid* were not treaties, but "executive agreements"—based on legal authority emanating from pre-existing treaties (*see infra*, this Chapter, Sec. 7). Does that weaken *Reid* as a precedent that *treaties* concluded under Article II, Section 2, cannot contravene the Constitution? The *Reid* plurality saw no significance in the fact that the agreements before the Court were executive agreements and cited cases, such as *De Geofroy v. Riggs*, 133 U.S. 258 (1890), in which the Court had declared the supremacy of the Constitution over a treaty.

How broad, then, is the rule in *Reid*? Relying upon *Reid*, the *Restatement of the Law (Third), The Foreign Relations Law of the United States*, § 302(2)

(1987) states: "No provision of an agreement may contravene any of the prohibitions or limitations of the Constitution applicable to the exercise of authority by the United States"; see also *id.*, reporters' note 1. Thus it is generally accepted that a treaty that contravenes the first eight amendments of the Bill of Rights (safeguarding individual rights), the Eleventh Amendment (limiting suits against the several states), or the Fourteenth Amendment (applying Bill of Rights protections to the states) would be invalid as a matter of U.S. law (though it may still bind the United States under international law). Likewise, a treaty that sought to reallocate constitutional power (*e.g.*, transferring the power to declare war from Congress to the president) likely would be struck down by U.S. courts. Is this more or less what Justice Holmes had in mind? Recall that, in *Missouri v. Holland,* the Court stated that a treaty cannot stand in the face of "prohibitory words" contained in the Constitution.

3. *Relationship to Treaty Ratification.* Since *Reid* indicates that the Constitution "trumps," or supersedes, treaties, the U.S. government is wary of joining treaties that will obligate the United States internationally but cannot be fulfilled as a matter of U.S. constitutional law. Thus, for example, the United States has declined to join the Convention on the Rights of the Child, Nov. 20, 1989, 1577 U.N.T.S. 3, arguing that doing so would intrude inappropriately into core matters of family law that are constitutionally reserved to the several states. Even when the United States has joined treaties, it often files reservations, understandings, or declarations (RUDs) designed to protect existing constitutional rights or state prerogatives. The RUDs filed by the United States when ratifying the Convention Against Torture have already been noted (*see supra*, this Chapter, Sec. 2). The United States took similar precautions in ratifying the International Covenant on Civil and Political Rights (ICCPR), Dec. 16, 1966, 999 U.N.T.S. 171, and the International Convention on the Elimination of All Forms of Racial Discrimination (CERD), Dec. 21, 1965, 660 U.N.T.S. 195: for each, the United States declared that the treaty's substantive rights were not self-executing, and included an understanding that recognized the role of federalism in U.S. law.

4. *Treaties and Government Interests.* U.S. treaty practice appears to accommodate constitutional interests, even if they fall short of establishing a direct conflict with treaty obligations. What of the interest in abiding by treaties? In the Religious Freedom Restoration Act (RFRA), Congress prohibited the federal government from substantially burdening a person's exercise of religion except when the Government can demonstrate that such burden furthers a compelling government interest and is the least restrictive means of doing so. 42 U.S.C. §§ 2000bb–1(a), –1(b) (2012). In *Gonzales v. O Centro Espirita Beneficiente Uniao do Vegetal*, 546 U.S. 418 (2006), the Supreme Court considered whether the U.S. government could regulate the use of hallucinogenic tea by an American branch of a religious sect based in the Amazon rainforest. Members of the church (UDV) receive communion by drinking a sacramental tea brewed from hoasca. The U.S. government maintained that the tea, which contains a drug called dimethyltryptamine (DMT), violated U.S. narcotics laws and U.S. obligations under the U.N.

Convention on Psychotropic Substances, which prohibit importation of DMT. The Supreme Court held that—absent evidence regarding the consequences of a breach—compliance did not by itself establish a compelling government interest warranting the regulation of religious liberty. *Id.* at 438.

5. *Altering Constitutional Allocation of Power.* Notwithstanding U.S. caution about entering treaties, domestic critics regard some of its agreements as risking alteration of the constitutional allocation of power. Consider, for example, international panels charged with reviewing domestic administrative decisions under the North American Free Trade Agreement, U.S.-Can.-Mex., Dec. 17, 1992, 32 I.L.M. 289 & 605 [hereinafter NAFTA]. Previously, final determinations by the U.S. Department of Commerce regarding antidumping and countervailing duty matters were appealed solely within the U.S. national legal system to the U.S. Court of International Trade. To alleviate concerns about bias in national courts, Chapter 19 of NAFTA—like a similar provision in the U.S.-Canada Free Trade Agreement, Can.-U.S., Jan. 2, 1988, 27 I.L.M. 281 (1988) [FTA]—provides that U.S. final determinations (like their Canadian and Mexican counterparts) could be appealed by Canada or Mexico to arbitral panels charged with deciding whether they were consistent with U.S. law. Those panels could uphold a final determination or remand for further proceedings, but a panel decision was in either respect binding on the parties with respect to that matter. NAFTA arts. 1904(8), (9).

Beginning with use of the Chapter 19 mechanism in the FTA, members of Congress saw it as constitutionally suspect. They pointed to a denial of due-process rights and structural concerns in (1) the unique "supranational" nature of the international panels; (2) the procedure for appointing the panelists; (3) perhaps most seriously, the panels' ability to interpret national law and to make binding, nonreviewable determinations of decisions by U.S. administrative agencies, functions normally vested in Article III courts. *See United States-Canada Free-Trade Agreement: Hearing Before the Senate Comm. on the Judiciary*, 100th Cong. (1988); H.R. REP. NO. 100–816, pt. 4 (1988). Ultimately, however, as a House report put it, Congress was convinced that "[i]t is in large part the international context of this Agreement—impinging on the regulation of both foreign affairs and foreign commerce—that makes the binational panel review process constitutional." It also cited the authority of Congress to remove government-created "public rights" from ordinary judicial review, and due process protections in the panel system that were appropriate to the questions at issue. H.R. REP. NO. 100–816, pt. 4, at 4–5 (1988).

Similar concerns surfaced when NAFTA was concluded. Like the FTA, NAFTA is a "congressional-executive agreements" rather than a treaty; this means that it was authorized by a majority vote of both Houses of Congress, rather than by a two-thirds majority of the Senate (*see infra*, this Chapter, Sec. 7), and each became part of U.S. law when implemented by statute. United States-Canada Free-Trade Agreement Implementation Act of 1988, Pub. L. No. 100–449, 102 Stat. 1851 (1988); North American Free Trade Agreement Implementation Act of 1993, Pub L. No. 103–182, 107 Stat. 2057 (1993).

Binational panels have been convened under both the FTA and NAFTA. For example, a NAFTA panel ordered the Department of Commerce's International Trade Commission (ITC) to revoke its "threat of material injury" finding in antidumping and countervailing duty cases on Canadian softwood lumber. Certain Softwood Lumber Products from Canada: Final Affirmative Threat of Injury Determination (NAFTA Ch. 19 Panel. Aug. 31, 2004). In September 2004, the ITC revoked its finding and, after several rounds of administrative review by both nations, the U.S. Trade Representative and Canada's Minister for International Trade signed the Softwood Lumber Agreement 2006 to settle lingering litigation. While a constitutional challenge had been proceeding in U.S. court, pursuant to a special statutory provision establishing original jurisdiction in the D.C. Circuit over such a matter, see 19 U.S.C. § 1516a(g)(4)(A), it was dismissed in light of the settlement. *Coalition for Fair Lumber Imports v. United States*, 471 F.3d 1329 (D.C. Cir. 2006). Pending matters were ultimately dismissed from the NAFTA panel in January 2009. Certain Softwood Lumber Products from Canada; Final Results of Countervailing Duty Administrative Review and Rescission of Certain Company-Specific Reviews (NAFTA Ch. 19 Panel. Jan. 30, 2009). For an analysis that finds such adjudication constitutionally permissible, see Henry Paul Monaghan, *Article III and Supranational Review*, 107 COLUM. L. REV. 833 (2007).

6. Missouri v. Holland*'s Continued Vitality*. Subsequent Supreme Court decisions cited *Missouri v. Holland*, but until *Bond v. United States*—which followed recent cases limiting national authority and protecting state sovereignty—the Court had little opportunity to directly reconsider its decision's merits. In *Bond*, the majority interpreted the implementing statute so as to avoid addressing the scope of *Missouri v. Holland* or whether it should be overruled; Justice Scalia, writing for himself and Justice Thomas, would have overruled read the statute more broadly, confronted *Missouri v. Holland*, and overruled it. Was Justice Scalia's critique convincing? Assess the options that U.S. treaty-makers would face were his approach adopted. For broader examination of how Missouri had fared before *Bond*, see *Symposium: Return to* Missouri v. Holland*: Federalism and International Law*, 73 MO. L. REV. 921 et seq. (2008); for an assessment of Bond, see *Symposium: The Treaty Power after Bond v. United States*, 90 NOTRE DAME L. REV. 1415 et seq. (2015).

7. *What About Treaties Versus Statutes?* *Bond v. United States* involved the relationship between a treaty and a statute implementing that treaty. What of the relationship between treaties and other statutes? If the Constitution always prevails in the event of a conflict with a treaty, what about when a treaty conflicts with a Federal statute? The next case and the following notes address that question.

WHITNEY V. ROBERTSON

124 U.S. 190, 190–95 (1888).

MR. JUSTICE FIELD delivered the opinion of the court.

The plaintiffs are merchants, doing business in the city of New York, and in August, 1882, they imported a large quantity of "centrifugal and molasses sugars," the produce and manufacture of the island of San Domingo.[1] These goods were similar in kind to sugars produced in the Hawaiian Islands, which are admitted free of duty under the treaty with the king of those islands, and the act of Congress, passed to carry the treaty into effect. They were duly entered at the custom house at the port of New York, the plaintiffs claiming that by the treaty with the Republic of San Domingo the goods should be admitted on the same terms, that is, free of duty, as similar articles, the produce and manufacture of the Hawaiian Islands. The defendant, who was at the time collector of the port, refused to allow this claim, treated the goods as dutiable articles under the acts of Congress, and exacted duties on them to the amount of $21,936. . . .

The treaty with the king of the Hawaiian Islands provides for the importation into the United States, free of duty, of various articles, the produce and manufacture of those islands, in consideration, among other things, of like exemption from duty, on the importation into that country, of sundry specified articles which are the produce and manufacture of the United States. 19 Stat. 625. The language of the first two articles of the treaty, which recite the reciprocal engagements of the two countries, declares that they are made in consideration "of the rights and privileges" and "as an equivalent therefor," which one concedes to the other.

The plaintiffs rely for a like exemption of the sugars imported by them from San Domingo upon the ninth article of the treaty with the Dominican Republic, which is as follows: "No higher or other duty shall be imposed on the importation into the United States of any article the growth, produce, or manufacture of the Dominican Republic, or of her fisheries; and no higher or other duty shall be imposed on the importation into the Dominican Republic of any article, the growth, produce, or manufacture of the United States, or their fisheries, than are or shall be payable on the like articles, the growth, produce, or manufacture of any other foreign country, or its fisheries." 15 St. 473, 478. . . .

. . . The act of Congress under which the duties were collected, authorized their exaction. It is of general application, making no exception in favor of goods of any country. It was passed after the treaty with the

[1] [Authors' Note: The island of Hispaniola lies west of Puerto Rico and east of Cuba. In 1697, Spain recognized French dominion over the western third of the island, which in 1804 became Haiti. The remainder of the island, known as "Santo Domingo" or "San Domingo," was conquered by Haiti in 1821. In 1844, it attained independence as the "Dominican Republic," with a capital named "Santo Domingo."]

Dominican Republic, and, if there be any conflict between the stipulations of the treaty and the requirements of the law, the latter must control. A treaty is primarily a contract between two or more independent nations, and is so regarded by writers on public law. . . . When the stipulations are not self-executing they can only be enforced pursuant to legislation to carry them into effect, and such legislation is as much subject to modification and repeal by Congress as legislation upon any other subject. If the treaty contains stipulations which are self-executing, that is, require no legislation to make them operative, to that extent they have the force and effect of a legislative enactment. Congress may modify such provisions, so far as they bind the United States, or supersede them altogether. By the Constitution a treaty is placed on the same footing, and made of like obligation, with an act of legislation. Both are declared by that instrument to be the supreme law of the land, and no superior efficacy is given to either over the other. When the two relate to the same subject, the courts will always endeavor to construe them so as to give effect to both, if that can be done without violating the language of either; but if the two are inconsistent, the one last in date will control the other, provided always the stipulation of the treaty on the subject is self-executing. If the country with which the treaty is made is dissatisfied with the action of the legislative department, it may present its complaint to the executive head of the government, and take such other measures as it may deem essential for the protection of its interests. The courts can afford no redress. . . .

. . . The duty of the courts is to construe and give effect to the latest expression of the sovereign will. In *Head-Money Cases*, 112 U.S. 580 . . . , it was objected to an act of Congress that it violated provisions contained in treaties with foreign nations, but the court replied that so far as the provisions of the act were in conflict with any treaty, they must prevail in all the courts of the country; and, after a full and elaborate consideration of the subject, it held that "so far as a treaty made by the United States with any foreign nation can be the subject of judicial cognizance in the courts of this country, it is subject to such acts as Congress may pass for its enforcement, modification, or repeal."

Judgment affirmed.

NOTES

1. *The Basic Doctrine. Whitney v. Robertson* articulates the "later-in-time" doctrine, which is based on a reading of the Supremacy Clause that views treaty law on the same footing (neither higher nor lower) as federal statutory law. Thus, either may repeal the other. As noted in *Whitney v. Robertson*, the doctrine was also considered in the *Head Money Cases* (*supra*, this Chapter, Sec. 4); an earlier case applying the "last-in-time" doctrine is *The Cherokee Tobacco,* 78 U.S. (11 Wall.) 616 (1871). In that case the Supreme Court was faced with a conflict between an 1866 U.S.-Cherokee Nation treaty and the

Internal Revenue Act of July 20, 1868. The Court said: "Undoubtedly one or the other must yield. The repugnancy is clear and cannot stand together. . . . The effect of treaties and acts of Congress, when in conflict, is not settled by the Constitution. But the question is not involved in any doubt as to its proper solution. A treaty may supersede a prior act of Congress, and an act of Congress may supersede a prior treaty." *Id.* at 620–21 (footnote omitted).

Later, the "Chinese Exclusion" case (*Chae Chan Ping v. United States*, 130 U.S. 581 (1889)) (*see* Chapter 1, Sec. 1) held that the fact that treaties with China were violated by the Chinese Exclusion Act of 1888 is no objection to the later statute's validity. That law had been enacted by Congress to prevent Chinese immigration at the time of the gold rush, when their willingness to work cheaply provoked fierce objection and public disturbances. 130 U.S. at 595. The 1888 Act did not merely stanch immigration; it also denied re-entry to any Chinese laborers who were outside the United States at the time of the passage of the law, and precluded subsequent departure and return, with the effect of expelling those returning to visit their families. The Supreme Court said, in part:

> It must be conceded that the act of 1888 is in contravention of express stipulations of the treaty of 1868 and of the supplemental treaty of 1880, but it is not on that account invalid, or to be restricted in its enforcement. The treaties were of no greater legal obligation than the act of Congress. . . . A treaty . . . is in its nature a contract between nations and is often merely promissory in its character, requiring legislation to carry its stipulations into effect. Such legislation will be open to future repeal or amendment. If the treaty operates by its own force, and relates to a subject within the power of Congress, it can be deemed in that particular only the equivalent of a legislative act, to be repealed or modified at the pleasure of Congress. In either case the last expression of the sovereign will must control.

Id. at 600.

For a contemporary formulation, including details concerning how to assess which instrument arises later, see *Restatement of the Law (Fourth), The Foreign Relations Law of the United States: Treaties* § 109 (Tentative Draft No. 1, 2016).

2. *Relationship to Constitutional Supremacy*. Interestingly, the Supreme Court in *Reid v. Covert* relied upon its holding in *Whitney* to support the proposition that the Constitution was supreme over treaties. The *Reid* Court stated:

> This Court has also repeatedly taken the position that an Act of Congress which must comply with the Constitution, is on a full parity with a treaty, and that when a statute which is subsequent in time is inconsistent with a treaty, the statute to the extent of a conflict renders the treaty null. It would be completely anomalous to say that a treaty need not comply with the Constitution when such an

agreement can be overridden by a statute that must conform to that instrument.

354 U.S. at 18.

3. *Interpreting Statutes and Treaties so as to Avoid a Conflict.* In *Whitney v. Robertson*, the Court stated that "the courts will always endeavor to construe [a potentially conflicting statute and treaty] so as to give effect to both, if that can be done without violating the language of either. . . ." How hard should a court work to do so? In a recent case, the D.C. Circuit decided, contrary to prior dicta in that circuit, that textual ambiguity was not required—such that a court was still obligated to interpret a later statute to avoid conflict with an earlier-arising treaty obligation even if the statutory language was clear. That statute required the Secretary of Transportation to require all commercial vehicle operators "to have a current valid medical certificate," separate from their commercial licenses and issued by a person on a national registry, see 49 U.S.C. §§ 31136, 31149 (2012); nonetheless, mindful of earlier executive agreements with Canada and Mexico for reciprocal recognition of commercial drivers' licenses, when those two countries lacked separate medical certification, the Secretary and the Federal Motor Carrier Safety Administration exempted Canadian and Mexican drivers from otherwise applicable registration requirements. National Registry of Certified Medical Examiners, 77 Fed. Reg. 24,104 (Apr. 20, 2012). The D.C. Circuit denied a petition for review. While the court conceded the "textually unambiguous terms," it sought a "clear statement" of an intention to violate the earlier agreements, noting that "if Congress or the President understood the Act to be a repudiation of the federal government's obligations to Mexico and Canada, someone would have said something." *Owner-Operator Indep. Drivers Ass'n v. U.S. Dep't of Transp.*, 724 F.3d 230, 234, 237 (D.C. 2013). Dissenting, Judge Sentelle objected to requiring that "Congress must use some additional magic words to give the admittedly clear statute effect," and argued that the majority's approach "elevates treaties above statutes by making it more difficult for Congress to abrogate prior treaties than prior statutes." He found it particularly unsatisfactory given that the Supremacy Clause did not "expressly encompass international agreements of the type at issue" (executive agreements, addressed *infra*, this Chapter, Sec. 7), thereby making it "harder for Congress to overrule two letters exchanged between mid-level administrative functionaries than it would be for Congress to overrule a statute passed by a majority of the people's representatives and signed by the President." 724 F.3d at 240–41 (Sentelle, J., dissenting).

Owner-Operator concerned the application of a general statute to an international matter. What about when Congress is directly contemplating international application (even controversy), but not necessarily breach of an agreement? In 1947, the United States and the United Nations concluded an Agreement Regarding the Headquarters of the United Nations, July 26, 1947, 61 Stat. 3416, 11 U.N.T.S. 11, obligating the United States to permit unimpeded transit, entry and access to the U.N. headquarters district for representatives of members and others persons invited by the United Nations.

Invited persons include permanent observers. In 1974, the Palestine Liberation Organization (PLO) was designated as permanent observer and allowed to establish a permanent observer Mission in New York, thereby securing rights of access under the Headquarters Agreement. In 1987, Congress enacted an Anti-Terrorism Act (ATA), which was designed, in part, to force the closure of all PLO offices located in the United States. The ATA determined that the PLO was "a terrorist organization and a threat to the interests of the United States, its allies, and to international law and should not benefit from operating in the United States." 22 U.S.C. § 5201(b) (2012). Consequently, the ATA provided that

> It shall be unlawful, if the purpose be to further the interests of the Palestinian Liberation Organization . . . notwithstanding any provision of law to the contrary, to establish or maintain an office, headquarters, premises, or other facilities or establishments within the jurisdiction of the United States at the behest or direction of, or with funds provided by the Palestinian Liberation Organization.

22 U.S.C. § 5202 (2012).

When the U.S. government thereafter sought to close the PLO Mission in New York, the PLO maintained that doing so violated the Headquarters Agreement. In *United States v. Palestine Liberation Organization,* 695 F. Supp. 1456 (S.D.N.Y. 1988), the district court found the ATA inapplicable to the PLO Mission due to the lack of a "clear legislative intent that the Congress was directing the Attorney General, the State Department or this Court to act in contravention of the Headquarters Agreement"—principally because the statute failed to mention either the Mission or the Headquarters Agreement, and "any law to the contrary" did not (as it did elsewhere in the statute) specifically "purport to apply notwithstanding any *treaty*." *Id.* at 1468–69. Is the court's approach more or less indulgent of treaties than that taken in *Owner-Operator*? After the district court's decision, the U.S. government decided not to appeal the decision and not to pursue further the closure of the PLO Mission. Congress did not react, and the dispute quietly ended.

4. *Questioning the Doctrine*. Do you think the later-in-time doctrine is a good one? Some commentators have expressed concern that federal statutes can be subsequently repealed by treaties. Professor Akhil Reed Amar writes:

> By allowing federal treaties to repeal federal statutes . . . the modern judiciary has paid insufficient heed to the text of Article VI itself, ignoring the apparent legal hierarchy implicit in that text. In *Marbury v. Madison*, Chief Justice Marshall, in emphasizing the legal priority of the Constitution, deemed it "not entirely unworthy of observation" that the Article VI supremacy clause listed the Constitution *first*. Isn't it likewise worthy of notice that this very same clause listed federal statutes *ahead of* federal treaties, thereby implying a rank order between the two? . . .

> . . . [T]he Constitution deserved priority over lesser laws because of its superior democratic pedigree. A similar argument would seem to support the priority of federal statutes over federal treaties. After all, treaties cut the House of Representatives out of the loop.

Akhil Reed Amar, *America's Constitution: A Biography* 303 (2005). Consider, in this connection, that even treaty provisions deemed to be non-self-executing appear to be subject to the interpretive principle suggested in *Whitney v. Robertson* and other cases. *Restatement of the Law (Fourth), The Foreign Relations Law of the United States: Treaties* § 109 (Tentative Draft No. 1, 2016).

Other commentators, however, have expressed concern at the prospect that treaties can be repealed—in their domestic legal effect—by subsequent federal statutes. Professor Louis Henkin writes:

> [O]ne might well argue . . . that a treaty should prevail as law even in the face of a subsequent statute. The international obligations of the United States are the responsibility of the treaty-makers. The Senate was given a part in the process, but the House, and Congress as a whole, were purposely denied any voice in it. Congress . . . has a constitutional obligation to implement the treaties which the President and the Senate make; it is anomalous to accord it power to disregard a treaty obligation, compel its violation, and put the United States in default. . . . [I]nconsistent legislation by Congress not only violates international obligations but ruptures international consensus which the President-and-Senate helped achieve. . . .

Louis Henkin, *Foreign Affairs and the Constitution* 210–11 (2d ed. 1996). How far is this accommodated by the fact that—perhaps contrary to what *Whitney v. Robertson* suggests—statutes are often interpreted to accommodate treaties, but not the converse? Evaluate why this might be so when considering the materials *infra*, this Chapter, Sec. 9.

5. *Practice of Other Countries.* In some countries, treaties are paramount even with respect to subsequent legislation. For example, the French Constitution provides: "Duly ratified or approved treaties or agreements shall, upon their publication, override laws, subject, for each agreement or treaty, to its application by the other party." CONSTITUTION OF FRANCE, art. 55 (1958). Similarly, the Dutch Constitution provides: "Statutory regulations in force within the Kingdom shall not be applicable if such application is in conflict with provisions of treaties that are binding on all persons or of resolutions by international institutions." GRONDWET [CONSTITUTION OF THE KINGDOM OF THE NETHERLANDS], art. 94 (1983).

NOTE: CAN A LATER-IN-TIME CUSTOMARY INTERNATIONAL LAW RULE "TRUMP" A TREATY OR STATUTE?

We know, then, that for purposes of U.S. law, a treaty must yield to a later-in-time statute and vice-versa. What about a later-in-time rule of customary international law? In other words, if it appears that a rule of customary international law has crystallized in recent years, and the United States has not persistently objected to the rule, can it have the effect of superseding earlier U.S. treaties (or statutes) under U.S. law?

Consider the following example. In 1961, the United States ratified the Convention on the Territorial Sea and Contiguous Zone, Apr. 29, 1958, 15 U.S.T. 1606, 516 U.N.T.S. 205. Article 24(2) of that Convention provides that a state's contiguous zone (a zone outside the territorial sea in which the coastal State can enforce certain types of its laws, such as on customs) may not extend beyond twelve miles from the coast. Thus, the treaty precluded the United States from declaring a contiguous zone beyond twelve miles from U.S. shores. The 1982 Law of the Sea Convention, to which the United States is not a party, permits the contiguous zone to be as much as twenty-four nautical miles from the coast, and many states (either as parties or non-parties) began claiming a contiguous zone of that distance.

In 1989, the U.S. Department of State Office of the Legal Adviser advised that a 24 nautical-mile contiguous zone was now permitted under customary international law and assessed the repercussions of the new rule's emergence on U.S. obligations under the 1958 treaty. As you read the explanation of the U.S. legal position below—the U.S. Department of Justice Office of Legal Counsel later indicated that it deferred on this matter, see Letter from John O. McGinnis, Deputy Assistant Attorney General, U.S. Department of Justice, to Alan Kreczko, Deputy Legal Adviser, U.S. Department of State (July 1, 1991)—note that much of the analysis turns on the president's power to terminate treaties, discussed in greater depth *infra* this Chapter, Sec. 10. Consider whether the remaining analysis turns more on presidential power than anything about customary international law. Could a sole executive agreement (an agreement based solely on the Executive's power, without consent from Congress) can also alter an existing treaty?

MEMORANDUM OF THE U.S. DEPARTMENT OF STATE OFFICE OF THE LEGAL ADVISER REGARDING THE TERRITORIAL SEA CONVENTION

(Apr. 5, 1989) available at http://www.state.gov/s/l/65626.htm, [https://perma.cc/T4YV-QPDQ].

As a general matter, the President has "the power to determine how far this country will claim territorial rights in the marginal sea as against other nations." *United States v. Louisiana*, 363 U.S. 1, 35 (1960); *see also* Proclamation 5928, December 27, 1988 (extending the U.S. territorial sea to 12 nautical miles). *A fortiori*, the President has the power to extend a maritime jurisdiction under international law which is less than full sovereignty, such as the contiguous zone. This has been done by Presidential action with respect to the exclusive economic zone. Proclamation 5030, March 10, 1983.

The question has been raised, however, whether Article 24(2) of the 1958 Territorial Sea Convention limits the President's authority to extend the contiguous zone beyond 12 nautical miles. That it does not do so in present circumstances flows from two constitutional considerations: first, the President may unilaterally determine for the United States that Article 24(2) no longer binds the United States as a matter of international law; and second, a treaty provision's force in domestic law is generally no greater than its international law force.

A. PRESIDENTIAL AUTHORITY TO ACT ON THE INTERNATIONAL PLANE

It is well-established that the President is "the sole organ of the federal government in the field of international relations." *United States v. Curtiss-Wright Export Corp.*, 299 U.S. 304, 320 (1936) . . .

The President's constitutional authority to act for the United States in international relations includes the power to engage in state practice that contributes to or dissents from the establishment of customary norms, as well as the power to assess the customary norms relevant to United States action. As a leading scholar has stated,

> "It is principally the President, 'sole organ' of the United States in its international relations, who is responsible for the behavior of the United States in regard to international law, and who participates on her behalf in the indefinable process by which customary international law is made, unmade, remade. He makes legal claims for the United States and reacts to the claims of others; he performs acts reflecting views on legal questions and justifies them under the law, in diplomatic exchange, in judicial or arbitral proceedings, in international organizations or in the public forum."

L. Henkin, *Foreign Affairs and the Constitution* 188 (1972). His constitutional authority also includes significant power with relation to the operation of treaties. As Alexander Hamilton stated:

> "[The President's] power of determining virtually upon the operation of national treaties, as a consequence of the power to receive public ministers, is an important instance of the right of the executive to decide upon the obligations of the country with regard to foreign nations. Hence . . . , treaties can only be made by the President and Senate jointly, but their activity may be continued or suspended by the President alone."

A. Hamilton, *Letters of Pacificus and Helvidius on the Proclamation of Neutrality of 1793*, at 12–13 (Gideon ed. 1845). *But cf. Taylor v. Morton*, 23 Fed. Cas. 784, 786 (C.C. Mass. 1855); 4 Moore, *Digest of International Law* 321 (1906) (quoting Jan. 2, 1791, letter of James Madison intimating that Senate must participate in decision to declare a treaty void).

At the extreme, it is often asserted that a President has the general authority to terminate treaties on behalf of the United States. . . .

Acts in exercise of the foreign relations power may contribute to the modification or termination of a treaty provision. For example, when another party acts inconsistently with a treaty provision, it is the President who must determine whether it constitutes a material breach. Since such breach renders a treaty voidable but not void, a decision must also be made on the appropriate response under international law, *e.g.*, suspension or termination of the agreement in whole or in part or acquiescence or waiver on behalf of the United States. It is settled that the President has the power to waive the right of the United States to terminate a treaty for breach by another party. . . . Implicit in this is the view that the executive can exercise the U.S. right rather than waive it. . . . If he acquiesces in general violations of the treaty by the other parties, this can have the effect of terminating the treaty obligation. *See* 5 Hackworth, *Digest of International Law* 340–41; 14 M. Whiteman, *Digest of International Law* 441 (1970). . . .

The Court has also deferred to the executive branch in determining whether a treaty was abrogated due to the outbreak of war, *Clark v. Allen*, 331 U.S. 503, 508–09 (1947) (although the outbreak of war does not "necessarily suspend or abrogate treaty provisions," the executive may formulate a national policy "inconsistent with the enforcement of a treaty in whole or in part"), or was abrogated by the operation of law, due to the absorption of the other party into another state, *Terlinden v. Ames*, 184 U.S. 270 (1902) (Court was without power to review the validity of a treaty if the practice of the parties indicated that they recognized the treaty as in force). Similarly, during World War II, the Attorney General ruled that the President had the authority to suspend or declare inoperative a peacetime treaty on the grounds of *rebus sic stantibus*. 40 *Op. Att'y Gen.* 119 (1941). . . .

Another relevant and more routinely exercised aspect of the President's foreign affairs power is that the President has the initial and primary responsibility to interpret and apply treaty provisions. The President has submitted treaty construction issues to the Senate only in exceptional instances. S. Crandall, *Treaties, Their Making and Enforcement* 369 (2d ed. 1916). While courts may interpret treaty provisions in the context of cases properly before them, they have traditionally given great weight to the interpretations of the Executive Branch. . . . Were the issue to arise before our courts, substantial deference would be given to the Executive Branch view that the 1958 Territorial Sea Convention was adopted as a law-stating treaty and was not intended to constitute a special regime, particularly given that no contrary interpretation was presented to the Senate during the ratification process. . . .

Thus, in the context of the contiguous zone extension, the President, as the "sole organ of the United States in its external relations," has the constitutional authority (1) to determine that customary international law now permits a 24 nautical mile Contiguous zone, (2) to assess the intent of the 1958 Convention parties regarding the preservation of Article 24(2) as a special regime, (3) to acquiesce in conduct by other parties inconsistent with the wording of the 1958 Territorial Sea Convention, thereby leading to the termination of Article 24(2) by estoppel and (4) to decide that Article 24(2) no longer is operative under international law for the United States.

B. TREATIES AS DOMESTIC LAW

Article VI of the Constitution declares that treaties are among the "supreme law of the land." . . .

The status of treaties as law of the land, however, does not mean that they are in all respects equivalent to statutes. Treaties are, at root, compacts among sovereigns. *Head Money Cases*, 112 U.S. 580, 598 (1884); *Federalist* No. 75. They become the law of the land through the combined action of the President and Senate—the "fourth branch of government" as Hamilton called it. *See* L. Henkin, *supra*, at 130. More importantly, their status as "law of the land" depends on their status as international law. Except perhaps with respect to treaties that create vested rights, "[a] rule of international law or an international agreement has no status as law of the United States if the United States is not in fact bound by it: for example, . . . a provision in a treaty that is invalid or has been terminated or suspended." *Restatement (Third)*, at § 111, comment b; *see also id.* at § 339, Reporters' Note 1; L. Henkin, *supra*, at 160 ("The status of a treaty as law of the land derives from and depends on its status as a valid, living treaty of the United States. . . . It is not law of the land if it is not an effective treaty of the United States internationally because it is not binding, or is invalid under international law, or because it has expired, or has been terminated or destroyed by breach, whether by the United States or the other party.") . . .

Based on these principles, it follows that, if Article 24(2) of the 1958 Territorial Sea Convention has been superseded on the international plane by a new rule of customary international law permitting a 24 nautical mile contiguous zone, then Article 24(2) no longer has effect as a law of the United States and need not be "faithfully executed" by the President. . . .

It is important to note that to reach this conclusion one need not reach the question of whether customary international law will supersede a statute. *See Paquete Habana*, 175 U.S. 677, 700 (1900) (only resort to customary international law if there is "no controlling executive or legislative act"). Treaty and custom both operate on the international plane and, on that plane, the customary norm can supersede the treaty norm; this terminates the domestic legal effects of the treaty because those effects are derivative of the treaty's status as binding under international law. In contrast, statutes derive their effect from independent action of domestic institutions. The effect of changed custom on an earlier statute involves a different constitutional question, whether domestic and customary international law have the same status or whether they stand in a hierarchical relationship.

While it has not been authoritatively determined that the emergence of a new rule of customary international law which supersedes a treaty provision on the international plane also has the effect of superseding the treaty provision as a matter of domestic law, there seems, not surprisingly, to be no authority for the contrary proposition. It would be anomalous to have our domestic law on the obligations of the United States vis-a-vis other nations derive from but become more restrictive than our international law obligations. Where (i) the treaty has not created vested rights, (ii) the new rule of customary international law is clearly recognized as internationally controlling by the executive and (iii) there were no contrary assurances on which the Senate relied in granting advice and consent, there is no good reason to adopt a constitutional rule creating such an anomaly. Because treaties are, at root, compacts among sovereigns, it is appropriate that the President, "sole organ" of the United States in its foreign relations, have wider powers with respect to treaties than statutes.

C. CONCLUSION

In light of the international legal considerations set forth in the first section of this memorandum, Article 24(2) has lost its controlling effect internationally for the United States.

The Constitution does not provide Article 24(2) with independent continuing legal force and, therefore, does not require the President to refrain from exercising his foreign affairs power to extend the contiguous zone of the United States beyond the 12 nautical mile limited stated in that Article.

7. EXECUTIVE AGREEMENTS

The Constitution nowhere makes provision for the president to conclude international agreements other than by an Article II treaty. It does recognize (Article I, Section 10) the right of a state of the Union to enter into an "agreement or compact with another State or with a foreign power" if it has obtained the consent of Congress, while prohibiting any state from entering into a "treaty, alliance, or confederation. . . ." (*See* Chapter 6, Sec. 7). From this it may be argued either:

(1) that the drafters understood a distinction between "treaties" and other kinds of agreements, and chose not to create a federal "agreement" power distinct from the treaty power; or

(2) that the drafters could not reasonably be assumed to have denied to the federal government a power which (within restrictions) was accorded to the states.[53]

While the Constitution may be ambiguous, the Executive's right to enter into agreements even without the advice and consent of the Senate has long been recognized both in practice and by the courts.[54] Indeed, the "executive agreement" has come to occupy a prominent place in the arsenal of diplomatic tools of the U.S. government.

Pre-Constitutional Practice

The earliest American executives were, primarily, the colonial Governors commissioned by the British Government. The discharge of their duties was subject to royal approval. Nevertheless, as the interests of the colonies often differed from their colonizers, the colonies often entered into engagements with sovereign entities—including other colonies, particularly to establish reciprocal trading privileges, and with Indian tribes—by means that bypassed seeking formal approval from London.[55] A similar inattention to formalities was sometimes observed by the government under the Articles of Confederation, which (for example) entered a commercial accord with France and a ship-signal arrangement with Morocco without the use of a formal treaty; although the Articles lacked any "executive" to conclude such agreements, their use may at least be analogized to the turn to executive agreements under the Constitution.[56]

Early Practice Under the Constitution

On April 22, 1793, President Washington issued a proclamation that stated the U.S. policy of neutrality in the recently begun war between Great Britain and France. The president's assertion of authority to affect U.S. rights and obligations, though it took the form of a declaration, had important implications for the power to enter into executive agreements.[57] In a series of articles in *The Gazette of the United States,* Alexander Hamilton, writing as "Pacificus," defended the proclamation against critics who saw it as beyond the president's competence. Hamilton asked "what department of our government is the proper one to make a declaration of neutrality." Answering, he reported that a "correct mind will discern at once that it . . . must belong to the executive," since "[t]he Legislative

---

53 *See* 14 Marjorie M. Whiteman, *Digest of International Law* 193–216 (1970); Myres McDougal & Asher Lans, *Treaties and Congressional-Executive or Presidential Agreements: Interchangeable Instruments of National Policy,* 54 YALE L.J. 181–351 (1945).

54 *See* Edwin S. Corwin, *The Constitution of the United States of America, Analysis and Interpretation*, S. DOC. NO. 82–170, at 433 (1953).

55 Max Savelle, *The Origins of American Diplomacy: The International History of Angloamerica 1492–1763*, at 159 (1968).

56 Wallace McClure, *International Executive Agreements: Democratic Procedure Under the Constitution of the United States* 35 (1941) (footnote omitted) [hereinafter "*McClure*"].

57 *Id.* at 37.

Department is not the *organ* of intercourse between the UStates and foreign Nations" and "is charged neither with *making* nor *interpreting* Treaties"—and "therefore [is] not naturally that Organ of the Government which is to pronounce the existing condition of the Nation, with regard to foreign Powers . . ."[58]

Arguably, this broad, residual executive power also supported the ability to enter into executive agreements with foreign nations. The earliest executive agreements under the Constitution were the Postal Acts of the Washington Administration—which were later authorized by Congress, but suggested the possibility of concluding international engagements outside the formal treaty-making process. Later, a 1817 executive agreement between Great Britain and the United States for determining the naval armaments maintained by them on the Great Lakes and Lake Champlain was made immediately effective upon the exchange of diplomatic notes. John Quincy Adams, then Secretary of State, recorded that some months later British Foreign Minister Charles Bagot asked him whether the president intended to communicate to Congress this "sort of treaty." Adams spoke to the president, "who did not think it necessary that they should be communicated," though later it was in fact sent to the Senate, which duly provided its advice and consent.[59] Do these experiences illustrate a presidential power, or suggest that presidents ultimately acknowledged the need to regularize agreements by securing approval of the Senate or, at least, Congress?

Frequency of Executive Agreements

Whatever early precedents signaled, in practice—as reflected in the following table, which compares 50-year intervals since the founding—the vast majority of international agreements concluded by the United States have been done *without* securing a two-thirds vote of the U.S. Senate.

TREATIES AND EXECUTIVE AGREEMENTS CONCLUDED BY THE UNITED STATES, 1789–1999[60]

Period	Number of Treaties	Number of Executive Agreements
1789–1839	60	27
1839–1889	215	238
1889–1939	524	917
1939–1989	702	11,698
Total	1,501	12,880

58 15 *The Papers of Alexander Hamilton* 33–43 (Harold C. Syrett ed., 1969).

59 *McClure, supra* note 5, at 31, 38.

60 Treaties and Other International Agreements: The Role of the United States Senate, S. Prt. 106–71, at 39 (2001).

This trend continues to hold. Data for shorter intervals can be misleading, since treaties need not be submitted to the Senate, let alone considered, in the same year they are concluded. But in the ten-year period from 1990–1999, the United States concluded 249 treaties and 2,857 agreements; the proportion of treaties to executive agreements appeared to be even lower in the Bush and Obama administrations.[61]

The persistent and growing use of executive agreements ultimately resulted in the adoption of two important regulatory instruments, excerpted below. First, the Department of State adopted a "Circular 175" Procedure, designed to ensure that the Department consider carefully whether an agreement should be concluded as a treaty and, if not, the exact legal basis for concluding the agreement as an executive agreement. Second, the Case-Zablocki Act requires that all executive agreements be transmitted to Congress upon their completion, thereby allowing Congress to monitor their use. Following the Case-Zablocki Act is an example of how the Office of the Legal Adviser determines whether certain specific executive agreements may be negotiated and concluded. As you read these materials, consider whether they provide sufficient guidance to the executive branch and Congress.

U.S. DEPARTMENT OF STATE CIRCULAR 175 PROCEDURE

11 Foreign Affairs Manual (FAM) 721–726 (Sept. 25, 2006)
(internal notation omitted).

11 FAM 723.2 Constitutional Requirements

There are two procedures under the Constitution through which the United States becomes a party to an international agreement. Those procedures and the constitutional parameters of each are found below.

11 FAM 723.2–1 Treaties

International agreements (regardless of their title, designation, or form) whose entry into force with respect to the United States takes places only after the Senate has given its advice and consent are treaties. The President, with the advice and consent of two-thirds of the Senators present, may enter into an international agreement on any subject genuinely of concern in foreign relations, so long as the agreement does not contravene the United States Constitution; and

11 FAM 723.2–2 International Agreements Other than Treaties

International agreements brought into force with respect to the United States on a constitutional basis other than with the advice and consent of

---

[61] *Id.* (reporting data through 2009); Jeffrey S. Peake, Presidential Unilateralism in an Era of Polarization: The End of the Treaty Power? at Table 1 (American Political Science Association, Philadelphia, Sep. 1, 2016); *see also* Glen S. Krutz & Jeffrey S. Peake, *Treaty Politics and the Rise of Executive Agreements: International Commitments in a System of Shared Powers* (2009).

the Senate are international agreements other than treaties. (The term sole executive agreement is appropriately reserved for agreements made solely on the basis of the constitutional authority of the President.) There are three constitutional bases for international agreements other than treaties as set forth below. An international agreement may be concluded pursuant to one or more of these constitutional bases: (1) Treaty; (2) Legislation; (3) Constitutional authority of the President.

11 FAM 723.2–2(A) Agreements Pursuant to Treaty

The President may conclude an international agreement pursuant to a treaty brought into force with the advice and consent of the Senate, the provisions of which constitute authorization for the agreement by the Executive without subsequent action by the Congress.

11 FAM 723.2–2(B) Agreements Pursuant to Legislation

The President may conclude an international agreement on the basis of existing legislation, or subject to legislation to be adopted by the Congress, or upon the failure of Congress to adopt a disapproving joint or concurrent resolution within designated time periods.

11 FAM 723.2–2(C) Agreements Pursuant to the Constitutional Authority of the President

The President may conclude an international agreement on any subject within his constitutional authority so long as the agreement is not inconsistent with legislation enacted by the Congress in the exercise of its constitutional authority. The constitutional sources of authority for the President to conclude international agreements include:

(1) The President's authority as Chief Executive to represent the nation in foreign affairs;

(2) The President's authority to receive ambassadors and other public ministers, and to recognize foreign governments;

(3) The President's authority as Commander-in-Chief; and

(4) The President's authority to take care that the laws be faithfully executed.

11 FAM 723.3 Considerations for Selecting Among Constitutionally Authorized Procedures

In determining a question as to the procedure which should be followed for any particular international agreement, due consideration is given to the following factors along with those in 11 FAM 723.2:

(1) The extent to which the agreement involves commitments or risks affecting the nation as a whole;

(2) Whether the agreement is intended to affect state laws;

(3) Whether the agreement can be given effect without the enactment of subsequent legislation by the Congress;

(4) Past U.S. practice as to similar agreements;

(5) The preference of the Congress as to a particular type of agreement;

(6) The degree of formality desired for an agreement;

(7) The proposed duration of the agreement, the need for prompt conclusion of an agreement, and the desirability of concluding a routine or short-term agreement; and

(8) The general international practice as to similar agreements.

In determining whether an international agreement should be brought into force as a treaty or as an international agreement other than a treaty, the utmost care is to be exercised to avoid any invasion or compromise of the constitutional powers of the President, the Senate, and the Congress as a whole.

11 FAM 723.4 Questions as to Type of Agreement to Be Used; Consultation with Congress

a. All legal memoranda accompanying Circular 175 requests . . . will discuss thoroughly the legal authorities underlying the type of agreement recommended.

b. When there is any question whether an international agreement should be concluded as a treaty or as an international agreement other than a treaty, the matter is brought to the attention, in the first instance, of the Legal Adviser for Treaty Affairs. . . . Every practicable effort will be made to identify such questions at the earliest possible date so that consultations may be completed in sufficient time to avoid last-minute consideration.

c. Consultations on such questions will be held with congressional leaders and committees as may be appropriate. . . .

CASE-ZABLOCKI ACT

1 U.S.C. § 112b (2012).

(a) The Secretary of State shall transmit to the Congress the text of any international agreement (including the text of any oral international agreement, which agreement shall be reduced to writing), other than a treaty, to which the United States is a party as soon as practicable after such agreement has entered into force with respect to the United States but in no event later than sixty days thereafter. However, any such agreement the immediate public disclosure of which would, in the opinion of the President, be prejudicial to the national security of the United States shall not be so transmitted to the Congress but shall be transmitted to the Committee on Foreign Relations of the Senate and the Committee on International Relations of the House of Representatives under an appropriate injunction of secrecy . . .

(b) Not later than March 1, 1979, and at yearly intervals thereafter, the President shall, under his own signature, transmit to the Speaker of the House of Representatives and the chairman of the Committee on Foreign Relations of the Senate a report with respect to each international agreement which, during the preceding year, was transmitted to the Congress after the expiration of the 60-day period referred to in the first sentence of subsection (a), describing fully and completely the reasons for the late transmittal.

(c) Notwithstanding any other provision of law, an international agreement may not be signed or otherwise concluded on behalf of the United States without prior consultation with the Secretary of State. Such consultation may encompass a class of agreements rather than a particular agreement.

(d)(1) The Secretary of State shall annually submit to Congress a report that contains an index of all international agreements . . . that the United States—

> (A) has signed, proclaimed, or with reference to which any other final formality has been executed, or that has been extended or otherwise modified, during the preceding calendar year; and
>
> (B) has not been published, or is not proposed to be published, in the compilation entitled "United States Treaties and Other International Agreements".

(2) The report described in paragraph (1) may be submitted in classified form.

(e)(1) Subject to paragraph (2), the Secretary of State shall determine for and within the executive branch whether an arrangement constitutes an international agreement within the meaning of this section. . . .

DEPARTMENT OF STATE CIRCULAR 175 LEGAL MEMORANDUM REGARDING A REQUEST FOR USAID TO NEGOTIATE AND CONCLUDE CERTAIN INTERNATIONAL AGREEMENTS

(August 15, 2002), available at http://www.usaid.gov/policy/ads/300/349maa.pdf, [https://perma.cc/6ED4-AQ7M].

[On August 15, 2002, Secretary Colin Powell approved a request from the Administrator of the U.S. Agency for International Development (USAID) for "blanket" authority (*i.e.*, authority not specific to any particular country) to negotiate and conclude certain bilateral agreements with countries that are recipients of U.S. foreign aid. Attached to the "action memo" from USAID to the Secretary requesting such authority was a memorandum of law prepared by the Office of the Legal Adviser addressing the legal authority for concluding such agreements.]

Memorandum of Law

SUBJECT: *Circular 175: U.S. Agency for International Development ("USAID") Request for Blanket Authorization to Negotiate and Conclude Certain International Agreements*

In accordance with thc Circular 175 procedure, 11 FAM 700 *et seq.*, the accompanying action memorandum requests blanket authority for USAID to negotiate and conclude certain classes of international agreements for its foreign assistance and food aid programs. . . .

USAID is currently operating under a blanket authorization from the Secretary [of State] issued on July 27, 1956, to USAID's predecessor agency, the International Cooperation Agency. The present C-175 request is designed to address the extensive changes to the format, scope and content of USAID agreements and to be more consistent with current USAID operations, for example with respect to privileges and immunities as well as fiscal privileges granted the USAID mission and its personnel.

The agreements subject to the accompanying Circular 175 authority fall into two broad categories: (a) framework agreements that establish the USAID Mission as a special mission in another country, where the other party commits to provide the mission with specific privileges and immunities for USAID, USAID personnel, contractors and recipients, as well as USAID-financed supplies and services; and (b) implementing agreements that govern the provision of foreign assistance, in the form of a particular grant or a program to the other party.

The framework agreement generally involves unilateral non-reciprocal commitments by the other government to the United States. It contains no ongoing USG commitments to provide foreign assistance, in any form (*e.g.*, either by grants or program activities); but rather apply to such assistance as may be given subject to U.S. law. The implementing agreements may apply to grants of amounts stated therein. They are carefully and appropriately caveated that the provision of any assistance generally be subject to U.S. law, including that the provision in specified amounts be subject to the availability of funds to USAID for this purpose. Such assistance funds are appropriated in annual Foreign Operations, Export Financing and Related Programs Appropriations Acts.

Accordingly, the authority to negotiate and conclude such agreements is derived from the President's Constitutional Powers (Article II), including his authority to represent the nation in foreign affairs, as delegated to the Secretary of State on a day-to-day basis (22 U.S.C. 2656). Furthermore, additional authority exists under the Foreign Assistance Act and the Agricultural Trade Development and Assistance Act of 1954—the statutes pursuant to which USAID conducts its foreign assistance and food aid programs, respectively—for the President to enter into agreements concerning the provision of foreign assistance. Specifically, section 635(b) of the Foreign Assistance Act of 1961, as amended, ("FAA"), 22 U.S.C. § 2151 *et seq.* provides legal authority for the negotiation and conclusion of executive agreements. Section 635 (b) provides:

> The President may make loans, advances, and grants to, make and perform agreements and contracts with, or enter into other transactions with, any individual, corporation, or other body of persons, friendly government or government agency, whether within or without the United States, and international organizations in furtherance of the purposes and within the limitations of this Act.

This authority was delegated to the Secretary of State in Executive Order 12163, as amended (March 31, 1999). The Secretary specifically delegated to the Administrator of USAID in Delegation of Authority No. 145 the authority to negotiate, sign and terminate international agreements for USAID programs, subject to the Circular 175 procedure.

Similarly, Titles II and III of the Agricultural Trade Development and Assistance Act of 1954, as amended, ("P.L. 480"), 7 U.S.C. § 1691 *et seq.* authorize the President in Sections 201 and 202 of Title II, to "establish a program to provide agricultural commodities to foreign countries"; to provide emergency assistance "through governments and public or private agencies, including intergovernmental organizations"; and to provide non-emergency assistance through intergovernmental organizations. 7 U.S.C §§ 1721 and 1722. To this end, section 301(b) of Title III, 7 U.S.C. § 1727 (b) provides that the Administrator of USAID "may negotiate and execute agreements with less developed countries to provide commodities to such countries on a grant basis."

The authority to implement Titles II and III of P.L. 480 is delegated to the Administrator of USAID by the President in Executive Order 12752 (February 25, 1991).

Only implementing agreements involving specific grants of assistance greater than $25 million are considered subject to the accompanying Circular 175 request. The Department has taken the position that grant agreements involving less than $25 million are not considered international agreements . . .

At the same time, framework agreements and implementing agreements in excess of $25 million will generally be considered international agreements, within the meaning established in 22 C.F.R. 181.2. As such, USAID will transmit these agreements to the Department as they are concluded so that they can be reported to Congress consistent with the requirements of the Case Act, 1 U.S.C. 112b. Finally, as noted in the action memorandum, agreements relating to assistance or less than $25 million may be considered international agreements if they present issues of a non-routine nature (*e.g.*, political), and hence any such non-routine agreements, regardless of the value of the assistance with which they are associated, shall be considered international agreements requiring a separate Circular 175 authorization. The Office of General Counsel at USAID has advised that there are no legal impediments to concluding such agreements.

On the basis of these considerations, I conclude that there are no legal objections to granting USAID blanket authorization to negotiate and conclude the framework and implementing agreements described in the accompanying action memo and its attachments.

CAROL SCHWAB
ASSISTANT LEGAL ADVISER FOR
POLITICAL & MILITARY AFFAIRS

NOTES

1. *Nomenclature.* The typology and labeling of executive agreements vary, warranting care in appraisal. Nonetheless, the Circular 175 Procedure makes clear that there are different types that derive their authority from different sources—described below and in the accompanying chart.

- *Presidential-executive (or "sole executive") agreements.* These are entered into by the president solely in pursuance of the exercise of his plenary powers. To the extent textual authority has been marshaled, it has derived from the "vesting" of the executive power in the president and from extrapolations of the enumerated presidential powers as chief executive (Article II, Section 1) and commander-in-chief power (Article II, Section 2), presidential powers pertaining to the nomination (Article II, Section 2) and receiving (Article II, Section 3) of ambassadors, and the president's authority to "take care that the laws be faithfully executed" (Article II, Section 3).
- *Treaty-based executive agreements.* These are entered into by the president solely on the basis of authorization contained in an existing treaty. For example, in *Wilson v. Girard,* 354 U.S. 524 (1957), the Court based the validity of an agreement defining jurisdiction over offenses committed by U.S. military personnel in Japan on the authorization of such an agreement in Security Treaty, Sept. 8, 1951, U.S.-Jap., Art. III, 3 U.S.T. 3329, T.I.A.S. No. 2491.
- *Congressional-executive agreements.* These are entered into by the president solely on the basis of authorization from a simple

majority vote of *both* houses of Congress. Such authorization may arise from a standing statute authorizing the president to conclude an agreement or class of agreements, typically subject to certain conditions (sometimes called an "ex ante" congressional-executive agreement). Alternatively, the authorization may arise after the president completes negotiation of the agreement, by the president submitting the agreement for approval to both houses of Congress (sometimes called an "ex post" congressional-executive agreement).

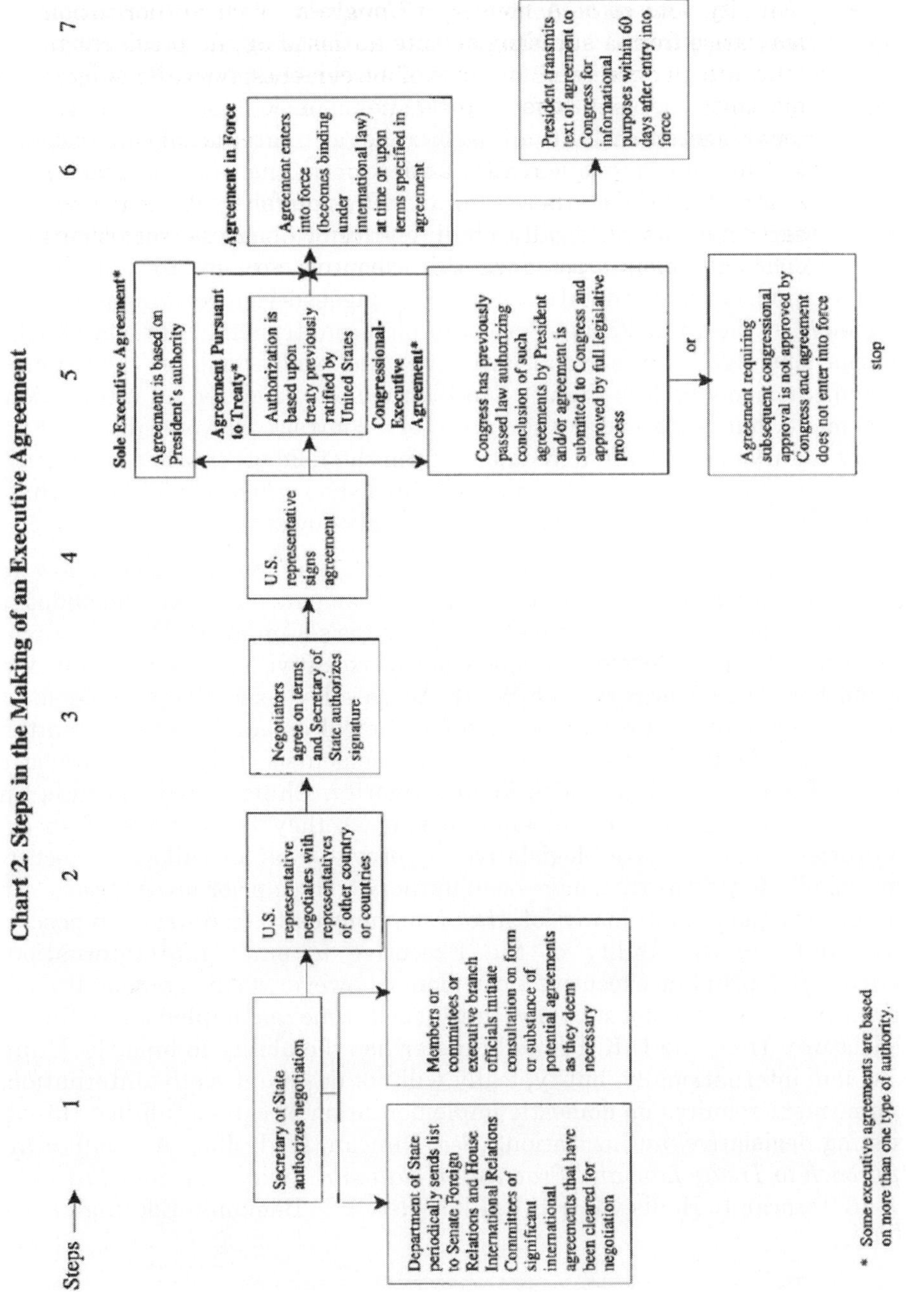

Which type best describes the AID agreements? Suppose that in the course of negotiating one of them, the foreign country insists upon reciprocity, such that any of its foreign aid personnel operating in the United States obtain the same privileges and immunities. Could the U.S. negotiators agree?

2. *The "International Agreement" Threshold.* This Section focuses on how certain international agreements may be based on authority other than the Treaty Clause. Section (e) of the Case-Zablocki Act, however, indicates that a threshold must be met before an instrument will be regarded as an "international agreement" at all (either as a treaty or as an executive agreement), and appears to leave that question in the first instances to the Secretary of State. Are there limits? Presumably an instrument or arrangement that has no legally binding effect will not be regarded as an international agreement (*see infra*, this Chapter, Sec. 8). In addition, the memorandum of law on the AID agreements suggests that certain instruments concluded by the United States with a foreign country might not qualify as an international agreements even though they are legally binding. Thus, a grant agreement involving less than $25 million is not considered an international agreement., but is instead in the nature of a contract. Do you think that this ability to carve out certain agreements from the field of "treaties or executive agreements" is appropriate as a matter of expediency? Or do you worry that it represents a further diminishment of the treaty power?

3. *Practice Abroad.* Some countries, such as Colombia, do not allow any executive agreements; all international agreements must be concluded as treaties, thus requiring approval by Colombia's Congress. Most countries, however, appear to allow for the conclusion of executive agreements of one kind or another. Thus, Germany and South Africa allow executive agreements so long as they only relate only to minor technical or administrative matters. Canada and Switzerland allow executive agreements so long as they are based on the Executive's sole constitutional authority. China, Egypt, France, and Russia allow executive agreements so long as they fall outside of specific categories that require legislative approval. Japan allows executive agreements so long as they have been authorized by a prior law or treaty. The United Kingdom and many of the Commonwealth countries impose no constraints on the ability of the Executive to enter into international agreements, including executive agreements; however, such agreements do not have the force of domestic law until such time as implemented by the legislature. Thus, the U.K. Prime Minister has the ability to bind the United Kingdom internationally, but typically will not do so unless the international commitment requires no domestic implementation or can be fulfilled through existing legislative authorization. *See* Duncan B. Hollis, *A Comparative Approach to Treaty Law and Practice, in National Treaty Law and Practice* 1, 24–26 (Duncan B. Hollis, Merritt R. Blakeslee, & L. Benjamin Ederington eds., 2005).

UNITED STATES V. BELMONT

301 U.S. 324, 325–32 (1937).

MR. JUSTICE SUTHERLAND delivered the opinion of the Court.

This is an action at law brought by petitioner against respondents in a federal district court to recover a sum of money deposited by a Russian corporation (Petrograd Metal Works) with August Belmont . . . Belmont died in 1924; and respondents are the duly-appointed executors of his will. . . .

The corporation had deposited with Belmont, prior to 1918, the sum of money which petitioner seeks to recover. In 1918, the Soviet Government duly enacted a decree by which it dissolved, terminated and liquidated the corporation (together with others), and nationalized and appropriated all of its property and assets of every kind and wherever situated, including the deposit account with Belmont. As a result, the deposit became the property of the Soviet Government, and so remained until November 16, 1933, at which time the Soviet Government released and assigned to petitioner all amounts due to that government from American nationals, including the deposit account of the corporation with Belmont. Respondents failed and refused to pay the amount upon demand duly made by petitioner.

The assignment was effected by an exchange of diplomatic correspondence between the Soviet Government and the United States. The purpose was to bring about a final settlement of the claims and counterclaims between the Soviet Government and the United States; and it was agreed that the Soviet Government would take no steps to enforce claims against American nationals; but all such claims were released and assigned to the United States, with the understanding that the Soviet Government was to be duly notified of all amounts realized by the United States from such release and assignment. The assignment and requirement for notice are parts of the larger plan to bring about a settlement of the rival claims of the high contracting parties. The continuing and definite interest of the Soviet Government in the collection of assigned claims is evident; and the case, therefore, presents a question of public concern, the determination of which well might involve the good faith of the United States in the eyes of a foreign government. The court below held that the assignment thus effected embraced the claim here in question; and with that we agree.

That court, however, took the view that the situs of the bank deposit was within the state of New York; that in no sense could it be regarded as an intangible property right within Soviet territory; and that the nationalization decree, if enforced, would put into effect an act of confiscation. And it held that a judgment for the United States could not be had, because, in view of that result, it would be contrary to the controlling public policy of the state of New York. The further contention is made by respondents that the public policy of the United States would likewise be infringed by such a judgment. The two questions thus presented are the only ones necessary to be considered.

First. We do not pause to inquire whether in fact there was any policy of the state of New York to be infringed, since we are of opinion that no state policy can prevail against the international compact here involved. . . .

We take judicial notice of the fact that coincident with the assignment set forth in the complaint, the President recognized the Soviet Government, and normal diplomatic relations were established between that government and the government of the United States, followed by an exchange of ambassadors. The effect of this was to validate, so far as this country is concerned, all acts of the Soviet Government here involved from the commencement of its existence. The recognition, establishment of diplomatic relations, the assignment, and agreements with respect thereto, were all parts of one transaction, resulting in an international compact between the two governments. That the negotiations, acceptance of the assignment and agreements and understandings in respect thereof were within the competence of the President may not be doubted. Governmental power over internal affairs is distributed between the national government and the several states. Governmental power over external affairs is not distributed, but is vested exclusively in the national government. And in respect of what was done here, the Executive had authority to speak as the sole organ of that government. The assignment and the agreements in connection therewith did not, as in the case of treaties, as that term is used in the treaty making clause of the Constitution (Art. II, § 2), require the advice and consent of the Senate.

A treaty signifies "a compact made between two or more independent nations, with a view to the public welfare." *Altman & Co. v. United States*, 224 U.S. 583, 600. But an international compact, as this was, is not always a treaty which requires the participation of the Senate. There are many such compacts, of which a protocol, a modus vivendi, a postal convention, and agreements like that now under consideration are illustrations. *See* 5 Moore, Int. Law Digest, 210–221. . . .

Plainly, the external powers of the United States are to be exercised without regard to state laws or policies. . . . In respect of all international negotiations and compacts, and in respect of our foreign relations generally, state lines disappear. As to such purposes the State of New York does not exist. Within the field of its powers, whatever the United States rightfully undertakes, it necessarily has warrant to consummate. And when judicial authority is invoked in aid of such consummation, state constitutions, state laws, and state policies are irrelevant to the inquiry and decision. It is inconceivable that any of them can be interposed as an obstacle to the effective operation of a federal constitutional power. *Cf. Missouri v. Holland*, 252 U.S. 416; *Asakura v. Seattle*, 265 U.S. 332, 341.

Second. The public policy of the United States relied upon as a bar to the action is that declared by the Constitution, namely, that private property shall not be taken without just compensation. But the answer is that our Constitution, laws, and policies have no extraterritorial operation, unless in respect of our own citizens. *Compare United States v. Curtiss-Wright Export Corp., supra*, 299 U.S. 304, at p. 318. What another country has done in the way of taking over property of its nationals, and especially of its corporations, is not a matter for judicial consideration here. Such nationals must look to their own government for any redress to which they may be entitled. So far as the record shows, only the rights of the Russian corporation have been affected by what has been done; and it will be time enough to consider the rights of our nationals when, if ever, by proper judicial proceeding, it shall be made to appear that they are so affected as to entitle them to judicial relief. The substantive right to the moneys, as now disclosed, became vested in the Soviet Government as the successor to the corporation; and this right that government has passed to the United States. It does not appear that respondents have any interest in the matter beyond that of a custodian. Thus far no question under the Fifth Amendment is involved. . . .

Judgment reversed.

DAMES & MOORE V. REGAN

453 U.S. 654, 659–90 (1981).

JUSTICE REHNQUIST delivered the opinion of the Court. . . .

. . . We are confined to a resolution of the dispute presented to us. That dispute involves various Executive Orders and regulations by which the President nullified attachments and liens on Iranian assets in the United States, directed that these assets be transferred to Iran, and suspended claims against Iran that may be presented to an International Claims Tribunal. This action was taken in an effort to comply with an Executive Agreement between the United States and Iran. . . .

I

On November 4, 1979, the American Embassy in Tehran was seized and our diplomatic personnel were captured and held hostage. In response to that crisis, President Carter, acting pursuant to the International Emergency Economic Powers Act, 91 Stat. 1626, 50 U.S.C. §§ 1701–1706 (1976 ed., Supp. III) (hereinafter IEEPA), declared a national emergency on November 14, 1979, and blocked the removal or transfer of "all property and interests in property of the Government of Iran, its instrumentalities and controlled entities and the Central Bank of Iran which are or become subject to the jurisdiction of the United States. . . ." Exec. Order No. 12170, 3 CFR 457 (1980), note following 50 U.S.C. § 1701 (1976 ed., Supp. III). President Carter authorized the Secretary of the Treasury to promulgate regulations carrying out the blocking order. On November 15, 1979, the Treasury Department's Office of Foreign Assets Control issued a regulation providing that "[u]nless licensed or authorized . . . any attachment, judgment, decree, lien, execution, garnishment, or other judicial process is null and void with respect to any property in which on or since [November 14, 1979] there existed an interest of Iran." 31 CFR § 535.203(e) (1980). The regulations also made clear that any licenses or authorizations granted could be "amended, modified, or revoked at any time." § 535.805.

On November 26, 1979, the President granted a general license authorizing certain judicial proceedings against Iran but which did not allow the "entry of any judgment or of any decree or order of similar or analogous effect. . . ." § 535.504(a). On December 19, 1979, a clarifying regulation was issued stating that "the general authorization for judicial proceedings contained in § 535.504(a) includes pre-judgment attachment." § 535.418. . . .

On January 20, 1981, the Americans held hostage were released by Iran pursuant to an Agreement entered into the day before and embodied in two Declarations of the Democratic and Popular Republic of Algeria[:]. Declaration of the Government of the Democratic and Popular Republic of Algeria, and Declaration of the Government of the Democratic and Popular Republic of Algeria Concerning the Settlement of Claims by the Government of the United States of America and the Government of the Islamic Republic of Iran. The Agreement stated that "[i]t is the purpose of [the United States and Iran] . . . to terminate all litigation as between the Government of each party and the nationals of the other, and to bring about the settlement and termination of all such claims through binding arbitration." In furtherance of this goal, the Agreement called for the establishment of an Iran-United States Claims Tribunal which would arbitrate any claims not settled within six months. Awards of the Claims Tribunal are to be "final and binding" and "enforceable . . . in the courts of any nation in accordance with its laws." Under the Agreement, the United States is obligated

> "to terminate all legal proceedings in United States courts involving claims of United States persons and institutions against Iran and its state enterprises, to nullify all attachments and judgments obtained therein, to prohibit all further litigation based on such claims, and to bring about the termination of such claims through binding arbitration."

In addition, the United States must "act to bring about the transfer" by July 19, 1981, of all Iranian assets held in this country by American banks. One billion dollars of these assets will be deposited in a security account in the Bank of England, to the account of the Algerian Central Bank, and used to satisfy awards rendered against Iran by the Claims Tribunal.

On January 19, 1981, President Carter issued a series of Executive Orders implementing the terms of the agreement. Exec. Orders Nos. 12276–12285, 46 Fed.Reg. 7913–7932. . . .

[Petitioner brought a claim in U.S. court against the government of Iran for its failure to pay for services rendered under a contract prior to its termination by Iran. Petitioner secured a pre-judgment attachment of certain Iranian assets and obtained a U.S. court judgment against Iran, but was prohibited from enforcing the judgment by the President's Executive Orders and the Treasury Department regulations.]

On April 28, 1981, petitioner filed this action in the District Court for declaratory and injunctive relief against the United States and the Secretary of the Treasury, seeking to prevent enforcement of the Executive Orders and Treasury Department regulations implementing the Agreement with Iran. In its complaint, petitioner alleged that the actions of the President and the Secretary of the Treasury implementing the Agreement with Iran were beyond their statutory and constitutional powers and, in any event, were unconstitutional to the extent they adversely affect petitioner's final judgment against the Government of Iran and the Atomic Energy Organization, its execution of that judgment in the State of Washington, its prejudgment attachments, and its ability to continue to litigate against the Iranian banks. On May 28, 1981, the District Court denied petitioner's motion for a preliminary injunction and dismissed petitioner's complaint for failure to state a claim upon which relief could be granted. . . .

II

The parties and the lower courts, confronted with the instant questions, have all agreed that much relevant analysis is contained in *Youngstown Sheet & Tube Co. v. Sawyer,* 343 U.S. 579 (1952). Justice Black's opinion for the Court in that case, involving the validity of President Truman's effort to seize the country's steel mills in the wake of a nationwide strike, recognized that "[t]he President's power, if any, to issue the order must stem either from an act of Congress or from the Constitution itself." *Id.,* at 585. . . .

IV

Although we have concluded that the IEEPA constitutes specific congressional authorization to the President to nullify the attachments and order the transfer of Iranian assets, there remains the question of the President's authority to suspend claims pending in American courts. Such claims have, of course, an existence apart from the attachments which accompanied them. In terminating these claims through Executive Order No. 12294, the President purported to act under authority of both the IEEPA and 22 U.S.C. § 1732, the so-called "Hostage Act." 46 Fed. Reg. 14111 (1981).

We conclude that although the IEEPA authorized the nullification of the attachments, it cannot be read to authorize the suspension of the claims. The claims of American citizens against Iran are not in themselves transactions involving Iranian property or efforts to exercise any rights with respect to such property. An *in personam* lawsuit, although it might eventually be reduced to judgment and that judgment might be executed upon, is an effort to establish liability and fix damages and does not focus on any particular property within the jurisdiction. The terms of the IEEPA therefore do not authorize the President to suspend claims in American courts. . . .

Although we have declined to conclude that the IEEPA or the Hostage Act directly authorizes the President's suspension of claims for the reasons noted, we cannot ignore the general tenor of Congress' legislation in this area in trying to determine whether the President is acting alone or at least with the acceptance of Congress. As we have noted, Congress cannot anticipate and legislate with regard to every possible action the President may find it necessary to take or every possible situation in which he might act. Such failure of Congress specifically to delegate authority does not, "especially . . . in the areas of foreign policy and national security," imply "congressional disapproval" of action taken by the Executive. *Haig v. Agee,* [453 U.S. 280,] 291. On the contrary, the enactment of legislation closely related to the question of the President's authority in a particular case which evinces legislative intent to accord the President broad discretion may be considered to "invite" "measures on independent presidential responsibility," *Youngstown,* 343 U.S., at 637 (Jackson, J., concurring). At least this is so where there is no contrary indication of legislative intent and when, as here, there is a history of congressional acquiescence in conduct of the sort engaged in by the President. It is to that history which we now turn.

Not infrequently in affairs between nations, outstanding claims by nationals of one country against the government of another country are "sources of friction" between the two sovereigns. *United States v. Pink,* 315 U.S. 203, 225. To resolve these difficulties, nations have often entered into agreements settling the claims of their respective nationals. As one treatise writer puts it, international agreements settling claims by nationals of one state against the government of another "are established international practice reflecting traditional international theory." L. Henkin, *Foreign Affairs and the Constitution* 262 (1972). Consistent with that principle, the United States has repeatedly exercised its sovereign authority to settle the claims of its nationals against foreign countries. Though those settlements have sometimes been made by treaty, there has also been a longstanding practice of settling such claims by executive agreement without the advice and consent of the Senate.[8] Under such agreements, the President has agreed to renounce or extinguish claims of United States nationals against foreign governments in return for lump-sum payments or the establishment of arbitration procedures. To be sure, many of these settlements were encouraged by the United States claimants themselves, since a claimant's only hope of obtaining any payment at all might lie in having his Government negotiate a diplomatic settlement on his behalf. But it is also undisputed that the "United States has sometimes disposed of the claims of its citizens without their consent, or even without consultation with them, usually without exclusive regard for their interests, as distinguished from those of the nation as a whole." Henkin, *supra,* at 262–263. . . .

Crucial to our decision today is the conclusion that Congress has implicitly approved the practice of claim settlement by executive agreement. This is best demonstrated by Congress' enactment of the International Claims Settlement Act of 1949, 64 Stat. 13, as amended, 22 U.S.C. § 1621 *et seq.* (1976 ed. and Supp. IV). The Act had two purposes: (1) to allocate to United States nationals funds received in the course of an executive claims settlement with Yugoslavia, and (2) to provide a procedure whereby funds resulting from future settlements could be distributed. To achieve these ends Congress created the International Claims Commission, now the Foreign Claims Settlement Commission, and gave it jurisdiction to make final and binding decisions with respect to claims by United States nationals against settlement funds. 22 U.S.C. § 1623(a). By creating a procedure to implement future settlement agreements, Congress placed its stamp of approval on such agreements. Indeed, the legislative history of the Act observed that the United States was seeking settlements with countries other than Yugoslavia and that the bill contemplated settlements of a similar nature in the future. H.R.Rep. No. 770, 81st Cong., 1st Sess., 4, 8 (1949).

Over the years Congress has frequently amended the International Claims Settlement Act to provide for particular problems arising out of settlement agreements, thus demonstrating Congress' continuing acceptance of the President's claim settlement authority. . . . Finally, the legislative history of the IEEPA further reveals that Congress has accepted the authority of the Executive to enter into settlement agreements. Though the IEEPA was enacted to provide for some limitation on the President's emergency powers, Congress stressed that "[n]othing in this act is intended . . . to interfere with the authority of the President to [block assets], or to

[8] At least since the case of the "Wilmington Packet" in 1799, Presidents have exercised the power to settle claims of United States nationals by executive agreement. *See* Lillich, *The Gravel Amendment to the Trade Reform Act of 1974*, 69 Am.J.Int'l L. 837, 844 (1975). In fact, during the period of 1817–1917, "no fewer than eighty executive agreements were entered into by the United States looking toward the liquidation of claims of its citizens." W. McClure, International Executive Agreements 53 (1941). *See also* 14 M. Whiteman, *Digest of International Law* 247 (1970).

impede the settlement of claims of U.S. citizens against foreign countries." S.Rep. No. 95–466, p. 6 (1977); 50 U.S.C. § 1706(a)(1) (1976 ed., Supp. III).

In addition to congressional acquiescence in the President's power to settle claims, prior cases of this Court have also recognized that the President does have some measure of power to enter into executive agreements without obtaining the advice and consent of the Senate. In *United States v. Pink,* 315 U.S. 203 (1942), for example, the Court upheld the validity of the Litvinov Assignment, which was part of an Executive Agreement whereby the Soviet Union assigned to the United States amounts owed to it by American nationals so that outstanding claims of other American nationals could be paid. The Court explained that the resolution of such claims was integrally connected with normalizing United States' relations with a foreign state . . .

In light of all of the foregoing—the inferences to be drawn from the character of the legislation Congress has enacted in the area, such as the IEEPA and the Hostage Act, and from the history of acquiescence in executive claims settlement—we conclude that the President was authorized to suspend pending claims pursuant to Executive Order No. 12294. As Justice Frankfurter pointed out in *Youngstown,* 343 U.S., at 610–611, "a systematic, unbroken, executive practice, long pursued to the knowledge of the Congress and never before questioned . . . may be treated as a gloss on 'Executive Power' vested in the President by § 1 of Art. II." Past practice does not, by itself, create power, but "long-continued practice, known to and acquiesced in by Congress, would raise a presumption that the [action] had been [taken] in pursuance of its consent. . . ." *United States v. Midwest Oil Co.,* 236 U.S. 459, 474 (1915). *See Haig v. Agee,* [453 U.S.], at 291, 292. Such practice is present here and such a presumption is also appropriate. In light of the fact that Congress may be considered to have consented to the President's action in suspending claims, we cannot say that action exceeded the President's powers.

Our conclusion is buttressed by the fact that the means chosen by the President to settle the claims of American nationals provided an alternative forum, the Claims Tribunal, which is capable of providing meaningful relief. The Solicitor General also suggests that the provision of the Claims Tribunal will actually *enhance* the opportunity for claimants to recover their claims, in that the Agreement removes a number of jurisdictional and procedural impediments faced by claimants in United States courts. Although being overly sanguine about the chances of United States claimants before the Claims Tribunal would require a degree of naiveté which should not be demanded even of judges, the Solicitor General's point cannot be discounted. Moreover, it is important to remember that we have already held that the President has the *statutory* authority to nullify attachments and to transfer the assets out of the country. The President's power to do so does not depend on his provision of a forum whereby claimants can recover on those claims. The fact that the President has provided such a forum here means that the claimants are receiving something in return for the suspension of their claims, namely, access to an international tribunal before which they may well recover something on their claims. Because there does appear to be a real "settlement" here, this case is more easily analogized to the more traditional claim settlement cases of the past.

Just as importantly, Congress has not disapproved of the action taken here. Though Congress has held hearings on the Iranian Agreement itself, Congress has not enacted legislation, or even passed a resolution, indicating its displeasure with the Agreement. Quite the contrary, the relevant Senate Committee has stated that the establishment of the Tribunal is "of vital importance to the United States." S.Rep. No. 97–71, p. 5 (1981).[13] We are thus clearly not confronted with a situation in which Congress has in some way resisted the exercise of Presidential authority.

Finally, we re-emphasize the narrowness of our decision. We do not decide that the President possesses plenary power to settle claims, even as against foreign governmental entities. . . . But where, as here, the settlement of claims has been determined to be a necessary incident to the resolution of a major foreign policy dispute between our country and another, and where, as here, we can conclude that Congress acquiesced in the President's action, we are not prepared to say that the President lacks the power to settle such claims. . . .

The judgment of the District Court is accordingly affirmed, and the mandate shall issue forthwith.

It is so ordered.

NOTES

1. *Congressional Authorization or Presidential Power? Dames & Moore* was criticized for striving to find implied congressional authorization for the president to suspend claims by removing them from the jurisdiction of U.S. courts, and doing so on the basis of legislative silence only. *See* Lee R. Marks & John C. Grabow, *The President's Foreign Economic Powers After* Dames & Moore v. Regan: *Legislation by Acquiescence,* 68 CORNELL L. REV. 68, 102–03 (1982). The authors also interpret the *Dames & Moore* decision as holding that the president "possesses no plenary power to make such a settlement. . . ." *Id.* If this is correct, could Congress prevent the president's action, as the authors suggest, "with an unambiguous expression of contrary intent"? *Id.*

[13] Contrast congressional reaction to the Iranian Agreements with congressional reaction to a 1973 Executive Agreement with Czechoslovakia. There the President sought to settle over $105 million in claims against Czechoslovakia for $20.5 million. Congress quickly demonstrated its displeasure by enacting legislation requiring that the Agreement be renegotiated. *See* Lillich, *supra,* n. 8, at 839–840. Though Congress has shown itself capable of objecting to executive agreements, it has rarely done so and has not done so in this case.

At least in the absence of such an expression, do *Belmont* and *Dames & Moore* actually support the proposition that there is a freestanding presidential power to make sole presidential executive agreements with the force of federal law? If so, does this power circumvent key political and procedural safeguards embedded in the Constitution, or can these precedents be construed more narrowly? *See* Bradford R. Clark, *Domesticating Sole Executive Agreements*, 93 VA. L. REV. 1573 (2007). The executive power to affect rights of citizens by the operation of an executive agreement usually does not present itself in stark form. Some color of explicit legislative authorization, or implicit legislative accommodation, is usually present to buttress the exercise of pure presidential power in making the agreement. It may also be unclear whether an actual property "right" has been affected by the operation of the executive agreement.

2. *Iranian Claims Return*. *Dames & Moore* accepted that the president could suspend claims in U.S. courts in favor of an international arbitral forum, the Iran-U.S. Claims Tribunal. But what if the Tribunal determined that it had no jurisdiction over a claim? The company Foremost-McKesson initially pursued in U.S. court a claim for unpaid cash dividends and expropriation. In light of the president's Executive Order and the Treasury Department regulations, the U.S. court suspended the claim and Foremost pursued the claim before the Tribunal. The Tribunal issued an award in favor of Foremost for the unpaid cash dividends, but dismissed the expropriation claim, saying that any expropriation had not ripened as of January 1981, the cut-off date for the Tribunal's jurisdiction. *Foremost Tehran v. Iran*, 10 Iran-U.S. Cl. Trib. Rep. 228 (1986). At Foremost's request, the U.S. district court reactivated the expropriation claim, allowed Foremost to amend its complaint to allege an expropriation ripening in April 1982, and subsequently determined that such an expropriation had occurred. *McKesson Corp. v. Iran*, No. Civ. A. 82–220, 1997 WL 361177 (D.D.C. June 23, 1997), *aff'd in part and rev'd in part*, 271 F.3d 1101 (D.C. Cir. 2001). For the Tribunal's consideration of this U.S. process for suspending/reactivating claims in U.S. courts, see *Iran v. United States*, Partial Award No. 590–A15(IV)–A/24–FT (Dec. 28, 1998).

3. *Claims Settlement Agreements and Takings*. The U.S. Court of Claims in *Shanghai Power v. United States,* 4 Cl.Ct. 237 (1983), considered the question of whether an unsatisfied (and, perhaps, unsatisfiable) claim by a U.S. citizen against a foreign government constitutes "property," making it subject to the protection of the Fifth Amendment of the Constitution. There, an executive agreement entered into by President Carter settled plaintiff's claim against the People's Republic of China as part of a general settlement of unsatisfied claims going back to the fall of the Nationalist regime. The settlement would have entitled the plaintiff to a fraction of the face value of its claim as it had been evaluated by the Foreign Claims Settlement Commission (FCSC). While the court found that the claim was "property" for purposes of the "just compensation clause," it found that there was no "taking" of that property by the executive agreement, explaining that every "U.S. national who trades in foreign commerce is a potential beneficiary of the President's authority to settle claims" and "it is frequently entirely fortuitous who will

benefit and who will suffer from any such presidential action." *Id.* at 247. Subsequent cases, however, have distinguished a plaintiff's claims when they are extinguished as part of a settlement but excluded from the resulting settlement process. *See, e.g., Aureus Asset Managers, Ltd. v. United States*, 121 Fed. Cl. 206, 211–43 (2015) (denying motion to dismiss claim where plaintiffs had cognizable property interest but "were excluded from receiving any just compensation whatsoever" under claims settlement agreement with Libya).

4. *Later-in-Time Executive Agreements.* As we have seen, later-in-time treaties can amend or repeal inconsistent earlier statutes. Do executive agreements have the same status? Courts (and even Congress) strive to avoid a conflict. In *Weinberger v. Rossi*, 456 U.S. 25 (1982), Justice Rehnquist found that a congressional-executive agreement on military bases between the United States and the Philippines and a subsequently negotiated presidential-executive agreement giving employment preferences to locals were not inconsistent with a U.S. statute prohibiting discriminatory hiring by the Department of Defense due to the "treaty" exception in that statute, which the court interpreted to include an executive agreement. By harmonizing the statute and the agreement, the court avoided deciding between them. To similar effect, see *Collins v. Weinberger,* 707 F.2d 1518 (D.C. Cir. 1983).

Should an earlier-in-time statute be trumped by a congressional-executive agreement (in which both Houses of Congress are involved), or by a presidential-executive agreement (in which neither House is involved)? According to the *Restatement (Third)*, executive agreements authorized by a federal statute or treaty have the same normative rank as the statute or treaty on which they are based, with the later-in-time having precedence. Presidential-executive agreements supersede inconsistent state laws, but may not prevail against a conflicting prior federal statute. *See* 1 *Restatement of the Law (Third), The Foreign Relations Law of the United States*, § 115 reporters' note 5 (1987).

5. *Constitution Versus Executive Agreement.* It would be natural to assume that if treaties cannot abridge constitutional rights, neither can presidential-executive agreements or congressional-executive agreements. *See Reid v. Covert* (*supra*, this Chapter, Sec. 6); *Holmes v. Laird*, 459 F.2d 1211, 1217 (D.C. Cir. 1972). In *Ozonoff v. Berzak,* 744 F.2d 224 (1st Cir. 1984), the First Circuit considered a "loyalty-screening" executive agreement concluded by the U.S. government with the World Health Organization (WHO) in 1953. Under the agreement, the WHO agreed not to hire a U.S. national until the United States first investigated that person's "loyalty" to the U. S. government (pursuant to Executive Order No. 10422, 18 Fed. Reg. 239 (1953) (*reprinted as amended at* 22 U.S.C. § 287 (2012))). When the U.S. national sued the U.S. government on First Amendment grounds, the government responded, in part, that the executive agreement validated such an exercise of presidential investigatory power. The First Circuit, holding for the plaintiff, found that the existence of the executive agreement did not provide adequate justification for the deprivation of free speech rights, absent showing "any tangible harm that might occur to United States security or foreign policy concerns if persons such

as [the plaintiff] are not subjected to sweeping, undirected inquiries of this type." 744 F.2d at 233. Is this reminiscent of the approach to treaties?

6. *Executive Agreements That Alter Treaties.* Can a congressional-executive agreement substantially modify the obligations that the United States would otherwise have under an existing treaty? The Office of Legal Counsel has reasoned that since a later-in-time statute can alter a treaty obligation (as a matter of U.S. law), a later-in-time executive agreement authorized by Congress should be able to do the same: "Accordingly, it lies within the power of Congress to modify the substantive obligations that a treaty imposed upon the United States, or to authorize the President to modify those obligations, insofar as those treaty obligations are binding as a matter of domestic or municipal law. The advice and consent of the Senate are not necessary to achieve this outcome." *See* Memorandum for Alan J. Kreczko, Special Assistant to the President and Legal Adviser to the National Security Council, Validity of Congressional-Executive Agreements That Substantially Modify the United States' Obligations Under an Existing Treaty, 20 U.S. Op. Off. Legal Counsel 389, *3 (Nov. 25, 1996). Can you anticipate any objections, or qualifications, to this view? Should a presidential-executive agreement also be able to alter a treaty obligation as a matter of U.S. law?

7. *Trade Agreements.* The Constitution gives Congress the authority to regulate foreign commerce, art. I, § 8, cl. 3, and to "lay and collect Taxes, Duties, Imposts and Excises," art. I, § 8, cl. 1. But the president has exercised, in practice, a great deal of control over international trade, sometimes asserting the Executive's inherent power to conduct foreign relations, and the president's express constitutional power to make treaties, art. II, § 2. Legislation authorizing the Executive to conduct international trade agreements minimizes potential friction, barring allegations that it has acted on the basis of that legislation but outside of its scope or within an area that Congress has comprehensively regulated. *See Consumers Union of the United States, Inc. v. Kissinger*, 506 F.2d 136, 141–44 (D.C. Cir. 1974).

The president has long enjoyed "fast-track" or "trade-promotion" procedures to conduct international trade negotiations. Initially enacted in the Trade Act of 1974, and modified and renewed thereafter, "trade-promotion" authority permits expedited congressional treatment for international trade agreements negotiated by the president that harmonize, reduce, or eliminate barriers to trade. When an agreement reaches Congress, it is guaranteed, within a set time period, automatic discharge from committee, limited floor debate, and an up-or-down vote without amendment. In exchange for Congress's accelerated treatment, the president is required: (1) to consult with relevant House and Senate committees for sixty days before notifying Congress of intent to enter an agreement; and (2) to notify these same committees at least ninety days before entering an agreement. During these periods either committee may object to the negotiations, derailing the agreement from fast-track consideration. Congress is also free to set time limits on negotiations, specify negotiation objectives, and require executive consultation with congressional and private trade experts. *See, e.g.*, Bipartisan Congressional

Trade Priorities and Accountability Act of 2015, Pub. L. No. 114–26, 129 Stat 320 (2015) (codified at 17 U.S.C. §§ 4201–4210). Such authority was used, for example, in the United States-Canada-Mexico North American Free Trade Agreement (NAFTA), Dec. 17, 1992, 32 I.L.M. 289 & 605 (1993).

Unsurprisingly, providing expedited procedures for sometimes controversial agreements has sometimes been challenged, including on constitutional grounds. Some commentators have questioned whether the House Ways and Means and Senate Finance Committees' ability to derail executive negotiations by a single committee's objection amounts to an informal "legislative veto" of the kind declared unconstitutional in *I.N.S. v. Chadha* (Chapter 1, Sec. 2) (Powell, J. concurring) ("The Court's decision . . . apparently will invalidate every use of the legislative veto."). *See generally* Harold Hongju Koh, *Congressional Controls on Presidential Trade Policymaking After* I.N.S. v. Chadha, 18 N.Y.U. J. INT'L L. & POLITICS 1191 (1986).

8. CHOICE OF INSTRUMENTS

As is clear from the prior Sections of this Chapter, an international agreement might be concluded as a "treaty" within the meaning of the U.S. Constitution, in which case it is submitted to the U.S. Senate for advice and consent by means of a two-thirds majority vote. (Thereafter, further international agreements might be concluded in implementation of the treaty without additional approval by Congress.) Alternatively, an international agreement might be concluded as a congressional-executive agreement, in which case it must be supported by a majority vote in both houses of Congress, either in advance of or after its negotiation. Finally, an international agreement may be concluded as a presidential-executive agreement, based solely on the president's own constitutional authority.

When may each be used? Is the president free to choose whichever of these alternatives he or she finds most suitable? Obviously, if an international agreement cannot be based solely on the president's own constitutional authority, then a presidential-executive agreement will not be available. But is it within the president's discretion—even then—to submit an international agreement to the Senate for consideration as a treaty or to Congress for consideration as a congressional-executive agreement? Recall that the Circular 175 Procedure (excerpted *supra*, this Chapter, Sec. 7) sets forth certain "considerations" when deciding how to proceed. It does not, however, actually indicate which method of making an international agreement is favored after analyzing those considerations; moreover, Circular 175 is an internal State Department administrative provision, not a source of law binding upon the president.

There may be situations when the president thinks that the agreement will not obtain majority approval in the House, but can secure a two-thirds vote in the Senate. There may be other situations when the president thinks that the agreement cannot obtain a super-majority vote in the Senate, but can achieve a simple majority in both houses. Is the president allowed to choose whichever route he or she regards as politically feasible? Does allowing presidential discretion in this area trample certain important allocations of power established in the U.S. constitutional scheme?

The treatment of trade agreements in U.S. law provides a prism for considering this issue. Though early trade agreements were concluded by the United States as treaties, by the 1930s most trade agreements were being approved as congressional-executive agreements. By the 1980s, the multilateral trade system began expanding dramatically to cover not just trade in goods, but trade in services, intellectual property, and investment, areas of considerable importance for economic activity at all levels of the U.S. economy. Treaties such as the North American Free Trade Agreement (NAFTA) and the Uruguay Round Agreements (establishing the World Trade Organization and amending the General Agreement on Tariffs and Trade (GATT)) came under considerable fire on policy grounds, and prompted many legal analysts to reconsider whether trade agreements should be concluded as congressional-executive agreements. Professor Laurence Tribe of Harvard Law School asserted that such agreements had to be concluded as treaties. Other prominent academics disagreed, and the Justice Department's Office of the Legal Counsel (headed by a longtime professor of constitutional law) defended the practice.

LAURENCE H. TRIBE, PREPARED STATEMENT BEFORE THE SENATE COMMITTEE ON COMMERCE, SCIENCE AND TRANSPORTATION

Hearing on S. 2467, GATT Implementing Legislation,
S. Hrg. 103–623, at 298–310 (1994).

Although it is remarkable that such basic constitutional argument need even be made, I begin by defending the view that the Constitution provides that certain agreements with foreign nations may be entered into only "with the Advice and Consent of the Senate," culminating in approval by two-thirds of those Senators present. U.S. Const., Art. II, § 2, cl. 2. Contrary to the claims of some scholars and political leaders, the Constitution's requirement of Senate supermajority approval of treaties is not simply an alternative procedure to be followed only if the president and Senate find it expedient to do so. Rather, the Treaty Clause provides an exclusive procedure for treaty approval.

The Constitution certainly does not mandate that all international agreements be subject to the requirements of the Treaty Clause. The Constitution uses an array of terms to describe a variety of international agreements, including "Agreement[s]," "Compact[s]," and "Treat[ies]," Art. I, § 10, cl. 1, 3. The Constitution makes absolutely clear that these are not completely interchangeable terms, but represent discrete categories of agreements subject to distinct constitutional requirements. For example, although each of the fifty states may, with congressional approval, enter into "agreements" and "compacts" with foreign countries, *see* Art. I, § 10, cl. 3, no state may enter a "treaty" with a foreign nation under any circumstances, *see* Art. I, § 10, cl. 1. . . .

In countering the claims of those who argue that congressional-executive agreements and treaties are wholly interchangeable, I find support in a variety of sources:

- In the leading Supreme Court case on treaties, *Missouri v. Holland*, 252 U.S. 416 (1920), the Court made clear—as everyone understands—that the treaty power and Congress's legislative power are not coextensive. The Constitution permits treaties to accomplish things that cannot be achieved through mere legislation. *See id.* at 433. It necessarily follows that the treaty form and the congressional-executive agreement are not wholly interchangeable.
- The United States Supreme Court has noted that, "[u]nder the Constitution . . . the word 'treaty' has a far more restrictive meaning" than it does under international law, *Weinberger v. Rossi*, 456 U.S. 25, 29 (1982), and has spoken of agreements "possessing the dignity of one requiring ratification by the Senate," *B. Altman & Co. v. United States*, 224 U.S. 583, 601 (1912) (emphasis added).
- Controversy over the Senate Foreign Relations Committee's one-time insistence that the term "treaties" in the Vienna Convention on the Law of Treaties be equated with the constitutional treaty category has been a primary reason for the Senate's failure to approve the Convention. . . .
- The notes to the *Restatement (3d) of Foreign Relations Law of the United States* indicate that United States law differs from international law in that, under United States law, 'treaties' constitute one category of international agreement that constitutionally requires a particular process and has a particular status. . . .
- The State Department has issued guidelines for deciding whether a particular agreement should properly be negotiated and approved as a treaty. *See* 11 *Foreign Affairs Manual*, Chapter 700, § 721.3 (codifying State Department Circular 175, December 13, 1955, as amended).

All these sources support a conclusion that should be obvious from the mere existence of the Treaty Clause: the content and import of certain international agreements require that they be approved by two-thirds of Senators present. . . .

The paragraph of the Constitution that contains the Treaty Clause provides for the "Advice and Consent of the Senate" for both treaty-making and certain federal appointments, but there is a striking and telling difference between the Treaty Clause and the adjacent Appointments Clause, for only the Appointments Clause permits alternative procedures. *See* Art. II, § 2, cl. 2. The Appointments Clause provides for Senate majority approval of both principal and inferior officers, but specifically allows Congress to remove the requirement of Senate approval for inferior officers. The Supreme Court's interpretation of the Appointments Clause makes clear that the Constitution's senatorial advice and consent requirement may be replaced with alternative approval methods only where the Constitution specifically so provides. Principal officers, for example, must be confirmed by the Senate, even though the phrase of the Constitution providing for Senate confirmation does not include the word "only." *See Weiss v. United States*, 114 S. Ct. 752, 767 (1994) (Souter, J. concurring). It is inconceivable that the Constitution would permit or the Senate would agree to the Senate's surrender of its unique role in confirming Supreme Court Justices, for example, to allow the House of Representatives alone or perhaps even a committee of the House or Senate to confirm or reject presidential appointments of Supreme Court Justices. The Constitution's affirmative grant of permission to Congress to alter the procedures for appointing inferior officers indicates that the Constitution is explicit when prescribed methods of confirmation or approval are not exclusive. The Treaty Clause's provision for Senate ratification by supermajority must thus be understood as exclusive.

Some have argued, however, that Congress's broad powers under the Interstate and Foreign Commerce Clause and the Necessary and Proper Clause provide ample authority for the use of congressional-executive agreements to effect any change that a treaty might accomplish. This argument is flawed for two basic reasons. First, it begs the central question at issue here. The Necessary and Proper Clause authorizes Congress "[t]o make all Laws" necessary to execute its powers, but it does not mention treaties. Art. I, § 8, cl. 18. The Necessary and Proper Clause, then, cannot be read to authorize bicameral legislative adoption of measures that properly fall within the Constitution's "treaty" category. Second, the function of the Necessary and Proper Clause, which extends congressional power over all fields fairly related to Congress's enumerated powers, does not speak at all to the structural or procedural requirements for passage of measures. In *INS v. Chadha*, 462 U.S. 919 (1983), the Supreme Court's historic decision to invalidate federal legislative veto provisions, the Court made clear that Congress may not abandon the Constitution's prescribed structural and procedural requirements even to regulate a field properly within the legislative power of Congress. The Necessary and Proper Clause no more provides a circuitous route for the approval of treaties than it authorizes a legislative veto in violation of the Constitution's requirements of bicameralism and presentment. . . .

What the text of the Treaty Clause will not permit cannot be validated by so-called congressional "precedent." The *Chadha* case provides strong support for the proposition that congressional practice alone cannot justify abandonment of the Constitution's structural provisions. The Supreme Court was willing to invalidate the legislative veto in *Chadha* even though such provisions had been inserted in hundreds of statutes since 1932. As the Supreme Court has often recognized, congressional "precedent" is most persuasive as an argument for the constitutionality of a practice when the practice extends back to our nation's earliest days under the Constitution. *See, e.g.*, *Field v. Clark*, 143 U.S. 649, 683 (1892). Late-breaking developments, however, can easily be signs of unconstitutional innovation. . . . [T]he adoption of important congressional-executive agreements after World War II was part of a "constitutional transformation." . . .

. . . [T]he Supreme Court cases that are sometimes trotted out for the proposition that any executive agreement can become "the supreme Law of the Land" through majority approval of the House and Senate in fact establish no such thing. . . . These cases often deal with the very different issues of unilateral presidential settlement or suspension of claims against foreign nations, *see, e.g.*, *United States v. Pink*, 315 U.S. 203 (1942); *United States v. Belmont*, 301 U.S. 324 (1937), or proclamation statutes, by which Congress authorizes the president to take certain actions upon making particular findings, *see, e.g.*, *United States v. Curtis-Wright*, 299 U.S. 304 (1936); *Field v. Clark*, 143 U.S. 649 (1892). The Supreme Court has never addressed directly the constitutionality of using the congressional-executive agreement to deal with matters that fall within the Constitution's "treaty" category. On the contrary, . . . at least prior to World War II, there really was no congressional or Supreme Court precedent for any attempt to read the Treaty Clause as purely optional and to regard congressionally approved executive agreements as fully interchangeable with Senate-ratified treaties. . . .

. . . The Uruguay Round presents the Senate with an opportunity either to repeat or to avoid the mistakes of the past. If political considerations lead the Senate to abdicate its constitutional role "just this once," its practice with regard to an agreement whose ardent supporters call the most significant international trade agreement ever will forever be cited as support for the proposition that no treaty need be submitted for supermajority approval by the Senate. . . .

When I first entered this national debate, it was to add a perspective that I felt was missing: the Uruguay Round's impositions on state sovereignty are so serious as to require the protection of states as equal sovereigns that is embodied in the Treaty Clause's provision for supermajority Senate approval. . . . [S]uch impositions on state sovereignty so deeply implicate the normal lawmaking process of our political system that they are impermissible if the safeguards of the Treaty Clause are not followed.

The Uruguay Round's establishment of the World Trade Organization and its dispute resolution mechanisms represents a significant departure from prior versions of GATT. Under the Uruguay Round, the United States will commit itself to "ensure the conformity of its laws, regulations and administrative procedures with its obligations as provided" in the Uruguay Round agreements. Agreement Establishing the World Trade Organizations (WTO Agreement), Art. XVI, ¶ 4. This commitment applies not only to those laws directed related to trade, but to any measure with even an indirect impact on trade that would be inconsistent with the provision of the Uruguay Round. Under the Uruguay Round, any nation's complaint against a United States law or regulation could require the United States to submit to the authority of the WTO's Dispute Settlement Body or Appellate Body. Were a panel of the DSB (or the Appellate Body on appeal) to find a United States law "GATT-illegal," the United States would be bound by that decision unless it could persuade the entire GATT membership by consensus to overturn the adverse decision. The United States would then be faced with the choice of either changing the challenged law to bring it into conformity with the panel or Appellate Body decision, or accepting the imposition of trade sanctions. With the commitment of the United States to confirm its every law and administrative regulation to GATT, with more than 120 member nations entitled to challenge American law, and with the United States deprived of any veto power over the decisions of the dispute settlement bodies, our participation in the WTO makes very real the prospect of serious economic sanctions imposed in accord with an international regime that will be binding on the United States—sanctions, therefore, against which we will not be in a position to retaliate lawfully.

This prospect seems an inevitability when one considers that the Uruguay Round establishes that its provisions and dispute resolution mechanisms will apply not only to federal laws and regulations, but to all state and local measures as well. See WTO Agreement, Annex 2, Understanding on Rules and Procedures Governing the Settlement of Disputes (Dispute Settlement Understanding), Art. 22, ¶ 9. Like the federal government, states must also bring their laws into conformity with the Uruguay Round agreements. They too must submit to the authority of the WTO dispute resolution system.

The position of the states under the Uruguay Round, however, is decidedly more precarious than that of the federal government. Whereas Congress may choose between a GATT-illegal federal law and WTO-imposed sanctions, a state whose law has been found in violation of GATT provisions will know that if it does not change its law, one of the following will occur: Congress may preempt the offending state law; the Executive Branch may bring an action against the state and persuade a court to strike the law down under GATT; or the nation as a whole will be subject to retaliatory sanctions. If the state does not wish to change its law, the consequences are left to federal officials and to other nations.

This imposes upon states considerable new burdens and vulnerabilities—vulnerabilities that are exacerbated by the secretive dispute resolution procedures of the WTO, in which states may not participate directly. In the dispute resolution process, states to a significant degree will be forced to place their fates under the Uruguay Round in the hands of the Executive Branch, which may have incentives counter to those of particular states in the context of particular disputes. . . . Because approval of the Uruguay Round will powerfully curtail state sovereignty and shift power from the states to the federal government, this trade agreement calls for the precautions of the Treaty Clause to be followed. . . .

Although I do not offer a comprehensive set of criteria for defining the boundary between treaties and other international agreements, it is clear to me that, whatever the precise contours of the treaty category, an agreement warrants the high level of consensus mandated by the Treaty Clause and may not escape classification as a treaty if it (1) creates a governing entity with a "legal personality" and legal powers capable of affecting the lives of all United States citizens by affecting state and federal lawmaking efforts; (2) provides for ongoing cooperation and reciprocal commitments among more than 120 nations; (3) accedes to the more than theoretical possibility of the United States being subjected to substantial international sanctions against which the United States cannot retaliate without placing itself in violation of the agreement; and (4) accordingly contemplates wide-reaching effects on the legal, economic, and political life of every state.

The combination of these factors in a single agreement would seem to compel the conclusion that the agreement warrants the high level of deliberation and consensus that the formal requirements of the Treaty Clause guarantee. This agreement will help shape the future of American trade with nearly every nation on earth and will likely have a significant impact on the efforts of state to regulate their own industries, environment and public safety. The very idea that the creation of a World Trade Organization—an international governance body with real powers—would not require approval as a treaty is remarkable, to say the least.

DEPARTMENT OF JUSTICE, OFFICE OF LEGAL COUNSEL, MEMORANDUM TO AMBASSADOR MICHAEL KANTOR, U.S. TRADE REPRESENTATIVE

Re: Whether Uruguay Round Agreements Require Ratification as a Treaty, Nov. 22, 1994 18 U.S. Op. Off. Legal Counsel 232 (1994).

I. THE TREATY CLAUSE

. . . Like Professor Tribe, we find that neither the text of the Constitution, nor the materials surrounding its drafting and ratification, nor subsequent Supreme Court case law interpreting it, provide clear-cut tests for deciding when an international agreement must be regarded as a "treaty" in the constitutional sense, and submitted to the Senate for its "Advice and Consent" under the Treaty Clause, U.S. Const. art. II, § 2, cl. 2. In such circumstances, a significant guide to the interpretation of the Constitution's requirements is the practical construction placed on it by the Executive and Legislative Branches acting together. . . . Indeed, the Court has been particularly willing to rely on the practical statesmanship of the political branches when considering constitutional questions that involve foreign relations. *See, e.g., United States v. Verdugo-Urquidez*, 494 U.S. 259, 273 (1990); *Dames & Moore v. Regan*, 453 U.S. 654, 686 (1981). . . .

Such practical construction has long established (and Professor Tribe acknowledges) that "there are many classes of agreements with foreign countries which are not required to be formulated as treaties" for constitutional purposes. Most pertinently here, practice under the Constitution has established that the United States can assume major international trade obligations such as those found in the Uruguay Round Agreements when they are negotiated by the President and approved and implemented by Act of Congress pursuant to procedures such as those set forth in 19 U.S.C. §§ 2902 & 2903. In following these procedures, Congress acts under its broad Foreign Commerce Clause powers, and the President acts pursuant to his constitutional responsibility for conducting the Nation's foreign affairs. The use of these procedures, in which both political branches deploy sweeping constitutional powers, fully satisfies the Constitution's requirements; the Treaty Clause's provision for concurrence by two-thirds of the Senators present is not constitutionally mandatory for international agreements of this kind.

Professor Tribe recognizes the existence of these decades-old practices, which have resulted in the approval of such fundamental trade pacts as the North American Free Trade Agreement (the "NAFTA"). But he disparages the use of Congressional-Executive agreements as merely a matter of "political leaders' casual approach to the Constitution." This dismissive characterization gives virtually no weight to the considered constitutional judgments of the political branches. We believe that that approach is mistaken. Disagreements and uncertainties surrounding the scope of the

Treaty Clause—including its interaction with Congress's power to regulate commerce—are two centuries old. . . . Congress's Foreign Commerce Clause authority and the President's responsibility for foreign affairs are unquestionably broad. In such circumstances, the political branches can fairly conclude—and have in fact concluded—that even major trade agreements such as the Uruguay Round Agreements may be approved and implemented by Acts of Congress, rather than ratified as treaties. Indeed, Professor Tribe himself wrote in 1988 that "it does appear settled that a hybrid form of international agreement—that in which the President is supported by a Joint Resolution of Congress—*is coextensive with the treaty power*. Such Congressional-Executive agreements are the law of the land, superseding inconsistent state or federal laws." Laurence H. Tribe, *American Constitutional Law* 228 n.18 (2d ed. 1988) (emphasis added).

Historically, the scope of the Treaty Clause, and its interplay with other constitutional clauses, have provoked controversies of several different kinds. . . .

One recurring kind of dispute over the Treaty Clause has been whether international agreements could be given effect by Executive action alone, or whether they required submission to the Senate for its concurrence. *See, e.g.*, 2 *Messages and Papers of the Presidents* 33 (James D. Richardson ed., 1896) (President Monroe's message to the Senate of April 6, 1818, expressing uncertainty whether the Executive alone could make an international agreement for the naval disarmament of the Great Lakes, or whether Senate advice and consent was required). A second type of recurring dispute, more pertinent here, centered on the respective powers of the Senate and the House of Representatives in such areas as the regulation of foreign trade, where different clauses of the Constitution assign responsibilities either to one House alone or to both Houses together. . . .

From time to time, the House of Representatives has . . . insisted that a treaty be made dependent on the consent of both Houses of Congress. This has occurred when, for example, the House's power over appropriations has been at issue, as in the Gadsden purchase treaty of 1853 and the Alaskan purchase treaty of 1867. . . .

In 1898, the United States annexed Hawaii by joint resolution, Joint Res. 55, 30 Stat. 750 (1898), even though the Senate had previously rejected an annexation treaty, and even though opponents of the measure argued strenuously both in Congress and in the press that such an annexation could by accomplished only by treaty, and not by a simple legislative act. . . .

In general, these inter- and intra-branch disputes over the scope of the Treaty Clause have been resolved through the political process, occasionally with marked departures from prior practices. . . . For example, after the House of Representatives objected to the concentration of power over Indian affairs in the hands of the Senate through the Treaty Clause, Congress in 1871 enacted a rider to an Indian appropriation bill declaring that no fresh treaties were to be made with the Indian nations. 16 Stat. 544, 566 (1871). Although the United States had been making Indian treaties for almost a century before that enactment, *see United States v. Kagama*, 118 U.S. 375, 382 (1886), after 1871 "the federal government continued to make agreements with Indian tribes, many similar to treaties, that were approved by both Senate and House," but "the House's action sounded the death knell for treaty making." Felix S. Cohen, *Handbook of Federal Indian Law* 107 & n.370 (1982 ed.). The policy of the 1871 enactment remains in effect. *See* 25 U.S.C. § 71. We are uncertain whether this longstanding legislation would be constitutional by Professor Tribe's lights. . . .

Finally, Professor Tribe's newly-crafted account of the treaty power entails that the Federal Government may diminish State sovereignty by employing the Treaty Clause to ratify an international agreement, but not by using any other constitutional procedure for giving such an agreement effect. Basic to Professor Tribe's analysis is the assumption that *some* "set of intrusions on state sovereignty is sufficiently grave to trigger the requirements of the Treaty Clause." . . . On this view, the Federal Government is not constitutionally prohibited from curtailing State sovereignty to a certain degree, but it may not accomplish such a curtailment by the ordinary Article I process of legislation. We find that conclusion odd and unconvincing. If the Federal Government may not trespass on State sovereignty beyond certain limits, then the attempt to do so by making a treaty would not remove the constitutional infirmity: it is by now well-established that treaties may not violate basic constitutional ordinances, including the principles of federalism. *See, e.g., Reid v. Covert*, 354 U.S. 1 (1957); *see also* Laurence H. Tribe, *American Constitutional Law* at 228. On the other hand, if it *does* lie within the Federal Government's power to curtail State sovereignty under an international agreement, we see no reason why the Government may not invoke Article I procedures for giving effect to that agreement. In short, if the Uruguay Round Agreements unduly invade State sovereignty, ratification as a treaty will not save them from unconstitutionality; if they are not an undue invasion, they can be given effect by Act of Congress.

II. THE URUGUAY ROUND AGREEMENTS AND PRESIDENTIAL POWER

In considering Professor Tribe's critique of the Uruguay Round Agreements—which focuses on the asserted impairment that the agreement causes to State sovereignty—it should be borne in mind that judicial decisions have treated GATT as effectively a "Treat[y]," and hence "supreme Law," within the meaning of the Supremacy Clause, U.S. Const., art. VI, § 2, and have held provisions of State law to be superseded by the

GATT when in conflict with it. It is also important to remember that the existing GATT arrangements include dispute resolution procedures, which often involve referring disputes to panels of individuals, who act in an individual and not a governmental capacity. Professor Tribe does not contend that the existing version of GATT or the dispute resolution procedures that have developed under it are unconstitutional as applied to the Federal or State governments of this country; rather, he alleges that "[t]he Uruguay Round's establishment of the World Trade Organization [the WTO] and its dispute resolution mechanisms represents a [constitutionally] significant departure from prior versions of GATT." . . .

We do not understand why Professor Tribe finds constitutional significance in the Uruguay Round's "reverse consensus" requirement. Under the *current* version of GATT, the States could equally well be said to be "in the hands of the Executive," for the simple reason that the President, as the sole constitutional actor who may represent the United States abroad, alone speaks for the United States in the GATT organization. Thus, the *President*, through his delegate, possesses the "veto" over the outcome of a dispute resolution under existing GATT practice, and *may refuse to exercise it*. In other words, State laws may, even under the current version of GATT, be finally determined to be "GATT-illegal" unless the Executive Branch takes affirmative action to prevent that result.

Moreover, it is misleading to suggest that the WTO procedures of the Uruguay Round Agreements place State law "at the mercy of the Executive Branch and the Trade Representative." As Professor Tribe himself explains, even if the Executive Branch decides to bring an action against a State for the purpose of having a State law declared invalid for inconsistency with the Uruguay Round Agreements, the implementing legislation explicitly precludes the WTO panel's (or Appellate Body's) report from being considered "binding or otherwise accorded deference" by the court that hears the case. *See* S. 2467, § 102(b)(2)(B)(i). Thus, the State law cannot be declared invalid by the Executive Branch acting unilaterally, even if the Executive is armed with a WTO report that has found the State law GATT-illegal; rather, the independent action of another branch of the government—the courts—is required.

Furthermore, given the breadth of the joint authority of Congress and the President in the field of foreign relations, it would be the truly extraordinary case indeed in which Presidential action in that area, when supported by an Act of Congress, could amount to an unconstitutional invasion of State sovereignty. *See Youngstown Sheet & Tube Co. v. Sawyer*, 343 U.S. at 635 (Jackson, J., concurring) (Presidential power in such cases is "at its maximum"). The Supreme Court has held that even *unilateral* Executive action, relying on the President's inherent constitutional powers alone, may constitute a "treaty" for purposes of the Supremacy Clause, and hence supersede contrary State law. Thus, in *United States v. Belmont*, 301 U.S. 324, 331–32 (1937), the Court upheld a unilateral Executive agreement in the face of contrary State law. . . .

Accordingly, we cannot agree that the powers assigned to the President by the Uruguay Round Agreements and their implementing legislation would be unconstitutional (unless the agreement were ratified as a treaty) because they might be exercised in a manner that persuaded the courts to rule that State laws were superseded. Against the massive powers of Congress and the President, acting together, to control the Nation's foreign policy and commerce, the claims of State sovereignty have little force.

III. THE WORLD TRADE ORGANIZATION

Professor Tribe has also argued that the Uruguay Round Agreements must be ratified as a treaty because its WTO dispute settlement procedures undermines State sovereignty *directly*, rather than by vesting the power to do so in the President. Unfortunately, Professor Tribe's description of the WTO's powers, scope and functions is mistaken. The proposed arrangements for the WTO do *not* represent an invasion of State sovereignty that can be cured only if the Uruguay Round Agreements are ratified as a treaty; rather, the Uruguay Round Agreements are similar in kind to earlier, Congressionally-approved trade pacts, including NAFTA and the Tokyo Round Codes, that were not, and that did not have to be, ratified as treaties. . . .

Neither the WTO, nor any dispute settlement panels, will have the authority to enter injunctions or impose monetary sanctions against member countries. Nor will they be able to order any member country that has a federal system to change its component governments' laws. While a WTO dispute settlement may opine on whether a law is inconsistent with a member's obligations under the Uruguay Round Agreements, it is up to the parties to decide how to resolve the situation. The complaining country may suspend reciprocal trade concessions if alternative forms of settlement—*e.g.*, compensation in the form of additional trade concessions, or a change in the defending country's domestic law—are not made. . . . Because our foreign trading partners would be able to increase tariffs on American goods even more easily in the absence of a trade agreement, it is hard to see how the attempt in the Uruguay Round Agreements to resolve trade disputes between member countries and to prevent the unilateral imposition of retaliatory tariffs could amount to an unconstitutional invasion of State or local sovereignty.

Professor Tribe objects that it is "no answer that the United States might choose to pay whatever fine is levied by the WTO rather than sacrifice the sovereignty of one of the fifty States, for that makes each State's sovereignty a hostage to the Federal Government's willingness to impose a tax burden on the Nation as a whole. It also puts each State in the dilemma of either accepting the tax burden on its citizens entailed by having the United States pay a WTO fine, or protecting its citizens from that burden by lobbying against the fine and urging instead that the offending State be brought to heel." Setting apart the factual error of assuming that the WTO has the power to "lev[y]" a "fine," Professor Tribe's argument buries the critical point that it is only *the United States*, not the WTO, that would wield the power to limit or displace State law. Even if United States participation in the WTO's dispute resolution procedure might create incentives that would otherwise not exist to set aside some State laws, Congress can certainly structure the range of its future choices in a way that tends to have that effect. There is in such a decision no "meaningful shift of control over state sovereignty to foreign tribunals."

CONCLUSION

We remain persuaded that, in deciding not to submit the Uruguay Round Agreements to the Senate for the concurrence of two-thirds of the Senators present, the President is acting in a wholly proper and constitutional manner. Like other recent trade agreements, including NAFTA, the United States-Canada Free Trade Agreement, the United States-Israel Free Trade Agreement and the Tokyo Round Agreement, the Uruguay Round Agreements may constitutionally be executed by the President and approved and implemented by Act of Congress.

WALTER DELLINGER
Assistant Attorney General

NOTES

1. *Availability of Congressional-Executive Agreements.* The dispute concerning the use of congressional-executive agreements continued in more academic form. *Compare* Laurence H. Tribe, *Taking Text and Structure Seriously: Reflections on Free-Form Method in Constitutional Interpretation*, 108 HARV. L. REV. 1221 (1995), *with* Bruce Ackerman & David Golove, *Is NAFTA Constitutional?*, 108 HARV. L. REV. 799 (1995). Other academics have argued that nearly all agreements can, and should, be done in the form of congressional-executive agreement, so as to make U.S. engagement with international law more sensible, effective, and democratic. *See* Oona Hathaway, *Treaties' End: The Past, Present, and Future of International Lawmaking in the United States*, 117 YALE L.J. 1236 (2008).

2. *Availability of Presidential-Executive Agreements.* When U.S. military and civilian personnel are deployed abroad, an agreement is often concluded with the host government concerning the status of those forces within the country. Such "status of forces agreements" (SOFAs) typically address issues such as privileges and immunities of the personnel, the ability to import and export goods and services in support of the personnel, and exemptions from local taxation for the force component. When the Bush

administration concluded in 2008 a SOFA with the government of Iraq on the presence of U.S. forces, controversy arose as to whether the agreement required congressional approval. *See* Agreement On the Withdrawal of United States Forces from Iraq and the Organization of Their Activities during Their Temporary Presence in Iraq, U.S.-Iraq, Nov. 17, 2008, Hein's No. KAV 8551.

The signed SOFA was submitted to the Iraqi Parliament and the Iraqi Presidency Council for approval. It was not submitted to the U.S. Senate or to both houses of the U.S. Congress. Professor Oona Hathaway argued:

> The Administration has asserted that the bilateral agreement with Iraq is simply a status of forces agreement (SOFA), more than a hundred of which have been concluded as sole executive agreements. That is incorrect. Although it has been called a SOFA, it includes provisions that have never been a part of any prior SOFA—most notably, provisions granting the authority for U.S. troops to engage in military operations, the grant of power over military operations to a joint U.S.-Iraq Committee, and a specification of timetables for military operations. These commitments go beyond the President's own constitutional authority and must be approved by Congress.

Renewing the United Nations Mandate for Iraq: Plans and Prospects: Hearing Before the Subcomm. on Int'l Orgs., Human Rights, and Oversight of the House Comm. on Foreign Affairs. 110th Cong. 117 (2008) (statement of Oona A. Hathaway). Do these lines seem appropriate, and likely to constrain the executive branch? Do they suggest an approach applicable outside of SOFAs?

3. *Choosing to Commit by Other Means*. What options exist besides treaties and the various types of executive agreement? As the president considers the type of agreement that might be used, other choices might include: (1) declaring that an international agreement, which binds other states as a matter of treaty law, reflects customary international law; (2) declaring that the United States will adhere on a provisional or similar basis to an international agreement (for example, in the period prior to consent by the Senate); or (3) negotiating a non-legally binding instrument, even if that instrument appears to address rights and obligations. The remaining Notes consider each possibility in turn.

4. *Using Customary International Law*. The president might seek to avoid the burden of ever soliciting Senate advice and consent by simply declaring all or part of a new international agreement to be declaratory of customary international law. For example, a comprehensive treaty on the law of the sea—the U.N. Convention on the Law of the Sea, 1833 U.N.T.S. 3—was adopted at a conference in 1982 by an overwhelming margin (130 states in favor, 4 against, and 17 abstentions) and subsequently opened for signature and ratification. *See* 82 DEP'T STATE BULL. NO. 2067, at 48 (1982). The U.S. executive branch took the position that the United States would not ratify the treaty, principally because of a few unacceptable provisions relating to seabed mining, but it also asserted that many things in the treaty restated or clarified customary law, or were useful and acceptable developments. *See* President's

Statement on United States Oceans Policy, 19 WEEKLY COMP. PRES. DOC. 383–84 (March 14, 1983). The Convention has since come into force, with (as of 2017) 168 parties; the United States has neither ratified nor changed its view that much of the Convention is customary international law. Does maintaining this position evade the role of the Senate under Article II, Section 2? For example, does it function like an offer to other states for the United States to be bound by almost all parts of the treaty, except those applicable to seabed mining (to which the United States objects), so long as those states reciprocate?

5. *Provisionally Committing to an International Agreement.* As discussed *supra*, this Chapter, Sec. 2, the United States, by signing an international agreement, assumes under international law an interim obligation to not to interfere with its object and purpose; the decision to sign is one committed to the discretion of the executive branch. Is a more comprehensive undertaking possible? Given that there will be a lag time between when negotiations are concluded on a treaty and the date the United States can ratify the treaty, the president might by some means commit the United States to abiding immediately by the treaty, pending Senate approval.

A number of international agreements contain provisions providing for the provisional application of some or all of the agreement prior to its entry into force, including as a consequence of signature. For example, when President Obama and Russian President Medvedev signed the "New START" Treaty, they also signed a protocol which provided that "[u]ntil entry into force of the Treaty, the provisions of the Treaty and this Protocol, listed in this Part, shall apply provisionally from the date of signature of the Treaty." *See* Treaty on Measures for the Further Reduction and Limitation of Strategic Offensive Arms, U.S.-Russ., Apr. 8, 2010, S. TREATY DOC. NO. 111–5, at Protocol, pt. 8 (2010); *see generally* Congressional Research Service, *The New START Treaty: Central Limits and Key Provisions,* CRS Rep. R41219 (Apr. 21, 2011). The GATT is another important example. The Protocol for Provisional Application of the General Agreement on Tariffs and Trade (GATT), Oct. 30, 1947, art. 1, 55 U.N.T.S. 308. Provisional application is subject to conditions established by the agreement, but is binding as a matter of international law, as the United States has acknowledged; as a matter of domestic law, the president's capacity for applying any treaty provision domestically depends on whether there is statutory or constitutional authority for doing so. *See, e.g.*, Three Treaties Establishing Maritime Boundaries Between the United States and Mexico, Venezuela and Cuba: Hearing Before the S. Comm. on Foreign Relations, 99th Cong. at 19, 27 (1980) (responses of the Deputy Legal Adviser, Department of State to questions submitted by Sen. Javits), *reprinted in* 1980 *Digest of United States Practice in International Law* 413–14; *see generally Restatement of the Law (Fourth), The Foreign Relations Law of the United States: Treaties* § 104 (Tentative Draft No. 2, 2017).

Is it objectionable as an encroachment on legislative authority when an agreement is provisionally applied for a prolonged period of time? The United States and Cuba signed a maritime boundary agreement providing for a two-year period of provisional application, see U.S.-Cuba Maritime Boundary

Agreement, Dec. 16, 1977, art. V, T.I.A.S. No. 12–208.1; that has been periodically extended, and there is as yet no definitive action in the Senate, which has been asked for advice and consent. Would it matter if the treaty had received advice and consent, and the president was simply asserting that it should be adhered to for a period after its expiration?

6. *Opting for a Political Agreement.* The president might decide to adhere to an instrument—sometimes referred to as non-binding agreements, gentlemen's agreements, joint statements or declarations—that the parties do not intent to be legally binding. *See* Robert E. Dalton, Assistant Legal Adviser for Treaty Affairs, U.S. Department of State, *Memorandum on International Documents of a Non-Legally Binding Character*, 88 AM. J. INT'L L. 515 (1994); Duncan Hollis & Joshua Newcomer, *Political Commitments and the Constitution*, 49 VA. J. INT'L L. 507 (2009).

A recent and significant example concerns the Joint Comprehensive Plan of Action, July 14, 2015, 55 I.L.M. 80 (2016), an agreement concluded among the permanent members of the Security Council (including the United States), Germany, the European Union, and Iran, to regulate Iran's uranium enrichment program in exchange for the easing of nuclear-related sanctions imposed on it. Executive branch officials emphasized that the Plan was designed to be nonbinding. *See* Kristina Daugirdas & Julian Davis Mortenson, *Contemporary Practice of the United States*, 109 AM. J. INT'L L. 649 (2015) (describing agreement and its depiction by administration officials). Indeed, the Plan's preface described its measures as "voluntary," avoided imperative language like "shall," and eschewed conventional formalities both in naming and concluding the agreement. On the other hand, it involved specific sanctions, a precise timetable, a dispute resolution mechanism, and purported to govern U.S. sanctions for 15 years—and there were indications that Iran might not share the U.S. understanding. *See* Michael D. Ramsey, *Evading the Treaty Power?: The Constitutionality of Nonbinding Agreements*, 11 FIU L. REV. 371, 377–80 (2016).

Critics were not mollified. Members of Congress (while describing the Plan as an "executive agreement") emphasized that the agreement did not bind future presidents in an open letter directed to Iran's leadership, suggesting their concerns regarding the agreement and the avoidance of legislative approval. Senator Tom Cotton, et al., An Open Letter to the Leaders of the Islamic Republic of Iran (Mar. 9, 2015), available at https://www.cotton.senate.gov/?p=press_release&id=120, [https://perma.cc/C752-4PMT]. Subsequently, Congress enacted the Iran Nuclear Agreement Review Act of 2015 (INARA), which provided a mechanism for reviewing the finalized deal with Iran and delayed presidential implementation, principally by requiring President Obama to give Congress sixty days to review the deal once signed before he might waive statutory sanctions (as existing statutes permitted him to do). Atomic Energy Act of 1954, 42 U.S.C. § 2160e, amended by Iran Nuclear Agreement Review Act of 2015, Pub. L. No. 114–17, 129 Stat. 201 (2015). INARA provided that Congress could during this period pass a joint resolution of disapproval, which would engender further delays, but that did not come to pass—though President Obama had threatened to veto it in the event it did. The Plan and an attendant measure by the Security Council, which had been adapted to accommodate INARA-based delays, went into effect. Kristina Daugirdas & Julian Davis Mortenson, *Contemporary Practice of the United States*, 109 AM. J. INT'L L. 874 (2015).

Those concerned about the Iran deal might have been skeptical that it was genuinely nonbinding, and regarded assertions about its nonbinding character as a way to blunt objections that—if it were binding—President Obama lacked constitutional authority to conclude ~~an agreement~~ the agreement. Others argued that—even conceding that President Obama possessed statutory authority to lift sanctions as the Plan contemplated—it was constitutionally defensible as a continuing proposition only if it were accepted that the agreement itself lacked domestic legal force, did not constrain future presidents ("even informally"), and was "clearly and unequivocally nonbinding under international law." Ramsey, *supra*, at 375–81. Do these criteria seem defensible, and do you agree that the Plan might have lacked sufficient clarity from the agreement itself that it was nonbinding? Or does the Plan further undermine the formal distinctions among the forms of international agreements under U.S. law? Former State Department Legal Advisor Harold Koh has suggested that future analysis avoid such distinctions, while taking into account "(1) whether the agreement entails new, legally binding obligations; (2) the degree of congressional approval for the executive lawmaking; and (3) the constitutional allocation of institutional authority over the subject matter area at issue." Harold Koh, *Triptych's End: A Better Framework to Evaluate 21st Century International Lawmaking,* 126 YALE L.J. F. 338, 345–49 (2017); *id.* at 352–55 (indicating that the Iran deal would be constitutional, and not require further congressional approval, under that approach).

Adding further complexity, many agreements—like the Paris Agreement on climate change, see Adoption of the Paris Agreement, annex, U.N. Doc. FCCC/CP/2015/L.9 (Dec. 12, 2015), are best understood as having some provisions that are legally binding and some that are not. This complicates attempts to analyze such an agreement as a mere political commitment. Compare, for example, Ramsey, *supra*, at 381–87 (concluding, tentatively, that the Paris Agreement was unconstitutional, based on criteria for executive agreements mixing binding and nonbinding provisions), with Koh, *supra*, at 352 (concluding that it "seems plain that the Paris Accord is lawful, inasmuch as it is adopted within the framework of an Article II treaty, the [United Nations Framework Convention on Climate Change (UNFCCC)], which the United States ratified [in 1992]; follows broad congressional directives in the Clean Air Act and the Global Climate Protection Act; and mostly assumes obligations that, while new, are not legally binding under domestic law"). As noted below *infra,* this Chapter, Sec. 10, however, the Paris Agreement also raised questions about the distinctiveness of nonbinding or political commitments for purposes of termination.

9. TREATY INTERPRETATION

United States constitutional law thus distinguishes between the treaties and executive agreements, but international law does not. The Vienna Convention on the Law of Treaties, May 23, 1969, 1155 U.N.T.S. 331, provides in Article 2 that a "treaty" (for purposes of the Convention only) is an international agreement concluded between States in written form and governed by international law, whether embodied in a single instrument or in two or more related instruments and whatever its particular designation. Article 2 defines its terms "without prejudice to the use of those terms or to the meanings which may be given them in the internal law of any State."

The Vienna Convention entered into force on January 27, 1980. As of mid-2017, it has 114 State parties. The United States signed the Vienna Convention on April 24, 1970, but has not ratified it. This failure to ratify arises from several factors. An initial problem was that the Senate Foreign Relations Committee

> sought to equate "treaties" as used in the Convention with "treaties" in the United States Constitution, and to declare that every agreement that is a "treaty" under the Convention can be concluded by the United States only by the process prescribed for "treaties" in the Constitution. That position has been rejected by the Executive Branch. . . .[62]

More recently, the failure to ratify the Convention may be attributed to a more general resistance of the United States to entering into wide-ranging multilateral instruments and the desire of the executive branch to focus on more high-profile agreements.

Despite this, the executive branch has repeatedly taken the position that the Vienna Convention "is already generally recognized as the authoritative guide to current treaty law and practice."[63] The Department has also specifically referred to certain articles of the Convention as illustrating its view of the Convention "as reflecting generally accepted norms of international law."[64] The Supreme Court has sometimes cited the Convention, as have lower courts. *See, e.g.*, *Weinberger v. Rossi*, 456 U.S. 25, 29 n. 5 (1982) (referring to Article 2 of the Vienna Convention as denying international importance to the distinction between treaties and other international agreements).

One important component of the Vienna Convention concerns treaty interpretation, which is addressed in Articles 31–32, reprinted below.

---

[62] *Restatement of the Law (Third), The Foreign Relations Law of the United States*, pt. III, introductory note 146 n. 4 (1987).

[63] Letter of Submittal, S. EXEC. REP., NO. 92–L, at 1 (1971).

[64] U.S. Department of State, 1979 *Digest of United States Practice of International Law* 692–93, 703–05, 767, 769 (1983).

Other relevant articles include Article 33, on interpreting treaties authenticated in two or more languages.

VIENNA CONVENTION ON THE LAW OF TREATIES, ARTICLES 31–32

May 23, 1969, 1155 U.N.T.S. 331.

ARTICLE 31

General rule of interpretation

1. A treaty shall be interpreted in good faith in accordance with the ordinary meaning to be given to the terms of the treaty in their context and in the light of its object and purpose.

2. The context for the purpose of the interpretation of a treaty shall comprise, in addition to the text, including its preamble and annexes:

(a) any agreement relating to the treaty which was made between all the parties in connection with the conclusion of the treaty;

(b) any instrument which was made by one or more parties in connection with the conclusion of the treaty and accepted by the other parties as an instrument related to the treaty.

3. There shall be taken into account, together with the context:

(a) any subsequent agreement between the parties regarding the interpretation of the treaty or the application of its provisions;

(b) any subsequent practice in the application of the treaty which establishes the agreement of the parties regarding its interpretation;

(c) any relevant rules of international law applicable in the relations between the parties.

4. A special meaning shall be given to a term if it is established that the parties so intended.

ARTICLE 32

Supplementary means of interpretation

Recourse may be had to supplementary means of interpretation, including the preparatory work of the treaty and the circumstances of its conclusion, in order to confirm the meaning resulting from the application of article 31, or to determine the meaning when the interpretation according to article 31:

(a) leaves the meaning ambiguous or obscure; or

(b) leads to a result which is manifestly absurd or unreasonable.

NOTE: TREATY INTERPRETATION BY U.S. COURTS

Article 31(1) of the Vienna Convention points to different elements of treaty interpretation. First, it calls for focusing on the "ordinary meaning" of treaty provision, which U.S. lawyers might refer to as the "plain meaning" when engaged in statutory interpretation. Second, it calls for considering that ordinary meaning "in context"—which, as Article 31(2) indicates, requires consulting other treaty provisions, its preamble, and annexes. Third, it calls for interpretation in light of the "object and purpose" of the treaty. Article 31(3) appears to favor consideration of subsequent practice of the treaty parties, while resort to the negotiating history (often referred to as the "travaux prėparatoires") appears to have a secondary status in Article 32.

Does this approach comport with your sense of how U.S. courts normally interpret a constitutional provision? A statutory provision? A contract? In those contexts, to what degree do you think U.S. courts follow a theory of textualism, a theory of originalism, or a theory of teleology (focusing on achieving the purposes underlying the text)? Detlev Vagts suggests that:

> None of these theories in fact represent the practice of the Supreme Court in interpreting the Constitution. A more modest claim would be that cases tend to follow a hierarchy of indicia, starting, as does the Vienna Convention, with the ordinary meaning and moving to evidence of intent and historical meaning, and then to teleology. In addition the Supreme Court places an emphasis on previous case-law, which is an approach that international courts do not and cannot share, given their light case load.

Detlev Vagts, *Treaty Interpretation and the New American Ways of Law Reading*, 4 EUR. J. INT'L L. 472, 493–95 (1993).

While it may be difficult to identify the exact theory by which U.S. courts approach interpretation in domestic contexts, the same difficulty arises with respect to treaty interpretation. U.S. courts do not habitually invoke the methodological approach of the Vienna Convention on the Law of Treaties, though it would be perfectly plausible to do so: (1) as a matter of convenience; (2) promote uniformity with other national courts that also engage in interpreting the same treaty; (3) to promote conformity of U.S. law with international law, per the *Charming Betsy* doctrine (*see* Chapter 2, Sec. 2); or (4) as a matter of law, if the Vienna Convention rules have domestic status derived from customary international law.

As you read the next case and accompanying notes, consider the following:

- Is the U.S. Supreme Court using a textualist, originalist, or teleological approach to treaty interpretation—or all three?
- Should treaties be interpreted like contracts, or is a different approach warranted? If given special treatment, should treaties be construed more cautiously (since it is a matter of inter-governmental relations) or more liberally (so as to help advance

transnational relations)? Should the Court be guided by a principle of good faith towards U.S. treaty partners?

- How does the Court evaluate practice prior to and after the conclusion of a treaty? What kind of practice is deemed relevant?
- To what extent is the Court interested in the interpretations reached by the executive branch? Interpretations reached by foreign courts?

OLYMPIC AIRWAYS V. HUSAIN

540 U.S. 644 (2004).

JUSTICE THOMAS delivered the opinion of the Court.

Article 17 of the Warsaw Convention (Convention) imposes liability on an air carrier for a passenger's death or bodily injury caused by an "accident" that occurred in connection with an international flight. . . . The issue we must decide is whether the "accident" condition precedent to air carrier liability under Article 17 is satisfied when the carrier's unusual and unexpected refusal to assist a passenger is a link in a chain of causation resulting in a passenger's pre-existing medical condition being aggravated by exposure to a normal condition in the aircraft cabin. We conclude that it is.

I

. . . In December 1997, Dr. Abid Hanson and his wife, Rubina Husain (hereinafter respondent), traveled with their children and another family from San Francisco to Athens and Cairo for a family vacation. During a stopover in New York, Dr. Hanson learned for the first time that petitioner allowed its passengers to smoke on international flights. Because Dr. Hanson had suffered from asthma and was sensitive to secondhand smoke, respondent requested and obtained seats away from the smoking section. Dr. Hanson experienced no problems on the flights to Cairo.

For the return flights, Dr. Hanson and respondent arrived early at the Cairo airport in order to request non-smoking seats. Respondent showed the check-in agent a physician's letter explaining that Dr. Hanson "has [a] history of recurrent anaphylactic reactions," and asked the agent to ensure that their seats were in the non-smoking section. The flight to Athens was uneventful.

After boarding the plane for the flight to San Francisco, Dr. Hanson and respondent discovered that their seats were located only three rows in front of the economy-class smoking section. Respondent advised Maria Leptourgou, a flight attendant for petitioner, that Dr. Hanson could not sit in a smoking area, and said, " 'You have to move him.' " The flight attendant told her to " 'have a seat.' " After all the passengers had boarded but prior to takeoff, respondent again asked Ms. Leptourgou to move Dr.

Hanson, explaining that he was " 'allergic to smoke.' " Ms. Leptourgou replied that she could not reseat Dr. Hanson because the plane was " 'totally full' " and she was "too busy" to help.

[Dr. Hanson was soon "surrounded by ambient cigarette smoke" and repeatedly, but unsuccessfully, asked to be seated elsewhere.]

About two hours into the flight, the smoking noticeably increased in the rows behind Dr. Hanson. Dr. Hanson asked respondent for a new inhaler because the one he had been using was empty. Dr. Hanson then moved toward the front of the plane to get some fresher air. While he was leaning against a chair near the galley area, Dr. Hanson gestured to respondent to get his emergency kit. Respondent returned with it and gave him a shot of epinephrine. . . . Dr. Hanson died shortly thereafter. . . .

II

A

Neither party here contests *Saks*' definition of the term "accident" under Article 17 of the Convention. Rather, the parties differ as to which event should be the focus of the "accident" inquiry. The Court's reasoning in *Saks* sheds light on whether the flight attendant's refusal to assist a passenger in a medical crisis is the proper focus of the "accident" inquiry.

. . . .

The Court [in *Saks*] focused its analysis on determining "what causes can be considered accidents," and observed that Article 17 "embraces causes of injuries" that are "unexpected or unusual." The Court did not suggest that only one event could constitute the "accident," recognizing that "[a]ny injury is the product of a chain of causes." Thus, for purposes of the "accident" inquiry, the Court stated that a plaintiff need only be able to prove that "some link in the chain was an unusual or unexpected event external to the passenger."

B

Petitioner argues that the "accident" inquiry should focus on the "injury producing event," which, according to petitioner, was the presence of ambient cigarette smoke in the aircraft's cabin. Because petitioner's policies permitted smoking on international flights, petitioner contends that Dr. Hanson's death resulted from his own internal reaction—namely, an asthma attack—to the normal operation of the aircraft. . . .

Petitioner's focus on the ambient cigarette smoke as the injury producing event is misplaced. We do not doubt that the presence of ambient cigarette smoke in the aircraft's cabin during an international flight might have been "normal" at the time of the flight in question. But petitioner's "injury producing event" inquiry—which looks to "the precise factual 'event' that caused the injury"—neglects the reality that there are often multiple interrelated factual events that combine to cause any given injury. In *Saks*, the Court recognized that any one of these factual events or happenings may be a link in the chain of causes and—so long as it is unusual or unexpected—could constitute an "accident" under Article 17. Indeed, the very fact that multiple events will necessarily combine and interrelate to cause any particular injury makes it difficult to define, in any coherent or non-question-begging way, any single event as the "injury producing event." . . . .

And petitioner's argument that the flight attendant's failure to act cannot constitute an "accident" because only affirmative acts are "event[s] or happening[s]" under *Saks* is unavailing. The distinction between action and inaction, as petitioner uses these terms, would perhaps be relevant were this a tort law negligence case. But respondents do not advocate, and petitioner vigorously rejects, that a negligence regime applies under Article 17 of the Convention. The relevant "accident" inquiry under Saks is whether there is "an unexpected or unusual event or happening." The rejection of an explicit request for assistance would be an "event" or "happening" under the ordinary and usual definitions of these terms. See *American Heritage Dictionary* 635 (3d ed. 1992) ("event": "[s]omething that takes place; an occurrence"); *Black's Law Dictionary* 554–555 (6th ed. 1990) ("event": "Something that happens"); *Webster's New International Dictionary* 885 (2d ed. 1957) ("event": "The fact of taking place or occurring; occurrence" or "[t]hat which comes, arrives, or happens").[9] . . .

Confirming this interpretation, other provisions of the Convention suggest that there is often no distinction between action and inaction on the issue of ultimate liability. For example, Article 25 provides that Article 22's liability cap does not apply in the event of "wilful misconduct or . . . such default on [the carrier's] part as, in accordance with the law of the court to which the case is submitted, is considered to be equivalent to wilful

---

[9] The dissent cites two cases from our sister signatories United Kingdom and Australia—*Deep Vein Thrombosis and Air Travel Group Litigation*, [2003] EWCA Civ. 1005, 2003 WL 21353471, *650 (July 3, 2003), and *Qantas Ltd. v. Povey*, [2003] VSCA 227, ¶ 17, 2003 WL 23000692, ¶ 17 (Dec. 23, 2003) (Ormiston, J. A.), respectively—and suggests that we should simply defer to their judgment on the matter. But our conclusion is not inconsistent with *Deep Vein Thrombosis and Air Travel Litigation*, where the United Kingdom Court of Appeals commented on the District Court and Court of Appeals opinions in this case, and agreed that Dr. Hanson's death had resulted from an accident. The United Kingdom court reasoned: "The refusal of the flight attendant to move Dr. Hanson cannot properly be considered as mere inertia, or a non-event. It was a refusal to provide an alternative seat which formed part of a more complex incident, whereby Dr. Hanson was exposed to smoke in circumstances that can properly be described as unusual and unexpected." EWCA Civ. 1005, ¶ 50, 2003 WL 21353471, at *664, ¶ 50.

To the extent that the precise reasoning used by the courts in *Deep Vein Thrombosis and Air Travel Group Litigation* and *Povey* is inconsistent with our reasoning, we reject the analysis of those cases for the reasons stated in the body of this opinion. In such a circumstance, we are hesitant to "follo[w]" the opinions of intermediate appellate courts of our sister signatories, *post*, at 2 (Scalia, J., dissenting). This is especially true where there are substantial factual distinctions between these cases . . . and where the respective courts of last resort—the House of Lords and High Court of Australia—have yet to speak.

misconduct." 49 Stat. 3020 (emphasis added).[11] Because liability can be imposed for death or bodily injury only in the case of an Article 17 "accident" and Article 25 only lifts the caps once liability has been found, these provisions read together tend to show that inaction can give rise to liability. Moreover, Article 20(1) makes clear that the "due care" defense is unavailable when a carrier has failed to take "all necessary measures to avoid the damage." These provisions suggest that an air carrier's inaction can be the basis for liability. . . .

For the foregoing reasons, we conclude that the conduct here constitutes an "accident" under Article 17 of the Warsaw Convention. Accordingly, the judgment of the Court of Appeals is affirmed.

It is so ordered.

JUSTICE SCALIA, with whom JUSTICE O'CONNOR joins . . . dissenting.

When we interpret a treaty, we accord the judgments of our sister signatories " 'considerable weight.' " *Air France v. Saks*, 470 U.S. 392, 404 . . . (1985). True to that canon, our previous Warsaw Convention opinions have carefully considered foreign case law. *See, e.g., El Al Israel Airlines, Ltd. v. Tsui Yuan Tseng*, 525 U.S. 155, 173–174 . . . (1999); *Eastern Airlines, Inc. v. Floyd*, 499 U.S. 530, 550–551 . . . (1991); *Saks, supra*, at 404. . . . Today's decision stands out for its failure to give any serious consideration to how the courts of our treaty partners have resolved the legal issues before us.

This sudden insularity is striking, since the Court in recent years has canvassed the prevailing law in other nations (at least Western European nations) to determine the meaning of an American Constitution that those nations had no part in framing and that those nations' courts have no role in enforcing. *See Atkins v. Virginia*, 536 U.S. 304, 316–317, n.21 . . . (2002) (whether the Eighth Amendment prohibits execution of the mentally retarded); *Lawrence v. Texas*, . . . [539 U.S. 558, 578] . . . (2003) (whether the Fourteenth Amendment prohibits the criminalization of homosexual conduct). One would have thought that foreign courts' interpretations of a treaty that their governments adopted jointly with ours, and that they have an actual role in applying, would be (to put it mildly) all the more relevant.

The Court's new abstemiousness with regard to foreign fare is not without consequence: Within the past year, appellate courts in both

---

[11] The Montreal Protocol No. 4 to Amend the Convention for the Unification of Certain Rules relating to International Carriage by Air (1975) amends Article 25 by replacing "wilful misconduct" with the language "done with intent to cause damage or recklessly and with knowledge that damage would probably result," as long as the airline's employee or agent was acting "within the scope of his employment." S. Exec. Rep. No. 105–20, p. 29 (1998). In 1998, the United States gave its advice and consent to ratification of the protocol, and it entered into force in the United States on March 4, 1999. *See El Al Israel Airlines, Ltd. v. Tsui Yuan Tseng*, 525 U.S. 155, 174, n.14 (1999). Because the facts here took place in 1997–1998, Montreal Protocol No. 4 does not apply.

England and Australia have rendered decisions squarely at odds with today's holding. . . .

. . . In *Deep Vein Thrombosis and Air Travel Group Litigation*, [2003] EWCA Civ. 1005, 2003 WL 21353471 (July 3, 2003), England's Court of Appeal, in an opinion by the Master of the Rolls that relied heavily on *Abramson v. Japan Airlines Co.*, 739 F.2d 130 (C.A.3 1984), and analyzed more than a half-dozen other non-English decisions, held as follows:

> "A critical issue in this appeal is whether a failure to act, or an omission, can constitute an accident for the purposes of Article 17. Often a failure to act results in an accident, or forms part of a series of acts and omissions which together constitute an accident. In such circumstances it may not be easy to distinguish between acts and omissions. I cannot see, however, how inaction itself can ever properly be described as an accident. It is not an event; it is a non-event. Inaction is the antithesis of an accident." [2003] EWCA Civ. 1005, ¶ 25, 2003 WL 21353471 (Lord Phillips, M. R.).

Six months later, the appellate division of the Supreme Court of Victoria, Australia, in an opinion that likewise gave extensive consideration to American and other foreign decisions, agreed . . .

We can, and should, look to decisions of other signatories when we interpret treaty provisions. Foreign constructions are evidence of the original shared understanding of the contracting parties. Moreover, it is reasonable to impute to the parties an intent that their respective courts strive to interpret the treaty consistently. (The Warsaw Convention's preamble specifically acknowledges "the advantage of regulating *in a uniform manner* the conditions of . . . the liability of the carrier." 49 Stat. 3014 (emphasis added).) Finally, even if we disagree, we surely owe the conclusions reached by appellate courts of other signatories the courtesy of respectful consideration. . . .

Tragic though Dr. Hanson's death may have been, it does not justify the Court's putting us in needless conflict with other signatories to the Warsaw Convention. I respectfully dissent.

NOTES

1. *Supreme Court and Treaty Interpretation*. In light of *Olympic Airways*, how would you answer the questions posed at the beginning of this Section? Does the Court's approach seem to you coherent, and complete?

In *Chew Heong v. United States*, the Supreme Court stated: " 'Treaties of every kind . . . are to receive a fair and liberal interpretation, according to the intention of the contracting parties, and are to be kept in the most scrupulous good faith. . . .' [T]he court cannot be unmindful of the fact that the honor of the government and people of the United States is involved in every inquiry whether rights secured by [treaty] stipulations shall be recognized and protected." 112 U.S. 536, 540 (1884). Is this an operative principle upon which U.S. courts should interpret treaties and, if so, what consequences should flow from it? *See* Michael P. Van Alstine, *The Death of Good Faith in Treaty Jurisprudence and a Call for Resurrection*, 93 GEO. L.J. 1885 (2005).

2. *Use of International Court Decisions When Interpreting Treaties.* Should U.S. courts follow the interpretations placed upon treaties by international courts (as opposed to foreign courts operating in national legal systems)? The International Court of Justice (ICJ) in the period prior to the *Medellín* case, *supra,* this Chapter, Sec. 4, interpreted the Vienna Convention on Consular Relations as precluding the application of State "procedural default" rules to claims brought under Article 36 of the Convention. While the U.S. Supreme Court stated that the International Court's treaty interpretation deserved "respectful consideration," in *Sanchez-Llamas v. Oregon*, 548 U.S. 331 (2006), the Supreme Court declined to adopt that interpretation.

> Under our Constitution, "[t]he judicial Power of the United States" is "vested in one supreme Court, and in such inferior Courts as the Congress may from time to time ordain and establish." Art. III, § 1. That "judicial Power . . . extend[s] to . . . Treaties." *Id.*, § 2. And, as Chief Justice Marshall famously explained, that judicial power includes the duty "to say what the law is." *Marbury v. Madison*, 1 Cranch 137, 177 . . . (1803). If treaties are to be given effect as federal law under our legal system, determining their meaning as a matter of federal law "is emphatically the province and duty of the judicial department," headed by the "one supreme Court" established by the Constitution. *Ibid.* . . . It is against this background that the United States ratified, and the Senate gave its advice and consent to, the various agreements that govern referral of Vienna Convention disputes to the ICJ.
>
> Nothing in the structure or purpose of the ICJ suggests that its interpretations were intended to be conclusive on our courts. The ICJ's decisions have "*no binding force* except between the parties and in respect of that particular case," Statute of the International Court of Justice, Art. 59, 59 Stat. 1062, T. S. No. 993 (1945) (emphasis added). Any interpretation of law the ICJ renders in the course of resolving particular disputes is thus not binding precedent *even as to the ICJ itself*; there is accordingly little reason to think that such interpretations were intended to be controlling on our courts. The ICJ's principal purpose is to arbitrate particular disputes between national governments. . . .

NOTE ON TREATY INTERPRETATION BY THE EXECUTIVE BRANCH

Interpretation of treaties is often undertaken by the executive branch in the course of its day-to-day implementation of treaties without the matter ending up before a U.S. court. *See, e.g.,* U.S. Department of State, *Digest of*

United States Practice in International Law 2001, at 219 (Sally J. Cummins & David P. Stewart eds., 2001). For matters arising in litigation, courts often signal deference to executive branch interpretations, usually while finding support on other bases as well. *See, e.g., Abbott v. Abbott*, 560 U.S. 1, 15 (2010) ("This Court's conclusion that Mr. Abbott possesses a right of custody under the Convention is supported and informed by the State Department's view on the issue. . . . It is well settled that the Executive Branch's interpretation of a treaty 'is entitled to great weight.' There is no reason to doubt that this well-established canon of deference is appropriate here.") (citations omitted).

At the same time, U.S. courts do not always defer to the executive branch's interpretation of a treaty, particularly in recent years. Deborah N. Pearlstein notes that

> the Court has invoked a *Marbury*-based insistence on asserting its own formal interpretive authority. . . . [I]n a series of decisions involving national security, the Court has been anything but deferential to the executive's interpretation of the relevant statute or treaty. In *Rasul v. Bush*, *Hamdi v. Rumsfeld*, *Hamdan v. Rumsfeld*, and *Boumediene v. Bush*, the Court has swept aside vigorous arguments by the executive that it refrain from engagement on abstention or political question grounds. Moreover, the Court has scarcely noted any doctrinal tradition of interpretive "deference" on the meaning of the laws.

Deborah N. Pearlstein, *After Deference: Formalizing the Judicial Power for Foreign Relations Law*, 159 U. PA. L. REV. 783, 793–801 (2011).

Should courts defer to the executive branch, and on what basis? If the justification is relative expertise, should the degree of deference depend on the regulatory context, including the relative expertise of the executive branch? Ganesh Sitaraman & Ingrid Wuerth, *The Normalization of Foreign Relations Law*, 128 HARV. L. REV. 1897 (2015). Should the degree of deference be mitigated by the degree of 'executive self-interest" in a particular outcome? *See* Scott M. Sullivan, *Rethinking Treaty Interpretation*, 86 TEX. L. REV. 777 (2008). Should it depend on formal or informal signals from Congress as to whether it shares the executive branch interpretation? And should Congress itself defer to the executive branch as to the interpretation of a treaty?

The respective roles of the Senate and president came to a head in the mid-1980s over the executive branch's interpretation of the 1972 Anti-Ballistic Missile Treaty (ABM Treaty). *See* Treaty on the Limitation of Anti-Ballistic Missile Systems, May 26, 1972, U.S.-U.S.S.R., 23 U.S.T. 3435. For the first decade of its existence, the ABM Treaty had been interpreted as imposing a blanket prohibition on the development of anti-ballistic missile systems, except for very limited land-based systems (the theory being that neither the United States nor the Soviet Union would initiate a nuclear attack if it were unable to defend itself against subsequent retaliation that almost certainly would ensue). Thus, the Treaty was interpreted "narrowly," in the sense that it only allowed limited exceptions.

In March 1983, however, President Ronald Reagan announced his intention to pursue a "Strategic Defense Initiative" (also known as "SDI," or "Star Wars"), which would be a ground-based and space-based system to protect the United States from attack by strategic nuclear ballistic missiles. The Reagan Administration offered an alternative interpretation of the ABM Treaty—a "broad" interpretation—that would allow such development and testing, but not deployment. In advancing such an interpretation, it relied in part on information contained in a secret negotiating record that was not provided to the Senate at the time of its advice and consent to ratification.

The Senate Foreign Relations Committee and the Senate Judiciary Committee held joint hearings on this effort to "reinterpret" the ABM Treaty. Then-Senator Joseph Biden introduced Senate Resolution 167 (reprinted in part below). As you review the materials (focusing on the general principles, rather than the intricacies of the ABM Treaty) consider several issues. First, when is "reinterpretation" of a treaty more or less an amendment (or a new treaty altogether), and how would you compare such a development to other ways in which treaties evolve? Second, what weight is to be accorded to the negotiating record of a treaty—and what difference does it make if that record was not transmitted to the Senate at the time it approved the treaty? Third, when the negotiating record is not transmitted (most are not), what weight is to be accorded the Senate's *implicit* understanding concerning the meaning of a treaty (gleaned, for example, from statements made by senators during committee hearings or on the Senate floor), as opposed to *explicit* reservations, understandings, or declarations?

THE ABM TREATY AND THE CONSTITUTION: JOINT HEARINGS ON SENATE RESOLUTION 167 BEFORE THE SENATE COMMITTEE ON FOREIGN RELATIONS AND THE SENATE COMMITTEE ON THE JUDICIARY

100th Cong. at 229–31, 236–37, 317–20, 355–64, 415–19 (1987).

. . . .

THE TREATY POWER

SEC. 2. The Senate finds as follows:

(1)(A) Article II, section 2, clause 2 of the United States Constitution provides that the President "shall have power, by and with the advice and consent of the Senate, to make treaties, provided two-thirds of the Senators present concur".

(B) If, following Senate advice and consent, the President proceeds to ratify a treaty, the President may ratify only the treaty to which the Senate advised and consented.

(2)(A) Under the United States Constitution, during the period in which a treaty is in force, the meaning of that treaty is what the Senate understands the treaty to mean when it gives its advice and consent, a meaning which is informed by reference to expressions of intent by the Senate as well as Senate acquiescence in any interpretation communicated by the Executive.

(B) In the absence of any evidence concerning how the Senate understands such treaty, it is properly interpreted by reference to its text, as reasonably construed, in light of its context and object and purpose.

(C) To the extent the meaning of a treaty is clear under subparagraphs (A) and (B), anything not transmitted to the Senate at such time, including the negotiating record, is not relevant to the meaning of the treaty.

(3) The President may not amend a treaty without the agreement of the Parties and the advice and consent of the Senate.

(4)(A) Under Article II, section 3, clause 4 of the Constitution, the President is required to "take care that the laws be faithfully executed".

(B) For purposes of such provision, during the period in which a treaty is in force, it constitutes a law.

(C) The President is required to take care that each such treaty be faithfully executed. . . .

PREPARED STATEMENT OF PROFESSOR LOUIS HENKIN TO THE SENATE FOREIGN RELATIONS COMMITTEE

(Mar. 11, 1987).

. . . For present purposes, one may reduce [Article II, Section 2] to a simple proposition: the President can make a treaty if the Senate has consented to it. Of course, the President can only make the treaty to which the Senate consented; he cannot make a treaty other than the one to which the Senate consented. Therefore, the President cannot make a treaty with a text different from the one to which the Senate consented; he cannot make a treaty with a meaning different from the one to which the Senate consented.

In considering treaties for possible consent, the Senate has on numerous occasions expressed itself on the meaning of one provision or another [through reservations or understandings]. . . .

The principle that the President can only make a treaty as it is understood by the Senate would govern even if the Senate had given no indication of its understanding of the treaty. In that event, it must be assumed—in the absence of any evidence to the contrary—that the Senate understood the treaty to mean what it would be understood to mean by reasonable people, reading the text of the treaty in good faith in accordance with the ordinary meaning to be given to the terms of the treaty, in their context and in the light of their object and purpose. . . .

PREPARED STATEMENT OF U.S. STATE DEPARTMENT LEGAL ADVISER ABRAHAM D. SOFAER TO THE SENATE FOREIGN RELATIONS COMMITTEE

(Mar. 26, 1987).

. . . Let me say, at the outset, that I fully agree with the proposition expressed in Section 2(1)(B) that "the President may ratify only the treaty to which the Senate advised and consented." . . . The issue, always, in the context of our international obligations, is: What is that treaty to which the Senate advised and consented? . . .

The Resolution misstates the law [in certain regards]. It is wrong, first, in the special weight it seeks to accord to what it defines as "Senate acquiescence in any interpretation communicated by the Executive." It is also wrong in attempting to mandate that, "to the extent the meaning of a treaty is clear" from how the Senate understands it and from the treaty's text, "anything not transmitted to the Senate" during the process of advice and consent, "including the negotiating record, is not relevant to the meaning of the treaty." These standards are inconsistent with established practice, and their adoption could have no effect internationally other than occasionally to bind the United States to standards of conduct which our treaty partners are free to ignore. Moreover, while these standards may appear to protect the prerogatives of the Senate, they would seriously undermine the Constitution's real purpose in assigning to the Senate the power of advice and consent.

. . . In each instance, the Senate acts, not merely to protect its own prerogatives, but as a partner with the President in forming an international contract. A treaty is a law, and in some respects it has purely domestic effects that lead to its being applied in the way any law is applied. But a treaty is also more than a law. It is an international contract, and the Senate is as responsible as the President for making sure that the contracts made in behalf of the U.S. are mutually enforceable and do not create unilateral duties.

In implementing its important powers, therefore, over the meaning of treaties, the Senate has developed a set of practices to ensure that the Senate's determinations and opinions have the same degree of binding effect on our treaty partners as they do upon the United States. Thus, the Senate acts to incorporate its proposed interpretations as amendments, reservations, understandings, or other conditions in the Senate's resolution of ratification. The resolution of ratification is the document by which the Senate formally grants advice and consent, and it typically requires the President to take appropriate action in connection with ratification to ensure that the other party is officially informed of the Senate's input on the terms of the international contract, and is mutually bound.

In the case of a bilateral treaty, the practice of the Executive Branch has generally been to seek the express agreement of the other party to all the conditions in the Senate's resolution of ratification which affect the rights and obligations of the parties. The Executive then incorporates all such conditions into the U.S. instrument of ratification. The Senate is well aware of the importance of this process, and has occasionally concerned itself in great detail with the precise manner in which the Executive Branch would ensure that our treaty partners are legally bound with respect to the Senate's understandings or conditions. . . .

In sharp contrast to Senate actions that are contained in the resolution of ratification and formally communicated to treaty partners, interpretations of a treaty merely discussed before, or presented by Executive witnesses to, the Senate in general have far less weight in the process of treaty interpretation. This does not mean that such interpretive statements have no probative value on the issue of the treaty's international meaning and effect.

Their probative value for this purpose, however, is far less certain than statements placed in ratification resolutions, and depends upon a variety of factors, including the degree to which the Senate evidenced an intent to adopt the interpretation as a condition to its assent to the treaty, whether and the manner in which the treaty partner is put officially on notice of such statements, and the extent and manner in which the treaty partner responds.

How the record of internal ratification proceedings fits into the scheme of the Vienna Convention on Treaties is unclear. The internal ratification proceedings of one of the parties to a treaty may shed light on that party's understanding of the meaning intended by its terms and the object and purpose of the treaty. Standing alone, however, such proceedings would not appear to be part of the context of a treaty, or the materials cited in Article 31. Such evidence might, however, qualify under Article 32 as "supplementary materials", and appear to have been treated as such by various scholars. Assuming that internal ratification records are, at best, "supplementary" means of interpretation, they are therefore no higher in status in the interpretation of treaties for international purposes than the negotiating record.

The Convention does not indicate what relative probative weight should be given to ratification proceedings; presumably this would depend on their content, significance, and all other relevant circumstances. But the content of such proceedings must always be considered with caution, in that they reflect the views expressed in the internal processes of only one of the parties.

NOTES

1. *Denouement to the ABM Treaty Confrontation.* On May 19, 1987, the Senate Foreign Relations Committee voted to recommend favorably Senate Resolution 167, but the resolution was never brought for consideration by the Senate as a whole. Subsequently, Congress sought to limit SDI funding to programs that the Congress and Executive had determined to be within the "original interpretation" of the Treaty. The Reagan Administration decided that it would not violate the boundaries of the "original interpretation" as a matter of policy, while maintaining that it did not feel compelled as a matter of law. For commentary on the dispute, see Joseph R. Biden & John B. Ritch, III, *The Treaty Power: Upholding a Constitutional Partnership,* 137 U. PA. L. REV. 1529 (1989); Lawrence J. Block, Lee A. Casey & David B. Rivkin, *The Senate's Pie-in-the-Sky Treaty Interpretation: Power and the Quest for Legislative Supremacy,* 137 U. PA. L. REV. 1481 (1989); David A. Koplow, *Constitutional Bait and Switch: Executive Reinterpretation of Arms Control Treaties,* 137 U. PA. L. REV. 1353 (1989); Eugene V. Rostow, *The Reinterpretation Debate and Constitutional Law,* 137 U. PA. L. REV. 1451 (1989).

The United States withdrew from the ABM Treaty in 2002. (*See infra*, this Chapter, Sec. 10). Similar issues arose, however, in relation to other arms control treaties. *See* Phillip R. Trimble & Alexander W. Koff, *All Fall Down: The Treaty Power in the Clinton Administration*, 16 BERKELEY J. INT'L L. 55, 62–63 (1998) (discussing the Senate adoption of a declaration embodying the Biden Condition in relation to the Treaty on Conventional Armed Forces in Europe (CFE)); John Love, Note, *On The Record: Why the Senate Should Have Access to Treaty Negotiating Documents*, 113 COLUM. L. REV. 483, 499–500 (2013) (discussing Obama's refusal to turn over negotiating records before New START was approved by the Senate).

2. *The Evolutionary Nature of (Some?) Treaties.* Are some treaties of a nature that they must be allowed to be reinterpreted in an organic way over time because they were meant to evolve? Consider the following depiction of the U.N. Charter:

> What emerges from the vast legacy of recorded debates and decisions of the principal political organs is that they tend to treat the Charter not as a static formula, but as a constitutive instrument capable of organic growth. Borrowing a phrase coined by the Imperial Privy Council speaking of the Canadian constitution, the Charter is "a living tree."
>
> Ordinary treaties are not "living trees" but international contracts to be construed in strict accord with the black-letter text. Not so the Charter. The Charter also differs from most treaties not only in enumerating rights and duties but also in elaborating institutions to carry them into effect. . . .

> Further, the Charter makes allowance for its interpretation through state practice. . . .
>
> Each principal organ and the members thus continuously interpret the Charter and do so in accordance with the requisites of ever-changing circumstances. This necessarily means that the Charter text is always evolving.

Thomas M. Franck, *Recourse to Force: State Action against Threats and Armed Attacks* 6–7 (2002).

Is the UN Charter really so distinctive? What of human rights treaties, or environmental treaties that evolve dynamically? (Or certain laws of war treaties that contain provisions that, in the view of the executive branch, are now "quaint" and of no further relevance to contemporary conflicts?) For the relevant class of treaties, does it make sense for the Senate's original understanding of the meaning of a treaty to govern the Executive thereafter? Does it matter whether at the time of ratification it was understood, or should have been understood, that the treaty will be a "living tree"?

10. TREATY TERMINATION

Congress has a role in U.S. adherence to many international agreements, either through the Senate alone (for a treaty) or through both Houses acting together (in the case of a congressional-executive agreement). Yet if the president wishes to terminate (or perhaps suspend) an international agreement to which Congress has assented, must he obtain congressional consent to do so?

The Supreme Court has addressed that question when Congress specifically authorized termination, but saw no cause to address presidential power in the absence of such authorization. *Van Der Weyde v. Ocean Transp. Co.*, 297 U.S. 114, 117 (1936). The opportunity arose much later, as the United States made arrangements to recognize the communist government of the People's Republic of China (located in Beijing). As a precondition, President Jimmy Carter unilaterally terminated a 25-year-old mutual defense treaty with the Republic of China, whose nationalist government was based in Taiwan. He did so without obtaining congressional consent, and in the teeth of a sense-of-Congress resolution relating that "that there should be prior consultation between the Congress and the executive branch on any proposed policy changes affecting the continuation in force of the Mutual Defense Treaty of 1954." International Security Assistance Act of 1978, Pub. L. 95–384, § 26, 92.

Eight senators, one former senator, and sixteen House members sued the president, claiming that they were being denied their constitutional role under the Treaty Clause.

GOLDWATER V. CARTER

481 F.Supp. 949, 950–65 (D.D.C. 1979).

MEMORANDUM

GASCH, DISTRICT JUDGE.

. . . Since the first treaty to which the United States was a party was terminated in 1798 by an act of Congress, a variety of means have been used to terminate treaties: by statute directing the President to deliver notice of termination; by the President acting pursuant to a joint resolution of Congress or otherwise acting with the concurrence of both houses of Congress; by the President acting with senatorial consent; and by the President acting alone. The final method of termination is of particular relevance here, but the precedents involving unilateral executive action are of only marginal utility. None of these examples involves a mutual defense treaty, nor any treaty whose national and international significance approaches that of the 1954 Mutual Defense Treaty. Virtually all of them, moreover, can be readily distinguished on the basis of some triggering factor not present here.

The great majority of the historical precedents involve some form of mutual action, whereby the President's notice of termination receives the affirmative approval of the Senate or the entire Congress. Taken as a whole, the historical precedents support rather than detract from the position that the power to terminate treaties is a power shared by the political branches of this government.

A.

. . . An attempt to justify a unilateral presidential power to terminate treaties by analogy to the Supreme Court's treatment of the removal power in *Myers* [*v. United States,* 272 U.S. 52 (1926)] is unpersuasive. The power to remove executive personnel cannot be compared with the power to terminate an important international treaty. The removal power is restricted in its exercise to "purely executive officers" charged with a duty unrelated to the legislative or judicial power. It concerns the President's administrative control over his subordinates and flows from the President's obligations to see that the laws are faithfully executed. By contrast, treaty termination impacts upon the substantial role of Congress in foreign affairs—especially in the context of a mutual defense pact involving the potential exercise of congressional war powers—and is a contradiction rather than a corollary of the Executive's enforcement obligation. . . .

B.

The termination of a treaty is not a single act entrusted by the Constitution to one or the other of our political branches. Like treaty formation, treaty termination is comprised of a series of acts that seek to maintain a constitutional balance. Initially, a policy determination must be made concerning whether the treaty should be terminated and the appropriate negotiations to effect termination undertaken. Such actions are clearly within the competency of the executive branch. Similarly, the communication of the message terminating a treaty, as here by delivery of formal notice to the other party pursuant to the terms of the agreement, is committed to the President as the sole representative of our country in foreign affairs.

But these purely executive functions are not the only elements involved in treaty termination. Termination of a treaty also involves a repeal of the "law of the land" established by the agreement. It is in this area that congressional participation is required under the present circumstances. The mere fact that the President has the authority to make an initial policy determination regarding the exercise of an option to terminate, and to notify the foreign state of termination, does not vest him with the unilateral power to complete the termination process and thereby effect the abrogation of the treaty. As two scholars have recently noted, "[i]t is inherently inconceivable that . . . a constitutional policy requiring joint action for external agreement and internal legislation could allow that agreement and law to be terminated by the president alone, against the intentions of the legislature."

This conclusion is dictated by several constitutional factors: the status of treaties as the supreme law of the land, together with the obligation of the President to faithfully execute those laws; the implications to be derived from the constitutionally delineated role of the Senate in treaty formation; and the fundamental doctrine of separation of powers. It is further bolstered by the historical experience represented by constitutional interpretation and practice.

. . . Defendants argue . . . that the 1954 Mutual Defense Treaty is not a "law of the land" for supremacy clause purposes. They assert that only those treaties that are self-executing, and thus become effective as domestic law at the time the agreement goes into effect, constitute the supreme law of the land. Careful consideration of the provisions of the Mutual Defense Treaty establishes that a number of its provisions are self-executing and that still others have been implemented by subsequent legislation. In light of the terms and conditions of the Treaty, as well as the acts subsequently taken by the Congress and the President which have fixed and defined the nation's responsibilities under it, it is now far too late to assert that this Treaty fails to have the status of the supreme law of the land under Article VI. Moreover, none of the factors that would impair that status are involved here.

Article II, section three of the Constitution requires that the President "shall take care that the Laws be faithfully executed." This constitutional responsibility clearly extends to all laws of the land, including in this instance the Mutual Defense Treaty. The President cannot faithfully execute that treaty by abrogating it any more than he can faithfully execute by failing to administer. He alone cannot effect the repeal of a law of the land which was formed by joint action of the executive and legislative branches, whether that law be a statute or a treaty. The limits upon his authority are in no way altered by the inclusion of a termination provision in Article X of the Mutual Defense Treaty, allowing either party to terminate upon one year notice. The President's powers of administering the Treaty do not include the power to terminate in accordance with the provisions of Article X. The "party" to which the termination provision refers is the United States, not the President alone, and such termination can only be effectuated in accordance with United States constitutional processes.

The requirements imposed by the Supremacy Clause and the President's responsibility to faithfully execute the laws are further supported by the doctrine of separation of powers and its corollary concept of checks and balances, which lies at the heart of our constitutional system. In the treaty formation process, the Constitution expressly limits the Executive's role by requiring the advice and consent of two-thirds of the Senate. This constitutional requirement reflects the concern of the Founding Fathers that neither political branch possess unchecked power. . . .

The predominate United States' practice in terminating treaties, including those containing notice provisions, has involved mutual action by the executive and legislative branches. In most instances, the President's notice of termination has received the affirmative approval of either the Senate or the entire Congress. Although no one constitutional interpretation has been accepted, nor has a definitive procedure emerged, the weight of historical precedent clearly supports the view that some form of congressional concurrence is required. Support can be found for requiring either of two alternatives: 1) the approval of a majority of both houses of Congress, or 2) the consent of two-thirds of the Senate. The latter is of course the most analogous to the treaty-making power, while the former is based primarily on congressional authority to repeal a law of the land. . . .

In view of the foregoing, it is the declaration of this Court that the President's notice of termination must receive the approval of two-thirds of the United States Senate or a majority of both houses of Congress for it to be effective under our Constitution to terminate the Mutual Defense Treaty of 1954. It is further ordered that the Secretary of State and his subordinate officers are hereby enjoined from taking any action to implement the President's notice of termination unless and until that notice is so approved.

GOLDWATER V. CARTER

617 F.2d 697, 699–716 (D.C. Cir. 1979) (en banc).

PER CURIAM:

. . . The preliminary questions we confront are, first, whether the District Court was without jurisdiction because appellees lacked standing, and, second, whether it should in any event have declined to exercise jurisdiction by reason of the political nature of the question it was called upon to decide. Since a majority of the court does not exist to dispose of the appeal on either of these bases, we reach the merits and reverse. . . .

3. The constitutional institution of advice and consent of the Senate, provided two-thirds of the Senators concur, is a special and extraordinary condition of the exercise by the President of certain specified powers under Article II. It is not lightly to be extended in instances not set forth in the Constitution. Such an extension by implication is not proper unless that implication is unmistakably clear.

The District Court's absolutist extension of this limitation to termination of treaties, irrespective of the particular circumstances involved, is not sound. The making of a treaty has the consequences of an entangling alliance for the nation. Similarly, the amending of a treaty merely continues such entangling alliances, changing only their character, and therefore also requires the advice and consent of the Senate. It does not follow, however, that a constitutional provision for a special concurrence (two-thirds of the Senators) prior to entry into an entangling alliance necessarily applies to its termination in accordance with its terms.

4. . . . [T]he powers conferred upon Congress in Article I of the Constitution are specific, detailed, and limited, while the powers conferred upon the President by Article II are generalized in a manner that bespeaks no such limitation upon foreign affairs powers. "Section 1. The executive Power shall be vested in a President. . . ." Although specific powers are listed in Section 2 and Section 3, these are in many instances not powers necessary to an Executive, while "The executive Power" referred to in Section 1 is nowhere defined. There is no required two-thirds vote of the Senate conditioning the exercise of any power in Section 1.

In some instances this difference is reflective of the origin of the particular power in question. In general, the powers of the federal government arise out of specific grants of authority delegated by the states—hence the enumerated powers of Congress in Article I, Section 8. The foreign affairs powers, however, proceed directly from the sovereignty of the Union. "[I]f they had never been mentioned in the Constitution, [they] would have vested in the federal government as necessary concomitants of nationality." *United States v. Curtiss-Wright Export Corp.*, 299 U.S. 304, 318 . . . (1936).

The President is the constitutional representative of the United States with respect to external affairs. It is significant that the treaty power appears in Article II of the Constitution, relating to the executive branch, and not in Article I, setting forth the powers of the legislative branch. It is the President as Chief Executive who is given the constitutional authority to enter into a treaty; and even after he has obtained the consent of the Senate it is for him to decide whether to ratify a treaty and put it into effect. Senatorial confirmation of a treaty concededly does not obligate the President to go forward with a treaty if he concludes that it is not in the public interest to do so.

Thus, in contrast to the lawmaking power, the constitutional initiative in the treaty-making field is in the President, not Congress. It would take an unprecedented feat of judicial construction to read into the Constitution an absolute condition precedent of congressional or Senate approval for termination of all treaties, similar to the specific one relating to initial approval. And it would unalterably affect the balance of power between the two Branches laid down in Articles I and II.

5. Ultimately, what must be recognized is that a treaty is *sui generis*. It is not just another law. It is an international compact, a solemn obligation of the United States and a "supreme Law" that supersedes state policies and prior federal laws. For clarity of analysis, it is thus well to distinguish between treaty-making as an international act and the consequences which flow domestically from such act. In one realm the Constitution has conferred the primary role upon the President; in the other, Congress retains its primary role as lawmaker. The fact that the Constitution, statutes, and treaties are all listed in the Supremacy Clause as being superior to any form of state law does not mean that the making and unmaking of treaties can be analogized to the making and unmaking of domestic statutes any more than it can be analogized to the making or unmaking of a constitutional amendment. . . .

6. If we were to hold that under the Constitution a treaty could only be terminated by exactly the same process by which it was made, we would be locking the United States into all of its international obligations, even if the President and two-thirds of the Senate minus one firmly believed that the proper course for the United States was to terminate a treaty. Many of our treaties in force, such as mutual defense treaties, carry potentially dangerous obligations. These obligations are terminable under international law upon breach by the other party or change in circumstances that frustrates the purpose of the treaty. In many of these situations the President must take immediate action. The creation of a constitutionally obligatory role in all cases for a two-thirds consent by the Senate would give to one-third plus one of the Senate the power to deny the President the authority necessary to conduct our foreign policy in a rational and effective manner.

7. Even as to the formal termination of treaties, as the District Court pointed out, "a variety of means have been used to terminate treaties." . . .

. . . Yet we think it is not without significance that out of all the historical precedents brought to our attention, in no situation has a treaty been continued in force over the opposition of the President.

There is on the other hand widespread agreement that the President has the power as Chief Executive under many circumstances to exercise functions regarding treaties which have the effect of either terminating or continuing their vitality. Prominent among these is the authority of the President as Chief Executive (1) to determine whether a treaty has terminated because of a breach, *Charlton v. Kelly,* 229 U.S. 447, 473–476 . . . (1913); and (2) to determine whether a treaty is at an end due to changed circumstances.

In short, the determination of the conduct of the United States in regard to treaties is an instance of what has broadly been called the "foreign affairs power" of the President. We have no occasion to define that term, but we do take account of its vitality. The *Curtiss-Wright* opinion, written by a Justice who had served in the United States Senate, declares in oft-repeated language that the President is "the sole organ of the federal government in the field of international relations." That status is not confined to the service of the President as a channel of communication, as the District Court suggested, but embraces an active policy determination as to the conduct of the United States in regard to a treaty in response to numerous problems and circumstances as they arise. . . .

9. The circumstances involved in the termination of the Mutual Defense Treaty with the Republic of China include a number of material and unique elements. Prominent is assertion by the officials of both the Republic of China and the People's Republic of China that each of them is the government of China, intending the term China to comprehend both the mainland of China and the island of Taiwan. In the 1972 Shanghai Communique, the United States acknowledged that position and did not challenge it. It is in this context that the recent Joint Communique set forth as of January 1, 1979 that the United States recognizes the People's Republic of China as "the sole legal government of China." This action made reference to "the people of Taiwan," stating that the peoples of the United States and Taiwan "will maintain cultural, commercial and other unofficial relations." This formulation was confirmed by the Taiwan Relations Act.

It is undisputed that the Constitution gave the President full constitutional authority to recognize the PRC and to derecognize the ROC. What the United States has evolved for Taiwan is a novel and somewhat indefinite relationship, namely, of unofficial relations with the people of Taiwan. The subtleties involved in maintaining amorphous relationships are often the very stuff of diplomacy—a field in which the President, not Congress, has responsibility under our Constitution. The President makes a responsible claim that he has authority as Chief Executive to determine that there is no meaningful vitality to a mutual defense treaty when there is no recognized state. That is not to say that the recognition power automatically gives the President authority to take any action that is required or requested by the state being recognized. We do not need to reach this question. Nevertheless, it remains an important ingredient in the case at bar that the President has determined that circumstances have changed so as to preclude continuation of the Mutual Defense Treaty with the ROC; diplomatic recognition of the ROC came to an end on January 1, 1979, and now there exists only "cultural, commercial and other unofficial relations" with the "people on Taiwan."

10. Finally, and of central significance, the treaty here at issue contains a termination clause. The existence of Article X of the ROC treaty, permitting termination by either party on one year's notice, is an overarching factor in this case, which in effect enables all of the other considerations to be knit together. . . .

As already noted, we have no occasion to decide whether this factor would be determinative in a case lacking other factors identified above, *e. g.*, under a notice of withdrawal from the NATO treaty unaccompanied by derecognition of the other signatories. No specific restriction or condition on the President's action is found within the Constitution or this treaty itself. The termination clause is without conditions and without designation as to who shall act to terminate it. No specific role is spelled out in either the Constitution or this treaty for the Senate or the Congress as a whole. That power consequently devolves upon the President, and there is no basis for a court to imply a restriction on the President's power to terminate not contained in the Constitution, in this treaty, or in any other authoritative source. . . .

. . . [T]he court is not to be taken as minimizing the role of the legislature in foreign affairs. The legislature's powers, including prominently its dominant status in the provision of funds, and its authority to investigate the Executive's functioning, establish authority for appropriate legislative participation in foreign affairs. The question of whether the Senate may be able to reserve to itself in particular treaties, at the time of their original submission, a specific role in their termination is not presented by the record in this appeal and we decide nothing with respect to it. The matter before us is solely one of whether the Constitution nullifies the procedure followed by the President in this instance. We find the President did not exceed his authority when he took action to withdraw from the ROC treaty, by giving notice under Article X of the Treaty, without the consent of the Senate or other legislative concurrences.

GOLDWATER V. CARTER

444 U.S. 996, 996–1007 (1979).

Certiorari granted, judgment vacated, and case remanded with directions to dismiss the complaint. MR. JUSTICE MARSHALL concurs in the result. MR. JUSTICE POWELL concurs in the judgment and filed a statement. MR. JUSTICE REHNQUIST concurs in the judgment and filed a statement in which THE CHIEF JUSTICE, MR. JUSTICE STEWART, and MR. JUSTICE STEVENS join. MR. JUSTICE WHITE and MR. JUSTICE BLACKMUN join in the grant of the petition for a writ of certiorari but would set the case for argument and give it plenary consideration. MR. JUSTICE BLACKMUN filed a statement in which MR. JUSTICE WHITE joins. MR. JUSTICE BRENNAN would grant the petition for writ of certiorari and affirm the judgment of the Court of Appeals and filed a statement. . . .

MR. JUSTICE POWELL, concurring in the judgment.

Although I agree with the result reached by the Court, I would dismiss the complaint as not ripe for judicial review.

I

. . . Prudential considerations persuade me that a dispute between Congress and the President is not ready for judicial review unless and until each branch has taken action asserting its constitutional authority. Differences between the President and the Congress are commonplace under our system. The differences should, and almost invariably do, turn on political rather than legal considerations. The Judicial Branch should not decide issues affecting the allocation of power between the President and Congress until the political branches reach a constitutional impasse. Otherwise, we would encourage small groups or even individual Members of Congress to seek judicial resolution of issues before the normal political process has the opportunity to resolve the conflict.

In this case, a few Members of Congress claim that the President's action in terminating the treaty with Taiwan has deprived them of their constitutional role with respect to a change in the supreme law of the land. Congress has taken no official action. In the present posture of this case, we do not know whether there ever will be an actual confrontation between the Legislative and Executive Branches. Although the Senate has considered a resolution declaring that Senate approval is necessary for the termination of any mutual defense treaty, *see* 125 Cong. Rec. 13672, 13695–13697 (1979), no final vote has been taken on the resolution. *See id.*, at 32522–32531. Moreover, it is unclear whether the resolution would have retroactive effect. *See id.*, at 13711–13721; *id.*, at 15210. It cannot be said that either the Senate or the House has rejected the President's claim. If the Congress chooses not to confront the President, it is not our task to do so. I therefore concur in the dismissal of this case.

II

MR. JUSTICE REHNQUIST suggests, however, that the issue presented by this case is a nonjusticiable political question which can never be considered by this Court. I cannot agree. In my view, reliance upon the political-question doctrine is inconsistent with our precedents. As set forth in the seminal case of *Baker v. Carr,* 369 U.S. 186, 217 (1962), the doctrine incorporates three inquiries: (i) Does the issue involve resolution of questions committed by the text of the Constitution to a coordinate branch of Government? (ii) Would resolution of the question demand that a court move beyond areas of judicial expertise? (iii) Do prudential considerations counsel against judicial intervention? In my opinion the answer to each of these inquiries would require us to decide this case if it were ready for review.

First, . . . [n]o constitutional provision explicitly confers upon the President the power to terminate treaties. Further, Art. II, § 2, of the Constitution authorizes the President to make treaties with the advice and consent of the Senate. Article VI provides that treaties shall be a part of the supreme law of the land. These provisions add support to the view that the text of the Constitution does not unquestionably commit the power to terminate treaties to the President alone. *Cf. Gilligan v. Morgan,* 413 U.S. 1, 6 (1973); *Luther v. Borden,* 7 How. 1, 42 (1849).

Second, there is no "lack of judicially discoverable and manageable standards for resolving" this case; nor is a decision impossible "without an initial policy determination of a kind clearly for nonjudicial discretion." *Baker v. Carr, supra,* at 217. We are asked to decide whether the President may terminate a treaty under the Constitution without congressional approval. Resolution of the question may not be easy, but it only requires us to apply normal principles of interpretation to the constitutional provisions at issue. . . .

A simple hypothetical demonstrates the confusion that I find inherent in MR. JUSTICE REHNQUIST'S opinion concurring in the judgment. Assume that the President signed a mutual defense treaty with a foreign country and announced that it would go into effect despite its rejection by the Senate. Under MR. JUSTICE REHNQUIST'S analysis that situation would present a political question even though Art. II, § 2, clearly would resolve the dispute. . . . In both cases, the Court would interpret the Constitution to decide whether congressional approval is necessary to give a Presidential decision on the validity of a treaty the force of law. . . .

Finally, the political-question doctrine rests in part on prudential concerns calling for mutual respect among the three branches of Government. . . .

If this case were ripe for judicial review . . . these prudential considerations would [not] be present. Interpretation of the Constitution does not imply lack of respect for a coordinate branch. *Powell v. McCormack, supra,* at 548. If the President and the Congress had reached irreconcilable positions, final disposition of the question presented by this case would eliminate, rather than create, multiple constitutional interpretations. The specter of the Federal Government brought to a halt because of the mutual intransigence of the President and the Congress would require this Court to provide a resolution pursuant to our duty " 'to say what the law is.' " *United States v. Nixon,* 418 U.S. 683, 703 (1974), quoting *Marbury v. Madison,* 1 Cranch 137, 177 (1803). . . .

MR. JUSTICE REHNQUIST, with whom THE CHIEF JUSTICE, MR. JUSTICE STEWART, and MR. JUSTICE STEVENS join, concurring in the judgment. . . .

Mr. Chief Justice Hughes' opinion [in *Coleman v. Miller,* 307 U.S. 433 (1939), "a case in which members of the Kansas Legislature brought an action attacking a vote of the State Senate in favor of the ratification of the Child Labor Amendment"] concluded that "Congress in controlling the promulgation of the adoption of a constitutional amendment has the final determination of the question whether by lapse of time its proposal of the amendment had lost its vitality prior to the required ratifications." *Id.,* at 456.

I believe it follows *a fortiori* from *Coleman* that the controversy in the instant case is a nonjusticiable political dispute that should be left for resolution by the Executive and Legislative Branches of the Government. Here, while the Constitution is express as to the manner in which the Senate shall participate in the ratification of a treaty, it is silent as to that body's participation in the abrogation of a treaty. . . .

I think that the justifications for concluding that the question here is political in nature are even more compelling than in *Coleman* because it involves foreign relations—specifically a treaty commitment to use military force in the defense of a foreign government if attacked. . . .

The present case differs in several important respects from *Youngstown Sheet & Tube Co. v. Sawyer,* 343 U.S. 579 (1952) . . . In *Youngstown,* private litigants brought a suit contesting the President's authority under his war powers to seize the Nation's steel industry, an action of profound and demonstrable domestic impact. Here, by contrast, we are asked to settle a dispute between coequal branches of our Government, each of which has resources available to protect and assert its interests, resources not available to private litigants outside the judicial forum. Moreover, as in *Curtiss-Wright,* the effect of this action, as far as we can tell, is "entirely external to the United States, and [falls] within the category of foreign affairs." . . .

MR. JUSTICE BLACKMUN, with whom MR. JUSTICE WHITE joins, dissenting in part.

. . . I would set the case for oral argument and give it the plenary consideration it so obviously deserves.

MR. JUSTICE BRENNAN, dissenting.

I respectfully dissent . . .

The constitutional question raised here is prudently answered in narrow terms. Abrogation of the defense treaty with Taiwan was a necessary incident to Executive recognition of the Peking Government, because the defense treaty was predicated upon the now-abandoned view that the Taiwan Government was the only legitimate political authority in China. Our cases firmly establish that the Constitution commits to the President alone the power to recognize, and withdraw recognition from, foreign regimes. . . .

NOTES

1. Goldwater's *Legacy for Judicial Review of Termination*. The district court and the court of appeals clearly viewed matters differently—which do you think had the better of the dispute? Was one view or the other aided by the Supreme Court proceedings? As one court subsequently remarked, given the four opinions by the Supreme Court—two concurring in the judgment and two dissenting—"there is no obviously binding holding in *Goldwater.*" *Kucinich v. Bush*, 236 F. Supp. 2d 1, 13 (D.D.C. 2002). The Court did suggest, at least, the difficulty of establishing circumstances in which judicial resolution of a termination controversy would be appropriate. Are there circumstances under which you think it might well be possible for the Supreme Court to reach the merits of this issue, and even possible for the Court to find against the president? For example, recall that the circuit court in *Goldwater* said that it was not deciding "whether the Senate may be able to reserve to itself in particular treaties, at the time of their original submission, a specific role in their termination. . . ."

2. *Restatement (Third) and Restatement (Fourth)*. The *Restatement of the Law (Third), The Foreign Relations Law of the United States* § 339 (1987) states that the president has the power to:

> (a) to suspend or terminate an agreement in accordance with its terms;
>
> (b) to make the determination that would justify the United States in terminating or suspending an agreement because of its violation by another party or because of supervening events, and to proceed to terminate or suspend the agreement on behalf of the United States; or
>
> (c) to elect in a particular case not to suspend or terminate an agreement.

(Copyright (c) 1987 by The American Law Institute. Reproduced with permission.) The *Restatement (Fourth)* likewise, concludes that the president has the authority to act for the United States in suspending or terminating a treaty on the basis of terms in the treaty or otherwise arising under international law that would allowing such action. *Restatement of the Law (Fourth), The Foreign Relations Law of the United States: Treaties* § 113 (Tentative Draft No. 2, 2017). Unlike the *Restatement (Third)*, however, the *Restatement (Fourth)* does not purport to address the termination of non-Article II agreements, an issue noted below. Given the absence of judicial precedent, on what authority are the *Restatement* pronouncements based?

3. *Termination of Treaties Since* Goldwater. According to executive branch estimates, between 1980 and 2002, the president terminated about thirty bilateral and multilateral treaties without the Senate's consent. *See* U.S. Department of State, *Digest of United States Practice in International Law 2002* (Sally J. Cummins & David P. Stewart eds., 2003). As noted in *Kucinich*, a high-profile bilateral treaty that was terminated was the Treaty of Friendship, Commerce, and Navigation, U.S.-Nicar., Jan. 21, 1956, 9 U.S.T. 449, T.I.A.S. No. 4024. On May 1, 1985, the Department of State gave one year's notice to Nicaragua that the United States would be terminating the treaty as of May 1, 1986. *See Beacon Prods Corp. v. Reagan*, 633 F. Supp. 1191, 1199 (D.Mass. 1986), *aff'd,* 814 F.2d 1 (1st Cir. 1987) (dismissing challenge to administration's unilateral termination of treaty with Nicaragua). Some terminations of multilateral treaties took the form of withdrawal from the constituent instruments of international organizations. For example, in December 1996, the United States withdrew from both the Statute of the World Tourism Organization, Sept. 27, 1970, 27 U.S.T. 2211, and the Constitution of the U.N. Industrial Development Organization, Apr. 8, 1979, S. TREATY DOC. NO. 97–19 (1981). The United States has also withdrawn its acceptance of the jurisdiction of the International Court of Justice over certain types of cases, include where this entails terminating a treaty protocol to which the U.S. Senate had consented. On March 7, 2005, the U.S. Government informed the U.N. Secretary-General that it had terminated its adherence to the Optional Protocol Concerning Compulsory Settlement of Disputes to the Vienna Convention on Consular Relations, Apr. 24, 1963, 21 U.S.T. 325, 596 U.N.T.S. 487. *See* Journal of the United Nations: Programme of Meetings and Agenda, No. 2005/48, at 13 (Mar. 12, 2005) (reporting receipt of the withdrawal on Mar. 7); *see* Charles Lane, *U.S. Quits Pact Used in Capital Cases*, WASH. POST, Mar. 10, 2005, at A1. Should the Senate have been involved in such decisions?

4. *Terminating a Treaty Outside Its Terms*. Does the *Restatement* and subsequent executive branch practice suggest that *Goldwater v. Carter* stands for the proposition that the president has the power to terminate (or modify) treaties regardless of whether the treaty permits such action? The 1954 mutual defense treaty with nationalist China was terminated by President Carter in 1979 by giving one year's notice *as required by the termination clause of the treaty*. (This created an anomalous situation because the United States was obliged to defend Taiwan for twelve months after recognition had been withdrawn from the nationalist regime and switched to the regime in Beijing.) The decision to proceed by notice, rather than by immediate termination, was

obviously taken deliberately. Why might this have been the preferred method of termination? Would the outcome of the *Goldwater v. Carter* litigation have been any different had the president decided to terminate the treaty instantly, in violation of its notice requirement? In short, may the president, on his own authority, terminate a treaty in violation of it?

Consider the following positions. The U.S. Department of Justice Office of Legal Counsel (OLC) issued opinions in 2001 and 2002 addressing whether the president could decide, on his own, that the 1949 Geneva Conventions were suspended with respect to the armed conflict in Afghanistan, especially as they might relate to the detention and trial of members of Al Qaeda and the Taliban militia. OLC asserted that the president, under U.S. law, has unconstrained discretion to suspend U.S. treaty obligations at any time and for any reason as an aspect of the "executive Power" vested in him by the Constitution. *See* Memorandum for John B. Bellinger III, Legal Adviser to the National Security Council, from John C. Yoo, Deputy Assistant Attorney General, and Robert J. Delahunty, Special Counsel, Office of Legal Counsel, Authority of the President to Suspend Certain Provisions of the ABM Treaty, at 12, 13, 2001 WL 36190673 (Nov. 15, 2001) ("11/15/01 ABM Suspension Opinion") ("The President's power to suspend treaties is wholly discretionary, and may be exercised whenever he determines that it is in the national interest to do so. While the President will ordinarily take international law into account when deciding whether to suspend a treaty in whole or in part, his constitutional authority to suspend a treaty provision does not hinge on whether such suspension is or is not consistent with international law."); Memorandum for Alberto R. Gonzales, Counsel to the President, and William J. Haynes II, General Counsel, Department of Defense, from Jay S. Bybee, Assistant Attorney General, Office of Legal Counsel, Application of Treaties and Laws to al Qaeda and Taliban Detainees at 11–13 (Jan. 22, 2002) ("1/22/02 Treaties Opinion") (reasoning that the President has "unrestricted discretion, as a matter of domestic law, in suspending treaties").

In 2009, after the assumption of office by President Barack Obama, OLC issued a new memorandum, indicating that

> Presidents have traditionally suspended treaties where authorized by Congress or where suspension was authorized by the terms of the treaty or under recognized principles of international law, such as where another party has materially breached the treaty or where there has been a fundamental change in circumstances. . . . [The relevant portions of the 2001 and 2002 OLC opinions] do not reflect the current views of this Office and should not be treated as authoritative, and . . . appropriate caution should be exercised before relying upon these opinions in other respects.

Memorandum for the Files from Steven G. Bradbury, Principal Deputy Assistant Attorney General, Status of Certain OLC Opinions Issued in the Aftermath of the Terrorist Attacks of September 11, 2001 at 8–9, 2009 WL 1267352 (Jan. 15, 2009).

Do you think that the president can either suspend or terminate a treaty without the consent of the Senate, even if it is done outside the terms of the treaty and for a reason not sanctioned by international treaty law?

5. *Terminating Executive Agreements and Political Commitments.* Article II treaties may be distinctive as regards termination. It is widely assumed, for example, that the president lacks the authority to terminate congressional-executive agreements, which—because of their statutory form—would require a later-in-time treaty or statute. *See* Kristen E. Eichensehr, *Treaty Termination and the Separation of Powers*, 53 VA. J. INT'L L. 247, 299–301 (2013). *But see* Curtis A. Bradley, Exiting Congressional-Executive Agreements (October 7, 2017 draft). available at https://ssrn.com/abstract=3049279 (suggesting that the president's unilateral power to terminate a congressional-executive agreement should in fact be congruent with that for treaties). In contrast, a presidential-executive (or "sole executive") agreement would not require legislative consent, because neither the Senate nor Congress as a whole was involved in establishing the agreement. Likewise, it would appear, presidents would be free to terminate a nonbinding or political commitment. Does this affect your appreciation of their interchangeability, as considered *supra*, this Chapter, Sec. 8?

Do you think that the president can either suspend or terminate a treaty without the consent of the Senate [illegible] is done outside the terms of the treaty and for a reason not sanctioned by international law?

CHAPTER 4

WAR POWERS

■ ■ ■

1. CONSTITUTIONAL ORIGINS

Though it is not the most commonly invoked power in the field of foreign relations law (thankfully), the power to initiate war is of extraordinary importance. With the strongest military in the world, the United States is capable of unleashing tremendous firepower by land, sea, and air across the globe in a matter of minutes. That power may be used to protect the American homeland, to assist an endangered ally, or to help quell civil unrest in troubled lands. Exercise of the war-initiation power often raises the most turbulent of policy debates. What American values and interests merit endangering American soldiers? When have diplomatic efforts proven ineffective? To what extent should allies be enlisted in the recourse to force? To what extent should the support of the United Nations or regional organizations be secured before acting? Rarely does use of war powers find unanimous support from the American polity; usually there are strong views on both sides.

In tandem with disagreements over policy, there are also often disagreements over the constitutional allocation of the powers to initiate and to prosecute war. What exactly is included in Congress's power to "declare War" or to "support" the army and "provide" a navy? What exactly is the president's role as "Commander in Chief"? Did the founding fathers seek to mimic the royal prerogatives of the King in this area or did they choose a different path? Regardless of what path they chose in the Constitution, in what direction has the course of American history taken the war powers? Is it a course well-chosen or is there something amiss that should be corrected? If the latter, how should any change be accomplished?

The Constitution addresses war powers in two sets of provisions. The first (under Article I) relates to congressional power; the second (under Article II) relates to executive power. Based on the text of the Constitution, which war powers appear to be plenary? Where do Congress and the president seem to share concurrent war powers? What were the views of the founders regarding these powers? What were they trying to accomplish?

LOUIS FISHER, PRESIDENTIAL WAR POWER

4–5 (3rd rev. 2013).*

On numerous occasions the delegates to the constitutional convention emphasized that the power of peace and war associated with monarchy would not be given to the President. On June 1, 1787, Charles Pinckney said he was for "a vigorous Executive but was afraid the Executive powers of <the existing> Congress might extend to peace & war & c which would render the Executive a Monarchy, of the worst kind, towit an elective one." John Rutledge wanted the executive power placed in a single person, "tho' he was not for giving him the power of war and peace." Roger Sherman considered "the Executive magistracy as nothing more than an institution for carrying the will of the Legislature into effect." James Wilson also preferred a single executive but "did not consider the Prerogatives of the British Monarch as a proper guide in defining the Executive powers. Some of these prerogatives were of a Legislative nature. Among others that of war & peace & c."

Edmund Randolph worried about executive power, calling it "the foetus of monarchy." The delegates to the Philadelphia convention, he said, had "no motive to be governed by the British Governmt. as our prototype." If the United States had no other choice he might adopt the British model, but "the fixt genius of the people of America required a different form of Government." Wilson agreed that the British model "was inapplicable to the situation of this Country; the extent of which was so great, and the manners so republican, that nothing but a great confederated Republic would do for it."

In a lengthy speech on June 18, Alexander Hamilton set forth his principles of government. Although later associated with vigorous and independent presidential power, he too jettisoned the British model of executive prerogatives in foreign affairs and the war power. Explaining that in his "private opinion he had no scruple in declaring . . . that the British Govt. was the best in the world," he nonetheless discarded the Blackstonian and Lockean models. He proposed that the President would have "with the advice and approbation of the Senate" the power of making treaties, the Senate would have the "sole power of declaring war," and the President would be authorized to have "the direction of war when authorized or begun."

* *Presidential War Power, Third Edition, Revised* by Louis Fisher, published by the University Press of Kansas, © 2013. www.Kansaspress.ku.edu. Used by permission of the publisher.

THE CONSTITUTION OF THE UNITED STATES

ARTICLE I

Section 8. [1] The Congress shall have Power to lay and collect Taxes, Duties, Imposts and Excises, to pay the Debts and provide for the Common Defence and general Welfare of the United States; but all Duties, Imposts and Excises shall be uniform throughout the United States; . . .

[10] To define and punish Piracies and Felonies committed on the High Seas, and Offenses against the Law of Nations;

[11] To declare War, grant Letters of Marque and Reprisal, and make Rules concerning Captures on Land and Water;

[12] To raise and support Armies, but no Appropriation of Money to that Use shall be for a longer Term than two Years;

[13] To provide and maintain a Navy;

[14] To make Rules for the Government and Regulation of the land and naval Forces;

[15] To provide for calling forth the Militia to execute the Laws of the Union, suppress Insurrections and repel Invasions;

[16] To provide for organizing, arming, and disciplining, the Militia, and for governing such Part of them as may be employed in the Service of the United States, reserving to the States respectively, the Appointment of the Officers, and the Authority of training the Militia according to the discipline prescribed by Congress; . . . [and]

[18] To make all Laws which shall be necessary and proper for carrying into Execution the foregoing Powers, and all other Powers vested by this Constitution in the Government of the United States, or in any Department or Officer thereof. . . .

ARTICLE II

Section 1. [1] The executive Power shall be vested in a President of the United States of America. . . .

[7] Before he enter on the Execution of his Office, he shall take the following Oath or Affirmation: "I do solemnly swear (or affirm) that I will faithfully execute the Office of President of the United States, and will to the best of my Ability, preserve, protect and defend the Constitution of the United States.". . .

Section 2. [1] The President shall be Commander in Chief of the Army and Navy of the United States, and of the Militia of the several States, when called into the actual Service of the United States; he may require the Opinion, in writing, of the principal Officer in each of the executive Departments, upon any Subject relating to the Duties of their respective

Offices, and he shall have Power to grant Reprieves and Pardons for Offenses against the United States, except in Cases of Impeachment.

THE FEDERALIST PAPERS NO. 69 (HAMILTON)

(Clinton Rossiter ed., 1961).

The President is to be the "commander-in-chief of the army and navy of the United States, and of the militia of the several States, when called into the actual service of the United States. . . ." In most of these particulars, the power of the President will resemble equally that of the king of Great Britain and of the governor of New York. The most material points of difference are these:—*First.* The President will have only the occasional command of such part of the militia of the nation as by legislative provision may be called into the actual service of the Union. The king of Great Britain and the governor of New York have at all times the entire command of all the militia within their several jurisdictions. In this article, therefore, the power of the President would be inferior to that of either the monarch or the governor. *Second.* The President is to be commander-in-chief of the army and navy of the United States. In this respect his authority would be nominally the same with that of the king of Great Britain, but in substance much inferior to it. It would amount to nothing more than the supreme command and direction of the military and naval forces, as first general and admiral of the Confederacy; while that of the British king extends to the *declaring* of war and to the *raising* and *regulating* of fleets and armies—all which, by the Constitution under consideration, would appertain to the legislature. The governor of New York, on the other hand, is by the constitution of the State vested only with the command of its militia and navy. But the constitutions of several of the States expressly declare their governors to be commanders-in-chief, as well of the army as navy; and it may well be a question whether those of New Hampshire and Massachusetts, in particular, do not, in this instance, confer larger powers upon their respective governors than could be claimed by a President of the United States. . . .

REPORT OF THE SENATE FOREIGN RELATIONS COMMITTEE ON THE WAR POWERS ACT

S. REP. NO. 220, 93rd Cong., 1st Sess. (1973).

BACKGROUND AND COMMITTEE ACTION

A. THE INTENT OF THE FRAMERS

The Founding Fathers had been much dismayed by the power of the British Crown to commit Great Britain—and its American colonies—to war. They were also fearful of the danger of large standing armies and of the possible defiance of civilian authority by military leaders. In order to alleviate the threat of militarism and of the possible resurgence of monarchical tendencies in the new Republic, the [*sic*] Article I, Section 8 the framers vested the authority to initiate war in the legislature, and in the legislature alone, and established the framework for tight Congressional control over the military establishment.

The absence of extended debate over the war powers in the Constitutional Convention attests to the near unanimity of the Founding Fathers as to where that authority was meant to be placed. There was some discussion as to whether the war power should be vested in the Congress as a whole or only the Senate, but only one delegate, Pierce Butler of South Carolina, favored vesting the war power in the President.

The Constitutional Convention at first proposed to give Congress the power to "make" war but changed this to "declare" war, not, however, because it was desired to enlarge Presidential power but in order to permit the President to take action to repel sudden attacks. Madison's notes on the proceedings of the Convention report the change of wording as follows: "Mr. Madison and Mr. Gerry *moved* to insert 'declare,' striking out '*make*' war; leaving to the executive the power to repel sudden attacks." It is noteworthy that the delegates who spoke on this change of wording all expressed concern with the possible enlargement of Presidential power. Elbridge Gerry, for example, declared that he "never expected to hear in a republic a motion to empower the Executive talons to declare war." George Mason firmly expressed himself as "against giving the power of war to the executive," on the ground that he was "not to be trusted with it."

A closely related concern of the framers was to make it more difficult to start a war than to stop one. It was essentially for this reason that the power to authorize hostilities was vested in the Congress rather than in the President as successor to the British Crown. It was also for this reason that the war power was vested in the two Houses of the Congress rather than in the Senate alone. As Oliver Ellsworth told his fellow delegates, it "should be more easy to get out of war, than into it"; and as George Mason said, he was "for clogging rather than facilitating war; but for facilitating peace."

2. EARLY CASE LAW

The undeclared naval war fought with France in 1798–1800 raised for the first time the question whether Congress could authorize hostilities falling short of all-out war. International law had long drawn a distinction between "perfect" and "imperfect" war; did the domestic separation of powers reflect this distinction? By granting Congress the power to "declare" perfect war, did the Constitution implicitly leave to the president the power to use military force in "imperfect" wars, when war was not formally declared? Can Congress authorize the use of force without formally declaring war? If Congress authorizes limited, "imperfect" war, is the president bound by those limits?

BAS V. TINGY

4 U.S. (4 Dall.) 37 (1800).

[T]he defendant, in error, had filed a libel in the District Court, as commander of the public armed ship the *Ganges,* for himself and others against the ship *Eliza, John Bas, master,* her cargo, & c. in which he set forth that the said ship and cargo belonged to citizens of the *United States*; that they were taken on the high seas by a *French* privateer, on the 31st of *March,* 1799; and that they were re-taken by the libellant, on the 21st of *April* following, after having been above ninety-six hours in possession of the captors. The libel prayed for salvage conformably to the acts of congress; and the facts being admitted by the answer of the respondents, the District Court decreed to the libellants one half of the whole value of ship and cargo. . . .

The controversy involved a consideration of the following sections in two acts of congress: By an act of the 28th of *June* 1798, (4 *vol. p.* 154, *s.* 2.) it is declared, "That whenever any vessel the property of, or employed by, any citizen of the *United States,* or person resident therein, or any goods or effects belonging to any such citizen, or resident, shall be re-captured by any public armed vessel of the *United States,* the same shall be restored to the former owner, or owners, upon due proof, he or they paying and allowing, as and for salvage to the re-captors, one-eighth part of the value of such vessel, goods and effects, free from all deduction and expenses."

By an act of the 2d of *March,* 1799 (4 *vol. p.* 472) it is declared, "That for the ships or goods belonging to the citizens of the *United States,* or to the citizens, or subjects, of any nation in amity with the *United States,* if re-taken from *the enemy* within twenty-four hours, the owners are to allow one-eighth part of the whole value for salvage, & c. and if above ninety-six hours one-half, all of which is to be paid without any deduction whatsoever, & c." . . . The JUDGES delivered their opinions *seriatim* in the following manner. . . .

WASHINGTON, JUSTICE. It is admitted, on all hands, that the defendant in error is entitled to some compensation; but the plaintiff in error contends, that the compensation should be regulated by the act of the 28th *June* 1798, (4 *vol. p.* 154, *s.* 2.) which allows only one-eighth for salvage; while the defendant in error refers his claim to the act of the 2d *March,* (*ibid.* 456. *s.* 7.) which makes an allowance of one-half, upon a re-capture from *the enemy,* after an adverse possession of ninety-six hours.

If the defendant's claim is well founded, it follows, that the latter law must virtually have worked a repeal of the former; but this has been denied, for a variety of reasons:

1st. Because the former law relates to re-captures from *the French,* and the latter law relates to re-captures from *the enemy*; and, it is said, that "*the enemy*" is not descriptive of *France,* or of her armed vessels, according to the correct and technical understanding of the word.

The decision of this question must depend upon another; which is, whether, at the time of passing the act of congress of the 2d of *March* 1799, there subsisted a state of war between the two nations? It may, I believe, be safely laid down, that every contention by force between two nations, in external matters, under the authority of their respective governments, is not only war, but public war. If it be declared in form, it is called *solemn,* and is of the perfect kind; because one whole nation is at war with another whole nation; and *all* the members of the nation declaring war, are authorised to commit hostilities against all the members of the other, in every place, and under every circumstance. In such a war all the members act under a general authority, and all the rights and consequences of war attach to their condition.

But hostilities may subsist between two nations more confined in its nature and extent; being limited as to places, persons, and things; and this is more properly termed *imperfect war*; because not solemn, and because those who are authorised to commit hostilities, act under special authority, and can go no farther than to the extent of their commission. Still, however, it is *public war,* because it is an external contention by force, between some of the members of the two nations, authorised by the legitimate powers. It is a war between the two nations, though all the members are not authorised to commit hostilities such as in a solemn war, where the government restrain the general power.

Now, if this be the true definition of war, let us see what was the situation of the *United States* in relation to *France.* In *March* 1799, congress had raised an army; stopped all intercourse with *France*; dissolved our treaty; built and equipt ships of war; and commissioned private armed ships; enjoining the former, and authorising the latter, to defend themselves against the armed ships of *France,* to attack them on the high seas, to subdue and take them as prize, and to re-capture armed vessels found in their possession. Here, then, let me ask, what were the technical characters of an *American* and *French* armed vessel, combating on the high seas, with a view the one to subdue the other, and to make prize of his property? They certainly were not friends, because there was a contention by force; nor were they private enemies, because the contention was external, and authorised by the legitimate authority of the two governments. If they were not our enemies, I know not what constitutes an enemy.

CHASE, JUSTICE. . . . Congress is empowered to declare a general war, or congress may wage a limited war; limited in place, in objects, and in time. If a general war is declared, its extent and operations are only restricted and regulated by the *jus belli,* forming a part of the law of nations; but if a partial war is waged, its extent and operation depend on our municipal laws.

What, then, is the nature of the contest subsisting between *America* and *France*? In my judgment, it is a limited, partial, war. Congress has not declared war in general terms; but congress has authorised hostilities on the high seas by certain persons in certain cases. There is no authority given to commit hostilities on land; to capture unarmed *French* vessels, nor even to capture *French* armed vessels lying in a *French* port; and the authority is not given, indiscriminately, to every citizen of *America,* against every citizen of *France*; but only to citizens appointed by commissions, or exposed to immediate outrage and violence. So far it is, unquestionably, a partial war; but, nevertheless, it is a public war, on account of the public authority from which it emanates.

LITTLE V. BARREME

6 U.S. (2 Cranch) 170 (1804).

[Review again this decision, which appears in Chapter 1, Sec. 2].

BROWN V. UNITED STATES

12 U.S. (8 Cranch) 110 (1814).

[Spurred by British restrictions on neutral trade with Napoleonic Europe and by the impressments of thousands of American sailors into the Royal Navy, a divided Congress declared war on Britain on June 18, 1812. The British responded by blockading much of the Atlantic coast. One American merchantman, the *Emulous,* was trapped in port with a cargo of pine timber bound for Plymouth, England. In 1814, Chief Justice John Marshall turned to the question of whether Congress's declaration of war implicitly authorized the "seizure and condemnation" of "enemy property," such as the pine timber carried by the *Emulous*.]

MARSHALL, CH. J., delivered the opinion of the Court, as follows:

The material facts in this case are these:

The *Emulous* owned by John Delano and others citizens of the United States, was chartered to a company carrying on trade in Great Britain, one of whom was an American citizen, for the purpose of carrying a cargo from Savannah to Plymouth. After the cargo was put on board, the vessel was stopped in port by the embargo of the 4th of April, 1812. On the 25th of the same month, it was agreed between the master of the ship and the agent of the shippers, that she should proceed with her cargo to New Bedford, where her owners resided, and remain there without prejudice to the charter party. In pursuance of this agreement, the *Emulous* proceeded to

New Bedford, where she continued until after the declaration of war. In October or November, the ship was unloaded, and the cargo, except the pine timber, was landed. The pine timber was floated up a salt water creek, where, at low tide, the ends of the timber rested on the mud, where it was secured from floating out with the tide, by impediments fastened in the entrance of the creek. . . . On the 19th of April, a libel was filed by the attorney for the United States, in the district Court of Massachusetts, against the said cargo, as well on behalf of the United States of America as for and in behalf of John Delano and of all other persons concerned. It does not appear that this seizure was made under any instructions from the president of the United States; nor is there any evidence of its having his sanction, unless the libels being filed and prosecuted by the law officer who represents the government, must imply that sanction.

The questions to be decided by the Court are:

1st. May enemy's property, found on land at the commencement of hostilities, be seized and condemned as a necessary consequence of the declaration of war?

2d. Is there any legislative act which authorizes such seizure and condemnation?

Since, in this country, from the structure of our government, proceedings to condemn the property of an enemy found within our territory at the declaration of war, can be sustained only upon the principle that they are instituted in execution of some existing law, we are led to ask,

Is the declaration of war such a law? Does that declaration, by its own operation, so vest the property of the enemy in the government, as to support proceedings for its seizure and confiscation, or does it vest only a right, the assertion of which depends on the will of the sovereign power?

The universal practice of forbearing to seize and confiscate debts and credits, the principle universally received, that the right to them revives on the restoration of peace, would seem to prove that war is not an absolute confiscation of this property, but simply confers the right of confiscation.

Between debts contracted under the faith of laws, and property acquired in the course of trade, on the faith of the same laws, reason draws no distinction; and, although, in practice, vessels with their cargoes, found in port at the declaration of war, may have been seized, it is not believed that modern usage would sanction the seizure of the goods of an enemy on land, which were acquired in peace in the course of trade. Such a proceeding is rare, and would be deemed a harsh exercise of the rights of war. But although the practice in this respect may not be uniform, that circumstance does not essentially affect the question. The inquiry is, whether such property vests in the sovereign by the mere declaration of war, or remains subject to a right of confiscation, the exercise of which depends on the national will: and the rule which applies to one case, so far as respects the operation of a declaration of war on the thing itself, must apply to all others over which war gives an equal right. The right of the sovereign to confiscate debts being precisely the same with the right to confiscate other property found in the country, the operation of a declaration of war on debts and on other property found within the country must be the same. What then is this operation?

Even *Bynkershoek*, who maintains the broad principle, that in war every thing done against an enemy is lawful; that he may be destroyed, though unarmed and defenceless; that fraud, or even poison, may be employed against him; that a most unlimited right is acquired to his person and property; admits that war does not transfer to the sovereign a debt due to his enemy; and, therefore, if payment of such debt be not exacted, peace revives the former right of the creditor; "because," he says, "the occupation which is had by war consists more in fact than in law." He adds to his observations on this subject, "let it not, however, be supposed that it is only true of actions, that they are not condemned *ipso jure,* for other things also belonging to the enemy may be concealed and escape condemnation."

Vattel says, that "the sovereign can neither detain the persons nor the property of those subjects of the enemy who are within his dominions at the time of the declaration."

It is true that this rule is, in terms, applied by *Vattel* to the property of those only who are personally within the territory at the commencement of hostilities; but it applies equally to things in action and to things in possession; and if war did, of itself, without any further exercise of the sovereign will, vest the property of the enemy in the sovereign, his presence could not exempt it from this operation of war. Nor can a reason be perceived for maintaining that the public faith is more entirely pledged for the security of property trusted in the territory of the nation in time of peace, if it be accompanied by its owner, than if it be confided to the care of others. . . .

The modern rule then would seem to be, that tangible property belonging to an enemy and found in the country at the commencement of war, ought not to be immediately confiscated; and in almost every commercial treaty an article is inserted stipulating for the right to withdraw such property.

This rule appears to be totally incompatible with the idea, that war does of itself vest the property in the belligerent government. It may be considered as the opinion of all who have written on the *jus belli,* that war gives the right to confiscate, but does not itself confiscate the property of the enemy; and their rules go to the exercise of this right.

The constitution of the United States was framed at a time when this rule, introduced by commerce in favor of moderation and humanity, was received throughout the civilized world. In expounding that constitution, a construction ought not lightly to be admitted, which would give to a declaration of war an effect in this country it does not possess elsewhere, and which would fetter that exercise of entire discretion respecting enemy property, which may enable the government to apply to the enemy the rule that he applies to us.

If we look to the constitution itself, we find this general reasoning much strengthened by the words of that instrument.

That the declaration of war has only the effect of placing the two nations in a state of hostility, of producing a state of war, of giving those rights which war confers; but not of operating, by its own force, any of those results, such as a transfer of property, which are usually produced by ulterior measures of government, is fairly deducible from the enumeration of powers which accompanies that of declaring war. "Congress shall have power" "to declare war, grant letters of marque and reprisal, and make rules concerning captures on land and water."

It would be restraining this clause within narrower limits than the words themselves import, to say that the power to make rules concerning captures on land and water, is to be confined to captures which are [extra-territorial]. If it extends to rules respecting enemy property found within the territory, then we perceive an express grant to congress of the power in question as an independent substantive power, not included in that of declaring war.

The acts of congress furnish many instances of an opinion that the declaration of war does not, of itself, authorize proceedings against the persons or property of the enemy found, at the time, within the territory.

War gives an equal right over persons and property: and if its declaration is not considered as prescribing a law respecting the person of an enemy found in our country, neither does it prescribe a law for his property. The act concerning alien enemies, which confers on the president very great discretionary powers respecting their persons, affords a strong implication that he did not possess those powers by virtue of the declaration of war.

The "act for the safe keeping and accommodation of prisoners of war," is of the same character. . . .

It appears to the Court, that the power of confiscating enemy property is in the legislature, and that the legislature has not yet declared its will to confiscate property which was within our territory at the declaration of war. The Court is therefore of opinion that there is error in the sentence of condemnation pronounced in the Circuit Court in this case, and doth direct that the same be reversed and annulled, and that the sentence of the District Court be affirmed.

STORY, J. [*dissenting.*]

It seems to have been taken for granted in the argument of counsel that the opinion held in the Circuit Court proceeded, in some degree, upon a supposition that a declaration of war operates *per se* an *actual confiscation* of enemy's property found within our territory. To me, this is a perfectly novel doctrine. It was not argued, on either side, in the Circuit Court, and certainly never received the slightest countenance from the Court. . . . All that I contend for is, that a declaration of war gives a right to confiscate enemies' property, and enables the power to whom the execution of the laws and the prosecution of the war are confided, to enforce that right. If, indeed, there be a limit imposed as to the extent to which hostilities may be carried by the executive, I admit that the executive cannot lawfully transcend that limit; but if no such limit exist, the war may be carried on according to the principles of the modern law of nations, and enforced when, and where, and on what property the executive chooses. . . .

My argument proceeds upon the ground, that when the legislative authority, to whom the right to declare war is confided, has declared war in its most unlimited manner, the executive authority, to whom the execution of the war is confided, is bound to carry it into effect. He has a discretion vested in him, as to the manner and extent; but he cannot lawfully transcend the rules of warfare established among civilized nations. He cannot lawfully exercise powers or authorize proceedings which the civilized world repudiates and disclaims. The sovereignty as to declaring war and limiting its effects, rests with the legislature. The sovereignty, as to its execution, rests with the president. If the legislature do not limit the nature of the war, all the regulations and rights of general war attach upon it. I do not, therefore, contend that modern usage of nations constitutes a rule acting on enemies' property, so as to produce confiscation of itself, and not through the sovereign power: on the contrary, I consider enemies' property in no case whatsoever confiscated by the mere declaration of war; it is only liable to be confiscated at the discretion of the sovereign power having the conduct and execution of the war. The modern usage of nations is resorted to, merely as a limitation of this discretion, not as conferring the authority to exercise it. The sovereignty to execute it is supposed already to exist in the president, by the very terms of the constitution: and I would again ask, if this general power to confiscate enemies' property does not exist in the executive, to be exercised in his discretion, how is it possible that he can have authority to seize and confiscate any enemies' property coming into the country since the war, or found in the enemies' territory?—Yet, I understood the opinion of my brethren to proceed upon the tacit acknowledgment that the executive may seize and confiscate such property, under the circumstances which I have stated.

On the whole, I am still of opinion, that the judgment of the Circuit Court was correct, and ought to be affirmed.

It is due, however, to myself to state, that, at the trial in the Circuit Court, it was agreed that the timber had always been afloat on tide waters; and the affidavit by which it is proved to have rested on land at low tide, was not taken until after the hearing and decision of the cause.

In the opinion which I have expressed I am authorized to state that I have the concurrence of one of my brethren.

ABRAHAM D. SOFAER, WAR, FOREIGN AFFAIRS AND CONSTITUTIONAL POWER: THE ORIGINS*

145–66, 274–75 (1976).

Soon [after *Bas v. Tingy*] the Court was presented—in *Talbot v. Seeman*—with a case in which an American commander was denied salvage for rescuing a vessel owned by citizens of a neutral nation. The Court agreed that no salvage could be paid for an unlawful recapture, but concluded that the recapture was lawful because authorized by Congress. "The whole powers of war being, by the constitution of the United States, vested in congress," wrote Chief Justice Marshall, "the acts of that body can alone be resorted to as our guides in this enquiry." No one denied that Congress could authorize general or limited hostilities; the issue was whether the limited hostilities authorized included the recapture of a neutral vessel, and Marshall found that they did.

In *Little v. Barreme* the Court faced a more difficult controversy—whether a seizure pursuant to an executive instruction was invalid because the instruction exceeded the power delegated by Congress. . . .

The Supreme Court made clear that it regarded Congress as the ultimate source of authority on whether and how the nation would make war. It granted relief against a seizure that exceeded the limits of authority implied by a statute, strongly suggesting that Congress has power to control the conduct of war, even over a subject—the seizure of American merchant vessels trading with an enemy—that Chief Justice Marshall suggested might well have come within the President's authority, in the absence of any legislative regulation. Both branches could act, in other words, but Congress had the final say. . . .

One limited but significant restraint on executive power to act under broad delegations was imposed by the Supreme Court in *Brown v. United States*. After war against Britain was formally declared, an attorney for the United States seized some British owned timber landed in Massachusetts before the declaration of war. The local United States Attorney relied on the declaration of war as authority for the seizure, and in at least one prior

* Reprinted with permission from Abraham D. Sofaer.

case the Court had suggested that a declaration allowed any and all acts of hostility. But the Court ruled this seizure unauthorized. The Constitution was a document imbued with moderation, concluded the majority, and should be read to require the legislature more specifically to authorize a measure in conflict with the law of nations. The express grant to Congress of power to "make rules concerning captures on land and water" was read to apply to domestic captures as well as those abroad, and required Congress to promulgate the rules more specifically. That Congress had frequently legislated with specificity concerning enemy individuals and property, the majority found, was evidence supporting its decision. Justice Story dissented vigorously, contending that the executive could seize an enemy alien's property when war was generally declared, though not moneys owed him; Story agreed, however, that Congress could have limited and regulated the President's authority in pursuing a general war.

NOTES

1. *Congressional Power over War Initiation.* Is Congress's power to declare "war" limited to the power to establish a formal state of "war" within the meaning of international law (sometimes referred to as "perfect" war) or does it encompass all types of military coercion, formal or informal (sometimes referred to as "imperfect" war)? Or is the power granted to Congress merely that of making a legal declaration? *See* John Yoo, *The Powers of War and Peace: The Constitution and Foreign Affairs After 9/11*, 143–60 (2005) (arguing that Congress's role in declaring war was meant to be limited to the formal declaration of war itself). What do the Marshall Court cases say or suggest about congressional power over war initiation? The text of the Constitution gives Congress the power to "grant Letters of Marque and Reprisal, and make Rules concerning Captures on Land and Water." How are these powers related to the Declare War Clause? *See* Ingrid Wuerth, *The Captures Clause*, 76 U. CHI. L. REV. 1683 (2009). Congress also has the power to appropriate funds for the military. Are appropriations a more important check on presidential war initiation than the Declare War Clause? Does it matter that war has become less costly over time in relation to the overall budget of the military and that conscription has been eliminated? These developments arguably mean that "critical features of the [ ] constitutional equilibrium, which largely controlled the war power even in the absence of formally declared hostilities, have come undone." Lucas Issacharoff & Samuel Issacharoff, *Constitutional Implications of the Cost of War*, 83 U. CHI. L. REV. 169 (2016).

2. *Scope of Authorizations to Use Force.* Assuming that Congress initiates military action that falls short of a formal declaration of war, what consequences flow from that action, given the reasoning in *Brown v. United States*? Must Congress be more specific about the effects of a declaration of informal/imperfect war than would be the case for a formal declaration of war? Compare the Supreme Court's opinions in *Hamdan v. Rumsfeld*, 548 U.S. 557 (2006) and *Hamdi v. Rumsfeld*, 542 U.S. 507 (2004), construing the breadth of

presidential authority conferred by the Authorization to Use Military Force statute. (*See* Chapter 1, Sec. 3 and *infra,* this Chapter, Sec. 7). Consider also the following reasoning:

> Finally, we note that the AUMF itself contains nothing that transforms a civilian into a combatant subject to indefinite military detention. Indeed, the AUMF contains only a broad grant of war powers and lacks any specific language authorizing detention. For this reason, the *Hamdi* plurality explained that its opinion "only finds legislative authority to detain under the AUMF once it is sufficiently clear that the individual *is*, in fact, an enemy combatant." *Hamdi,* 542 U.S. at 523 (emphasis added). Although the military detention of enemy combatants like Hamdi is certainly "a fundamental incident of waging war," *id.* at 519, the military detention of civilians like al-Marri just as certainly is not. Notably, even the Government does not contend that the AUMF transforms civilians into combatants or authorizes the President to classify civilians as enemy combatants and so detain them in military custody.
>
> Moreover, assuming the Constitution permitted Congress to grant the President such an awesome and unprecedented power, if Congress intended to grant this authority it could and would have said so explicitly. The AUMF lacks the particularly clear statement from Congress that would, at a minimum, be necessary to authorize the classification and indefinite military detention of *civilians* as "enemy combatants." *See, e.g., Ex Parte Endo,* 323 U.S. 283, 300 (1944) (rejecting Government argument that a "wartime" executive order and statute permitted detention of citizen of Japanese heritage when neither "use[d] the language of detention"); [additional citations omitted]. We are exceedingly reluctant to infer a grant of authority that is so far afield from anything recognized by precedent or law-of-war principles, especially given the serious constitutional concerns it would raise.

Al-Marri v. Wright, 487 F.3d 160, 188–89 (4th Cir. 2007). Sitting *en banc*, the Fourth Circuit vacated the opinion from which this excerpt was taken and held that assuming the government's allegations were true, Congress had authorized al-Marri's detention. *Al-Marri v. Pucciarelli*, 534 F.3d 213 (2008) (en banc), *vacated sub nom. Al-Marri v. Spagone*, 555 U.S. 1220 (2009).

3. *Justice Story*. Justice Story was not just an influential member of the Supreme Court, but an outstanding constitutional and private law scholar. Consider the following excerpt from his classic treatise on the U.S. Constitution:

> The power of declaring war is not only the highest sovereign prerogative; . . . it is in its own nature and effects so critical and calamitous, that it requires the utmost deliberation, and the successive review of all the councils of the nations. War, in its best estate, never fails to impose upon the people the most burdensome

> taxes, and personal sufferings. It is always injurious, and sometimes subversive of the great commercial, manufacturing, and agricultural interests. Nay, it always involves the prosperity, and not infrequently the existence, of a nation. It is sometimes fatal to public liberty itself, by introducing a spirit of military glory, which is ready to follow, wherever a successful commander will lead; . . . It should therefore be difficult in a republic to declare war; but not to make peace. . . . The cooperation of all the branches of the legislative power ought, upon principle, to be required in this the highest act of legislation.

Joseph Story, *Commentaries on the Constitution of the United States* 60–61 (1833).

DURAND V. HOLLINS

8 F.Cas. 111 (C.C.S.D.N.Y. 1860) (No. 4,186).

[In 1854, following an incident in which a bottle was thrown at an American diplomat in Greytown, Nicaragua, the Secretary of the Navy ordered the *Cyane* to bombard the town. Among the property damaged was a building owned by Durand, an American citizen, who sued Hollins, the commander of the *Cyane*. The facts arguably presented "no question of emergency intervention to save American citizens; it was rather a calculated retaliation after the fact." A. Schlesinger, *The Imperial Presidency* 55–57 (1973).]

NELSON, CIRCUIT JUSTICE. The principal ground of objection to the pleas, as a defence of the action, is, that neither the president nor the secretary of the navy had authority to give the orders relied on to the defendant, and, hence, that they afford no ground of justification.

The executive power, under the constitution, is vested in the president of the United States (article 2, § 1). He is commander-in-chief of the army and navy, (Id. § 2), and has imposed upon him the duty to "take care that the laws be faithfully executed" (Id. § 3). In organizing a government under the constitution, an executive department, called the "Department of Foreign Affairs," was established, and a principal officer, called the "Secretary for the Department of Foreign Affairs," placed at its head, to "execute such duties as shall, from time to time, be enjoined on or intrusted to him by the president of the United States, agreeable to the constitution, relative to correspondences, commissions, or instructions to or with public ministers or consuls from the United States, or to negotiations with public ministers from foreign states or princes, or to memorials or other applications from foreign public ministers or other foreigners, or to such other matters respecting foreign affairs as the president of the United States shall assign to the said department; and, furthermore, that the said principal officer shall conduct the business of the said department in such manner as the president of the United States shall from time to time order or instruct." Act Cong. July 27, 1789, § 1 (1 Stat. 28). By a subsequent act, this department has been denominated the "Department of State," and the head of it the "Secretary of State." There was also established another executive department, denominated the "Department of the Navy," the chief officer of which is called the "Secretary of the Navy," "whose duty it shall be to execute such orders as he shall receive from the president of the United States. . . ."

As the executive head of the nation, the president is made the only legitimate organ of the general government, to open and carry on correspondence or negotiations with foreign nations, in matters concerning the interests of the country or of its citizens. It is to him, also, the citizens abroad must look for protection of person and of property, and for the faithful execution of the laws existing and intended for their protection. For this purpose, the whole executive power of the country is placed in his hands, under the constitution, and the laws passed in pursuance thereof; and different departments of government have been organized, through which this power may be most conveniently executed, whether by negotiation or by force—a department of state and a department of the navy.

Now, as it respects the interposition of the executive abroad, for the protection of the lives or property of the citizen, the duty must, of necessity, rest in the discretion of the president. Acts of lawless violence, or of threatened violence to the citizen or his property, cannot be anticipated and provided for; and the protection, to be effectual or of any avail, may, not unfrequently, require the most prompt and decided action. Under our system of government, the citizen abroad is as much entitled to protection as the citizen at home. The great object and duty of government is the protection of the lives, liberty, and property of the people composing it, whether abroad or at home; and any government failing in the accomplishment of the object, or the performance of the duty, is not worth preserving.

I have said, that the interposition of the president abroad, for the protection of the citizen, must necessarily rest in his discretion; and it is quite clear that, in all cases where a public act or order rests in executive discretion neither he nor his authorized agent is personally civilly responsible for the consequences. . . . The question whether it was the duty of the president to interpose for the protection of the citizens at Greytown against an irresponsible and marauding community that had established itself there, was a public political question, in which the government, as well as the citizens whose interests were involved, was concerned, and which belonged to the executive to determine; and his decision is final and conclusive, and justified the defendant in the execution of his orders given through the secretary of the navy.

INTRODUCTORY NOTE TO THE PRIZE CASES

Professor John Hart Ely wrote as follows: "President Lincoln's actions at the outset of the Civil War are sometimes cited as precedent for presidential military ventures. Although Lincoln did engage in a number of unconstitutional acts during this period, . . . usurpation of the war power was not among them. The important fact is not that Congress retroactively authorized what Lincoln had done (since that shouldn't count) but rather that for constitutional purposes a domestic rebellion is quite different from a foreign war. Article II provides that the president 'shall take Care that the Laws be faithfully executed,' . . . and beyond that, though it shouldn't be necessary, congressional acts of 1795 and 1807 had empowered him to use the military to suppress insurrection against the government of the United States." John Hart Ely, *Suppose Congress Wanted a War Powers Act that Worked,* 88 COLUM. L. REV. 1379, 1390 n. 34 (1988) (reprinted with permission of Columbia Law Review, permission conveyed through Copyright Clearance Center, Inc.); *see also* John Hart Ely, *War and Responsibility: Constitutional Lessons of Vietnam and its Aftermath* (1993).

THE PRIZE CASES

67 U.S. (2 Black) 365 (1862).

These were cases in which the vessels named, together with their cargoes, were severally captured and brought in as prizes by public ships of the United States. The libels were filed by the proper District Attorneys, on behalf of the United States and on behalf of the officers and crews of the ships, by which the captures were respectively made. In each case the District Court pronounced a decree of condemnation, from which the claimants took an appeal. . . .

MR. JUSTICE GRIER. . . .

Had the President a right to institute a blockade of ports in possession of persons in armed rebellion against the Government, on the principles of international law, as known and acknowledged among civilized States? . . .

Neutrals have a right to challenge the existence of a blockade *de facto,* and also the authority of the party exercising the right to institute it. They have a right to enter the ports of a friendly nation for the purposes of trade and commerce, but are bound to recognize the rights of a belligerent engaged in actual war, to use this mode of coercion, for the purpose of subduing the enemy.

That a blockade *de facto* actually existed, and was formally declared and notified by the President on the 27th and 30th of April, 1861, is an admitted fact in these cases.

That the President, as the Executive Chief of the Government and Commander-in-chief of the Army and Navy, was the proper person to make such notification, has not been, and cannot be disputed.

The right of prize and capture has its origin in the "*jus belli,*" and is governed and adjudged under the law of nations. To legitimate the capture of a neutral vessel or property on the high seas, a war must exist *de facto,* and the neutral must have a knowledge or notice of the intention of one of the parties belligerent to use this mode of coercion against a port, city, or territory, in possession of the other.

Let us enquire whether, at the time this blockade was instituted, a state of war existed which would justify a resort to these means of subduing the hostile force.

War has been well defined to be, "That state in which a nation prosecutes its right by force."

The parties belligerent in a public war are independent nations. But it is not necessary to constitute war, that both parties should be acknowledged as independent nations or sovereign States. A war may exist where one of the belligerents, claims sovereign rights as against the other.

Insurrection against a government may or may not culminate in an organized rebellion, but a civil war always begins by insurrection against the lawful authority of the Government. A civil war is never solemnly declared; it becomes such by its accidents—the number, power, and organization of the persons who originate and carry it on. When the party in rebellion occupy and hold in a hostile manner a certain portion of territory; have declared their independence; have cast off their allegiance; have organized armies; have commenced hostilities against their former sovereign, the world acknowledges them as belligerents, and the contest a *war. They* claim to be in arms to establish their liberty and independence, in order to become a sovereign State, while the sovereign party treats them as insurgents and rebels who owe allegiance, and who should be punished with death for their treason. . . .

As a civil war is never publicly proclaimed, *eo nomine* against insurgents, its actual existence is a fact in our domestic history which the Court is bound to notice and to know.

The true test of its existence, as found in the writings of the sages of the common law, may be thus summarily stated: "When the regular course of justice is interrupted by revolt, rebellion, or insurrection, so that the Courts of Justice cannot be kept open, *civil war exists* and hostilities may be prosecuted on the same footing as if those opposing the Government were foreign enemies invading the land."

By the Constitution, Congress alone has the power to declare a national or foreign war. It cannot declare war against a State, or any number of States, by virtue of any clause in the Constitution. The Constitution confers on the President the whole Executive power. He is bound to take care that the laws be faithfully executed. He is Commander-in-chief of the Army and Navy of the United States, and of the militia of the several States when called into the actual service of the United States. He has no power to initiate or declare a war either against a foreign nation or a domestic State. But by the Acts of Congress of February 28th, 1795, and 3d of March, 1807, he is authorized to called out the militia and use the military and naval forces of the United States in case of invasion by foreign nations, and to suppress insurrection against the government of a State or of the United States.

If a war be made by invasion of a foreign nation, the President is not only authorized but bound to resist force by force. He does not initiate the war, but is bound to accept the challenge without waiting for any special legislative authority. And whether the hostile party be a foreign invader, or States organized in rebellion, it is none the less a war, although the declaration of it be "*unilateral.*" Lord Stowell (1 Dodson, 247) observes, "It is not the less a war on *that account,* for war may exist without a declaration on either side. It is so laid down by the best writers on the law of nations. A declaration of war by one country only, is not a mere challenge to be accepted or refused at pleasure by the other."

The battles of Palo Alto and Resaca de la Palma had been fought before the passage of the Act of Congress of May 13th, 1846, which recognized "*a state of war as existing by the act of the Republic of Mexico.*" This act not only provided for the future prosecution of the war, but was itself a vindication and ratification of the Act of the President in accepting the challenge without a previous formal declaration of war by Congress.

This greatest of civil wars was not gradually developed by popular commotion, tumultuous assemblies, or local unorganized insurrections. However long may have been its previous conception, it nevertheless sprung forth suddenly from the parent brain, a Minerva in the full panoply of *war*. The President was bound to meet it in the shape it presented itself, without waiting for Congress to baptize it with a name; and no name given to it by him or them could change the fact.

It is not the less a civil war, with belligerent parties in hostile array, because it may be called an "insurrection" by one side, and the insurgents be considered as rebels or traitors. It is not necessary that the independence of the revolted province or State be acknowledged in order to constitute it a party belligerent in a war according to the law of nations. Foreign nations acknowledge it as war by a declaration of neutrality. The condition of neutrality cannot exist unless there be two belligerent parties. In the case of the *Santissima Trinidad,* (7 Wheaton, 337,) this Court say: "The Government of the United States has recognized the existence of a civil war between Spain and her colonies, and has avowed her determination to remain neutral between the parties. Each party is therefore deemed by us a belligerent nation, having, so far as concerns us, the sovereign rights of war." . . .

The law of nations is also called the law of nature; it is founded on the common consent as well as the common sense of the world. It contains no such anomalous doctrine as that which this Court are now for the first time desired to pronounce, to wit: That insurgents who have risen in rebellion against their sovereign, expelled her Courts, established a revolutionary government, organized armies, and commenced hostilities, are not *enemies* because they are *traitors;* and a war levied on the Government by traitors, in order to dismember and destroy it, is not a *war* because it is an "insurrection."

Whether the President in fulfilling his duties, as Commander-in-chief, in suppressing an insurrection, has met with such armed hostile resistance, and a civil war of such alarming proportions as will compel him to accord to them the character of belligerents, is a question to be decided *by him,* and this Court must be governed by the decisions and acts of the political department of the Government to which this power was entrusted. "He must determine what degree of force the crisis demands." The proclamation of blockade is itself official and conclusive evidence to the Court that a state of war existed which demanded and authorized a recourse to such a measure, under the circumstances peculiar to the case. . . .

And finally, in 1861, we find Congress "*ex majore cautela*" and in anticipation of such astute objections, passing an act "approving, legalizing, and making valid all the acts, proclamations, and orders of the President, & c., as if they had been *issued and done under the previous express authority* and direction of the Congress of the United States."

Without admitting that such an act was necessary under the circumstances, it is plain that if the President had in any manner assumed powers which it was necessary should have the authority or sanction of Congress, that on the well known principle of law, "*omnis ratihabitio retrotrahitur et mandato equiparatur,*" this ratification has operated to perfectly cure the defect. In the case of *Brown vs. United States,* (8 Cr., 131, 132, 133,) Mr. Justice Story treats of this subject, and cites numerous authorities to which we may refer to prove this position, and concludes, "I am perfectly satisfied that no subject can commence hostilities or capture property of an enemy, when the sovereign has prohibited it. But suppose he did, I would ask if the sovereign may not ratify his proceedings, and thus by a retroactive operation give validity to them?"

Although Mr. Justice Story dissented from the majority of the Court on the whole case, the doctrine stated by him on this point is correct and fully substantiated by authority.

The objection made to this act of ratification, that it is *ex post facto,* and therefore unconstitutional and void, might possibly have some weight on the trial of an indictment in a criminal Court. But precedents from that source cannot be received as authoritative in a tribunal administering public and international law.

On this first question therefore we are of the opinion that the President had a right, *jure belli,* to institute a blockade of ports in possession of the States in rebellion, which neutrals are bound to regard.

MR. JUSTICE NELSON, dissenting. . . .

Another objection taken to the seizure of this vessel and cargo is, that there was no existing war between the United States and the States in insurrection within the meaning of the law of nations, which drew after it the consequences of a public or civil war. A contest by force between independent sovereign States is called a public war; and, when duly commenced by proclamation or otherwise, it entitles both of the belligerent parties to all the rights of war against each other, and as respects neutral nations. Chancellor Kent observes, "Though a solemn declaration, or previous notice to the enemy, be now laid aside, it is essential that some formal public act, proceeding directly from the competent source, should announce to the people at home their new relations and duties growing out of a state of war, and which should equally apprize neutral nations of the fact, to enable them to conform their conduct to the rights belonging to the new state of things." "Such an official act operates from its date to legalize all hostile acts, in like manner as a treaty of peace operates from its date to annul them." He further observes, "as war cannot lawfully be commenced on the part of the United States without an act of Congress, such act is, of course, a formal notice to all the world, and equivalent to the most solemn declaration."

The legal consequences resulting from a state of war between two countries at this day are well understood, and will be found described in every approved work on the subject of international law. The people of the two countries become immediately the enemies of each other—all intercourse commercial or otherwise between them unlawful—all contracts existing at the commencement of the war suspended, and all made during its existence utterly void. The insurance of enemies' property, the drawing of bills of exchange or purchase on the enemies' country, the remission of bills or money to it are illegal and void. Existing partnerships between citizens or subjects of the two countries are dissolved, and, in fine, interdiction of trade and intercourse direct or indirect is absolute and complete by the mere force and effect of war itself. All the property of the people of the two countries on land or sea are subject to capture and confiscation by the adverse party as enemies' property, with certain qualifications as it respects property on land, (*Brown vs. United States,* 8 Cranch, 110,) all treaties between the belligerent parties are annulled; The ports of the respective countries may be blockaded, and letters of marque and reprisal granted as rights of war, and the law of prizes as defined by the law of nations comes into full and complete operation, resulting from maritime captures *jure belli.* War also effects a change in the mutual relations of all States or countries, not directly, as in the case of the belligerents, but immediately and indirectly, though they take no part in the contest, but remain neutral.

This great and pervading change in the existing condition of a country, and in the relations of all her citizens or subjects, external and internal, from a state of peace, is the immediate effect and result of a state of war: and hence the same code which has annexed to the existence of a war all these disturbing consequences has declared that the right of making war belongs exclusively to the supreme or sovereign power of the State.

This power in all civilized nations is regulated by the fundamental laws or municipal constitution of the country.

By our Constitution this power is lodged in Congress. Congress shall have power "to declare war, grant letters of marque and reprisal, and make rules concerning captures on land and water."

We have thus far been considering the status of the citizens or subjects of a country at the breaking out of a public war when recognized or declared by the competent power.

In the case of a rebellion or resistance of a portion of the people of a country against the established government, there is no doubt, if in its progress and enlargement the government thus sought to be overthrown sees fit, it may by the competent power recognize or declare the existence of a state of civil war, which will draw after it all the consequences and rights of war between the contending parties as in the case of a public war. Mr. Wheaton observes, speaking of civil war, "But the general usage of nations regards such a war as entitling both the contending parties to all the rights of war as against each other, and even as respects neutral nations." It is not to be denied, therefore, that if a civil war existed between that portion of the people in organized insurrection to overthrow this Government at the time this vessel and cargo were seized, and if she was guilty of a violation of the blockade, she would be lawful prize of war. But before this insurrection against the established Government can be dealt with on the footing of a civil war, within the meaning of the law of nations and the Constitution of the United States, and which will draw after it belligerent rights, it must be recognized or declared by the war-making power of the Government. No power short of this can change the legal status of the Government or the relations of its citizens from that of peace to a state of war, or bring into existence all those duties and obligations of neutral third parties growing out of a state of war. The war power of the Government must be exercised before this changed condition of the Government and people and of neutral third parties can be admitted. There is no difference in this respect between a civil or a public war. . . .

Now, in one sense, no doubt this is war, and may be a war of the most extensive and threatening dimensions and effects, but it is a statement simply of its existence in a material sense, and has no relevancy or weight when the question is what constitutes war in a legal sense, in the sense of the law of nations, and of the Constitution of the United States? For it must be a war in this sense to attach to it all the consequences that belong to belligerent rights. Instead, therefore, of inquiring after armies and navies, and victories lost and won, or organized rebellion against the general Government, the inquiry should be into the law of nations and into the municipal fundamental laws of the Government. For we find there that to constitute a civil war in the sense in which we are speaking, before it can exist, in contemplation of law, it must be recognized or declared by the sovereign power of the State, and which sovereign power by our Constitution is lodged in the Congress of the United States—civil war, therefore, under our system of government, can exist only by an act of Congress, which requires the assent of two of the great departments of the Government, the Executive and Legislative.

We have thus far been speaking of the war power under the Constitution of the United States, and as known and recognized by the law of nations. But we are asked, what would become of the peace and integrity of the Union in case of an insurrection at home or invasion from abroad if this power could not be exercised by the President in the recess of Congress, and until that body could be assembled?

The framers of the Constitution fully comprehended this question, and provided for the contingency. Indeed, it would have been surprising if they had not, as a rebellion had occurred in the State of Massachusetts while the Convention was in session, and which had become so general that it was quelled only by calling upon the military power of the State. The Constitution declares that Congress shall have power "to provide for calling forth the militia to execute the laws of the Union, suppress insurrections, and repel invasions." Another clause, "that the President shall be Commander-in-chief of the Army and Navy of the United States, and of the militia of the several States when called into the actual service of the United States;" and, again, "He shall take care that the laws shall be faithfully executed." . . .

The last Act provided that whenever the United States shall be invaded or be in imminent danger of invasion from a foreign nation, it shall be lawful for the President to call forth such number of the militia most convenient to the place of danger, and in case of insurrection in any State against the Government thereof, it shall be lawful for the President, on the application of the Legislature of such State, if in session, or if not, of the Executive of the State, to call forth such number of militia of any other State or States as he may judge sufficient to suppress such insurrection.

The 2d section provides, that when the laws of the United States shall be opposed, or the execution obstructed in any State by combinations too powerful to be suppressed by the course of judicial proceedings, it shall be lawful for the President to call forth the militia of such State, or of any other State or States as may be necessary to suppress such combinations; and by the Act 3 March, 1807, (2 U.S. Laws, 443,) it is provided that in case of insurrection or obstruction of the laws, either in the United States or of any State or Territory, where it is lawful for the President to call forth the militia for the purpose of suppressing such insurrection, and causing the laws to be executed, it shall be lawful to employ for the same purpose such part of the land and naval forces of the United States as shall be judged necessary.

It will be seen, therefore, that ample provision has been made under the Constitution and laws against any sudden and unexpected disturbance of the public peace from insurrection at home or invasion from abroad. . . .

I am compelled to the conclusion that no civil war existed between this Government and the States in insurrection till recognized by the Act of Congress 13th of July, 1861; that the President does not possess the power under the Constitution to declare war or recognize its existence within the meaning of the law of nations, which carries with it belligerent rights, and thus change the country and all its citizens from a state of peace to a state of war; that this power belongs exclusively to the Congress of the United States, and, consequently, that the President had no power to set on foot a blockade under the law of nations, and that the capture of the vessel and cargo in this case, and in all cases before us in which the capture occurred before the 13th of July, 1861, for breach of blockade, or as enemies' property, are illegal and void, and that the decrees of condemnation should be reversed and the vessel and cargo restored.

MR. CHIEF JUSTICE TANEY, MR. JUSTICE CATRON and MR. JUSTICE CLIFFORD, concurred in the dissenting opinion of MR. JUSTICE NELSON.

NOTES

1. *In re Neagle*. In 1889, the U.S. Attorney General assigned Deputy U.S. Marshal David Neagle to protect Circuit Judge Stephen J. Field while the judge rode circuit in California. On August 14 of that year, a disappointed litigant before the judge, David S. Terry, burst into a room where Neagle and

Judge Field were having breakfast, and proceeded to assault the Judge. Neagle shot Terry twice with his revolver, killing him instantly.

Later that day, the Sheriff of San Joaquin County, California, arrested Neagle on charges of murder. The U.S. government filed a writ of *habeas corpus* in an effort to have Neagle released. Among other things, Neagle argued that "in killing Terry under the circumstances [he was acting] in the discharge of his duty as an officer of the United States." Congress, however, had never actually enacted a statute authorizing such protection. In deciding for Neagle, Justice Samuel F. Miller wrote:

> Is [the president's duty to "take care that the laws be faithfully executed"] limited to the enforcement of acts of Congress or of treaties of the United States according to their *express terms*, or does it include the rights, duties and obligations growing out of the Constitution itself, our international relations, and all the protection implied by the nature of the government under the Constitution?
>
> One of the most remarkable episodes in the history of our foreign relations, and which has become an attractive historical incident, is the case of Martin Koszta, a native of Hungary, who, though not fully a naturalized citizen of the United States, had in due form of law made his declaration of intention to become a citizen. While in Smyrna he was seized by command of the Austrian consul general at that place, and carried on board the *Hussar*, an Austrian vessel, where he was held in close confinement. Captain Ingraham, in command of the American sloop of war *St. Louis*, arriving in port at that critical period, and ascertaining that Koszta had with him his naturalization papers, demanded his surrender to him, and was compelled to train his guns upon the Austrian vessel before his demands were complied with. It was, however, to prevent bloodshed, agreed that Koszta should be placed in the hands of the French consul subject to the result of diplomatic negotiations between Austria and the United States. The celebrated correspondence between Mr. Marcy, Secretary of State, and Chevalier Hulsemann, the Austrian minister at Washington, which arose out of this affair, and resulted in the release and restoration to liberty of Koszta, attracted a great deal of public attention, and the position assumed by Mr. Marcy met the approval of the country and of Congress, who voted a gold medal to Captain Ingraham for his conduct in the affair. Upon what act of Congress then existing can any one lay his finger in support of the action of our government in this matter?

In re Neagle, 135 U.S. 1 (1890). Are Justice Miller's statements on the Koszta Affair part of the holding or are they dicta? Do they have precedential significance? The constitutional power exercised in *In re Neagle* is sometimes referred to as the "protective power." *See* Henry P. Monaghan, *The Protective Power of the Presidency*, 93 COLUM. L. REV. 1, 62 (1993). What is the scope of this power? How is it related to the "emergency powers" of the executive branch, if there are any such powers?

2. *Congressional and Presidential Power over the use of Military Force.* In both *Durand* and the *Prize Cases*, courts rejected challenges to the president's use of military force without congressional authorization. Why? Are these decisions consistent with the text of the Constitution, the Federalist Papers, and other materials from the founding? Are they consistent with the Marshall court cases? Consider the following evaluation of the Constitution's original meaning:

> The Constitution's text provides that the president is commander-in-chief of the U.S. military and that Congress has power to "declare War." Most war powers scholars agree on a set of core propositions: that, as an original matter, these provisions gave Congress an exclusive power to decide on the initiation of material hostilities with foreign states, while leaving to the president the direction of U.S. forces once Congress had authorized hostilities (subject to statutory limitation), and some independent ability to respond to attacks on the United States. Beyond this general agreement, there is substantial uncertainty at the margins, including:
>
> (1) What sorts of attacks and threats may trigger the president's power to respond?;
>
> (2) How far may the president go in responding to an attack?;
>
> (3) How is power allocated with respect to using force against nonstate actors?;
>
> (4) What are the president's powers over military deployments not immediately resulting in hostilities or made in support of the local sovereign government?;
>
> (5) To what extent may Congress give unspecific, open-ended authorizations for use of force by the president?; and
>
> (6) What level of force may be so *de minimus* that it does not amount to war in the constitutional sense?

Michael D. Ramsey, *Constitutional War Initiation and the Obama Presidency*, 110 AM. J. INT'L L. 701 (2016) (reprinted with permissions of the American Society of International Law, permission conveyed throught Copyright Clearance Center, Inc.). Do the early cases and ratification-related materials support the foregoing argument about the Constitution's original meaning? Note that some scholars argue, contrary to Professor Ramsey, that it is difficult or impossible to ascertain the original meaning of the Constitution. Is the "substantial uncertainty" that the author describes really "at the margins"? Do the mid-nineteenth century cases resolve—or heighten—any of the uncertainty around these six issues? As you read the following Section on more recent historical practice, consider whether use of force by the president is consistent with the "set of core propositions" and the uncertainties identified by Professor Ramsey.

3. HISTORICAL PRACTICE

What does historical practice suggest about the allocation of war powers between Congress and the president? Over the hundreds of instances in which U.S. armed forces have been deployed abroad, Congress has declared war only eleven times in five conflicts. At the same time, Congress has authorized most major post-World War II conflicts by statute, including the deployment of U.S. forces to Afghanistan in 2001 and Iraq in 2003. Does the history suggest a settled view that congressional approval is constitutionally required for all uses of U.S. military force? For only uses of U.S. military force that rise above a certain threshold level of significance? Can the president act on his own authority when necessary to respond to a sudden threat to U.S. national security? Does the historical practice show that today approval by Congress is never constitutionally required?

CONGRESSIONAL RESEARCH SERVICE, INSTANCES OF USE OF UNITED STATES ARMED FORCES ABROAD, 1798–2016

CRS Rep. R42738 (Oct. 7, 2016) available at https://fas.org/sgp/crs/natsec/R42738.pdf, [https://perma.cc/ZD7S-XAH7].

This report lists hundreds of instances in which the United States has used its Armed Forces abroad in situations of military conflict or potential conflict or for other than normal peacetime purposes. It was compiled in part from various older lists and is intended primarily to provide a rough survey of past U.S. military ventures abroad, without reference to the magnitude of the given instance noted. The listing often contains references, especially from 1980 forward, to continuing military deployments, especially U.S. military participation in multinational operations associated with NATO or the United Nations. Most of these post-1980 instances are summaries based on presidential reports to Congress related to the War Powers Resolution. A comprehensive commentary regarding any of the instances listed is not undertaken here.

The instances differ greatly in number of forces, purpose, extent of hostilities, and legal authorization. . . .

Some of the instances were extended military engagements that might be considered undeclared wars. These include the Undeclared Naval War with France from 1798 to 1800; the First Barbary War from 1801 to 1805; the Second Barbary War of 1815; the Korean War of 1950–1953; the Vietnam War from 1964 to 1973; the Persian Gulf War of 1991; global actions against foreign terrorists after the September 11, 2001, attacks on the United States; and the war with Iraq in 2003. With the exception of the

Korean War, all of these conflicts received congressional authorization in some form short of a formal declaration of war. Other, more recent instances have often involved deployment of U.S. military forces as part of a multinational operation associated with NATO or the United Nations.

The majority of the instances listed prior to World War II were brief Marine Corps or Navy actions to protect U.S. citizens or promote U.S. interests. A number were engagements against pirates or bandits. Covert operations, disaster relief, and routine alliance stationing and training exercises are not included here, nor are the Civil and Revolutionary Wars and the continual use of U.S. military units in the exploration, settlement, and pacification of the western part of the United States. . . .

LISTING OF NOTABLE DEPLOYMENTS OF U.S. MILITARY FORCES OVERSEAS, 1798–2016

1798–1800 Undeclared Naval War with France. This contest included land actions, such as that in the Dominican Republic, city of Puerto Plata, where marines captured a French privateer under the guns of the forts. Congress authorized military action through a series of statutes.

1801–1805 Tripoli. The First Barbary War included the USS George Washington and Philadelphia affairs and the Eaton expedition, during which a few marines landed with United States Agent William Eaton to raise a force against Tripoli in an effort to free the crew of the Philadelphia. Tripoli declared war on the United States on May 10, 1801, and although Congress authorized U.S. military action by statute, they never voted on a formal declaration of war.

1806 Mexico (Spanish territory). Captain Z. M. Pike, with a platoon of troops, invaded Spanish territory at the headwaters of the Rio Grande on orders from General James Wilkinson. He was made prisoner without resistance at a fort he constructed in present-day Colorado, taken to Mexico, and later released after seizure of his papers.

1806–1810 Gulf of Mexico. American gunboats operated from New Orleans against Spanish and French privateers off the Mississippi Delta, chiefly under Captain John Shaw and Master Commandant David Porter.

1810 West Florida (Spanish territory). Governor William Charles Cole Claiborne of Louisiana, on orders of the President, occupied with troops territory in dispute east of the Mississippi River as far as the Pearl River, later the eastern boundary of Louisiana. He was authorized to seize as far east as the Perdido River.

1812 Amelia Island and other parts of east Florida, then under Spain. Temporary possession was authorized by President Madison and by Congress, to prevent occupation by any other power; but possession was obtained by General George Matthews in so irregular a manner that his measures were disavowed by the President.

1812–1815 War of 1812. On June 18, 1812, the United States declared war between the United States and the United Kingdom of Great Britain and Ireland. Among the issues leading to the war were British interception of neutral ships and blockades of the United States during British hostilities with France.

1813 West Florida (Spanish territory). On authority given by Congress, General Wilkinson seized Mobile Bay in April with 600 soldiers. A small Spanish garrison gave way. The United States advanced into disputed territory to the Perdido River, as projected in 1810. No fighting.

1813–1814 Marquesas Islands. U.S. forces built a fort on the Pacific island of Nuku Hiva, the largest of the Marquesas, to protect three prize ships which had been captured from the British.

1814 Spanish Florida. General Andrew Jackson took Pensacola Bay and drove out the British, in September 1814 with whom the United States was at war and pacified the Spanish governor of Florida. This capture of Pensacola was crucial to Jackson securing victory during the battle of New Orleans in November 1814.

1814–1825 Caribbean. Engagements between pirates and American ships or squadrons took place repeatedly, especially ashore and offshore about Cuba, Puerto Rico, Santo Domingo, and Yucatan. Three thousand pirate attacks on merchantmen were reported between 1815 and 1823. In 1822, Commodore James Biddle deployed a squadron of two frigates, four sloops of war, two brigs, four schooners, and two gunboats in the West Indies.

1815 Algiers. The second Barbary War was declared against the United States by the Dey of Algiers of the Barbary states, an act not reciprocated by the United States. Congress did authorize a military expedition by statutes. A large fleet under U.S. Commodore Stephen Decatur attacked Algiers and obtained indemnities.

Tripoli. After securing an agreement from Algiers, Decatur demonstrated with his squadron at Tunis and Tripoli, where he secured indemnities for offenses during the War of 1812.

1816 Spanish Florida. United States forces destroyed Nicholls Fort, also called Negro Fort, located in present Franklin County, Florida, which harbored raiders making forays into United States territory.

1816–1818 Spanish Florida—First Seminole War. The Seminole Indians, whose area was a haven for escaped slaves and border ruffians, were attacked by troops under Generals Andrew Jackson and Edmund P. Gaines and pursued into northern Florida. Spanish posts were attacked and occupied, British citizens executed. In 1819, the Floridas were ceded to the United States. . . .

[Authors' Note: The list continues with hundreds of similar incidents from 1817 to 2006, most of which are excluded here in the interest of brevity. Notable incidents after 1817 include the following:]

1844 Mexico. U.S. President John Tyler deployed U.S. forces to protect Texas against Mexico, pending Senate approval of a treaty of annexation (later rejected). He defended his action against a Senate resolution of inquiry.

1846–1848 Mexican War. On May 13, 1846, the United States recognized the existence of a state of war with Mexico. After the annexation of Texas in 1845, the United States and Mexico failed to resolve a boundary dispute, and U.S. President James K. Polk said that it was necessary to deploy forces in Mexico to meet a threatened invasion.

1853–1854 Japan. Commodore Matthew C. Perry and his naval expedition made a display of force leading to the "opening of Japan." Ryukyu and Bonin Islands. Commodore Perry on three visits before going to Japan and while waiting for a reply from Japan made a naval demonstration, landing marines twice, and secured a coaling concession from the ruler of Naha on Okinawa. Perry also held a naval demonstration in the Bonin Islands, an archipelago of over 30 subtropical and tropical islands over 600 miles south of Tokyo, with the purpose of securing facilities for commerce.

1898 The Spanish-American War. On April 25, 1898, the United States declared war with Spain. The war followed a Cuban insurrection against Spanish rule and the sinking of the USS Maine in the harbor at Havana.

1903–1914 Panama. U.S. forces sought to protect American interests and lives during and following the revolution for independence from Colombia over construction of the Isthmian Canal. With brief intermissions, United States Marines were stationed on the Isthmus from November 4, 1903, to January 21, 1914, to guard American interests.

1912–1941 China. The disorders which began with the overthrow of the dynasty during Kuomintang rebellion in 1912, which were redirected by the invasion of China by Japan, led to demonstrations and landing parties for the protection of U.S. interests in China continuously and at many points from 1912 on to 1941. The guard at Peking and along the route to the sea was maintained until 1941. In 1927, the United States had 5,670 troops ashore in China and 44 naval vessels in its waters. In 1933 the United States had 3,027 armed men ashore. The protective action was generally based on treaties with China concluded from 1858 to 1901.

1917–1918 World War I. On April 6, 1917, the United States declared war with Germany and on December 7, 1917, with Austria-Hungary. Entrance of the United States into the war was precipitated by Germany's submarine warfare against neutral shipping.

1941–1945 World War II. On December 8, 1941, the United States declared war with Japan, on December 11 with Germany and Italy, and on June 5, 1942, with Bulgaria, Hungary, and Romania. The United States declared war against Japan after the surprise bombing of Pearl Harbor, and against Germany and Italy after those nations, under the dictators Hitler and Mussolini, declared war against the United States. The United States declared war against Bulgaria, Hungary, and Romania in response to the declarations of war by those nations against the United States.

1950–1953 Korean War. The United States responded to North Korean invasion of South Korea by going to its assistance, pursuant to United Nations Security Council resolutions. U.S. forces deployed in Korea exceeded 300,000 during the last year of the conflict. Over 36,600 U.S. military were killed in action.

1964–1973 Vietnam War. U.S. military advisers had been in South Vietnam for a decade, and their numbers had been increased as the military position of the Saigon government became weaker. After citing what he termed were attacks on U.S. destroyers in the Tonkin Gulf, President Johnson asked in August 1964 for a resolution expressing U.S. determination to support freedom and protect peace in Southeast Asia. Congress responded with the Tonkin Gulf Resolution, expressing support for "all necessary measures" the President might take to repel armed attack against U.S. forces and prevent further aggression. Following this resolution, and following a Communist attack on a U.S. installation in central Vietnam, the United States escalated its participation in the war to a peak of 543,000 military personnel by April 1969.

1980 Iran. On April 26, 1980, President Carter reported the use of six U.S. transport planes and eight helicopters in an unsuccessful attempt to rescue American hostages being held in Iran.

1987–1988 Persian Gulf. After the Iran-Iraq War resulted in several military incidents in the Persian Gulf, the United States increased U.S. joint military forces operations in the Persian Gulf and adopted a policy of reflagging and escorting Kuwaiti oil tankers through the Gulf. President Reagan reported that U.S. Navy ships had been fired upon or struck mines or taken other military action on September 23, October 10, and October 20, 1987, and April 19, July 4, and July 14, 1988. The United States gradually reduced its forces after a cease-fire between Iran and Iraq on August 20, 1988.

1988 Panama. In mid-March and April 1988, during a period of instability in Panama and as pressure grew for Panamanian military leader General Manuel Noriega to resign, the United States sent 1,000 troops to Panama, to "further safeguard the canal, U.S. lives, property and interests in the area." The forces supplemented 10,000 U.S. military personnel already in Panama.

[Authors' Note: Recent incidents are discussed *infra*, this Chapter, Sec. 5].

NOTES

1. *Reading the Tea Leaves*. What significance do the incidents described above have in shaping the contours of executive and congressional war powers? Do the incidents above represent, in Justice Frankfurter's words, "a gloss on executive power vested in the President," meaning that they show a robust ability of the president to engage in uses of military force without formal approval from Congress? *Youngstown Sheet & Tube Co. v. Sawyer*, 343 U.S. 579, 611 (1952) (Frankfurter, J., concurring). Or are they simply, as Jules Lobel argued during a district court hearing in *Dellums v. Bush*, "very minor uses of force to chase out some mobs [and] to protect some citizens. . . ," which should not be regarded as relevant when considering the power to deploy military forces on a large scale?

2. *Practical Consequences*. Are there any practical consequences that flow from the president acting pursuant to a "declaration of war," pursuant to an "authorization to use military force," or without any Congressional action? Consider the following:

> With respect to domestic law, a declaration of war automatically triggers many standby statutory authorities conferring special powers on the President with respect to the military, foreign trade, transportation, communications, manufacturing, alien enemies, etc. In contrast, no standby authorities appear to be triggered automatically by an authorization for the use of force, although the executive branch has argued, with varying success, that the authorization to use force in response to the terrorist attacks of 2001 provided a statutory exception to certain statutory prohibitions.
>
> Most statutory standby authorities do not expressly require a declaration of war to be actualized but can be triggered by a declaration of national emergency or simply by the existence of a state of war; however, courts have sometimes construed the word "war" in a statute as implying a formal declaration, leading Congress to enact clarifying amendments in two cases. Declarations of war and authorizations for the use of force waive the time limitations otherwise applicable to the use of force imposed by the War Powers Resolution.

CRS Report, *Declarations of War and Authorizations for the Use of Military Force: Historical Background and Legal Implications*, Rep. 31133 (Mar. 17, 2011).

3. *Looking Ahead*. Consider the use of U.S. armed forces to combat terrorism threats following 9/11. Does the expansiveness of the operations (e.g., Afghanistan, Djibouti, Eritrea, Ethiopia, Georgia, Iraq, Pakistan, the Philippines, Kenya, Yemen, Libya, etc.) represent a departure from past precedent? Does it suggest a need for the president to act on his own in subtle,

careful, and expeditious ways? Or does it suggest that even small combat operations have an important overall effect on U.S. national security, including the potential for inflaming terrorism or antagonizing U.S. allies, such that Congress must play a role in approving deployments?

4. *Covert Operations.* Note that the introduction to the CRS report stipulates that the list of incidents, "[c]overt operations, disaster relief, and routine alliance stationing and training exercises are not included here, nor are the Civil and Revolutionary Wars and the continual use of U.S. military units in the exploration, settlement, and pacification of the western part of the United States." What bearing do such actions have in assessing customary war powers practice?

4. WAR POWERS RESOLUTION

REPORT OF THE SENATE FOREIGN RELATIONS COMMITTEE ON THE WAR POWERS ACT

S. REP. NO. 220, 93rd Cong., 1st Sess. (1973).

Prior to the Second World War, Presidential use of the armed forces without Congressional authorization was confined for the most part to the Western Hemisphere, primarily to Mexico and the Caribbean. President McKinley's participation, in the Boxer expedition in China in 1900 was a noteworthy exception. Only since the Second World War have American Presidents claimed, and exercised, the power to commit the armed forces to full-scale and extend warfare overseas. The kind of foreign military intervention we have witnessed in the last quarter century is, in the words of Henry Steel Commager, Professor Emeritus of History, Almost College, "if not wholly unprecedented, clearly a departure from a long and deeply-rooted tradition."

Professor Alexander Bickel of the Yale Law School made the same point in his testimony before the Committee:

> [T]he decisions discussed as early as 1964, made in the first half of 1965, and executed thereafter, to commit the moral and material resources of this Nation to full-scale war in Vietnam seem to me the mark the farthest, and really an unprecedented, extension of Presidential power. Certainly the power of the President in matters of war and peace has grown steadily for over a century. The decisions of 1965 may have differed only in degree from earlier stages in this process of growth. But there comes a point when a difference of degree achieves the magnitude of a difference in kind. The decisions of 1965 amounted to an all but explicit transfer of the power to declare war from Congress, where the Constitution lodged it, to the President, on whom the framers explicitly refused to confer it.

The transfer from Congress to the executive of the actual power—as distinguished from the constitutional authority—to initiate war has been one of the most remarkable developments in the constitutional history of the United States. For this change Congress as well as the Executive bears a heavy burden of responsibility.

When President Truman committed the armed forces to Korea in 1950 without Congressional authorization, scarcely a voice of dissent was raised in Congress. Senator Watkins of Utah challenged the President's authority to commit the country to war without consulting the Congress, even in compliance with a resolution of the United Nations Security Council, and said that, if he were President, he ". . . would have sent a message to the Congress of the United States setting forth the situation and asking for authority to go ahead and do whatever was necessary to protect the situation." Senator Taft also challenged President Truman's action but not until January 1951. "The President," he said, "simply usurped authority, in violation of the laws and the Constitution, when he sent troops to Korea to carry out the resolution of the United Nations in an undeclared war."

The isolated voices of Watkins and Taft were ineffectual against the accelerating tide of growing executive power. Secretary of State Acheson virtually threw down the gauntlet to Congress—although few at that time were disposed to pick it up—when he testified before the Committee on Foreign Relations and Armed Services Committee in 1951 in support of President Truman's plan to station six divisions of American soldiers in Europe. He said on that occasion:

> Not only has the President the authority to use the Armed Forces in carrying out the broad foreign policy of the United States and implementing treaties, but it is equally clear that this authority may not be interfered with by the Congress in the exercise of powers which it has under the Constitution.

In the course of the Vietnam war, the Johnson Administration reconfirmed the executive's claim to unilateral authority in the use of the armed forces. Secretary of State Acheson virtually threw down the gauntlet to Congress—although few at that time were disposed to pick it up—when he testified before the Committee on Foreign Relations and Armed Services Committee in 1951 in support of President Truman's plan to station six divisions of American soldiers in Europe. He said on that occasion:

> Not only has the President the authority to use the Armed Forces in carrying out the broad foreign policy of the United States and implementing treaties, but it is equally clear that this authority may not be interfered with by the Congress in the exercise of powers which it has under the Constitution.

In the course of the Vietnam war, the Johnson Administration reconfirmed the executive's claim to unilateral authority in the use of the armed forces. In his now famous testimony of August 1967, Under Secretary of State Katzenbach contended that the Gulf of Tonkin Resolution was "as broad an authorization for the use of armed forces for a purpose as any declaration of war so-called could be in terms of our internal constitutional process." In fact, the Johnson Administration went farther.

Whereas Mr. Katzenbach at least claimed the existence of legislative authority, the President himself contended that no such authority was required. Speaking of the Gulf of Tonkin Resolution in his news conference of August 18, 1967, President Johnson said,

> We stated then, and we repeat now, we did not think the resolution was necessary to do what we did and what we're doing. But we thought it was desirable and we thought if we were going to ask them [Congress] to stay the whole route and if we expected them to be there on the landing we ought to ask them to be there on the takeoff.

Making the same claim in more formal language, the Legal Advisor to the Department of State had written in March 1966,

> There can be no question in present circumstances of the President's authority to commit U.S. forces to the defense of South Vietnam. The grant of authority to the President in Article II of the Constitution extends to the actions of the United States currently undertaken in Vietnam.

[I]t is far more difficult to reassert a power which has been permitted to atrophy than to defend one which has been habitually used. The Congress accordingly bears a heavy responsibility for its passive acquiescence in the unwarranted expansion of Presidential power. As the late Justice Robert H. Jackson pointed out in his concurring opinion in *Youngstown v. Sawyer,* there is a "zone of twilight" between the discrete areas of Presidential and Congressional power. Politics, like nature, abhors a vacuum. When Congress created a vacuum by failing to defend and exercise its powers, the President inevitably hastened to fill it. As Justice Jackson commented, "Congressional inertia, indifference or quiescence may sometimes, at least as a practical matter, enable, if not invite, measures on independent Presidential responsibility. . . ."

The Nixon Administration has shown that it shares the expansive view of the President's power as Commander-in-Chief held by preceding Administrations. The commitment of American military forces to Cambodia in 1970, and to Laos in 1971, demonstrated the present Administration's determination to initiate new foreign military actions solely on its own authority. . . .

Congress, in the Committee's view, can take no more useful and needed step toward the restoration of constitutional balance than to enact legislation to confirm and codify the intent of the framers of the Constitution with respect to the war power. The President, as Professor Bickel and as Mr. George Reedy, formerly of the White House staff, pointed out in their testimony before the Committee in 1971, is in many respects a remote and almost royal figure, shielded from direct personal participation in the adversary politics of democracy. "Under the American system," as one political scientist points out, "the executive is virtually *prevented* from engaging in public debate on policy by the institutional setting of his office; under the British system he is expected and, in fact, *compelled* to engage continually in it." The processes through which the President reaches decisions are largely personal and private, beyond the reach of direct institutional accountability.

Congress, on the other hand, makes its decisions almost entirely in the open and under public scrutiny. The President is subject to quadrennial plebiscite, but Congress provides the American people with points of access through which they can hold their Government to day-to-day account and thereby participate in it. Inefficient and shortsighted though it sometimes is, Congress provides the only feasible means under the American constitutional system of drawing the President, at least indirectly, into the adversary processes of democracy. The executive branch is endowed with organizational discipline and legions of experts, but Congressmen and Senators have a unique asset when it comes to playing an effective, democratic role in the making of foreign policy: the power to speak and act freely from an independent political base.

WAR POWERS RESOLUTION

50 U.S.C. §§ 1541–1548 (2006).

§ 1541. Purpose and policy [§ 2]

(a) Congressional declaration

It is the purpose of this chapter to fulfill the intent of the framers of the Constitution of the United States and insure that the collective judgment of both the Congress and the President will apply to the introduction of United States Armed Forces into hostilities, or into situations where imminent involvement in hostilities is clearly indicated by the circumstances, and to the continued use of such forces in hostilities or in such situations.

(b) Congressional legislative power under necessary and proper clause

Under article I, section 8, of the Constitution, it is specifically provided that the Congress shall have the power to make all laws necessary and proper for carrying into execution, not only its own powers but also all other powers vested by the Constitution in the

Government of the United States, or in any department or officer thereof.

(c) Presidential executive power as Commander-in-Chief; limitation

The constitutional powers of the President as Commander-in-Chief to introduce United States Armed Forces into hostilities, or into situations where imminent involvement in hostilities is clearly indicated by the circumstances, are exercised only pursuant to (1) a declaration of war, (2) specific statutory authorization, or (3) a national emergency created by attack upon the United States, its territories or possessions, or its armed forces.

§ 1542. Consultation; initial and regular consultations [§ 3]

The President in every possible instance shall consult with Congress before introducing United States Armed Forces into hostilities or into situations where imminent involvement in hostilities is clearly indicated by the circumstances, and after every such introduction shall consult regularly with the Congress until United States Armed Forces are no longer engaged in hostilities or have been removed from such situations.

§ 1543. Reporting requirement [§ 4]

(a) Written report; time of submission; circumstances necessitating submission; information reported.

In the absence of a declaration of war, in any case in which United States Armed Forces are introduced—

(1) into hostilities or into situations where imminent involvement in hostilities is clearly indicated by the circumstances;

(2) into the territory, airspace or waters of a foreign nation, while equipped for combat, except for deployments which relate solely to supply, replacement, repair, or training of such forces; or

(3) in numbers which substantially enlarge United States Armed Forces equipped for combat already located in a foreign nation;

the President shall submit within 48 hours to the Speaker of the House of Representatives and to the President pro tempore of the Senate a report, in writing, setting forth—

(A) the circumstances necessitating the introduction of United States Armed Forces;

(B) the constitutional and legislative authority under which such introduction took place; and

(C) the estimated scope and duration of the hostilities or involvement.

(b) Other information reported

The President shall provide such other information as the Congress may request in the fulfillment of its constitutional responsibilities with respect to committing the Nation to war and to the use of United States Armed Forces abroad.

(c) Periodic reports; semiannual requirement

Whenever United States Armed Forces are introduced into hostilities or into any situation described in subsection (a) of this section, the President shall, so long as such armed forces continue to be engaged in such hostilities or situation, report to the Congress periodically on the status of such hostilities or situation as well as on the scope and duration of such hostilities or situation, but in no event shall he report to the Congress less often than once every six months.

§ 1544. Congressional action [§ 5] . . .

(b) Termination of use of United States Armed Forces; exceptions; extension period

Within sixty calendar days after a report is submitted or is required to be submitted pursuant to section [4(a)(1)], whichever is earlier, the President shall terminate any use of United States Armed Forces with respect to which such report was submitted (or required to be submitted), unless the Congress (1) has declared war or has enacted a specific authorization for such use of United States Armed Forces, (2) has extended by law such sixty-day period, or (3) is physically unable to meet as a result of an armed attack upon the United States. Such sixty-day period shall be extended for not more than an additional thirty days if the President determines and certifies to the Congress in writing that unavoidable military necessity respecting the safety of United States Armed Forces requires the continued use of such armed forces in the course of bringing about a prompt removal of such forces.

(c) Concurrent resolution for removal by President of United States Armed Forces

Notwithstanding subsection (b) of this section, at any time that United States Armed Forces are engaged in hostilities outside the territory of the United States, its possessions and territories without a declaration of war or specific statutory authorization, such forces shall be removed by the President if the Congress so directs by concurrent resolution. . . .

§ 1547. Interpretation of joint resolution [§ 8]

(a) Inferences from any law or treaty

Authority to introduce United States Armed Forces into hostilities or into situations wherein involvement in hostilities is clearly indicated by the circumstances shall not be inferred—

(1) from any provision of law (whether or not in effect before November 7, 1973), including any provision contained in any appropriation Act, unless such provision specifically authorizes the introduction of United States Armed Forces into hostilities or into such situations and states that it is intended to constitute specific statutory authorization within the meaning of this chapter; or

(2) from any treaty heretofore or hereafter ratified unless such treaty is implemented by legislation specifically authorizing the introduction of United States Armed Forces into hostilities or into such situations and stating that it is intended to constitute specific statutory authorization within the meaning of this chapter. . . .

(d) Constitutional authorities or existing treaties unaffected; construction against grant of Presidential authority respecting use of United States Armed Forces

Nothing in this chapter—

(1) is intended to alter the constitutional authority of the Congress or of the President, or the provisions of existing treaties; or

(2) shall be construed as granting any authority to the President with respect to the introduction of United States Armed Forces into hostilities or into situations wherein involvement in hostilities is clearly indicated by the circumstances which authority he would not have had in the absence of this chapter.

§ 1548. Separability [§ 9]

If any provision of this chapter or the application thereof to any person or circumstance is held invalid, the remainder of the chapter and the application of such provision to any other person or circumstance shall not be affected thereby.

PRESIDENT NIXON'S VETO OF THE WAR POWERS RESOLUTION

1973 Pub. Papers 311 (Oct. 24, 1973).

To the House of Representatives

I hereby return without my approval House Joint Resolution 542—the War Powers Resolution. While I am in accord with the desire of the Congress to assert its proper role in the conduct of our foreign affairs, the restrictions which this resolution would impose upon the authority of the President are both unconstitutional and dangerous to the best interests of our Nation.

The proper roles of the Congress and the Executive in the conduct of foreign affairs have been debated since the founding of our country. Only recently, however, has there been a serious challenge to the wisdom of the Founding Fathers in choosing not to draw a precise and detailed line of demarcation between the foreign policy powers of the two branches.

The Founding Fathers understood the impossibility of foreseeing every contingency that might arise in this complex area. They acknowledged the need for flexibility in responding to changing circumstances. They recognized that foreign policy decisions must be made through close cooperation between the two branches and not through rigidly codified procedures.

These principles remain as valid today as they were when our Constitution was written. Yet House Joint Resolution 542 would violate those principles by defining the President's powers in ways which would strictly limit his constitutional authority.

CLEARLY UNCONSTITUTIONAL

House Joint Resolution 542 would attempt to take away, by a mere legislative act, authorities which the President has properly exercised under the Constitution for almost 200 years. One of its provisions would automatically cut off certain authorities after sixty days unless the Congress extended them. Another would allow the Congress to eliminate certain authorities merely by the passage of a concurrent resolution—an action which does not normally have the force of law, since it denies the President his constitutional role in approving legislation.

I believe that both these provisions are unconstitutional. The only way in which the constitutional powers of a branch of the Government can be altered is by amending the Constitution—and any attempt to make such alterations by legislation alone is clearly without force.

UNDERMINING OUR FOREIGN POLICY

While I firmly believe that a veto of House Joint Resolution 542 is warranted solely on constitutional grounds, I am also deeply disturbed by the practical consequences of this resolution. For it would seriously undermine this Nation's ability to act decisively and convincingly in times of international crisis. As a result, the confidence of our allies in our ability to assist them could be diminished and the respect of our adversaries for our deterrent posture could decline. A permanent and substantial element of unpredictability would be injected into the world's assessment of American behavior, further increasing the likelihood of miscalculation and war.

If this resolution had been in operation, America's effective response to a variety of challenges in recent years would have been vastly complicated or even made impossible. We may well have been unable to respond in the way we did during the Berlin crisis of 1961, the Cuban missile crisis of 1962, the Congo rescue operation in 1964, and the Jordanian crisis of 1970—to mention just a few examples. In addition, our recent actions to bring about a peaceful settlement of the hostilities in the Middle East would have been seriously impaired if this resolution had been in force.

While all the specific consequences of House Joint Resolution 542 cannot yet be predicted, it is clear that it would undercut the ability of the United States to act as an effective influence for peace. For example, the provision automatically cutting off certain authorities after 60 days unless they are extended by the Congress could work to prolong or intensify a crisis. Until the Congress suspended the deadline, there would be at least a chance of United States withdrawal and an adversary would be tempted therefore to postpone serious negotiations until the 60 days were up. Only after the Congress acted would there be a strong incentive for an adversary to negotiate. In addition, the very existence of a deadline could lead to an escalation of hostilities in order to achieve certain objectives before the 60 days expired.

The measure would jeopardize our role as a force for peace in other ways as well. It would, for example, strike from the President's hand a wide range of important peace-keeping tools by eliminating his ability to exercise quiet diplomacy backed by subtle shifts in our military deployments. It would also cast into doubt authorities which Presidents have used to undertake certain humanitarian relief missions in conflict areas, to protect fishing boats from seizure, to deal with ship or aircraft hijackings, and to respond to threats of attack. Not the least of the adverse consequences of this resolution would be the prohibition contained in section 8 against fulfilling our obligations under the NATO treaty as ratified by the Senate. Finally, since the bill is somewhat vague as to when the 60 day rule would apply, it could lead to extreme confusion and dangerous disagreements concerning the prerogatives of the two branches, seriously damaging our ability to respond to international crises.

FAILURE TO REQUIRE POSITIVE CONGRESSIONAL ACTION

I am particularly disturbed by the fact that certain of the President's constitutional powers as Commander in Chief of the Armed Forces would terminate automatically under this resolution 60 days after they were invoked. No overt Congressional action would be required to cut off these powers—they would disappear automatically unless the Congress extended them. In effect, the Congress is here attempting to increase its policy-making role through a provision which requires it to take absolutely no action at all.

In my view, the proper way for the Congress to make known its will on such foreign policy questions is through a positive action, with full debate on the merits of the issue and with each member taking the responsibility of casting a yes or no vote after considering those merits. The authorization and appropriations process represents one of the ways in which such influence can be exercised. I do not, however, believe that the Congress can responsibly contribute its considered, collective judgment on such grave questions without full debate and without a yes or no vote. Yet this is precisely what the joint resolution would allow. It would give every future Congress the ability to handcuff every future President merely by doing nothing and sitting still. In my view, one cannot become a responsible partner unless one is prepared to take responsible action.

RICHARD NIXON

The White House,
October 24, 1973.

JOHN HART ELY, SUPPOSE CONGRESS WANTED A WAR POWERS ACT THAT WORKED

88 Colum. L. Rev. 1379, 1386–98 (1988).*

[Like] other recent "framework" legislation, the War Powers Resolution is designed to force a decision regarding matters that Congress has in the past shown itself unwilling to face up to. Unlike Gramm-Rudman-Hollings, however, it does not push the tough decisions onto somebody else (such as the Comptroller General) but rather provides that once the Resolution is triggered by the commitment of troops, Congress itself has 60 days to make the critical decision on war and peace. However, "[p]ost-Watergate congressional bravado had a way of sputtering out in the face of crisis," and thanks to a combination of presidential defiance, congressional irresolution, and judicial abstention the War Powers Resolution has not worked. Repeatedly—as in the last stages of the war in IndoChina, the attempt to free our hostages in Iran, and in Lebanon,

Central America, Grenada, and Tripoli—the President either has not reported under section 4(a) or has failed to specify that what he is filing is a section 4(a)(1) "hostilities" report, thus avoiding the 60-day clock. Congress has responded to this evasion only once, in connection with the Lebanon crisis, when after much hemming and hawing it negotiated a "compromise" recognizing the applicability of the War Powers Resolution (which recognition President Reagan immediately repudiated) and extending the period the troops could remain in Lebanon for 18 months. . . .

C. Section 2(c)

[Section 2(c)] ended up in the Resolution as a result of a compromise between the Senate and House forces. The House's approach had been more procedural—not telling the President when he could and could not introduce forces into hostilities but rather instructing him that when he did, he had to report to Congress and withdraw if their use was not then approved. The Senate's more "substantive" approach is captured by the quoted language.

Despite the inclusion of the Senate's language, it is the House approach that prevailed. The heart of the Resolution resides in the combination of sections 4(a)(1) and 5(b). Section 2(c) appears in a part of the Resolution entitled "Purpose and Policy," where all agree it is operational only to the extent the President chooses voluntarily to comply. Unsurprisingly, therefore, Presidents have ignored it. Grenada, Tripoli, and the Mayaguez rescue operation are patent noncompliers, to name just three, and even such strong supporters of the Senate approach as Senators Javits and Eagleton admitted subsequent to passage that 2(c) had ended up too narrow. This section too thus helps breed contempt for the entire Resolution, which suggests that repeal may be in order.

That is not the only possible response, however, and some commentators have suggested that the cure for the Resolution's anemia may lie in taking 2(c) out of the "Purpose and Policy" section and making it legally "binding." I can certainly understand the impulse, but for two reasons this seems a bad idea.

The first is that 2(c) not only is too restrictive of necessary presidential authority, but is almost inevitably so. Virtually everyone agrees that it should have included the protection of American citizens as one of the justifications for presidential military action. That omission could be remedied, but it would not do the trick. The President and his advisers would then only come up with a list of other situations that should have been covered (and proceed to intervene should they arise). Monroe Leigh, State Department Legal Adviser in the Ford Administration, testified:

Besides the three situations listed in subsection 2(c) . . . it appears that the President has the constitutional authority to use the Armed Forces to rescue American citizens abroad, to rescue foreign nationals where such action directly facilitates the rescue of U.S. citizens abroad, to protect U.S. Embassies and Legations abroad, to suppress civil insurrection, to implement and administer the terms of an armistice or cease-fire designed to terminate hostilities involving the United States, and to carry out the terms of security commitments contained in treaties. We do not, however, believe that any such list can be a complete one, just as we do not believe that any single definitional statement can clearly encompass every conceivable situation in which the President's Commander in Chief authority could be exercised.

Neither is this enumeration recklessly open-ended, as it truly is impossible to predict and specify all the possible situations in which the President will need to act to protect the nation's security but will not have time to consult Congress. (I can't, for example, make the Cuban missile crisis of 1962 fit comfortably even on Leigh's list.) Indeed, if one were to insist on having such a "substantive" section, what it would most sensibly say is just this—that the President can use military force without prior congressional approval only when the national security is at stake and there is not time to consult Congress. That, however, would simply reiterate the command of the Constitution properly understood. Including it would therefore not only be redundant but also sacrifice the Resolution's contribution of giving more concrete meaning to the generalities of the original document. In other sections the Resolution may have succeeded in this quest. Here, however, complete advance specification seems impossible, which suggests that no President is likely to pay attention to any such list, which in turn serves only to decrease respect for the Resolution generally.

Even if a tolerable approximation of a satisfactory list could be constructed, however, it would remain a bad idea to attempt to make section 2(c) "operational." For even if it were moved out of the Purpose and Policy section, it would very likely remain unenforceable. Experience suggests that even if the list were expanded, the President would not be likely to obey it voluntarily: if Presidents won't acknowledge an imminent danger of hostilities in the Persian Gulf and similar situations, they are most unlikely to recognize any substantive limits on their authority. The same experience teaches that Congress cannot be counted on to enforce any such set of limits either. That seems to leave the courts, and of them we will have a good deal to say later on. This, however, does not seem the optimal place to expect them to take a stand. Judicial enforcement of an "operational" section 2(c) would take the form of a finding that the President had exceeded the legal justifications for intervention and a consequent order that he remove the troops. Such an order may not be unthinkable, but it is one that courts would understandably be very reluctant to enter. Judicial intervention seems much more likely in support of the House of Representatives' "procedural" approach. For if the order is simply that section 4(a)(1) has been satisfied and the clock has thus been started, the effect will be to "remand" to Congress the question whether the troops stay.

Experience thus suggests that if there is to be enforcement of the War Powers Resolution the judiciary must become involved, and common sense suggests that judicial assistance is more likely to be forthcoming in support of the House approach. Since section 2(c) cannot plausibly be made enforceable, its continued presence does more harm than good, and it too should probably be repealed.

D. Section 5(c)

All "procedural" approaches are not created equal, and not all of those contained in the existing War Powers Resolution are equally susceptible to being made workable. Section 5(c) provides that within the 60-day period, Congress can by concurrent resolution direct the President to remove troops he has committed to hostilities. A plausible argument can be made that this section was rendered invalid by the Supreme Court's 1983 decision in *INS v. Chadha*. For this reason, it too provides an excuse to condemn the entire Resolution as "unconstitutional." Since Congress's proclivities in this area virtually insure that 5(c) never would have been invoked anyhow, it too should be removed.

In fact, section 5(c) does not appear to be unconstitutional. Even assuming that *Chadha* makes sense, it seems distinguishable. (Indeed it is a little bizarre to regard this congressional effort to reassert its constitutional authority to decide on war and peace as a violation of either the separation of powers or the system of checks and balances.) Section 5(c) does not fit the profile of a standard "legislative veto" wherein Congress has delegated certain powers to the executive branch and then attempted to pull them back by reserving a right to veto executive exercises of the delegation. Instead, it should be read in the context of sections 4(a)(1) and 5(b), as part of a package attempting in concrete terms to approximate the accommodation reached by the Constitution's framers, that the President could act militarily in an emergency but was obligated to cease and desist in the event Congress did not approve as soon as it had a reasonable opportunity to do so.

Sixty days is essentially defined by the Resolution as the outer limit of the time Congress can reasonably be supposed to need to decide. (The additional 30 days for "unavoidable military necessity" is there to enable our troops to be withdrawn without getting killed.) However, it patently is not the notion of the Resolution that 60 days will always be necessary for such a decision. The scheme contemplates that sometime within that 60 days, whenever under the specific circumstances presented Congress can get its act together, it can either authorize continued military activity under 5(b) or indicate, under 5(c), that it is not prepared to do so. Section

5(c) thus resembles only distantly the sort of legislative veto to which the Chadha litigation was addressed.

However, *Chadha* is "a work of mechanical simplicity" that suggests no inclination to distinguish among provisions that bear any resemblance to that involved in the case, a reading buttressed by the sweeping references of the concurrence and dissent. There is thus a significant possibility that in the event section 5(c) ever got to court, it would be invalidated. We need not shed many tears over this possibility, however, as experience suggests that Congress would be most unlikely ever to try to invoke it. If it won't acknowledge that hostilities exist in situations like the Persian Gulf and thereby start the clock for its further decision, it certainly isn't going to order the President to remove the troops cold turkey within 60 days of his having committed them.

Such an apparently useless and arguably unconstitutional provision is likely only to provide an excuse for denunciation and defiance of the entire Resolution, and it too should be repealed. In one sense this surely seems a pity, since we can understand the motivation that drove 5(c), a desire to avoid giving the President carte blanche to keep troops he has committed on his own motion in the field for the 60 or 90 days the clock is running.

NOTES

1. *Override of the Veto.* On October 24, 1973, the Congress overrode President Nixon's veto and the joint resolution became law. Its passage in the face of presidential disapproval reflected the deep discontent within Congress and the public with the continuing U.S. involvement in the Vietnam War, as well as a weakened presidency from the unfolding of the Watergate scandal. For legislative history in the House of Representatives, *see House Reports,* No. 93–287 (Comm. on Foreign Affairs) and No. 93–541 (Comm. of Conference).

2. *Constitutionality.* Is the War Powers Resolution unconstitutional? Are any constitutional difficulties diminished by explicit reliance, in § 2(b), upon the Constitution's Necessary and Proper Clause? By a disclaimer of any intent (in § 8(d)(2)) "to alter the constitutional authority of the Congress or the President"? Can a statute alter the president's constitutional authority? For an affirmative answer, *see* Presidential Power to Use the Armed Forces Abroad Without Statutory Authorization, 4A Op. Office of the Legal Counsel, Dep't of Justice 185, 190 (1980) (upholding validity of the sixty-day period).

3. *Scope of Presidential Power.* Is the scope of presidential power recognized in § 2(c) correct? Are there situations not set out in that section in which the president can introduce the armed forces into hostilities without statutory authority? Are there limits upon constitutional presidential power that are *not* recognized in that section? If the use of force is permissible *ab initio,* does the Constitution impose any limits upon the *amount* of force that may be employed? If the president has constitutional power as Commander in Chief to use force in specified circumstances, as Congress acknowledges in

§ 2(c), how can it constitutionally require (in § 3) the president to consult in advance before using force in those circumstances, or (in § 5(b)) to terminate use of force in those circumstances?

4. *Triggering of Reporting Requirements*. What constitutes introducing U.S. armed forces into "hostilities" for purposes of the reporting requirement imposed on the president in § 4(a)(1)? Is it only when U.S. forces are sent into actual armed combat? What if they are sent to a border region where armed conflict might occur, such as sending U.S. forces to Saudi Arabia after Iraq's invasion of Kuwait? What if U.S. forces are sent to engage in mine laying or mine sweeping? What about launching U.S. air strikes or the launching of a missile from a submarine? Reconnaissance flights? Should the likelihood or number of casualties matter? Should the term be defined?

5. *Triggering Termination of the Use of U.S. Forces*. How is it determined whether a report is "required to be submitted" under § 5(b) for purposes of starting the clock for termination of the use of U.S. armed forces? Is § 5(c) constitutional in light of *INS v. Chadha* (*see* Chapter 1, Sec. 2)? If it is not, how is the rest of the War Powers Resolution affected given the separability clause (§ 9)? Do you think that § 9 accurately states Congress's intent? Might Congress, in other words, have viewed the Resolution as an integral package, and have preferred that the entire Resolution be swept away if the legislative veto were invalidated?

6. *A Judicial Trigger?* Should the War Powers Resolution be amended to ensure that the 60-day clock is triggered under appropriate circumstances, even if the president has not filed a § 4(a)(1) report? An amendment could provide that if the president does not start the clock, members of Congress would have standing to bring suit to do so, thus requiring federal courts to decide the issue whether hostilities (or the imminent likelihood thereof) exist. John Hart Ely, *Suppose Congress Wanted a War Powers Act That Worked*, 88 COLUM. L. REV. 1379, 1406–07 (1988). Are there any limits on congressional power to create standing through a federal statute? *See Spokeo, Inc. v. Robins*, 136 S. Ct. 1540 (2016).

7. *Implied Statutory and Treaty Authorization*. Section 8(a) of the War Powers Resolution stipulates that the authority to introduce U.S. forces into hostilities shall not be inferred from statutory or treaty provisions unless certain conditions are met. Why was § 1547(a) included in the WPR? Is it constitutional? Consider this argument:

> To the extent, however, that [Section 8(a)] would take from Congress a constitutionally permissible method of authorizing war, it runs afoul of the axiom that one Congress cannot bind a later Congress. *See, e.g., Marbury v. Madison*, 5 U.S. (1 Cranch) 137, 177 (1803) (noting that, in contrast to a constitution, legislative acts are "alterable when the legislature shall please to alter [them]"); *Fletcher v. Peck*, 10 U.S. (6 Cranch) 87, 135 (1810) (noting that "[t]he correctness of [the] principle," "that one legislature is competent to repeal any [law] which a former legislature was competent to pass,

> and that one legislature cannot abridge the powers of a succeeding legislature," "can never be controverted"). . . .
>
> If section 8(a)(1) were read to block all possibility of inferring congressional approval of military action from any appropriation, unless that appropriation referred in terms to the WPR and stated that it was intended to constitute specific authority for the action under that statute, then it would be unconstitutional. . . . [U]nder the Constitution, Congress can authorize or ratify presidential engagement in hostilities through an appropriation law. One statute, such as the WPR, cannot mandate that certain types of appropriation statutes that would otherwise constitute authorization for conflict cannot do so simply because a subsequent Congress does not use certain "magical passwords."

Memorandum for the Attorney General on Authorization for Continuing Hostilities in Kosovo available at https://www.justice.gov/file/19306/download, [https://perma.cc/99UZ-R2SS] (Dec. 19, 2000) (footnotes omitted). How convincing is this argument? Note that section 8(a)(1) can be repealed, so in that sense it does not bind later Congresses. Is the limitation best understood as a "canon of construction" which makes clear congressional intent not to infer authorization for the use of force from appropriations legislation? *See* Michael J. Glennon, *Applying the War Powers Resolution to the War on Terrorism, Testimony Before the Subcommittee on the Constitution of the U.S. Senate Committee on the Judiciary* (Apr. 17, 2002). Implied authorization by treaty is also relevant to the discussion of U.N. Security Council Resolutions in Section 5(C) of this Chapter.

8. *Nomenclature.* The War Powers Resolution is not properly cited as the War Powers *Act.* It is a joint resolution; a joint resolution, upon enactment, remains a joint resolution. A bill, upon enactment, becomes an "act." The House version of the Resolution was a bill, and the conference committee considered the issue, focusing upon the seeming formality of the term "act" versus "resolution." In light of the Resolution's history, did the conference committee err in choosing "Resolution"? Does that term reinforce a public perception that the measure is non-binding, or, in any event, somehow weaker than an "act"?

9. *A Better Way?* Analytically, three principal approaches are available for limiting the use of force by the president. First, a statute might identify circumstances in which the use of force is permissible, and prohibit any non-specified use. This "prior restraints" approach was embodied in the Senate version of the Resolution, which was rejected by the conference committee. Second, a statute might remain silent with respect to circumstances in which the use of force is permissible, and prohibit any use of force exceeding a "subsequent limitation," such as a durational limit. This was the approach of the House bill and is the approach of the Resolution. Third, a statute might affirmatively authorize use of force in specified circumstances and prohibit any unauthorized use of force. This is the approach of the draft "Use of Force Act," set forth in a Committee Print considered by the Senate Foreign Relations

Committee's Subcommittee on War Powers in 1988. Is any approach more constitutionally sound than the others? Which finds the broadest support in the case law? Does the third approach, for example, permit greater reliance upon "authorizing" cases such as *Bas v. Tingy, supra* this Chapter, Sec. 2? Which approach is preferable from a policy perspective?

10. *Reporting Requirement in Practice.* The Congressional Research Service describes compliance with the reporting requirements of the War Powers Resolution in the following terms:

> From 1975 through March 2015, Presidents have submitted 160 reports as the result of the War Powers Resolution, but only one, the 1975 Mayaguez seizure, cited Section 4(a)(1), which triggers the 60-day withdrawal requirement, and in this case the military action was completed and U.S. armed forces had disengaged from the area of conflict when the report was made. The reports submitted by the President since enactment of the War Powers Resolution cover a range of military activities, from embassy evacuations to full-scale combat military operations, such as the Persian Gulf conflict, and the 2003 war with Iraq, the intervention in Kosovo, and the anti-terrorism actions in Afghanistan. In some instances, U.S. Armed Forces have been used in hostile situations without formal reports to Congress under the War Powers Resolution.

Congressional Research Service, *The War Powers Resolution: Concepts and Practice, Summary and Appendix A*, April 3, 2015.

5. RECENT MAJOR INCIDENTS

A. THE FIRST AND SECOND GULF WARS WITH IRAQ (1990–1991 AND 2003–2010)

On August 2, 1990, Iraqi forces under Saddam Hussein invaded Kuwait and swiftly overwhelmed the Kuwaiti military. Thereafter, Iraq declared that it had annexed Kuwait. The same day, the U.N. Security Council adopted Resolution 660 (Aug. 2, 1990) condemning the invasion and demanding that Iraq withdraw immediately and unconditionally. On August 6, 1990, U.S. Secretary of Defense Dick Cheney met with King Fahd bin Abdul Aziz Al Saud in Riyadh to pledge that the United States would defend Saudi Arabia in the event of an attack by Iraq. King Fahd agreed to the deployment of American and allied troops in Saudi Arabia under what became known as Operation Desert Shield. By early 1991, the allied multinational force had swollen to nearly 500,000 soldiers.

Diplomatic efforts through the fall of 1990, including a series of increasingly stringent Security Council resolutions, failed to secure an Iraqi withdrawal. In November 1990, the Security Council adopted Resolution 678 authorizing states cooperating with Kuwait to "use all necessary means to uphold and implement" the Security Council's resolutions, unless Iraq complied by January 15, 1991.

In late 1990, President Bush made a number of statements suggesting that congressional authority was not necessary to authorize U.S. military intervention to expel Iraq from Kuwait. Based on the Constitution, early case law, and historical practice, do you agree with that position?

U.N. SECURITY COUNCIL RESOLUTION 678

(Nov. 29, 1990).

The Security Council, . . .

Acting under Chapter VII of the Charter,

1. *Demands* that Iraq comply fully with resolution 660 (1990) [demanding immediate and unconditional withdrawal of forces from Kuwait] and all subsequent relevant resolutions, and decides, while maintaining all its decisions, to allow Iraq one final opportunity, as a pause of goodwill, to do so;

2. *Authorizes* Member States co-operating with the Government of Kuwait, unless Iraq on or before 15 January 1991 fully implements, as set forth in paragraph 1 above, the above-mentioned resolutions, to use all necessary means to uphold and implement resolution 660 (1990) and all subsequent relevant resolutions and to restore international peace and security in the area;

3. *Requests* all States to provide appropriate support for the actions undertaken in pursuance of paragraph 2 above;

4. *Requests* the States concerned to keep the Security Council regularly informed on the progress of actions undertaken pursuant to paragraphs 2 and 3 above;

5. *Decides* to remain seized of the matter.

TRANSCRIPT OF HEARING BEFORE JUDGE HAROLD H. GREENE IN *DELLUMS V. BUSH*

Transcript at 37–54 (D.D.C. Dec. 4, 1990).

MR. (JULES) LOBEL [CENTER FOR CONSTITUTIONAL RIGHTS]: Your Honor, the question before this court is straightforward: can the President initiate a war against Iraq for the purpose of driving it from Kuwait without first obtaining the prior authorization of Congress. The President says he can; the Constitution says he cannot.

Here the threat that an explicit constitutional provision will be violated is clear. The President has repeatedly threatened Iraq with attack unless it withdraws from Kuwait. Just yesterday, Secretary Cheney said,

"We cannot wait for sanctions to work. We must have the option to use force."

Secondly, we are putting into place all of the means for driving Iraq out of Kuwait. We have sent close to 400,000 troops to the Persian Gulf in order to, in the President's words, "develop an adequate offensive military option."

We have traversed the globe and obtained United Nations authority to use force. In short, we have done everything necessary to put into place an offensive military action against Iraq except for one thing, and that is obtained the necessary congressional authority under our Constitution. . . .

THE COURT: How does this situation differ from the fighting in Korea?

MR. LOBEL: Your Honor, it may very well be that the Korean War was unconstitutional. It is a position that I will take, that I have written about, and most legal scholars and most people who have thought about the issue would say it was unconstitutional.

However, even in that situation, there is some distinction. There, the President was responding to a surprise attack by North Korea which threatened immediately to totally overwhelm South Korea. There was some time urgency. Here there is no time urgency.

Secondly, that unconstitutional war was not challenged prior to its initiation. [Within weeks] Congress met, and they approved budgetary authorizations, and therefore the question became different. Your Honor, we are here faced with a situation where the plaintiffs are coming in prior to the initiation of war, and saying, we must vote on it before war begins.

THE COURT: I take it you're not conceding that budgetary authorization is the equivalent of a declaration of war.

MR. LOBEL: I certainly am not. It's precisely for that reason, and precisely for what this court said in Mitchell v. Laird that every schoolboy knows, that once we are in war there is tremendous pressure on Congress to fund the troops who are out there fighting and dying, that this court must act now before we get into war and before Congress is faced, and this country is faced, and the courts will be faced with that impossible dilemma. It is that reason that the Constitution grants Congress the power to decide whether to go to war prior to its initiation.

Now, the defendant here doesn't like the way the Constitution reads. He would rather the Constitution read, the President can go to war subject to whatever after-the-fact ratification that Congress wants to address. But fortunately, I think for our country and for our history and for our constitutional government, the framers thought otherwise, and this court should act to affirm the explicit command of the Constitution.

We are not talking here about constitutional silence. This case does not raise the question of the silences of the Constitution in the areas of overlapping jurisdiction on foreign affairs. This case raises an explicit constitutional command, which every one of the framers knew what it meant, and that is we cannot go to war without congressional authorization. . . .

The Constitution requires an affirmative vote of Congress before we go to war. Therefore, if Congress is silent, the Constitution tells us we cannot go to war for whatever reason: Congress may be divided, Congress may be uncertain, Congress may not want to move. The explicit command of the Constitution is that absent affirmative authorization, the nation cannot be put in a state of war. . . .

We are not talking about some minor use of force. We are not talking about something that could be argued about. We are talking about, in the words of the Chairman of the Joint Chiefs of Staff, a war, a substantial war, a war which will be coordinated by land, sea, and air forces, designed to drive the fourth largest army in the world out of territory it now occupies.

I don't see how there can be any argument, by any reasonable person, that that decision is for Congress to make. I think the President is simply snubbing his nose at Congress, and I think that the court must say he cannot continue to do so. . . .

MR. GERSON [U.S. DEPT. OF JUSTICE]: Needless to say, I view Constitutional language and Constitutional history somewhat differently than my brother. Disputes of the sort that are embodied in this lawsuit are far from novel and were well within the compass of understanding and address of the Constitution's framers. From the earliest days of the republic, which saw Washington's pursuit of the undeclared Indian wars, and Jefferson's campaign against the Barbary Pirates, to McKinley's unilateral dispatch of troops to China to help put down the Boxer Rebellion, to Franklin D. Roosevelt's deviations from Congressional neutrality policy to aid those fighting Hitler before war was declared, to events relating to the military conduct of all nine of the Presidents since then, there have been disputes growing out of the tension between the President's powers as commander in chief and director of the nation's foreign affairs and—

THE COURT: Are you suggesting that the War Power's clause at Article I, Section 8, Clause 11, I think it is, means nothing?

MR. GERSON: No, I'm not suggesting that at all.

THE COURT: When does it apply?

MR. GERSON: Well, what the framers did in Article I, Section 8, which was understood then and now in the context of the vast international expectations and consequences, both internationally and domestic civil rights and the like of [what] a declared war constitutes, they set forth covalent powers, which to declare a war and carry one out had to be jointly exercised. Under this formulation, each branch might advance its conduct in support of belligerency ahead of the other: the President undertaking it, Congress in declaring it. But each could check the other, Congress securing its position through the power of the purse. . . .

I suggested earlier that the provision for declaring war is not superfluous, that a declared war always has been going back, really, to the 16th century, and before it, but in terms of the development of modern law, been understood to carry grave consequence. Title 50 of the United States Code consists of five or six volumes that are full of the consequences to the application of domestic law and sovereign immunity that occur during a declared war.

Internationally the consequences are grave. What was understood internationally, both at the time of the framers and ever since, is when both political branches of the government are acting in synchronization going forward exercising the declaring war power, the war-making power, the raising and support armies and navies, the power of the purse and the diplomatic power, that the entire fortune of the nation, and, indeed, its existence has been pledged. Just as the risk is the same on the other side, the juridical consequences of a declared war are immense. The term means a great deal. . . .

THE COURT: Isn't there some historical evidence, legislative history, so to speak, indicating that one reason for this clause was to make certain that one person does not get the country involved in a war? . . .

MR. GERSON: Well, I wish I could say, with absolute certainty, that we could know the answer to that, but let me tell you what I think the evidence is and, in doing so, rebut some of the points that the plaintiffs make about it. They cite Madison and his offering of an amendment to change making war to declaring war, declare war ultimately getting into the Constitution.

What they neglect to point out is following Madison's offering it and reciting a rationale that's very much the same as what your Honor described, that the Convention didn't support him, that they voted it down. It was only at a later time when I believe Rufus King raised a similarly worded provision but advanced the argument that it was the President who should carry out this form of activity—in other words, the individual—that the amendment passed and the language got into the Constitution. At the least, it's not at all certain, and I believe I am accurately quoting the history.

What we can say, and I believe that this runs true all the way through, the conduct of belligerency without a declaration of war was well-known to the framers. It existed for a long period of time throughout history. The events which followed the Constitution are so repetitive, where a vast majority of the Presidents have undertaken activities of this kind, that it vindicates what the framers said and did.

This was well within the compass of their expectation and understanding. They differentiated a declared war from the conduct of a number of kinds of activities, including offensive ones. There are checks in there. There are ways that a Congress could withdraw and paralyze the executive from acting, and that was well understood.

Again, I think that since the plaintiffs cited the source, they ought to have to live with it. If they believe that the War Powers Resolution is authority for any position that they are stating here, they well ought to look at its literal language which allows for the introduction of troops into hostilities. In other words, the conduct of offensive military action, without a war being declared. A number of requirements are then set out in the War Powers Resolution, some of them, as I say, posing significant legal and constitutional difficulty. But nevertheless, it was well within the compass of the understanding of the Congress in general that passed the act that you could have lawful offensive hostilities without a declaration of war. It then came Congress's time to decide whether or not one would be declared, which raises another point.

One can safely say, since the Constitution says it, that it is the role of the Congress to declare war, but in analyzing the right to vote of these plaintiffs, let's note that there is nothing in the Constitution that says when that vote has to take place or when that declaration has to take place. Again, I want to address your point of the consequence and the significance of the declaration. There just isn't any. The Constitution does not say war must be declared in advance of hostilities.

As I say, the historical understanding was otherwise. The historical experience since then has been otherwise. The understanding of Congress within the last few decades is different from that.

CONGRESSIONAL DEBATE ON THE AUTHORIZATION FOR USE OF MILITARY FORCE AGAINST IRAQ

102nd Cong., 1st Sess., 137 Cong. Rec. S110, S146, S365, H180 (daily ed. Jan. 10, 1991 and Jan. 12, 1991).

[SENATOR MOYNIHAN]: . . .

This is an idea—that Congress decides whether to go to war—that simply eroded in the cold war with the prospect of nuclear confrontation, permitting no time for reflection and consultation. The New York Times wrote this morning, very ably, I think, that Congress' constitutional warmaking authority fell into disuse during the cold war, so much that we can scarcely even remember the number of times that we have declared war. There is a notion that we declared war once during World War II. We declared war three times against six different countries in one form or another.

In the aftermath of the cold war, what we find is a kind of time warp in which we are acting in an old mode in response to a new situation. . . .

[SENATOR EXON]:

The prevalence of warmaking without a decree has led many in the present day to conclude that the President, therefore, has de facto power to declare war. To the contrary, repeated violation of the constitutional separation of powers is not synonymous with an invalidation or rewriting of the Constitution. If historically the executive branch has exceeded its powers in this respect, so must the Congress share responsibility. As John Hart Ely, a law professor at Stanford University, writes:

A Congress that lets the President call the shots on war and peace, and devotes itself instead to the construction of private political bomb shelters, is not what the Framers of the Constitution had in mind in vesting the war power in the legislative process. . . .

[SENATOR INOUYE]: Mr. President, I have read the arguments regarding the inherent powers of the Commander in Chief and I know there have been instances when Presidents have committed U.S. forces to combat without first receiving the assent of Congress. Most frequently these lapses have occurred when U.S. forces in the field were reeling under the armed assault of a foreign foe and were, in fact, already at war. I believe, however, that these were exceptional circumstances which in no way negate or diminish the authority of this body nor its responsibility to the people of the United States. It may be that our predecessors were not sufficiently vigilant in defending the constitutional authority of the Congress to declare war. There is no reason, however, why we in this Chamber today must repeat the errors of the past. To meet our responsibilities, we must insist that the Congress must give its explicit authorization for the use of force before the President can enter into battle.

AUTHORIZATION FOR USE OF MILITARY FORCE AGAINST IRAQ

H.J. Res. 77, Pub. L. No. 102–1, 105 Stat. 3 (Jan. 14, 1991).

JOINT RESOLUTION

To authorize the use of United States Armed Forces pursuant to United Nations Security Council Resolution 678.

Whereas the Government of Iraq without provocation invaded and occupied the territory of Kuwait on August 2, 1990;

Whereas both the House of Representatives (in H.J. Res. 658 of the 101st Congress) and the Senate (in S. Con. Res. 147 of the 101st Congress) have condemned Iraq's invasion of Kuwait and declared their support for international action to reverse Iraq's aggression;

Whereas, Iraq's conventional, chemical, biological, and nuclear weapons and ballistic missile programs and its demonstrated willingness to use weapons of mass destruction pose a grave threat to world peace;

Whereas the international community has demanded that Iraq withdraw unconditionally and immediately from Kuwait and that Kuwait's independence and legitimate government be restored;

Whereas the United Nations Security Council repeatedly affirmed the inherent right of individual or collective self-defense in response to the armed attack by Iraq against Kuwait in accordance with Article 51 of the United Nations Charter;

Whereas, in the absence of full compliance by Iraq with its resolutions, the United Nations Security Council in Resolution 678 has authorized member states of the United Nations to use all necessary means, after January 15, 1991, to uphold and implement all relevant Security Council resolutions and to restore international peace and security in the area; and

Whereas Iraq has persisted in its illegal occupation of, and brutal aggression against Kuwait:

Now, therefore, be it

Resolved by the Senate and House of Representatives of the United States of America in Congress assembled,

SEC. 1. SHORT TITLE.

This joint resolution may be cited as the "Authorization for Use of Military Force Against Iraq Resolution".

SEC. 2. AUTHORIZATION FOR USE OF UNITED STATES ARMED FORCES.

(a) AUTHORIZATION.—The President is authorized, subject to subsection (b), to use United States Armed Forces pursuant to United Nations Security Council Resolution 678 (1990) in order to achieve implementation of Security Council Resolutions 660, 661, 662, 664, 665, 666, 667, 669, 670, 674, and 677.

(b) REQUIREMENT FOR DETERMINATION THAT USE OF MILITARY FORCE IS NECESSARY.—Before exercising the authority granted in subsection (a), the President shall make available to the Speaker of the House of Representatives and the President pro tempore of the Senate his determination that—

(1) the United States has used all appropriate diplomatic and other peaceful means to obtain compliance by Iraq with the United Nations Security Council resolutions cited in subsection (a); and

(2) that those efforts have not been and would not be successful in obtaining such compliance.

(c) WAR POWERS RESOLUTION REQUIREMENTS.—

(1) SPECIFIC STATUTORY AUTHORIZATION.—Consistent with section 8(a)(1) of the War Powers Resolution, the Congress declares that this section is intended to constitute specific statutory authorization within the meaning of section 5(b) of the War Powers Resolution.

(2) APPLICABILITY OF OTHER REQUIREMENTS.—Nothing in this resolution supersedes any requirement of the War Powers Resolution.

SEC. 3. REPORTS TO CONGRESS.

At least once every 60 days, the President shall submit to the Congress a summary on the status of efforts to obtain compliance by Iraq with the resolutions adopted by the United Nations Security Council in response to Iraq's aggression.

MICHAEL J. GLENNON, THE GULF WAR AND THE CONSTITUTION

70 Foreign Affairs 84, 84–90 (Spring 1991).

During the January 1991 debate on whether to go to war in the Persian Gulf, many members of Congress were delighted at the legislature's response. "The Constitution, the American people and the cause of freedom have been served well," House minority leader Robert Michel (R-Ill.) said. Senator Strom Thurmond (R-S.C.) commented, "We have demonstrated to the world the meaning of democracy." Senator Sam Nunn (D-Ga.) rose to "commend President Bush for recognizing Congress' constitutional role." And House Foreign Affairs Committee Chairman Dante Fascell (D-Fla.) exclaimed: "He [the president] acknowledged the principle! . . . This is very important. By specific language, Congress authorized the war!" After four months of controversy about the allocation of the power to make war, it seemed easy to conclude, as did Representative Richard Durbin (D-Ill.), that "the United States Constitution had prevailed."

Easy, but wrong.

Starting from President Bush's unilateral commitment to defend Saudi Arabia and proceeding to Congress' jury-rigged approval, the episode represented a textbook example of how an audacious executive, acquiescent legislature and deferential judiciary have pushed the Constitution's system of separation of powers steadily backwards toward the monopolistic system of King George III. When President Bush finally requested legislative approval in a letter to Congress January 8, 1991, he never acknowledged that statutory authorization was constitutionally required. In fact, the president said that he still believed he had the authority to act without legislative authorization. "I don't think I need it," he said the next day, and White House aides hinted that the administration had the right to defy any restrictions that Congress might impose. . . .

The congressional debate on explicit authorization for the Gulf War was effectively over long before it began. It should have begun on August 7, 1990, the day after Secretary of Defense Dick Cheney announced the U.S. commitment to defend Saudi Arabia in the event of an attack by Iraq, which had overrun Kuwait four days earlier. John Kelly, assistant secretary of state for near eastern and south Asian affairs, had previously reminded a House Foreign Affairs subcommittee that the United States had no mutual security treaty with Kuwait, and the same applied to other gulf states.

The commitment was thus made as a sole executive agreement—an agreement more sweeping in its terms than any of the seven mutual security treaties to which the United States is party, for none of those contains an ironclad commitment to go to war. The administration could have easily, and probably successfully, sought congressional approval for sending troops to the gulf. Congress was in session and was willing and able to act quickly. In fact, each house adopted measures condemning the August 2 invasion on the very day it occurred.

The train was set in motion, therefore, by a promise of dubious constitutionality. Alexander Hamilton spoke for many of the Founding Fathers when he described the requirement of Senate advice and consent to a treaty as one of the "best digested and unexceptional parts of the plan," since it was "unsafe and improper to entrust that power to an elective magistrate of four years' duration." "The history of human conduct," Hamilton believed, "does not warrant that exalted opinion of human virtue which would make it wise in a nation to commit interests of so delicate and momentous a kind as those which concern its intercourse with the rest of the world to the sole disposal of a magistrate, created and circumstanced, as would be a president of the United States." Time-honored custom reinforced the proposition that a mutual security commitment could be made only with the advice and consent of two-thirds of the Senate—a requirement that cannot be dispensed with by calling a treaty something other than a treaty.

But nary a word was heard from Congress. It mattered naught that the United States was now committed to defend a feudal monarchy where women could not drive cars, adulterers were stoned and American chaplains would be forced to cover their religious insignia and conduct services clandestinely. Instead, members had nothing but praise for the president's bold response. When on August 5 President Bush announced—again with no congressional consultation, let alone approval—that Iraq's invasion of Kuwait "will not stand," members of Congress applauded. Few then cared how this invasion would be undone, or when and even whether Congress might be asked to approve its undoing. David Boren (D-Okla.), chairman of the Senate Intelligence Committee, was asked on September 12 whether the president should have at least consulted Congress before sending troops to the gulf. "No, I think the president should be supported on that point," he said. "It is extremely important that we project absolute unity." Only on November 8, when the president claimed the need for an "adequate offensive military option" and decided to double to nearly half a million the number of U.S. troops in Saudi Arabia, did congressional voices ask from what source the chief executive drew this extraordinary authority to place the nation at war without legislative approval. . . .

[The] observations of the framers are familiar. That their judgment retains wisdom for contemporary policymakers is suggested by the functional attributes of the two branches. One obvious advantage that Congress brings to the decision to go to war is diversity of opinion. Lincoln knew the value of diverse opinion and legislative deliberation. He said:

> In a certain sense, and to a certain extent, [the president] is the representative of the people. He is elected by them, as well as Congress is. But can he, in the nature [of] things, know the wants of the people, as well as three hundred other men, coming from all the various localities of the nation? If so, where is the propriety of having a Congress?

The safety and well-being of the U.S. forces engaged in combat are enhanced if adversaries as well as allies understand that the American public is resolutely behind them. It has been said often but is worth repeating: if a war—or any other foreign policy—cannot be sold to Congress, it cannot be sold to the American people. The national interest is ill served when a president embarks on a military initiative that lacks public support and, for political reasons, must be curtailed.

Congressional participation in a decision to use offensive force against Iraq would of course not preclude error. Congress is not immune to war-making blunders, nor is it necessarily more disinclined to use force; indeed, Capitol Hill is not territory foreign to hawkish hysteria. Yet history has provided little reason for heavier reliance on presidential judgment in war-powers matters. Lincoln said:

> The provision of the Constitution giving the war-making power to Congress, was dictated, as I understand it, by the following reasons. Kings had always been involving and impoverishing their people in wars, pretending generally, if not always, that the good of the people was the object. This our convention understood to be the most oppressive of all kingly oppressions; and they resolved to so frame the Constitution that

no one man should hold the power of bringing this oppression upon us.

Counterposed against these considerations are the advantages of sole presidential control over the decision to go to war. Few would contest the proposition that the presidency is institutionally better suited than Congress to respond to emergencies. But no emergency confronted the nation when President Bush announced the November buildup in Saudi Arabia. Whatever exigency may have attended the initial deployment of forces to that region had ended.

NOTES

1. *Form of Congressional Approval.* As indicated above, in January 1991 Congress engaged in a spirited debate about whether the United States should resort to war against Iraq, and ultimately authorized the president to use force to implement the Security Council's resolutions. When Iraq failed to withdraw from Kuwait by the deadline, allied forces began an air campaign against Iraq code-named Operation Desert Storm. On February 27, after Iraqi forces had been driven from Kuwait in a ground war lasting less than 100 hours, President Bush declared a cease-fire. Since the Congress did not formally declare war, was the president's resort to war lawful?

2. *Lack of Congressional Approval.* The congressional vote authorizing the president to act was 52–47 in the Senate and 250–183 in the House—the closest margin in authorizing force by the Congress since the War of 1812. What if the vote had fallen short and Congress never enacted H.J. Res. 77: could President Bush have ordered air strikes against Iraq? If so, under what authority? Perhaps Security Council Resolution 678, in conjunction with the U.N. Charter? Would it make a difference if Congress adopted an alternative joint resolution prohibiting the president from acting?

3. *The Slippery Slope.* Should it be permissible for the executive to undertake the sort of pledge made by Secretary of Defense Cheney to King Fahd on August 6, 1990? How is Cheney's pledge distinguished from more formal mutual security pacts entered into by the United States over the past 50 years? Are such formal "guarantees" any more binding under U.S. law? Separate from any such pledge, should it be permissible for the executive to deploy a half a million soldiers across the globe prior to obtaining any congressional authorization? Do such acts at some point make it extremely difficult for Congress to say "no" to military action and, if so, should Congress be expected to step up to the plate at some point early in the process? How can Congress act early in the process when it is unclear how events, including diplomacy, will unfold?

4. *Dellums v. Bush.* The Court rejected the government's argument that the political branches, not the courts, should determine how the war is initiated. Judge Greene reasoned that "[i]f the Executive had the sole power to

determine that any particular offensive military operation, no matter how vast, does not constitute war-making but only an offensive military attack, the congressional power to declare war will be at the mercy of a semantic decision by the Executive. Such an 'interpretation' would evade the plain language of the Constitution, and it cannot stand." Judge Greene also said that deference to the political branches might be appropriate if "the issue is factually close or ambiguous or fraught with intricate technical military and diplomatic baggage" but that here "the forces involved are of such magnitude and significance as to present no serious claim that a war would not ensue if they became engaged in combat." *Dellums v. Bush*, 752 F. Supp. 1141, 1143–45 (D.D.C. 1990). The judge concluded, however, that the action was not ripe for adjudication. Should the Court have dismissed the case for lack of standing? As a political question? Does it matter that the case sought injunctive relief, not damages? (*See* Chapter 7).

NOTE ON THE SECOND GULF WAR

Twelve years after his father took the United States to war against Iraq, President George W. Bush ordered the commencement of Operation Iraqi Freedom on March 20, 2003. Massive explosions erupted over Baghdad as allied coalition forces (the vast majority American) stormed across the border into Iraq. Within a little over a month, President Bush announced "the end of major combat operations" aboard the U.S.S. *Abraham Lincoln*.

Congress had authorized the use of force against Iraq in October, 2002. The Bush Administration justified intervention in Iraq mainly on the ground that Saddam Hussein's government had been pursuing weapons of mass destruction (WMD) in violation of multiple U.N. Security Council resolutions. Such weapons, it was argued, might ultimately fall into the hands of terrorist groups like Al Qaeda. In actuality, WMD were never discovered in Iraq. And despite early military triumphs, the United States soon found itself faced with a spiraling sectarian conflict.

In 2007, in what became known as the "surge," President Bush increased U.S. force levels in key areas of Iraq in order to combat sectarian violence and provide an atmosphere in which the Iraqi political process could move forward. Over the next few years, violence declined and the political process did move forward, though, as of mid-2011, it still faced significant hurdles.

On August 31, 2010, President Obama announced the end of United States combat operations in Iraq. Six conventional brigades and 4,500 special operations forces remained in Iraq to train Iraqi troops. Under a bilateral agreement between the United States and Iraq, all U.S. forces were required to leave Iraq by the end of 2011. 4,487 U.S. soldiers died in the Second Gulf War, making it the deadliest U.S. conflict since the war in Vietnam. That figure does not include Iraqi military and police (12,000 deaths), U.S. contractors (3,480 deaths) and Iraqi civilians (165,000 deaths). *See* Watson Institute for International & Public Affairs, Costs of War. As of 2017, the U.S. has more than 5,000 troops in Iraq to assist in the fight against ISIL. (*See infra*, this Chapter, Sec. 5(D)).

LORI FISLER DAMROSCH, WAR AND UNCERTAINTY

114 Yale L.J. 1405, 1408, 1414 (2005).

Congress has not had a good track record in establishing forensic truth at the times that it has authorized the President to proceed with military action. The disabilities under which Congress labors include a reliance on the executive branch for most of the information on which judgments about a military situation are based, an absence of procedures (adversarial or otherwise) to test the reliability of that information, and a tendency to accept the Executive's assertions about the need for urgent action. Even if Congress could improve its fact-finding capabilities—for example, by seeking alternative sources of information from outside the executive branch, through subpoena powers if appropriate; by subjecting executive representations to processes analogous to cross-examination instead of accepting them at face value; or by deliberating at a length appropriate to the gravity of the matter instead of yielding to the Executive's view on urgency—Congress is still not institutionally well suited to becoming a retrospective trier of fact and can hardly be expected to succeed at a task so far from its own institutional competence. The facts it ought to concentrate on developing (in war-and-peace decisions even more than in ordinary legislative enactments) are those that have relevance and salience for the charting of future policy directions.

NOTES

1. *Deciding to Use Force.* Is Congress or is the president better-qualified to make use-of-force decisions? Does your answer depend on what kind of error in decision-making is most likely? Note that there are two kinds of potential errors. The U.S. might err by entering into a conflict in which the costs outweigh the benefits, or it might err by not entering into a conflict in which the benefits outweigh the costs. Jide Nzelibe & John Yoo, *Rational War and Constitutional Design*, 115 YALE L. J. 2512 (2006).

2. *Intelligence and the War Power.* The United States now has a total of sixteen executive branch intelligence agencies under the umbrella of the Directorate of National Intelligence (DNI). To what extent should Congress take a more proactive role in providing oversight of the U.S. intelligence community given the importance of reliable information when resorting to war? What form should any additional oversight take? In 1977, the Carter Administration proposed setting up a "crisis consultative committee," consisting of the leadership of each house. A similar suggestion was made in 1988 by Senators Byrd, Nunn, Warner, and Mitchell in proposing to amend the War Powers Resolution. *See* MICHAEL J. GLENNON, CONSTITUTIONAL DIPLOMACY 307–313 (1990). What are some of the advantages and

disadvantages to such proposals? How much authority could a "crisis consultative committee" exercise after *Chadha* (*see* Chapter 1, Sec. 2)? Is Congress institutionally qualified to judge the reliability of intelligence estimates or is it better suited, as Professor Lori Damrosh writes, to "clarify the policy context" in which intelligence is analyzed?

B. ATTACKS OF SEPTEMBER 11, 2001 ("9/11")

On September 11, 2001, nineteen men affiliated with the terrorist group Al Qaeda hijacked four passenger aircraft, crashing two into New York's World Trade Center and one into the Pentagon (the fourth crashed in the Pennsylvania countryside). Almost 3,000 people died in the attack, making 9/11 the deadliest foreign attack on U.S. soil in American history.

In response to 9/11, President George W. Bush addressed a joint session of Congress on September 20, 2001. "Our war on terror begins with Al Qaeda," he declared, "but it does not end there. It will not end until every terrorist group of global reach has been found, stopped and defeated." On October 7, 2001, Operation Enduring Freedom commenced in Afghanistan, a longtime sanctuary for Al Qaeda. By spring 2002, most elements of the ruling Taliban regime had been driven from power.

AUTHORIZATION FOR USE OF MILITARY FORCE AGAINST THE PERPETRATORS OF 9/11 ("AUMF")

S.J. Res. 23, Pub. L. No. 107–40, 115 Stat. 224 (Sept. 18, 2001).

Joint Resolution

To authorize the use of United States Armed Forces against those responsible for the recent attacks launched against the United States.

Whereas, on September 11, 2001, acts of treacherous violence were committed against the United States and its citizens; and

Whereas, such acts render it both necessary and appropriate that the United States exercise its rights to self-defense and to protect United States citizens both at home and abroad; and

Whereas, in light of the threat to the national security and foreign policy of the United States posed by these grave acts of violence; and

Whereas, such acts continue to pose an unusual and extraordinary threat to the national security and foreign policy of the United States; and

Whereas, the President has authority under the Constitution to take action to deter and prevent acts of international terrorism against the United States:

Now, therefore, be it

Resolved by the Senate and House of Representatives of the United States of America in Congress assembled,

SEC. 1. SHORT TITLE.

This joint resolution may be cited as the "Authorization for Use of Military Force".

SEC. 2. AUTHORIZATION FOR USE OF UNITED STATES ARMED FORCES.

(a) In General.—That the President is authorized to use all necessary and appropriate force against those nations, organizations, or persons he determines planned, authorized, committed, or aided the terrorist attacks that occurred on September 11, 2001, or harbored such organizations or persons, in order to prevent any future acts of international terrorism against the United States by such nations, organizations or persons.

(b) War Powers Resolution Requirements.—

(1) Specific Statutory Authorization.—Consistent with section 8(a)(1) of the War Powers Resolution, the Congress declares that this section is intended to constitute specific statutory authorization within the meaning of section 5(b) of the War Powers Resolution.

(2) Applicability of Other Requirements.—Nothing in this resolution supercedes any requirement of the War Powers Resolution.

The 2001 AUMF provided the legal basis for combat in Afghanistan, but also for the 2011 ground operation that killed Osama Bin-Laden, and for air operations including drone strikes, in other countries such as Pakistan, Philippines, Yemen, Somalia and Libya. Fifteen years after its enactment, the AUMF today provides the legal basis for an ever-wider range of operations against various terrorist organizations in the Middle East. As you read the following materials, consider the language of the AUMF itself and how that language should be applied to new groups with unclear links to the Al Qaeda of 2001.

EXPANDING BOMBINGS IN YEMEN TAKES WAR TOO FAR

By Bruce Ackerman April 20, 2012, Washington Post.

CIA Director David H. Petraeus is asking the administration to expand the bombing campaign in Yemen. If President Obama approves this request, he will be breaking the legal barrier that Congress erected to prevent the White House from waging an endless war on terrorism.

Just days after the Sept. 11, 2001, attacks, Congress authorized the use of force against groups and countries that had supported the terrorist strikes on the United States. But lawmakers did not give President George W. Bush everything he wanted. When the White House first requested congressional support, the president demanded an open-ended military authority "to deter and preempt any future acts of terrorism or aggression against the United States."

Even at this moment of panic, Congress refused to hand Bush a blank check: "Given the breadth of activities potentially encompassed by the term 'aggression,' the President might never again have had to seek congressional authorization for the use of force to combat terrorism," David Abramowitz, chief counsel to what was then the House Committee on International Relations, wrote in a Harvard legal journal in 2002. Congress's final resolution eliminated the offending language and authorized the use of force against groups and countries that were involved in "the terrorist attacks on September 11th." The effect was to require the president to return to Congress, and the American people, for another round of express support for military campaigns against other terrorist threats.

The Petraeus proposal, reported this week by The Post, assaults this fundamental principle. Up to now, the CIA's drone campaign in Yemen has kept close to the legal line by restricting strikes to terrorist leaders, like the American Anwar al-Awlaki. Such leaders may have had personal links to the original al-Qaeda group, based in South Asia, that targeted New York and Washington in 2001. But now Petraeus is seeking permission to expand bombing raids whenever there is "suspicious behavior" at sites known to be controlled by a terrorist group—al-Qaeda in the Arabian Peninsula—that did not exist on Sept. 11.

Before the death of Osama bin Laden, it would have been plausible for the administration to suggest that the al-Qaeda terrorists in Afghanistan and Pakistan were giving orders to the group's namesake in Yemen. But al-Qaeda's failure to replace bin Laden with a credible leadership structure underscores the fact that the Yemeni group is on its own. In fact, The Post reported that the administration is weighing expansion of the CIA program precisely because it considers Yemen to pose the world's most serious terrorist threat.

The risk of attacks from Yemen may be real. But the 2001 resolution doesn't provide the president with authority to respond to these threats without seeking further congressional consent.

Congress hasn't reversed itself in the years since it authorized the use of military force. While lawmakers recently elaborated on the president's powers over captive terrorists in the military appropriations act of 2012, that legislation declared that "[n]othing in this section is intended to . . . expand the authority of the President or the scope of the Authorization for Use of Military Force [of September 2001]." If the administration wishes to escalate the fight against terrorists in Yemen, it should return to Congress for express approval.

Obama has an option. He has avoided Bush-era claims that he has the unilateral power as commander in chief to open up new fronts in an endless war against terrorism, independently of Congress. As a constitutional lawyer, he recognizes the weakness of such claims. As a politician he recognizes that they would profoundly alienate his base just when he needs it.

But unless Obama is prepared to cross this particular Rubicon, he should reject Petraeus's proposal. The president should not try to sleep-walk the United States into a permanent state of war by pretending that Congress has given him authority that Bush clearly failed to obtain at the height of the panic after Sept. 11.

AQAP IS NOT BEYOND THE AUMF: A RESPONSE TO ACKERMAN

By Robert Chesney, Lawfare, April 24, 2012
available at lawfareblog.com, [https://perma.cc/6JNK-6BPH].

Is al Qaeda in the Arabian Peninsula (AQAP) so distinct from the original al Qaeda network ("core al Qaeda") that the use of force against AQAP cannot be justified, as a matter of U.S. domestic law, under the 9/18/01 AUMF? More to the point, would President Obama necessarily have to rely upon a claim of independent Article II authority were he to grant an apparent request from CIA Director Petraeus for permission to use the "signature strike" model for targeting in Yemen? So argues Bruce Ackerman in this op-ed, which ran in the Washington Post this weekend. Ackerman adds that it would be a mistake, and unjustifiable, to make such an Article II claim.

I think that Ackerman is mistaken on both counts.

AQAP as Part-and-Parcel of Core Al Qaeda. Ackerman begins from the premise that the existing 9/18/01 AUMF was meant by Congress not to apply to all terrorist threats, but rather to the entity responsible for 9/11 and those harboring that entity. I agree with that reading up to a point; the AUMF on its face is certainly not a blanket authorization to use force against just any terrorist threat. But it does not follow that an attack directed at AQAP lies beyond the AUMF's scope.

AQAP is not some entirely distinct entity that simply happens to be like-minded and has decided to adopt core al Qaeda's brand for cache's sake. It is, rather, the direct and immediate manifestation of core al Qaeda's long-standing operational presence in Yemen. Over the years, core al Qaeda dispatched no small number of operatives to Yemen and Saudi Arabia, with varied results over time in the face of varied efforts by the regimes in Sana'a and Riyadh to suppress them. Efforts by these individuals to build a sustained organizational presence have waxed and waned, and gone under different names along the away. AQAP is the most recent name, and by far the most successful effort to date, expanding its ranks through local recruitment and building complex ties to local tribal leaders who share an antipathy for the central government's authority. In keeping with core al Qaeda's emerging (and necessity-driven) strategy of decentralization, it seems clear that AQAP does not think it necessary to obtain core al Qaeda's approval for its day-to-day operations (nor could it easily do so, given the successful efforts of the United States and others to make such communication as risky as possible). Yet there in no mistaking the continuing ties and fealty that run from AQAP to the core leadership. Before his death, for example, AQAP reportedly sought bin Laden's approval to elevate Anwar al-Awlaki's status within the group—approval that bin Laden denied. More recently, and more to the point, AQAP's emir Nasir al Wuyashi (himself an al Qaeda member who previously served directly under bin Laden) had this to say to Ayman al Zawahiri after bin Laden's death:

I give you allegiance of obedience in good and hard times, in ease and difficulty, in following the Book of Allah and the Sunnah [traditions] of Allah's Messenger, Allah's peace and prayer be upon him, and in fighting the enemies of Allah as much as I can—myself and . . . your loyal soldiers who are with me in the front of the Arabian Peninsula. . . ."

I don't mean to deny that there are hard questions about how one defines the boundaries of al Qaeda in light of its clandestine nature and diffuse organizational structure. Indeed, in cases like that of al Shabaab I think this difficulty is very significant. But AQAP is, relatively speaking, an easier case.

AQAP as an "associated force" encompassed by the AUMF. If AQAP is not best understood to be part-and-parcel of core al Qaeda, it does not follow automatically that AQAP is beyond the scope of the AUMF. The question then becomes whether the AUMF is best read to encompass, implicitly, those entities that join al Qaeda as "associated forces" functioning as co-belligerents in fighting the United States, and if so whether AQAP is such a group. Whether the AUMF does include an "associated forces" has certainly occasioned much debate, and important questions remain to be addressed as to the boundaries of the concept. But it is worth noting that in the few GTMO habeas cases to present the question, the courts have construed the AUMF to include an "associated force" concept encompassing at least those groups other than core al Qaeda and the Afghan Taliban who are engaged in conflict against U.S. forces in Afghanistan (see here for the D.C. Circuit's easy embrace of the concept as applied to the forces of Gulbuddin Hekmatyar, for example). The issue this leaves open is whether the same model should apply by extension to groups located outside Afghanistan whose attacks on America occur away from the hot battlefield. I think there is room and need for debate on that topic, but for now the important point is that it is far from obvious that the situation is excluded under the AUMF.

Criticizing the proposed strikes as being beyond the AUMF requires similarly criticizing many of the numerous strikes in Yemen that have occurred over the past few years. Because he frames his argument around the CIA request for signature-strike authority, Ackerman is in the awkward position of explaining why the numerous airstrikes already conducted (by both the CIA and the US military) against AQAP targets in Yemen over the past several years (at least 12 already this year, and at least 29 since late 2009) did not raise this same issue. His answer is that the prior strikes were limited to persons who "may have had personal links to the original al-Qaeda group, based in South Asia, that targeted New York and Washington in 2001," and by way of example cites Anwar al-Awlaki. But the al-Awlaki example cuts the other way. He had no such direct links to core al Qaeda (not beyond the links inherent in being part of AQAP, at any rate). The most accurate characterization of the existing set of strikes, I think, is to say that some did indeed targeted individuals with a personal and direct tie to core al Qaeda (such as Abdul Mun'im Salim al Fatahani, linked to the attack on the Cole in 2000), but many targeted leading AQAP figures who lacked such personal ties (such as al-Awlaki) and many others targeted mere AQAP "foot soldiers." Put simply, the Obama administration has long since crossed the line that Ackerman would draw with respect to the AUMF. (Interestingly, I note that the pattern of US strikes in Somalia may actually fit Ackerman's model—i.e., those strikes may indeed be limited to al Shabaab members who are in fact identifiable as core al Qaeda operatives).

Which way does the NDAA FY '12 cut? The NDAA famously confers explicit detention authority not just as to al Qaeda but also as to "associated forces." Ackerman suggests that one cannot infer anything from this since the NDAA states that "[n]othing in this section is intended to ... expand the authority of the President or the scope of the Authorization for Use of Military Force [of September 2001]." But given that the administration for a few years now has been using deadly force against AQAP under color of the AUMF on the theory that AQAP is either part of or an associated force of al Qaeda—and given that Congress was certainly aware of this at the time it enacted the NDAA—the language Ackerman quotes if anything seems to cut the other direction, favoring the conclusion that Congress does not view AQAP as beyond the original AUMF.

THE LEGAL FRAMEWORK FOR THE UNITED STATES' USE OF MILITARY FORCE SINCE 9/11

As Delivered by Stephen W. Preston, Dept. of Defense General Counsel
Annual Meeting of the American Society of International Law
Washington, DC, April 10, 2015
available at https://www.defense.gov/News/Speeches/Speech-View/Article/606662/, [https://perma.cc/K8US-66PA].

Although the 2001 AUMF was not unlimited, enacted as it was just a short time after the attacks, it was necessarily drafted in broad terms. Shortly after President Obama came into office, his Administration filed a memorandum in Guantanamo habeas litigation offering the new President's interpretation of his statutory authority to detain enemy forces as an aspect of his authority to use force under the 2001 AUMF. That memorandum explained that the statute authorized the detention of "persons who were part of, or substantially supported, Taliban or al Qaida forces or associated forces that are engaged in hostilities against the United States or its coalition partners, including any person who has committed a belligerent act, or has directly supported hostilities, in aid of such enemy armed forces." Moreover, it stated that "[p]rinciples derived from law-of-war rules governing international armed conflicts . . . must inform the interpretation of the detention authority Congress has authorized" under the AUMF.

This interpretation of the 2001 AUMF was adopted by the D.C. Circuit and, in 2011, it was expressly endorsed by Congress in the context of detention. The National Defense Authorization Act for Fiscal Year 2012 reaffirmed the authority to detain "person who was a part of or substantially supported al-Qaeda, the Taliban, or associated forces that are engaged in hostilities against the United States or its coalition partners, including any person who has committed a belligerent act or has directly supported such hostilities in aid of such enemy forces." It also reaffirmed that dispositions of such individuals are made "under the law of war." Thus, a decade after the conflict began, all three branches of the government weighed in to affirm the ongoing relevance of the 2001 AUMF and its application not only to those groups that perpetrated the 9/11 attacks or provided them safe haven, but also to certain others who were associated with them.

My predecessor, Jeh Johnson, later elaborated on the concept of associated forces. In a speech at Yale Law School in February 2012, he explained that the concept of associated forces is not open-ended. He pointed out that, consistent with international law principles, an associated force must be both (1) an organized, armed group that has entered the fight alongside al-Qa'ida, and (2) a co-belligerent with al-Qa'ida in hostilities against the United States or its coalition partners. This means that not every group that commits terrorist acts is an associated force. Nor is a group an associated force simply because it aligns with al-Qa'ida. Rather, a group must have also entered al-Qa'ida's fight against the United States or its coalition partners.

More recently, during a public hearing before the Senate Foreign Relations Committee in May 2014, I discussed at some length the Executive branch's interpretation of the 2001 AUMF and its application by the Department of Defense in armed conflict. In my testimony, I described in detail the groups and individuals against which the U.S. military was taking direct action (that is, capture or lethal operations) under the authority of the 2001 AUMF, including associated forces. Those groups and individuals are: al-Qa'ida, the Taliban and certain other terrorist or insurgent groups in Afghanistan; al-Qa'ida in the Arabian Peninsula (AQAP) in Yemen; and individuals who are part of al-Qa'ida in Somalia and Libya. In addition, over the past year, we have conducted military operations under the 2001 AUMF against the Nusrah Front and, specifically, those members of al-Qa'ida referred to as the Khorasan Group in Syria. We have also resumed such operations against the group we fought in Iraq when it was known as al-Qa'ida in Iraq, which is now known as ISIL.

The concept of associated forces under the 2001 AUMF does not provide the President with unlimited flexibility to define the scope of his statutory authority. Our government monitors the threats posed to the United States and maintains the capacity to target (or stop targeting) groups covered by the statute as necessary and appropriate. But identifying a new group as an associated force is not done lightly. The determination that a particular group is an associated force is made at the most senior levels of the U.S. Government, following reviews by senior government lawyers and informed by departments and agencies with relevant expertise and institutional roles, including all-source intelligence from the U.S. intelligence community. In addition, military operations against these groups are regularly briefed to Congress. There are no other groups—other than those publicly identified, as I have just described—against which the U.S. military is currently taking direct action under the authority of the 2001 AUMF.

NOTES

1. *The Scope of the 9/11 AUMF.* The AUMF authorized the president to use military force to invade Afghanistan and neutralize any further threats from Al Qaeda. How far does the authorization extend beyond these targets? What is its geographic scope? Does it apply outside areas of active hostilities? Of what relevance is international law? Is it significant that Congress has authorized funding for military operations consistent with the president's interpretation of the AUMF? What does the War Powers Resolution say about congressional authorization through appropriations bills?

2. *The Forever War.* Does the AUMF have any temporal limitations? Will the conflict with Al Qaeda come to a clear end? What does the Constitution say about terminating war? Of what relevance is the Treaty Clause? If Al Qaeda itself is extinguished, would the AUMF continue to apply to associated forces? With respect to detention, the Supreme Court's plurality opinion reasoned in *Hamdi v. Rumsfeld*, 542 U.S. 507, 520 (2004) that "it is a clearly established principle of the law of war that detention may last no longer than active hostilities." Consistent with the Court's approach, the Obama Administration has interpreted the AUMF as informed by these international law principles, reasoning that as long as "armed conflict remains ongoing and active hostilities have not ceased, it is clear that congressional authorization to detain and use military force under the 2001 AUMF continues." *See The Legal Framework for the United States' Use of Military Force Since 9/11, As Delivered by Stephen W. Preston, April 10, 2015. See Hamdi, infra* this Chapter, Sec. 7.

3. *Constraints on the Executive Branch?* The Bush and Obama administrations both argued that the 9/11 AUMF extends to "co-belligerents" who join Al Qaeda and the Taliban in fighting the United States and its allies. Although the government maintains that there is a well-established concept of co-belligerency in international law, scholars have noted that the test for classification of groups as "associated forces" or "co-belligerents" is ambiguous, apparently falling somewhere between covering only groups that directly engage in active hostilities against the United States and a lower standard covering groups that provide support to Al Qaeda, such as weapons or sharing of training camps. The concept accordingly preserves broad interpretive authority for the executive branch. *See* Rebecca Ingber, *Co-Belligerency*, 42 YALE J. INT'L L. (2017).

4. *The Killing of Osama bin Laden.* On May 1, 2011, the founder of Al Qaeda, Osama bin Laden, was shot and killed inside a private residential compound in Abbottabad, Pakistan, by U.S. Navy SEALs and CIA operatives. Abbottabad is a city fully under the control of the government of Pakistan; indeed, it hosts a military facility for the training of new recruits. By most accounts, the government of Pakistan was unaware of bin Laden's presence in Abbottabad. The covert operation was ordered by President Barack Obama apparently without the participation or consent of the government of Pakistan, so as to prevent Al Qaeda from learning of the planned operation. Was there any need for the president to obtain special congressional authorization for the operation? Any need for the president to determine that Pakistan was harboring or supporting bin Laden? Is such a killing consistent with international law? In a blog posting on the web site *Opinio Juris*, the U.S. Department of State Legal Adviser, Harold Koh, wrote the following:

> Given bin Laden's unquestioned leadership position within al Qaeda and his clear continuing operational role, there can be no question that he was the leader of an enemy force and a legitimate target in our armed conflict with al Qaeda. In addition, bin Laden continued to pose an imminent threat to the United States that engaged our

> right to use force, a threat that materials seized during the raid have only further documented. Under these circumstances, there is no question that he presented a lawful target for the use of lethal force. * * * Moreover, the manner in which the U.S. operation was conducted—taking great pains both to distinguish between legitimate military objectives and civilians and to avoid excessive incidental injury to the latter—followed the principles of distinction and proportionality described above, and was designed specifically to preserve those principles, even if it meant putting U.S. forces in harm's way. Finally, consistent with the laws of armed conflict and U.S. military doctrine, the U.S. forces were prepared to capture bin Laden if he had surrendered in a way that they could safely accept.

Harold Hongju Koh, *The Lawfulness of the U.S. Operation Against Osama bin Laden*, Opinio Juris (May 19, 2011), available at http://opiniojuris.org, [https://perma.cc/BC9P-QMBK].

5. *Targeting Outside Areas of Active Hostilities*. Between January 20, 2009, and December 31, 2015, the U.S. government undertook 473 strikes against terrorist targets outside "areas of active hostilities," meaning outside of Afghanistan, Iraq, and Syria. The strikes, which took place primarily in Pakistan, Somalia, and Yemen, killed between 2,372 and 2,581 combatants and between 64 and 116 non-combatants, according to the government. Estimates of civilian deaths by other organizations are higher. Beginning in 2013, the Obama Administration put in place Presidential Policy Guidance (PPG) for actions against terrorist targets located outside the United States and areas of "active hostilities." Why distinguish between areas inside and outside of "active hostilities"? The procedures apply to lethal and non-lethal uses of force. They include very detailed interagency planning and approval processes, and they require after-action reports. Critics acknowledge that the review process ensures that many senior officials are involved in key decisions, but also note that the "document drives home how bureaucratized, and therefore normalized, this practice of killing people away from conventional battlefields has become." Charlie Savage, *U.S. Releases Rules for Airstrike Killings of Terror Suspects*, N.Y. TIMES, Aug. 6, 2016, at A10 (quoting Jameel Jaffer, Deputy Legal Director of the ACLU).

6. *Drone Strikes*. Do drone strikes present special legal or policy problems? The PPG includes the following necessary preconditions for taking lethal action against high value targets:

> Lethal action requires that the individual may lawfully be targeted under existing authorities and that any conditions established in the appropriate operational plan. including those set forth in Section I.C.8, are met. The preconditions set forth in Section I.C.8 for the use of lethal force are as follows: (a) near certainly that an identified [High Value Target] is present; (b) near certainty that non-combatants will not be injured or killed; (c) [redacted]; (d) an assessment that capture is not feasible at the time of operation: (e)

an assessment that the relevant governmental authorities in the country where action is contemplated cannot or will not effectively address the threat to U.S. persons: and (f) an assessment that no other reasonable alternatives to lethal action exist to effectively address the threat to U.S. persons.

Are these precautions sufficient? Note that the PPG is an executive order not required by statute. Why did President Obama impose these limitations on his administration? As a matter of domestic law and policy, does it matter if targeted killings are conducted by the military or the Central Intelligence Agency? Robert Chesney, *Military-Intelligence Convergence and the Law of the Title 10/Title 50 Debate*, 5 J. OF NATIONAL SECURITY LAW & POLICY 539 (2012). Are targeted killings outside the area of active hostilities governed by the international law of war or by (the far more restrictive) international human rights law? For an overview of the international legal issues raised by drone strikes see Ryan J. Vogel, *Drone Warfare and the Law of Armed Conflict*, 39 DENV. J. INT'L L. & POL'Y 101 (2010) and Jelena Pejic, *Extraterritorial Targeting by Means of Armed Drones: Some Legal Implications*, 893 INT'L REV. RED CROSS (2015). For a discussion of the legal issues raised by targeted strikes against U.S. citizens see *infra,* this Chapter, Sec. 7.

C. AIRSTRIKES IN LIBYA, 2011

DEPARTMENT OF JUSTICE, OFFICE OF LEGAL COUNSEL, MEMORANDUM FOR THE ATTORNEY GENERAL

Authority to Use Military Force in Libya, April 1, 2011, 35 Op. O.L.C. 1 (2011).

This memorandum memorializes advice this Office provided to you, prior to the commencement of recent United States military operations in Libya, regarding the President's legal authority to conduct such operations. For the reasons explained below, we concluded that the President had the constitutional authority to direct the use of force in Libya because he could reasonably determine that such use of force was in the national interest. We also advised that prior congressional approval was not constitutionally required to use military force in the limited operations under consideration.

I.

In mid-February 2011, amid widespread popular demonstrations seeking governmental reform in the neighboring countries of Tunisia and Egypt, as well as elsewhere in the Middle East and North Africa, protests began in Libya against the autocratic government of Colonel Muammar Qadhafi, who has ruled Libya since taking power in a 1969 coup. Qadhafi moved swiftly in an attempt to end the protests using military force. Some Libyan government officials and elements of the Libyan military left the Qadhafi regime, and by early March, Qadhafi had lost control over much of the eastern part of the country, including the city of Benghazi. The

Libyan government's operations against its opponents reportedly included strafing of protesters and shelling, bombing, and other violence deliberately targeting civilians. Many refugees fled to Egypt and other neighboring countries to escape the violence, creating a serious crisis in the region.

The Libyan government's violence against civilians continued, and even escalated, despite condemnation by the UNSC and strong expressions of disapproval from other regional and international bodies. On March 1, 2011, the United States Senate passed by unanimous consent Senate Resolution 85. Among other things, the Resolution "strongly condemn[ed] the gross and systematic violations of human rights in Libya, including violent attacks on protesters demanding democratic reforms," "call[ed] on Muammar Gadhafi to desist from further violence," and "urge[d] the United Nations Security Council to take such further action as may be necessary to protect civilians in Libya from attack, including the possible imposition of a no-fly zone over Libyan territory." S. Res. 85, 112th Cong. §§ 2, 3, 7 (as passed by Senate, Mar. 1, 2011). On March 12, the Council of the League of Arab States similarly called on the UNSC "to take the necessary measures to impose immediately a no-fly zone on Libyan military aviation" and "to establish safe areas in places exposed to shelling as a precautionary measure that allows the protection of the Libyan people and foreign nationals residing in Libya, while respecting the sovereignty and territorial integrity of neighboring States."

By March 17, 2011, Qadhafi's forces were preparing to retake the city of Benghazi. Pledging that his forces would begin an assault on the city that night and show "no mercy and no pity" to those who would not give up resistance, Qadhafi stated in a radio address: "We will come house by house, room by room. It's over. The issue has been decided." See Dan Bilefsky & Mark Landler, *Military Action Against Qaddafi Is Backed by U.N.*, N.Y. Times, Mar. 18, 2011, at A1. Qadhafi, President Obama later noted, "compared [his people] to rats, and threatened to go door to door to inflict punishment. . . . We knew that if we . . . waited one more day, Benghazi, a city nearly the size of Charlotte, could suffer a massacre that would have reverberated across the region and stained the conscience of the world." . . .

[T]he UNSC determined that the "situation" in Libya "continues to constitute a threat to international peace and security" and "demand[ed] the immediate establishment of a cease-fire and a complete end to violence and all attacks against, and abuses of, civilians." S.C. Res. 1973. Resolution 1973 authorized member states, acting individually or through regional organizations, "to take all necessary measures . . . to protect civilians and civilian populated areas under threat of attack in the Libyan Arab Jamahiriya, including Benghazi, while excluding a foreign occupation force of any form on any part of Libyan territory." . . .

Despite a statement from Libya's Foreign Minister that Libya would honor the requested ceasefire, the Libyan government continued to conduct offensive operations, including attacks on civilians and civilian-populated areas. . . . In response, on March 19, 2011, the United States, with the support of a number of its coalition partners, launched airstrikes against Libyan targets to enforce Resolution 1973. Consistent with the reporting provisions of the War Powers Resolution, 50 U.S.C. § 1543(a) (2006), President Obama provided a report to Congress less than forty-eight hours later, on March 21, 2011. The President explained:

> At approximately 3:00 p.m. Eastern Daylight Time, on March 19, 2011, at my direction, U.S. military forces commenced operations to assist an international effort authorized by the United Nations (U.N.) Security Council and undertaken with the support of European allies and Arab partners, to prevent a humanitarian catastrophe and address the threat posed to international peace and security by the crisis in Libya. As part of the multilateral response authorized under U.N. Security Council Resolution 1973, U.S. military forces, under the command of Commander, U.S. Africa Command, began a series of strikes against air defense systems and military airfields for the purposes of preparing a no-fly zone. These strikes will be limited in their nature, duration, and scope. Their purpose is to support an international coalition as it takes all necessary measures to enforce the terms of U.N. Security Council Resolution 1973. These limited U.S. actions will set the stage for further action by other coalition partners.
>
> Obama March 21, 2011 Report to Congress. . . .

A.

Earlier opinions of this Office and other historical precedents establish the framework for our analysis. As we explained in 1992, Attorneys General and this Office "have concluded that the President has the power to commit United States troops abroad," as well as to "take military action," "for the purpose of protecting important national interests," even without specific prior authorization from Congress. *Authority to Use United States Military Forces in Somalia,* 16 Op. O.L.C. 6, 9 (1992) (*"Military Forces in Somalia"*). This independent authority of the President, which exists at least insofar as Congress has not specifically restricted it, *see Deployment of United States Armed Forces into Haiti*, 18 Op. O.L.C. 173, 176 n.4, 178 (1994) (*"Haiti Deployment"*), derives from the President's "unique responsibility," as Commander in Chief and Chief Executive, for "foreign and military affairs," as well as national security. *Sale v. Haitian Centers Council, Inc.*, 509 U.S. 155, 188 (1993); U.S. Const. art. II, § 1, cl. 1, § 2, cl. 2.

The Constitution, to be sure, divides authority over the military between the President and Congress, assigning to Congress the authority to "declare War," "raise and support Armies," and "provide and maintain a Navy," as well as general authority over the appropriations on which any military operation necessarily depends. U.S. Const. art. I, § 8, cl. 1, 11–14. Yet, under "the historical gloss on the 'executive Power' vested in Article II of the Constitution," the President bears the " 'vast share of responsibility for the conduct of our foreign relations,' " *Am. Ins. Ass'n v. Garamendi*, 539 U.S. 396, 414 (2003) (quoting *Youngstown Sheet & Tube Co. v. Sawyer*, 343 U.S. 579, 610–11 (1952) (Frankfurter, J., concurring)), and accordingly holds "independent authority 'in the areas of foreign policy and national security.' " *Id.* at 429 (quoting *Haig v. Agee*, 453 U.S. 280, 291 (1981)); *see also, e.g., Youngstown Sheet & Tube Co.*, 343 U.S. at 635–36 n.2 (Jackson, J., concurring) (noting President's constitutional power to "act in external affairs without congressional authority"). Moreover, the President as Commander in Chief "superintend[s] the military," *Loving v. United States*, 517 U.S. 748, 772 (1996), and "is authorized to direct the movements of the naval and military forces placed by law at his command." *Fleming v. Page*, 50 U.S. (9 How.) 603, 615 (1850); *see also Placing of United States Armed Forces Under United Nations Operational or Tactical Control*, 20 Op. O.L.C. 182, 184 (1996). The President also holds "the implicit advantage . . . over the legislature under our constitutional scheme in situations calling for immediate action," given that imminent national security threats and rapidly evolving military and diplomatic circumstances may require a swift response by the United States without the opportunity for congressional deliberation and action. *Presidential Power to Use the Armed Forces Abroad Without Statutory Authorization*, 4A Op. O.L.C. 185, 187 (1980) (*"Presidential Power"*); *see also Haig*, 453 U.S. at 292 (noting " 'the changeable and explosive nature of contemporary international relations, and the fact that the Executive is immediately privy to information which cannot be swiftly presented to, evaluated by, and acted upon by the legislature' " (quoting *Zemel v. Rusk*, 381 U.S. 1, 17 (1965)). Accordingly, as Attorney General (later Justice) Robert Jackson observed over half a century ago, "the President's authority has long been recognized as extending to the dispatch of armed forces outside of the United States, either on missions of goodwill or rescue, or for the purpose of protecting American lives or property or American interests." *Training of British Flying Students in the United States*, 40 Op. Att'y Gen. 58, 62 (1941).

This understanding of the President's constitutional authority reflects not only the express assignment of powers and responsibilities to the President and Congress in the Constitution, but also, as noted, the "historical gloss" placed on the Constitution by two centuries of practice. *Garamendi*, 539 U.S. at 414. "Our history," this Office observed in 1980, "is replete with instances of presidential uses of military force abroad in the absence of prior congressional approval." *Presidential Power*, 4A Op. O.L.C.

at 187; see generally Richard F. Grimmett, Cong. Research Serv., R41677, *Instances of Use of United States Armed Forces Abroad*, 1798–2010 (2011). Since then, instances of such presidential initiative have only multiplied, with Presidents ordering, to give just a few examples, bombing in Libya (1986), an intervention in Panama (1989), troop deployments to Somalia (1992), Bosnia (1995), and Haiti (twice, 1994 and 2004), air patrols and airstrikes in Bosnia (1993–1995), and a bombing campaign in Yugoslavia (1999), without specific prior authorizing legislation. *See* Grimmett, *supra*, at 13–31. This historical practice is an important indication of constitutional meaning, because it reflects the two political branches' practical understanding, developed since the founding of the Republic, of their respective roles and responsibilities with respect to national defense, and because "[m]atters intimately related to foreign policy and national security are rarely proper subjects for judicial intervention." Haig, 453 U.S. at 292. In this context, the "pattern of executive conduct, made under claim of right, extended over many decades and engaged in by Presidents of both parties, 'evidences the existence of broad constitutional power.'" *Haiti Deployment*, 18 Op. O.L.C. at 178 (quoting *Presidential Power*, 4A Op. O.L.C. at 187); *see also Proposed Deployment of United States Armed Forces into Bosnia*, 19 Op. O.L.C. 327, 330–31 (1995) (*"Proposed Bosnia Deployment"*) (noting that "[t]he scope and limits" of Congress's power to declare war "are not well defined by constitutional text, case law, or statute," but the relationship between that power and the President's authority as Commander in Chief and Chief Executive has been instead "clarified by 200 years of practice").

Indeed, Congress itself has implicitly recognized this presidential authority. The War Powers Resolution ("WPR"), 50 U.S.C. §§ 1541–1548 (2006), a statute Congress described as intended "to fulfill the intent of the framers of the Constitution of the United States," *id.* § 1541(a), provides that, in the absence of a declaration of war, the President must report to Congress within 48 hours of taking certain actions, including introduction of U.S. forces "into hostilities or into situations where imminent involvement in hostilities is clearly indicated by the circumstances." *Id.* § 1543(a). The Resolution further provides that the President generally must terminate such use of force within 60 days (or 90 days for military necessity) unless Congress extends this deadline, declares war, or "enact[s] a specific authorization." *Id.* § 1544(b). As this Office has explained, although the WPR does not itself provide affirmative statutory authority for military operations, *see id.* § 1547(d)(2), the Resolution's "structure . . . recognizes and presupposes the existence of unilateral presidential authority to deploy armed forces" into hostilities or circumstances presenting an imminent risk of hostilities. . . .

We have acknowledged one possible constitutionally-based limit on this presidential authority to employ military force in defense of important national interests—a planned military engagement that constitutes a "war" within the meaning of the Declaration of War Clause may require prior congressional authorization. *See Proposed Bosnia Deployment*, 19 Op. O.L.C. at 331; *Haiti Deployment*, 18 Op. O.L.C. at 177. But the historical practice of presidential military action without congressional approval precludes any suggestion that Congress's authority to declare war covers every military engagement, however limited, that the President initiates. In our view, determining whether a particular planned engagement constitutes a "war" for constitutional purposes instead requires a fact-specific assessment of the "anticipated nature, scope, and duration" of the planned military operations. *Haiti Deployment*, 18 Op. O.L.C. at 179. This standard generally will be satisfied only by prolonged and substantial military engagements, typically involving exposure of U.S. military personnel to significant risk over a substantial period. . . .

B.

Under the framework of these precedents, the President's legal authority to direct military force in Libya turns on two questions: first, whether United States operations in Libya would serve sufficiently important national interests to permit the President's action as Commander in Chief and Chief Executive and pursuant to his authority to conduct U.S. foreign relations; and second, whether the military operations that the President anticipated ordering would be sufficiently extensive in "nature, scope, and duration" to constitute a "war" requiring prior specific congressional approval under the Declaration of War Clause.

In prior opinions, this Office has identified a variety of national interests that, alone or in combination, may justify use of military force by the President. In 2004, for example, we found adequate legal authority for the deployment of U.S. forces to Haiti based on national interests in protecting the lives and property of Americans in the country, preserving "regional stability," and maintaining the credibility of United Nations Security Council mandates. Memorandum for Alberto R. Gonzales, Counsel to the President, from Jack L. Goldsmith III, Assistant Attorney General, Office of Legal Counsel, *Re: Deployment of United States Armed Forces to Haiti* at 3–4 (Mar. 17, 2004) ("2004 Haiti Opinion"), available at http://www.justice.gov/olc/opinions.htm, [https://perma.cc/C9RE-UTLM]. In 1995, we similarly concluded that the President's authority to deploy approximately 20,000 ground troops to Bosnia, for purposes of enforcing a peace agreement ending the civil war there, rested on national interests in completing a "pattern of inter-allied cooperation and assistance" established by prior U.S. participation in NATO air and naval support for peacekeeping efforts, "preserving peace in the region and forestalling the threat of a wider conflict," and maintaining the credibility of the UNSC. *Proposed Bosnia Deployment*, 19 Op. O.L.C. at 332–33. And in 1992, we explained the President's authority to deploy troops in Somalia in terms of national interests in providing security for American civilians and military personnel involved in UNSC-supported humanitarian relief efforts and (once again) enforcing UNSC mandates. *Military Forces in Somalia*, 16 Op. O.L.C. at 10–12.2.

In our view, the combination of at least two national interests that the President reasonably determined were at stake here—preserving regional stability and supporting the UNSC's credibility and effectiveness—provided a sufficient basis for the President's exercise of his constitutional authority to order the use of military force. First, the United States has a strong national security and foreign policy interest in security and stability in the Middle East that was threatened by Qadhafi's actions in Libya. As noted, we recognized similar regional stability interests as justifications for presidential military actions in Haiti and Bosnia. . . .

Qadhafi's actions not only endangered regional stability by increasing refugee flows and creating a humanitarian crisis, but, if unchecked, also could have encouraged the repression of other democratic uprisings that were part of a larger movement in the Middle East, thereby further undermining United States foreign policy goals in the region. Against the background of widespread popular unrest in the region, events in Libya formed "just one more chapter in the change that is unfolding across the Middle East and North Africa." Obama March 18, 2011 Remarks. Qadhafi's campaign of violence against his own country's citizens thus might have set an example for others in the region, causing "[t]he democratic impulses that are dawning across the region [to] be eclipsed by the darkest form of dictatorship, as repressive leaders concluded that violence is the best strategy to cling to power." Obama March 28, 2011 Address. At a minimum, a massacre in Libya could have imperiled transitions to democratic government underway in neighboring Egypt and Tunisia by driving "thousands of additional refugees across Libya's borders." *Id.* Based on these factors, we believe the President could reasonably find a significant national security interest in preventing Libyan instability from spreading elsewhere in this critical region.

The second important national interest implicated here, which reinforces the first, is the longstanding U.S. commitment to maintaining the credibility of the United Nations Security Council and the effectiveness of its actions to promote international peace and security. Since at least the Korean War, the United States government has recognized that " '[t]he continued existence of the United Nations as an effective international organization is a paramount United States interest.' " *Military Forces in Somalia*, 16 Op. O.L.C. at 11 (quoting *Authority of the President to Repel the Attack in Korea*, 23 Dep't St. Bull. 173, 177 (1950)). Accordingly, although of course the President is not required to direct the use of military force simply because the UNSC has authorized it, this Office has recognized that " 'maintaining the credibility of United Nations Security

Council decisions, protecting the security of United Nations and related relief efforts, and ensuring the effectiveness of United Nations peacekeeping operations can be considered a vital national interest' " on which the President may rely in determining that U.S. interests justify the use of military force. *Proposed Bosnia Deployment*, 19 Op. O.L.C. at 333 (quoting *Military Forces in Somalia*, 16 Op. O.L.C. at 11). Here, the UNSC's credibility and effectiveness as an instrument of global peace and stability were at stake in Libya once the UNSC took action to impose a no-fly zone and ensure the safety of civilians—particularly after Qadhafi's forces ignored the UNSC's call for a cease fire and for the cessation of attacks on civilians. . . .

We conclude, therefore, that the use of military force in Libya was supported by sufficiently important national interests to fall within the President's constitutional power. At the same time, turning to the second element of the analysis, we do not believe that anticipated United States operations in Libya amounted to a "war" in the constitutional sense necessitating congressional approval under the Declaration of War Clause. . . .

As in the case of the no-fly zone patrols and periodic airstrikes in Bosnia before the deployment of ground troops in 1995 and the NATO bombing campaign in connection with the Kosovo conflict in 1999—two military campaigns initiated without a prior declaration of war or other specific congressional authorization—President Obama determined that the use of force in Libya by the United States would be limited to airstrikes and associated support missions; the President made clear that "[t]he United States is not going to deploy ground troops in Libya." Obama March 18, 2011 Remarks. The planned operations thus avoided the difficulties of withdrawal and risks of escalation that may attend commitment of ground forces—two factors that this Office has identified as "arguably" indicating "a greater need for approval [from Congress] at the outset," to avoid creating a situation in which "Congress may be confronted with circumstances in which the exercise of its power to declare war is effectively foreclosed." *Proposed Bosnia Deployment*, 19 Op. O.L.C. at 333. Furthermore, also as in prior operations conducted without a declaration of war or other specific authorizing legislation, the anticipated operations here served a "limited mission" and did not "aim at the conquest or occupation of territory." *Id.* at 332. President Obama directed United States forces to "conduct[ ] a limited and well-defined mission in support of international efforts to protect civilians and prevent a humanitarian disaster"; American airstrikes accordingly were to be "limited in their nature, duration, and scope." Obama March 21, 2011 Report to Congress. As the President explained, "we are not going to use force to go beyond [this] well-defined goal." Obama March 18, 2011 Remarks. And although it might not be true here that "the risk of sustained military conflict was negligible," the anticipated operations also did not involve a "preparatory bombardment" in anticipation of a ground invasion—a form of military operation we distinguished from the deployment (without preparatory bombing) of 20,000 U.S. troops to Haiti in concluding that the latter operation did not require advance congressional approval. *Haiti Deployment*, 18 Op. O.L.C. at 176, 179. Considering the historical practice of even intensive military action—such as the 17-day-long 1995 campaign of NATO airstrikes in Bosnia and some two months of bombing in Yugoslavia in 1999—without specific prior congressional approval, as well as the limited means, objectives, and intended duration of the anticipated operations in Libya, we do not think the "anticipated nature, scope, and duration" of the use of force by the United States in Libya rose to the level of a "war" in the constitutional sense, requiring the President to seek a declaration of war or other prior authorization from Congress.

Accordingly, we conclude that President Obama could rely on his constitutional power to safeguard the national interest by directing the anticipated military operations in Libya—which were limited in their nature, scope, and duration—without prior congressional authorization.

NOTES

1. *Is the OLC's Libya Memorandum Convincing?* Consider this analysis:

> The OLC's Libya memorandum [ ]greatly overstated the support from past practice. [O]nly one post-Vietnam conflict materially resembled Libya: Clinton's Kosovo campaign. The OLC memorandum's other supposed precedents were inapplicable because they involved distinct circumstances: either they were principally peacekeeping missions not opposed by the local sovereign (Bosnia, Lebanon, Somalia) or they had been defended as necessary to rescue Americans or respond to attacks (Grenada, Panama, the Iran hostage rescue). To be sure, the Kosovo precedent was highly analogous, and thus the Libya intervention did not break entirely new ground. But the Libya intervention reinforced what had been the single expansive post-Vietnam precedent. (The president arguably operated under more constraint in Libya, as the operation was approved by the UN Security Council, but the president did not emphasize that in his defense.) As a result, Libya represents a potentially significant expansion of presidential war-initiation power.

Michael D. Ramsey, *Constitutional War Initiation and the Obama Presidency*, Michael D. Ramsey, 110 AM. J. INT'L L. 701, 712 (2016) (reprinted with permission of the American Society of International Law, permission conveyed through Copyright Clearance Center, Inc.).

2. *Relevance of the United Nations Security Council Resolution.* To what extent can the president rely upon a treaty as a source of domestic legal authority to use military force? The question arises in two contexts. First, does

a resolution of the U.N. Security Council serve as a substitute for statutory authorization by Congress? Note that U.N. Security Council Resolutions do not require the use of force by the United States, but they can make it permissible as a matter of international law. Second, if a mutual defense treaty commits the United States to defend an ally in case of attack, as NATO does, may the president rely on the treaty commitment as authorization? Is it relevant that the Constitution's framers considered and rejected a proposal to give the Senate alone the power to make war? *See* Michael Glennon, *Constitutional Diplomacy* 195, 204–205, 202–203 (1990). Assuming that the U.N. Charter was originally intended by the Senate to delegate to the president the power to use military force under the direction of the United Nations, would such a delegation be constitutional? *See* Thomas M. Franck & Faiza Patel, *UN Police Action in Lieu of War: "The Old Order Changeth,"* 85 AM. J. INT'L L. 63 (1991).

3. *War Powers Resolution.* Various members of Congress challenged President Obama's failure to seek authorization from Congress, both prior to the initial deployment and prior to the expiration of the sixty-day period envisaged in the War Powers Resolution. For example, a letter from six U.S. senators to the president on May 18, 2011, argued as follows:

> On March 19, 2011, you introduced the United States Armed Forces into hostilities in Libya. That action was taken without regard to or compliance with the requirement of section 2(c) of the War Powers Resolution that the United States Armed Forces only be introduced into hostilities or situations where imminent involvement in hostilities is clearly indicated by the circumstances "pursuant to (1) a declaration of war, (2) specific statutory authorization, or (3) a national emergency created by attack upon the United States, its territories or possessions, or its armed forces.
>
> Since that time, numerous aircraft and ships have been deployed and engaged in hostilities and remain in situations where imminent involvement in hostilities is clearly indicated by the circumstances. Secretary of Defense Robert Gates reports that operations in Libya have cost the Pentagon at least $750 million. . . .
>
> Congress received your report pursuant to section 4(a)(1) of the War Powers Resolution on March 21, 2011. Friday is the final day of the statutory sixty-day period for you to terminate the use of the United States Armed Forces in Libya under the War Powers Resolution. As recently as last week your Administration indicated use of the United States Armed Forces will continue indefinitely. Therefore, we are writing to ask whether you intend to comply with the requirements of the War Powers Resolution. We await your response.

If the War Powers Resolution did require authorization from Congress within sixty days (or cessation of U.S. military operations), that deadline passed without congressional action. *See* Charlie Savage, *Libya Effort Is Called Violation of War Act*, N.Y. TIMES, May 26, 2011, at A8. With continuing criticism from members of Congress, U.S. State Department Legal Adviser Harold Koh appeared before the Senate Foreign Relations to explain in greater depth the administration's legal position.

TESTIMONY BY U.S. DEPARTMENT OF STATE LEGAL ADVISER HAROLD HONGJU KOH ON LIBYA AND WAR POWERS

Testimony before the Senate Foreign Relations Committee, at 3–4, (June 28, 2011), available at http://foreign.senate.gov, [http://perma.cc/SE3Q-7E27].

Throughout the Libya episode, the President has never claimed the authority to take the nation to war without Congressional authorization, to violate the War Powers Resolution or any other statute, to violate international law, to use force abroad when doing so would not serve important national interests, or to refuse to consult with Congress on important war powers issues. . . .

The legal debate has focused on the Resolution's 60-day clock, which directs the President—absent express Congressional authorization (or the applicability of other limited exceptions) and following an initial 48-hour reporting period—to remove United States Armed Forces within 60 days from "hostilities" or "situations where imminent involvement in hostilities is clearly indicated by the circumstances." But as virtually every lawyer recognizes, the operative term, "hostilities," is an ambiguous standard, which is nowhere defined in the statute. Nor has this standard ever been defined by the courts or by Congress in any subsequent war powers legislation. Indeed, the legislative history of the Resolution makes clear there was no fixed view on exactly what the term "hostilities" would encompass. Members of Congress understood that the term was vague, but specifically declined to give it more concrete meaning, in part to avoid unduly hampering future Presidents by making the Resolution a "one size fits all" straitjacket that would operate mechanically, without regard to particular circumstances.

From the start, lawyers and legislators have disagreed about the meaning of this term and the scope of the Resolution's 60-day pullout rule. Application of these provisions often generates difficult issues of interpretation that must be addressed in light of a long history of military actions abroad, without guidance from the courts, involving a Resolution passed by a Congress that could not have envisioned many of the operations in which the United States has since become engaged. Because the War Powers Resolution represented a broad compromise between competing views on the proper division of constitutional authorities, the question whether a particular set of facts constitutes "hostilities" for purposes of the Resolution has been determined more by inter branch practice than by a narrow parsing of dictionary definitions. Both branches have recognized that different situations may call for different responses, and that an overly mechanical reading of the statute could lead to unintended automatic cutoffs of military involvement in cases where more flexibility is required. . . .

[A] combination of four factors present in Libya suggests that the current situation does not constitute the kind of "hostilities" envisioned by the War Powers Resolution's 60-day automatic pullout provision.

First, the *mission* is limited: By Presidential design, U.S. forces are playing a constrained and supporting role in a NATO-led multinational civilian protection operation, which is implementing a U.N. Security Council Resolution tailored to that limited purpose. This is a very unusual set of circumstances, not found in any of the historic situations in which the "hostilities" question was previously debated, from the deployment of U.S. armed forces to Lebanon, Grenada, and El Salvador in the early 1980s, to the fighting with Iran in the Persian Gulf in the late 1980s, to the use of ground troops in Somalia in 1993. Of course, NATO forces as a whole are more deeply engaged in Libya than are U.S. forces, but the War Powers Resolution's 60-day pullout provision was designed to address the activities of the latter.

Second, the *exposure* of our armed forces is limited: To date, our operations have not involved U.S. casualties or a threat of significant U.S. casualties. Nor do our current operations involve active exchanges of fire with hostile forces, and members of our military have not been involved in significant armed confrontations or sustained confrontations of any kind with hostile forces. Prior administrations have not found the 60-day rule to apply even in situations where significant fighting plainly did occur, as in Lebanon and Grenada in 1983 and Somalia in 1993. By highlighting this point, we in no way advocate a legal theory that is indifferent to the loss of non-American lives. But here, there can be little doubt that the greatest threat to Libyan civilians comes not from NATO or the United States military, but from Qadhafi. The Congress that adopted the War Powers Resolution was principally concerned with the safety of *U.S. forces*, and with the risk that the President would entangle them in an overseas conflict from which they could not readily be extricated. In this instance, the absence of U.S. ground troops, among other features of the Libya operation, significantly reduces both the risk to U.S. forces and the likelihood of a protracted entanglement that Congress may find itself practically powerless to end.

Third, the *risk of escalation* is limited: U.S. military operations have not involved the presence of U.S. ground troops, or any significant chance of escalation into a broader conflict characterized by a large U.S. ground presence, major casualties, sustained active combat, or expanding geographical scope. Contrast this with the 1991 Desert Storm operation, which although also authorized by a United Nations Security Council

Resolution, presented "over 400,000 [U.S.] troops in the area—the same order of magnitude as Vietnam at its peak—together with concomitant numbers of ships, planes, and tanks." Prior administrations have found an absence of "hostilities" under the War Powers Resolution in situations ranging from Lebanon to Central America to Somalia to the Persian Gulf tanker controversy, although members of the United States Armed Forces were repeatedly engaged by the other side's forces and sustained casualties in volatile geopolitical circumstances, in some cases running a greater risk of possible escalation than here.

Fourth and finally, the *military means* we are using are limited: This situation does not present the kind of "full military engagement[ ] with which the [War Powers] Resolution is primarily concerned." The violence that U.S. armed forces have directly inflicted or facilitated after the handoff to NATO has been modest in terms of its frequency, intensity, and severity. The air-to-ground strikes conducted by the United States in Libya are a far cry from the bombing campaign waged in Kosovo in 1999, which involved much more extensive and aggressive aerial strike operations led by U.S. armed forces. The U.S. contribution to NATO is likewise far smaller than it was in the Balkans in the mid-1990s, where U.S. forces contributed the vast majority of aircraft and air strike sorties to an operation that lasted over two and a half years, featured repeated violations of the no-fly zone and episodic firefights with Serb aircraft and gunners, and paved the way for approximately 20,000 U.S. ground troops. Here, by contrast, the bulk of U.S. contributions to the NATO effort has been providing intelligence capabilities and refueling assets. A very significant majority of the overall sorties are being flown by our coalition partners, and the overwhelming majority of strike sorties are being flown by our partners. American strikes have been confined, on an as-needed basis, to the suppression of enemy air defenses to enforce the no-fly zone, and to limited strikes by Predator unmanned aerial vehicles against discrete targets in support of the civilian protection mission; since the handoff to NATO, the total number of U.S. munitions dropped has been a tiny fraction of the number dropped in Kosovo. All NATO targets, moreover, have been clearly linked to the Qadhafi regime's systematic attacks on the Libyan population and populated areas, with target sets engaged only when strictly necessary and with maximal precision.

Had any of these elements been absent in Libya, or present in different degrees, a different legal conclusion might have been drawn. But the unusual confluence of these four factors, in an operation that was expressly designed to be limited—limited in mission, exposure of U.S. troops, risk of escalation, and military means employed—led the President to conclude that the Libya operation did not fall within the War Powers Resolution's automatic 60-day pullout rule.

NOTES

1. *The Meaning of "Hostilities."* Do you view the position taken by Legal Adviser Koh as correct or are you inclined to support those in Congress that were critical of the Obama Administration's position? If Koh is correct, then will most uses of U.S. force abroad likely fall within or outside the scope of the War Powers Resolution? Koh's argument was accepted by President Obama, but it was rejected by top lawyers at the Pentagon and the Justice Department who told the White House that they believed that the United States military's activities in the NATO-led air war amounted to "hostilities." How should the executive branch structure its legal decision-making? Does this disagreement undermine the legal basis or the legitimacy of the U.S. use of force in Libya? How much transparency about executive-branch decision-making is desirable? *See* Bob Bauer, *The National Security Lawyer in Crisis: When the 'Best View' of the Law May Not Be the Best View* (March 1, 2017), NYU School of Law, Public Law Research Paper No. 17–08, available at https://ssrn.com/abstract=2931165, [https://perma.cc/H24Y-HSL4].

2. *Where You Sit May Determine Where You Stand.* Presidential candidate Senator Barack Obama stated to the *Boston Globe* in 2007 that "[t]he president does not have power under the Constitution to unilaterally authorize a military attack in a situation that does not involve stopping an actual or imminent threat to the nation." Those who were to become members of President Obama's cabinet expressed similar positions. Senator Joseph Biden, who later became vice president, stated: "The Constitution is clear: Except in response to an attack or the imminent threat of attack, only Congress may authorize war and the use of force." Senator Hillary Clinton, who later became Secretary of State, asserted: "I do not believe that the President can take military action—including any kind of strategic bombing—against Iran without congressional authorization." *See* Glenn Kessler, *Fact Checker: President's war authority*, WASH. POST, Apr. 3, 2011, at A15. Was the view of President Barack Obama consistent with that of Senator Barack Obama? If not, which one was right?

D. ISLAMIC STATE OF IRAQ AND LEVANT, 2014

TEXT OF A LETTER FROM THE PRESIDENT TO THE SPEAKER OF THE HOUSE OF REPRESENTATIVES AND THE PRESIDENT PRO TEMPORE OF THE SENATE

August 8, 2014.

available at https://obamawhitehouse.archives.gov/the-press-office/2014/08/08/letter-president-war-powers-resolution-regarding-iraq, [https://perma.cc/A43V-6C35].

Dear Mr. Speaker: (Dear Mr. President:) As I announced publicly on August 7, 2014, I have authorized the U.S. Armed Forces to conduct targeted airstrikes in Iraq. These military operations will be limited in their scope and duration as necessary to protect American personnel in Iraq by stopping the current advance on Erbil by the terrorist group Islamic

State of Iraq and the Levant and to help forces in Iraq as they fight to break the siege of Mount Sinjar and protect the civilians trapped there. Pursuant to this authorization, on August 8, 2014, U.S. military forces commenced targeted airstrike operations in Iraq. In addition, I have authorized U.S. Armed Forces to provide humanitarian assistance in Iraq in an operation that commenced on August 7, 2014. These operations will also be limited to supporting the civilians trapped on Mount Sinjar. I have directed these actions, which are in the national security and foreign policy interests of the United States, pursuant to my constitutional authority to conduct U.S. foreign relations and as Commander in Chief and Chief Executive. These actions are being undertaken in coordination with the Iraqi government. I am providing this report as part of my efforts to keep the Congress fully informed, consistent with the War Powers Resolution (Public Law 93–148). I appreciate the support of the Congress in this action.

Sincerely, BARACK OBAMA

THE LEGAL FRAMEWORK FOR THE UNITED STATES' USE OF MILITARY FORCE SINCE 9/11

As Delivered by Stephen W. Preston, Dept. of Defense General Counsel
Annual Meeting of the American Society of International Law,
Washington, DC, April 10, 2015
available at https://www.defense.gov/News/Speeches/Speech-View/Article/606662/,
[http://perma.cc/K8US-66PA].

First, a word about this group we call ISIL, referred to variously as ISIS, the Islamic State or Daesh (its acronym in Arabic). In 2003, a terrorist group founded by Abu Mu'sab al-Zarqawi—whose ties to bin Laden dated from al-Zarqawi's time in Afghanistan and Pakistan before 9/11—conducted a series of sensational terrorist attacks in Iraq. These attacks prompted bin Laden to ask al-Zarqawi to merge his group with al-Qa'ida. In 2004, al-Zarqawi publicly pledged his group's allegiance to bin Laden, and bin Laden publicly endorsed al-Zarqawi as al-Qa'ida's leader in Iraq. For years afterwards, al-Zarqawi's group, often referred to as al-Qa'ida in Iraq, or AQI for short, conducted numerous deadly terrorist attacks against U.S. and coalition forces, as well as Iraqi civilians, using suicide bombers, car bombs and executions. In response to these attacks, U.S. forces engaged in combat—at times, near daily combat—with the group from 2004 until U.S. and coalition forces left Iraq in 2011. Even since the departure of U.S. forces from Iraq, the group has continued to plot attacks against U.S. persons and interests in Iraq and the region—including the brutal murder of kidnapped American citizens in Syria and threats to U.S. military personnel in Iraq.

The 2001 AUMF has authorized the use of force against the group now called ISIL since at least 2004, when bin Laden and al-Zarqawi brought their groups together. The recent split between ISIL and current al-Qa'ida leadership does not remove ISIL from coverage under the 2001 AUMF, because ISIL continues to wage the conflict against the United States that it entered into when, in 2004, it joined bin Laden's al-Qa'ida organization in its conflict against the United States. As AQI, ISIL had a direct relationship with bin Laden himself and waged that conflict in allegiance to him while he was alive. ISIL now claims that it, not al-Qa'ida's current leadership, is the true executor of bin Laden's legacy. There are rifts between ISIL and parts of the network bin Laden assembled, but some members and factions of al-Qa'ida-aligned groups have publicly declared allegiance to ISIL. At the same time, ISIL continues to denounce the United States as its enemy and to target U.S. citizens and interests.

In these circumstances, the President is not divested of the previously available authority under the 2001 AUMF to continue protecting the country from ISIL—a group that has been subject to that AUMF for close to a decade—simply because of disagreements between the group and al-Qa'ida's current leadership. A contrary interpretation of the statute would allow the enemy—rather than the President and Congress—to control the scope of the AUMF by splintering into rival factions while continuing to prosecute the same conflict against the United States.

Some initially greeted with skepticism the President's reliance on the 2001 AUMF for authority to renew military operations against ISIL last year. To be sure, we would be having a different conversation if ISIL had emerged out of nowhere a year ago, having no history with bin Laden and no more connection to current al-Qa'ida leadership than it has today, or if the group once known as AQI had, for example, renounced terrorist violence against the United States at some point along the way. But ISIL did not spring fully formed from the head of Zeus a year ago, and the group certainly has never laid down its arms in its conflict against the United States.

The name may have changed, but the group we call ISIL today has been an enemy of the United States within the scope of the 2001 AUMF continuously since at least 2004. A power struggle may have broken out within bin Laden's jihadist movement, but this same enemy of the United States continues to plot and carry out violent attacks against us to this day. Viewed in this light, reliance on the AUMF for counter-ISIL operations is hardly an expansion of authority. After all, how many new terrorist groups have, by virtue of this reading of the statute, been determined to be among the groups against which military force may be used? The answer is zero.

The President's authority to fight ISIL is further reinforced by the 2002 authorization for the use of military force against Iraq (referred to as the 2002 AUMF). That AUMF authorized the use of force to, among other things, "defend the national security of the United States against the continuing threat posed by Iraq." Although the threat posed by Saddam

Hussein's regime in Iraq was the primary focus of the 2002 AUMF, the statute, in accordance with its express goals, has always been understood to authorize the use of force for the related purposes of helping to establish a stable, democratic Iraq and addressing terrorist threats emanating from Iraq. After Saddam Hussein's regime fell in 2003, the United States, with its coalition partners, continued to take military action in Iraq under the 2002 AUMF to further these purposes, including action against AQI, which then, as now, posed a terrorist threat to the United States and its partners and undermined stability and democracy in Iraq. Accordingly, the 2002 AUMF authorizes military operations against ISIL in Iraq and, to the extent necessary to achieve these purposes, in Syria.

Beyond the domestic legal authorities, our military operations against ISIL have a firm foundation in international law, as well. The U.S. Government remains deeply committed to abiding by our obligations under the applicable international law governing the resort to force and the conduct of hostilities. In Iraq, of course, the United States is operating against ISIL at the request and with the consent of the Government of Iraq, which has sought U.S. and coalition support in its defense of the country against ISIL. In Syria, the United States is using force against ISIL in the collective self-defense of Iraq and U.S. national self-defense, and it has notified the UN Security Council that it is taking these actions in Syria consistent with Article 51 of the UN Charter. Under international law, states may defend themselves, in accordance with the inherent right of individual and collective self-defense, when they face armed attacks or the imminent threat of armed attacks and the use of force is necessary because the government of the state where the threat is located is unwilling or unable to prevent the use of its territory for such attacks.

The inherent right of self-defense is not restricted to threats posed by states, and over the past two centuries states have repeatedly invoked the right of self-defense in response to attacks by non-state actors. Iraq has been clear, including in letters it has submitted to the UN Security Council, that it is facing a serious threat of continuing armed attacks from ISIL coming out of safe havens in Syria, and it has asked the United States to lead international efforts to strike ISIL sites and strongholds in Syria in order to end the continuing armed attacks on Iraq, to protect Iraqi citizens and ultimately enable Iraqi forces to regain control of Iraqi borders. ISIL is a threat not only to Iraq and our partners in the region, but also to the United States. Finally, the Syrian government has shown that it cannot and will not confront these terrorist groups effectively itself.

WILLIAM S. CASTLE, THE ARGUMENT FOR A NEW AND FLEXIBLE AUTHORIZATION FOR THE USE OF MILITARY FORCE

38 Harv. J.L. & Pub. Pol'y 509, 509–11 (2015).

I agree with President Obama's assertion that he has the constitutional authority to conduct military operations against IS. In addition to this Article II power, President Obama was appropriate in invoking the 2001 Authorization for the Use of Military Force (2001 AUMF) and the 2002 Authorization for Use of Military Force Against Iraq Resolution (2002 AUMF) as additional bases for using force against IS.

Nevertheless, the President continues to insist on limiting the types of strategies and tactics that can be utilized by our forces against this new enemy. The Administration's initial policy was to prohibit "boots on the ground" in Iraq and Syria. With the publication of the President's AUMF proposal, this position appears to have been modified so as to prohibit "the use of the United States Armed Forces in enduring offensive ground combat operations." Additionally, the President's proposal would cap the new authorization at three years.

The importance of maintaining legal flexibility for the possible use of additional military capabilities against IS was underscored by former Defense Secretary Robert Gates's recent warning that "there will be boots on the ground if there is to be any hope of success in the strategy." This point was echoed by General David Petraeus in his admonition that defeating IS will take "months and years, not days or weeks."

But just as the President appears to have changed his position from a policy of prohibiting "boots on the ground" to not authorizing an "enduring offensive ground combat operation," the Administration has on a number of occasions revised its interpretation of the existing AUMFs over the past two years. This fluctuation could lead to questions as to the legitimacy of using the 2001 and 2002 AUMFs as the basis for the use of force against IS. Though the President has ample war powers to confront IS, Congress should follow the President's adjure and enact a third AUMF to address any lingering concerns and ensure there is no legal doubt that our military has maximum flexibility to eliminate IS. However, it is of vital importance that any new AUMF not create the artificial and potentially harmful limitations which are unfortunately a hallmark of the President's proposal.

SENATOR TIM KAINE
WEDNESDAY, NOVEMBER 30, 2016

available at https://www.kaine.senate.gov/press-releases/kaine-renews-call-for-congress-to-vote-on-war-against-isil-encourages-new-debate-on-changing-security-challenges, [https://perma.cc/C4QE-QFF6].

Since the war against ISIL began in August of 2014, more than 5,000 members of the U.S. military have served in Operation Inherent Resolve either in Iraq or Syria. . . . The U.S. military has launched over 12,600 airstrikes. We're carrying out Special Forces operations. We're assisting the Iraqi military, Syrians fighting against the Islamic State in Syria, as well as the Kurdish Peshmerga in the northern part of the Iraq. . . . The war has cost $10 billion, 800 days of operations, an average of $12 million a day, and I began honoring Scott Dayton, but Scott Dayton is not the only military member who's lost his life in this war. Five have been killed in combat. In total 28 American service members have lost their lives supporting Operation: Inherent Resolve.

As we speak, there are more than 300 Special Forces now in Syria fighting in a very complex battlefield where Turkish, Syrian, Russian, Iranian, Lebanese Hezbollah, and Kurdish forces are operating in close proximity as evidenced by recent developments in the growing humanitarian catastrophe in Aleppo. . . .

The President maintains that he can conduct this war without a new authorization from Congress, relying upon an authorization that was passed on September 14, 2001. When the new Congress is sworn in in early January, I think 80% of the members of Congress were not here when the September 14, 2001 authorization was passed. So the 80% of us that were not here in 2001 have never had a meaningful debate or vote upon this war against ISIL. . . .

It should never be an easy vote. It should be a hard vote but it should be a necessary vote. . . .

[I]f we're unwilling to have the debate and have the vote it seems to me to be almost the height of public immorality to force people to risk and give their lives in support for a mission we're unwilling to discuss.

NOTES

1. *Why not Article II?* President Obama at first relied on his constitutional powers as the legal basis for U.S. operations against the Islamic State. During 2014 and 2015, as the fight against ISIL spread, the president abandoned the constitutional rationale and relied instead on congressional authorization based on either the 9/11 AUMF or the 2002 authorization for the Iraq war. How strong was the president's claim to independent Article II power? Under what circumstances could the attacks on ISIL be

constitutionally justified? Why would the president abandon the Article II argument?

2. *The Scope of Congressional Authorization*. Did Congress authorize military action against ISIL? Critics have argued that the 9/11 AUMF does not provide authorization because ISIL was formed after 9/11, had no connections to the 9/11 attacks, and by 2014 had renounced any relationship with Al Qaeda. How convincing are Stephen Preston's counterarguments? Critics have also argued that the 2002 Iraq AUMF does not authorize the use of force against ISIL because it was aimed at the regime of Saddam Hussein. The text of the 2002 AUMF authorizes military action "against the continuing threat posed by Iraq."

3. *Smith v. Obama*. A U.S. Army captain sued President Obama seeking a declaration that Congress did not authorize the hostilities against ISIL in Iraq and Syria and that therefore the War Powers Resolution requires the president to withdraw U.S. forces. The government argued that actions against ISIL were authorized through the 2016 Consolidated Appropriations bill which provides money "for payments to reimburse key cooperating nations for logistical, military, and other support, including access, provided to United States military and stability operations in Afghanistan and to counter the Islamic State of Iraq and the Levant." The Explanatory Statement for the Act notes the threat posed by the "rise of [ISIL]," and notes that the Act "moves funding from the base appropriation to the [overseas contingency operations] appropriation to provide additional funding for the Army, Navy, Marine Corps, and Air Force" in order to "conduct counter-ISIL operations," among other things. Is that argument consistent with Section 8(a)(1) of the War Powers Resolution? *See* Marty Lederman, *DOJ's Motion to Dismiss in* Smith v. Obama, *the case challenging the legality of the war against ISIL,* JustSecurity (July 14, 2016), available at https://www.justsecurity.org/, [https://perma.cc/CB8C-X528]. The case was dismissed for lack of standing and under the political question doctrine. *Smith v. Obama*, 217 F. Supp. 3d 283 (D.D.C. 2016).

4. *A New AUMF?* President Obama sought a new AUMF. Congress did not pass one, although the fight against ISIL had broad public support. What political obstacles prevented enactment of a new AUMF? Do congressional inaction and the administration's very broad interpretation of the 2001 AUMF suggest that the constitutional system regulating the use of force is no longer working?

E. SYRIA: THE "RED LINE" AND 2017 AIRSTRIKES

The Obama administration used military strikes against ISIL in Syria starting in 2014, as described above, and it also provided varying levels of support to Syrian rebels seeking to overthrow the government of Bashar al Assad starting in 2011. During the summer of 2013, as the civil war in Syria escalated, reports emerged that the government had used chemical weapons against rebel forces. In response, the Obama administration began to contemplate publicly the use of military force directly against the

Syrian regime. President Obama had already said that if the Syrian government used chemical weapons it would cross a "red line." More than 100 members of Congress, including 98 Republicans and 18 Democrats formally requested that President Obama seek congressional approval for any military response to the use of chemical weapons in Syria. Although President Obama said that he had the constitutional authority to respond without congressional authorization, he eventually did seek approval. A political deal was ultimately brokered by Russia; Congress did not vote.

The issue arose again under the Trump Administration when the Syrian government deployed chemical weapons against its own people, killing more than 80 civilians. Two days later, on April 6, 2017, President Trump used airstrikes against the air base in Syria from which the chemical attack was launched. President Trump said this about the airstrikes:

> There can be no dispute that Syria used banned chemical weapons, violated its obligations under the Chemical Weapons Convention, and ignored the urging of the UN Security Council. Years of previous attempts at changing Assad's behavior have all failed, and failed very dramatically. As a result, the refugee crisis continues to deepen and the region continues to destabilize, threatening the United States and its allies. Tonight, I call on all civilized nations to join us in seeking to end the slaughter and bloodshed in Syria, and also to end terrorism of all kinds and all types.

The United Nations Security Council did not authorize the use of force against Syria. After the April 6, 2017 airstrikes, Russia vetoed a Security Council resolution which would have condemned Syrian use of chemical weapons. Russia argued that there was not enough evidence that the Assad regime carried out the chemical weapons attack.

In 2013, U.N. Security Council Resolution 2118 had endorsed the Russian-brokered Framework for the Elimination of Syrian Chemical Weapons and a related procedure for destroying Syrian chemical weapons. That resolution provided "that the use of chemical weapons anywhere constitutes a threat to international peace and security" and that non-compliance would result in the imposition of "measures under Chapter VII of the United Nations Charter." Russia and China vetoed subsequent resolutions which would have sanctioned Syria for using chemical weapons.

NOTES

1. *The Libya Precedent.* Consider President Trump's airstrikes in Syria in light of the Office of Legal Counsel's memorandum on the legal basis for President Obama's use of force in Libya. Neither action was authorized by

Congress. How similar are the "national interests" at issue? Do the roles of regional organizations and the United Nations differ? Considered together, do Syria and Libya mark a sharp departure from prior practice?

2. *International Law.* U.S. and NATO intervention in Libya was authorized by the U.N. Security Council and therefore did not violate international law. The Syrian airstrikes were not, by contrast, authorized by the U.N. Security Council. Although the airstrikes violated international law, the use of force for humanitarian purposes was not unprecedented. The 1999 NATO bombing in Kosovo, for example, also lacked U.N. Security Council approval and was defended by some States—including Belgium and the United Kingdom—as lawful because it served humanitarian purposes. How relevant is a potential violation of international law to the domestic statutory and constitutional issues? Compare the discussion of the U.N. Security Council authorization in the materials on Libya. Does it matter that international law may be undergoing a transition towards allowing "humanitarian intervention"? Is it relevant that the U.S. has not defended the Kosovo or the Syrian airstrikes as consistent with existing or emerging international law?

6. THE COMMANDER-IN-CHIEF POWER

As Commander in Chief, the president has at least some power to introduce U.S. troops into armed conflict. For example, as we have seen, the president has the constitutional power to repel armed attacks. The Commander-in-Chief power also, however, gives the president power to prosecute war once it has been authorized. As Hamilton wrote in Federalist 69, the president as Commander in Chief has "the supreme command and direction of the military and naval forces, as first general and admiral of the Confederacy." How far does the power to prosecute or execute war extend? To what extent is it exclusive to the president and to what extent is it shared with Congress? Writing in 1915, William Howard Taft argued that the president's Commander-in-Chief power means that "Congress could not order battles to be fought on a certain plan, and could not direct parts of the army to be moved from one part of the country to another." William Howard Taft, *The Boundaries Between the Executive, the Legislative and the Judicial Branches of the Government*, 25 YALE L.J. 599, 610 (1916).

The president's power to prosecute war has already been addressed at various points in the course. Of what significance was the Commander-in-Chief power in the *Youngstown* and *Little v. Barrame* cases from Chapter 1, Sec. 2? In *Brown v. United States* from Section 2 of this Chapter? Also re-read the U.S. Department of Justice Office of Legal Counsel 2002 Memorandum on Interrogation from Chapter 3, Sec. 3. To what extent is the approach in the 2002 Memorandum repudiated by the 2009 Memorandum on Interrogation? The president's power to conduct war is also relevant to the following Section on the detention and trial of detainees and to the discussion in Chapter 5, Sec. 3 of Congress's power to compel withdrawal of the armed forces through funding restrictions.

EXCERPTS, 1974 HOUSE HEARINGS

War Powers: A Test of Compliance: Hearings Before the Subcommittee on International Security and Scientific Affairs, House Committee on International Relations. 94th Cong., 1st Sess. (June 4, 1974).

Mr. SOLARZ. . . .

Would it be fair to say in your judgment, from a legal and constitutional point of view, the evacuation of American nationals from Vietnam authorized by the President was essentially the same as his justification for the rescue of the crew of the *Mayaguez,* that his determination to use American forces in both instances rested on essentially the same legal and constitutional foundations?

Mr. LEIGH [State Dep't Legal Adviser]. Yes; I agree with that. I think that the legal situation was more complicated in the case of the rescue operation of the refugees and—well, Saigon.

Mr. SOLARZ. Because of the fact that foreign nationals were involved?

Mr. LEIGH. Intermingled.

Mr. SOLARZ. Yes. I understand it is your position that the amendments restricting American paramilitary action in Indochina were not applicable in this instance. Is that essentially because the legislative history behind those amendments to the law clearly indicated that they were not intended to prevent this kind of operation?

Mr. LEIGH. Yes.

Mr. SOLARZ. Or is it because you take the position that the President has an inherent constitutional authority to rescue American nationals that have been captured on the high seas and regardless of the legislative history of those particular provisions the President had the right to do it from a constitutional point of view anyway?

Mr. LEIGH. Yes; I would take that as the ultimate position but here they tend to merge because my understanding of the reasons which were given at the time of the enactment of the funds limitation provisions was that they did not go so far as to prevent the President from exercising his constitutional authority to rescue American citizens simply because those citizens happened to be in Indochina. So it was understood, I think fairly clearly, both from the legislative history and also from the constitutional doctrine which lay back of it, that the Congress did not intend to foreclose the use of Armed Forces to rescue Americans in Indochina.

Mr. SOLARZ. That was part of it. I was not there at the time although I have read your memo. My understanding is while the President may have authority to send in American troops to rescue American nationals, that the Congress has an inherent authority to refuse to fund such an operation, and that therefore if the Congress enacted legislation prohibiting the use of American tax dollars to support an operation for rescue for, say, American nationals in some area of the world, that the President would not be able to pay the troops who he sent in to accomplish that objective.

Mr. LEIGH. I think that is correct.

Mr. SOLARZ. So that your position with respect to the inapplicability of the existing restrictions in the law has to do essentially with the legislative history of those provisions which in your judgment would not clearly indicate that they were not designed to prohibit this kind of action.

Mr. LEIGH. That is right.

Mr. SOLARZ. If the legislative history indicated otherwise, then they would be applicable?

Mr. LEIGH. They would be applicable subject to possible constitutional difficulties.

Mr. SOLARZ. Yes; but if I understand your testimony correctly you are saying that Congress does have the constitutional authority to cut off funding for such an operation.

Mr. LEIGH. I see what you mean. Well, certainly if Congress is able to cut off the funding, there is no question that the President has no funds to use. It does not always arise as easily as that because Congress usually has appropriated the money. The President has the appropriation, he is in the process of expending it and he has to face the question whether the particular limitation is constitutional.

Now I see that I should have made a distinction in the first instance in answering your question between a limitation which is a condition subsequent and a failure of Congress to provide appropriations when all other appropriations have run out. My testimony when we were previously in a colloquy on this was that I was not sure that the Congress by imposing a condition subsequent on an appropriation which has not yet been fully expended could limit the President's power to carry out certain constitutional duties such as to defend the United States from hostile attack against its mainland territory. There is obviously no judicial decision on this but I would think that there would be a serious doubt as to the constitutionality of such a limitation if it were applied to prevent the President from defending the mainland territory of the United States from attack.

Mr. SOLARZ. In your judgment, how far does the President's inherent authority to use American troops to rescue American nationals extend in terms of the uses to which such troops can be put? For instance, does the military action have to clearly be related to the rescue of the individuals involved?

Mr. LEIGH. To take your first more general question first, I think it is very difficult to lay down any rule of thumb because one of the fascinating things about our constitutional system is that it is constantly producing different kinds of questions which even the brightest people were not able to foresee in advance, so I would be very reluctant to try to specify.

I notice that Professor Bickel when he testified in hearings similar to this took the same position. It is almost impossible to give a rigid and precise definition of what the President's constitutional powers are as Commander in Chief, so that would be my general answer to your general question.

Now I believe in theory that the President, if he has the money, as Chief Justice Taft said on one occasion, to support troops could constitutionally send them anywhere. On the other hand, I think this is really in the area of the political accommodation that has to exist between the executive branch and the legislative branch, and I think you ought to count on the President not really doing wildly foolish things with the power that the Constitution gives him as Commander in Chief. I realize this is a controversial discussion in the wake of the Cambodian situation but that is my technical view. . . .

Mr. SOLARZ. . . .

Do you believe that in a situation where the President would commit American troops into combat pursuant to what he believed was his inherent constitutional authority that the Congress, if it determined that it did not want the troops there—would the Congress have the authority, in your judgment, to pass a law cutting off funding for the troops and thereby in effect requiring the President to withdraw them?

Mr. LEIGH. Again, I make the distinction as between the condition subsequent in an appropriation not yet completely spent and new appropriations.

Mr. SOLARZ. I have to confess that without a legal background—

Mr. LEIGH. If he has used up all the money appropriated and then Congress refuses to provide any more, I think the Congress has effectively stopped the President from continuing the military action. I don't know how he can go on. If, on the other hand, he still had moneys that were unexpended, he could continue to spend those until such time as there was a court challenge and the court found that he was acting illegally.

NOTES

1. *Congressional Abdication?* In light of situations such as the intervention in Libya, do you think Congress has abdicated its role over U.S. resort to war? Or is Congress simply choosing to regulate such conduct in ways other than always expressly authorizing or not authorizing the use of force? Consider the following view:

> Since at least the Vietnam War, discussions of constitutional war powers have consistently depicted a Congress so fearful of taking responsibility for wartime judgments that it hardly acts at all. Although there is an important element of truth in this common understanding, it is also misleading. In particular, whatever utility the scholarly paradigm of congressional abdication might once have had, it is inadequate in the special context of the so-called "war on terrorism." . . . Moreover, the congressional abdication paradigm is not even adequate to explain important war powers issues that now often arise in more traditional military contexts. . . .
>
> [W]e disclaim the traditional assumption that Congress has ceded the field to the President when it comes to war, and proceed from a contrary premise: that even when hostilities are underway, the Commander in Chief often operates in a legal environment instinct with legislatively imposed limitations.
>
> Thus, the war powers issue that is now at the forefront of the most important clashes between the political branches . . . is the one Justice Jackson famously described in *Youngstown Sheet & Tube Co. v. Sawyer* as arising when the President's authority as Commander in Chief is at its "lowest ebb," namely, when the chief executive acts contrary to congressional will.
>
> [N]othing approaching a constitutional consensus, either among the branches or within the executive branch itself, has emerged to support the view that the President has the power to defy statutes that interfere with his preferred manner of prosecuting a military conflict.

David J. Barron & Martin S. Lederman, *The Commander in Chief at the Lowest Ebb-Framing the Problem, Doctrine, and Original Understanding*, 121 HARV. L. REV. 692, 692–694, 697 (2008) (reprinted with permission of Harvard Law Review, permissions conveyed through Copyright Clearance Center, Inc.).

2. *Neutrality Act.* Section 5 of the Neutrality Act of 1794, 18 U.S.C. § 960, forbids the planning of, provision for, or participation in "any military or naval expedition or enterprise to be carried on" from the United States "against the territory or dominion of any foreign prince or state . . . with whom the United States is at peace." The Neutrality Act was intended to protect the

independence of the United States from foreign entanglements and to encourage the non-interference by foreign governments in U.S. affairs. *See* Jules Lobel, *The Rise and Decline of the Neutrality Act: Sovereignty and Congressional War Powers in United States Foreign Policy*, 24 HARV. INT'L L.J. 1, 1–39 (1983). Could the Act be applied to government officials? *See Dellums v. Smith*, 577 F. Supp. 1449 (N.D. Cal. 1984); Application of the Neutrality Act to Official Gov't Activities, 8 U.S. Op. Off. Legal Counsel 58, 80 (1984).

7. DETENTION AND PROSECUTION OF ENEMY COMBATANTS

This Section considers the legal issues that arise when individuals are detained or prosecuted during time of war. Chapters 2 and 3 considered the general application within the U.S. legal system of customary international law and of international agreements. Those Chapters are relevant here because both customary international law and treaties regulate some aspects of the detention and possible prosecution of enemy combatants. For example, when an armed conflict arises, who may be detained: Enemy soldiers? Enemy spies? Civilians who take up arms against the United States? What if the "enemy" is not a foreign country but, instead, a terrorist group? Do the same rules apply? Of what relevance is international law to questions of the president's statutory and constitutional authority?

An enemy combatant cannot be prosecuted simply because he sought to kill U.S. soldiers or otherwise engaged in conduct permitted under the laws of war. However, any enemy combatant can be prosecuted for violating the laws of war, such as intentionally attacking civilian, rather than military, targets. When the United States detains such a combatant, three options arise. First, the prosecution might proceed in regular U.S. criminal courts, with the full panoply of rights normally accorded in those courts, assuming that the relevant court has subject matter jurisdiction over the alleged crime. Second, the prosecution might proceed in the same U.S. military courts that prosecute U.S. military personnel for misconduct, pursuant to the Uniform Code of Military Justice (UCMJ), 10 U.S.C. §§ 801 et seq. (2006) (previously known as the "Articles of War"). Third, the prosecution might proceed before *ad hoc* "military commissions" established by the president for use during a particular armed conflict, in accordance with whatever procedural and evidentiary rules are established for those commissions. Though they are unusual in nature, military commissions are recognized in passing by the UCMJ, and have long been used by the United States in times of war to try captured enemies for war crimes. Those commissions, however, are not subject to the full breadth of constitutional protections that apply in civilian courts nor to the relatively robust protections now embedded in the UCMJ for prosecution of U.S. military personnel.

Rules on detention and prosecution of combatants can be difficult to apply even in traditional inter-state conflicts. For example, do spies and saboteurs receive the same protections as uniformed soldiers? The rules become even more challenging to apply in the context of a conflict with a non-State actor, such as a terrorist organization. Is such a conflict an "armed conflict" within the meaning of the laws of war? If so, are captured terrorists to be treated as prisoners of war or as unprivileged combatants? If prosecuted before a military commission, can the detainee challenge a conviction before regular U.S. courts? In considering whether the detainee should be prosecuted in or otherwise have access to U.S. courts, does it matter where the detainee is located? When is congressional approval required for either detention or prosecution? Does it matter if the detainee is a U.S. citizen? Is a U.S. citizen who is captured or targeted entitled to due process protections? If so, to what is he or she entitled?

EX PARTE QUIRIN

317 U.S. 1 (1942).

MR. CHIEF JUSTICE STONE delivered the opinion of the Court. . . .

The following facts appear from the petitions or are stipulated. Except as noted they are undisputed.

All the petitioners were born in Germany; all have lived in the United States. All returned to Germany between 1933 and 1941. All except petitioner Haupt are admittedly citizens of the German Reich, with which the United States is at war. Haupt came to this country with his parents when he was five years old; it is contended that he became a citizen of the United States by virtue of the naturalization of his parents during his minority and that he has not since lost his citizenship. The Government, however, takes the position that on attaining his majority he elected to maintain German allegiance and citizenship, or in any case that he has by his conduct renounced or abandoned his United States citizenship. . . .

After the declaration of war between the United States and the German Reich, petitioners received training at a sabotage school near Berlin, Germany, where they were instructed in the use of explosives and in methods of secret writing. Thereafter petitioners, with a German citizen, Dasch, proceeded from Germany to a seaport in Occupied France, where petitioners Burger, Heinck and Quirin, together with Dasch, boarded a German submarine which proceeded across the Atlantic to Amagansett Beach on Long Island, New York. The four were there landed from the submarine in the hours of darkness, on or about June 13, 1942, carrying with them a supply of explosives, fuses, and incendiary and timing devices. While landing they wore German Marine Infantry uniforms or parts of uniforms. Immediately after landing they buried their uniforms and the other articles mentioned, and proceeded in civilian dress to New York City.

The remaining four petitioners at the same French port boarded another German submarine, which carried them across the Atlantic to Ponte Vedra Beach, Florida. On or about June 17, 1942, they came ashore during the hours of darkness, wearing caps of the German Marine Infantry and carrying with them a supply of explosives, fuses, and incendiary and timing devices. They immediately buried their caps and the other articles mentioned, and proceeded in civilian dress to Jacksonville, Florida, and thence to various points in the United States. All were taken into custody in New York or Chicago by agents of the Federal Bureau of Investigation. All had received instructions in Germany from an officer of the German High Command to destroy war industries and war facilities in the United States, for which they or their relatives in Germany were to receive salary payments from the German Government. They also had been paid by the German Government during their course of training at the sabotage school and had received substantial sums in United States currency, which were in their possession when arrested. The currency had been handed to them by an officer of the German High Command, who had instructed them to wear their German uniforms while landing in the United States.

The President, as President and Commander in Chief of the Army and Navy, by Order of July 2, 1942, appointed a Military Commission and directed it to try petitioners for offenses against the law of war and the Articles of War, and prescribed regulations for the procedure on the trial and for review of the record of the trial and of any judgment or sentence of the Commission.

On July 3, 1942, the Judge Advocate General's Department of the Army prepared and lodged with the Commission the following charges against petitioners, supported by specifications:

1. Violation of the law of war.
2. Violation of Article 81 of the Articles of War, defining the offense of relieving or attempting to relieve, or corresponding with or giving intelligence to, the enemy.
3. Violation of Article 82, defining the offense of spying.
4. Conspiracy to commit the offenses alleged in charges 1, 2 and 3.

Petitioners' main contention is that the President is without any statutory or constitutional authority to order the petitioners to be tried by military tribunal for offenses with which they are charged; that in consequence they are entitled to be tried in the civil courts with the safeguards, including trial by jury, which the Fifth and Sixth Amendments guarantee to all persons charged in such courts with criminal offenses. In any case it is urged that the President's Order, in prescribing the procedure of the Commission and the method for review of its findings and sentence, and the proceedings of the Commission under the Order, conflict with Articles of War adopted by Congress—particularly Articles 38, 43, 46, 50 1/2 and 70—and are illegal and void. . . .

By the Articles of War, 10 U.S.C. §§ 1471–1593, Congress has provided rules for the government of the Army. It has provided for the trial and punishment, by courts martial, of violations of the Articles by members of the armed forces and by specified classes of persons associated or serving with the Army. Arts. 1, 2. But the Articles also recognize the "military commission" appointed by military command as an appropriate tribunal for the trial and punishment of offenses against the law of war not ordinarily tried by court martial. *See* Arts. 12, 15. . . .

From the very beginning of its history this Court has recognized and applied the law of war as including that part of the law of nations which prescribes, for the conduct of war, the status, rights and duties of enemy nations as well as of enemy individuals. By the Articles of War, and especially Article 15, Congress has explicitly provided, so far as it may constitutionally do so, that military tribunals shall have jurisdiction to try offenders or offenses against the law of war in appropriate cases. Congress, in addition to making rules for the government of our Armed Forces, has thus exercised its authority to define and punish offenses against the law of nations by sanctioning, within constitutional limitations, the jurisdiction of military commissions to try persons for offenses which, according to the rules and precepts of the law of nations, and more particularly the law of war, are cognizable by such tribunals. And the President, as Commander in Chief, by his Proclamation in time of war has invoked that law. By his Order creating the present Commission he has undertaken to exercise the authority conferred upon him by Congress, and also such authority as the Constitution itself gives the Commander in Chief, to direct the performance of those functions which may constitutionally be performed by the military arm of the nation in time of war.

An important incident to the conduct of war is the adoption of measures by the military command not only to repel and defeat the enemy, but to seize and subject to disciplinary measures those enemies who in their attempt to thwart or impede our military effort have violated the law of war. It is unnecessary for present purposes to determine to what extent the President as Commander in Chief has constitutional power to create military commissions without the support of Congressional legislation. For here Congress has authorized trial of offenses against the law of war before such commissions. We are concerned only with the question whether it is within the constitutional power of the National Government to place petitioners upon trial before a military commission for the offenses with which they are charged. We must therefore first inquire whether any of the acts charged is an offense against the law of war cognizable before a military tribunal, and if so whether the Constitution prohibits the trial. We may assume that there are acts regarded in other countries, or by some writers on international law, as offenses against the law of war which would not be triable by military tribunal here, either because they are not recognized by our courts as violations of the law of war or because they are of that class of offenses constitutionally triable only by a jury. It was upon such grounds that the Court denied the right to proceed by military tribunal in *Ex parte Milligan, supra.* But as we shall show, these petitioners were charged with an offense against the law of war which the Constitution does not require to be tried by jury.

It is no objection that Congress in providing for the trial of such offenses has not itself undertaken to codify that branch of international law or to mark its precise boundaries, or to enumerate or define by statute all the acts which that law condemns. An Act of Congress punishing "the crime of piracy, as defined by the law of nations" is an appropriate exercise of its constitutional authority, Art. I, § 8, cl. 10, "to define and punish" the offense, since it has adopted by reference the sufficiently precise definition of international law. *United States v. Smith,* 5 Wheat. 153. . . . Similarly, by the reference in the 15th Article of War to "offenders or offenses that . . . by the law of war may be triable by such military commissions," Congress has incorporated by reference, as within the jurisdiction of military commissions, all offenses which are defined as such by the law of war (*compare Dynes v. Hoover,* 20 How. 65, 82), and which may constitutionally be included within that jurisdiction. Congress had the choice of crystallizing in permanent form and in minute detail every offense against the law of war, or of adopting the system of common law applied by military tribunals so far as it should be recognized and deemed applicable by the courts. It chose the latter course.

By universal agreement and practice, the law of war draws a distinction between the armed forces and the peaceful populations of belligerent nations and also between those who are lawful and unlawful combatants. Lawful combatants are subject to capture and detention as prisoners of war by opposing military forces. Unlawful combatants are likewise subject to capture and detention, but in addition they are subject to trial and punishment by military tribunals for acts which render their belligerency unlawful. The spy who secretly and without uniform passes the military lines of a belligerent in time of war, seeking to gather military information and communicate it to the enemy, or an enemy combatant who without uniform comes secretly through the lines for the purpose of waging war by destruction of life or property, are familiar examples of belligerents who are generally deemed not to be entitled to the status of prisoners of war, but to be offenders against the law of war subject to trial and punishment by military tribunals. *See* Winthrop, Military Law, 2d ed., pp. 1196–97, 1219–21; Instructions for the Government of Armies of the

United States in the Field, approved by the President, General Order No. 100, April 24, 1863, §§ IV and V.

Such was the practice of our own military authorities before the adoption of the Constitution, and during the Mexican and Civil Wars. . . .

Specification 1 states that petitioners, "being enemies of the United States and acting for . . . the German Reich, a belligerent enemy nation, secretly and covertly passed, in civilian dress, contrary to the law of war, through the military and naval lines and defenses of the United States . . . and went behind such lines, contrary to the law of war, in civilian dress . . . for the purpose of committing . . . hostile acts, and, in particular, to destroy certain war industries, war utilities and war materials within the United States."

This specification so plainly alleges violation of the law of war as to require but brief discussion of petitioners' contentions. As we have seen, entry upon our territory in time of war by enemy belligerents, including those acting under the direction of the armed forces of the enemy, for the purpose of destroying property used or useful in prosecuting the war, is a hostile and warlike act. It subjects those who participate in it without uniform to the punishment prescribed by the law of war for unlawful belligerents. . . .

Citizenship in the United States of an enemy belligerent does not relieve him from the consequences of a belligerency which is unlawful because in violation of the law of war. Citizens who associate themselves with the military arm of the enemy government, and with its aid, guidance and direction enter this country bent on hostile acts, are enemy belligerents within the meaning of the Hague Convention and the law of war. . . .

Presentment by a grand jury and trial by a jury of the vicinage where the crime was committed were at the time of the adoption of the Constitution familiar parts of the machinery for criminal trials in the civil courts. But they were procedures unknown to military tribunals, which are not courts in the sense of the Judiciary Article, *Ex parte Vallandigham,* 1 Wall. 243; *In re Vidal,* 179 U.S. 126, 21 S.Ct. 48; cf. *Williams v. United States,* 289 U.S. 553, and which in the natural course of events are usually called upon to function under conditions precluding resort to such procedures. As this Court has often recognized, it was not the purpose or effect of § 2 of Article III, read in the light of the common law, to enlarge the then existing right to a jury trial. The object was to preserve unimpaired trial by jury in all those cases in which it had been recognized by the common law and in all cases of a like nature as they might arise in the future, *District of Columbia v. Colts,* 282 U.S. 63, but not to bring within the sweep of the guaranty those cases in which it was then well understood that a jury trial could not be demanded as of right.

The Fifth and Sixth Amendments, while guaranteeing the continuance of certain incidents of trial by jury which Article III, § 2 had left unmentioned, did not enlarge the right to jury trial as it had been established by that Article. *Callan v. Wilson,* 127 U.S. 540, 549. . . .

NOTES

1. Quirin: *Not a Happy Precedent*? The Nazi saboteurs were tried by a military commission in closed courtroom during July, 1942. The Supreme Court was called into special session on July 29 and on July 31 it issued a short per curium order upholding the legality of the military commissions. Six of the convicted saboteurs were put to death on August 3, 1942. The Court's opinion was issued months later, after sharp disagreement emerged among the Justices as to whether the military commission ordered by the president followed the procedures required by the Articles of War and whether Congress could, as a matter of constitutional law, limit the president's use of military commissions during war. The final opinion, excerpted above, did not resolve these issues. *See* G. Edward White, *Felix Frankfurter's "Soliloquy" in* Ex parte Quirin, 5 GREEN BAG 2d 423 (2002). Does the president's Commander-in-Chief power allow him to disregard congressional limitation on the use of military commissions? How relevant is Congress's power to "make Rules for the Government and Regulation of the land and naval Forces"?

2. *Enemy Alien Detainees and the Right of* Habeas Corpus. Why were the *Quirin* petitioners entitled to petition a federal court at all? In *Johnson v. Eisentrager*, 339 U.S. 763 (1950), the Supreme Court held that twenty-one German nationals captured in China were "enemy aliens" who had violated the laws of war by continuing military activity after the surrender of Germany, and were not entitled to the *habeas corpus* rights for which they had petitioned. The *Eisentrager* petitioners were convicted and sentenced in China by a U.S. military commission of violating the laws of war. At the time they lodged their *habeas* petition, they were held by the U.S. Army in a U.S.-occupied part of Germany. Their *habeas* action sought to argue in U.S. court that their trial, conviction and punishment violated Articles I and III, and the Fifth Amendment of the U.S. Constitution. How do the *Quirin* petitioners differ from the *Eisentrager* petitioners? Keep that question in mind as you read the rest of this Section, which considers the scope of the right to petition a federal court for a writ of *habeas corpus*, as well as the constitutional limits on the use of military commissions.

NOTE ON GUANTÁNAMO DETAINEES: HABEAS RIGHTS AND MILITARY COMMISSIONS

Following the attacks of September 11, 2001, a large number of individuals were detained as suspected terrorists at the U.S. naval base at Guantánamo Bay, Cuba. According to the Bush Administration, these "combatants" could be held for the duration of the hostilities with Al Qaeda, but would not be accorded the status of "prisoners of war" since the means and methods of their warfare made them "unlawful" or "unprivileged" combatants. Could these individuals challenge in U.S. courts the fact of their detention, such as on grounds of mistaken identity?

Further, President Bush issued a "military order" providing for prosecution for war crimes of some of those suspects before newly established military commissions, rather than in U.S. civilian courts or regular U.S. military courts. Military Order of November 13, 2001, 66 Fed. Reg. 57,833 (Nov. 16, 2001). The military order and its implementing regulations called for a military judge to preside over a trial of the detainee on charges of war crimes, with special rules on evidence and hearsay, before a panel of U.S. service members who would decide whether to convict and, if so, the appropriate sentence, including the possibility of the death penalty. Could these individuals challenge in U.S. courts the military order, its implementing regulations, and the decisions reached during the trials?

Because the detainees were held outside the territory of the United States, the executive branch, relying upon *Eisentrager,* argued that they were not entitled to the right of *habeas corpus*. In *Rasul v. Bush*, 542 U.S. 466 (2004), the Supreme Court held that U.S. district courts had jurisdiction under the federal *habeas* statute to hear the claims of detainees (in that case, two Australians and twelve Kuwaitis). The Court distinguished *Eisentrager*:

> Petitioners in these cases differ from the *Eisentrager* detainees in important respects: They are not nationals of countries at war with the United States, and they deny that they have engaged in or plotted acts of aggression against the United States; they have never been afforded access to any tribunal, much less charged with and convicted of wrongdoing; and for more than two years they have been imprisoned in territory over which the United States exercises exclusive jurisdiction and control.
>
> Not only are petitioners differently situated from the *Eisentrager* detainees, but the Court in *Eisentrager* made quite clear that all six of the facts critical to its disposition were relevant only to the question of the prisoners' *constitutional* entitlement to *habeas* corpus. *Id.,* at 777. The Court had far less to say on the question of the petitioners' *statutory* entitlement to *habeas* review. Its only statement on the subject was a passing reference to the absence of statutory authorization: "Nothing in the text of the Constitution extends such a right, nor does anything in our statutes." *Id.,* at 768.

542 U.S. at 476, 478. Statutory *habeas* rights, the *Rasul* Court held, applied in any territory over which the United States had "exclusive jurisdiction and control," which included Guantánamo Bay. *Id.* at 476.

In the wake of the decision in *Rasul*, the executive branch instituted a process for reviewing whether each detainee was properly regarded as a "combatant" against the United States. These Combatant Status Review Tribunals (CSRTs) provided for an individualized assessment of each detainee, but were criticized for lax evidentiary standards, the inability of detainees to retain their own counsel, and their inability to call as witnesses persons who could testify as to their innocence. Separately, the executive branch also commenced an administrative process for "continuing threat" assessments, in which the government would determine whether a combatant was no longer a threat to the United States, and thus could be released. What standards should be applied when considering whether to release such individuals? For a discussion, see Sean D. Murphy, *Evolving Geneva Convention Paradigms in the "War on Terrorism:" Applying the Core Rules to the Release of Persons Deemed "Unprivileged Combatants,"* 75 GEO. WASH. L. REV. 1105 (2007).

In 2005, Congress enacted the Detainee Treatment Act of 2005, Pub. L. No. 109–148 (2005) (DTA), which revoked the statutory basis for federal court jurisdiction over *habeas* claims by the detainees (at least with respect to claims not already pending). Instead, the DTA created jurisdiction in the D.C. Circuit Court of Appeals only to hear appeals of final decisions of the military commissions.

Decisions such as *Eisentrager, Quirin*, and *Rasul* set the stage for the Supreme Court's consideration of the legality of prosecutions of the detainees before military commissions established by the president's military order. In *Hamdan v. Rumsfeld*, 548 U.S. 557 (2006), the Supreme Court decided that the military commission convened to try Hamdan lacked the power to proceed because its structure and procedures violated an existing statute, the UCMJ. The DTA did not deprive the court of *habeas* jurisdiction because the *Hamdan* case was already pending. On the constitutional issue, the Court reasoned the president does have the constitutional power to convene military commissions, but that power is shared with Congress, and Congress may impose limitations on the exercise of the power. Although the UCMJ largely regulates the conduct of regular military courts (courts martial), it also imposes two important limitations on the president's power to convene military commissions.

First, the military commissions should not deviate unnecessarily from the procedures by which courts martial operate; military commission procedures must be uniform with those of courts martial insofar as practical. 10 U.S.C. § 836 (2006). In this case, the Court found that the procedures governing Hamdan's military commission did deviate in significant ways without justification, such as by allowing the accused to be excluded from the proceedings even in the absence of any disruptive conduct.

Second, the military commissions must operate in accordance with the "laws of war," including the 1949 Geneva Conventions and customary international law. 10 U.S.C. § 821 (2006). To what extent did the conflict with Al Qaeda fall within the scope of the 1949 Geneva Conventions, which only addresses "armed conflicts"? Since Al Qaeda is not a State, arguably the conflict at issue was not an inter-state armed conflict of the kind regulated by the Conventions. However, the Court found that the conflict between the United States and Al Qaeda is an "armed conflict not of an international character" that falls within the scope of Common Article 3 of the 1949 Geneva

Conventions. *See* Geneva Convention (III) Relative to the Treatment of Prisoners of War, Aug. 12, 1949, art. 3, 6 U.S.T. 3316, 75 U.N.T.S. 135. That article prohibits "the passing of sentences and the carrying out of executions without previous judgment pronounced by a regularly constituted court affording all the judicial guarantees which are recognized as indispensable by civilized peoples." *Id.* art. 3(1)(d). According to the Court, the Hamdan military commission was not such a court since it had not been established by congressional statute. Among other things, the Court stated:

> For, regardless of the nature of the rights conferred on Hamdan, cf. *United States v. Rauscher,* 119 U.S. 407 (1886), they are, as the Government does not dispute, part of the law of war. *See Hamdi,* 542 U.S., at 520–21 (plurality opinion). And compliance with the law of war is the condition upon which the authority set forth in Article 21 is granted. . . .
>
> Common Article 3, then, is applicable here and, as indicated above, requires that Hamdan be tried by a "regularly constituted court affording all the judicial guarantees which are recognized as indispensable by civilized peoples." 6 U.S.T., at 3320 (Art. 3, ¶ 1(d)). . . .

548 U.S. at 628, 631. Writing for four Justices, Justice Stevens also stated:

> We agree with JUSTICE KENNEDY that the procedures adopted to try Hamdan deviate from those governing courts-martial in ways not justified by any "evident practical need," *post,* at 2805, and for that reason, at least, fail to afford the requisite guarantees. *See post,* at 2803, 2804–2808. We add only that, as noted in Part VI-A, *supra,* various provisions of Commission Order No. 1 dispense with the principles, articulated in Article 75 and indisputably part of the customary international law, that an accused must, absent disruptive conduct or consent, be present for his trial and must be privy to the evidence against him. . . .
>
> Common Article 3 obviously tolerates a great degree of flexibility in trying individuals captured during armed conflict; its requirements are general ones, crafted to accommodate a wide variety of legal systems. But *requirements* they are nonetheless. The commission that the President has convened to try Hamdan does not meet those requirements.

548 U.S. at 634–35.

Moreover, customary international law also featured in the Court's reasoning. A plurality of the Court also based its decision on the trial guarantees contained in Article 75 of Protocol I to the Geneva Conventions, a treaty which the U.S. has *not* ratified, but whose provisions have come to constitute customary international law. *See id.* at 633. Justice Stevens wrote:

> Inextricably intertwined with the question of regular constitution is the evaluation of the procedures governing the

> tribunal and whether they afford "all the judicial guarantees which are recognized as indispensable by civilized peoples." 6 U.S.T., at 3320 (Art. 3, ¶ 1(d)). Like the phrase "regularly constituted court," this phrase is not defined in the text of the Geneva Conventions. But it must be understood to incorporate at least the barest of those trial protections that have been recognized by customary international law. Many of these are described in Article 75 of Protocol I to the Geneva Conventions of 1949, adopted in 1977 (Protocol I). Although the United States declined to ratify Protocol I, its objections were not to Article 75 thereof. Indeed, it appears that the Government "regard[s] the provisions of Article 75 as an articulation of safeguards to which all persons in the hands of an enemy are entitled." Taft, The Law of Armed Conflict After 9/11: Some Salient Features, 28 Yale J. Int'l L. 319, 322 (2003). Among the rights set forth in Article 75 is the "right to be tried in [one's] presence." Protocol I, Art. 75(4)(e). [footnote omitted].

Id. at 633.

It is not clear from the opinion whether the Court believes that the custom evolved from State practice in conformity with the treaty provisions, or whether it was a separate and existing norm in customary international law. Does consistent State practice in conformity with multilateral treaty obligations establish new customary international law obligations? Will U.S. courts enforce this customary law even in the face of resistance by the U.S. government? Does such resistance rise to the level of persistent objector status?

In his concurrence in *Hamdan*, Justice Kennedy reasoned that the president had acted within Justice Jackson's third category, where the power of the president "is at its lowest ebb":

> In this case, as the Court observes, the President has acted in a field with a history of congressional participation and regulation. In the Uniform Code of Military Justice (UCMJ), 10 U.S.C. § 801 *et seq.*, which Congress enacted, building on earlier statutes, in 1950, see Act of May 5, 1950, ch. 169, 64 Stat. 107, and later amended, see, *e.g.*, Military Justice Act of 1968, 82 Stat. 1335, Congress has set forth governing principles for military courts. The UCMJ as a whole establishes an intricate system of military justice. It authorizes courts-martial in various forms; it regulates the organization and procedure of those courts; it defines offenses and rights for the accused; and it provides mechanisms for appellate review. As explained below, the statute further recognizes that special military commissions may be convened to try war crimes. While these laws provide authority for certain forms of military courts, they also impose limitations, at least two of which control this case. If the President has exceeded these limits, this becomes a case of conflict

> between Presidential and congressional action—a case within Justice Jackson's third category, not the second or first. . . .
>
> [A]s presently structured, Hamdan's military commission exceeds the bounds Congress has placed on the President's authority in §§ 836 and 821 of the UCMJ. Because Congress has prescribed these limits, Congress can change them, requiring a new analysis consistent with the Constitution and other governing laws. At this time, however, we must apply the standards Congress has provided. By those standards the military commission is deficient.

Hamdan, 548 U.S. at 638–39, 653.

By contrast, Justice Thomas in dissent saw Jackson's first category as the relevant one; he focuses on a different statute, one that authorized the use of military force in response to the September 11 attacks:

> [T]he President's decision to try Hamdan before a military commission for his involvement with al Qaeda is entitled to a heavy measure of deference. In the present conflict, Congress has authorized the President "to use all necessary and appropriate force against those nations, organizations, or persons *he determines* planned, authorized, committed, or aided the terrorist attacks that occurred on September 11, 2001 . . . in order to prevent any future acts of international terrorism against the United States by such nations, organizations or persons." Authorization for Use of Military Force (AUMF) 115 Stat. 224, note following 50 U.S.C. § 1541 (2000 ed., Supp. III) (emphasis added). As a plurality of the Court observed in *Hamdi*, the "capture, detention, and *trial* of unlawful combatants, by 'universal agreement and practice,' are 'important incident[s] of war,'" *Hamdi*, 542 U.S., at 518 (quoting *Quirin*, *supra*; emphasis added), and are therefore "an exercise of the 'necessary and appropriate force' Congress has authorized the President to use." *Hamdi*, 542 U.S., at 518; *id.*, at 587 (THOMAS, J., dissenting). *Hamdi*'s observation that military commissions are included within the AUMF's authorization is supported by this Court's previous recognition that "[a]n important incident to the conduct of war is the adoption of measures by the military commander, not only to repel and defeat the enemy, but to seize and subject to disciplinary measures those enemies who, in their attempt to thwart or impede our military effort, have violated the law of war." *In re Yamashita*, 327 U.S. 1 (1946). . . .

Id. at 680–81.

Who do you think had the better argument? How should courts ascertain Congress's posture for *Youngstown* purposes when there are potentially different statutes in play, enacted at different points in time?

In response to the Court's decision in *Hamdan*, Congress and the president collaborated to ground the president's military commissions in a new statute, the Military Commissions Act of 2006, Pub. L. No. 109–366, 120 Stat. 2600 (Oct. 17, 2006). The MCA largely maintained the structure and process for the commissions that had been developed by the executive branch. While some modifications were made to the prior scheme, modeled after rules contained in the UCMJ, the MCA still exempted the military commissions from certain key UCMJ rules, including the defendant's right to a speedy trial and the right to be warned about the possibility of self-incrimination. Importantly, the MCA clarified that persons exposed to the jurisdiction of the commissions were not just those who engaged in hostilities against the United States or its allies, but also those who purposefully and materially supported such hostilities. Further, the MCA created an executive branch Court of Military Commission Review, to which a final decision of a military commission on an issue of law could be appealed. If that appeal failed, the accused could appeal the decision to the D.C. Circuit Court of Appeals, which in turn could be reviewed by the Supreme Court.

As noted above, the DTA revoked federal court jurisdiction over *habeas* claims by the detainees, an approach maintained under the MCA. Nevertheless, the Guantánamo detainees still sought to bring *habeas corpus* actions in U.S. courts, challenging the fact of their detention and, in some instances, their prosecution before the re-engineered military commissions. Should such detainees have a constitutional right to bring petitions for *habeas corpus* in U.S. courts, notwithstanding Congress and the president's decision to the contrary?

Before turning to the constitutional rights of Guantánamo detainees to bring *habeas* petitions, consider the following case on the extraterritorial application of the Fourth Amendment.

UNITED STATES V. VERDUGO-URQUIDEZ

494 U.S. 259 (1990).

[In this case, a Mexican citizen transported to the United States to stand trial for drug-related crimes sought to quash the evidence obtained from a search and seizure of his home in Mexico. The search was conducted by the Drug Enforcement Agency and Mexican officials without a U.S.-issued warrant. The Court advanced a narrow view of the Fourth Amendment language which protects "the right of the people," reasoning that this language was limited to "a class of persons who are part of a national community or who have otherwise developed sufficient connection with this country to be considered part of that community."]

The global view taken by the Court of Appeals of the application of the Constitution is also contrary to this Court's decisions in the *Insular Cases*, which held that not every constitutional provision applies to governmental activity even where the United States has sovereign power. . . . In *Dorr*, we declared the general rule that in an unincorporated territory—one not clearly destined for statehood—Congress was not required to adopt "a system of laws which shall include the right of trial by jury, and that *the Constitution does not, without legislation and of its own force, carry such right to territory so situated.*" 195 U.S., at 149 (emphasis added). Only "fundamental" constitutional rights are guaranteed to inhabitants of those territories. *Id.*, at 148. . . . If that is true with respect to territories ultimately governed by Congress, respondent's claim that the protections of the Fourth Amendment extend to aliens in foreign nations is even weaker. And certainly, it is not open to us in light of the *Insular Cases* to endorse the view that every constitutional provision applies wherever the United States Government exercises its power.

Indeed, we have rejected the claim that aliens are entitled to Fifth Amendment rights outside the sovereign territory of the United States. . . . If such is true of the Fifth Amendment, which speaks in the relatively universal term of "person," it would seem even more true with respect to the Fourth Amendment, which applies only to "the people."

To support his all-encompassing view of the Fourth Amendment, respondent points to language from the plurality opinion in *Reid v. Covert*, 354 U.S. 1 (1957). *Reid* involved an attempt by Congress to subject the wives of American servicemen to trial by military tribunals without the protection of the Fifth and Sixth Amendments. The Court held that it was unconstitutional to apply the Uniform Code of Military Justice to the trials of the American women for capital crimes. Four Justices "reject[ed] the idea that when the United States acts *against citizens* abroad it can do so free of the Bill of Rights." *Id.*, at 5 (emphasis added). The plurality went on to say:

> The United States is entirely a creature of the Constitution. Its power and authority have no other source. It can only act in accordance with all the limitations imposed by the Constitution. When the Government reaches out to punish a *citizen* who is abroad, the shield which the Bill of Rights and other parts of the Constitution provide to protect his life and liberty should not be stripped away just because he happens to be in another land." *Id.*, at 5–6 (emphasis added) (footnote omitted).

Respondent urges that we interpret this discussion to mean that federal officials are constrained by the Fourth Amendment wherever and against whomever they act. But the holding of *Reid* stands for no such sweeping proposition: it decided that United States citizens stationed abroad could invoke the protection of the Fifth and Sixth Amendments. The concurrences by Justices Frankfurter and Harlan in *Reid* resolved the case on much narrower grounds than the plurality and declined even to hold that United States citizens were entitled to the full range of constitutional protections in all overseas criminal prosecutions. . . . Since respondent is not a United States citizen, he can derive no comfort from the *Reid* holding.

Verdugo-Urquidez also relies on a series of cases in which we have held that aliens enjoy certain constitutional rights. . . . These cases, however, establish only that aliens receive constitutional protections when they have come within the territory of the United States and developed substantial connections with this country. . . . Respondent is an alien who has had no previous significant voluntary connection with the United States, so these cases avail him not.

JUSTICE KENNEDY concurred, but wrote separately, reasoning in part that:

The conditions and considerations of this case would make adherence to the Fourth Amendment's warrant requirement impracticable and anomalous. Just as the Constitution in the *Insular Cases* did not require Congress to implement all constitutional guarantees in its territories because of their "wholly dissimilar traditions and institutions," the Constitution does not require United States agents to obtain a warrant when searching the foreign home of a nonresident alien. If the search had occurred in a residence within the United States, I have little doubt that the full protections of the Fourth Amendment would apply. But that is not this case. The absence of local judges or magistrates available to issue warrants, the differing and perhaps unascertainable conceptions of reasonableness and privacy that prevail abroad, and the need to cooperate with foreign officials all indicate that the Fourth Amendment's warrant requirement should not apply in Mexico as it does in this country. For this reason, in addition to the other persuasive justifications stated by the Court, I agree that no violation of the Fourth Amendment has occurred in the case before us. The rights of a citizen, as to whom the United States has continuing obligations, are not presented by this case.

BOUMEDIENE V. BUSH

553 U.S. 723 (2008).

JUSTICE KENNEDY delivered the opinion of the Court.

Petitioners are aliens designated as enemy combatants and detained at the United States Naval Station at Guantanamo Bay, Cuba. There are others detained there, also aliens, who are not parties to this suit.

Petitioners present a question not resolved by our earlier cases relating to the detention of aliens at Guantanamo: whether they have the constitutional privilege of *habeas corpus*, a privilege not to be withdrawn except in conformance with the Suspension Clause, Art. I, § 9, cl. 2. We hold these petitioners do have the *habeas corpus* privilege. Congress has enacted a statute, the Detainee Treatment Act of 2005 (DTA), 119 Stat. 2739, that provides certain procedures for review of the detainees' status. We hold that those procedures are not an adequate and effective substitute for *habeas corpus*. Therefore § 7 of the Military Commissions Act of 2006

(MCA), 28 U.S.C.A. § 2241(e) (Supp. 2007), operates as an unconstitutional suspension of the writ. We do not address whether the President has authority to detain these petitioners nor do we hold that the writ must issue. These and other questions regarding the legality of the detention are to be resolved in the first instance by the District Court. . . .

The Government's formal sovereignty-based test raises troubling separation-of-powers concerns as well. The political history of Guantanamo illustrates the deficiencies of this approach. The United States has maintained complete and uninterrupted control of the bay for over 100 years. . . . [A]lthough it recognized, by entering into the 1903 Lease Agreement, that Cuba retained "ultimate sovereignty" over Guantanamo, the United States continued to maintain the same plenary control it had enjoyed since 1898. Yet the Government's view is that the Constitution had no effect there, at least as to noncitizens, because the United States disclaimed sovereignty in the formal sense of the term. The necessary implication of the argument is that by surrendering formal sovereignty over any unincorporated territory to a third party, while at the same time entering into a lease that grants total control over the territory back to the United States, it would be possible for the political branches to govern without legal constraint.

Our basic charter cannot be contracted away like this. The Constitution grants Congress and the President the power to acquire, dispose of, and govern territory, not the power to decide when and where its terms apply. Even when the United States acts outside its borders, its powers are not "absolute and unlimited" but are subject "to such restrictions as are expressed in the Constitution." Abstaining from questions involving formal sovereignty and territorial governance is one thing. To hold the political branches have the power to switch the Constitution on or off at will is quite another. The former position reflects this Court's recognition that certain matters requiring political judgments are best left to the political branches. The latter would permit a striking anomaly in our tripartite system of government, leading to a regime in which Congress and the President, not this Court, say "what the law is." *Marbury v. Madison,* 1 Cranch 137 (1803). . . .

[T]he outlines of a framework for determining the reach of the Suspension Clause are suggested by the factors the Court relied upon in *Eisentrager*. In addition to the practical concerns discussed above, the *Eisentrager* Court found relevant that each petitioner:

> "(a) is an enemy alien; (b) has never been or resided in the United States; (c) was captured outside of our territory and there held in military custody as a prisoner of war; (d) was tried and convicted by a Military Commission sitting outside the United States; (e) for

offenses against laws of war committed outside the United States;
(f) and is at all times imprisoned outside the United States."

Based on this language from *Eisentrager,* and the reasoning in our other extraterritoriality opinions, we conclude that at least three factors are relevant in determining the reach of the Suspension Clause: (1) the citizenship and status of the detainee and the adequacy of the process through which that status determination was made; (2) the nature of the sites where apprehension and then detention took place; and (3) the practical obstacles inherent in resolving the prisoner's entitlement to the writ.

Applying this framework, we note at the onset that the status of these detainees is a matter of dispute. Petitioners, like those in *Eisentrager,* are not American citizens. But the petitioners in *Eisentrager* did not contest, it seems, the Court's assertion that they were "enemy alien[s]." In the instant cases, by contrast, the detainees deny they are enemy combatants. They have been afforded some process in CSRT proceedings to determine their status; but, unlike in *Eisentrager,* there has been no trial by military commission for violations of the laws of war. The difference is not trivial. The records from the *Eisentrager* trials suggest that, well before the petitioners brought their case to this Court, there had been a rigorous adversarial process to test the legality of their detention. The *Eisentrager* petitioners were charged by a bill of particulars that made detailed factual allegations against them. To rebut the accusations, they were entitled to representation by counsel, allowed to introduce evidence on their own behalf, and permitted to cross-examine the prosecution's witnesses.

In comparison the procedural protections afforded to the detainees in the CSRT hearings are far more limited, and, we conclude, fall well short of the procedures and adversarial mechanisms that would eliminate the need for habeas corpus review. Although the detainee is assigned a "Personal Representative" to assist him during CSRT proceedings, the Secretary of the Navy's memorandum makes clear that person is not the detainee's lawyer or even his "advocate." The Government's evidence is accorded a presumption of validity. The detainee is allowed to present "reasonably available" evidence, but his ability to rebut the Government's evidence against him is limited by the circumstances of his confinement and his lack of counsel at this stage. And although the detainee can seek review of his status determination in the Court of Appeals, that review process cannot cure all defects in the earlier proceedings.

As to the second factor relevant to this analysis, the detainees here are similarly situated to the *Eisentrager* petitioners in that the sites of their apprehension and detention are technically outside the sovereign territory of the United States. As noted earlier, this is a factor that weighs against finding they have rights under the Suspension Clause. But there are critical differences between Landsberg Prison, circa 1950, and the United States Naval Station at Guantanamo Bay in 2008. Unlike its present control over the naval station, the United States' control over the prison in Germany was neither absolute nor indefinite. Like all parts of occupied Germany, the prison was under the jurisdiction of the combined Allied Forces. The Allies had not planned a long-term occupation of Germany, nor did they intend to displace all German institutions even during the period of occupation. The Court's holding in *Eisentrager* was thus consistent with the Insular Cases, where it had held there was no need to extend full constitutional protections to territories the States did not intend to govern indefinitely. Guantanamo Bay, on the other hand, is no transient possession. In every practical sense Guantanamo is not abroad; it is within the constant jurisdiction of the United States.

As to the third factor, we recognize, as the Court did in *Eisentrager,* that there are costs to holding the Suspension Clause applicable in a case of military detention abroad. Habeas corpus proceedings may require expenditure of funds by the Government and may divert the attention of military personnel from other pressing tasks. While we are sensitive to these concerns, we do not find them dispositive. Compliance with any judicial process requires some incremental expenditure of resources. Yet civilian courts and the Armed Forces have functioned along side each other at various points in our history. The Government presents no credible arguments that the military mission at Guantanamo would be compromised if habeas corpus courts had jurisdiction to hear the detainees' claims. And in light of the plenary control the United States asserts over the base, none are apparent to us.

It is true that before today the Court has never held that noncitizens detained by our Government in territory over which another country maintains de jure sovereignty have any rights under our Constitution. But the cases before us lack any precise historical parallel. They involve individuals detained by executive order for the duration of a conflict that, if measured from September 11, 2001, to the present, is already among the longest wars in American history. See Oxford Companion to American Military History 849 (1999). The detainees, moreover, are held in a territory that, while technically not part of the United States, is under the complete and total control of our Government. Under these circumstances the lack of a precedent on point is no barrier to our holding.

We hold that Art. I, § 9, cl. 2, of the Constitution has full effect at Guantanamo Bay. If the privilege of *habeas corpus* is to be denied to the detainees now before us, Congress must act in accordance with the requirements of the Suspension Clause. *Cf. Hamdi*, 542 U.S., at 564 (SCALIA, J., dissenting) ("[I]ndefinite imprisonment on reasonable suspicion is not an available option of treatment for those accused of aiding the enemy, absent a suspension of the writ"). This Court may not impose a de facto suspension by abstaining from these controversies. *See Hamdan*, 548 U.S., at 585, n.16 ("[A]bstention is not appropriate in cases . . . in which the legal challenge 'turn[s] on the status of the persons as to whom the military asserted its power' " (quoting *Schlesinger v. Councilman*, 420 U.S. 738, 759 (1975))). The MCA does not purport to be a formal suspension of the writ; and the Government, in its submissions to us, has not argued that it is. Petitioners, therefore, are entitled to the privilege of *habeas corpus* to challenge the legality of their detention. . . .

Our opinion does not undermine the Executive's powers as Commander in Chief. On the contrary, the exercise of those powers is vindicated, not eroded, when confirmed by the Judicial Branch. Within the Constitution's separation-of-powers structure, few exercises of judicial power are as legitimate or as necessary as the responsibility to hear challenges to the authority of the Executive to imprison a person. Some of these petitioners have been in custody for six years with no definitive judicial determination as to the legality of their detention. Their access to the writ is a necessity to determine the lawfulness of their status, even if, in the end, they do not obtain the relief they seek.

It bears repeating that our opinion does not address the content of the law that governs petitioners' detention. That is a matter yet to be determined. We hold that petitioners may invoke the fundamental procedural protections of *habeas corpus*. The laws and Constitution are designed to survive, and remain in force, in extraordinary times. Liberty and security can be reconciled; and in our system they are reconciled within the framework of the law. The Framers decided that *habeas corpus*, a right of first importance, must be a part of that framework, a part of that law.

JUSTICE SCALIA, with whom THE CHIEF JUSTICE, JUSTICE THOMAS, and JUSTICE ALITO join, dissenting.

Today, for the first time in our Nation's history, the Court confers a constitutional right to *habeas corpus* on alien enemies detained abroad by our military forces in the course of an ongoing war. The Chief Justice's dissent, which I join, shows that the procedures prescribed by Congress in the Detainee Treatment Act provide the essential protections that *habeas corpus* guarantees; there has thus been no suspension of the writ, and no basis exists for judicial intervention beyond what the Act allows. My problem with today's opinion is more fundamental still: The writ of *habeas corpus* does not, and never has, run in favor of aliens abroad; the Suspension Clause thus has no application, and the Court's intervention in this military matter is entirely *ultra vires*.

I shall devote most of what will be a lengthy opinion to the legal errors contained in the opinion of the Court. Contrary to my usual practice, however, I think it appropriate to begin with a description of the disastrous consequences of what the Court has done today.

I

America is at war with radical Islamists. The enemy began by killing Americans and American allies abroad: 241 at the Marine barracks in Lebanon, 19 at the Khobar Towers in Dhahran, 224 at our embassies in Dar es Salaam and Nairobi, and 17 on the USS Cole in Yemen. See National Commission on Terrorist Attacks upon the United States, The 9/11 Commission Report, pp. 60–61, 70, 190 (2004). On September 11, 2001, the enemy brought the battle to American soil, killing 2,749 at the Twin Towers in New York City, 184 at the Pentagon in Washington, D. C., and 40 in Pennsylvania. *See id.*, at 552, n. 9. It has threatened further attacks against our homeland; one need only walk about buttressed and barricaded Washington, or board a plane anywhere in the country, to know that the threat is a serious one. Our Armed Forces are now in the field against the enemy, in Afghanistan and Iraq. Last week, 13 of our countrymen in arms were killed.

The game of bait-and-switch that today's opinion plays upon the Nation's Commander in Chief will make the war harder on us. It will almost certainly cause more Americans to be killed. That consequence would be tolerable if necessary to preserve a time-honored legal principle vital to our constitutional Republic. But it is this Court's blatant abandonment of such a principle that produces the decision today. The President relied on our settled precedent in *Johnson v. Eisentrager*, 339 U.S. 763 (1950), when he established the prison at Guantanamo Bay for enemy aliens. . . .

In the long term, then, the Court's decision today accomplishes little, except perhaps to reduce the well-being of enemy combatants that the Court ostensibly seeks to protect. In the short term, however, the decision is devastating. At least 30 of those prisoners hitherto released from Guantanamo Bay have returned to the battlefield. *See* S. Rep. No. 110–90, pt. 7, p. 13 (2007) (Minority Views of Sens. Kyl, Sessions, Graham, Cornyn, and Coburn) (hereinafter Minority Report). Some have been captured or killed. *See ibid.; see also* Mintz, Released Detainees Rejoining the Fight, Washington Post, Oct. 22, 2004, pp. A1, A12. But others have succeeded in carrying on their atrocities against innocent civilians. . . .

These, mind you, were detainees whom the *military* had concluded were not enemy combatants. Their return to the kill illustrates the incredible difficulty of assessing who is and who is not an enemy combatant in a foreign theater of operations where the environment does not lend itself to rigorous evidence collection. Astoundingly, the Court today raises the bar, requiring military officials to appear before civilian courts and defend their decisions under procedural and evidentiary rules that go beyond what Congress has specified. . . .

[E]ven when the military has evidence that it can bring forward, it is often foolhardy to release that evidence to the attorneys representing our enemies. And one escalation of procedures that the Court is clear about is affording the detainees increased access to witnesses (perhaps troops serving in Afghanistan?) and to classified information. During the 1995 prosecution of Omar Abdel Rahman, federal prosecutors gave the names of 200 unindicted co-conspirators to the "Blind Sheik's" defense lawyers; that information was in the hands of Osama Bin Laden within two weeks. *See* Minority Report 14–15. . . .

And today it is not just the military that the Court elbows aside. A mere two Terms ago in *Hamdan v. Rumsfeld*, 548 U.S. 557 (2006), when the Court held (quite amazingly) that the Detainee Treatment Act of 2005 had not stripped *habeas* jurisdiction over Guantanamo petitioners' claims, four Members of today's five-Justice majority joined an opinion saying the following:

"Nothing prevents the President from returning to Congress to seek the authority [for trial by military commission] he believes necessary.

"Where, as here, no emergency prevents consultation with Congress, judicial insistence upon that consultation does not weaken our Nation's ability to deal with danger. To the contrary, that insistence strengthens the Nation's ability to determine—through democratic means—how best to do so. The Constitution places its faith in those democratic means." *Id.*, at 636 (BREYER, J., concurring).

Turns out they were just kidding. For in response, Congress, at the President's request, quickly enacted the Military Commissions Act, emphatically reasserting that it did not want these prisoners filing *habeas* petitions. It is therefore clear that Congress and the Executive—*both* political branches—have determined that limiting the role of civilian courts in adjudicating whether prisoners captured abroad are properly detained is important to success in the war that some 190,000 of our men and women are now fighting. . . .

But it does not matter. The Court today decrees that no good reason to accept the judgment of the other two branches is "apparent." *Ante*, at 40. "The Government," it declares, "presents no credible arguments that the military mission at Guantanamo would be compromised if *habeas corpus* courts had jurisdiction to hear the detainees' claims." *Id.*, at 39. What competence does the Court have to second-guess the judgment of Congress and the President on such a point? None whatever. But the Court blunders in nonetheless. Henceforth, as today's opinion makes unnervingly clear, how to handle enemy prisoners in this war will ultimately lie with the branch that knows least about the national security concerns that the subject entails.

NOTES

1. *Lingering Issues.* Arguably, *Boumediene* represents the only time in history that the Court has, during a time of armed conflict, invalidated a major national security policy backed by both Congress and the president. In so doing, *Boumediene* left many questions unanswered. For example, the Court suggested that *habeas* might not be constitutionally required if "suitable alternative processes" were in place. What might those be? For analysis of the case and its implications, see Congressional Research Service, *Closing the Guantanamo Detention Center: Legal Issues*, CRS Rep. R40139 (Feb. 11, 2011); Stephen I. Vladeck, *The D.C. Circuit After* Boumediene, 42 SETON HALL L. REV. 1451 (2011). *Boumediene* also left open whether other constitutional rights in addition to *habeas*, such as the right to due process, apply to Guantánamo detainees. What does the reasoning in *Boumediene* suggest? The D.C. Circuit held that Guantánamo detainees can challenge the conditions of their confinement in a *habeas* petition. *Aamer v. Obama*, 742 F.3d 1023 (D.C. Cir. 2014). *See* Mary Van Houten, *The Post-*Boumediene *Paradox: Habeas Corpus or Due Process?* 67 STAN. L. REV. ONLINE 9 (2014).

What are the implications of the case, now and in the future, for detainees held in places other than Guantánamo, such as in Iraq or Afghanistan? In *Al Maqaleh v. Gates*, 605 F.3d 84 (D.C. Cir. 2010), the D.C. Circuit ruled that Bagram Air Base in Afghanistan, while also a U.S. military base abroad, was not sufficiently analogous to Guantánamo so as to require that *habeas* rights be accorded to the alien detainees held there. For analysis, see Kal Raustiala, Al Maqaleh v. Gates, 104 AM. J. INT'L L. 647 (2010). By contrast, the Supreme Court has said that the *habeas corpus* statute does extend to U.S. nationals held at a U.S. base abroad whenever in the custody of U.S. forces who are subject to a U.S. chain of command, even if acting as part of a multi-national coalition. *Munaf v. Geren*, 553 U.S. 674 (2008). If future prisoners of war who are detained by the United States, following a classic battlefield conflict, can demand *habeas* proceedings, will it create an incentive for the U.S. military to transfer prisoners to allies who might treat them less humanely? Or is such a risk outweighed by the value of ensuring, through judicial review, that the United States treats them properly?

Assuming that a Guantánamo detainee is successful in convincing a U.S. court that he is not a combatant and therefore should be released, what happens if his country will not take him back or if he cannot be repatriated for fear of persecution or torture in his home country? Can the detainee seek an order from the court that he be released into the United States? *See Kiyemba v. Obama*, 555 F.3d 1022 (D.C. Cir. 2009) (the decision to allow such a detainee to enter U.S. territory is a matter for the political branches and not the courts).

Suppose Congress formally suspends the writ of *habeas corpus* for such detainees; what exactly does that empower the president to do? For an argument that exercise of the suspension power only provides narrow authority to restore order and preserve the existence of the government in times of rebellion or invasion, see Amanda Tyler, *Suspension as an Emergency Power*, 118 YALE L.J. 600 (2009).

2. *Reengagement of Guantánamo Detainees.* Justice Scalia warned that the Court's decision would lead to the release of Guantánamo detainees who would re-engage in armed conflict against the United States. According to the Director of National Intelligence, as of late 2017, 714 detainees have been transferred out of Guantánamo, of whom 29% are confirmed or suspected of re-engaging. Those numbers have decreased, however. Of the 182 detainees released since January 2009, only 12% are confirmed or suspected of re-engaging. As of late 2017, 41 detainees remain at Guantánamo.

3. *Should Congress Take Center Stage?* Rather than allowing the courts to resolve these issues piecemeal, should Congress step up to the plate and enact a comprehensive statutory framework, one that addresses issues of coercive interrogation, trial, preventive detention, and related issues? For an argument to that effect, see Benjamin Wittes, *Law and the Long War: The Future of Justice in the Age of Terror* (2008). Wittes notes that in doing so, Congress might well get it wrong, or a statutory scheme that works today might become deficient as social mores, surveillance technology, or other factors change over time. If so, Congress can always re-write the rules. By contrast, when the courts take on the job with a blank legislative slate, they may feel they need to check executive overreaching through resort to the Constitution. That basically means writing the rules in stone, which makes adaptation and revision virtually impossible. Are you persuaded? Or do you think that the process that unfolded post-2001, with the executive branch acting, the courts reacting, and Congress intermittently participating, provides the appropriate inter-branch, incremental process for moving forward? Even if you agree with Wittes, do you think that, politically, Congress is capable of mustering the requisite votes (if necessary, over a presidential veto) for a comprehensive statute?

After taking office in January 2009, President Obama issued an executive order suspending military commission proceedings. Later that year, he signed into law the Military Commissions Act of 2009, Pub. L. 111–84, 123 Stat. 2190 (2009), which amended the Military Commissions Act of 2006 in various respects, but still retained the basic structure of the military commissions. In 2011, after the adoption of new implementing rules and procedures, President Obama lifted his suspension of the military commission proceedings. As of late 2017, eight people have been convicted, either through trial or plea bargain. Those convictions have raised a host of constitutional issues, as the following case illustrates.

BAHLUL V. UNITED STATES

840 F.3d 757 (D.C. Cir. 2016).

PER CURIAM: Bahlul is a member of al Qaeda who assisted Osama bin Laden in planning the September 11, 2001, attacks on the United States.

Bahlul was convicted by a U.S. military commission of the offense of conspiracy to commit war crimes, among other offenses. The U.S. Court of Military Commission Review affirmed Bahlul's conviction. . . .

In this en banc case, Bahlul argues that Articles I and III of the Constitution bar Congress from making conspiracy an offense triable by military commission, because conspiracy is not an offense under the international law of war.

We affirm the judgment of the U.S. Court of Military Commission Review upholding Bahlul's conspiracy conviction. Six judges . . . have voted to affirm. [Four] would affirm because they conclude that, consistent with Articles I and III of the Constitution, Congress may make conspiracy to commit war crimes an offense triable by military commission. They would uphold Bahlul's conspiracy conviction on that basis. [The dissenting judges] conclude that Article III of the Constitution bars Congress from making inchoate conspiracy an offense triable by a law-of-war military commission.

KAVANAUGH, CIRCUIT JUDGE, with whom CIRCUIT JUDGES BROWN and GRIFFITH join, concurring:

This case [raises] one central legal question: Under the U.S. Constitution, may Congress establish military commissions to try unlawful enemy combatants for the offense of conspiracy to commit war crimes, even if conspiracy is not an offense under the international law of war? The answer is yes. We know that from the text and original understanding of the Constitution; the structure of the Constitution; landmark Supreme Court precedent; longstanding congressional practice, as reflected in venerable and contemporary federal statutes; and deeply rooted Executive Branch practice, from the 1800s to the present. . . .

The premise of Bahlul's Article I argument is that Congress's *sole* source of constitutional authority to make offenses triable by military commission is the Define and Punish Clause of Article I. That Clause grants Congress authority to "define and punish . . . Offences against the Law of Nations." U.S. CONST. art. I, § 8, cl. 10. Bahlul argues that the "law of nations" is a synonym for international law, and further contends that conspiracy is not an offense under the international law of war. Therefore, according to Bahlul, Congress lacks power under Article I, Section 8 to make conspiracy an offense triable by military commission.

We need not decide the scope of the Define and Punish Clause in this case. That is because the premise of Bahlul's Article I argument is flawed. Regardless of the scope of the Define and Punish Clause, an issue we do not decide, Congress's Article I authority to establish military commissions—including its authority to determine which crimes may be tried by military commission—does not derive exclusively from that Clause.

Rather, the war powers clauses in Article I, Section 8—including the Declare War Clause and the Captures Clause, together with the Necessary and Proper Clause—supply Congress with ample authority to establish military commissions and make offenses triable by military commission. And the Declare War Clause and the other war powers clauses in Article I do not refer to international law or otherwise impose international law as a constraint on Congress's authority to make offenses triable by military commission.

As the Supreme Court has long recognized, a congressional authorization of war pursuant to the Declare War Clause is understood "by universal agreement and practice" to encompass all of the traditional incidents of war—including the power to kill, capture, and detain enemy combatants, and most relevant here, the power to try unlawful enemy combatants by military commission for war crimes. As Colonel William Winthrop, described by the Supreme Court as the "Blackstone of Military Law," *Reid v. Covert,* 354 U.S. 1, 19 n.38 (1957) (plurality opinion), summarized it: "[I]n general, it is those provisions of the Constitution which empower Congress to 'declare war' and 'raise armies,' and which, in authorizing the initiation of *war*, authorize the employment of all necessary and proper agencies for its due prosecution, from which this tribunal derives its original sanction. . . . The commission is simply an instrumentality for the more efficient execution of the war powers vested in Congress and the power vested in the President as Commander-in-chief in war." . . .

[T]he historical practice in the Executive Branch demonstrates that international law is not a constraint on which offenses may be tried by military commissions. Indeed, perhaps the most telling factor when considering this constitutional question is the deeply rooted history of U.S. military commission trials of the offense of conspiracy, which is not and has never been an offense under the international law of war.

The two most important military commission precedents in U.S. history—the trials of the Lincoln conspirators and the Nazi saboteurs—were trials for the offense of conspiracy.

Consider the trial of the Lincoln conspirators. After seeking the advice of the Attorney General, President Andrew Johnson decided to try the Lincoln conspirators by military commission rather than by criminal trial in civilian court. See Military Commissions, 11 Op. Attorney Gen. 297, 298 (1865). The Lincoln conspirators were expressly charged with and convicted of conspiracy—in that case, conspiracy to violate the law of war by killing the President and Commander in Chief of the Union Army, Abraham Lincoln. Indeed, conspiracy was the only offense charged against them. After an extensive multi-week trial that gripped the Nation and after vigorous argument about the facts and the commission's jurisdiction, numerous conspirators were convicted of conspiracy.

The joint dissent tries to cast doubt on whether the Lincoln conspirators were actually tried for conspiracy. There is no doubt. Consider what a contemporary court said in response to a habeas petition filed by three of the Lincoln conspirators: "[T]he prisoners are guilty of the charge on which they were convicted—of a conspiracy to commit the military crime which one of their number did commit, and some of them of more or less participation." *Ex parte Mudd*, 17 F.Cas. 954 (S.D. Fla. 1868). Indeed, in the prior en banc decision in this case, our Court (joined by one of the judges who joins the joint dissent today) described the Lincoln case as a trial for conspiracy and stated that "the sole offense alleged was conspiracy." *Al Bahlul v. United States*, 767 F.3d 1, 25 (D.C. Cir. 2014) (en banc). Our en banc Court explained that the Lincoln case was a "particularly significant precedent" and a "high-profile example of a conspiracy charge tried by a military commission." *Id.*; *see also Al Bahlul v. United States*, 792 F.3d 1, 59–61 (D.C. Cir. 2015) (Henderson, J., dissenting). . . .

Bahlul also contends that Article III of the U.S. Constitution confines U.S. military commissions to international law of war offenses.

This iteration of Bahlul's argument begins with the premise that Article III vests the judicial power in Article III courts and requires crimes to be tried by jury, not before military commissions.

Based solely on the text of Article III, Bahlul might have a point. But the Supreme Court has long recognized an exception to Article III for military commissions to try enemy war crimes. *See Ex parte Quirin*, 317 U.S. 1, 38–45 (1942); *see also Hamdan v. Rumsfeld*, 548 U.S. 557 (2006).

As explained in Part I of this opinion, the history of U.S. military commissions trying non-international-law-of-war offenses is extensive and dates from the beginning of the Republic. That historical practice therefore amply demonstrates that Article III is not a barrier to U.S. military commission trials of non-international-law-of-war offenses, including the offense of conspiracy to commit war crimes.

Notwithstanding that history, Bahlul says that *Quirin* already considered the military commission exception to Article III and limited the exception to international law of war offenses.

Bahlul's reading of *Quirin* is incorrect. In *Quirin*, the Nazi saboteur defendants claimed that they had a right under Article III to be tried by jury in an Article III federal court and therefore could not be tried by military commission. At some length, the *Quirin* Court specifically considered and rejected the defendants' Article III objection. The Court explained that Article III did not "enlarge the then existing right to a jury trial" beyond the right as it existed at common law. Because the common law did not preclude trial by military commission for war crimes, Article III "cannot be taken to have extended the right to demand a jury to trials by military commission, or to have required that offenses against the law of war not triable by jury at common law be tried only in the civil courts."

As explained above, in reaching its conclusion on the Article III issue, the *Quirin* Court emphasized that Congress—exercising its Article I powers—had made spying an offense triable by military commission since the earliest days of the Republic. The Court stated that the early Congress's enactment of the spying statute "must be regarded as a contemporary construction" of Article III "as not foreclosing trial by military tribunals, without a jury, of offenses against the law of war committed by enemies not in or associated with our Armed Forces." "Such a construction," the Court said, "is entitled to the greatest respect."

The Supreme Court's analysis in *Quirin* is instructive for present purposes because, as noted above, the offense of spying on which the *Quirin* Court relied to answer the Article III objection was not (and is not) an offense under the international law of war. It thus makes little sense to read *Quirin* as barring military commission trials of non-international-law-of-war offenses when *Quirin*, in rejecting a jury trial objection to military commissions, expressly relied on a longstanding statute making spying—a non-international-law-of-war offense—triable by military commission.

In addition, as previously discussed, nothing about the Court's reasoning in *Quirin* rested on whether the offense tried by a military commission was an international law of war offense. The Court never suggested that military commissions are constitutionally permitted only for international law of war offenses. Nor has the Court ever said anything like that in its several later military commission cases. One would have expected the Court to say as much if the Court actually thought as much.

To be sure, the *Quirin* Court referred to international law authorities. But as noted above, the Court discussed those authorities in part because an offense's status as an international law offense is sufficient but not necessary to make an offense triable by military commission under 10 U.S.C. § 821, the statute that used the broad term "law of war" to define offenses triable by military commission.

In short, Article III does not limit U.S. military commissions to international law of war offenses or otherwise foreclose trial of the offense of conspiracy to commit war crimes before U.S. military commissions.

All of that said, the Constitution does not grant Congress unlimited authority to designate crimes as triable by military commission. At oral argument, the Government stated that the charges must at least involve an enemy combatant who committed a proscribed act during or in relation to hostilities against the United States. See Tr. of Oral Arg. at 37. In general, if an offense is an international law of war offense or has historically been tried by U.S. military commission, that is sufficient to uphold Congress's constitutional authority to make the offense triable by military commission. As Winthrop explained, the war crimes triable by U.S. military commission are "derived from International Law, supplemented by acts and orders of the military power and a few legislative provisions."

But is one of those conditions necessary? In other words, what if an offense is neither an international law of war offense nor historically rooted in U.S. military commission practice? Consider a hypothetical new statute that makes cyber-attacks by enemy forces a war crime triable by military commission. *Quirin* stated that Article III does "not restrict whatever authority was conferred by the Constitution to try offenses against the law of war by military commission," and does not bar "the practice of trying, before military tribunals without a jury, offenses committed by enemy belligerents against the law of war." Perhaps that language suggests that Article III permits what Article I authorizes with respect to which enemy war crimes may be tried by U.S. military commission. But we need not answer that hypothetical in this case and need not define with precision the outer limits of the Constitution in this context, other than to say that international law is not such a limit. Wherever one might ultimately draw the outer boundaries of Congress's authority to establish offenses triable by military commission, the historically rooted offense of conspiracy to commit war crimes is well within those limits. An enemy of the United States who engages in a conspiracy to commit war crimes—in Bahlul's case, by plotting with Osama bin Laden to murder thousands of American civilians—may be tried by a U.S. military commission for conspiracy to commit war crimes.

NOTES

1. *Historical Practice*. The Lincoln and *Ex parte Quirin* precedents involved completed war crimes rather than just conspiracy charges, and both were responses to attacks or armed conflict on U.S. soil. Are these distinctions relevant? Are those two precedents enough to demonstrate a historical practice that creates an exception to the normal requirements of Article III? The dissent in *Bahlul* argued that there is a limited exception to Article III for prosecutions by military commissions of internationally-recognized war crimes (which *Quirin* reasoned included spying), but that the exception should not be expanded to include prosecution of inchoate conspiracy charges that do not violate international law.

2. *Additional Constitutional Issues*. Bahlul argued that his prosecution by military commission violated the Ex Post Facto Clause because the Military Commissions Act, pursuant to which he was prosecuted for conspiracy, was enacted five years after he was charged. Lower courts held that he forfeited this objection. Defendants facing trial at Guantánamo have also argued that

the system of military commissions, which applies only to non-citizens, violates equal protection because an across-the-board distinction between citizens and non-citizens is not rationally related to any national security purpose. *See Al Bahlul v. U.S.*, 767 F.3d 1, 75 (D.C. Cir. 2014) (rejecting that argument). Decisions of the military commissions can be appealed to the Court of Military Commission Review ("CMCR"), which may include as judges persons who are already appellate military judges and who are assigned to the CMCR by the Secretary of Defense. The reassignment may violate the Appointments Clause. *See In re al-Nashiri*, 791 F.3d 71 (D.C. Cir. 2015).

3. *Military Commissions v. Federal Courts*. Lawyers for detainees facing military commission prosecutions argue that the cases should be tried in federal court instead. Federal courts have tried more than 480 terrorism cases since the Sept. 11 attacks. Evidence against Bahlul was presented by law enforcement agencies and the tribunals themselves are not operated by battlefield commanders but instead by a civilian bureaucracy. Critics argue that the commissions are an improper shadow justice system, especially when used to try crimes that are violations of domestic but not international law. Do the military commissions pose a threat to the integrity of Article III courts?

NOTE ON DETAINING AND TARGETING U.S. NATIONALS AS "ENEMY COMBATANTS"

In some situations, persons detained or targeted by the U.S. government as suspected terrorists turned out to be U.S. nationals. Detainees who are U.S. citizens were not held at Guantánamo Bay. Can the president, constitutionally, detain a U.S. national in the United States as an "enemy combatant," and thereby deny to him the normal rights of being released if not charged with a crime and, if charged, a speedy trial before a jury of his peers?

HAMDI V. RUMSFELD

542 U.S. 507 (2004).

JUSTICE O'CONNOR announced the judgment of the Court and delivered an opinion, in which THE CHIEF JUSTICE, JUSTICE KENNEDY, and JUSTICE BREYER join.

[For the basic facts of this case, see the excerpt provided in Chapter 1, Sec. 3.]. . .

II

The threshold question before us is whether the Executive has the authority to detain citizens who qualify as "enemy combatants." There is some debate as to the proper scope of this term, and the Government has never provided any court with the full criteria that it uses in classifying individuals as such. It has made clear, however, that, for purposes of this case, the "enemy combatant" that it is seeking to detain is an individual who, it alleges, was " 'part of or supporting forces hostile to the United

States or coalition partners' " in Afghanistan and who " 'engaged in an armed conflict against the United States' " there. Brief for Respondents 3. We therefore answer only the narrow question before us: whether the detention of citizens falling within that definition is authorized.

The Government maintains that no explicit congressional authorization is required, because the Executive possesses plenary authority to detain pursuant to Article II of the Constitution. We do not reach the question whether Article II provides such authority, however, because we agree with the Government's alternative position, that Congress has in fact authorized Hamdi's detention, through the [Authorization to Use Military Force Statute (AUMF), Pub. L. No. 107–40, 115 Stat. 224 (2001)]. . . .

Our analysis on that point, set forth below, substantially overlaps with our analysis of Hamdi's principal argument for the illegality of his detention. He posits that his detention is forbidden by 18 U.S.C. § 4001(a). Section 4001(a) states that "[n]o citizen shall be imprisoned or otherwise detained by the United States except pursuant to an Act of Congress." Congress passed § 4001(a) in 1971 as part of a bill to repeal the Emergency Detention Act of 1950, 50 U.S.C. § 811 *et seq.,* which provided procedures for executive detention, during times of emergency, of individuals deemed likely to engage in espionage or sabotage. Congress was particularly concerned about the possibility that the Act could be used to reprise the Japanese-American internment camps of World War II. H.R. Rep. No. 92–116 (1971); *id.,* at 4 ("The concentration camp implications of the legislation render it abhorrent"). . . . [F]or the reasons that follow, we conclude that the AUMF is explicit congressional authorization for the detention of individuals in the narrow category we describe (assuming, without deciding, that such authorization is required), and that the AUMF satisfied § 4001(a)'s requirement that a detention be "pursuant to an Act of Congress" (assuming, without deciding, that § 4001(a) applies to military detentions).

The AUMF authorizes the President to use "all necessary and appropriate force" against "nations, organizations, or persons" associated with the September 11, 2001, terrorist attacks. 115 Stat. 224. There can be no doubt that individuals who fought against the United States in Afghanistan as part of the Taliban, an organization known to have supported the al Qaeda terrorist network responsible for those attacks, are individuals Congress sought to target in passing the AUMF. We conclude that detention of individuals falling into the limited category we are considering, for the duration of the particular conflict in which they were captured, is so fundamental and accepted an incident to war as to be an exercise of the "necessary and appropriate force" Congress has authorized the President to use.

The capture and detention of lawful combatants and the capture, detention, and trial of unlawful combatants, by "universal agreement and practice," are "important incident[s] of war." *Ex parte Quirin,* 317 U.S., at 28. . . .

There is no bar to this Nation's holding one of its own citizens as an enemy combatant. In *Quirin,* one of the detainees, Haupt, alleged that he was a naturalized United States citizen. 317 U.S., at 20. . . . We held that "[c]itizens who associate themselves with the military arm of the enemy government, and with its aid, guidance and direction enter this country bent on hostile acts, are enemy belligerents within the meaning of . . . the law of war." *Id.,* at 37–38. . . . While Haupt was tried for violations of the law of war, nothing in *Quirin* suggests that his citizenship would have precluded his mere detention for the duration of the relevant hostilities. Nor can we see any reason for drawing such a line here. A citizen, no less than an alien, can be "part of or supporting forces hostile to the United States or coalition partners" and "engaged in an armed conflict against the United States," Brief for Respondents 3; such a citizen, if released, would pose the same threat of returning to the front during the ongoing conflict.

Hamdi objects, nevertheless, that Congress has not authorized the *indefinite* detention to which he is now subject. The Government responds that "the detention of enemy combatants during World War II was just as 'indefinite' while that war was being fought." *Id.,* at 16. We take Hamdi's objection to be not to the lack of certainty regarding the date on which the conflict will end, but to the substantial prospect of perpetual detention. We recognize that the national security underpinnings of the "war on terror," although crucially important, are broad and malleable. As the Government concedes, "given its unconventional nature, the current conflict is unlikely to end with a formal cease-fire agreement." *Ibid.* The prospect Hamdi raises is therefore not far-fetched. If the Government does not consider this unconventional war won for two generations, and if it maintains during that time that Hamdi might, if released, rejoin forces fighting against the United States, then the position it has taken throughout the litigation of this case suggests that Hamdi's detention could last for the rest of his life.

It is a clearly established principle of the law of war that detention may last no longer than active hostilities. *See* Article 118 of the Geneva Convention (III) Relative to the Treatment of Prisoners of War, Aug. 12, 1949, [1955] 6 U.S.T. 3316, 3406, T.I.A.S. No. 3364 ("Prisoners of war shall be released and repatriated without delay after the cessation of active hostilities"). . . .

[W]e understand Congress' grant of authority for the use of "necessary and appropriate force" to include the authority to detain for the duration of the relevant conflict, and our understanding is based on longstanding law-of-war principles. If the practical circumstances of a given conflict are entirely unlike those of the conflicts that informed the development of the law of war, that understanding may unravel. But that is not the situation we face as of this date. . . . The United States may detain, for the duration of these hostilities, individuals legitimately determined to be Taliban combatants who "engaged in an armed conflict against the United States." If the record establishes that United States troops are still involved in active combat in Afghanistan, those detentions are part of the exercise of "necessary and appropriate force," and therefore are authorized by the AUMF.

Ex parte Milligan, 4 Wall. 2, 125 (1866), does not undermine our holding about the Government's authority to seize enemy combatants, as we define that term today. In that case, the Court made repeated reference to the fact that its inquiry into whether the military tribunal had jurisdiction to try and punish Milligan turned in large part on the fact that Milligan was not a prisoner of war, but a resident of Indiana arrested while at home there. *Id.,* at 118, 131. That fact was central to its conclusion. Had Milligan been captured while he was assisting Confederate soldiers by carrying a rifle against Union troops on a Confederate battlefield, the holding of the Court might well have been different. The Court's repeated explanations that Milligan was not a prisoner of war suggest that had these different circumstances been present he could have been detained under military authority for the duration of the conflict, whether or not he was a citizen.[1]. . .

To the extent that JUSTICE SCALIA accepts the precedential value of *Quirin,* he argues that it cannot guide our inquiry here because "[i]n *Quirin* it was uncontested that the petitioners were members of enemy forces," while Hamdi challenges his classification as an enemy combatant. *Post,* at 571. But it is unclear why, in the paradigm outlined by JUSTICE SCALIA, such a concession should have any relevance. JUSTICE SCALIA envisions a system in which the only options are congressional suspension of the writ of *habeas corpus* or prosecution for treason or some other crime. *Post,* at 554. He does not explain how his historical analysis supports the addition of a third option—detention under some other process after concession of enemy-combatant status—or why a concession should carry any different effect than proof of enemy-combatant status in a proceeding that comports with due process. To be clear, our opinion only finds legislative authority to detain under the AUMF once it is sufficiently clear that the individual is, in fact, an enemy combatant; whether that is established by concession

[1] Here the basis asserted for detention by the military is that Hamdi was carrying a weapon against American troops on a foreign battlefield; that is, that he was an enemy combatant. The legal category of enemy combatant has not been elaborated upon in great detail. The permissible bounds of the category will be defined by the lower courts as subsequent cases are presented to them.

or by some other process that verifies this fact with sufficient certainty seems beside the point.

Moreover, JUSTICE SCALIA presumably would come to a different result if Hamdi had been kept in Afghanistan or even Guantanamo Bay. *See post,* at 577. This creates a perverse incentive. Military authorities faced with the stark choice of submitting to the full-blown criminal process or releasing a suspected enemy combatant captured on the battlefield will simply keep citizen-detainees abroad. Indeed, the Government transferred Hamdi from Guantanamo Bay to the United States naval brig only after it learned that he might be an American citizen. It is not at all clear why that should make a determinative constitutional difference.

III

Even in cases in which the detention of enemy combatants is legally authorized, there remains the question of what process is constitutionally due to a citizens who disputes his enemy-combatant status. [The Court then decided that Hamdi could not be stripped of his *habeas corpus* rights, and that his due process right should be measured by the balancing test enunciated in *Mathews v. Eldridge*: private liberty interests versus public necessity. The Court concluded that the detainees seeking to challenge their status should receive notice of the basis of their classification and an opportunity to challenge the government before a "neutral decisionmaker."]

NOTES

1. Hamdi *Aftermath.* As noted in Chapter 1, Sec. 3, in the fall of 2004 the U.S. government brokered a deal in which Hamdi—a U.S. citizen born in Saudi Arabia—was freed from detention in exchange for agreeing to return to Saudi Arabia, renouncing his American citizenship, and adhering to prescribed travel restrictions.

2. *Ambit of the Ability to Detain.* Notice Justice O'Connor's emphasis on Hamdi's capture "on the battlefield" in Afghanistan. Is the Court signaling discomfort with applying the laws of war, as they pertain to detention and incapacitation, to an indefinite "war on terrorism" beyond the hostilities in Afghanistan? If so, is that discomfort only arising with respect to U.S. nationals, such as Hamdi, or to all persons?

3. *Scope of Congressional Authorization.* How does Justice O'Connor's opinion interpret the AUMF? Is her approach similar to the Court's interpretation of the declaration of war in *Brown v. United States*?

4. *Due Process.* To what due process protections are U.S. citizens entitled when they are captured on the battlefield? Re-read the *Hamdi* excerpt from Chapter 1. The plurality applied the *Mathews v. Eldridge* balancing test to analyze Hamdi's Fifth Amendment due process rights, explaining that "the process due in any given instance is determined by weighing 'the private

interest that will be affected by the official action' against the Government's asserted interest, 'including the function involved' and the burdens the Government would face in providing greater process." To what kind of hearing was *Hamdi* constitutionally entitled? The due process question also arises when the U.S. government targets U.S. citizens, including through drone strikes. In the excerpt below, the Office of Legal Counsel considers the due process rights of Anwar al-Aulaqi, a Muslim cleric born in New Mexico. Al-Aulaqi, a spokesperson for Al Qaeda in the Arabian Peninsula, was located in Yemen.

DEPARTMENT OF JUSTICE, OFFICE OF LEGAL COUNSEL, MEMORANDUM FOR THE ATTORNEY GENERAL

Re: Applicability of Federal Criminal Laws and the Constitution to Contemplated Lethal Action against Shaykh Anwar al-Aulaqi, July 16, 2010. available at https://www.justice.gov/sites/default/files/olc/pages/attachments/2015/04/02/2010-07-16_-_olc_aaga_barron_-_al-aulaqi.pdf, [https://perma.cc/5ZJH-B87R].

As explained above, on the facts represented to us, a decision-maker could reasonably decide that the threat posed by al-Aulaqi's activities to United States persons is "continued" and "imminent" [material redacted]

In addition to the nature of the threat posed by al-Aulaqi's activities, both agencies here have represented that they intend to capture rather than target al-Aulaqi if feasible; yet we also understand that an operation by either agency to capture al-Aulaqi in Yemen would be infeasible at this time. [material redacted] *Cf., e.g., Public Committee Against Torture in Israel v. Government of Israel,* HCJ 769/02 40, 46 I.L.M. 375, 394 (Israel Supreme Court sitting as the High Court of Justice, 2006) (although arrest, investigation and trial "might actually be particularly practical under the conditions of belligerent occupation, in which the army controls the area in which the operation takes place," such alternatives "are not means which can always be used," either because they are impossible or because they involve a great risk to the lives of soldiers).

Although in the "circumstances of war," as the *Hamdi* plurality observed, the risk of erroneous deprivation of a citizen's liberty in the absence of sufficient process . . . is very real," 542 U.S. at 530, the plurality also recognized that "the realities of combat" render certain uses of force "necessary and appropriate," including against U.S. citizens who have become part of enemy forces-and that "due process analysis need not blink at those realities," *id.* at 531. [material redacted].

We conclude that at least where, as here, the target's activities pose a "continued and imminent threat of violence or death" to U.S. persons, "the highest officers in the Intelligence Community have reviewed the factual basis" for the lethal operation, and a capture operation would be infeasible-and where the CIA and DoD "continue to monitor whether changed circumstances would permit such an alternative," [material redacted] see also DoD May 18 Memorandum for OLC at 2—the "realities of combat" and the weight of the government's interest in using an authorized means of lethal force against this enemy are such that the Constitution would not require the government to provide further process to the U.S. person before using such force. *Cf. Hamdi* 542 U.S. at 535 (noting that Court "accord[s] the greatest respect and consideration to the judgments of military authorities in matters relating to the actual prosecution of war, and . . . the scope of that discretion is wide") (plurality opinion).

NOTES

1. *Targeting U.S. Citizens.* How convincing is the OLC's analysis of Anwar al-Aulaqi's due process rights? How would the analysis change if capture were feasible? How would the analysis change if he were located outside the Middle East? How "imminent" a threat must the targeted citizen pose? Al-Aulaqi had overseen a plot to detonate explosive devices on cargo planes bound for the United States, and he was involved in a Christmas-day attempt to detonate a bomb in a passenger plane landing in Detroit, Michigan. The government alleged that he was also involved in other plots against the United States. Is this an adequate showing of imminence?

2. *Checks on the Executive Branch's Due Process Analysis?* Does it matter that courts have not scrutinized the factual basis upon which the government's due process analysis was based? Note that the Obama administration refused to release the 2010 OLC Memo and did so only after losing a lawsuit brought by press and civil liberties organizations. Al-Aulaqi was killed by a U.S. drone strike in September, 2011. A suit filed on al-Aulaqi's behalf while he was still alive challenged the government's plans to kill him in a targeted strike. That suit was dismissed for lack of standing and under the political question doctrine. *Al-Aulaqi v. Obama*, 727 F. Supp. 2d 1, 11 (D.D.C. 2010). A suit filed after al-Aulaqi was killed was dismissed because even assuming his due process rights were violated, the law provided no remedy for that harm. *Al-Aulaqi v. Panetta*, 35 F. Supp. 3d 56 (D.D.C. 2014).

CHAPTER 5

THE POWER OF THE PURSE

■ ■ ■

1. THE APPROPRIATIONS POWER IN FOREIGN AFFAIRS: TRUMP CARD, BALANCER, OR ILLUSION?

The Constitution assigns to Congress the "power of the purse" in one succinct sentence. Article I, Section 9, Clause 7 provides that "No Money shall be drawn from the Treasury, but in Consequence of Appropriations made by Law. . . ." To this may be added, Article I, Section 7, Clause 1, which provides: "All bills for raising Revenue shall originate in the House of Representatives; but the Senate may propose or concur with amendments as on other Bills." Such provisions prompted Madison in the *Federalist Papers* No. 48 (Clinton Rossiter ed., 1961) to observe that "the legislative department alone has access to the pockets of the people."

A centerpiece of exercising this appropriations power in the field of U.S. foreign relations is the 1961 Foreign Assistance Act (FAA).[1] Among other things, the FAA reorganized U.S. foreign assistance programs so as to separate military and non-military aid. Military aid was expected to help U.S. allies defend themselves from attack and participate in collective security arrangements. Non-military aid was expected to foster economic growth and democracy in the developing world, combat the perceived spread of ideological threats such as communism, and address the threat of instability arising from poverty. As originally enacted in 1961, the FAA contained few restrictions on how assistance was to be provided and only general factors were to be taken into account prior to the provision of assistance. Over time, however, the FAA has been amended repeatedly to contain restrictions on the conduct of the Executive Branch and to adjust the purposes for which military and non-military aid may be dispensed. Further, the FAA must now be read in conjunction with other statutes, such as the Arms Export Control Act (AECA),[2] which contains important restrictions on the end use and retransfer of arms sold to U.S. allies.

Annual and biennial authorization and appropriations statutes are also important means for congressional regulation and oversight of

---

1 Pub. L. No. 87–195, 75 Stat. 424 (1961) (codified as amended in scattered sections of 22 U.S.C.).

2 Pub. L. No. 90–629, 82 Stat. 1320 (1968), as amended.

executive branch action in the field of foreign affairs. The Foreign Relations Authorization Act—covering one or two fiscal years—falls under the authority of the Senate Foreign Relations and House International Relations committees. The principal annual appropriations legislation—the Foreign Operations, Export Financing, and Related Appropriations Act, and the Commerce, State, and Justice departments' appropriations legislation—fall under the authority of the Senate and House Appropriations committees. Other authorization and appropriations statutes, such as those relating to the Department of Defense, often include important provisions on the conduct of U.S. foreign relations. The annual or biennial adoption of these statutes entails a process of negotiation among congressional representatives, and between Congress and the executive branch, by which important initiatives in U.S. foreign relations are discussed and addressed.

Failure to comply with such statutes entails risks for executive branch personnel; the Anti-Deficiency Act makes it a crime to spend funds in a manner not authorized by Congress, while the Miscellaneous Receipts Statute prohibits U.S. government personnel from lending or using public money without authorization.[3]

At the same time, when Congress adopts legislation that imposes restrictions or requirements on executive branch conduct, the president might view the legislation as intruding upon the president's constitutional powers. If so, the president might veto the legislation and, unless his veto is overridden, that ends the matter. Since the provision might be embedded in lengthy legislation containing numerous non-controversial provisions, however, the president may decide to sign the legislation into law, yet with a signing statement indicating that he regards the controversial provision to be unconstitutional. In so doing, the president might state that he views the congressional restriction or requirement as simply advisory in nature.

A good example of this may be seen in the events preceding the *Zivitofsky* case (*see* Chapter 1, Sec. 2). In 2002, Congress adopted the Foreign Relations Authorization Act, Fiscal Year 2003, which provided in section 214(d) that: "For purposes of the registration of birth, certification of nationality, or issuance of a passport of a United States citizen born in the city of Jerusalem, the Secretary [of State] shall, upon the request of the citizen or the citizen's legal guardian, record the place of birth as Israel."[4] Although President George W. Bush signed the legislation into law, he issued a statement indicating that section 214(d) was an impermissible interference "with the President's constitutional authority to conduct the

---

[3] *See* Anti-Deficiency Act, 31 U.S.C. §§ 1341–42, 1350 (2012); Miscellaneous Receipts Statute, 31 U.S.C. 3302 (2012).

[4] 7 U.S.C. § 1765d–1 (2012) (now repealed).

Nation's foreign affairs and to supervise the unitary executive branch."[5] Thereafter, the executive branch declined to issue passports in those circumstances recording the place of birth as Israel, such as was requested by the parents of Menachem Zivotofsky. Ultimately, the Supreme Court ruled that the provision did violate the president's power to recognize foreign States and governments (*see* Chapter 7, Sec. 1).

Is such a step by the president constitutionally permissible and indeed desirable as a matter of transparency? Or does it raise constitutional concerns? *See American Bar Association Task Force on Presidential Signing Statements and the Separation of Powers Doctrine, Report and Recommendations* 1 (2006) (asserting that "the American Bar Association opposes, as contrary to the rule of law and our constitutional system of separation of powers, the issuance of presidential signing statements that claim the authority or state the intention to disregard or decline to enforce all or part of a law the president has signed, or to interpret such a law in a manner inconsistent with the clear intent of Congress"); Louis Fisher, *Signing Statements: Constitutional and Practical Limits*, 16 WM. & MARY BILL RTS. J. 183 (2007). If constitutionally suspect, what standards should be applied when assessing such signing statements? Does the president's use of signing statements to set aside or alter a statutory provision fall within Justice Jackson's third category in *Youngstown*, where the president's power is at its lowest?

The U.S. Government Accountability Office (GAO), a non-partisan congressional investigating body, conducted a study of presidential signing statements concerning fiscal year 2006 appropriations acts of all kinds (not just foreign relations laws). The GAO study found that, in 11 signing statements, the president singled out 160 specific provisions as ones to which he was not necessarily bound. The study further examined 19 of those provisions to determine whether the executive agencies responsible for their execution in fact carried out the provisions as written in the law. Of those 19 provisions, the GAO found that 10 provisions were executed as written, 6 were not, and 3 were not triggered and so there was no agency action to examine. *See* Government Accountability Office, *Presidential Signing Statements Accompanying the Fiscal Year 2006 Appropriations Acts*, Study No. B–308603 (June 18, 2007), available at http://www.gao.gov/decisions/appro/308603.pdf, [https://perma.cc/B56E-NK79].

When is it that congressional exercise of the power of the purse in the field of foreign affairs is constitutional? When is it unconstitutional? Many scholars have wrestled with this issue. *See, e.g.,* William C. Banks & Peter Raven-Hansen, *National Security Law and the Power of the Purse* (1994); John F. Cogan, Timothy J. Muris & Allen Schick, *The Budget Puzzle: Understanding Federal Spending* (1994); Louis Fisher, "The Spending

[5] Statement on Signing the Foreign Relations Authorization Act, Fiscal Year 2003, Public Papers of the Presidents, George W. Bush, Vol. 2, Sept. 30, 2002, p. 1698 (2005).

Power," in *The Constitution and the Conduct of American Foreign Policy* 227 (David Gray Adler & Larry N. George eds., 1996); Louis Fisher, *Congressional Abdication on War and Spending* (2000).

In reviewing the materials in this Chapter, focus on three recurring questions that arise. First, in separation-of-power disputes, emphasis is often placed upon the plenary character of the presidential power in question. However, Congress's power over the purse is also plenary; the constitutional text grants only the Congress power to authorize the withdrawal of funds from the treasury. Absent congressional approval, the president has no power under the appropriations clause to order a withdrawal. The difficult question posed by these materials involves a clash between the "immovable object" of a plenary presidential power, such as the negotiations power or the commander-in-chief power, and the "irresistible force" of Congress's plenary appropriations power. On what principled basis can one plenary power be seen to trump another? What principle emerges that might resolve such conflicts? If the principle is, for example, that Congress must fund "core functions" of the executive branch, how are such functions identified?

Second, rather than attempting to draw an inevitably arbitrary line, is it less capricious to conclude that Congress's power over the purse is co-extensive with its legislative powers, *i.e.*, that Congress can impose no check on executive power through its appropriations power that it cannot impose through its share of the war power, commerce power, or other powers set out in Article I, Section 8 of the Constitution? But if this were true, would the appropriations power not be robbed of all meaning as an independent check on presidential power?

Third, it might be equally principled to avoid drawing such a line by concluding that an exercise of Congress's appropriations power *always* trumps the exercise of *any* presidential power, whether that presidential power is plenary or concurrent. But would not this view rob the notion of plenary presidential power of all meaning? To what extent can Congress formulate the exercise of virtually any legislative power as an exercise of its power over the purse thus defeating any arrow in the Executive's quiver?

KATE STITH, CONGRESS' POWER OF THE PURSE

97 Yale L.J. 1343, 1350–52 (1988).

Limits on Congress' appropriations power derive from limitations on, and obligations of, the government expressed elsewhere in the Constitution. Thus, the First Amendment imposes a limitation upon the exercise of all government powers, including Congress' appropriations power. Significantly, Congress is obliged to provide public funds for constitutionally mandated activities—both obligations imposed upon the government generally and independent constitutional activities of the President. For instance, in the area of foreign affairs, Congress itself would violate the Constitution if it refused to appropriate funds for the President to receive foreign ambassadors or to make treaties. . . .

At the same time, the appropriations clause enjoins the President to spend funds in the name of the United States only as appropriated by Congress. Even where the President believes that Congress has transgressed the Constitution by failing to provide funds for a particular activity, the President has no constitutional authority to draw funds from the Treasury to finance the activity. Spending in the absence of appropriations is ultra vires. Of course, where an emergency exists, the President might decide that principles more fundamental than the Constitution's appropriations requirement justify spending. The constitutional processes for resolving such situations, as well as cases where Congress fails to appropriate money for an inherent executive activity, are political.

Although Congress may not completely frustrate the exercise of the President's constitutional duties, this is but a marginal circumscription of Congress' power over the purse and its other legislative powers.

J. GREGORY SIDAK, THE PRESIDENT'S POWER OF THE PURSE

1989 Duke L.J. 1162, 1183–98 (1989).

The responsibilities of the Executive under the Constitution can be grouped into two categories. In the first category are the duties that article II explicitly imposes on the President. In the second category are the President's prerogatives, also enumerated in article II. . . . [T]he President has the right under the Constitution to perform these explicit duties and exercise these explicit prerogatives even if Congress has not appropriated funds for him to do so. The Constitution commands the President to act with respect to the subjects listed in article II—even if, as in the case of the President's prerogatives, the command is to exercise discretion. The Constitution does not condition its commands in article II on Congress periodically granting the President permission to act. This insight leads to the conclusion that the President has an implicit power to encumber the Treasury in the name of carrying out the responsibilities assigned to him by the plain text of article II.

In the alternative, one might argue that, even accepting that Congress cannot withhold appropriations for article II duties and prerogatives, it does not follow that the President may spend money in the absence of appropriations. Under the system of checks and balances, one branch can frustrate another's ability to fulfill its constitutional functions, as when Congress refuses to confirm the President's nominees, the President declines to enforce laws he disfavors, or the Judiciary strikes down an act of Congress. Recent Supreme Court decisions on the separation of powers have emphasized two themes in disputes between Congress and the President. First, the Court has looked to the interference another branch suffers in its ability to perform constitutionally assigned functions. *Morrison v. Olson,* [487 U.S. 654 (1988),] for example, established that congressional efforts to impede the President's performance of his duty to faithfully execute the law do not violate the principle of separation of powers if they do not (1) "impermissibly undermine" the powers of the Executive Branch, or (2) prevent the Executive Branch from "accomplishing its constitutionally assigned functions." The second theme concerns the aggrandizement of one branch by its acquiring powers assigned to the other branches. . . .

Given this, one could hardly assert, as the Court concluded of the independent counsel law in *Morrison,* that denying the President the funds with which to perform a duty or exercise a prerogative specified by article II "does not involve an attempt by Congress to increase its own power at the expense of the Executive Branch." . . . Therefore, I do not believe that Congress may impose conditions on the funding of article II duties and prerogatives; nor do I believe that such conditions lie in some indeterminate zone of action whose propriety is judged by the current balance of political power between Congress and the President rather than the language of the Constitution and the separation of powers that its structure is intended to effect. . . .

. . . The assignment to the President of enumerated duties and prerogatives in article II implicitly conferred on the President the ability to have the funding necessary for him to carry out those duties and prerogatives. So, for example, Hamilton specifically believed that the Constitution's grant to the President of powers and prerogatives in foreign affairs precluded Congress from having any discretion to withhold funding for the execution of treaties as a means of controlling the Executive in foreign policy. Likening Congress's lack of discretion in this respect to its inability to manipulate the salaries of federal judges, Hamilton wrote that the House of Representatives "cannot deliberate whether they will appropriate and pay the money" for the execution of treaties; rather "the *mode* of raising and appropriating the money only remains [a] matter of deliberation."[122]

. . . Therefore, I believe that a President who acts to discharge his article II duties when Congress has failed or refused to provide him appropriations for that purpose does not violate the appropriations clause. He need not cite necessity or any other legal defense to justify his

[122] Letter from Alexander Hamilton to William Smith (Mar. 10, 1796), *reprinted in* 20 THE PAPERS OF ALEXANDER HAMILTON 72 (H. Syrett ed. 1974) . . .

expenditure of funds to the extent necessary to execute the particular duty at issue.

. . . The prerogatives of the President in article II also have a textual basis for their implicit source of funding. The pardon power, the power to negotiate treaties, and the power to make recess appointments are all preceded by the following words: The President (or "he") "shall have Power . . . to" perform the function. Although it is a fine point, this language is considerably more specific than simply saying "the President *may* grant pardons" or "the President *is authorized* to negotiate treaties." The text of article II makes clear that the people have given the President something more than merely the permission or the authority to perform these functions. He "shall have *Power* to" perform them as well. Indeed, John Locke's *Second Treatise on Government,* which influenced the Framers' thinking on separation of powers, defined executive prerogative to be "nothing but the Power of doing public good without a Rule." The Constitution itself must give the President the ability to fund the exercise of his enumerated prerogatives, for otherwise the recurring statement in article II that the President "shall have Power" to perform certain explicit responsibilities would become meaningless whenever Congress refused him the necessary appropriation of funds. The power to negotiate treaties, for example, would be reduced to the precatory statement that it would be nice if the President could negotiate treaties now and then. Of course, this reasoning holds *a fortiori* in the case of the explicit duties imposed on the President by article II. . . .

[Under the appropriations clause] the President has an implied power to incur claims against the Treasury to the extent minimally necessary to perform his duties and exercise his prerogatives under article II. The rule of law implies that some principle must limit the President's implied power to spend, but it is hardly obvious from the text of the Constitution what that principle would be. . . .

[The] potential for the Executive to abuse its implied spending power must be evaluated in terms of the likelihood that the power would have to be exercised and the means available to Congress and the people for containing such spending if it did occur. On the first point, I would expect that unappropriated spending by the President would be the rare exception and not the general practice. Although the text and history of the appropriations clause does not demonstrate an intent by the Framers to create a legislative veto, they obviously do demonstrate an intent to give Congress the principal and recurring responsibility for raising public funds and directing their use. The primary value of the President's implied power to fund his duties and prerogatives, therefore, is like that of the veto: It is a strategic deterrent to opportunistic behavior by Congress, one that consequently gives the President bargaining strength *vis-a-vis* Congress in the ordinary course of setting the direction and magnitude of specific national policies.

In the first instance, therefore, the political process imposes a limiting principle on the President's unappropriated spending. . . . Like any rarely used but strategically potent constitutional power (such as the power to suspend habeas corpus, exercised by Lincoln), the President must be able, as a political matter, to persuade the people (from whom, of course, all powers under the Constitution have been delegated to the federal government) that his actions are necessary and proper to carrying out a responsibility that article II plainly imposes on him. In an era that has witnessed Presidents Johnson, Nixon, Ford, and Carter either denied reelection or driven from office (and President Reagan politically immobilized for the remainder of his second term once the story of arms shipments to Iran broke in the fall of 1986), there should be little doubt that the electoral process will provide a check on the President (and his party) if such an assertion of spending power appears to be unsupportable. . . .

In addition to these political constraints, there are two legal principles that limit the President's ability to spend in the absence of appropriations. . . . First, the *object* of the unappropriated spending must be a textually demonstrable duty or prerogative of the President under article II, such as the duty to faithfully execute the laws or the prerogative to negotiate treaties. . . .

Second, the *extent* to which the President may spend public funds in furtherance of such an object is defined by the minimum amount necessary to successfully produce the desired public good. . . .

[I]t serves no useful purpose for the President to make disbursements of an amount of unappropriated funds that is too little to successfully discharge his duty or exercise his prerogative under article II. It makes no sense to disburse funds to send an envoy only as far as Paris if the arms reduction negotiations to which the President wishes to send his envoy are taking place in Geneva. Thus, the President must be permitted to spend enough unappropriated funds to produce the minimally necessary level of public output required by the faithful performance of his article II duties or the reasonable exercise of this article II prerogatives.

In other words, the President must identify the necessary level of public output implied by article II and then seek to minimize the cost of producing that level of output. . . .

2. SETTING FOREIGN POLICY BY RESTRICTING FUNDING FOR EMBASSIES ABROAD

The United States maintains embassies or consulates in every country with which it has diplomatic relations. Building and maintaining those diplomatic properties, and the staffing of them, requires funding, and is in part the subject of annual appropriations bills. Can Congress impose restrictions on the availability of such funds so as to achieve certain foreign policy ends? For example, could Congress limit the total number of personnel employed at a particular embassy to ten persons? Does it matter if Congress's objective is (1) to save money; (2) to signal to the host country that U.S. relations with it are minimal; or (3) to prevent the president from engaging in extensive diplomatic contacts with the host country?

Can Congress condition the availability of funds on the construction of an embassy in a location that it views as less-costly? More safe? Politically important? In 1995, Congress adopted and President Clinton signed into law the Jerusalem Embassy Act of 1995, which declared the policy of the United States that Jerusalem should be recognized as the capital of the State of Israel and that the U.S. Embassy should be moved from Tel Aviv to Jerusalem no later than May 31, 1999. Pub. L. No. 104–45, § 3, 109 Stat. 398, 399 (1995). Further, the law limited the funds available to the Department of State for acquisition and maintenance of buildings abroad pending the opening of the embassy in Jerusalem, but allowed the president to suspend such limitation if necessary to protect national security interests. *Id.* §§ 3(b), 7. Thereafter, Presidents Clinton, Bush and Obama all exercised the waiver and declined to move the U.S. Embassy to Jerusalem. Although Donald J. Trump, on the presidential election campaign trail, repeatedly stated his intention to move the embassy, he too signed such a waiver in May 2017. *See* Memorandum on Suspension of Limitations Under the Jerusalem Embassy Act, 2017 DAILY COMP. PRES. DOC. 372 (May 31, 2017). How far may Congress go with such restrictions?

SECTION 609 OF THE FISCAL YEAR 1996 OMNIBUS APPROPRIATIONS ACT

Pub. L. No. 104–134, 110 Stat. 1321 (1996).

None of the funds appropriated or otherwise made available by this Act may be obligated or expended to pay for any cost incurred for (1) opening or operating any United States diplomatic or consular post in the Socialist Republic of Vietnam that was not operating on July 11, 1995; (2) expanding any United States diplomatic or consular post in the Socialist Republic of Vietnam that was operating on July 11, 1995; or (3) increasing the total number of personnel assigned to United States diplomatic or consular posts in the Socialist Republic of Vietnam above the levels existing on July 11, 1995, unless the President certifies within 60 days, based upon all information available to the United States Government that the Government of the Socialist Republic of Vietnam is cooperating in full faith with the United States in the following four areas:

(1) Resolving discrepancy cases, live sightings and field activities,

(2) Recovering and repatriating American remains,

(3) Accelerating efforts to provide documents that will help lead to the fullest possible accounting of POW/MIA's,

(4) Providing further assistance in implementing trilateral investigations with Laos.

MEMORANDUM FOR CONRAD HARPER, DEPARTMENT OF STATE LEGAL ADVISER, FROM WALTER DELLINGER, ASSISTANT ATTORNEY GENERAL

(May 15, 1996), available at https://www.hsdl.org/?view&did=742136, [https://perma.cc/EJL4-CBCK].

[S]ection 609's prohibition on the use of appropriated funds to maintain diplomatic relations with Vietnam unless the President provides Congress with a detailed certification is an unconstitutional condition on the exercise of the President's power to control the recognition and non-recognition of foreign governments—a power that flows directly from his textually-committed authority to receive ambassadors, U.S. Const., art. II, § 3. It is by now firmly established that "[p]olitical recognition is exclusively a function of the Executive." *Banco Nacional de Cuba v. Sabbatino*, 376 U.S. 398, 410 (1964). As President Woodrow Wilson (himself a leading constitutional scholar) stated in a message to Congress in 1919, "the initiative in directing the relations of our Government with foreign governments is assigned by the Constitution to the Executive, and to the Executive only." Accordingly, Congress may not determine the conditions that a foreign government must satisfy in order to be recognized by, or to enter into normal diplomatic relations with, the United States.

The Executive's recognition power necessarily subsumes within itself the power to withhold or deny recognition, to determine the conditions on which recognition will be accorded, and to define the nature and extent of diplomatic contacts with an as-yet unrecognized government. The United States' diplomatic history has illustrated, on many occasions, the importance of the Executive's powers to withhold or condition recognition. Just as Congress may not usurp the Executive's power by attempting to compel the President affirmatively to recognize a particular government as the sole sovereign of a disputed area, so also it may not ordain that the Executive is to withhold recognition, or that the Executive is not to accord recognition unless the foreign government concerned complies with requirements that Congress, rather than the Executive, imposes. Were Congress to seek to direct and control the exercise of the recognition power in any of these ways, it would violate separation of powers principles.

The Supreme Court has identified two fashions in which Congress may impermissibly encroach on the Executive power. First, Congress may attempt to exercise itself one of the functions that the Constitution commits solely to the Executive, thus "pos[ing] a 'danger of congressional usurpation of Executive Branch functions.'" *Morrison v. Olson*, 487 U.S. 654, 694 (1988) (quoting *Bowsher v. Synar*, 478 U.S. 714, 727 (1986)). Second, Congress may not attempt to " 'impermissibly undermine' the powers of the Executive Branch, [*Commodity Futures Trading Comm'n v.] Schor*, [478 U.S. 833 (1986)] at 856, or 'disrupt[ ] the proper balance between the coordinate branches [by] prevent[ing] the Executive Branch from accomplishing its constitutionally assigned functions,' Nixon *v. Administrator of General Services*, [433 U.S. 425 (1977)] at 433." *Morrison*, 487 U.S. at 695.

Section 609 both poses a "danger of congressional usurpation" of the Executive function of recognition, and "impermissibly undermine[s]" that authority. In effect, section 609 requires the President either (1) to reduce our diplomatic presence in, and contacts with, Vietnam to the levels that existed immediately before his July 11, 1995 offer to normalize relations, or else (2) to go forward with normalizing relations, but only if Vietnam satisfies specific conditions that Congress, rather than the Executive, demands. This Congress may not do: if the United States is to impose conditions precedent on Vietnam for being recognized, it is for the President, not Congress, to decide what those conditions are.

Specifically, section 609 purports to impose a certification requirement on the availability of funds (1) to "open[ ] or operat[e]" a diplomatic or consular post in Vietnam that was not operating on the date the President offered to establish diplomatic relations with that country, (2) to "expand[ ]" any such post that was operating in Vietnam before that date, or (3) to augment the number of personnel assigned to United States diplomatic or consular posts in Vietnam before that date. In our view, each of these three restrictions is unconstitutional. That the first two restrictions (on opening, operating or expanding any diplomatic or consular post in Vietnam) overtly infringe on the President's recognition power is, we think, clear. While the unconstitutionality of the third restriction (on the number of personnel assigned to such posts) may be less patent, we think that, in the particular context surrounding the enactment of section 609, it too impermissibly invades a core Presidential power. As we have explained, section 609 was enacted against the backdrop of the progress that the Government of Vietnam had made between July, 1993 and July, 1995 in resolving POW/MIA issues, the President's July 11, 1995 offer to the Government of Vietnam, that government's response to it, and the ensuing diplomatic dealings between the two nations. Indeed, one of the signatories of the Congressional Letter [sent just after Section 609 was signed into law] explicitly stated that the purpose of a prior version of section 609 was to "bar[ ] the use of Federal funds for implementing the President's ill-considered, pre-mature [sic] decision to expand diplomatic relations with Vietnam." 141 Cong. Rec. H7765 (daily ed. July 26, 1995) (remarks of Rep. Gilman). Thus, the unmistakeable [sic] intent and effect of section 609's restrictions, taken as a whole, are to return the United States' diplomatic relations with Vietnam to the very limited level that existed before the President's offer, or else to require that Vietnam demonstrably satisfy requirements imposed by legislative mandate. Thus, even if Congress may, for reasons of economy or efficiency, reduce the size of embassy staff, it may not do so as part of an effort, as here, to direct and control the recognition power in a particular instance. . . .

The fact that in section 609 Congress is seeking to control the exercise of the Presidential recognition power indirectly, through the appropriations process, rather than as a direct mandate, does not change our conclusion. Broad as Congress' spending power undoubtedly is, it is clear that Congress may not deploy it to accomplish unconstitutional ends. In particular, as our Office has insisted over the course of several Administrations, "Congress may not use its power over appropriation of public funds 'to attach conditions to Executive Branch appropriations requiring the President to relinquish his constitutional discretion in foreign affairs.'" 16 Op. O.L.C. 18, 30 (1992) (preliminary print) (quoting 14 Op. O.L.C. 38, 42 n.3 (1990)) (preliminary print) (quoting 13 Op. O.L.C. 311, 315 (1989) (preliminary print)).

Indeed, it has long been established that the spending power may not be deployed to invade core Presidential prerogatives in the conduct of diplomacy. As early as 1818, an attempt by Representative Henry Clay to use an appropriations bill rider to compel the recognition of a South American government was criticized by other members of Congress as a violation of separation of powers principles, and it soon proved to be abortive. . . .

Accordingly, Congress may not attempt indirectly, through the use of its spending power, to control the exercise of the President's exclusive right to grant or withhold political recognition. Section 609 is such an attempt; thus, it is an unconstitutional encroachment on the President's power. . . .

Because section 609 is, in our view, invalid, we regard it as being without legal force or effect.

The past practice of the Executive branch demonstrates its refusal to comply with unconstitutional spending conditions that trench on core Executive powers. Particularly pertinent in this regard is an opinion written in 1960 by Attorney General William Rogers for President Eisenhower concerning such an unconstitutional condition.

Attorney General Rogers' opinion dealt with a provision of a statute that directed that certain expenses of a State Department office be charged to certain appropriations, provided that all documents relating to activities of that office were furnished upon request to Congress. A related statute provided for termination of funds if all documents were not produced, unless the President certified that he had forbidden the disclosure of the documents to protect the public interest. The State Department refused to furnish a number of documents requested by a House subcommittee, and the President certified that he had forbidden their disclosure. The Comptroller General, interpreting the former statute as not incorporating a "public interest" exception permitting the President to withhold the documents from Congress, directed that funds not be made available to liquidate obligations incurred from the following day forward. The Attorney General concluded that the statute should be construed to include a "public interest" exception because, as applied under the circumstances, it would otherwise embody an unconstitutional condition. He based this conclusion in part on the reasoning that:

> the Constitution does not permit any indirect encroachment by Congress upon this authority of the President through resort to conditions attached to appropriations such as are contended to be contained in . . . the act.

Further, the Attorney General concluded that "the Comptroller General's view that the proviso . . . has cut off funds under the circumstances disclosed here is an erroneous interpretation of the meaning of this statute," and that "if this view of the Comptroller General as to the meaning of this statute is correct, the proviso is unconstitutional." He stated that, despite the Comptroller General's view that appropriated funds had been cut off, the funds "continue to be available as heretofore."

Accordingly, we conclude that funds elsewhere appropriated in the Act for State Department diplomatic activities abroad may lawfully be obligated or expended for diplomatic relations with the Government of Vietnam if those funds are otherwise available for that purpose, without the President's having to certify that Vietnam has met the conditions purportedly imposed by section 609.

NOTES

1. *Congressional Control on Funding the Embassy in Vietnam.* Do you think that Congress can constitutionally refuse to fund the U.S. Embassy in Vietnam? If not, can it refuse to fund the Embassy beyond a core staff (e.g., an Ambassador, a Deputy Chief of Mission, and a secretary)? If not, can it refuse

to fund an Embassy larger than twenty persons? If not, is the president able to operate diplomatic functions abroad at whatever level he deems necessary?

2. *Drawing the Line.* Does it matter the reason stated by Congress for the limitation? For example, is it constitutionally problematic to condition the funding on a particular foreign policy objective (such as demanding cooperation from a foreign government in determining the fate of soldiers who are missing in action), but not problematic to limit funding due to congressional concern with the national debt? If so, does Congress simply need to say the right thing in the preamble to the legislation?

What two-part test does the Justice Department see in prior Supreme Court jurisprudence? What exactly is the core presidential function that the Justice Department asserts is being usurped by Congress? Do you agree? Does it matter that the president's power to appoint ambassadors to foreign countries is a power shared with the Senate, which must consent to such appointments? Further, note that the Justice Department seems to suggest that funds can be denied for reasons of efficiency and economy.

3. *"Unitary Executive."* In some instances, the president has declared that a foreign relations appropriations provision is unconstitutional because it impinges upon the "unitary executive." The theory of the unitary executive is apparently grounded in the vesting of the executive power in the president under Article II of the Constitution and Article II's direction that the president "take Care that the Laws be faithfully executed." According to the Justice Department:

> Because no one individual could personally carry out all executive functions, the President delegates many of these functions to his subordinates in the executive branch. But because the Constitution vests this power in him alone, it follows that he is solely responsible for supervising and directing the activities of his subordinates in carrying out executive functions.

Office of the Legal Counsel, Opinion on Statute Limiting the President's Authority to Supervise the Director of the Centers for Disease Control in the Distribution of an AIDS Pamphlet, 12 Op. Off. Legal Counsel 47, 48 (1988).

This theory of the unitary executive can affect statutory foreign relations law in at least three ways. The president may invoke the theory to declare unconstitutional a foreign relations provision that requires some type of communication from an executive branch employee to Congress, that requires consultation with Congress, or that requires the executive branch to make legislative recommendations to Congress.

For example, in 2005 Congress adopted a provision of the Foreign Operations, Export Financing, and Related Programs appropriations legislation for fiscal year 2006 that required consultations with Congress before certain funds could be used. Specifically, § 534(k) of the statute provided:

> Middle East Foundation.—Of the funds appropriated by this Act under the heading "Economic Support Fund" that are available for the Middle East Partnership Initiative, up to $35,000,000 may be made available, including as an endowment, notwithstanding any other provision of law and *following consultations with the Committees on Appropriations*, to establish and operate a Middle East Foundation, or any other similar entity, whose purpose is to support democracy, governance, human rights, and the rule of law in the Middle East region. . . .

Foreign Operations, Export Financing, and Related Programs Appropriations Act, 2006, § 534(k), Pub. L. No. 109–102, 119 Stat. 2172, 2210–11 (Nov. 14, 2005) (emphasis added).

Although President Bush signed the legislation into law, he stated:

> The Executive Branch shall . . . construe certain provisions of the Act that purport to make consultation with the Congress a precondition to the execution of the law as calling for, but not mandating, such consultation, as is consistent with the Constitution's provisions concerning the separate powers of the Congress to legislate and of the President to execute the laws. Such provisions include section . . . 534(k). . . .

Statement on Signing the Foreign Operations, Export Financing, and Related Programs Appropriations Act, 2006, 41 WEEKLY COMP. PRES. DOC. 1718 (Nov. 21, 2005). Despite this statement, the Department of State did—prior to expending such funds—consult with the relevant committees. *See* Government Accountability Office, *Presidential Signing Statements Accompanying the Fiscal Year 2006 Appropriations Acts*, Study No. B–308603, at 20–21 (June 18, 2007), available at http://www.gao.gov/decisions/appro/308603.pdf, [https://perma.cc/B56E-NK79]. To what extent do you think the Constitution draws clear lines in this area, as opposed to providing a general framework in which political power operates?

For further reading on the theory, see Christopher S. Yoo, Steven Calabresi, & Anthony J. Colangelo, *The Unitary Executive in the Modern Era, 1945–2004*, 90 IOWA L. REV. 601 (2005); Christopher S. Yoo, Steven G. Calabresi, & Laurence D. Nee, *The Unitary Executive During the Third Half-Century, 1889–1945*, 80 NOTRE DAME L. REV. 1 (2004).

3. COMPELLING THE WITHDRAWAL OF U.S. MILITARY FORCES THROUGH FUNDING RESTRICTIONS

In October 2002, Congress authorized the president to use U.S. armed forces "as he determines to be necessary and appropriate" to "defend the national security of the United States against the continuing threat posed by Iraq" and "enforce all relevant United Nations Security Council resolutions regarding Iraq." Authorization for Use of Military Force Against Iraq Resolution of 2002, Pub. L. No. 107–243, 116 Stat. 1498 (2002). In March 2003, the United States, with a small coalition of other states, invaded Iraq, asserting that Iraq had failed to abide by its obligations under Security Council resolutions to cooperate in the elimination of its weapons of mass destruction. The coalition quickly defeated Iraq's military forces and toppled the Iraqi government. (*See* Chapter 4, Sec. 5(A)).

The United States and United Kingdom, operating as "occupying powers under a unified command," initially governed Iraq through an entity known as the Coalition Provisional Authority (CPA). *See* S.C. Res. 1483 (May 22, 2003). In June 2004, governing authority in Iraq was transferred to a new Iraqi government and the CPA ceased to exist. Neither the CPA nor the new Iraqi government, however, were able to restore order in Iraq in the aftermath of the war. Extensive "asymmetric warfare" existed, involving an insurgency against the new government, civil war between Sunni and Shia Iraqis, and paramilitary operations by groups linked to the terrorist organization al-Qaeda. Consequently, U.S. military forces remained in Iraq at the request of the Iraqi government, mired in an effort to restore order.

By 2007, more than 3,000 U.S. soldiers had been killed since the commencement of the invasion, and both houses of Congress had turned Democratic in the November 2006 mid-term elections, based largely on popular discontent with the war. Consequently, Congress began to move toward restricting funds for continued military operations in Iraq, raising once again the question of the division of constitutional authority in this area.

In the materials below, consider the different views expressed in congressional testimony on the respective roles of the president and the Congress. Which views do you find the most persuasive? If Congress has a role in denying funds for U.S. military operations, what is the scope of that role? Can Congress deny all funds immediately, even when U.S. forces are already in the field? Can (or must) Congress deny funds pursuant to a gradual schedule for withdrawal of those troops? Can that schedule be contingent upon certain events occurring? If you were trying to restrict U.S. military operations through a statute, how would you do it?

2007 SENATE JUDICIARY COMMITTEE HEARINGS ON EXERCISING CONGRESS'S CONSTITUTIONAL POWER TO END A WAR

S. Hrg. 110–902, 110th Cong., 1st Sess. (Jan. 30, 2007).

SEN. FEINGOLD . . .

It is often said in this era of ubiquitous public opinion polls that the only poll that really matters is the one held on election day. On November 7, 2006, we had such a poll, and all across this country, the American people expressed their opinion on the war in Iraq in the most significant and meaningful way possible—they voted. And with those votes, they sent a clear message that they disagree with this war and they want our involvement in it to stop.

The President has chosen to ignore that message. So it is up to Congress to act.

The Constitution gives Congress the explicit power "[to] declare War," "[t]o raise and support Armies," "[t]o provide and maintain a Navy," and "[t]o make Rules for the Government and Regulation of the land and naval Forces." In addition, under Article I, "No Money shall be drawn from the Treasury, but in Consequence of Appropriations made by Law." These are direct quotes from the Constitution of the United States. Yet to hear some in the Administration talk, it is as if these provisions were written in invisible ink. They were not. These powers are a clear and direct statement from the founders of our republic that Congress has authority to declare, to define, and ultimately, to end a war.

Our founders wisely kept the power to fund a war separate from the power to conduct a war. In their brilliant design of our system of government, Congress got the power of the purse, and the President got the power of the sword. As James Madison wrote, "Those who are to conduct a war cannot in the nature of things, be proper or safe judges, whether a war ought to be commenced, continued or concluded."

The President has made the wrong judgment about Iraq time and again, first by taking us into war on a fraudulent basis, then by keeping our brave troops in Iraq for nearly four years, and now by proceeding despite the opposition of the Congress and the American people to put 21,500 more American troops into harm's way.

If and when Congress acts on the will of the American people by ending our involvement in the Iraq war, Congress will be performing the role assigned it by the founding fathers—defining the nature of our military commitments and acting as a check on a President whose policies are weakening our nation.

There is little doubt that decisive action from the Congress is needed. Despite the results of the election, and two months of study and supposed consultation—during which experts and members of Congress from across the political spectrum argued for a new policy—the President has decided to escalate the war. When asked whether he would persist in this policy despite congressional opposition, he replied: "Frankly, that's not their responsibility."

Last week Vice President Cheney was asked whether the non-binding resolution passed by the Foreign Relations Committee that will soon be considered by the full Senate would deter the President from escalating the war. He replied: "It's not going to stop us."

In the United States of America, the people are sovereign, not the President. It is Congress' responsibility to challenge an administration that persists in a war that is misguided and that the country opposes. We cannot simply wring our hands and complain about the Administration's policy. We cannot just pass resolutions saying "your policy is mistaken." And we can't stand idly by and tell ourselves that it's the President's job to fix the mess he made. It's our job to fix the mess, and if we don't do so we are abdicating our responsibilities. . . .

There is plenty of precedent for Congress exercising its constitutional authority to stop U.S. involvement in armed conflict.

In late December 1970, Congress prohibited the use of funds to finance the introduction of United States ground combat troops into Cambodia or to provide U.S. advisors to or for Cambodian military forces in Cambodia.

In late June 1973, Congress set a date to cut off funds for combat activities in South East Asia. . . .

More recently, President Clinton signed into law language that prohibited funding after March 31, 1994, for military operations in Somalia, with certain limited exceptions. And in 1998, Congress passed legislation including a provision that prohibited funding for Bosnia after June 30, 1998, unless the President made certain assurances.

Our witnesses today are well aware of this history, and I look forward to hearing their analysis of it as they discuss Congress's power in this area. They are legal scholars, not military or foreign policy experts. We are here to find out from them not what Congress should do, but what Congress can do. Ultimately, it rests with Congress to decide whether to use its constitutional powers to end the war.

The answer should be clear. Since the President is adamant about pursuing his failed policies in Iraq, Congress has the duty to stand up and use its power to stop him. If Congress doesn't stop this war, it's not because it doesn't have the power. It's because it doesn't have the will.

MR. [BRADFORD] BERENSON[1] . . .

Although the President and the Congress each have important exclusive powers in the field of warfare—Congress primarily as provisioner and rulemaker for the armed forces and the President primarily as wielder of the forces thus created and governed—there are important areas of war power where the Constitution is silent as to which branch is to exercise power. In my view, these include most of the areas in which the Congress is now considering legislation. For example, the Constitution does not specify how an armed conflict is to be terminated. It does not specify who is to decide whether war aims are worth pursuing, or whether the cost of pursuing them at a given moment in time is too high. It does not say whether the President or the Congress is to determine what levels of national military and economic resources may be expended in the pursuit of those aims.

In these areas, I believe the power is shared—that is, both the Congress and the President have legitimate authority to express and give effect to their preferences, and national policy is ultimately set through the interplay between the two branches. See generally *United States v. Curtiss-Wright Export Co.*, 299 U.S. 304 (1936). But the power is shared in a particular way—the interplay results in a particular balance between Congress and the President—which makes both constitutional and functional sense.

The first principle defining this interplay is that the President is the first mover. This means that, in the absence of contrary legislation, the President is entitled to set policy on these subjects, which fall into spheres where the institutional advantages of the Executive over a deliberative and legislative body such as the Congress make the President presumptively the best choice to guide the nation. . . . Unlike Congress, whose powers are limited to those enumerated, the President, through the Vesting Clause, is endowed with the whole of the "Executive power." . . . The Vesting Clause provides the President a vast reserve of implied authority to do whatever may be necessary in executing the laws and governing the nation. . . . This plainly encompasses making the ongoing, critical decisions and judgments necessary to safeguard the national security and guide our relations, friendly or hostile, with foreign nations and foreign powers. Unlike the Congress, which must follow a constitutionally prescribed and somewhat cumbersome procedure for effecting its will, the President may simply decide and act in these spheres of his international and national security authority. As the Supreme Court has recognized on numerous occasions, the President's inherent authority is especially broad, and his primacy especially clear, in the realm of foreign affairs, military affairs, and intelligence activities. *See, e.g., Department of the Navy v. Egan*, 484 U.S.

1 [Authors' Note: From January 2001 through January 2003, Mr. Berenson served as Associate Counsel to the President of the United States].

518, 529 (1988); *Harlow v. Fitzgerald*, 457 U.S. 800, 812 n. 19 (1982); *Ludecke v. Watkins*, 335 U.S. 160, 173 (1948); *Curtiss-Wright Export Co.*, 299 U.S. at 320.

But unlike the President's core Commander in Chief powers, the broader policy decisions relating to military affairs and the nation's overall defense posture are subject to review and, if legislation can be enacted, control by the Congress. Congress derives its authority in these areas from two principal sources: the Necessary and Proper Clause, and the Spending Clause. Through the Necessary and Proper Clause, Congress has general, residual authority to "make all laws which shall be necessary and proper for carrying into execution the foregoing powers" and all other powers vested in the United States government. . . . More than two centuries of constitutional history make clear that this power is not narrowly limited to the specific powers enumerated in Article I but rather extends to any power of the government as a whole . . . and, more broadly, to furthering by rational means legitimate constitutional ends of government not forbidden to the Congress, see *M'Culloch v. Maryland*, 17 U.S. (4 Wheat.) 316, 421 (1819). Congress's power of the purse also gives it an abundant reserve of authority in the realm of military and defense matters. Pursuant to the Spending Clause, U.S. Const., art. I, sec. 8, cl. 1, Congress may generally control the levels of spending on various governmental functions, including military spending, as well as the purposes for which federal tax dollars may be expended. Indeed, Congress's power of the purse is so broad that virtually all military activities directed by the President are inevitably, if implicitly, authorized by the Congress through its decisions to fund and not interfere with those activities.

The need to enact legislation to override the President's initial policy choices in these areas of shared power informs the second major principle of the interbranch interplay in this arena: when the Congress and the President disagree on important matters of defense or military policy, Congress can only bind the President if it assembles a veto-proof majority in favor of its view. Nothing short of legislation that complies with the presentment requirements of Article I, section 7, clause 2 of the Constitution could require the President to desist from his preferred course and obey that chosen by the Congress. See generally *INS v. Chadha*, 462 U.S. 919 (1983). Thus, where the President disagrees strongly enough with the contrary views of the Congress, he may veto the legislation setting forth those views, obliging the Congress to override his veto by a two-thirds majority of each House.

This produces a functionally sensible process and result. It means that in areas of shared war power where there is substantial interbranch disagreement, the President has strong incentives to engage in a public dialogue and debate with the Congress. He will have every reason to share what he knows with the legislature and explain his thinking and that of his military commanders, and to answer the objections and doubts raised by the Members. If disagreement nonetheless persists, a tie or anything close to it goes to the Executive, whose overall constitutional primacy in military matters will therefore be respected. But if the President is unable to convince even a third of a single House of Congress that his position is correct—i.e., if there is a substantial consensus among legislators in both Houses of Congress that the President has chosen the wrong course—then the system will override the normal presumption in favor of the President's views and assume that, despite his institutional advantages, he is incorrect. In that case, Congress will set policy for the nation, and the President will be obliged to comply with that policy in all its constitutional applications.

This does not mean, of course that the President must obey whatever Congress enacts. As we have seen, it is possible that Congress could overstep its bounds and enact a restriction on military activity that would amount to a usurpation of the President's role as Commander in Chief of the nation's military. Neither the Necessary and Proper Clause nor the Spending Clause gives the Congress any power to contravene otherwise applicable constitutional requirements or to invade spheres of authority reserved to other branches of government. . . . To take a hypothetical example, if Congress were to enact a law providing that no American soldier could be sent into combat without body armor, there would be a strong argument that such an enactment impermissibly interferes with the Commander in Chief's discretion to order lightly armed or lightly equipped troops to proceed by stealth into battle in appropriate circumstances. Or if Congress purported to forbid the President from sending particular units to Iraq, that, too, would likely be an unconstitutional infringement of the President's power as Commander in Chief. But in my judgment, if the Congress could muster sufficient strength to enact a mandatory termination of the Iraq War over the President's veto, for example through a de-funding of the war effort, such an enactment would be facially constitutional.

Should the Congress attempt to enact restrictions on the President's ability to conduct the Iraq War—whether in the form of a blanket prohibition on continued hostilities or, more likely, through somewhat more limited or nuanced restrictions—careful analysis would be required to evaluate their constitutionality. Because the outer boundaries of the President's Commander in Chief powers are so poorly defined, it is exceedingly difficult to assess these questions in the abstract. And there may still be considerable uncertainty and room for reasonable, good faith disagreement as to specific proposals.

Moreover, even as to a restriction that all reasonable people could agree was constitutional on its face, it is important to recognize and remember that such a law might be unconstitutional in some of its applications. Precisely because it is impossible to envision all possible developments or events in a field of endeavor as chaotic and fast-moving as warfare, it is essential to retain a degree of humility and flexibility in assessing how the President implements such a law. It would ill serve the national interest for every instance of presidential non-compliance with laws in this area to be decried as presidential "lawbreaking," invoking the familiar tropes about the President not being above the law. I can assure you that the President does not regard himself as being above the law, but he does regard himself, properly, as having an overriding constitutional responsibility to protect our citizens, whether civilian or military. Notwithstanding anything the Congress may enact, the President as Commander in Chief at all times retains authority to direct actions that may be necessary to protect troops in field or to repel sudden attacks or deal with military exigencies. . . .

MR. [LOUIS] FISHER[2] . . .

Congress is not merely a "coequal" branch of government. The framers vested the decisive and ultimate powers of war and spending in the legislative branch. We start with that basic understanding. American democracy places the sovereign power in the people and entrusts to them the temporary delegation of their power to elected Senators and Representatives. Members of Congress take an oath of office to defend the Constitution, not the President. Their primary allegiance is to the people and the constitutional principles of checks and balances and separation of power. Any interpretation of presidential power that fails to take account of those basic concepts is contrary to the democratic system established in the United States.

The legislative judgment to take the country to war carries with it a duty throughout the conflict to decide that military force remains in the national interest. As with any other statute, Congress is responsible for monitoring what it has set in motion. In the midst of war, there are no grounds for believing that the President's judgment for continuing the war is superior to the collective judgment of elected representatives. Congress has both the constitutional authority and the responsibility to retain control and recalibrate national policy whenever necessary. . . .

The need to keep the purse and the sword in separate hands was a bedrock principle for the framers. They recalled the efforts of English kings who, denied funds from Parliament, decided to rely on outside sources of revenue for their military expeditions. The result was civil war and the loss of Charles I of both his office and his head. The growth of democratic government is directly tied to legislative control over all expenditures, including those for foreign and military affairs.

---

[2] [Authors' Note: Mr. Fisher was a Senior Specialist in the Government and Finance Division of the Congressional Research Service of the Library of Congress.]

The U.S. Constitution attempted to avoid the British history of civil war and bloodshed by vesting the power of the purse wholly in Congress. Under Article I, Section 9, "No Money shall be drawn from the Treasury, but in Consequence of Appropriations made by Law." In Federalist No. 48, Madison explained that "the legislative department alone has access to the pockets of the people." The President gained the title of Commander in Chief but Congress retained the power to finance military operations. For Madison, it was a fundamental principle of democratic government that "[t]hose who are to conduct a war cannot in the nature of things, be proper or safe judges, whether a war ought to be commenced, continued, or concluded. They are barred from the latter functions by a great principle in free government, analogous to that which separates the sword from the purse, or the power of executing from the power of enacting laws." This understanding of the war power was widely understood. Jefferson praised the transfer of the war power "from the executive to the Legislative body, from those who are to spend to those who are to pay." . . .

In recent years, advocates of presidential authority have argued that the title "Commander in Chief" empowers the President to initiate military operations against other countries and to continue unless Congress cut off all funds, presumably by mustering a two-thirds majority in each House to overcome an expected presidential veto. Such a scenario means that a President could start and continue a war so long as he had at least one-third plus one in a single chamber of Congress. Nothing in the writings of the framers, the debates at Philadelphia and the ratifying conventions, or the text of the Constitution supports that theory.

Article II reads: "The President shall be Commander in Chief of the Army and Navy of the United States, and of the Militia of the several States, when called into the actual Service of the United States." Here is one constitutional check. Congress, not the President, does the calling. Article I gives to Congress the power to provide "for calling forth the Militia to execute the Laws of the Union, suppress Insurrections and repel Invasions." Under Article I, Congress raises and supports armies and provides and maintains a navy. It makes rules for the government and regulation of the land and naval forces. It provides for organizing, arming, and disciplining the militia.

The Constitution does not empower the President as Commander in Chief to initiate and continue wars. In Federalist No. 74, Hamilton explained part of the purpose for making the President Commander in Chief: unity of command. The direction of war "most peculiarly demands those qualities which distinguish the exercise of power by a single head." The power of directing war and emphasizing the common strength "forms a usual and essential part in the definition of the executive authority." The President's authority to bring unity of purpose in military command does not deprive Congress of its constitutional responsibility to monitor war and decide whether to restrict or terminate military operations.

A third quality attaches to the Commander in Chief Clause. Giving that title to the President represents an important technique for preserving civilian supremacy over the military. The person leading the armed forces would be the civilian President, not a military officer. In 1861, Attorney General Edward Bates explained that the President is Commander in Chief not because he is "skilled in the art of war and qualified to marshal a host in the field of battle." He is Commander in Chief for a different reason. Whatever soldier leads U.S. armies to victory against an enemy, "he is subject to the orders of the civil magistrate, and he and his army are always 'subordinate to the civil power.'" Just as military officers are subject to the direction and command of the President, so is the President subject to the direction and command of Members of Congress, because they are the representative of the sovereign people. To allow a President to conduct a war free of legislative constraints, or free of constraints unless both Houses muster a two-thirds majority to override a veto, would violate fundamental principles of republican government. . . .

Congress has often enacted legislation to restrict and limit military operations by the President, selecting both appropriations bills and authorizing legislation to impose conditions and constraints. The Congressional Research Service recently prepared a lengthy study that lists these statutory provisions. A major cutoff of funds occurred in 1973, when Congress passed legislation to deny funds for the war in Southeast Asia. After President Nixon vetoed the bill, the House effort to override failed on a vote of 241 to 173, or 35 votes short of the necessary two-thirds majority. A lawsuit by Representative Elizabeth Holtzman asked the courts to determine that President Nixon could not engage in combat operations in Cambodia and elsewhere in Indochina in the absence of congressional authorization. A federal district court held that Congress had not authorized the bombing of Cambodia. Its inability to override the veto and the subsequent adoption of an August 15 deadline for the bombing could not be taken as an affirmative grant of legislative authority: "It cannot be the rule that the President needs a vote of only one-third plus one of either House in order to conduct a war, but this would be the consequence of holding that Congress must override a presidential veto in order to terminate hostilities which it had not authorized." Appellate courts mooted the case because the August 15 compromise settled the dispute between the two branches and terminated funding for the war.

Through its power to authorize programs and appropriate funds, Congress can define and limit presidential military actions. Some claim that the power of the purse is an ineffective and impractical method of restraining presidential wars. Senator Jacob Javits said that Congress "can hardly cut off appropriations when 500,000 American troops are fighting for their lives, as in Vietnam." The short answer is that Congress can, and has, used the power of the purse to restrict and terminate presidential wars. If Congress is concerned about the safety of American troops, those lives are not protected by voting additional funds for a war it does not support.

A proper and responsible action, when war has declining value or purpose, is to reevaluate the commitment by placing conditions on appropriations, terminating funding, moving U.S troops to a more secure location, and taking other legislative steps. There is one central and overriding question: Is the continued use of military force in the nation's interest? If not, then U.S. soldiers need to be safely withdrawn and redeployed. Answering that difficult question is not helped by speculation about whether congressional action might "embolden the enemy."

Other examples of congressional intervention can be cited. In 1976, Congress prohibited the CIA from conducting military or paramilitary operations in Angola and denied any appropriated funds to finance directly or indirectly any type of military assistance to Angola. In 1984, Congress adopted the Boland Amendment to prohibit assistance of any kind to support the Contras in Nicaragua. No constitutional objection to this provision was ever voiced publicly by President Reagan, the White House, the Justice Department, or any other agency of the executive branch.

Congress has options other than a continuation of funding or a flat cutoff. In 1986, Congress restricted the President's military role in Central America by stipulating that U.S. personnel "may not provide any training or other service, or otherwise participate directly or indirectly in the provision of any assistance, to the Nicaraguan democratic resistance pursuant to this title within those land areas of Honduras and Costa Rica which are within 20 miles of the border with Nicaragua." In 1991, when Congress authorized President George H. W. Bush to use military force against Iraq, the authority was explicitly linked to UN Security Council Resolution 678, which was adopted to expel Iraq from Kuwait. Thus, the legislation did not authorize any wider action, such as using U.S. forces to invade and occupy Iraq. In 1993, Congress established a deadline for U.S. troops to leave Somalia. No funds could be used for military action after March 31, 1994, unless the President requested an extension from Congress and received prior legislative priority.

NOTE ON THE FUNDING OF THE SECOND WAR IN IRAQ

On March 20, 2007, the U.S. Troop Readiness, Veteran's Care, Katrina Recovery, and Iraq Appropriations Act, H.R. 1591, 110th Cong., 1st Sess. (2007), was introduced in the House of Representatives. Among other things, the legislation would require the president to determine by July 1 "whether the Government of Iraq has given United States Armed Forces and Iraqi Security Forces the authority to pursue all extremists" and "whether the

Government of Iraq and United States Armed Forces are making substantial progress in reducing the level of sectarian violence in Iraq." If the president failed to make such determinations, then "the Secretary of Defense shall commence the redeployment of the Armed Forces from Iraq no later than July 1, 2007, with a goal of completing such redeployment within 180 days." If the president made the determinations, "the Secretary of Defense shall commence the redeployment of the Armed Forces from Iraq not later than October 1, 2007, with a goal of completing such redeployment within 180 days."

The legislation passed the House on March 23 by a vote of 218–212, passed the Senate on March 29 by a vote of 51–47, and, after certain differences were resolved in conference on April 25–26, was sent to the White House. In vetoing the bill, President Bush stated:

> It makes no sense to tell the enemy when you plan to start withdrawing. All the terrorists would have to do is mark their calendars and gather their strength and begin plotting how to overthrow the Government and take control of the country of Iraq. I believe setting a deadline for withdrawal would demoralize the Iraqi people, would encourage killers across the broader Middle East, and send a signal that America will not keep its commitments. Setting a deadline for withdrawal is setting a date for failure, and that would be irresponsible.

President Bush's Remarks on Returning Without Approval to the House of Representatives, U.S. Troop Readiness, Veteran's Care, Katrina Recovery, and Iraq Appropriations Act, 2007, 43 WEEKLY COMP. PRES. DOC. 558–59 (May 1, 2007). In the course of the negotiations between the White House and the Congress over the legislation, White House officials made various statements that Congressional efforts to include dates for the withdrawal of U.S. troops from Iraq were not just misguided but also unconstitutional. Do you agree?

After President Bush's veto, the House of Representatives on May 2 attempted an override, but failed. Thereafter, both Houses approved, and the president signed into law, the U.S. Troop Readiness, Veteran's Care, Katrina Recovery, and Iraq Appropriations Act, 2007, H.R. 2206, Pub. L. No. 110–28, 121 Stat. 112 (HR 2206) (May 25, 2007). Section 1314 of the law established certain "benchmarks" that the Government of Iraq was required to meet and provided that economic support funds would be denied to Iraq unless the president certified that the benchmarks were being met, though the law also allowed the president to waive this restriction so long as he provided a written justification to Congress. Among other things, the law also contained the following provision:

> The President of the United States, in respecting the sovereign rights of the nation of Iraq, shall direct the orderly redeployment of elements of U.S. forces from Iraq, if the components of the Iraqi government, acting in strict accordance with their respective powers given by the Iraqi Constitution, reach a consensus as recited in a resolution, directing a redeployment of U.S. forces.

Id. at § 1314(d).

Does comparing the legislation that failed (H.R. 1591) and the legislation that succeeded (Pub. L. No. 110–28) provide a window on the allocation of constitutional responsibilities in this area? Or is this outcome simply a reflection of the politics of the day?

At a news conference, President Bush was asked about the matter, prompting the following exchange:

> *Question.* When Congress has linked war funding with a timetable, you have argued micromanagement. When they've linked it to unrelated spending, you've argued porkbarrel. But now there's talk from [Senate majority leader] Harry Reid and others that if you veto this bill, they may come back and just simply cut off funding. Wouldn't that be a legitimate exercise of a congressional authority, which is the power of the purse?
>
> *The President.* The Congress is exercising its legitimate authority as it sees fit right now. I just disagree with their decisions. I think setting an artificial timetable for withdrawal is a significant mistake. It . . . sends mixed signals, bad signals to the region and to the Iraqi citizens.

The President's News Conference, 43 WEEKLY COMP. PRES. DOC. 409, 415 (Apr. 3, 2007); *see also* Michael Abramowitz, *Bush Acknowledges Congress' Right to Weigh in on War*, WASH. POST, Apr. 16, 2007, at A15. For further analysis, see Charles Tiefer, *Can Appropriation Riders Speed Our Exit From Iraq?*, 42 STAN. J. INT'L L. 291, 298–317 (2006) (concluding that "there is no principled basis on which the President can usurp Congress' power of the purse, and expend the nation's resources, in Iraq differently than in past wars, if the nation, through Congress, decides to limit the scope of what it will authorize and fund").

4. FUNDING RESTRICTIONS AND THE "IRAN-CONTRA" AFFAIR

During the first term of the Reagan administration (1981–85), there existed a civil war in Nicaragua between the Marxist Sandinista government and the "Contra" rebels. With congressional support, the Reagan administration began supporting the Contras. However, when certain acts of sabotage by the Central Intelligence Agency in support of the Contras were not properly reported to Congress, the Congress was outraged and enacted, beginning in 1982, a series of provisions referred to as the "Boland Amendments" (after Representative Edward Boland, a Massachusetts Democrat) to restrict U.S. support for the Contras. They were:

- *Department of Defense Appropriations Act, 1983, Pub. L. No. 97–377, § 793, 96 Stat. 1865 (1982):*

  None of the funds provided in this Act may be used by the Central Intelligence Agency or the Department of Defense to furnish military equipment, military training or advice, or other support for military activities, to any group or individual, not part of a country's armed forces, for the purpose of overthrowing the Government of Nicaragua or provoking a military exchange between Nicaragua and Honduras.

- *Intelligence Authorization for Fiscal Year 1984, Pub. L. No. 98–215, § 108, 97 Stat. 1473 (1983):*

  During fiscal year 1984, not more than $24,000,000 of the funds available to the Central Intelligence Agency, the Department of Defense, or any other agency or entity of the United States involved in intelligence activities may be obligated or expended for the purpose or which would have the effect of supporting, directly or indirectly, military or paramilitary operations in Nicaragua by any nation, group, organization, movement, or individual.

- *Continuing Appropriations Act for Fiscal Year 1985, Pub. L. No. 98–473, § 8066(a), 98 Stat. 1837 (1984):*

  During fiscal year 1985, no funds available to the Central Intelligence Agency, the Department of Defense, or any other agency or entity of the United States involved in intelligence activities may be obligated or expended for the purpose or which would have the effect of supporting, directly or indirectly, military or paramilitary operations in Nicaragua by any nation, group, organization, movement, or individual.

After enactment of the Boland Amendments, employees of President Reagan's National Security Council engaged in a scheme whereby anti-tank and anti-aircraft missiles were surreptitiously sold to the Government of Iran (with whom the United States had no diplomatic relations) and the funds from those sales, as well as funds raised from private donors and foreign countries, were channeled to support the Contras. Thus, the funding involved non-appropriated money and was provided to the Contras by an office of the president, not by U.S. intelligence agencies. When the "Iran-Contra" scheme became public in 1986, many in Congress declared that the scheme violated the Boland Amendments, while the Reagan Administration maintained that no violation had occurred. The Reagan Administration argued that the Boland Amendments were not a comprehensive ban on support for the Contras; they covered only appropriated funds spent by intelligence agencies (such as the CIA).

Thereafter, no court ever determined whether the Boland Amendments were violated by the Iran-Contra scheme, nor was anyone ever convicted of doing so. (National Security Adviser John Poindexter and an assistant, Oliver North, were convicted on other charges, which were overturned on appeal.)

Assuming that the Boland Amendments *did* preclude any and all support for the Contras, were they an unconstitutional interference in the president's ability to conduct foreign policy? Can Congress not only preclude the expenditure of funds from in the U.S. treasury, but also funds that might be raised by the president from private entities or foreign governments? To address those and other issues, joint House and Senate committees jointly convened to investigate the affair.

REPORT OF THE CONGRESSIONAL COMMITTEES INVESTIGATING THE IRAN-CONTRA AFFAIR

S. Rep. No. 216, H. Rep. No. 433, 100th Cong., 1st Sess., at 406–07, 475–76 (1987).

THE REPORT . . .

The Administration only recently has asserted that Congress lacked the authority to restrict the President's options in Nicaragua in the manner it did. . . . [A]t no time prior to public disclosure of alleged violations of the Boland Amendments did the Administration come forward to challenge their constitutionality. On the contrary, Congress and the American people were routinely being assured that the statutes were being observed, "in letter and in spirit." As President Reagan himself stated during a press conference on April 14, 1983, "But what I might wish or our government might wish still would not justify us violating the law of the land."[116]

Surely an Administration should identify in a timely fashion those laws it claims a constitutional prerogative to ignore or subvert. But even beyond the aura of disingenuousness, the attack on the constitutionality of the Boland Amendment falls, in the Committees' collective opinion, far short of the mark.

The analysis must begin, of course, with an appropriate statement of what is, and is not, in issue. Some have attempted, for example, to cast the Boland Amendments as violative of the Supreme Court's famous dictum in *United States v. Curtiss-Wright Export Corp.,*[117] referring to:

> the very delicate, plenary and exclusive power of the President as the sole organ of the federal government in the field of international relations—a power which does not require as a basis for its exercise an act of Congress . . .

---

116 Public Papers of the President: Ronald Reagan, 1983, at 541.

117 299 U.S. 304, 319–20 (1936).

But one does not have to be a proponent of an imperial Congress to see that this language has little application to the situation presented here. We are not confronted with a situation where the President is claiming inherent constitutional authority in the absence of an Act of Congress. Instead, to succeed on this argument the Administration must claim it retains authority to proceed in derogation of an Act of Congress—and not just any act, at that. Here, Congress relied on its traditional authority over appropriations, the "power of the purse," to specify that no funds were to be expended by certain entities in a certain fashion.

Bearing this in mind, the Committees believe a more instructive decision than *Curtiss-Wright* is *Dames & Moore v. Regan*.[118] There, the Supreme Court upheld Executive Orders issued by President Carter to govern the treatment of claims against Iran after resolution of the hostage crisis 1979 and 1980. Chief Justice Rehnquist, then an associate justice, wrote for the Court and quoted portions of a concurring opinion filed by Justice Jackson in [*Youngstown Sheet & Tube Co. v. Sawyer*]. According to Chief Justice Rehnquist:

> When the President acts pursuant to an express or implied authorization from Congress, he exercises not only his powers but also those delegated by Congress. In such a case the executive action "would be supported by the strongest presumptions and widest latitude of judicial interpretation, and the burden of persuasion would rest heavily upon any who might attack it." When the President acts in the absence of congressional authorization he may enter a "zone of twilight in which he and Congress may have concurrent authority, or in which its distribution is uncertain." In such a case, the analysis becomes more complicated, and the validity of the President's action, at least so far as separation-of-powers principles are concerned, hinges on a consideration of all the circumstances which might shed light on the views of the Legislative Branch toward such action, including "congressional inertia, indifference or quiescence." Finally, *when the President acts in contravention of the will of Congress, "his power is at its lowest ebb"* and the Court can sustain his actions "only by disabling the Congress from action on the subject."[120]

As the Committees have already noted, the Administration's activities in support of the Contras were conducted in direct contravention of the will of Congress. It follows, then, that the President's constitutional authority to conduct those activities was "at its lowest ebb."

---

[118] 453 U.S. 654 (1981).

[120] 453 U.S. at 668–69 (emphasis supplied; quoting in part from Jackson, J., concurring in *Youngstown Sheet & Tube Co. v. Sawyer*, 343 U.S. at 637–38).

It strains credulity to suggest that the President has the constitutional prerogative to staff and fund a military operation without the knowledge of Congress and in direct disregard of contrary legislation. To endorse such a prerogative would, in the language of *Dames & Moore,* "[disable] the Congress from action on the subject" and leave the Administration entirely unaccountable for such clandestine initiatives.

In Federalist 75, Alexander Hamilton cautioned against granting the President too much authority over foreign affairs:

> The history of human conduct does not warrant that exalted opinion of human virtue which would make it wise in a nation to commit interests so delicate and momentous a kind as those which concern its intercourse with the rest of the world to the sole disposal of a magistrate, created and circumstanced, as would be a president of the United States.

While each branch of our Government undoubtedly has primacy in certain spheres, none can function in secret disregard of the others in any sphere. That, in essence, was the Administration's attempt here.

Congress must be able to depend upon the President for the execution of laws. It cannot be thrust into an adversarial role in which it must treat representations from the President's staff with skepticism and incredulity. If the President believes that a law has provisions that are unconstitutional, he must either veto it or put Congress on notice of his position. . . . The one option the executive branch does not have is to pretend that it is executing the law when it is, in fact, evading it.

The American system works well only when its branches of government trust one another. The Iran-Contra Affair is a perfect example of how to destroy that trust. . . .

THE MINORITY REPORT . . .

[Past] court decisions demonstrate that the President was meant to have a substantial degree of discretionary power to do many of the kinds of things President Reagan did in Iran and Central America. They do not suggest that a President can do anything he wants. Congress and President were given different resources and different modes of influencing the same policy arenas. Both President and Congress can sway the U.S. posture toward Nicaragua or Iran, for example, but each have their own characteristic tools to bring to bear on the subject. What the Constitutional separation of powers protects is not the President's or Congress's precise sway over particular events. That is for the individual occupants of each branch to earn. But the Constitution does prevent either branch from using its own powers, or modes of activity, to deprive the other branch of its central functions.

The Iranian arms sales, for example, involved sales of U.S. assets. As such, the sales were governed either by the Arms Export Control Act, or by the Economy Act and National Security Act. These laws clearly affect one method a President may wish to use to protect American lives abroad. Nevertheless, the constitutionality of the legislation seems assured both by Congress's power to regulate foreign commerce (Article I, Sec. 8) and, perhaps, by Congress's power to set rules for disposing of U.S. property. More importantly, the legislation would withstand constitutional challenge because Congress acted to pursue an explicit grant of legislative power without undermining or negating the President's equally important inherent power to protect American lives and safety.

Similarly, we grant without argument that Congress may use its power over appropriations, and its power to set rules for statutorily created agencies, to place significant limits on the methods a President may use to pursue objectives the Constitution put squarely within the executive's discretionary power. For example, . . . we have no doubt that Congress has the constitutional power to enact a statute that would cut off all military and financial aid to the [*Contras*], except those that fall under the constitutionally protected rubric of information-sharing and diplomatic communication.

The question thus is not whether Congress has any power overlapping the President's, but what boundaries the Constitution places on congressional attempts to limit the President. The most obvious limit is that just as Congress cannot tell the President to do something unconstitutional, neither can it impose an unconstitutional requirement as a condition for granting a privilege. It therefore may not insist that the President forego some of his constitutionally protected power to get appropriations. The most recent major case on this point is the "legislative veto" decision of *INS v. Chadha,* in which the Supreme Court held that Congress cannot demand that the President give up his power to sign, or refuse to sign, legislative decisions—even if the President agreed to the original bill that set up the procedure to bypass the so-called "presentment" requirement. . . .

In other words, Congress may not use its control over appropriations, including salaries, to prevent the executive or judiciary from fulfilling Constitutionally mandated obligations. The implication for the Boland amendments is obvious. If any part of the amendments would have used Congress's control over salaries to prevent executive actions that Congress may not prohibit directly, the amendments would be just as unconstitutional as if they had dealt with the subject directly.

There is one other important way the Constitution circumscribes legislative limitations on the executive. To explain the way it works, it is easiest to begin with a quotation from the 1893 case of *Swaim v. U.S.*:

> Congress may increase the Army, or reduce the Army, or abolish it altogether; but so long as we have a military force Congress cannot take away from the President the supreme command. . . . Congress can not in the disguise of 'rules for the government' of the Army impair the authority of the President as commander in chief.[24]

The same argument extends by analogy to all of the President's inherent powers under Article II. Congress does not have to create a State Department or an intelligence agency. Once such departments are created, however, the Congress may not prevent the President from using his executive branch employees from serving as the country's "eyes and ears" in foreign policy. Even if Congress refuses to fund such departments, it may not prevent the President from doing what he can without funds to act as the nation's "sole organ" in foreign affairs. Even the final report of the Church committee acknowledged this point.

In the same vein, Congress does not have to appropriate any funds for covert operations. Or, it may decide to give funds only for specified operations one at a time. Since 1789, however, Congress has chosen to give the President a contingency reserve fund for secret agents and operations. The existence of such a fund is obviously crucial, because without it Congress would have to make individual appropriations for each action and thereby harm the country's ability to respond to breaking events during a fiscal year without compromising the secrecy of the operation. Nevertheless, even though a contingency fund is an essential tool for foreign policy, there is nothing in the Constitution requiring Congress to set one up. Once Congress makes the decision to establish such a fund, therefore, it may as a quid pro quo set rules for its use.

However, there are some limits to the rules Congress may thereby impose. For example, Congress may not insist, and has never insisted upon giving advance approval to covert operations because such a requirement would be the functional equivalent of a legislative veto. Similarly, Congress may not condition an authorization or appropriation upon any other procedural requirements that would negate powers granted to the President by the Constitution. What Congress grants by statute may be taken away by statute. But Congress may not ask the President to give up a power he gets from the Constitution, as opposed to one he gets from Congress, as a condition for getting something, whether money or some other good or power from Congress.

---

24 *Swaim v. U.S.*, 28 Ct. Cl. 173, 221 (1893).

LOUIS FISHER, HOW TIGHTLY CAN CONGRESS DRAW THE PURSE STRINGS?*

83 AM. J. INT'L L. 758 (1989).

Of all the revelations emanating from the Iran-contra hearings, the most startling constitutional claim was the assertion that Congress cannot control foreign affairs by withholding appropriations. According to the argument advanced by some administration officials, if Congress prohibits the use of appropriations for foreign policy objectives—as it did with the Boland amendment—the President can nevertheless continue his goals by soliciting funds from the private sector and from foreign countries. If one well dries up, tap another. This theory has profound implications for executive-legislative relations and constitutional government. . . .

. . . When President Reagan signed the continuing resolution that contained the strict language of the Boland amendment, he did not issue a statement claiming that Congress had overstepped its powers and that the administration would pursue its course in Nicaragua. The Attorney General did not challenge the constitutionality of the Boland amendment. The Office of Legal Counsel in the Justice Department did not conclude in any internal memorandum or report that the amendment was invalid or nonbinding.

Nevertheless, . . . executive branch officials were actively soliciting funds from private parties and from foreign governments to assist the contras. Working closely with the White House and the National Security Council, private citizens raised money from private contributors to provide military weapons and supplies to the contras. Administration officials also made repeated efforts to obtain funds from foreign governments. . . .

Only one document from the administration asserted that the Boland amendment permitted some executive officials to assist the contras. Bretton G. Sciaroni, counsel to the President's Intelligence Oversight Board, issued a memorandum on September 12, 1985, concluding that the National Security Council was not covered by the Boland amendment. This memorandum was never made available to Congress or to the public; its existence was revealed only after the Iran-contra affair became public in November 1986. If the legal analysis in the memorandum is correct, John Poindexter, Robert McFarlane, Oliver North and other members of the NSC staff could do what the intelligence community, the Defense Department and "any other agency or entity" had been prohibited from doing by the Boland amendment.

The Sciaroni memorandum is deficient in several respects. First, under the terms of the Boland amendment, the NSC is an "entity . . . involved in intelligence activities." The National Security Act provides that there "is established under the National Security Council a Central Intelligence Agency." How can a subordinate body (the CIA) be involved in intelligence activities but not the controlling agency (the NSC)? Second, the NSC-CIA relationship is elaborated in Executive Order No. 12,333, issued by President Reagan on December 4, 1981. The order states that the NSC "shall act as the highest Executive Branch entity that provides review of, guidance for and direction to the conduct of all national foreign intelligence, counterintelligence, and special activities [covert operations], and attendant policies and programs." This provides clear evidence that the NSC is "involved in intelligence activities" within the meaning of the Boland amendment. Moreover, as defined in the order, the Director of Central Intelligence "shall be responsible directly to the President and the NSC." The CIA shall "conduct services of common concern for the Intelligence Community as directed by the NSC." The principal responsibility for implementing the order, entitled "United States Intelligence Activities," falls to the NSC. Third, even if one rejects this line of argument, the plain fact is that the NSC under North and company *was* "involved in intelligence activities."

The idea that North and other members of the NSC could carry out a covert operation to assist the contras is inconsistent with another section of Executive Order No. 12,333. No agency except the CIA "may conduct any special activity [covert operation] unless the President determines that another agency is more likely to achieve a particular objective." President Reagan never determined that the NSC should conduct a covert action to replace the CIA. Such a determination would have deliberately undermined the Boland amendment, shifting the operating responsibility from an agency proscribed by law to one that attempts, by stealth and proxy, to achieve an end prohibited by Congress. Had Reagan used the NSC as a substitute for the CIA, I think that he would have committed an impeachable offense. . . .

The Framers did more than place the power of the purse with Congress. They deliberately divided government by making the President the commander in chief and reserving to Congress the power to finance military expeditions. The Framers rejected a government in which a single branch could both make war and fund it. . . .

Madison warned against placing the power of commander in chief in the same hands as the power to go to war:

> Those who are to *conduct a war* cannot in the nature of things, be proper or safe judges, whether *a war ought* to be *commenced, continued,* or *concluded.* They are barred from the latter functions by a great principle in free government, analogous to that which

> separates the sword from the purse, or the power of executing from the power of enacting laws.[24]

George Mason advised his colleagues at the Philadelphia convention in 1787 that the "purse & the sword ought never to get into the same hands <whether Legislative or Executive>."[25]

The congressional power of the purse is not unlimited. Congress cannot use appropriations bills to enact bills of attainder, to restrict the President's pardon power or to establish a national religion. The Constitution prohibits Congress from diminishing the salaries of the President or federal judges. Congress would overstep its boundaries if it "refused to appropriate funds for the President to receive foreign ambassadors or to make treaties."[28] It is conventional to say that Congress, in adding conditions and provisos to appropriations bills, may not achieve unconstitutional results. But this merely restates the issue. What types of conditions are unconstitutional? It is false to assume that conditions on appropriations bills are proper for domestic legislation but impermissible for legislation governing foreign affairs and the war power. In foreign affairs as in domestic affairs, Presidents acknowledge that Congress can use conditions to tailor its spending power. . . .

The CIA uses a contingency fund to initiate covert operations before notifying Congress. If administrations abuse this authority and claim a constitutional right not to notify Congress, even within 48 hours or some minimal period, Congress can abolish the contingency fund and force the President to seek congressional approval in advance for each covert action. . . .

It is possible to conduct federal operations with private and foreign funds, but only when authorized by Congress. Statutes have created trust funds to receive gifts from the private sector and from foreign governments. Gift funds must be placed in the Treasury Department and spent only for objects defined by Congress. The purpose is to "ensure that the executive branch remains dependent upon the congressional appropriations process."[39]

Beginning with the Neutrality Act of 1794, Congress has specifically forbidden private citizens from organizing military expeditions against a foreign government. U.S. foreign policy must be conducted through political institutions, not private parties. A Department of Justice analysis in 1979 concluded that the legislative history of the Neutrality Act "clearly shows that the evil it proscribed was precisely and exclusively one which

---

24 6 THE WRITINGS OF JAMES MADISON 148 (G. Hunt ed. 1906).

25 1 THE RECORDS OF THE FEDERAL CONVENTION OF 1787, at 139–40 (M. Farrand ed. 1937).

28 Stith, *Congress' Power of the Purse*, 97 YALE L.J. 1343, 1351 (1988). . . .

39 U.S. GENERAL ACCOUNTING OFFICE, PRINCIPLES OF FEDERAL APPROPRIATIONS LAW 5–65 (1982). . . .

threatens the ability of the Government to carry on a coherent foreign policy."[41]

Despite these precedents and principles, Colonel North asserted that the President "could authorize and conduct covert operations with nonappropriated funds."[42] He was asked at the hearings: "[I]f Congress told the President he could not ask foreign countries or private individuals for financial or other official assistance for the Contras, there would be serious doubt whether Congress had exceeded its constitutional power, correct?" North replied: "If Congress passed such a measure, it would clearly, in my opinion, be unconstitutional."[43]

This argument suffers from weaknesses both political and constitutional. If President Reagan had defied the Boland amendment by seeking financial or other assistance from foreign countries or private individuals, at a minimum this would have subjected the United States to ridicule and humiliation. Having been rebuffed by Congress, the President would go, hat in hand, to foreign governments and private citizens for assistance in implementing the administration's foreign policy. Such conduct would risk a major collision with Congress, with the President acting in the face of a congressional policy enacted into law. In such circumstances, I believe a President would invite, and deserve, impeachment proceedings. He would fail in his constitutional duty to see that the laws are faithfully executed, and he would precipitate a constitutional crisis by merging the power of the sword with the power of the purse.

Moreover, soliciting funds from foreign governments to promote U.S. foreign policy opens the door to widespread compromise and corruption. Admiral Poindexter testified that the administration could withhold information from Congress because the contras were being assisted with nonappropriated funds: "we weren't using appropriated funds. They were private, third-country funds."[44] Accepting funds from foreign governments to sustain U.S. policy creates an implicit quid pro quo, requiring the United States to reciprocate by giving contributing countries extra consideration in the form of foreign assistance, military assistance, arms sales and trade concessions. . . .

For reasons that have both constitutional and practical dimensions, U.S. foreign policy must be conducted only with funds appropriated by Congress. Allowing the President to carry out foreign policy with private or foreign contributions would create what the Framers feared most: the

[41] Office of Legal Counsel, U.S. Department of Justice, Applicability of the Neutrality Act to Activities of the Central Intelligence Agency, memorandum from Larry L. Sims to Philip B. Heymann, Assistant Attorney General, Criminal Division, at 5 (Oct. 10, 1979).

[42] 100–7 *Iran-Contra Hearings*, . . . pt. II at 37.

[43] *Id.*, pt. I at 207.

[44] 100–8 *id.* at 158.

union of the purse and the sword. The Framers deliberately separated those powers to protect individual liberties. Fusing the powers in today's world creates dangers far greater than in 1787. At the Iran-contra hearings, Secretary of State George Shultz repudiated the idea of using nonappropriated funds for foreign policy: "You cannot spend funds that the Congress doesn't either authorize you to obtain or appropriate. That is what the Constitution says, and we have to stick with it."[46]

NOTES

1. *Standing for Private Litigants?* As the materials in this Chapter indicate, the field of foreign relations law as it relates to the appropriations power is not case-driven. One problem for private litigants in bringing such cases is establishing their standing to do so. For example, in *United States v. Richardson*, 418 U.S. 166 (1974), a taxpayer brought an action in mandamus to compel the Secretary of the Treasury to publish an accounting of the receipts and expenditures of the Central Intelligence Agency. In dismissing the case due to lack of standing, the Supreme Court stated at footnote 11:

> Although we need not reach or decide precisely what is meant by a "regular Statement and Account," it is clear that Congress has plenary power to exact any reporting and accounting it considers appropriate in the public interest. It is therefore open to serious question whether the Framers of the Constitution ever imagined that general directives to the Congress or the Executive would be subject to enforcement by an individual citizen. While the available evidence is neither qualitatively nor quantitatively conclusive, historical analysis of the genesis of cl. 7 suggests that it was intended to permit some degree of secrecy of governmental operations. The ultimate weapon of enforcement available to the Congress would, of course, be the "power of the purse." Independent of the statute here challenged by respondent, Congress could grant standing to taxpayers or citizens, or both, limited, of course, by the "cases" and "controversies" provisions of Art. III.

The Court stated further that:

> It can be argued that if respondent is not permitted to litigate this issue, no one can do so. In a very real sense, the absence of any particular individual or class to litigate these claims gives support to the argument that the subject matter is committed to the surveillance of Congress, and ultimately to the political process. Any other conclusion would mean that the Founding Fathers intended to set up something in the nature of an Athenian democracy or a New England town meeting to oversee the conduct of the National Government by means of lawsuits in federal courts. The Constitution created a *representative* Government with the representatives directly

[46] 100–9 *id.* at 75.

> responsible to their constituents at stated periods of two, four, and six years; that the Constitution does not afford a judicial remedy does not, of course, completely disable the citizen who is not satisfied with the "ground rules" established by the Congress for reporting expenditures of the Executive Branch. Lack of standing within the narrow confines of Art. III jurisdiction does not impair the right to assert his views in the political forum or at the polls. Slow, cumbersome, and unresponsive though the traditional electoral process may be thought at times, our system provides for changing members of the political branches when dissatisfied citizens convince a sufficient number of their fellow electors that elected representatives are delinquent in performing duties committed to them.

Id. at 179.

Do you think only Congress should have standing to challenge whether the executive branch is properly expending appropriated funds in the field of foreign affairs? Is Congress in fact exercising such oversight?

2. *Further Reading.* For further background and analysis of the Iran-Contra affair, see Theodore Draper, *A Very Thin Line: The Iran-Contra Affairs* (1991); Andrew W. Hayes, *The Boland Amendments and Foreign Affairs Deference*, 88 COLUM. L. REV. 1534 (1988); Harold Hongju Koh, *The National Security Constitution: Sharing Power After the Iran-Contra Affair* (1990); Harold Hongju Koh, *Why the President (Almost) Always Wins in Foreign Affairs: Lessons of the Iran-Contra Affair*, 97 YALE L.J. 1255 (1988); Peter E. Quint, *Reflections on the Separation of Powers and Judicial Review at the End of the Reagan Era*, 57 GEO. WASH. L. REV. 427 (1989).

CHAPTER 6

FEDERALISM

■ ■ ■

1. RELEVANCE OF FEDERALISM TO FOREIGN AFFAIRS

"Federalism" is concerned with the proper allocation of authority between the federal and state governments. Consequently, the materials in this Chapter deal with the constitutional propriety of actions by state and local governmental units affecting foreign relations. James Madison in Federalist No. 44 contemplated how the United States might have functioned had state constitutions been held out of the Supremacy Clause, saying "the world would have seen, for the first time, a system of government founded on an inversion of the fundamental principles of all government; it would have seen the authority of the whole society everywhere subordinate to the authority of the parts; it would have seen a monster, in which the head was under the direction of the members." Given that the state constitutions were not exempted, some have contended that the U.S. Constitution vested plenary and exclusive power concerning foreign relations with the national government, as may be seen in the *Curtiss-Wright* case (Chapter 1, Sec. 1). Yet neither vision (complete state independence or exclusive federal control) seems borne out in practice; the reality lies somewhere in between.

First, while the federal government is the focal point of U.S. foreign policy, a significant amount of activity relating to foreign affairs occurs at the state and local levels without overt opposition from the federal government. Such activities may take many different forms. State legislatures have enacted laws, state courts have issued decisions, and state governors have used their executive powers to implement U.S. treaty obligations and customary international law.[1] Further, the adoption and amendment of state constitutions have been influenced by developments in

---

[1] *See* Earl H. Fry, *The Expanding Role of State and Local Governments in U.S. Foreign Affairs* (1998); Julian G. Ku, *The State of New York Does Exist: How the States Control Compliance with International Law*, 82 N.C. L. REV. 457 (2004); Julian G. Ku, *Gubernatorial Foreign Policy*, 115 YALE L.J. 2380 (2006); Michael J. Glennon & Robert D. Sloane, *Foreign Affairs Federalism: The Myth of National Exclusivity* (2016); Chad G. Marzen, *The Application of International Law in State Courts: The Case of Florida*, U. TOLEDO L. REV. (forthcoming). Marzen recounts how Florida courts in recent years have decided cases involving sovereign immunity, international aviation, law of the sea, international child abduction, consular relations, service of documents abroad, and human rights.

the field of international law, such as human rights law.[2] In this way, state-level activity may be seen as reinforcing and assisting in the foreign-relations activities of the federal government. Should Congress act proactively to adopt laws that provide guidance to states as to their optimal role in foreign affairs?[3]

Further, in situations where the federal government has declined to adopt an international standard, some states or cities have chosen to do so on their own. Thus, San Francisco passed legislation in 1998 implementing portions of the Convention on the Elimination of All Forms of Discrimination Against Women (CEDAW),[4] even though the U.S. Senate has been unwilling to consent to U.S. ratification of CEDAW.[5] Likewise, even though the U.S. government chose not to join the Kyoto Protocol to the United Nations Framework Convention on Climate Change,[6] some 185 cities nevertheless implemented or modeled local laws on the Protocol. Indeed, nine Northeastern states (Connecticut, Delaware, Maine, Maryland, Massachusetts, New Hampshire, New York, Rhode Island, and Vermont) established a Regional Greenhouse Gas Initiative (RGGI) as the first mandatory market based program in the United States to reduce greenhouse gas emissions. RGGI, which became operative in 2009, establishes a regional cap on the amount of carbon dioxide emissions that power plants can emit, but allows for a limited number of tradable allowances, an approach modeled after the Kyoto Protocol.[7] Similarly, in 2006 five governors from Western states agreed on a plan to cut emissions of greenhouse gases by their states, including through a regional carbon-trading system.[8]

States and cities also have adopted measures that conflict with federal law and policy. For example, state legalization of marijuana arguably places the United States in breach of treaty obligations regulating narcotic

---

[2] *See* Vicki Jackson, *Constitutional Dialogue and Human Dignity: States and Transnational Constitutional Discourse*, 65 MONT. L. REV. 15, 21–27 (2004); Martha F. Davis, *The Spirit of Our Times: State Constitutions and International Human Rights*, 30 N.Y.U. REV. L. & SOC. CHANGE 359 (2006).

[3] For a positive response, see Ryan Baasch & Saikrishna B. Prakash, *Congress and the Reconstruction of Foreign Affairs Federalism*, 115 MICH. L. REV. 47 (2016).

[4] Dec. 18, 1979, 1249 U.N.T.S. 13.

[5] *See* Stacy Laira Lozner, *Diffusion of Local Regulatory Innovations: The San Francisco CEDAW Ordinance and the New York City Human Rights Initiative*, 104 COLUM. L. REV. 768 (2004); *see also* Elizabeth M. Schneider, *Transnational Law as a Domestic Resource: Thoughts on the Case of Women's Rights*, 38 NEW ENG. L. REV. 689, 721 n. 201 (2004) (listing other cities that urged national ratification of CEDAW). For the San Francisco ordinance, see San Francisco, Cal., Administrative Code, ch. 12K (2001).

[6] Dec. 10, 1997, 37 I.L.M. 22 (1998).

[7] *See* Regional Greenhouse Gas Initiative, at http://www.rggi.org; Judith Resnik, Joshua Civin & Joseph Frueh, *Ratifying Kyoto at the Local Level: Sovereigntism, Federalism, and Translocal Organizations of Local Actors (TOGAs)*, 50 ARIZ. L. REV. 709 (2008).

[8] *See* Juliet Eilperin, *Western States Agree to Cut Greenhouse Gases*, WASH. POST, Feb. 27, 2007, at A8.

drugs.[9] With respect to policy, in late 2005 the Massachusetts government and Venezuela's state-owned oil company entered into an agreement for Venezuela to supply oil at highly subsidized prices to low-income Massachusetts families and organizations serving low income communities. This agreement took place even though Venezuelan President Hugo Chavez was a major critic of the Bush Administration's foreign policies, was very friendly with Cuba, and was peddling "21st century socialism" as an alternative model to U.S. "free market" policies. The unusual agreement (involving a developing country providing aid to U.S. citizens) was negotiated with Chavez by Congressman William Delahunt, and was viewed by some as an effort by Chavez to embarrass the Bush administration.[10]

Second, when a federal challenge is brought against state laws (or other measures) relating to the field of foreign affairs, the state law might be struck down on a variety of theories. The state law or measure might be invalidated because of an express prohibition in the U.S. Constitution, such as the prohibitions in Article I, Section 10 against states entering into any treaty or, without the consent of Congress, any "Agreement or Compact" with a "foreign Power." (While states have been allowed to enter into agreements with foreign nations or sub-national units on certain local issues (*e.g.*, on the building of transboundary bridges or highways), a state would not be permitted to conclude a peace treaty with another country.[11]) Alternatively, a state law or measure might be preempted by a federal statute, such as with respect to the imposition of sanctions on a foreign nation, or by a treaty concluded by the president with the advice and consent of the Senate under Article II, Section 2. Even if there is no affirmative measure taken at the federal level, a state law might be struck down as running afoul of the "dormant" foreign commerce power found in Article I, Section 8 or based on what is sometimes referred to as the "dormant" foreign affairs power. Since customary international law is a part of federal common law, in theory it too can preempt conflicting state law. The Supremacy Clause (Article VI, Clause 2), however, does not expressly include customary international law. (*See* Chapter 2, Sec. 2).

Third, as seen in the materials below, federal power in this area is routinely (although not unfailingly) upheld. Often, courts make reference to the importance of the nation speaking with "one voice" in foreign policy matters.[12] While "uniformity" in foreign relations is widely regarded as

---

[9] *See* Jonathan R. Nash, *Doubly Uncooperative Federalism and the Challenge of U.S. Treaty Compliance*, 55 COLUM. J. TRANSNAT'L L. 3, 21–23 (2016); Jean Gailbraith, *Cooperative and Uncooperative Foreign Affairs Federalism*, 130 HARV. L. REV. 2131 (2017).

[10] *See* Justin Blum, *Chavez Pushes Petro-Diplomacy*, WASH. POST, Nov. 22, 2005, at A22.

[11] *See infra,* this Chapter, Sec. 7 on the Compact Clause.

[12] *See, e.g.*, *Holmes v. Jennison*, 39 U.S. (14 Pet.) 540, 575, 10 L.Ed. 579 (1840) (finding that it "was one of the main objects of the Constitution to make us, so far as regarded our foreign relations, one people and one nation. . . .").

desirable, are there some situations where states and cities should be allowed to experiment with different ways of handling transnational matters? In other words, are there some questions about whether it is better to "let a thousand flowers bloom," to allow states and cities to lay the groundwork simultaneously for alternative, possibly antithetical, policies to those of the federal government? And who is empowered to answer that question? Congress? The president? The president acting in conjunction with the Senate? Federal courts? The several states? As you proceed through the following sections, note that the United States itself rarely initiates a legal challenge to state authority. Rather, litigation is usually brought by private parties who prefer the substance of the federal policy (or inaction) to the substance of state policies, and who are only derivatively concerned with the underlying constitutional principles. Does that affect your appraisal?

Fourth, although the focus in this Chapter is on current U.S. doctrine, federalism issues can be placed in a somewhat broader context. Numerous other federal systems—including Australia, Brazil, Canada, Germany, India, Malaysia, Nigeria, Russia, and Switzerland—have grappled with the distribution of lawmaking between the center and quasi-autonomous regions. One common challenge has been the increased use of multilateral conventions to address human rights, criminal law, copyright, air pollution, and other subjects, which has often moved into the federal domain issues previously within the purview of the states or provinces. In some countries (*e.g.*, Australia, Switzerland, and the United States), treaties or their implementing statutes may upset authority previously exercised by the states or provinces, yet this is not true of all nations. In Canada, for instance, the federal treaty-implementing power is limited to those areas in which the central government can legislate absent a treaty, such that adoption of some treaties by the federal government may require concurrent action by provincial legislatures; the federal authorities may not simply proceed on their own. A useful compendium is *National Treaty Law and Practice* (Duncan B. Hollis et al. eds., 2005), which analyzes the law and practice of nineteen nations, several of which have federal systems.

The historical context is also important. Since the ratification of the U.S. Constitution, the power of the federal government to regulate on matters traditionally left to the states has increased dramatically, particularly since the New Deal in the 1930s. Congress's power under the Commerce Clause has supported extensive federal regulation in domestic matters once regarded as quintessentially local in nature, as witnessed by the Civil Rights Act of 1964. Contemporaneously, the U.S. emergence as a superpower in World War II has expanded national activity in the field of foreign affairs.

From the late 1930s to the early 1990s, the courts imposed few limits on the federal power to preempt state laws under the Commerce Clause.

See, e.g., *Garcia v. San Antonio Metropolitan Transit Authority*, 469 U.S. 528 (1985) (overruling *National League of Cities v. Usery*, 426 U.S. 833 (1976)). However, more recent Supreme Court cases establish that there are some limits to federal power—in effect, Congress cannot regulate matters that are "truly local." Thus, the Court found that Congress lacked the power to criminalize the "purely intrastate" possession of a gun near a school, since the matter was noneconomic in nature and not part of a larger regulation of economic activity, and since the statute contained no jurisdictional element that would ensure a case-by-case inquiry into whether a particular firearm possession affected interstate commerce. *See United States v. Lopez*, 514 U.S. 549 (1995). Under similar reasoning, a federal civil remedy for gender-motivated crimes was struck down. *See United States v. Morrison*, 529 U.S. 598 (2000). The Court also found that Congress lacks the power under the Commerce Clause to abrogate a state's constitutional immunity from suit under the Eleventh Amendment. *See Seminole Tribe of Florida v. Florida*, 517 U.S. 44 (1996). Further, Congress is limited in its ability to restrict a state's freedom to enforce a federal statute on religious freedom by means the state deems most appropriate. *See City of Boerne v. Flores*, 521 U.S. 507 (1997). On the other hand, Congress may criminalize the purely local cultivation, possession, and use of marijuana for medicinal purposes—even in the face of a California statute allowing such conduct—since failure to do so would undercut congressional regulation of the interstate market. *See Gonzales v. Raich*, 545 U.S. 1 (2005). Further, Congress can abrogate a state's immunity if it is acting to enforce the Fourteenth Amendment. *See Fitzpatrick v. Bitzer*, 427 U.S. 445 (1976).

To date, the Supreme Court has not found that these decisions have direct implications for federalism in the field of foreign relations. When Congress passes a statute purportedly on a matter of foreign relations, or the federal government ratifies an international agreement, is the matter *ipso facto* not "truly local"? Put another way, are such acts *ipso facto* part of a broader scheme of regulation that falls within the realm of federal constitutional power? Interest in whether the Court's jurisprudence suggests limits on the federal foreign relations power has given rise to a veritable cottage industry of scholarship. For a sampling, see Martin S. Flaherty, *Are We to Be a Nation?: Federal Power vs. "States' Rights" in Foreign Affairs*, 70 U. COLO. L. REV. 1277 (1999); Michael D. Ramsey, *The Power of the States in Foreign Affairs: The Original Understanding of Foreign Policy Federalism*, 75 NOTRE DAME L. REV. 341 (1999).

2. PREEMPTION OF STATE LAW BY FEDERAL STATUTE

TARBLE'S CASE

80 U.S. (13 Wall.) 397, 401–09 (1871).

[Edward Tarble was a U.S. soldier being held in military custody. Tarble's father claimed that his son had enlisted in the U.S. army before his eighteenth birthday without the father's consent. A Wisconsin state court commissioner issued a writ of *habeas corpus* directing the army to release Tarble. The army produced Tarble, but protested that the commissioner had no jurisdiction to issue the writ. According to the army, Tarble had enlisted as a U.S. soldier for a period of five years and had taken the oath required by the law and regulations of the army. Further, the army maintained that Tarble deserted, but was captured and confined pending trial by the proper military authorities. Upon appeal, the Wisconsin Supreme Court upheld the commissioner's writ.]

MR. JUSTICE FIELD . . . delivered the opinion of the court, as follows:

. . . There are within the territorial limits of each State two governments [*i.e.*, the U.S. government and the state government], restricted in their spheres of action, but independent of each other, and supreme within their respective spheres. Each has its separate departments; each has its distinct laws, and each has its own tribunals for their enforcement. Neither government can intrude within the jurisdiction, or authorize any interference therein by its judicial officers with the action of the other. The two governments in each State stand in their respective spheres of action in the same independent relation to each other, except in one particular, that they would if their authority embraced distinct territories. That particular consists in the supremacy of the authority of the United States when any conflict arises between the two governments. The Constitution and the laws passed in pursuance of it, are declared by the Constitution itself to be the supreme law of the land, and the judges of every State are bound thereby, "anything in the constitution or laws of any State to the contrary notwithstanding." Whenever, therefore, any conflict arises between the enactments of the two sovereignties, or in the enforcement of their asserted authorities, those of the National government must have supremacy until the validity of the different enactments and authorities can be finally determined by the tribunals of the United States. This temporary supremacy until judicial decision by the National tribunals, and the ultimate determination of the conflict by such decision, are essential to the preservation of order and peace, and the avoidance of forcible collision between the two governments. "The Constitution," as said by Mr. Chief Justice Taney, "was not framed merely to guard the States against danger from abroad, but chiefly to secure union and harmony at home; and to accomplish this end it was deemed necessary, when the Constitution was framed, that many of the rights of sovereignty which the States then possessed should be ceded to the General government; and that in the sphere of action assigned to it, it should be supreme and strong enough to execute its own laws by its own tribunals, without interruption from a State, or from State authorities." And the judicial power conferred extends to all cases arising under the Constitution, and thus embraces every legislative act of Congress, whether passed in pursuance of it, or in disregard of its provisions. The Constitution is under the view of the tribunals of the United States when any act of Congress is brought before them for consideration.

Such being the distinct and independent character of the two governments, within their respective spheres of action, it follows that neither can intrude with its judicial process into the domain of the other, except so far as such intrusion may be necessary on the part of the National government to preserve its rightful supremacy in cases of conflict of authority. In their laws, and mode of enforcement, neither is responsible to the other. How their respective laws shall be enacted; how they shall be carried into execution; and in what tribunals, or by what officers; and how much discretion, or whether any at all shall be vested in their officers, are matters subject to their own control, and in the regulation of which neither can interfere with the other.

Now, among the powers assigned to the National government, is the power "to raise and support armies," and the power "to provide for the government and regulation of the land and naval forces." The execution of these powers falls within the line of its duties; and its control over the subject is plenary and exclusive. It can determine, without question from any State authority, how the armies shall be raised, whether by voluntary enlistment or forced draft, the age at which the soldier shall be received, and the period for which he shall be taken, the compensation he shall be allowed, and the service to which he shall be assigned. And it can provide the rules for the government and regulation of the forces after they are raised, define what shall constitute military offences, and prescribe their punishment. No interference with the execution of this power of the National government in the formation, organization, and government of its armies by any State officials could be permitted without greatly impairing the efficiency, if it did not utterly destroy, this branch of the public service. . . . It is manifest that the powers of the National government could not be exercised with energy and efficiency at all times, if its acts could be interfered with and controlled for any period by officers or tribunals of another sovereignty. . . .

The conclusion we have reached renders it unnecessary to consider how far the declaration of the prisoner as to his age, in the oath of enlistment, is to be deemed conclusive evidence on that point on the return to the writ.

Judgment reversed.

CROSBY V. NATIONAL FOREIGN TRADE COUNCIL

530 U.S. 363, 366–88 (2000).

JUSTICE SOUTER delivered the opinion of the Court.

The issue is whether the Burma law of the Commonwealth of Massachusetts, restricting the authority of its agencies to purchase goods or services from companies doing business with Burma, is invalid under the Supremacy Clause of the National Constitution owing to its threat of frustrating federal statutory objectives. We hold that it is.

I

In June 1996, Massachusetts adopted "An Act Regulating State Contracts with Companies Doing Business with or in Burma (Myanmar)," 1996 Mass. Acts 239, ch. 130 (codified at Mass. Gen. Laws §§ 7:22G–7:22M, 40 F. 1/2 (1997)). The statute generally bars state entities from buying goods or services from any person (defined to include a business organization) identified on a "restricted purchase list" of those doing business with Burma. §§ 7:22H(a), 7:22J. Although the statute has no general provision for waiver or termination of its ban, it does exempt from boycott any entities present in Burma solely to report the news, § 7:22H(e), or to provide international telecommunication goods or services, *ibid.*, or medical supplies, § 7:22I. . . .

In September 1996, three months after the Massachusetts law was enacted, Congress passed a statute imposing a set of mandatory and conditional sanctions on Burma. *See* Foreign Operations, Export Financing, and Related Programs Appropriations Act, 1997, § 570, 110 Stat. 3009–166 to 3009–167 (enacted by the Omnibus Consolidated Appropriations Act, 1997, § 101(c), 110 Stat. 3009–121 to 3009–172). The federal Act has five basic parts, three substantive and two procedural.

First, it imposes three sanctions directly on Burma. It bans all aid to the Burmese Government except for humanitarian assistance, counternarcotics efforts, and promotion of human rights and democracy. § 570(a)(1). The statute instructs United States representatives to international financial institutions to vote against loans or other assistance to or for Burma, § 570(a)(2), and it provides that no entry visa shall be issued to any Burmese Government official unless required by treaty or to staff the Burmese mission to the United Nations, § 570(a)(3). These restrictions are to remain in effect "[u]ntil such time as the President determines and certifies to Congress that Burma has made measurable and substantial progress in improving human rights practices and implementing democratic government." § 570(a).

Second, the federal Act authorizes the President to impose further sanctions subject to certain conditions. He may prohibit "United States persons" from "new investment" in Burma, and shall do so if he determines and certifies to Congress that the Burmese Government has physically harmed, rearrested, or exiled Daw Aung San Suu Kyi (the opposition leader selected to receive the Nobel Peace Prize), or has committed "large-scale repression of or violence against the Democratic opposition." § 570(b). "New investment" is defined as entry into a contract that would favor the "economical development of resources located in Burma," or would provide ownership interests in or benefits from such development, § 570(f)(2), but the term specifically excludes (and thus excludes from any Presidential prohibition) "entry into, performance of, or financing of a contract to sell or purchase goods, services, or technology," *ibid.*

Third, the statute directs the President to work to develop "a comprehensive, multilateral strategy to bring democracy to and improve human rights practices and the quality of life in Burma." § 570(c). He is instructed to cooperate with members of the Association of Southeast Asian Nations (ASEAN) and with other countries having major trade and investment interests in Burma to devise such an approach, and to pursue the additional objective of fostering dialogue between the ruling State Law and Order Restoration Council (SLORC) and democratic opposition groups. *Ibid.*

As for the procedural provisions of the federal statute, the fourth section requires the President to report periodically to certain congressional committee chairmen on the progress toward democratization and better living conditions in Burma as well as on the development of the required strategy. § 570(d). And the fifth part of the federal Act authorizes the President "to waive, temporarily or permanently, any sanction [under the federal Act] . . . if he determines and certifies to Congress that the application of such sanction would be contrary to the national security interests of the United States." § 570(e).

On May 20, 1997, the President issued the Burma Executive Order, Exec. Order No. 13047, 3 CFR 202 (1997 Comp.). He certified for purposes of § 570(b) that the Government of Burma had "committed large-scale repression of the democratic opposition in Burma" and found that the Burmese Government's actions and policies constituted "an unusual and extraordinary threat to the national security and foreign policy of the United States," a threat characterized as a national emergency. The President then prohibited new investment in Burma "by United States persons," Exec. Order No. 13047, § 1, any approval or facilitation by a United States person of such new investment by foreign persons, § 2(a), and any transaction meant to evade or avoid the ban, § 2(b). The order generally incorporated the exceptions and exemptions addressed in the statute. §§ 3, 4. Finally, the President delegated to the Secretary of State the tasks of working with ASEAN and other countries to develop a strategy for democracy, human rights, and the quality of life in Burma, and of making the required congressional reports. § 5.

II

Respondent National Foreign Trade Council (Council) is a nonprofit corporation representing companies engaged in foreign commerce; 34 of its members were on the Massachusetts restricted purchase list in 1998. . . . Three withdrew from Burma after the passage of the state Act, and one member had its bid for a procurement contract increased by 10 percent under the provision of the state law allowing acceptance of a low bid from a listed bidder only if the next-to-lowest bid is more than 10 percent higher. *Ibid.*

In April 1998, the Council filed suit in the United States District Court for the District of Massachusetts, seeking declaratory and injunctive relief against the petitioner state officials charged with administering and enforcing the state Act (whom we will refer to simply as the State). . . .

III

A fundamental principle of the Constitution is that Congress has the power to preempt state law. Art. VI, cl. 2; *Gibbons v. Ogden*, 9 Wheat. 1, 211 (1824); *Savage v. Jones*, 225 U.S. 501, 533 (1912); *California v. ARC America Corp.*, 490 U.S. 93, 101 (1989). Even without an express provision for preemption, we have found that state law must yield to a congressional Act in at least two circumstances. When Congress intends federal law to "occupy the field," state law in that area is preempted. *Id.*, at 100; *cf. United States v. Locke,* 529 U.S. 89, 115 (2000) (citing *Charleston & Western Carolina R. Co. v. Varnville Furniture Co.*, 237 U.S. 597, 604 (1915)). And even if Congress has not occupied the field, state law is naturally preempted to the extent of any conflict with a federal statute. *Hines v. Davidowitz*, 312 U.S. 52, 66–67 (1941); *ARC America Corp., supra,* at 100–101; *Locke, supra,* at 109. We will find preemption where it is impossible for a private party to comply with both state and federal law, *see, e.g., Florida Lime & Avocado Growers, Inc. v. Paul,* 373 U.S. 132, 142–43 (1963), and where "under the circumstances of [a] particular case, [the challenged state law] stands as an obstacle to the accomplishment and execution of the full purposes and objectives of Congress." *Hines, supra,* at 67. What is a sufficient obstacle is a matter of judgment, to be informed by examining the federal statute as a whole and identifying its purpose and intended effects. . . .

Applying this standard, we see the state Burma law as an obstacle to the accomplishment of Congress's full objectives under the federal Act. We find that the state law undermines the intended purpose and "natural effect" of at least three provisions of the federal Act, that is, its delegation of effective discretion to the President to control economic sanctions against Burma, its limitation of sanctions solely to United States persons and new investment, and its directive to the President to proceed diplomatically in developing a comprehensive, multilateral strategy toward Burma.

A

First, Congress clearly intended the federal Act to provide the President with flexible and effective authority over economic sanctions against Burma. Although Congress immediately put in place a set of initial sanctions (prohibiting bilateral aid, § 570(a)(1), support for international financial assistance, § 570(a)(2), and entry by Burmese officials into the United States, § 570(a)(3)), it authorized the President to terminate any and all of those measures upon determining and certifying that there had been progress in human rights and democracy in Burma. § 570(a). It invested the President with the further power to ban new investment by United States persons, dependent only on specific Presidential findings of repression in Burma. § 570(b). And, most significantly, Congress empowered the President "to waive, temporarily or permanently, any sanction [under the federal Act] . . . if he determines and certifies to Congress that the application of such sanction would be contrary to the national security interests of the United States." § 570(e).

This express investiture of the President with statutory authority to act for the United States in imposing sanctions with respect to the Government of Burma, augmented by the flexibility to respond to change by suspending sanctions in the interest of national security, recalls Justice Jackson's observation in *Youngstown Sheet & Tube Co. v. Sawyer,* 343 U.S. 579, 635 (1952): "When the President acts pursuant to an express or implied authorization of Congress, his authority is at its maximum, for it includes all that he possesses in his own right plus all that Congress can delegate." . . . Within the sphere defined by Congress, then, the statute has placed the President in a position with as much discretion to exercise economic leverage against Burma, with an eye toward national security, as our law will admit. And it is just this plenitude of Executive authority that we think controls the issue of preemption here. The President has been given this authority not merely to make a political statement but to achieve a political result, and the fullness of his authority shows the importance in the congressional mind of reaching that result. It is simply implausible that Congress would have gone to such lengths to empower the President if it had been willing to compromise his effectiveness by deference to every provision of state statute or local ordinance that might, if enforced, blunt the consequences of discretionary Presidential action.

B

Congress manifestly intended to limit economic pressure against the Burmese Government to a specific range. The federal Act confines its reach to United States persons, § 570(b), imposes limited immediate sanctions, § 570(a), places only a conditional ban on a carefully defined area of "new investment," § 570(f)(2), and pointedly exempts contracts to sell or purchase goods, services, or technology, § 570(f)(2). These detailed provisions show that Congress's calibrated Burma policy is a deliberate effort "to steer a middle path,". . . .

The State has set a different course, and its statute conflicts with federal law at a number of points by penalizing individuals and conduct that Congress has explicitly exempted or excluded from sanctions. . . .

C

Finally, the state Act is at odds with the President's intended authority to speak for the United States among the world's nations in developing a "comprehensive, multilateral strategy to bring democracy to and improve human rights practices and the quality of life in Burma." § 570(c). Congress called for Presidential cooperation with members of ASEAN and other countries in developing such a strategy, *ibid.,* directed the President to encourage a dialogue between the Government of Burma and the democratic opposition, *ibid.,* and required him to report to the Congress on the progress of his diplomatic efforts, § 570(d). As with Congress's explicit delegation to the President of power over economic sanctions, Congress's express command to the President to take the initiative for the United States among the international community invested him with the maximum authority of the National Government, *cf. Youngstown Sheet & Tube Co.,* 343 U.S., at 635, in harmony with the President's own constitutional powers, U.S. Const., Art. II, § 2, cl. 2 ("[The President] shall have Power, by and with the Advice and Consent of the Senate, to make Treaties" and "shall appoint Ambassadors, other public Ministers and Consuls"); § 3 ("[The President] shall receive Ambassadors and other public Ministers"). This clear mandate and invocation of exclusively national power belies any suggestion that Congress intended the President's effective voice to be obscured by state or local action. . . .

V

Because the state Act's provisions conflict with Congress's specific delegation to the President of flexible discretion, with limitation of sanctions to a limited scope of actions and actors, and with direction to develop a comprehensive, multilateral strategy under the federal Act, it is preempted, and its application is unconstitutional, under the Supremacy Clause.

ARIZONA V. UNITED STATES

567 U.S. 387 (2012).

JUSTICE KENNEDY delivered the opinion of the Court. . . .

To address pressing issues related to the large number of aliens within its borders who do not have a lawful right to be in this country, the State of Arizona in 2010 enacted a statute called the Support Our Law Enforcement and Safe Neighborhoods Act. The law is often referred to as S.B. 1070, the version introduced in the state senate. Its stated purpose is to "discourage and deter the unlawful entry and presence of aliens and economic activity by persons unlawfully present in the United States." The law's provisions establish an official state policy of "attrition through enforcement." The question before the Court is whether federal law preempts and renders invalid four separate provisions of the state law.

I

The United States filed this suit against Arizona, seeking to enjoin S.B. 1070 as preempted. Four provisions of the law are at issue here. Two create new state offenses. Section 3 makes failure to comply with federal alien-registration requirements a state misdemeanor. Section 5, in relevant part, makes it a misdemeanor for an unauthorized alien to seek or engage in work in the State; this provision is referred to as § 5(C). Two other provisions give specific arrest authority and investigative duties with respect to certain aliens to state and local law enforcement officers. Section 6 authorizes officers to arrest without a warrant a person "the officer has probable cause to believe . . . has committed any public offense that makes the person removable from the United States." Section 2(B) provides that officers who conduct a stop, detention, or arrest must in some circumstances make efforts to verify the person's immigration status with the Federal Government.

The United States District Court for the District of Arizona issued a preliminary injunction preventing the four provisions at issue from taking effect. The Court of Appeals for the Ninth Circuit affirmed. . . .

II

A

The Government of the United States has broad, undoubted power over the subject of immigration and the status of aliens. See *Toll v. Moreno*, 458 U.S. 1, 10 (1982); see generally S. Legomsky & C. Rodríguez, Immigration and Refugee Law and Policy 115–132 (5th ed. 2009). This authority rests, in part, on the National Government's constitutional power to "establish an uniform Rule of Naturalization," U.S. Const., Art. I, § 8, cl. 4, and its inherent power as sovereign to control and conduct relations with foreign nations, see *Toll, supra*, at 10 (citing *United States v. Curtiss-Wright Export Corp.*, 299 U.S. 304, 318 (1936)).

The federal power to determine immigration policy is well settled. Immigration policy can affect trade, investment, tourism, and diplomatic relations for the entire Nation, as well as the perceptions and expectations of aliens in this country who seek the full protection of its laws. Perceived mistreatment of aliens in the United States may lead to harmful reciprocal treatment of American citizens abroad.

It is fundamental that foreign countries concerned about the status, safety, and security of their nationals in the United States must be able to confer and communicate on this subject with one national sovereign, not the 50 separate States. This Court has reaffirmed that "[o]ne of the most important and delicate of all international relationships . . . has to do with the protection of the just rights of a country's own nationals when those nationals are in another country." *Hines v. Davidowitz*, 312 U.S. 52, 64 (1941).

Federal governance of immigration and alien status is extensive and complex. Congress has specified categories of aliens who may not be admitted to the United States. See 8 U.S.C. § 1182. Unlawful entry and unlawful reentry into the country are federal offenses. §§ 1325, 1326. Once here, aliens are required to register with the Federal Government and to carry proof of status on their person. See §§ 1301–1306. Failure to do so is a federal misdemeanor. §§ 1304(e), 1306(a). Federal law also authorizes States to deny noncitizens a range of public benefits, § 1622; and it imposes sanctions on employers who hire unauthorized workers, § 1324a.

Congress has specified which aliens may be removed from the United States and the procedures for doing so. Aliens may be removed if they were inadmissible at the time of entry, have been convicted of certain crimes, or meet other criteria set by federal law. See § 1227. Removal is a civil, not criminal, matter. A principal feature of the removal system is the broad discretion exercised by immigration officials. See Brief for Former Commissioners of the United States Immigration and Naturalization Service as Amici Curiae 8–13 (hereinafter Brief for Former INS Commissioners). Federal officials, as an initial matter, must decide whether it makes sense to pursue removal at all. If removal proceedings commence, aliens may seek asylum and other discretionary relief allowing them to remain in the country or at least to leave without formal removal. See § 1229a(c)(4); see also, e.g., §§ 1158 (asylum), 1229b (cancellation of removal), 1229c (voluntary departure).

Discretion in the enforcement of immigration law embraces immediate human concerns. Unauthorized workers trying to support their families, for example, likely pose less danger than alien smugglers or aliens who commit a serious crime. The equities of an individual case may turn on many factors, including whether the alien has children born in the United States, long ties to the community, or a record of distinguished military service. Some discretionary decisions involve policy choices that bear on this Nation's international relations. Returning an alien to his own country may be deemed inappropriate even where he has committed a removable offense or fails to meet the criteria for admission. The foreign state may be mired in civil war, complicit in political persecution, or enduring conditions that create a real risk that the alien or his family will be harmed upon return. The dynamic nature of relations with other countries requires the Executive Branch to ensure that enforcement policies are consistent with this Nation's foreign policy with respect to these and other realities.

Agencies in the Department of Homeland Security play a major role in enforcing the country's immigration laws. United States Customs and Border Protection (CBP) is responsible for determining the admissibility of aliens and securing the country's borders. In 2010, CBP's Border Patrol apprehended almost half a million people. Immigration and Customs Enforcement (ICE), a second agency, "conducts criminal investigations involving the enforcement of immigration-related statutes." ICE also operates the Law Enforcement Support Center. LESC, as the Center is known, provides immigration status information to federal, state, and local officials around the clock. ICE officers are responsible "for the identification, apprehension, and removal of illegal aliens from the United States." Hundreds of thousands of aliens are removed by the Federal Government every year.

B

The pervasiveness of federal regulation does not diminish the importance of immigration policy to the States. Arizona bears many of the consequences of unlawful immigration. Hundreds of thousands of deportable aliens are apprehended in Arizona each year. Unauthorized aliens who remain in the State comprise, by one estimate, almost six percent of the population. And in the State's most populous county, these aliens are reported to be responsible for a disproportionate share of serious crime. . . .

These concerns are the background for the formal legal analysis that follows. The issue is whether, under preemption principles, federal law permits Arizona to implement the state-law provisions in dispute.

III

Federalism, central to the constitutional design, adopts the principle that both the National and State Governments have elements of sovereignty the other is bound to respect. From the existence of two sovereigns follows the possibility that laws can be in conflict or at cross-purposes. The Supremacy Clause provides a clear rule that federal law "shall be the supreme Law of the Land; and the Judges in every State shall be bound thereby, any Thing in the Constitution or Laws of any State to the Contrary notwithstanding." Art. VI, cl. 2. Under this principle,

Congress has the power to preempt state law. See *Crosby v. National Foreign Trade Council*, 530 U.S. 363, 372 (2000). . . .

State law must also give way to federal law in at least two other circumstances. First, the States are precluded from regulating conduct in a field that Congress, acting within its proper authority, has determined must be regulated by its exclusive governance. The intent to displace state law altogether can be inferred from a framework of regulation "so pervasive . . . that Congress left no room for the States to supplement it" or where there is a "federal interest . . . so dominant that the federal system will be assumed to preclude enforcement of state laws on the same subject." *Rice v. Santa Fe Elevator Corp.*, 331 U.S. 218, 230 (1947).

Second, state laws are preempted when they conflict with federal law. *Crosby*, *supra*, at 372. This includes cases where "compliance with both federal and state regulations is a physical impossibility," *Florida Lime & Avocado Growers, Inc. v. Paul*, 373 U.S. 132, 142–143 (1963), and those instances where the challenged state law "stands as an obstacle to the accomplishment and execution of the full purposes and objectives of Congress," *Hines*, 312 U.S., at 67. . . .

The four challenged provisions of the state law each must be examined under these preemption principles.

IV

A

Section 3

Section 3 of S.B. 1070 creates a new state misdemeanor. It forbids the "willful failure to complete or carry an alien registration document . . . in violation of 8 United States Code section 1304(e) or 1306(a)." In effect, § 3 adds a state-law penalty for conduct proscribed by federal law. . . .

The present regime of federal regulation is . . . comprehensive. Federal law now includes a requirement that aliens carry proof of registration. . . . Aliens who remain in the country for more than 30 days must apply for registration and be fingerprinted. Detailed information is required, and any change of address has to be reported to the Federal Government. The statute provide[s] penalties for the willful failure to register.

The framework enacted by Congress leads to the conclusion . . . that the Federal Government has occupied the field of alien registration. The federal statutory directives provide a full set of standards governing alien registration, including the punishment for noncompliance. . . . Where Congress occupies an entire field, as it has in the field of alien registration, even complementary state regulation is impermissible. Field preemption reflects a congressional decision to foreclose any state regulation in the area, even if it is parallel to federal standards. . . .

Arizona contends that § 3 can survive preemption because the provision has the same aim as federal law and adopts its substantive standards. This argument not only ignores the basic premise of field preemption—that States may not enter, in any respect, an area the Federal Government has reserved for itself—but also is unpersuasive on its own terms. Permitting the State to impose its own penalties for the federal offenses here would conflict with the careful framework Congress adopted. Were § 3 to come into force, the State would have the power to bring criminal charges against individuals for violating a federal law even in circumstances where federal officials in charge of the comprehensive scheme determine that prosecution would frustrate federal policies. . . .

These specific conflicts between state and federal law simply underscore the reason for field preemption. . . . Section 3 is preempted by federal law.

B

Section 5(C)

Unlike § 3, which replicates federal statutory requirements, § 5(C) enacts a state criminal prohibition where no federal counterpart exists. The provision makes it a state misdemeanor for "an unauthorized alien to knowingly apply for work, solicit work in a public place or perform work as an employee or independent contractor" in Arizona. Violations can be punished by a $2,500 fine and incarceration for up to six months. The United States contends that the provision upsets the balance struck by the Immigration Reform and Control Act of 1986 (IRCA) and must be preempted as an obstacle to the federal plan of regulation and control. . . .

[IRCA's] comprehensive framework does not impose federal criminal sanctions on the employee side (*i.e.*, penalties on aliens who seek or engage in unauthorized work). Under federal law some civil penalties are imposed instead. With certain exceptions, aliens who accept unlawful employment are not eligible to have their status adjusted to that of a lawful permanent resident. Aliens also may be removed from the country for having engaged in unauthorized work. In addition to specifying these civil consequences, federal law makes it a crime for unauthorized workers to obtain employment through fraudulent means. Congress has made clear, however, that any information employees submit to indicate their work status "may not be used" for purposes other than prosecution under specified federal criminal statutes for fraud, perjury, and related conduct.

The legislative background of IRCA underscores the fact that Congress made a deliberate choice not to impose criminal penalties on aliens who seek, or engage in, unauthorized employment. A commission established by Congress to study immigration policy and to make recommendations concluded these penalties would be "unnecessary and unworkable." Proposals to make unauthorized work a criminal offense were debated and discussed during the long process of drafting IRCA. But Congress rejected them. In the end, IRCA's framework reflects a considered judgment that making criminals out of aliens engaged in unauthorized work—aliens who already face the possibility of employer exploitation because of their removable status—would be inconsistent with federal policy and objectives. . . .

The ordinary principles of preemption include the well-settled proposition that a state law is preempted where it "stands as an obstacle to the accomplishment and execution of the full purposes and objectives of Congress." *Hines*, 312 U.S., at 67. Under § 5(C) of S.B. 1070, Arizona law would interfere with the careful balance struck by Congress with respect to unauthorized employment of aliens. Although § 5(C) attempts to achieve one of the same goals as federal law—the deterrence of unlawful employment—it involves a conflict in the method of enforcement. The Court has recognized that a "[c]onflict in technique can be fully as disruptive to the system Congress enacted as conflict in overt policy." *Motor Coach Employees v. Lockridge*, 403 U.S. 274, 287 (1971). The correct instruction to draw from the text, structure, and history of IRCA is that Congress decided it would be inappropriate to impose criminal penalties on aliens who seek or engage in unauthorized employment. It follows that a state law to the contrary is an obstacle to the regulatory system Congress chose. Section 5(C) is preempted by federal law.

C

Section 6

Section 6 of S.B. 1070 provides that a state officer, "without a warrant, may arrest a person if the officer has probable cause to believe . . . [the person] has committed any public offense that makes [him] removable from the United States." The United States argues that arrests authorized by this statute would be an obstacle to the removal system Congress created.

As a general rule, it is not a crime for a removable alien to remain present in the United States. If the police stop someone based on nothing more than possible removability, the usual predicate for an arrest is absent. When an alien is suspected of being removable, a federal official issues an administrative document called a Notice to Appear. The form does not authorize an arrest. Instead, it gives the alien information about the proceedings, including the time and date of the removal hearing. If an alien fails to appear, an *in absentia* order may direct removal.

The federal statutory structure instructs when it is appropriate to arrest an alien during the removal process. For example, the Attorney General can exercise discretion to issue a warrant for an alien's arrest and detention "pending a decision on whether the alien is to be removed from the United States." 8 U.S.C. § 1226(a). And if an alien is ordered removed after a hearing, the Attorney General will issue a warrant. In both instances, the warrants are executed by federal officers who have received training in the enforcement of immigration law. If no federal warrant has been issued, those officers have more limited authority. They may arrest an alien for being "in the United States in violation of any [immigration] law or regulation," for example, but only where the alien "is likely to escape before a warrant can be obtained." § 1357(a)(2).

Section 6 attempts to provide state officers even greater authority to arrest aliens on the basis of possible removability than Congress has given to trained federal immigration officers. Under state law, officers who believe an alien is removable by reason of some "public offense" would have the power to conduct an arrest on that basis regardless of whether a federal warrant has issued or the alien is likely to escape. This state authority could be exercised without any input from the Federal Government about whether an arrest is warranted in a particular case. This would allow the State to achieve its own immigration policy. The result could be unnecessary harassment of some aliens (for instance, a veteran, college student, or someone assisting with a criminal investigation) whom federal officials determine should not be removed.

This is not the system Congress created. . . .

Congress has put in place a system in which state officers may not make warrantless arrests of aliens based on possible removability except in specific, limited circumstances. By nonetheless authorizing state and local officers to engage in these enforcement activities as a general matter, § 6 creates an obstacle to the full purposes and objectives of Congress. Section 6 is preempted by federal law.

D

Section 2(B)

Section 2(B) of S.B. 1070 requires state officers to make a "reasonable attempt . . . to determine the immigration status" of any person they stop, detain, or arrest on some other legitimate basis if "reasonable suspicion exists that the person is an alien and is unlawfully present in the United States." The law also provides that "[a]ny person who is arrested shall have the person's immigration status determined before the person is released." The accepted way to perform these status checks is to contact ICE, which maintains a database of immigration records.

Three limits are built into the state provision. First, a detainee is presumed not to be an alien unlawfully present in the United States if he or she provides a valid Arizona driver's license or similar identification. Second, officers "may not consider race, color or national origin . . . except to the extent permitted by the United States [and] Arizona Constitution[s]." Third, the provisions must be "implemented in a manner consistent with federal law regulating immigration, protecting the civil rights of all persons and respecting the privileges and immunities of United States citizens."

The United States and its amici contend that, even with these limits, the State's verification requirements pose an obstacle to the framework Congress put in place. The first concern is the mandatory nature of the status checks. The second is the possibility of prolonged detention while the checks are being performed.

1

Consultation between federal and state officials is an important feature of the immigration system. Congress has made clear that no formal agreement or special training needs to be in place for state officers to "communicate with the [Federal Government] regarding the immigration status of any individual, including reporting knowledge that a particular alien is not lawfully present in the United States." And Congress has obligated ICE to respond to any request made by state officials for verification of a person's citizenship or immigration status. ICE's Law Enforcement Support Center operates "24 hours a day, seven days a week, 365 days a year" and provides, among other things, "immigration status, identity information and real-time assistance to local, state and federal law enforcement agencies."

The United States argues that making status verification mandatory interferes with the federal immigration scheme. It is true that § 2(B) does not allow state officers to consider federal enforcement priorities in deciding whether to contact ICE about someone they have detained. . . .

Congress has done nothing to suggest it is inappropriate to communicate with ICE in these situations, however. Indeed, it has encouraged the sharing of information about possible immigration violations. A federal statute regulating the public benefits provided to qualified aliens in fact instructs that "no State or local government entity may be prohibited, or in any way restricted, from sending to or receiving from [ICE] information regarding the immigration status, lawful or unlawful, of an alien in the United States." The federal scheme thus leaves room for a policy requiring state officials to contact ICE as a routine matter.

2

Some who support the challenge to § 2(B) argue that, in practice, state officers will be required to delay the release of some detainees for no reason other than to verify their immigration status. Detaining individuals solely to verify their immigration status would raise constitutional concerns. And it would disrupt the federal framework to put state officers in the position of holding aliens in custody for possible unlawful presence without federal direction and supervision. The program put in place by Congress does not allow state or local officers to adopt this enforcement mechanism.

But § 2(B) could be read to avoid these concerns. To take one example, a person might be stopped for jaywalking in Tucson and be unable to produce identification. The first sentence of § 2(B) instructs officers to make a "reasonable" attempt to verify his immigration status with ICE if there is reasonable suspicion that his presence in the United States is unlawful. The state courts may conclude that, unless the person continues to be suspected of some crime for which he may be detained by state officers, it would not be reasonable to prolong the stop for the immigration inquiry. . . .

However the law is interpreted, if § 2(B) only requires state officers to conduct a status check during the course of an authorized, lawful detention or after a detainee has been released, the provision likely would survive preemption—at least absent some showing that it has other consequences that are adverse to federal law and its objectives. There is no need in this case to address whether reasonable suspicion of illegal entry or another immigration crime would be a legitimate basis for prolonging a detention, or whether this too would be preempted by federal law.

The nature and timing of this case counsel caution in evaluating the validity of § 2(B). The Federal Government has brought suit against a sovereign State to challenge the provision even before the law has gone into effect. There is a basic uncertainty about what the law means and how it will be enforced. At this stage, without the benefit of a definitive interpretation from the state courts, it would be inappropriate to assume § 2(B) will be construed in a way that creates a conflict with federal law. As a result, the United States cannot prevail in its current challenge. This opinion does not foreclose other preemption and constitutional challenges to the law as interpreted and applied after it goes into effect.

V . . .

The United States has established that §§ 3, 5(C), and 6 of S.B. 1070 are preempted. It was improper, however, to enjoin § 2(B) before the state courts had an opportunity to construe it and without some showing that enforcement of the provision in fact conflicts with federal immigration law and its objectives.

JUSTICE SCALIA, concurring in part and dissenting in part. . . .

As a sovereign, Arizona has the inherent power to exclude persons from its territory, subject only to those limitations expressed in the Constitution or constitutionally imposed by Congress. That power to exclude has long been recognized as inherent in sovereignty. Emer de Vattel's seminal 1758 treatise on the Law of Nations stated:

> "The sovereign may forbid the entrance of his territory either to foreigners in general, or in particular cases, or to certain persons, or for certain particular purposes, according as he may think it

> advantageous to the state. There is nothing in all this, that does not flow from the rights of domain and sovereignty: every one is obliged to pay respect to the prohibition; and whoever dares violate it, incurs the penalty decreed to render it effectual." The Law of Nations, bk. II, ch. VII, § 94, p. 309 (B. Kapossy & R. Whatmore eds. 2008).

See also I R. Phillimore, *Commentaries upon International Law*, pt. III, ch. X, p. 233 (1854) ("It is a received maxim of International Law that, the Government of a State may prohibit the entrance of strangers into the country"). . . .

In light of the predominance of federal immigration restrictions in modern times, it is easy to lose sight of the States' traditional role in regulating immigration—and to overlook their sovereign prerogative to do so. I accept as a given that State regulation is excluded by the Constitution when (1) it has been prohibited by a valid federal law, or (2) it conflicts with federal regulation—when, for example, it admits those whom federal regulation would exclude, or excludes those whom federal regulation would admit.

Possibility (1) need not be considered here: there is no federal law prohibiting the States' sovereign power to exclude (assuming federal authority to enact such a law). The mere existence of federal action in the immigration area—and the so-called field preemption arising from that action, upon which the Court's opinion so heavily relies, cannot be regarded as such a prohibition. We are not talking here about a federal law prohibiting the States from regulating bubble-gum advertising, or even the construction of nuclear plants. We are talking about a federal law going to the core of state sovereignty: the power to exclude. Like elimination of the States' other inherent sovereign power, immunity from suit, elimination of the States' sovereign power to exclude requires that "Congress . . . unequivocally expres[s] its intent to abrogate," *Seminole Tribe of Fla. v. Florida*, 517 U.S. 44, 55 (1996) (internal quotation marks and citation omitted). Implicit "field preemption" will not do.

Nor can federal power over illegal immigration be deemed exclusive because of what the Court's opinion solicitously calls "foreign countries['] concern[s] about the status, safety, and security of their nationals in the United States". The Constitution gives all those on our shores the protections of the Bill of Rights—but just as those rights are not expanded for foreign nationals because of their countries' views (some countries, for example, have recently discovered the death penalty to be barbaric), neither are the fundamental sovereign powers of the States abridged to accommodate foreign countries' views. Even in its international relations, the Federal Government must live with the inconvenient fact that it is a Union of independent States, who have their own sovereign powers. This is not the first time it has found that a nuisance and a bother in the conduct of foreign policy. Four years ago, for example, the Government importuned us to interfere with thoroughly constitutional state judicial procedures in the criminal trial of foreign nationals because the international community, and even an opinion of the International Court of Justice, disapproved them. See *Medellín v. Texas*, 552 U.S. 491 (2008). We rejected that request, as we should reject the Executive's invocation of foreign-affairs considerations here. Though it may upset foreign powers—and even when the Federal Government desperately wants to avoid upsetting foreign powers—the States have the right to protect their borders against foreign nationals, just as they have the right to execute foreign nationals for murder.

What this case comes down to, then, is whether the Arizona law conflicts with federal immigration law—whether it excludes those whom federal law would admit, or admits those whom federal law would exclude. It does not purport to do so. It applies only to aliens who neither possess a privilege to be present under federal law nor have been removed pursuant to the Federal Government's inherent authority. . . .

Arizona has moved to protect its sovereignty—not in contradiction of federal law, but in complete compliance with it. The laws under challenge here do not extend or revise federal immigration restrictions, but merely enforce those restrictions more effectively. If securing its territory in this fashion is not within the power of Arizona, we should cease referring to it as a sovereign State. I dissent.

JUSTICE THOMAS, concurring in part and dissenting in part.

I agree with JUSTICE SCALIA that federal immigration law does not pre-empt any of the challenged provisions of S.B. 1070. I reach that conclusion, however, for the simple reason that there is no conflict between the "ordinary meanin[g]" of the relevant federal laws and that of the four provisions of Arizona law at issue here. *Wyeth v. Levine*, 555 U.S. 555, 588 (2009) (Thomas, J., concurring in judgment) ("Pre-emption analysis should not be a freewheeling judicial inquiry into whether a state statute is in tension with federal objectives, but an inquiry into whether the ordinary meanings of state and federal law conflict" (brackets and internal quotation marks omitted)). . . .

Despite the lack of any conflict between the ordinary meaning of the Arizona law and that of the federal laws at issue here, the Court holds that various provisions of the Arizona law are pre-empted because they "stan[d] as an obstacle to the accomplishment and execution of the full purposes and objectives of Congress." I have explained that the "purposes and objectives" theory of implied pre-emption is inconsistent with the Constitution because it invites courts to engage in freewheeling speculation about congressional purpose that roams well beyond statutory text. Under the Supremacy Clause, pre-emptive effect is to be given to congressionally enacted laws, not to judicially divined legislative purposes. Thus, even assuming the existence of some tension between Arizona's law and the supposed "purposes and objectives" of Congress, I would not hold that any of the provisions of the Arizona law at issue here are pre-empted on that basis.

JUSTICE ALITO, concurring in part and dissenting in part. . . .

While I agree with the Court on § 2(B) and § 3, I part ways on § 5(C) and § 6. The Court's holding on § 5(C) is inconsistent with *De Canas v. Bica*, 424 U.S. 351 (1976), which held that employment regulation, even of aliens unlawfully present in the country, is an area of traditional state concern. Because state police powers are implicated here, our precedents require us to presume that federal law does not displace state law unless Congress' intent to do so is clear and manifest. I do not believe Congress has spoken with the requisite clarity to justify invalidation of § 5(C). Nor do I believe that § 6 is invalid. Like § 2(B), § 6 adds virtually nothing to the authority that Arizona law enforcement officers already exercise. And whatever little authority they have gained is consistent with federal law.

NOTES

1. *Constitutional Bases for Federal Enactments*. Federal statutes and regulations in the field of foreign affairs must rest, of course, on the constitutional powers accorded to the federal government. In *Tarble*, the military laws and regulations rested upon Congress's power to raise and regulate an army. In *Crosby*, the statute imposing sanctions on Burma (Myanmar) rested principally upon Congress's power to regulate foreign commerce and the president's power to engage in foreign diplomacy. In *Arizona v. United States*, the statute rested largely upon Congress's power to regulate immigration. So long as the federal law or regulation is constitutional, it preempts conflicting state law under the Supremacy Clause.

2. *Varieties of Preemption*. When a state's exercise of its police power is challenged under the Supremacy Clause, the Supreme Court has stated that preemption may be either express or implied.

Express preemption involves an explicit direction from Congress that state authority is being ousted. *See, e.g.*, War and National Defense Act, Pub. L. 96–72, § 8, Sept. 29, 1979, 93 Stat. 521, *codified at* 50 U.S.C. app. § 2407(c) (2006) (providing that the statutory section and implementing regulations "shall preempt any law, rule, or regulation of any of the several States or the District of Columbia, or any of the territories or possessions of the United States, or of any governmental subdivision thereof, which law, rule, or regulation pertains to participation in, compliance with, implementation of, or the furnishing of information regarding restrictive trade practices or boycotts fostered or imposed by foreign countries against other countries"). Does the fact that express preemption is relatively unusual in the foreign affairs context suggest anything?

Implied preemption can occur in one of two ways: (1) *conflict preemption* (where compliance with both the federal and state statute is impossible, or "state law 'stands as an obstacle to the accomplishment and execution of the full purposes and objectives of Congress.' "); or (2) *field preemption* (where the federal scheme is so pervasive as to make reasonable the inference that Congress has preempted state law). *Gade v. Nat'l Solid Wastes Mgmt. Ass'n*, 505 U.S. 88, 98 (1992). How clear or direct must such preemption be, taking into account the dissents of Justices Thomas and Alito in *Arizona v. United States*?

3. *Presumptions About Preemption*. If the information before the court is ambiguous, should the court employ a presumption either against implied preemption or in favor of it? The Supreme Court normally begins with a presumption that Congress has *not* intended to preempt state law. *See Medtronic, Inc. v. Lohr*, 518 U.S. 470, 485 (1996); *Rice v. Santa Fe Elevator Corp.*, 331 U.S. 218, 230 (1947).

However, in *United States v. Locke*, the Supreme Court stated that such a presumption was inappropriate in the context of considering state law restrictions affecting international maritime commerce, since this was an area in which historically Congress had had a significant presence. *See United States v. Locke*, 529 U.S. 89, 108–10 (2000). When statutes concern foreign relations matters, should courts begin with a presumption that Congress has intended to preempt state law? *See* Erwin Chemerinsky, *Empowering States When It Matters: A Different Approach to Preemption*, 69 BROOK. L. REV. 1313 (2004) (arguing against a presumption of preemption); *see also* Jack Goldsmith, *Statutory Foreign Affairs Preemption*, 2000 SUP. CT. REV. 175; Harold G. Maier, *Preemption of State Law: A Recommended Analysis*, 83 AM. J. INT'L L. 832 (1989).

Although the Massachusetts statute in *Crosby* preceded the federal statute by three months, the federal statute contained no reference to existing state or local measures directed against Burma. Thus, Congress did not expressly preempt the Massachusetts statute. Massachusetts argued that Congress's silence should be read as implicit acceptance of the state law, and that the state law could supplement and assist the federal sanctions program. Nevertheless, the Massachusetts statute was found to be preempted. Had the Supreme Court not found Massachusetts' law preempted, the president might have been in a position of being able to waive federal sanctions against Burma (to reward good behavior), but not those of Massachusetts. In *Crosby*, the Court stated that the conflict between the state and federal law was so clear that it would "leave for another day a consideration in this context of a presumption against preemption." 530 U.S. at 374 n. 8.

Do you think presumptions implicitly played a role in the differences between the majority opinion in *Arizona v. United States* and the views of the three dissenting judges? Recall that Justice Kennedy begins the majority opinion stating that "[t]he federal power to determine immigration policy is well settled," while Justice Scalia begins his dissent arguing that as "a sovereign, Arizona has the inherent power to exclude persons from its territory, subject only to those limitations expressed in the Constitution or constitutionally imposed by Congress." For an argument that courts should vary the operative presumption depending on the circumstances, see Daniel Abebe & Aziz Z. Huq, *Foreign Affairs Federalism: A Revisionist Approach*, 66 VAND. L. REV. 723 (2013).

Although the Court in *Arizona* upheld the most controversial requirement of the Arizona law (sometimes referred to as a "show me your papers" requirement), the judgment has been viewed as a rebuke to sweeping State immigration power. *See, e.g.*, Lucas Guttentag, *Immigration Preemption and the Limits of State Power: Reflections on* Arizona v. United States, 9 STAN. J. CIV. RTS. & CIV. LIBERTIES 1 (2013); Catherine Y. Kim, *Immigration Separation of Powers and the President's Power to Preempt*, 90 NOTRE DAME L. REV. 691 (2014). For cases in which federal immigration law preempted state regulation, see *United States v. Alabama*, 691 F.3d 1269 (2012); *Lozano v. City of Hazleton*, 724 F.3d 297 (2013); *but see Keller v. City of Fremont*, 719 F.3d 931 (2013) (upholding city ordinance requiring prospective tenants to obtain occupancy licenses identifying their citizenship and immigration status); *Equal Access Educ. v. Merten*, 305 F. Supp. 2d 585 (E.D. Va. 2004) (Virginia policy denying post-secondary school admission to illegal aliens was not preempted by federal authority to regulate immigration and did not violate the dormant Foreign Commerce Clause); *Martinez v. Regents of Univ. of Cal.*, 50 Cal.4th 1277 (Cal. 2010) (upholding California law exempting certain nonresident aliens, including unlawful aliens, from paying nonresident tuition).

4. *Statutory Authorization*. What about the opposite of statutory preemption—statutory authorization for states to engage in foreign relations matters? In 2011, the Supreme Court reviewed another deeply controversial Arizona law (the "Legal Arizona Workers Act") providing for the suspension or revocation of licenses of state employers that knowingly or intentionally employ unauthorized aliens, and which requires that state employers use an internet-based system for checking the work authorization status of their employees. *Chamber of Commerce v. Whiting*, 563 U.S. 582 (2011). Business and civil rights organizations challenged the compatibility of the Arizona law with the Immigration Reform and Control Act (IRCA), which makes it unlawful for employers and other entities "to hire, or to recruit or refer for a fee, for employment in the United States an alien knowing the alien is an unauthorized alien." 8 U.S.C. § 1324a(a)(1)(A). IRCA restricts the ability of States to combat employment of unauthorized workers; it expressly preempts "any State or local law imposing civil or criminal sanctions (*other than through licensing and similar laws*) upon those who employ, or recruit or refer for a fee for employment, unauthorized aliens." § 1324a(h)(2) (emphasis added).

Once the Supreme Court determined that the Arizona law was not expressly preempted (since it was styled as a licensing law), a plurality of the justices further rejected the argument that the law was impliedly preempted on the ground that "Arizona's procedures simply implement the sanctions that Congress expressly allowed Arizona to pursue through licensing laws. Given that Congress specifically preserved such authority for the States, it stands to reason that Congress did not intend to prevent the States from using appropriate tools to exercise that authority." 563 U.S. at 600–01 (Roberts, C.J.) (plurality op.). An exemption from express preemption, in other words, served equally as an exemption from implied preemption.

Can statutory authorization do more than insulate states from statutory preemption? In 2007, Congress enacted the Sudan Accountability and Divestment Act of 2007, Pub. L. No. 110–174, 121 Stat. 2516 (2007) (codified as amended at 15 U.S.C. § 80a–13, 50 U.S.C. § 1701), which among other things permitted states and municipalities to adopt and enforce measures that divested state and local government assets or prohibited the investment of state and local government assets from certain business operations in the Sudan. How completely does this immunize states and localities from claims that the states are intruding on foreign prerogatives? Would it matter if the federal government established the list of implicated business operations in Sudan? If the federal government left it to the states to determine those operations?

President George W. Bush issued a signing statement providing that:

> This Act purports to authorize State and local governments to divest from companies doing business in named sectors in Sudan and thus risks being interpreted as insulating from Federal oversight State and local divestment actions that could interfere with implementation of national foreign policy. However, as the Constitution vests the exclusive authority to conduct foreign relations with the Federal Government, the executive branch shall construe and enforce this legislation in a manner that does not conflict with that authority.

Statement on Signing the Sudan Accountability and Divestment Act of 2007, 43 WEEKLY COMP. PRES. DOC. (Dec. 31, 2007). Was President Bush's concern well founded? You may be best positioned to evaluate this later in this Chapter, after contemplating the scope of the dormant foreign affairs power.

5. *Relevance of Foreign Protests to State Laws.* In considering whether the Massachusetts statute in *Crosby* conflicted with the federal statute's objective, the Supreme Court noted that protests against the Massachusetts statute had been made to the United States by Japan, the Association of Southeast Asian Nations (ASEAN), and the European Community. Further, the Court noted that the European Community and Japan had filed complaints with the World Trade Organization. For the Court, these protests demonstrated that the Massachusetts law had "complicated [the federal government's] dealings with foreign sovereigns and proven an impediment to accomplishing objectives assigned it by Congress." 530 U.S. at 383. Such

language might be read as simply reinforcing the explicit basis for the decision in *Crosby*—preemption by a statute.

Yet is the Court really limiting itself to preemption by statute, or is there an "extra-statutory solicitude for formal diplomatic interaction with foreign powers, and for the president's presumptively exclusive ability to engage in it"? Edward T. Swaine, *Crosby as Foreign Relations Law*, 41 VA. J. INT'L L. 481, 502 (2001); *see* Carlos Manuel Vázquez, *W(h)ither Zschernig?*, 46 VILL. L. REV. 1259, 1287–1304 (2001) (arguing that the Court's approach in *Crosby* would have led to preemption even in the absence of a federal statute); Sarah H. Cleveland, *Crosby and the "One-Voice" Myth in U.S. Foreign Relations*, 46 VILL. L. REV. 975, 976 (2001) (arguing that the Court's use of the "one voice" doctrine in statutory preemption analysis "contravened the federal government's longstanding deference to the states in this area.").

6. *Relevance of a Treaty Regime to Statutory Preemption*. The *Crosby* decision referred to the Court's earlier decision in *United States v. Locke*, 529 U.S. 89 (2000). In that case, an association of tanker owners asked a federal court to strike down a regulatory regime of the State of Washington that was aimed at preventing, and providing remedies for, oil spills by oceangoing oil tankers. The Supreme Court found that the federal government's overall regulation in this area clearly invalidated various regulations of the State of Washington due to "field preemption." In doing so, the Court did not find it necessary to decide whether international treaties and instruments had a direct preemptive effect on the state regulatory scheme. The Court noted, however, that the "existence of the treaties and agreements on standards of shipping is of relevance, of course, for these agreements give force to the longstanding rule that the enactment of a uniform federal scheme displaces state law, and the treaties indicate Congress will have demanded national uniformity regarding maritime commerce." *Id.* at 103. The next Section considers the issue of preemption of state law by international agreement.

3. PREEMPTION OF STATE LAW BY INTERNATIONAL AGREEMENT

THE FEDERALIST PAPERS NO. 22 (HAMILTON)

(Clinton Rossiter ed., 1961).

The treaties of the United States under the present [Articles of Confederation] are liable to the infractions of thirteen different legislatures, and as many different courts of final jurisdiction, acting under the authority of those legislatures. The faith, the reputation, the peace of the whole Union are thus continually at the mercy of the prejudices, the passions, and the interests of every member of which it is composed. Is it possible that foreign nations can either respect or confide in such a government? Is it possible that the people of America will longer consent to trust their honor, their happiness, their safety, on so precarious a foundation?

WARE V. HYLTON

3 U.S. (3 Dall.) 199, 220–77 (1796).

[The 1783 Treaty of Paris, which ended the American Revolution and was concluded during the period of the Articles of Confederation, provided that British creditors would "meet with no lawful Impediment to the Recovery" of their debts, and would be paid not in state currency but in the equivalent of gold. *See* Definitive Treaty of Peace, art. IV, Sept. 3, 1783, U.S.-Gr. Brit., *reprinted in* 2 *Treaties and Other International Acts of the United States of America* 151 (Hunter Miller ed., 1931) (Treaty of Paris). After the U.S. Constitution took effect in 1789, a Virginian refused to pay a debt owed to a British subject. An administrator acting on behalf of the British subject sued in U.S. federal court to recover the debt. Virginia state law, enacted in 1777, provided for the confiscation of debts owed to enemy aliens. Consequently, the case presented the question of whether, under the new Constitution, the Treaty of Paris could override an otherwise valid state law. The Supreme Court reached a unanimous holding. Justice Samuel Chase wrote the lead opinion, and the other justices wrote separately, following the British custom of the day.]

CHASE, JUSTICE. . . .

If the legislature of Virginia could not, by ordinary acts of legislation, do these things, yet, possessing the supreme sovereign power of the state, she certainly could do them, by a treaty of peace; if she had not parted with the power of making such treaty. If Virginia had such power, before she delegated it to congress [under the Articles of Confederation], it follows, that afterwards, that body possessed it. Whether Virginia parted with the power of making treaties of peace, will be seen by a perusal of the 9th article of the [Articles of Confederation] (ratified by all the states, on the first of March 1781), in which it was declared, "that the United States in congress assembled, shall have the sole and exclusive right and power of determining on peace or war, except in the two cases mentioned in the 6th article; and of entering into treaties and alliances, with a proviso, when made, respecting commerce." This grant has no restriction, nor is there any limitation on the power in any part of the confederation. A right to make peace, necessarily includes the power of determining on what terms peace shall be made. A power to make treaties must, of necessity, imply a power to decide the terms on which they shall be made: a war between two nations can only be concluded by treaty.

Surely, the sacrificing [of] public or private property, to obtain peace, cannot be the cases in which a treaty would be void. . . . It seems to me, that treaties made by congress, according to the confederation, were superior to the laws of the states; because the confederation made them obligatory on all the states. They were so declared by congress on the 13th of April 1787; were so admitted by the legislatures and executives of most of the states; and were so decided by the judiciary of the general government, and by the judiciaries of some of the state governments.

If doubts could exist, before the establishment of the present national government, they must be entirely removed by the 6th article of the [U.S.] constitution, which provides "That all treaties made, or which shall be made, under the authority of the United States, shall be the supreme law of the land; and the judges in every state shall be bound thereby, anything in the constitution or laws of any state to the contrary notwithstanding." There can be no limitation on the power of the people of the United States. By their authority, the state constitutions were made, and by their authority the constitution of the United States was established; and they had the power to change or abolish the state constitutions, or to make them yield to the general government, and to treaties made by their authority. A treaty cannot be the supreme law of the land, that is, of all the United States, if any act of a state legislature can stand in its way. If the constitution of a state (which is the fundamental law of the state, and paramount to its legislature) must give way to a treaty, and fall before it; can it be questioned, whether the less power, an act of the state legislature, must not be prostrate? It is the declared will of the people of the United States, that every treaty made by the authority of the United States, shall be superior to the constitution and laws of any individual state; and their will alone is to decide. If a law of a state, contrary to a treaty, is not void, but voidable only, by a repeal, or nullification by a state legislature, this certain consequence follows, that the will of a small part of the United States may control or defeat the will of the whole. . . .

IREDELL, JUSTICE. . . .

The opinion I have long entertained and still do entertain . . . [is] that the stipulation in favor of creditors, so as to enable them to bring suits, and recover the full value of their debts, could not, at that time [of the Articles of Confederation], be carried into effect, in any other manner, than by a repeal of the statutes of the different states, constituting the impediments to their recovery, and the passing of such other acts as might be necessary to give the recovery entire efficacy, in execution of the treaty. . . .

Requisitions formerly [by Congress, under the Articles of Confederation,] were made binding in point of moral obligation, (so far as the amount of money was concerned, of which congress was the constitutional judge,) but the right and the power being separated, it was found often impracticable to make them act in conjunction. To obviate this difficulty, which every one knows had been the means of greatly distressing the Union, and injuring its public credit, a power was given [under the U.S.

Constitution] to the representatives of the whole Union to raise taxes, by their own authority, for the good of the whole. Similar embarrassments had been found about the treaty [power]: this was binding in moral obligation, but could not be constitutionally carried into effect (at least in the opinion of many), so far as acts of legislation then in being constituted an impediment, but by a repeal. The extreme inconveniences felt from such a system dictated the remedy which the constitution has now provided, "that all treaties made or which shall be made under the authority of the United States, shall be the supreme law of the land; and that the judges in every state shall be bound thereby, anything in the constitution or laws of any state to the contrary notwithstanding." Under this constitution, therefore, so far as a treaty constitutionally is binding, upon principles of moral obligation, it is also, by the vigor of its own authority, to be executed in fact. It would not otherwise be the supreme law, in the new sense provided for, and it was so before, in a moral sense.

The provision extends to subsisting as well as to future treaties. I consider, therefore, that when this constitution was ratified, the case as to the treaty in question stood upon the same footing, as if every act constituting an impediment to a creditor's recovery had been expressly repealed, and any further act passed, which the public obligation had before required, if a repeal alone would not have been sufficient.

KOLOVRAT V. OREGON

366 U.S. 187, 190–98 (1961).

[A national and resident of communist Yugoslavia sought to collect an inheritance in Oregon. The state courts denied his claim under an Oregon probate statute that required him to show that he would enjoy the inheritance "without confiscation" and that U.S. nationals had a reciprocal ability to inherit property in the claimant's country. The Oregon Supreme Court found that reciprocity did not exist because Yugoslavian law gave discretion to Yugoslavian authorities to control foreign exchange payments in a way that might prevent Americans from receiving the full value of Yugoslavian inheritances.]

MR. JUSTICE BLACK delivered the opinion of the Court. . . .

[R]ecognizing quite properly that state policies as to the rights of aliens to inherit must give way under our Constitution's Supremacy Clause to "overriding" federal treaties and conflicting arrangements, the state court considered petitioners' contention, supported in this Court by the Government as *amicus curiae*, that petitioners were entitled to inherit this personal property because of an 1881 Treaty between the United States and Serbia, which country is now a part of Yugoslavia. The state court rejected this contention on the basis of its interpretation of the Treaty although it correctly recognized that the Treaty is still in effect between the United States and Yugoslavia. The state court also rejected petitioners' contention that their claims could not be defeated solely because of the possible effect of the Yugoslavian Foreign Exchange Laws and Regulations since those laws and regulations admittedly meet the requirements of the Bretton Woods Agreement of 1945, to which both Yugoslavia and the United States are signatories. We granted certiorari because the cases involve important rights asserted in reliance upon federal treaty obligations. . . .

The 1881 Treaty clearly declares its basic purpose to bring about "reciprocally full and entire liberty of commerce and navigation" between the two signatory nations so that their citizens "shall be at liberty to establish themselves freely in each other's territory." Their citizens are also to be free to receive, hold and dispose of property by trading, donation, marriage, inheritance or any other manner "under the same conditions as the subjects of the most favored nation." Thus, both paragraphs of Art. II of the Treaty which have pertinence here contain a "most favored nation" clause with regard to "acquiring, possessing or disposing of every kind of property." This clause means that each signatory grants to the other the broadest rights and privileges which it accords to any other nation in other treaties it has made or will make. . . .

The International Monetary Fund (Bretton Woods) Agreement of 1945, *supra*, to which Yugoslavia and the United States are signatories, comprehensively obligates participating countries to maintain only such monetary controls as are consistent with the terms of that Agreement. The Agreement's broad purpose, as shown by Art. IV, § 4, is "to promote exchange stability, to maintain orderly exchange arrangements with other members, and to avoid competitive exchange alterations." Article VI, § 3, forbids any participating country from exercising controls over international capital movements "in a manner which will restrict payments for current transactions or which will unduly delay transfers of funds in settlement of commitments. . . ." Article 8 of the Yugoslavian laws regulating payment transactions with other countries expressly recognizes the authority of "the provisions of agreements with foreign countries which are concerned with payments." In addition to all of this, an Agreement of 1948 between our country and Yugoslavia obligated Yugoslavia, in the words of the Senate Report on the Agreement, "to continue to grant most-favored-nation treatment to Americans in ownership and acquisition of assets in Yugoslavia . . . [and] Yugoslavia is required, by article 10, to authorize persons in Yugoslavia to pay debts to United States nationals, firms, or agencies, and, so far as feasible, to permit dollar transfers for such purpose."

These treaties and agreements show that this Nation has adopted programs deemed desirable in bringing about, so far as can be done, stability and uniformity in the difficult field of world monetary controls and exchange. These arrangements have not purported to achieve a sufficiently rigid valuation of moneys to guarantee that foreign exchange payments will at all times, at all places and under all circumstances be based on a "definitely ascertainable" valuation measured by the diverse currencies of the world. Doubtless these agreements may fall short of that goal. But our National Government's powers have been exercised so far as deemed desirable and feasible toward that end, and the power to make policy with regard to such matters is a national one from the compulsion of both necessity and our Constitution. After the proper governmental agencies have selected the policy of foreign exchange for the country as a whole, Oregon of course cannot refuse to give foreign nationals their treaty rights because of fear that valid international agreements might possibly not work completely to the satisfaction of state authorities. Our National Government's assent to these international agreements, coupled with its continuing adherence to the 1881 Treaty, precludes any State from deciding that Yugoslavian laws meeting the standards of those agreements can be the basis for defeating rights conferred by the 1881 Treaty.

The judgment of the Supreme Court of Oregon is reversed and the cause remanded for proceedings not inconsistent with this opinion.

Reversed and remanded.

NOTES

1. *Supremacy of Treaties over State Law.* Justices Chase and Iredell in *Ware v. Hylton* agreed that the Treaty of Peace was a self-executing obligation that, under the U.S. Constitution, superseded the conflicting Virginia state law. While they differed over whether treaties under the Articles of Confederation were similarly self-executing, it is generally accepted that one of the problems with the Articles of Confederation was the inability of Congress to compel the several states to comply with treaties. *See* Carlos Manuel Vázquez, *Treaty-Based Rights and Remedies of Individuals*, 92 COLUM. L. REV. 1082, 1101–04 (1992). That is why Hamilton in *The Federalist Papers* No. 22 and Madison in *The Federalist Papers* No. 42 (*see* Chapter 1, Sec. 1) heralded the need for a new treaty power, one that would not allow treaties to "be substantially frustrated by regulations of the States." *Ware v. Hylton* was the first case to establish federal judicial review of state laws, and preceded *Marbury v. Madison* (establishing federal judicial review of federal statutes and executive acts) by seven years.

2. *Scope of the Treaty Power.* As was discussed in Chapter 3, the scope of the treaty power has been regarded by the Supreme Court as quite broad, resulting in the preemption of various state laws. In the case of *Missouri v. Holland*, 252 U.S. 416 (1920) (*see* Chapter 3, Sec. 6), the Supreme Court endorsed the proposition that the president and the Senate together may achieve via the treaty power what Congress and the president cannot do by statute under Article I, Section 8 of the Constitution. In that case, the Supreme

Court found that even if Congress could not by a statute, enacted solely under Article I, impose restrictions on the several states regarding the hunting of migratory birds, such restrictions could be imposed by a statute that implemented a treaty (in that case, the U.S.-U.K. Migratory Bird Treaty).

According to the *Restatement of the Law (Fourth), The Foreign Relations Law of the United States* (Tentative Draft No. 2, 2017), § 112:

> The treaty power conferred by Article II of the Constitution may be used to enter into treaties addressing matters that would fall outside of Congress's legislative authority in the absence of the treaty;
>
> Congress has the constitutional authority to enact legislation that is necessary and proper to implement treaties, even if such legislation addresses matters that would otherwise fall outside of Congress's legislative authority.

Yet even if the scope of the federal treaty power is broader than the scope of Congress's powers under Article I, is the exercise of that power as against the several states still constrained by principles of federalism? *See* Curtis A. Bradley, *Federalism, Treaty Implementation, and Political Process:* Bond v. United States, 108 AM. J. INT'L L. 486 (2014) (finding the principles of federalism are still relevant, both as a matter of law and politics).

3. *Preemption by Executive Agreement.* Chapter 3, Sec. 7, noted that many international agreements concluded by the United States are not done in the form of a "treaty" as that term is understood in the U.S. Constitution. Some agreements are concluded by the president based on authorization from a majority of both Houses of Congress (congressional-executive agreements) or based solely on the president's own constitutional powers (presidential-executive agreements). In *United States v. Belmont*, 301 U.S. 324 (1937) and *Dames & Moore v. Regan*, 453 U.S. 654 (1981), the Supreme Court upheld the constitutionality of such agreements even in the face of contrary state laws or rules.

In *Belmont*, the president had concluded an executive agreement that, among other things, recognized Soviet ownership rights in expropriated property and transferred those rights to the U.S. government. If the Supreme Court had applied New York law in *Belmont,* certain creditors would have had priority to the property rather than the federal government (the state of New York had refused to recognize the validity of the Soviet expropriation). Instead, the Court looked to the executive agreement as the controlling law, and therefore found that the U.S. government and not the creditors were entitled to the property.

Dames & Moore upheld the president's authority under a sole-executive agreement to transfer claims pending in both U.S. federal and state courts to an international arbitral tribunal, notwithstanding any state laws or rules to the contrary. In *American Insurance Ass'n v. Garamendi*, 539 U.S. 396, 416 (2003) (excerpted in Section 5 below), the Supreme Court stated that "valid executive agreements are fit to preempt state law, just as treaties are. . . ."

These cases have led most authorities to conclude that executive agreements supersede state law in the same manner as treaties. *See, e.g.*, 1 *Restatement of the Law (Third), The Foreign Relations Law of the United States* § 302(d) (1987); Bruce Ackerman & David Golove, *Is NAFTA Constitutional?*, 108 HARV. L. REV. 799 (1995). Nevertheless, at least one commentator maintains that legislative-executive agreements must remain within the scope of Congress's enumerated powers, see John C. Yoo, *Laws as Treaties?: The Constitutionality of Congressional-Executive Agreements*, 99 MICH. L. REV. 757 (2001), others contend that sole-executive agreements should not be allowed to supersede state law, see Michael D. Ramsey, *Executive Agreements and the (Non)Treaty Power*, 77 N.C. L. REV. 133 (1998), while still others maintain that sole-executive agreements should only be allowed to supercede state law in particular areas, such as claims settlements, see Bradford R. Clark, *Domesticating Sole Executive Agreements*, 93 VA. L. REV. 1573 (2007). Thus far, U.S. courts have not adopted one of these theories. Do you think they should?

4. PREEMPTION OF STATE LAW BY THE DORMANT FOREIGN COMMERCE CLAUSE

U.S. Constitution, Article I, Section 8, Clause 3 provides: "The Congress shall have Power . . . To regulate Commerce with foreign Nations, and among the several states, and with the Indian Tribes. . . ." U.S. courts have found that the Commerce Clause and the Foreign Commerce Clause are not only "positive" grants of power to Congress, but are also "negative" constraints upon the several states. In other words, U.S. courts have developed a doctrine of the "dormant" Commerce Clause and "dormant" Foreign Commerce Clause, which can have the effect of striking down state regulation even in situations where Congress has not expressly or implicitly preempted the state. What is "dormant" is the congressional exercise of the power (not the clauses themselves). Situations where the dormant Foreign Commerce Clause may be implicated include state taxation of foreign business and restrictions by states on their governments or companies doing business with foreign nations. The U.S. Supreme Court has addressed this issue on more than one occasion in the context of state taxation of foreign business.

As you read *Barclays Bank PLC*, which concerns a corporate franchise tax, consider the following questions. What four requirements must be met for a state tax law to survive a Commerce Clause challenge? What two additional requirements must be met for a state tax law to survive a Foreign Commerce Clause challenge? Why have those additional requirements? In the *Natsios* case that follows, what standard is applied when reviewing a state law that imposes a sanction on foreign commerce?

BARCLAYS BANK PLC V. FRANCHISE TAX BOARD

512 U.S. 298, 301–31 (1994).

JUSTICE GINSBURG delivered the opinion of the Court.

Eleven years ago, in *Container Corp. of America v. Franchise Tax Bd.*, 463 U.S. 159 (1983), this Court upheld California's income-based corporate franchise tax, as applied to a multinational enterprise, against a comprehensive challenge made under the Due Process and Commerce Clauses of the Federal Constitution. *Container Corp.* involved a corporate taxpayer domiciled and headquartered in the United States; in addition to its stateside components, the taxpayer had a number of overseas subsidiaries incorporated in the countries in which they operated. The Court's decision in *Container Corp.* did not address the constitutionality of California's taxing scheme as applied to "domestic corporations with foreign parents or [to] foreign corporations with either foreign parents or foreign subsidiaries." *Id.*, at 189, n. 26. In the consolidated cases before us, we return to the taxing scheme earlier considered in *Container Corp.* and resolve matters left open in that case.

The petitioner in No. 92–1384, Barclays Bank PLC (Barclays), is a United Kingdom corporation in the Barclays Group, a multinational banking enterprise. The petitioner in No. 92–1839, Colgate-Palmolive Co. (Colgate), is the United States-based parent of a multinational manufacturing and sales enterprise. Each enterprise has operations in California. During the years here at issue, California determined the state corporate franchise tax due for these operations under a method known as "worldwide combined reporting." California's scheme first looked to the worldwide income of the multinational enterprise, and then attributed a portion of that income (equal to the average of the proportions of worldwide payroll, property, and sales located in California) to the California operations. The State imposed its tax on the income thus attributed to Barclays' and Colgate's California business.

Barclays urges that California's tax system distinctively burdens foreign-based multinationals and results in double international taxation, in violation of the Commerce and Due Process Clauses. Both Barclays and Colgate contend that the scheme offends the Commerce Clause by frustrating the Federal Government's ability to "speak with one voice when regulating commercial relations with foreign governments." *Japan Line, Ltd. v. County of Los Angeles*, 441 U.S. 434, 449 (1979) (internal quotation marks omitted). . . .

The Commerce Clause expressly gives Congress power "[t]o regulate Commerce with foreign Nations, and among the several States." U.S. Const., Art. I, 8, cl. 3. It has long been understood, as well, to provide "protection from state legislation inimical to the national commerce [even] where Congress has not acted. . . ." . . . The Clause does not shield interstate (or foreign) commerce from its "fair share of the state tax burden." . . . Absent congressional approval, however, a state tax on such commerce will not survive Commerce Clause scrutiny if the taxpayer demonstrates that the tax (1) applies to an activity lacking a substantial nexus to the taxing State; (2) is not fairly apportioned; (3) discriminates against interstate commerce; *or* (4) is not fairly related to the services provided by the State. *Complete Auto Transit, Inc. v. Brady*, 430 U.S. 274, 279 (1977).

In "the unique context of foreign commerce," a State's power is further constrained because of "the special need for federal uniformity." *Wardair Canada, Inc. v. Florida Dept. of Revenue*, 477 U.S. 1, 8 (1986). " 'In international relations and with respect to foreign intercourse and trade the people of the United States act through a single government with unified and adequate national power.' " *Japan Line, Ltd. v. County of Los Angeles*, 441 U.S., at 448. . . . A tax affecting *foreign* commerce therefore raises two concerns in addition to the four delineated in *Complete Auto*. The first is prompted by "the enhanced risk of multiple taxation." *Container Corp.*, 463 U.S., at 185. The second relates to the Federal Government's capacity to " 'speak with one voice when regulating commercial relations with foreign governments.' " *Japan Line*, 441 U.S., at 449, quoting *Michelin Tire Corp. v. Wages*, 423 U.S. 276, 285 (1976). . . .

Satisfied that California's corporate franchise tax is "proper and fair" as tested under *Complete Auto*'s guides, . . . we proceed to the "additional scrutiny" required when a State seeks to tax *foreign* commerce. . . . First of the two additional considerations is "the enhanced risk of multiple taxation." . . .

In *Container Corp.*, we upheld application of California's combined reporting obligation to "foreign subsidiaries of *domestic* corporations," . . . against a charge that such application unconstitutionally exposed those subsidiaries to a risk of multiple international taxation. . . .

Container Corp.'s holding on multiple taxation relied on two considerations: first, that multiple taxation was not the "inevitable result" of the California tax; and, second, that the "alternativ[e] reasonably available to the taxing State" (*i.e.*, some version of the separate accounting/"arm's length" approach),[1] . . . "could not eliminate the risk of double taxation" and might in some cases enhance that risk. . . . We

[1] [Authors' Note: Under a "separate accounting/arm's-length" approach to taxation, the taxing state treats each corporate entity within a conglomerate separately for the purpose of determining income tax liability (rather than trying to look at the range of related local and foreign corporate entities). The risk in separate accounting is that the conglomerate may manipulate transfers of value among its corporate entities to minimize its total tax liability (*i.e.*, use accounting techniques to move profits to the jurisdiction where taxes are the lowest). To prevent such manipulation, transactions between affiliated corporations need to be scrutinized to ensure that they are reported on an "arm's-length" basis, *i.e.*, at a price reflecting their true market value. California chose not to follow this approach.]

underscored that "even though most nations have adopted the arm's-length approach in its general outlines, the precise rules under which they reallocate income among affiliated corporations often differ substantially, and *whenever that difference exists, the possibility of double taxation also exists.*" . . .

These considerations are not dispositively diminished when California's tax is applied to the components of foreign, as opposed to domestic, multinationals. Multiple taxation of such entities because of California's scheme is not "inevitable"; the existence *vel non* of actual multiple taxation of income remains, as in *Container Corp.*, dependent "on the facts of the individual case." . . . And if, as we have held, adoption of a separate accounting system does not dispositively lessen the risk of multiple taxation of the income earned by foreign affiliates of domestic-owned corporations, we see no reason why it would do so in respect of the income earned by foreign affiliates of foreign-owned corporations. . . .

We turn, finally, to the question ultimately and most energetically presented: Did California's worldwide combined reporting requirement, as applied to Barcal, BBI, and Colgate, "impair federal uniformity in an area where federal uniformity is essential," *Japan Line*, 441 U.S., at 448; in particular, did the State's taxing scheme "preven[t] the Federal Government from 'speaking with one voice' in international trade"? . . .

Two decisions principally inform our judgment: first, this Court's 1983 determination in *Container Corp.*; and second, our decision three years later in *Wardair Canada, Inc. v. Florida Dept. of Revenue*, 477 U.S. 1 (1986). *Container Corp.* held that California's worldwide combined reporting requirement, as applied to domestic corporations with foreign subsidiaries, did not violate the "one voice" standard. *Container Corp.* bears on Colgate's case, but not Barclays' or BBI's, to this extent: "[T]he tax [in *Container Corp.*] was imposed not on a foreign entity . . . , but on a domestic corporation." 463 U.S., at 195. Other factors emphasized in *Container Corp.*, however, are relevant to the complaints of all three taxpayers in the consolidated cases now before us. Most significantly, the Court found no "specific indications of congressional intent" to preempt California's tax. . . .

The Court again confronted a "one voice" argument in *Wardair Canada, Inc. v. Florida Dept. of Revenue*, 477 U.S. 1 (1986), and there rejected a Commerce Clause challenge to Florida's tax on the sale of fuel to common carriers, including airlines. Air carriers were taxed on all aviation fuel purchased in Florida, without regard to the amount the carrier consumed within the State or the amount of its in-state business. The carrier in *Wardair*, a Canadian airline that operated charter flights to and from the United States, conceded that the challenged tax satisfied the *Complete Auto* criteria and entailed no threat of multiple international taxation. Joined by the United States as *amicus curiae*, however, the carrier urged that Florida's tax "threaten[ed] the ability of the Federal Government to 'speak with one voice.'" 477 U.S., at 9. There is "a federal policy," the carrier asserted, "of reciprocal tax exemptions for aircraft, equipment, and supplies, including aviation fuel, that constitute the instrumentalities of international air traffic"; this policy, the carrier argued, "represents the statement that the 'one voice' of the Federal Government wishes to make," a statement "threatened by [Florida's tax]." *Ibid.*

This Court disagreed, observing that the proffered evidence disclosed no federal policy of the kind described, and indeed demonstrated that the Federal Government intended to *permit* the States to impose sales taxes on aviation fuel. The international convention and resolution and more than 70 bilateral treaties on which the carrier relied to show a United States policy of tax exemption for the instrumentalities of international air traffic, the Court explained, in fact indicated far less: "[W]hile there appears to be an international *aspiration* on the one hand to eliminate all impediments to foreign air travel—including taxation of fuel—the *law* as it presently stands acquiesces in taxation of the sale of that fuel by political subdivisions of countries." *Id.*, at 10 (emphasis in original). . . .

As in *Container Corp.* and *Wardair*, we discern no "specific indications of congressional intent" to bar the state action here challenged. Our decision upholding California's franchise tax in *Container Corp.* left the ball in Congress' court; had Congress, the branch responsible for the regulation of foreign commerce, *see* U.S. Const., Art. I, § 8, cl. 3, considered nationally uniform use of separate accounting "essential," *Japan Line*, 441 U.S., at 448, it could have enacted legislation prohibiting the States from taxing corporate income based on the worldwide combined reporting method. In the 11 years that have elapsed since our decision in *Container Corp.*, Congress has failed to enact such legislation. . . .

The Constitution does "'not make the judiciary the overseer of our government.'" *Dames & Moore v. Regan*, 453 U.S. 654, 660 (1981). . . . Having determined that the taxpayers before us had an adequate nexus with the State, that worldwide combined reporting led to taxation which was fairly apportioned, nondiscriminatory, fairly related to the services provided by the State, and that its imposition did not result inevitably in multiple taxation, we leave it to Congress—whose voice, in this area, is the Nation's—to evaluate whether the national interest is best served by tax uniformity, or state autonomy. Accordingly, the judgments of the California Court of Appeal are

Affirmed.

NATIONAL FOREIGN TRADE COUNCIL V. NATSIOS

181 F.3d 38, 44–67 (1st Cir. 1999).

LYNCH, CIRCUIT JUDGE.

[In *Crosby v. National Foreign Trade Council* (excerpted *supra* Section 2), the U.S. Supreme Court found that a Massachusetts statute imposing sanctions on Burma (Myanmar) was directly preempted by a federal statute. The Court did not reach the issue of whether the Massachusetts statute was also invalid under the dormant Foreign Commerce Clause. The First Circuit Court of Appeals, however, had reached that issue (the case name changed on appeal to the Supreme Court).]

Massachusetts puts forth two arguments to support its claim that its law does not violate the Foreign Commerce Clause. First, Massachusetts contends that the law does not discriminate between domestic and foreign companies. Second, Massachusetts argues that its law does not impair the federal government's ability to speak with one voice regarding foreign commerce. Under standard Commerce Clause analysis, a statute that facially discriminates against interstate or foreign commerce will, in most cases, be found unconstitutional. *See, e.g., Oregon Waste Systems, Inc. v. Department of Environmental Quality*, 511 U.S. 93, 99 . . . (1994) ("If a restriction on commerce is discriminatory, it is virtually *per se* invalid. By contrast, nondiscriminatory regulations that have only incidental effects on interstate commerce are valid unless 'the burden imposed on such commerce is clearly excessive in relation to the putative local benefits.'" . . . (emphasis in original) (citation omitted)). Even under that analysis, we find that the [Massachusetts] law is discriminatory and violates the Foreign Commerce Clause. Although the law does not discriminate against foreign companies, it does discriminate against foreign commerce. Also, the law impedes the federal government's ability to speak with one voice in foreign affairs, and amounts to an attempt to regulate conduct outside of Massachusetts and outside of this country's borders. For these three reasons, we hold that the Massachusetts law violates the Foreign Commerce Clause.

NOTE: PREEMPTION OF STATE LAW BY THE DORMANT FOREIGN COMMERCE CLAUSE

Clearly the U.S. Constitution does not prohibit every state law or measure that has an effect on interstate or foreign commerce. Analysis under the dormant Commerce Clause and the dormant Foreign Commerce Clause seeks to identify situations where state action is so burdensome on commerce that it should be struck down, even in the absence of a conflicting federal law. As indicated in *Barclays Bank PLC* and *Natsios*, a threshold issue is whether the state law discriminates against interstate or foreign commerce (either facially or by substantial effects). In the particular situation of a state tax, the courts focus on whether the tax: (1) applies to an activity with a substantial nexus to the taxing state; (2) is fairly apportioned; and (3) is fairly related to the services provided by the state. In the context of foreign commerce cases, however, the Supreme Court imposes an additional layer of scrutiny: whether the state law prevents the federal government from "speaking with one voice" in international trade. For tax cases, such scrutiny includes whether there is an enhanced risk of multiple taxation.

5. PREEMPTION OF STATE LAW UNDER THE DORMANT FOREIGN AFFAIRS POWER

ZSCHERNIG V. MILLER

389 U.S. 429, 430–41 (1968).

MR. JUSTICE DOUGLAS delivered the opinion of the Court.

This case concerns the disposition of the estate of a resident of Oregon who died there intestate in 1962. Appellants are decedent's sole heirs and they are residents of East Germany. Appellees include members of the [Oregon] State Land Board that petitioned the Oregon probate court for the escheat of the net proceeds of the estate under the provisions of Ore. Rev. Stat. § 111.070 (1957), which provides for escheat in cases where a nonresident alien claims real or personal property unless three requirements are satisfied:

> (1) the existence of a reciprocal right of a United States citizen to take property on the same terms as a citizen or inhabitant of the foreign country;
>
> (2) the right of United States citizens to receive payment here of funds from estates in the foreign country; and
>
> (3) the right of the foreign heirs to receive the proceeds of Oregon estates "without confiscation." . . .

[W]e conclude that the history and operation of this Oregon statute make clear that § 111.070 is an intrusion by the State into the field of foreign affairs which the Constitution entrusts to the President and the Congress. *See Hines v. Davidowitz*, 312 U.S. 52, 63.

As already noted, one of the conditions of inheritance under the Oregon statute requires "proof that such foreign heirs, distributees, devisees or legatees may receive the benefit, use or control of money or property from estates of persons dying in this state without confiscation, in whole or in part, by the governments of such foreign countries," the burden being on the nonresident alien to establish that fact.

This provision came into Oregon's law in 1951. Prior to that time the rights of aliens under the Oregon statute were defined in general terms of reciprocity, similar to the California Act which we had before us in *Clark v. Allen*, 331 U.S., at 506, n. 1.

We held in *Clark v. Allen* that a general reciprocity clause did not on its face intrude on the federal domain. 331 U.S., at 516–517. We noted that the California statute, then a recent enactment, would have only "some incidental or indirect effect in foreign countries." *Id.*, at 517.[5]

Had that case appeared in the posture of the present one, a different result would have obtained. We were there concerned with the words of a statute on its face, not the manner of its application. State courts, of course, must frequently read, construe, and apply laws of foreign nations. It has never been seriously suggested that state courts are precluded from performing that function, albeit there is a remote possibility that any holding may disturb a foreign nation—whether the matter involves commercial cases, tort cases, or some other type of controversy. At the time *Clark v. Allen* was decided, the case seemed to involve no more than a routine reading of foreign laws. It now appears that in this reciprocity area under inheritance statutes, the probate courts of various States have launched inquiries into the type of governments that obtain in particular foreign nations—whether aliens under their law have enforceable rights, whether the so-called "rights" are merely dispensations turning upon the whim or caprice of government officials, whether the representation of consuls, ambassadors, and other representatives of foreign nations is credible or made in good faith, whether there is in the actual administration in the particular foreign system of law any element of confiscation.

In a California case, involving a reciprocity provision, the United States made the following representation:

> "The operation and effect of the statute is inextricably enmeshed in international affairs and matters of foreign policy. The statute does not work disinheritance of, or affect ownership of property in California by, any group or class, but on the contrary operates in fields exclusively for, and preempted by, the United States;

---

5 In *Clark v. Allen*, 331 U.S. 503, the District Court had held the California reciprocity statute unconstitutional because of legislative history indicating that the purpose of the statute was to prevent American assets from reaching hostile nations preparing for wars on this country. *Crowley v. Allen*, 52 F. Supp. 850, 853 (D. C. N. D. Calif.). But when the case reached this Court, petitioner contended that the statute was invalid, not because of the legislature's motive, but because on its face the statute constituted "an invasion of the exclusively Federal field of control over our foreign relations." In discussing how the statute was applied, petitioner noted that a California court had accepted as conclusive proof of reciprocity the statement of a foreign ambassador that reciprocal rights existed in his nation. Brief for petitioner in *Clark v. Allen*, No. 626, October Term 1946, pp. 73–74. Thus we had no reason to suspect that the California statute in *Clark v. Allen* was to be applied as anything other than a general reciprocity provision requiring just matching of laws. Had we been reviewing the later California decision of *Estate of Gogabashvele*, . . . 16 Cal. Rptr. 77, *see* n.6, *infra*, the additional problems we now find with the Oregon provision would have been presented.

namely, the control of the international transmission of property, funds, and credits, and the capture of enemy property. The statute is not an inheritance statute, but a statute of confiscation and retaliation." *In re Bevilacqua's Estate*, 161 P. 2d 589, 593 (Dist. Ct. App. Cal. [1945]), superseded by . . . 191 P. 2d 752.

In its brief *amicus curiae*, the Department of Justice states that: "The government does not . . . contend that the application of the Oregon escheat statute in the circumstances of this case unduly interferes with the United States' conduct of foreign relations."

The Government's acquiescence in the ruling of *Clark v. Allen* certainly does not justify extending the principle of that case, as we would be required to do here to uphold the Oregon statute as applied; for it has more than "some incidental or indirect effect in foreign countries," and its great potential for disruption or embarrassment makes us hesitate to place it in the category of a diplomatic bagatelle.

As we read the decisions that followed in the wake of *Clark v. Allen*, we find that they radiate some of the attitudes of the "cold war," where the search is for the "democracy quotient" of a foreign regime as opposed to the Marxist theory.[6] The Oregon statute introduces the concept of "confiscation," which is of course opposed to the Just Compensation Clause of the Fifth Amendment. And this has led into minute inquiries concerning the actual administration of foreign law, into the credibility of foreign diplomatic statements, and into speculation whether the fact that some received delivery of funds should "not preclude wonderment as to how many may have been denied 'the right to receive'. . . ." *See State Land Board v. Kolovrat*, . . . 349 P. 2d 255, 262, *rev'd sub nom. Kolovrat v. Oregon*, 366 U.S. 187, on other grounds.

That kind of state involvement in foreign affairs and international relations—matters which the Constitution entrusts solely to the Federal Government—is not sanctioned by *Clark v. Allen*. Yet such forbidden state activity has infected each of the three provisions of § 111.070, as applied by Oregon.

---

[6] *See Estate of Gogabashvele*, . . . 16 Cal. Rptr. 77, *disapproved in Estate of Larkin*, . . . 416 P. 2d 473, and *Estate of Chichernea*, . . . 424 P. 2d 687. One commentator has described the *Gogabashvele* decision in the following manner:

> "The court analyzed the general nature of rights in the Soviet system instead of examining whether Russian inheritance rights were granted equally to aliens and residents. The court found Russia had no separation of powers, too much control in the hands of the Communist Party, no independent judiciary, confused legislation, unpublished statutes, and unrepealed obsolete statutes. Before stating its holding of no reciprocity, the court also noted Stalin's crimes, the Beria trial, the doctrine of crime by analogy, Soviet xenophobia, and demonstrations at the American Embassy in Moscow unhindered by the police. The court concluded that a leading Soviet jurist's construction of article 8 of the law enacting the R. S. F. S. R. Civil Code seemed modeled after Humpty Dumpty, who said, 'When I use a word . . . , it means just what I choose it to mean—neither more nor less.' " Note, 55 Calif. L. Rev. 592, 594–595, n. 10 (1967).

In *State Land Board v. Pekarek*, . . . 378 P.2d 734, the Oregon Supreme Court in ruling against a Czech claimant because he had failed to prove the "benefit" requirement of subsection (1)(c) of the statute said:

> "Assuming, without deciding, that all of the evidence offered by the legatees was admissible, it can be given relatively little weight. The statements of Czechoslovakian officials must be judged in light of the interest which they had in the acquisition of funds for their government. Moreover, in judging the credibility of these witnesses we are entitled to take into consideration the fact that declarations of government officials in communist-controlled countries as to the state of affairs existing within their borders do not always comport with the actual facts." . . . 378 P.2d, at 738.

Yet in *State Land Board v. Schwabe*, . . . 400 P.2d 10, where the certificate of the Polish Ambassador was tendered against the claim that the inheritance would be confiscated abroad, the Oregon court, appraising the current attitude of Washington, D.C., toward Warsaw, accepted the certificate as true. . . . 400 P.2d at 11. . . .

As one reads the Oregon decisions, it seems that foreign policy attitudes, the freezing or thawing of the "cold war," and the like are the real desiderata.[8] Yet they of course are matters for the Federal Government, not for local probate courts.

This is as true of (1) (a) of § 111.070 as it is of (1) (b) and (1) (c). In *Clostermann v. Schmidt*, . . . 332 P.2d 1036, the court—applying the predecessor of (1) (a)—held that not only must the foreign law give inheritance rights to Americans, but the political body making the law must have "membership in the family of nations" (. . . 332 P.2d, at 1041), because the purpose of the Oregon provision was to serve as "an inducement to foreign nations to so frame the inheritance laws of their respective countries in a manner which would insure to Oregonians the same opportunities to inherit and take personal property abroad that they enjoy in the state of Oregon." . . . 332 P.2d, at 1042. . . .

---

[8] Such attitudes are not confined to the Oregon courts. Representative samples from other States would include statements in the New York courts, such as "This court would consider sending money out of this country and into Hungary tantamount to putting funds within the grasp of the Communists," and "If this money were turned over to the Russian authorities, it would be used to kill our boys and innocent people in Southeast Asia. . . ." Heyman, The Nonresident Alien's Right to Succession Under the "Iron Curtain Rule," 52 Nw. U. L. Rev. 221, 234 (1957). In Pennsylvania, a judge stated at the trial of a case involving a Soviet claimant that "If you want to say that I'm prejudiced, you can, because when it comes to Communism I'm a bigoted anti-Communist." And another judge exclaimed, "I am not going to send money to Russia where it can go into making bullets which may one day be used against my son." A California judge, upon being asked if he would hear argument on the law, replied, "No, I won't send any money to Russia." The judge took "judicial notice that Russia kicks the United States in the teeth all the time," and told counsel for the Soviet claimant that "I would think your firm would feel it honor bound to withdraw as representing the Russian government. No American can make it too strong." Berman, Soviet Heirs in American Courts, 62 Col. L. Rev. 257, and n.3 (1962).

In short, it would seem that Oregon judges in construing § 111.070 seek to ascertain whether "rights" protected by foreign law are the same "rights" that citizens of Oregon enjoy. If, as in the *Rogers* case, the alleged foreign "right" may be vindicated only through Communist-controlled state agencies, then there is no "right" of the type § 111.070 requires. The same seems to be true if enforcement may require approval of a Fascist dictator. . . . The statute as construed seems to make unavoidable judicial criticism of nations established on a more authoritarian basis than our own.

It seems inescapable that the type of probate law that Oregon enforces affects international relations in a persistent and subtle way. The practice of state courts in withholding remittances to legatees residing in Communist countries or in preventing them from assigning them is notorious. The several States, of course, have traditionally regulated the descent and distribution of estates. But those regulations must give way if they impair the effective exercise of the Nation's foreign policy. *See* Miller, The Corporation as a Private Government in the World Community, 46 Va. L. Rev. 1539, 1542–1549 (1960). Where those laws conflict with a treaty, they must bow to the superior federal policy. *See Kolovrat v. Oregon*, 366 U.S. 187. Yet, even in absence of a treaty, a State's policy may disturb foreign relations. As we stated in *Hines v. Davidowitz*, *supra*, at 64: "Experience has shown that international controversies of the gravest moment, sometimes even leading to war, may arise from real or imagined wrongs to another's subjects inflicted, or permitted, by a government." Certainly a State could not deny admission to a traveler from East Germany nor bar its citizens from going there. *Passenger Cases*, 7 How. 283; *cf. Crandall v. Nevada*, 6 Wall. 35; *Kent v. Dulles*, 357 U.S. 116. If there are to be such restraints, they must be provided by the Federal Government. The present Oregon law is not as gross an intrusion in the federal domain as those others might be. Yet, as we have said, it has a direct impact upon foreign relations and may well adversely affect the power of the central government to deal with those problems.

The Oregon law does, indeed, illustrate the dangers which are involved if each State, speaking through its probate courts, is permitted to establish its own foreign policy.

Reversed.

AMERICAN INSURANCE ASSOCIATION V. GARAMENDI

539 U.S. 396, 401–27 (2003).

JUSTICE SOUTER delivered the opinion of the Court.

California's Holocaust Victim Insurance Relief Act of 1999 (HVIRA or Act), Cal. Ins. Code Ann. §§ 13800–13807 (West Cum. Supp. 2003), requires any insurer doing business in that State to disclose information about all policies sold in Europe between 1920 and 1945 by the company itself or any one "related" to it. The issue here is whether HVIRA interferes with the National Government's conduct of foreign relations. We hold that it does, with the consequence that the state statute is preempted. . . .

The Nazi Government of Germany engaged not only in genocide and enslavement but theft of Jewish assets, including the value of insurance policies, and in particular policies of life insurance, a form of savings held by many Jews in Europe before the Second World War. Early on in the Nazi era, loss of livelihood forced Jews to cash in life insurance policies prematurely, only to have the government seize the proceeds of the repurchase, and many who tried to emigrate from Germany were forced to liquidate insurance policies to pay the steep "flight taxes" and other levies imposed by the Third Reich to keep Jewish assets from leaving the country. . . . Before long, the Reich began simply seizing the remaining policies outright. . . . After the war, even a policy that had escaped confiscation was likely to be dishonored, whether because insurers denied its existence or claimed it had lapsed from unpaid premiums during the persecution, or because the government would not provide heirs with documentation of the policyholder's death. . . . Responsibility as between the government and insurance companies is disputed, but at the end of the day, the fact is that the value or proceeds of many insurance policies issued to Jews before and during the war were paid to the Reich or never paid at all.

These confiscations and frustrations of claims fell within the subject of reparations, which became a principal object of Allied diplomacy soon after the war. At the Potsdam Conference, the United States, Britain, and the Soviet Union took reparations for wartime losses by seizing industrial assets from their respective occupation zones, putting into effect the plan originally envisioned at the Yalta Conference months before. . . . A year later, the United States was among the parties to an agreement to share seized assets with other western allies as settlement, as to each signatory nation, of "all its claims and those of its nationals against the former German Government and its Agencies, of a governmental or private nature, arising out of the war." Agreement on Reparation from Germany, on the Establishment of Inter-Allied Reparation Agency and Restitution of Monetary Gold, 61 Stat. 3163, Art. 2(A), T. I. A. S. No. 1655 (hereinafter Paris Agreement).

The effect of the Paris Agreement was curtailed, however, and attention to reparations intentionally deferred, when the western allies moved to end their occupation and reestablish a sovereign Germany as a buffer against Soviet expansion. They worried that continued reparations would cripple the new Federal Republic of Germany economically, and so decided in the London Debt Agreement to put off "[c]onsideration of claims arising out of the second World War by countries which were at war with or were occupied by Germany during that war, and by nationals of such countries, against the Reich and agencies of the Reich . . . until the final settlement of the problem of reparation." Agreement on German External Debts, Feb. 27, 1953, 4 U. S. T. 443, 449, T. I. A. S. No. 2792. . . .

In the meantime, the western allies placed the obligation to provide restitution to victims of Nazi persecution on the new West German Government. . . . West Germany enacted its own restitution laws in 1953 and 1956, . . . and signed agreements with 16 countries for the compensation of their nationals. . . . Despite a payout of more than 100 billion deutsch marks as of 2000, . . . these measures left out many claimants and certain types of claims, and when the agreement reunifying East and West Germany . . . was read by the German courts as lifting the London Debt Agreement's moratorium on Holocaust claims by foreign nationals, class-action lawsuits for restitution poured into United States courts against companies doing business in Germany during the Nazi era. . . .

These suits generated much protest by the defendant companies and their governments, to the point that the Government of the United States took action to try to resolve "the last great compensation related negotiation arising out of World War II." . . . From the beginning, the Government's position . . . stressed mediated settlement "as an alternative to endless litigation" promising little relief to aging Holocaust survivors. . . . Ensuing negotiations at the national level produced the German Foundation Agreement, signed by President Clinton and German Chancellor Schröder in July 2000, in which Germany agreed to enact legislation establishing a foundation funded with 10 billion deutsch marks contributed equally by the German Government and German companies, to be used to compensate all those "who suffered at the hands of German companies during the National Socialist era." Agreement Concerning the Foundation "Remembrance, Responsibility and the Future," 39 Int'l Legal Materials 1298 (2000).

The willingness of the Germans to create a voluntary compensation fund was conditioned on some expectation of security from lawsuits in United States courts, and after extended dickering President Clinton put his weight behind two specific measures toward that end. . . . First, the Government agreed that whenever a German company was sued on a Holocaust-era claim in an American court, the Government of the United States would submit a statement that "it would be in the foreign policy interests of the United States for the Foundation to be the exclusive forum and remedy for the resolution of all asserted claims against German companies arising from their involvement in the National Socialist era and World War II." 39 Int'l Legal Materials, at 1303. Though unwilling to guarantee that its foreign policy interests would "in themselves provide an independent legal basis for dismissal," that being an issue for the courts, the Government agreed to tell courts "that U.S. policy interests favor dismissal on any valid legal ground." *Id.*, at 1304. On top of that undertaking, the Government promised to use its "best efforts, in a manner it considers appropriate," to get state and local governments to respect the foundation as the exclusive mechanism. *Id.*, at 1300.

As for insurance claims specifically, both countries agreed that the German Foundation would work with the International Commission on Holocaust Era Insurance Claims (ICHEIC), a voluntary organization formed in 1998 by several European insurance companies, the State of Israel, Jewish and Holocaust survivor associations, and the National Association of Insurance Commissioners, the organization of American state insurance commissioners. The job of the ICHEIC, chaired by former Secretary of State Eagleburger, includes negotiation with European insurers to provide information about unpaid insurance policies issued to Holocaust victims and settlement of claims brought under them. It has thus set up procedures for handling demands against participating insurers, including "a reasonable review . . . of the participating companies' files" for production of unpaid policies, "an investigatory process to determine the current status" of insurance policies for which claims are filed, and a "claims and valuation process to settle and pay individual claims," employing "relaxed standards of proof." . . .

The German Foundation pact has served as a model for similar [U.S. executive] agreements with Austria and France, and the United States Government continues to pursue comparable agreements with other countries. . . .

While these international efforts were underway, California's Department of Insurance began its own enquiry into the issue of unpaid claims under Nazi-era insurance policies, prompting state legislation designed to force payment by defaulting insurers. In 1998, the state legislature made it an unfair business practice for any insurer operating in the State to "fai[l] to pay any valid claim from Holocaust survivors." Cal. Ins. Code Ann. § 790.15(a) (West Cum. Supp. 2003). The legislature placed "an affirmative duty" on the Department of Insurance "to play an independent role in representing the interests of Holocaust survivors," including an obligation to "gather, review, and analyze the archives of insurers . . . to provide for research and investigation" into unpaid insurance claims. §§ 12967(a)(1), (2).

State legislative efforts culminated the next year with passage of Assembly Bill No. 600, 1999 Cal. Stats. ch. 827, the first section of which amended the State's Code of Civil Procedure to allow state residents to sue in state court on insurance claims based on acts perpetrated in the Holocaust and extended the governing statute of limitations to December 31, 2010. Cal. Civ. Proc. Code Ann. § 354.5 (West Cum. Supp. 2003). The section of the bill codified as HVIRA, at issue here, requires "[a]ny insurer currently doing business in the state" to disclose the details of "life, property, liability, health, annuities, dowry, educational, or casualty insurance policies" issued "to persons in Europe, which were in effect between 1920 and 1945." Cal. Ins. Code Ann. § 13804(a) (West Cum. Supp. 2003). . . . The mandatory penalty for default is suspension of the company's license to do business in the State, § 13806, and there are misdemeanor criminal sanctions for falsehood in certain required representations about whether and to whom the proceeds of each policy have been distributed, § 13804(b). . . .

[S]everal American and European insurance companies and the American Insurance Association (a national trade association), filed suit for injunctive relief against respondent insurance commissioner of California, challenging the constitutionality of HVIRA. . . .

The principal argument for preemption made by petitioners and the United States as *amicus curiae* is that HVIRA interferes with foreign policy of the Executive Branch, as expressed principally in the executive agreements with Germany, Austria, and France. The major premises of the argument, at least, are beyond dispute. There is, of course, no question that at some point an exercise of state power that touches on foreign relations must yield to the National Government's policy, given the "concern for uniformity in this country's dealings with foreign nations" that animated the Constitution's allocation of the foreign relations power to the National Government in the first place. *Banco Nacional de Cuba v. Sabbatino*, 376 U.S. 398, 427, n.25 (1964); *see Crosby v. National Foreign Trade Council*, 530 U.S. 363, 381–382, n. 16 (2000) (" '[T]he peace of the WHOLE ought not to be left at the disposal of a PART' " (quoting *The Federalist* No. 80, pp. 535–536 (J. Cooke ed. 1961) (A. Hamilton))); *Id.*, No. 44, p. 299 (J. Madison) (emphasizing "the advantage of uniformity in all points which relate to foreign powers"); *Id.*, No. 42, p. 279 (J. Madison) ("If we are to be one nation in any respect, it clearly ought to be in respect to other nations"); *see also First Nat. City Bank v. Banco Nacional de Cuba*, 406 U.S. 759, 769 (1972) (plurality opinion) (act of state doctrine was "fashioned because of fear that adjudication would interfere with the conduct of foreign relations"); *Japan Line, Ltd. v. County of Los Angeles*, 441 U.S. 434, 449 (1979) (negative Foreign Commerce Clause protects the National Government's ability to speak with "one voice" in regulating commerce with foreign countries (internal quotation marks omitted)).

Nor is there any question generally that there is executive authority to decide what that policy should be. Although the source of the President's power to act in foreign affairs does not enjoy any textual detail, the historical gloss on the "executive Power" vested in Article II of the Constitution has recognized the President's "vast share of responsibility for the conduct of our foreign relations." *Youngstown Sheet & Tube Co. v.*

Sawyer, 343 U.S. 579, 610–611 (1952) (Frankfurter, J., concurring). While Congress holds express authority to regulate public and private dealings with other nations in its war and foreign commerce powers, in foreign affairs the President has a degree of independent authority to act. . . .

Generally, . . . valid executive agreements are fit to preempt state law, just as treaties are, and if the agreements here had expressly preempted laws like HVIRA, the issue would be straightforward. . . . But petitioners and the United States as *amicus curiae* both have to acknowledge that the agreements include no preemption clause, and so leave their claim of preemption to rest on asserted interference with the foreign policy those agreements embody. Reliance is placed on our decision in *Zschernig v. Miller*, 389 U.S. 429 (1968). . . .

The *Zschernig* majority relied on statements in a number of previous cases open to the reading that state action with more than incidental effect on foreign affairs is preempted, even absent any affirmative federal activity in the subject area of the state law, and hence without any showing of conflict. The Court cited the pronouncement in *Hines v. Davidowitz*, 312 U.S. 52, 63 (1941), that "[o]ur system of government is such that the interest of the cities, counties and states, no less than the interest of the people of the whole nation, imperatively requires that federal power in the field affecting foreign relations be left entirely free from local interference." *See* 389 U.S., at 432; *id.*, at 442–443 (Stewart, J., concurring) (setting out the foregoing quotation). Likewise, Justice Stewart's concurring opinion viewed the Oregon statute as intruding "into a domain of exclusively federal competence." *Id.*, at 442; *see also Belmont*, 301 U.S., at 331 ("[C]omplete power over international affairs is in the national government and is not and cannot be subject to any curtailment or interference on the part of the several states" (citing *Curtiss-Wright Export Corp.*, 299 U.S., at 316 et seq.)).

Justice Harlan, joined substantially by Justice White, disagreed with the *Zschernig* majority on this point, arguing that its implication of preemption of the entire field of foreign affairs was at odds with some other cases suggesting that in the absence of positive federal action "the States may legislate in areas of their traditional competence even though their statutes may have an incidental effect on foreign relations." 389 U.S., at 459 (opinion concurring in result) (citing cases); see *id.*, at 462 (White, J., dissenting). Thus, for Justice Harlan it was crucial that the challenge to the Oregon statute presented no evidence of a "specific interest of the Federal Government which might be interfered with" by the law. *Id.*, at 459 (opinion concurring in result); see *id.*, at 461 (finding "no evidence of adverse effect in the record"). He would, however, have found preemption in a case of "conflicting federal policy," see *id.*, at 458–459, and on this point the majority and Justices Harlan and White basically agreed: state laws "must give way if they impair the effective exercise of the Nation's foreign

policy," *id.*, at 440 (opinion of the Court). *See also Pink*, 315 U.S., at 230–231 ("[S]tate law must yield when it is inconsistent with, or impairs . . . the superior Federal policy evidenced by a treaty or international compact or agreement"); *id.*, at 240 (Frankfurter, J., concurring) (state law may not be allowed to "interfer[e] with the conduct of our foreign relations by the Executive").

It is a fair question whether respect for the executive foreign relations power requires a categorical choice between the contrasting theories of field and conflict preemption evident in the *Zschernig* opinions,[11] but the question requires no answer here. For even on Justice Harlan's view, the likelihood that state legislation will produce something more than incidental effect in conflict with express foreign policy of the National Government would require preemption of the state law. And since on his view it is legislation within "areas of . . . traditional competence" that gives a State any claim to prevail, 389 U.S., at 459, 88 S.Ct. 664, it would be reasonable to consider the strength of the state interest, judged by standards of traditional practice, when deciding how serious a conflict must be shown before declaring the state law preempted. *Cf. Southern Pacific Co. v. Arizona ex rel. Sullivan*, 325 U.S. 761, 768–769 (1945) (under negative Commerce Clause, "reconciliation of the conflicting claims of state and national power is to be attained only by some appraisal and accommodation of the competing demands of the state and national interests involved"); Henkin, Foreign Affairs and the United States Constitution, at 164 (suggesting a test that "balance[s] the state's interest in a regulation against the impact on U.S. foreign relations"); Maier, Preemption of State Law: A Recommended Analysis, 83 Am. J. Int'l L. 832, 834 (1989) (similar). Judged by these standards, we think petitioners and the Government have demonstrated a sufficiently clear conflict to require finding preemption here. . . .

To begin with, resolving Holocaust-era insurance claims that may be held by residents of this country is a matter well within the Executive's responsibility for foreign affairs. Since claims remaining in the aftermath of hostilities may be "sources of friction" acting as an "impediment to

---

[11] The two positions can be seen as complementary. If a State were simply to take a position on a matter of foreign policy with no serious claim to be addressing a traditional state responsibility, field preemption might be the appropriate doctrine, whether the National Government had acted and, if it had, without reference to the degree of any conflict, the principle having been established that the Constitution entrusts foreign policy exclusively to the National Government. *See, e.g., Hines v. Davidowitz*, 312 U.S. 52, 63 (1941). Where, however, a State has acted within what Justice Harlan called its "traditional competence," 389 U.S., at 459, but in a way that affects foreign relations, it might make good sense to require a conflict, of a clarity or substantiality that would vary with the strength or the traditional importance of the state concern asserted. Whether the strength of the federal foreign policy interest should itself be weighed is, of course, a further question. *Cf. Rice v. Santa Fe Elevator Corp.*, 331 U.S. 218, 230 (1947) (congressional occupation of the field is not to be presumed "in a field which the States have traditionally occupied"); *Boyle v. United Technologies Corp.*, 487 U.S. 500, 507–508 (1988) ("In an area of uniquely federal interest," "[t]he conflict with federal policy need not be as sharp as that which must exist for ordinary pre-emption").

resumption of friendly relations" between the countries involved, . . . there is a "longstanding practice" of the national Executive to settle them in discharging its responsibility to maintain the Nation's relationships with other countries. . . .

The exercise of the federal executive authority means that state law must give way where, as here, there is evidence of clear conflict between the policies adopted by the two. The foregoing account of negotiations toward the three settlement agreements is enough to illustrate that the consistent Presidential foreign policy has been to encourage European governments and companies to volunteer settlement funds in preference to litigation or coercive sanctions. . . . As for insurance claims in particular, the national position, expressed unmistakably in the executive agreements signed by the President with Germany and Austria, has been to encourage European insurers to work with the ICHEIC to develop acceptable claim procedures, including procedures governing disclosure of policy information. . . . This position, of which the agreements are exemplars, has also been consistently supported in the high levels of the Executive Branch. . . . The approach taken serves to resolve the several competing matters of national concern apparent in the German Foundation Agreement: the national interest in maintaining amicable relationships with current European allies; survivors' interests in a "fair and prompt" but nonadversarial resolution of their claims so as to "bring some measure of justice . . . in their lifetimes"; and the companies' interest in securing "legal peace" when they settle claims in this fashion. 39 Int'l Legal Materials, at 1304. . . .

California has taken a different tack of providing regulatory sanctions to compel disclosure and payment, supplemented by a new cause of action for Holocaust survivors if the other sanctions should fail. The situation created by the California legislation calls to mind the impact of the Massachusetts Burma law on the effective exercise of the President's power, as recounted in the statutory preemption case, *Crosby v. National Foreign Trade Council*, 530 U.S. 363 (2000). HVIRA's economic compulsion to make public disclosure, of far more information about far more policies than ICHEIC rules require, employs "a different, state system of economic pressure," and in doing so undercuts the President's diplomatic discretion and the choice he has made exercising it. *Id.*, at 376. . . .

The basic fact is that California seeks to use an iron fist where the President has consistently chosen kid gloves. We have heard powerful arguments that the iron fist would work better, and it may be that if the matter of compensation were considered in isolation from all other issues involving the European allies, the iron fist would be the preferable policy. But our thoughts on the efficacy of the one approach versus the other are beside the point, since our business is not to judge the wisdom of the National Government's policy; dissatisfaction should be addressed to the

President or, perhaps, Congress. The question relevant to preemption in this case is conflict, and the evidence here is "more than sufficient to demonstrate that the state Act stands in the way of [the President's] diplomatic objectives." *Crosby, supra*, at 386.

NOTES

1. Zschernig*'s Dormant Foreign Affairs Power*. In *Zschernig*, there was no federal statute either directly preempting the state statute or occupying the field. A national and resident of communist East Germany sought to collect an inheritance, but Oregon state courts denied his claim under the same Oregon probate statute at issue in *Kolovrat v. Oregon* (*see supra,* this Chapter, Sec. 4). This time, however, there was no treaty precluding operation of the state statute, at least as it applied to personal property. So, in striking down the state statute, the Court relied simply on what might be called a "dormant foreign affairs power," meaning a power not actually exercised by the federal government, but which nevertheless precludes state action.

The dormant foreign affairs power in *Zschernig* has been regarded as a form of federal common law. Prior to *Garamendi*, some commentators speculated that the *Zschernig* doctrine of preemption by a dormant foreign affairs power was on its way out, since the Supreme Court had not returned to it despite opportunities to do so. *See, e.g.*, Peter J. Spiro, *Foreign Relations Federalism*, 70 U. COLO. L. REV. 1223 (1999). For critics of *Zschernig,* although the Constitution expressly excludes the states from certain activities relating to foreign affairs, it allows them to continue others. As such, while there is a valid basis under the U.S. Constitution for preemption by statute (or even by the dormant Foreign Commerce Clause), there is no such basis for preemption by an unenumerated, dormant foreign affairs power. Preemption should only occur where there is an express prohibition on the states in the Constitution, or an affirmative decision by the political branches to preempt; it should not be left to unelected judges to decide whether state action conflicts with U.S. foreign policy. *See, e.g.*, Jack L. Goldsmith, *Federal Courts, Foreign Affairs, and Federalism*, 83 VA. L. REV. 1617 (1997); Michael D. Ramsey, *The Power of States in Foreign Affairs: The Original Understanding of Foreign Policy Federalism*, 75 NOTRE DAME L. REV. 341, 392–93 (1999).

Given the extensive activity of states relating to foreign relations and the globalization of all manner of activities, how might states know when they have "crossed the line" and violated the dormant foreign affairs power? One commentator argues that the Court should narrow the *Zschernig* doctrine to the following proposition: "[S]tate sanctions that single out foreign states (or their citizens or those who do business with them) for unfavorable treatment are categorically forbidden unless affirmatively authorized by Congress." Carlos Manuel Vázquez, *W(h)ither* Zschernig?, 46 VILL. L. REV. 1259, 1316 (2001). Does this standard capture what *Zschernig* and its progeny seek to accomplish? Alternatively, one commentator favors shifting to a "dormant treaty power." *See* Edward T. Swaine, *Negotiating Federalism: State*

Bargaining and the Dormant Treaty Power, 49 DUKE L.J. 1127 (2000). A dormant treaty power would preclude states from bargaining with, or applying measures contingent on the behavior of, foreign governments, except in limited circumstances (*e.g.*, when such action is deemed unobjectionable by the federal government).

2. *Relevance of the Executive Branch's Views*. In an earlier case, *Clark v. Allen*, 331 U.S. 503 (1947), the Court upheld a similar California probate statute. Why the difference in *Zschernig*? (Only four of the eight Justices participating in *Zschernig* were confident that the Court's results could be reconciled). *Compare Zschernig*, 389 U.S. at 433–35 (refusing the invitation to reexamine the Court's ruling in *Clark v. Allen*), *with id.* at 443 (Stewart, J., concurring, joined by Brennan, J.) ("To the extent that *Clark v. Allen* is inconsistent with these views, I would overrule that decision."), and *id.* at 458 (Harlan, J., concurring) ("It seems to me impossible to distinguish the present case from *Clark v. Allen* in this respect in any convincing way."), and *id.* at 462 (White, J., dissenting) (indicating agreement with the relevant portion of Justice Harlan's concurrence). How much was the Court engaging in speculation about the effects of state action on foreign affairs? To the extent that the Court was engaging in speculative reasoning, do you think that it would be best for the Court to defer to the political branches on such matters? As noted in the Court's decision, the executive branch in *Zschernig* filed an amicus brief that stated: "The government does not . . . contend that the application of the Oregon escheat statute in the circumstances of this case unduly interferes with the United States' conduct of foreign relations." 539 U.S. at 434. Should the Court have regarded that position as dispositive on the issue of undue effects on U.S. foreign affairs? Or did the Court go too far in *Garamendi* in crediting the executive branch's views?

3. *Foreign Policymaking and the Dormant Foreign Affairs Power*. Whatever credence may be given to executive branch submissions in the course of litigation, the hallmark of the dormant foreign affairs power is the absence of any conflicts arising from formal federal lawmaking. The Court's opinion in *Garamendi*, which appeared reluctant to rely on *Zschernig* overtly, straddled the line in this regard. On the one hand, the case involved no statute or international agreement preempting state law (and did not turn on application of the dormant foreign commerce power). At the same time, the Court relied on conflict with a foreign policy established by the executive branch, as "embod[ied]" in executive agreements that merely lacked preemption clauses, thus arguably occupying space somewhere between a dormant foreign affairs power and preemption by lawmaking. Indeed, the Court seemed to distinguish circumstances involving "field preemption" arising regardless "whether the National Government had acted and, if it had, without reference to the degree of any conflict." 539 U.S. at 420 n.11.

The reference to field preemption in *Garamendi* was confusing, insofar as it left unclear what kinds of state laws are preempted by the federal government's foreign policy. In *Von Saher v. Norton Simon Museum of Art at Pasadena*, 592 F.3d 954 (9th Cir. 2010), the court of appeals held that a

California statute addressing the recovery of art looted by the Nazis was preempted, agreeing with the district court's conclusion that the statute "intrudes on the power to make and resolve war." *Id.* at 965–66. In reaching this conclusion, which followed *Garamendi*'s invitation to apply a field preemption analysis, *id.* at 965, the court found its conclusion "buttressed by the documented history of federal action addressing the subject of Nazi-looted art" which was "so comprehensive and pervasive as to leave no room for state legislation." *Id.* at 966. On remand, however, plaintiffs pursued their claims based on an amended California statute of general applicability and, unlike in *Garamendi*, sought relief solely from a U.S. museum allegedly possessing art looted by the Nazis but otherwise that had no connection to Holocaust-era injustices. This time the court of appeals found that the claims did not conflict with federal policy, given that "there is no Holocaust-specific legislation at issue." *Von Saher v. Norton Simon Museum of Art*, 754 F.3d 712, 723 (2014); *see also Cassirer v. Thyssen-Bornemisza Collection Foundation*, 737 F.3d 613 (9th Cir. 2013) (likewise upholding against a dormant foreign affairs challenge claims brought under the California statute of general applicability); *Museum of Fine Arts Boston v. Seger-Thomschitz*, 623 F.3d 1, 12–13 (1st Cir. 2010) (upholding against dormant foreign affairs challenge a Massachusetts statute of limitations applicable to Nazi-era artwork claim in part on the basis that, in contrast to *Garamendi*, there is "no comparably express federal policy bearing on the issues").

The Ninth Circuit Court of Appeals initially upheld against a preemption challenge a California statute that extended the statute of limitations for claims arising out of life insurance policies issued to victims of the "Armenian genocide." *Movsesian v. Victoria Versicherung AG*, 629 F.3d 901 (9th Cir. 2010). That decision found that there was no "clear, express federal policy" that prohibited California from referring to an "Armenian genocide." *Id.* at 907–08. On rehearing *en banc*, however, the court of appeals decided that the California statute did not concern an area of traditional state responsibility, intruded on the federal government's foreign affairs power, and therefore was preempted. *Movsesian v. Victoria Versicherung AG*, 670 F.3d 1067 (9th Cir. 2012). Among other things, the court stated that California's statute expressed "a distinct political point of view on a specific matter of foreign policy" by imposing "the politically charged label of 'genocide' on the actions of the Ottoman Empire (and consequently, present-day Turkey)" and required courts to decide whether persons "escaped to avoid persecution" from the Ottoman Empire. *Id.* at 1076. *But see Gingery v. City of Glendale*, 831 F.3d 1222 (9th Cir. 2016) (city's installation of a monument to Korean women who allegedly were forced by Japan to serve as "comfort women" before and during World War II not preempted by foreign affairs power).

4. *"Traditional State Responsibility" and the Dormant Foreign Affairs Power*. The Court in *Garamendi* found relevant whether the state was acting in an area of traditional state competence. First, "[i]f a State were simply to take a position on a matter of foreign policy with no serious claim to be addressing a traditional state responsibility, field preemption might be the

appropriate doctrine" regardless of whether the federal government had acted and, if it had, without regard to the degree of any conflict. 539 U.S. at 419 n.11. Second, where there was a conflict with "express foreign policy" (albeit not in the form of a preemptive law), "the strength of the state interest, judged by standards of traditional practice," was relevant when "deciding how serious a conflict must be shown before declaring the state law preempted." *Id.* at 420. Do you think that courts are well-equipped to gauge the seriousness and strength of the state's interests?

6. PREEMPTION OF STATE LAW BY CUSTOMARY INTERNATIONAL LAW

Chapter 2 discussed in detail the manner in which the "law of nations," or customary international law, is a part of U.S. law. For purposes of this Chapter, we return briefly to the issue so as to focus on whether customary international law can preempt state law. To the extent that customary international law is regarded as a part of federal common law (*see Sosa v. Alvarez-Machain*, Chapter 2, Sec. 6), it seems appropriate that customary international law would preempt conflicting state law. Note, however, that the U.S. Constitution does not expressly provide for such preemption. Article VI, Section 2 (the Supremacy Clause) specifically states that "treaties" are supreme over state law, but there is no reference to the "law of nations" (even though elsewhere in the Constitution, in Article I, Section 8, the "law of nations" is contemplated). Since the "Laws of the United States" referred to in the Supremacy Clause are those "made in Pursuance" of the Constitution, viewing customary international law (which is made, or results from, the practice of nations) as falling within that portion of the Supremacy Clause is problematic.

Nevertheless, there is reason to think that the framers expected the law of nations to preempt state law. In *The Federalist Papers* No. 80, Alexander Hamilton spoke about the need for the federal judicial power to extend to application of the law of nations, because "the peace of the WHOLE ought not to be left at the disposal of a PART"—warranting jurisdiction over cases in which foreign citizens were concerned, at least for "cases arising upon treaties and the law of nations." *The Federalist Papers,* No. 80, at 475–78 (Hamilton) (Clinton Rossiter ed., 1961). Likewise, John Jay in *The Federalist Papers* No. 3 saw a need for federal courts to apply the law of nations to avoid inconsistencies by the several states. *The Federalist Papers, supra,* No. 3, at 43 (Jay).

But if the framers intended to allow the law of nations to supersede state law, why was it not made express in the Supremacy Clause? Professor Louis Henkin offered the following explanation:

> [T]here is nothing to suggest that the Framers intended higher constitutional status for treaties than for customary law, and

> much to suggest that they expected the United States to honor both scrupulously. Their commitment was to "the law of nations" which for them was essentially customary law, including, notably, a state's obligation under customary law to carry out treaties. Their reticence about customary international law in contrast to the several references to treaties did not bespeak a judgment as to their comparative constitutional significances, but had other explanation. The Constitution had to determine who could make treaties for the United States; it sought to deny any treaty power to the states. The Framers wrote treaties explicitly into the Supremacy Clause because the supremacy of treaties to state law was a major issue that had to be resolved, and accepted by the states. Cases arising under treaties were declared to be within the judicial power of the United States because such cases were to be expected; the Framers probably did not anticipate cases or controversies arising under international law until Congress defined offenses under that law or enacted other legislation to implement international law, and cases arising under international law would then be cases arising under the laws of the United States.

Louis Henkin, *Foreign Affairs and the U.S. Constitution* 237–38 (2d ed. 1996). Thus, Henkin asserted that the framers chose not to write "the law of nations" into the Supremacy Clause because they likely assumed that such law would first be reduced to legislation by Congress, at which point it would qualify as "Laws of the United States." If this is right, then should the Constitution be read as only allowing the "law of nations" to supersede state law in situations where Congress has legislated on the matter? This would be acceptable to many critics of the so-called "modern position." *See* Chapter 2, Sec. 2. Note that in establishing the jurisdiction of federal courts in Article III, the framers did not assume that certain important matters associated with the law of nations (admiralty and maritime issues) would necessarily fall within the scope of the "Laws of the United States." If they took the trouble in Article III to make sure federal courts could hear some matters relating to the law of nations, even if not reduced to federal legislation, why did they not address the law of nations in the Supremacy Clause?

There are no cases squarely addressing whether state law is preempted by customary international law, although U.S. courts have referred to the practice of foreign nations in the course of preempting state law as inconsistent with the U.S. Constitution. (*See* Chapter 2, Sec. 4.)

7. THE COMPACT CLAUSE

Article I, Section 10, clause 1, of the U.S. Constitution prohibits states from entering "into any Treaty, Alliance, or Confederation." At the same time, Clause 3 (the "Compact Clause") provides that "No state shall, without the consent of Congress, . . . enter into any Agreement or Compact with another State, or with a foreign Power. . . ." Thus, the Constitution provides that states may not enter into a "treaty," but may enter into an "agreement" or "compact" with a "foreign power" if so authorized by Congress.

Despite the language of the Compact Clause, the U.S. Supreme Court has stated that certain compacts may be concluded among the several states ("inter-state compacts") without the approval of Congress. *See Virginia v. Tennessee*, 148 U.S. 504 (1893). In that case, Justice Field said that the test is whether the agreement tends to increase the political power of the states such that it encroaches upon or interferes with the just supremacy of the United States.

The only Supreme Court case addressing state-foreign country compacts is *Holmes v. Jennison*, 39 U.S. (14 Pet.) 540 (1840). In that case, the Court (per Justice Taney) struck down a Vermont governor's agreement with Canada regarding the extradition of an individual because the agreement had not been approved by Congress. Yet, in light of the Supreme Court's subsequent decision in *Virginia v. Tennessee*, at least one state court has found that a state-foreign country compact was permissible even without congressional consent. *See McHenry County v. Brady*, 37 N.D. 59, 163 N.W. 540 (1917). In, 1978, the Supreme Court in *United States Steel Corp. v. Multistate Tax Commission,* 434 U.S. 452, 473 (1978) maintained the position it took in *Virginia v. Tennessee*, but in doing so underlined that Justice Field's statement in *Virginia v. Tennessee* was in the context of a state-state agreement and not a state-foreign country agreement.

If there are certain compacts that the several states may conclude among themselves without any congressional authorization, do you think that the same conditions apply for compacts concluded with foreign countries or their political sub-divisions ("state-foreign country compacts")? In practice, many such agreements exist. For example, from 2007 to 2011 seven U.S. states and four Canadian provinces cooperated on identifying, evaluating and implementing regulations and policies to address climate change, through an agreement called the "Western Climate Initiative."[13] In 2014, California and Quebec reached an agreement linking their cap-and-trade markets for greenhouse gas emissions.[14] Such agreements might be challenged under preemption doctrines relating to federal environmental statutes, the dormant foreign commerce power, or the

---

[13] *See* Alexander Kazazis, Note, *The Western Climate Initiative: The Fate of an Experiment in Subnational Cross-Border Environmental Collaboration*, 37 BROOK. J. INT'L L. 1177 (2012).

[14] *See* David V. Wright, *Cross-Border Constraints on Climate Change Agreements: Legal Risks in the California-Quebec Cap-and-Trade Linkage*, 46 ENVTL. L. REP. NEWS & ANALYSIS 10478 (2016).

dormant foreign affairs power. Yet might such an agreement also be challenged as a violation of the Compact Clause?

Consider a memorandum of understanding of January 25, 2001, between the State of Missouri and the Canadian province of Manitoba. As background, you should know that for about 800 years, Devils Lake in North Dakota has had no natural outlet. Consequently, its waters have continually risen, resulting in periodic flooding of the surrounding areas. In the early 2000s, North Dakota began constructing a fourteen-mile open channel and pipeline to drain water from Devils Lake to the Sheyenne River. From there, the water would flow into the Red River, which flows north into Canada.

The flood-mitigation project was strongly opposed by Canada, which believed that North Dakota had not adequately studied the project's environmental impact, including the possibility of introducing invasive species and pollutants (such as phosphorous) into Canada's Hudson Bay watershed in Manitoba province. Fierce lobbying broke out in Washington, D.C., with Canada trying to convince the federal government to have the project reviewed by a U.S.-Canadian boundary water commission. Canada sought to secure allies among various states operating within the same water basin, including Minnesota, Ohio, and Missouri.[15]

Upon the conclusion of a Memorandum of Understanding (MOU) between Manitoba and Missouri, U.S. Senator Byron L. Dorgan (of North Dakota) wrote to the U.S. Department of State Legal Adviser, expressing the position that the MOU was inconsistent with the Constitution and soliciting a reaction.

U.S. DEPARTMENT OF STATE ANALYSIS OF THE MISSOURI-MANITOBA MEMORANDUM OF UNDERSTANDING

(Nov. 20, 2001).

THE MOU AND THE COMPACT CLAUSE

. . . [I]t appears that two questions need to be asked to determine whether it triggers the Compact Clause's requirement for congressional approval. First, is the MOU a "compact or agreement" for constitutional purposes? Second, if so, does it belong to that class of agreements that the Supreme Court has determined require congressional consent?

As for the first question, to qualify as a "compact or agreement" the Department traditionally has looked to whether the text in question is intended to be legally binding. The form and the content of this MOU suggest that Missouri and Manitoba likely intended to conclude such a

[15] For background, see Joseph M. Flanders, *Transboundary Water Disputes on an International and State Platform: A Controversial Resolution to North Dakota's Devils Lake Dilemma*, 82 N.D. L. REV. 997 (2006).

legal agreement. The MOU is structured as an agreement with a title, preamble, specific commitments and a signature block. The terminology used (e.g., "agree" and "ensure") is consistent with legally binding intent. . . .

The fact that the two parties condition their cooperation on existing law and treaties does not preclude a finding that the MOU is intended to be legally binding. The United States has concluded a number of treaties and other international agreements in which a particular provision or the agreement as a whole is subject to the parties' laws or international commitments. In such circumstances, although the parties can avoid their obligations based on an existing law or treaty, they may not avoid such obligations simply because, from a policy perspective, they no longer desire to comply with them.

Ultimately, however, the legal status of an instrument such as the MOU may not itself be determinative of whether the document qualifies as a compact. As the Supreme Court reasoned in *U.S. Steel Corp.* "the mere form of the interstate agreement cannot be dispositive." [*U.S. Steel Corp. v. Multistate Tax Comm.*, 434 U.S. 452, 470 (1978).] In other words, even in the absence of a legally binding agreement, the Compact Clause may be implicated. In *Northeast Bancorp, Inc.*, for example, the Court undertook a Compact Clause analysis of reciprocal state banking legislation even where there was no evidence of a legal agreement between the states to enact such legislation. Instead, the Court looked for "several of the classic indicia" of a Compact: e.g., establishment of a joint organization or a body; some restriction on the state's ability to withdraw from the arrangements by repealing or modifying its law unilaterally; or a requirement that limitations on state action are reciprocal. [*Northeast Bancorp, Inc. v. Board of Governors of the Fed. Reserve System*, 472 U.S. 159, 175 (1985)]. Although these factors seem particularly relevant where a court has to determine if independent state statutes constitute a compact, the Court has not to our knowledge addressed whether such indicia are also required where in fact a legal agreement exists. At a minimum, however, assuming that the same indicia applicable to interstate compacts apply to state compacts with foreign powers, these indicia are useful in evaluating the MOU.

Whether the "indicia" cited in *Northeast Bancorp, Inc.* are present in the MOU is not immediately apparent. Missouri and Manitoba have had at least one meeting "under" the MOU, but it is not clear if such meetings would constitute the "joint organization" referred to by the Supreme Court. Another question is whether Manitoba could argue that Missouri had violated the MOU if Missouri announced that it supported inter-basin water transfer (à la a repeal in legislation). Similarly, *Northeast Bancorp, Inc.* would ask whether the obligation of Missouri to cooperate in opposing inter-basin water-transfers is contingent on Manitoba's performance of similar obligations. Firm answers to such questions would require further factual development of what actions the parties understood as being required by their agreement "to work cooperatively to the fullest possible extent consistent with law and existing treaties . . . to oppose [inter-basin] water transfers."

Assuming for purposes of analysis that the MOU constitutes a "compact or agreement," the next question is whether it is the sort of compact or agreement for which congressional consent is required. As stated above, the Department traditionally applies the standard laid out in *Virginia—i.e.*, whether a compact is "directed to the formation of any combination tending to the increase of political power in the states, which may encroach upon or interfere with the just supremacy of the United States." Evidence of an actual impact on the federal government's supremacy has traditionally not been required; it is the potential impact of the compact that has led the Department to point out the need for congressional consent.

Examining the MOU in light of *Virginia* and its progeny, the Department would look to whether the MOU (a) impacts other U.S. states; (b) interferes with the federal government's interests in inter-basin water transfers; (c) deals solely with local matters; or (d) involves activities that could be carried out by Missouri even in the absence of the MOU. The following discussion briefly reviews each of these factors.

First, with respect to the effects on other states, the water in the Missouri and Hudson Bay watersheds that is the subject of the MOU borders or supplies water for numerous states. Missouri and Manitoba are therefore not the only parties interested in how those watersheds are treated. Missouri's alliance with Manitoba to support each other's effort to oppose inter-basin water-transfers could affect the interest of other states both as to the outcome and the process leading to decisions on how these waters are managed.

Second, in terms of the federal government's role, Congress has indicated an express interest in the inter-basin transfers at issue in the MOU. Two statutes—the Dakota Waters Resources Act of 2000 ("DWRA"), which amended the Garrison Diversion Reformulation Act of 1986 ("Garrison Act") and the Garrison Act itself—address inter-basin water transfer directly. . . . The DWRA provides a comprehensive set of procedures for the Secretary of the Interior to follow in order to study and possibly construct projects involving inter-basin transfers in the Red River Valley (part of the Hudson Bay watershed), with both federal and state involvement in the review process. Ultimately, the DWRA reserves to Congress the final decision on whether a transfer will be authorized, but any such transfers are limited to those that the Executive branch determines comport with 1909 U.S.-Canada Boundary Waters Treaty's restrictions on activities that might pollute or otherwise affect the level or flow of boundary waters.

Given such federal interest, applications of the *Virginia* standard would require an analysis of whether the MOU encroaches on the political power of the federal government to address inter-basin water-transfers. It is not enough to show simply that the federal government has competence over these matters. Rather, one must ask whether Missouri's enlistment of Manitoba's support in the MOU to oppose particular transfers potentially operates to the legal detriment of the federal government by interfering with the decision-making scheme set out in the federal legislation or, where decisions have been made, in their effective implementation. A secondary question is whether the MOU could interfere with administration of the Boundary Waters Treaty. That Treaty affords the United States and Canada, not Missouri or Manitoba, the right to interpret and apply the Treaty as well as to refer matters to the International Joint Commission.

As indicated above, a third factor the Department would customarily examine is the question of whether the MOU deals only with matters of local policy. Some state arrangements with foreign powers dealing with water use issues have been deemed to be solely of local interest for Compact Clause purposes. This was true of the drainage basin at issue in *McHenry County* and the Vermont-Quebec International Water District, which had "no political function." The MOU in this case, in contrast, addresses cooperation between a U.S. state and a Canadian province to work together to oppose the possibility of inter-basin water transfers that could affect other states of the United States and which are to be considered pursuant to federal statute.

Fourth, the Department would assess the implications of the Supreme Court's decision in *Multistate Tax Commission*, which highlighted that congressional consent to an interstate compact is not required so long as the state is free to undertake the contemplated activities in the absence of the MOU, on a proposed arrangement. Thus, if one could show in this case that activities contemplated under the MOU—*i.e.*, sharing information on actions contemplated under the DWRA, opposing inter-basin water transfers and communicating concerns about such transfers to the federal government—are actions that Missouri has the authority to carry out irrespective of an MOU, it would argue against applying the Compact Clause.

A key inquiry for this purpose is the extent to which the MOU calls for "mutually supportive" cooperation which might be understood as cooperation that cannot occur without another party. This would pose two issues: first, the extent to which such activities are possible even in the absence of the MOU, and secondly, whether this kind of activity impinges upon the "exclusive foreign relations power expressly reserved to the federal government," and therefore falls outside the *Multistate Tax Commission* authorization for interstate compacts to be concluded without Congressional approval.

Finally, in addition to these four factors, evidence of agreement on concrete actions by the parties undertaken pursuant to the MOU could assist in ascertaining whether the MOU impacts our federal structure. The MOU, however, is not so specific as to require either party to cooperate in ways that must physically manifest themselves (*i.e.*, constructing a facility, etc.) nor does it appear to require them to enact any reciprocal obligations into law. This is presumably because the objects and purpose of the MOU seems to be to commit Missouri and Manitoba to oppose the actions of others; *i.e.*, to oppose what the federal government is studying, and in some cases, doing, with respect to inter-basin water transfers. Thus, any interference that the MOU might cause to the federal government's supremacy would likely be procedural rather that substantive in nature. For example, if the MOU requires Missouri to operate not only on its own behalf, but also on Manitoba's behalf, in attempting to influence federal water management policy, would that interfere with the federal government's ability to implement the DWRA, the Garrison Act and the 1909 Boundary Waters Treaty? As discussed below, in the event Missouri sought to undertake concrete actions with respect to such water management issues, a strong argument can be made that such actions would be pre-empted by the DWRA, the Garrison Act, and the 1909 Boundary Waters Treaty.

Because of the expressions of federal policy, in addition to Compact Clause considerations, the MOU also potentially implicates the more general constitutional issues of federal preemption and the foreign affairs powers of the federal government. This memorandum therefore provides some additional background on these separate constitutional issues.

THE MOU, THE SUPREMACY CLAUSE AND THE FOREIGN AFFAIRS POWER

The Supreme Court decision in *Crosby v. National Foreign Trade Council*, [530 U.S. 363 (2000)] illustrates the Court's most recent views on federal preemption in a foreign affairs context. In *Crosby*, the Court held unanimously that Massachusetts law imposing sanctions on Burma was invalid under the Supremacy Clause of the Constitution "owing to its threat of frustrating federal statutory objectives." . . .

In examining the issue, the Court emphasized that "[I]t is simply implausible that Congress would have gone to such lengths to empower the President had it been willing to compromise the effectiveness by deference to every provision of state statute or local ordinance that might, if enforced, blunt the consequences of discretionary Presidential action." Referring to the foreign affairs context of the statute, the Court also stressed that Massachusetts' independent actions threatened the ability of the United

States to speak effectively with one voice on the international plane, noting that "the President's maximum power to persuade rest[s] on his capacity to bargain for the benefits of access to the entire national economy without exception for enclaves fenced off willy-nilly by inconsistent political tactics."

As far as the Department is aware the courts have not had occasion to consider the applicability of these principles to a state agreement with a foreign power, rather than a state statute. It would seem, however, that the logic of *Crosby* would prohibit states from accomplishing, via agreement with foreign states, what they are not able to accomplish by their own statutes. Therefore, it would appear relevant to assess the MOU's operation in light of federal preemption principles.

The central issue would be the MOU's compatibility with the federal statutory scheme for addressing the inter-basin water issue covered by the MOU. The NAWS project, for example, will involve such a transfer and has already been approved by the federal government in accordance with the terms of the Garrison Act. As for the DWRA, it is as comprehensive, if not more so, than the federal sanctions at issue in *Crosby*. Under the DWRA, the Secretary of Interior is charged with preparing a comprehensive report for Congress studying the Red River Valley's water needs and options for fulfilling them. The Secretary is required to solicit input from states that may be impacted by possible options. Environmental impact assessments of all feasible options are mandated by the statute. Within the statutory scheme, the Secretary of Interior is given some responsibility for selecting among potential projects, with the notable exception that any project that would require transfer of water from the Missouri River or its tributaries must be submitted to Congress for specific approval by an Act of Congress.

Given this comprehensive scheme, it is plain that Congress intended, in enacting the DWRA, to ensure that the decision making process about water allocation to the Red River Valley be centrally coordinated at the federal level. State input is recognized by the DWRA as an important piece of the process, but it is clearly subsumed into a federal decision-making process that reserves all final decision-making authority to the federal government. . . . As such, the statute appears to be designed to "occupy the field" when it comes to major decisions impacting certain water resources across several states.

Analogizing to the logic in *Crosby*, it is difficult to believe that Congress would have enacted the DWRA "had it been willing to compromise the effectiveness by deference to every provision of state statute or legal ordinance" that might, if enforced, interfere with [the] overall purpose of the scheme. Any concrete actions by Missouri to oppose inter-basin water transfers outside of this scheme would likely be preempted in that they would interfere with federal policies and programs.

On the other hand, Missouri is not precluded from expressing its own viewpoint on the resolution of federal water management issues; to the contrary, the DWRA explicitly allows Missouri such a role. Thus, the question under *Crosby* is whether through the MOU Missouri is seeking to afford a surrogate voice for Manitoba in the federal government's decision-making and implementation process that would interfere with the scheme envisioned by Congress.

Besides such principles of federal preemption, the courts have also confirmed the exclusive assignment of foreign affairs responsibilities to the federal government under the U.S. Constitution. Although the Court in *Crosby* did not reach the question of whether the Massachusetts statute unconstitutionally interfered in foreign affairs, both the district court and the appeals court held that it did, based on the decision by the Supreme Court in *Zschernig v. Miller*. The appellate court opined that "*Zschernig* stands for the principle that there is a threshold level of involvement in and impact on foreign affairs which the states may not exceed." The court held that while the boundaries of *Zschernig* were unclear, the Massachusetts law was clearly inconsistent with the principle in *Zschernig*. The court rejected arguments by Massachusetts to the effect that courts must balance the interests in a unified foreign policy against the particular interests of an individual state. Rather, quoting from *Zschernig*, the court reiterated that "[state] regulations must give away if they impair the effective exercise of the nation's foreign policy." A similar ruling was recently issued by the U.S. District Court for the Northern District of California. In that case, the Court found *Zschernig* applicable where a state was conducting its own foreign policy.

Thus, depending on the extent of its actual interference with U.S. foreign policy efforts in managing the water resources of the Hudson Bay watershed shared with Canada, the Missouri-Manitoba MOU would need to be evaluated for whether it constitutes an unconstitutional disruption of the federal government's foreign affairs power.

CONCLUSION

In light of the DWRA, the Garrison Act, the Boundary Waters Treaty and relevant practice, the Missouri-Manitoba MOU potentially implicates several constitutional doctrines. First, if the MOU is intended to be an instrument that could interfere with the just supremacy of the federal government, issues are raised as to the necessity for congressional consent under the Compact Clause. Given Congress's occupation of the field of inter-basin water transfers by statute (e.g., the DWRA), there are further issues under *Crosby* which set out the standards for determining when a state statute is preempted under the Supremacy Clause. Finally, to the extent the MOU may potentially interfere with the foreign affairs power more generally it would need to be evaluated for its consistency with principles set out in *Zschernig*.

NOTES

1. *Post-Script*. In August 2005, North Dakota, Minnesota, Manitoba and the U.S. and Canadian federal governments reached an accord on guidelines allowing North Dakota to operate the new outlet. The agreement, which was not legally binding, provided that the two federal governments would design and build a filtration system for the diverted waters. *See* U.S. Dep't of State, Joint Press Statement on Devils Lake Flooding and Ecological Protection by the United States and Canada, North Dakota, Minnesota and Manitoba (Aug. 5, 2005).

2. *Great Lakes Compact to Limit Water Diversion*. In December 2005, the governors of eight U.S. states in the Great Lakes region (Illinois, Indiana, Michigan, Minnesota, New York, Ohio, Pennsylvania, and Wisconsin) and the premiers of two Canadian provinces (Ontario and Quebec) entered into an agreement that severely limited diversions of water to areas outside the Great Lakes-St. Lawrence River basin. The agreement, called The Great Lakes-St. Lawrence River Basin Sustainable Water Resources Agreement, says that the states and provinces "agree" to adopt and implement various measures necessary to limit water diversion. Article 700(2) of the Agreement states: "This Agreement is not intended to infringe upon the treaty power of the United States of America, nor shall any term hereof be construed to alter or amend any treaty or term thereof that has been or may hereafter be executed by the United States of America." Does Article 700(2) satisfy completely any constitutional concerns about the agreement?

8. VIENNA CONVENTION ON CONSULAR RELATIONS, THE DEATH PENALTY, AND FEDERALISM

From 1998 to 2004, the International Court of Justice considered three cases filed against the United States by Paraguay (the *Breard* case), Germany (the *LaGrand* case), and Mexico (the *Avena* case) concerning the treatment of aliens on death row in the United States. A central issue in these cases was that U.S. law enforcement personnel repeatedly failed to advise aliens upon their arrest of the right to have their consulate notified, a right contained in Article 36 of the Vienna Convention on Consular Relations (VCCR). That failure is perhaps not surprising given the distribution of law enforcement authority in the United States, which is predominantly exercised at the state and local level. A further issue was whether, as a remedy for violation of the VCCR, state courts should review and reconsider the death sentences, to determine whether the lack of consular access prejudiced the aliens (*i.e.*, whether the inability to have consular assistance impaired the alien from undertaking a strong defense).

One problem that many aliens faced was that they only became aware of the protections contained in the VCCR after the trial stage and were therefore bared under the "procedural default rule" contained in many state laws from raising the issue for the first time in state appellate proceedings or collateral federal proceedings.

In all three cases, the International Court ordered provisionally that the United States "take all measures at its disposal to ensure" (*Breard*, *LaGrand*) or "all measures necessary to ensure" (*Avena*) that the relevant aliens not be executed pending a final decision by the Court. *Vienna Convention on Consular Relations* (Para. v. U.S.), Provisional Measures, 1998 I.C.J. 248 (Apr. 9); *LaGrand Case* (Ger. v. U.S.), Provisional Measures, 1999 I.C.J. 9 (Mar. 3); *Avena and Other Mexican Nationals* (Mex. v. U.S.), Provisional Measures, 2003 I.C.J. 6 (Feb. 5). The position of the U.S. government in the *Breard* and *LaGrand* cases, however, was that such I.C.J. provisional orders were not binding upon the United States under the U.N. Charter, I.C.J. Statute, or VCCR optional protocol.

After the provisional-measures order was issued in *Breard*, the U.S. Secretary of State sent a letter to the governor of Virginia (where Breard was on death row). The Secretary requested that the governor stay Breard's execution since the

> execution of Mr. Breard in the face of the Court's April 9 action could be seen as a denial by the United States of the significance of international law and the Court's processes in its international relations and thereby limit our ability to ensure that Americans are protected when living or traveling abroad.

Letter from Madeleine K. Albright, U.S. Sec'y of State, to James S. Gilmore III, Gov. of Virginia (Apr. 13, 1998), *partially reprinted in* 92 AM. J. INT'L L. 671–72 (1998). In declining to intervene in the case, the U.S. Supreme Court stated that it was "clear that Breard procedurally defaulted his claim, if any, under the VCCR by failing to raise that claim in the state courts." *Breard v. Greene*, 523 U.S. 371, 375 (1998). Further, the Court stated:

> [W]hile we should give respectful consideration to the interpretation of an international treaty rendered by an international court with jurisdiction to interpret such, it has been recognized in international law that, absent a clear and express statement to the contrary, the procedural rules of the forum State govern the implementation of the treaty in that State.

Id. Thereafter, the governor of Virginia decided not to stay the execution, and Breard was executed.

After the provisional-measures order was issued in *LaGrand*, the U.S. government transmitted the order to the governor of Arizona (where

LaGrand was on death row). Again, the U.S. Supreme Court declined to intervene, *Federal Republic of Germany v. United States*, 526 U.S. 111 (1999), and the governor of Arizona decided not to stay LaGrand's execution.

After Breard was executed, Paraguay withdrew its case from the International Court. Germany, however, continued its case even after LaGrand was executed. In a judgment on the merits, the Court found that by not immediately informing LaGrand (and his brother who was executed prior to the I.C.J.'s provisional-measures order) of the right of consular notification, the United States breached its obligations under the VCCR. The U.S. failure to provide judicial review of the conviction and sentence in light of the lack of notification constituted a further breach. The Court also found that its provisional orders are binding on states and that the United States violated the Court's provisional order by failing to take all measures at its disposal to ensure that LaGrand was not executed pending a final decision by the Court.

Noting the steps already taken by the United States to improve implementation of its VCCR obligations, the Court did not order it to provide a general assurance of nonrepetition (Germany did not request reparation in the form of compensation). The Court did find, however, that "should nationals of the Federal Republic of Germany nonetheless be sentenced to severe penalties" without their right to consular notification having been respected, the United States, "by means of its own choosing, shall allow the review and reconsideration of the conviction and sentence by taking account of the violation of the rights set forth" in the VCCR. *LaGrand* (Ger. v. U.S.), Judgment, 2001 I.C.J. 466, 516, para. 128(7) (June 27).

In the *Avena* case, Mexico also pursued a decision on the merits, this time on behalf of more than fifty Mexicans on death row.

CASE CONCERNING AVENA AND OTHER MEXICAN NATIONALS (MEX. V. U.S.)

2004 I.C.J. 12 (Mar. 31).

1. On 9 January 2003 the United Mexican States (hereinafter referred to as "Mexico") filed in the Registry of the Court an Application instituting proceedings against the United States of America (hereinafter referred to as the "United States") for "violations of the Vienna Convention on Consular Relations" of 24 April 1963 (hereinafter referred to as the "Vienna Convention") allegedly committed by the United States.

In its Application, Mexico based the jurisdiction of the Court on Article 36, paragraph 1, of the Statute of the Court and on Article I of the Optional Protocol concerning the Compulsory Settlement of Disputes, which accompanies the Vienna Convention (hereinafter referred to as the "Optional Protocol"). . . .

19. The underlying facts alleged by Mexico may be briefly described as follows: some are conceded by the United States, and some disputed. Mexico states that all the individuals the subject of its claims were Mexican nationals at the time of their arrest. It further contends that the United States authorities that arrested and interrogated these individuals had sufficient information at their disposal to be aware of the foreign nationality of those individuals. According to Mexico's account, in 50 of the specified cases, Mexican nationals were never informed by the competent United States authorities of their rights under Article 36, paragraph 1 *(b)*, of the Vienna Convention and, in the two remaining cases, such information was not provided "without delay", as required by that provision. Mexico has indicated that in 29 of the 52 cases its consular authorities learned of the detention of the Mexican nationals only after death sentences had been handed down. In the 23 remaining cases, Mexico contends that it learned of the cases through means other than notification to the consular post by the competent United States authorities under Article 36, paragraph 1 *(b)*. It explains that in five cases this was too late to affect the trials, that in 15 cases the defendants had already made incriminating statements, and that it became aware of the other three cases only after considerable delay. . . .

111. The "procedural default" rule in United States law has already been brought to the attention of the Court in the *LaGrand* case. The following brief definition of the rule was provided by Mexico in its Memorial in this case and has not been challenged by the United States: "a defendant who could have raised, but fails to raise, a legal issue at trial will generally not be permitted to raise it in future proceedings, on appeal or in a petition for a writ of *habeas corpus*". The rule requires exhaustion of remedies, *inter alia*, at the state level and before a *habeas corpus* motion can be filed with federal courts. In the *LaGrand* case, the rule in question was applied by United States federal courts; in the present case, Mexico also complains of the application of the rule in certain state courts of criminal appeal. . . .

115. Having concluded that in most of the cases brought before the Court by Mexico in the 52 instances, there has been a failure to observe the obligations prescribed by Article 36, paragraph 1 *(b)*, of the Vienna Convention, the Court now proceeds to the examination of the legal consequences of such a breach and of what legal remedies should be considered for the breach. . . .

131. In stating in its Judgment in the *LaGrand* case that "the United States of America, *by means of its own choosing*, shall allow the review and reconsideration of the conviction and sentence" (*I.C.J. Reports 2001*, p. 516, para. 128; emphasis added), the Court acknowledged that the concrete

modalities for such review and reconsideration should be left primarily to the United States. It should be underlined, however, that this freedom in the choice of means for such review and reconsideration is not without qualification: as the passage of the Judgment quoted above makes abundantly clear, such review and reconsideration has to be carried out "by taking account of the violation of the rights set forth in the Convention" (*I.C.J. Reports 2001*, p. 514, para. 125), including, in particular, the question of the legal consequences of the violation upon the criminal proceedings that have followed the violation. . . .

133. However, the Court wishes to point out that the current situation in the United States criminal procedure, as explained by the Agent at the hearings, is that "If the defendant alleged at trial that *a failure of consular information resulted in harm to a particular right essential to a fair trial*, an appeals court can *review how the lower court handled that claim of prejudice*", but that "*If the foreign national did not raise his Article 36 claim at trial, he may face procedural constraints* [*i.e.*, the application of the procedural default rule] on raising that particular claim in direct or collateral judicial appeals" (emphasis added). As a result, a claim based on the violation of Article 36, paragraph 1, of the Vienna Convention, however meritorious in itself, could be barred in the courts of the United States by the operation of the procedural default rule (see paragraph 111 above). . . .

138. The Court would emphasize that the "review and reconsideration" prescribed by it in the *LaGrand* case should be effective. Thus it should "tak[e] account of the violation of the rights set forth in [the] Convention" (*I.C.J. Reports 2001*, p. 516, para. 128 (7)) and guarantee that the violation and the possible prejudice caused by that violation will be fully examined and taken into account in the review and reconsideration process. Lastly, review and reconsideration should be both of the sentence and of the conviction.

139. Accordingly, in a situation of the violation of rights under Article 36, paragraph 1, of the Vienna Convention, the defendant raises his claim in this respect not as a case of "harm to a particular right essential to a fair trial"—a concept relevant to the enjoyment of due process rights under the United States Constitution—but as a case involving the infringement of his rights under Article 36, paragraph 1. The rights guaranteed under the Vienna Convention are treaty rights which the United States has undertaken to comply with in relation to the individual concerned, irrespective of the due process rights under United States constitutional law. In this regard, the Court would point out that what is crucial in the review and reconsideration process is the existence of a procedure which guarantees that full weight is given to the violation of the rights set forth in the Vienna Convention, whatever may be the actual outcome of such review and reconsideration.

140. . . . [T]he Court is of the view that, in cases where the breach of the individual rights of Mexican nationals under Article 36, paragraph 1 *(b)*, of the Convention has resulted, in the sequence of judicial proceedings that has followed, in the individuals concerned being subjected to prolonged detention or convicted and sentenced to severe penalties, the legal consequences of this breach have to be examined and taken into account in the course of review and reconsideration. The Court considers that it is the judicial process that is suited to this task.

141. The Court in the *LaGrand* case left to the United States the choice of means as to how review and reconsideration should be achieved, especially in the light of the procedural default rule. Nevertheless, the premise on which the Court proceeded in that case was that the process of review and reconsideration should occur within the overall judicial proceedings relating to the individual defendant concerned. . . .

[The United States had informed the Court that it was focusing on clemency proceedings as the best route for "review and reconsideration" because the U.S. government saw clemency as effective and as not hampered by legal constraints such as the procedural default rule.]

143. It may be true, as the United States argues, that in a number of cases "clemency in fact results in pardons of convictions as well as commutations of sentences". In that sense and to that extent, it might be argued that the facts demonstrated by the United States testify to a degree of effectiveness of the clemency procedures as a means of relieving defendants on death row from execution. The Court notes, however, that the clemency process, as currently practised within the United States criminal justice system, does not appear to meet the requirements described in paragraph 138 above and that it is therefore not sufficient in itself to serve as an appropriate means of "review and reconsideration" as envisaged by the Court in the *LaGrand* case. The Court considers nevertheless that appropriate clemency procedures can supplement judicial review and reconsideration, in particular where the judicial system has failed to take due account of the violation of the rights set forth in the Vienna Convention. . . .

153. For these reasons,

THE COURT, ...

(4) By fourteen votes to one,

Finds that, by not informing, without delay upon their detention, the 51 Mexican nationals referred to in paragraph 106(1) above of their rights under Article 36, paragraph 1(b), of the Vienna Convention on Consular Relations of 24 April 1963, the United States of America breached the obligations incumbent upon it under that subparagraph; . . . .

(5) By fourteen votes to one,

Finds that, by not notifying the appropriate Mexican consular post without delay of the detention of the 49 Mexican nationals referred to in paragraph 106(2) above and thereby depriving the United Mexican States of the right, in a timely fashion, to render the assistance provided for by the Vienna Convention to the individuals concerned, the United States of America breached the obligations incumbent upon it under Article 36, paragraph 1(b); . . . .

(6) By fourteen votes to one,

Finds that, in relation to the 49 Mexican nationals referred to in paragraph 106(3) above, the United States of America deprived the United Mexican States of the right, in a timely fashion, to communicate with and have access to those nationals and to visit them in detention, and thereby breached the obligations incumbent upon it under Article 36, paragraph 1(a) and (c), of the Convention;

(7) By fourteen votes to one,

Finds that, in relation to the 34 Mexican nationals referred to in paragraph 106(4) above, the United States of America deprived the United Mexican States of the right, in a timely fashion, to arrange for legal representation of those nationals, and thereby breached the obligations incumbent upon it under Article 36, paragraph 1(c), of the Convention; . . . .

(8) By fourteen votes to one,

Finds that, by not permitting the review and reconsideration, in the light of the rights set forth in the Convention, of the conviction and sentences of Mr. César Roberto Fierro Reyna, Mr. Roberto Moreno Ramos and Mr. Osvaldo Torres Aguilera, after the violations referred to in subparagraph (4) above had been established in respect of those individuals, the United States of America breached the obligations incumbent upon it under Article 36, paragraph 2, of the Convention; . . . .

(9) By fourteen votes to one,

Finds that the appropriate reparation in this case consists in the obligation of the United States of America to provide, by means of its own choosing, review and reconsideration of the convictions and sentences of the Mexican nationals referred to in subparagraphs (4), (5), (6) and (7) above, by taking account both of the violation of the rights set forth in Article 36 of the Convention and of paragraphs 138 to 141 of this Judgment; . . . .

(10) Unanimously,

Takes note of the commitment undertaken by the United States of America to ensure implementation of the specific measures adopted in performance of its obligations under Article 36, paragraph 1 (b), of the

Vienna Convention; and *finds* that this commitment must be regarded as meeting the request by the United Mexican States for guarantees and assurances of non-repetition;

(11) Unanimously,

Finds that, should Mexican nationals nonetheless be sentenced to severe penalties, without their rights under Article 36, paragraph 1 (b), of the Convention having been respected, the United States of America shall provide, by means of its own choosing, review and reconsideration of the conviction and sentence, so as to allow full weight to be given to the violation of the rights set forth in the Convention, taking account of paragraphs 138 to 141 of this Judgment.

*NOTE ON POST-*AVENA *REMEDIES*

After issuance of *Avena*, aliens on death row in the United States sought to use the decision to obtain review and reconsideration of their death sentences. For example, Osbaldo Torres, one of the fifty-one Mexican nationals at issue in *Avena*, had been scheduled for execution on May 18, 2004. After issuance of the I.C.J.'s *Avena* decision, Torres filed a new request for post-conviction relief in the Oklahoma Court of Criminal Appeals and a stay of his execution. On May 13, the court granted the stay and remanded the case to a lower court for an evidentiary hearing. *See Torres v. Oklahoma*, No. PCD–04–442, 2004 WL 3711623 (Okla. Crim. App. May 13, 2004), *reprinted in* 43 I.L.M. 1227 (2004). In doing so, one of the judges stated in an unpublished concurrence that "we are bound to give full faith and credit to the *Avena* decision." *Id.* at 1229 (Chapel, J., specially concurring). Among other things, Judge Chapel noted:

> I am not suggesting that the International Court of Justice has jurisdiction over this Court—far from it. However, in these unusual circumstances the issue of whether this Court must abide by that court's opinion in Torres's case is not ours to determine. The United States Senate and the President have made that decision for us. The Optional Protocol . . . provides that the International Court of Justice is the forum for resolution of disputes under the Vienna Convention.

Id. (footnote omitted).

On a separate track, the U.S. Department of State Legal Adviser on May 11, 2004, wrote a letter to the governor of Oklahoma describing and transmitting a copy of the I.C.J.'s decision in *Avena*. The letter to the governor requested "that in your review of the case you give careful consideration to the pending clemency request of Mr. Torres, including by considering the failure to provide Mr. Torres with consular information and notification pursuant to Article 36 of the VCCR and whether that failure should be regarded as having ultimately led to his conviction and sentence." Letter from Department of State Legal Adviser William H. Taft, IV, to Governor of Oklahoma Brad Henry, at 2 (May 11, 2004). On May 13, the governor of Oklahoma commuted Torres's penalty to life without parole, thus ending the matter. For background, see Janet Koven Levit, *A Tale of International Law in the Heartland: Torres and the Role of State Courts in Transnational Legal Conversation*, 12 TULSA J. COMP. & INT'L L. 163 (2004–2005); *see also Torres v. State of Oklahoma*, 120 P.3d 1184 (Ct. of Crim. App. 2005).

Other courts, however, did not see the *Avena* decision as altering the alien's rights in U.S. courts, including in the case of a Mexican national named José Ernesto Medellín. The Bush Administration moved to alter the terms of the debate by issuance of a presidential memorandum designed to implement the *Avena* decision for the Mexican nationals implicated by that decision.

MEMORANDUM OF PRESIDENT GEORGE W. BUSH TO THE U.S. ATTORNEY GENERAL ALBERTO GONZALES

44 I.L.M. 950 (2005).

SUBJECT: Compliance with the Decision of the International Court of Justice in *Avena*

The United States is a party to the Vienna Convention on Consular Relations (the "Convention") and the Convention's Optional Protocol Concerning the Compulsory Settlement of Disputes (Optional Protocol), which gives the International Court of Justice (ICJ) jurisdiction to decide disputes concerning the "interpretation and application" of the Convention.

I have determined, pursuant to the authority vested in me as President by the Constitution and the laws of the United States of America, that the United States will discharge its international obligations under the decision of the International Court of Justice in the *Case Concerning Avena and Other Mexican Nationals (Mexico v. United States of America) (Avena)*, 2004 ICJ 128 (Mar. 31), by having State courts give effect to the decision in accordance with general principles of comity in cases filed by the 51 Mexican nationals addressed in that decision.

GEORGE BUSH

MEDELLÍN V. TEXAS

552 U.S. 491 (2008).

[For a brief summary of the facts and excerpts from Parts I and II of the majority opinion addressing whether the international obligation of the United States to comply with the ICJ judgment in *Avena* was self-executing, as well as relevant portions of the dissent, see Chapter 3, Sec. 4.]

CHIEF JUSTICE ROBERTS delivered the opinion of the Court. . . .

III

Medellín next argues that the ICJ's judgment in *Avena* is binding on state courts by virtue of the President's February 28, 2005 Memorandum. The United States contends that while the *Avena* judgment does not of its own force require domestic courts to set aside ordinary rules of procedural default, that judgment became the law of the land with precisely that effect pursuant to the President's Memorandum and his power "to establish binding rules of decision that preempt contrary state law." Brief for United States as *Amicus Curiae* 5. Accordingly, we must decide whether the President's declaration alters our conclusion that the *Avena* judgment is not a rule of domestic law binding in state and federal courts.[13]

A

The United States maintains that the President's constitutional role "uniquely qualifies" him to resolve the sensitive foreign policy decisions that bear on compliance with an ICJ decision and "to do so expeditiously." Brief for United States as *Amicus Curiae* 11, 12. We do not question these propositions. . . . In this case, the President seeks to vindicate United States interests in ensuring the reciprocal observance of the Vienna Convention, protecting relations with foreign governments, and demonstrating commitment to the role of international law. These interests are plainly compelling.

Such considerations, however, do not allow us to set aside first principles. The President's authority to act, as with the exercise of any governmental power, "must stem either from an act of Congress or from the Constitution itself." *Youngstown, supra,* at 585; *Dames & Moore v. Regan,* 453 U.S. 654, 668 (1981).

Justice Jackson's familiar tripartite scheme provides the accepted framework for evaluating executive action in this area. First, "[w]hen the President acts pursuant to an express or implied authorization of Congress, his authority is at its maximum, for it includes all that he possesses in his own right plus all that Congress can delegate." *Youngstown,* 343 U.S., at 635 (Jackson, J., concurring). Second, "[w]hen the President acts in absence of either a congressional grant or denial of authority, he can only rely upon his own independent powers, but there is a zone of twilight in which he and Congress may have concurrent authority, or in which its distribution is uncertain." *Id.,* at 637. In this circumstance, Presidential authority can

[13] The dissent refrains from deciding the issue, but finds it "difficult to believe that in the exercise of his Article II powers pursuant to a ratified treaty, the President can *never* take action that would result in setting aside state law." *Post,* at 1390. We agree. The questions here are the far more limited ones of whether he may unilaterally create federal law by giving effect to the judgment of this international tribunal pursuant to this non-self-executing treaty, and, if not, whether he may rely on other authority under the Constitution to support the action taken in this particular case. Those are the only questions we decide.

derive support from "congressional inertia, indifference or quiescence." *Id.* Finally, "[w]hen the President takes measures incompatible with the expressed or implied will of Congress, his power is at its lowest ebb," and the Court can sustain his actions "only by disabling the Congress from acting upon the subject." *Id.*, at 637–638.

B

The United States marshals two principal arguments in favor of the President's authority "to establish binding rules of decision that preempt contrary state law." Brief for United States as *Amicus Curiae* 5. The Solicitor General first argues that the relevant treaties give the President the authority to implement the *Avena* judgment and that Congress has acquiesced in the exercise of such authority. The United States also relies upon an "independent" international dispute-resolution power wholly apart from the asserted authority based on the pertinent treaties. Medellín adds the additional argument that the President's Memorandum is a valid exercise of his power to take care that the laws be faithfully executed.

1

The United States maintains that the President's Memorandum is authorized by the Optional Protocol and the U.N. Charter. Brief for United States as *Amicus Curiae* 9. That is, because the relevant treaties "create an obligation to comply with *Avena*," they "*implicitly* give the President authority to implement that treaty-based obligation." *Id.*, at 11 (emphasis added). As a result, the President's Memorandum is well grounded in the first category of the *Youngstown* framework.

We disagree. The President has an array of political and diplomatic means available to enforce international obligations, but unilaterally converting a non-self-executing treaty into a self-executing one is not among them. The responsibility for transforming an international obligation arising from a non-self-executing treaty into domestic law falls to Congress. *Foster,* 2 Pet., at 315; *Whitney,* 124 U.S., at 194; *Igartua-De La Rosa,* 417 F.3d, at 150. As this Court has explained, when treaty stipulations are "not self-executing they can only be enforced pursuant to legislation to carry them into effect." *Whitney, supra,* at 194. Moreover, "[u]ntil such act shall be passed, the Court is not at liberty to disregard the existing laws on the subject." *Foster, supra,* at 315.

The requirement that Congress, rather than the President, implement a non-self-executing treaty derives from the text of the Constitution, which divides the treaty-making power between the President and the Senate. The Constitution vests the President with the authority to "make" a treaty. Art. II, § 2. If the Executive determines that a treaty should have domestic effect of its own force, that determination may be implemented "in mak[ing]" the treaty, by ensuring that it contains language plainly providing for domestic enforceability. If the treaty is to be self-executing in this respect, the Senate must consent to the treaty by the requisite two-thirds vote, *ibid.*, consistent with all other constitutional restraints.

Once a treaty is ratified without provisions clearly according it domestic effect, however, whether the treaty will ever have such effect is governed by the fundamental constitutional principle that " '[t]he power to make the necessary laws is in Congress; the power to execute in the President.' " *Hamdan v. Rumsfeld,* 548 U.S. 557, 591 (2006) (quoting *Ex parte Milligan,* 4 Wall. 2, 139 (1866) (opinion of Chase, C. J.)); *see* U.S. Const., Art. I, § 1 ("All legislative Powers herein granted shall be vested in a Congress of the United States"). As already noted, the terms of a non-self-executing treaty can become domestic law only in the same way as any other law-through passage of legislation by both Houses of Congress, combined with either the President's signature or a congressional override of a Presidential veto. *See* Art. I, § 7. Indeed, "the President's power to see that the laws are faithfully executed refutes the idea that he is to be a lawmaker." *Youngstown,* 343 U.S., at 587.

A non-self-executing treaty, by definition, is one that was ratified with the understanding that it is not to have domestic effect of its own force. That understanding precludes the assertion that Congress has implicitly authorized the President—acting on his own—to achieve precisely the same result. We therefore conclude, given the absence of congressional legislation, that the non-self-executing treaties at issue here did not "express[ly] or implied[ly]" vest the President with the unilateral authority to make them self-executing. *See id.,* at 635 (Jackson, J., concurring). Accordingly, the President's Memorandum does not fall within the first category of the *Youngstown* framework.

Indeed, the preceding discussion should make clear that the non-self-executing character of the relevant treaties not only refutes the notion that the ratifying parties vested the President with the authority to unilaterally make treaty obligations binding on domestic courts, but also implicitly prohibits him from doing so. When the President asserts the power to "enforce" a non-self-executing treaty by unilaterally creating domestic law, he acts in conflict with the implicit understanding of the ratifying Senate. His assertion of authority, insofar as it is based on the pertinent non-self-executing treaties, is therefore within Justice Jackson's third category, not the first or even the second. *See id.,* at 637–638.

Each of the two means described above for giving domestic effect to an international treaty obligation under the Constitution-for making law-requires joint action by the Executive and Legislative Branches: The Senate can ratify a self-executing treaty "ma[de]" by the Executive, or, if the ratified treaty is not self-executing, Congress can enact implementing legislation approved by the President. It should not be surprising that our Constitution does not contemplate vesting such power in the Executive alone. As Madison explained in The Federalist No. 47, under our constitutional system of checks and balances, "[t]he magistrate in whom the whole executive power resides cannot of himself make a law." J. Cooke ed., p. 326 (1961). That would, however, seem an apt description of the asserted executive authority unilaterally to give the effect of domestic law to obligations under a non-self-executing treaty.

The United States nonetheless maintains that the President's Memorandum should be given effect as domestic law because "this case involves a valid Presidential action in the context of Congressional 'acquiescence'." Brief for United States as *Amicus Curiae* 11, n. 2. Under the *Youngstown* tripartite framework, congressional acquiescence is pertinent when the President's action falls within the second category—that is, when he "acts in absence of either a congressional grant or denial of authority." 343 U.S., at 637 (Jackson, J., concurring). Here, however, as we have explained, the President's effort to accord domestic effect to the *Avena* judgment does not meet that prerequisite.

In any event, even if we were persuaded that congressional acquiescence could support the President's asserted authority to create domestic law pursuant to a non-self-executing treaty, such acquiescence does not exist here. The United States first locates congressional acquiescence in Congress's failure to act following the President's resolution of prior ICJ controversies. A review of the Executive's actions in those prior cases, however, cannot support the claim that Congress acquiesced in this particular exercise of Presidential authority, for none of them remotely involved transforming an international obligation into domestic law and thereby displacing state law.[14]

---

[14] Rather, in the *Case Concerning Military and Paramilitary Activities in and Against Nicaragua* (*Nicar. v. U.S.*), 1986 I.C.J. 14 (Judgment of June 27), the President determined that the United States would *not* comply with the ICJ's conclusion that the United States owed reparations to Nicaragua. In the *Case Concerning Delimitation of the Maritime Boundary in the Gulf of Maine Area* (*Can.v.U.S.*), 1984 I.C.J. 246 (Judgment of Oct. 12), a federal agency-the National Oceanic and Atmospheric Administration-issued a final rule which complied with the ICJ's boundary determination. The *Case Concerning Rights of Nationals of the United States of America in Morocco* (*Fr.v.U.S.*), 1952 I.C.J. 176 (Judgment of Aug. 27), concerned the legal status of United States citizens living in Morocco; it was not enforced in United States courts.

The final two cases arose under the Vienna Convention. In the *Lagrand Case* (*F.R. G.v.U.S.*), 2001 I.C.J. 466 (Judgment of June 27), the ICJ ordered the review and reconsideration of convictions and sentences of German nationals denied consular notification. In response, the State Department sent letters to the States "encouraging" them to consider the Vienna Convention in the clemency process. Brief for United States as *Amicus Curiae* 20–21. Such encouragement did not give the ICJ judgment direct effect as domestic law; thus, it cannot serve as precedent for doing so in which Congress might be said to have acquiesced. In the *Case Concerning the Vienna Convention on Consular Relations* (*Para.v.U.S.*), 1998 I.C.J. 248 (Judgment of Apr. 9), the ICJ issued a provisional order, directing the United States to "*take all measures at its disposal* to ensure that [Breard] is not executed pending the final decision in [the ICJ's] proceedings." *Breard*, 523 U.S., at 374 (internal quotation marks omitted). In response, the Secretary of State sent a letter to the Governor of Virginia requesting that he stay Breard's execution. *Id.*, at 378. When Paraguay sought a stay of execution from this Court, the United States argued that it had taken every measure at its disposal: because "our federal system imposes limits on the federal government's ability to interfere with the criminal justice systems of the States," those measures

The United States also directs us to the President's "related" statutory responsibilities and to his "established role" in litigating foreign policy concerns as support for the President's asserted authority to give the ICJ's decision in *Avena* the force of domestic law. Brief for United States as *Amicus Curiae* 16–19. Congress has indeed authorized the President to represent the United States before the United Nations, the ICJ, and the Security Council, 22 U.S.C. § 287, but the authority of the President to represent the United States before such bodies speaks to the President's *international* responsibilities, not any unilateral authority to create domestic law. The authority expressly conferred by Congress in the international realm cannot be said to "invite" the Presidential action at issue here. *See Youngstown, supra,* at 637 (Jackson, J., concurring). At bottom, none of the sources of authority identified by the United States supports the President's claim that Congress has acquiesced in his asserted power to establish on his own federal law or to override state law.

None of this is to say, however, that the combination of a non-self-executing treaty and the lack of implementing legislation precludes the President from acting to comply with an international treaty obligation. It is only to say that the Executive cannot unilaterally execute a non-self-executing treaty by giving it domestic effect. That is, the non-self-executing character of a treaty constrains the President's ability to comply with treaty commitments by unilaterally making the treaty binding on domestic courts. The President may comply with the treaty's obligations by some other means, so long as they are consistent with the Constitution. But he may not rely upon a non-self-executing treaty to "establish binding rules of decision that preempt contrary state law." Brief for United States as *Amicus Curiae* 5.

2

We thus turn to the United States' claim that—independent of the United States' treaty obligations—the Memorandum is a valid exercise of the President's foreign affairs authority to resolve claims disputes with foreign nations. *Id.,* at 12–16. The United States relies on a series of cases in which this Court has upheld the authority of the President to settle foreign claims pursuant to an executive agreement. *See Garamendi,* 539 U.S., at 415; *Dames & Moore,* 453 U.S., at 679–680; *United States v. Pink,* 315 U.S. 203, 229 (1942); *United States v. Belmont,* 301 U.S. 324, 330 (1937). In these cases this Court has explained that, if pervasive enough, a history of congressional acquiescence can be treated as a "gloss on 'Executive Power' vested in the President by § 1 of Art. II." *Dames & Moore, supra,* at 686 (some internal quotation marks omitted).

---

included "only persuasion," not "legal compulsion." Brief for United States as *Amicus Curiae,* O.T.1997, No. 97-8214, p. 51. This of course is precedent contrary to the proposition asserted by the Solicitor General in this case.

This argument is of a different nature than the one rejected above. Rather than relying on the United States' treaty obligations, the President relies on an independent source of authority in ordering Texas to put aside its procedural bar to successive habeas petitions. Nevertheless, we find that our claims-settlement cases do not support the authority that the President asserts in this case.

The claims-settlement cases involve a narrow set of circumstances: the making of executive agreements to settle civil claims between American citizens and foreign governments or foreign nationals. *See, e.g., Belmont, supra,* at 327. They are based on the view that "a systematic, unbroken, executive practice, long pursued to the knowledge of the Congress and never before questioned," can "raise a presumption that the [action] had been [taken] in pursuance of its consent." *Dames & Moore, supra,* at 686 (some internal quotation marks omitted). . . .

Even still, the limitations on this source of executive power are clearly set forth and the Court has been careful to note that "[p]ast practice does not, by itself, create power." *Dames & Moore, supra,* at 686.

The President's Memorandum is not supported by a "particularly longstanding practice" of congressional acquiescence, see *Garamendi, supra,* at 415, but rather is what the United States itself has described as "unprecedented action," Brief for United States as *Amicus Curiae* in *Sanchez-Llamas,* O.T.2005, Nos. 05–51 and 04–10566, pp. 29–30. Indeed, the Government has not identified a single instance in which the President has attempted (or Congress has acquiesced in) a Presidential directive issued to state courts, much less one that reaches deep into the heart of the State's police powers and compels state courts to reopen final criminal judgments and set aside neutrally applicable state laws. . . .

3

Medellín argues that the President's Memorandum is a valid exercise of his "Take Care" power. Brief for Petitioner 28. The United States, however, does not rely upon the President's responsibility to "take Care that the Laws be faithfully executed." U.S. Const., Art. II, § 3. We think this a wise concession. This authority allows the President to execute the laws, not make them. For the reasons we have stated, the *Avena* judgment is not domestic law; accordingly, the President cannot rely on his Take Care powers here. . . .

JUSTICE STEVENS, concurring in the judgment.

[Justice Stevens concurred in the judgment; in relevant part, his opinion suggested that it was Texas' responsibility to comply, and in view of developments in the case of Osbaldo Torres, one of the Mexican nationals involved in the *Avena* judgment (*see supra*), he remarked that this "minimal" cost is one "that the State of Oklahoma unhesitatingly assumed."]

JUSTICE BREYER, with whom JUSTICE SOUTER and JUSTICE GINSBURG join, dissenting. . . .

III

Because the majority concludes that the Nation's international legal obligation to enforce the ICJ's decision is not automatically a domestic legal obligation, it must then determine whether the President has the constitutional authority to enforce it. And the majority finds that he does not. *See* Part III, *ante.*

In my view, that second conclusion has broader implications than the majority suggests. The President here seeks to implement treaty provisions in which the United States agrees that the ICJ judgment is binding with respect to the *Avena* parties. Consequently, his actions draw upon his constitutional authority in the area of foreign affairs. In this case, his exercise of that power falls within that middle range of Presidential authority where Congress has neither specifically authorized nor specifically forbidden the Presidential action in question. *See Youngstown Sheet & Tube Co. v. Sawyer,* 343 U.S. 579 (1952) (Jackson, J., concurring). At the same time, if the President were to have the authority he asserts here, it would require setting aside a state procedural law.

It is difficult to believe that in the exercise of his Article II powers pursuant to a ratified treaty, the President can *never* take action that would result in setting aside state law. *Cf. United States v. Pink,* 315 U.S. 203, 233 (1942) ("No State can rewrite our foreign policy to conform to its own domestic policies"). Suppose that the President believes it necessary that he implement a treaty provision requiring a prisoner exchange involving someone in state custody in order to avoid a proven military threat. *Cf. Ware,* 3 Dall., at 205. Or suppose he believes it necessary to secure a foreign consul's treaty-based rights to move freely or to contact an arrested foreign national. *Cf.* Vienna Convention, Art. 34, 21 U.S.T., at 98. Does the Constitution require the President in each and every such instance to obtain a special statute authorizing his action? On the other hand, the Constitution must impose significant restrictions upon the President's ability, by invoking Article II treaty-implementation authority, to circumvent ordinary legislative processes and to pre-empt state law as he does so.

Previously this Court has said little about this question. It has held that the President has a fair amount of authority to make and to implement executive agreements, at least in respect to international claims settlement, and that this authority can require contrary state law to be set aside. *See, e.g., Pink, supra,* at 223, 230–231, 233–234; *United States v. Belmont,* 301 U.S. 324, 326–327. It has made clear that principles of foreign sovereign immunity trump state law and that the Executive, operating without explicit legislative authority, can assert those principles in state court. *See Ex parte Peru,* 318 U.S. 578, 588 (1943). It has also made clear that the Executive has inherent power to bring a lawsuit "to carry out treaty obligations." *Sanitary Dist. of Chicago v. United States,* 266 U.S. 405, 425, 426 (1925). But it has reserved judgment as to "the scope of the President's power to preempt state law pursuant to authority delegated by . . . a ratified treaty"—a fact that helps to explain the majority's inability to find support in precedent for its own conclusions. *Barclays Bank PLC v. Franchise Tax Bd. of Cal.,* 512 U.S. 298, 329 (1994).

Given the Court's comparative lack of expertise in foreign affairs; given the importance of the Nation's foreign relations; given the difficulty of finding the proper constitutional balance among state and federal, executive and legislative, powers in such matters; and given the likely future importance of this Court's efforts to do so, I would very much hesitate before concluding that the Constitution implicitly sets forth broad prohibitions (or permissions) in this area. *Cf. ante,* at 1367, n. 13 (stating that the Court's holding is "limited" by the facts that (1) this treaty is non-self-executing and (2) the judgment of an international tribunal is involved).

I would thus be content to leave the matter in the constitutional shade from which it has emerged. Given my view of this case, I need not answer the question. And I shall not try to do so. That silence, however, cannot be taken as agreement with the majority's Part III conclusion.

NOTES

1. *Authority for the President's Memorandum.* What exactly is the constitutional basis for the president's memorandum? Consider the strengths and weaknesses of the various grounds reviewed by the Supreme Court, both from the president's perspective and as a matter of dispassionate constitutional analysis. For example, one ground urged by Medellín—but not by the executive branch—was that the president's memorandum effectuated his responsibility to "take Care that the Laws be faithfully executed." U.S. Const., Art. II, § 3. From the president's perspective, such an argument had definite drawbacks; can you imagine what they are? Do they bear any relation to the Court's analysis? For contemporaneous commentary on the strengths and weaknesses of the arguments considered in *Medellín*, see Margaret E. McGuinness, *Medellín, Norm Portals, and the Horizontal Integration of International Human Rights*, 82 NOTRE DAME L. REV. 755 (2006); Edward T. Swaine, *Taking Care of Treaties*, 108 COLUM. L. REV. 331 (2008); Michael P. Van Alstine, *Executive Aggrandizement in Foreign Affairs Lawmaking*, 54 U.C.L.A. L. REV. 309 (2006).

One of the Court's most important conclusions, one bearing on all the potential bases for presidential authority was its understanding of the implications of non-self-execution: namely, that only congressional legislation could implement a non-self-executing treaty, and that for this reason, the conclusion that a treaty was non-self-executing implicitly negated presidential authority, leaving it to be analyzed within the third tier of Justice Jackson's *Youngstown* framework. Do you think this accords with the meaning of non-self-execution preceding *Medellín*? For a criticism, see Edward T. Swaine, *The Political Economy of* Youngstown, 83 S. CAL. L. REV. 263, 329–33 (2010). When the Supreme Court insists that its view does not deprive the executive branch of the authority to direct compliance with the international obligations of the United States, what might it mean?

Yet more broadly, some have speculated that the result in *Medellín* undermines the broader language relating to preemptive executive branch authority in *American Ins. Ass'n v. Garamendi*. A. Mark Weisburd, *Medellín, the President's Foreign Affairs Power and Domestic Law,* 28 PENN ST. INT'L L.REV. 595, 625 (2010). *But cf. Museum of Fine Arts Boston v. Seger-Thomschitz,* 623 F.3d 1, 12 n.12 (1st Cir. 2010) (distinguishing *Garamendi* on other grounds, and noting post-*Medellín* case applying broad understanding of *Garamendi).*

2. *Alternative Remedies.* Commandments by the Supreme Court or the president are not the only possible means of remedying a treaty violation. As noted earlier, both Oklahoma's courts and its governor proved receptive on at least one occasion to the claims that Article 36 violations should bear upon an alien's conviction and sentence. Others who were denied their consular rights have been less fortunate. *Another Mexican National Executed in Texas in Defiance of Avena Decision*, 108 AM. J. INT'L L. 322 (2014).

Another avenue, of course, is Congress. There have been several attempts to generate congressional interest in legislating a remedy to Article 36 violations in general or to *Avena* in particular. In late spring 2011, Senator Leahy introduced a bill backed by the Obama Administration, entitled the "Consular Notification Compliance Act of 2011," that would have implemented the Article 36 obligation as a matter of federal law and provided federal jurisdiction to the review the merits of petitions alleging Article 36 violations that caused actual prejudice to a criminal conviction or sentence. The bill would have afforded one year for filing a petition of review alleging such violations and, while not generally relieving petitioners of the rules for federal *habeas* petitions, would have effectively relieved procedural limitations that would have inhibited petitioners whose applications would otherwise have been due before or shortly after enactment. S. 1194, 112th Cong., 157 Cong. Rec. S3779 (daily ed. June 14, 2011). Such legislation, however, was not enacted into law.

Last, but not least, should an alien who is not notified of his or her right to contact his or her consulate be able to sue state law enforcement officials for damages? *Compare Cornejo v. San Diego*, 504 F.3d 853 (9th Cir. 2007) (finding that the VCCR does not create judicially enforceable private rights pursuant to 42 U.S.C. § 1983), *with Jogi v. Voges*, 480 F.3d 822, 824–25 (7th Cir. 2007)

("[R]ather than wade into the treacherous waters of implied remedies, we have concluded that Jogi's action rests on a more secure footing as one under 42 U.S.C. § 1983. At bottom, he is complaining about police action, under color of state law, that violates a right secured to him by a federal law (here, a treaty). We can safely leave for another day the question whether the Vienna Convention would directly support a private remedy.").

CHAPTER 7

THE JUDICIARY

■ ■ ■

Many issues in U.S. foreign relations law are addressed, if not completely resolved, by the judiciary, and the foregoing Chapters illustrate the courts' ongoing struggle to say what the law is while respecting the function of other actors in the constitutional system—not to mention international actors.

While the relative capacity and expertise of courts comes up frequently in the foreign relations doctrines considered elsewhere in this text, questions of justiciability—essentially, a set of doctrines designed to ensure that Article III courts in the United States only hear "cases or controversies"—arise distinctly in U.S. judicial proceedings. Various discrete concepts operate within the realm of justiciability, such as the political question doctrine, ripeness, mootness, and standing (including, in the foreign relations context, whether a foreign government that has not been "recognized" by the U.S. government has standing to sue or be sued).

Justiciability issues have frequently barred U.S. courts from reaching the merits of foreign relations cases, and the materials in the first six Sections of this Chapter analyze this phenomenon, with a particular focus on how these hurdles differ in this field. The remaining Sections then address two additional issues, immunities and the act of state doctrine, that have undoubtedly had a substantial influence on the functioning of courts in these areas.

1. POLITICAL QUESTION DOCTRINE GENERALLY

ZIVOTOFSKY EX REL. ZIVOTOFSKY V. CLINTON

566 U.S. 189 (2012).

[In 2002, Congress enacted the Foreign Relations Authorization Act for Fiscal Year 2003. Section 214 of the Act was entitled "United States Policy with Respect to Jerusalem as the Capital of Israel." One of its provisions, § 214(d) (entitled "Record of Place of Birth as Israel for Passport Purposes") provided that "[f]or purposes of the registration of birth, certification of nationality, or issuance of a passport of a United States citizen born in the city of Jerusalem, the Secretary [of State] shall, upon the request of the citizen or the citizen's legal guardian, record the place of birth as Israel."

By contrast, the State Department's Foreign Affairs Manual provides that "[w]here the birthplace of the applicant is located in territory disputed by another country, the city or area of birth may be written in the passport." Further, the manual specifically directs that passport officials should enter "Jerusalem" and should "not write Israel or Jordan" when recording the birthplace of a person born in Jerusalem on a passport.

When signing the Act into law, President George W. Bush stated his belief that § 214 "impermissibly interferes with the President's constitutional authority to conduct the Nation's foreign affairs and to supervise the unitary executive branch." He added that if the section is "construed as mandatory," then it would "interfere with the President's constitutional authority to formulate the position of the United States, speak for the Nation in international affairs, and determine the terms on which recognition is given to foreign states." *See* Statement on Signing the Foreign Relations Authorization Act, Fiscal Year 2003, Public Papers of the Presidents, George W. Bush, Vol. 2, Sept. 30, 2002, p. 1698 (2005).

Menachem Binyamin Zivotofsky was born in Jerusalem in 2002 shortly after § 214(d) was enacted. Zivotofsky's parents were U.S. citizens and he accordingly was as well, by virtue of congressional enactment. Zivotofsky's mother filed an application for a consular report of birth abroad and a U.S. passport, requesting that his place of birth be listed as "Jerusalem, Israel" on both documents. U.S. officials informed Zivotofsky's mother that State Department policy prohibits recording "Israel" as Zivotofsky's place of birth. Pursuant to that policy, Zivotofsky was issued both documents listing only "Jerusalem."

Zivotofsky's parents filed a complaint in federal court on his behalf against the Secretary of State, seeking declaratory and injunctive relief. Although Zivotofsky was found by the lower courts to have standing, his complaint was dismissed as presenting a nonjusticiable political question.]

CHIEF JUSTICE ROBERTS delivered the opinion of the Court.

Congress enacted a statute providing that Americans born in Jerusalem may elect to have "Israel" listed as the place of birth on their passports. The State Department declined to follow that law, citing its longstanding policy of not taking a position on the political status of Jerusalem. When sued by an American who invoked the statute, the Secretary of State argued that the courts lacked authority to decide the case because it presented a political question. The Court of Appeals so held. . . .

In general, the Judiciary has a responsibility to decide cases properly before it, even those it "would gladly avoid." *Cohens v. Virginia*, 6 Wheat. 264, 404 (1821). Our precedents have identified a narrow exception to that rule, known as the "political question" doctrine. *See, e.g., Japan Whaling Assn. v. American Cetacean Soc.*, 478 U.S. 221, 230 (1986). We have explained that a controversy "involves a political question . . . where there is 'a textually demonstrable constitutional commitment of the issue to a coordinate political department; or a lack of judicially discoverable and manageable standards for resolving it.'" *Nixon v. United States*, 506 U.S. 224, 228 (1993) (quoting *Baker v. Carr*, 369 U.S. 186, 217 (1962)). In such a case, we have held that a court lacks the authority to decide the dispute before it.

The lower courts ruled that this case involves a political question because deciding Zivotofsky's claim would force the Judicial Branch to interfere with the President's exercise of constitutional power committed to him alone. The District Court understood Zivotofsky to ask the courts to "decide the political status of Jerusalem." 511 F.Supp.2d, at 103. This misunderstands the issue presented. Zivotofsky does not ask the courts to determine whether Jerusalem is the capital of Israel. He instead seeks to determine whether he may vindicate his statutory right, under § 214(d), to choose to have Israel recorded on his passport as his place of birth.

For its part, the D.C. Circuit treated the two questions as one and the same. That court concluded that "[o]nly the Executive—not Congress and not the courts—has the power to define U.S. policy regarding Israel's sovereignty over Jerusalem," and also to "decide how best to implement that policy." 571 F.3d, at 1232. Because the Department's passport rule was adopted to implement the President's "exclusive and unreviewable constitutional power to keep the United States out of the debate over the status of Jerusalem," the validity of that rule was itself a "nonjusticiable political question" that "the Constitution leaves to the Executive alone." *Id.*, at 1231–1233. Indeed, the D.C. Circuit's opinion does not even mention § 214(d) until the fifth of its six paragraphs of analysis, and then only to dismiss it as irrelevant: "That Congress took a position on the status of Jerusalem and gave Zivotofsky a statutory cause of action . . . is of no moment to whether the judiciary has [the] authority to resolve this dispute. . . ." *Id.*, at 1233.

The existence of a statutory right, however, is certainly relevant to the Judiciary's power to decide Zivotofsky's claim. The federal courts are not being asked to supplant a foreign policy decision of the political branches with the courts' own unmoored determination of what United States policy toward Jerusalem should be. Instead, Zivotofsky requests that the courts enforce a specific statutory right. To resolve his claim, the Judiciary must decide if Zivotofsky's interpretation of the statute is correct, and whether the statute is constitutional. This is a familiar judicial exercise.

Moreover, because the parties do not dispute the interpretation of § 214(d), the only real question for the courts is whether the statute is constitutional. At least since *Marbury v. Madison*, 1 Cranch 137 (1803), we have recognized that when an Act of Congress is alleged to conflict with the

Constitution, "[i]t is emphatically the province and duty of the judicial department to say what the law is." *Id.*, at 177. That duty will sometimes involve the "[r]esolution of litigation challenging the constitutional authority of one of the three branches," but courts cannot avoid their responsibility merely "because the issues have political implications." *INS v. Chadha*, 462 U.S. 919, 943 (1983).

In this case, determining the constitutionality of § 214(d) involves deciding whether the statute impermissibly intrudes upon Presidential powers under the Constitution. If so, the law must be invalidated and Zivotofsky's case should be dismissed for failure to state a claim. If, on the other hand, the statute does not trench on the President's powers, then the Secretary must be ordered to issue Zivotofsky a passport that complies with § 214(d). Either way, the political question doctrine is not implicated. "No policy underlying the political question doctrine suggests that Congress or the Executive . . . can decide the constitutionality of a statute; that is a decision for the courts." *Id.*, at 941–942.

The Secretary contends that "there is 'a textually demonstrable constitutional commitment' " to the President of the sole power to recognize foreign sovereigns and, as a corollary, to determine whether an American born in Jerusalem may choose to have Israel listed as his place of birth on his passport. Perhaps. But there is, of course, no exclusive commitment to the Executive of the power to determine the constitutionality of a statute. The Judicial Branch appropriately exercises that authority, including in a case such as this, where the question is whether Congress or the Executive is "aggrandizing its power at the expense of another branch." *Freytag v. Commissioner*, 501 U.S. 868, 878 (1991).

Our precedents have also found the political question doctrine implicated when there is " 'a lack of judicially discoverable and manageable standards for resolving' " the question before the court. *Nixon, supra*, at 228 (quoting *Baker, supra*, at 217). Framing the issue as the lower courts did, in terms of whether the Judiciary may decide the political status of Jerusalem, certainly raises those concerns. They dissipate, however, when the issue is recognized to be the more focused one of the constitutionality of § 214(d). Indeed, both sides offer detailed legal arguments regarding whether § 214(d) is constitutional in light of powers committed to the Executive, and whether Congress's own powers with respect to passports must be weighed in analyzing this question.

For example, the Secretary reprises on the merits her argument on the political question issue, claiming that the Constitution gives the Executive the exclusive power to formulate recognition policy. She roots her claim in the Constitution's declaration that the President shall "receive Ambassadors and other public Ministers." U.S. Const., Art. II, § 3. According to the Secretary, "[c]enturies-long Executive Branch practice, congressional acquiescence, and decisions by this Court" confirm that the "receive Ambassadors" clause confers upon the Executive the exclusive power of recognition. . . .

For his part, Zivotofsky argues that, far from being an exercise of the recognition power, § 214(d) is instead a "legitimate and permissible" exercise of Congress's "authority to legislate on the form and content of a passport." He points the Court to Professor Louis Henkin's observation that " 'in the competition for power in foreign relations,' Congress has 'an impressive array of powers expressly enumerated in the Constitution.' " Zivotofsky suggests that Congress's authority to enact § 214(d) derives specifically from its powers over naturalization, U.S. Const., Art. I, § 8, cl. 4, and foreign commerce, *id.*, § 8, cl. 3. According to Zivotofsky, Congress has used these powers to pass laws regulating the content and issuance of passports since 1856. . . .

Recitation of these arguments—which sound in familiar principles of constitutional interpretation—is enough to establish that this case does not "turn on standards that defy judicial application." *Baker*, 369 U.S., at 211. Resolution of Zivotofsky's claim demands careful examination of the textual, structural, and historical evidence put forward by the parties regarding the nature of the statute and of the passport and recognition powers. This is what courts do. The political question doctrine poses no bar to judicial review of this case. . . .

The judgment of the Court of Appeals for the D.C. Circuit is vacated, and the case is remanded for further proceedings consistent with this opinion. [For the Court's decision on the merits, see Chapter 1, Sec. 2].

JUSTICE SOTOMAYOR, with whom JUSTICE BREYER joins as to Part I, concurring in part and concurring in the judgment.

As this case illustrates, the proper application of *Baker*'s six factors has generated substantial confusion in the lower courts. I concur in the Court's conclusion that this case does not present a political question. I write separately, however, because I understand the inquiry required by the political question doctrine to be more demanding than that suggested by the Court.

I

The political question doctrine speaks to an amalgam of circumstances in which courts properly examine whether a particular suit is justiciable—that is, whether the dispute is appropriate for resolution by courts. The doctrine is "essentially a function of the separation of powers," *Baker v. Carr*, 369 U.S. 186, 217 (1962), which recognizes the limits that Article III imposes upon courts and accords appropriate respect to the other branches' exercise of their own constitutional powers.

In *Baker*, this Court identified six circumstances in which an issue might present a political question: (1) "a textually demonstrable constitutional commitment of the issue to a coordinate political department"; (2) "a lack of judicially discoverable and manageable standards for resolving it"; (3) "the impossibility of deciding without an initial policy determination of a kind clearly for nonjudicial discretion"; (4) "the impossibility of a court's undertaking independent resolution without expressing lack of the respect due coordinate branches of government"; (5) "an unusual need for unquestioning adherence to a political decision already made"; or (6) "the potentiality of embarrassment from multifarious pronouncements by various departments on one question." *Baker* established that "[u]nless one of these formulations is inextricable from the case at bar, there should be no dismissal for nonjusticiability." But *Baker* left unanswered when the presence of one or more factors warrants dismissal, as well as the interrelationship of the six factors and the relative importance of each in determining whether a case is suitable for adjudication.

In my view, the *Baker* factors reflect three distinct justifications for withholding judgment on the merits of a dispute. When a case would require a court to decide an issue whose resolution is textually committed to a coordinate political department, as envisioned by *Baker* 's first factor, abstention is warranted because the court lacks authority to resolve that issue. In such cases, the Constitution itself requires that another branch resolve the question presented.

The second and third *Baker* factors reflect circumstances in which a dispute calls for decisionmaking beyond courts' competence. " 'The judicial Power' created by Article III, § 1, of the Constitution is not whatever judges choose to do," but rather the power "to act in the manner traditional for English and American courts." *Vieth v. Jubelirer*, 541 U.S. 267, 278 (2004) (plurality opinion). That traditional role involves the application of some manageable and cognizable standard within the competence of the Judiciary to ascertain and employ to the facts of a concrete case. When a court is given no standard by which to adjudicate a dispute, or cannot resolve a dispute in the absence of a yet-unmade policy determination charged to a political branch, resolution of the suit is beyond the judicial role envisioned by Article III. This is not to say, of course, that courts are incapable of interpreting or applying somewhat ambiguous standards using familiar tools of statutory or constitutional interpretation. But where an issue leaves courts truly rudderless, there can be "no doubt of [the] validity" of a court's decision to abstain from judgment. *Ibid.*

The final three *Baker* factors address circumstances in which prudence may counsel against a court's resolution of an issue presented. Courts should be particularly cautious before forgoing adjudication of a dispute on the basis that judicial intervention risks "embarrassment from multifarious pronouncements by various departments on one question," would express a "lack of the respect due coordinate branches of government," or because there exists an "unusual need for unquestioning adherence to a political decision already made." 369 U.S., at 217, 82 S.Ct. 691. We have repeatedly rejected the view that these thresholds are met whenever a court is called upon to resolve the constitutionality or propriety of the act of another branch of Government. A court may not refuse to adjudicate a dispute merely because a decision "may have significant political overtones" or affect "the conduct of this Nation's foreign relations," *Japan Whaling Assn. v. American Cetacean Soc.*, 478 U.S. 221, 230 (1986). Nor may courts decline to resolve a controversy within their traditional competence and proper jurisdiction simply because the question is difficult, the consequences weighty, or the potential real for conflict with the policy preferences of the political branches. The exercise of such authority is among the "gravest and most delicate dut[ies] that this Court is called on to perform," *Blodgett v. Holden*, 275 U.S. 142, 148 (1927) (Holmes, J., concurring), but it is the role assigned to courts by the Constitution. "Questions may occur which we would gladly avoid; but we cannot avoid them. All we can do is, to exercise our best judgment, and conscientiously to perform our duty." *Cohens v. Virginia*, 6 Wheat. 264, 404 (1821).

Rare occasions implicating *Baker* 's final factors, however, may present an " 'unusual case' " unfit for judicial disposition. 369 U.S., at 218, 82 S.Ct. 691. Because of the respect due to a coequal and independent department, for instance, courts properly resist calls to question the good faith with which another branch attests to the authenticity of its internal acts. Likewise, we have long acknowledged that courts are particularly ill suited to intervening in exigent disputes necessitating unusual need for "attributing finality to the action of the political departments," *Coleman v. Miller*, 307 U.S. 433, 454 (1939), or creating acute "risk [of] embarrassment of our government abroad, or grave disturbance at home," *Baker*, 369 U.S., at 226. Finally, it may be appropriate for courts to stay their hand in cases implicating delicate questions concerning the distribution of political authority between coordinate branches until a dispute is ripe, intractable, and incapable of resolution by the political process. *See Goldwater v. Carter*, 444 U.S. 996, 997 (1979) (Powell, J., concurring in judgment). Abstention merely reflects that judicial intervention in such cases is "legitimate only in the last resort," *Chicago & Grand Trunk R. Co. v. Wellman*, 143 U.S. 339, 345 (1892), and is disfavored relative to the prospect of accommodation between the political branches.

When such unusual cases arise, abstention accommodates considerations inherent in the separation of powers and the limitations envisioned by Article III, which conferred authority to federal courts against a common-law backdrop that recognized the propriety of abstention in exceptional cases. The political questions envisioned by *Baker*'s final categories find common ground, therefore, with many longstanding doctrines under which considerations of justiciability or comity lead courts to abstain from deciding questions whose initial resolution is better suited to another time.

To be sure, it will be the rare case in which *Baker*'s final factors alone render a case nonjusticiable. But our long historical tradition recognizes that such exceptional cases arise, and due regard for the separation of powers and the judicial role envisioned by Article III confirms that abstention may be an appropriate response.

II

The court below held that this case presented a political question because it thought petitioner's suit asked the court to decide an issue "textually committed" to a coordinate branch—namely, "to review a policy of the State Department implementing the President's decision" to keep the United States out of the debate over the status of Jerusalem. 571 F.3d 1227, 1231–1232 (C.A.D.C.2009). Largely for the reasons set out by the Court, I agree that the Court of Appeals misapprehended the nature of its task. In two respects, however, my understanding of the political question doctrine might require a court to engage in further analysis beyond that relied upon by the Court.

First, the Court appropriately recognizes that petitioner's claim to a statutory right is "relevant" to the justiciability inquiry required in this case. In order to evaluate whether a case presents a political question, a court must first identify with precision the issue it is being asked to decide. Here, petitioner's suit claims that a federal statute provides him with a right to have "Israel" listed as his place of birth on his passport and other related documents. To decide that question, a court must determine whether the statute is constitutional, and therefore mandates the Secretary of State to issue petitioner's desired passport, or unconstitutional, in which case his suit is at an end. Resolution of that issue is not one "textually committed" to another branch; to the contrary, it is committed to this one. In no fashion does the question require a court to review the wisdom of the President's policy toward Jerusalem or any other decision committed to the discretion of a coordinate department. For that reason, I agree that the decision below should be reversed.

That is not to say, however, that no statute could give rise to a political question. It is not impossible to imagine a case involving the application or even the constitutionality of an enactment that would present a nonjusticiable issue. Indeed, this Court refused to determine whether an Ohio state constitutional provision offended the Republican Guarantee Clause, Art. IV, § 4, holding that "the question of whether that guarantee of the Constitution has been disregarded presents no justiciable controversy." *Ohio ex rel. Davis v. Hildebrant*, 241 U.S. 565, 569 (1916). A similar result would follow if Congress passed a statute, for instance, purporting to award financial relief to those improperly "tried" of impeachment offenses. To adjudicate claims under such a statute would require a court to resolve the very same issue we found nonjusticiable in *Nixon*. Such examples are atypical, but they suffice to show that the foreclosure altogether of political question analysis in statutory cases is unwarranted.

Second, the Court suggests that this case does not implicate the political question doctrine's concern with issues exhibiting " 'a lack of judicially discoverable and manageable standards,' " because the parties' arguments rely on textual, structural, and historical evidence of the kind that courts routinely consider. But that was equally true in *Nixon*, a case in which we found that "the use of the word 'try' in the first sentence of the Impeachment Trial Clause lacks sufficient precision to afford any judicially manageable standard of review of the Senate's actions." 506 U.S., at 230. We reached that conclusion even though the parties' briefs focused upon the text of the Impeachment Trial Clause, "the Constitution's drafting history," "contemporaneous commentary," "the unbroken practice of the Senate for 150 years," contemporary dictionary meanings, "Hamilton's Federalist essays," and the practice in the House of Lords prior to ratification. Such evidence was no more or less unfamiliar to courts than that on which the parties rely here.

In my view, it is not whether the evidence upon which litigants rely is common to judicial consideration that determines whether a case lacks judicially discoverable and manageable standards. Rather, it is whether that evidence in fact provides a court a basis to adjudicate meaningfully the issue with which it is presented. The answer will almost always be yes, but if the parties' textual, structural, and historical evidence is inapposite or wholly unilluminating, rendering judicial decision no more than guesswork, a case relying on the ordinary kinds of arguments offered to courts might well still present justiciability concerns.

In this case, however, the Court of Appeals majority found a political question solely on the basis that this case required resolution of an issue "textually committed" to the Executive Branch. Because there was no such textual commitment, I respectfully concur in the Court's decision to reverse the Court of Appeals.

JUSTICE BREYER, dissenting.

I join Part I of JUSTICE SOTOMAYOR's opinion. As she points out, *Baker v. Carr*, set forth several categories of legal questions that the Court had previously held to be "political questions" inappropriate for judicial determination. . . .

JUSTICE SOTOMAYOR adds that the circumstances in which these prudential considerations lead the Court not to decide a case otherwise properly before it are rare. But in my view we nonetheless have before us such a case. Four sets of prudential considerations, taken together, lead me to that conclusion.

First, the issue before us arises in the field of foreign affairs. . . . The Constitution primarily delegates the foreign affairs powers "to the political departments of the government, Executive and Legislative," not to the Judiciary. *Chicago & Southern Air Lines, Inc. v. Waterman S.S. Corp.*, 333 U.S. 103, 111 (1948); *see also Marbury v. Madison*, 1 Cranch 137, 166 (1803) (noting discretionary foreign affairs functions of Secretary of State as beyond the power of the Judiciary to review). And that fact is not surprising. Decisionmaking in this area typically is highly political. It is "delicate" and "complex." *Chicago & Southern Air Lines*, 333 U.S., at 111. It often rests upon information readily available to the Executive Branch and to the intelligence committees of Congress, but not readily available to the courts. It frequently is highly dependent upon what Justice Jackson called "prophecy." *Ibid.* And the creation of wise foreign policy typically lies well beyond the experience or professional capacity of a judge. At the same time, where foreign affairs is at issue, the practical need for the United States to speak "with one voice and ac[t] as one," is particularly important. *See United States v. Pink*, 315 U.S. 203, 242 (1942) (Frankfurter, J., concurring).

The result is a judicial hesitancy to make decisions that have significant foreign policy implications, as reflected in the fact that many of the cases in which the Court has invoked the political-question doctrine have arisen in this area, e.g., cases in which the validity of a treaty depended upon the partner state's constitutional authority, or upon its continuing existence; cases concerning the existence of foreign states, governments, belligerents, and insurgents; and cases concerning the territorial boundaries of foreign states.

Second, if the courts must answer the constitutional question before us, they may well have to evaluate the foreign policy implications of foreign policy decisions. . . .

Were the statutory provision undisputedly concerned only with purely administrative matters (or were its enforcement undisputedly to involve only major foreign policy matters), judicial efforts to answer the constitutional question might not involve judges in trying to answer questions of foreign policy. But in the Middle East, administrative matters can have implications that extend far beyond the purely administrative. Political reactions in that region can prove uncertain. And in that context it may well turn out that resolution of the constitutional argument will require a court to decide how far the statute, in practice, reaches beyond the purely administrative, determining not only whether but also the extent to which enforcement will interfere with the President's ability to make significant recognition-related foreign policy decisions.

Certainly the parties argue as if that were so. Zivotofsky, for example, argues that replacing "Jerusalem" on his passport with "Israel" will have no serious foreign policy significance. . . . Moreover, Zivotofsky says, it is unfair to allow the 100,000 or so Americans born in cities that the United States recognizes as under Israeli sovereignty, such as Tel Aviv or Haifa, the right to a record that mentions Israel, while denying that privilege to the 50,000 or so Americans born in Jerusalem.

At the same time, the Secretary argues that listing Israel on the passports (and consular birth reports) of Americans born in Jerusalem will have significantly adverse foreign policy effects. She says that doing so would represent " 'an official decision by the United States to begin to treat Jerusalem as a city located within Israel,' " that it "would be interpreted as an official act of recognizing Jerusalem as being under Israeli sovereignty," and that our "national security interests" consequently "would be significantly harmed". . . .

A judge's ability to evaluate opposing claims of this kind is minimal. At the same time, a judicial effort to do so risks inadvertently jeopardizing sound foreign policy decisionmaking by the other branches of Government. How, for example, is this Court to determine whether, or the extent to which, the continuation of the adjudication that it now orders will itself have a foreign policy effect?

Third, the countervailing interests in obtaining judicial resolution of the constitutional determination are not particularly strong ones. Zivotofsky does not assert the kind of interest, *e.g.*, an interest in property or bodily integrity, which courts have traditionally sought to protect. Nor, importantly, does he assert an interest in vindicating a basic right of the kind that the Constitution grants to individuals and that courts traditionally have protected from invasion by the other branches of Government. And I emphasize this fact because the need for judicial action in such cases can trump the foreign policy concerns that I have mentioned. . . .

The interest that Zivotofsky asserts, however, is akin to an ideological interest. And insofar as an individual suffers an injury that is purely ideological, courts have often refused to consider the matter, leaving the injured party to look to the political branches for protection. This is not to say that Zivotofsky's claim is unimportant or that the injury is not serious or even that it is purely ideological. It is to point out that those suffering somewhat similar harms have sometimes had to look to the political branches for resolution of relevant legal issues.

Fourth, insofar as the controversy reflects different foreign policy views among the political branches of Government, those branches have nonjudicial methods of working out their differences. The Executive and Legislative Branches frequently work out disagreements through ongoing contacts and relationships, involving, for example, budget authorizations, confirmation of personnel, committee hearings, and a host of more informal contacts, which, taken together, ensure that, in practice, Members of Congress as well as the President play an important role in the shaping of foreign policy. Indeed, both the Legislative Branch and the Executive Branch typically understand the need to work each with the other in order to create effective foreign policy. In that understanding, those related contacts, and the continuous foreign policy-related relationship lies the possibility of working out the kind of disagreement we see before us. . . .

The upshot is that this case is unusual both in its minimal need for judicial intervention and in its more serious risk that intervention will bring about "embarrassment," show lack of "respect" for the other branches, and potentially disrupt sound foreign policy decisionmaking. For these prudential reasons, I would hold that the political-question doctrine bars further judicial consideration of this case. And I would affirm the Court of Appeals' similar conclusion.

With respect, I dissent.

NOTES

1. Zivotofsky *on the Merits*. For the Supreme Court's resolution of this dispute on the merits, see Chapter 1, Sec. 2.

2. *Political Question Doctrine in Theory*. What is the exact nature of the political question doctrine? In one formulation, the doctrine is a finding by the court that the question before it has been constitutionally allocated exclusively to one or both of the other branches of the federal government, *i.e.*, the political branches. In this sense, the court does not assert nonjusticiability but, employing the appropriate level of judicial review, implicitly reaches the merits and decides that the government has acted constitutionally.

In another formulation, the doctrine is a finding by the court that the question before it, while normally within the scope of its review, will nevertheless not be adjudicated due to a lack of judicial capacity or out of prudence. In this sense, the court is extraordinarily asserting nonjusticiability. Unlike a determination of lack of standing, which only affects the individual litigants, a finding of a political question preempts all future judicial inquiry into the subject matter. The court is thus eschewing its pervasive role to "say what the law is." *Marbury v. Madison,* 5 U.S. (1 Cranch) 13 (1803).

Both interpretations of the political question doctrine have received scholarly support. Arguing for the constitutionally-allocated position, Herbert Wechsler wrote that "the only proper judgment that may lead to an abstention from decision is that the Constitution has committed the determination of the issue to another agency of government than the courts," a judgment he described as completely "different from a broad discretion to abstain or intervene." Herbert Wechsler, *Toward Neutral Principles of Constitutional Law,* 73 HARV. L. REV. 1, 9 (1959).

In response, Alexander Bickel argued for the prudential position:

> Such is the basis of the political-question doctrine: the court's sense of lack of capacity, compounded in unequal parts of the strangeness of the issue and the suspicion that it will have to yield more often and more substantially to expediency than to principle; the sheer momentousness of it, which unbalances judgment and prevents one from subsuming the normal calculations of probabilities; the anxiety not so much that judicial judgment will be ignored, as that perhaps it should be, but won't; finally and in sum ("in a mature democracy"), the inner vulnerability of an institution which is electorally irresponsible and has no earth to draw strength from.

Alexander M. Bickel, *The Supreme Court, 1960 Term—Foreword: The Passive Virtues,* 75 HARV. L. REV. 40, 75 (1961).

Some academics have urged the elimination of the doctrine or tried to redesign its application. Louis Henkin, rejecting the prudential formulation and viewing the constitutionally-allocated formulation as congruent with the normal scope of judicial review, suggested scrapping the doctrine—to the extent it really existed at all. *See* Louis Henkin, *Is There a "Political Question" Doctrine?,* 85 YALE L.J. 597 (1976). In its place, he discerned discrete components now mixed in the doctrine: ordinary judicial respect for the coordinate branches of government, discretionary refusal of a court of equity to issue relief, and lack of a private cause of action.

Finding Henkin's position too extreme, Linda Champlin and Alan Schwarz argued that, correctly understood, the political question doctrine results from a judicial assumption of validity dictated by an overwhelming need for finality. Linda Champlin & Alan Schwarz, *Political Question Doctrine and Allocation of the Foreign Affairs Power,* 13 HOFSTRA L. REV. 215 (1985). According to them, such a need arises only in the context of foreign affairs and only when the political branches have acted jointly. If the two branches dispute the allocation of foreign affairs power, the judiciary should decide the matter. Champlin and Schwarz maintain that preservation of order is the underlying rationale of the political question doctrine and that this goal is not furthered by inter-branch battles left unresolved by judicial abstention.

Others have defended the doctrine. Peter Mulhern argued that the political question doctrine is a useful tool for demarcating the responsibility to interpret the Constitution that is shared by the courts and the political branches. He claimed that criticism of the doctrine relies on the invalid assumptions that the judiciary has a "monopoly" on constitutional interpretation and that limiting this monopoly would undermine the rule of law. J. Peter Mulhern, *In Defense of the Political Question Doctrine,* 137 U. PA.

L. REV. 97 (1988); *see also* Jesse H. Choper, *The Political Question Doctrine: Suggested Criteria*, 54 DUKE L.J. 1457 (2005).

3. *Political Question Doctrine in Practice.* In practice, the Supreme Court only rarely has disposed of litigation solely on the basis of the political question doctrine—with its most common application being to the guarantee clause (the Article IV, Section 4 requirement that "[t]he United States shall guarantee to every State in this Union a Republican Form of Government") or similar questions that are literally political in character. *See, e.g., Luther v. Borden*, 48 U.S. (7 How.) 1 (1849) (dismissing as a political question a dispute as to which government of Rhode Island was the legitimate government during the Dorr rebellion); *Pacific States Telephone & Telegraph Co. v. Oregon*, 223 U.S. 118 (1912) (dismissing as a political question a dispute concerning whether direct popular initiatives and referenda violated the guarantee clause); *Coleman v. Miller*, 307 U.S. 433 (1939) (efficacy of state ratification of proposed constitutional amendment a political question).

As indicated by *Zivotofsky,* the case most commonly cited as having set out the standard for the political question doctrine is *Baker v. Carr,* 369 U.S. 186 (1962). The first two of the six categories identified in *Baker* are sometimes considered as referring to "classical" textual constraints (*i.e.*, allocation of decisions to the political branches), while the other four categories are explained as addressing prudential concerns. Do you think the majority in *Zivotofsky* ignored the prudential factors altogether, essentially characterizing political questions as concerned only with textual constraints? *See* Note, *Political Questions, Public Rights, and Sovereign Immunity*, 130 HARV. L. REV. 723 (2016).

In *Baker*, the Court actually managed to reach the merits of a voting district case and, in effect, reversed *Colegrove v. Green*, 328 U.S. 549 (1946). The Court rested its decision on its duty to give effect to the equal protection clause, insisting that a claim based solely on the guarantee clause would have presented a political question.

Later cases continued to apply the doctrine warily. For instance, in *Powell v. McCormack,* the Court avoided application of the political question doctrine in a case involving the refusal of the House of Representatives to seat Adam Clayton Powell. *Powell v. McCormack*, 395 U.S. 486, 518–49 (1969) (concluding that, despite claims that the decision whether to seat an elected member was constitutionally allocated to the House under Article I, Section 5, only refusals premised on the criteria of Article I, Section 2 (*i.e.*, age, citizenship, and residence) would be a political question); *see also Davis v. Bandemer*, 478 U.S. 109, 118–27 (refusing to apply the political question doctrine to political gerrymandering claims); *United States v. Munoz-Flores*, 495 U.S. 385, 389–96 (1990) (holding that a lawsuit seeking to invalidate a law on Origination Clause grounds presents no political question). *But see Gilligan v. Morgan*, 413 U.S. 1 (1973) (finding that evaluation of the training, procedures and weaponry of the Ohio National Guard was a political question).

Given the dearth of cases accepting political question objections, even before *Zivotofsky*, some academics have begun writing its obituary. *See* Rachel E. Barkow, *More Supreme Than Court? The Fall of the Political Question Doctrine and the Rise of Judicial Supremacy*, 102 COLUM. L. REV. 237, 273–317 (2002); Martin H. Redish, *Judicial Review and the "Political Question"*, 79 NW. L. REV. 1031 (1985); Mark Tushnet, *Law and Prudence in the Law of Justiciability: The Transformation and Disappearance of the Political Question Doctrine*, 80 N.C. L. REV. 1203, 1230–31 (2002).

4. *Political Question Doctrine and Foreign Affairs*. In the context of foreign affairs, the political question doctrine has displayed some greater vitality, particularly among the lower federal courts. Both concepts of the doctrine have been employed: that the handling of foreign affairs is allocated to the political branches of the government; and that judicial meddling into foreign affairs could involve determining issues controlled by judicially unassessable facts or making determinations which might be of great detrimental consequence to the United States in its foreign relations. For commentary, see, e.g., Harold Hongju Koh, *Why the President (Almost) Always Wins in Foreign Affairs: Lessons of the Iran-Contra Affair,* 97 YALE L.J. 1255 (1988); Lisa Rudikoff Price, *Banishing the Specter of Judicial Foreign Policymaking: A Competence-Based Approach to the Political Question Doctrine*, 38 N.Y.U. J. INT'L L. & POL. 323 (2005–2006).

Even before *Baker*, the Supreme Court endorsed these premises. In *Oetjen v. Central Leather Co.,* the Court stated: "The conduct of the foreign relations of our Government is committed by the Constitution to the Executive and Legislative—'the political'—Departments of the Government, and the propriety of what may be done in the exercise of this political power is not subject to judicial inquiry or decision." 246 U.S. 297, 302 (1918). In *United States v. Curtiss-Wright Export Corp.,* 299 U.S. 304 (1936), Justice Sutherland, for the Court, announced the expansive *dicta* which has so often been cited to advance the prudential abstention of the judiciary in foreign affairs-based cases: "In this vast external realm, with its important, complicated, delicate and manifold problems, the President alone has the power to speak or listen as a representative of the nation." *Id.* at 319. The Court further spoke of the "very delicate, plenary and exclusive power of the President as the sole organ of the federal government in the field of international relations" even though the very exercise of "plenary" power under consideration was one as to which Congress had already legislated without constitutional challenge. *Id.* at 319–20. In *Chicago & S. Air Lines, Inc. v. Waterman S.S. Corp.,* Justice Jackson again articulated the Court's reluctance to decide issues involving foreign policy:

> Such decisions are wholly confided by our Constitution to the political departments of the government, Executive and Legislative. They are delicate, complex, and involve large elements of prophecy. They are and should be undertaken only by those directly responsible to the people whose welfare they advance or imperil. They are decisions of a kind for which the Judiciary has neither aptitude, facilities nor

> responsibility and which has long been held to belong in the domain of political power not subject to judicial intrusion or inquiry.

333 U.S. 103, 111 (1948) (citations omitted).

In *Baker v. Carr*, Justice Brennan also referred to the unique nature of foreign affairs issues: "Not only does resolution of such issues frequently turn on standards that defy judicial application, or involve the exercise of a discretion demonstrably committed to the executive or legislature," he said, "but many such questions uniquely demand single-voiced statement of the Government's views." 369 U.S. 186, 211. Yet, significantly, he went on to caution that "it is error to suppose that every case or controversy which touches foreign relations lies beyond judicial cognizance." *Id.* Brennan then arrived at his classic formulation of what factors give rise to political questions.

Since *Baker*, the Supreme Court has adjudicated several issues that touch upon foreign affairs. Recall that in *Goldwater v. Carter,* 444 U.S. 996 (1979), a plurality of the Court invoked the doctrine to dismiss a challenge to the president's authority to terminate a treaty without Senate ratification. *See* Chapter 3, Sec. 10.

In *Japan Whaling Ass'n v. American Cetacean Society,* 478 U.S. 221 (1986) (cited above in *Zivotofsky*), several wildlife conservation groups claimed that congressional amendments required the Secretary of Commerce, upon certain findings of fact, to certify that Japan's whaling practices "diminish the effectiveness" of the International Convention for the Regulation of Whaling (ICRW) because Japan's annual harvest exceeded quotas established under the ICRW. Under the law, such a finding would have triggered U.S. import restrictions. Prior to the suit, the Secretary had negotiated an executive agreement with Japan that provided for reduced whaling harvests but did not bring Japan into immediate compliance with the ICRW. Nevertheless, the Secretary refused to certify noncompliance. The district court ordered the Secretary to do so, 604 F.Supp. 1398 (D.D.C. 1985), and the Court of Appeals affirmed, 768 F.2d 426 (D.C. Cir. 1985), but the Supreme Court reversed. Writing for the majority, Justice White determined that the Secretary's decision to secure Japan's gradual compliance with the ICRW through an executive agreement rather than certification was a "reasonable construction" of the amendments. 478 U.S. at 223. However, regarding the Japanese petitioners' claim that a federal court lacks the judicial power to command the Secretary to repudiate the executive agreement with Japan because to do so might create "embarrassment from multifarious pronouncements by various departments on one question," *id.* at 229 (quoting *Baker v. Carr,* 369 U.S. at 217), the Court responded:

> The political question doctrine excludes from judicial review those controversies which revolve around policy choices and value determinations constitutionally committed for resolution to the halls of Congress or the confines of the Executive Branch. The Judiciary is particularly ill suited to make such decisions, as "courts are

> fundamentally underequipped to formulate national policies or develop standards for matters not legal in nature." . . .
>
> As *Baker* plainly held, however, the courts have the authority to construe treaties and executive agreements, and it goes without saying that interpreting congressional legislation is a recurring and accepted task for the federal courts. It is also evident that the challenge to the Secretary's decision not to certify Japan for harvesting whales in excess of [ICRW] quotas presents a purely legal question of statutory interpretation. The Court must first determine the nature and scope of the duty imposed upon the Secretary by the Amendments, a decision which calls for applying no more than the traditional rules of statutory construction, and then applying this analysis to the particular set of facts presented below. We are cognizant of the interplay between these Amendments and the conduct of this Nation's foreign relations, and we recognize the premier role which both Congress and the Executive play in this field. But under the Constitution, one of the Judiciary's characteristic roles is to interpret statutes, and we cannot shirk this responsibility merely because our decision may have significant political overtones.

478 U.S. at 229–30 (footnote omitted).

Do the Court's decisions in *Japan Whaling* and *Zivotofsky* suggest that courts must always retain the power to interpret the legality of executive policy when there is a statute or treaty to guide the exercise of executive discretion? Does this limit the political question doctrine to cases in which the Executive is acting under a constitutional authority unfettered by statute or treaty? Or do you agree with Justices Sotomayor and Breyer that even in circumstances where there is a statute or treaty, the political question doctrine may sometimes have salience? If those two Justices agreed on the applicable law, why did they disagree on the outcome in *Zivotofsky*?

Notwithstanding the outcome in *Zivotofsky*, some U.S. courts have applied the political question doctrine so as to dismiss cases relating to foreign affairs, even in situations where the application of a statute is at issue. *See, e.g., Smith v. Obama*, 217 F. Supp. 3d 283 (D.D.C. 2016) (dismissing a claim against the president seeking a declaration that U.S. military action in Iraq and Syria was unconstitutional because Congress had not authorized it); *Mobarez v. Kerry*, 187 F. Supp. 3d 85 (D.D.C. 2016) (dismissing a claim seeking compliance with an alleged duty of the U.S. government to evacuate U.S. citizens from Yemen).

5. *Legislating the Political Question Doctrine*. Whether Congress may circumscribe the courts' recourse to the political question doctrine depends on the basis of the doctrine. If the doctrine is an interpretation of the Constitution's allocation of powers, then legislation seeking to alter or repeal an aspect of it would be unconstitutional. If the "prudential" formulation is correct—that is, if the doctrine is merely an instance of the courts' recourse to what Alexander Bickel has called "the passive virtues"—then legislation might compel justiciability. One article suggested that the Hickenlooper Amendment

to the Foreign Assistance Act of 1961—which requires courts to decide claims alleging foreign expropriation of U.S.-owned assets "on the merits giving effect to the principles of international law," 22 U.S.C. § 2370(e)(2) (2012), thus limiting the act of state doctrine—suggests that Congress might require the adjudication of cases otherwise falling within the political question doctrine. Thomas M. Franck & Clifford A. Bob, *The Return of Humpty-Dumpty: Foreign Relations Law After the* Chadha *Case*, 79 AM. J. INT'L L. 912, 957–59 (1985); *see Banco Nacional de Cuba v. Farr*, 383 F.2d 166, 181 n.18 (2d Cir. 1967) (leaving open "whether there might be a constitutional compulsion that the courts accept the direction of Congress even as to issues the Court has held to be nonjusticiable because they are 'political questions.' ").

2. POLITICAL QUESTION DOCTRINE AND THE WAR POWER

CAMPBELL V. CLINTON

203 F.3d 19 (D.C. Cir. 2000).

[Before reading this case, revisit the War Powers Resolution, 50 U.S.C. §§ 1541–1548, reprinted in Chapter 4, Sec. 4. The War Powers Resolution was a joint resolution passed by Congress over President Nixon's veto in 1973, in the wake of the Vietnam War. The Resolution addressed the issue of declaration of war by other means, enacting a framework for congressional involvement and approval of the use of force initiated unilaterally by the president. Some of Nixon's successors as president have also objected to the Resolution; its constitutionality and effectiveness remain a source of heated debate.]

SILBERMAN, CIRCUIT JUDGE:

A number of congressmen, led by Tom Campbell of California, filed suit claiming that the President violated the War Powers Resolution and the War Powers Clause of the Constitution by directing U.S. forces' participation in the recent NATO campaign in Yugoslavia. The district court dismissed for lack of standing. We agree with the district court and therefore affirm.

I.

On March 24, 1999, President Clinton announced the commencement of NATO air and cruise missile attacks on Yugoslav targets. Two days later he submitted to Congress a report, "consistent with the War Powers Resolution," detailing the circumstances necessitating the use of armed forces, the deployment's scope and expected duration, and asserting that he had "taken these actions pursuant to [his] authority . . . as Commander in Chief and Chief Executive." On April 28, Congress voted on four resolutions related to the Yugoslav conflict: It voted down a declaration of war 427 to 2 and an "authorization" of the air strikes 213 to 213, but it also voted against requiring the President to immediately end U.S. participation in the NATO operation and voted to fund that involvement. The conflict between NATO and Yugoslavia continued for 79 days, ending on June 10 with Yugoslavia's agreement to withdraw its forces from Kosovo and allow deployment of a NATO-led peacekeeping force. Throughout this period Pentagon, State Department, and NATO spokesmen informed the public on a frequent basis of developments in the fighting.

Appellants, 31 congressmen opposed to U.S. involvement in the Kosovo intervention, filed suit prior to termination of that conflict seeking a declaratory judgment that the President's use of American forces against Yugoslavia was unlawful under both the War Powers Clause of the Constitution and the War Powers Resolution ("the WPR"). *See* 50 U.S.C. § 1541 *et seq.* The WPR requires the President to submit a report within 48 hours "in any case in which United States Armed Forces are introduced . . . into hostilities or into situations where imminent involvement in hostilities is clearly indicated by the circumstances," and to "terminate any use of United States Armed Forces with respect to which a report was submitted (or required to be submitted), unless the Congress . . . has declared war or has enacted a specific authorization for such use of United States Armed Forces" within 60 days. Appellants claim that the President did submit a report sufficient to trigger the WPR on March 26, or in any event was required to submit a report by that date, but nonetheless failed to end U.S. involvement in the hostilities after 60 days. The district court granted the President's motion to dismiss, *see Campbell v. Clinton*, 52 F. Supp. 2d 34 (D.D.C. 1999), and this appeal followed.

II.

The government does not respond to appellants' claim on the merits. Instead the government challenges the jurisdiction of the federal courts to adjudicate this claim on three separate grounds: the case is moot; appellants lack standing, as the district court concluded; and the case is nonjusticiable. Since we agree with the district court that the congressmen lack standing it is not necessary to decide whether there are other jurisdictional defects. [For the Court's analysis of the standing issue, see *infra*, this Chapter, Sec. 5.] . . .

Accordingly, the district court is affirmed; appellants lack standing.

SILBERMAN, CIRCUIT JUDGE, concurring:

Appellants argued that we should consider in our standing analysis that if congressmen lack standing only military personnel might be able to challenge a President's arguably unlawful use of force, and it would be undesirable to put the armed forces in such a position. Although that is not a consideration that bears on standing, *see Schlesinger v. Reservists Comm. to Stop the War*, 418 U.S. 208, 227 (1974), that argument leads me to observe that, in my view, no one is able to bring this challenge because the two claims are not justiciable. We lack "judicially discoverable and manageable standards" for addressing them, and the War Powers Clause claim implicates the political question doctrine. *See Baker v. Carr*, 369 U.S. 186, 217 (1962).

Prior litigation under the WPR has turned on the threshold test whether U.S. forces are engaged in hostilities or are in imminent danger of hostilities. But the question posed by appellants—whether the President's refusal to discontinue American activities in Yugoslavia violates the WPR—necessarily depends on the statute having been triggered in the first place. It has been held that the statutory threshold standard is not precise enough and too obviously calls for a political judgment to be one suitable for judicial determinations. *See, e.g., Sanchez-Espinoza v. Reagan*, 770 F.2d 202, 209 (D.C. Cir. 1985) (aid to Contras); *Crockett v. Reagan*, 720 F.2d 1355, 1356–57 (D.C. Cir. 1983) (U.S. advisors in El Salvador); *see also Ange v. Bush,* 752 F. Supp. 509, 514 (D.D.C. 1990) (pre-Gulf War buildup); *Lowry v. Reagan,* 676 F. Supp. 333, 340 n. 53 (D.D.C. 1987) (reflagging operations in the Persian Gulf). I think that is correct. Appellants point to a House Report suggesting that hostilities for purposes of the WPR include all situations "where there is a reasonable expectation that American military personnel will be subject to hostile fire." See H.R. REP. NO. 287, 93rd Cong., 1st Sess. 7 (1973). That elaboration hardly helps. It could reasonably be thought that anytime American soldiers are confronted by armed or potentially armed forces of a non-ally there is a reasonable expectation that they will be subject to hostile fire. Certainly any competent military leader will assume that to be so.

Appellants argue that here there is no real problem of definition because this air war was so overwhelming and indisputable. It is asserted that the President implicitly conceded the applicability of the WPR by sending the report to Congress. In truth, the President only said the report was "consistent" with the WPR. In any event, I do not think it matters how clear it is in any particular case that "hostilities" were initiated if the statutory standard is one generally unsuited to judicial resolution.

Nor is the constitutional claim justiciable. Appellants contend this case is governed by *Mitchell v. Laird*, 488 F.2d 611, 614 (D.C. Cir. 1973), where we said that "[t]here would be no insuperable difficulty in a court determining whether" the Vietnam conflict constituted a war in the Constitutional sense. *See also Dellums v. Bush,* 752 F. Supp. 1141, 1146 (D.D.C. 1990) ("[T]he Court has no hesitation in concluding that an offensive entry into Iraq by several hundred thousand United States servicemen . . . could be described as a 'war' within the meaning . . . of the Constitution."). But a careful reading of both cases reveals that the language upon which appellants rely is only dicta. (In *Laird* the Court ultimately held that the resolution of the issues was a political question. *See* 488 F.2d at 616.).[1]

Appellants cannot point to any constitutional test for what is war. *See, e.g., Holtzman v. Schlesinger*, 414 U.S. 1316 (1973) (Justice Douglas, in chambers, vacating order of Court of Appeals granting stay of district court's injunction against bombing of Cambodia), 414 U.S. at 1321 (1973) (Justice Marshall, in chambers, granting stay the same day with the concurrence of the other Justices); *Holtzman v. Schlesinger,* 484 F.2d 1307 (2d Cir. 1973) (holding legality of Cambodia bombing nonjusticiable because courts lack expertise to determine import of various military actions). Instead, appellants offer a rough definition of war provided in 1994 by an Assistant Attorney General to four Senators with respect to a planned intervention in Haiti, as well as a number of law review articles each containing its own definition of war. I do not think any of these sources, however, offers a coherent test for judges to apply to the question what constitutes war, a point only accentuated by the variances, for instance, between the numerous law review articles. For that reason, I disagree with Judge Tatel's assertion that we can decide appellants' constitutional claim because it is somehow obvious in this case that our country fought a war. . . . *Baker v. Carr* speaks of a case involving "a lack of judicially discoverable and manageable standards for resolving" the issue presented, *see* 369 U.S. at 217, not just a case the facts of which are obscure; the focus is on the standards. Even if this court knows all there is to know about the Kosovo conflict, we still do not know what standards to apply to those facts.

Judge Tatel points to numerous cases in which a court has determined that our nation was at war, but none of these cases involved the question whether the President had "declared war" in violation of the Constitution. For instance, in *Bas v. Tingy*, 4 U.S. (4 Dall.) 37 (1800), the question whether there was a "war" was only relevant to determining whether France was an "enemy" within the meaning of a prize statute. *See id.* at 37 ("[T]he argument turned, principally, upon two inquiries: 1st. Whether the Act of March 1799, applied only to the event of a future general war? 2d. Whether France was *an enemy* of the United States, within the meaning of the law?"). Indeed, Justice Washington's opinion in that case, upon which Judge Tatel principally relies, suggests that whether there was a war in the constitutional sense was irrelevant. *See id.* at 42 ("Besides, it may be

1 The additional cases upon which Judge Tatel relies with respect to this point were also held to present political questions. *See Massachusetts v. Laird,* 451 F.2d 26, 34 (1st Cir. 1971) ("All we hold here is that in a situation of prolonged but undeclared hostilities, where the executive continues to act not only in the absence of any conflicting congressional claim of authority but with steady congressional support, the Constitution has not been breached."); *Orlando v. Laird,* 443 F.2d 1039, 1043 (2d Cir. 1971) (whether Vietnam conflict required a declaration of war was a political question); *Berk v. Laird,* 429 F.2d 302 (2d Cir. 1970) (denying a preliminary injunction against dispatch of soldier to Vietnam because whether Congress had authorized conflict was a political question).

asked, why should the rate of salvage be different in such a war as the present, from the salvage in a war more solemn [*i.e.,* a declared war] or general?"). It is similarly irrelevant that courts have determined the existence of a war in cases involving insurance policies and other contracts, the Federal Tort Claims Act, and provisions of the military criminal code applicable in "time of war." *See infra* . . . (Tatel, J., concurring). None of these cases asked whether there was a war as the Constitution uses that word, but only whether a particular statutory or contractual provision was triggered by some instance of fighting. Comparing *Bas v. Tingy*'s lengthy discussion whether our quarrel with France constituted a solemn or imperfect, general or limited war, *see* 4 U.S. at 40–41, with today's propensity to label any widespread conflict an undifferentiated war, it would not be surprising if an insurance contract's "war" provisions, or even a statute's for that matter, were triggered before the Constitution's.

Even assuming a court could determine what "war" is, it is important to remember that the Constitution grants Congress the power to declare war, which is not necessarily the same as the power to determine whether U.S. forces will fight in a war. This distinction was drawn in the *Prize Cases*, 67 U.S. (2 Black) 635 (1862). There, petitioners challenged the authority of the President to impose a blockade on the secessionist States, an act of war, where Congress had not declared war against the Confederacy. The Court, while recognizing that the President "has no power to initiate or declare a war," observed that "war may exist without a declaration on either side." *Id.* at 668. In instances where war is declared against the United States by the actions of another country, the President "does not initiate the war, but is bound to accept the challenge without waiting for any special legislative authority." *Id.* Importantly, the Court made clear that it would not dispute the President on measures necessary to repel foreign aggression. The President alone

> must determine what degree of force the crisis demands. The proclamation of blockade is itself official and conclusive evidence to the Court that a state of war existed which demanded and authorized a recourse to such a measure, under the circumstances peculiar to the case.

Id. at 670.[2] And, to confirm the independent authority of the President to meet foreign aggression, the Court noted that while Congress had

---

[2] Judge Tatel's reliance on the *Prize Cases* as an example of the Court concluding a war exists is misplaced because the Court itself did not label the Civil War such, but instead deferred to the President's determination that the country was at war. *See* 67 U.S. (2 Black) at 670 ("Whether the President in fulfilling his duties, as Commander-in-chief . . . has met with such armed hostile resistance . . . as will compel him to accord to them the character of belligerents, is a question to be decided by *him*, and this Court must be governed by the decisions and acts of the political department of the Government to which this power was entrusted") (emphasis in original). Therefore, the Court's assertion that "it is bound to notice and to know" the war, *see id.* at 667, provides no support for the proposition that a court itself may decide when in fact there is one. The *Prize Cases* thus refute the suggestion in *Talbot v. Seeman,* 5 U.S. (1 Cranch) 1, 28 (1801),

authorized the war, it may not have been required to: "*If* it were necessary to the technical existence of a war, that it should have a legislative sanction, we find it. . . ." *Id.* (emphasis added).

I read the *Prize Cases* to stand for the proposition that the President has independent authority to repel aggressive acts by third parties even without specific congressional authorization, and courts may not review the level of force selected. *See* Geoffrey Corn, *Presidential War Power: Do the Courts Offer Any Answers?,* 157 MIL. L. REV. 180, 214 (1998); J. Gregory Sidak, *To Declare War,* 41 DUKE L.J. 27, 54 (1991); Cyrus R. Vance, *Striking the Balance: Congress and the President Under the War Powers Resolution*, 133 U. PA. L. REV. 79, 85 (1984). Therefore, I assume, *arguendo*, that appellants are correct and only Congress has authority to *initiate* "war." If the President may direct U.S. forces in response to third-party initiated war, then the question any plaintiff who challenges the constitutionality of a war must answer is, who started it? The question of who is responsible for a conflict is, as history reveals, rather difficult to answer, and we lack judicial standards for resolving it. *See, e.g., Greenham Women Against Cruise Missiles v. Reagan*, 591 F. Supp. 1332, 1337–38 (S.D.N.Y. 1984) (court lacked judicially manageable standards to decide if placement of U.S. cruise missiles in England was a war-like, "aggressive" act). Then there is the problem of actually discovering the necessary information to answer the question, when such information may be unavailable to the U.S. or its allies, or unavailable to courts due to its sensitivity. *See id.* at 1338. Perhaps Yugoslavia did pose a threat to a much wider region of Europe and to U.S. civilian and military interests and personnel there.

Judge Tatel does not take into account the *Prize Cases* when he concludes that the President was not exercising his independent authority to respond to foreign aggression because "in fact, the Kosovo issue had been festering for years." *See infra* . . . (Tatel, J., concurring). As quoted above the President alone "must determine what degree of force the crisis demands." *See* 67 U.S. at 670. Judge Tatel would substitute our judgment for the President's as to the point at which an intervention for reasons of national security is justified, after which point—when the crisis is no longer acute—the President must obtain a declaration of war. One should bear in mind that Kosovo's tensions antedate the creation of this republic.

In most cases this will also be an issue of the greatest sensitivity for our foreign relations. Here, the President claimed on national television that our country needed to respond to Yugoslav aggression to protect our trading interests in Europe, and to prevent a replay of World War I. A pronouncement by another branch of the U.S. government that U.S. participation in Kosovo was "unjustified" would no doubt cause strains

that only acts of Congress are evidence of the existence of a war. *See infra* . . . (Tatel, J., concurring).

within NATO. *Cf. United States v. New*, 50 M.J. 729, 739–40 (Army Ct. Crim. App.1999) (lawfulness of U.N. peacekeeping operation in Macedonia was a political question).

In sum, there are no standards to determine either the statutory or constitutional questions raised in this case, and the question of whether the President has intruded on the war-declaring authority of Congress fits squarely within the political question doctrine. We therefore have another basis for our affirming the district court's dismissal of appellants' case. . . .

TATEL, CIRCUIT JUDGE, concurring:

Although I agree with Judge Silberman that *Raines v. Byrd*, 521 U.S. 811 (1997), as interpreted by this court in *Chenoweth v. Clinton*, 181 F.3d 112 (D.C. Cir. 1999), deprives plaintiffs of standing to bring this action, I do not share his view that the case poses a nonjusticiable political question. *See supra* (Silberman, J., concurring). In my view, were this case brought by plaintiffs with standing, we could determine whether the President, in undertaking the air campaign in Yugoslavia, exceeded his authority under the Constitution or the War Powers Resolution.

To begin with, I do not agree that courts lack judicially discoverable and manageable standards for "determining the existence of a 'war.' " Brief of Appellee at 36. *See also supra* . . . (Silberman, J., concurring). Whether the military activity in Yugoslavia amounted to "war" within the meaning of the Declare War Clause, U.S. CONST. art. I, § 8, cl. 11, is no more standardless than any other question regarding the constitutionality of government action. Precisely what police conduct violates the Fourth Amendment guarantee "against unreasonable searches and seizures?" When does government action amount to "an establishment of religion" prohibited by the First Amendment? When is an election district so bizarrely shaped as to violate the Fourteenth Amendment guarantee of "equal protection of the laws?" Because such constitutional terms are not self-defining, standards for answering these questions have evolved, as legal standards always do, through years of judicial decisionmaking. Courts have proven no less capable of developing standards to resolve war powers challenges.

Since the earliest years of the nation, courts have not hesitated to determine when military action constitutes "war." In *Bas v. Tingy*, 4 U.S. (4 Dall.) 37 (1800), the Supreme Court had to decide whether hostilities between France and the United States amounted to a state of war in order to resolve disputes over captured ships. Because outright war had not been declared, the justices examined both the facts of the conflict ("the scene of bloodshed, depredation and confiscation, which has unhappily occurred," *id.* at 39) and the acts of Congress that had authorized limited military action:

> In March 1799, congress had raised an army; stopped all intercourse with France; dissolved our treaty; built and equipt ships of war; and commissioned private armed ships; enjoining the former, and authorising the latter, to defend themselves against the armed ships of France, to attack them on the high seas, to subdue and take them as prize, and to re-capture armed vessels found in their possession.

Id. at 41. Given these events, Justice Bushrod Washington concluded that France and the United States were at war both "[i]n fact and in law." *Id.* at 42. "If they were not our enemies," he said, "I know not what constitutes an enemy." *Id.* at 41. One year later, Chief Justice Marshall, focusing on the same conflict with France, said: "The whole powers of war being, by the constitution of the United States, vested in congress, the acts of that body can alone be resorted to as our guides in this enquiry. . . . To determine the real situation of America in regard to France, the acts of congress are to be inspected." *Talbot v. Seeman*, 5 U.S. (1 Cranch) 1, 28 (1801).

Half a century later, in *The Prize Cases*, 67 U.S. (2 Black) 635, 666 (1862), the Court had to determine whether a state of war, though undeclared, existed "*de facto*" between the United States and the confederacy, and if so, whether it justified the U.S. naval blockade of confederate ports. "As a civil war is never publicly proclaimed, . . . its actual existence is a fact in our domestic history which the Court is bound to notice and to know." *Id.* at 667. There was no formal declaration of war, the Court explained, because the Constitution does not permit Congress to "declare war against a State, or any number of States." *Id.* at 668. Yet the Court, guided by the definition of war as "[t]hat state in which a nation prosecutes its right by force," *id.* at 666, determined that a state of war actually existed.

> A civil war is never solemnly declared; it becomes such by its accidents—the number, power, and organization of the persons who originate and carry it on. When the party in rebellion occupy and hold in a hostile manner a certain portion of territory; have declared their independence; have cast off their allegiance; have organized armies; have commenced hostilities against their former sovereign, the world acknowledges them as belligerents, and the contest *a war*.

Id. at 666–67. In making this determination, the Court looked to the facts of the conflict, *id.*, to the acts of foreign governments recognizing the war and declaring their neutrality, *id.* at 669, and to congressional action authorizing the President's use of force, *id.* at 670–71. Given these facts, the Court refused "to affect a technical ignorance of the existence of a war, which all the world acknowledges to be the greatest civil war known in the history of the human race." *Id.* at 669.

More recent cases have also recognized the competence of courts to determine whether a state of war exists. Responding to a challenge to the constitutionality of the Vietnam War, this circuit confronted "the critical question . . . whether the hostilities in Indo-China constitute *in the Constitutional sense* a 'war,' both within and beyond the meaning of that term in Article I, Section 8, Clause 11." *Mitchell v. Laird,* 488 F.2d 611, 614 (D.C. Cir. 1973) (emphasis added). The court found "no insuperable difficulty in a court determining whether," given the extent of the hostilities, "there has been a war in Indo-China." *Id.* Once the war was recognized as such, the court saw no problem in "facing up to the question as to whether because of the war's duration and magnitude the President is or was without power to continue the war without Congressional approval," or "whether Congress has given, in a Constitutionally satisfactory form, the approval requisite for a war of considerable duration and magnitude." *Id.* Nor did the court hesitate to determine that once the Gulf of Tonkin resolution had been repealed, later congressional actions appropriating funds for the war and extending the draft were insufficient to "serve as a valid assent to the Vietnam war." *Id.* at 615. Given this absence of congressional approval for the war's continuation, the President had a duty to try "in good faith and to the best of his ability, to bring the war to an end as promptly as was consistent with the safety of those fighting and with a profound concern for the durable interests of the nation—its defense, its honor, its morality." *Id.* at 616. Although the court ultimately declined to answer the question whether President Nixon was in fact fulfilling his duty to end the Vietnam War, *see id.*, it nonetheless made clear that courts are competent to adjudge the existence of war and the allocation of war powers between the President and Congress. Regardless of whether this language is dicta, *see supra* . . . (Silberman, J., concurring), *Mitchell* supports my view that this court could resolve the war powers claims presented here. *See also, e.g., Massachusetts v. Laird,* 451 F.2d 26, 34 (1st Cir. 1971) ("The war in Vietnam is a product of the jointly supportive actions of the two branches to whom the congeries of the war powers have been committed. Because the branches are not in opposition, there is no necessity of determining boundaries. Should either branch be opposed to the continuance of hostilities, however, and present the issue in clear terms, a court might well take a different view."); *Orlando v. Laird,* 443 F.2d 1039, 1042 (2d Cir. 1971) ("[T]he constitutional delegation of the war-declaring power to the Congress contains a discoverable and manageable standard imposing on the Congress a duty of mutual participation in the prosecution of war. Judicial scrutiny of that duty, therefore, is not foreclosed by the political question doctrine."); *Berk v. Laird,* 429 F.2d 302, 305 (2d Cir. 1970) ("History makes clear that the congressional power 'to declare War' conferred by Article I, section 8, of the Constitution was intended as an explicit restriction upon the power of the Executive to initiate war on his own prerogative which was enjoyed by the

British sovereign. . . . [E]xecutive officers are under a threshold constitutional duty which can be judicially identified and its breach judicially determined.") (internal quotation marks and brackets omitted).

Without undue difficulty, courts have also determined whether hostilities amount to "war" in other contexts. These have included insurance policies and other contracts, *see, e.g., Western Reserve Life Ins. Co. v. Meadows,* 152 Tex. 559, 567, 261 S.W.2d 554, 559 (1953) ("We are unwilling in deciding this case to shut our eyes to what everyone knows, that there has been . . . actually and in reality a war in Korea in which the United States has been seriously engaged."); *Pan Am. World Airways, Inc. v. Aetna Casualty & Sur. Co.,* 505 F.2d 989, 1012–15 (2d Cir. 1974); *Navios Corp. v. The Ulysses II,* 161 F. Supp. 932 (D. Md. 1958), *aff'd,* 260 F.2d 959 (4th Cir. 1958), the Federal Tort Claims Act, *see, e.g., Koohi v. United States,* 976 F.2d 1328 (9th Cir. 1992) (noting that even absent a formal declaration, "no one can doubt that a state of war existed when our armed forces marched first into Kuwait and then into Iraq"); *Rotko v. Abrams,* 338 F. Supp. 46, 47–48 (D. Conn. 1971), *aff'd,* 455 F.2d 992 (2d Cir. 1972), and provisions of military criminal law applicable "in time of war," *see, e.g., United States v. Anderson,* 17 U.S.C.M.A. 588, 1968 WL 5425 (1968); *United States v. Ayers,* 4 U.S.C.M.A. 220, 1954 WL 2280 (1954).

Although courts have thus determined the existence of war as defined by the Constitution, statutes, and contracts, in this case plaintiffs' War Powers Resolution claim would not even require that we do so. We would need to ask only whether, and at what time, "United States Armed Forces [were] introduced into hostilities or into situations where imminent involvement in hostilities [was] clearly indicated by the circumstances." 50 U.S.C. § 1543(a)(1). On this question, the record is clear. In his report to the Speaker of the House and the President pro tempore of the Senate, transmitted "consistent with the War Powers Resolution," President Clinton stated: "on March 24, 1999, U.S. military forces, at my direction . . . began a series of air strikes in the Federal Republic of Yugoslavia. . . ." 35 Weekly Comp. Pres. Doc. 527 (March 26, 1999), available at 1999 WL 12654381. Pursuant to the priority procedures of the War Powers Resolution, 50 U.S.C. §§ 1545–46, both houses of Congress responded by expediting consideration of resolutions to declare war, H.J. Res 44, to authorize airstrikes, S.J. Res. 20, and to withdraw troops, H. Con. Res. 82. Defense Secretary William Cohen told the Senate Armed Services Committee: "We're certainly engaged in hostilities, we're engaged in combat." Hearing on Kosovo, Senate Armed Services Comm., 106th Cong., April 15, 1999, 1999 WL 221637 (testimony of William Cohen, Secretary of Defense). President Clinton issued an Executive Order designating the region a U.S. combat zone and March 24 as "the date of the commencement of combatant activities in such zone." Exec. Order No. 13,119, 64 Fed. Reg. 18797 (Apr. 13, 1999).

The undisputed facts of this case are equally compelling with respect to plaintiffs' constitutional claim. If in 1799 the Supreme Court could recognize that sporadic battles between American and French vessels amounted to a state of war, and if in 1862 it could examine the record of hostilities and conclude that a state of war existed with the confederacy, then surely we, looking to similar evidence, could determine whether months of daily airstrikes involving 800 U.S. aircraft flying more than 20,000 sorties and causing thousands of enemy casualties amounted to "war" within the meaning of Article I, section 8, clause 11.

Determining whether a state of war exists would certainly be more difficult in situations involving more limited military force over a shorter period of time. But just as we never shrink from deciding a First Amendment case simply because we can imagine a more difficult one, the fact that a challenge to a different military action might present a closer question would not justify abdicating our responsibility to construe the law and apply it to the facts of this case.

Nor is the question nonjusticiable because the President, as Commander in Chief, possesses emergency authority to use military force to defend the nation from attack without obtaining prior congressional approval. Judge Silberman's suggestion notwithstanding, *see supra.* (Silberman, J., concurring), President Clinton does not claim that the air campaign was necessary to protect the nation from imminent attack. In his report to Congress, the President explained that the military action was "in response to the FRY government's continued campaign of violence and repression against the ethnic Albanian population in Kosovo." 35 Weekly Comp. Pres. Doc. 527 (Mar. 26, 1999), available at 1999 WL 12654381. Although the President also said that military action would prevent an expanded war in Europe, *see* Radio Address of the President to the Nation, March 27, 1999, available at 1999 WL 170552, he never claimed that an emergency required him to act without congressional authorization; in fact, the Kosovo issue had been festering for years. . . .

The government also claims that this case is nonjusticiable because it "requires a political, not a judicial, judgment." The government has it backwards. Resolving the issue in this case would require us to decide not whether the air campaign was wise—a "policy choice[ ] and value determination [ ] constitutionally committed for resolution to the halls of Congress or the confines of the Executive Branch," *Japan Whaling Ass'n v. American Cetacean Soc'y*, 478 U.S. 221, 230 (1986)—but whether the President possessed legal authority to conduct the military operation. Did the President exceed his constitutional authority as Commander in Chief? Did he intrude on Congress's power to declare war? Did he violate the War Powers Resolution? Presenting purely legal issues, these questions call on us to perform one of the most important functions of Article III courts: determining the proper constitutional allocation of power among the branches of government. Although our answer could well have political implications, "the presence of constitutional issues with significant political overtones does not automatically invoke the political question doctrine. Resolution of litigation challenging the constitutional authority of one of the three branches cannot be evaded by courts because the issues have political implications. . . ." *INS v. Chadha,* 462 U.S. 919, 942–43 (1983). *See also Baker v. Carr,* 369 U.S. 186, 217 (1962) ("The doctrine . . . is one of 'political questions,' not one of 'political cases.' The courts cannot reject as 'no law suit' a bona fide controversy as to whether some action denominated 'political' exceeds constitutional authority."). This is so even where, as here (and as in the other cases discussed above), the issue relates to foreign policy. *See Baker,* 369 U.S. at 211 ("[I]t is error to suppose that every case or controversy which touches foreign relations lies beyond judicial cognizance"). If "we cannot shirk [our] responsibility" to decide whether an Act of Congress requires the President to impose economic sanctions on a foreign nation for diminishing the effectiveness of an international treaty, a question rife with "political overtones," *Japan Whaling Ass'n,* 478 U.S. at 230, then surely we cannot shirk our responsibility to decide whether the President exceeded his constitutional or statutory authority by conducting the air campaign in Yugoslavia.

The Government's final argument—that entertaining a war powers challenge risks the government speaking with "multifarious voices" on a delicate issue of foreign policy—fails for similar reasons. Because courts are the final arbiters of the constitutionality of the President's actions, "there is no possibility of 'multifarious pronouncements' on this question." *Chadha,* 462 U.S. at 942. Any short-term confusion that judicial action might instill in the mind of an authoritarian enemy, or even an ally, is but a small price to pay for preserving the constitutional separation of powers and protecting the bedrock constitutional principle that "[i]t is emphatically the province and duty of the judicial department to say what the law is." *Marbury v. Madison*, 5 U.S. (1 Cranch) 137 (1803).

NOTES

1. *Suing to Challenge Uses of Force That Violate U.S. Law.* Throughout the lengthy and controversial period of the Vietnam War, various lower courts confronted cases challenging the war as unconstitutional, which in turn produced several distinct theories as to the basis for, and extent of, the political question doctrine. *Luftig v. McNamara,* 373 F.2d 664, 665–66 (D.C. Cir. 1967) (per curiam); *Mora v. McNamara,* 387 F.2d 862 (D.C. Cir. 1967) (per curiam); *Orlando v. Laird*, 443 F.2d 1039 (2d Cir. 1971); *DaCosta v. Laird*, 448 F.2d 1368 (2d Cir. 1971); *Holtzman v. Schlesinger*, 484 F.2d 1307 (2d Cir. 1973). Throughout this period, the Supreme Court successfully evaded the issue denying certiorari to the appeals of *Luftig*, *Mora*, *Orlando*, *DaCosta* (I) and *Holtzman*. Justice Douglas often dissented, noting his *Baker v. Carr* concurrence that "[t]he category of the 'political' question is, in my view,

narrower than the decided cases indicate." 369 U.S. 186, 246 n. 3 (1962). In *DaCosta*, he stated:

> This Court, of course, should give deference to the coordinate branches of the Government. But we did not defer in the *Prize Cases*, 2 Black 635, 17 L.Ed. 459, when the issue was presidential power as Commander in Chief to order a blockade. We did not defer in the *Steel Seizure Case,* when the issue was presidential power, in time of armed international conflict, to order the seizure of domestic steel mills. Nor should we defer here, when the issue is presidential power to seize, not steel, but people. See *Mass. I, supra*, at 891–900.
>
> The Constitution gives Congress the power "To declare War," Art. I, § 8; and it is argued that the Constitution gives to Congress the *exclusive* power to determine when it has declared war. But if there is such a "textually demonstrable constitutional commitment," *Baker v. Carr,* 369 U.S. 186, 217, it is for this Court to determine its scope. *Powell v. McCormack,* 395 U.S. 486, 521. See *Mass. I, supra*, at 892.
>
> While we debate whether to decide the constitutionality of this war, our countrymen are daily compelled to undergo the physical and psychological tortures of armed combat on foreign soil. Families and careers are disrupted; young men maimed and disfigured; lives lost. The issues are large; they are precisely framed; we should decide them.

405 U.S. 979, 979–81 (1972) (footnotes omitted).

While *Clinton v. Campbell* ultimately turned on an issue of standing, the political question doctrine nevertheless featured in the case, as it has in other circumstances where the president has resorted to a use of military force in the absence of congressional authorization. For example, in *Lowry v. Reagan,* suit was brought by members of Congress to enforce the War Powers Resolution with respect to U.S. deployments in the so-called "tanker war" in the Persian Gulf in the 1980s, charging that U.S. involvement constituted military actions that must be approved by Congress. In finding that the case presented a non-justiciable political question, the Court of Appeals stated:

> Appellants' first claim, that United States Armed Forces are currently involved in present or imminent hostilities in the Persian Gulf, presents a nonjusticiable political question. The claim is in essence that hostilities remain present or imminent because the Gulf cease-fire is unstable. An assessment of the cease-fire's stability, however, would require an inquiry into the likely intentions of the Iranian and Iraqi governments. Although we express no view as to the justiciability of other claims under § 4(a)(1), we hold that an inquiry of this sort is beyond the judicial competence.

Lowry v. Reagan, No. 87–5426 (D.C. Cir. Oct. 1, 1988) (per curiam).

2. *Suing to Challenge Uses of Force That Violate International Law*. Can a suit (or a defensive claim) be brought in U.S. court challenging whether the federal government is violating international law in resorting to the use of armed force? For example, should the judiciary entertain complaints arising from U.S. Armed Forces' negligent exercise of police protection during occupation of a foreign territory? *See Industria Panificadora v. United States*, 763 F.Supp. 1154, 1159–61 (D.D.C. 1991) (dismissing as political question suit by Panamanian corporations to recover for damage to property, which was looted or destroyed by Panamanian civilians during the American military operation to remove General Noriega); *see also Nejad v. United States*, 724 F.Supp. 753, 755 (C.D. Cal. 1989) (dismissing as political question suit by families and dependents of passengers who died aboard Iranian airliner shot down by missile from U.S.S. *Vincennes*); *Chaser Shipping Corp. v. United States*, 649 F.Supp. 736, 737–40 (S.D.N.Y. 1986), *aff'd mem.*, 819 F.2d 1129 (2d Cir. 1987) (dismissing as political question suit by shipowners whose vessels were damaged by U.S. mines in Nicaraguan port).

As a part of the defense in his criminal trial in U.S. court, deposed Panamanian leader Manuel Noriega sought to argue that the U.S. invasion of Panama in 1989 was unlawful. The court responded:

> Noriega does not, and legally cannot, allege that President Bush exceeded his powers as Commander-in-Chief in ordering the invasion of Panama. Rather, he asks this Court to find that the deaths of innocent civilians and destruction of private property is "shocking to the conscience and in violation of the laws and norms of humanity." At bottom, then, Noriega's complaint is a challenge to the very morality of war itself. This is a political question in its most paradigmatic and pristine form. It raises the specter of judicial management and control of foreign policy and challenges in a most sweeping fashion the wisdom, propriety, and morality of sending armed forces into combat—a decision which is constitutionally committed to the executive and legislative branches and hence beyond judicial review. Questions such as under what circumstances armed conflict is immoral, or whether it is always so, are not ones for the courts, but must be resolved by the political branches entrusted by the Constitution with the awesome responsibility of committing this country to battle.

United States v. Noriega, 746 F.Supp. 1506, 1538–39 (S.D. Fla. 1990), *aff'd*, 117 F.3d 1206 (11th Cir. 1997).

3. *Suing Against U.S. Military Goals, Directives, or Tactics*. In general, courts refuse to hear challenges to the military establishment, its goals, directives, or tactics. *See Gilligan v. Morgan*, 413 U.S. 1, 5–12 (1973) (congressional and executive authority to prescribe and regulate training, weaponry, programs, and standing orders of the National Guard precludes any form of judicial regulation). In other cases nearly unreviewable discretion is found vested in the political branches. *See, e.g., Chappell v. Wallace*, 462 U.S.

296, 300 (1983) (Court refused to entertain suit to recover damages by enlisted military personnel against a superior officer for alleged constitutional violations since the special nature of the military requires two systems of justice and the judiciary is ill-equipped to regulate military discipline); *Parker v. Levy,* 417 U.S. 733, 749–56 (1974) (special nature and needs that differentiate military society from civil society barred court consideration of legality of more encompassing regulations defining criminal conduct and restricting First Amendment rights in the military); *Orloff v. Willoughby*, 345 U.S. 83, 90 (1953) (commissioning of officers in Army is matter of discretion within the province of the president over which the courts have no control); *Bancoult v. McNamara*, 445 F.3d 427 (D.C. Cir. 2006) (forced depopulation of an island in the Chagos archipelago in the Indian Ocean for construction of a U.S. naval base is a nonreviewable political question).

In 2006, the D.C. Circuit refused to entertain a petition for a writ of *habeas corpus* by a U.S. servicemember who was convicted by a court-martial for violating an order to add the U.N. insignia to his uniform when he was deployed as part of a peacekeeping force in Macedonia, a mission he viewed as unlawful. The decision conveyed a willingness to defer broadly to a military court's application of the political question doctrine.

> Two of the canonical factors from *Baker v. Carr,* 369 U.S. 186, 217 (1962), "an unusual need for unquestioning adherence to a political decision already made," 369 U.S. at 217, and "the potentiality of embarrassment from multifarious pronouncements by various departments on one question," *id.,* are uniquely powerful when the context is a soldier's use of the "self-help remedy of disobedience." Also supporting a broader sweep to the political question doctrine in military trials is the point made by Judge Effron in his concurring opinion-that the doctrine "ensur[es] that courts-martial do not become a vehicle for altering the traditional relationship between the armed forces and the civilian policymaking branches of government" by adjudicating the legality of political decisions. *Id.* at 110. Thus we find no defect in the Court of Appeals' application of the political question doctrine, even though that application might be highly contestable in another context. Compare *Campbell v. Clinton,* 203 F.3d 19, 24–28 (D.C. Cir. 2000) (Silberman, J., concurring) (finding that no "judicially discoverable and manageable standards" exist for application of the Constitution's war powers clause or the War Powers Resolution, 50 U.S.C. § 1541 *et seq.*), with *id.* at 37–41 (Tatel, J., concurring) (concluding that such standards do exist). Given the threat to military discipline, see Court-Martial Transcript at 433, we have no difficulty accepting the military courts' reliance on the doctrine.

United States ex rel. New v. Rumsfeld, 448 F.3d 403, 411 (D.C. Cir. 2006).

At the same time, a challenge by press members to media pool regulations promulgated by armed forces overseas during the First Gulf War did not present a political question. *Nation Magazine v. United States Department of Defense,* 762 F.Supp. 1558, 1566–68 (S.D.N.Y. 1991). The central issues involved press access and inequality of treatment, which have only an incidental relationship to American foreign policy; they raise claims judicially enforceable under the First and Fifth Amendments. For commentary, see Tom Dienes, *When the First Amendment Is Not Preferred: The Military and Other "Special Contexts,"* 56 U. CINN. L. REV. 779 (1988); Note, *Judicial Review of Constitutional Claims against the Military,* 84 COLUM. L. REV. 387 (1984); Note, *Judicial Review and Soldiers' Rights: Is the Principle of Deference a Standard of Review?,* 17 HOFSTRA L. REV. 465 (1989).

4. *Suing for Wrongful Acts of Foreign Forces.* Should the political question analysis be affected if the alleged misconduct was committed by another country's armed forces? *See In re Korean Air Lines Disaster,* 597 F.Supp. 613, 616–17 (D.D.C. 1984) (dismissing as political question suits arising from deaths of passengers aboard a Korean airliner allegedly shot down by Soviet military aircraft). A key problem in bringing such a suit is not just justiciability, but sovereign immunity as well. *See infra*, this Chapter, Sec. 7.

5. *Commentary.* For further commentary, see David Cole, *Challenging Covert War: The Politics of the Political Question Doctrine,* 26 HARV. INT'L L.J. 155 (1985); Michael Ratner & David Cole, *The Force of Law: Judicial Enforcement of the War Powers Resolution,* 17 LOY. L.A.L. REV. 715 (1984); Patrick Robbins, *The War Powers Resolution After Fifteen Years: A Reassessment*, 38 AM. U.L. REV. 141 (1988); Note, *Covert Wars and Presidential Power: Judicial Complicity in a Realignment of Constitutional Power,* 14 HASTINGS CONST. L.Q. 683 (1987); Jonathan L. Entin, *The Dog That Rarely Barks: Why the Courts Won't Resolve the War Powers Debate*, 47 CASE W. RES. L. REV. 1305 (1997); John C. Yoo, *Judicial Review and the War on Terrorism*, 72 GEO. WASH. L. REV. 427 (2003); Jonathan L. Entin, *War Powers, Foreign Affairs, and the Courts: Some Institutional Considerations*, 45 CASE W. RES. J. INT'L L. 443 (2012).

3. POLITICAL QUESTION DOCTRINE WHEN PROTECTING RIGHTS OF INDIVIDUALS

AL SHIMARI V. CACI PREMIER TECHNOLOGY

840 F.3d 147 (4th Cir. 2016).

BARBARA MILANO KEENAN, CIRCUIT JUDGE:

Suhail Al Shimari, Taha Rashid, Salah Al-Ejaili, and Asa'ad Al-Zuba'e (the plaintiffs), four Iraqi nationals, alleged that they were abused while detained in the custody of the United States Army at Abu Ghraib prison, located near Baghdad, Iraq, in 2003 and 2004. They were detained beginning in the fall of 2003, and ultimately were released without being charged with a crime. In 2008, they filed this civil action against CACI

Premier Technology, Inc. (CACI), which provided contract interrogation services for the military at the time of the alleged mistreatment.

In their third amended complaint, the plaintiffs alleged pursuant to the Alien Tort Statute (ATS), 28 U.S.C. § 1350, that CACI employees committed acts involving torture and war crimes, and cruel, inhuman, or degrading treatment. The plaintiffs also asserted various tort claims under the common law, including assault and battery, sexual assault and battery, and intentional infliction of emotional distress. . . .

The political question doctrine derives from the principle of separation of powers, and deprives courts of jurisdiction over "controversies which revolve around policy choices and value determinations constitutionally committed" to Congress or, as alleged in this case, to the executive branch. *Japan Whaling Ass'n v. Am. Cetacean Soc'y*, 478 U.S. 221, 230 (1986). This doctrine is a "narrow exception" to the judiciary's general obligation to decide cases properly brought before the courts. *Zivotofsky v. Clinton*, 566 U.S. 189 (2012). Although most military decisions are committed exclusively to the executive branch, a claim is not shielded from judicial review merely because it arose from action taken under orders of the military.

The Supreme Court established a six-factor test in *Baker v. Carr*, 369 U.S. 186 (1962) (the *Baker* factors), to aid courts in determining whether a case presents a political question. . . .

In *Taylor v. Kellogg Brown & Root Services, Inc.*, 658 F.3d 402 (4th Cir. 2011), we considered the proper application of the Baker factors to cases involving the civil liability of a government contractor in a negligence case. We distilled the *Baker* factors into two questions for consideration in determining whether a court has subject matter jurisdiction in a suit against a government contractor. We first asked "whether the government contractor was under the 'plenary' or 'direct' control of the military" (direct control). Second, we asked whether "national defense interests were 'closely intertwined' with military decisions governing the contractor's conduct, such that a decision on the merits of the claim 'would require the judiciary to question actual, sensitive judgments made by the military.' " An affirmative response to either of the two *Taylor* factors, namely, the fact of direct control or the need to question sensitive military judgments, generally triggers application of the political question doctrine. . . .

[Authors' Note: The appeals court concluded that the district court had not adequately assessed the two *Taylor* factors.] Accordingly, on remand, the district court will be required to determine which of the alleged acts, or constellations of alleged acts, violated settled international law and criminal law governing CACI's conduct and, therefore, are subject to judicial review. The district court also will be required to identify any "grey area" conduct that was committed under the actual control of the military or involved sensitive military judgments and, thus, is protected under the political question doctrine. . . .

Distinct from its holding of non-justiciability under *Taylor*, the district court separately concluded under the second *Baker* factor that the case lacked manageable standards for judicial resolution of the plaintiffs' claims. The court emphasized that its general lack of expertise in applying international law, and the difficulty of determining the constraints of such law, also rendered the case non-justiciable. We disagree with the district court's conclusion.

Unlike in negligence cases calling into question military standards of conduct, the district court in the present case is called upon to interpret statutory terms and established international norms to resolve the issues presented by the ATS claims.

With regard to the present case, the terms "torture" and "war crimes" are defined at length in the United States Code and in international agreements to which the United States government has obligated itself. *See, e.g.*, 18 U.S.C. §§ 2340–2340A (implementing the United States' obligations as a signatory of the Convention Against Torture and Other Cruel, Inhuman or Degrading Treatment or Punishment); 18 U.S.C. § 2441 (prescribing criminal penalties under the United States Code for "war crimes," including "grave breaches" of the Geneva Conventions). Courts also have undertaken the challenge of evaluating whether particular conduct amounts to torture, war crimes, or cruel, inhuman, or degrading treatment. *See, e.g.*, *United States v. Belfast*, 611 F.3d 783, 828 (11th Cir. 2010) (torture); *Kadic* [*v. Karadzic*], 70 F.3d at 243 (war crimes and torture); *Xuncax v. Gramajo*, 886 F.Supp. 162, 187 (D. Mass. 1995) (torture and cruel, inhuman, or degrading treatment). Likewise, in his common law claims, Al Shimari has alleged familiar torts based on long-standing common law principles.

Although the substantive law applicable to the present claims may be unfamiliar and complicated in many respects, we cannot conclude that we lack manageable standards for their adjudication justifying invocation of the political question doctrine. In reaching this conclusion, we agree with the observation that courts may not "decline to resolve a controversy within their traditional competence and proper jurisdiction simply because the question is difficult, the consequences weighty, or the potential real for conflict with the policy preferences of the political branches." *Zivotofsky*, 132 S.Ct. at 1432 (Sotomayor, J., concurring in part and concurring in the judgment); *cf. Hamdi*, 542 U.S. at 536 ("Whatever power the United States Constitution envisions for the Executive in its exchanges with other nations or with enemy organizations in times of conflict, it most assuredly envisions a role for all three branches when individual liberties are at stake.") (opinion of O'Connor, J.). . . .

We recognize that the legal issues presented in this case are indisputably complex, but we nevertheless cannot abdicate our judicial role in such cases. Nor will we risk weakening prohibitions under United States and international law against torture and war crimes by questioning the justiciability of a case merely because the case involves the need to define such terms. The political question doctrine does not shield from judicial review intentional acts by a government contractor that were unlawful at the time they were committed.

Accordingly, we vacate the district court's judgment, and remand this case for further proceedings consistent with the principles and instructions stated in this opinion.

NOTES

1. *The Distinct Treatment of Individual and Constitutional Rights.* As the *Al Shimari* case demonstrates, some complaints alleging violations of individual or constitutional rights by government action have been found appropriate for judicial review, even though they implicate the conduct of foreign relations. Chief Justice Marshall first made this distinction in *Marbury v. Madison,* qualifying his assertion of absolute executive discretion in political subjects:

> It follows then that the question, whether the legality of an act of the head of a department be examinable in a court of justice or not, must always depend on the nature of that act.
>
> If some acts be examinable, and others not, there must be some rule of law to guide the court in the exercise of its jurisdiction.
>
> In some instances there may be difficulty in applying the rule to particular cases; but there cannot, it is believed, be much difficulty in laying down the rule.
>
> By the constitution of the United States, the President is invested with certain important political powers, in the exercise of which he is to use his own discretion, and is accountable only to his country in his political character, and to his own conscience. To aid him in the performance of these duties, he is authorized to appoint certain officers, who act by his authority and in conformity with his orders.
>
> In such cases, their acts are his acts; and whatever opinion may be entertained of the manner in which executive discretion may be used, still there exists, and can exist, no power to control that discretion. The subjects are political. They respect the nation, not individual rights, and being entrusted to the executive, the decision of the executive is conclusive. The application of this remark will be perceived by adverting to the act of congress for establishing the department of foreign affairs. This officer, as his duties were prescribed by that act, is to conform precisely to the will of the

> President. He is the mere organ by whom that will is communicated. The acts of such an officer, as an officer, can never be examinable by the courts.
>
> But when the legislature proceeds to impose on that officer other duties; when he is directed peremptorily to perform certain acts; when the rights of individuals are dependent on the performance of those acts; he is so far the officer of the law; is amenable to the laws for his conduct; and cannot at his discretion sport away the vested rights of others.

1 Cranch (5 U.S.) 137, 165–66 (1803). Is it fair to say that "there cannot . . . be much difficulty in laying down the rule," insofar as it depends on the presence or absence of the rights of individuals? How narrowly, or broadly, should we construe Marshall's reference to "the act of congress for establishing the department of foreign affairs"?

Although it is hazardous to generalize, it would appear that courts have been more reluctant to embrace the political question doctrine in cases involving alleged constitutional violations. *See, e.g., Lamont v. Woods*, 948 F.2d 825, 831–34 (2d Cir. 1991) (Walker, J., concurring in the result) (permitting federal taxpayers' Establishment Clause challenge to the appropriation and expenditure of public funds by the United States for the construction, maintenance and operation of foreign religious schools); *Ukrainian-American Bar Ass'n v. Baker*, 893 F.2d 1374, 1380 (D.C. Cir. 1990) (permitting claim by organization seeking to integrate persons of Ukrainian descent into the United States that it has a First Amendment right to provide counsel to aliens from Soviet or Eastern Bloc countries seeking asylum); *Planned Parenthood Fed'n, Inc. v. AID*, 838 F.2d 649, 653–54 (2d Cir. 1988) (permitting First Amendment challenge to clause inserted by the executive branch in family planning grants barring federal assistance to foreign nongovernmental organizations that perform abortions); *Langenegger v. United States,* 756 F.2d 1565, 1568–70 (Fed. Cir. 1985) (permitting claim regarding whether the United States had effected an illegal taking of a citizen's coffee plantation in El Salvador by prompting expropriation of the plantation by the Government of El Salvador); *Ramirez de Arellano v. Weinberger*, 745 F.2d 1500 (D.C. Cir. 1984) (similar claim concerning illegal taking in Honduras).

At the same time, "[t]he political question doctrine bars . . . review of claims that, regardless of how they are styled, call into question the prudence of the political branches in matters of foreign policy or national security committed to their discretion"—suggesting that the mere fact that a case involves individual rights, even those of private citizens, should not be dispositive. *El-Shifa Pharmaceutical Indus. v. United States*, 607 F.3d 836, 842 (D.C. Cir. 2010). *El-Shifa* stemmed from an American cruise missile strike on a Sudanese pharmaceutical plant that the United States believed to be associated with Osama bin Laden. The plaintiffs, the company owning the plant and its individual owner, sued under the Federal Tort Claims Act seeking compensation for the plant's destruction and for retraction of associated allegations that they were involved in terrorism. The en banc majority held that whether compensation was due because the plant's destruction was " 'mistaken and not justified'," and whether the government's justifications for the attack were false and defamatory, ultimately called into question the decision to launch a military strike abroad and posed nonjusticiable political questions. *Id.* at 844–49. Did the court err? Three judges concurred in the judgment on the ground that the plaintiffs' claims were so legally insubstantial as to deprive the federal courts of subject matter jurisdiction. As to the political question analysis, however, they stressed that the complaint had not alleged the violation of constitutional rights, but only "that the Executive Branch violated congressionally enacted statutes that purportedly constrain the Executive," and that "[t]he Supreme Court has never applied the political question doctrine in cases involving statutory claims of this kind." *Id.* at 852, 855 (Kavanaugh, J., concurring in the judgment). As the opinion explained, applying the political question doctrine under such circumstances would at least implicitly decide that Congress was without capacity to constrain the executive branch and "would systematically favor the Executive Branch over the Legislative Branch—without the courts' acknowledging as much or grappling with the critical separation of powers and Article II issues." *Id.* at 857. Do you find this position persuasive, both in its distinction of statutory rights and its interrogation of the result? Would the concurrence's dismissal for lack of subject matter jurisdiction, which the majority critiqued as expanding that avenue considerably, *id.* at 849–50, accomplish the same thing under a different guise?

2. *The Distinct Character of Alien Tort Statute Cases*. As the *Al Shimari* case suggests, the political question doctrine arises with some frequency in Alien Tort Statute (ATS) cases. Such cases often entail a wariness by courts toward claims predicated on customary international law, and the Supreme Court's suggestion—not formalized, or tied directly to the political question doctrine—of a possible limitation consisting of "case-specific deference to the political branches." *Sosa v. Alvarez-Machain*, 542 U.S. 692, 733 n.21 (2004); *see* Chapter 2, Sec. 6.

Before and after *Sosa*, the lower courts have struggled to distinguish and apply these objections to adjudicating ATS claims. *See, e.g., Gonzalez-Vera v. Kissinger*, 449 F.3d 1260, 1262–64 (D.C. Cir. 2006) (dismissing on political question grounds claims brought, *inter alia*, under the ATS, against the former Secretary of State and National Security Adviser based on human rights abuses allegedly carried out by Chilean government); *Schneider v. Kissinger*, 412 F.3d 190 (D.C. Cir. 2005) (similar); *In re XE Services Alien Tort Litigation*, 665 F. Supp. 2d 569, 601–02 (E.D. Va. 2009) (declining to dismiss on political question grounds action brought by Iraqi nationals against eleven business entities under, *inter alia*, the ATS, in part because while the defendants allegedly killed or seriously injured the plaintiffs while providing security services for United States government, adjudication of the claims would not require "second-guessing the battlefield procedures, plans, or decisions of the United States Armed Forces, or of any government entity"); *Lizarbe v. Rondon*,

642 F. Supp. 2d 473, 485–87 (D. Md. 2009) (declining to dismiss on political question grounds action brought against a former Peruvian Army officer under, *inter alia*, the ATS, because allegations of extrajudicial killing, torture, and war crimes arising out of a massacre in a Peruvian village during a civil war did not relate to any policy decision of the United States or any conduct of U.S. armed forces), *aff'd on other grounds,* 402 Fed. Appx. 834 (4th Cir. 2010) (unpublished op.); *In re South African Apartheid Litigation*, 617 F. Supp. 2d 228, 283–85 (S.D.N.Y. 2009) (declining to dismiss on political question grounds an action brought on behalf of individuals who suffered damages as result of crimes of apartheid in South Africa).

Some courts have indicated that the political question doctrine is less germane because separation of powers principles are not implicated when actions are brought against private parties—at least so long as the private parties were not carrying out policies of the United States. Indeed, the private party may have been acting contrary to those policies. *See Al-Quraishi v. Nakhla*, 728 F. Supp. 2d 702, 726–32 (D. Md. 2010) (declining to dismiss on political question grounds action by Iraqi citizens formerly detained at various military prisons in Iraq against military contractor under, *inter alia*, the ATS, and discussing comparable cases). Of course, determining whether the complained-of acts were within the scope of U.S. policy may be difficult and sensitive. *See, e.g., Corrie v. Caterpillar, Inc.*, 503 F.3d 974, 979–84 (9th Cir. 2007) (dismissing on political question grounds claims against U.S. manufacturer of bulldozers used by Israeli Defense Forces to demolish homes in the Palestinian Territories and financed by Foreign Military Financing program adopted by Congress and administered by the executive branch).

Other courts have been guided by statements of interest filed by the executive branch that support dismissal. *See, e.g., Matar v. Dichter*, 500 F. Supp. 2d 284, 293–96 (S.D.N.Y. 2007) (holding nonjusticiable as political question a class action brought by citizens injured or killed in bombing of Gaza apartment building against former head of Israeli General Security Service (GSS) under, *inter alia*, the ATS, because the claims implicated anti-terrorism policies and diplomacy and "elicited request for dismissal from Department of State and Israel"), *aff'd on other grounds*, 563 F.3d 9 (2d Cir. 2009); *Mujica v. Occidental Petroleum Corp.*, 381 F. Supp. 2d 1164 (C.D. Cal. 2005) (dismissing on political question grounds action brought, *inter alia*, under the ATS, by Colombian citizens against oil company and private security firm based on bombing of village by Colombian military, in part because the United States had already expressed its disapproval of Colombian military's actions by ending military assistance to unit involved in bombing and the State Department submitted that litigation would interfere with its approach to encouraging protection of human rights in Colombia), *vacated and remanded on other grounds*, 564 F.3d 1190 (9th Cir. 2009). Courts have also been guided by statements of interest that declined to support dismissal on political question grounds or that appeared equivocal. *See, e.g., Kadic v. Karadzic*, 70 F.3d 232, 248–50 (2d Cir. 1995) (declining to dismiss on political question grounds action against self-proclaimed president of unrecognized Bosnian-

Serb entity under, *inter alia*, the ATS, and noting that the State Department's statement of interest expressly disclaimed suggesting the political question doctrine should be invoked).

One interesting borderline case is *Doe v. Exxon Mobil Corp.*, 473 F.3d 345 (D.C. Cir. 2007), which involved a suit by Indonesian villagers who claimed that Exxon had employed as its security forces Indonesian military members who subjected the villagers to various human rights abuses. The district court solicited a letter from the State Department's Legal Adviser as to whether adjudication of plaintiffs' claims would adversely impact U.S. foreign policy interests. The Legal Adviser subsequently advised that the litigation "would in fact risk a potentially serious adverse impact on significant interests of the United States," principally by harming U.S. relations with Indonesia and discouraging foreign investment in Indonesia; however, the letter cautioned that these potential effects on U.S.-Indonesian relations "cannot be determined with certainty." 473 F.3d at 347. When the lower court refused to dismiss the plaintiffs' common law tort claims as raising non-justiciable political questions, 393 F. Supp. 2d 20 (D.D.C. 2005), Exxon-Mobil filed an interlocutory appeal. The D.C. Circuit Court of Appeals found that the district court's decision was not an immediately appealable collateral order, and that Exxon could not be granted its requested writ of mandamus because the district court had not clearly and indisputably exceeded its jurisdiction by refusing dismissal on political question grounds, explaining that:

> We interpret the State Department's letter not as an unqualified opinion that this suit must be dismissed, but rather as a word of caution to the district court alerting it to the State Department's concerns. Indeed, the fact that the letter refers to "how the case might unfold in the course of the litigation" shows that the State Department did not necessarily expect the district court to immediately dismiss the case in its entirety. Thus, we need not decide what level of deference would be owed to a letter from the State Department that *unambiguously* requests that the district court dismiss a case as a non-justiciable political question. *See Sosa v. Alvarez-Machain,* 542 U.S. 692, 733 n. 21 (2004) (suggesting that when the State Department files a statement of interest "there is a strong argument that federal courts should give serious weight to the Executive Branch's view of the case's impact on foreign policy"). Of course, if we have misinterpreted this letter, or if the State Department has additional concerns about this litigation, it is free to file further letters or briefs with the district court expressing its views. *Cf. Republic of Austria v. Altmann,* 541 U.S. 677, 701 (2004) (noting that "nothing in our holding prevents the State Department from filing statements of interest suggesting that courts decline to exercise jurisdiction in particular cases implicating foreign sovereign immunity"). But given the letter before us in the record, we cannot say it is "indisputable" that the district court erroneously failed to dismiss the plaintiffs' claims under the political question doctrine, no

matter what level of deference is owed to the State Department's letter.

Id. at 354.

If the State Department's letter was an unqualified opinion that the suit must be dismissed, should a federal court be bound to defer to that opinion? (And would it matter if the letter cited as a basis the political question doctrine, or the *Sosa* footnote concerning "case-specific deference to the political branches"?) Should a court be bound by a letter that is an unqualified opinion that the suit must go forward? Would it matter if the U.S. government were a party in the case? Should a letter sent to the court on behalf of Congress calling either for or against dismissal also be given deference? What if the political branches are in conflict?

In reviewing the issue subsequent to its decision on interlocutory appeal, the D.C. Circuit stood by its analysis and refused to dismiss on political question grounds. *Doe v. Exxon Mobil Corp.*, 654 F.3d 11 (D.C. Cir. 2011). Ultimately, after the Supreme Court's 2013 decision in *Kiobel v. Royal Dutch Petroleum Co.,* 569 U.S. 108 (2013) (*see* Chapter 2, Sec. 6), the district court refused to dismiss on political question grounds because "there [was an] insufficiently recent and definite statement from the Executive that this case interfere[d] with the foreign policy of the United States." *Doe v. Exxon Mobil Corp.*, 69 F. Supp. 3d 75, 92 (D.D.C. 2014).

3. *The Distinct Character of Political Question Determinations.* Although courts may be reluctant to deem nonjusticiable cases involving individual and constitutional rights, decisions on the merits often give considerable deference to government explanations for challenged governmental conduct. *See Haig v. Agee*, 453 U.S. 280 (1981) (president, through Secretary of State, has authority to revoke passport in order to restrict holder's ability to travel to foreign countries where his activities may damage national security or foreign policy of the United States). The courts' reasoning often reflects traditional political question concerns. In the context of immigration and naturalization, the Supreme Court has stated that "any policy toward aliens is vitally and intricately interwoven with contemporaneous policies in regard to the conduct of foreign relations, the war power, and the maintenance of a republican form of government. Such matters are so exclusively trusted to the political branches of government as to be largely immune from judicial inquiry or interference." *Harisiades v. Shaughnessy*, 342 U.S. 580, 588–89 (1952); *see also Mathews v. Diaz*, 426 U.S. 67, 81 (1976) (in cases involving rights of aliens courts should use a narrow standard of review to allow for "flexibility in policy choices rather than the rigidity often characteristic of constitutional adjudication"). One Supreme Court case suggested in a footnote that it was an open question "whether there may be actions of the Congress with respect to aliens that are so essentially political in character as to be non-justiciable." *Fiallo v. Bell*, 430 U.S. 787, 793 n.5 (1977).

Just as some merits decisions may conceal political question concerns, cases nominally decided on political question grounds may just as easily be depicted as involving the merits. *See, e.g., Smith v. Reagan,* 844 F.2d 195, 198–200 (4th Cir. 1988) (dismissing as political question a challenge to the adequacy of the president's efforts, required by the Hostage Act, to secure release of American citizens who remain in captivity in Southeast Asia).

4. *Detainees, Habeas, and the Political Question Doctrine.* Many cases in the "War on Terror" hinge on the justiciability of *habeas corpus* petitions, both statutory and constitutional. In cases such as *Hamdi, Hamdan,* and *Rasul* (*see* Chapter 2, Sec. 7), the Supreme Court has remained remarkably silent on the issue of justiciability, including the political question doctrine. One case overtly addressing the political question doctrine in this context was *Omar v. Harvey*, 479 F.3d 1 (D.C. Cir. 2007), which confronted a petition for a writ of *habeas corpus* from a dual American-Jordanian citizen arrested in Iraq and held at first at various military detention facilities there. The petitioner challenged his detention, on the ground that it violated the U.S. Constitution, federal law, Army regulations, and international law; he also challenged plans to transfer him to Iraqi custody, arguing that the military lacked statutory or treaty authorization to do so and that transferring him to a government likely to torture him would violate the Constitution. The court of appeals concluded that both claims were justiciable. As to detention, it relied primarily on *Hamdi*, acknowledging that *Hamdi* did not directly involve a political question issue. As to transfer, the court held that whether the executive branch possessed the necessary statutory or treaty authorization, or needed it, presented difficult questions of constitutional law that could be "resolve[d] without making any judgments about foreign policy or the war in Iraq."

The Supreme Court later vacated the court of appeals decision. *Munaf v. Geren*, 553 U.S. 674 (2008). The Court concluded that jurisdiction was properly exercised over *habeas corpus* petitions by U.S. citizens challenging their detention by multinational forces operating under the direction of U.S. military leaders in Iraq. *Id.* at 685–88 (distinguishing *Hirota v. MacArthur*, 338 U.S. 197 (1948)). However, it also held that this jurisdiction was not properly exercised to enjoin the U.S. military from "transferring individuals detained within another sovereign's territory to that sovereign's government for criminal prosecution," bearing in mind both the need to avoid intruding on executive branch authority in military and national security matters and the respect owed Iraq's right to punish criminal offenses committed within its territory. *Id.* at 689, 692–700. Regarding the claim that the transferees would be mistreated, the Court noted that the U.S. government had not determined there to be a likelihood of torture and that second-guessing that conclusion would undermine the capacity of the United States to speak with one voice in foreign affairs. *Id.* at 702–03. At bottom, did the Supreme Court's emphasis on separation of power considerations and the need to defer to the executive branch differ so radically from accepting a political question defense to the transfer claim?

4. RIPENESS AND MOOTNESS

In addition to the political question doctrine, other judicial doctrines may also come into play in the context of foreign affairs litigation. The doctrines of ripeness and mootness generally determine whether judicial review is appropriate as a temporal matter. Specifically, the doctrine of ripeness focuses on whether certain cases are premature for review because the injury is speculative or may even never occur. The doctrine of mootness focuses on whether there still exists a true case or controversy; that is, whether a decision of the court will have any practical significance.

DOE V. BUSH

323 F.3d 133, 134–39 (1st Cir. 2003).

LYNCH, CIRCUIT JUDGE.

Plaintiffs are active-duty members of the military, parents of military personnel, and members of the U.S. House of Representatives.[1] They filed a complaint in district court seeking a preliminary injunction to prevent the defendants, President George W. Bush and Secretary of Defense Donald Rumsfeld, from initiating a war against Iraq. They assert that such an action would violate the Constitution. The district court dismissed the suit, and plaintiffs appeal. We affirm the dismissal.

In October 2002, Congress passed the Authorization for Use of Military Force Against Iraq Resolution of 2002 (the "October Resolution"), Pub L. No. 107–243, 116 Stat. 1498. Plaintiffs argue that the October Resolution is constitutionally inadequate to authorize the military offensive that defendants are now planning against Iraq. *See* U.S. Const. art. I, § 8, cl. 11 (granting Congress the power "[t]o declare war"). They base this argument on two theories. They argue that Congress and the President are in collision—that the President is about to act in violation of the October Resolution. They also argue that Congress and the President are in collusion—that Congress has handed over to the President its exclusive power to declare war.

In either case, plaintiffs argue, judicial intervention is necessary to preserve the principle of separation of powers which undergirds our constitutional structure. Only the judiciary, they argue, has the constitutionally assigned role and the institutional competence to police the boundaries of the constitutional mandates given to the other branches:

---

1 The military personnel and some of the parents are proceeding under pseudonyms, pursuant to an order by the district court that is not before us. The members of the House of Representatives are John Conyers, Dennis Kucinich, Jesse Jackson, Jr., Sheila Jackson Lee, Jim McDermott, José E. Serrano, Danny K. Davis, Maurice D. Hinchey, Carolyn Kilpatrick, Pete Stark, Diane Watson, and Lynn C. Woolsey. We also acknowledge the assistance provided by amicus curiae on behalf of the plaintiffs.

Congress alone has the authority to declare war and the President alone has the authority to make war.

The plaintiffs argue that important and increasingly vital interests are served by the requirement that it be Congress which decides whether to declare war. Quoting Thomas Jefferson, they argue that congressional involvement will slow the "dogs of war"; that Congress, the voice of the people, should make this momentous decision, one which will cost lives; and that congressional support is needed to ensure that the country is behind the war, a key element in any victory. They also argue that, absent an attack on this country or our allies, congressional involvement must come prior to war, because once war has started, Congress is in an uncomfortable default position where the use of its appropriations powers to cut short any war is an inadequate remedy.

The defendants are equally eloquent about the impropriety of judicial intrusion into the "extraordinarily delicate foreign affairs and military calculus, one that could be fatally upset by judicial interference." Such intervention would be all the worse here, defendants say, because Congress and the President are in accord as to the threat to the nation and the legitimacy of a military response to that threat.

The case before us is a somber and weighty one. We have considered these important concerns carefully, and we have concluded that the circumstances call for judicial restraint. The theory of collision between the legislative and executive branches is not suitable for judicial review, because there is not a ripe dispute concerning the President's acts and the requirements of the October Resolution passed by Congress. By contrast, the theory of collusion, by its nature, assumes no conflict between the political branches, but rather a willing abdication of congressional power to an emboldened and enlarged presidency. That theory is not fit for judicial review for a different, but related, reason: Plaintiffs' claim that Congress and the President have transgressed the boundaries of their shared war powers, as demarcated by the Constitution, is presently insufficient to present a justiciable issue. Common to both is our assessment that, before courts adjudicate a case involving the war powers allocated to the two political branches, they must be presented with a case or controversy that clearly raises the specter of undermining the constitutional structure.[2]

I.

Tensions between the United States and Iraq have been high at least since Iraq invaded neighboring Kuwait in 1990. In 1991, the United States

---

[2] We do not reach all the issues concerning the justiciability of the case, including the question of the parties' standing. There is no required sequence to the consideration of the various non-merits issues presented here. *See Ruhrgas AG v. Marathon Oil Co.*, 526 U.S. 574, 584–85 (1999); *In re Middlesex Power Equip. & Marine, Inc.*, 292 F.3d 61, 66 n. 1 (1st Cir. 2002).

led an international coalition in the Persian Gulf War, which drove Iraqi forces from Kuwait. Before that conflict, Congress passed a resolution quite similar to the October Resolution. *See* Pub. L. No. 102–1, 105 Stat. 3 (1991). As part of the ceasefire ending the Gulf War, Iraq agreed to United Nations Security Council Resolution 687, which required that Iraq end the development of nuclear, biological, and chemical weapons, destroy all existing weapons of this sort and their delivery systems, and allow United Nations weapons inspections to confirm its compliance with these terms. *See* S.C. Res. 687, U.N. SCOR, 46th Sess., 2981st mtg., U.N. Doc. S/RES/687 (1991). Since that time, Iraq has repeatedly been in breach of this agreement by, among other things, blocking inspections and hiding banned weapons. Iraq ended cooperation with the weapons inspection program in 1998. Since 1991, the United States and other nations have enforced a no-fly zone near the Kuwaiti border and on several occasions have launched missile strikes against Iraq.

Congress has been engaged in the American response to Iraqi noncompliance throughout this period. It was well-informed about ongoing American military activities, enforcement of the no-fly zone, and the missile strikes. In 1998, Congress passed a joint resolution which chronicled Iraqi noncompliance and declared that "the Government of Iraq is in material and unacceptable breach of its international obligations, and therefore the President is urged to take appropriate action, in accordance with the Constitution and relevant laws of the United States, to bring Iraq into compliance with its international obligations." Pub. L. No. 105–235, 112 Stat. 1538, 1541 (1998). Later that year, Congress also passed the Iraq Liberation Act of 1998, Pub. L. No. 105–338, 112 Stat. 3178. This statute authorized assistance, including military equipment and training, for "Iraqi democratic opposition organizations," and declared that it should be United States policy to remove Iraqi leader Saddam Hussein from power. *Id.* §§ 3, 4, 112 Stat. at 3179.[3]

The United Nations has also remained engaged in the dispute ever since the Persian Gulf War. It supervised weapons inspections, supported economic sanctions against Iraq, and, through the Security Council, repeatedly passed resolutions declaring that Iraq was not fulfilling the conditions of Resolution 687. On September 12, 2002, President Bush addressed the United Nations General Assembly. There he called for a renewed effort to demand Iraqi disarmament and indicated that he thought military force would be necessary if diplomacy continued to fail. In response, Iraq agreed to allow inspectors back into the country, but it has failed to comply fully with the earlier Security Council resolutions.

---

[3] Another provision of the Iraq Liberation Act stated that, other than the military assistance provision in § 4(a)(2), the Act should not "be construed to authorize or otherwise speak to the use of United States Armed Forces." § 8, 112 Stat. at 3181. Nonetheless, this statute provides important context.

The week after his September 12 speech at the United Nations, President Bush proposed language for a congressional resolution supporting the use of force against Iraq. Detailed and lengthy negotiations between and among congressional leaders and the Administration hammered out a revised and much narrower version of the resolution. The House of Representatives passed this measure by a vote of 296 to 133 on October 10, 2002; the Senate followed suit on October 11 by a vote of 77 to 23. The full text of the October Resolution is attached as an appendix to this opinion.

On November 8, 2002, the Security Council passed Resolution 1441, which declared that Iraq remained in material breach of its obligations and offered "a final opportunity to comply with its disarmament obligations." S.C. Res. 1441, U.N. SCOR, 57th Sess., 4644th mtg., U.N. Doc. S/RES/1441 (2002). It also noted that "the Council has repeatedly warned Iraq that it will face serious consequences as a result of its continued violations of its obligations." *Id.* In diplomatic parlance, the phrase "serious consequences" generally refers to military action. More than 200,000 United States troops are now deployed around Iraq, preparing for the possibility of an invasion.

The complaint was filed, along with motions for preliminary injunction and expedited hearing, on February 13, 2003. The district court heard oral argument on February 24 and denied the motion in an order issued that day. The court released a more detailed written opinion on February 27. *See Doe v. Bush,* 240 F. Supp. 2d 95 (D. Mass. 2003). Plaintiffs appealed and this court expedited consideration, hearing oral argument on March 4, 2003 and receiving additional briefing on March 11. Because the case was dismissed on a pretrial motion, we independently review the claims afresh.

II.

The Constitution reserves the war powers to the legislative and executive branches. This court has declined the invitation to become involved in such matters once before. Over thirty years ago, the First Circuit addressed a war powers case challenging the constitutionality of the Vietnam War on the basis that Congress had not declared war. *Massachusetts v. Laird*, 451 F.2d 26 (1st Cir. 1971). The court found that other actions by Congress, such as continued appropriations to fund the war over the course of six years, *id.* at 34, provided enough indication of congressional approval to put the question beyond the reach of judicial review:

> The war in Vietnam is a product of the jointly supportive actions of the two branches to whom the congeries of the war powers have been committed. Because the branches are not in opposition, there is no necessity of determining boundaries. Should either branch be opposed to the continuance of hostilities, however, and present

> the issue in clear terms, a court might well take a different view. This question we do not face.

Id. Applying this precedent to the case at hand today, the district court concluded, "[T]here is a day to day fluidity in the situation that does not amount to resolute conflict between the branches—but that does argue against an uninformed judicial intervention," *Doe*, 240 F. Supp. 2d at 96. *See Drinan v. Nixon*, 364 F. Supp. 854, 858 (D. Mass. 1973); *see also DaCosta v. Laird,* 471 F.2d 1146, 1157 (2d Cir. 1973); *Orlando v. Laird,* 443 F.2d 1039, 1043 (2d Cir. 1971); *cf. United States v. Kin-Hong*, 110 F.3d 103, 111 (1st Cir. 1997) (drawing support from political question doctrine in case where "questions involve an evaluation of contingent political events").

The lack of a fully developed dispute between the two elected branches, and the consequent lack of a clearly defined issue, is exactly the type of concern which causes courts to find a case unripe. In his concurring opinion in *Goldwater v. Carter*, 444 U.S. 996 (1979), Justice Powell stated that courts should decline, on ripeness grounds, to decide "issues affecting the allocation of power between the President and Congress until the political branches reach a constitutional impasse." *Id.* at 997 (Powell, J., concurring). A number of courts have adopted Justice Powell's ripeness reasoning in cases involving military powers. *See Greenham Women Against Cruise Missiles v. Reagan*, 755 F.2d 34, 37 (2d Cir. 1985) (per curiam); *Dellums v. Bush,* 752 F.Supp. 1141, 1150 & nn. 23–25 (D.D.C. 1990); *see also Sanchez-Espinoza v. Reagan,* 770 F.2d 202, 210–11 (D.C. Cir. 1985) (R. Ginsburg, J., concurring).

Ripeness doctrine involves more than simply the timing of the case. It mixes various mutually reinforcing constitutional and prudential considerations. *See Mangual v. Rotger-Sabat*, 317 F.3d 45, 59 (1st Cir. 2003). One such consideration is the need "to prevent the courts, through avoidance of premature adjudication, from entangling themselves in abstract disagreements." *Abbott Labs. v. Gardner*, 387 U.S. 136, 148 (1967). Another is to avoid unnecessary constitutional decisions. *Reg'l Rail Reorganization Act Cases,* 419 U.S. 102, 138 (1974). A third is the recognition that, by waiting until a case is fully developed before deciding it, courts benefit from a focus sharpened by particular facts. *See Ohio Forestry Ass'n v. Sierra Club,* 523 U.S. 726, 736 (1998). The case before us raises all three of these concerns.

These rationales spring, in part, from the recognition that the scope of judicial power is bounded by the Constitution. "It is a principle of first importance that the federal courts are courts of limited jurisdiction." C.A. Wright & M.K. Kane, *Law of Federal Courts* 27 (6th ed. 2002). Article III of the Constitution limits jurisdiction to "cases" and "controversies," and prudential doctrines may counsel additional restraint.

The ripeness of a dispute is determined de novo. *Stern v. U.S. Dist. Court,* 214 F.3d 4, 10 (1st Cir. 2000). Ripeness is dependent on the circumstances of a particular case. *See Ernst & Young v. Depositors Econ. Prot. Corp.*, 45 F.3d 530, 535 (1st Cir. 1995) ("[T]he various integers that enter into the ripeness equation play out quite differently from case to case. . . ."). Two factors are used to evaluate ripeness: "the fitness of the issues for judicial decision and the hardship to the parties of withholding court consideration." *Abbott Labs.,* 387 U.S. at 149. Ordinarily, both factors must be present. *Ernst & Young,* 45 F.3d at 535.

The hardship prong of this test is most likely satisfied here; the current mobilization already imposes difficulties on the plaintiff soldiers and family members, so that they suffer "present injury from a future contemplated event." *McInnis-Misenor v. Me. Med. Ctr.*, 319 F.3d 63, 70 (1st Cir. 2003). Plaintiffs also lack a realistic opportunity to secure comparable relief by bringing the action at a later time. *See Ohio Forestry,* 523 U.S. at 734.[4]

The fitness inquiry here presents a greater obstacle. Fitness "typically involves subsidiary queries concerning finality, definiteness, and the extent to which resolution of the challenge depends upon facts that may not yet be sufficiently developed." *Ernst & Young*, 45 F.3d at 535. The baseline question is whether allowing more time for development of events would "significantly advance our ability to deal with the legal issues presented [or] aid us in their resolution." *Duke Power Co. v. Carolina Envtl. Study Group*, 438 U.S. 59, 82 (1978); *see Ohio Forestry*, 523 U.S. at 737; *Regional Rail,* 419 U.S. at 144–45; *Gun Owners' Action League v. Swift,* 284 F.3d 198, 208–09 (1st Cir. 2002); *R.I. Ass'n of Realtors v. Whitehouse*, 199 F.3d 26, 34 (1st Cir. 1999). "[T]he question of fitness does not pivot solely on whether a court is capable of resolving a claim intelligently, but also involves an assessment of whether it is appropriate for the court to undertake the task." *Ernst & Young,* 45 F.3d at 537. These prudential considerations are particularly strong in this case, which presents a politically-charged controversy involving momentous issues, both substantively (war and peace) and constitutionally (the powers of coequal branches). *See Dellums*, 752 F. Supp. at 1149.

One thrust of the plaintiffs' argument is that the October Resolution only permits actions sanctioned by the Security Council.[5] In plaintiffs'

[4] Defendants, citing *Ange v. Bush,* 752 F.Supp. at 515, assert that no claim can ever be ripe until an attack has actually occurred. We would be reluctant to accept this assertion; it would seem to say that a case cannot be ripe on the basis of reasonably predictable future injury. This is not the law. "[T]he doctrine of ripeness . . . asks whether an injury that has not yet happened is sufficiently likely to happen to warrant judicial review." *Gun Owners' Action League v. Swift,* 284 F.3d 198, 205 (1st Cir. 2002) (internal quotation omitted).

[5] Plaintiffs argue that § 3(a) of the October Resolution, which authorizes use of force to "defend the national security of the United States . . . and . . . enforce all relevant United Nations Security Council resolutions," 116 Stat. at 1501, excludes any action that is not called for by a

view, the Resolution's authorization is so narrow that, even with Security Council approval of military force, Congress would need to pass a new resolution before United States participation in an attack on Iraq would be constitutional. At a minimum, according to plaintiffs, the October Resolution authorizes no military action "outside of a United Nations coalition."

For various reasons, this issue is not fit now for judicial review. For example, should there be an attack, Congress may take some action immediately. The purported conflict between the political branches may disappear. "[T]hat the future event may never come to pass augurs against a finding of fitness." *McInnis-Misenor,* 319 F.3d at 72.

Many important questions remain unanswered about whether there will be a war, and, if so, under what conditions. Diplomatic negotiations, in particular, fluctuate daily. The President has emphasized repeatedly that hostilities still may be averted if Iraq takes certain actions. The Security Council is now debating the possibility of passing a new resolution that sets a final deadline for Iraqi compliance. United Nations weapons inspectors continue their investigations inside Iraq. Other countries ranging from Canada to Cameroon have reportedly pursued their own proposals to broker a compromise. As events unfold, it may become clear that diplomacy has either succeeded or failed decisively. The Security Council, now divided on the issue, may reach a consensus. To evaluate this claim now, the court would need to pile one hypothesis on top of another. We would need to assume that the Security Council will not authorize war, and that the President will proceed nonetheless. *See id.* at 72–73 (outlining chain of uncertain events necessary to make case ripe); *Ernst & Young,* 45 F.3d at 538 (same).

Thus, even assuming that plaintiffs correctly interpret the commands of the legislative branch, it is impossible to say yet whether or not those commands will be obeyed. As was the situation in *Goldwater*, "[i]n the present posture of this case, we do not know whether there will ever be an actual confrontation between the Legislative and Executive Branches." 444 U.S. at 998 (Powell, J., concurring).

Dismissal of the complaint is *affirmed.*

WHITNEY V. OBAMA

845 F.Supp.2d 136 (D.D.C. 2012).

RICHARD W. ROBERTS, DISTRICT JUDGE.

Plaintiff Mark Whitney brought this action for declaratory and injunctive relief against President Barack Obama and the United States,

---

Security Council resolution. They support their reading by reference to the October Resolution's preamble and to legislative history.

challenging under the War Powers Resolution the President's authority to deploy United States armed forces to Libya. The defendants have filed a suggestion of mootness, arguing that the military activity of which the plaintiff complains ended in 2011. . . .

BACKGROUND

On March 17, 2011, the United Nations Security Council approved Resolution 1973 (2011), which imposed a no-fly zone over Libya and authorized "all necessary measures" other than foreign occupation to "end . . . the current attacks against civilians" in that country. By March 28, 2011, President Obama "commit[ted] U.S. forces to the U.N.-authorized military mission in Libya[.]" He announced that the U.S. would "play 'a supporting role—including intelligence, logistical support, search-and-rescue assistance, and capabilities to jam regime communications[.]' " "[F]ollowing the death of [Libyan leader] Muammar Qaddafi and the defeat of Qaddafi-regime forces" on October 23, "the [U.S.] ceased air operations in support of" Operation Unified Protector on October 31. The U.S. military personnel remaining in Libya are there to support the diplomatic mission. . . .

I. THE MOOTNESS BAR

"It is a basic constitutional requirement that a dispute before a federal court be 'an actual controversy . . . extant at all stages of review, [and] not merely at the time the complaint is filed.' " *Newdow v. Roberts*, 603 F.3d 1002, 1008 (D.C.Cir. 2010). " '[W]hat makes [a judicial pronouncement] a proper judicial resolution of a "case or controversy" rather than an advisory opinion [ ] is in the settling of some dispute *which affects the behavior of the defendant towards the plaintiff.*' " *Nat'l Ass'n of Home Builders v. Salazar*, 827 F.Supp.2d 1, 7–8, Civil Action No. 10–832(GK), 2011 WL 6097988, at *6 (D.D.C. Dec. 8, 2011) (emphasis in original). If " 'the issues presented are no longer "live" or the parties lack a legally cognizable interest in the outcome[,]' " the case is considered moot. *Honeywell Int'l, Inc. v. Nuclear Regulatory Comm'n*, 628 F.3d 568, 576 (D.C.Cir.2010)). Moot cases "must be dismissed[,]" *id.*, where "events outrun the controversy such that the court can grant no meaningful relief," *Del Monte Fresh Produce Co. v. United States*, 570 F.3d 316, 326 (D.C.Cir.2009) (Sentelle, J., dissenting).

The defendants, who bear the "heavy burden" of establishing mootness, *Honeywell*, 628 F.3d at 576, describe how the actions Whitney challenged in 2011 had ceased by 2012. Whitney sought to enjoin the defendants from continuing U.S. military participation in NATO Operation Unified Protector, which was undertaken to "protect civilians from attack or the threat of attack in Libya." In October of 2011, President Obama recognized the Libyan Transitional National Council's declaration of liberation, and NATO announced that the "Alliance's job to protect civilians from the threat of attack [wa]s done." The United Nations Security Council likewise terminated the "use-of-force provisions of resolution 1973 (2011)," effective October 31, 2011. Since "the alleged 'hostilities' that formed the basis for plaintiff's challenges in his Complaint[ ] have ended[ ]", the defendants conclude that Whitney's challenge to "[U.S.] support for these international operations in Libya is moot[.]" . . .

The D.C. Circuit found a similar challenge to be moot in 1985. *Conyers v. Reagan*, 765 F.2d 1124 (D.C.Cir.1985). In *Conyers*, eleven members of Congress challenged the military invasion of Grenada in October of 1983 as violative of the War Powers Clause of the United States Constitution. The President, who "stated that he ordered the invasion to protect innocent lives," withdrew all combat troops by December 15 of that year. However, "[a]pproximately 300 United States military personnel remained in Grenada to maintain order and assist in training the Grenadian police force." By the time the case reached the D.C. Circuit, "the actions complained of ha[d] long since ended[.]" Accordingly, the D.C. Circuit dismissed the appeal as moot and remanded the case for the district court to vacate its judgment. The court also described as "dubious" the plaintiffs' "attempt to avoid mootness" by arguing "that the mere presence of military personnel in Grenada, under peaceful circumstances, continues to violate the War Powers Clause."

In light of *Conyers*, Whitney's claims have become moot. . . .

II. THE EXCEPTION TO THE BAR

The D.C. Circuit has recognized the "capable of repetition, yet evading review" exception to the mootness doctrine when "intervening events beyond the [parties'] control . . . appear to have rendered the claims moot." *Conyers*, 765 F.2d at 1128 n. 9. "[A] controversy is capable of repetition, yet evading review where both of the following two requirements are met: 1) the challenged action [is] in its duration too short to be fully litigated prior to its cessation or expiration, and 2) there [is] a reasonable expectation that the same complaining party [will] be subjected to the same action again." *Habitat for Horses v. Salazar*, No. 10 Civ. 7684, 2011 WL 4343306, at *4 (S.D.N.Y. Sept. 7, 2011). Under the evading review prong, courts must "determine whether the activity challenged is 'inherently' of a sort that evades review[.]" *Campbell v. Clinton*, 203 F.3d 19, 34 (D.C.Cir.2000) (citation omitted) (Randolph, J., concurring). Since "offensive wars initiated without congressional approval are not in th[is] category[,]" neither are mere military missions "inherently short in duration." *Id.*; *Conyers*, 765 F.2d at 1128. Whitney has not demonstrated that this dispute evades review.

Neither does Whitney satisfy the "capable of repetition" prong, since there is no "reasonable expectation" that Whitney will suffer the same alleged violation of the War Powers Resolution again. *Honeywell*, 628 F.3d at 576. . . .

CONCLUSION

The military activities Whitney sought to enjoin have ended. The case is moot, and Whitney has established no applicable exception to the mootness bar. Accordingly, the complaint will be dismissed.

NOTES

1. *Ripeness*. Do you find the court's decision in *Doe v. Bush* convincing? Is it not better for a court to contemplate the legality of the resort to war in a setting where an attack is *not* imminent, in order to provide suitable time for briefing by the parties and careful deliberation by the court? If the bombers are about to take off and the ballistic missiles are being warmed up, is it not a bit late for judicial intervention? Or is the court right that it would be premature to act before that point, since perhaps the rumor of war will prove only to be a rumor?

The plaintiffs' second claim in *Doe v. Bush* stated that Congress and the president were in "collusion" to effect a "willing abdication of congressional power to an emboldened and enlarged presidency." This the court refused to entertain on justiciability grounds, though it did not explicitly invoke the political question doctrine:

> In this zone of shared congressional and presidential responsibility, courts should intervene only when the dispute is clearly framed. . . .
>
> Questions about the structure of congressional power can be justiciable under the proper circumstances. But courts are rightly hesitant to second-guess the form or means by which the coequal political branches choose to exercise their textually committed constitutional powers. As the circumstances presented here do not warrant judicial intervention, the appropriate recourse for those who oppose war with Iraq lies with the political branches.

323 F.3d at 143–44 (internal citations omitted). Plaintiffs' subsequent petition for a rehearing based on intervening events was dismissed on March 18. The court found that "the case continues not to be fit for judicial review." *John Doe I v. Bush*, 322 F.3d 109, 110 (1st Cir. 2003).

2. *Mootness*. Do you find the court's decision in *Whitney v. Obama* convincing? Does the outcome suggest that short-term uses of force by the president may never be capable of judicial review?

Section 2 above contained excerpts from the case of *Campbell v. Clinton*, 203 F.3d 19 (D.C. Cir. 2000), with respect to the political question doctrine. Recall that in *Campbell*, certain members of Congress argued that a presidential decision to conduct airstrikes against Yugoslavia conflicted with the War Powers Resolution. Although the D.C. Circuit dismissed the case on the basis of the political question doctrine, the U.S. government argued in the alternative that it should be dismissed on grounds of mootness. Judge Randolph in his concurring opinion addressed that argument:

> The amended complaint, filed on May 19, 1999, sought a declaratory judgment "that no later than May 25, 1999, the President must terminate the involvement of the United States Armed Forces in such hostilities unless Congress declares war, or enacts other explicit authorization, or has extended the sixty day period." Amended Complaint at 12; *see* 50 U.S.C. § 1544(b)(1)–(2). All agree that the "hostilities" ended by June 21, 1999, after NATO's Secretary General announced the official termination of the air campaign and Secretary of Defense Cohen announced the redeployment of more than 300 U.S. aircraft back to their home bases.
>
> To save their case from mootness, plaintiffs therefore invoke the rule regarding issues "capable of repetition, yet evading review." *Southern Pacific Terminal Co. v. ICC,* 219 U.S. 498, 515 (1911); *Christian Knights of the Ku Klux Klan v. District of Columbia*, 972 F.2d 365, 369–71 (D.C. Cir. 1992). Plaintiffs must, but cannot, satisfy both elements to prevail. Their constitutional and statutory claims are at cross purposes.
>
> The "evading review" part of the formulation is temporal. How quickly must an activity begin and end to evade judicial review? This depends on which court does the reviewing. The Supreme Court has treated the matter in terms of itself. Hence evading review means evading Supreme Court review, *see Christian Knights,* 972 F.2d at 369, which can be (though usually is not) swift review. *See, e.g., New York Times Co. v. United States*, 403 U.S. 713 (1971); *Buckley v. Valeo*, 424 U.S. 1 (1976). Some undeclared wars, or in the euphemism of the day, "hostilities," are over quickly; others, like the Korean War and the war in Vietnam, last for years. Circuit precedent requires us to determine whether the activity challenged is "inherently" of a sort that evades review; circuit precedent also holds that "offensive wars initiated without congressional approval" are not in that category. *Conyers v. Reagan*, 765 F.2d 1124, 1128 (D.C. Cir. 1985). That holding, which remains the law of the circuit, means that we must treat plaintiffs' claims as moot.
>
> Plaintiffs' statutory claim—that President Clinton continued the war for more than 60 days without congressional authorization, in violation of the War Powers Resolution—also may not satisfy the "capable of repetition" element. There is an aspect of probability involved here. "By 'capable of repetition' the Supreme Court means 'a reasonable expectation that the same complaining party would be subject to the same action again.' " *Christian Knights,* 972 F.2d at 370 (quoting *Weinstein v. Bradford*, 423 U.S. 147, 149 (1975) (per

> curiam)).[14] This introduces some complications. Who should be considered the "same complaining parties"? And what is the "same action again"?
>
> The same "complaining parties" must refer to the individual Members of Congress who brought this suit. They have sued in their official capacity and, as in *Karcher v. May*, 484 U.S. 72, 79–81 (1987), the injury they allege relates to their conduct as legislators. Thus, in assessing the likelihood of a recurrence of "the same action," the inquiry must be restricted only to the period in which these Congressmen would likely remain in office. As to the "same action," this refers to President Clinton's alleged violation of the War Powers Resolution by continuing hostilities for more than 60 days without Congress's affirmative approval. How likely is that to recur? Not very, if history is any guide. The War Powers Resolution has been in effect for a quarter of a century. Yet President Clinton is the first President who arguably violated the 60-day provision. In order to show why their claims will "evade review," plaintiffs tell us that, in modern times, United States attacks on foreign nations will be over quickly, by which they mean less than 60 days.[15] Accepting that prediction as accurate dooms their case. It means that the likelihood of this President, or some other, violating the 60-day provision of the War Powers Resolution is remote, not only because we can expect other Presidents to obtain congressional approval for wars lasting more than 60 days, but also because most military actions in the future (as plaintiffs agree) will be over before the 60-day limit for undeclared or unauthorized wars has been exceeded.

203 F.3d 19, 33–34 (D.C. Cir. 2000) (Randolph, J., concurring). Does the pairing of ripeness and mootness alter the appeal of one or the other? Should those doctrines be managed so as to ensure an adequate opportunity for review?

5. STANDING

The concept of "standing" encompasses both constitutional doctrine and prudential concerns. To meet the minimum requirements of Article III, a litigant must

---

[14] The Supreme Court recently stated that "a defendant claiming that its voluntary compliance moots a case bears the formidable burden of showing that it is absolutely clear the allegedly wrongful behavior could not reasonably be expected to recur." *Friends of the Earth*, 528 U.S. at 190 (citing *United States v. Concentrated Phosphate Export Ass'n*, 393 U.S. 199, 203 (1968)). The president's cessation of the attack on Yugoslavia was not "voluntary" within the Court's meaning; the war ended because the United States won, not because the president sought to avoid litigation.

[15] "The 1998 air attack against Afghanistan and Sudan, the December 1998 air attacks against Iraq, the 1995 air assault against the Bosnian Serbs, the 1994 Haitian invasion, the 1991 Persian Gulf War, the 1989 Panama invasion, the 1986 air attack against Libya, the 1983 Grenada attack were all completed in less than 60 days." Reply Brief for Plaintiffs-Appellants at 5–6.

> show [1] that he personally has suffered some actual or threatened injury as a result of the putatively illegal conduct of the defendant, and that the injury [2] fairly can be traced to the challenged action and [3] is likely to be redressed by a favorable decision.

Valley Forge Christian College v. Americans United for Separation of Church & State, Inc., 454 U.S. 464, 472 (1982) (citations and internal quotations omitted); *see also Lujan v. Defenders of Wildlife*, 504 U.S. 555 (1992); *Massachusetts v. EPA*, 549 U.S. 497 (2007). The prudential limits self-imposed by the judiciary in this area include a "general prohibition on a litigant's raising another person's legal rights, the rule barring adjudication of generalized grievances more appropriately addressed in the representative branches, and the requirement that a plaintiff's complaint fall within the zone of interests protected by the law invoked." *Allen v. Wright*, 468 U.S. 737, 751 (1984).

These requirements make judicial enforcement of non-individualized, abstract rights problematic. To take a domestic example, what if the president, by executive order, created titles of nobility, and bestowed knighthood upon some favored cronies? The Constitution, art. I, § 9, cl. 8, directly forbids this action; Hamilton termed this prohibition a "Cornerstone of Republican government." *Federalist Papers* No. 84, at 512 (Clinton Rossiter ed., 1961). Nonetheless, would any potential litigant have suffered the requisite particularized injury to have standing to challenge the action? If no one has standing, is the ostensible constitutional prohibition only precatory? Would it make any difference if the plaintiff was a member of Congress or a private individual?

Unlike the political question doctrine, a dismissal based on standing merely indicates that the suit could not be brought by that particular plaintiff, rather than a general determination that the court could not adjudicate the merits of such a case. In this sense, it is a narrower doctrine. Nonetheless, it can have very significant implications for the ability of plaintiffs to bring suit regarding foreign affairs issues. Plaintiffs who bring suit against the government in matters of foreign policy tend to fall into three main categories: (1) members of the U.S. Congress; (2) U.S. servicemembers and their families; and (3) concerned citizens. In the last few decades, members of Congress have regularly requested judicial relief for alleged harms to them in their official capacities. Some of the cases discussed below do not involve foreign affairs, but congressional plaintiffs in those instances of domestic litigation are asserting similar institutional rights and face the same standing difficulties as do those who sue to alter foreign policy.

The Supreme Court first addressed the standing of legislators in *Coleman v. Miller,* 307 U.S. 433 (1939), which concerned the standing of Kansas state legislators. When the Kansas State Senate voted twenty for and twenty against the Child Labor Amendment, the Lieutenant Governor, the presiding officer of the Senate, broke the deadlock and voted for it. The twenty senators who voted against (along with another senator and three members of the House of Representatives) contested, *inter alia,* this procedure, demanding a court ruling that the resolution concerning the Amendment had not been effectively passed. On appeal from the Kansas Supreme Court, the U.S. Supreme Court found in favor of standing, but divided into three positions. Chief Justice Hughes, joined by Justices Stone and Reed, granted the plaintiffs standing but then held the political question doctrine prevented judicial examination of the merits. Justices Butler and McReynolds granted standing but dissented, arguing on other grounds that the resolution was invalid. Justice Frankfurter, joined by Justices Roberts, Black and Douglas, argued that standing should not be granted. Chief Justice Hughes, in support of granting standing, wrote:

> Here, the plaintiffs include twenty senators, whose votes against ratification have been overridden and virtually held for naught although if they are right in their contentions their votes would have been sufficient to defeat ratification. We think that these senators have a plain, direct and adequate interest in maintaining the effectiveness of their votes.

307 U.S. at 438. Justice Frankfurter responded:

> What is their distinctive claim to be here, not possessed by every Kansan? What is it that they complain of, which could not be complained of here by all their fellow citizens? . . .
>
> . . . The fact that these legislators are part of the ratifying mechanism while the ordinary citizen of Kansas is not, is wholly irrelevant to this issue. . . .

Id. at 464 (Frankfurter, J., concurring). Frankfurter supported the English tradition of leaving "intra-parliamentary controversies to parliaments and outside the scrutiny of law courts." *Id.* at 469.

In 1997, the Supreme Court again addressed legislator standing, dismissing a suit brought by six members of Congress for lack of standing. *Raines v. Byrd*, 521 U.S. 811 (1997). In *Raines*, the six members had voted against passage of the Line Item Veto Act, and brought suit alleging that the Act was an unconstitutional expansion of the president's powers in violation of Article I of the Constitution. The members claimed that they had been injured "directly and concretely . . . in their official capacities." *Id.* at 816. Justice Rehnquist, writing for the Court, found that, unlike in *Coleman,* the votes of the legislators in *Raines* had not been "completely nullified."

> In the vote on the Act, their votes were given full effect. They simply lost that vote. . . .

> There is a vast difference between the level of vote nullification at issue in *Coleman* and the abstract dilution of institutional legislative power that is alleged here. To uphold standing here would require a drastic extension of *Coleman*. We are unwilling to take that step.
>
> We therefore hold that these individual members of Congress do not have a sufficient "personal stake" in this dispute and have not alleged a sufficiently concrete injury to have established Article III standing. The judgment of the District Court is vacated, and the case is remanded with instructions to dismiss the complaint for lack of jurisdiction.

521 U.S. at 824–30 (footnotes omitted). *See also* Neal Devins & Michael A. Fitts, *The Triumph of Timing:* Raines v. Byrd *and the Modern Supreme Court's Attempts to Control Constitutional Confrontations*, 86 GEO. L.J. 351 (1997). Subsequently, when the president exercised his line-item authority, different plaintiffs directly affected by the president's cancellation decisions—the City of New York, hospitals and hospital associations, unions, farmers and a farmer's cooperative—were held to have standing, and the Supreme Court further held that the statute violated the Presentment Clause of the Constitution (Art. I, § 7, cl. 2). *Clinton v. City of New York*, 524 U.S. 417 (1998).

Since 1997, the District Court for the District of Columbia has invoked *Raines* in dismissing for lack of standing various suits brought by members of Congress. For example, in *Kucinich v. Bush*, 236 F. Supp. 2d 1 (D.D.C. 2002), the court dismissed an action brought by members of Congress over the president's unilateral withdrawal from the Anti-Ballistic Missile Treaty. Should members of Congress have standing to challenge the president's use of military force without obtaining congressional consent?

CAMPBELL V. CLINTON

203 F.3d 19 (D.C. Cir. 2000).

SILBERMAN, CIRCUIT JUDGE:

A number of congressmen, led by Tom Campbell of California, filed suit claiming that the President violated the War Powers Resolution and the War Powers Clause of the Constitution by directing U.S. forces' participation in the recent NATO campaign in Yugoslavia. The district court dismissed for lack of standing. We agree with the district court and therefore affirm. . . .

[For additional facts on this case, see *supra*, this Chapter, Sec. 2].

The question whether congressmen have standing in federal court to challenge the lawfulness of actions of the executive was answered, at least in large part, in the Supreme Court's recent decision in *Raines v. Byrd*, 521

U.S. 811 (1997). *Raines* involved a constitutional challenge to the President's authority under the short-lived Line Item Veto Act. Individual congressmen claimed that under that Act a President could veto (unconstitutionally) only part of a law and thereby diminish the institutional power of Congress. Observing it had never held that congressmen have standing to assert an institutional injury as against the executive, *see id.* at 821,[2] the Court held that petitioners in the case lacked "legislative standing" to challenge the Act. The Court noted that petitioners already possessed an adequate political remedy, since they could vote to have the Line Item Veto Act repealed, or to provide individual spending bills with a statutory exemption. *See id.* at 829.

Thereafter in *Chenoweth v. Clinton,* 181 F.3d 112, 115 (D.C. Cir. 1999), emphasizing the separation-of-powers problems inherent in legislative standing, we held that congressmen had no standing to challenge the President's introduction of a program through executive order rather than statute. As in *Raines*, appellants contended that the President's action inflicted an institutional injury upon Congress, in this case by circumventing its legislative authority, but, we said,

> It is uncontested that the Congress could terminate the [contested program] were a sufficient number in each House so inclined. Because the parties' dispute is therefore fully susceptible to political resolution, we would [under circuit precedent] dismiss the complaint to avoid "meddl[ing] in the internal affairs of the legislative branch." Applying *Raines*, we would reach the same conclusion.

Id. at 116 (citation omitted).

There remains, however, a soft spot in the legal barrier against congressional legal challenges to executive action, and it is a soft spot that appellants sought to penetrate. In 1939 the Supreme Court in *Coleman v. Miller* voted 5–4 to recognize the standing of Kansas State legislators in the Supreme Court to challenge the actions of the Kansas Secretary of State and the Secretary of the State Senate. *See* 307 U.S. 433 (1939). That case arose out of a State Senate vote on the ratification of a constitutional amendment, the Child Labor Amendment, proposed by Congress in 1924. The State Senate split 20 to 20, and the Lieutenant Governor, the presiding officer of the Senate, then cast a deciding vote in favor. The State House subsequently also passed a ratification resolution. Thereupon the twenty State Senators who voted against ratification plus one more (who

---

2 The Court noted that it had found standing for a congressman in *Powell v. McCormack,* 395 U.S. 486 (1969), where he was unconstitutionally excluded from Congress, thus depriving him of a salary and the House seat he was constitutionally due, both personal injuries. The Court did not decide whether congressmen would have standing to challenge actions of Congress which diminished their institutional role. *Cf. Michel v. Anderson,* 14 F.3d 623 (D.C. Cir. 1994) (congressmen had standing to challenge House rule which diluted their vote in Committee of the Whole).

presumably had voted for the resolution) brought a mandamus action in the State Supreme Court challenging the Lieutenant Governor's right to vote.[3] They sought an order compelling the Secretary of the Senate to erase the endorsement on the resolution and restraining the Secretary of State from authenticating the resolution and passing it on to the Governor. The Supreme Court of Kansas entertained the action but ruled against the plaintiffs on the merits. Granting certiorari, the United States Supreme Court determined that "at least the twenty senators whose votes, if their contention were sustained, would have been sufficient to defeat the resolution . . . have an interest . . . sufficient to give the Court jurisdiction," *id.* at 446, because they have a legal interest "in maintaining the effectiveness of their votes." *Id.* at 438.

In *Raines* the plaintiff congressmen had relied on *Coleman* to argue that they had standing because the presidential veto had undermined the "effectiveness of their votes." The Supreme Court noted that *Coleman* might be distinguished on grounds that the federal constitutional separation of powers concerns that underlay its decision in *Raines* (and which we emphasized in *Chenoweth*) were not present, or that if the Court in *Coleman* had not taken the case a question of federal law—the ratification *vel non* by the Kansas Legislature—would remain as decided by the Kansas Court. *But cf. Coleman,* 307 U.S. at 465–66 (opinion of Frankfurter, J.). But the Court thought it unnecessary to cabin *Coleman* on those grounds. *See Raines*, 521 U.S. at 824 n. 8. Instead, the Court emphasized that the congressmen were not asserting that their votes had been "completely nullified":

> They have not alleged that they voted for a specific bill, that there were sufficient votes to pass the bill, and that the bill was nonetheless deemed defeated. . . .
>
> Nor can they allege that the Act will nullify their votes in the future in the same way that the votes of the *Coleman* legislators had been nullified. . . .
>
> In addition, a majority of Senators and Congressmen can vote to repeal the Act, or to exempt a given appropriations bill. . . .

Id. at 824.

Here the plaintiff congressmen, by specifically defeating the War Powers Resolution authorization by a tie vote and by defeating a declaration of war, sought to fit within the *Coleman* exception to the *Raines*

---

[3] The government also challenges the congressmen's standing on the basis that they do not constitute a majority of the Congress. In *Raines* the Supreme Court did "attach some importance to the fact that appellees have not been authorized to represent their respective Houses of Congress in this action," but it declined to say how much importance. *Raines,* 521 U.S. at 829–30. Because we find that appellants lack standing for another reason, we need not discuss that issue.

rule. This parliamentary tactic led to an extensive argument before us as to exactly what the Supreme Court meant by a claim that a legislator's vote was completely "nullified."

It is, to be sure, not readily apparent what the Supreme Court meant by that word. It would seem the Court used nullify to mean treating a vote that did not pass as if it had, or vice versa. The "nullification" alleged in this case therefore differs from *Coleman* in a significant respect. In that case state officials endorsed a defeated ratification, treating it as approved, while the President here did not claim to be acting pursuant to the defeated declaration of war or a statutory authorization, but instead "pursuant to [his] constitutional authority to conduct U.S. foreign relations and as Commander-in-Chief and Chief Executive." *See* Letter to Congressional Leaders Reporting on Airstrikes Against Serbian Targets in the Federal Republic of Yugoslavia (Serbia and Montenegro), 35 Weekly Comp. Pres. Doc. 528 (March 26, 1999). The Court did not suggest in *Raines* that the President "nullifies" a congressional vote and thus legislators have standing whenever the government does something Congress voted against, still less that congressmen would have standing anytime a President allegedly acts in excess of statutory authority. As the government correctly observes, appellants' statutory argument, although cast in terms of the nullification of a recent vote, essentially is that the President violated the quarter-century old War Powers Resolution. Similarly, their constitutional argument is that the President has acted illegally—in excess of his authority—because he waged war in the constitutional sense without a congressional delegation. Neither claim is analogous to a *Coleman* nullification.

We think the key to understanding the Court's treatment of *Coleman* and its use of the word nullification is its implicit recognition that a ratification vote on a constitutional amendment is an unusual situation. It is not at all clear whether once the amendment was "deemed ratified," *see Raines*, 521 U.S. at 822, the Kansas Senate could have done anything to reverse that position.[4] We think that must be what the Supreme Court implied when it said the *Raines* plaintiffs could not allege that the "[Line Item Veto Act] would nullify their votes *in the future*," and that, after all, a majority of senators and congressmen could always repeal the Line Item Veto Act. *Id.* at 824 (emphasis added). The *Coleman* senators, by contrast, may well have been powerless to rescind a ratification of a constitutional amendment that they claimed had been defeated. In other words, they had no legislative remedy. Under that reading—which we think explains the very narrow possible *Coleman* exception to *Raines*—appellants fail because

4 *See Coleman,* 307 U.S. at 450 ("[T]he question of the efficacy of ratifications of state legislatures, in the light of . . . attempted withdrawal, should be regarded as a political question. . . .").

they continued, after the votes, to enjoy ample legislative power to have stopped prosecution of the "war."

In this case, Congress certainly could have passed a law forbidding the use of U.S. forces in the Yugoslav campaign; indeed, there was a measure—albeit only a concurrent resolution—introduced to require the President to withdraw U.S. troops. Unfortunately, however, for those congressmen who, like appellants, desired an end to U.S. involvement in Yugoslavia, this measure was *defeated* by a 139 to 290 vote. Of course, Congress always retains appropriations authority and could have cut off funds for the American role in the conflict. Again there was an effort to do so but it failed; appropriations were authorized. And there always remains the possibility of impeachment should a President act in disregard of Congress' authority on these matters. . . .

Appellants' constitutional claim stands on no firmer footing. Appellants argue that the War Powers Clause of the Constitution proscribes a President from using military force except as is necessary to repel a sudden attack. But they also argue that the WPR "implements" or channels congressional authority under the Constitution. It may well be then that since we have determined that appellants lack standing to enforce the WPR there is nothing left of their constitutional claim. Assuming, however, that appellants' constitutional claim should be considered separately, the same logic dictates they do not have standing to bring such a challenge. That is to say Congress has a broad range of legislative authority it can use to stop a President's war making, *see generally* John C. Yoo, *The Continuation of Politics by Other Means: The Original Understanding of War Powers*, 84 CAL. L. REV. 167 (1996), and therefore under *Raines* congressmen may not challenge the President's war-making powers in federal court.

Judge Randolph asserts that appellants lack standing because they do not claim that the President violated various statutes that depend on the existence of a war or the *imminence* of war. But that position sidesteps appellants' basic claim that the President unconstitutionally conducted a war without authority, and the logic of Judge Randolph's reasoning ("There is no suggestion that despite the vote, President Clinton *invaded* Yugoslavia by land or took some other action authorized only during a declared war.") is that if there had been a "war" appellants would have had standing. *See infra* at 31 (Randolph, J., concurring).[5] He therefore presents as an alternate reason for denying standing that the President did not "nullify" the vote against the declaration of war because he did not take any actions that constitute "war" in the constitutional sense. *See id.* at 29–31. That analysis, however, conflates standing with the merits. At the

---

[5] It is certainly not logically necessary for appellants to assert a violation of the statutes (three of which do not even depend on a declaration of war) relied upon by the concurrence in order to make their constitutional claim.

standing stage we must take as correct appellants' claim that the President violated the Constitution simply by ordering U.S. forces to attack Yugoslavia.

In our view Judge Randolph's criticism of our analysis does not give sufficient attention to *Raines*' focus on the political self-help available to congressmen. *See infra* at 22 (Randolph, J., concurring). Even though the congressmen in *Raines* sought review before the Court of what was soon after determined in *Clinton v. City of New York,* 524 U.S. 417 (1998), to be an unconstitutional statute, the Court denied them standing as congressmen because they possessed political tools with which to remedy their purported injury. Our colleague notes a distinction drawn by *Raines* between "the right to vote in the future [and] the nullification of a vote in the past," *see infra* at 22 (Randolph, J., concurring), and asserts that the former does not remedy the latter. But *Raines* rejected this argument, which is why the congressmen in *Raines* lacked standing whereas petitioners in *New York* were allowed to contest the President's "nullification" of particular appropriations line items. Indeed, *Raines* explicitly rejected Judge Randolph's argument that legislators should not be required to turn to politics instead of the courts for their remedy. Although the plaintiff legislators in *Raines* had already failed to stop passage of the Line Item Veto Act, the Court's response was the equivalent of "if at first you don't succeed, try and try again"—either work for repeal of the Act, or seek to have individual spending bills made exempt. *See Raines*, 521 U.S. at 824–25, 825 n. 9, 830. Judge Randolph overlooks this key portion of *Raines* when he disagrees with our conclusion that plaintiffs lack standing because they may "fight again tomorrow." *Infra* at 22 (Randolph, J., concurring).[6] . . .

RANDOLPH, CIRCUIT JUDGE, concurring in the judgment:

The majority opinion does not, I believe, correctly analyze plaintiffs' standing to sue. It misconceives the holding of *Raines v. Byrd,* 521 U.S. 811 (1997), and conflicts with the law of this circuit. I believe plaintiffs lack

[6] Judge Randolph also contends that our opinion is in conflict with *Chenoweth v. Clinton,* 181 F.3d 112, 116–17 (D.C. Cir. 1999). But as we have already described that opinion, *see supra* at 21, it too focused on the political options available to congressmen when denying them standing. *Chenoweth* did not hold, as Judge Randolph would have it, that *Kennedy v. Sampson*, 511 F.2d 430 (D.C. Cir. 1974), survived *Raines.* Instead, we stressed the increased emphasis placed by such post-*Kennedy* cases as *Raines* on separation of powers concerns. *See Chenoweth*, 181 F.3d at 113–15. Although appellants' injury in *Chenoweth* was "precisely the harm we held in . . . *Kennedy* to be cognizable under Article III," it was also "identical to the injury the Court in *Raines* deprecated as 'widely dispersed' and 'abstract,' " and therefore we affirmed the district court's dismissal for lack of standing. *Id.* We only suggested tentatively that "*Kennedy may* remain good law . . . as a peculiar application of the narrow rule announced in" *Coleman. See id.* at 116 (emphasis added). Indeed, Judge Tatel understandably read our opinion to "essentially overrule[ ] the theory of legislative standing recognized in *Kennedy*. . . ." *See id.* at 117 (Tatel, J., concurring). In any event, *Chenoweth's* discussion of *Kennedy's* fate after *Raines* was dicta, and we need not decide for purposes of this case if *Kennedy,* which involved the special question of a pocket veto, survived *Raines.*

standing, at least to litigate their constitutional claim, but for reasons the majority opinion neglects. I also believe that the case is moot, an optional disposition of the appeal.[1] The serious questions about the constitutionality of the War Powers Resolution[2] must therefore be put off for still another day.

I. STANDING

The Constitution reserves the power to declare "war"[3] to Congress and delegates the power to conduct war to the President. *Compare* U.S. CONST. art. I, § 8, cl. 11, *with id.* art. II, § 2. When President Clinton committed armed forces to the attack on the Federal Republic of Yugoslavia, he did so without a declaration of war from Congress. On April 28, 1999, after air operations and missile strikes were underway, the House of Representatives voted 427 to 2 against a declaration of war. *See* H.R.J. Res. 44, 106th Cong. (1999); 126 CONG. REC. H2440–41 (daily ed. Apr. 28, 1999).

The War Powers Resolution, passed over President Nixon's veto in 1973, implements Congress's power to declare war under the Constitution. *See* 50 U.S.C. § 1541(a)–(b). It commands the President to "terminate any use of United States Armed Forces" within sixty days "unless the Congress (1) has declared war or has enacted a specific authorization for such use of United States Armed Forces, (2) has extended by law such sixty-day period, or (3) is physically unable to meet as a result of an armed attack upon the United States." 50 U.S.C. § 1544(b). The Senate, on March 23, 1999, passed a concurrent resolution providing that "the President of the United States is authorized to conduct military air operations and missile strikes in cooperation with our NATO allies against the Federal Republic of Yugoslavia." S. Con. Res. 21, 106th Cong. (1999); 145 CONG. REC. S3118 (daily ed. Mar. 23, 1999). The House rejected that measure by a tie vote on April 28, 1999. *See* 126 CONG. REC. H2451–52 (daily ed. Apr. 28, 1999).

---

[1] While we may be required to decide jurisdictional issues before disposing of a case on the merits, we are not required to decide jurisdictional questions in any particular order. *See Arizonans for Official English v. Arizona,* 520 U.S. 43, 66–67 (1997); *Galvan v. Federal Prison Indus., Inc.,* 199 F.3d 461 (D.C. Cir. 1999) (citing *Steel Co. v. Citizens for a Better Environment,* 523 U.S. 83, 94–95 (1998); *Ruhrgas A.G. v. Marathon Oil Co.*, 526 U.S. 574 (1999)). Specifically, we may assume standing when dismissing a case as moot. *See Friends of the Earth, Inc. v. Laidlaw Envtl. Servs.,* 528 U.S. at 180, 120 S.Ct. 693, 703–04 (2000) (citing *Arizonans*, 520 U.S. at 66–67).

[2] I include as an Addendum to this opinion President Nixon's 1973 message to the House of Representatives explaining why he vetoed the War Powers Resolution on the grounds of its unconstitutionality.

[3] *War* may be defined [as] the exercise of violence under sovereign command against withstanders; force, authority and resistance being the essential parts thereof. Violence, limited by authority, is sufficiently distinguished from robbery, and like outrages; yet consisting in relation towards others, it necessarily requires a supposition of resistance, whereby the force of *war* becomes different from the violence inflicted upon slaves or yielding malefactors.

SAMUEL JOHNSON, A DICTIONARY OF THE ENGLISH LANGUAGE (facsimile ed., Times Books, Ltd., London 1978) (1755). *See United States v. Bajakajian,* 524 U.S. 321, 335 (1998) (citing *Johnson*); *Nixon v. United States,* 506 U.S. 224, 229–30 (1993) (same); *see also Bas v. Tingy,* 4 U.S. (4 Dall.) 37 (1800) (relying on Blackstone and other commentators to distinguish between perfect and imperfect wars).

The Members of Congress appearing as plaintiffs contend that President Clinton violated the Constitution and the War Powers Resolution and that they are entitled to a judicial declaration so stating. They have standing, they say, because President Clinton's prosecution of the war "completely nullified" their votes against declaring war and against authorizing a continuation of the hostilities. *See* Amended Complaint ¶ 18; Brief for Plaintiffs-Appellants at 8, 16.

A.

The quoted phrase—"completely nullified"—is from *Raines v. Byrd,* 521 U.S. 811, 823 (1997), giving the Court's appraisal of the rule in *Coleman v. Miller*, 307 U.S. 433 (1939). The majority opinion in our case seems to assume that the only thing left of legislative standing is whatever *Raines* preserves. I will not quarrel with the assumption, at least for cases in which a legislator is claiming that his vote has been illegally nullified.[4] The heart of the *Raines* decision is this: "legislators whose votes would have been sufficient to defeat (or enact) a specific legislative act have standing to sue if that legislative action goes into effect (or does not go into effect), on the ground that their votes have been completely nullified." 521 U.S. at 823.[5]

Here, plaintiffs had the votes "sufficient to defeat" "a specific legislative action"—they defeated a declaration of war (their constitutional claim) and they blocked a resolution approving the President's continuation of the war (their statutory claim). To follow precisely the formulation in *Raines*, they would have standing only if the legislative actions they defeated went "into effect." Obviously, this did not happen: war was not declared, and the President never maintained that he was prosecuting the war with the House's approval.

Plaintiffs' reply is that the President's military action against Yugoslavia without congressional authorization had the effect of completely nullifying their votes, of making their votes worthless. With respect to their vote against declaring war, that clearly is not true. A congressional declaration of war carries with it profound consequences.[6]

---

[4] The Court has "recognized that state legislators have standing to contest a decision holding a state statute unconstitutional if state law authorizes legislators to represent the State's interests," *Arizonans*, 520 U.S. at 65 (citing *Karcher v. May*, 484 U.S. 72, 82 (1987)). Compare *INS v. Chadha*, 462 U.S. 919, 930 n. 5, 939–40 (1983), in which the "Court held Congress to be a proper party to defend [a] measure's validity where both Houses, by resolution, had authorized intervention in the lawsuit," and the executive branch refused to defend the one-House veto provision. 520 U.S. at 65 n. 20.

[5] A vote is "completely nullified" when it is "deprived of all validity," *Raines*, 521 U.S. at 822, "overridden and virtually held for naught," *id.* at 822–23, or "stripped of its validity," *id.* at 824 n. 7.

[6] Although the United States has committed its armed forces into combat more than a hundred times, Congress has declared war only five times: the War of 1812, the Mexican-American War of 1848, the Spanish-American War of 1898, World War I, and World War II. *See* CONGRESSIONAL RESEARCH SERVICE, INSTANCES OF USE OF UNITED STATES ARMED FORCES ABROAD, 1789–1989 (Ellen C. Collier ed., 1989), *reprinted in* THOMAS M. FRANCK & MICHAEL J.

The United States Code is thick with laws expanding executive power "in time of war." *See* OFFICE OF THE JUDGE ADVOCATE GENERAL, UNITED STATES AIR FORCE, DIGEST OF WAR AND EMERGENCY LEGISLATION AFFECTING THE DEPARTMENT OF DEFENSE 171–84 (1996) (listing statutes "effective in time of war"); *cf. id.* at 185–91 (listing statutes "effective in time of national emergency declared by the President"); id. at 192–98 (listing statutes "effective in time of national emergency declared by Congress").[7] Under these laws, the President's authority over industries, the use of land, and the terms and conditions of military employment is greatly enhanced.[8] A declaration of war may also have the effect of decreasing commercial choices and curtailing civil liberties.[9] *See* WILLIAM H. REHNQUIST, ALL THE LAWS BUT ONE: CIVIL LIBERTIES IN WARTIME 218–19 (1998) ("Without question the government's authority to engage in conduct that infringes civil liberty is greatest in time of declared war—the *Schenck* and *Hirabayashi* opinions make this clear. . . . [B]ut from the point of view of governmental authority under the Constitution, it is clear that the President may do many things in carrying out a congressional directive that he may not be able to do on his own.").

The vote of the House on April 28, 1999, deprived President Clinton of these powers. The vote against declaring war followed immediately upon

---

GLENNON, FOREIGN RELATIONS AND NATIONAL SECURITY LAW 650 (2d ed.1993); OFFICE OF THE LEGAL ADVISER, U.S. DEPARTMENT OF STATE, THE LEGALITY OF UNITED STATES PARTICIPATION IN THE DEFENSE OF VIETNAM (1966), *reprinted in* 1 THE VIETNAM WAR AND INTERNATIONAL LAW 583, 597 (Richard A. Falk ed., 1968) (listing 125 incidents prior to the Vietnam Conflict).

7 In the early days of the Republic, the power of the executive in time of war was constrained by an absence of legislation. For example, in *Brown v. United States*, 12 U.S. (8 Cranch) 110 (1814), the Court rejected the argument that the President had the authority to confiscate enemy property found within the United States without explicit statutory authority even during a declared war. See id. at 129. The same reasoning was applied to the taking of ships on the high seas in *Little v. Barreme*, 6 U.S. (2 Cranch) 170 (1804). Even in the wake of World War II, after Congress passed a large number of war-related measures, the Court strictly construed the President's authority. The most notable example, of course, is *Youngstown Sheet & Tube Co. v. Sawyer*, 343 U.S. 579, 585 (1952) ("The President's power, if any, to issue the order must stem either from an act of Congress or from the Constitution itself."); *cf. also Dames & Moore v. Regan,* 453 U.S. 654 (1981).

8 *See, e.g.,* 10 U.S.C. § 2538 (authorizing the President to "take immediate possession of any plant that is equipped to manufacture, or that . . . is capable of manufacturing" war material "in time of war or when war is imminent"); 10 U.S.C. § 2644 ("In time of war, the President, through the Secretary of Defense, may take possession and assume control of all or part of any system of transportation to transport troops, war material, and equipment, or for other purposes related to the emergency."); 10 U.S.C. § 2663(b) ("In time of war or when war is imminent, the United States may, immediately upon the filing of a petition for condemnation under subsection (a), take and use the land to the extent of the interest sought to be acquired."); 50 U.S.C. § 1829 ("Notwithstanding any other provision of law, the President, through the Attorney General, may authorize physical searches without a court order . . . to acquire foreign intelligence information for a period not to exceed 15 calendar days following a declaration of war by the Congress.").

9 *See, e.g.,* 18 U.S.C. § 2388(a) ("Whoever, when the United States is at war, willfully causes or attempts to cause insubordination, disloyalty, mutiny, or refusal of duty, in the military or naval forces of the United States, or willfully obstructs the recruiting or enlistment service of the United States, to the injury of the service or the United States, or attempts to do so—Shall be fined under this title or imprisoned not more than twenty years, or both."); 18 U.S.C. § 3287 (tolling statute of limitations for any offense involving fraud against the property of the United States until three years after the termination of hostilities).

the vote not to require immediate withdrawal. Those who voted against a declaration of war did so to deprive the President of the authority to expand hostilities beyond the bombing campaign and, specifically, to deprive him of the authority to introduce ground troops into the conflict. *See* 145 CONG. REC. H2427–41 (daily ed. Apr. 28, 1999). There is no suggestion that despite the vote, President Clinton invaded Yugoslavia by land or took some other action authorized only during a declared war. It follows that plaintiffs' votes against declaring war were not for naught. For that reason, plaintiffs do not have standing to sue on their constitutional claim.

As to their claim under the War Powers Resolution, the beauty of this measure, or one of its defects (see the Addendum to this opinion), is in its automatic operation: unless a majority of both Houses declares war, or approves continuation of hostilities beyond 60 days, or Congress is "physically unable to meet as a result of an armed attack upon the United States," the Resolution requires the President to withdraw the troops. 50 U.S.C. § 1544(b). The President has nothing to veto. Congress may allow the time to run without taking any vote, or it may—as the House did here—take a vote and fail to muster a majority in favor of continuing the hostilities.

To put the matter in terms of *Raines* once again, plaintiffs had the votes "sufficient to defeat" "a specific legislative action"—they blocked a resolution authorizing the President's continuation of the war with Yugoslavia—but it is not true, in the language of *Raines*, that this "legislative action" nevertheless went "into effect." Congressional authorization simply did not occur. The President may have acted as if he had Congress's approval, or he may have acted as if he did not need it. Either way, plaintiffs' real complaint is not that the President ignored their votes; it is that he ignored the War Powers Resolution, and hence the votes of an earlier Congress, which enacted the law over President Nixon's veto. It is hard for me to see that this amounts to anything more than saying: "We, the members of Congress, have standing because the President violated one of our laws." To hold that Members of Congress may litigate on such a basis strikes me as highly problematic, not only because the principle is unconfined but also because it raises very serious separation-of-powers concerns. *See Raines*, 521 U.S. at 825 n. 8; *Barnes v. Kline*, 759 F.2d 21, 41 (D.C. Cir. 1985) (Bork, J., dissenting), *vacated as moot*, 479 U.S. 361 (1987). But because the case is moot, I need say no more.

B.

The majority opinion analyzes standing rather differently than I do. It says plaintiffs lack standing to pursue their statutory claim because "they continued, after the votes, to enjoy ample legislative power to have stopped prosecution of the 'war.'" Maj. op. at 23. For specifics, the opinion points out that Congress defeated House Concurrent Resolution 82, a resolution requiring immediate disengagement from the conflict in Yugoslavia; that "Congress always retains appropriations authority and could have cut off funds for the American role in the conflict";[10] and that "there always remains the possibility of impeachment." *Id.*[11] The same reason—the possibility of future legislative action—is used to defeat plaintiffs' standing with respect to their constitutional claim. *Id.* at 23.

The majority has, I believe, confused the right to vote in the future with the nullification of a vote in the past, a distinction *Raines* clearly made. See 521 U.S. at 824. To say that your vote was not nullified because you can vote for other legislation in the future is like saying you did not lose yesterday's battle because you can fight again tomorrow. The Supreme Court did not engage in such illogic. When the Court in *Raines* mentioned the possibility of future legislation, it was addressing the argument that "the [Line Item Veto] Act will nullify the [Congressmen's] votes in the future. . . ." *Id.* This part of the Court's opinion, which the majority adopts here, is quite beside the point to our case. No one is claiming that their votes on future legislation will be impaired or nullified or rendered ineffective.

Besides, as long as Congress and the Constitution exist, Members will always be able to vote for legislation. And so the majority's decision is tantamount to a decision abolishing legislative standing. I have two problems with this. First, if we are going to get rid of legislative standing altogether, we ought to do so openly and not under the cover of an interpretation, or rather misinterpretation, of a phrase in *Raines*. If the Supreme Court had meant to do away with legislative standing, it would have said so and it would have given reasons for taking that step.

My second problem is just as serious, perhaps more so: the majority's decision conflicts with this court's latest legislative standing decision. In

---

10 The majority attaches some importance to Congress's decision to authorize funding for Operation Allied Force and argues that Congress could have denied funding if it wished to end the war. However, in *Mitchell v. Laird,* 488 F.2d 611, 616 (D.C. Cir.1 973), we held that, as "every schoolboy knows," Congress may pass such legislation, not because it is in favor of continuing the hostilities, but because it does not want to endanger soldiers in the field. The War Powers Resolution itself makes the same point: "Authority to introduce United States Armed Forces into hostilities or into situations wherein involvement in hostilities is clearly indicated by the circumstances *shall not be inferred* . . . from any provision of law (whether or not in effect before November 7, 1973), *including any provision contained in any appropriation Act,* unless such provision specifically authorizes the introduction of United States Armed Forces into hostilities or into such situations and states that it is intended to constitute specific statutory authorization within the meaning of this chapter." 50 U.S.C. § 1547(a)(1) (emphasis added). Those portions of the Emergency Supplemental Appropriations Act, Pub. L. No. 106–31, 113 Stat. 57, relating to the attacks on Yugoslavia specified the limited purpose for the emergency appropriations, but contained no language even roughly approximating that required by the War Powers Resolution. *See id.,* ch. 3, 113 Stat. 76–83.

11 These are not the only possibilities. "It has been thought that Congress could constitutionally cut the President's salary in half and auction off the White House, reduce the President's staff to one secretary, and limit her or him to answering personal correspondence." A. Raymond Randolph, *Introduction-Disciplining Congress: The Boundaries of Legislative Power,* 13 J.L. & POL. 585, 586 (1997).

Chenoweth v. Clinton, 181 F.3d 112, 116–17 (D.C. Cir. 1999), we interpreted *Raines* consistently with my analysis in this case and concluded that a previous legislative standing decision of this court—*Kennedy v. Sampson*, 511 F.2d 430 (D.C. Cir. 1974)—upholding legislative standing to challenge the legality of a pocket veto was still good law. The plaintiff in *Kennedy* had standing under the proper interpretation of *Raines*, we held, because the "pocket veto challenged in that case had made ineffective a bill that both houses of the Congress had approved. Because it was the President's veto—not a lack of legislative support—that prevented the bill from becoming law (either directly or by the Congress voting to override the President's veto), those in the majority could plausibly describe the President's action as a complete nullification of their votes." 181 F.3d at 116–17. If *Chenoweth* is correct, the majority opinion in this case must be wrong. If *Chenoweth* is correct, it is no answer to say—as the majority says in this case—that standing is lacking because, despite the pocket veto, Congress could pass the same law again, or it could retaliate by cutting off appropriations for the White House or it could impeach the President.

C.

My position, the majority complains, "sidesteps" plaintiffs' merits "claim that the President unconstitutionally conducted a war without authority," Maj. op. at 23. This is meant to be criticism? A properly-conducted standing analysis almost always avoids—sidesteps—a decision on the merits.[12] In the next breath, the majority turns around and contradicts itself, proclaiming that my analysis "conflates standing with the merits." *Id.* I am familiar with what I have written. I do not recall having rendered a judgment about whether the President violated the Constitution. The careful reader will, I think, agree with me. Nor do I present "as an alternative reason for denying standing that the President did not . . . take any actions constituting war in the constitutional sense." *Id.* The majority's sentence is doubly misleading. Here is my alternative reason for denying standing, pure and simple: regardless whether President Clinton waged a "war," plaintiffs never claimed that he exercised statutory authority reserved to him only when Congress has declared a war; and so their votes against declaring war cannot be considered a nullity. Thus, one, I have taken no position on whether the President engaged in a "war," and two, I say only that plaintiffs never *alleged* that the President utilized these statutory powers. Too often a strategy in legal

[12] The majority drops this footnote: "It is certainly not logically necessary for appellants to assert a violation of the statutes . . . relied upon by the concurrence in order to make their constitutional claim." Maj. op. at 23 n.5. How strange a statement. I refer to the statutes not in the context of plaintiffs' making their constitutional claim, but in regard to their standing to litigate that claim. It is as if the majority had made this brow-furrowing statement: "in order to make out their constitutional claim, it is not logically necessary for plaintiffs to assert that their votes were nullified within the meaning of *Raines*."

argumentation is to pretend to answer an argument by misstating it.[13] My argument remains unanswered. All the majority has done is to misstate it almost as badly as it has misread *Raines*.

NOTES

1. *Standing Cases and Contemporary Military Actions*. How would you characterize the difference in views between the majority in *Campbell* and Judge Randolph? Who do you think has the better position? For a similar case, see *Kucinich v. Obama*, 821 F.Supp.2d 110 (D.D.C. 2011) (members of the House of Representatives found to lack standing in a case against the president and secretary of defense alleging the 2011 U.S. military action in Libya violated the War Powers Clause and the War Powers Resolution).

2. *Standing Cases in the Vietnam War Era*. Challenges to the constitutionality of the Vietnam War frequently encountered two justiciability hurdles: standing and the political question doctrine. *See supra,* this Chapter, Sec. 2. For individual litigants, standing was usually granted only to a party "under orders to fight in the combat in which he objects." *Holtzman v. Schlesinger*, 484 F.2d 1307, 1315 (2d Cir. 1973). *See Berk v. Laird*, 429 F.2d 302 (2d Cir. 1970); *Massachusetts v. Laird*, 451 F.2d 26 (1st Cir. 1971). As the Second Circuit explained, being a draftee or draft registrant was insufficient:

> Regardless of the proof that appellant might present to demonstrate the correlation between the Selective Service and our nation's efforts in Vietnam, as a matter of law the congressional power "to raise and support armies" and "to provide and maintain a navy" is a matter quite distinct from the use which the Executive makes of those who have been found qualified and who have been inducted into the Armed Forces.

United States v. Mitchell, 369 F.2d 323, 324 (2d Cir. 1966). *See also Ashton v. United States*, 404 F.2d 95 (8th Cir. 1968); *United States v. Battaglia,* 410 F.2d 279 (7th Cir. 1969); *United States v. Rehfield*, 416 F.2d 273 (9th Cir.1969); *Mottola v. Nixon*, 464 F.2d 178 (9th Cir. 1972). *But see United States v. Sisson*, 294 F.Supp. 511 (D. Mass. 1968) (draftee granted standing).

While many suits challenging the Vietnam War were brought by servicemembers, members of Congress also brought suits to protect their institutional rights in response to the Vietnam War. *See, e.g.*, *Mitchell v. Laird*, 488 F.2d 611 (D.C. Cir. 1973) (Court, *sua sponte,* proposed a very weak test for congressional standing; plaintiffs, though granted standing, were precluded from adjudication on basis of political question doctrine); *Holtzman v. Schlesinger*, 484 F.2d 1307, 1315 (2d Cir. 1973) (Congresswoman Holtzman, among others, having asked that the bombing of Cambodia be enjoined, was

---

[13] See also the sentence attributing to me the "argument that legislators should not be required to turn to politics instead of the courts for their remedy." Maj. op. at 24. There are other examples not worth mentioning.

denied standing); *Harrington v. Schlesinger,* 528 F.2d 455 (4th Cir. 1975) (plaintiffs denied standing).

Attempts by citizen-taxpayers to litigate the constitutionality of the Vietnam war were unsuccessful. In *Velvel v. Nixon,* the Tenth Circuit examined a law school professor's complaint in terms of *Flast v. Cohen*, 392 U.S. 83 (1968), then the leading Supreme Court case on taxpayer standing:

> [T]he first requirement of *Flast* is that the taxpayer challenge "exercises of congressional power under the taxing and spending clause. . . ." 392 U.S. at 102. Since congressional appropriations for the war are made under authority of the powers "to raise and support Armies" and "to provide and maintain a Navy," such expenditures are not exercises of the power to spend for the general welfare, but rather, represent exercises of power under the later enumerated powers, powers which are separate and distinct from the grant of authority to tax and spend for the general welfare. *United States v. Butler,* 297 U.S. 1, 65 (1936). It follows then that appellant has not satisfied the first criterion of *Flast* and therefore lacks standing to sue.
>
> Even if we were to assume that the first criterion for standing had been met, the Court's discussion of *Frothingham v. Mellon* would still require a finding that the appellant must fail. The Court in *Flast* noted that although the taxpayer in *Frothingham* complied with the first criterion by attacking a federal spending program, she nonetheless lacked standing because her constitutional complaint was not based on an allegation that Congress had breached a *specific* limitation upon its taxing and spending power. Instead, the taxpayer alleged essentially that Congress in enacting the challenged program, had exceeded the general powers delegated to it by Art. I, § 8, and thereby invaded the legislative province of the states. Similarly, in the case at bar the appellant is attempting to assert the congressional interest in its legislative prerogatives, and just as was the case of the taxpayer in *Frothingham,* this is "not a federal taxpayer's interest in being free of taxing and spending in contravention of specific constitutional limitations imposed upon Congress' taxing and spending power." Thus, the appellant will not be permitted "to employ a federal court as a forum in which to air his generalized grievances about the conduct of government or the allocation of power in the Federal System." 392 U.S. at 106.

Velvel v. Nixon, 415 F.2d 236, 239 (10th Cir. 1969). *See also Kalish v. United States,* 411 F.2d 606 (9th Cir. 1969); *Pietsch v. President of the United States*, 434 F.2d 861 (2d Cir. 1970). As to whether a state has standing, representing its citizens as *parens patriae,* see *Massachusetts v. Laird,* 400 U.S. 886 (1970) (Douglas, J., dissenting); *Massachusetts v. Laird,* 451 F.2d 26 (1st Cir. 1971).

3. *Further Reading*. For further analysis of the doctrine of standing, see David J. Weiner, *The New Law of Legislative Standing*, 54 STAN. L. REV. 205 (2001); John O. McGinnis, *Constitutional Review by the Executive in Foreign*

Affairs and War Powers: A Consequence of Rational Choice in the Separation of Powers, 56 LAW. & CONTEMP. PROBS. 293, 319–320 (1993); Carlin Meyer, *Imbalance of Powers: Can Congressional Lawsuits Serve as Counterweight?*, 54 U. PITT. L. REV. 63 (1992); Theodore Y. Blumoff, *Judicial Review, Foreign Affairs and Legislative Standing,* 25 GA. L. REV. 227 (1991); R. Lawrence Dessem, *Congressional Standing to Sue: Whose Vote Is This Anyway?,* 62 NOTRE DAME L. REV. 1 (1986); Note, *The Burger Court's Unified Approach to Standing And Its Impact on Congressional Plaintiffs,* 60 NOTRE DAME L. REV. 1187 (1985); Note, *The Justiciability of Congressional-Plaintiff Suits,* 82 COLUM. L. REV. 526 (1982); Note, *Congressional Access to the Federal Courts,* 90 HARV. L. REV. 1632 (1977).

6. UNRECOGNIZED GOVERNMENTS IN U.S. COURTS

Recognition of foreign governments in U.S. courts is distinct from recognition on the international plane, but understanding the international context is important. In international legal theory, three concepts need to be distinguished: (1) recognition of a State, (2) recognition of a government, and (3) establishment of diplomatic relations.

At its simplest, *recognition of a State* is the affirmation, usually by the government of another State, that a new nation has come into existence which, at least as far as the recognizer is concerned, is subject to all the rights and duties of a State in international law. *Recognition of a government* is the affirmation, by the government of an existing State, of a regime's entitlement to the rights and duties accruing to governments under international law. A form of recognition may also be extended by an international organization when it admits a State to membership, and again, when it accepts the credentials of the representatives of the member State. The *establishment of diplomatic relations* is accomplished by accrediting an ambassador or lower level diplomat who is received by the government of the State to whom he or she is accredited, and, usually, by establishing a diplomatic mission, often on a reciprocal basis, at the seat of the recognized government. Note, however, that an ambassador may be accredited to several (usually small, neighboring) states and that one embassy may serve several capitals.

These three different events—recognition of State, recognition of government, and establishment of diplomatic relations—often occur simultaneously. There is no inherent reason, however, why this should be so. The coming into existence of a new State, in theory, could be recognized even though there are several contenders for its leadership. In such circumstances, recognition of government may be withheld until the outcome of the civil contest is clarified by events. The overthrow of the recognized government of an established State may cause other governments for a time to withhold recognition of the usurpers for various reasons, including plain pique, while still recognizing the State itself. And there is no legal requirement that any government must maintain diplomatic relations with any other, even one it has recognized. The United States did not have formal diplomatic relations with the government of Cuba from 1961 to 2015, but this in no way diminished the U.S. government's recognition of that government and of the Cuban State. On the other hand, the establishing of diplomatic relations does, of course, presume recognition.

U.S. courts generally encounter the issue of recognition in three contexts:

> (1) cases where the foreign government (or its instrumentality) appears as a plaintiff in a suit, usually for purposes of vindicating a contract right or claiming State assets located in the United States;
>
> (2) cases where the foreign government is sued as a defendant and wishes to claim immunity from suit, an issue that is now governed by the Foreign Sovereign Immunities Act; and
>
> (3) cases where the foreign government itself does not appear in a U.S. court but its acts or laws are at issue with respect to persons or chattels before the court.
>
> In each of these kinds of cases the court must ask whether the foreign government is an entity entitled to standing or entitled to acceptance of its acts as a sovereign government.

Mary Beth West & Sean D. Murphy, *The Impact on U.S. Litigation of Non-Recognition of Foreign Governments*, 26 STAN. J. INT'L L. 435, 440 (1990).

The "diversity" jurisdiction clause of the U.S. Constitution (Article III, § 2), gives federal courts jurisdiction over all cases in law and equity "between a State, or the Citizens thereof, and foreign States, Citizens or Subjects." What constitutes a foreign State—and, consequently whether a citizen or subject is of a foreign State—thus has important implications for litigants. Should U.S. courts decide on their own that a foreign entity is a "State" or a "government" of a State or should such matters be determined by the executive branch? If the latter, what should happen if no such determination is forthcoming; may the courts proceed on their own based on collaterally-ascertained facts and "common sense"?

Consider the following cases involving foreign governments as plaintiffs. At the time of the cases, the U.S. government: did not recognize the foreign government (Russia); recognized the foreign government but did not have diplomatic relations with it (Cuba); and both recognized and had diplomatic relations with the foreign government (India).

RUSSIAN SOCIALIST FEDERATED SOVIET REPUBLIC V. CIBRARIO

235 N.Y. 255, 260–65 (1923).

ANDREWS, J. . . .

[Established in 1917 after the Bolshevik revolution in Russia, the Russian Soviet Federated Socialist Republic (RSFSR) was the largest and most populous of the fifteen Soviet republics, which became part of the Soviet Union in 1922. The United States initially refused to recognize the new communist regime as the lawful government in Russia (eventually U.S. recognition and opening of diplomatic relations occurred in 1933). In this case, the RSFSR sought to bring an action in New York state court against an individual, but it was dismissed by the lower court.]

Does any rule of comity . . . require us to permit a suit by an unrecognized power? In view of the attitude of our government should we permit an action to be brought by the Soviet government? To both queries we must give a negative answer.

We may state at the outset that we find no precedent that a power not recognized by the United States may seek relief in our courts. Such intimations as exist are to the contrary. . . .

What then is the meaning and effect of recognition in its relation to comity? It is difficult to find a clear discussion of this question, either in reports or in textbooks. Where a new government has seized power "no official intercourse is possible between the powers refusing recognition and the state concerned." "Through recognition the other states declare that they are ready to negotiate with such individual (a new ruler) as the highest organ of his state." *(Oppenheim International Law* [3d ed.], vol. 1, sections 77, 342.) Speaking of the recognition of a new state Wheaton (*International Law* [2d ed.], p. 39) says: "So long, indeed, as the new state confines its action to its own citizens and to the limits of its own territory, it may well dispense with such recognition. But if it desires to enter into the great society of nations, all the members of which recognize rights to which they are mutually entitled, and duties which they may be called upon reciprocally to fulfil, such recognition becomes essentially necessary to the complete participation of the new state in all the advantages of this society. . . . The new state becomes entitled to the exercise of its external sovereignty as to those states only by whom that sovereignty has been recognized." In Hyde's *International Law* (Vol. 1, sec. 37) is the statement that "the mode of recognition is not material, provided there be an unequivocal act indicating clearly that the new state is dealt with as such and is deemed to be entitled to exercise the privileges of statehood in the society of nations."

More assistance may be found in the reasons underlying various decisions of the courts as to the effect to be given to the acts of foreign governments. This effect depends upon our acknowledgment of the comity of nations. "The principle that the conduct of one independent government cannot be successfully questioned in the courts of another is as applicable to a case involving the title to property brought within the custody of a court such as we have here, as it was held to be to the cases cited, in which claims for damages were based upon acts done in a foreign country, for it rests at last upon the highest considerations of international comity and expediency." (*Oetjen v. Central Leather Co.*, 246 U.S. 297, 303. . . .) Therefore, where comity exists between two nations and no question of public policy arises this rule is invariable. Yet in specific cases the question of recognition is thought controlling—recognition existing at the time the alleged wrongful act was done, or recognition later which relates back to that time. *Oetjen v. Central Leather Co.*, supra. . . .

We reach the conclusion, therefore, that a foreign power brings an action in our courts not as a matter of right. Its power to do so is the creature of comity. Until such government is recognized by the United States no such comity exists. The plaintiff concededly has not been so recognized. There is, therefore, no proper party before us. We may add that recognition and consequently the existence of comity is purely a matter for the determination of the legislative or executive departments of the government. Who is the sovereign of a territory is a political question. In any case where that question is in dispute the courts are bound by the decision reached by those departments. (*Jones v. U.S.*, 137 U.S. 202; *Luther v. Sagor*, [3 K.B. 1921 532], 556). It is not for the courts to say whether the present governments of Russia or Mexico or Great Britain should or should not be recognized. They are or they are not. That is as far as we may inquire. Nor is anything here decided inconsistent with *Wulfsohn v. Soviet Republic*. . . . Upon the facts in that case, if the defendant was not an existing government it might not be sued. There was no party before the court. If it were, as was alleged and admitted, the same result followed not because of comity, but because an independent government is not answerable for its acts to our courts.

We are the more ready to reach this conclusion because to hold otherwise might tend to nullify the rule that public policy must always prevail over comity. More than once during the last seventy years our relations with one or another existing but unrecognized government have been of so critical a character that to permit it to recover in our courts funds which might strengthen it or which might even be used against our interests would be unwise. We should do nothing to thwart the policy which the United States has adopted. Yet unless recognition is the test of the right to sue we do not see why Maximilian as emperor of Mexico might not have maintained an action here.

With regard to the present Russian government the case is still stronger, even did comity not depend on recognition. We not only refuse to recognize it. Our State Department gives the reasons. Secretary Colby has stated them in an official note, dated August 10, 1920. He begins by saying that our government will not participate in any plan for the expansion of the armistice negotiations between Russia and Poland into a general European conference, "which would in all probability involve two results, from both of which this country strongly recoils, viz.: The recognition of the Bolshevist régime and a settlement of the Russian problem almost inevitably upon the basis of a dismemberment of Russia." He continues:

> "We are unwilling that while it is helpless in the grip of a nonrepresentative government whose only sanction is brutal force, Russia shall be weakened still further by a policy of dismemberment, conceived in other than Russian interests.... The Bolsheviki, although in number an inconsiderable minority of the people, by force and cunning seized the powers and machinery of government, and have continued to use them with savage oppression to maintain themselves in power.... It is not possible for the government of the United States to recognize the present rulers of Russia as a government with which the relations common to friendly governments can be maintained.... The existing régime in Russia is based upon the negation of every principle of honor and good faith, and every usage and convention, underlying the whole structure of international law, the negation, in short, of every principle upon which it is possible to base harmonious and trustful relations, whether of nations or of individuals. The responsible leaders of the régime have frequently and openly boasted that they are willing to sign agreements and undertakings with foreign powers while not having the slightest intention of observing such undertakings or carrying out such agreements.... They have made it quite plain that they intend to use every means ... to promote revolutionary movements in other countries.... In the view of this government, there cannot be any common ground upon which it can stand with a power whose conceptions of international relations are so entirely alien to its own, so utterly repugnant to its moral sense. There can be no mutual confidence or trust, no respect even, if pledges are to be given and agreements made with a cynical repudiation of their obligations already in the mind of one of the parties. We cannot recognize, hold official relations with, or give friendly reception to the agents of a government which is determined and bound to conspire against our institutions, whose diplomats will be the agitators of dangerous revolt, whose spokesmen say that they sign agreements with no intention of keeping them." ...

The judgment appealed from should be affirmed, with costs.

BANCO NACIONAL DE CUBA V. SABBATINO

376 U.S. 398, 410–412 (1964).

[As discussed in greater depth *infra*, this Chapter, Sec. 8, in this case an instrumentality of the Cuban government brought suit in U.S. court against a commodities broker for conversion of bills of lading and against a receiver for certain injunctive relief. The defendants responded in part by challenging the ability of the Cuban government (or its instrumentalities) to appear in U.S. court, since there were no diplomatic relations between the United States and Cuba. Although no such relations existed, the United States did recognize Cuba as a sovereign state and did recognize the government of Fidel Castro as the government of Cuba.]

Respondents, pointing to the severance of diplomatic relations, commercial embargo, and freezing of Cuban assets in this country, contend that relations between the United States and Cuba manifest such animosity that unfriendliness is clear, and that the courts should be closed to the Cuban Government. We do not agree. This Court would hardly be competent to undertake assessments of varying degrees of friendliness or its absence, and, lacking some definite touchstone for determination, we are constrained to consider any relationship, short of war, with a recognized sovereign power as embracing the privilege of resorting to United States courts. Although the severance of diplomatic relations is an overt act with objective significance in the dealings of sovereign states, we are unwilling to say that it should inevitably result in the withdrawal of the privilege of bringing suit. Severance may take place for any number of political reasons, its duration is unpredictable, and whatever expression of animosity it may imply does not approach that implicit in a declaration of war.

It is perhaps true that nonrecognition of a government in certain circumstances may reflect no greater unfriendliness than the severance of diplomatic relations with a recognized government, but the refusal to recognize has a unique legal aspect. It signifies this country's unwillingness to acknowledge that the government in question speaks as the sovereign authority for the territory it purports to control, see *Russian Republic v. Cibrario*, . . . 235 N.Y. at 260–263. Political recognition is exclusively a function of the Executive. The possible incongruity of judicial "recognition," by permitting suit, of a government not recognized by the Executive is completely absent when merely diplomatic relations are broken.[12]

---

[12] The doctrine that nonrecognition precludes suit by the foreign government in every circumstance has been the subject of discussion and criticism. See, *e.g.*, Hervey, The Legal Effects of Recognition in International Law (1928) 112–119; Jaffe, Judicial Aspects of Foreign Relations

The view that the existing situation between the United States and Cuba should not lead to a denial of status to sue is buttressed by the circumstance that none of the acts of our Government have been aimed at closing the courts of this country to Cuba, and more particularly by the fact that the Government has come to the support of Cuba's "act of state" claim in this very litigation.

Respondents further urge that reciprocity of treatment is an essential ingredient of comity generally, and, therefore, of the privilege of foreign states to bring suit here. Although *Hilton v. Guyot*, 159 U.S. 113, contains some broad language about the relationship of reciprocity to comity, the case in fact imposed a requirement of reciprocity only in regard to conclusiveness of judgments, and even then only in limited circumstances. *Id.*, at 170–171. In *Direction der Disconto-Gesellschaft v. United States Steel Corp.*, 300 F. 741, 747 (D.C.S.D.N.Y.), Judge Learned Hand pointed out that the doctrine of reciprocity has apparently been confined to foreign judgments.

There are good reasons for declining to extend the principle to the question of standing of sovereign states to sue. Whether a foreign sovereign will be permitted to sue involves a problem more sensitive politically than whether the judgments of its courts may be re-examined, and the possibility of embarrassment to the Executive Branch in handling foreign relations is substantially more acute. Re-examination of judgments, in principle, reduces rather than enhances the possibility of injustice being done in a particular case; refusal to allow suit makes it impossible for a court to see that a particular dispute is fairly resolved. The freezing of Cuban assets exemplifies the capacity of the political branches to assure, through a variety of techniques . . . , that the national interest is protected against a country which is thought to be improperly denying the rights of United States citizens.

Furthermore, the question whether a country gives *res judicata* effect to United States judgments presents a relatively simple inquiry. The precise status of the United States Government and its nationals before foreign courts is much more difficult to determine. To make such an investigation significant, a court would have to discover not only what is provided by the formal structure of the foreign judicial system, but also what the practical possibilities of fair treatment are. The courts, whose powers to further the national interest in foreign affairs are necessarily

(1933) 148–156; Borchard, The Unrecognized Government in American Courts, 26 Am. J. Int'l L. 261 (1932); Dickinson, The Unrecognized Government or State in English and American Law, 22 Mich. L. Rev. 118 (1923); Fraenkel, The Juristic Status of Foreign States, Their Property and Their Acts, 25 Col. L. Rev. 544, 547–552 (1925); Lubman, The Unrecognized Government in American Courts: Upright v. Mercury Business Machines, 62 Col. L. Rev. 275 (1962). In this litigation we need intimate no view on the possibility of access by an unrecognized government to United States courts, except to point out that even the most inhospitable attitude on the matter does not dictate denial of standing here.

circumscribed as compared with those of the political branches, can best serve the rule of law by not excluding otherwise proper suitors because of deficiencies in their legal systems.

We hold that this petitioner is not barred from access to the federal courts.

PFIZER INC. V. INDIA

434 U.S. 308, 318–20 (1978).

[In this case, the governments of several foreign countries, as purchasers of antibiotics, brought antitrust treble damage suits against major pharmaceutical firms in the United States. The Eighth Circuit Court of Appeals found that the governments had standing to pursue the claim and the case was appealed.]

. . . This Court has long recognized the rule that a foreign nation is generally entitled to prosecute any civil claim in the courts of the United States upon the same basis as a domestic corporation or individual might do. "To deny him this privilege would manifest a want of comity and friendly feeling." *The Sapphire,* 11 Wall. 164, 167; *Monaco v. Mississippi,* 292 U.S. 313, 323 n.2; *Banco Nacional de Cuba v. Sabbatino,* 376 U.S. 398, 408–409; see U.S. Const., Art. III, § 2, cl. 1.[19] To allow a foreign sovereign to sue in our courts for treble damages to the same extent as any other person injured by an antitrust violation is thus no more than a specific application of a long-settled general rule. To exclude foreign nations from the protections of our antitrust laws would, on the other hand, create a conspicuous exception to this rule, an exception that could not be justified in the absence of clear legislative intent.

[T]he result we reach does not require the Judiciary in any way to interfere in sensitive matters of foreign policy.[20] It has long been established that only governments recognized by the United States and at peace with us are entitled to access to our courts, and that it is within the exclusive power of the Executive Branch to determine which nations are entitled to sue. *Jones v. United States,* 137 U.S. 202, 212; *Guaranty Trust*

---

[19] Congress has explicitly conferred jurisdiction upon the federal courts to entertain such suits:

> "The district courts shall have original jurisdiction of all civil actions where the matter in controversy exceeds the sum or value of $10,000, exclusive of interest and costs, and is between—. . .
>
> "(4) a foreign state . . . as plaintiff and citizens of a State or of different States." 28 U.S.C. § 1332(a)(4) (1976 ed.). . . .

[20] In a letter that was presented to the Court of Appeals when it reconsidered this case en banc, the Legal Adviser of the Department of State advised "that the Department of State would not anticipate any foreign policy problems if . . . foreign governments [were held to be] 'persons' within the meaning of Clayton Act § 4." A copy of this letter is contained in the Memorandum for the United States as *Amicus Curiae* in opposition to the petition for a writ of certiorari filed in this Court.

Co. v. United States, 304 U.S. 126, 137–138; *Banco Nacional de Cuba v. Sabbatino, supra*, at 408–412. Nothing we decide today qualifies this established rule of complete judicial deference to the Executive Branch.

We hold today only that a foreign nation otherwise entitled to sue in our courts is entitled to sue for treble damages under the antitrust laws to the same extent as any other plaintiff. Neither the fact that the respondents are foreign nor the fact that they are sovereign is reason to deny them the remedy of treble damages Congress afforded to "any person" victimized by violations of the antitrust laws.

Accordingly, the judgment of the Court of Appeals is

Affirmed.

NOTES

1. *Executive Communication to the Judiciary*. The method by which courts learn the executive branch's official recognition policy has changed from independent judicial determinations to specific State Department instructions.

In the first half of the 20th century, courts usually took "judicial notice" of official policy. Given the public nature of recognition, discerning the position of the executive was not difficult. The Supreme Court sanctioned this method when it took judicial notice of U.S. recognition of the Mexican Carranza government. *Oetjen v. Central Leather Co.,* 246 U.S. 297, 301 (1918). The New York *Cibrario* court (extracted above) quoted public pronouncements concerning U.S. nonrecognition of the Soviet Union by the Secretary of State. In *Guaranty Trust Co. of New York v. United States,* the State Department reaffirmed the diplomatic status of a Kerensky official at the time crucial for purposes of the litigation. 304 U.S. 126, 138 n. 4 (1938).

After World War II, perhaps to ensure that executive and judicial positions did not diverge, the State Department often issued specific "suggestions" or instructions to courts, frequently prompted by the requests of individual litigants. Courts sometimes compared these State Department submissions to public pronouncements (not made with a particular litigation in mind) to see whether they were congruent. *See, e.g., Latvian State Cargo & Passenger S.S. Line v. McGrath,* 188 F.2d 1000, 1003 (D.C. Cir. 1951).

Most contemporary cases, however, have relied on the Department's "suggestions" whenever these have been forthcoming. This is in part due to the fact that U.S. policy has shifted away from formal recognition after a change in government. In 1977, the State Department announced that it would thenceforth focus on the existence of diplomatic relations with new governments, rather than on formal recognition or nonrecognition of those governments—a gesture that can be particularly freighted when a government that is nondemocratic or authoritarian comes to power. 77 DEP'T ST. BULL. 462 (1977). Consequently, very few putative States today are publicly identified by the State Department as "recognized" or "not recognized".

Yet if formal recognition of a foreign government is no longer standard practice, then what is the touchstone for determining whether a foreign government may sue in U.S. courts? As suggested by the *National Petrochemical Company of Iran* case (below), the courts must look to other factors. In particular, the diminished interest in formal recognition or non-recognition has caused courts to rely increasingly on interventions by the State Department on a case-by-case basis. *See* Mary Beth West & Sean D. Murphy, *The Impact on U.S. Litigation of Non-Recognition of Foreign Governments,* 26 STAN. J. INT'L L. 435, 456 (1990).

NATIONAL PETROCHEMICAL COMPANY OF IRAN V. M/T STOLT SHEAF

860 F.2d 551 (2d Cir. 1988).

CARDAMONE, CIRCUIT JUDGE:

The sole question presented on this appeal is whether National Petrochemical Company of Iran (NPC), a foreign corporation wholly owned by the government of Iran, is entitled to bring suit as a plaintiff in a diversity action in federal court. To answer such a question in this shoalstrewn area of the law, it is wise for courts to have in mind, like doctors taking the Hippocratic oath, that they must "first, do no harm." For the reasons that follow, we hold that NPC may maintain its action in the courts of the United States.

I

A brief background is necessary. In November of 1979 militants loyal to the Ayatollah Khomeini seized the United States Embassy in Tehran and took 52 American diplomatic personnel hostage. With the embassy and its personnel still in the militants' hands, on April 7, 1980 President Carter severed diplomatic relations with Iran and issued Executive Order No. 12,205, 45 Fed.Reg. 24,099 (1980), barring the sale to it of American products. As a result, NPC—which is a subsidiary of the National Iranian Oil Company that in turn is wholly owned by the government of Iran—found itself unable to procure essential chemicals such as ethylhexanol, orthoxylene, and ethylene dichloride from its usual sources in the United States. NPC's attempts to circumvent President Carter's trade embargo resulted in the transactions that brought about the instant litigation.

In the spring of 1980, NPC agreed to buy the needed chemicals from Monnris Enterprises (Monnris) of Dubai, United Arab Emirates. Monnris arranged to purchase them from Rotexchemie Brunst & Co. of Hamburg (Rotex), which contracted with United States sellers through its Geneva affiliate, Formula, S.A. (Formula). Rotex and Formula apparently fabricated shipping documents that concealed both the origin of the chemical cargo and its destination, and by such illegal methods were able to draw on the letters of credit issued by NPC before the cargoes were even shipped.

In August, 1980 Rotex chartered the defendant M/T Stolt Sheaf from the Liberian defendant Parcel Tankers, Inc. to carry the chemicals from Houston, Texas to Iran, via Barcelona, Spain. The remaining defendants are United States and Norwegian companies affiliated with Parcel Tankers and the M/T Stolt Sheaf. Rotex planned to deliver the embargoed goods to NPC in Iran, but when war broke out between Iran and Iraq in September, 1980 the chemicals were diverted to Taiwan, where Rotex resold them.

NPC thereupon instituted civil and criminal suits against the middlemen in Hamburg and Rotterdam to recover the losses it incurred in its scheme to skirt the American trade embargo. Because these suits were unsuccessful, plaintiff filed a complaint on September 30, 1986 in the United States District Court for the Southern District of New York (Owen, J.) alleging that the above named defendants had participated with the middlemen in fraud, conversion, falsifying bills of lading, all in breach of their duties and obligations under the bills of lading and the law. In a published decision, 671 F. Supp. 1009 (S.D.N.Y. 1987), Judge Owen concluded—based upon a United States State Department letter written in connection with an unrelated case, *Iran Handicraft & Carpet Export Center v. Marjan Int'l Corp.*, 655 F. Supp. 1275 (S.D.N.Y. 1987)—that the United States has not recognized the Khomeini government of Iran. The district court therefore held that because NPC is a wholly-owned entity of an unrecognized foreign government, it is not entitled to bring suit in the courts of the United States. It dismissed NPC's complaint with prejudice. 671 F.Supp. at 1010.

On NPC's appeal from dismissal of its complaint, the United States has, for the first time, entered the litigation, submitting a brief as Amicus Curiae signed by attorneys from the Justice and State Departments, urging that NPC be granted access to the courts of the United States in this case.

II

We turn to an analysis of the law. Article III of the United States Constitution extends the federal judicial power to "all Cases . . . between a State, or the Citizens thereof, and foreign States, Citizens or Subjects." U.S. Const., art. III, § 2, cl. 1. To effectuate this power, the United States Judicial Code provides diversity jurisdiction over any civil action arising between "a foreign state . . . as plaintiff and citizens of a State or of different States." 28 U.S.C. § 1332(a)(4) (1982).

To determine whether NPC as a wholly-owned entity of the Khomeini government of Iran should be granted access to federal court under § 1332(a)(4), it is helpful to review several well-established rules in this area of the law. In order to take advantage of diversity jurisdiction, a foreign state and the government representing it must be "recognized" by the United States. *See Pfizer Inc. v. India,* 434 U.S. 308, 319–20 (1978); *Calderone v. Naviera Vacuba S/A,* 325 F.2d 76, 77 (2d Cir. 1963); *Land Oberoesterreich v. Gude,* 109 F.2d 635, 637 (2d Cir.), *cert. denied,* 311 U.S. 670 (1940). As an incident to the President's express constitutional powers to appoint, U.S. Const., art. II, § 2, and to receive ambassadors, *id.* § 3, and to his implied power to maintain international relations, *United States v. Curtiss-Wright Export Corp.,* 299 U.S. 304, 318–20 (1936), the Supreme Court has acknowledged the President's exclusive authority to recognize or refuse to recognize a foreign state or government and to establish or refuse to establish diplomatic relations with it. *See Banco Nacional de Cuba v. Sabbatino,* 376 U.S. 398, 410 (1964); *Guaranty Trust Co. v. United States,* 304 U.S. 126, 137 (1938); *see also Restatement (Third) of the Foreign Relations Law of the United States* § 204 (1987) (*Restatement 3d*).

For our purposes in this case, we also note that, under international law, a "state" is generally defined as "an entity that has a defined territory and a permanent population, under the control of its own government, and that engages in, or has the capacity to engage in, formal relations with other such entities." *Restatement 3d* § 201; *see Texas v. White,* 74 U.S. (7 Wall.) 700, 720 (1868). Although international law purports to require recognition of "states" that satisfy the elements of this definition, recognition of the particular government in control of another state is not mandatory. Further, a state *derecognizes* a governmental regime when it recognizes another regime as the legitimate government of that state. For example, when the United States recognized the People's Republic of China it derecognized the regime of the Taiwanese "Republic of China" which the United States had previously treated as the Chinese government. *See Restatement 3d* § 203, Cmt. f.

A break in diplomatic relations with another government does not automatically signify denial of access to federal courts. *See Sabbatino*, 376 U.S. 408–12. As the Supreme Court has observed, courts are hardly competent to assess how friendly or unfriendly our relationship with a foreign government is at any given moment, and absent some "definite touchstone for determination, we are constrained to consider any relationship, short of war, with a recognized sovereign power as embracing the privilege of resorting to United States courts." *Id.* at 410; *see Pfizer Inc.,* 434 U.S. at 319–20. With these general rules in mind, we consider the circumstance of the instant case.

III

A. Recognition For Purposes of Federal Diversity Jurisdiction

The United States, as noted, severed diplomatic relations with Iran in 1980. In addition, NPC and Amicus concede that the President has never formally recognized the Khomeini government of Iran. The district court relied on a letter from the Assistant Legal Advisor for Management of the Department of State clarifying Iran's diplomatic status in connection with *Iran Handicraft & Carpet Export Center v. Marjan Int'l Corp.*, 655 F. Supp. 1275 (S.D.N.Y. 1987). The letter, dated December 26, 1985, stated in part:

In response to your letter of December 13, 1985, the questions you posed and the answers of the State Department are as follows:

"1. Has the United States recognized the Khomeini government of the Islamic Republic of Iran?"

Answer: No.

Id. at 1280 n. 4. Amicus contends that this response referred merely to the absence of formal recognition and was not intended to foreclose courts from entertaining suits by the Khomeini regime. NPC and Amicus argue that the Executive Branch has not prohibited the Khomeini regime's access to federal courts, and that the Executive Branch may recognize a government for the purposes of bringing suit despite the absence of formal recognition.

Appellees assert, to the contrary, that unlike diplomatic relations, the President's formal statement of recognition of a foreign government is a necessary condition to permitting it to sue in federal court. Certain language in the Supreme Court's decisions arguably supports such a requirement. *See, e.g., Sabbatino*, 376 U.S. at 410 ("[T]he refusal to recognize has a unique legal aspect. It signifies this country's unwillingness to acknowledge that the government in question speaks . . . for the territory it purports to control.") (citations omitted); *Guaranty Trust*, 304 U.S. at 137 ("[I]n conformity to generally accepted principles, the Soviet Government could not maintain a suit in our courts before its recognition by the political department of the Government."). Thus, appellees urge that NPC must be denied access to federal court based on the President's failure to extend formal recognition to the Khomeini government. We disagree and hold that the absence of formal recognition does not necessarily result in a foreign government being barred from access to United States courts.

Two reasons support this holding. First, as this century draws to a close, the practice of extending formal recognition to new governments has altered: The United States Department of State has sometimes refrained from announcing recognition of a new government because grants of recognition have been misinterpreted as pronouncements of approval. *See 77 State Dep't Bull.* 462–63 (Oct. 10, 1977) ("In recent years, U.S. practice has been to deemphasize and avoid the use of recognition in cases of changes of governments. . . ."); *Restatement 3d* § 203, reporter's note 1 (commenting on recent deemphasis of formal recognition). As a result, the absence of formal recognition cannot serve as the touchstone for determining whether the Executive Branch has "recognized" a foreign nation for the purpose of granting that government access to United States courts.

Second, the power to deal with foreign nations outside the bounds of formal recognition is essential to a president's implied power to maintain international relations. *Cf. United States v. Curtiss-Wright Export Corp.*, 299 U.S. 304, 318–20 (1936). As part of this power, the Executive Branch must have the latitude to permit a foreign nation access to U.S. courts, even if that nation is not formally recognized by the U.S. government. This is because the president alone—as the constitutional guardian of foreign policy—knows what action is necessary to effectuate American relations with foreign governments. *Cf. Sabbatino*, 376 U.S. at 411 n. 12 (citing criticisms of any policy which would mandate formal recognition before a foreign nation could sue in U.S. courts).

This case serves as an excellent example. Relations between the United States and Iran over the past eight years have been less than friendly. Yet, the status of that relationship has not been unchanging. There have been periods of improvement, for example, release of the embassy hostages, and periods of worsening relations, most recently occasioned by the unfortunate downing of an Iranian civilian airliner by the U.S.S. Vincennes. It is evident that in today's topsy-turvy world governments can topple and relationships can change in a moment. The Executive Branch must therefore have broad, unfettered discretion in matters involving such sensitive, fast-changing, and complex foreign relationships. *See Guaranty Trust*, 304 U.S. at 137 ("What government is to be regarded here as representative of a foreign sovereign state is a political rather than a judicial question, and is to be determined by the political department of the government."); *Sabbatino*, 376 U.S. at 410 ("This Court would hardly be competent to undertake assessments of varying degrees of friendliness or its absence. . . ."); *Curtiss-Wright,* 299 U.S. at 319 ("In this vast external realm, with its important, complicated, delicate and manifold problems, the President alone has the power to speak or listen as a representative of the nation.").

B. Deference to the Executive Branch

Determining that formal recognition is not necessary for Iran to gain access to U.S. courts does not end our inquiry. We must also consider whether the Executive Branch—despite its withholding of formal recognition—has evinced a willingness to permit Iran to litigate its claims in the U.S. forum. Several facts persuasively indicate such a willingness. For example, Iran and the United States entered into the Algerian Accords to resolve the embassy personnel hostage crisis; an ongoing Iran-United States Claims Tribunal at the Hague continues to adjudicate disputes between the two countries; and the 1955 Treaty of Amity, Economic Relations and Consular Rights between the United States and Iran remains in full force and effect. Standing alone, none of these indicia of Executive Branch willingness to allow Iran to proceed as a plaintiff in the United States courts would necessarily persuade us to reverse the district court and grant access. Considering these factors in the aggregate, and not in isolation, as integral components of the United States overall relationship to Iran, the above recited connections strongly suggest that the Executive Branch has evinced an implicit willingness to permit the government of Iran to avail itself of a federal forum.

It is unnecessary to go further in examining other treaties, documents, or ties in order to ascertain the Executive Branch's intentions regarding Iran's access to the federal courts. The United States has submitted a Statement of Interest pursuant to 28 U.S.C. § 517 (1982) stating that "it is the position of the Executive Branch that the Iranian government and its instrumentality should be afforded access to our courts for purposes of resolution of the instant dispute." Because this Statement was not filed with Judge Owen, he was not apprised of the Executive Branch's position prior to ruling.

Appellees protest that for us to defer to what they term an "*ad hoc, pro hac vice*" directive to allow NPC's suit will encourage arbitrary and unpredictable pronouncements on the status of foreign governments, but we need not reach that question here because there is no indication that this is an arbitrary or *ad hoc* directive. This is not a case where the Executive Branch is attempting to prohibit a formally recognized government from bringing a single suit in the United States courts, nor is it a case where the Executive is arbitrarily allowing some suits by an unrecognized nation while disallowing others. Rather, here the Executive Branch—after entering into treaties with Iran, after establishing a claims tribunal to adjudicate disputes between the two countries, and after complying with U.S.-Iran agreements—expressly entered this case as Amicus requesting that Iran be given access to our courts. Under such circumstances, and as the sole branch authorized to conduct relations with foreign countries, the Executive clearly did not act arbitrarily. Accordingly, we hold that, for all the reasons stated, NPC must be permitted to proceed with its diversity suit in the Southern District of New York.

NOTES

1. *Recognized Governments as Defendants.* A recognized foreign government is entitled to immunity from judicial process in U.S. courts for certain of its public (or sovereign) acts. (*See infra*, this Chapter, Sec. 7); Foreign Sovereign Immunities Act of 1976, 28 U.S.C. § 1604 (2012).

2. *Unrecognized Governments as Defendants.* The cases extracted above (*Cibrario, Sabbatino, Pfizer, and National Petrochemical Company of Iran*) involved governments (or their agencies or instrumentalities) appearing in

U.S. courts as plaintiffs. What happens if an unrecognized government is sued as a defendant?

One approach might be to regard the foreign entity, though not recognized as a foreign sovereign, as nevertheless being immune from suit. Recall that in the *Cibrario* case, the court noted a prior decision in *Wulfsohn v. Russian Socialist Federated Soviet Republic,* 234 N.Y. 372 (1923). In that case, the Court of Appeals of New York held that the Soviet government's existence "whenever it becomes material may probably be proved in other ways" than by reference to the State Department's recognition policy. *Id.* at 375. The court's result "depends upon more basic considerations than recognition or nonrecognition by the United States. Whether or not a government exists clothed with the power to enforce its authority within its own territory, obeyed by the people over whom it rules, capable of performing the duties and fulfilling the obligations of an independent power, able to enforce its claims by military force, is a fact, not a theory." *Id.* The plaintiff "may not bring a foreign sovereign before our bar, not because of comity, but because he has not submitted himself to our laws. Without his consent he is not subject to them. Concededly that is so as to a foreign government that has received recognition. . . . But whether recognized or not, the evil of such an attempt would be the same." *Id.* at 376 (citations omitted).

Consider the court's reasoning about this "evil." It said that it would "vex the peace of nations" and "the hands of the State Department would be tied." *Id.* Why? Does it matter that in *Wulfsohn* the property, which plaintiff alleged had been wrongfully seized by the Soviet government, was in territory under its control? If the court had reached the conclusion that the Soviet defendant, being unrecognized, was not entitled to immunity, would that have made it an entity capable of being sued? In passing, the court says of the question at issue: "Here, however, we need no proof. The fact is conceded. We have an existing government sovereign within its own territories." *Id.*

Yet another approach might be to regard the foreign entity as not entitled to immunity as a foreign sovereign but, rather, as simply a person (albeit in the form of an organization) that is capable of being sued just like any other person, subject to the normal rules on jurisdiction. How might such an approach unfold?

WALDMAN V. PALESTINE LIBERATION ORGANIZATION

835 F.3d 317 (2d Cir. 2016).

JOHN G. KOELTL, DISTRICT JUDGE:

In this case, eleven American families sued the Palestine Liberation Organization ("PLO") and the Palestinian Authority ("PA") (collectively, "defendants") under the Anti-Terrorism Act ("ATA"), 18 U.S.C. § 2333(a), for various terror attacks in Israel that killed or wounded the plaintiffs-appellees-cross-appellants ("plaintiffs") or their family members. . . .

After a seven-week trial, a jury found that the defendants, acting through their employees, perpetrated the attacks and that the defendants knowingly provided material support to organizations designated by the United States State Department as foreign terrorist organizations. The jury awarded the plaintiffs damages of $218.5 million, an amount that was trebled automatically pursuant to the ATA, 18 U.S.C. § 2333(a), bringing the total award to $655.5 million.

On appeal, the defendants seek to overturn the jury's verdict by arguing that the United States Constitution precludes the exercise of personal jurisdiction over them. . . .

The PA was established by the 1993 Oslo Accords as the interim and non-sovereign government of parts of the West Bank and the Gaza Strip (collectively referred to here as "Palestine"). The PA is headquartered in the city of Ramallah in the West Bank, where the Palestinian President and the PA's ministers reside.

The PLO was founded in 1964. At all relevant times, the PLO was headquartered in Ramallah, the Gaza Strip, and Amman, Jordan. Because the Oslo Accords limit the PA's authority to Palestine, the PLO conducts Palestine's foreign affairs.

During the relevant time period for this action, the PLO maintained over 75 embassies, missions, and delegations around the world. The PLO is registered with the United States Government as a foreign agent. The PLO has two diplomatic offices in the United States: a mission to the United States in Washington, D.C. and a mission to the United Nations in New York City. The Washington, D.C. mission had fourteen employees between 2002 and 2004, including two employees of the PA, although not all at the same time. . . .

Courts have repeatedly held that neither the PA nor the PLO is a "State" under United States or international law. *See Klinghoffer v. S.N.C. Achille Lauro*, 937 F.2d 44, 47–48 (2d Cir. 1991) (holding the PLO, which had no defined territory or permanent population and did not have capacity to enter into genuine formal relations with other nations, was not a "State" for purposes of the Foreign Sovereign Immunities Act); *Estates of Ungar v. Palestinian Auth.*, 315 F.Supp.2d 164, 178–86 (D.R.I. 2004) (holding that neither the PA nor the PLO is a State entitled to sovereign immunity under the Foreign Sovereign Immunities Act because neither entity has a defined territory with a permanent population controlled by a government that has the capacity to enter into foreign relations); *see also Knox v. Palestine Liberation Org.*, 306 F.Supp.2d 424, 431 (S.D.N.Y. 2004) (holding that neither the PLO nor the PA was a "State" for purposes of the Foreign Sovereign Immunities Act).

While the United States does not recognize Palestine or the PA as a sovereign government, *see Sokolow v. Palestine Liberation Org.*, 583

F.Supp.2d 451, 457–58 (S.D.N.Y. 2008) ("Palestine, whose statehood is not recognized by the United States, does not meet the definition of a 'state,' under United States and international law. . . .") (collecting cases), the PA is the governing authority in Palestine and employs tens of thousands of security personnel in Palestine. . . .

. . . [T]he plaintiffs argue that the defendants have no due process rights because the defendants are foreign governments and share many of the attributes typically associated with a sovereign government. Foreign sovereign states do not have due process rights but receive the protection of the Foreign Sovereign Immunities Act. The plaintiffs argue that entities, like the defendants, lack due process rights, because they . . . are treated as a foreign government in other contexts. The plaintiffs do not cite any cases indicating that a non-sovereign entity with governmental attributes lacks due process rights. All the cases cited by the plaintiffs stand for the proposition that sovereign governments lack due process rights, and these cases have not been extended beyond the scope of entities that are separate sovereigns, recognized by the United States government as sovereigns, and therefore enjoy foreign sovereign immunity. . . .

Pursuant to the due process clauses of the Fifth and Fourteenth Amendments, there are two parts to the due process test for personal jurisdiction as established by *International Shoe [Co. v. Washington]*, 326 U.S. 310, 66 S.Ct. 154 [(1945)], and its progeny: the "minimum contacts" inquiry and the "reasonableness" inquiry. The minimum contacts inquiry requires that the court determine whether a defendant has sufficient minimum contacts with the forum to justify the court's exercise of personal jurisdiction over the defendant. *See Daimler [AG v. Bauman]*, 134 S.Ct. [746] at 754 [(2014)]. The reasonableness inquiry requires the court to determine whether the assertion of personal jurisdiction over the defendant comports with " 'traditional notions of fair play and substantial justice' " under the circumstances of the particular case. *Daimler*, 134 S.Ct. at 754.

International Shoe distinguished between two exercises of personal jurisdiction: general jurisdiction and specific jurisdiction. . . .

The district court concluded that it had general jurisdiction over the defendants; however, that conclusion relies on a misreading of the Supreme Court's decision in *Daimler*. . . .

As the District Court for the District of Columbia observed, "[i]t is common sense that the single ascertainable place where a government such a[s] the Palestinian Authority should be amenable to suit for all purposes is the place where it governs. Here, that place is the West Bank, not the United States." *Livnat*, 82 F.Supp.3d at 30. The same analysis applies equally to the PLO, which during the relevant period maintained its headquarters in Palestine and Amman, Jordan. *See Klieman*, 82 F.Supp.3d at 245 ("Defendants' alleged contacts . . . do not suffice to render the PA and the PLO 'essentially at home' in the United States.")

The activities of the defendants' mission in Washington, D.C.—which the district court concluded simultaneously served as an office for the PLO and the PA—were limited to maintaining an office in Washington, promoting the Palestinian cause in speeches and media appearances, and retaining a lobbying firm.

These contacts with the United States do not render the PA and the PLO "essentially at home" in the United States. The commercial contacts that the district court found supported general jurisdiction are like those rejected as insufficient by the Supreme Court in *Daimler*. . . .

The district court did not rule explicitly on whether it had specific personal jurisdiction over the defendants, but the question was sufficiently briefed and argued to allow us to reach that issue. . . .

. . . [B]ecause the terror attacks in Israel at issue here were not expressly aimed at the United States and because the deaths and injuries suffered by the American plaintiffs in these attacks were "random [and] fortuitous" and because lobbying activities regarding American policy toward Israel are insufficiently "suit-related conduct" to support specific jurisdiction, the Court lacks specific jurisdiction over these defendants.

* * *

The terror machine gun attacks and suicide bombings that triggered this suit and victimized these plaintiffs were unquestionably horrific. But the federal courts cannot exercise jurisdiction in a civil case beyond the limits prescribed by the due process clause of the Constitution, no matter how horrendous the underlying attacks or morally compelling the plaintiffs' claims.

The district court could not constitutionally exercise either general or specific personal jurisdiction over the defendants in this case. Accordingly, this case must be dismissed.

NOTE ON GIVING EFFECT TO ACTS OF UNRECOGNIZED GOVERNMENTS

The cases extracted for this Chapter addressed situations where an unrecognized foreign government is either the plaintiff or defendant in a case before a U.S. court. What if the unrecognized government is not a party in the case, but the legal effects of its acts are at issue before the U.S. court?

There is considerable variation in how courts deal with the fact of nonrecognition in deciding whether to give effect to acts of the unrecognized governments. Courts seem sometimes to give effect to such acts due to a perceived compatibility of so doing with the purposes behind the executive's policy of nonrecognition. Conversely, among the reasons given by courts for *not* giving effect to such decrees is the incompatibility of doing so with the perceived intent of the executive's nonrecognition policy. How do the courts know whether a presidential policy of nonrecognition would or would not be frustrated by giving effect to any particular decree of the foreign regime? If the courts, as they constantly protest in these cases, are unequipped to make foreign policy, what equips them to determine whether a particular policy would be helped or hindered by departing from, or applying, the strict letter of that policy in a particular case?

In some instances, the State Department will attempt to provide the courts with information as to whether its nonrecognition policy should be applied to the circumstances of a case. *See The Rogdai*, 278 Fed. 294 (N.D. Cal. 1920). Or the courts may take "judicial notice" of the actions of the executive that seem controlling, even if only a general press release. *See The Penza*, 277 Fed. 91 (E.D.N.Y. 1921). Particularly "when the executive branch of the Government has determined upon a foreign policy, which can be and is ascertained, and the nonrecognition of specific foreign decrees is deliberate and is shown to be part of that policy, such nonrecognition must be given effect by the courts." *Latvian State Cargo & Passenger S.S. Line v. McGrath*, 188 F.2d 1000 (D.C. Cir. 1951) (refusing to recognize confiscations effectuated by nationalization decrees of Latvia in light of affidavits by the Secretary of State addressing both nonrecognition in general and the decrees in particular).

Should some acts that are less politically significant or that do not offend public policy be given effect? Is it practical or appropriate to withhold effect for certain types of private rights and acts, such as government-sanctioned marriages or divorces?

In *Sokoloff v. National City Bank,* 239 N.Y. 158 (1924), the Court of Appeals of New York (Cardozo, J.) stated that a plaintiff who paid money into the defendant U.S. bank to open an account at its branch in Petrograd could recover the deposit even though the Petrograd branch and its accounts had been expropriated by the unrecognized Soviet government. The court said, in part:

> We think the case at hand is not so governed by authority but that it may be dealt with upon principle.
>
> Juridically, a government that is unrecognized may be viewed as no government at all, if the power withholding recognition chooses thus to view it. In practice, however, since juridical conceptions are seldom, if ever, carried to the limit of their logic, the equivalence is not absolute, but is subject to self-imposed limitations of common sense and fairness, as we learned in litigations following our Civil War. In those litigations acts or decrees of the rebellious governments, which, of course, had not been recognized as governments de facto, were held to be nullities when they worked injustice to citizens of the Union, or were in conflict with its public policy. *Williams v. Bruffy*, 96 U.S. 176, 187. On the other hand, acts or decrees that were just in operation and consistent with public

policy, were sustained not infrequently to the same extent as if the governments were lawful. *U.S. v. Insurance Companies*, 22 Wall. 99; *Sprott v. U.S.*, 20 Wall. 459; *Texas v. White*, 7 Wall. 700, 733; *Mauran v. Alliance Ins. Co.*, 6 Wall. 1; *Baldy v. Hunter*, 171 U.S. 388; cf. Dickinson, Unrecognized Governments, 22 Mich. L. R. 29, 42. These analogies suggest the thought that, subject to like restrictions, effect may at times be due to the ordinances of foreign governments which, though formally unrecognized, have notoriously an existence as governments de facto. Consequences appropriate enough when recognition is withheld on the ground that rival factions are still contending for the mastery, may be in need of readjustment before they can be fitted to the practice, now a growing one, of withholding recognition whenever it is thought that a government, functioning unhampered, is unworthy of a place in the society of nations. Limitations upon the general rule may be appropriate for the protection of one who has been the victim of spoliation though they would be refused to the spoliator or to others claiming under him. We leave these questions open. At the utmost, they suggest the possibility that a body or group which has vindicated by the course of events its pretensions to sovereign power, but which has forfeited by its conduct the privileges or immunities of sovereignty, may gain for its acts and decrees a validity quasi-governmental, if violence to fundamental principles of justice or to our own public policy might otherwise be done.

. . . The *res* belonging to the plaintiff was not a physical object committed to the defendant's keeping, but an intangible right, a chose in action, the right to receive rubles in the future under an executory contract. This contract the defendant has not performed, yet it refuses to return the dollars that were paid to it by the plaintiff upon its promise of performance. Two acts that must be kept distinct in thought are said to justify this refusal. One is the decree nationalizing the banks of Russia with the accompanying seizure of their assets. The other is the later decree confiscating the accounts of the depositors as a "revolutionary tax."

The defendant's liability was unaffected by the attempt to terminate its existence and the seizure of its assets. A government of Russia could not terminate its existence either by dissolution or by merger, for it was a corporation formed under our laws, and its corporate life continued until the law of its creation declared that it should end. What a Russian government could do was to deprive it of the privilege of doing business upon Russian soil. But the ending of its Russian business was not the ending of its duty to make restitution for benefits received without requital. . . .

239 N.Y. at 165–67.

7. IMMUNITIES

Justiciability questions do not exhaust the kinds of issues posed directly to the judiciary. A longstanding feature of the international legal system is the immunity of foreign diplomatic, consular, and other personnel and property from proceedings before national courts or other authorities. Such immunity contributes to friendly relations among States by allowing State officials to perform their functions without the risk of being exposed to national proceedings, which in some instances might be a form of harassment or retaliation. The contours of these immunities, and the kinds of law from which they derive, depend on the type of official concerned.

Diplomatic Immunities. In general, once a government (the "sending State") accredits a person as a diplomat to another government (the "receiving State"), that person is immune with respect to acts or omissions in the exercise of his or her official functions and in other circumstances in which lack of immunity would be inconsistent with diplomatic status. The diplomat is also immune from criminal process and most civil process in the receiving State. *See Restatement (Third)* § 464.

Customary international law governing the treatment of diplomats and diplomatic property is now codified in the Vienna Convention on Diplomatic Relations (VCDR), Apr. 18, 1961, 23 U.S.T. 3227, 500 U.N.T.S. 95. The VCDR has been ratified by 191 States as of mid-2017, including the United States. Under the VCDR, the "person" of the diplomat is inviolable, and the receiving State has an affirmative duty to protect each diplomat from an attack "on his person, freedom or dignity." *Id.*, art. 29. The receiving State may neither arrest nor detain the diplomat, and the diplomat is immune from criminal laws as well as from civil and administrative jurisdiction. *Id.*, art. 31(1). Diplomats may not be compelled to give evidence, and they are immune from personal service, most taxes, social security provisions, and customs duties and inspections. *Id.*, arts. 31(2), 33–36. Diplomatic immunity also extends to the diplomat's family members. *Id.*, art. 37. *See generally* Eileen Denza, *Diplomatic Law: Commentary on the Vienna Convention on Diplomatic Relations* (4th ed. 2016); Grant V. McClanahan, *Diplomatic Immunity: Principles, Practices, Problems* (1989).

For the role of the president in the provision of such immunities, see section 4 of the Diplomatic Relations Act of 1978, 22 U.S.C. § 254c (2016). Subsection (a) provides that the "President may, on the basis of reciprocity and under such terms and conditions as he may determine, specify privileges and immunities for the mission, the members of the mission, their families, and the diplomatic couriers which result in more favorable treatment or less favorable treatment than is provided under the Vienna Convention."

Consular Immunities. Customary international law governing the treatment of consular officers and consulates is codified in the Vienna Convention on Consular Relations (VCCR), Apr. 24, 1963, 21 U.S.T. 77, 596 U.N.T.S. 261. The VCCR has been ratified by 179 States as of mid-2017, including the United States. It prohibits the arrest or detention of consular officers except for grave crimes and under court order. *Id.*, art. 41. Consular officers are not subject to judicial jurisdiction "in respect of acts performed in the exercise of consular functions," although they may be required to give evidence, and their privileges may be waived by the sending State. *Id.*, arts. 43–45; *see Restatement (Third)* § 465; Luke T. Lee, *Consular Law and Practice* (3d ed. 2008).

The VCCR also obligates States, when they arrest a foreign national, to notify the national of a right to have his or her consulate informed. The failure to notify foreigners of this right has been used to challenge their convictions and sentences in U.S. court, in the Inter-American Commission on Human Rights, and in cases before the International Court of Justice. (*See* Chapter 6, Sec. 8).

International Civil Servant Immunities. Civil servants employed by international organizations typically enjoy a variety of immunities. They are usually exempted from alien registration acts and generally have personal immunities similar to those accorded diplomats and consuls. For the United Nations, the relevant multilateral treaty is the General Convention on the Privileges and Immunities of the United Nations, Feb. 13, 1946, 21 U.S.T. 1418, 1 U.N.T.S. 15. The General Convention provides for immunity from personal arrest and protects papers, documents, and courier bags. Further, since the U.N. headquarters is in the United States, certain privileges and immunities are accorded U.N. personnel pursuant to a bilateral U.S.-U.N. Headquarters Agreement, June 26, 1947, 61 Stat. 3416, 11 U.N.T.S. 11.

The United States implements many of its obligations toward international civil servants via the International Organizations Immunities Act (IOIA), Pub. L. No. 79–291, 59 Stat. 669 (1945) (codified at 22 U.S.C. §§ 288–288k (2012)). The statute grants to presidentially-designated international organizations the same immunity enjoyed by foreign governments. *Id.* § 288a(b). (The scope of foreign government immunity, as opposed to foreign *official* immunity, is considered later in this Section.) The statute also provides to persons designated by foreign governments as their representatives and the officers and employees of those organizations (and their immediate families, other than U.S. nationals) the same privileges, exemptions, and immunities enjoyed by officers and employees of foreign governments (and their families) in relation to entry, departure, and registration requirements. More important, it provides representatives, officers, and employees immunity from "suit and legal process relating to acts performed by them in their official capacity and falling within their functions . . . except insofar as such immunity may be waived by the foreign government or international organization concerned." *Id.* § 288d(b).

Head-of-State Immunity. Separate from the immunities accorded to diplomats, consular officials, and international civil servants, international law also provides "head-of-state" immunity. Since there is no multilateral treaty addressing this type of immunity, head-of-state immunity in the United States is a part of federal common law derived in part from customary international law.

As the cases below indicate, when foreign officials are sued or prosecuted in U.S. courts, they will often raise head-of-state immunity as a defense. Sometimes immunity is granted, whereas other times it is rejected. *Compare United States v. Noriega*, 117 F.3d 1206, 1212 (11th Cir. 1997) (rejecting head-of-state immunity for Panamanian military leader being prosecuted on drug charges) *and Kadic v. Karadzic*, 70 F.3d 232, 248 (2d Cir. 1995) (rejecting head-of-state immunity for civilian leader of Serbs in Bosnia) *with Habyarimana v. Kagame*, 696 F. 3d 1029 (10th Cir. 2012) (accepting head-of-state immunity for sitting president of Rwanda). Such immunity may be waived by an individual's government. *See, e.g., Doe v. United States*, 860 F.2d 40, 44–46 (2d Cir. 1988) (finding no head-of-state immunity for former Philippine leader and his wife in light of waiver by the Philippine government).

When reading the following case, consider the role of customary international law. If customary international law governs the immunity issue, should U.S. courts defer to the executive branch in determining whether head-of-state immunity should be accorded? Is deference being granted because the president is best placed to interpret international law or for some other reason?

MOTIONS OR SUGGESTIONS OF IMMUNITY

22 U.S.C. § 254d (2012).

Dismissal on motion of action against individual entitled to immunity

Any action or proceeding brought against an individual who is entitled to immunity with respect to such action or proceeding under the Vienna Convention on Diplomatic Relations . . . or under any other laws extending diplomatic privileges and immunities, shall be dismissed. Such immunity may be established upon motion or suggestion by or on behalf of the individual, or as otherwise permitted by law or applicable rules of procedure.

YE V. ZEMIN

383 F.3d 620 (7th Cir. 2004).

MANION, CIRCUIT JUDGE.

Jiang Zemin served as President of China for approximately ten years, from March 1993 to March 15, 2003. During part of his tenure as President, he also served as the Secretary General of the Central Committee of the Chinese Communist Party (the head of the Party). President Jiang stepped down as head of the Party on November 15, 2002.

Beginning in 1999, the Chinese government and the Party took steps to crack down on Falun Gong. Falun Gong, formed in 1992 by a former Chinese soldier, Li Hongzhi, "combin[es] traditional Buddhist teachings and predictions about the end of the world with meditation and martial arts discipline as a prescription for physical and spiritual well-being. Falun Gong teaches that illness stems from evil and that by following the principles of 'truth, compassion and forbearance,' one can attain clairvoyance and other preternatural faculties." The Chinese government and the Party see things differently. They have denounced the movement as a cult and have accused it of seeking to subvert or overthrow the government and the Party's grip on power. According to at least one news report, President Jiang himself declared that suppressing Falun Gong was one of the " 'three major political struggles' of 1999."

To that end, on June 10, 1999, President Jiang established, as part of the Party's apparatus, the Falun Gong Control Office. The Office is known as "Office 6/10" after the date of its creation. In July 1999, President Jiang issued an edict outlawing Falun Gong. . . .

The appellants filed this lawsuit against President Jiang and Office 6/10 on October 18, 2002. The appellants' complaint, recites, *inter alia,* claims of torture, genocide, arbitrary arrest and imprisonment, as well as other claims related to the appellants' freedom of conscience, movement, and religion. . . .

Because President Jiang was scheduled to be in Chicago on October 22 and 23 on his way to visit with United States President George W. Bush in Washington, D.C., the appellants moved *ex parte* for leave from the district court to effect service on President Jiang (and by extension Office 6/10) while he was in Chicago. The district court granted this motion and entered an order permitting service by delivery of a copy of the summons and complaint "to any of the security agents or hotel staff helping to guard" President Jiang. The appellants contend that service was complete when they delivered a copy of these documents to a Chicago police officer and agents of the United States Secret Service detail stationed at the hotel at which President Jiang was staying in Chicago.

Neither President Jiang nor a representative of the Chinese government or Office 6/10 responded to the complaint, and the appellants moved for an entry of default. The United States, however, intervened pursuant to 28 U.S.C. § 517 and moved to vacate the service order or, in the alternative, to assert head-of-state immunity for President Jiang. The United States further argued that President Jiang was personally inviolable and, therefore, incapable of being served in any capacity. Specifically, the government argued that President Jiang could not be served as an agent of Office 6/10.

The district court accepted the United States' assertion of head-of-state immunity on behalf of President Jiang and dismissed the appellants' claims against him. The district court rejected, however, the government's argument of personal inviolability. Instead, the district court found that service of process on Office 6/10 could not be achieved through President Jiang because the appellants had not shown that President Jiang was either an agent or an officer of Office 6/10. Further, the district court held that, even assuming service of process on Office 6/10 could be effectuated through President Jiang, it lacked personal jurisdiction to hear claims against it. The district court, therefore, dismissed the appellants' complaint in its entirety. This appeal followed.

II.

The appellants raise three issues on appeal. First, they argue that the district court erred when it accepted, as controlling, the United States' assertion of head-of-state immunity on behalf of President Jiang. Second, the appellants argue that the district court erred when it determined that President Jiang could not be served as an agent of Office 6/10. Finally, the appellants argue that the district court erred when it held that it lacked personal jurisdiction over Office 6/10. . . .

B. The Present Case

In this case the Executive Branch entered a suggestion of immunity. The appellants argue, however, that the Executive Branch has no power to immunize a head of state (or any person for that matter) for acts that violate *jus cogens* norms of international law. We have explained *jus cogens* norms before:

> A *jus cogens* norm is a special type of customary international law. A *jus cogens* norm " 'is a norm accepted and recognized by the international community of states as a whole as a norm from which no derogation is permitted and which can be modified only by a subsequent norm of general international law having the same character.' " *See Siderman de Blake v. Republic of Argentina,* 965 F.2d 699, 714 (9th Cir. 1992) (*quoting* Vienna Convention on the Law of Treaties, art. 53, May 23, 1969, 1155 U.N.T.S. 332, 8 I.L.M. 679). Most famously, *jus cogens* norms

> supported the prosecutions in the Nuremberg trials. *See Siderman,* 965 F.2d at 715 (9th Cir. 1992) ("The universal and fundamental rights of human beings identified by Nuremberg—rights against genocide, enslavement, and other inhumane acts . . .—are the direct ancestors of the universal and fundamental norms recognized as jus cogens.").

Sampson v. Federal Republic of Germany, 250 F.3d 1145, 1149–50 (7th Cir. 2001).

The appellants' position, therefore, is that, in at least a particular class of cases (those involving *jus cogens* norms), a court cannot defer to the position of the Executive Branch with respect to immunity for heads of states. The Supreme Court has held, however, that the Executive Branch's suggestion of immunity is conclusive and not subject to judicial inquiry. *See Ex Parte Republic of Peru,* 318 U.S. 578, 589 . . . (1943) ("The certification and the request that the vessel be declared immune *must be accepted by the courts as a conclusive determination* by the political arm of the Government that the continued retention of the vessel interferes with the proper conduct of our foreign relations.") (emphasis added); *Compañia Española de Navegacion Maritima, S.A. v. The Navemar,* 303 U.S. 68, 74 . . . (1938) ("If [a claim of immunity by a foreign government] is recognized and allowed by the Executive Branch of the government, *it is then the duty of the courts* to release the vessel upon appropriate suggestion by the Attorney General of the United States, or other officer acting under his discretion.") (emphasis added); *see also Spacil v. Crowe,* 489 F.2d 614, 617 (5th Cir. 1974) ("The precedents are overwhelming. For more than 160 years American courts have consistently applied the doctrine of sovereign immunity when requested to do so by the executive branch. Moreover, they have done so with no further review of the executive's determination."); *Isbrandtsen Tankers, Inc. v. President of India,* 446 F.2d 1198, 1201 (2d Cir. 1971) ("The State Department is to make [an immunity determination] in light of the potential consequences to our own international position. Hence once the State Department has ruled in a matter of this nature, the judiciary will not interfere."); *Rich v. Naviera Vacuba S.A.,* 295 F.2d 24, 26 (4th Cir. 1961) ("[W]e conclude that the certificate and grant of immunity issued by the Department of State should be accepted by the court without further inquiry. We think that the doctrine of the separation of powers under our Constitution requires us to assume that all pertinent considerations have been taken into account by the Secretary of State in reaching his conclusion.") (internal citations omitted).

The appellants present their argument as one of international law—under customary international law, a state cannot provide immunity to a defendant accused of violating *jus cogens* norms. Our first concern, however, is to ascertain the proper relationship between the Executive and Judicial Branches insofar as the immunity of foreign leaders is concerned.

The obligation of the Judicial Branch is clear—a determination by the Executive Branch that a foreign head of state is immune from suit is conclusive and a court must accept such a determination without reference to the underlying claims of a plaintiff. *See Spacil*, 489 F.2d at 618 ("[W]e are analyzing here the proper allocation of functions of the branches of government in the scheme of the United States. We are not analyzing the proper scope of sovereign immunity under international law.").

Our deference to the Executive Branch is motivated by the caution we believe appropriate of the Judicial Branch when the conduct of foreign affairs is involved. *Cf. Republic of Mexico v. Hoffman*, 324 U.S. 30, 35 . . . (1945) ("[I]t is a guiding principle in determining whether a court should [recognize a suggestion of immunity] in such cases, that the courts should not so act as to embarrass the executive arm in its conduct of foreign affairs. 'In such cases the judicial department of this government follows the action of the political branch, and will not embarrass the latter by assuming an antagonistic jurisdiction.' ") (quoting *United States v. Lee*, 106 U.S. 196, 209 . . . (1882)); *Spacil,* 489 F.2d at 619 ("Separation-of-powers principles impel a reluctance in the judiciary to interfere with or embarrass the executive in its constitutional role as the nation's primary organ of international policy."). The determination to grant (or not grant) immunity can have significant implications for this country's relationship with other nations. A court is ill-prepared to assess these implications and resolve the competing concerns the Executive Branch is faced with in determining whether to immunize a head of state.

Although our decision in *Sampson* was one of statutory interpretation, we believe it is also instructive here. In *Sampson* we held that the [Foreign Sovereign Immunities Act of 1976, 28 U.S.C. §§ 1602 et seq. (2000) (FSIA)] did not include an implied exception to its general grant of sovereign immunity to foreign states where a foreign state was accused of violating *jus cogens* norms. [250 F.3d] at 1156. Because the FSIA contained no such exception, Germany was immune from suit brought by a survivor of Auschwitz in the Northern District of Illinois.

Our interpretation of the FSIA confirmed that Congress could grant immunity to a foreign state for acts that amounted to violations of *jus cogens* norms. Just as the FSIA is the Legislative Branch's determination that a nation should be immune from suit in the courts of this country, the immunity of foreign leaders remains the province of the Executive Branch. The Executive Branch's determination that a foreign leader should be immune from suit even when the leader is accused of acts that violate *jus cogens* norms is established by a suggestion of immunity. We are no more free to ignore the Executive Branch's determination than we are free to ignore a legislative determination concerning a foreign state. *Cf. Hoffman*, 324 U.S. at 35 . . . (1945) ("It is . . . not for the courts to deny an immunity which our government has seen fit to allow, or to allow an immunity on new grounds which the government has not seen fit to recognize."). Pursuant to their respective authorities, Congress or the Executive Branch can create exceptions to blanket immunity. In such cases the courts would be obliged to respect such exceptions. In the present case the Executive Branch has recognized the immunity of President Jiang from the appellants' suit. The district court was correct to accept this recognition as conclusive.

C. Service of Process on President Jiang to Reach Third Parties

We turn next to Office 6/10. The appellants maintain that service on Office 6/10 was complete when President Jiang was served during his stay in Chicago. As recounted above, the United States argues that President Jiang's immunity extends to service aimed not at him, but at a third party.

The district court rejected the United States' immunity argument but, nonetheless, held that service on President Jiang was insufficient to reach Office 6/10 because the appellants had provided only conclusory evidence that President Jiang was, at the time of service, an officer or agent of Office 6/10. The district court also held that "even if Jiang was an agent or officer of Office 6/10 and thus capable of receiving service on its behalf, such service was insufficient to confer personal jurisdiction over Office 6/10 because the Office is not subject to the jurisdiction of Illinois courts."

Although the district court reached the correct result, it erred when it rejected the United States' argument concerning the scope of President Jiang's immunity. Because the Executive Branch has recognized President Jiang's immunity from suit, President Jiang could not be used as an involuntary agent of the appellants to effect service on Office 6/10. We need not therefore consider whether President Jiang was acting as an agent or officer of Office 6/10 or whether the district court had personal jurisdiction over Office 6/10.

We agree with the Executive Branch that its power to recognize the immunity of a foreign head of state includes the power to preclude service of process in that same suit on the head of state even where that service is intended to reach third parties.

Recognizing the immunity of a head of state and precluding service of process on a head of state are motivated by the same concern for the effective conduct of this nation's foreign affairs. As emphasized above, this responsibility is left to the political branches of this government. The Executive Branch has represented to this court that permitting service of process is often viewed by foreign governments and their heads of state "as an affront to the dignity of both the leader and the state." The Executive Branch has also indicated that "the potential for insult is the same, regardless of whether the service relates to the visiting head of state himself, or to service on the visiting leader in some purported representational or agency capacity." Finally, the Executive Branch has indicated that "[s]uch attacks on the dignity of a visiting head of state can easily frustrate our President's ability to reach this Nation's diplomatic objectives. . . ." The deference we extend the Executive Branch with regard to its determination of immunity, *see supra,* is equally appropriate here. The Executive Branch is better equipped than this court or the district court to assess the consequences for our foreign policy of permitting service of process on visiting heads of state, and it is the Executive Branch in its dealings with China that will confront, in the first instance, the consequences of that determination. *Cf. Hellenic Lines, Ltd. v. Moore*, 345 F.2d 978, 980–81 (D.C. Cir. 1965) (holding that the Ambassador of Tunisia was not properly subject to service directed to Tunisia after the State Department informed the court that "service would prejudice the United States foreign relations and would probably impair the performance of diplomatic functions."); *see also Spacil,* 489 F.2d at 619 ("[I]n the chess game that is diplomacy only the executive has a view of the entire board and an understanding of the relationship between isolated moves. Will granting immunity serve as a bargaining counter in complex diplomatic negotiations? Will it preclude a significant diplomatic advance; perhaps a detente between this country and one with whom we are not on the best speaking terms? These are questions for the executive, not the judiciary.") (internal citation omitted).

Also important to our decision is the treatment accorded the President of the United States in his travels abroad. The Executive Branch has stated that it would be a "great offense if foreign states and their courts were to encourage process servers to hound our President when he is abroad to conduct important negotiations with his foreign counterparts." Such concerns must weigh heavily in our determination that service of process should not be permitted on foreign heads of state visiting this country in the circumstances of this case. . . .

III.

In this case the Executive Branch has recognized President Jiang's immunity from the appellants' suit. We are required to defer to the decision of the Executive Branch. The Executive Branch has also determined that service of process by the appellants on President Jiang in order to reach an intended co-defendant in the same suit could frustrate this Nation's diplomatic objectives. It is appropriate to defer to that decision as well. Because we do so, service on Office 6/10 could not be effectuated through President Jiang. We need not reach, therefore, the question of whether President Jiang was, at the time of service, an officer or agent of Office 6/10 or whether the district court had personal jurisdiction over Office 6/10.

We conclude by stating that we are not unsympathetic to the appellants' claims. For the reasons stated above, however, we cannot permit this suit to go forward. The Executive Branch has stated it is working to persuade the government of China to put an end to the human rights violations it has inflicted on its people for more than half a century. Success depends on diplomacy, not United States courts.

Affirmed

NOTES

1. *Immunity for Heads of State.* The scope of head-of-state immunity under customary international law was clarified somewhat by the International Court of Justice (ICJ) in a case involving an arrest warrant issued by a Belgian court for the detention of the then-foreign affairs minister of the Democratic Republic of the Congo (DRC). The minister was accused of committing war crimes and crimes against humanity—acts committed prior to assuming his post, which he held at the time of the issuance of the warrant but which he relinquished prior to the announcement of the ICJ's judgment—by making speeches that incited the massacre of civilians. Belgium asserted that the exercise of its national criminal law over such conduct was permissible under international law because of the principle of "universal jurisdiction."

Without speaking to the issue of whether such jurisdiction was permissible under international law, the Court asserted "that in international law it is firmly established that, as also diplomatic and consular agents, certain holders of high-ranking office in a State, such as the Head of State, Head of Government and Minister for Foreign Affairs, enjoy immunities from jurisdiction in other States, both civil and criminal." *Arrest Warrant of 11 April 2000* (Congo v. Belg.), Judgment, 2002 I.C.J. 3, 20–21 (Feb. 14). As such, the ICJ held that Belgium's warrant violated customary international law, because it failed to respect the incumbent minister's inviolability and immunity from criminal jurisdiction.

The U.N. International Law Commission in 2013 provisionally adopted a draft article providing that "Heads of State, Heads of Government and Ministers for Foreign Affairs enjoy immunity *ratione personae* from the exercise of foreign criminal jurisdiction." *See* Report of the International Law Commission on the Work of Its Sixty-Fifth Session, UN GAOR, 68th Sess., Supp. No. 10, at 52, UN Doc. A/68/10 (2013).

Similar immunity has been accorded by U.S. courts. *See, e.g., Tachiona v. Mugabe*, 169 F.Supp.2d 259, 296–97 (S.D.N.Y. 2001) (dismissing case against a Zimbabwe foreign minister, in accordance with State Department suggestion of immunity), *aff'd in part on other grounds, rev'd in part,* 386 F.3d 205 (2d Cir. 2004); *Kilroy v. Windsor (Prince Charles, The Prince of Wales)*, Civ. No. C–78–291 (N.D.Ohio 1978), *excerpted in* U.S. Dept. of State, *Digest of United States Practice in International Law* 641–43 (1978) (dismissing suit against Prince Charles, in accordance with State Department suggestion of immunity); *Philippines v. Marcos*, 665 F. Supp. 793, 799 (N.D.Cal.1987) (dismissing suit against Philippines solicitor general, in accordance with State Department suggestion of immunity). If you were a lawyer for the U.S. government, which officials would you regard as being entitled to head-of-state immunity?

2. *Special Missions Immunity.* Foreign officials (other than accredited diplomats) who are engaged in diplomatic activities are sometimes described as serving "special missions" in their host States. Those missions may be entitled to "special missions" immunity under customary international law or pursuant to the Convention on the Prevention and Punishment of Crimes Against Internationally Protected Persons including Diplomatic Agents, Dec. 14, 1973, 28 U.S.T. 1975, 1035 U.N.T.S. 167. Although not a party to that convention, the U.S. government has effectively recognized instances of special mission immunity.

For example, a visiting Chinese Commerce Minister was served with process for actions he took as a provincial governor. As such, his status both when he acted and when he was served was not that of a head of State (or foreign minister), nor was he an accredited diplomat. Nonetheless, the State Department suggested immunity on the ground that the minister was serving as a diplomatic envoy at the time process was served. The district court agreed and dismissed the action. *Weixum v. Xilai*, 568 F.Supp.2d 35 (D.D.C. 2008). In addition, cases like *Kilroy v. Windsor* and *Tachiona v. Mugabe* involved suggestions of immunity for officials who not only held high office, but who were also present in the United States and served with process while performing diplomatic or other similar official functions.

3. *Official Immunity and Former Heads of State.* In the *Arrest Warrant* case, the ICJ found that the issuance of an arrest warrant against a then-incumbent foreign minister violated Belgium's international legal obligations. Because the head-of-state immunity to which a foreign minister was entitled was absolute in character, it protected against "any act of authority of another State which would hinder him or her in the performance of his or her duties." 2002 I.C.J. at 22. It was irrelevant, then, whether the warrant related to acts undertaken by the minister in an official or private capacity, whether those acts occurred before the minister even assumed office, or whether the acts were especially severe or heinous under international law. *Id.*

At the same time, the Court emphasized that the minister would potentially be vulnerable to prosecution under other circumstances. The DRC could choose itself to prosecute him or to waive immunity so as to enable prosecution by another State. The minister might also be subject to prosecution by certain international criminal tribunals with jurisdiction over the matter. Last, but not least, absolute immunity was effective only for the period in which the minister held office: afterward, he might be prosecuted by Belgium or another State for acts committed prior or subsequent to the minister's period of office, as well as for private acts committed during his or her tenure, so long as the prosecuting State's asserted jurisdiction was consistent with international law. *Id.* at 26–27. Head-of-state immunity is a status-based or *in personae* form of immunity; the immunity enjoyed by former heads of States and by other sitting and former officials is a conduct-based or *ratione materiae* form of immunity.

On remand following the Supreme Court's decision in *Samantar v. Yousuf*, 560 U.S. 305 (2010) (holding that the immunity of foreign officials is governed by common law), the question arose whether a former Somali vice president, minister of defense, and prime minister was entitled to immunity from civil suit for acts he asserted had been taken in an official capacity. The State Department filed a statement of interest determining that the official in question did not enjoy immunity, emphasizing in particular that because the United States did not recognize a government of Somalia, there was no government to assert immunity on the official's behalf or to express a position as to whether the acts concerned were taken in an official capacity. Further, the Department argued that the defendant official was now a resident of the United States. Statement of Interest of the United States of America, *Yousuf v. Samantar*, No. 1:04 CV 1360 (LMV) (E.D. Va.). The Court of Appeals held that Samantar was not entitled to official immunity in part for the reasons given by the government but also because he allegedly committed *jus cogens* violations, reasoning that although *jus cogens* violations "may well be committed under color of law and, in that sense, constitute actions performed in the court of the foreign officials employment," they are "as a matter of international and domestic law" by definition acts "not officially authorized by the Sovereign." *Yousuf v. Samantar*, 699 F. 3d 763 (4th Cir. 2012). Is this reasoning consistent with *Ye v. Zemin*? *See also* Matar v. Dichter, 563 F.3d 9, 14–15 (2d Cir. 2009); *Giraldo v. Drummond Co.*, 493 Fed. Appx. 106 (D.C. Cir. 2012) (granting immunity to a foreign official even in the face of allegations of *jus cogens* violations).

4. *The Role of the Courts*. The Foreign Sovereign Immunities Act governs the immunity of foreign States before courts in the United States, but it does not address the immunity of individuals. *Samantar v. Yousuf*, 560 U.S. 305 (2010). Must U.S. courts accept as binding the State Department's decision as to whether a foreign government official is to be accorded immunity? *See, e.g., Matar v. Dichter*, 563 F.3d 9, 13–14 (2d Cir. 2009) (dismissing suit against former director of security and intelligence service, in accordance with State Department suggestion of immunity). Note that the executive branch's view might turn on several different factors: whether the person in question is the head of State (or other high-ranking official) of a government; whether that government is recognized by the United States; whether that official because of his or her position qualifies for head-of-state immunity; whether that official because of his or work qualifies for special mission immunity; and whether, if that immunity only extends to acts undertaken in an official capacity, the acts in question were of that nature. Should conclusive effect be given by U.S. courts for all or just some of those factors? For criticism of the judiciary's reliance on executive branch determinations, see Ingrid B. Wuerth, *Foreign Official Immunity Determinations in U.S. Courts: The Case Against the State Department*, 51 VA. J. INT'L L. 915 (2011).

For example, should the judiciary exercise any greater degree of independent judgment with respect to the claims of special mission immunity than is the case for head-of-state immunity? Is it troubling to depart from an approach that limits immunity to only a relatively small number of high-level officials (head-of-state immunity) to a different approach (special missions immunity) that potentially immunizes a wide range of individuals at the wholesale discretion of the executive branch? Or is it preferable to focus less on the position of the person and more on whether diplomatic activity is being performed, a matter best left to executive scrutiny? On remand in *Yousuf v. Samantar*, the Court of Appeals held that the State Department's position on status-based immunity doctrines, including head-of-state immunity, are binding on the courts but that the State Department's decision on conduct-based immunity is entitled only to "substantial weight." It drew the distinction based on the president's constitutional power to recognize foreign governments, including heads of State. *Yousuf v. Samantar*, 699 F.3d 763, 772 (4th Cir. 2012). Is this reasoning convincing? Or should courts treat as conclusive the president's determination about who is a foreign head of State, but not the domestic legal consequences (such as immunity) that follow from that status? *Cf. Manoharan v. Rajapaska*, 711 F.3d 178, 179 (D.C. Cir. 2013) (holding that courts should accept State Department suggestions of head-of-state immunity as a matter of "common law").

Are there any limitations on the power of the executive branch to determine which individual is the head of State? Consider the following case. The president of Haiti, Jean-Bertrand Aristide, was exiled to the United States after a military coup. When sued for human rights violations allegedly committed during his tenure as president, Aristide moved to dismiss the action based on a suggestion of immunity filed by the U.S. government asserting that Aristide was entitled to head-of-state immunity. Although Aristide was no longer actually in power, the U.S. government continued to recognize him as the lawful president of Haiti. The plaintiff pointed to a letter purportedly signed by Aristide relinquishing his title as president and to the election of a new president by the Haitian Parliament under control of the military regime to show that Aristide was not entitled to immunity as head of State. The plaintiff also argued that the new government had implicitly waived any immunity to which Aristide was entitled. The judge rejected these arguments, holding that the determination of who qualifies as head of State (and thus who may waive immunity) is not a factual issue but a determination made by the executive branch. *Lafontant v. Aristide*, 844 F. Supp. 128 (E.D.N.Y. 1994). How are the issues in *Lafontant* related to the Court's more recent decision in *Zivotofsky v. Kerry*, 135 S.Ct. 2076 (2015), which is excerpted in Chapter 1, Sec. 2?

NOTE ON THE PROTECTION OF DIPLOMATS VERSUS FREE SPEECH

18 U.S.C. § 112 (2012) subjects to criminal punishment willful acts or attempts to "intimidate, coerce, threaten, or harass a foreign official or an official guest or obstruct a foreign official in the performance of his duties." Can this statute be used to preclude persons from picketing foreign embassies in

the United States, since protesting the policies of foreign countries constitutes a form of "harassment"?

In *CISPES v. Federal Bureau of Investigation,* 770 F.2d 468 (5th Cir. 1985), the Fifth Circuit Court of Appeals upheld the constitutionality of that statute against a challenge by the Committee in Solidarity with the People of El Salvador (CISPES), which had sought a confrontation with the Honduran Consul in New Orleans, including a picket line in front of the main entrance to the consulate. The FBI had ordered the picket dissolved on the basis of the statute. The court found that the law "is a legislative effort to implement various international obligations of the United States government." *Id.* at 472. These obligations were found to include the norms established by the Convention to Prevent and Punish the Acts of Terrorism Taking the Form of Crimes against Persons and Related Extortion That Are of International Significance, adopted by the Organization of American States, and the Convention on the Prevention and Punishment of Crimes against Internationally Protected Persons, adopted by the United Nations. *Id.* at 472 n. 5. Since peaceful picketing is normally regarded as an activity protected by the First Amendment, is the court demonstrating a willingness to tolerate what amounts to prior restraint on such activity because of the government's interest in upholding its international legal obligations?

BOOS V. BARRY

485 U.S. 312 (1988).

JUSTICE O'CONNOR delivered the opinion of the Court, except as to Part II-A.

The question presented in this case is whether a provision of the District of Columbia Code, § 22–1115, violates the First Amendment. This section prohibits the display of any sign within 500 feet of a foreign embassy if that sign tends to bring that foreign government into "public odium" or "public disrepute." It also prohibits any congregation of three or more persons within 500 feet of a foreign embassy.

I

Petitioners are three individuals who wish to carry signs critical of the Governments of the Soviet Union and Nicaragua on the public sidewalks within 500 feet of the embassies of those Governments in Washington, D.C. Petitioners Bridget M. Brooker and Michael Boos, for example, wish to display signs stating "RELEASE SAKHAROV" and "SOLIDARITY" in front of the Soviet Embassy. Petitioner J. Michael Waller wishes to display a sign reading "STOP THE KILLING" within 500 feet of the Nicaraguan Embassy. All of the petitioners also wish to congregate with two or more other persons within 500 feet of official foreign buildings.

Asserting that D.C. Code § 22–1115 (1981) prohibited them from engaging in these expressive activities, petitioners, together with respondent Father R. David Finzer, brought a facial First Amendment challenge to that provision in the District Court for the District of Columbia. . . .

Congress enacted § 22–1115 in 1938, S.J. Res. 191, ch. 29, § 1, 52 Stat. 30 (1938), pursuant to its authority under Article I, § 8, cl. 10, of the Constitution to "define and punish . . . Offenses against the Law of Nations." . . .

The first portion of this statute, the "display" clause, applies to signs tending to bring a foreign government into public odium or public disrepute, such as signs critical of a foreign government or its policies. The display clause applies only to the display of signs, not to the spoken word. . . . The second portion of the statute, the "congregation" clause, addresses a different concern. It prohibits congregation, which District of Columbia common law defines as an assemblage of three or more people. . . . Both of these prohibitions generally operate within a 500-foot zone surrounding embassies or consulates owned by foreign governments, but the statute also can extend to other buildings if foreign officials are inside for some official purpose. . . .

The Court of Appeals . . . concluded that the display clause was a content-based restriction on speech. Relying, however, upon our decisions in *Perry Education Assn. v. Perry Local Educators' Assn.,* 460 U.S. 37, 45 (1983), and *Carey v. Brown*, 447 U.S. 455, 461–462 (1980), the court nonetheless found it constitutional because it was justified by a compelling governmental interest and was narrowly drawn to serve that interest. Second, the Court of Appeals concluded that the congregation clause should be construed to authorize an order to disperse "only when the police reasonably believe that a threat to the security or peace of the embassy is present," and that as construed, the congregation clause survived First Amendment scrutiny. 255 U.S. App. D.C., at 40, 798 F.2d, at 1471.

We granted certiorari, 479 U.S. 1083 (1987). We now reverse the Court of Appeals' conclusion as to the display clause, but affirm as to the congregation clause.

II

A

Analysis of the display clause must begin with several important features of that provision. First, the display clause operates at the core of the First Amendment by prohibiting petitioners from engaging in classically political speech. . . .

Second, the display clause bars such speech on public streets and sidewalks, traditional public fora that "time out of mind, have been used for purposes of assembly, communicating thoughts between citizens, and discussing public questions." *Hague v. CIO,* 307 U.S. 496, 515 (1939)

(Roberts, J.). In such places, which occupy a "special position in terms of First Amendment protection," *United States v. Grace*, 461 U.S., at 180, the government's ability to restrict expressive activity "is very limited." Id., at 177.

Third, § 22–1115 is content based. Whether individuals may picket in front of a foreign embassy depends entirely upon whether their picket signs are critical of the foreign government or not. One category of speech has been completely prohibited within 500 feet of embassies. Other categories of speech, however, such as favorable speech about a foreign government or speech concerning a labor dispute with a foreign government, are permitted. *See* D.C. Code § 22–1116 (1981).

. . . Both respondents and the United States . . . contend that the statute is not content based because the government is not itself selecting between viewpoints; the permissible message on a picket sign is determined solely by the policies of a foreign government.

We reject this contention, although we agree the provision is not viewpoint based. The display clause determines which viewpoint is acceptable in a neutral fashion by looking to the policies of foreign governments. While this prevents the display clause from being directly viewpoint based, a label with potential First Amendment ramifications of its own, . . . it does not render the statute content neutral. Rather, we have held that a regulation that "does not favor either side of a political controversy" is nonetheless impermissible because the "First Amendment's hostility to content-based regulation extends . . . to prohibition of public discussion of an entire topic." . . .

B

Our cases indicate that as a *content-based* restriction on *political speech* in a *public forum*, § 22–1115 must be subjected to the most exacting scrutiny. Thus, we have required the State to show that the "regulation is necessary to serve a compelling state interest and that it is narrowly drawn to achieve that end." . . .

We first consider whether the display clause serves a compelling governmental interest in protecting the dignity of foreign diplomatic personnel. Since the dignity of foreign officials will be affronted by signs critical of their governments or governmental policies, we are told, these foreign diplomats must be shielded from such insults in order to fulfill our country's obligations under international law.

As a general matter, we have indicated that in public debate our own citizens must tolerate insulting, and even outrageous, speech in order to provide "adequate 'breathing space' to the freedoms protected by the First Amendment." . . .

We are not persuaded that the differences between foreign officials and American citizens require us to deviate from these principles here. The dignity interest is said to be compelling in this context primarily because its recognition and protection is part of the United States' obligations under international law. The Vienna Convention on Diplomatic Relations, April 18, 1961, [1972] 23 U.S.T. 3227, T.I.A.S. No. 7502, which all parties agree represents the current state of international law, imposes on host states

> "[the] special duty to take all appropriate steps to protect the premises of the mission against any intrusion or damage and to prevent any disturbance of the peace of the mission or impairment of its dignity." *Id.*, at 3237–3238, Art. 22.

As a general proposition, it is of course correct that the United States has a vital national interest in complying with international law. The Constitution itself attempts to further this interest by expressly authorizing Congress "[t]o define and punish Piracies and Felonies committed on the high Seas, and Offenses against the Law of Nations." U.S. Const., Art. I, § 8, cl. 10. Cf. The Federalist No. 3, p. 43 (C. Rossiter ed. 1961) (J. Jay). Moreover, protecting foreign emissaries has a long history and noble purpose. In this country national concern for the protection of ambassadors and foreign ministers even predates the Constitution. In 1781 the Continental Congress adopted a resolution calling on the States to enact laws punishing "infractions of the immunities of ambassadors and other public ministers, authorised and received as such by the United States in Congress assembled," targeting in particular "violence offered to their persons, houses, carriages and property." 21 J. Continental Cong. 1136–1137 (G. Hunt ed. 1912).

The need to protect diplomats is grounded in our Nation's important interest in international relations. As a leading commentator observed in 1758, "[i]t is necessary that nations should treat and hold intercourse together, in order to promote their interests,—to avoid injuring each other,—and to adjust and terminate their disputes." E. Vattel, The Law of Nations 452 (J. Chitty ed. 1844) (translation). This observation is even more true today given the global nature of the economy and the extent to which actions in other parts of the world affect our own national security. Diplomatic personnel are essential to conduct the international affairs so crucial to the well-being of this Nation. In addition, in light of the concept of reciprocity that governs much of international law in this area, *see* C. Wilson, Diplomatic Privileges and Immunities 32 (1967), we have a more parochial reason to protect foreign diplomats in this country. Doing so ensures that similar protections will be accorded those that we send abroad to represent the United States, and thus serves our national interest in protecting our own citizens. Recent history is replete with attempts, some unfortunately successful, to harass and harm our ambassadors and other diplomatic officials. These underlying purposes combine to make our national interest in protecting diplomatic personnel powerful indeed.

At the same time, it is well established that "no agreement with a foreign nation can confer power on the Congress, or on any other branch of Government, which is free from the restraints of the Constitution." *Reid v. Covert*, 354 U.S. 1, 16 (1957). *See* 1 *Restatement of Foreign Relations Law of the United States* § 131, Comment a, p. 53 (Tent. Draft No. 6, Apr. 12, 1985) ("[R]ules of international law and provisions of international agreements of the United States are subject to the Bill of Rights and other prohibitions, restrictions or requirements of the Constitution and cannot be given effect in violation of them").

Thus, the fact that an interest is recognized in international law does not automatically render that interest "compelling" for purposes of First Amendment analysis. We need not decide today whether, or to what extent, the dictates of international law could ever require that First Amendment analysis be adjusted to accommodate the interests of foreign officials. Even if we assume that international law recognizes a dignity interest and that it should be considered sufficiently "compelling" to support a content-based restriction on speech, we conclude that § 22–1115 is not narrowly tailored to serve that interest. *See, e.g., Perry Education Assn.*, 460 U.S., at 45; *Board of Airport Comm'rs of Los Angeles*, 482 U.S., at 573.

The most useful starting point for assessing § 22–1115 is to compare it with an analogous statute adopted by Congress, which is the body primarily responsible for implementing our obligations under the Vienna Convention. Title 18 U.S.C. § 112(b)(2) subjects to criminal punishment willful acts or attempts to "intimidate, coerce, threaten, or harass a foreign official or an official guest or obstruct a foreign official in the performance of his duties."

Its legislative history reveals that § 112 was developed as a deliberate effort to implement our international obligations. *See, e.g.*, 118 Cong. Rec. 27112–27113 (1972). At the same time, the history reflects a substantial concern with the effect of any such legislation on First Amendment freedoms. . . . After the 1972 passage of § 112 [ ], congressional concerns about its impact on First Amendment freedoms apparently escalated rather than abated. In 1976, Congress revisited the area and repealed the antipicketing provision, leaving in place only the current prohibition on willful acts or attempts to "intimidate, coerce, threaten, or harass a foreign official." § 112(b)(2). In modifying § 112, Congress was motivated by First Amendment concerns:

> "This language [of the original antipicketing provision] raises serious Constitutional questions because it appears to include within its purview conduct and speech protected by the First

Amendment." S. Rep. No. 94–1273, p. 8, n. 9 (1976); H.R. Rep. No. 94–1614, p. 6, n. 9 (1976).

Thus, after a careful balancing of our country's international obligations with our Constitution's protection of free expression, Congress has determined that § 112 adequately satisfies the Government's interest in protecting diplomatic personnel outside the District of Columbia. It is the necessary, "appropriate" step that Congress has enacted to fulfill our international obligations. Cf. Vienna Convention on Diplomatic Relations, Art. 22, § 2, 23 U.S.T., at 3237 ("special duty to take all appropriate steps").

Section 112 applies to all conduct "within the United States but outside the District of Columbia." § 112(b)(3). In the legislative history, the exclusion of the District from the statute's reach is explained with reference to § 22–1115; Congress was informed that a "similar" statute already applied inside the District. S. Rep. No. 92–1105, *supra,* at 19; H.R. Rep. No. 92–1268, p. 5 (1972). The two statutes, however, are not identical, and the differences between them are constitutionally significant. In two obvious ways, § 112 is considerably less restrictive than the display clause of § 22–1115. First and foremost, § 112 is not narrowly directed at the content of speech but at any activity, including speech, that has the prohibited effects. Moreover, § 112, unlike § 22–1115, does not prohibit picketing; it only prohibits activity undertaken to "intimidate, coerce, threaten, or harass." Indeed, unlike the display clause, even the repealed antipicketing portion of § 112 permitted peaceful picketing.

Given this congressional development of a significantly less restrictive statute to implement the Vienna Convention, there is little force to the argument that we should give deference to a supposed congressional judgment that the Convention demands the more problematic approach reflected in the display clause. If § 112 is all that is necessary in the rest of the country, petitioners contend it should be all that is necessary in the District of Columbia. The only counter-argument offered by respondents is that the District has a higher concentration of foreign embassies than other locales and that a more restrictive statute is therefore necessary. But this is arguably factually incorrect (New York City is reported to have a greater number of foreign embassies, missions, or consulates than does the District of Columbia, *see* Note, Regulating Embassy Picketing in the Public Forum, 55 Geo. Wash. L. Rev. 908, 928, n. 140 (1987)), and logically beside the point since the need to protect "dignity" is equally present whether there is one embassy or mission or one hundred. The United States points to Congress' exclusive legislative authority over the District of Columbia, U.S. Const., Art. I, § 8, cl. 17, and argues that this justifies more extensive measures. We fail to see, however, why the potential legislative power to enact more extensive measures makes such measures necessary.

V.

We conclude that the display clause of § 22–1115 is unconstitutional on its face. It is a content-based restriction on political speech in a public forum, and it is not narrowly tailored to serve a compelling state interest. We also conclude that the congregation clause, as narrowed by the Court of Appeals, is not facially unconstitutional. Accordingly, the judgment of the Court of Appeals is reversed in part and affirmed in part.

It is so ordered.

NOTE ON INTERNATIONAL IMMUNITIES FOR FOREIGN STATES

The acknowledgement by U.S. courts of the immunity due to foreign officials (whether diplomats, consular officials, international civil servants, heads of state, or otherwise) shares its roots with the immunity conferred on foreign sovereigns as a whole. For much of U.S. history, U.S. courts adhered to an "absolute" theory of immunity, meaning that foreign sovereigns were completely immune from the jurisdiction of U.S. courts, except in very limited circumstances that rarely arose. By the first half of the twentieth century, the adherence to the absolute theory of immunity became increasingly problematic, especially as foreign governments began to engage in activities that were more commercial in nature, and as the U.S. government began waiving aspects of its own sovereign immunity in U.S. courts. In 1952, Acting Legal Adviser of the State Department, Jack Tate, wrote to the Acting Attorney General announcing the United States' adherence to the "restrictive theory" of sovereign immunity, which afforded immunity to a foreign state for its public acts, but not for its commercial acts.

Beginning in 1952 with the Tate Letter and continuing for nearly twenty-five years, the U.S. Department of State and the U.S. Department of Justice attempted to administer a scheme for determining whether a foreign government's request for immunity should be accepted and for reporting that conclusion to the relevant court. *See* Harold Hongju Koh, *Foreign Official Immunity After Samantar: A United States Government Perspective*, 44 VAND. J. TRANSNAT'L L. 1141, 1144 (2011). State Department control over the immunity of foreign states proved unsatisfactory. Critics argued that immunity determinations were made based on foreign policy, not law, and that the State Department process did not adequately consider all of the facts in many cases. At times the State Department made no decision on immunity one way or the other, which left courts in the difficult position of trying to apply precedent from prior State Department decisions. The process also subjected the State Department to intense pressure from foreign governments on questions of immunity. *See Verlinden B.V. v. Central Bank of Nigeria*, 461 U.S. 480, 487–88 (1983).

With the support of the State Department, Congress passed the Foreign Sovereign Immunities Act of 1976 (FSIA) (excerpted below), which both defined the kinds of activity by governments and state enterprises that were entitled to immunity in civil actions and transferred to the federal courts full responsibility for making the relevant determinations. As you read the excerpts from the FSIA, note that there is a general accordance of immunity (§ 1604) and then a series of exceptions when immunity will not be accorded (§ 1605). Why do you think these exceptions were adopted? What are some of the important limitations on the way the exceptions operate? Does the statute distinguish between the ability to bring an action to obtain a judgment and the ability to attach assets and enforce the judgment? If so, why make such a distinction? Are some assets of a foreign government completely off-limits from actions in U.S. courts? If so, why?

FOREIGN SOVEREIGN IMMUNITIES ACT OF 1976, AS AMENDED

28 U.S.C. §§ 1330, 1602–1605A, 1609–1611 (2012).

§ 1330. Actions against Foreign States

(a) The district courts shall have original jurisdiction without regard to amount in controversy of any nonjury civil action against a foreign state as defined in section 1603(a) of this title as to any claim for relief in personam with respect to which the foreign state is not entitled to immunity either under sections 1605–1607 of this title or under any applicable international agreement.

(b) Personal jurisdiction over a foreign state shall exist as to every claim for relief over which the district courts have jurisdiction under subsection (a) where service has been made under section 1608 of this title.

(c) For purposes of subsection (b), an appearance by a foreign state does not confer personal jurisdiction with respect to any claim for relief not arising out of any transaction or occurrence enumerated in sections 1605–1607 of this title.

§ 1602. Findings and Declaration of Purpose

The Congress finds that the determination by United States courts of the claims of foreign states to immunity from the jurisdiction of such courts would serve the interests of justice and would protect the rights of both foreign states and litigants in United States courts. Under international law, states are not immune from the jurisdiction of foreign courts insofar as their commercial activities are concerned, and their commercial property may be levied upon for the satisfaction of judgments rendered against them in connection with their commercial activities. Claims of foreign states to immunity should henceforth be decided by courts of the United States and of the States in conformity with the principles set forth in this chapter.

§ 1603. Definitions

For purposes of this chapter—

(a) A "foreign state", except as used in section 1608 of this title, includes a political subdivision of a foreign state or an agency or instrumentality of a foreign state as defined in subsection (b).

(b) An "agency or instrumentality of a foreign state" means any entity—

(1) which is a separate legal person, corporate or otherwise, and

(2) which is an organ of a foreign state or political subdivision thereof, or a majority of whose shares or other ownership interest is owned by a foreign state or political subdivision thereof, and

(3) which is neither a citizen of a State of the United States as defined in section 1332(c) and (e) of this title, nor created under the laws of any third country.

(c) The "United States" includes all territory and waters, continental or insular, subject to the jurisdiction of the United States.

(d) A "commercial activity" means either a regular course of commercial conduct or a particular commercial transaction or act. The commercial character of an activity shall be determined by reference to the nature of the course of conduct or particular transaction or act, rather than by reference to its purpose.

(e) A "commercial activity carried on in the United States by a foreign state" means commercial activity carried on by such state and having substantial contact with the United States.

§ 1604. Immunity of a Foreign State from Jurisdiction

Subject to existing international agreements to which the United States is a party at the time of enactment of this Act a foreign state shall be immune from the jurisdiction of the courts of the United States and of the States except as provided in sections 1605 to 1607 of this chapter.

§ 1605. General Exceptions to the Jurisdictional Immunity of a Foreign State

(a) A foreign state shall not be immune from the jurisdiction of courts of the United States or of the States in any case—

(1) in which the foreign state has waived its immunity either explicitly or by implication, notwithstanding any withdrawal of the waiver which the foreign state may purport to effect except in accordance with the terms of the waiver;

(2) in which the action is based upon a commercial activity carried on in the United States by the foreign state; or upon an act

performed in the United States in connection with a commercial activity of the foreign state elsewhere; or upon an act outside the territory of the United States in connection with a commercial activity of the foreign state elsewhere and that act causes a direct effect in the United States;

(3) in which rights in property taken in violation of international law are in issue and that property or any property exchanged for such property is present in the United States in connection with a commercial activity carried on in the United States by the foreign state; or that property or any property exchanged for such property is owned or operated by an agency or instrumentality of the foreign state and that agency or instrumentality is engaged in a commercial activity in the United States;

(4) in which rights in property in the United States acquired by succession or gift or rights in immovable property situated in the United States are in issue;

(5) not otherwise encompassed in paragraph (2) above, in which money damages are sought against a foreign state for personal injury or death, or damage to or loss of property, occurring in the United States and caused by the tortious act or omission of that foreign state or of any official or employee of that foreign state while acting within the scope of his office or employment; except this paragraph shall not apply to—

(A) any claim based upon the exercise or performance or the failure to exercise or perform a discretionary function regardless of whether the discretion be abused, or

(B) any claim arising out of malicious prosecution, abuse of process, libel, slander, misrepresentation, deceit, or interference with contract rights;

(6) in which the action is brought, either to enforce an agreement made by the foreign state with or for the benefit of a private party to submit to arbitration all or any differences which have arisen or which may arise between the parties with respect to a defined legal relationship, whether contractual or not, concerning a subject matter capable of settlement by arbitration under the laws of the United States, or to confirm an award made pursuant to such an agreement to arbitrate, if (A) the arbitration takes place or is intended to take place in the United States, (B) the agreement or award is or may be governed by a treaty or other international agreement in force for the United States calling for the recognition and enforcement of arbitral awards, (C) the underlying claim, save for the agreement to arbitrate, could have been brought in a United States court under this section or

section 1607, or (D) paragraph (1) of this subsection is otherwise applicable. . . .

§ 1605A. Terrorism Exception to the Jurisdictional Immunity of a Foreign State

(a) In general.—

(1) No immunity.—A foreign state shall not be immune from the jurisdiction of courts of the United States or of the States in any case not otherwise covered by this chapter in which money damages are sought against a foreign state for personal injury or death that was caused by an act of torture, extrajudicial killing, aircraft sabotage, hostage taking, or the provision of material support or resources for such an act if such act or provision of material support or resources is engaged in by an official, employee, or agent of such foreign state while acting within the scope of his or her office, employment, or agency.

(2) Claim heard.—The court shall hear a claim under this section if—

(A)(i)(I) the foreign state was designated as a state sponsor of terrorism at the time the act described in paragraph (1) occurred, or was so designated as a result of such act, and, subject to subclause (II), either remains so designated when the claim is filed under this section or was so designated within the 6-month period before the claim is filed under this section; or

(II) in the case of an action that is refiled under this section by reason of section 1083(c)(2)(A) of the National Defense Authorization Act for Fiscal Year 2008 or is filed under this section by reason of section 1083(c)(3) of that Act, the foreign state was designated as a state sponsor of terrorism when the original action or the related action under section 1605(a)(7) (as in effect before the enactment of this section) or section 589 of the Foreign Operations, Export Financing, and Related Programs Appropriations Act, 1997 (as contained in section 101(c) of division A of Public Law 104–208) was filed;

(ii) the claimant or the victim was, at the time the act described in paragraph (1) occurred—

(I) a national of the United States;

(II) a member of the armed forces; or

(III) otherwise an employee of the Government of the United States, or of an individual performing a contract awarded by the United States Government, acting within the scope of the employee's employment; and

(iii) in a case in which the act occurred in the foreign state against which the claim has been brought, the claimant has afforded the foreign state a reasonable opportunity to arbitrate the claim in accordance with the accepted international rules of arbitration; or

(B) the act described in paragraph (1) is related to Case Number 1:00CV03110 (EGS) in the United States District Court for the District of Columbia.

(b) Limitations.—An action may be brought or maintained under this section if the action is commenced, or a related action was commenced under section 1605(a)(7) (before the date of the enactment of this section) or section 589 of the Foreign Operations, Export Financing, and Related Programs Appropriations Act, 1997 (as contained in section 101(c) of division A of Public Law 104–208) not later than the latter of—

(1) 10 years after April 24, 1996; or

(2) 10 years after the date on which the cause of action arose.

(c) Private right of action.—A foreign state that is or was a state sponsor of terrorism as described in subsection (a)(2)(A)(i), and any official, employee, or agent of that foreign state while acting within the scope of his or her office, employment, or agency, shall be liable to—

(1) a national of the United States,

(2) a member of the armed forces,

(3) an employee of the Government of the United States, or of an individual performing a contract awarded by the United States Government, acting within the scope of the employee's employment, or

(4) the legal representative of a person described in paragraph (1), (2), or (3),

for personal injury or death caused by acts described in subsection (a)(1) of that foreign state, or of an official, employee, or agent of that foreign state, for which the courts of the United States may maintain jurisdiction under this section for money damages. In any such action, damages may include economic damages, solatium, pain and suffering, and punitive damages. In any such action, a foreign state shall be vicariously liable for the acts of its officials, employees, or agents. . . .

(h) Definitions.—For purposes of this section—

(1) the term "aircraft sabotage" has the meaning given that term in Article 1 of the Convention for the Suppression of Unlawful Acts Against the Safety of Civil Aviation;

(2) the term "hostage taking" has the meaning given that term in Article 1 of the International Convention Against the Taking of Hostages;

(3) the term "material support or resources" has the meaning given that term in section 2339A of title 18;

(4) the term "armed forces" has the meaning given that term in section 101 of title 10;

(5) the term "national of the United States" has the meaning given that term in section 101(a)(22) of the Immigration and Nationality Act (8 U.S.C. 1101(a)(22));

(6) the term "state sponsor of terrorism" means a country the government of which the Secretary of State has determined, for purposes of section 6(j) of the Export Administration Act of 1979 (50 U.S.C. App. 2405(j)), section 620A of the Foreign Assistance Act of 1961 (22 U.S.C. 2371), section 40 of the Arms Export Control Act (22 U.S.C. 2780), or any other provision of law, is a government that has repeatedly provided support for acts of international terrorism; and

(7) the terms "torture" and "extrajudicial killing" have the meaning given those terms in section 3 of the Torture Victim Protection Act of 1991 (28 U.S.C. 1350 note).

§ 1605B. Responsibility of Foreign States for International Terrorism against the United States

(a) Definition.—In this section, the term "international terrorism"—

(1) has the meaning given the term in section 2331 of title 18, United States Code; and

(2) does not include any act of war (as defined in that section).

(b) Responsibility of Foreign States.—A foreign state shall not be immune from the jurisdiction of the courts of the United States in any case in which money damages are sought against a foreign state for physical injury to person or property or death occurring in the United States and caused by—

(1) an act of international terrorism in the United States; and

(2) a tortious act or acts of the foreign state, or of any official, employee, or agent of that foreign state while acting within the scope of his or her office, employment, or agency, regardless where the tortious act or acts of the foreign state occurred.

(c) Claims by Nationals of the United States.—Notwithstanding section 2337(2) of title 18, a national of the United States may bring a claim against a foreign state in accordance with section 2333 of that title if the foreign state would not be immune under subsection (b).

(d) Rule of Construction.—A foreign state shall not be subject to the jurisdiction of the courts of the United States under subsection (b) on the basis of an omission or a tortious act or acts that constitute mere negligence.

§ 1609. Immunity from Attachment and Execution of Property of a Foreign State

Subject to existing international agreements to which the United States is a party at the time of enactment of this Act the property in the United States of a foreign state shall be immune from attachment, arrest and execution except as provided in sections 1610 and 1611 of this chapter.

§ 1610. Exceptions to the Immunity from Attachment or Execution

(a) The property in the United States of a foreign state, as defined in section 1603(a) of this chapter, used for a commercial activity in the United States, shall not be immune from attachment in aid of execution, or from execution, upon a judgment entered by a court of the United States or of a State after the effective date of this Act, if—

(1) the foreign state has waived its immunity from attachment in aid of execution or from execution either explicitly or by implication, notwithstanding any withdrawal of the waiver the foreign state may purport to effect except in accordance with the terms of the waiver, or

(2) the property is or was used for the commercial activity upon which the claim is based, or

(3) the execution relates to a judgment establishing rights in property which has been taken in violation of international law or which has been exchanged for property taken in violation of international law, or

(4) the execution relates to a judgment establishing rights in property—

(A) which is acquired by succession or gift, or

(B) which is immovable and situated in the United States: *Provided*, That such property is not used for purposes of maintaining a diplomatic or consular mission or the residence of the Chief of such mission, or

(5) the property consists of any contractual obligation or any proceeds from such a contractual obligation to indemnify or hold harmless the foreign state or its employees under a policy of automobile or other liability or casualty insurance covering the claim which merged into the judgment, or

(6) the judgment is based on an order confirming an arbitral award rendered against the foreign state, provided that attachment in aid of execution, or execution, would not be inconsistent with any provision in the arbitral agreement, or

(7) the judgment relates to a claim for which the foreign state is not immune under section 1605A or section 1605(a)(7) (as such section was in effect on January 27, 2008), regardless of whether the property is or was involved with the act upon which the claim is based.

(b) In addition to subsection (a), any property in the United States of an agency or instrumentality of a foreign state engaged in commercial activity in the United States shall not be immune from attachment in aid of execution, or from execution, upon a judgment entered by a court of the United States or of a State after the effective date of this Act, if—

(1) the agency or instrumentality has waived its immunity from attachment in aid of execution or from execution either explicitly or implicitly, notwithstanding any withdrawal of the waiver the agency or instrumentality may purport to effect except in accordance with the terms of the waiver, or

(2) the judgment relates to a claim for which the agency or instrumentality is not immune by virtue of section 1605(a)(2), (3), or (5), 1605(b), or 1605A of this chapter, regardless of whether the property is or was involved in the act upon which the claim is based, or

(3) the judgment relates to a claim for which the agency or instrumentality is not immune by virtue of section 1605A of this chapter or section 1605(a)(7) of this chapter (as such section was in effect on January 27, 2008), regardless of whether the property is or was involved in the act upon which the claim is based.

(c) No attachment or execution referred to in subsections (a) and (b) of this section shall be permitted until the court has ordered such attachment and execution after having determined that a reasonable period of time has elapsed following the entry of judgment and the giving of any notice required under section 1608(e) of this chapter.

(d) The property of a foreign state, as defined in section 1603(a) of this chapter, used for a commercial activity in the United States, shall not be immune from attachment prior to the entry of judgment in any action brought in a court of the United States or of a State, or prior to the elapse of the period of time provided in subsection (c) of this section, if—

(1) the foreign state has explicitly waived its immunity from attachment prior to judgment, notwithstanding any withdrawal of the waiver the foreign state may purport to effect except in accordance with the terms of the waiver, and

(2) the purpose of the attachment is to secure satisfaction of a judgment that has been or may ultimately be entered against the foreign state, and not to obtain jurisdiction. . . .

REPUBLIC OF ARGENTINA V. WELTOVER

504 U.S. 607 (1992).

[In this case, the Supreme Court heard claims arising from Argentina's default on certain bonds issued to foreign creditors, which it claimed were issued in order to alleviate "a domestic credit crisis, and as a component of a program designed to control that nation's critical shortage of foreign exchange." 504 U.S. at 616. Argentina argued that its actions were distinctly political and not commercial and thus it should be entitled to sovereign immunity.]

JUSTICE SCALIA delivered the opinion of the court. . . .

[W]e conclude that when a foreign government acts, not as regulator of a market, but in the manner of a private player within it, the foreign sovereign's actions are "commercial" within the meaning of the FSIA. Moreover, because the Act provides that the commercial character of an act is to be determined by reference to its "nature" rather than its "purpose," 28 U.S.C. § 1603(d), the question is not whether the foreign government is acting with a profit motive or instead with the aim of fulfilling uniquely sovereign objectives. Rather, the issue is whether the particular actions that the foreign state performs (whatever the motive behind them) are the *type* of actions by which a private party engages in "trade and traffic or commerce," Black's Law Dictionary 270 (6th ed. 1990). . . .

The commercial character of the Bonods [bonds] is confirmed by the fact that they are in almost all respects garden-variety debt instruments: They may be held by private parties; they are negotiable and may be traded on the international market (except in Argentina); and they promise a future stream of cash income. We recognize that, prior to the enactment of the FSIA, there was authority suggesting that the issuance of public debt instruments did not constitute a commercial activity. *Victory Transport*, 336 F.2d, at 360 (dicta). There is, however, nothing distinctive about the state's assumption of debt (other than perhaps its purpose) that would cause it always to be classified as *jure imperii,* and in this regard it is significant that *Victory Transport* expressed confusion as to whether the "nature" or the "purpose" of a transaction was controlling in determining commerciality, *id.,* at 359–360. Because the FSIA has now clearly established that the "nature" governs, we perceive no basis for concluding that the issuance of debt should be treated as categorically different from other activities of foreign states. . . .

Argentina argues that the Bonods differ from ordinary debt instruments in that they "were created by the Argentine Government to fulfill its obligations under a foreign exchange program designed to address a domestic credit crisis, and as a component of a program designed to control that nation's critical shortage of foreign exchange." In this regard, Argentina relies heavily on *De Sanchez v. Banco Central de Nicaragua,* 770 F.2d 1385 (1985), in which the Fifth Circuit took the view that "[o]ften, the essence of an act is defined by its purpose"; that unless "we can inquire into the purposes of such acts, we cannot determine their nature"; and that, in light of its purpose to control its reserves of foreign currency, Nicaragua's refusal to honor a check it had issued to cover a private bank debt was a sovereign act entitled to immunity. *Id.,* at 1393. Indeed, Argentina asserts that the line between "nature" and "purpose" rests upon a "formalistic distinction [that] simply is neither useful nor warranted." We think this line of argument is squarely foreclosed by the language of the FSIA. However difficult it may be in some cases to separate "purpose" (*i.e.,* the *reason* why the foreign state engages in the activity) from "nature" (*i.e.,* the outward form of the conduct that the foreign state performs or agrees to perform), the statute unmistakably commands that to be done, 28 U.S.C. § 1603(d). We agree with the Court of Appeals, *see* 941 F.2d, at 151, that it is irrelevant *why* Argentina participated in the bond market in the manner of a private actor; it matters only that it did so. We conclude that Argentina's issuance of the Bonods was a "commercial activity" under the FSIA. . . .

The remaining question is whether Argentina's unilateral rescheduling of the Bonods had a "direct effect" in the United States, 28 U.S.C. § 1605(a)(2). In addressing this issue, the Court of Appeals rejected the suggestion in the legislative history of the FSIA that an effect is not "direct" unless it is both "substantial" and "foreseeable." That suggestion is found in the House Report, which states that conduct covered by the third clause of § 1605(a)(2) would be subject to the jurisdiction of American courts "consistent with principles set forth in section 18, Restatement of the Law, Second, Foreign Relations Law of the United States (1965)." Section 18 states that American laws are not given extraterritorial application except with respect to conduct that has, as a "direct and foreseeable result," a "substantial" effect within the United States. Since this obviously deals with jurisdiction to *legislate* rather than jurisdiction to *adjudicate,* this passage of the House Report has been charitably described as "a bit of a *non sequitur,*" *Texas Trading & Milling Corp. v. Federal Republic of Nigeria,* 647 F.2d 300, 311 (CA2 1981), cert. denied, 454 U.S. 1148 (1982). Of course the generally applicable principle *de minimis non curat lex* ensures that jurisdiction may not be predicated on purely trivial effects in the United States. But we reject the suggestion that § 1605(a)(2) contains any unexpressed requirement of "substantiality" or "foreseeability." As the Court of Appeals recognized, an effect is "direct" if it follows "as an immediate consequence of the defendant's . . . activity."

The Court of Appeals concluded that the rescheduling of the maturity dates obviously had a "direct effect" on respondents. It further concluded that that effect was sufficiently "in the United States" for purposes of the FSIA, in part because "Congress would have wanted an American court to entertain this action" in order to preserve New York City's status as "a preeminent commercial center." The question, however, is not what Congress "would have wanted" but what Congress enacted in the FSIA. Although we are happy to endorse the Second Circuit's recognition of "New York's status as a world financial leader," the effect of Argentina's rescheduling in diminishing that status (assuming it is not too speculative to be considered an effect at all) is too remote and attenuated to satisfy the "direct effect" requirement of the FSIA.

We nonetheless have little difficulty concluding that Argentina's unilateral rescheduling of the maturity dates on the Bonods had a "direct effect" in the United States. Respondents had designated their accounts in New York as the place of payment, and Argentina made some interest payments into those accounts before announcing that it was rescheduling the payments. Because New York was thus the place of performance for Argentina's ultimate contractual obligations, the rescheduling of those obligations necessarily had a "direct effect" in the United States: Money that was supposed to have been delivered to a New York bank for deposit was not forthcoming. We reject Argentina's suggestion that the "direct effect" requirement cannot be satisfied where the plaintiffs are all foreign corporations with no other connections to the United States.

HELMERICH & PAYNE INT'L DRILLING CO. V. VENEZUELA

784 F.3d 804 (D.C. Cir. 2015).

TATEL, CIRCUIT JUDGE: . . .

For more than half a century, Oklahoma-based Helmerich & Payne International Drilling Co. (H&P-IDC) successfully operated an oil-drilling business in Venezuela through a series of subsidiaries. Incorporated under Venezuelan law, the most recent subsidiary, Helmerich & Payne de Venezuela (H&P-V), provided drilling services for the Venezuelan government. Having nationalized its oil industry in the mid-70s, Venezuela now controls exploration, production, and exportation of oil through two state-owned corporations: Petro□leos de Venezuela, S.A. (PDVSA) and PDVSA Petro□leo, known collectively as PDVSA. From its creation in 1975 through 2010, PDVSA depended on H&P-V's highly valuable and rare drilling rigs because they were capable of reaching depths of more than four miles. Those rigs were originally purchased by H&P-IDC and then transferred to its subsidiary H&P-V. At issue here are ten contracts executed in 2007 between H&P-V and PDVSA, each involving one of these rigs—nine in Venezuela's eastern region and one in the west. The contracts initially covered periods ranging from five months to one year, though all were subsequently extended.

Soon after signing the contracts, PDVSA fell substantially behind in its payments. By August 2008, unpaid invoices totaled $63 million. PDVSA never denied its contractual debt; quite to the contrary, it repeatedly reassured H&P-V that payment would be forthcoming. But no payments were made, and after overdue receivables topped $100 million, H&P-V announced in January 2009 that it would not renew the contracts absent "an improvement in receivable collections." By November of that year, H&P-V had fulfilled all of its contractual obligations, disassembled its drilling rigs, and stacked the equipment in its yards pending payment by PDVSA.

PDVSA made no further payments. Instead, on June 12, 2010, PDVSA employees, assisted by armed soldiers of the Venezuelan National Guard, blockaded H&P-V's premises in western Venezuela, and then did the same to the company's eastern properties on June 13 and 14. PDVSA acknowledged that it erected the blockade to "prevent H&P-V from removing its rigs and other assets from its premises, and to force H&P-V to negotiate new contract terms immediately."

In the wake of the blockade, PDVSA issued a series of press releases that are central to H&P-V's expropriation claim. The first, issued on June 23, stated that "[t]he Bolivarian Government, through [PDVSA had] nationalized 11 drilling rigs belonging to the company Helmerich & Payne[ ], a U.S. transnational firm." A second press release, dated June 25, declared that PDVSA's "workers are guarding the drills" and that:

> The nationalization of the oil production drilling rigs from the American contractor H&P not only will result in an increase of oil and gas production in the country, but also in the release of more than 600 workers and the increase of new sources of direct and indirect employment in the hydrocarbon sector.

The June 25 release also "emphatically reject[ed] statements made by spokesmen of the American empire—traced [*sic*] in our country by means of the oligarchy." Another press release, this one undated, stated that the nationalization would "guarantee that the drills will be operated by PDVSA as a company of all Venezuelans, . . . ensur [ing] the rights of former employees of H & P, who a year ago were exploited and then dismissed by this American company, but now they will become part of PDVSA." . . .

The FSIA, "establishes a comprehensive framework for determining whether a court in this country, state or federal, may exercise jurisdiction over a foreign state." *Republic of Argentina v. Weltover, Inc.*, 504 U.S. 607, 610 (1992). The Act provides that "a foreign state *shall* be immune from the jurisdiction of the courts of the United States and of the States," 28 U.S.C. § 1604 (emphasis added), unless one of several exceptions applies, *id.* §§ 1605–07. H & P-V and H & P-IDC invoke the expropriation exception for their takings claim. H & P-V invokes the commercial activity exception for its breach of contract claim. We address each in turn.

Expropriation Exception

This exception, contained in FSIA section 1605(a)(3), denies foreign sovereign immunity "in any case . . . in which rights in property taken in violation of international law are in issue." 28 U.S.C. § 1605(a)(3). According to Venezuela, the exception is inapplicable here for two reasons. First, as a Venezuelan national, H & P-V may not claim a taking in violation of *international* law. Second, under generally applicable corporate law principles, H & P-IDC has no "rights in property" belonging to its subsidiary and thus lacks standing . . .

As to the first inquiry, the parties begin on common ground. All agree that for purposes of international law, "a corporation has the nationality of the state under the laws of which the corporation is organized," Restatement (Third) of Foreign Relations Law § 213 (1987), and that generally, a foreign sovereign's expropriation of its own national's property does not violate international law, *United States v. Belmont*, 301 U.S. 324, 332 (1937). The Supreme Court has summarized the latter principle, known as the "domestic takings rule," this way: "What another country has done in the way of taking over property of its nationals, and especially of its corporations, is not a matter for judicial consideration here. Such nationals must look to their own government for any redress to which they may be entitled."

According to Venezuela, the domestic takings rule ends this case because H & P-V, as a Venezuelan national, may not seek redress in an American court for wrongs suffered in its home country. This argument has a good deal of appeal. Having freely chosen to incorporate under Venezuelan law, H & P-V operated in that country for many years and reaped the benefits of its choice, including several extremely lucrative contracts with the Venezuelan government. Given this, and especially given that H & P-V expressly agreed that these contracts would be governed by Venezuelan law in Venezuelan courts, one might conclude that H & P-V should live with the consequences of its bargain.

According to H & P-V, however, this case is not so simple. It argues that Venezuela has unreasonably discriminated against it on the basis of its sole shareholder's nationality, thus implicating an exception to the domestic takings rule. In support, H & P-V cites *Banco Nacional de Cuba v. Sabbatino*, 307 F.2d 845, 861 (2d Cir.1962), in which the Second Circuit determined that the Cuban government's expropriation of a Cuban corporation's property qualified as a taking in violation of international law. More than 90% of the Cuban corporation's shares were owned by Americans, and the official expropriation decree "clearly indicated that the property was seized because [the corporation] was owned and controlled by Americans." This, the Second Circuit held, justified disregarding the domestic takings rule: "When a foreign state treats a corporation in a particular way because of the nationality of its shareholders, it would be inconsistent for [the court] in passing on the validity of that treatment to look only to the nationality of the corporate fiction." Although the Supreme Court vacated this decision on other grounds, the Second Circuit later reiterated "with emphasis" its decision to disregard the domestic takings rule in the face of Cuba's anti-American discrimination. *Banco Nacional de Cuba v. Farr*, 383 F.2d 166, 185 (2d Cir.1967).

H & P-V also relies on the most recent Restatement of Foreign Relations Law, which recognizes discriminatory takings as a violation of international law. Specifically, section 712 suggests that "a program of taking that singles out aliens generally, or aliens of a particular nationality, or particular aliens, would violate international law." Restatement (Third) of Foreign Relations Law § 712 cmt. f. (1987). "Discrimination," the Restatement continues, "implies *unreasonable* distinction," and so "[t]akings that invidiously single out property of persons of a particular nationality would be [discriminatory]," whereas "classifications, even if based on nationality, that are rationally related to the state's security or economic policies might not be [discriminatory]" and thus not in violation of international law. *Id.*(emphasis added). The reporter's notes to section 712 cite *Sabbatino* as an example of a discriminatory taking, explaining that Cuba's express "purpose was to retaliate against United States nationals for acts of their Government, and was directed against United States nationals exclusively." *Id.* § 712 reporter's note 5.

H & P-V insists that its complaint, which emphasizes the Venezuelan government's well-known anti-American sentiment, as well as PDVSA's statements decrying the "American empire," successfully pleads a discriminatory takings claim. For its part, Venezuela urges us not to "be the first to revive the overturned Second Circuit precedent" because "there is no internationally recognized exception—based on 'discrimination' or otherwise—to the domestic takings rule." Dated and uncited as it may be, however, *Sabbatino* remains good law. Although "we are not *bound* by the decisions of other circuits," we may "of course . . . find the reasons given for such [decisions] persuasive," especially where, as here, our circuit has yet to consider the issue. Moreover, neither Venezuela nor the dissent cites any decision from any circuit that so completely forecloses H & P-V's discriminatory takings theory as to "*inescapably* render the claim[ ] frivolous" and "*completely* devoid of merit." Given this, and given the Restatement's recognition of discriminatory takings claims, we believe that H & P-V has satisfied this Circuit's forgiving standard for surviving a motion to dismiss in an FSIA case.

Alternatively, Venezuela claims that even if international law recognizes discriminatory takings, "plaintiffs have failed to plead facts to support it" because "the motivation for the expropriation was Venezuela's need for H & P-V's uniquely powerful rigs." As it points out, the official decrees cited only the scarcity of these powerful rigs as the reason for the expropriation. The Bill of Agreement, for example, declared H & P-V's drilling rigs necessary for Venezuela's "public benefit and good," and President Chavez's decree stated that "the lack thereof would affect [Venezuela's national oil drilling] Plan." Based on these statements, it may well be, as the Restatement puts it, that the taking was "rationally related to [Venezuela's] security or economic policies." *Restatement (Third) of Foreign Relations Law* § 712 cmt. f (1987).

Other statements, however, went well beyond Venezuela's economic and security needs and could be viewed as demonstrating "unreasonable distinction" based on nationality. PDVSA's press release referred to the "American empire," and a National Assembly member warned that opponents of the expropriation were supporting America's mission of "war[ ] . . . through the large military industry[ ] of the Empire and its allies." At this stage of the litigation, where we view the complaint "in the light most favorable to the plaintiff," these statements are sufficient to plead a "non-frivolous" discriminatory takings claim.

We turn next to Venezuela's argument that H & P-IDC may not invoke the FSIA's expropriation exception because it has no rights in H & P-V's property. By its terms, the expropriation exception applies only to plaintiffs having "rights in property" taken in violation of international law. Moreover, and quite apart from the FSIA, plaintiffs must demonstrate Article III standing by asserting their "own legal rights and interests" rather than resting "claim[s] to relief on the legal rights or interests of third parties." *Warth v. Seldin*, 422 U.S. 490, 499 (1975). The "shareholder standing rule" is an example of this latter principle. Because corporations are legally distinct from their shareholders, the rule "prohibits shareholders from initiating actions to enforce the rights of the corporation unless the corporation's management has refused to pursue the same action for reasons other than good-faith business judgment." *Franchise Tax Board of California v. Alcan Aluminium Limited*, 493 U.S. 331, 336 (1990). Combining both of these principles, Venezuela argues that as a mere shareholder, H & P-IDC has no rights in the property of its subsidiary and thus lacks standing.

In support of this argument, Venezuela relies almost entirely on *Dole Food Co. v. Patrickson*, 538 U.S. 468 (2003), an FSIA case in which the Supreme Court held that "[a] corporate parent which owns the shares of a subsidiary does not, for that reason alone, own or have legal title to the assets of the subsidiary." This, according to Venezuela, means that "in enacting the FSIA, Congress specifically intended that basic corporate law concepts inform the interpretation of the statute," and thus "rights in property" must mean corporate ownership.

Contrary to Venezuela's assertion, however, *Dole Food* does not represent a wholesale incorporation of corporate law into the FSIA. The issue in that case was whether a corporate subsidiary qualified as an instrumentality of a foreign state under the FSIA where the foreign state did not own a majority of the subsidiary's shares but did own a majority of the corporate parent's shares. Answering that question in the negative, the Court focused on FSIA section 1603(b)(2), which defines "instrumentality" as "an organ of a foreign state or political subdivision thereof, or a majority of whose shares or other ownership interest is owned by a foreign state or political subdivision thereof[.]" Given this definition, the Court refused to "ignore corporate formalities not because the FSIA generally incorporates corporate law principles, but because section 1603(b)(2) expressly "speaks of ownership."

By contrast, FSIA section 1605(a)(3), the expropriation exception, speaks only of "rights in property" generally, not ownership in shares. The Supreme Court's analysis of another FSIA exception is instructive. In *Permanent Mission of India to the United Nations v. City of New York,* the Court examined the FSIA's abrogation of sovereign immunity in cases involving "rights in immovable property situated in the United States." 551 U.S. 193 (2007) (quoting 28 U.S.C. § 1605(a)(4)). An instrumentality of the Indian government argued that the FSIA "limits the reach of the exception to actions contesting ownership or possession." *Id.* Seeing no such limitation in the statute's text, the Court concluded that "the exception focuses more broadly on 'rights in' property."

So too here. The expropriation exception requires only that "rights in property . . . are in issue," § 1605(a)(3), and we have recognized that corporate ownership aside, shareholders may have rights in corporate property. In *Ramirez de Arellano v. Weinberger,* for example, we considered whether an American citizen, the sole shareholder of three Honduran corporations, had a "cognizable property interest" in land owned by the Honduran corporations and seized by the United States government. Whether Ramirez had property rights in the land, we held, "does *not* turn on whether certain rights which may belong *only* to the Honduran corporation may be asserted 'derivatively' by the sole United States shareholders." Instead, property rights depend upon whether the shareholders have "rights *of their own,* which exist by virtue of their exclusive beneficial ownership, control, and possession of the properties and businesses allegedly seized." We thus concluded that notwithstanding corporate ownership, Ramirez had property rights in the Honduran property that he "personally controlled and managed . . . for over 20 years." "The corporate ownership of land and property," we held, "does not deprive the sole beneficial owners—United States citizens—of a property interest." . . . .

Ramirez is especially persuasive in this case because H&P-IDC, like the American citizen in *Ramirez*, was the foreign subsidiary's sole shareholder. Moreover, H&P-IDC provided the rigs central to this dispute, and as a result of the expropriation, has suffered a total loss of control over its subsidiary, which has ceased operating as an ongoing enterprise because *all* of its assets were taken. Under these circumstances, H&P-IDC has "put its rights in property in issue in a non-frivolous way." No more is required to survive a motion to dismiss under the FSIA. . . .

This brings us, finally, to H & P-V's argument that the FSIA's commercial activity exception extends to its breach of contract claim against PDVSA. . . . Because this case involves a contract executed and performed outside the United States, our analysis focuses on the exception's third clause—specifically, whether Venezuela's breach of the drilling contracts "cause[d] a direct effect in the United States." *Id.* A direct effect "is one which has no intervening element, but, rather, flows in a straight line without deviation or interruption." *Princz v. Federal Republic of Germany*, 26 F.3d 1166, 1172 (D.C.Cir.1994). H & P-V alleges three such effects.

First, relying on our decision in *Cruise Connections Charter Management v. Canada*, 600 F.3d 661 (D.C.Cir.2010), H & P-V argues that its contracts with third-party vendors in the United States, made pursuant to the drilling contracts, constitute a direct effect. In *Cruise Connections,* we found a "direct effect" where the Royal Canadian Mounted Police (RCMP) cancelled a contract with a U.S. corporation to provide cruise ships during the 2010 Winter Olympics. H & P-V argues that just as in *Cruise Connections,* where the RCMP contract "required . . . subcontract[s] with two U.S.-based cruise lines," *id.,* its agreements with PDVSA required contracts with U.S.-based companies for various drilling rig parts. PDVSA responds that even if H & P-V subcontracted with U.S. vendors, nothing in the drilling contracts obligated them to do so.

We need not resolve this dispute, however, because even assuming that the drilling contracts required subcontracts with American companies, those contracts had no direct effect in the United States. Our holding in *Cruise Connections* rested not on the mere formation of third-party contracts in the United States, but rather on "*losses* caused by the *termination* of [the] contract with [Royal Canadian Mounted Police]." *Cruise Connections*, 600 F.3d at 664 (emphases added); see also *id.* at 666 (noting that the "alleged breach resulted in the direct loss of millions of dollars worth of business in the United States."). Here, H & P-V concedes that none of the third-party contracts was breached. As a result, no losses, and therefore no "direct effect," occurred in the United States.

We are unpersuaded by H & P-V's argument that its inability to renew the third-party contracts constitutes a direct effect caused by PDVSA's breach. As noted above, H & P-V had already performed all of its obligations under the existing third-party contracts. Its claim of third-party loss is therefore based on expected loss from *future* contracts that H & P-V says it would have entered into had PDVSA renewed its own contracts with H & P-V instead of breaching them. But H & P-V makes no allegation that PDVSA had an *obligation* to renew its contracts.. Accordingly, any losses to third parties based on expected future contracts were not a direct effect of PDVSA's breach, but rather of PDVSA's contractually permitted decision not to renew its agreement with H & P-V. . . .

Relying on the Supreme Court's decision in *Republic of Argentina v. Weltover*, H & P-V claims a second effect in the United States: that PDVSA made payments to Helmerich & Payne's Oklahoma bank account. In *Weltover,* Argentina had issued bonds providing for payment through a currency transfer on the London, Frankfurt, Zurich, or New York markets at the discretion of the creditor. Two Panamanian bondholders demanded payment in New York, and when Argentina failed to pay, brought suit in the United States, claiming jurisdiction under the commercial activity exception. The Court had "little difficulty" finding a direct effect because, as a result of Argentina's failure to meet its payment obligations, a contractually required payment into an American bank was not made. Relying on *Weltover,* H & P-V emphasizes that both the eastern and western contracts permitted PDVSA to pay a portion of invoiced amounts in U.S. dollars into an American bank—indeed, PDVSA ultimately paid $65 million this way. As in *Weltover,* then, PDVSA's breach meant that money "that was supposed to have been delivered to [an American] bank for deposit was not forthcoming." But as PDVSA points out, the contracts gave H & P-V no power to demand payment in the United States. Rather, under both the eastern and western contracts, PDVSA could choose to deposit payments in bolivars in Venezuelan banks whenever, in its "exclusive discretion" and "judgment," it "deem[ed] it discretionally convenient."

This case presents facts akin to those we examined in *Goodman Holdings v. Rafidain Bank*, 26 F.3d 1143, 1144 (D.C.Cir.1994), in which an Iraqi bank failed to pay on letters of credit, and the payee claimed that the bank's prior payments from its accounts in the United States constituted a direct effect. We rejected this contention because pursuant to the letters of credit, Iraq "might well have paid . . . from funds in United States banks but it might just as well have done so from accounts located outside of the United States." *Id.* at 1146–47. Such unlimited discretion, we concluded, meant that unlike in *Weltover,* no money was " 'supposed' to have been paid" in the United States. *Id.* at 1146 (quoting *Weltover*, 504 U.S. at 608).

In other words, where, as here, the alleged effect depends solely on a foreign government's discretion, we cannot say that it "flows in a straight line without deviation or interruption."

Finally, relying on *McKesson Corp. v. Islamic Republic of Iran*, 52 F.3d 346 (D.C.Cir.1995), H & P-V contends that PDVSA's breach halted a flow of commerce between Venezuela and the United States, thus causing a direct effect. McKesson, an American corporation, alleged that the Iranian government had illegally divested it of its investment in a dairy located in Iran. In doing so, we concluded, Iran halted a "constant flow of capital, management personnel, engineering data, machinery, equipment, materials and packaging, between the United States and Iran to support the operation of [the dairy]," thereby causing a direct effect. H & P-V insists that the same is true here. We think not. Iran's actions in "freezing-out American corporations in their ownership of [the dairy]" had the direct and immediate effect of halting a flow of resources and capital between the United States and Iran. *Id.* By contrast, any interruptions in commerce between the United States and PDVSA flowed immediately not from PDVSA's breach of contract, but rather from Helmerich & Payne's decision to cease business in Venezuela. And, given that the contracts were for set periods of time ranging from five months to one year, there was no guarantee of future business between Helmerich & Payne and PDVSA beyond those contracts.

NOTES

1. *Definition of Commercial Activity.* Recall the definition of "commercial activity" contained in 28 U.S.C. § 1603(d): "The commercial character of an activity shall be determined by reference to the *nature* of the course of conduct or particular transaction or act, rather than by reference to its *purpose*" (emphasis added). How does a determination of commercial "purpose" differ, in practice, from a determination of commercial "nature"? Do you agree with the Court's assessment in *Republic of Argentina v. Weltover* that the actions taken by Argentina were commercial in nature?

The following year, in a case brought by a United States citizen who had been severely beaten and tortured after whistle-blowing about the practices of a Saudi hospital in which he worked, the Supreme Court declined to characterize the Saudi Arabian government's activity as "commercial" and upheld the state's sovereign immunity. *Saudi Arabia v. Nelson*, 507 U.S. 349 (1993). Nelson was an American recruited to work in Saudi hospitals by an independent corporation, under an agreement signed by the Saudi government. When he discovered safety hazards in some of the hospital's medical equipment and reported the defects, he was arrested by Saudi police and taken to a cell where he alleged that he was tortured and beaten for a prolonged period of time. In bringing suit, Nelson claimed jurisdiction under the FSIA's commercial-activity exception to sovereign immunity, arguing that a nexus existed between the commercial activities of the hospital recruitment and employment and the Saudi government's tortious actions against him. The Court, invoking the "nature" vs. "purpose" reasoning in *Weltover,* rejected this reasoning:

> The conduct boils down to abuse of the power of its police by the Saudi Government, and however monstrous such abuse undoubtedly may be, a foreign state's exercise of the power of its police has long been understood for purposes of the restrictive theory as peculiarly sovereign in nature. . . . Exercise of the powers of police and penal officers is not the sort of action by which private parties can engage in commerce.

507 U.S. at 361–62. Do you agree?

2. *Pleading Standards and the Expropriation Exception.* In the *Helmerich* case, the Court of Appeals held that plaintiffs only needed to plead a "non-frivolous" discriminatory takings claim in order to defeat a motion to dismiss for lack of jurisdiction. The Court of Appeals used the "non-frivolous argument" standard because it is used to evaluate subject matter jurisdiction under 28 U.S.C. § 1332, and the FSIA confers subject matter jurisdiction on federal courts if an exception to immunity applies. The Supreme Court vacated and remanded, holding that the exception only applies if property was taken in violation of international law and that courts must decide whether this standard has been met as part of the jurisdictional inquiry, even if doing so also involves resolving the merits of the case. *Bolivarian Republic of Venezuela v. Helmerich & Payne Int'l Drilling Co.*, 137 S.Ct. 1312 (2017). How do you think the case should be resolved on remand applying the new pleading standard?

3. *The Domestic Takings Exception to the Expropriation Exception.* What is the purpose of the "domestic takings" rule in the international law on expropriation? Under what circumstances can it be overcome based on the reasoning in *Helmerich & Payne*? Note that the dissenting Court of Appeals judge in *Helmerich & Payne* argued that the domestic takings rule should apply in that case because the subsidiary had chosen to incorporate in Venezuela and thus should be subject to the burdens as well as the benefits of Venezuelan citizenship. U.S. courts have occasionally held the domestic takings rule inapplicable in certain human rights cases. *See, e.g., Simon v. Hungary*, 812 F.3d 127 (D.C. Cir. 2016) (holding that the expropriations themselves constituted genocide and accordingly violated international law irrespective of the citizenship of the property owner); *Cassier v. Kingdom of Spain,* 461 F.Supp. 2d 1157 (C.D. Cal. 2006); *aff'd in part, rev'd in part on other grounds,* 580 F.3d 1048 (9th Cir. 2009); *reh'ing en banc,* 616 F.3d 1019 (9th Cir. 2010) (reasoning that a German-Jewish victim's heir could sue for the expropriation of a painting because the Nazi government did not consider Jews to be German citizens).

4. *Based Upon.* The commercial activity exception has three clauses. Review § 1605(a)(2). How do the three clauses differ? Which were at issue in *Weltover*, *Nelson*, and *Helmerich & Payne*? Why? Note that all three require

that the action be "based upon" an act or activity. Is the action "based upon" activity that provides the basis for one element of the cause of action? Or is a closer nexus between the activity and the action required? Consider that question as you read the following case on the non-commercial tort exception to foreign sovereign immunity.

KIDANE V. FEDERAL DEMOCRATIC REPUBLIC OF ETHIOPIA

851 F.3d 7 (D.C. Cir. 2017).

KAREN LECRAFT HENDERSON, C.J.

Plaintiff John Doe—proceeding pseudonymously as "Kidane"—claims he was tricked into downloading a computer program. The program allegedly enabled the Federal Democratic Republic of Ethiopia (Ethiopia) to spy on him from abroad. He wants to sue the Republic of Ethiopia. . . .

Unless an exception applies, "a foreign state shall be immune from the jurisdiction of the courts of the United States." 28 U.S.C. § 1604. One of those exceptions is the noncommercial-tort exception. It abrogates immunity from an action involving "personal injury or death, or damage to or loss of property, occurring in the United States and caused by the tortious act or omission of [a] foreign state or of any official or employee of that foreign state while acting within the scope of his office or employment[.]" *Id.* § 1605(a)(5). The phrase "occurring in the United States" is no mere surplusage. " '[T]he entire tort'—including not only the injury but also the act precipitating that injury—must occur in the United States." *Jerez v. Republic of Cuba*, 775 F.3d 419, 424 (D.C. Cir. 2014) (quoting *Asociacion de Reclamantes v. United Mexican States*, 735 F.2d 1517, 1525 (D.C. Cir. 1984)).

In *Jerez*, the plaintiff (Jerez) alleged he was intentionally injected with hepatitis C while imprisoned in Cuba. He sued Cuba, relying on the noncommercial-tort exception. We found the exception inapplicable. As we explained, the alleged injection of hepatitis C occurred abroad and we rejected Jerez's argument that a separate tort occurred each time the virus replicated in his body. Replication showed only that Jerez suffered an "ongoing injury," not that the tort's precipitating act also occurred in the United States. *Id.* (emphasis omitted). To support his replication theory, Jerez "analogiz[ed] the defendants' actions to a foreign agent's delivery into the United States of an anthrax package or a bomb." That analogy was flawed, we explained, because "the defendants' infliction of injury . . . occurred entirely in Cuba, whereas the infliction of injury by the hypothetical anthrax package or bomb would occur entirely in the United States."

Kidane argues that Ethiopia's tort is akin to the anthrax hypothetical. But the hypothetical was dictum and . . . *Jerez*'s holding hardly helps Kidane. *Jerez* squarely held that "the *entire* tort . . . must occur in the

United States" for the noncommercial-tort exception to apply. Here, at least a portion of Ethiopia's alleged tort occurred abroad.

Maryland's intrusion-upon-seclusion tort shows why that is so. The tort covers "[o]ne who intentionally intrudes, physically or otherwise, upon the solitude or seclusion of another or his private affairs or concerns, [making the intruder] subject to liability to the other for invasion of his privacy, if the intrusion would be highly offensive to a reasonable person." *Bailer v. Erie Ins. Exch.*, 687 A.2d 1375, 1380–81 (Md. 1997) (emphasis and internal quotation marks omitted). There is thus no tort without intentional intrusion. But whether in London, Ethiopia or elsewhere, the tortious intent aimed at Kidane plainly lay abroad and the tortious acts of computer programming likewise occurred abroad. Moreover, Ethiopia's placement of the FinSpy virus on Kidane's computer, although completed in the United States when Kidane opened the infected e-mail attachment, began outside the United States. It thus cannot be said that the entire tort occurred in the United States. . . .

Kidane also directs us to the FSIA's *commercial* activity exception to illuminate section 1605(a)(5)'s boundaries. The commercial activity exception authorizes claims "based upon a commercial activity carried on in the United States by [a] foreign state[.]" 28 U.S.C. § 1605(a)(2). He observes that the Supreme Court, interpreting this provision, found instructive the "point of contact" between the tort and its victim in determining where the tort occurred. *OBB Personenverkehr AG v. Sachs*, 577 U.S. ___, ___ (2015) (internal quotation marks omitted). But *Sachs* underscores why the commercial activity exception is of limited usefulness here. There, the American plaintiff purchased a European rail travel pass from a Massachusetts travel agent. When she used the pass to board the defendant Austrian state-owned railway's train in Innsbruck, Austria, she fell onto the tracks, where the moving train crushed her legs. She sued, invoking the FSIA's commercial activity exception. The Supreme Court concluded, however, that her lawsuit was not "based upon" the domestic sale of the rail pass. It noted that "an action is based upon the particular conduct that constitutes the gravamen of the suit." It explained that "the conduct constituting the gravamen of [her] suit plainly occurred abroad." But *Sachs* interpreted the commercial activity exception. And unlike the commercial activity exception, the noncommercial-tort exception does not ask where the "gravamen" occurred, instead, it asks where the "*entire* tort" occurred.

BANK MARKAZI V. PETERSON

136 S.Ct. 1310 (2016).

We set out here statutory provisions relevant to this case. American nationals may file suit against state sponsors of terrorism in the courts of the United States. See 28 U.S.C. § 1605A. Specifically, they may seek "money damages . . . against a foreign state for personal injury or death that was caused by" acts of terrorism, including "torture, extrajudicial killing, aircraft sabotage, hostage taking, or the provision of material support" to terrorist activities. § 1605A(a)(1). This authorization—known as the "terrorism exception"—is among enumerated exceptions prescribed in the Foreign Sovereign Immunities Act of 1976 (FSIA) to the general rule of sovereign immunity.

After gaining a judgment [ ]plaintiffs proceeding under the terrorism exception "have often faced practical and legal difficulties" at the enforcement stage. Subject to stated exceptions, the FSIA shields foreign-state property from execution. § 1609. When the terrorism exception was adopted, only foreign-state property located in the United States and "used for a commercial activity" was available for the satisfaction of judgments. § 1610(a)(7), (b)(3). Further limiting judgment-enforcement prospects, the FSIA shields from execution property "of a foreign central bank or monetary authority held for its own account." § 1611(b)(1).

To lessen these enforcement difficulties, Congress enacted the Terrorism Risk Insurance Act of 2002 (TRIA), which authorizes execution of judgments obtained under the FSIA's terrorism exception against "the blocked assets of [a] terrorist party (including the blocked assets of any agency or instrumentality of that terrorist party)." § 201(a), 116 Stat. 2337, note following 28 U.S.C. § 1610. A "blocked asset" is any asset seized by the Executive Branch pursuant to either the Trading with the Enemy Act (TWEA), 40 Stat. 411, 50 U.S.C.App. 1 et seq., or the International Emergency Economic Powers Act (IEEPA), 91 Stat. 1625, 50 U.S.C. § 1570 *et seq.* See TRIA § 201(d)(2). Both measures, TWEA and IEEPA, authorize the President to freeze the assets of "foreign enemy state[s]" and their agencies and instrumentalities. These blocking regimes "put control of foreign assets in the hands of the President so that he may dispose of them in the manner that best furthers the United States' foreign-relations and national-security interests."

Invoking his authority under the IEEPA, the President, in February 2012, issued an Executive Order blocking "[a]ll property and interests in property of any Iranian financial institution, including the Central Bank of Iran, that are in the United States." Exec. Order No. 13599, 3 CFR 215 (2012 Comp.). The availability of these assets for execution, however, was contested.

To place beyond dispute the availability of some of the Executive Order No. 13599-blocked assets for satisfaction of judgments rendered in terrorism cases, Congress passed the statute at issue here: § 502 of the Iran Threat Reduction and Syria Human Rights Act of 2012, 126 Stat. 1258, 22 U.S.C. § 8772. Enacted as a freestanding measure, not as an amendment to the FSIA or the TRIA, § 8772 provides that, if a court makes specified findings, "a financial asset . . . shall be subject to execution . . . in order to satisfy any judgment to the extent of any compensatory damages awarded against Iran for damages for personal injury or death caused by" the acts of terrorism enumerated in the FSIA's terrorism exception. § 8772(a)(1). Section 8772(b) defines as available for execution by holders of terrorism judgments against Iran "the financial assets that are identified in and the subject of proceedings in the United States District Court for the Southern District of New York in *Peterson et al. v. Islamic Republic of Iran et al.*, Case No. 10 Civ. 4518(BSJ)(GWG), that were restrained by restraining notices and levies secured by the plaintiffs in those proceedings."

Respondents are victims of Iran-sponsored acts of terrorism, their estate representatives, and surviving family members. Numbering more than 1,000, respondents rank within 16 discrete groups, each of which brought a lawsuit against Iran pursuant to the FSIA's terrorism exception. . . The majority of respondents sought redress for injuries suffered in connection with the 1983 bombing of the U.S. Marine barracks in Beirut, Lebanon. "Together, [respondents] have obtained billions of dollars in judgments against Iran, the vast majority of which remain unpaid." The validity of those judgments is not in dispute. . . .

Although the enforcement proceeding was initiated prior to the issuance of Executive Order No. 13599 and the enactment of § 8772, the judgment holders updated their motions in 2012 to include execution claims under § 8772. Making the findings necessary under § 8772, the District Court ordered the requested turnover.

In reaching its decision, the court reviewed the financial history of the assets and other record evidence showing that Bank Markazi owned the assets. Since at least early 2008, the court recounted, the bond assets have been held in a New York account at Citibank directly controlled by Clearstream Banking, S.A. (Clearstream), a Luxembourg-based company that serves "as an intermediary between financial institutions worldwide." Initially, Clearstream held the assets for Bank Markazi and deposited interest earned on the bonds into Bank Markazi's Clearstream account. At some point in 2008, Bank Markazi instructed Clearstream to position another intermediary—Banca UBAE, S.p.A., an Italian bank—between the bonds and Bank Markazi. Thereafter, Clearstream deposited interest payments in UBAE's account, which UBAE then remitted to Bank Markazi.

Resisting turnover of the bond assets, Bank Markazi and Clearstream, as the District Court observed, "filled the proverbial kitchen sink with arguments." They argued, *inter alia,* the absence of subject-matter and personal jurisdiction, asserting that the blocked assets were not assets "of" the Bank, and that the assets in question were located in Luxembourg, not

New York. Several of their objections to execution became irrelevant following enactment of § 8772, which, the District Court noted, "sweeps away . . . any . . . federal or state law impediments that might otherwise exist, so long as the appropriate judicial determination is made." § 8772(a)(1) (Act applies "notwithstanding any other provision of law"). After § 8772's passage, Bank Markazi changed its defense. It conceded that Iran held the requisite "equitable title to, or beneficial interest in, the assets," § 8772(a)(2)(A), but maintained that § 8772 could not withstand inspection under the separation-of-powers doctrine.

"[I]n passing § 8772," Bank Markazi argued, "Congress effectively dictated specific factual findings in connection with a specific litigation—invading the province of the courts." The District Court disagreed. The ownership determinations § 8772 required, the court said, "[were] not mere fig leaves," for "it [was] quite possible that the [c]ourt could have found that defendants raised a triable issue as to whether the [b]locked [a]ssets were owned by Iran, or that Clearstream and/or UBAE ha[d] some form of beneficial or equitable interest." Observing from the voluminous filings that "[t]here [was] . . . plenty . . . to [litigate]," the court described § 8772 as a measure that "merely chang[es] the law applicable to pending cases; it does not usurp the adjudicative function assigned to federal courts." Further, the court reminded, "Iran's liability and its required payment of damages was . . . established years prior to the [enactment of § 8772]"; "[a]t issue [here] is merely execution [of judgments] on assets present in this district." . . .

Citing *United States v. Klein*, 13 Wall. 128 (1872), Bank Markazi urges a further limitation. Congress treads impermissibly on judicial turf, the Bank maintains, when it "prescribe[s] rules of decision to the Judicial Department . . . in [pending] cases." . . .

Klein involved Civil War legislation providing that persons whose property had been seized and sold in wartime could recover the proceeds of the sale in the Court of Claims upon proof that they had "never given any aid or comfort to the present rebellion." Ch. 120, § 3, 12 Stat. 820. In 1863, President Lincoln pardoned "persons who . . . participated in the . . . rebellion" if they swore an oath of loyalty to the United States. Presidential Proclamation No. 11, 13 Stat. 737. One of the persons so pardoned was a southerner named Wilson, whose cotton had been seized and sold by Government agents. Klein was the administrator of Wilson's estate. In *United States v. Padelford*, 9 Wall. 531, 543 (1870), this Court held that the recipient of a Presidential pardon must be treated as loyal, *i.e.,* the pardon operated as "a complete substitute for proof that [the recipient] gave no aid or comfort to the rebellion." Thereafter, Klein prevailed in an action in the Court of Claims, yielding an award of $125,300 for Wilson's cotton.

During the pendency of an appeal to this Court from the Court of Claims judgment in *Klein,* Congress enacted a statute providing that no pardon should be admissible as proof of loyalty. Moreover, acceptance of a pardon without disclaiming participation in the rebellion would serve as conclusive evidence of disloyalty. The statute directed the Court of Claims and the Supreme Court to dismiss for want of jurisdiction any claim based on a pardon. 16 Stat. 235; R. Fallon, J. Manning, D. Meltzer, & D. Shapiro, Hart and Wechsler's *The Federal Courts and the Federal System* 323, n. 29 (7th ed. 2015) (Hart and Wechsler). Affirming the judgment of the Court of Claims, this Court held that Congress had no authority to "impai[r] the effect of a pardon," for the Constitution entrusted the pardon power "[t]o the executive alone." The Legislature, the Court stated, "cannot change the effect of . . . a pardon any more than the executive can change a law." Lacking authority to impair the pardon power of the Executive, Congress could not "direc[t] [a] court to be instrumental to that end." In other words, the statute in *Klein* infringed the judicial power, not because it left too little for courts to do, but because it attempted to direct the result without altering the legal standards governing the effect of a pardon—standards Congress was powerless to prescribe.

Bank Markazi, as earlier observed, argues that § 8772 conflicts with [*United States* v. *Klein,* 13 Wall. 128 (1872)]. The Bank points to a statement in the *Klein* opinion questioning whether "the legislature may prescribe rules of decision to the Judicial Department . . . in cases pending before it." One cannot take this language from *Klein* "at face value," however, "for congressional power to make valid statutes retroactively applicable to pending cases has often been recognized." As we explained in *Landgraf v. USI Film Products*, 511 U.S. 244, 267 (1994), the restrictions that the Constitution places on retroactive legislation "are of limited scope":

> "The *Ex Post Facto* Clause flatly prohibits retroactive application of penal legislation. Article I, § 10, cl. 1, prohibits States from passing . . . laws 'impairing the Obligation of Contracts.' The Fifth Amendment's Takings Clause prevents the Legislature (and other government actors) from depriving private persons of vested property rights except for a 'public use' and upon payment of 'just compensation.' The prohibitions on 'Bills of Attainder' in Art. I, §§ 9–10, prohibit legislatures from singling out disfavored persons and meting out summary punishment for past conduct. The Due Process Clause also protects the interests in fair notice and repose that may be compromised by retroactive legislation; a justification sufficient to validate a statute's prospective application under the Clause 'may not suffice' to warrant its retroactive application." Id., at 266–267, 114 S.Ct. 1483 (citation and footnote omitted).

"Absent a violation of one of those specific provisions," when a new law makes clear that it is retroactive, the arguable "unfairness of retroactive civil legislation is not a sufficient reason for a court to fail to give [that law] its intended scope." So yes, we have affirmed, Congress may indeed direct courts to apply newly enacted, outcome-altering legislation in pending civil cases. . . .

Bank Markazi argues most strenuously that § 8772 did not simply amend pre-existing law. Because the judicial findings contemplated by § 8772 were "foregone conclusions," the Bank urges, the statute "effectively" directed certain fact findings and specified the outcome under the amended law. Recall that the District Court, closely monitoring the case, disagreed. . . .

In any event, a statute does not impinge on judicial power when it directs courts to apply a new legal standard to undisputed facts. "When a plaintiff brings suit to enforce a legal obligation it is not any less a case or controversy upon which a court possessing the federal judicial power may rightly give judgment, because the plaintiff's claim is uncontested or incontestable." In *Schooner Peggy*, 1 Cranch, at 109–110, for example, this Court applied a newly ratified treaty that, by requiring the return of captured property, effectively permitted only one possible outcome. And in [*Robertson v. Seattle Audobon Soc'y*], 503 U.S. 429, 434–435, 438–439 (1992), a statute replaced governing environmental-law restraints on timber harvesting with new legislation that permitted harvesting in all but certain designated areas. Without inquiring whether the new statute's application in pending cases was a "foregone conclusio[n]," we upheld the legislation because it left for judicial determination whether any particular actions violated the new prescription. In short, § 8772 changed the law by establishing new substantive standards, entrusting to the District Court application of those standards to the facts (contested or uncontested) found by the court.

Resisting this conclusion, The Chief Justice compares § 8772 to a hypothetical "law directing judgment for Smith if the court finds that Jones was duly served with notice of the proceedings." Of course, the hypothesized law would be invalid—as would a law directing judgment for Smith, for instance, if the court finds that the sun rises in the east. For one thing, a law so cast may well be irrational and, therefore, unconstitutional for reasons distinct from the separation-of-powers issues considered here. For another, the law imagined by the dissent does what *Robertson* says Congress cannot do: Like a statute that directs, in "Smith v. Jones," "Smith wins," it "compel[s] . . . findings or results under old law," for it fails to supply any new legal standard effectuating the lawmakers' reasonable policy judgment. By contrast, § 8772 provides a new standard clarifying that, if Iran owns certain assets, the victims of Iran-sponsored terrorist attacks will be permitted to execute against those assets. Applying laws implementing Congress' policy judgments, with fidelity to those judgments, is commonplace for the Judiciary. . . .

Section 8772 remains "unprecedented," Bank Markazi charges, because it "prescribes a rule for a single pending case—identified by caption and docket number." The amended law in *Robertson,* however, also applied to cases identified by caption and docket number, and was nonetheless upheld. Moreover, § 8772, as already described, facilitates execution of judgments in 16 suits, together encompassing more than 1,000 victims of Iran-sponsored terrorist attacks. Although consolidated for administrative purposes at the execution stage, the judgment-execution claims brought pursuant to Federal Rule of Civil Procedure 69 were not independent of the original actions for damages and each claim retained its separate character. . . .

The Bank's argument is further flawed, for it rests on the assumption that legislation must be generally applicable, that "there is something wrong with particularized legislative action." *Plaut* [*v. Spendthrift Farm, Inc.*], 514 U.S. 211, 239, n. 9 (1995). We have found that assumption suspect:

> "While legislatures usually act through laws of general applicability, that is by no means their only legitimate mode of action. Private bills in Congress are still common, and were even more so in the days before establishment of the Claims Court. Even laws that impose a duty or liability upon a single individual or firm are not on that account invalid—or else we would not have the extensive jurisprudence that we do concerning the Bill of Attainder Clause, including cases which say that [the Clause] requires not merely 'singling out' but also *punishment. Ibid.*

This Court and lower courts have upheld as a valid exercise of Congress' legislative power diverse laws that governed one or a very small number of specific subjects. . . . We stress, finally, that § 8772 is an exercise of congressional authority regarding foreign affairs, a domain in which the controlling role of the political branches is both necessary and proper. See, *e.g., Zivotofsky v. Kerry*, 576 U.S. ___, ___, 135 S.Ct. 2076, 2090–2091 (2015). In furtherance of their authority over the Nation's foreign relations, Congress and the President have, time and again, as exigencies arose, exercised control over claims against foreign states and the disposition of foreign-state property in the United States. See *Dames & Moore v. Regan*, 453 U.S. 654, 673–674, 679–681 (1981) (describing this history). In pursuit of foreign policy objectives, the political branches have regulated specific foreign-state assets by, *inter alia,* blocking them or governing their availability for attachment. Such measures have never been rejected as invasions upon the Article III judicial power. *Cf. id.*, at 674, 101 S.Ct. 2972 (Court resists the notion "that the Federal Government as a whole lacked the power" to "nullif[y] . . . attachments and orde[r] the transfer of [foreign-state] assets.").

Particularly pertinent, the Executive, prior to the enactment of the FSIA, regularly made case-specific determinations whether sovereign immunity should be recognized, and courts accepted those determinations as binding. As this Court explained in *Republic of Mexico v. Hoffman*, 324 U.S. 30, 35 (1945), it is "not for the courts to deny an immunity which our government has seen fit to allow, or to allow an immunity on new grounds which the government has not seen fit to recognize." This practice, too, was never perceived as an encroachment on the federal courts' jurisdiction.

Enacting the FSIA in 1976, Congress transferred from the Executive to the courts the principal responsibility for determining a foreign state's amenability to suit. But it remains Congress' prerogative to alter a foreign state's immunity and to render the alteration dispositive of judicial proceedings in progress. By altering the law governing the attachment of particular property belonging to Iran, Congress acted comfortably within the political branches' authority over foreign sovereign immunity and foreign-state assets. . . .

For the reasons stated, we are satisfied that § 8772—a statute designed to aid in the enforcement of federal-court judgments—does not offend "separation of powers principles . . . protecting the role of the independent Judiciary within the constitutional design." The judgment of the Court of Appeals for the Second Circuit is therefore affirmed.

NOTES

1. *Nexus to the United States.* Both the "entire tort" limitation to the noncommercial tort exception and the "based upon" language in the commercial activity exception require a nexus between the United States and the conduct of the foreign state in order for the exception to apply. Re-read §§ 1605 (a)(2) and (a)(5). Should courts interpret these exceptions to require a close relationship between the conduct and the territory of the United States? Does the same reasoning apply to the "direct effect" language in § 1605(a)(2)? Consider the following hypothetical discussed at oral argument in *OBB Personenverkehr v. Sachs:* an airline employee negligently sets the landing gear of an airplane as it is departing from New York. Upon landing in Vienna, the landing gear does not function correctly and someone is injured. Where is the "gravamen" of the suit? Can a suit have more than one "gravamen"? Is the "entire tort" requirement satisfied? Why have different tests for commercial and noncommercial torts? Does the focus on U.S. territory make sense in today's world of hacking and cyber-crime? Is it compelled by the language of the FSIA?

2. *Terrorism and the FSIA.* Beginning in 1996, Congress has repeatedly amended the FSIA and passed other legislation to permit suits and the execution of judgments against states that engage in or support acts of

terrorism. Note that jurisdiction to adjudicate is distinct from jurisdiction to execute, so that jurisdiction to enter judgment does not mean jurisdiction to enforce that judgment. *See* 28 U.S.C. §§ 1609–1611. Some of the terrorism-related immunity legislation is described in the excerpt from the *Bank Markazi* case. Unlike most other exceptions to immunity (compare § 1605(a)(6)), these statutes generally require no relationship between the terrorism-related action of the foreign state and the territory of the United States. Also unlike other exceptions, the terrorism statutes have generally been enacted over the objection of the State Department. They also, however, applied only against foreign states that were designated by the State Department as "state sponsors of terrorism." As of 2017, Iran, Sudan, and Syria have this designation.

3. *International Reaction to Terrorism Litigation Against Foreign States.* The terrorism exceptions to immunity from jurisdiction and from enforcement may violate customary international law that affords states immunity in foreign domestic courts, subject to some exceptions. *See Restatement of the Law (Fourth), The Foreign Relations Law of the United States: Sovereign Immunity* § 460, reporters' note 10 (Tentative Draft No. 1, 2015); *see generally* Hazel Fox & Philippa Webb, *The Law of State Immunity* (3d ed. 2015). After the Supreme Court upheld the district court's turnover order against Bank Markazi, Iran instituted proceedings against the United States before the International Court of Justice. Iran maintains that U.S. courts have awarded over $56 billion in damages against Iran for alleged involvement in acts of terrorism (mostly outside of the United States) in violation of the 1955 Treaty of Amity between the U.S. and Iran. Iran's application specifically alleges that the U.S. "abrogate[ed] [ ]immunities to which Iran and Iranian State-owned companies, including Bank Markazi, and their property, are entitled under customary international law and as required by the Treaty of Amity." *See* Application Instituting Proceedings, Certain Iranian Assets (Islamic Republic of Iran v. United States of America) ¶ 6 (14 June 2016).

4. *Justice Against Sponsors of Terrorism Act.* Partly in order to allow victims of the 9/11 attacks to sue Saudi Arabia, in 2016 Congress passed the Justice against State Sponsors of Terrorism Act which lifts immunity and creates a cause of action against any foreign states for injury occurring in the United States caused by an act of international terrorism in the United States and by a "tortious act or acts of the foreign state," regardless of where the tortious act by the foreign state occurred and not limited to state sponsors of terrorism. President Obama vetoed the legislation, citing concerns about putting foreign policy "in the hands of private litigants and courts," and about reciprocity, international principles, and other national interests. *See* The White House, Veto Message from the President, Sept. 23, 2016 available at https://obamawhitehouse.archives.gov/the-press-office/2016/09/23/veto-message-president-s2040. Congress overrode the veto.

5. *Separation of Powers.* Chief Justice Roberts, joined by Justice Sotomayor, dissented in *Bank Markazi v. Peterson*, arguing that the statute was unconstitutional. Consider the hypothetical "Smith Statute" posited by

Roberts and discussed in the majority opinion. Is the Court's analysis convincing? In 2017 the Supreme Court granted certiorari in *Patchak v. Zinke* on whether "a statute directing the federal courts to 'promptly dismiss a pending lawsuit following substantive determinations by the courts (including this Court's determination that the 'suit may proceed')—without amending underlying substantive or procedural laws—violates the Constitution's separation of powers principles." How do you think the Court will resolve the case? *See Patchak v. Jewell*, 828 F.3d 995 (D.C. Cir. 2016).

8. ACT OF STATE DOCTRINE

The "act of state doctrine" is essentially a rule of judicial self-restraint that has developed in the United States. Under this rule, U.S. courts decline to "sit in judgment" on the acts of a foreign government when those acts are taken within the foreign government's territory. The principal motivation for this self-restraint appears to be a desire that disputes involving the acts of foreign governments in their own territories be resolved through diplomatic means, not through litigation in national courts. *See Restatement (Third)* § 443, reporters' note 12 (1987). While the doctrine may not be compelled by customary international law, it is certainly used by many other states in one form or another. Robert Jennings & Arthur Watts eds., *Oppenheim's International Law* 365–71 (9th ed. 1992).

An early application of this doctrine in the United States is illustrated in *Underhill v. Hernandez*, 168 U.S. 250 (1897). In 1892, revolution broke out in Venezuela, led by General Hernandez, who assumed control of the city of Bolivar. Underhill, a U.S. national, wished to leave the city, but was prevented by Hernandez because Underhill had constructed the city's waterworks and was needed to help operate the system. Eventually the revolutionaries succeeded in seizing control of the entire country, and Underhill was able to leave Venezuela. Upon his return to the United States, he sued Hernandez for violations of Venezuelan tort law. The U.S. Supreme Court viewed Hernandez's action as that of a sovereign and so affirmed the dismissal of the case based on the act of state doctrine.

> Every sovereign State is bound to respect the independence of every other sovereign State, and the courts of one country will not sit in judgment on the acts of the government of another done within its own territory. Redress of grievances by reason of such acts must be obtained through the means open to be availed of by sovereign powers as between themselves.

Id. at 252. Later cases have suggested that the doctrine either was required by principles of comity, see, e.g., *Oetjen v. Central Leather Co.*, 246 U.S. 297 (1918); *Ricaud v. American Metal Co.*, 246 U.S. 304 (1918), or was a special choice of law rule, see, e.g., *American Banana Co. v. United Fruit Co.*, 213 U.S. 347 (1909).

Since the act of state doctrine is frequently invoked in cases in U.S. courts involving foreign governments, discussion of the doctrine is often coupled with discussion of sovereign immunity. It must be emphasized, however, that the act of state doctrine is potentially relevant in *any case* where the validity of a foreign government's act, taken in its own territory, is at issue. Hence, such cases may arise even when the foreign government itself is not a party.

BANCO NACIONAL DE CUBA V. SABBATINO

376 U.S. 398 (1964).

MR. JUSTICE HARLAN delivered the opinion of the Court.

The question which brought this case here, and is now found to be the dispositive issue, is whether the so-called act of state doctrine serves to sustain petitioner's claims in this litigation. Such claims are ultimately founded on a decree of the Government of Cuba expropriating certain property, the right to the proceeds of which is here in controversy. The act of state doctrine in its traditional formulation precludes the courts of this country from inquiring into the validity of the public acts a recognized foreign sovereign power committed within its own territory.

I.

[In 1960 President Eisenhower, acting pursuant to permission from Congress, reduced the sugar quota for Cuba. Cuba retaliated by adopting "Law No. 851," which called the U.S. reduction an "act of aggression" and granted discretionary power to the Cuban President and Prime Minister to nationalize property or enterprises in which American nationals had an interest. The U.S. State Department called this law "manifestly in violation" of international law and "in its essence discriminatory, arbitrary and confiscatory." In August 1960 Cuba seized a sugar shipment belonging to C.A.V., a company in which U.S. nationals had an interest. The sugar had been contracted for by an American commodity broker, Farr, Whitlock & Co, which was then forced to make a new agreement to buy the sugar from an instrumentality of the Cuban government. Upon receiving the shipment in New York, Farr, Whitlock accepted the shipping documents and negotiated the bills of lading to its customers, but refused to deliver the proceeds to Cuba. Instead, it handed the proceeds to Sabbatino, the temporary receiving agent for C.A.V., in exchange for C.A.V.'s promise of indemnity. Cuba's national bank then instituted this proceeding in Federal District Court for the Southern District of New York, alleging conversion of the bills of lading and seeking an injunction against Sabbatino to prevent him from taking the proceeds from the sugar sale.] . . .

Upon motions to dismiss and for summary judgment, the District Court, 193 F.Supp. 375, sustained federal *in personam* jurisdiction despite state control of the funds. It found that the sugar was located within Cuban territory at the time of expropriation and determined that under merchant law common to civilized countries Farr, Whitlock could not have asserted ownership of the sugar against C.A.V. before making payment. It concluded that C.A.V. had a property interest in the sugar subject to the territorial jurisdiction of Cuba. The court then dealt with the question of Cuba's title to the sugar, on which rested petitioner's claim of conversion. While acknowledging the continuing vitality of the act of state doctrine, the court believed it inapplicable when the questioned foreign act is in violation of international law. Proceeding on the basis that a taking invalid under international law does not convey good title, the District Court found the Cuban expropriation decree to violate such law in three separate respects: it was motivated by a retaliatory and not a public purpose; it discriminated against American nationals; and it failed to provide adequate compensation. Summary judgment against petitioner was accordingly granted.

The Court of Appeals, 307 F.2d 845, affirming the decision on similar grounds, relied on two letters (not before the District Court) written by State Department officers which it took as evidence that the Executive Branch had no objection to a judicial testing of the Cuban decree's validity. The court was unwilling to declare that any one of the infirmities found by the District Court rendered the taking invalid under international law, but was satisfied that in combination they had that effect. We granted certiorari because the issues involved bear importantly on the conduct of the country's foreign relations and more particularly on the proper role of the Judicial Branch in this sensitive area. 372 U.S. 905. For reasons to follow we decide that the judgment below must be reversed.

[For the Court's discussion of whether there is standing in U.S. court for the instrumentality of a government with whom the United States has no diplomatic relations, see *supra*, this Chapter, Sec. 6.] . . .

IV.

The classic American statement of the act of state doctrine, which appears to have taken root in England as early as 1674, *Blad v. Bamfield,* 3 Swans. 604, 36 Eng. Rep. 992, and began to emerge in the jurisprudence of this country in the late eighteenth and early nineteenth centuries, *see e.g., Ware v. Hylton*, 3 Dall. 199, 230; *Hudson v. Guestier*, 4 Cranch 293, 294; *The Schooner Exchange v. M'Faddon,* 7 Cranch 116, 135, 136; *L'Invincible,* 1 Wheat. 238, 253; *The Santissima Trinidad*, 7 Wheat. 283, 336, is found in *Underhill v. Hernandez*, 168 U.S. 250, where Chief Justice Fuller said for a unanimous Court (p. 252):

> "Every sovereign State is bound to respect the independence of every other sovereign State, and the courts of one country will not sit in judgment on the acts of the government of another done within its own territory. Redress of grievances by reason of such

acts must be obtained through the means open to be availed of by sovereign powers as between themselves." . . .

None of this Court's subsequent cases in which the act of state doctrine was directly or peripherally involved manifest any retreat from *Underhill*. *See American Banana Co. v. United Fruit Co.*, 213 U.S. 347; *Oetjen v. Central Leather Co.*, 246 U.S. 297; *Ricaud v. American Metal Co.*, 246 U.S. 304; *Shapleigh v. Mier*, 299 U.S. 468; *United States v. Belmont*, 301 U.S. 324; *United States v. Pink*, 315 U.S. 203. On the contrary in two of these cases, *Oetjen* and *Ricaud*, the doctrine as announced in *Underhill* was reaffirmed in unequivocal terms. . . .

The outcome of this case, therefore, turns upon whether any of the contentions urged by respondents against the application of the act of state doctrine in the premises is acceptable: (1) that the doctrine does not apply to acts of state which violate international law, as is claimed to be the case here; (2) that the doctrine is inapplicable unless the Executive specifically interposes it in a particular case; and (3) that, in any event, the doctrine may not be invoked by a foreign government plaintiff in our courts.

V.

Preliminarily, we discuss the foundations on which we deem the act of state doctrine to rest, and more particularly the question of whether state or federal law governs its application in a federal diversity case.

We do not believe that this doctrine is compelled either by the inherent nature of sovereign authority, as some of the earlier decisions seem to imply, *see Underhill, supra; American Banana, supra; Oetjen, supra,* at 303, or by some principle of international law. If a transaction takes place in one jurisdiction and the forum is in another, the forum does not by dismissing an action or by applying its own law purport to divest the first jurisdiction of its territorial sovereignty; it merely declines to adjudicate or makes applicable its own law to parties or property before it. The refusal of one country to enforce the penal laws of another . . . is a typical example of an instance when a court will not entertain a cause of action arising in another jurisdiction. While historic notions of sovereign authority do bear upon the wisdom of employing the act of state doctrine, they do not dictate its existence.

That international law does not require application of the doctrine is evidenced by the practice of nations. Most of the countries rendering decisions on the subject fail to follow the rule rigidly.[21] No international

[21] In English jurisprudence, in the classic case of *Luther v. James Sagor & Co.*, (1921) 3 K.B. 532, the act of state doctrine is articulated in terms not unlike those of the United States cases. *See Princess Paley Olga v. Weisz*, [1929] 1 K.B. 718. But see *Anglo-Iranian Oil Co. v. Jaffrate*, [1953] 1 Weekly L.R. 246, [1953] Int'l L. Rep. 316 (Aden Sup. Ct.) (exception to doctrine if foreign act violates international law). Civil law countries, however, which apply the rule make exceptions for acts contrary to their sense of public order. *See, e.g., Ropit* case, Cour de Cassation (France), [1929] Recueil General Des Lois et Des Arrets (Sirey) Part I, 217; 55 Journal Du Droit

arbitral or judicial decision discovered suggests that international law prescribes recognition of sovereign acts of foreign governments, see 1 Oppenheim's International Law, § 115aa (Lauterpacht, 8th ed. 1955), and apparently no claim has ever been raised before an international tribunal that failure to apply the act of state doctrine constitutes a breach of international obligation. If international law does not prescribe use of the doctrine, neither does it forbid application of the rule even if it is claimed that the act of state in question violated international law. The traditional view of international law is that it establishes substantive principles for determining whether one country has wronged another. Because of its peculiar nation-to-nation character the usual method for an individual to seek relief is to exhaust local remedies and then repair to the executive authorities of his own state to persuade them to champion his claim in diplomacy or before an international tribunal. *See United States v. Diekelman,* 92 U.S. 520, 524. Although it is, of course, true that United States courts apply international law as a part of our own in appropriate circumstances, *Ware v. Hylton*, 3 Dall. 199, 28; *The Nereide*, 9 Cranch 388, 423; *The Paquete Habana*, 175 U.S. 677, 700, the public law of nations can hardly dictate to a country which is in theory wronged how to treat that wrong within its domestic borders.

Despite the broad statement in *Oetjen* that "The conduct of the foreign relations of our Government is committed by the Constitution to the Executive and Legislative . . . Departments," 246 U.S. at 302, it cannot of course be thought that "every case or controversy which touches foreign relations lies beyond judicial cognizance." *Baker v. Carr,* 369 U.S. 186, 211. The text of the Constitution does not require the act of state doctrine; it does not irrevocably remove from the judiciary the capacity to review the validity of foreign acts of state.

The act of state doctrine does, however, have "constitutional" underpinnings. It arises out of the basic relationships between branches of government in a system of separation of powers. It concerns the competency of dissimilar institutions to make and implement particular kinds of decisions in the area of international relations. The doctrine as formulated in past decisions expresses the strong sense of the Judicial Branch that its engagement in the task of passing on the validity of foreign

---

International (Clunet) 674 (1928), [1927–1928] Ann. Dig., No. 43; Graue, Germany: Recognition of Foreign Expropriations, 3 Am. J. Comp.L. 93 (1954); Domke, Indonesian Nationalization Measures Before Foreign Court, 54 Am. J. Int'l L. 305 (1960) (discussion of and excerpts from opinions of the District Court in Bremen and the Hanseatic Court of Appeals in *N.V. Verenigde Deli-Maatschapijen v. Deutsch-Indonesische Tabak-Handelsgesellschaft m.b.H.,* and of the Amsterdam District Court and Appellate Court in *Senembah Maatschappij N.V. v. Republiek Indonesie Bank Indonesia*); Massouridis, The Effects of Confiscation, Expropriation, and Requisition by a Foreign Authority, 3 Revue Hellenique De Droit International 62, 68 (1950) (recounting a decision of the court of the first instance of Piraeus); *Anglo-Iranian Oil Co. v. S.U.P.O.R. Co.,* [1955] Int'l L. Rep. 19, (Ct. of Venice), 78 Il Foro Italiano Part I, 719; 40 Blatter fur Zurcherische Rechtsprechung No. 65, 172–173 (Switzerland). *See also Anglo-Iranian Oil Co. v. Idemitsu Kosan Kabushiki Kaisha,* [1953] Int'l L. Rep. 312 (High Ct. of Tokyo).

acts of state may hinder rather than further this country's pursuit of goals both for itself and for the community of nations as a whole in the international sphere. . . .

We could perhaps in this diversity action avoid the question of deciding whether federal or state law is applicable to this aspect of the litigation. New York has enunciated the act of state doctrine in terms that echo those of federal decisions decided during the reign of *Swift v. Tyson*, 16 Pet. 1 . . . Thus our conclusions might well be the same whether we dealt with this problem as one of state law, *see Erie R. Co. v. Tompkins*, 304 U.S. 64; *Klaxon Co. v. Stentor Elec. Mfg. Co.*, 313 U.S. 487; *Griffin v. McCoach,* 313 U.S. 498, or federal law.

However, we are constrained to make it clear that an issue concerned with a basic choice regarding the competence and function of the Judiciary and the National Executive in ordering our relationships with other members of the international community must be treated exclusively as an aspect of federal law. It seems fair to assume that the Court did not have rules like the act of state doctrine in mind when it decided *Erie R. Co. v. Tompkins*. Soon thereafter, Professor Philip C. Jessup, now a judge of the International Court of Justice, recognized the potential dangers were *Erie* extended to legal problems affecting international relations.[24] He cautioned that rules of international law should not be left to divergent and perhaps parochial state interpretations. His basic rationale is equally applicable to the act of state doctrine.

The Court in the pre-*Erie* act of state cases, although not burdened by the problem of the source of applicable law, used language sufficiently strong and broad-sweeping to suggest that state courts were not left free to develop their own doctrines (as they would have been had this Court merely been interpreting common law under *Swift v. Tyson, supra*). The Court of Appeals in the first *Bernstein* case, *supra*, a diversity suit, plainly considered the decisions of this Court, despite the intervention of *Erie*, to be controlling in regard to the act of state question, at the same time indicating that New York law governed other aspects of the case. We are not without other precedent for a determination that federal law governs; there are enclaves of federal judge-made law which bind the States. A national body of federal-court-built law has been held to have been contemplated by § 301 of the Labor Management Relations Act, *Textile Workers Union of America v. Lincoln Mills*, 353 U.S. 448. Principles formulated by federal judicial law have been thought by this Court to be necessary to protect uniquely federal interests, *D'Oench, Duhme & Co. v. Federal Deposit Ins. Corp.*, 315 U.S. 447; *Clearfield Trust Co. v. United States*, 318 U.S. 363. Of course the federal interest guarded in all these cases is one the ultimate statement of which is derived from a federal

[24] The Doctrine of Erie Railroad v. Tompkins Applied to International Law, 33 Am. J. Int'l L. 740 (1939).

statute. Perhaps more directly in point are the bodies of law applied between States over boundaries and in regard to the apportionment of interstate waters.

In *Hinderlider v. La Plata River Co.*, 304 U.S. 92, 110, in an opinion handed down the same day as *Erie* and by the same author, Mr. Justice Brandeis, the Court declared, "For whether the water of an interstate stream must be apportioned between the two States is a question of 'federal common law' upon which neither the statutes nor the decisions of either State can be conclusive." Although the suit was between two private litigants and the relevant States could not be made parties, the Court considered itself free to determine the effect of an interstate compact regulating water apportionment. The decision implies that no State can undermine the federal interest in equitably apportioned interstate waters even if it deals with private parties. This would not mean that, absent a compact, the apportionment scheme could not be changed judicially or by Congress, but only that apportionment is a matter of federal law. *Cf. State of Arizona v. State of California*, 373 U.S. 546, 597–598. The problems surrounding the act of state doctrine are, albeit for different reasons, as intrinsically federal as are those involved in water apportionment or boundary disputes. The considerations supporting exclusion of state authority here are much like those which led the Court in *United States v. California*, 332 U.S. 19, to hold that the Federal Government possessed paramount rights in submerged lands though within the three-mile limit of coastal States. We conclude that the scope of the act of state doctrine must be determined according to federal law.[25]

VI.

If the act of state doctrine is a principle of decision binding on federal and state courts alike but compelled by neither international law nor the Constitution, its continuing vitality depends on its capacity to reflect the proper distribution of functions between the judicial and political branches of the Government on matters bearing upon foreign affairs. It should be apparent that the greater the degree of codification or consensus concerning a particular area of international law, the more appropriate it is for the judiciary to render decisions regarding it, since the courts can then focus on the application of an agreed principle to circumstances of fact rather than on the sensitive task of establishing a principle not inconsistent with the national interest or with international justice. It is also evident that some aspects of international law touch much more

[25] Various constitutional and statutory provisions indirectly support this determination, *see* U.S. Const., Art I, § 8, cls. 3, 10; Art. II, §§ 2, 3; Art. III, § 2; 28 U.S.C. §§ 1251(a)(2), (b)(1), (b)(3), 1332(a)(2), 1333, 1350–1351, by reflecting a concern for uniformity in this country's dealings with foreign nations and indicating a desire to give matters of international significance to the jurisdiction of federal institutions. *See* Comment, The Act of State Doctrine—Its Relation to Private and Public International Law, 62 Col. L. Rev., 1278, 1297, n. 123; *cf. United States v. Belmont, supra; United States v. Pink, supra.*

sharply on national nerves than do others; the less important the implications of an issue are for our foreign relations, the weaker the justification for exclusivity in the political branches. The balance of relevant considerations may also be shifted if the government which perpetrated the challenged act of state is no longer in existence . . . for the political interest of this country may, as a result, be measurably altered. Therefore, rather than laying down or reaffirming an inflexible and all-encompassing rule in this case, we decide only that the Judicial Branch will not examine the validity of a taking of property within its own territory by a foreign sovereign government, extant and recognized by this country at the time of suit, in the absence of a treaty or other unambiguous agreement regarding controlling legal principles, even if the complaint alleges that the taking violates customary international law.

There are few if any issues in international law today on which opinion seems to be so divided as the limitations on a state's power to expropriate the property of aliens.[26] . . .

It is difficult to imagine the courts of this country embarking on adjudication in an area which touches more sensitively the practical and ideological goals of the various members of the community of nations.[34]

When we consider the prospect of the courts characterizing foreign expropriations, however justifiably, as invalid under international law and ineffective to pass title, the wisdom of the precedents is confirmed. While each of the leading cases in this Court may be argued to be distinguishable on its facts from this one—*Underhill* because sovereign immunity provided an independent ground and *Oetjen, Ricaud,* and *Shapleigh* because there was actually no violation of international law—the plain implication of all these opinions . . . is that the act of state doctrine is applicable even if international law has been violated. . . .

The possible adverse consequences of a conclusion to the contrary of that implicit in these cases is highlighted by contrasting the practices of the political branch with the limitations of the judicial process in matters of this kind. Following an expropriation of any significance, the Executive engages in diplomacy aimed to assure that United States citizens who are harmed are compensated fairly. Representing all claimants of this country,

---

[26] *Compare, e.g.,* Friedman, Expropriation in International Law 206–211 (1953); Dawson and Weston, "Prompt, Adequate and Effective": A Universal Standard of Compensation? 30 Fordham L. Rev. 727 (1962), with Note from Secretary of State Hull to Mexican Ambassador, August 22, 1938, V Foreign Relations of the United States 685 (1938); Doman, Postwar Nationalization of Foreign Property in Europe, 48 Col. L. Rev. 1125, 1127 (1948). We do not, of course, mean to say that there is no international standard in this area; we conclude only that the matter is not [meant] for adjudication by domestic tribunals.

[34] There are, of course, areas of international law in which consensus as to standards is greater and which do not represent a battleground for conflicting ideologies. This decision in no way intimates that the courts of this country are broadly foreclosed from considering questions of international law.

it will often be able, either by bilateral or multilateral talks, by submission to the United Nations, or by the employment of economic and political sanctions, to achieve some degree of general redress. Judicial determinations of invalidity of title can, on the other hand, have only an occasional impact, since they depend on the fortuitous circumstance of the property in question being brought into this country. Such decisions would, if the acts involved were declared invalid, often be likely to give offense to the expropriating country; since the concept of territorial sovereignty is so deep seated, any state may resent the refusal of the courts of another sovereign to accord validity to acts within its territorial borders. Piecemeal dispositions of this sort involving the probability of affront to another state could seriously interfere with negotiations being carried on by the Executive Branch and might prevent or render less favorable the terms of an agreement that could otherwise be reached. Relations with third countries which have engaged in similar expropriations would not be immune from effect.

The dangers of such adjudication are present regardless of whether the State Department has, as it did in this case, asserted that the relevant act violated international law. If the Executive Branch has undertaken negotiations with an expropriating country, but has refrained from claims of violation of the law of nations, a determination to that effect by a court might be regarded as a serious insult, while a finding of compliance with international law would greatly strengthen the bargaining hand of the other state with consequent detriment to American interests.

Even if the State Department has proclaimed the impropriety of the expropriation, the stamp of approval of its view by a judicial tribunal, however impartial, might increase any affront and the judicial decision might occur at a time, almost always well after the taking, when such an impact would be contrary to our national interest. Considerably more serious and far-reaching consequences would flow from a judicial finding that international law standards had been met if that determination flew in the face of a State Department proclamation to the contrary. When articulating principles of international law in its relations with other states, the Executive Branch speaks not only as an interpreter of generally accepted and traditional rules, as would the courts, but also as an advocate of standards it believes desirable for the community of nations and protective of national concerns. In short, whatever way the matter is cut, the possibility of conflict between the Judicial and Executive Branches could hardly be avoided. . . .

Against the force of such considerations, we find respondents' countervailing arguments quite unpersuasive. Their basic contention is that United States courts could make a significant contribution to the growth of international law, a contribution whose importance, it is said, would be magnified by the relative paucity of decisional law by international bodies. But given the fluidity of present world conditions, the effectiveness of such a patchwork approach toward the formulation of an acceptable body of law concerning state responsibility for expropriations is, to say the least, highly conjectural. Moreover, it rests upon the sanguine presupposition that the decisions of the courts of the world's major capital exporting country and principal exponent of the free enterprise system would be accepted as disinterested expressions of sound legal principle by those adhering to widely different ideologies. . . .

However offensive to the public policy of this country and its constituent States an expropriation of this kind may be, we conclude that both the national interest and progress toward the goal of establishing the rule of law among nations are best served by maintaining intact the act of state doctrine in this realm of its application.

W.S. KIRKPATRICK & CO. V. ENVIRONMENTAL TECTONICS CORP.

493 U.S. 400 (1990).

[According to respondent's complaint, petitioners obtained a construction contract from the Nigerian Government by bribing Nigerian officials. Nigerian law prohibits both the payment and the receipt of such bribes. Respondent, an unsuccessful bidder for the contract, filed an action for damages against petitioners and others under various federal and state statutes. The District Court ruled that the suit was barred by the act of state doctrine, which in its view precluded judicial inquiry into the motivation of a sovereign act that would result in embarrassment to the sovereign, or constitute interference with the conduct of United States foreign policy. The court granted summary judgment for petitioners because resolution of the case in favor of respondent would require imputing to foreign officials an unlawful motivation (the obtaining of bribes), and accordingly might embarrass the executive branch in its conduct of foreign relations. The Court of Appeals reversed and remanded the case for trial, holding that on the facts of this case the doctrine of sovereign immunity did not apply because no embarrassment of the executive in its conduct of foreign affairs was evident. Indeed, the court found that a Department of State letter indicating that a decision would not result in embarrassment to the executive branch was entitled to substantial respect.]

JUSTICE SCALIA delivered the opinion of the Court.

In this case we must decide whether the act of state doctrine bars a court in the United States from entertaining a cause of action that does not rest upon the asserted invalidity of an official act of a foreign sovereign, but that does require imputing to foreign officials an unlawful motivation (the obtaining of bribes) in the performance of such an official act. . . .

II

This Court's description of the jurisprudential foundation for the act of state doctrine has undergone some evolution over the years. We once viewed the doctrine as an expression of international law, resting upon "the highest considerations of international comity and expediency," *Oetjen v. Central Leather Co.*, 246 U.S. 297, 303–304 (1918). We have more recently described it, however, as a consequence of domestic separation of powers, reflecting "the strong sense of the Judicial Branch that its engagement in the task of passing on the validity of foreign acts of state may hinder" the conduct of foreign affairs, *Banco Nacional de Cuba v. Sabbatino*, 376 U.S. 398, 423 (1964). Some Justices have suggested possible exceptions to application of the doctrine, where one or both of the foregoing policies would seemingly not be served: an exception, for example, for acts of state that consist of commercial transactions, since neither modern international comity nor the current position of our Executive Branch accorded sovereign immunity to such acts, see *Alfred Dunhill of London, Inc. v. Republic of Cuba*, 425 U.S. 682, 695–706 (1976) (opinion of WHITE, J.); or an exception for cases in which the Executive Branch has represented that it has no objection to denying validity to the foreign sovereign act, since then the courts would be impeding no foreign policy goals, see *First National City Bank v. Banco Nacional de Cuba*, 406 U.S. 759, 768–770 (1972) (opinion of REHNQUIST, J.).

The parties have argued at length about the applicability of these possible exceptions, and, more generally, about whether the purpose of the act of state doctrine would be furthered by its application in this case. We find it unnecessary, however, to pursue those inquiries, since the factual predicate for application of the act of state doctrine does not exist. Nothing in the present suit requires the court to declare invalid, and thus ineffective as "a rule of decision for the courts of this country," *Ricaud v. American Metal Co.*, 246 U.S. 304, 310 (1918), the official act of a foreign sovereign.

In every case in which we have held the act of state doctrine applicable, the relief sought or the defense interposed would have required a court in the United States to declare invalid the official act of a foreign sovereign performed within its own territory. In *Underhill v. Hernandez*, 168 U.S. 250, 254 (1897), holding the defendant's detention of the plaintiff to be tortious would have required denying legal effect to "acts of a military commander representing the authority of the revolutionary party as government, which afterwards succeeded and was recognized by the United States." In *Oetjen v. Central Leather Co., supra*, and in *Ricaud v. American Metal Co., supra*, denying title to the party who claimed through purchase from Mexico would have required declaring that government's prior seizure of the property, within its own territory, legally ineffective. *See Oetjen, supra*, 246 U.S., at 304; *Ricaud, supra*, 246 U.S., at 310. In *Sabbatino*, upholding the defendant's claim to the funds would have required a holding that Cuba's expropriation of goods located in Havana was null and void. In the present case, by contrast, neither the claim nor any asserted defense requires a determination that Nigeria's contract with Kirkpatrick International was, or was not, effective.

Petitioners point out, however, that the facts necessary to establish respondent's claim will also establish that the contract was unlawful. Specifically, they note that in order to prevail respondent must prove that petitioner Kirkpatrick made, and Nigerian officials received, payments that violate Nigerian law, which would, they assert, support a finding that the contract is invalid under Nigerian law. Assuming that to be true, it still does not suffice. The act of state doctrine is not some vague doctrine of abstention but a "principle of decision binding on federal and state courts alike." *Sabbatino, supra*, 376 U.S., at 427 (emphasis added). As we said in *Ricaud*, "the act within its own boundaries of one sovereign State . . . becomes . . . a rule of decision for the courts of this country." 246 U.S., at 310. Act of state issues only arise when a court must decide—that is, when the outcome of the case turns upon—the effect of official action by a foreign sovereign. When that question is not in the case, neither is the act of state doctrine. That is the situation here. Regardless of what the court's factual findings may suggest as to the legality of the Nigerian contract, its legality is simply not a question to be decided in the present suit, and there is thus no occasion to apply the rule of decision that the act of state doctrine requires. *Cf. Sharon v. Time, Inc.*, 599 F.Supp. 538, 546 (SDNY 1984) ("The issue in this litigation is not whether [the alleged] acts are valid, but whether they occurred").

In support of their position that the act of state doctrine bars any factual findings that may cast doubt upon the validity of foreign sovereign acts, petitioners cite Justice Holmes' opinion for the Court in *American Banana Co. v. United Fruit Co.*, 213 U.S. 347 (1909). That was a suit under the United States antitrust laws, alleging that Costa Rica's seizure of the plaintiff's property had been induced by an unlawful conspiracy. In the course of a lengthy opinion Justice Holmes observed, citing *Underhill*, that "a seizure by a state is not a thing that can be complained of elsewhere in the courts." *Id.*, at 357–358. The statement is concededly puzzling. *Underhill* does indeed stand for the proposition that a seizure by a state cannot be complained of elsewhere—in the sense of being sought to be declared ineffective elsewhere. The plaintiff in *American Banana*, however, like the plaintiff here, was not trying to undo or disregard the governmental action, but only to obtain damages from private parties who had procured it. Arguably, then, the statement did imply that suit would not lie if a foreign state's actions would be, though not invalidated, impugned.

Whatever Justice Holmes may have had in mind, his statement lends inadequate support to petitioners' position here, for two reasons. First, it was a brief aside, entirely unnecessary to the decision. *American Banana* was squarely decided on the ground (later substantially overruled, see *Continental Ore Co. v. Union Carbide & Carbon Corp.*, 370 U.S. 690, 704–705 (1962)) that the antitrust laws had no extraterritorial application, so that "what the defendant did in Panama or Costa Rica is not within the scope of the statute." 213 U.S., at 357. Second, whatever support the dictum might provide for petitioners' position is more than overcome by our later holding in *United States v. Sisal Sales Corp.*, 274 U.S. 268 (1927). There we held that, *American Banana* notwithstanding, the defendant's actions in obtaining Mexico's enactment of "discriminating legislation" could form part of the basis for suit under the United States antitrust laws. 274 U.S., at 276. Simply put, *American Banana* was not an act of state case; and whatever it said by way of dictum that might be relevant to the present case has not survived *Sisal Sales*.

Petitioners insist, however, that the policies underlying our act of state cases—international comity, respect for the sovereignty of foreign nations on their own territory, and the avoidance of embarrassment to the Executive Branch in its conduct of foreign relations—are implicated in the present case because, as the District Court found, a determination that Nigerian officials demanded and accepted a bribe "would impugn or question the nobility of a foreign nation's motivations," and would "result in embarrassment to the sovereign or constitute interference in the conduct of foreign policy of the United States." 659 F.Supp., at 1392–1393. The United States, as *amicus curiae*, favors the same approach to the act of state doctrine, though disagreeing with petitioners as to the outcome it produces in the present case. We should not, the United States urges, "attach dispositive significance to the fact that this suit involves only the 'motivation' for, rather than the 'validity' of, a foreign sovereign act," Brief for United States as *Amicus Curiae* 37, and should eschew "any rigid formula for the resolution of act of state cases generally," id., at 9. In some future case, perhaps, "litigation . . . based on alleged corruption in the award of contracts or other commercially oriented activities of foreign governments could sufficiently touch on 'national nerves' that the act of state doctrine or related principles of abstention would appropriately be found to bar the suit," *id.*, at 40 (quoting *Sabbatino*, 376 U.S., at 428), and we should therefore resolve this case on the narrowest possible ground, viz., that the letter from the legal advisor to the District Court gives sufficient indication that, "in the setting of this case," the act of state doctrine poses no bar to adjudication. . . .

These urgings are deceptively similar to what we said in *Sabbatino*, where we observed that sometimes, even though the validity of the act of a foreign sovereign within its own territory is called into question, the policies underlying the act of state doctrine may not justify its application. We suggested that a sort of balancing approach could be applied—the balance shifting against application of the doctrine, for example, if the government that committed the "challenged act of state" is no longer in existence. 376 U.S., at 428. But what is appropriate in order to avoid unquestioning judicial acceptance of the acts of foreign sovereigns is not similarly appropriate for the quite opposite purpose of expanding judicial incapacities where such acts are not directly (or even indirectly) involved. It is one thing to suggest, as we have, that the policies underlying the act of state doctrine should be considered in deciding whether, despite the doctrine's technical availability, it should nonetheless not be invoked; it is something quite different to suggest that those underlying policies are a doctrine unto themselves, justifying expansion of the act of state doctrine (or, as the United States puts it, unspecified "related principles of abstention") into new and uncharted fields.

The short of the matter is this: Courts in the United States have the power, and ordinarily the obligation, to decide cases and controversies properly presented to them. The act of state doctrine does not establish an exception for cases and controversies that may embarrass foreign governments, but merely requires that, in the process of deciding, the acts of foreign sovereigns taken within their own jurisdictions shall be deemed valid. That doctrine has no application to the present case because the validity of no foreign sovereign act is at issue.

The judgment of the Court of Appeals for the Third Circuit is *affirmed*.

NOTES

1. *Rationale for the Doctrine*. According to the *Restatement (Third)*:

> The rationale for the doctrine has been variously described. The doctrine was developed by the Court on its own authority, as a principle of judicial restraint, essentially to avoid disrespect for foreign states. "To permit the validity of the acts of one sovereign State to be reexamined and perhaps condemned by the courts of another would very certainly 'imperil the amicable relations between governments and vex the peace of nations.' " *Oetjen v. Central Leather Co.*, 246 U.S. 297, 304 (1918). Thus, the doctrine is related in spirit to the rules of international law that accord to foreign sovereigns large immunity from adjudication in domestic courts. *See* Reporters' Note 11; *see also* §§ 451–460. In *Sabbatino*, the Court said that the act of state doctrine is compelled neither by international law nor by the Constitution, but that it has "constitutional underpinnings," 376 U.S. at 423. The Court referred to the doctrine as "concerned with a basic choice regarding the competence and function of the Judiciary and the National Executive in ordering our relationships with other members of the international community." 376 U.S. at 425. The Court's statement in *Underhill* implies that disputes arising out of foreign acts of state should be resolved between governments. The act

> of state doctrine therefore also reflects deference to the Executive Branch, akin to the political question doctrine. . . . Where the act of a foreign state is challenged under international law, as in *Sabbatino*, the lack of consensus on the relevant content of that law has contributed to the Court's reluctance to entertain such a challenge. . . . Courts and commentators have stressed one or another of these bases for the doctrine, and the weight given to the different bases may determine possible limitations or exceptions. . . .

Restatement of the Law (Third), The Foreign Relations Law of the United States § 443 comment a (1987) (Copyright (c) 1987 by The American Law Institute. Reproduced with permission.)

2. *Congress's Ability to Set Aside the Doctrine.* Can Congress by statute direct federal courts in some instances not to apply the act of state doctrine? After the *Sabbatino* case was decided by the Supreme Court, Congress enacted the "Second Hickenlooper Amendment," Pub. L. No. 88–633, § 302(d)(2) (1964), amended and codified at 22 U.S.C. § 2370(e)(2) (2012), which states:

> Notwithstanding any other provision of law, no court in the United States shall decline on the ground of the federal act of state doctrine to make a determination on the merits giving effect to the principles of international law in a case in which a claim of title or other rights to property is asserted by any party including a foreign state (or a party claiming through such state) based upon (or traced through) a confiscation or other taking after January 1, 1959, by an act of that state in violation of the principles of international law, including the principles of compensation and the other standards set out in this subsection: *Provided*, That this subparagraph shall not be applicable (1) in any case in which an act of a foreign state is not contrary to international law or with respect to a claim of title or other right to property acquired pursuant to an irrevocable letter of credit of not more than 180 days duration issued in good faith prior to the time of the confiscation or other taking, or (2) in any case with respect to which the President determines that application of the act of state doctrine is required in that particular case by the foreign policy interests of the United States and a suggestion to this effect is filed on his behalf in that case with the court.

Courts have upheld the constitutionality of the Hickenlooper Amendment. The matter was considered in *Banco Nacional de Cuba v. Farr,* 243 F.Supp. 957 and 272 F.Supp. 836 (S.D.N.Y. 1965), *aff'd*, 383 F.2d 166 (2d Cir. 1967). The district court found that eliminating the act of state doctrine in the areas of foreign investment and international trade and commerce, except by contrary presidential determination, was wholly within the powers of Congress under its commerce-clause authority as well as under the necessary-and-proper clause, Art. I, § 8, cl. 18. The court hinted that such powers were also granted under the define-and-punish clause, Art. I, § 8, cl. 10, or "within the ambit of implied congressional power over foreign relations." Looking to these additional sources was unnecessary, however: "congressional power under the commerce clause is so clear that to discuss these less obvious questions would be merely gilding the lily." The court further rejected the contention that the amendment impinged on the president's foreign relations powers and thus violated separation of powers. 243 F.Supp. at 972–73. If the act of state doctrine is a constitutionally based rule of judicial restraint, can Congress alter such a rule? If it is not constitutionally based, what is it? Note that a foreign national complaining as to a taking of property by his own government cannot take advantage of the Hickenlooper Amendment if such taking is not viewed as a violation of *international* law. *See Mezerhane v. Republica Bolivariana de Venezuela*, 785 F.3d 545 (11th Cir. 2015).

Likewise, when enacting the Torture Victim Protection Act, 28 U.S.C. § 1350 note (2012)—which, as discussed in Chapter 3, Sec. 4, provides a civil remedy to persons who suffer torture or extrajudicial killing by, or under the authority of, a foreign government—a congressional committee indicated that it did not intend the act of state doctrine to apply to such claims. *See* S. REP. NO. 102–249, at 8 (1991).

A third example concerns the Cuban Liberty and Democratic Solidarity (Libertad) Act, Pub. L. No. 104–114, 110 Stat. 785, 104th Cong. 2d Sess. (1996), better known as the "Helms-Burton Act." Title III of the Act provides a civil remedy against those "trafficking" in property formerly owned by U.S. citizens and confiscated by the Cuban government on or after January 1, 1959. "Trafficking" was described quite broadly in the Act. In § 302(a)(6), 22 U.S.C. § 6082(a)(6) (2012), the Act precludes courts in the United States from using the act of state doctrine as justification for declining to adjudicate the merits of such cases. The Helms-Burton Act provoked intense opposition from foreign states, which viewed it as an impermissible extension of U.S. jurisdiction. Since the law was passed in 1996, successive presidents have applied consistent waivers of Title III's controversial provisions, as permitted under 22 U.S.C. § 6085(b) (2012).

3. *Executive's Ability to Set Aside the Doctrine (The "Bernstein" Exception).* In the interplay between courts and the executive over recognition policy, courts follow executive policy, often receiving specific instructions from the Department of State. (*See supra*, this Chapter, Sec. 6). These instructions as to recognition can also determine the application of act of state doctrine since the doctrine can be applied only to the acts of recognized governments. *Sabbatino, supra*, 376 U.S. at 428. A broader question is whether the executive can generally command the non-application of the act of state doctrine.

The Second Circuit followed executive instructions during the course of the *Bernstein* litigation. Bernstein, a German Jew, brought suits after the Second World War to recover damages for property that Nazi officials had compelled him to transfer to third parties. At first, he was unsuccessful because the courts invoked the act of state doctrine. *Bernstein v. Van Heyghen Freres S.A.*, 163 F.2d 246 (2d Cir. 1947); *Bernstein v. N.V. Nederlandsche-Amerikaansche Stoomvaart-Maatschappij*, 173 F.2d 71 (2d Cir. 1949).

Bernstein then procured a letter from the State Department advising that: "The policy of the Executive, with respect to claims asserted in the United States for the restitution of identifiable property (or compensation in lieu thereof) lost through force, coercion, or duress as a result of Nazi persecution in Germany, is to relieve American courts from any restraint upon the exercise of their jurisdiction to pass upon the acts of Nazi officials." 20 DEP'T STATE BULL. 592, 593 (1949).

The Second Circuit, "in view of this supervening expression of Executive policy," remanded the case to the district court, expressly accepting that the act of state doctrine was no longer a hindrance. *Bernstein v. N.V. Nederlandsche-Amerikaansche Stoomvaart-Maatschappij*, 210 F.2d 375 (2d Cir. 1954). In light of this case, the executive's ability to set aside the doctrine is sometimes referred to as the "*Bernstein* exception" to the doctrine. However, the *Bernstein* holding can be, and later was, limited to its facts: the Nazi government was both defunct (and therefore could not be offended by U.S. judicial action) and, uniquely, had been condemned universally. *See, e.g.*, *Sabbatino, supra*, 376 U.S. at 428.

In *First National City Bank v. Banco Nacional de Cuba,* the Supreme Court reached the *Bernstein* exception issue. 406 U.S. 759 (1972). The litigation involved a loan, secured by collateral, by First National to the pre-revolutionary Cuban government. In 1960, the Castro regime confiscated First National property in Cuba. In retaliation, First National cashed in the collateral, receiving more than was due on the outstanding loan (but less than the Bank's total loss due to confiscation). Banco Nacional brought suit to recover this excess. First National, on the basis of the other confiscations, counterclaimed to the extent of the Cuban claim. The Second Circuit, reversing the district court, asserted that *Sabbatino* prevented judicial consideration of the U.S. bank's counterclaim. *Banco Nacional de Cuba v. First National City Bank of New York,* 431 F.2d 394 (2d Cir. 1970). The Hickenlooper law did not reverse this result since it only applied to confiscated property brought into the United States. *Id.* at 399–402.

While appeal to the Supreme Court was pending, the State Department intervened. The Department wrote to the Court that "the act of state doctrine should not be applied to bar consideration of a defendant's counterclaim or set-off against the Government of Cuba in this or like cases." *Reprinted in* 442 F.2d at 538. In response, the Supreme Court vacated the circuit court decision and remanded the case. *First National City Bank v. Banco Nacional de Cuba*, 400 U.S. 1019 (1971). Despite the letter, the Second Circuit, re-asserting its previous position in the case, refused to follow the State Department's suggestion. It limited the *Bernstein* exception to its specific circumstances. *Banco Nacional de Cuba v. First National City Bank of New York*, 442 F.2d 530, 534 (2d Cir. 1971).

On appeal, the Supreme Court reversed in a 5–4 decision. *First National City Bank v. Banco Nacional de Cuba,* 406 U.S. 759 (1972). The five justices voting for reversal offered divergent rationales. Justice Rehnquist, joined by

Chief Justice Burger and Justice White, approved the *Bernstein* exception: "We conclude that where the Executive Branch, charged as it is with primary responsibility for the conduct of foreign affairs, expressly represents to the Court that application of act of state doctrine would not advance the interests of American foreign policy, that doctrine should not be applied by the courts." 406 U.S. at 759, 768. Justice Douglas, concurring, based his opinion on *National City Bank v. Republic of China,* 348 U.S. 356 (1955), elaborating that to allow Cuba to enter U.S. courts and make its claim without that claim being subject to setoff "would permit Cuba to have its cake and eat it too." 406 U.S. at 772. He continued, "It is that principle, not the *Bernstein* exception, which should govern here." *Id.* at 772–73 (footnote omitted). Justice Powell, concurring, also disavowed the *Bernstein* exception, reporting that he "would be uncomfortable with a doctrine which would require the judiciary to receive the Executive's permission before invoking its jurisdiction." *Id.* at 773. The problem for Powell was that he believed *Sabbatino* itself to have been wrongly decided. *Id.* at 774–75. He concluded that "federal courts have an obligation to hear cases such as this . . . [u]nless it appears that an exercise of jurisdiction would interfere with delicate foreign relations conducted by the political branches." *Id.* at 775–76.

The dissent, authored by Justice Brennan, calculated that a majority of the Court had rejected the *Bernstein* exception. *Id.* at 776–77. It also argued that *Sabbatino* had implicitly rejected the *Bernstein* exception and, applying Harlan's reasoning in *Sabbatino,* argued that, although the executive had urged that the act of state doctrine not be applied, it had done so only because it "anticipate[d] a favorable ruling," and if the Court upset that expectation, its ruling would "frustrate the conduct of this country's foreign relations." *Id.* at 783–84. Second, the rationale for applying the act of state doctrine included other concerns: for example, the lack of international consensus with respect to the law applicable to expropriation, the respect due to an existing and recognized foreign government, and the ability of the executive to negotiate an overall settlement. *Id.* at 788.

4. *Other Limitations to the Doctrine.* In addition to situations where non-application of the act of state doctrine is directed by Congress (note 2 above) or by the executive (note 3 above), there are circumstances where courts have declined to apply the doctrine or declared its inherent limitations.

First, the act at issue must be an *official act* of a foreign sovereign. In declining to apply the act of state doctrine in a claim by a U.S. company (McKesson) against the government of Iran for the taking of a dairy (Pak) in Iran, the court of appeals stated:

> The facts allege a pattern of conduct by Iran's agents that cannot fairly be characterized as public or official acts of a sovereign government. Iran did not pass a law, issue an edict or degree, or engage in formal governmental action explicitly taking McKesson's property for the benefit of the Iranian public. Instead, it allegedly took control of Pak's board of directors and abused its position as

> majority shareholder, making McKesson's claims "akin to a corporate dispute between majority and minority shareholders." . . . This is not the type of "*public* act [ ] [of] a foreign sovereign power" to which the act of state doctrine applies. *Sabbatino,* 376 U.S. at 401. . . .

McKesson Corp. v. Iran, 672 F.3d 1066, 1074 (D.C. Cir. 2012).

Second, the *validity* of the public act must be at issue before the court for the act of state doctrine to come into play. In *W.W. Kirkpatrick*, the issue before the court was not the validity of the Nigerian official's act but, rather, whether a particular motivation could be imputed to the foreign official in the performance of his duties so as to satisfy U.S. requirements for a civil recovery by the plaintiff.

Third, the official act must be undertaken *within the foreign sovereign's territory*. Prior case law has established that the act of state doctrine does not apply where the foreign government seeks to affect property located outside its territory. *See Republic of Iraq v. First Nat'l City Bank*, 353 F.2d 47 (2d Cir. 1965). Situs questions become particularly important in cases involving actions against intangibles, such as credits, debts, or securities.

Fourth, a clear and countervailing international law principle may contraindicate application of the act of state doctrine. *Sabbatino, supra*, explained that "the greater the degree of codification or consensus concerning a particular area of international law, the more appropriate it is for the judiciary to render decisions regarding it." 376 U.S. at 428. Even the expropriation issue in *Sabbatino* was susceptible to reconsideration under the appropriate circumstances.

In *Kalamazoo Spice Extraction Co. v. Ethiopia*, 729 F.2d 422 (6th Cir. 1984), the district court was asked to decide a counterclaim by a U.S. defendant for the expropriation of his property by the revolutionary government of Ethiopia. Although the U.S.-Ethiopia Treaty of Amity and Economic Relations, U.S.-Eth., Sept. 7, 1951, 4 U.S.T. 2134, 206 U.N.T.S. 41, included a standard of "prompt payment of just and effective compensation" in the event that one party expropriated property belonging to nationals of the other, the district court applied the act of state doctrine and dismissed the case. 543 F.Supp. 1224 (W.D.Mich. 1982). Before the appeal was heard, the Department of State transmitted a letter to the Sixth Circuit stating: "When, as in this case, there is a controlling legal standard for compensation, we believe that adjudication would not be inconsistent with foreign policy interests under the Act of State Doctrine." On appeal, the Sixth Circuit accepted the position expressed in the letter.

The presence of a "controlling legal standard" is cited as a basis for resisting application of the act of state doctrine to cases alleging human rights violations by a foreign government in its territory. *See, e.g., Doe I v. Unocal Corp.*, 395 F.3d 932, 959 (9th Cir. 2002) ("[b]ecause *jus cogens* violations are, by definition, internationally denounced, there is a high degree of international consensus against them"); *Kadic v. Karadzic*, 70 F.3d 232, 250 (2d Cir. 1995) (claiming that "it would be a rare case in which the act of state doctrine precluded suit under [the Alien Tort Statute, 28 U.S.C. § 1350]"). Some courts have explained similar results by claiming that at least some acts—for example, torture, extrajudicial killing, and crimes against humanity—"committed in violation of the norms of customary international law, are not deemed official acts for purposes of the act of state doctrine." *Lizarbe v. Rondon*, 642 F.Supp.2d 473, 488 (D. Md. 2009); *see Sarei v. Rio Tinto*, 487 F.3d 1193, 1208–10 (9th Cir. 2007) (suggesting that *jus cogens* norms, including claims of racial discrimination, are not public acts subjected to the act of state doctrine, but other customary international law violations may be), *vacated*, 499 F.3d 923 (9th Cir. 2007).

Fifth, *Sabbatino* advised that "the balance of relevant considerations may also be shifted if the government which perpetrated the challenged act of state is no longer in existence." 376 U.S. at 428*; see Bigio v. Coca-Cola Co.*, 239 F.3d 440, 453 (2d Cir. 2001) (declining to dismiss on act of state grounds an Alien Tort Statute action alleging nationalization by the Egyptian government during the 1960s, over thirty years prior to suit); *but see Konowaloff v. Metropolitan Museum of Art*, 702 F.3d 140 (2d Cir. 2012) (rejecting an argument that the act of state doctrine should not be applied because the U.S.S.R. no longer exists, given that its successor has not renounced expropriations that occurred in 1918).

Sixth, *Sabbatino* observed that "the less important the implications of an issue are for our foreign relations, the weaker the justification for exclusivity in the political branches." 376 U.S. at 428. How adept are courts likely to be at this inquiry?

Seventh, it has been suggested that the act of state doctrine may not be invoked by a foreign government in instances where it availed itself of U.S. courts. In *First National City Bank v. Banco Nacional de Cuba*, *supra*, a foreign government filed a claim, and a U.S. national responded with a counterclaim. The foreign government raised the act of state doctrine as a defense to the counterclaim. The Supreme Court declined to apply the doctrine. Justice Douglas took the position that the act of state doctrine should not be applied to counterclaims. 406 U.S. at 770–73 (citing to *National City Bank v. China*, 348 U.S. 356 (1955)). None of the other justices, however, found that issue dispositive.

Eighth, in *Alfred Dunhill of London, Inc. v. Cuba*, 425 U.S. 682 (1976), three justices argued that the act of state doctrine did not apply to a foreign sovereign's *commercial* acts, even though those acts were done within its own territory. According to those justices, such acts are incapable of examination in U.S. courts only if U.S. jurisdiction over the conduct is limited under international jurisdictional principles. This possible exception has occasionally been suggested since, but without evident success. *See, e.g.*, *In re Refined Petroleum Products Antitrust Litigation*, 649 F.Supp.2d 572, 595 (S.D. Tex. 2009) (rejecting such a "commercial activities" exception, and noting that "[a]part from *Dunhill*, plaintiffs cite no judicial authority in support of their argument that the act of state doctrine is inapplicable under the facts of this case because the acts of which they complain are purely commercial acts as opposed to sovereign—i.e., governmental—acts.").

5. *Complaints and Criticisms*. Despite the several decades-long history of the act of state doctrine and its perhaps diminishing importance in U.S. foreign relations law, some basic questions remain unsettled. Critics have often pointed to the shifting and not-altogether-clear rationales for the act of state doctrine; in general, courts seem to have moved from an international comity rationale to a separation-of-powers rationale. *See, e.g.*, *Sabbatino, supra*; *Restatement of the Law (Third), The Foreign Relations Law of the United States*, § 443, reporters' note 2 (1987). Which is a more convincing rationale for the act of state doctrine? One way of thinking about the issue that combines both rationales is to realize that in terms of comity, states "sit in judgment" of the actions of other states under international law all the time—but this judgment is usually exercised by the executive branch in its diplomatic dealings with other nations, rather than by the judiciary. Is this as it should be? Why?

Critics also bemoan the lack of a bright-line rule for courts as to when and whether to apply the act of state doctrine. Would a clear rule be preferable, thereby increasing consistency and predictability (especially for those wishing to engage in commercial transactions involving foreign states), or is judicial discretion appropriate in determining when the court should make forays into the realm of sensitive foreign policy issues, even at some cost to predictability?

APPENDIX I

U.S. CONSTITUTION

■ ■ ■

[On September 17, 1787, the U.S. Constitution was adopted by the framers meeting in convention in Philadelphia. The Convention transmitted the Constitution to the Congress then operating under the Articles of Confederation, which approved it. The Congress, in turn, submitted the Constitution to the thirteen states for ratification. After the ninth state (New Hampshire) ratified the Constitution on June 21, 1788, the requirements were met for its entry into force (eventually all thirteen states ratified). On March 4, 1789, the new federal government began operating under the Constitution. Today, the U.S. Constitution is the oldest written constitution that is still in use.

The text that is reproduced below does not include text that has been repealed, but does include amendments adopted since its entry into force. For ease of reference, individual clauses are numbered using square brackets.]

We the People of the United States, in Order to form a more perfect Union, establish Justice, insure domestic Tranquility, provide for the common defence, promote the general Welfare, and secure the Blessings of Liberty to ourselves and our Posterity, do ordain and establish this Constitution for the United States of America.

Article I

Section 1

All legislative Powers herein granted shall be vested in a Congress of the United States, which shall consist of a Senate and House of Representatives.

Section 2

[1] The House of Representatives shall be composed of Members chosen every second Year by the People of the several States, and the Electors in each State shall have the Qualifications requisite for Electors of the most numerous Branch of the State Legislature.

[2] No Person shall be a Representative who shall not have attained to the Age of twenty five Years, and been seven Years a Citizen of the United States, and who shall not, when elected, be an Inhabitant of that State in which he shall be chosen.

[3] Representatives and direct Taxes shall be apportioned among the several States which may be included within this Union, according to their respective Numbers, which shall be determined by adding to the whole Number of free Persons, including those bound to Service for a Term of Years, and excluding Indians not taxed, three fifths of all other Persons. The actual Enumeration shall be made within three Years after the first Meeting of the Congress of the United States, and within every subsequent Term of ten Years, in such Manner as they shall by Law direct. The Number of Representatives shall not exceed one for every thirty Thousand, but each State shall have at Least one Representative; and until such enumeration shall be made, the State of New Hampshire shall be entitled to choose three, Massachusetts eight, Rhode Island and Providence Plantations one, Connecticut five, New York six, New Jersey four, Pennsylvania eight, Delaware one, Maryland six, Virginia ten, North Carolina five, South Carolina five, and Georgia three.

[4] When vacancies happen in the Representation from any State, the Executive Authority thereof shall issue Writs of Election to fill such Vacancies.

[5] The House of Representatives shall choose their Speaker and other Officers; and shall have the sole Power of Impeachment.

Section 3

[1] The Senate of the United States shall be composed of two Senators from each State, chosen by the Legislature thereof, for six Years; and each Senator shall have one Vote.

[2] Immediately after they shall be assembled in Consequence of the first Election, they shall be divided as equally as may be into three Classes. The Seats of the Senators of the first Class shall be vacated at the Expiration of the second Year, of the second Class at the Expiration of the fourth Year, and of the third Class at the Expiration of the sixth Year, so that one third may be chosen every second Year; and if Vacancies happen by Resignation, or otherwise, during the Recess of the Legislature of any State, the Executive thereof may make temporary Appointments until the next Meeting of the Legislature, which shall then fill such Vacancies.

[3] No person shall be a Senator who shall not have attained to the Age of thirty Years, and been nine Years a Citizen of the United States, and who shall not, when elected, be an Inhabitant of that State for which he shall be chosen.

[4] The Vice President of the United States shall be President of the Senate, but shall have no Vote, unless they be equally divided.

[5] The Senate shall choose their other Officers, and also a President pro tempore, in the Absence of the Vice President, or when he shall exercise the Office of President of the United States.

[6] The Senate shall have the sole Power to try all Impeachments. When sitting for that Purpose, they shall be on Oath or Affirmation. When the President of the United States is tried, the Chief Justice shall preside: And no Person shall be convicted without the Concurrence of two thirds of the Members present.

[7] Judgment in Cases of Impeachment shall not extend further than to removal from Office, and disqualification to hold and enjoy any Office of honor, Trust or Profit under the United States: but the Party convicted shall nevertheless be liable and subject to Indictment, Trial, Judgment and Punishment, according to Law.

Section 4

[1] The Times, Places and Manner of holding Elections for Senators and Representatives, shall be prescribed in each State by the Legislature thereof; but the Congress may at any time by Law make or alter such Regulations, except as to the Place of choosing Senators.

[2] The Congress shall assemble at least once in every Year, and such Meeting shall be on the first Monday in December, unless they shall by Law appoint a different Day.

Section 5

[1] Each House shall be the Judge of the Elections, Returns and Qualifications of its own Members, and a Majority of each shall constitute a Quorum to do Business; but a smaller Number may adjourn from day to day, and may be authorized to compel the Attendance of absent Members, in such Manner, and under such Penalties as each House may provide.

[2] Each House may determine the Rules of its Proceedings, punish its Members for disorderly Behavior, and, with the Concurrence of two thirds, expel a Member.

[3] Each House shall keep a Journal of its Proceedings, and from time to time publish the same, excepting such Parts as may in their Judgment require Secrecy; and the Yeas and Nays of the Members of either House on any question shall, at the Desire of one fifth of those Present, be entered on the Journal.

[4] Neither House, during the Session of Congress, shall, without the Consent of the other, adjourn for more than three days, nor to any other Place than that in which the two Houses shall be sitting.

Section 6

[1] The Senators and Representatives shall receive a Compensation for their Services, to be ascertained by Law, and paid out of the Treasury of the United States. They shall in all Cases, except Treason, Felony and Breach of the Peace, be privileged from Arrest during their Attendance at the Session of their respective Houses, and in going to and returning from

the same; and for any Speech or Debate in either House, they shall not be questioned in any other Place.

[2] No Senator or Representative shall, during the Time for which he was elected, be appointed to any civil Office under the Authority of the United States which shall have been created, or the Emoluments whereof shall have been increased during such time; and no Person holding any Office under the United States, shall be a Member of either House during his Continuance in Office.

Section 7

[1] All bills for raising Revenue shall originate in the House of Representatives; but the Senate may propose or concur with amendments as on other Bills.

[2] Every Bill which shall have passed the House of Representatives and the Senate, shall, before it become a Law, be presented to the President of the United States; If he approve he shall sign it, but if not he shall return it, with his Objections to that House in which it shall have originated, who shall enter the Objections at large on their Journal, and proceed to reconsider it. If after such Reconsideration two thirds of that House shall agree to pass the Bill, it shall be sent, together with the Objections, to the other House, by which it shall likewise be reconsidered, and if approved by two thirds of that House, it shall become a Law. But in all such Cases the Votes of both Houses shall be determined by Yeas and Nays, and the Names of the Persons voting for and against the Bill shall be entered on the Journal of each House respectively. If any Bill shall not be returned by the President within ten Days (Sundays excepted) after it shall have been presented to him, the Same shall be a Law, in like Manner as if he had signed it, unless the Congress by their Adjournment prevent its Return, in which Case it shall not be a Law.

[3] Every Order, Resolution, or Vote to which the Concurrence of the Senate and House of Representatives may be necessary (except on a question of Adjournment) shall be presented to the President of the United States; and before the Same shall take Effect, shall be approved by him, or being disapproved by him, shall be repassed by two thirds of the Senate and House of Representatives, according to the Rules and Limitations prescribed in the Case of a Bill.

Section 8

[1] The Congress shall have Power To lay and collect Taxes, Duties, Imposts and Excises, to pay the Debts and provide for the common Defence and general Welfare of the United States; but all Duties, Imposts and Excises shall be uniform throughout the United States;

[2] To borrow Money on the credit of the United States;

[3] To regulate Commerce with foreign Nations, and among the several States, and with the Indian Tribes;

[4] To establish an uniform Rule of Naturalization, and uniform Laws on the subject of Bankruptcies throughout the United States;

[5] To coin Money, regulate the Value thereof, and of foreign Coin, and fix the Standard of Weights and Measures;

[6] To provide for the Punishment of counterfeiting the Securities and current Coin of the United States;

[7] To establish Post Offices and Post Roads;

[8] To promote the Progress of Science and useful Arts, by securing for limited Times to Authors and Inventors the exclusive Right to their respective Writings and Discoveries;

[9] To constitute Tribunals inferior to the supreme Court;

[10] To define and punish Piracies and Felonies committed on the high Seas, and Offences against the Law of Nations;

[11] To declare War, grant Letters of Marque and Reprisal, and make Rules concerning Captures on Land and Water;

[12] To raise and support Armies, but no Appropriation of Money to that Use shall be for a longer Term than two Years;

[13] To provide and maintain a Navy;

[14] To make Rules for the Government and Regulation of the land and naval Forces;

[15] To provide for calling forth the Militia to execute the Laws of the Union, suppress Insurrections and repel Invasions;

[16] To provide for organizing, arming, and disciplining the Militia, and for governing such Part of them as may be employed in the Service of the United States, reserving to the States respectively, the Appointment of the Officers, and the Authority of training the Militia according to the discipline prescribed by Congress;

[17] To exercise exclusive Legislation in all Cases whatsoever, over such District (not exceeding ten Miles square) as may, by Cession of particular States, and the Acceptance of Congress, become the Seat of the Government of the United States, and to exercise like Authority over all Places purchased by the Consent of the Legislature of the State in which the Same shall be, for the Erection of Forts, Magazines, Arsenals, dock-Yards, and other needful Buildings; and

[18] To make all Laws which shall be necessary and proper for carrying into Execution the foregoing Powers, and all other Powers vested

by this Constitution in the Government of the United States, or in any Department or Officer thereof.

Section 9

[1] The Migration or Importation of such Persons as any of the States now existing shall think proper to admit, shall not be prohibited by the Congress prior to the Year one thousand eight hundred and eight, but a Tax or Duty may be imposed on such Importation, not exceeding ten dollars for each Person.

[2] The Privilege of the Writ of Habeas Corpus shall not be suspended, unless when in Cases of Rebellion or Invasion the public Safety may require it.

[3] No Bill of Attainder or ex post facto Law shall be passed.

[4] No Capitation, or other direct Tax shall be laid, unless in Proportion to the Census or Enumeration herein before directed to be taken.

[5] No Tax or Duty shall be laid on Articles exported from any State.

[6] No Preference shall be given by any Regulation of Commerce or Revenue to the Ports of one State over those of another: nor shall Vessels bound to, or from, one State, be obliged to enter, clear, or pay Duties in another.

[7] No Money shall be drawn from the Treasury, but in Consequence of Appropriations made by Law; and a regular Statement and Account of the Receipts and Expenditures of all public Money shall be published from time to time.

[8] No Title of Nobility shall be granted by the United States: And no Person holding any Office of Profit or Trust under them, shall, without the Consent of the Congress, accept of any present, Emolument, Office, or Title, of any kind whatever, from any King, Prince or foreign State.

Section 10

[1] No State shall enter into any Treaty, Alliance, or Confederation; grant Letters of Marque and Reprisal; coin Money; emit Bills of Credit; make any Thing but gold and silver Coin a Tender in Payment of Debts; pass any Bill of Attainder, ex post facto Law, or Law impairing the Obligation of Contracts, or grant any Title of Nobility.

[2] No State shall, without the Consent of the Congress, lay any Imposts or Duties on Imports or Exports, except what may be absolutely necessary for executing its inspection Laws: and the net Produce of all Duties and Imposts, laid by any State on Imports or Exports, shall be for the Use of the Treasury of the United States; and all such Laws shall be subject to the Revision and Control of the Congress.

[3] No State shall, without the Consent of Congress, lay any Duty of Tonnage, keep Troops, or Ships of War in time of Peace, enter into any Agreement or Compact with another State, or with a foreign Power, or engage in War, unless actually invaded, or in such imminent Danger as will not admit of delay.

Article II

Section 1

[1] The executive Power shall be vested in a President of the United States of America. He shall hold his Office during the Term of four Years, and, together with the Vice President chosen for the same Term, be elected, as follows:

[2] Each State shall appoint, in such Manner as the Legislature thereof may direct, a Number of Electors, equal to the whole Number of Senators and Representatives to which the State may be entitled in the Congress: but no Senator or Representative, or Person holding an Office of Trust or Profit under the United States, shall be appointed an Elector.

[3] The Electors shall meet in their respective States, and vote by Ballot for two Persons, of whom one at least shall not be an Inhabitant of the same State with themselves. And they shall make a List of all the Persons voted for, and of the Number of Votes for each; which List they shall sign and certify, and transmit sealed to the Seat of the Government of the United States, directed to the President of the Senate. The President of the Senate shall, in the Presence of the Senate and House of Representatives, open all the Certificates, and the Votes shall then be counted. The Person having the greatest Number of Votes shall be the President, if such Number be a Majority of the whole Number of Electors appointed; and if there be more than one who have such Majority, and have an equal Number of Votes, then the House of Representatives shall immediately choose by Ballot one of them for President; and if no Person have a Majority, then from the five highest on the List the said House shall in like Manner choose the President. But in choosing the President, the Votes shall be taken by States, the Representation from each State having one Vote; a quorum for this Purpose shall consist of a Member or Members from two thirds of the States, and a Majority of all the States shall be necessary to a Choice. In every Case, after the Choice of the President, the Person having the greatest Number of Votes of the Electors shall be the Vice President. But if there should remain two or more who have equal Votes, the Senate shall choose from them by Ballot the Vice President.

[4] The Congress may determine the Time of choosing the Electors, and the Day on which they shall give their Votes; which Day shall be the same throughout the United States.

[5] No Person except a natural born Citizen, or a Citizen of the United States, at the time of the Adoption of this Constitution, shall be eligible to the Office of President; neither shall any Person be eligible to that Office who shall not have attained to the Age of thirty-five Years, and been fourteen Years a Resident within the United States.

[6] In Case of the Removal of the President from Office, or of his Death, Resignation, or Inability to discharge the Powers and Duties of the said Office, the Same shall devolve on the Vice President, and the Congress may by Law provide for the Case of Removal, Death, Resignation or Inability, both of the President and Vice President, declaring what Officer shall then act as President, and such Officer shall act accordingly, until the Disability be removed, or a President shall be elected.

[7] The President shall, at stated Times, receive for his Services, a Compensation, which shall neither be increased nor diminished during the Period for which he shall have been elected, and he shall not receive within that Period any other Emolument from the United States, or any of them.

[8] Before he enter on the Execution of his Office, he shall take the following Oath or Affirmation: "I do solemnly swear (or affirm) that I will faithfully execute the Office of President of the United States, and will to the best of my Ability, preserve, protect and defend the Constitution of the United States."

Section 2

[1] The President shall be Commander in Chief of the Army and Navy of the United States, and of the Militia of the several States, when called into the actual Service of the United States; he may require the Opinion, in writing, of the principal Officer in each of the executive Departments, upon any Subject relating to the Duties of their respective Offices, and he shall have Power to Grant Reprieves and Pardons for Offenses against the United States, except in Cases of Impeachment.

[2] He shall have Power, by and with the Advice and Consent of the Senate, to make Treaties, provided two thirds of the Senators present concur; and he shall nominate, and by and with the Advice and Consent of the Senate, shall appoint Ambassadors, other public Ministers and Consuls, Judges of the supreme Court, and all other Officers of the United States, whose Appointments are not herein otherwise provided for, and which shall be established by Law: but the Congress may by Law vest the Appointment of such inferior Officers, as they think proper, in the President alone, in the Courts of Law, or in the Heads of Departments.

[3] The President shall have Power to fill up all Vacancies that may happen during the Recess of the Senate, by granting Commissions which shall expire at the End of their next Session.

Section 3

He shall from time to time give to the Congress Information of the State of the Union, and recommend to their Consideration such Measures as he shall judge necessary and expedient; he may, on extraordinary Occasions, convene both Houses, or either of them, and in Case of Disagreement between them, with Respect to the Time of Adjournment, he may adjourn them to such Time as he shall think proper; he shall receive Ambassadors and other public Ministers; he shall take Care that the Laws be faithfully executed, and shall Commission all the Officers of the United States.

Section 4

The President, Vice President and all Civil Officers of the United States, shall be removed from Office on Impeachment for, and Conviction of, Treason, Bribery, or other high Crimes and Misdemeanors.

Article III

Section 1

The judicial Power of the United States, shall be vested in one supreme Court, and in such inferior Courts as the Congress may from time to time ordain and establish. The Judges, both of the supreme and inferior Courts, shall hold their Offices during good Behavior, and shall, at stated Times, receive for their Services a Compensation which shall not be diminished during their Continuance in Office.

Section 2

[1] The judicial Power shall extend to all Cases, in Law and Equity, arising under this Constitution, the Laws of the United States, and Treaties made, or which shall be made, under their Authority; to all Cases affecting Ambassadors, other public Ministers and Consuls; to all Cases of admiralty and maritime Jurisdiction; to Controversies to which the United States shall be a Party; to Controversies between two or more States; between a State and Citizens of another State; between Citizens of different States; between Citizens of the same State claiming Lands under Grants of different States, and between a State, or the Citizens thereof, and foreign States, Citizens or Subjects.

[2] In all Cases affecting Ambassadors, other public Ministers and Consuls, and those in which a State shall be Party, the supreme Court shall have original Jurisdiction. In all the other Cases before mentioned, the supreme Court shall have appellate Jurisdiction, both as to Law and Fact, with such Exceptions, and under such Regulations as the Congress shall make.

[3] The Trial of all Crimes, except in Cases of Impeachment, shall be by Jury; and such Trial shall be held in the State where the said Crimes

shall have been committed; but when not committed within any State, the Trial shall be at such Place or Places as the Congress may by Law have directed.

Section 3

[1] Treason against the United States, shall consist only in levying War against them, or in adhering to their Enemies, giving them Aid and Comfort. No Person shall be convicted of Treason unless on the Testimony of two Witnesses to the same overt Act, or on Confession in open Court.

[2] The Congress shall have Power to declare the Punishment of Treason, but no Attainder of Treason shall work Corruption of Blood, or Forfeiture except during the Life of the Person attainted.

Article IV

Section 1

Full Faith and Credit shall be given in each State to the public Acts, Records, and judicial Proceedings of every other State. And the Congress may by general Laws prescribe the Manner in which such Acts, Records and Proceedings shall be proved, and the Effect thereof.

Section 2

[1] The Citizens of each State shall be entitled to all Privileges and Immunities of Citizens in the several States.

[2] A Person charged in any State with Treason, Felony, or other Crime, who shall flee from Justice, and be found in another State, shall on Demand of the executive Authority of the State from which he fled, be delivered up, to be removed to the State having Jurisdiction of the Crime.

[3] No Person held to Service or Labour in one State, under the Laws thereof, escaping into another, shall, in Consequence of any Law or Regulation therein, be discharged from such Service or Labour, but shall be delivered up on Claim of the Party to whom such Service or Labour may be due.

Section 3

[1] New States may be admitted by the Congress into this Union; but no new States shall be formed or erected within the Jurisdiction of any other State; nor any State be formed by the Junction of two or more States, or parts of States, without the Consent of the Legislatures of the States concerned as well as of the Congress.

[2] The Congress shall have Power to dispose of and make all needful Rules and Regulations respecting the Territory or other Property belonging to the United States; and nothing in this Constitution shall be so construed as to Prejudice any Claims of the United States, or of any particular State.

Section 4

The United States shall guarantee to every State in this Union a Republican Form of Government, and shall protect each of them against Invasion; and on Application of the Legislature, or of the Executive (when the Legislature cannot be convened) against domestic Violence.

Article V

The Congress, whenever two thirds of both Houses shall deem it necessary, shall propose Amendments to this Constitution, or, on the Application of the Legislatures of two thirds of the several States, shall call a Convention for proposing Amendments, which, in either Case, shall be valid to all Intents and Purposes, as Part of this Constitution, when ratified by the Legislatures of three fourths of the several States, or by Conventions in three fourths thereof, as the one or the other Mode of Ratification may be proposed by the Congress; Provided that no Amendment which may be made prior to the Year One thousand eight hundred and eight shall in any Manner affect the first and fourth Clauses in the Ninth Section of the first Article; and that no State, without its Consent, shall be deprived of its equal Suffrage in the Senate.

Article VI

[1] All Debts contracted and Engagements entered into, before the Adoption of this Constitution, shall be as valid against the United States under this Constitution, as under the Confederation.

[2] This Constitution, and the Laws of the United States which shall be made in Pursuance thereof; and all Treaties made, or which shall be made, under the Authority of the United States, shall be the supreme Law of the Land; and the Judges in every State shall be bound thereby, any Thing in the Constitution or Laws of any State to the Contrary notwithstanding.

[3] The Senators and Representatives before mentioned, and the Members of the several State Legislatures, and all executive and judicial Officers, both of the United States and of the several States, shall be bound by Oath or Affirmation, to support this Constitution; but no religious Test shall ever be required as a Qualification to any Office or public Trust under the United States.

Article VII

The Ratification of the Conventions of nine States, shall be sufficient for the Establishment of this Constitution between the States so ratifying the Same.

Done in Convention by the Unanimous Consent of the States present the Seventeenth Day of September in the Year of our Lord one thousand seven hundred and Eighty seven and of the Independence of the United States of America the Twelfth.

In Witness whereof We have hereunto subscribed our Names.

George Washington—President and deputy from Virginia

New Hampshire—John Langdon, Nicholas Gilman

Massachusetts—Nathaniel Gorham, Rufus King

Connecticut—William Samuel Johnson, Roger Sherman

New York—Alexander Hamilton

New Jersey—William Livingston, David Brearley, William Paterson, Jonathan Dayton

Pennsylvania—Benjamin Franklin, Thomas Mifflin, Robert Morris, George Clymer, Thomas FitzSimons, Jared Ingersoll, James Wilson, Gouvernour Morris

Delaware—George Read, Gunning Bedford Jr., John Dickinson, Richard Bassett, Jacob Broom

Maryland—James McHenry, Daniel of St Thomas Jenifer, Daniel Carroll

Virginia—John Blair, James Madison Jr.

North Carolina—William Blount, Richard Dobbs Spaight, Hugh Williamson

South Carolina—John Rutledge, Charles Cotesworth Pinckney, Charles Pinckney, Pierce Butler

Georgia—William Few, Abraham Baldwin

Attest: William Jackson, Secretary

Amendment 1 [1791]

Congress shall make no law respecting an establishment of religion, or prohibiting the free exercise thereof; or abridging the freedom of speech, or of the press; or the right of the people peaceably to assemble, and to petition the Government for a redress of grievances.

Amendment 2 [1791]

A well regulated Militia, being necessary to the security of a free State, the right of the people to keep and bear Arms, shall not be infringed.

Amendment 3 [1791]

No Soldier shall, in time of peace be quartered in any house, without the consent of the Owner, nor in time of war, but in a manner to be prescribed by law.

Amendment 4 [1791]

The right of the people to be secure in their persons, houses, papers, and effects, against unreasonable searches and seizures, shall not be violated, and no Warrants shall issue, but upon probable cause, supported by Oath or affirmation, and particularly describing the place to be searched, and the persons or things to be seized.

Amendment 5 [1791]

No person shall be held to answer for a capital, or otherwise infamous crime, unless on a presentment or indictment of a Grand Jury, except in cases arising in the land or naval forces, or in the Militia, when in actual service in time of War or public danger; nor shall any person be subject for the same offence to be twice put in jeopardy of life or limb; nor shall be compelled in any criminal case to be a witness against himself, nor be deprived of life, liberty, or property, without due process of law; nor shall private property be taken for public use, without just compensation.

Amendment 6 [1791]

In all criminal prosecutions, the accused shall enjoy the right to a speedy and public trial, by an impartial jury of the State and district wherein the crime shall have been committed, which district shall have been previously ascertained by law, and to be informed of the nature and cause of the accusation; to be confronted with the witnesses against him; to have compulsory process for obtaining witnesses in his favor, and to have the Assistance of Counsel for his defence.

Amendment 7 [1791]

In Suits at common law, where the value in controversy shall exceed twenty dollars, the right of trial by jury shall be preserved, and no fact tried by a jury, shall be otherwise re-examined in any Court of the United States, than according to the rules of the common law.

Amendment 8 [1791]

Excessive bail shall not be required, nor excessive fines imposed, nor cruel and unusual punishments inflicted.

Amendment 9 [1791]

The enumeration in the Constitution, of certain rights, shall not be construed to deny or disparage others retained by the people.

Amendment 10 [1791]

The powers not delegated to the United States by the Constitution, nor prohibited by it to the States, are reserved to the States respectively, or to the people.

Amendment 11 [1798]

The Judicial power of the United States shall not be construed to extend to any suit in law or equity, commenced or prosecuted against one of the United States by Citizens of another State, or by Citizens or Subjects of any Foreign State.

Amendment 12 [1804]

The Electors shall meet in their respective states, and vote by ballot for President and Vice President, one of whom, at least, shall not be an inhabitant of the same state with themselves; they shall name in their ballots the person voted for as President, and in distinct ballots the person voted for as Vice President, and they shall make distinct lists of all persons voted for as President, and of all persons voted for as Vice President, and of the number of votes for each, which lists they shall sign and certify, and transmit sealed to the seat of the government of the United States, directed to the President of the Senate;

The President of the Senate shall, in the presence of the Senate and House of Representatives, open all the certificates and the votes shall then be counted;

The person having the greatest Number of votes for President, shall be the President, if such number be a majority of the whole number of Electors appointed; and if no person have such majority, then from the persons having the highest numbers not exceeding three on the list of those voted for as President, the House of Representatives shall choose immediately, by ballot, the President. But in choosing the President, the votes shall be taken by states, the representation from each state having one vote; a quorum for this purpose shall consist of a member or members from two-thirds of the states, and a majority of all the states shall be necessary to a choice. And if the House of Representatives shall not choose a President whenever the right of choice shall devolve upon them, before the fourth day of March next following, then the Vice President shall act as President, as in the case of the death or other constitutional disability of the President.

The person having the greatest number of votes as Vice President, shall be the Vice President, if such number be a majority of the whole number of Electors appointed, and if no person have a majority, then from the two highest numbers on the list, the Senate shall choose the Vice President; a quorum for the purpose shall consist of two-thirds of the whole number of Senators, and a majority of the whole number shall be necessary to a choice. But no person constitutionally ineligible to the office of President shall be eligible to that of Vice President of the United States.

Amendment 13 [1865]

Section 1. Neither slavery nor involuntary servitude, except as a punishment for crime whereof the party shall have been duly convicted, shall exist within the United States, or any place subject to their jurisdiction.

Section 2. Congress shall have power to enforce this article by appropriate legislation.

Amendment 14 [1868]

Section 1. All persons born or naturalized in the United States, and subject to the jurisdiction thereof, are citizens of the United States and of the State wherein they reside. No State shall make or enforce any law which shall abridge the privileges or immunities of citizens of the United States; nor shall any State deprive any person of life, liberty, or property, without due process of law; nor deny to any person within its jurisdiction the equal protection of the laws.

Section 2. Representatives shall be apportioned among the several States according to their respective numbers, counting the whole number of persons in each State, excluding Indians not taxed. But when the right to vote at any election for the choice of electors for President and Vice President of the United States, Representatives in Congress, the Executive and Judicial officers of a State, or the members of the Legislature thereof, is denied to any of the male inhabitants of such State, being twenty-one years of age, and citizens of the United States, or in any way abridged, except for participation in rebellion, or other crime, the basis of representation therein shall be reduced in the proportion which the number of such male citizens shall bear to the whole number of male citizens twenty-one years of age in such State.

Section 3. No person shall be a Senator or Representative in Congress, or elector of President and Vice President, or hold any office, civil or military, under the United States, or under any State, who, having previously taken an oath, as a member of Congress, or as an officer of the United States, or as a member of any State legislature, or as an executive or judicial officer of any State, to support the Constitution of the United States, shall have engaged in insurrection or rebellion against the same, or given aid or comfort to the enemies thereof. But Congress may by a vote of two-thirds of each House, remove such disability.

Section 4. The validity of the public debt of the United States, authorized by law, including debts incurred for payment of pensions and bounties for services in suppressing insurrection or rebellion, shall not be questioned. But neither the United States nor any State shall assume or pay any debt or obligation incurred in aid of insurrection or rebellion against the United States, or any claim for the loss or emancipation of any slave; but all such debts, obligations and claims shall be held illegal and void.

Section 5. The Congress shall have power to enforce, by appropriate legislation, the provisions of this article.

Amendment 15 [1870]

Section 1. The right of citizens of the United States to vote shall not be denied or abridged by the United States or by any State on account of race, color, or previous condition of servitude.

Section 2. The Congress shall have power to enforce this article by appropriate legislation.

Amendment 16 [1913]

The Congress shall have power to lay and collect taxes on incomes, from whatever source derived, without apportionment among the several States, and without regard to any census or enumeration.

Amendment 17 [1913]

The Senate of the United States shall be composed of two Senators from each State, elected by the people thereof, for six years; and each Senator shall have one vote. The electors in each State shall have the qualifications requisite for electors of the most numerous branch of the State legislatures.

When vacancies happen in the representation of any State in the Senate, the executive authority of such State shall issue writs of election to fill such vacancies: *Provided,* That the legislature of any State may empower the executive thereof to make temporary appointments until the people fill the vacancies by election as the legislature may direct.

This amendment shall not be so construed as to affect the election or term of any Senator chosen before it becomes valid as part of the Constitution.

Amendment 18 [1919]

[Prohibition on manufacture, sale, or transportation of intoxicating liquors, which was repealed by Amendment 21]

Amendment 19 [1920]

The right of citizens of the United States to vote shall not be denied or abridged by the United States or by any State on account of sex.

Congress shall have power to enforce this article by appropriate legislation.

Amendment 20 [1933]

Section 1. The terms of the President and Vice President shall end at noon on the 20th day of January, and the terms of Senators and Representatives at noon on the 3d day of January, of the years in which such terms would have ended if this article had not been ratified; and the terms of their successors shall then begin.

Section 2. The Congress shall assemble at least once in every year, and such meeting shall begin at noon on the 3d day of January, unless they shall by law appoint a different day.

Section 3. If, at the time fixed for the beginning of the term of the President, the President elect shall have died, the Vice President elect shall become President. If a President shall not have been chosen before the time fixed for the beginning of his term, or if the President elect shall have failed to qualify, then the Vice President elect shall act as President until a President shall have qualified; and the Congress may by law provide for the case wherein neither a President elect nor a Vice President elect shall have qualified, declaring who shall then act as President, or the manner in which one who is to act shall be selected, and such person shall act accordingly until a President or Vice President shall have qualified.

Section 4. The Congress may by law provide for the case of the death of any of the persons from whom the House of Representatives may choose a President whenever the right of choice shall have devolved upon them, and for the case of the death of any of the persons from whom the Senate may choose a Vice President whenever the right of choice shall have devolved upon them.

Section 5. Sections 1 and 2 shall take effect on the 15th day of October following the ratification of this article.

Section 6. This article shall be inoperative unless it shall have been ratified as an amendment to the Constitution by the legislatures of three-fourths of the several States within seven years from the date of its submission.

Amendment 21 [1933]

Section 1. The eighteenth article of amendment to the Constitution of the United States is hereby repealed.

Section 2. The transportation or importation into any State, Territory, or possession of the United States for delivery or use therein of intoxicating liquors, in violation of the laws thereof, is hereby prohibited.

Section 3. The article shall be inoperative unless it shall have been ratified as an amendment to the Constitution by conventions in the several States, as provided in the Constitution, within seven years from the date of the submission hereof to the States by the Congress.

Amendment 22 [1951]

Section 1. No person shall be elected to the office of the President more than twice, and no person who has held the office of President, or acted as President, for more than two years of a term to which some other person was elected President shall be elected to the office of the President more than once. But this Article shall not apply to any person holding the office of President, when this Article was proposed by the Congress, and shall not prevent any person who may be holding the office of President, or acting as President, during the term within which this Article becomes operative from holding the office of President or acting as President during the remainder of such term.

Section 2. This article shall be inoperative unless it shall have been ratified as an amendment to the Constitution by the legislatures of three-fourths of the several States within seven years from the date of its submission to the States by the Congress.

Amendment 23 [1961]

Section 1. The District constituting the seat of Government of the United States shall appoint in such manner as the Congress may direct:

A number of electors of President and Vice President equal to the whole number of Senators and Representatives in Congress to which the District would be entitled if it were a State, but in no event more than the least populous State; they shall be in addition to those appointed by the States, but they shall be considered, for the purposes of the election of President and Vice President, to be electors appointed by a State; and they shall meet in the District and perform such duties as provided by the twelfth article of amendment.

Section 2. The Congress shall have power to enforce this article by appropriate legislation.

Amendment 24 [1964]

Section 1. The right of citizens of the United States to vote in any primary or other election for President or Vice President, for electors for President or Vice President, or for Senator or Representative in Congress, shall not be denied or abridged by the United States or any State by reason of failure to pay any poll tax or other tax.

Section 2. The Congress shall have power to enforce this article by appropriate legislation.

Amendment 25 [1967]

Section 1. In case of the removal of the President from office or of his death or resignation, the Vice President shall become President.

Section 2. Whenever there is a vacancy in the office of the Vice President, the President shall nominate a Vice President who shall take office upon confirmation by a majority vote of both Houses of Congress.

Section 3. Whenever the President transmits to the President pro tempore of the Senate and the Speaker of the House of Representatives his written declaration that he is unable to discharge the powers and duties of his office, and until he transmits to them a written declaration to the contrary, such powers and duties shall be discharged by the Vice President as Acting President.

Section 4. Whenever the Vice President and a majority of either the principal officers of the executive departments or of such other body as Congress may by law provide, transmit to the President pro tempore of the Senate and the Speaker of the House of Representatives their written declaration that the President is unable to discharge the powers and duties of his office, the Vice President shall immediately assume the powers and duties of the office as Acting President.

Thereafter, when the President transmits to the President pro tempore of the Senate and the Speaker of the House of Representatives his written declaration that no inability exists, he shall resume the powers and duties of his office unless the Vice President and a majority of either the principal officers of the executive department or of such other body as Congress may by law provide, transmit within four days to the President pro tempore of the Senate and the Speaker of the House of Representatives their written declaration that the President is unable to discharge the powers and duties of his office. Thereupon Congress shall decide the issue, assembling within forty-eight hours for that purpose if not in session. If the Congress, within twenty-one days after receipt of the latter written declaration, or, if Congress is not in session, within twenty-one days after Congress is required to assemble, determines by two-thirds vote of both Houses that the President is unable to discharge the powers and duties of his office, the Vice President shall continue to discharge the same as Acting President; otherwise, the President shall resume the powers and duties of his office.

Amendment 26 [1971]

Section 1. The right of citizens of the United States, who are eighteen years of age or older, to vote shall not be denied or abridged by the United States or by any State on account of age.

Section 2. The Congress shall have power to enforce this article by appropriate legislation.

Amendment 27 [1992]

No law varying the compensation for the services of the Senators and Representatives shall take effect until an election of Representatives shall have intervened.

APPENDIX II

PRACTICE EXERCISES

■ ■ ■

PRACTICE EXERCISE FOR CHAPTER 2 (CUSTOMARY INTERNATIONAL LAW)

#1

U.S. relations with the State of Being, a nation in the Western Hemisphere, are in peril. Being's popularly elected government has maintained generally positive relations with the present U.S. administration. But Being suffers a military coup against its government, led by General Specific. The U.S. president has strongly denounced the coup—not least because he feared it would cascade into a series of bloody conflicts across the region—while conservative U.S. critics of the former government's socialist policies rejoiced.

What happened next surprised most observers. Senator Leghorn (South Carolina) summarized developments in the following remarks, delivered on the Senate floor:

> Ladies and Gentleman, the United States stands today in a position of unusual embarrassment. I speak, of course, of the Being situation, and with apologies to those of a tender disposition, let me catalog our offenses.
>
> As you are aware, General Specific was seized from the smoking lounge at Being's principal airport by a Trans American Airways crew, at the direction of Trans American's CEO—who was acting, let us be clear, at the prompting of the U.S. Secretary of Transportation and, I strongly suspect, our own president—and forced onto one of its planes. He was transported against his will to the United States and he is being held incommunicado at Andrews Air Force Base. This kidnaping and arbitrary detention clearly violated customary international law. The Constitution says, and the courts have made this perfectly clear, that customary international law is federal law that constrains every American. Our Secretary of Transportation and our president offended this law, and I have been advised that General Specific has filed suit against both to force his release. I am also informed that he has sued Trans American Airways and its CEO under

something called the Alien Tort Statute. It pains me to say that I wish him success in both endeavors.

Assuming the facts as stated by Senator Leghorn, what are the merits of the objections he has raised, and the strengths and weaknesses of the lawsuits he mentions? Students should assume the roles of: (a) Senator Leghorn; (b) White House Counsel; (c) counsel for General Specific; and (d) counsel for Trans American Airways. Be sure to consider whether there are additional facts you would need for your analysis.

#2

In 2016, Montana voters overwhelmingly approve the "Montana International Law Amendment" to the Montana Constitution. The Amendment reads:

> A. The judicial power of this State shall be vested in the Senate, sitting as a Court of Impeachment, a Supreme Court, the Court of Criminal Appeals, the Court on the Judiciary, and such intermediate appellate and lower courts as may be provided.
>
> B. The Courts provided for in subsection A of this section, when exercising their judicial authority, shall uphold and adhere to the law as provided in the United States Constitution, the Montana Constitution, the United States Code, federal regulations promulgated pursuant thereto, federal common law, Montana Statutes and rules promulgated pursuant thereto, and if necessary the law of another state of the United States provided the law of the other state does not include Sharia Law, in making judicial decisions. Under no circumstance shall such courts shall look to the legal precepts of other nations or cultures, including international or Sharia law.

Abdul Awad, the Executive Director of the Council on American-Islamic Relations in Montana, files a lawsuit against the State of Montana in the federal district court, requesting a preliminary injunction against implementation of the new Amendment and a ruling that the Amendment is unconstitutional. Awad attacks the constitutionality of the Amendment through two arguments. First, he maintains that the Amendment is unconstitutional because it denies the effect of international law as a part of U.S. law. Second, he contends the Amendment is problematic with respect to the freedom of religion clause of the U.S. Constitution. The district court indicates that it intends to proceed initially by only dealing with the first issue; the second issue will be addressed, if necessary, at a later stage in the proceedings.

Students should assume the roles of: (1) counsel for the Council on American-Islamic Relations in Montana (opposing the amendment); (2)

counsel representing the Montana Attorney-General's office (defending amendment); and (3) the federal district court judge.

#3

In March 2017, five men set off from Somalia in a heavily-armed seagoing vessel in search of a merchant ship to attack and plunder. Somewhere on the high seas between Somalia and the Seychelles, the men spot what they think is a merchant vessel. They approach the vessel and open fire upon it, but to their surprise, it turns out to be the USS *Intrepid*, a U.S. Navy frigate.

The *Intrepid* returns fire, gives chase, and eventually captures the five men. The men are brought to the United States and indicted under 18 U.S.C. § 1651. The defendants move to dismiss the charge, asserting that their attack on the USS *Nicholas* did not constitute "piracy" under the law of nations, since "piracy" requires a robbery or taking of property on the high seas, and no such robbery occurred. The district court issues an opinion agreeing with the defendants and dismissing the charge. The matter is then appealed to the Ninth Circuit Court of Appeals.

The U.S. president is troubled by the decision and sets up a Commission to propose a new statute (or series of statutes) to address piracy and privateering.

Students should assume the roles of: (1) counsel to the defendants (arguing that the district court decision was correct); (2) counsel for the government (arguing that the decision was incorrect); (3) counsel to the Commission (arguing in favor of and making concrete proposals for expansion and clarification of existing law); (4) counsel representing a group of foreign countries before the Commission (opposing greater extraterritorial application of U.S. law).

PRACTICE EXERCISE FOR CHAPTER 3 (TREATIES AND OTHER INTERNATIONAL AGREEMENTS)

On December 18, 1979, the General Assembly of the United Nations adopted a resolution accepting and commending for signature and ratification by U.N. members the Convention on the Elimination of All Forms of Discrimination Against Women (CEDAW).[92] Article 2 of CEDAW provides:

States Parties condemn discrimination against women in all its forms, agree to pursue by all appropriate means and without delay a policy of eliminating discrimination against women and, to this end, undertake:

(a) To embody the principle of the equality of men and women in their national constitutions or other appropriate legislation if not yet incorporated therein and to ensure, through

[92] 1249 U.N.T.S. 13.

law and other appropriate means, the practical realization of this principle;

(b) To adopt appropriate legislative and other measures, including sanctions where appropriate, prohibiting all discrimination against women;

(c) To establish legal protection of the rights of women on an equal basis with men and to ensure through competent national tribunals and other public institutions the effective protection of women against any act of discrimination;

(d) To refrain from engaging in any act or practice of discrimination against women and to ensure that public authorities and institutions shall act in conformity with this obligation;

(e) To take all appropriate measures to eliminate discrimination against women by any person, organization or enterprise;

(f) To take all appropriate measures, including legislation, to modify or abolish existing laws, regulations, customs and practices which constitute discrimination against women;

(g) To repeal all national penal provisions which constitute discrimination against women.

As of mid-2011, 186 countries (more than ninety-five percent of the members of the United Nations) are party to the Convention. Although the United States signed CEDAW in July 1980 and President Carter submitted it to the Senate for advice and consent, such consent has not been forthcoming.

The majority leader of the Senate has now decided to bring CEDAW before the full Senate for a vote. The majority leader is concerned, however, about the consequences of U.S. ratification on: (1) the constitutional rights of Congress; (2) the constitutional rights of the states; and (3) the constitutional rights of U.S. citizens. In particular, the majority leader is wondering whether the provisions of CEDAW Article 2, upon ratification, will become part of the supreme law of the United States, whether they are directly enforceable, and, if so, by whom; or whether, if they require implementing legislation, the implementing laws can be enacted by Congress in a form that would be constitutional.

A reservation to the resolution of acceptance has been offered by Senator Abigail Blaghard which states, in part, "None of the provisions of this Convention shall become part of the law of the United States or of the several states unless and until such provisions shall have been enacted into law by the United States or the several states in accordance with the constitutional powers allocated to each that would apply had the Convention not been ratified."

Members of the class are to assume the following roles in simulating a meeting of members of the majority leader's staff:

(1) A member of the staff who will examine the effect the Convention could have, if no reservations were added, on the constitutional rights and privileges of the states, the Congress and U.S. citizens.

(2) Another staffer who will examine whether any of the quoted provisions are self-executing and supreme law of the land, and what the consequences would be if (1) they, or any of them are self-executing; or (2) they are not self-executing. The same staffer shall consider what legislation Congress would have to enact to give effect domestically to the international legal obligations of the Convention and the constitutionality of such laws.

(3) A staffer who will examine the constitutionality and effect on the international legal obligation of the United States of the Blaghard Amendment. The same staffer shall consider what must be required of other states parties to the Convention by way of agreeing to such a reservation and what the legal position would be *vis-a-vis* parties to the Convention which do not agree to this reservation. The same staffer will also address the issue of whether there are alternative methods to achieve some or all of Senator Blaghard's purposes, should the reservation be unconstitutional in its present form.

The practice exercise consists of meetings between the three staffers and a caucus of interested Senators (i.e., the other members of the class). The Senators may question the staff on their findings, discuss their implications, propose and debate reservations, understandings, or declarations (RUDs), and, finally, indicate whether they intend to vote in favor of consent to CEDAW with such RUDs as command majority support.

PRACTICE EXERCISES FOR CHAPTER 4 (WAR POWERS)

#1

Moraine is a nation in the Middle East governed by Islamic radicals. Its record of human rights abuses is one of the worst in the world. It has verbally threatened other nations in the region, and intelligence reports indicate that it has acquired centrifuges with which it has begun to enrich uranium, although estimates are that Moraine will not have deliverable nuclear devices for at least eight years. Months of direct negotiations have not persuaded Moraine to give up its nuclear enrichment program. Assume that the use of force has not been authorized or prohibited by either statute or treaty. The president argues that he has constitutional power to use force against Moraine without congressional approval. The Senate Foreign Relations Committee has requested the opinion of its staff and the Department of State on whether the use of force under these circumstances would be constitutionally permissible.

Students should assume the roles of: (1) Committee counsel (arguing the negative); (2) the State Department Legal Adviser (arguing the affirmative); and (3) Committee members.

#2

Following the facts set out in practice exercise #1 above, the United States launches a preemptive strike against Moraine nuclear facilities. In response, Moraine artillery bombards neighboring Imman, a U.S. ally, and invading Moraine troops engage American ground forces stationed in Imman. Full-scale hostilities continue for 78 days following the date of the preemptive strike. Assume that the Senate Foreign Relations Committee is holding a hearing on the issue.

1. Constitutionally, must the president comply with the requirement of the War Powers Resolution to withdraw the armed forces prior to the ninetieth day?
2. If Congress were to adopt a concurrent resolution under section 5(c) of the War Powers Resolution, would the president constitutionally be required to comply with it and to withdraw U.S. forces from Imman?
3. Can the president infer congressional approval from the enactment of previous legislation appropriating funds for the stationing of U.S. troops in Imman, notwithstanding section 8(a)(1) of the War Powers Resolution?

Students should assume the roles of: (1) Committee counsel (arguing in favor of congressional power); (2) the State Department Legal Adviser (arguing in favor of presidential power); and (3) Committee members (from both parties, attempting to find the middle ground).

#3

Moraine is a nation in the Middle East governed by Islamic radicals. Its armed forces have attacked North Arabia. North Arabia is a party to the North Atlantic Treaty. The president argues that he has constitutional power to use force against Moraine without congressional approval because it is authorized by the NATO treaty. Moreover, the U.N. Security Council has adopted a resolution authorizing member States to use armed force against Moraine in defense of North Arabia. The Senate Foreign Relations Committee has requested the opinion of its staff and the Department of

State on whether the use of force under these circumstances would be constitutionally permissible.

Students should assume the roles of: (1) Committee counsel (arguing the negative); (2) the State Department Legal Adviser (arguing the affirmative); and (3) Committee members.

PRACTICE EXERCISE FOR CHAPTER 5 (THE POWER OF THE PURSE)

#1

In 2021, a newly-elected Congress is eager to demonstrate its willingness to reduce the federal deficit. At the same time, Congress is very disturbed about various classified documents that continue to be released by WikiLeaks, including a series of cables from the U.S. Embassy in Caracas demonstrating an executive branch willingness to cooperate with Venezuelan strongman Nicolás Maduro, rather than pressuring him to improve his human rights records, to allow for a more pluralist democracy, and to depart from his "socialist ways".

The Chair of the House Appropriations Subcommittee on State Department, Foreign Operations, and Related Programs is considering legislation that would:

1. reduce personnel at all U.S. embassies and consulates abroad by 50%, although in no instance would any embassy or consulate have less than 5 persons;
2. reduce personnel at the U.S. Embassy in Caracas by a further 30% (subject to the 5-person minimum), unless the president certifies in writing that U.S. policy to Venezuela seeks improve Venezuela's human rights record, to promote greater democratic participation in Venezuela, and to establish in Venezuela a free market economy; and
3. cut off all foreign aid to Venezuela until such time as the president certifies in writing that Venezuela engages in no significant human rights abuses.

The Chair of the Subcommittee has scheduled a hearing on whether any of these provisions, if enacted into law (perhaps over a presidential veto), would constitute an unconstitutional encroachment upon presidential power.

Students should assume the role of: (1) Committee counsel (arguing in favor of congressional power); (2) a representative from the Justice Department's Office of Legal Counsel (arguing in favor of presidential power); (3) an esteemed law professor (no predisposition).

#2

Narco-terrorism has become an enormous problem in Mexico, with transnational implications. For example, after Ricardo Valles de la Rosa, a native of Juárez, Mexico, committed a crime just across the river from Juárez in El Paso, Texas, he was caught and imprisoned in El Paso, where he came into contact with members of the Barrio Azteca, a Mexican narcotics gang. After serving his time, Valles de la Rosa was deported in 2014 from the United States back to Mexico, where he reportedly joined the ranks of Barrio Azteca. In 2016, he allegedly participated in an attempted attack in Juárez on an El Paso prison officer, who lives in Juárez with his wife. Although the prison officer survived the attack unscathed, his wife—an employee of the U.S. Consulate in Juárez—and two other employees of the U.S. Consulate were killed.

Reacting to this and other incidents, Congress adopts a statute in 2020, over the president's veto, entitled the Narcotics Trafficking in Mexico Act (NTMA). Among other things, the statute:

(1) authorizes and appropriates no more than $80 million for Department of Justice programs that train and equip Mexican police involved in anti-narcotics operations;

(2) prohibits the use of any funds in the relevant statute dealing with foreign embassies and consulates (the Foreign Operations, Export Financing, and Related Appropriations Act) for the operation of a consulate in Juárez, given the dangers to consular personnel posted there; and

(3) prohibits the use of any funds to support the sharing of U.S. intelligence information with the Mexican Government on narcotics trafficking in Mexico, due to a concern that such information is being leaked by unknown persons in the Mexican Government to the narcotics traffickers, thereby making it more difficult to thwart their activities.

Once the NTMA is adopted, the president indicates that he views the restrictions contained in the above provisions as "merely advisory in nature, given the inability of Congress to supercede the president's constitutional role as the 'sole voice' in matter of foreign relations." Your law school convenes a conference to hear views on the constitutionality of the statute.

Students should assume the roles of: (1) counsel to the Senate Majority leader; (2) White House counsel; (3) counsel for the Mexican Embassy in Washington, D.C.; and (4) counsel for the governor of Texas.

PRACTICE EXERCISE FOR CHAPTER 6 (FEDERALISM)

#1

A new Administration and Congress have taken office in Washington, D.C., and both are keenly interested in taking steps to protect the sanctity of life in all aspects. Among other things, the new federal officials note that aliens travel to and reside in the United States, where they are exposed to the death penalty, and where their unborn children have been aborted, and that such matters, as well as the practice of abortion and the death penalty as it affects Americans, have resulted in protests from various foreign governments. Conversely, U.S. nationals have traveled abroad, where they have been convicted and sentenced to death in unjust situations, as well as obtained abortions. The following steps are contemplated:

1. Enacting a federal statute that asserts the sense of the Congress that the practice of abortion and of the death penalty have caused extensive "friction" between the United States and the other nations of the world, and therefore the statute criminalizes such practice in the United States as a matter of federal law; or

2. Ratifying (a) the Second Optional Protocol to the International Covenant on Civil and Political Rights (ICCPR), Dec. 15, 1989, 29 I.L.M. 1464, which prohibits the death penalty; and (b) the American Convention on Human Rights, Nov. 22, 1969, 1144 U.N.T.S. 123, 9 I.L.M. 673, as amended, which provides that "[e]very person has the right to have his life protected . . . , in general, from the moment of conception," followed by enacting a federal statute that, in implementation of the American Convention, criminalizes all abortion; or

3. Having the president issue an executive order stating that it is the foreign policy of the United States to end abortion and the death penalty worldwide as a means of protecting Americans abroad, avoiding frictions with foreign governments regarding the treatment of aliens in the United States, and promoting a more stable and just world; or

4. Having the U.S. Department of State Legal Adviser issue a declaration that contemporary customary international law forbids the practice of abortion and of the death penalty, and then seeking leave for the Department of Justice to appear as amicus curiae in all cases in U.S. courts where such practice is at issue so as to urge the court to prevent the practice as prohibited under U.S. federal law.

Students should assume the roles of: (1) a U.S. Department of Justice Assistant Attorney-General: (2) the Attorney-General of the State of Texas; (3) a lawyer for a non-governmental organization (People for Choice) which favors a woman's right to choose whether to abort, but opposes the death penalty as a racially-biased and unjust form of punishment; and (4) a lawyer for a non-governmental organization (Stop Crime) which favors allowing the several states to choose whether to use the death penalty, but opposes abortion on moral grounds.

#2

Review the facts of the practice exercise for Chapter 5 (#2). Add to those facts that the Governor of Texas and the Governor of Chihuahua (the Mexican State where Juárez is located) sign an instrument that provides the following:

> WHEREAS the State of Texas and the State of Chihuahua are experiencing significant levels of violence by persons engaged in narcotics trafficking; and
>
> WHEREAS such persons often operate and cooperate across the border between the State of Texas and the State of Chihuahua in a manner that poses difficulties for police investigation and apprehension of such persons; and
>
> WHEREAS cooperation between police authorities of Texas and Chihuahua is necessary to ensure timely, accurate, and effective investigation of narcotics trafficking, as well as apprehension of those who violate narcotics laws;
>
> THEREFORE, the State of Texas and the State of Chihuahua agree to work cooperatively to the fullest extent possible consistent with their respective laws to ensure that:
>
> 1. Each State fully informs the other State regarding its respective investigation and apprehension of persons involved in narcotics trafficking that has a transborder dimension;
>
> 2. Each State cooperates on educating the other State about the organization, policies, and tactics of its respective police authorities in addressing narcotics trafficking that has a transborder dimension; and
>
> 3. Each State communicates to its national government both its concerns and any concerns of the other State relating to narcotics trafficking that has a transborder dimension.

The Speaker of the House of Representatives believes that the Texas-Chihuahua instrument—which was not authorized by Congress—is constitutionally impermissible. He convenes a hearing on the matter, at which various legal experts testify.

Students should assume the roles of: (1) counsel for the State of Texas; (2) counsel for the House Committee on Foreign Affairs; (2) counsel for the State of Chihuahua; and (4) counsel for the U.S. Department of State Office of the Legal Adviser.

PRACTICE EXERCISE FOR CHAPTER 7 (THE JUDICIARY)

#1

Congress has passed a law, over a presidential veto, which prohibits the president, or any official of the U.S. government, from assassinating, or planning or otherwise seeking to assassinate, any foreign head of State or of government or any other foreign government official.

The Washington *Tattler* last month carried a report that quotes a telephone call from the president to the Director of the Central Intelligence Agency in which the president reads him a secret directive ordering him to secure the death of Azam Mogul, the dictator of the north-central Asian Republic of Ishtar. Mogul has been responsible for the torture-death of thousands of Ishtar citizens and, most recently, has kidnapped and killed five American Episcopal nuns who had operated a medical facility in the capital, Ishtar City.

The Senate Foreign Relations Committee has held hearings to determine whether the president has acted in violation of the law. At a session with the CIA director, its chair demanded that the director produce any memoranda of this telephone conversation and a copy of the secret directive, if such exists. The director has refused to comply, giving the Committee a copy of a letter from the president claiming executive privilege.

The Senate Committee, last week, voted to bring an action against the president and the director of the CIA asking the U.S. District Court for the District of Columbia to issue an order to the defendants to comply with the Committee's request for production and ordering them also to desist from any actions vis à vis Ishtar in contravention of the law prohibiting assassinations.

Students should assume the roles of: (1) White House Counsel to the president; (2) General Counsel of the CIA; and (3) the Counsel to the Senate Foreign Relations Committee.

#2

In 2021, the Democratic Party controls a bare majority of both the Senate and the House of Representatives. The president is a Republican, and announces on April 1 that the United States will attack Iran with both

U.S. air and ground forces on May 1 to eliminate what appears to be a nascent Iranian nuclear weapons program that in the future might be used against the United States and its key allies, such as Israel.

On April 15, both Houses of Congress, by party-line vote, adopt resolutions stating that Congress opposes the president's use of such military force. Further, all Democratic Senate and House members join together to file a suit on April 25 in the District Court for the District of Columbia seeking an injunction that the president shall not proceed in the absence of a Congressional declaration of war or other authorization to use military force.

The District Court finds that the case is justiciable and that the plaintiffs have standing. That decision is taken up on expedited appeal directly to the Supreme Court, given the importance of the issue.

Drawing upon relevant Constitutional, statutory, judicial, or other precedent, students should assume the roles of: (1) counsel for Congress (arguing in favor of justiciability and standing); (2) counsel for the Justice Department (in opposition); (3) counsel for an independent legal think tank (submitting amicus views to the court).

#3

Baltasar Ramdan, a national of Syria, wins a University of Damascus prize to study at Columbia University in New York for one year. He travels to New York with his wife, Lilith, who is a dual U.S.-Syrian national. During that year, he learns about serious human rights abuses by the Syrian Government from reading reports in the Western media and attending academic conferences on the Middle East. Ramdan starts a blog entitled "Syrian Ghosts" in which he reveals extensive details about Syrian Government abuses and calls upon the people of Syria to rise up and depose the Syrian president.

One morning while riding his bicycle to class, Ramdan is gunned down near Columbus Circle by two masked assailants. Though the two men attempt to escape from the scene, they are stopped and apprehended by New York police officers who were having coffee in a nearby shop. The two assailants ultimately confess in great detail that they are agents of the Government of Syria, who were instructed to kill Ramdan by senior Syrian officials at a secret meeting in Damascus.

The next day, Lilith shows up in the law office of Smith & Wesson. She notes that the two men who confessed will be criminally prosecuted for their action, but bringing a civil action against them makes no sense because they are relatively poor and are simply "foot soldiers" of the government. Instead, she wants to sue in a U.S. court both the Government of Syria and the Syrian president. Smith & Wesson agrees to take the case and files suit under the Alien Tort Statute, the Torture Victim Protection

Act, and New York tort law. When the Syrian president arrives in New York one week later to attend a major fund-raising event for Middle East refugee camps, an employee of Smith & Wesson manages to serve him directly with the relevant court papers. At the same time, the relevant court papers are sent to the Syrian Embassy in Washington, D.C.

A meeting is convened among the relevant counsel to clarify their basic positions. Students should assume the role of: (1) counsel for Smith & Wesson (arguing why the U.S. court has jurisdiction and why plaintiff will prevail on the merits); (2) counsel for the Syrian president (opposing jurisdiction and the merits); (3) counsel for the Government of Syria (also opposing); (4) esteemed law professor (providing an objective view).

INDEX

References are to Pages